# CLASSIC THROUGH MODERN DRAMA

# CLASSIC
# THROUGH
# MODERN
# DRAMA

*An Introductory Anthology*

EDITED BY

OTTO REINERT

*University of Washington, Seattle*

LITTLE, BROWN AND COMPANY BOSTON

LIBRARY OF CONGRESS CATALOG CARD NO. 72-116980

SEVENTH PRINTING

*Printed simultaneously in Canada by*
*Little, Brown & Company (Canada) Limited*

PRINTED IN THE UNITED STATES OF AMERICA

# PREFACE

I have tried to follow here the same principles that guided my selection of plays for the earlier anthologies I have edited. Time and critical consensus have long certified the literary value of most of the plays; about the more recent ones I can only say that I think they are all worth seeing, reading, and talking about. Collectively, the fifteen plays illustrate a range of western drama, in time and kind.

Six of the plays have been retained from *Drama: An Introductory Anthology*. Of the other nine, two are included in *Drama: Alternate Edition,* and seven are new selections.

The general Introduction is a revised and expanded version of the introductions to the two predecessors of *Classic Through Modern Drama.* The major expansion is a new section on "Tragedy and Comedy." The Introduction still emphasizes the *literary* nature of drama in considering the relationship between written and performed drama and between drama and the other literary genres. It takes up some of the problems peculiar to reading drama, discusses dramatic conventions, defines some technical terms, and analyzes a single scene (the ending of Etherege's *The Man of Mode*) in some detail. In the comments on the individual plays I have tried to suggest their theatrical setting and their place in the history of drama, but my main concern has been with the plays as imaginative structures of language and action. I have tried to be specific and inclusive without being dogmatic and exhaustive. I hope that the comments – like the plays themselves – will invite a number of different approaches and raise more questions than they answer. The distinction of drama, I believe, is that it speaks with many voices that all claim our attention.

As in the earlier collections, the Appendix includes brief biographies of the playwrights and selective individual and general bibliographies. A new feature of the latter is the listing of recordings and screen versions (for rental or sale) of the plays for which they are available.

For his assistance with the Appendix and for his criticisms of the play commentaries I want to thank Robert W. Hermer of the English Department at the University of Washington. The book is better for his contributions. I would also like to thank Jane E. Aaron of Little, Brown and Company for her skillful editing of my manuscript.

# CONTENTS

# INTRODUCTION

## A DEFINITION OF DRAMA

Drama, like poetry and fiction, is an art of words, a genre of literature. In drama, the words are mainly dialogue: people talking is the basic dramatic action. The talk may be interrupted by wordless activity — swordplay, love-making, silence — but such activity will derive its significance from its context of dialogue. If not, we are dealing with pantomime and not with drama.

This is a distinction more meaningfully made in general theory than in dealing with individual works of dramatic art. Films, for example, generally subordinate dialogue to photography, and yet film scripts have been published to be read. At what point of verbal artistry do they cease being scenario and production notes and become drama? Conversely, to what extent is the concept of drama covered by the old definition of theater as "three boards and a passion"?

Such questions are posed by the double aspect of dramatic language. As written words, drama is literature; as spoken words in a spectacle, it is theater. A novel or a poem is read (or listened to in recital). A play can be either read or performed, but performance affects its status as literature. Dialogue can be performed directly, intact, but stage directions, however skillfully written, do not survive the transfer from script to stage. In fact, the more literary they are, the more they lose in the transfer. Their referents in performance — speech manner, movement, costume, set, etc. — are creations of the theater rather than of literature. The only way the audience can register what, in *Who's Afraid of Virginia Woolf?*, Albee describes as George's "put-upon" look at Martha and as "Not enough enthusiasm" in Nick's comment that Martha's father is "a remarkable man" is through the expression on the face of the actor playing George and through the voice inflection of the actor playing Nick. And the haggard looks of all the four characters at the end of the play, after a long night's drinking, can only be conveyed by a combination of acting and make-up. This is only to say that a performance of drama is much more than just an art of words. It is the joint product of many arts, of which direction, acting, and stage design are the most important. And since what the dramatist writes is a performable script, the images he works with make up, in Ronald Peacock's words, "a composite form, using different 'arts' to one end." The language of drama includes the idiom of the physical theater. The most dramatic dialogue, it could be argued, is that which Bertolt Brecht calls "gestic": speech so cadenced by natural rhythms that bodily postures, gestures, and movements naturally accompany the speech and reinforce the attitudes expressed by its semantics.

The fact that successful playwrights make more money in the box office than in the bookstores is evidence that for most people the theatrical medium of drama takes precedence over the literary one and that they find *reading* a play a pallid substitute for *seeing* it. As stage spectacle a play is intensely *there* — a three-dimensional and audible progress of absorbing physical action. While words are consecutive and reading is an act in the time dimension, seeing a play is an experience of both time and space. At any one moment the spectator may be simultaneously aware of weather or time of day, of rich or shabby furniture, or of one character speaking, another listening, and a third crawling noiselessly toward the speaker with a knife between his teeth. The spatial concreteness and immediacy of staged drama enlist the attention of a larger set of the spectator's sensory responses, and do so more intensely, than the purely imaginative evocations of a printed play ever can.

Still, the popular assumption that the theatrical medium of drama is primary may be challenged. Performance is no more the play than the concert is the symphony. Most plays — like symphonies — have been written to be performed, but the artistic construct exists complete in the written words, just as the melody, harmony, rhythm, tempo, and orchestration of the symphony "are" in the printed score. The only difference between a printed play and a printed musical composition in this respect is that for most of us it is easier to "see" and "hear" a play in the imagination than it is to "hear" the music in the read score. A play is a potential but never-to-be-realized performance, an "ideal" performance in the philosophical sense, inherent in the configuration of the playwright's words and independent of the artists of the theater whom it keeps challenging to produce performed drama. Items may be cut or added in the performance of a play, just as an enterprising editor may alter a text or a conductor a score, but this does not prove that the original work was not an autonomous artistic entity.

Drama is distinguished from the other forms of literature not just by performability but also by the objectivity and externality that performability implies. The statement "She is a woman without hope" is, as stage direction, undramatic. It could become a speech by one of the characters, or it could inspire an actress to perform an electrifying gesture of fluttering futility, but as *stage direction* it is novelistic. Not only does it not denote anything actable, it also violates the objectivity that is the condition for the playwright's craft: the tacit agreement between him and us that for the duration of the make-believe he does not exist at all, that the characters can be known only by what they reveal of themselves in speech and action. The play shows and tells itself; the characters speak for themselves.

The most elementary mistake a critic of drama can make is to confuse playwright and character. Neither Marat nor Sade can be taken to speak for the playwright in Weiss's play. To assume that Hamlet's advice to the players on the art of acting represents Shakespeare's own thoughts on his craft is, however attractive and plausible an assumption, irrelevant to an understanding of either Prince or play. And it is at least arguable that LeRoi Jones turns from drama to non-dramatic polemics when he puts what could be taken as the thesis of his whole play into Clay's long monologue near the end of *Dutchman.*

The theatricalist devices which certain plays (both old and new) deliberately use to distance the spectator from what happens on stage, reminding him that what he experiences is "only" theater, are themselves part of the dramatic spectacle. They should not be separated from the rest of the play as devices for editorial commentary by the playwright. The god Ra's Prologue in Shaw's *Cæsar and Cleopatra* and the narrative frame of Brecht's *The Caucasian Chalk Circle* sophisticate the stage-audience relationship, but Shaw's god and Brecht's Singer are just as much "characters" within the playwright's imaginative artifact of drama as are Hamlet and Hjalmar Ekdal within their formally simpler worlds. Even the play that by design expresses the playwright's inmost self or features a "playwright" (acted, it may be, by the playwright himself) as mouthpiece or commentator, who speaks directly to the audience on the significance of the "inner" play he shows us — can reach us only as objective stage reality, a dynamic spectacle of speakers of parts. Either the framing figure is simply a prologue-epilogue, in which case he is no integral part of the play, or he *is* part of the play, in which case he has exactly the same formal status as Shaw's Egyptian god and Brecht's Caucasian Singer. As a framing device he may make it necessary for us to distinguish between the play's "outer" and its "inner" action, but not to distinguish between drama and non-drama. The objectivity of drama is inviolate. Whatever he may be in his private life, the dramatist is, by definition, a man of multiple voice and vision. He has, in Keats's words, "as much delight in conceiving an Iago as an Imogen. What shocks the virtuous philosopher delights the chameleon poet." We can only tentatively infer his own convictions — if we can do so at all — from the values implicit in the total, integrated set of images, verbal and non-verbal, that constitutes "the world" on stage. And we are willing to accept that world as valid and relevant only if it offers itself, freely and directly, as an object for our interpretation and evaluation. Drama is suspended tension, open options, a dialectic in moving equilibrium.

Plays and movies based on novels prove that there is much that is performable in the other genres of literature as well. The art of poet and novelist, however, extends beyond dialogue and description of stageables. The lyric poet explores his own inner world of feeling and sensation, a world different in kind from the externalized world of drama. But even narrative, whether in prose or verse, is, despite an area of possible overlap, different from drama. A novelist or an epic poet can suspend action indefinitely, do without dialogue and physical setting and event altogether ("epics of the mind"), and discourse abstractly on any number of subjects in slow or quick sequence. He can judge and analyze his characters in authorial comment, enter at will into their hearts and souls by godlike ubiquity and omniscience, and just as easily exit back into straight narrative of external events. And if he never makes use of any of these novelistic freedoms, he is, in effect, a playwright, whether he calls his work a play or not.

Actually, this is a stricter definition of drama than many plays allow. Bernard Shaw, for example, often violates dramatic objectivity in stage directions that interpret his characters for us. Perhaps the most flagrant example is the ending of *Candida*. When the heroine has sent her would-be lover, a young poet, "into the night" and turns to her husband, Shaw tells us, "They embrace. But they do not know the secret in the poet's heart." The former of these two sentences is stageable, a genuine stage direction. But no theatrical ingenuity can stage the latter — except as words flashed on a screen, like the subtitles of old silent movies. The point is not that Shaw's plays occasionally include bits of novels; we are concerned here with isolating a quality that all plays have in common, the quality that makes them, distinctly, *drama*. Performability is that quality. The spectator is in the theater to watch and listen. Shaw's comments do not exist for him, except insofar as they may have been translated into the language of the theater: sights and sounds the audience can perceive through the senses. A reader of *Candida* will, of course, make Shaw's last sentence part of his experience of the play, and an important part, too. But that does not make it a sentence of drama. The distinction is, if one likes, "academic," "purely theoretical." It certainly does not turn *Candida* into something other than a play. But to abandon it is to abandon an effort to make a general distinction between drama and other forms of literature. We *want* to be "theoretical" at this point; we are trying to suggest the outlines of a theory of drama.

This is not to exclude from the genre of drama works that cannot, for technical reasons, be staged (or staged in their entirety) in any existing theater or that, if staged, would overtax the patience and subtlety of an audience. Not only are such pragmatic criteria obviously relative; there is also a sense in which dramatic poems like *Samson Agonistes, Prometheus Unbound,* and *Peer Gynt,* though not intended for the stage and in some respects unperformable (if only, perhaps, by being bad box office), are completely dramatic. That is, their form is a system of speaking parts developing a coherent action. Whatever abstracts their total meaning includes are expressed or implied in speech, and speech is performable by impersonators of the fictitious speakers.

The mode of drama is the objectivity of the performable. Movement, directness, concreteness are its characteristics. The dramatic experience, whether in the theater or over a printed page, is one of urgent immediacy, of watching and listening to human destinies in the making, here and now, which the novelist or the poet can evoke only by being, precisely, dramatic.

## DRAMA AND THE READER

From such a definition of drama it follows that in a skillful and successful reading of a play the mind is being filled with a sequence of vivid and relevant images, called up by speeches and stage directions. The reader translates everything performable into concretes that participate in the total, complex image of words, physical movement, and scene that makes up the drama being enacted in the infinitely resourceful and adaptable stage of his mind. Whatever is not performable, or whatever he cannot conceive of as being performable, he will also incorporate into his inclusive reading experience, though not, strictly speaking, as *drama.*

Basic to any kind of meaningful response to literature is understanding of the author's words in context and of the underlying conditions for action in the imagined world. "Understanding" depends on more than conscientious use of footnotes and dictionary; it entails a total response: intellectual, emotional, sensory. And though all readers cannot respond equally well, they can all make the effort to engage more than the top of their minds and the shallows of their souls. Generally, in the case of plays from ages and cultures different from our own, *some* awareness of cultural background will be imperative, and *more* desirable, but the line between some and more is hard to draw in given cases. For some readers, at least, certain plays will create their own climate of understanding.

Perhaps the ideal performance of the play, the standard by which both a theatrical production and a reading of it should be judged, will be thought of as the performance the playwright himself envisioned for his play. But this is neither a practicable nor even a really reasonable formula. There are playwrights who have left no record as to how they thought their plays should be produced, or whose ideas are too vague or incomplete to be of much help, or who refuse to answer when asked. And even if we assume that the original staging realized the playwright's ideal, for most older plays we can reconstruct it only by means of more or less inferential evidence, either within the play itself or supplied by research. Nor are the playwright's views, when available, necessarily more valid than someone else's — just as composers are not necessarily the best performers of their own works or even the best critics of the performance of their works by others. Intention is not accomplishment.

There is more force to the argument that a meaningful reading of a play requires knowledge of the kind of theater for which it was written. To read Sophocles or Shakespeare, the argument goes, we must know something about Greek and Elizabethan stagecraft, see productions that try to reproduce the contemporary performance, see models or pictures or diagrams of the playhouses, or at the very least read descriptions of them.

It is certainly true that the more knowledge the reader has of the culture — including the theatrical culture — reflected in what he reads, the more significant and enjoyable his reading will be. And the impossibility of ever knowing everything about a play and the fact that knowledge alone is insufficient for recreating the sense impressions, beliefs, attitudes, and moods of a bygone audience cannot invalidate the efforts of historians of drama and theater to know as much as possible. Though each culture, each age, each reader, even the same reader at different times, reads a literary work differently, knowledge of what can be factually known about it and its times is a protection against an anarchic subjectivity of interpretation that could eventually destroy its continuum of identity. This is part of the justification of scholarship.

But though knowledge of theatrical conditions, past or present, can discipline and enrich one's experience of a play, and though such knowledge is valuable for its own sake, it is still not a precondition for the dramatic imagination itself. The images that arise in the mind during the reading of drama can be translated into stage actualities, but they are not images of such actualities. The reader does not ordinarily imagine a staged scene but its real life counterpart — not a stage castle, crypt, or kitchen, but the real thing — Hamlet, not actor A or actor B impersonating Hamlet. The exceptions are the director, designer, or actor who read with a projected performance in mind and the reader — and he is the one who concerns us — who comes to his reading of the play fresh from an impressive performance of it. His reading experience will no doubt be more vivid than it otherwise would have been, but it will also be more limited. His imagination will be channeled by his memory of the hundreds of big and little details of voice and mimicry, movement and set, costume and light, that together make up any particular actualization of the ideal abstract the play is. Any one performance, however brilliant, is bound to be different from — both more and less than — the literary work that occasioned it, forever detached as the latter is from the impermanent particulars of the real. A good production may help a reader imagine what he found unimaginable as he read the play, or it may cool and contain an imagination that catches fire too easily, but a reader to whom a play is nothing but a blueprint for an evening in the theater has abdicated his rights as reader. It is only because most people *can* stage a play in their imagination, alive with the sights and sounds of reality, that drama is literature at all — that is, capable of being experienced through reading. The theater is the home of drama, and drama may be the occasion for theater, but all theater is not drama, nor is the drama lost without the theater.

## DRAMATIC CONVENTIONS

Understanding the underlying condition for action in the imagined world involves understanding dramatic conventions. These are the conditions which playwright and audience between them have implicitly (whether they are conscious of it or not) agreed to accept as reality in the play. In the sense that what is called for is a willingness to take the world of imagination as reality for the time being, acceptance of conventions enters into any kind of successful experience of figurative (representational, non-abstract) art. But because the theater makes tangible the forms of the make-believe, conventions operate with particular force in the experience of drama — most insistently in the theater, but also in reading. There is a widespread, though tacit and largely uninspected, assumption that drama is the most referential of the literary genres (*i.e.,* that it corresponds most closely to some real world of sensory phenomena) and the least purely expressive (*i.e.,* lyrical). For this the sensory immediacy of the performable must be responsible. And when an audience hesitates to accept a play that flouts all pretense to mirror an objective world of things and facts or that makes use of unfamiliar conventions, some form of the referential fallacy in the public concept of drama is likely to be involved. Among the dramatists represented in this collection, Sophocles, Shakespeare, and Ibsen all write plays that purport to record reality (though the nature of the realities they record differs), while the anonymous author of *Everyman,* Strindberg, Brecht, and Weiss exploit a convention by which a phase in the flux of phenomenal experience is transfixed and "seen" as pattern-with-meaning. This is, very roughly, the distinction between the "realistic" and the "expressionistic" conventions of drama.

Chorus, soliloquy, and aside are examples of conventions, mainly of older drama. They were no more everyday realities then than they are now, but as artistic devices they were given status as reality because they satisfied needs for dramatic expression without going beyond what the contemporary public was willing to accept as make-believe. Some conventions may have been means to achieve certain kinds of communication under the technically limiting conditions of older theater. For example, such "facts" of the imagined world as location and time of day, which in the modern theater can be established by sets and electric lights, were on the Elizabethan stage communicated by the dialogue itself. Hence the rather remarkable number of Shakespearean characters who mention time and place in their speeches, particularly in the opening of scenes (see, for example, Barnardo's and Francisco's opening speeches in Hamlet, I, 1, 1–13). To the extent that such information is for the benefit of the audience rather than for the listeners on stage, the device is conventional: a breach of reality for the sake of establishing, economically and often beautifully, "reality" within the play.

Conventions vary with time and place. Yesterday's conventions are today's absurdities and tomorrow's brilliant innovations. No play is without them. In the ceremonial tradition of drama (Greek, Elizabethan, neoclassical tragedy), ritualistic use of language in verse and imagery and of archetypal action of aristocratic agony raises life to a plane of greater dignity, significance, intensity, and eloquence than that of ordinary life lived on naturalistic terms (classical comedy). In the illusionistic tradition (some forms of older comedy, modern dramatic realism like Ibsen's and Chekhov's), convention ignores the theatrical situation and assumes the commonplace surface of stage life to be that of actuality. In the expressionistic tradition (allegorical and symbolic drama, some of Strindberg's and O'Neill's plays, the theatricalism of Brecht, Pirandello, and Weiss, aspects of contemporary absurd theater), scenic abstractionism and stylization, dream sequences of realistic or distorted fragments of reality, montage techniques, and freedom of time and place are conventional means to the end of insinuating the reality of the single, subjective consciousness.

The actor who uses the Stanislavsky "method" to create a role from within, seeking to lose his real-life, off-stage personality in that of the human being he is projecting – "to be" rather than "to act" – is engaged in an enterprise of illusionistic theater. The Brechtian actor who deliberately plays up his double function as both impersonator and professional mimic or (in Brecht's word) "demonstrator" of a fictitious personality is practicing non-illusionistic theater, what, in this book, we shall refer to as "theatricalism," i.e., the theater's frank acknowledgement of itself as a place for the production of artifact. Actually, of course, the Stanislavsky way of acting is no less artificial, no more natural, than the Brechtian. All art is, quite properly, "artificial," that is, literally, "made by art" as conscious craft. The two acting methods differ only in the kind of effect they seek to create and in the conventions by which they create that effect.

Because our popular theater of stage, film, and television is still very largely the heir of the realist tradition of the late nineteenth century, the modern reader or playgoer may at first find older drama and contemporary avant-garde experiments "odd," "unrealistic," "obscure." The distance between his own ordinary language and Elizabethan blank-verse rhetoric or the non-communication of absurdist dialogue may frustrate and alienate him, and he is not likely to be put at ease by the proposition that the spectacle has been put on not for its reality but for its art. Taking the conventions of realism for granted, he may fail to see that they *are* conventions. Or if he is sophisticated enough to recognize them for what they are, he may still feel they are the only "natural" conventions. But if he objects to the artificiality of the neoclassical convention of the three unities (which demanded that the action of the play be confined to a single plot, a single place, and a single day), he ought also to object to the convention of today's film and television that presents human beings as disembodied heads in facial close-ups and to the three-walled rooms of most post-Renaissance theater. And there is no reason to believe that playgoers of the past would have found a modern theater, with its artificially lighted box peeked into by a supposedly nonexistent audience, any less unnatural than we presume to find the choric rituals and public unburdenings of soul in soliloquy in their plays. If the naive or stubbornly literal-minded person is bothered by the hero's apparent deafness to the villain's stage whisper, by the scarcity of actors on stage during Shakespeare's battle scenes, or by the free and flexible treatment of time and place in a contemporary play like *The Caucasian Chalk Circle,* he simply fails to understand or accept dramatic convention.

## CHARACTER, PLOT, ACTION, CONFLICT

Like most serious writing, drama represents man's use of words to make sense out of the myriad perplexities that befall him. The dramatist sees the world not primarily as shapes and colors and feelings, or as an object for religious or philosophical or scientific contemplation, or as a market, or as a reluctant machine that challenges his skill and ingenuity to make it run better. He sees it rather as an arena for human action manifested in speech. The arena may be expansive and crowded, as in such panoramic plays as *Hamlet, Cæsar and Cleopatra,* and *The Caucasian Chalk Circle,* or it may be small, close, and sparsely populated, as in such focused plays as *Tartuffe, Riders to the Sea,* and *Who's Afraid of Virginia Woolf?* The speech may be the heightened utterance of verse or everyday, colloquial prose. Or a single play, such as *Hamlet,* may employ both media. In Shakespeare's *Othello,* the shifts from one to the other extend the antithesis between Iago's vulgarity and rationalism ("prose") and Othello's dignity and passion ("poetry") beyond characterization and overt action. In *The Caucasian Chalk Circle,* the shifts between realistic prose dialogue, on the one hand, and the songs and the Singer's free-verse chants, on the other, are a dramatic image that serves to remind us that the action of the play proceeds on two levels.

The newcomer to the reading of drama may at first find confusing the conversations of unknowns who are discovered in the embroilments of an existence about which he knows nothing. He may miss preliminary explanations, the novelist's guiding hand. And if he has had experience with performed drama, he may also miss the aid to understanding provided by the presences and the voices of actors and by the physical spectacle in which they appear. That he can be guided by stage directions and ponder the dialogue at his leisure he may feel to be poor compensation for the absence of the sights and sounds of performance.

What the characters say and do begins to make sense only as we learn more about them, but we learn more about them only by what they say and do. Gradually they become more than a list of names. They reveal their antecedents and their present situations, their motives and purposes, they assume plot identity and "character." We learn to respond to the revealing remark or gesture, to listen to the eloquence of their silence, to sense their continuous pressure on the plot. Among them, they define and develop the dramatic action.

Dramatic action is neither physical activity nor simply the sum of everything that happens on stage: conversation, eating, people running up and down staircases, laughter, doors closing, lights going on and off. These are part of the action, but in the traditional definition action itself is a more abstract and comprehensive concept.

In the *Poetics,* Aristotle (384–322 B.C.), the first and still the single most important theorist of drama, said that all poetry is an "imitation [*mimesis*] of men in action" and that drama differs from other kinds of poetry (i.e., imaginative literature) by its manner of imitation. Unlike the epic poet, the dramatist does not narrate a human action but "presents all his characters as living and moving before us." Drama for Aristotle, then, is a stageable story. Aristotle's "imitation" has always been a controversial concept, but the full context of the *Poetics* (in which it is the first term discussed) makes it clear that he used it to mean something different from just a mindless replica of actual human behavior. "Imitation" is not a mere slice of life. Rather, as applied to drama, it seems to denote a selection of images or representations of human actuality so arranged as to present a coherent course of events, an "action" (*praxis*) that illuminates and verifies the changeless physical, psychological, moral, and metaphysical laws – the principles of "Nature" in the inclusive sense – by which and under which men manifest their humanity, alone or in interaction with others. Drama, like other forms of literature, has a didactic function: it teaches men to orient themselves in reality. That something close to this was what Aristotle meant by dramatic "imitation" is supported by the probability that he wrote the *Poetics* in vindication of poetry against Plato's charge (mainly in *The Republic*) that its excitation of the imagination was a threat to the stability of the state and that its fictions had inferior status as images of reality.

A further set of definitions may be useful at this point. A play is a patterning of language, character, event, and spectacle, each element a function of the other three. When the elements are mutually appropriate, the play observes dramatic *decorum*. Speech should be suited to the character and circumstance of the speaker, style and tone should be proper to the level of the action ("high" in tragedy, "middle" or "low" in comedy), and manners should be made to accord with period and place and the characters' social class. The plot of the play is the particular sequence of events that gives it the coherence and movement toward a given end that could not inhere in a random aggregate of happenings. Plot is the way the playwright has chosen to tell his story, the detailed arrangement of incidents for maximum meaning or beauty or suspense. The action of the play is both the summation of the plot and the abstraction of its meaning, the distillation of the play's totality in a single phrase. "To give God an account of one's life" defines the action of *Everyman,* "to purge the rotten state of Denmark" that of *Hamlet,* "to control one's clique for power and pleasure" that of *The Man of Mode,* "to learn to live with death at sea" that of *Riders to the Sea,* and "to reenact the French Revolution" that of *Marat/Sade*. The advantage, as Francis Fergusson has pointed out, of defining dramatic action in infinitive phrases is that they call attention to purpose as the motor force of action. When we perceive action in this way we exercise what Fergusson calls our "histrionic sensibility": we respond to what happens on stage as to the expression of "the changing life of the psyche," the teleology of the self interacting with its environment.

The nature and function of plot differ in different plays. It may be a strong, causal story line which we find suspenseful and convincing because of constant interaction between character and event. The nature of Tartuffe's scheming against Orgon and his family is determined by his character and by his assessment of Orgon's character, but the events of the action, which follow the logic of the Tartuffe-Orgon relationship, keep revealing the character of schemer and victims alike, until all the characters in the play seem defined by the events. Successful plot manipulation makes a character's behavior seem surprising and inevitable at the same time. When Emperor Jones saunters out of his palace at the end of the first scene of O'Neill's play, the only reason to think that he will not succeed in escaping from his island empire is that we already guess that the miscarriage of his well-laid plans is going to be the ironic point of the play. But we are willing to accept the final irony only if the intervening plot makes his defeat seem plausibly in character. Given the island setting, the jungle journey is a plausible plot element; and given Jones's character, the jungle darkness is plausible both as setting for and cause of the regressive fantasies that accomplish his psychological disintegration.

In other plays plot is less a matter of dramatized narrative than of conveying a vivid sense of human presence. Molière in *The Misanthrope* and Chekhov in *The Three Sisters* do not base their dramas on the convenient convention that life runs in plots. They seek rather to illuminate a certain kind of human response to experience by means of juxtaposed scenes that subtly modify one another by discordant or mutually ironic styles, tones, and content. Molière takes Alceste through his paces, by turns admirable, ridiculous, and ominous, in an exposure of misanthropy in its several facets. Here plot is the display of a master passion in the round. *The Three Sisters* poses moments of emotional stasis against a background of moving time. The apparently arbitrary intermittence of the static moments and our simultaneous awareness of the resistless flow of time – and the contrast between them – constitute Chekhov's plot, in the sense that they give shape and point to the string of individual happenings. The "persecution and assassination of Jean-Paul Marat" provides Weiss's play with a kind of skeletal plot structure, but the structure is there only to be constantly fractured – by the deliberate stylization of the staged reenactment, by spontaneous, mad frenzy, and by digressive discussions and songs. The subversion of the plot turns the whole noisy, frantic spectacle into a chaos of conflicts, a symbol of the insanity of the historical process.

In traditional anatomies of drama, plot is usually divided into four parts: (1) the *exposition,* which introduces the characters, gives essential information about their pre-play background, sets the plot in motion, and informs us about important off-stage events; (2) the *complication,* usually the bulk of the play, interweaving the characters' shifting fortunes and including the *climax,* a point of tension and the critical juncture at which a decision or an event irretrievably determines the outcome; (3) the *reversal,* or peripety, the point at which the complication culminates in the resolution of the plot: the protagonist's fortune changing from good to bad (the *catastrophe* in tragedy) or from bad to good (comedy); and (4) the *denouement,* or unraveling, which presents the consequences of the reversal, ties up loose ends, and allows the audience time to regain emotional equilibrium. Exposition and complication are likely to be the longest phases of the dramatic progress, the denouement is normally shorter, and the reversal may be marked by a single speech or event that occurs, most often, quite late in the play.

The plays in which the four parts of the plot are neatly distinct and laid end to end are few and not likely to be of the highest order. Good plots are complex, organic structures, whose parts blend into one another, overlapping and alternating. Though the exposition in *Hamlet* is largely confined to Act I (the talk among the watchers for the Ghost, King Claudius's speech from the throne, Hamlet's soliloquy, the Ghost's revelation of the murder), there are expository details in later scenes as well, *e.g.,* Claudius's confession of guilt in an aside and Hamlet's account to Horatio about his adventures at sea. In *The Caucasian Chalk Circle* the rebellion scenes in the beginning of the play are expository relative to the story of Grusha and the child, but so are the flashback scenes of Azdak's judgeship, which follow the completion of the story of Grusha's journey. In *Tartuffe* and *Riders to the Sea,* important expository passages appear late in the plays. In *Oedipus Rex, The Wild Duck,* and *Who's Afraid of Virginia Woolf?,* fragments of explanation of past events responsible for the present crisis keep appearing almost throughout. As a result, all three plays seem retrospective in structure: on stage we see, not the past itself, but only the consequences of the presumably buried past rushing in to overwhelm the present. They are "fifth-act plays," dramas of ripe condition. To separate exposition from complication in such plays is not only difficult but senseless: exposition *is* complication. In fact, the traditional paradigm of formal plot analysis often seems to apply only partly, or insignificantly, or not at all, to individual plays in the heterogeneity and generic confusion of modern drama. To a contemporary, at least, the story of modern drama is to a very large extent the story of revolt and experimentation superseding a sense of formal tradition. Nothing precedes the complication in *Dutchman* and hardly anything in *The Ghost Sonata.* How do we distinguish climax from reversal in *The Caucasian Chalk Circle,* and how does traditional analysis deal with its play-within-a-play form? Does it apply at all to the apparently arbitrary selection of trivial social moments in *The Three Sisters* or to the enormously complicated time scheme and actor-audience relationships in *Marat/Sade*? We do not conclude that the traditional terms are useless but that they cannot be used indiscriminately or with equal relevance for all plays. Our lexicon of criticism is constantly being supplemented in response to new modes of literary expression. We may illustrate the use of the traditional terms in an analysis of the plot structure of a traditional play.

The *story* of *Oedipus Rex* is the entire chronicle of the fulfillment of the prophecy from the time it was first announced to Laïos and Iocaste until the moment when Oedipus exits, blind and banished. Most of the chronicle is not staged, for the play is concerned only with the fruition of the past in Oedipus's present, but the past is the subject of most of the dialogue. The *plot* is the tight, causal chain of events that gradually reveals the meaning of the past. The *action* is the quest for Laïos's murderer, the cause of the blight on Thebes. The *exposition,* as we noted above, can be said to continue right up to the *reversal:* Oedipus's fortune changes when he realizes that he, the seeker, is the man sought. In other words, it is because the revelation of the past – the function of exposition – fills the interval between Oedipus's first statement of purpose and the ironic accomplishment of it in the reversal, that we say that exposition and *complication* coincide in this play. The *climax* comes at the last moment at which Oedipus could still avoid the fatal self-discovery, the moment when in his pride of good fortune and anticipated achievement he refuses to listen to Iocaste's warning not to inquire further into his parentage. Beyond that point (the end of Scene III), his movement toward enlightenment is irreversible. The *denouement* is what follows Oedipus's discovery of his identity: the reports of Iocaste's suicide and of Oedipus's blinding himself, the dialogue between Oedipus and the Chorus, Oedipus's soliloquy, Creon's taking charge, the banishment of Oedipus, and the final choric statement of the moral of the play.

Plot generates and releases suspense, the feeling in the audience that keeps it wondering what happens next. One characteristic of great drama is that suspense survives knowledge of "how things come out," because our absorbed wait for what is going to happen concerns the outcome less than it concerns the happenings themselves and the patterns we see them forming. We may know exactly what happens in Sophocles's Theban plays and still attend, fascinated and moved, to every small step in Oedipus's movement toward tragic recognition in *Oedipus Rex* and toward apotheosis in *Oedipus at Colonus* and to the two diverging movements in *Antigone:* Antigone's to the triumph of deliberate martyrdom, and Creon's to humiliation, loss, and acceptance of guilt. In fact, superior plays have a way of seeming better in later readings. That is the reason we may rather want to see still another stage or screen production of *Hamlet* than a brand new play. What we lose in mere thrill we gain in understanding and enjoyment through our intimacy with the characters and our knowledge of events to come. Familiarity also increases our appreciation and enjoyment of dramaturgy: the exercise of the playwright's craft, the dexterous manipulation of plot and character in the integrated structure of successful dramatic action. As the football fan goes to the game not just to learn who wins and by what score but to enjoy the game being played and the skill of coach and players, so the lover of drama seeks vicarious experience of significant action in artistic form, and not just information about a result. The ideal spectator attends both kinds of play in a mood of disinterested fascination.

Conflict is the element in plot that creates suspense. It is what the plot is about. In *Oedipus Rex* the conflict may be variously defined. Most simply and obviously it is one between man and god (or fate), between Oedipus's commitment to the values of rationality and worldly duty and the mysterious, transcendent dimension in human existence. Or we may sense the conflict chiefly as irony: the distance between what Oedipus *thinks* his purpose – to purge the city – will accomplish for him personally ("By avenging the murdered king I protect myself") and what it *does* accomplish. To Oedipus himself, up until the moment when the final piece of the puzzle falls into place, the conflict appears as one between his intent and the human and circumstantial obstacles in its way.

Conflict may be multiple, a collection of variants of a many-sided subject, each presenting it in a new view, and all covered by a wider definition of the play's conflict. In Shakespeare's *King Lear* the main plot about Lear and his daughters and the subplot of Gloucester and his sons allow Shakespeare a fuller treatment of the theme of filial ingratitude than either plot alone would have allowed him, and the doubleness of the plot suggests the pervasiveness of the evil. In *Cæsar and Cleopatra* there is no subplot in this sense, but the conflicts of Rome against Egypt and of Cæsar against Pothinus are in the end seen to be, respectively, military and political variants of the moral conflict between Cæsar and Cleopatra and of the still more comprehensive conflict between saint and sinner, god and man, promoter and frustrater of the Life Force. In Chekhov, the situations of the several characters who fail in different ways to fulfil themselves, to achieve happiness, to establish human contact, and to take decisive action cohere in a single image of frustration, the clash of hope with reality. Plot unity is obviously not the same kind of thing in all plays. Contrasting the rambling diffuseness of small events in *The Three Sisters* with the closely woven plots of *Oedipus Rex, Tartuffe,* and *The Wild Duck* or with the complicated intrigues for sex and money in comedies of manners like Etherege's *The Man of Mode,* Congreve's *The Way of the World,* and Sheridan's *School for Scandal,* suggests the range in kinds and patterns of conflict.

Conflict is opposition of forces, one of which is likely to be a human will that is heroically uncompromising and therefore doomed in tragedy and abortive or reformable in comedy. Man against god, man against nature (a mountain, the sea, hunger), man against society, man against man, and man against himself represent (in rough terms) the five main kinds of conflict. Conflict may be as simple as it is in a fairy tale (bad queen against good princess, bad guy against good sheriff). It may be morally unequivocal as in *Tartuffe* and *The Caucasian Chalk Circle* or ambiguous as in *Oedipus Rex* and *The Man of Mode.* It may be elemental as in *Riders to the Sea,* political as in *Cæsar and Cleopatra,* or psychological as in *The Emperor Jones.* It may be allegorical as in *Everyman,* realistic as in *The Wild Duck,* or fantastic as in *The Ghost Sonata.* It may be of world significance as in *Cæsar and Cleopatra* or trivial and banal as in *The Three Sisters.* Drama without conflict is unthinkable. For the essence of the dramatic experience is the fascination with the progress of clashing forces toward resolution: the hero's death or enlightenment, the villain's defeat; the reintegration of a threatened social order in a wedding, a reconciliation, a verdict; the revelation of the transcendent nature that shapes our lives as order and meaning or as silence and darkness.

The spoken word is the medium of drama, the objectivity of the performable its mode or manner of being, the surrender of our imaginations to that of the playwright the condition for its existence for us, but the drama itself is the action of man in conflict. This action we witness partly as safe and superior deities, enjoying the pleasure of dramatic irony at the expense of people who do not know what is happening to them; partly as sympathetic observers, commiserating with the good, relishing the downfall of the bad; and partly as fellow fools and sufferers: there, but for the grace of God, *we* strut and fret.

## TRAGEDY AND COMEDY

Defining tragedies as plays that end unhappily and comedies as plays that end happily sounds like a more simpleminded distinction than it actually is. There are, of course, perspectives in which the two coalesce in a vision of human life as simultaneously terrible and joyous, but the mixed view does not invalidate the original distinction. There are those who argue that tragicomedy prevails in modern drama because skepticism has placed the awe that is at the heart of older tragedy beyond our reach and because the enormity of modern experience has killed the spirit of older comedy. But if this were altogether so, we would hardly continue to respond as we do to the great tragedies and comedies of the past.

Our age is not the first to have felt the irreducible ambivalence in the human condition. Both tragedy and comedy are thought to have originated in rites propitiating the powers controlling the natural cycles of night and day, growth and decay, life and death. In communal enactments of myths of redemptive sacrifice and orgiastic abandon man paid tribute to the gods, but the fixed forms of his mimetic art were also symbols of his mastery of all the patterns imposed upon his life. The Dionysiac theater in ancient Athens staged tragic suffering and obscene ribaldry as parts of the same production. Homer and Dante and Cervantes and Dr. Johnson knew as well as do Beckett and Ionesco today that the tragic and the comic worlds cannot be kept apart. There are clowns in Shakespeare's tragedies and tragic implications in some of his comedies. Molière's *The Misanthrope* is as much a tragicomedy as Ibsen's *The Wild Duck* and Chekhov's *The Three Sisters* and *The Cherry Orchard.* Our sensibility is not unique. We may see ourselves as exiles from the conceptual universe in which the writing of pure tragedy and pure comedy was possible, but the distinction between them still gives shape to our sense of both drama and life. It is a division which man in all ages reaches for when he tries to purify his human essence, to isolate the components of his psyche, to find clarity and order in the murky mess of his actual experience. The old dichotomies of tragedy and comedy, suffering and joy, tears and laughter, the sublime and the ludicrous, still name the deepest perceptions he derives from contemplating his strange and various lot.

Tragedy and comedy, then, are terms that do more than classify plays. They stand for ways, not so much contrasting as complementary, of perceiving life. In tragedy, man is a paradox in a paradoxical existence. Fallible and vulnerable in his mortal finity, he is yet capable of transcendent greatness. Freely exercising his will (a passive hero is pathetic rather than tragic), he is yet the plaything of destiny. Acting on his virtue, he incurs guilt. Divided within by impulses and imperatives in conflict and beset without by other wilful selves and by his physical environment, he pits his naked strength against forces that inhibit him and enrage him and that he can neither control nor understand. Flawed by his human nature, he is incapable of compromise. He demands that an imperfect world conform to his notions of right and good, and he is defeated because discord, injustice, pain, and moral evil are the world's warp and woof. The final paradox is man in his tragic vision saying, "I do not believe in the invincibility of evil but in the inevitability of defeat."

Why this is so is the question all tragedy asks and no tragedy answers. Plays that do answer, in vindication of the universe against man's ceaseless questioning, are moving away from tragedy proper toward religious drama. Aeschylus's *Agamemnon* is more tragic than his *Eumenides,* and *Hamlet* is more tragic than *Everyman.* Milton's *Samson Agonistes* is in form a perfect Greek tragedy, but as a "Christian tragedy" it is, perhaps, a contradiction in terms.

But in the absoluteness of his commitment, the tragic hero triumphs in the very inevitability of his defeat. Foolishly, pitifully, magnificently pressing his human potential beyond its limits, he asserts man's significance and dignity in the face of the unanswering unknown; tragic man matters. The hero's high social rank in traditional tragedy is not a sign of aristocratic prejudice but both a symbol of his superior human quality and a way of signifying that what happens to him affects others than himself. The metaphor of rank points up the grim irony that the very best specimens of mankind suffer most from the irremediableness of the human condition. Aristotle had both the moral and the social sense in mind when he distinguished tragedy from comedy by saying that "Comedy aims at representing men as worse, Tragedy as better, than in actual life." There is painful irony in this, too: in the implication that "goodness" meets disaster and "badness" survives and succeeds.

In the abstract (making allowance for intermediary and mixed types), tragedies are of two main kinds. One kind affirms the meaning and justice of the world order and gives compensation for the final calamity by the Aeschylean formula of "wisdom through suffering." In a scene of *anagnorisis* (recognition), the hero (and the spectator) understands what is happening to him and that he is responsible for it, and he and we accept his fate. In the worldly catastrophe there is an enlightenment of the spirit. If the ways of the gods are inscrutable and severe, their manifestations in human life testify to the existence of eternal laws and to man's capacity to suffer greatly and to learn from his suffering. We leave the play solemn but not depressed. This is tragedy of *catharsis:* purged of rebelliousness, fear, and self-pity, we submit to things as they mysteriously and immutably are. *Oedipus Rex* is one example, *Riders to the Sea* another.

In the other kind of tragedy, the dramatization of human suffering poses questions that challenge the order and justice of things. Why is there evil in the world? Why do the innocent suffer? Why does fineness of human qualities bring disaster? Why should we have to submit to laws that are capricious, indifferent, blindly mechanical, or malicious? We may call this kind existential or Promethean tragedy (from the demigod Prometheus in ancient myth, man's benefactor and champion who stole fire from the gods and gave it to man, thereby incurring Jove's wrath and punishment). It is tragedy that recognizes man's helplessness but asserts his dignity by protesting against it. Aeschylus's *Libation Bearers,* Euripides's *Bacchae* and *Medea,* Shakespeare's *Hamlet, Othello,* and *King Lear,* and Racine's *Phaedra* and *Berenice* are in some respects tragedies of this type. For more clear-cut examples of existential discontent in drama, we go — significantly, perhaps — to modern plays: Giraudoux's *Caligula,* Sartre's *The Flies,* Beckett's *Waiting for Godot* and *Endgame,* Weiss's *Marat/Sade,* and Stoppard's *Rosenkrantz and Guildenstern Are Dead.* In all of these, either the single tragic hero or the dialectic thrust of the whole play defies the arbitrary order in which evil and pain are undeserved or inflicted in excess of man's transgressions. The writer of Promethean tragedy withholds, on behalf of embattled mankind, resignation to the cruel discrepancy between intrinsic virtue and extrinsic evil. That he knows his refusal is absurd in its futility only stiffens his stance.

The domain of tragedy is metaphysics: solitary, unaccommodated, questing man confronting the contradictoriness and the ultimate mysteries of his being and circumstance. The domain of comedy is the physical and the social: man's triumphs and tribulations as gregarious animal. "The world," said Horace Walpole in the eighteenth century, "is a comedy to those that think, a tragedy to those that feel." He did not mean that tragedy is mindless and that comedy has no emotional appeal. He meant that the issues raised by tragedy cannot be resolved by rational analysis but relate to our awareness of our precarious position in a dark existence of uncertain meaning and purpose, in which selves may shatter in the division between passion and reason. And he meant that comedy addresses itself to our critical faculties, sharpening our perception of the ludicrous discrepancy between what man is and what he tries or pretends to be. The eccentric character, who foolishly and stubbornly deviates from sane and viable values — good nature, flexibility, moderation, social intelligence, love of others — and thereby opposes himself to the flow of life in all its varied fecundity, is a common figure in all comedy, not just in comedy of humors, where he is central. Comic laughter, said Henri Bergson, the French philosopher, follows our perception of "something mechanical encrusted upon the living": the incongruous spectacle of a human being reducing himself to a rigid automaton. Orgon in *Tartuffe* and Sir Fopling Flutter in *The Man of Mode* are good examples.

The spirit of comedy is the spirit that will tolerate everything except intolerance. The killjoy Malvolio in Shakespeare's *Twelfth Night* and Alceste, the man of uncompromising honesty, in Molière's *The Misanthrope* are its enemies. At the end, both alienate themselves from the social group. Comedy shows us the ridiculous posturings of the silly and the selfish, the vicious and the vain. It laughs folly and vice out of countenance. Its laughter is thoughtful but good-natured. It is capacious enough to welcome and absorb into its world the fool made wise and the sinner reformed. Where its laughter becomes shrill or bitter or sardonic, the comedy is about to turn into satire, for satire is inspired by righteous indignation rather than by tolerant amusement. Satire ridicules and contemns in order to expose and reform corruption. Comedy, too, recognizes imperfection but accepts it and exhibits it for our thoughtful amusement, reminding us of the vices and follies which we all share. Comedy, above everything, asserts the richness of human life, valuing food, drink, and sex no less than virtue and sentiment, courage and kindness, wit and fancy.

If satire marks one end of the comic spectrum, the festive marks the other. Satiric comedy tends toward "problem" comedy or tragicomedy in its vision of human depravity. Shakespeare's *Measure for Measure* and *Troilus and Cressida,* Ben Jonson's *The Alchemist* and *Volpone* and Molière's *Tartuffe* and *The Misanthrope* are on the very edge of comedy in this sense. Pure festive comedy, such as Shakespeare's *As You Like It,* tends toward romance in its vision of a redeemed world of love, innocence, and justice. Most comedies fall somewhere between the two poles. In *Tartuffe,* for example, the satire of Orgon, the tyrannical father foolishly gulled by Tartuffe, recedes when he recognizes his error at the end and bestows his grateful blessing on Valère's and Mariane's romance.

In its defeat of evil, repudiation of folly, and reconciliation of young love with old social authority, *Tartuffe* has an ending typical of comedy. The archetypal comic action harmonizes the sexual instinct with stable social norms. The plot shows young love overcoming obstacles, most often represented by one or more blocking characters: a parent figure (commonly, like Old Bellair in *The Man of Mode,* a father who is his son's rival in love), a vindictive mistress, an evil schemer. At the end, the authority figure relents and blesses the young couple, the mistress is cast out from the festive group or reconciled to it, the schemer is exposed and punished or forgiven. The lovers' faithful fortitude triumphs over lechery, deception, and greed; and they are rewarded with their rightful inheritance of wealth and with society's sanction of their happiness in marriage.

A final ceremony, a wedding, a banquet, a dance, reintegrates the social group and signifies general reconciliation, benevolence, and harmony. A society in bondage to the old and inflexible and unnatural regroups itself around the young couple, who represent freedom and flexibility and whose marriage promises the continuation of the life cycle. At the end of *The Man of Mode,* the rake Dorimant surrenders his liberty to his love for Harriet, and Old Bellair good-humoredly reconciles himself to the new and "right" order of things by calling for the fiddlers and a dance to celebrate the double triumph of young romance. In comedy, vice and folly are psychological and social rather than metaphysical realities, and the adaptive social structure survives the threat they have posed to the ongoing joy of human life. Like tragedy, comedy says that man endures.*

## ANATOMY OF A SCENE

A good plot does not just come to a stop; it concludes. The ending of Etherege's *The Man of Mode* releases suspense and disposes of the characters in a manner suitable to their story, to their human qualities, and to the values they represent. Because the basic structures of the play are a coherent story and consistent characterization, a closer look at its ending can illustrate an important aspect of the dominant dramaturgy in our tradition.

A successful plot resolution in this tradition is neither wholly predictable nor wholly surprising. If we correctly anticipate every final move and

* Dramatic criticism traditionally puts melodrama and farce, with their simpler images of life, below the genres of tragedy and comedy. Characters in melodrama are easily recognizable moral types: the lustful count, the chaste maid, the pathetic parent, the exploited orphan, the mad scientist, the brave and honest apprentice, the cruel capitalist. It uses such types not for their psychology but because they lend themselves to manipulation in suspenseful and sensational plots. Such plots are not necessarily without dramatic effectiveness, but they are simplistic in their moral judgments and their facile emotional appeal to stock responses. Farce is low comedy, capitalizing on slapstick, dialogue double-takes, and contrived intrigue moving at breakneck speed. As in melodrama, characterization is shallow and stereotyped, but the emphasis is not on moral absolutes but on people reduced to puppets, hilariously victimized by broad physical action, whims of coincidence, and their own and others' silliness.

There is a place in the dramatic repertory for both melodrama and farce. Superior plays in both genres often have strong and ingenious plots. Elements of both or either can often be found in tragedy and comedy. The story of the ruin of the Ekdal family in *The Wild Duck* is embryonic melodrama, and only Hjalmar's farcical rhetoric of ready-made sentiment tempers the melodrama of Hedvig's pathetic suicide to the demands of tragicomic irony. The wholesale dying at the end of *Hamlet* is not without an aspect of melodrama. Sir Fopling Flutter in *The Man of Mode* is a farcical figure, and so, at least in some of his scenes, is Azdak in *The Caucasian Chalk Circle*. There are moments of both verbal and physical farce in *Tartuffe* and *Who's Afraid of Virginia Woolf?,* and one could do worse than to say that a major point of *Marat/Sade* is its rendering an important historical event as grotesque farce. All of which goes to show that the world of drama is subtler and more complex than a set of discrete categories of plays.

sentiment, the ending becomes anticlimactic, a sign that the playwright has mismanaged his resources. But if the play ends in a new and quite unprepared-for collocation of sudden circumstances, the surprise becomes a cheat. Some kind of decorum – an ordering principle that makes for inner unity – must be observed. Different plays observe different rules, and it is perhaps possible to conceive of a dramatic world entirely ruled by whim. But in such a play, whimsical unpredictability would itself become an absolute law, and erratic incoherence would define dramatic decorum. Generally, we are not willing to accept an ending that violates the rules under which the rest of the play has been played. *Hamlet* cannot end in an election, *The Man of Mode* in murder, *The Wild Duck* in the apparition of a ghost, or *Marat/Sade* in the cure of all the lunatics. Such endings would break the imaginative logic by which the action has proceeded. If physical laws are suddenly to be suspended, if war becomes peace and a fantasy a documentary, if the lecher turns chaste and the buffoon hero, something in the play itself, some gathering momentum of event, imagery, psyche, or theme, must persuade us of the appropriateness of such wrenching changes. We want and expect to be able to accept the fictitious reality the dramatist makes, but there are conditions for our acceptance. As we rise from the play, it must hold our minds as a single, intact image. Only if the ending preserves the integrity of the imitation of life will the whole plot in a plotted play feel "right": complete without cracks and loose ends. Even when we know that the hero of the comedy will disentangle himself from his difficulties and win the girl, we insist on being taken through all the final paces of the plot. We refuse to be satisfied until the shape of the play completes itself in stage action, our expectations of laughter dissolve in laughter, and our enjoyment proves our understanding. The playwright has to earn his plot resolution.

Manipulated intrigue, which is what is concluded in Etherege's final scene, is not the only or even the most important mode of drama. The interweaving strands of Shakespearean imagery, the interplay of ideas in Shavian dialogue, and the separate moments of poignant realism in Chekhov do not depend on intrigue for their dramatic meaning and effectiveness. There are contemporary theatricalist and absurdist plays that do without both plot and character in the traditional sense, in successful defiance of the axiom that both are indispensable to good drama. Tight intrigue would obviously work against the nihilistic philosophy implied by Weiss's multileveled spectacle of violent disjunction in *Marat/Sade.* But intrigue turns up in plays as far apart in time and convention as *Oedipus Rex, Hamlet, The Wild Duck,* and *The Caucasian Chalk Circle.* The relentless logic of interlocking revelations that leads the foundling king in *Oedipus Rex* to the final, fearful question, "Who were my parents?", the cause-and-effect sequence of moves and countermoves in Hamlet's secret combat with Claudius, the tangle of past and present relationships between the Ekdal and the Werle families in *The Wild Duck,* and the long action leading up to the moment at the end of Section III of *The Caucasian Chalk Circle* when the Ironshirts ask Grusha if little Michael is her child and she and we both know that if she says yes she will lose Simon and if she says no she will lose Michael – these are all plot structures in which tensions self-generate and draw toward release. And because superior intrigue is a piece of fine literary machinery, it lends itself perhaps more readily than other modes of drama to an illustration of drama as technique.

The release of suspense and the settling of character destinies are not, however, the only functions of the last scene in *The Man of Mode*. Etherege's play should be conceived of as an elaborate dance, a kind of graceful and difficult minuet in which a false or awkward step exposes the dancer to scorn, rather than as an intricate sequence of moves in a game of conflict. The dance is a metaphor for the exercise of the particular kind of social intelligence that is Etherege's subject. Elegance of wit and manners conceals the successful libertine's grossness of appetite and aggressive mores – *that* is the ultimate irony of the play. And because the playwright is more intent on the exhibition of an ambivalent code of social conduct than on the thrilling dynamics of suspenseful intrigue, the texture of the scene is at least as important as its structure. Sir Fopling Flutter turns up at Lady Townley's at the end not just because he is needed for the resolution of one of the plot issues, but also because his arrival, as his hostess says, will "raise the mirth of the company." The presence of the disappointed fop in the final festive tableau is not a feature of Etherege's plot but an important tonal element in his image of a society whose artificial manners and cynical hedonism his whole play simultaneously espouses and exposes.

As plot conclusion, the last scene in *The Man of Mode* resolves both the main plot about Dorimant and the Bellair subplot.* The two plots are linked by their joint share in the intrigue motif of the duped parent. Young Bellair's and Emilia's secret marriage defeats Old Bellair's and Lady Woodvill's planned match of his son with her daughter and keeps Harriet available for Dorimant's further courtship. The two plots are further linked by parallel circumstances, for both parents are doubly duped: Old Bellair loses his own "sweetheart" and hoped-for bride, Emilia, to his son; and Lady Woodvill is taken in by Dorimant's false identity as "Mr. Courtage." And both at first refuse to forgive their wilful children.

Dramatic decorum dictates the ending of both plots. Plot decorum requires a happy conclusion to the Young Bellair-Emilia romance. Since they are already married, all that remains for a proper ending is the winning of Old Bellair's forgiveness and his blessings. The acerbic irony that

* The reader should turn to Act V, Scene 2 in *The Man of Mode* (p. 331) and read from the point at which Lady Townley enters "in haste" until the end of the play.

determines events in the comedy of manners requires a less conclusive, more ambivalent ending for the Dorimant plot. Its greater complexity of tone has a counterpart in its greater complexity of intrigue. There are three issues involved: Dorimant must come to some kind of settlement with his two ex-mistresses, Loveit and Bellinda; he must vindicate his reputation as witty and masterful seducer by publicly triumphing over Sir Fopling; and he must win the right to court Harriet honorably.

Before we consider the way in which Etherege achieves these various plot ends, let us look for a moment at an aspect of his skill in stagecraft. Instead of disposing of the issues one at a time, he keeps shifting his focus from one to another. The result is a kind of multiple stage action that furthers play economy, sustains several plot interests concurrently, and creates a scenic image of social bustle and mobility and of the intricacy of the characters' mutual entanglements that is central to Etherege's vision of the society he is scrutinizing.

As the concerns of one group of characters move toward resolution in audible forestage dialogue, those of another group proceed in conversational pantomime in the rear. No part of the on-stage cast remains idle, and groups keep breaking up and reforming in new constellations. The dance pattern is inclusive, and the dancers are in constant motion. After the clandestine marriage has been disclosed and just before the entry of Loveit and Bellinda, Old Bellair tells Lady Woodvill, "A dod, Madam, you shall hear me first." Two brief scenes, one between Lady Townley and Loveit and another between Harriet and Dorimant, successively take the front of the stage before we return to the duped parent intrigue and Lady Woodvill's "You need make no more apologies, Sir" tells us what the unheard conversation between her and Old Bellair has been about. Lady Woodvill's reaction to her discovery that "Mr. Courtage" is actually Dorimant is interrupted by a scene between Dorimant and Loveit. We return to Lady Woodvill only in time to hear the last of Medley's, Lady Townley's, and Harriet's speeches in what we now realize has been their concerted effort to convince the old lady that Dorimant's character is not so black as it has been painted. The scene ends with Lady Woodvill's petulant concession to her daughter's wayward love for Dorimant: "Upon yourself light your undoing!" Again the stage focus shifts, and the placating of Lady Woodvill is not finally concluded until, vanquished once more by Dorimant's charm, she declares, near the very end of the play, "If his occasions bring him that way, I have now so good an opinion of him, he shall be welcome."* (Her speech, incidentally, is subtly ironic. It does more

* Another fine example of Etherege's mastery of multiple stage action by furthering a single plot strand alternately in forestage dialogue and backstage pantomime is in Act IV, Scene 1 (p. 307). The reader may discover for himself how Etherege handles the "business" that young Bellair and Emilia have with Medley and how a little exchange between Young Bellair and Medley later in the same act and scene (p. 313) allows us to infer what the nature of "that business" has been.

than clear the way for Dorimant's country courtship of Harriet; it also completes another instance of social gulling in the very middle of the final scene of clarification and reconciliation.)

Let us now see how Etherege in the last part of Scene 2 in Act IV resolves the four connected but separate plot issues that we distinguished above: the reconciliation of the newlyweds, Young Bellair and Emilia, to Old Bellair (which is the only remaining issue in the Bellair plot); Dorimant's settlement of his affairs with Loveit and Bellinda; his public triumph over Sir Fopling; and his acceptance by both Harriet and old Lady Woodvill as the former's suitor.

The final, climactic movement in the dance begins when Lady Townley orders the chaplain, Mr. Smirk, out of the closet just before Old Bellair's arrival for what he thinks will be his son's and Harriet's wedding. The business with the concealed chaplain raises Harriet's suspicion that it is Dorimant who has placed him in the closet, confident of the "ease" with which she will be persuaded to marry him without her mother's consent. Her suspicion is allayed as soon as she learns that the romantic conspirators (Emilia, Young Bellair, Medley, and Lady Townley) have hidden Smirk, but for a few moments, at least, the incident raises another difficulty that Dorimant has to overcome in this last scene: Harriet must become convinced that he respects her filial piety. His problem solves itself when Harriet (with Old Bellair) gets the news about the marriage, and our interest can shift to the reconciliation issue and to Dorimant's wooing of Harriet.

The separate entries of Old Bellair, of Loveit and Bellinda, and of Sir Fopling "and's Page" mark the phases in the final resolution. At first, Old Bellair, angered by his son's disobedience, embarrassed vis-à-vis Lady Woodvill, and disappointed in his hope of marrying Emilia himself, refuses to forgive the young couple. The reconciliation is ultimately accomplished only in the second phase of the concluding action (just before Sir Fopling's entry) through the mediation of Medley and Lady Townley, Old Bellair's sister. Here, in the final development in the Bellair plot, she, like Medley, leaves her sophisticated role as "bare spectator" of the romantic intrigues and becomes the protectress and champion of young love.

But for the time being Etherege leaves the Bellair plot suspended on the sentimental impasse of the young lovers kneeling, in a tableau, before the irate father who announces he "will never forgive" them. Etherege turns instead to the complication of Dorimant's affairs with the entry of Loveit and Bellinda.

We can hardly relish what follows unless we have clearly in mind what has preceded. Dorimant's annoyed and perplexed aside, "Loveit and Bellinda! The devil owes me a shame today and I think never will have done paying it," should recall for us what a troubled morning he has had: his friends' interruption of his tender parting from Bellinda after their early morning tryst; Loveit's refusal to promise to snub Sir Fopling in public in order to clear his reputation, which has put him at the mercy of his friend Medley's scornful glee and by which he has incurred the risk of having his public image tarnished; the awkwardness of meeting Bellinda at Loveit's and his realization of her understandable resentment after he had promised her never to see Loveit again; his memory of the hollow bravado with which he "flung off" from the two jealous women; and, finally, his fears that their presence at Lady Townley's will ruin his chances with Harriet. All morning, Dorimant, the most accomplished dancer of them all, has felt himself losing control of his steps.

At the beginning of this second phase of the climactic scene, his worst fears seem to be coming true. Loveit happens to reveal his true identity to Lady Woodvill, who so far has known him only as the courtly "Mr. Courtage."* Realizing that she has been tricked both by him and by her daughter, Lady Woodvill angrily turns on Harriet and insists that they leave London immediately. The moment marks the low point in Dorimant's fortunes.

But almost immediately things begin to take a turn for the better. While Harriet seeks to placate her mother, Dorimant talks first with Loveit and then with Bellinda and succeeds in clearing himself of the infamy they came ready to accuse him of. Turning his apparent loss on one front into a gain on another, Dorimant gives Loveit the satisfaction of learning that her exposure of the counterfeit "Mr. Courtage" may have lost him Harriet. Her temper is further soothed when she lets herself be persuaded that Harriet was the "mask" for which he jilted her and that "interest" (i.e., money) rather than love has motivated his suit. Bellinda, who has overheard their conversation, is relieved to find that Dorimant is protecting both her reputation and her friendship with Loveit. If, in her ensuing talk with Dorimant, she refuses to let him clear himself with her as he did with Loveit, she *does* satisfy his curiosity by accounting for her unexpected presence at Loveit's earlier that morning. When Dorimant suggests a future meeting, her emphatic "Never!" is immediately qualified by her ambiguous, "When we do [meet], may I be as infamous as you are false." It is her last speech, and it suggests the dangerousness of the game she has allowed herself to be drawn into by falling in love with Dorimant and letting him make love to her. Bellinda's final situation, like Lady Woodvill's, is one of the circumstances that temper with tart and worldly irony the festiveness of the ending.

While Dorimant has been coming to at least a tentative and partial

* Since Loveit does not know about Dorimant's imposture, it is obvious that her disclosure here *is* fortuitous rather than a deliberate act of jealous revenge. To make a mistake about this is to misunderstand Etherege's use of Loveit in this last scene. Spiteful revenge on her part would be understandable, certainly, and her cleverly feigned infatuation with Sir Fopling in the Mall in Act III, Scene 3, shows her capable of that kind of dexterous malice. But Etherege designed her "counterplot" in Act III as a challenge to Dorimant's social *hubris*. What he now designs is a situation that will vindicate that *hubris* by demonstrating Dorimant's brilliant conquest on all fronts. A Loveit calm and resourceful enough to scheme further would diminish that effect.

understanding with his ex-mistresses, the conciliation of the two duped parents has reached its final stage. Lady Woodvill is about to be convinced by the others that Dorimant's notoriety as a rake is undeserved and to give her reluctant approval of Harriet's romance; and old Bellair is so impressed with Medley's worldly common sense that he yields to his plea for the newlyweds still on their knees before him and gives them his blessing. Medley and Lady Townley, the two conciliators, have succeeded in restoring harmony in both the Bellair and the Woodvill families.

All that remains to be shown is Dorimant's triumph over Sir Fopling, who, in the eyes of "the world," has been his apparently successful rival for Loveit's affection. By now, we feel that Dorimant's skillful encounters with Loveit and Bellinda have earned him a piece of sheer luck. It comes when the third and last phase in the resolution scene begins with Sir Fopling's timely entry and his instant resumption of his courtship of Loveit. Still frustrated by her loss of Dorimant and smarting under Harriet's taunt, Loveit would be in no mood to listen to the amorous pleasantries of a fop even if she thought that further pretense at welcoming his attentions would serve any purpose. She snubs him — just as Dorimant that morning tried to make her promise to do. She exits in a huff, and Medley pronounces Dorimant's reputation as conqueror of women clear: "henceforward when I would know anything of woman, I will consult no other oracle."

What follows Loveit's exit is largely social ceremony. Lady Woodvill, her reluctance gone, invites Dorimant to visit Harriet in Hampshire; Dorimant declares his devotion to Harriet; Harriet — playful to the end — pretends to find his sentiment "more dismal than the country!"; and Old Bellair calls for music and a dance in Harriet's honor. One hopes that Medley has the good grace to engage Bellinda.

It is, of course, an ending rich in irony: Sir Fopling, who has no identity except as social man *par excellence,* is solitary among the dancing couples; Bellinda is heartbroken and with a dubious future; and Dorimant, his rake's career brilliantly vindicated, is in the incongruous role of prospective wooer and later husband of a country heiress, but not above making gestures toward a resumption of his town amours.

What we enjoy here is our share in the playwright's detached, skeptical, and ironic view of a small group of people who simultaneously manipulate others in order to gratify their lust and greed and are the pawns of their own foibles and passions crossing their rational purpose. Dorimant is obviously the hero of *The Man of Mode* — he is the man of mode in the sense that he is the perfect gentleman by his society's norms — but while we laugh *with* him at those who are less graceful and who have been less successful than he, we also laugh *at* him. He, too, is comical as rake turned doting lover. In a spirit approaching that of satire we dissociate ourselves from the exclusive narrowness of his concerns and from the cruelties his pursuit of sex, wealth, and social power forces him to commit. With Etherege, we survey the entire pattern of Dorimant's and his set's stratagems and subterfuges, desires and disappointments. We see what they cannot see because they are entangled in the confused intrigues of their own vulnerable lives. We know more about them than they know themselves: much of the drama of the final scene of *The Man of Mode* is in our awareness of their unawareness.

Characters in literature are aware of themselves only as people in real life are aware of *them*selves. Even when we try to see ourselves as others see us, we can never, by the nature of things, attain the detached view-in-the-round available to others. We are disqualified as objective and all-informed observers by our own identities: we are that which we are trying to observe. But vis-à-vis characters in literature we enjoy absolute omniscience. We know all there is to be known about them, because they have no existence outside of the work in which they appear. Dorimant has no past (beyond an affair with a prostitute and the affair with Loveit) because Etherege tells us nothing about his past. He is a dazzling but momentary stance, isolated from any context except the immediate one on stage. He exists for the sole sake of sustaining his preeminent position in a social group that values exquisite manners, preciously clever wit, and the discreet mastery of sexual intrigue. That group ethos – the way of the world – determines the decorum of plot and character that Etherege has to observe. Dorimant, the dissembling sexual marauder, must emerge as a success from all his involvements. Anything less than success is failure – and not just his, but Etherege's as well. And this is so not because such success is inevitable or laudable in real life, but because it is the dramatically viable premise for Etherege's ambivalent study of the consummate libertine, his social circle, and the values they all live by.

Literary characters are, after all, only constituent moving parts in shaped patterns of action. And because they are, what happens to them can seem more meaningful than the random events that befall us, living as we are among the uncontrollable recalcitrance of the actual. Only if we see characters in this double aspect, as men and as artifacts mimicking men, can we experience their world as one made by art. Literature is not a daydream that substitutes for life. To ask if Dorimant and Harriet will get married and, if they do, if they will be happy together is to seek answers which Etherege's play quite properly does not provide.

# CLASSIC THROUGH MODERN DRAMA

# SOPHOCLES

# Oedipus Rex

*An English Version*
*by Dudley Fitts and Robert Fitzgerald*

PERSONS REPRESENTED

| | | |
|---|---|---|
| OEDIPUS | TEIRESIAS | SHEPHERD OF LAÏOS |
| A PRIEST | IOCASTE | SECOND MESSENGER |
| CREON | MESSENGER | CHORUS OF THEBAN ELDERS |

*The Scene: Before the palace of Oedipus, King of Thebes. A central door and two lateral doors open onto a platform which runs the length of the façade. On the platform, right and left, are altars; and three steps lead down into the* "orchestra," *or chorus-ground. At the beginning of the action these steps are crowded by* SUPPLIANTS *who have brought branches and chaplets of olive leaves and who lie in various attitudes of despair.* OEDIPUS *enters.*

## PROLOGUE

OEDIPUS: My children, generations of the living
In the line of Kadmos, nursed at his ancient hearth:
Why have you strewn yourselves before these altars
In supplication, with your boughs and garlands?
The breath of incense rises from the city 5
With a sound of prayer and lamentation.
Children,
I would not have you speak through messengers,
And therefore I have come myself to hear you —
I, Oedipus, who bear the famous name.
(*To a* PRIEST.) You, there, since you are eldest in the company,
Speak for them all, tell me what preys upon you, 10
Whether you come in dread, or crave some blessing:
Tell me, and never doubt that I will help you
In every way I can; I should be heartless
Were I not moved to find you suppliant here.
PRIEST: Great Oedipus, O powerful King of Thebes! 15
You see how all the ages of our people
Cling to your altar steps: here are boys
Who can barely stand alone, and here are priests
By weight of age, as I am a priest of God,
And young men chosen from those yet unmarried; 20
As for the others, all that multitude,
They wait with olive chaplets in the squares,
At the two shrines of Pallas, and where Apollo
Speaks in the glowing embers.
Your own eyes
Must tell you: Thebes is in her extremity 25
And can not lift her head from the surge of death.
A rust consumes the buds and fruits of the earth;
The herds are sick; children die unborn,
And labor is vain. The god of plague and pyre
Raids like detestable lightning through the city, 30
And all the house of Kadmos is laid waste,
All emptied, and all darkened: Death alone
Battens upon the misery of Thebes.

You are not one of the immortal gods, we know;
Yet we have come to you to make our prayer 35
As to the man of all men best in adversity
And wisest in the ways of God. You saved us

From the Sphinx, that flinty singer, and the tribute
We paid to her so long; yet you were never
Better informed than we, nor could we teach you: 40
It was some god breathed in you to set us free.

Therefore, O mighty King, we turn to you:
Find us our safety, find us a remedy,
Whether by counsel of the gods or men.
A king of wisdom tested in the past 45
Can act in a time of troubles, and act well.
Noblest of men, restore
Life to your city! Think how all men call you
Liberator for your triumph long ago;
Ah, when your years of kingship are remembered, 50
Let them not say *We rose, but later fell* —
Keep the State from going down in the storm!
Once, years ago, with happy augury,
You brought us fortune; be the same again!
No man questions your power to rule the land: 55
But rule over men, not over a dead city!
Ships are only hulls, citadels are nothing,
When no life moves in the empty passageways.

OEDIPUS: Poor children! You may be sure I know
All that you longed for in your coming here. 60
I know that you are deathly sick; and yet,
Sick as you are, not one is as sick as I.
Each of you suffers in himself alone
His anguish, not another's; but my spirit
Groans for the city, for myself, for you. 65

I was not sleeping, you are not waking me.
No, I have been in tears for a long while
And in my restless thought walked many ways.
In all my search, I found one helpful course,
And that I have taken: I have sent Creon, 70
Son of Menoikeus, brother of the Queen,
To Delphi, Apollo's place of revelation,
To learn there, if he can,
What act or pledge of mine may save the city.
I have counted the days, and now, this very day, 75
I am troubled, for he has overstayed his time.
What is he doing? He has been gone too long.
Yet whenever he comes back, I should do ill
To scant whatever hint the god may give.

PRIEST: It is a timely promise. At this instant 80
They tell me Creon is here.

OEDIPUS: O Lord Apollo!
May his news be fair as his face is radiant!
PRIEST: It could not be otherwise: he is crowned with bay,
The chaplet is thick with berries.
OEDIPUS: We shall soon know;
He is near enough to hear us now.

(*Enter* CREON.)

O Prince: 85
Brother: son of Menoikeus:
What answer do you bring us from the god?
CREON: It is favorable. I can tell you, great afflictions
Will turn out well, if they are taken well.
OEDIPUS: What was the oracle? These vague words 90
Leave me still hanging between hope and fear.
CREON: Is it your pleasure to hear me with all these
Gathered around us? I am prepared to speak,
But should we not go in?
OEDIPUS: Let them all hear it.
It is for them I suffer, more than for myself. 95
CREON: Then I will tell you what I heard at Delphi.

In plain words
The god commands us to expel from the land of Thebes
An old defilement that it seems we shelter.
It is a deathly thing, beyond expiation. 100
We must not let it feed upon us longer.
OEDIPUS: What defilement? How shall we rid ourselves of it?
CREON: By exile or death, blood for blood. It was
Murder that brought the plague-wind on the city.
OEDIPUS: Murder of whom? Surely the god has named him? 105
CREON: My lord: long ago Laïos was our king,
Before you came to govern us.
OEDIPUS: I know;
I learned of him from others; I never saw him.
CREON: He was murdered; and Apollo commands us now
To take revenge upon whoever killed him. 110
OEDIPUS: Upon whom? Where are they? Where shall we find a clue
To solve that crime, after so many years?
CREON: Here in this land, he said.
If we make enquiry,
We may touch things that otherwise escape us.
OEDIPUS: Tell me: Was Laïos murdered in his house, 115
Or in the fields, or in some foreign country?

CREON: He said he planned to make a pilgrimage.
He did not come home again.
OEDIPUS: And was there no one,
No witness, no companion, to tell what happened?
CREON: They were all killed but one, and he got away 120
So frightened that he could remember one thing only.
OEDIPUS: What was that one thing? One may be the key
To everything, if we resolve to use it.
CREON: He said that a band of highwaymen attacked them,
Outnumbered them, and overwhelmed the King. 125
OEDIPUS: Strange, that a highwayman should be so daring —
Unless some faction here bribed him to do it.
CREON: We thought of that. But after Laïos' death
New troubles arose and we had no avenger.
OEDIPUS: What troubles could prevent your hunting down the killers? 130
CREON: The riddling Sphinx's song
Made us deaf to all mysteries but her own.
OEDIPUS: Then once more I must bring what is dark to light.
It is most fitting that Apollo shows,
As you do, this compunction for the dead. 135
You shall see how I stand by you, as I should,
To avenge the city and the city's god,
And not as though it were for some distant friend,
But for my own sake, to be rid of evil.
Whoever killed King Laïos might — who knows? — 140
Decide at any moment to kill me as well.
By avenging the murdered king I protect myself.
Come, then, my children: leave the altar steps,
Lift up your olive boughs!
One of you go
And summon the people of Kadmos to gather here. 145
I will do all that I can; you may tell them that.

(*Exit a* PAGE.)

So, with the help of God,
We shall be saved — or else indeed we are lost.
PRIEST: Let us rise, children. It was for this we came,
And now the King has promised it himself. 150
Phoibos has sent us an oracle; may he descend
Himself to save us and drive out the plague.

(*Exeunt* OEDIPUS *and* CREON *into the palace by the central door. The* PRIEST *and the* SUPPLIANTS *disperse R and L. After a short pause the* CHORUS *enters the orchestra.*)

## PARODOS

[STROPHE 1

CHORUS: What is God singing in his profound
Delphi of gold and shadow?
What oracle for Thebes, the sunwhipped city?
Fear unjoints me, the roots of my heart tremble.
Now I remember, O Healer, your power, and wonder; 5
Will you send doom like a sudden cloud, or weave it
Like nightfall of the past?
Speak, speak to us, issue of holy sound:
Dearest to our expectancy: be tender!

[ANTISTROPHE 1

Let me pray to Athenê, the immortal daughter of Zeus, 10
And to Artemis her sister
Who keeps her famous throne in the market ring,
And to Apollo, bowman at the far butts of heaven –

O gods, descend! Like three streams leap against
The fires of our grief, the fires of darkness; 15
Be swift to bring us rest!

As in the old time from the brilliant house
Of air you stepped to save us, come again!

[STROPHE 2

Now our afflictions have no end,
Now all our stricken host lies down 20
And no man fights off death with his mind;

The noble plowland bears no grain,
And groaning mothers can not bear –

See, how our lives like birds take wing,
Like sparks that fly when a fire soars, 25
To the shore of the god of evening.

[ANTISTROPHE 2

The plague burns on, it is pitiless,
Though pallid children laden with death
Lie unwept in the stony ways,

And old gray women by every path 30
Flock to the strand about the altars

There to strike their breasts and cry
Worship of Phoibos in wailing prayers:
Be kind, God's golden child!

[STROPHE 3

There are no swords in this attack by fire, 35
No shields, but we are ringed with cries.
Send the besieger plunging from our homes
Into the vast sea-room of the Atlantic
Or into the waves that foam eastward of Thrace —
For the day ravages what the night spares — 40

Destroy our enemy, lord of the thunder!
Let him be riven by lightning from heaven!

[ANTISTROPHE 3

Phoibos Apollo, stretch the sun's bowstring,
That golden cord, until it sing for us,
Flashing arrows in heaven!
Artemis, Huntress, 45
Race with flaring lights upon our mountains!

O scarlet god, O golden-banded brow,
O Theban Bacchos in a storm of Maenads,

(*Enter* OEDIPUS, *C.*)

Whirl upon Death, that all the Undying hate!
Come with blinding cressets, come in joy! 50

## SCENE I

OEDIPUS: Is this your prayer? It may be answered. Come,
Listen to me, act as the crisis demands,
And you shall have relief from all these evils.

Until now I was a stranger to this tale,
As I had been a stranger to the crime. 5
Could I track down the murderer without a clue?
But now, friends,
As one who became a citizen after the murder,
I make this proclamation to all Thebans:
If any man knows by whose hand Laïos, son of Labdakos, 10
Met his death, I direct that man to tell me everything,
No matter what he fears for having so long withheld it.
Let it stand as promised that no further trouble
Will come to him, but he may leave the land in safety.

Moreover: If anyone knows the murderer to be foreign, 15
Let him not keep silent: he shall have his reward from me.
However, if he does conceal it; if any man

Fearing for his friend or for himself disobeys this edict,
Hear what I propose to do:

I solemnly forbid the people of this country, 20
Where power and throne are mine, ever to receive that man
Or speak to him, no matter who he is, or let him
Join in sacrifice, lustration, or in prayer.
I decree that he be driven from every house,
Being, as he is, corruption itself to us: the Delphic 25
Voice of Zeus has pronounced this revelation.
Thus I associate myself with the oracle
And take the side of the murdered king.

As for the criminal, I pray to God —
Whether it be a lurking thief, or one of a number — 30
I pray that that man's life be consumed in evil and wretchedness.
And as for me, this curse applies no less
If it should turn out that the culprit is my guest here,
Sharing my hearth.

You have heard the penalty.
I lay it on you now to attend to this 35
For my sake, for Apollo's, for the sick
Sterile city that heaven has abandoned.
Suppose the oracle had given you no command:
Should this defilement go uncleansed for ever?
You should have found the murderer: your king, 40
A noble king, had been destroyed!

Now I,
Having the power that he held before me,
Having his bed, begetting children there
Upon his wife, as he would have, had he lived —
Their son would have been my children's brother, 45
If Laïos had had luck in fatherhood!
(But surely ill luck rushed upon his reign) —
I say I take the son's part, just as though
I were his son, to press the fight for him
And see it won! I'll find the hand that brought 50
Death to Labdakos' and Polydoros' child,
Heir of Kadmos' and Agenor's line.
And as for those who fail me,
May the gods deny them the fruit of the earth,
Fruit of the womb, and may they rot utterly! 55
Let them be wretched as we are wretched, and worse!

For you, for loyal Thebans, and for all
Who find my actions right, I pray the favor
Of justice, and of all the immortal gods.

CHORAGOS: Since I am under oath, my lord, I swear 60
I did not do the murder, I can not name
The murderer. Might not the oracle
That has ordained the search tell where to find him?
OEDIPUS: An honest question. But no man in the world
Can make the gods do more than the gods will. 65
CHORAGOS: There is one last expedient —
OEDIPUS: Tell me what it is.
Though it seem slight, you must not hold it back.
CHORAGOS: A lord clairvoyant to the lord Apollo,
As we all know, is the skilled Teiresias.
One might learn much about this from him, Oedipus. 70
OEDIPUS: I am not wasting time:
Creon spoke of this, and I have sent for him —
Twice, in fact; it is strange that he is not here.
CHORAGOS: The other matter — that old report — seems useless.
OEDIPUS: Tell me. I am interested in all reports. 75
CHORAGOS: The King was said to have been killed by highwaymen.
OEDIPUS: I know. But we have no witnesses to that.
CHORAGOS: If the killer can feel a particle of dread,
Your curse will bring him out of hiding!
OEDIPUS: No.
The man who dared that act will fear no curse. 80

(*Enter the blind seer* TEIRESIAS, *led by a* PAGE.)

CHORAGOS: But there is one man who may detect the criminal.
This is Teiresias, this is the holy prophet
In whom, alone of all men, truth was born.
OEDIPUS: Teiresias: seer: student of mysteries,
Of all that's taught and all that no man tells, 85
Secrets of Heaven and secrets of the earth:
Blind though you are, you know the city lies
Sick with plague; and from this plague, my lord,
We find that you alone can guard or save us.

Possibly you did not hear the messengers? 90
Apollo, when we sent to him,
Sent us back word that this great pestilence
Would lift, but only if we established clearly
The identity of those who murdered Laïos.
They must be killed or exiled.
Can you use 95
Birdflight or any art of divination
To purify yourself, and Thebes, and me
From this contagion? We are in your hands.

There is no fairer duty
Than that of helping others in distress. 100
TEIRESIAS: How dreadful knowledge of the truth can be
When there's no help in truth! I knew this well,
But did not act on it: else I should not have come.
OEDIPUS: What is troubling you? Why are your eyes so cold?
TEIRESIAS: Let me go home. Bear your own fate, and I'll 105
Bear mine. It is better so: trust what I say.
OEDIPUS: What you say is ungracious and unhelpful
To your native country. Do not refuse to speak.
TEIRESIAS: When it comes to speech, your own is neither temperate
Nor opportune. I wish to be more prudent. 110
OEDIPUS: In God's name, we all beg you —
TEIRESIAS: You are all ignorant.
No; I will never tell you what I know.
Now it is my misery; then, it would be yours.
OEDIPUS: What! You do know something, and will not tell us?
You would betray us all and wreck the State? 115
TEIRESIAS: I do not intend to torture myself, or you.
Why persist in asking? You will not persuade me.
OEDIPUS: What a wicked old man you are! You'd try a stone's
Patience! Out with it! Have you no feeling at all?
TEIRESIAS: You call me unfeeling. If you could only see 120
The nature of your own feelings . . .
OEDIPUS: Why,
Who would not feel as I do? Who could endure
Your arrogance toward the city?
TEIRESIAS: What does it matter!
Whether I speak or not, it is bound to come.
OEDIPUS: Then, if "it" is bound to come, you are bound to tell me. 125
TEIRESIAS: No, I will not go on. Rage as you please.
OEDIPUS: Rage? Why not!
And I'll tell you what I think:
You planned it, you had it done, you all but
Killed him with your own hands: if you had eyes,
I'd say the crime was yours, and yours alone. 130
TEIRESIAS: So? I charge you, then,
Abide by the proclamation you have made:
From this day forth
Never speak again to these men or to me;
You yourself are the pollution of this country. 135
OEDIPUS: You dare say that! Can you possibly think you have
Some way of going free, after such insolence?
TEIRESIAS: I have gone free. It is the truth sustains me.
OEDIPUS: Who taught you shamelessness? It was not your craft.

TEIRESIAS: You did. You made me speak. I did not want to. 140
OEDIPUS: Speak what? Let me hear it again more clearly.
TEIRESIAS: Was it not clear before? Are you tempting me?
OEDIPUS: I did not understand it. Say it again.
TEIRESIAS: I say that you are the murderer whom you seek.
OEDIPUS: Now twice you have spat out infamy. You'll pay for it! 145
TEIRESIAS: Would you care for more? Do you wish to be really angry?
OEDIPUS: Say what you will. Whatever you say is worthless.
TEIRESIAS: I say you live in hideous shame with those
Most dear to you. You can not see the evil.
OEDIPUS: It seems you can go on mouthing like this for ever. 150
TEIRESIAS: I can, if there is power in truth.
OEDIPUS: There is:
But not for you, not for you,
You sightless, witless, senseless, mad old man!
TEIRESIAS: You are the madman. There is no one here
Who will not curse you soon, as you curse me. 155
OEDIPUS: You child of endless night! You can not hurt me
Or any other man who sees the sun.
TEIRESIAS: True: it is not from me your fate will come.
That lies within Apollo's competence,
As it is his concern.
OEDIPUS: Tell me: 160
Are you speaking for Creon, or for yourself?
TEIRESIAS: Creon is no threat. You weave your own doom.
OEDIPUS: Wealth, power, craft of statesmanship!
Kingly position, everywhere admired!
What savage envy is stored up against these, 165
If Creon, whom I trusted, Creon my friend,
For this great office which the city once
Put in my hands unsought — if for this power
Creon desires in secret to destroy me!

He has bought this decrepit fortune-teller, this 170
Collector of dirty pennies, this prophet fraud —
Why, he is no more clairvoyant than I am!
Tell us:
Has your mystic mummery ever approached the truth?
When that hellcat the Sphinx was performing here,
What help were you to these people? 175
Her magic was not for the first man who came along:
It demanded a real exorcist. Your birds —
What good were they? or the gods, for the matter of that?
But I came by,
Oedipus, the simple man, who knows nothing — 180

I thought it out for myself, no birds helped me!
And this is the man you think you can destroy,
That you may be close to Creon when he's king!
Well, you and your friend Creon, it seems to me,
Will suffer most. If you were not an old man, 185
You would have paid already for your plot.

CHORAGOS: We can not see that his words or yours
Have been spoken except in anger, Oedipus,
And of anger we have no need. How can God's will
Be accomplished best? That is what most concerns us. 190

TEIRESIAS: You are a king. But where argument's concerned
I am your man, as much a king as you.
I am not your servant, but Apollo's.
I have no need of Creon to speak for me.

Listen to me. You mock my blindness, do you? 195
But I say that you, with both your eyes, are blind:
You can not see the wretchedness of your life,
Nor in whose house you live, no, nor with whom.
Who are your father and mother? Can you tell me?
You do not even know the blind wrongs 200
That you have done them, on earth and in the world below.
But the double lash of your parents' curse will whip you
Out of this land some day, with only night
Upon your precious eyes.
Your cries then — where will they not be heard? 205
What fastness of Kithairon will not echo them?
And that bridal-descant of yours — you'll know it then,
The song they sang when you came here to Thebes
And found your misguided berthing.
All this, and more, that you can not guess at now, 210
Will bring you to yourself among your children.

Be angry, then. Curse Creon. Curse my words.
I tell you, no man that walks upon the earth
Shall be rooted out more horribly than you.

OEDIPUS: Am I to bear this from him? — Damnation 215
Take you! Out of this place! Out of my sight!

TEIRESIAS: I would not have come at all if you had not asked me.

OEDIPUS: Could I have told that you'd talk nonsense, that
You'd come here to make a fool of yourself, and of me?

TEIRESIAS: A fool? Your parents thought me sane enough. 220

OEDIPUS: My parents again! — Wait: who were my parents?

TEIRESIAS: This day will give you a father, and break your heart.

OEDIPUS: Your infantile riddles! Your damned abracadabra!

TEIRESIAS: You were a great man once at solving riddles.

OEDIPUS: Mock me with that if you like; you will find it true. 225
TEIRESIAS: It was true enough. It brought about your ruin.
OEDIPUS: But if it saved this town?
TEIRESIAS (*to the* PAGE):
Boy, give me your hand.
OEDIPUS: Yes, boy; lead him away.
— While you are here
We can do nothing. Go; leave us in peace.
TEIRESIAS: I will go when I have said what I have to say. 230
How can you hurt me? And I tell you again:
The man you have been looking for all this time,
The damned man, the murderer of Laïos,
That man is in Thebes. To your mind he is foreignborn,
But it will soon be shown that he is a Theban, 235
A revelation that will fail to please.
A blind man,
Who has his eyes now; a penniless man, who is rich now;
And he will go tapping the strange earth with his staff;
To the children with whom he lives now he will be
Brother and father — the very same; to her 240
Who bore him, son and husband — the very same
Who came to his father's bed, wet with his father's blood.

Enough. Go think that over.
If later you find error in what I have said,
You may say that I have no skill in prophecy. 245

(*Exit* TEIRESIAS, *led by his* PAGE. OEDIPUS *goes into the palace.*)

## ODE I

[STROPHE 1

CHORUS: The Delphic stone of prophecies
Remembers ancient regicide
And a still bloody hand.
That killer's hour of flight has come.
He must be stronger than riderless 5
Coursers of untiring wind,
For the son of Zeus armed with his father's thunder
Leaps in lightning after him;
And the Furies follow him, the sad Furies.

[ANTISTROPHE 1

Holy Parnassos' peak of snow 10
Flashes and blinds that secret man,

That all shall hunt him down:
Though he may roam the forest shade
Like a bull gone wild from pasture
To rage through glooms of stone. 15
Doom comes down on him; flight will not avail him;
For the world's heart calls him desolate,
And the immortal Furies follow, for ever follow.

[STROPHE 2

But now a wilder thing is heard
From the old man skilled at hearing Fate in the wingbeat of a bird. 20
Bewildered as a blown bird, my soul hovers and can not find
Foothold in this debate, or any reason or rest of mind.
But no man ever brought – none can bring
Proof of strife between Thebes' royal house,
Labdakos' line, and the son of Polybos; 25
And never until now has any man brought word
Of Laïos' dark death staining Oedipus the King.

[ANTISTROPHE 2

Divine Zeus and Apollo hold
Perfect intelligence alone of all tales ever told;
And well though this diviner works, he works in his own night; 30
No man can judge that rough unknown or trust in second sight,
For wisdom changes hands among the wise.
Shall I believe my great lord criminal
At a raging word that a blind old man let fall?
I saw him, when the carrion woman faced him of old, 35
Prove his heroic mind! These evil words are lies.

## SCENE II

CREON: Men of Thebes:
I am told that heavy accusations
Have been brought against me by King Oedipus.

I am not the kind of man to bear this tamely.

If in these present difficulties 5
He holds me accountable for any harm to him
Through anything I have said or done – why, then,
I do not value life in this dishonor.
It is not as though this rumor touched upon
Some private indiscretion. The matter is grave. 10
The fact is that I am being called disloyal
To the State, to my fellow citizens, to my friends.

CHORAGOS: He may have spoken in anger, not from his mind.
CREON: But did you not hear him say I was the one
Who seduced the old prophet into lying? 15
CHORAGOS: The thing was said; I do not know how seriously.
CREON: But you were watching him! Were his eyes steady?
Did he look like a man in his right mind?
CHORAGOS: I do not know.
I can not judge the behavior of great men.
But here is the King himself.

(*Enter* OEDIPUS.)

OEDIPUS: So you dared come back. 20
Why? How brazen of you to come to my house,
You murderer!
Do you think I do not know
That you plotted to kill me, plotted to steal my throne?
Tell me, in God's name: am I coward, a fool,
That you should dream you could accomplish this? 25
A fool who could not see your slippery game?
A coward, not to fight back when I saw it?
You are the fool, Creon, are you not? hoping
Without support or friends to get a throne?
Thrones may be won or bought: you could do neither. 30
CREON: Now listen to me. You have talked; let me talk, too.
You can not judge unless you know the facts.
OEDIPUS: You speak well: there is one fact; but I find it hard
To learn from the deadliest enemy I have.
CREON: That above all I must dispute with you. 35
OEDIPUS: That above all I will not hear you deny.
CREON: If you think there is anything good in being stubborn
Against all reason, then I say you are wrong.
OEDIPUS: If you think a man can sin against his own kind
And not be punished for it, I say you are mad. 40
CREON: I agree. But tell me: what have I done to you?
OEDIPUS: You advised me to send for that wizard, did you not?
CREON: I did. I should do it again.
OEDIPUS: Very well. Now tell me:
How long has it been since Laïos —
CREON: What of Laïos?
OEDIPUS: Since he vanished in that onset by the road? 45
CREON: It was long ago, a long time.
OEDIPUS: And this prophet,
Was he practicing here then?
CREON: He was; and with honor, as now.
OEDIPUS: Did he speak of me at that time?

CREON: He never did;
At least, not when I was present.
OEDIPUS: But . . . the enquiry?
I suppose you held one?
CREON: We did, but we learned nothing. 50
OEDIPUS: Why did the prophet not speak against me then?
CREON: I do not know; and I am the kind of man
Who holds his tongue when he has no facts to go on.
OEDIPUS: There's one fact that you know, and you could tell it.
CREON: What fact is that? If I know it, you shall have it. 55
OEDIPUS: If he were not involved with you, he could not say
That it was I who murdered Laïos.
CREON: If he says that, you are the one that knows it! —
But now it is my turn to question you.
OEDIPUS: Put your questions. I am no murderer. 60
CREON: First, then: You married my sister?
OEDIPUS: I married your sister
CREON: And you rule the kingdom equally with her?
OEDIPUS: Everything that she wants she has from me.
CREON: And I am the third, equal to both of you?
OEDIPUS: That is why I call you a bad friend. 65
CREON: No. Reason it out, as I have done.
Think of this first. Would any sane man prefer
Power, with all a king's anxieties,
To that same power and the grace of sleep?
Certainly not I. 70
I have never longed for the king's power — only his rights.
Would any wise man differ from me in this?
As matters stand, I have my way in everything
With your consent, and no responsibilities.
If I were king, I should be a slave to policy. 75

How could I desire a scepter more
Than what is now mine — untroubled influence?
No, I have not gone mad; I need no honors,
Except those with the perquisites I have now.
I am welcome everywhere; every man salutes me, 80
And those who want your favor seek my ear,
Since I know how to manage what they ask.
Should I exchange this ease for that anxiety?
Besides, no sober mind is treasonable.
I hate anarchy 85
And never would deal with any man who likes it.

Test what I have said. Go to the priestess
At Delphi, ask if I quoted her correctly.

And as for this other thing: if I am found
Guilty of treason with Teiresias, 90
Then sentence me to death! You have my word
It is a sentence I should cast my vote for —
But not without evidence!
You do wrong
When you take good men for bad, bad men for good.
A true friend thrown aside — why, life itself 95
Is not more precious!
In time you will know this well:
For time, and time alone, will show the just man,
Though scoundrels are discovered in a day.

CHORAGOS: This is well said, and a prudent man would ponder it.
Judgments too quickly formed are dangerous. 100

OEDIPUS: But is he not quick in his duplicity?
And shall I not be quick to parry him?
Would you have me stand still, hold my peace, and let
This man win everything, through my inaction?

CREON: And you want — what is it, then? To banish me? 105

OEDIPUS: No, not exile. It is your death I want,
So that all the world may see what treason means.

CREON: You will persist, then? You will not believe me?

OEDIPUS: How can I believe you?

CREON: Then you are a fool.

OEDIPUS: To save myself?

CREON: In justice, think of me. 110

OEDIPUS: You are evil incarnate.

CREON: But suppose that you are wrong?

OEDIPUS: Still I must rule.

CREON: But not if you rule badly.

OEDIPUS: O city, city!

CREON: It is my city, too!

CHORAGOS: Now, my lords, be still. I see the Queen,
Iocastê, coming from her palace chambers; 115
And it is time she came, for the sake of you both.
This dreadful quarrel can be resolved through her.

(*Enter* IOCASTE.)

IOCASTE: Poor foolish men, what wicked din is this?
With Thebes sick to death, is it not shameful
That you should rake some private quarrel up? 120
(*To* OEDIPUS.) Come into the house.
— And you, Creon, go now:
Let us have no more of this tumult over nothing.

CREON: Nothing? No, sister: what your husband plans for me
Is one of two great evils: exile or death.
OEDIPUS: He is right.
Why, woman I have caught him squarely 125
Plotting against my life.
CREON: No! Let me die
Accurst if ever I have wished you harm!
IOCASTE: Ah, believe it, Oedipus!
In the name of the gods, respect this oath of his
For my sake, for the sake of these people here! 130

[STROPHE 1

CHORAGOS: Open your mind to her, my lord. Be ruled by her, I beg you!
OEDIPUS: What would you have me do?
CHORAGOS: Respect Creon's word. He has never spoken like a fool,
And now he has sworn an oath.
OEDIPUS: You know what you ask?
CHORAGOS: I do.
OEDIPUS: Speak on, then.
CHORAGOS: A friend so sworn should not be baited so, 135
In blind malice, and without final proof.
OEDIPUS: You are aware, I hope, that what you say
Means death for me, or exile at the least.

[STROPHE 2

CHORAGOS: No, I swear by Helios, first in Heaven!
May I die friendless and accurst, 140
The worst of deaths, if ever I meant that!
It is the withering fields
That hurt my sick heart:
Must we bear all these ills,
And now your bad blood as well? 145
OEDIPUS: Then let him go. And let me die, if I must,
Or be driven by him in shame from the land of Thebes.
It is your unhappiness, and not his talk,
That touches me.
As for him —
Wherever he is, I will hate him as long as I live. 150
CREON: Ugly in yielding, as you were ugly in rage!
Natures like yours chiefly torment themselves.
OEDIPUS: Can you not go? Can you not leave me?
CREON: I can.
You do not know me; but the city knows me,
And in its eyes I am just, if not in yours. 155

(*Exit* CREON.)

[ANTISTROPHE 1

CHORAGOS: Lady Iocastê, did you not ask the King to go to his chambers?

IOCASTE: First tell me what has happened.

CHORAGOS: There was suspicion without evidence; yet it rankled
As even false charges will.

IOCASTE: On both sides?

CHORAGOS: On both.

IOCASTE: But what was said?

CHORAGOS: Oh let it rest, let it be done with! 160
Have we not suffered enough?

OEDIPUS: You see to what your decency has brought you:
You have made difficulties where my heart saw none.

[ANTISTROPHE 2

CHORAGOS: Oedipus, it is not once only I have told you —
You must know I should count myself unwise 165
To the point of madness, should I now forsake you —
You, under whose hand,
In the storm of another time,
Our dear land sailed out free.
But now stand fast at the helm! 170

IOCASTE: In God's name, Oedipus, inform your wife as well:
Why are you so set in this hard anger?

OEDIPUS: I will tell you, for none of these men deserves
My confidence as you do. It is Creon's work,
His treachery, his plotting against me. 175

IOCASTE: Go on, if you can make this clear to me.

OEDIPUS: He charges me with the murder of Laïos.

IOCASTE: Has he some knowledge? Or does he speak from hearsay?

OEDIPUS: He would not commit himself to such a charge,
But he has brought in that damnable soothsayer 180
To tell his story.

IOCASTE: Set your mind at rest.
If it is a question of soothsayers, I tell you
That you will find no man whose craft gives knowledge
Of the unknowable.
Here is my proof:

An oracle was reported to Laïos once 185
(I will not say from Phoibos himself, but from
His appointed ministers, at any rate)
That his doom would be death at the hands of his own son —
His son, born of his flesh and of mine!

Now, you remember the story: Laïos was killed 190

By marauding strangers where three highways meet;
But his child had not been three days in this world
Before the King had pierced the baby's ankles
And left him to die on a lonely mountainside.

Thus, Apollo never caused that child 195
To kill his father, and it was not Laïos' fate
To die at the hands of his son, as he had feared.
This is what prophets and prophecies are worth!
Have no dread of them.
It is God himself
Who can show us what he wills, in his own way. 200

OEDIPUS: How strange a shadowy memory crossed my mind,
Just now while you were speaking; it chilled my heart.
IOCASTE: What do you mean? What memory do you speak of?
OEDIPUS: If I understand you, Laïos was killed
At a place where three roads meet.
IOCASTE: So it was said; 205
We have no later story.
OEDIPUS: Where did it happen?
IOCASTE: Phokis, it is called: at a place where the Theban Way
Divides into the roads towards Delphi and Daulia.
OEDIPUS: When?
IOCASTE: We had the news not long before you came
And proved the right to your succession here. 210
OEDIPUS: Ah, what net has God been weaving for me?
IOCASTE: Oedipus! Why does this trouble you?
OEDIPUS: Do not ask me yet.
First, tell me how Laïos looked, and tell me
How old he was.
IOCASTE: He was tall, his hair just touched
With white; his form was not unlike your own. 215
OEDIPUS: I think that I myself may be accurst
By my own ignorant edict.
IOCASTE: You speak strangely.
It makes me tremble to look at you, my King.
OEDIPUS: I am not sure that the blind man can not see.
But I should know better if you were to tell me — 220
IOCASTE: Anything — though I dread to hear you ask it.
OEDIPUS: Was the King lightly escorted, or did he ride
With a large company, as a ruler should?
IOCASTE: There were five men with him in all: one was a herald;
And a single chariot, which he was driving. 225
OEDIPUS: Alas, that makes it plain enough!

But who —
Who told you how it happened?

IOCASTE: A household servant,
The only one to escape.

OEDIPUS: And is he still
A servant of ours?

IOCASTE: No; for when he came back at last
And found you enthroned in the place of the dead king, 230
He came to me, touched my hand with his, and begged
That I would send him away to the frontier district
Where only the shepherds go —
As far away from the city as I could send him.
I granted his prayer; for although the man was a slave, 235
He had earned more than this favor at my hands.

OEDIPUS: Can he be called back quickly?

IOCASTE: Easily.
But why?

OEDIPUS: I have taken too much upon myself
Without enquiry; therefore I wish to consult him.

IOCASTE: Then he shall come.
But am I not one also 240
To whom you might confide these fears of yours?

OEDIPUS: That is your right; it will not be denied you,
Now least of all; for I have reached a pitch
Of wild foreboding. Is there anyone
To whom I should sooner speak? 245
Polybos of Corinth is my father.
My mother is a Dorian: Meropê.
I grew up chief among the men of Corinth
Until a strange thing happened —
Not worth my passion, it may be, but strange. 250

At a feast, a drunken man maundering in his cups
Cries out that I am not my father's son!

I contained myself that night, though I felt anger
And a sinking heart. The next day I visited
My father and mother, and questioned them. They stormed, 255
Calling it all the slanderous rant of a fool;
And this relieved me. Yet the suspicion
Remained always aching in my mind;
I knew there was talk; I could not rest;
And finally, saying nothing to my parents, 260
I went to the shrine at Delphi.
The god dismissed my question without reply;

He spoke of other things.
Some were clear,
Full of wretchedness, dreadful, unbearable:
As, that I should lie with my own mother, breed 265
Children from whom all men would turn their eyes;
And that I should be my father's murderer.

I heard all this, and fled. And from that day
Corinth to me was only in the stars
Descending in that quarter of the sky, 270
As I wandered farther and farther on my way
To a land where I should never see the evil
Sung by the oracle. And I came to this country
Where, so you say, King Laïos was killed.

I will tell you all that happened there, my lady. 275

There were three highways
Coming together at a place I passed;
And there a herald came towards me, and a chariot
Drawn by horses, with a man such as you describe
Seated in it. The groom leading the horses 280
Forced me off the road at his lord's command;
But as this charioteer lurched over towards me
I struck him in my rage. The old man saw me
And brought his double goad down upon my head
As I came abreast.
He was paid back, and more! 285
Swinging my club in this right hand I knocked him
Out of his car, and he rolled on the ground.
I killed him.

I killed them all.
Now if that stranger and Laïos were – kin,
Where is a man more miserable than I? 290
More hated by the gods? Citizen and alien alike
Must never shelter me or speak to me –
I must be shunned by all.
And I myself
Pronounced this malediction upon myself!

Think of it: I have touched you with these hands, 295
These hands that killed your husband. What defilement!

Am I all evil, then? It must be so,
Since I must flee from Thebes, yet never again

See my own countrymen, my own country,
For fear of joining my mother in marriage 300
And killing Polybos, my father.
Ah,
If I was created so, born to this fate,
Who could deny the savagery of God?

O holy majesty of heavenly powers!
May I never see that day! Never! 305
Rather let me vanish from the race of men
Than know the abomination destined me!

CHORAGOS: We too, my lord, have felt dismay at this.
But there is hope: you have yet to hear the shepherd.

OEDIPUS: Indeed, I fear no other hope is left me. 310

IOCASTE: What do you hope from him when he comes?

OEDIPUS: This much:
If his account of the murder tallies with yours,
Then I am cleared.

IOCASTE: What was it that I said
Of such importance?

OEDIPUS: Why, "marauders," you said,
Killed the King, according to this man's story. 315
If he maintains that still, if there were several,
Clearly the guilt is not mine: I was alone.
But if he says one man, singlehanded, did it,
Then the evidence all points to me.

IOCASTE: You may be sure that he said there were several; 320
And can he call back that story now? He can not.
The whole city heard it as plainly as I.
But suppose he alters some detail of it:
He can not ever show that Laïos' death
Fulfilled the oracle: for Apollo said 325
My child was doomed to kill him; and my child —
Poor baby! — it was my child that died first.

No. From now on, where oracles are concerned,
I would not waste a second thought on any.

OEDIPUS: You may be right.
But come: let someone go 330
For the shepherd at once. This matter must be settled.

IOCASTE: I will send for him.
I would not wish to cross you in anything,
And surely not in this. — Let us go in.

*(Exeunt into the palace.)*

## ODE II

[STROPHE 1

CHORUS: Let me be reverent in the ways of right,
Lowly the paths I journey on;
Let all my words and actions keep
The laws of the pure universe
From highest Heaven handed down. 5
For Heaven is their bright nurse,
Those generations of the realms of light;
Ah, never of mortal kind were they begot,
Nor are they slaves of memory, lost in sleep:
Their Father is greater than Time, and ages not. 10

[ANTISTROPHE 1

The tyrant is a child of Pride
Who drinks from his great sickening cup
Recklessness and vanity,
Until from his high crest headlong
He plummets to the dust of hope. 15
That strong man is not strong.
But let no fair ambition be denied;
May God protect the wrestler for the State
In government, in comely policy,
Who will fear God, and on His ordinance wait. 20

[STROPHE 2

Haughtiness and the high hand of disdain
Tempt and outrage God's holy law;
And any mortal who dares hold
No immortal Power in awe
Will be caught up in a net of pain: 25
The price for which his levity is sold.
Let each man take due earnings, then,
And keep his hands from holy things,
And from blasphemy stand apart—
Else the crackling blast of heaven 30
Blows on his head, and on his desperate heart;
Though fools will honor impious men,
In their cities no tragic poet sings.

[ANTISTROPHE 2

Shall we lose faith in Delphi's obscurities,
We who have heard the world's core 35
Discredited, and the sacred wood

Of Zeus at Elis praised no more?
The deeds and the strange prophecies
Must make a pattern yet to be understood.
Zeus, if indeed you are lord of all, 40
Throned in light over night and day,
Mirror this in your endless mind:
Our masters call the oracle
Words on the wind, and the Delphic vision blind!
Their hearts no longer know Apollo, 45
And reverence for the gods has died away.

## SCENE III

*Enter* IOCASTE.

IOCASTE: Princes of Thebes, it has occurred to me
To visit the altars of the gods, bearing
These branches as a suppliant, and this incense.
Our King is not himself: his noble soul
Is overwrought with fantasies of dread, 5
Else he would consider
The new prophecies in the light of the old.
He will listen to any voice that speaks disaster,
And my advice goes for nothing.

(*She approaches the altar, R.*)

To you, then, Apollo,
Lycean lord, since you are nearest, I turn in prayer. 10
Receive these offerings, and grant us deliverance
From defilement. Our hearts are heavy with fear
When we see our leader distracted, as helpless sailors
Are terrified by the confusion of their helmsman.

(*Enter* MESSENGER.)

MESSENGER: Friends, no doubt you can direct me: 15
Where shall I find the house of Oedipus,
Or, better still, where is the King himself?
CHORAGOS: It is this very place, stranger; he is inside.
This is his wife and mother of his children.
MESSENGER: I wish her happiness in a happy house, 20
Blest in all the fulfillment of her marriage.
IOCASTE: I wish as much for you: your courtesy
Deserves a like good fortune. But now, tell me:
Why have you come? What have you to say to us?

MESSENGER: Good news, my lady, for your house and your husband. 25
IOCASTE: What news? Who sent you here?
MESSENGER: I am from Corinth.
The news I bring ought to mean joy for you,
Though it may be you will find some grief in it.
IOCASTE: What is it? How can it touch us in both ways?
MESSENGER: The people of Corinth, they say, 30
Intend to call Oedipus to be their king.
IOCASTE: But old Polybos – is he not reigning still?
MESSENGER: No. Death holds him in his sepulchre.
IOCASTE: What are you saying? Polybos is dead?
MESSENGER: If I am not telling the truth, may I die myself. 35
IOCASTE (*to a* MAIDSERVANT): Go in, go quickly; tell this to your master.

O riddlers of God's will, where are you now!
This was the man whom Oedipus, long ago,
Feared so, fled so, in dread of destroying him –
But it was another fate by which he died. 40

(*Enter* OEDIPUS, *C.*)

OEDIPUS: Dearest Iocastê, why have you sent for me?
IOCASTE: Listen to what this man says, and then tell me
What has become of the solemn prophecies.
OEDIPUS: Who is this man? What is his news for me?
IOCASTE: He has come from Corinth to announce your father's death! 45
OEDIPUS: Is it true, stranger? Tell me in your own words.
MESSENGER: I can not say it more clearly: the King is dead.
OEDIPUS: Was it by treason? Or by an attack of illness?
MESSENGER: A little thing brings old men to their rest.
OEDIPUS: It was sickness, then?
MESSENGER: Yes, and his many years. 50
OEDIPUS: Ah!
Why should a man respect the Pythian hearth, or
Give heed to the birds that jangle above his head?
They prophesied that I should kill Polybos,
Kill my own father; but he is dead and buried, 55
And I am here – I never touched him, never,
Unless he died of grief for my departure,
And thus, in a sense, through me. No. Polybos
Has packed the oracles off with him underground.
They are empty words.
IOCASTE: Had I not told you so? 60
OEDIPUS: You had; it was my faint heart that betrayed me.
IOCASTE: From now on never think of those things again.
OEDIPUS: And yet – must I not fear my mother's bed?

IOCASTE: Why should anyone in this world be afraid,
Since Fate rules us and nothing can be foreseen? 65
A man should live only for the present day.

Have no more fear of sleeping with your mother:
How many men, in dreams, have lain with their mothers!
No reasonable man is troubled by such things.

OEDIPUS: That is true; only — 70
If only my mother were not still alive!
But she is alive. I can not help my dread.

IOCASTE: Yet this news of your father's death is wonderful.

OEDIPUS: Wonderful. But I fear the living woman.

MESSENGER: Tell me, who is this woman that you fear? 75

OEDIPUS: It is Meropê, man; the wife of King Polybos.

MESSENGER: Meropê? Why should you be afraid of her?

OEDIPUS: An oracle of the gods, a dreadful saying.

MESSENGER: Can you tell me about it or are you sworn to silence?

OEDIPUS: I can tell you, and I will. 80
Apollo said through his prophet that I was the man
Who should marry his own mother, shed his father's blood
With his own hands. And so, for all these years
I have kept clear of Corinth, and no harm has come —
Though it would have been sweet to see my parents again. 85

MESSENGER: And is this the fear that drove you out of Corinth?

OEDIPUS: Would you have me kill my father?

MESSENGER: As for that
You must be reassured by the news I gave you.

OEDIPUS: If you could reassure me, I would reward you.

MESSENGER: I had that in mind, I will confess: I thought 90
I could count on you when you returned to Corinth.

OEDIPUS: No: I will never go near my parents again.

MESSENGER: Ah, son, you still do not know what you are doing —

OEDIPUS: What do you mean? In the name of God tell me!

MESSENGER: — If these are your reasons for not going home. 95

OEDIPUS: I tell you, I fear the oracle may come true.

MESSENGER: And guilt may come upon you through your parents?

OEDIPUS: That is the dread that is always in my heart.

MESSENGER: Can you not see that all your fears are groundless?

OEDIPUS: How can you say that? They are my parents, surely? 100

MESSENGER: Polybos was not your father.

OEDIPUS: Not my father?

MESSENGER: No more your father than the man speaking to you.

OEDIPUS: But you are nothing to me!

MESSENGER: Neither was he.

OEDIPUS: Then why did he call me son?

MESSENGER: I will tell you:
Long ago he had you from my hands, as a gift. 105
OEDIPUS: Then how could he love me so, if I was not his?
MESSENGER: He had no children, and his heart turned to you.
OEDIPUS: What of you? Did you buy me? Did you find me by chance?
MESSENGER: I came upon you in the crooked pass of Kithairon.
OEDIPUS: And what were you doing there?
MESSENGER: Tending my flocks. 110
OEDIPUS: A wandering shepherd?
MESSENGER: But your savior, son, that day.
OEDIPUS: From what did you save me?
MESSENGER: Your ankles should tell you that.
OEDIPUS: Ah, stranger, why do you speak of that childhood pain?
MESSENGER: I cut the bonds that tied your ankles together.
OEDIPUS: I have had the mark as long as I can remember. 115
MESSENGER: That was why you were given the name you bear.
OEDIPUS: God! Was it my father or my mother who did it?
Tell me!
MESSENGER: I do not know. The man who gave you to me
Can tell you better than I. 120
OEDIPUS: It was not you that found me, but another?
MESSENGER: It was another shepherd gave you to me.
OEDIPUS: Who was he? Can you tell me who he was?
MESSENGER: I think he was said to be one of Laïos' people.
OEDIPUS: You mean the Laïos who was king here years ago? 125
MESSENGER: Yes; King Laïos; and the man was one of his herdsmen.
OEDIPUS: Is he still alive? Can I see him?
MESSENGER: These men here
Know best about such things.
OEDIPUS: Does anyone here
Know this shepherd that he is talking about?
Have you seen him in the fields, or in the town? 130
If you have, tell me. It is time things were made plain.
CHORAGOS: I think the man he means is that same shepherd
You have already asked to see. Iocastê perhaps
Could tell you something.
OEDIPUS: Do you know anything
About him, Lady? Is he the man we have summoned? 135
Is that the man this shepherd means?
IOCASTE: Why think of him?
Forget this herdsman. Forget it all.
This talk is a waste of time.
OEDIPUS: How can you say that,
When the clues to my true birth are in my hands?

IOCASTE: For God's love, let us have no more questioning! 140
Is your life nothing to you?
My own is pain enough for me to bear.
OEDIPUS: You need not worry. Suppose my mother a slave,
And born of slaves: no baseness can touch you.
IOCASTE: Listen to me, I beg you: do not do this thing! 145
OEDIPUS: I will not listen; the truth must be made known.
IOCASTE: Everything that I say is for your own good!
OEDIPUS: My own good
Snaps my patience, then; I want none of it.
IOCASTE: You are fatally wrong! May you never learn who you are!
OEDIPUS: Go, one of you, and bring the shepherd here. 150
Let us leave this woman to brag of her royal name.
IOCASTE: Ah, miserable!
That is the only word I have for you now.
That is the only word I can ever have.

(*Exit into the palace.*)

CHORAGOS: Why has she left us, Oedipus? Why has she gone 155
In such a passion of sorrow? I fear this silence:
Something dreadful may come of it.
OEDIPUS: Let it come!
However base my birth, I must know about it.
The Queen, like a woman, is perhaps ashamed
To think of my low origin. But I 160
Am a child of Luck; I can not be dishonored.
Luck is my mother; the passing months, my brothers,
Have seen me rich and poor.
If this is so,
How could I wish that I were someone else?
How could I not be glad to know my birth? 165

## ODE III

[STROPHE

CHORUS: If ever the coming time were known
To my heart's pondering,
Kithairon, now by Heaven I see the torches
At the festival of the next full moon,
And see the dance, and hear the choir sing 5
A grace to your gentle shade:
Mountain where Oedipus was found,
O mountain guard of a noble race!

May the god who heals us lend his aid,
And let that glory come to pass 10
For our king's cradling-ground.

[ANTISTROPHE

Of the nymphs that flower beyond the years,
Who bore you, royal child,
To Pan of the hills or the timberline Apollo,
Cold in delight where the upland clears, 15
Or Hermês for whom Kyllenê's heights are piled?
Or flushed as evening cloud,
Great Dionysos, roamer of mountains,
He — was it he who found you there,
And caught you up in his own proud 20
Arms from the sweet god-ravisher
Who laughed by the Muses' fountains?

## SCENE IV

OEDIPUS: Sirs: though I do not know the man,
I think I see him coming, this shepherd we want:
He is old, like our friend here, and the men
Bringing him seem to be servants of my house.
But you can tell, if you have ever seen him. 5

(*Enter* SHEPHERD *escorted by servants.*)

CHORAGOS: I know him, he was Laïos' man. You can trust him.
OEDIPUS: Tell me first, you from Corinth: is this the shepherd
We were discussing?
MESSENGER: This is the very man.
OEDIPUS (*to* SHEPHERD): Come here. No, look at me. You must answer
Everything I ask. — You belonged to Laïos? 10
SHEPHERD: Yes: born his slave, brought up in his house.
OEDIPUS: Tell me: what kind of work did you do for him?
SHEPHERD: I was a shepherd of his, most of my life.
OEDIPUS: Where mainly did you go for pasturage?
SHEPHERD: Sometimes Kithairon, sometimes the hills near-by. 15
OEDIPUS: Do you remember ever seeing this man out there?
SHEPHERD: What would he be doing there? This man?
OEDIPUS: This man standing here. Have you ever seen him before?
SHEPHERD: No. At least, not to my recollection.
MESSENGER: And that is not strange, my lord. But I'll refresh 20
His memory: he must remember when we two

Spent three whole seasons together, March to September,
On Kithairon or thereabouts. He had two flocks;
I had one. Each autumn I'd drive mine home
And he would go back with his to Laïos' sheepfold. — 25
Is this not true, just as I have described it?
SHEPHERD: True, yes; but it was all so long ago.
MESSENGER: Well, then: do you remember, back in those days
That you gave me a baby boy to bring up as my own?
SHEPHERD: What if I did? What are you trying to say? 30
MESSENGER: King Oedipus was once that little child.
SHEPHERD: Damn you, hold your tongue!
OEDIPUS: No more of that!
It is your tongue needs watching, not this man's.
SHEPHERD: My King, my Master, what is it I have done wrong?
OEDIPUS: You have not answered his question about the boy. 35
SHEPHERD: He does not know . . . He is only making trouble . . .
OEDIPUS: Come, speak plainly, or it will go hard with you.
SHEPHERD: In God's name, do not torture an old man!
OEDIPUS: Come here, one of you; bind his arms behind him.
SHEPHERD: Unhappy king! What more do you wish to learn? 40
OEDIPUS: Did you give this man the child he speaks of?
SHEPHERD: I did.
And I would to God I had died that very day.
OEDIPUS: You will die now unless you speak the truth.
SHEPHERD: Yet if I speak the truth, I am worse than dead.
OEDIPUS: Very well; since you insist upon delaying — 45
SHEPHERD: No! I have told you already that I gave him the boy.
OEDIPUS: Where did you get him? From your house? From somewhere else?
SHEPHERD: Not from mine, no. A man gave him to me.
OEDIPUS: Is that man here? Do you know whose slave he was?
SHEPHERD: For God's love, my King, do not ask me any more! 50
OEDIPUS: You are a dead man if I have to ask you again.
SHEPHERD: Then . . . Then the child was from the palace of Laïos.
OEDIPUS: A slave child? or a child of his own line?
SHEPHERD: Ah, I am on the brink of dreadful speech!
OEDIPUS: And I of dreadful hearing. Yet I must hear. 55
SHEPHERD: If you must be told, then . . .
They said it was Laïos' child,
But it is your wife who can tell you about that.
OEDIPUS: My wife! — Did she give it to you?
SHEPHERD: My lord, she did.
OEDIPUS: Do you know why?
SHEPHERD: I was told to get rid of it.

OEDIPUS: An unspeakable mother!

SHEPHERD: There had been prophecies . . . 60

OEDIPUS: Tell me.

SHEPHERD: It was said that the boy would kill his own father.

OEDIPUS: Then why did you give him over to this old man?

SHEPHERD: I pitied the baby, my King,
And I thought that this man would take him far away
To his own country.
He saved him — but for what a fate! 65
For if you are what this man says you are,
No man living is more wretched than Oedipus.

OEDIPUS: Ah God!
It was true!
All the prophecies!
— Now,
O Light, may I look on you for the last time! 70
I, Oedipus,
Oedipus, damned in his birth, in his marriage damned,
Damned in the blood he shed with his own hand!

(*He rushes into the palace.*)

## ODE IV

[STROPHE 1

CHORUS: Alas for the seed of men.

What measure shall I give these generations
That breathe on the void and are void
And exist and do not exist?

Who bears more weight of joy 5
Than mass of sunlight shifting in images,
Or who shall make his thought stay on
That down time drifts away?

Your splendor is all fallen.

O naked brow of wrath and tears, 10
O change of Oedipus!
I who saw your days call no man blest —
Your great days like ghósts góne.

[ANTISTROPHE 1

That mind was a strong bow.
Deep, how deep you drew it then, hard archer, 15

At a dim fearful range,
And brought dear glory down!

You overcame the stranger —
The virgin with her hooking lion claws —
And though death sang, stood like a tower 20
To make pale Thebes take heart.

Fortress against our sorrow!

Divine king, giver of laws,
Majestic Oedipus!
No prince in Thebes had ever such renown, 25
No prince won such grace of power.

[STROPHE 2

And now of all men ever known
Most pitiful is this man's story:
His fortunes are most changed, his state
Fallen to a low slave's 30
Ground under bitter fate.

O Oedipus, most royal one!
The great door that expelled you to the light
Gave at night — ah, gave night to your glory:
As to the father, to the fathering son. 35

All understood too late.

How could that queen whom Laïos won,
The garden that he harrowed at his height,
Be silent when that act was done?

[ANTISTROPHE 2

But all eyes fail before time's eye, 40
All actions come to justice there.
Though never willed, though far down the deep past,
Your bed, your dread sirings,
Are brought to book at last.
Child by Laïos doomed to die, 45
Then doomed to lose that fortunate little death,
Would God you never took breath in this air
That with my wailing lips I take to cry:

For I weep the world's outcast.

I was blind, and now I can tell why: 50
Asleep, for you had given ease of breath
To Thebes, while the false years went by.

## EXODOS

*Enter, from the palace,* SECOND MESSENGER.

SECOND MESSENGER: Elders of Thebes, most honored in this land,
What horrors are yours to see and hear, what weight
Of sorrow to be endured, if, true to your birth,
You venerate the line of Labdakos!
I think neither Istros nor Phasis, those great rivers, 5
Could purify this place of the corruption
It shelters now, or soon must bring to light —
Evil not done unconsciously, but willed.

The greatest griefs are those we cause ourselves.
CHORAGOS: Surely, friend, we have grief enough already; 10
What new sorrow do you mean?
SECOND MESSENGER: The Queen is dead.
CHORAGOS: Iocastê? Dead? But at whose hand?
SECOND MESSENGER: Her own.
The full horror of what happened you can not know,
For you did not see it; but I, who did, will tell you
As clearly as I can how she met her death. 15

When she had left us,
In passionate silence, passing through the court,
She ran to her apartment in the house,
Her hair clutched by the fingers of both hands.
She closed the doors behind her; then, by that bed 20
Where long ago the fatal son was conceived —
That son who should bring about his father's death —
We heard her call upon Laïos, dead so many years,
And heard her wail for the double fruit of her marriage,
A husband by her husband, children by her child. 25

Exactly how she died I do not know:
For Oedipus burst in moaning and would not let us
Keep vigil to the end: it was by him
As he stormed about the room that our eyes were caught.
From one to another of us he went, begging a sword, 30
Cursing the wife who was not his wife, the mother
Whose womb had carried his own children and himself.
I do not know: it was none of us aided him,
But surely one of the gods was in control!
For with a dreadful cry 35
He hurled his weight, as though wrenched out of himself,
At the twin doors: the bolts gave, and he rushed in.

And there we saw her hanging, her body swaying
From the cruel cord she had noosed about her neck.
A great sob broke from him, heartbreaking to hear, 40
As he loosed the rope and lowered her to the ground.

I would blot out from my mind what happened next!
For the King ripped from her gown the golden brooches
That were her ornament, and raised them, and plunged them down
Straight into his own eyeballs, crying, "No more, 45
No more shall you look on the misery about me,
The horrors of my own doing! Too long you have known
The faces of those whom I should never have seen,
Too long been blind to those for whom I was searching!
From this hour, go in darkness!" And as he spoke, 50
He struck at his eyes — not once, but many times;
And the blood spattered his beard,
Bursting from his ruined sockets like red hail.

So from the unhappiness of two this evil has sprung,
A curse on the man and woman alike. The old 55
Happiness of the house of Labdakos
Was happiness enough: where is it today?
It is all wailing and ruin, disgrace, death — all
The misery of mankind that has a name —
And it is wholly and for ever theirs. 60

CHORAGOS: Is he in agony still? Is there no rest for him?

SECOND MESSENGER: He is calling for someone to lead him to the gates
So that all the children of Kadmos may look upon
His father's murderer, his mother's — no,
I can not say it!
And then he will leave Thebes, 65
Self-exiled, in order that the curse
Which he himself pronounced may depart from the house.
He is weak, and there is none to lead him,
So terrible is his suffering.
But you will see:
Look, the doors are opening; in a moment 70
You will see a thing that would crush a heart of stone.

(*The central door is opened;* OEDIPUS, *blinded, is led in.*)

CHORAGOS: Dreadful indeed for men to see.
Never have my own eyes
Looked on a sight so full of fear.

Oedipus! 75
What madness came upon you, what daemon

Leaped on your life with heavier
Punishment than a mortal man can bear?
No: I can not even
Look at you, poor ruined one. 80
And I would speak, question, ponder,
If I were able. No.
You make me shudder.

OEDIPUS: God. God.
Is there a sorrow greater? 85
Where shall I find harbor in this world?
My voice is hurled far on a dark wind.
What has God done to me?

CHORAGOS: Too terrible to think of, or to see.

[STROPHE 1

OEDIPUS: O cloud of night, 90
Never to be turned away: night coming on,
I can not tell how: night like a shroud!

My fair winds brought me here.
Oh God. Again
The pain of the spikes where I had sight,
The flooding pain 95
Of memory, never to be gouged out.

CHORAGOS: This is not strange.
You suffer it all twice over, remorse in pain,
Pain in remorse.

[ANTISTROPHE 1

OEDIPUS: Ah dear friend 100
Are you faithful even yet, you alone?
Are you still standing near me, will you stay here,
Patient, to care for the blind?
The blind man!
Yet even blind I know who it is attends me,
By the voice's tone – 105
Though my new darkness hide the comforter.

CHORAGOS: Oh fearful act!
What god was it drove you to rake black
Night across your eyes?

[STROPHE 2

OEDIPUS: Apollo. Apollo. Dear 110
Children, the god was Apollo.
He brought my sick, sick fate upon me.
But the blinding hand was my own!

How could I bear to see
When all my sight was horror everywhere? 115
CHORAGOS: Everywhere; that is true.
OEDIPUS: And now what is left?
Images? Love? A greeting even,
Sweet to the senses? Is there anything?
Ah, no, friends: lead me away. 120
Lead me away from Thebes.
Lead the great wreck
And hell of Oedipus, whom the gods hate.
CHORAGOS: Your fate is clear, you are not blind to that.
Would God you had never found it out!

[ANTISTROPHE 2

OEDIPUS: Death take the man who unbound 125
My feet on that hillside
And delivered me from death to life! What life?
If only I had died,
This weight of monstrous doom
Could not have dragged me and my darlings down. 130
CHORAGOS: I would have wished the same.
OEDIPUS: Oh never to have come here
With my father's blood upon me! Never
To have been the man they call his mother's husband!
Oh accurst! Oh child of evil, 135
To have entered that wretched bed —
the selfsame one!
More primal than sin itself, this fell to me.
CHORAGOS: I do not know how I can answer you.
You were better dead than alive and blind.
OEDIPUS: Do not counsel me any more. This punishment 140
That I have laid upon myself is just.
If I had eyes,
I do not know how I could bear the sight
Of my father, when I came to the house of Death,
Or my mother: for I have sinned against them both 145
So vilely that I could not make my peace
By strangling my own life.
Or do you think my children,
Born as they were born, would be sweet to my eyes?
Ah never, never! Nor this town with its high walls,
Nor the holy images of the gods.
For I, 150
Thrice miserable! — Oedipus, noblest of all the line

Of Kadmos, have condemned myself to enjoy
These things no more, by my own malediction
Expelling that man whom the gods declared
To be a defilement in the house of Laïos. 155
After exposing the rankness of my own guilt,
How could I look men frankly in the eyes?
No, I swear it,
If I could have stifled my hearing at its source,
I would have done it and made all this body 160
A tight cell of misery, blank to light and sound:
So I should have been safe in a dark agony
Beyond all recollection.
Ah Kithairon!
Why did you shelter me? When I was cast upon you,
Why did I not die? Then I should never 165
Have shown the world my execrable birth.

Ah Polybos! Corinth, city that I believed
The ancient seat of my ancestors: how fair
I seemed, your child! And all the while this evil
Was cancerous within me!
For I am sick 170
In my daily life, sick in my origin.

O three roads, dark ravine, woodland and way
Where three roads met: you, drinking my father's blood,
My own blood, spilled by my own hand: can you remember
The unspeakable things I did there, and the things 175
I went on from there to do?
O marriage, marriage!
The act that engendered me, and again the act
Performed by the son in the same bed —
Ah, the net
Of incest, mingling fathers, brothers, sons,
With brides, wives, mothers: the last evil 180
That can be known by men: no tongue can say
How evil!
No. For the love of God, conceal me
Somewhere far from Thebes; or kill me; or hurl me
Into the sea, away from men's eyes for ever.

Come, lead me. You need not fear to touch me. 185
Of all men, I alone can bear this guilt.

(*Enter* CREON.)

CHORAGOS: We are not the ones to decide; but Creon here

May fitly judge of what you ask. He only
Is left to protect the city in your place.
OEDIPUS: Alas, how can I speak to him? What right have I 190
To beg his courtesy whom I have deeply wronged?
CREON: I have not come to mock you, Oedipus,
Or to reproach you, either.
(*To* ATTENDANTS.) — You, standing there:
If you have lost all respect for man's dignity,
At least respect the flame of Lord Helios: 195
Do not allow this pollution to show itself
Openly here, an affront to the earth
And Heaven's rain and the light of day. No, take him
Into the house as quickly as you can.
For it is proper 200
That only the close kindred see his grief.
OEDIPUS: I pray you in God's name, since your courtesy
Ignores my dark expectation, visiting
With mercy this man of all men most execrable:
Give me what I ask — for your good, not for mine. 205
CREON: And what is it that you would have me do?
OEDIPUS: Drive me out of this country as quickly as may be
To a place where no human voice can ever greet me.
CREON: I should have done that before now — only,
God's will had not been wholly revealed to me. 210
OEDIPUS: But his command is plain: the parricide
Must be destroyed. I am that evil man.
CREON: That is the sense of it, yes; but things are,
We had best discover clearly what is to be done.
OEDIPUS: You would learn more about a man like me? 215
CREON: You are ready now to listen to the god.
OEDIPUS: I will listen. But it is to you
That I must turn for help. I beg you, hear me.

The woman in there —
Give her whatever funeral you think proper: 220
She is your sister.
— But let me go, Creon!
Let me purge my father's Thebes of the pollution
Of my living here, and go out to the wild hills,
To Kithairon, that has won such fame with me,
The tomb my mother and father appointed for me, 225
And let me die there, as they willed I should.
And yet I know
Death will not ever come to me through sickness
Or in any natural way: I have been preserved

For some unthinkable fate. But let that be. 230
As for my sons, you need not care for them.
They are men, they will find some way to live.
But my poor daughters, who have shared my table,
Who never before have been parted from their father —
Take care of them, Creon; do this for me. 235
And will you let me touch them with my hands
A last time, and let us weep together?
Be kind, my lord,
Great prince, be kind!
Could I but touch them,
They would be mine again, as when I had my eyes. 240

(*Enter* ANTIGONE *and* ISMENE, *attended.*)

Ah, God!
Is it my dearest children I hear weeping?
Has Creon pitied me and sent my daughters?
CREON: Yes, Oedipus: I knew that they were dear to you
In the old days, and know you must love them still. 245
OEDIPUS: May God bless you for this — and be a friendlier
Guardian to you than he has been to me!

Children, where are you?
Come quickly to my hands: they are your brother's —
Hands that have brought your father's once clear eyes 250
To this way of seeing —
Ah dearest ones,
I had neither sight nor knowledge then, your father
By the woman who was the source of his own life!
And I weep for you — having no strength to see you —,
I weep for you when I think of the bitterness 255
That men will visit upon you all your lives.
What homes, what festivals can you attend
Without being forced to depart again in tears?
And when you come to marriageable age,
Where is the man, my daughters, who would dare 260
Risk the bane that lies on all my children?
Is there any evil wanting? Your father killed
His father; sowed the womb of her who bore him;
Engendered you at the fount of his own existence!
That is what they will say of you.

Then, whom 265
Can you ever marry? There are no bridegrooms for you,
And your lives must wither away in sterile dreaming.
O Creon, son of Menoikeus!

You are the only father my daughters have,
Since we, their parents, are both of us gone for ever. 270
They are your own blood: you will not let them
Fall into beggary and loneliness;
You will keep them from the miseries that are mine!
Take pity on them; see, they are only children,
Friendless except for you. Promise me this, 275
Great Prince, and give me your hand in token of it.

(CREON *clasps his right hand.*)

Children:
I could say much, if you could understand me,
But as it is, I have only this prayer for you:
Live where you can, be as happy as you can — 280
Happier, please God, than God has made your father!

CREON: Enough. You have wept enough. Now go within.
OEDIPUS: I must; but it is hard.
CREON: Time eases all things.
OEDIPUS: But you must promise —
CREON: Say what you desire.
OEDIPUS: Send me from Thebes!
CREON: God grant that I may! 285
OEDIPUS: But since God hates me . . .
CREON: No, he will grant your wish.
OEDIPUS: You promise?
CREON: I can not speak beyond my knowledge.
OEDIPUS: Then lead me in.
CREON: Come now, and leave your children.
OEDIPUS: No! Do not take them from me!
CREON: Think no longer
That you are in command here, but rather think 290
How, when you were, you served your own destruction.

*(Exeunt into the house all but the* CHORUS; *the* CHORAGOS *chants directly to the audience.)*

CHORAGOS: Men of Thebes: look upon Oedipus.

This is the king who solved the famous riddle
And towered up, most powerful of men.
No mortal eyes but looked on him with envy, 295
Yet in the end ruin swept over him.
Let every man in mankind's frailty
Consider his last day; and let none
Presume on his good fortune until he find
Life, at his death, a memory without pain. 300

To an Athenian of the fifth century B.C. a theatrical performance was at the same time religious ritual, community service, and entertainment. The theater (from *theatron* = seeing place) was a place for the worship of Dionysus, god of fertility and rebirth, and participation in the production of plays in the god's honor was a privilege and obligation reserved for free citizens.* The most important of the Dionysiac festivals was the Greater or City Dionysia, celebrated for five or six days every spring. Three playwrights were chosen to compete for first prize with four plays each, three tragedies, sometimes but not always related in subject matter, and one satyr play, which burlesqued parts of the old myths dramatized in the tragedies.

"Tragedy" means literally "goat song," from its origin in the *dithyramb,* lyrical odes in praise of the god and chanted by a chorus dressed in goat skins and moving, dance-like, to music. Thespis, who lived in the sixth century, is said to have been the first writer of tragedy, but since his works are lost we know little of the transition from early to later forms. The performers of the primitive dithyrambs may have looked something like the chorus in the later satyr plays, who were costumed as satyrs, shaggy and obscene woodland creatures, half human and half animal. In the tetralogies of historical times the ribaldry of the satyr plays complemented the solemnity of the tragedies. We may think of them as the libidinal, orgiastic component in the celebration of the many ways in which the physical and psychic forces personified by anthropomorphic gods shaped human destiny.

Thus, the Dionysiac theater was a ceremony of word, song, and spectacle that united the entire community in a ritual expression of a range of religious experience—from springtime joy in nature's revived fecundity to pride and terror in man's capacity for good and evil, and awe before the vast mysteries behind his being. Most of the surviving Greek tragedies are not *about* Dionysus, but they all affirm the power of gods over men. When characters arrive with relevant news just when the plot calls for it, when the sole survivor of the old fight at the crossroads turns out to be the same man who saved the infant Oedipus from exposure on the Kithairon, when the shepherd is forced to recognize the messenger from Corinth who brings the news of King Polybus's death to Thebes as his fellow shepherd to whom he gave the baby, and when Iocaste prays to Apollo for "delivery from defilement" moments before the defiler is found and expelled from the city, a Greek spectator would not have felt these coincidences of timing and identity

* The origin of Greek drama in the cult of Dionysus has been disputed by some scholars, but there is general agreement that the Dionysiac festival was the exclusive setting for theatrical performance.

as outrageous implausibilities but as testimony to Apollo's direction of events and vindication of his oracle in Delphi and his priest Teiresias against Oedipus's and Iocaste's impious disbelief. Sophocles's rational control of the violent matter of the old myth is evident in the skill with which he has woven the intricate web of causality by which the plot moves, but his imagination is numinous, his argument metaphysical. In the twentieth century, Jean Cocteau has entitled his version of the story of Oedipus *The Infernal Machine,* in recognition of the same self-destructive pattern in Oedipus's life that informs Sophocles's treatment. And Cocteau's assigning responsibility for the train of events to a demonic rather than to a divine agent is proof, perhaps, not so much of a change in religious attitude as of the power of Sophocles's grim paganism to prompt modern questionings of the nature of a world order that victimizes heroic man.

Aristotle credits Aeschylus with the introduction of a second actor (*deuteragonist*) – a virtual prerequisite for the development of flexible dialogue and complex plot. (Plot, says Aristotle, some one hundred years after the great age of Greek tragedy, is "the soul of tragedy," and character is the second most important element.) Sophocles added a third actor, which Aeschylus also used in his last plays. In early tragedy the lyrical or choral element must have predominated over histrionics, and even in Sophocles the part of the chorus as the community voice, a kind of audience representative on stage – concerned but ignorant, affected by what happens but not directly participant in it – remains of crucial importance. Aeschylus reduced the number of the chorus from fifty to twelve; Sophocles raised it again to fifteen. The chorus moved in slow and stately measures to the accompaniment of flutes, while their leader, the *coryphaeus,* chanted the odes, reflective lyrics dealing with the inscrutable ways of gods with men and usually having specific reference to the action immediately preceding. The odes were divided into stanzas, called *strophes* and *antistrophes,* delivered, respectively, as the chorus moved first in one and then in the opposite direction. The odes alternated with *episodes,* in which the plot proper was carried forward. The first of the episodes was called the *prologos,* the last the *exodos.* It is probably an anachronism to think of the odes as having also the function of separating the different episodes, like a curtain in a modern theater, though no doubt that is one of the ways in which they work for a modern audience or reader.

We have only limited knowledge of the physical properties of the Dionysiac theater in Athens during the age of Aeschylus, Sophocles, and Euripides. The audience – perhaps as many as 15,000 – sat on benches in rising concentric half circles on the southern slope of the Acropolis. The plays were performed before a long, low, wooden building (*skene*) that served both as dressing room and as conventional backdrop for the action – thus in *Oedipus Rex* as the palace front. Before the skene was the main circular acting area, the *orchestra,* with an altar for Dionysus in the center. In the time of the great tragedians both actors and chorus almost certainly appeared in the orchestra; the raised stage separating the main from the choric action seems to have been a later development in stage architecture. Both actors and chorus wore masks, not for reasons of acoustics, as was once believed, but as stylized indicators of age, sex – men played women's parts – and temperament. They must also have created an effect of depersonalized, universal myth. The performers were dressed in long, colored robes. Elevated shoes (*kothurnoi*) came into use only after the great age of the classical Athenian theater was past. Performance of a complete tetralogy took most of the daylight hours.

*Oedipus Rex* was written about 430 B.C., when Sophocles was in his sixties. Though it deals with an earlier episode in the story of the House of Laïos, it followed *Antigone* in composition, and the two plays are not parts of the same tetralogy. Sophocles did not win the prize for the tetralogy to which *Oedipus Rex* belongs. In his *Poetics,* the most important classical treatment of the theory of tragedy, Aristotle discusses *Oedipus Rex* as a model tragedy: a unified dramatization of formal complexity of a story of a certain magnitude concerning a good but not perfect man who comes to grief because of some tragic flaw (*hamartia*) and which effects the purgation (*katharsis*) of the emotions of pity and fear in the audience. The exact meaning of catharsis has been much debated, but the medical denotation of Aristotle's term suggests that he had in mind some kind of soul therapy: witnessing the tragic action unfold to catastrophe in a scene of recognition (*anagnorisis*), the spectator harmlessly expends his subrational passions in vicarious suffering. Because moral enlightenment is the intended effect of this feeling of there-but-for-the-grace-of-God-go-I and because it depends on a degree of audience identification, the protagonist can be neither vicious nor perfect. Suffering vice commands no sympathy, and suffering perfection would seem merely preposterous.

When a playwright dramatizes a traditional story well known to his audience he must forego major plot invention and alteration and all attempts to surprise his audience in the more obvious ways. He is tied to the received facts. But in compensation he can dispense with the laborious exposition that clutters many an original play of more modern times. With the tragic myth given he can proceed at once to essentials: the dramatization not of a story but of its meaning. The old myth of man's vain effort to circumvent the divine will is in Sophocles's treatment a tautly suspenseful revelation of the unredeemability of the past, of the fateful continuity in a human life. There is the pathos of innocent ignorance and impotence in the scene where the two shepherds meet again, the Corinthian effusively reminiscing about the distant days when they tended their flocks together on the Kithairon, the Theban scared and reluctant at the approach of the disastrous revelation he sees coming. The retrospective structure orders the narrative into a metaphor for the way the past doesn't just *produce* but *is* the present. The hours on stage comprise all of Oedipus's life. It is difficult to think of another play in which unity of time as a formal property of the drama contributes more to the meaning. Every step Oedipus takes to solve the old murder mystery, every new confrontation with those he summons to appear with pieces of the past, every one of their chance disclosures, brings him closer both to the solution he seeks and to the self-discovery he does not foresee. When the last piece falls into place the detective has become the criminal, his success his doom, his happy ignorance tragic knowledge, and the evil without the evil within.

Such a summary description of the plot points up its heavily ironic nature. Dramatic irony operates whenever the audience is aware of some circumstance in plot or character that gives a speech a meaning beyond or at odds with that which the speaker consciously intends, or charges a situation with a significance unsuspected by the character caught in it. The more hostile the covert significance is to the unwitting ironist and the farther he is from realizing it, the more poignant the irony. In Oedipus's words to the citizen supplicants in Scene I, "Sick as you are, not one is as sick as I," we hear not just the king's concern for his stricken people and his self-involvement in their fate, we also perceive the dreadful accuracy of his description of himself. Our perception depends on our knowledge of the outcome, but the alert reader can anticipate the outcome in the persistent pattern of ironies – Oedipus cursing Laïos's murderer, promising to avenge the dead king "just as though I were his son," and berating Teiresias for his arrogance, mocking his blindness, and accusing him of complicity in the murder. Far from being an inept, premature giveaway of the plot, Sophocles's method engages our interest in the dramatic form as an image of the frailty of man's defenses, the folly of his feelings of security and power – *hubris* is the Greek word – and the strange inevitability of his fate. Our suspense concerning the manner in which the ironies will complete themselves in the unraveling of the directed past is of a subtler kind than that produced by ignorance of outcome. If we miss the grim geometry in all this, the plot will seem only like a set of brutal facts manipulated for shock effect – not so much an irrelevant as an inadequate response.

Irony is a rhetorical device for holding different or opposite truths in suspension, for focusing on the discrepancy between what seems to be and what is. It is therefore properly the sustaining mode of a tragedy of self-ignorance. At the beginning of the play Oedipus has a clear and single purpose: to find Laïos's murderer. When he later begins to pursue his own parentage the obvious irony is that this wise and self-assured man doesn't realize that his purpose has changed. The deeper irony is that it hasn't *really* changed, since the answer to the question of whose son he is is also the answer to the question of who killed Laïos. Pride motivates both quests. He undertakes the first because he pities his people and wants to protect himself against Laïos's fate but above all because he is King Oedipus "of the famous name," the conqueror of the Sphinx with a reputation as Thebes's savior to maintain, and sure of his own ability to discover the truth. That the Priest in the Prologue finds it proper to remind him that he is "not one of the immortal gods" says something perhaps about the respect he commands and expects to command. For the same reason he is later willing to risk learning that he is low-born; his achievements, he feels, will cancel any possible ignominy of birth. He is proud of being a self-made man, superior to what he takes to be Iocaste's aristocratic prejudice.

> How could I wish that I were someone else?
> How could I not be glad to know my birth?

His two quests turn out to have been one when he learns that he is the child not of "luck" but of the man he has slain and of the woman he has married. He was the one man clever enough to identify "man" from the clues in the Sphinx' riddle,* yet he has never known his own identity. The recognition scene imparts the old tragic wisdom that knowledge is suffering, an early, dark, and bitter variant of the Socratic "know thyself." One could define an abiding tension in western consciousness by these two views: faith in knowledge as a way to virtue and the good life, and the conviction that ultimate self-knowledge is painful. The Socratic ethic assumes progress through moral endeavor. Tragedy questions man's ability to perfect himself and his institutions through learning and self-discipline and demands a high price for enlightenment. The wage of noble striving is death. The tragic temper is devastating to a philosophy of amelioration and is hard to reconcile with a belief in a just and benevolent providence, but it is not unsupportable by the facts of history. Socrates was, as he recognized himself, a non-tragic figure. Coming to him — or to Plato's accounts of him — from Greek tragedy one is struck by a sense of the Socratic fallacy, a quality of innocence in his concept of man's nature.

Does Oedipus suffer justly? In committing parricide and incest he has violated the most sacred of the taboos governing family life. Freud used his name for the most primary of interpersonal conflicts, the child's sexual jealousy of the parent of his own sex, and equated his crime with each man's original sin. But since Oedipus is clearly inno-

* "Who moves on four in the morning, on two at noon, and on three in the evening?"

cent of evil intent, can the god be called just who exacts such suffering for crimes thus committed? How can he be held responsible for a destiny decreed for him before his birth and for the god's manipulation of events in such a way that the means by which he and his parents try to avert his destiny become the very means by which it is fulfilled? Why should Oedipus have to pay for his parents' impiety in ignoring Apollo's warning and in seeking to frustrate the god's will by abandoning their child? Does retribution in *Oedipus Rex* strike the right victim?

It does if we make a distinction between divine *foreknowledge* and divine *preordination.* The god in his wisdom, knowing the kind of man Oedipus was, could know what his destiny was. But the god did not *determine* or *order* that destiny. Related to this view is that which sees Oedipus as the maker of his own misfortune and the whole play as a critique of rationalism. It is not the acts themselves that cause his suffering, for he has lived happily for years after killing his father and marrying his mother; it is the finding out. He may have been doomed to do what he did but not to discover what he had done. He thinks he can outwit the god. Anger subverts his reason in his encounters with Laïos, Teiresias, and Creon. He fails to see the possible connection between the drunken Corinthian's taunt that he is the son of an unknown father and the words of the Delphic oracle. His purpose is diverted when his pride is involved. He refuses to heed Teiresias's and Iocaste's warning to leave the past alone. Intellectual pride and a hasty temper constitute his tragic flaw. Sophocles's tragedy, like so many of Shakespeare's, implies that character is fate. That Oedipus means well is true, but good intentions have never guaranteed protection against evil consequences.

That, however, is precisely the problem of divine justice in the play. If Oedipus regards the unsolved murder of Laïos as a challenge to his ingenuity and determination, he also undertakes the investigation because he is not callous enough to ignore his people's plea for help. He suffers not *in spite* of but *because* of his exercise of kingly responsibility. True, if he had not been king he would not have had the responsibility, and he became king because he was headstrong. But that is not the whole truth. When all his vulnerabilities of mind and temper have been listed there remains a sense in which he is the victim both of circumstances over which he had no control and of his own virtues.

But Oedipus blinds himself in an agony of shame and guilty horror. Beyond his bewildered, "What has the God done to me?" it doesn't occur to anyone to question the justice of his fate. He accepts the fact that he is a pollution of which Thebes must cleanse herself. The god's punishment of the city that has innocently harbored the violator of natural law is a blight of infertility on crops, beasts, and humans.

And at the end Oedipus's personal tragedy restores the city to health; once again he saves Thebes, just as he set out to do. We are aware in all of this of the workings of a supernatural order that is ruthless but neither arbitrary nor malign. That Oedipus is an abomination in the eyes of god and men alike is a matter neither of morality nor of justice, but it is a fact that must be heeded. The universe is not obliged to fit man's sense of fair play. The will of the gods is inscrutable, but it must be obeyed. "Neither destiny nor Oedipus is acquitted or condemned" is how one critic puts the affirmation in *Oedipus Rex* of an order that passes human understanding.

When enlightenment crashes in on Oedipus, he obliterates his sight of the world he thought he controlled. Like Shakespeare's Gloucester he learns that "he stumbled when he saw." And like Teiresias, Apollo's priest-prophet, whose experience of both male and female existence gives him an understanding that transcends that of ordinary men, and whose blindness is a symbol of inner vision, so Oedipus, too, at the end of his life is a figure whom great suffering has sanctified. In *Oedipus at Colonus* the aged king is still in exile and still irascible and imperious. But his destiny has taken him beyond tragedy, and his death is a holy mystery. Our questions of divine justice are not answered, but they are silenced. After Iocaste learns the truth in Scene III and realizes that she can't keep it from her still ignorant son-husband, she goes to her suicide without further words. And the messenger from Corinth, the cheerful bringer of good news who finds himself turning into an instrument of catastrophe, can only listen in silent, mounting horror as Oedipus examines the old shepherd. At the end we think of him as slinking away, shaken and ignored.

Human guilt and innocence are ambiguous and inextricable; before the absolute, pride and power and virtue are equally helpless. The voice that stays with us is that of the Chorus, lost, awed, grieving for humanity, recognizing its "blindness" "while the false years went by":

> What measure shall I give these generations
> That breathe on the void and are the void
> And exist and do not exist?

# ANONYMOUS

# Everyman

CHARACTERS

GOD

| | | | |
|---|---|---|---|
| MESSENGER | KINDRED | KNOWLEDGE | DISCRETION |
| DEATH | COUSIN | CONFESSION | FIVE WITS |
| EVERYMAN | GOODS | BEAUTY | ANGEL |
| FELLOWSHIP | GOOD DEEDS | STRENGTH | DOCTOR |

*Here Beginneth a Treatise how the High Father of Heaven Sendeth Death to Summon Every Creature to Come and Give Account of their Lives in this World, and is in Manner of a Moral Play.*

MESSENGER: I pray you all give your audience,
And hear this matter with reverence,
By figure[1] a moral play:
The *Summoning of Everyman* called it is,
That of our lives and ending shows 5
How transitory we be all day.
This matter is wondrous precious,
But the intent of it is more gracious,

From the book *Everyman and Medieval Miracle Plays,* edited by A. C. Cowley. Dutton Everyman Paperback. Reprinted by permission of E. P. Dutton & Co., Inc. Canadian rights granted by J. M. Dent & Sons Ltd.

[1] form

And sweet to bear away.
The story saith: Man, in the beginning 10
Look well, and take good heed to the ending,
Be you never so gay!
Ye think sin in the beginning full sweet,
Which in the end causeth the soul to weep,
When the body lieth in clay. 15
Here shall you see how Fellowship and Jollity,
Both Strength, Pleasure, and Beauty,
Will fade from thee as flower in May;
For ye shall hear how our Heaven King
Calleth Everyman to a general reckoning: 20
Give audience, and hear what he doth say. *(Exit.)*

(GOD *speaketh:*)

GOD: I perceive, here in my majesty,
How that all creatures be to me unkind,
Living without dread in worldly prosperity:
Of ghostly[2] sight the people be so blind, 25
Drowned in sin, they know me not for their God;
In worldly riches is all their mind,
They fear not my righteousness, the sharp rod.
My law that I showed, when I for them died,
They forget clean,[3] and shedding of my blood red; 30
I hanged between two, it cannot be denied;
To get them life I suffered[4] to be dead;
I healed their feet, with thorns hurt was my head.
I could do no more than I did, truly;
And now I see the people do clean forsake me: 35
They use the seven deadly sins damnable,
As pride, covetise, wrath, and lechery
Now in the world be made commendable;
And thus they leave of angels the heavenly company.
Every man liveth so after his own pleasure, 40
And yet of their life they be nothing[5] sure:
I see the more that I them forbear
The worse they be from year to year.
All that liveth appaireth[6] fast;
Therefore I will, in all the haste, 45
Have a reckoning of every man's person;
For, and[7] I leave the people thus alone
In their life and wicked tempests,

[2] spiritual
[3] completely, altogether
[4] allowed myself
[5] not at all
[6] becomes worse
[7] if

Verily they will become much worse than beasts;
For now one would by envy another up eat; 50
Charity they do all clean forget.
I hoped well that every man
In my glory should make his mansion,
And thereto I had them all elect;
But now I see, like traitors deject, 55
They thank me not for the pleasure that I to them meant,
Nor yet for their being I them have lent.
I proffered the people great multitude of mercy,
And few there be that asketh it heartily.
They be so cumbered with worldly riches 60
That needs on them I must do justice,
On every man living without fear.
Where art thou, Death, though mighty messenger?

(*Enter* DEATH.)

DEATH: Almighty God, I am here at your will,
Your commandment to fulfil. 65
GOD: Go thou to Everyman,
And show him, in my name,
A pilgrimage he must on him take,
Which he in no wise[8] may escape;
And that he bring with him a sure reckoning 70
Without delay or any tarrying. (GOD *withdraws.*)
DEATH: Lord, I will in the world go run overall,[9]
And cruelly outsearch both great and small;
Every man will I beset that liveth beastly
Out of God's laws, and dreadeth not folly. 75
He that loveth riches I will strike with my dart,
His sight to blind, and from heaven to depart[10] –
Except that alms be his good friend –
In hell for to dwell, world without end.
Lo, yonder I see Everyman walking. 80
Full little he thinketh on my coming;
His mind is on fleshly lusts and his treasure,
And great pain it shall cause him to endure
Before the Lord, Heaven King.

(*Enter* EVERYMAN.)

Everyman, stand still! Whither art thou going 85
Thus gaily? Hast thou thy Maker forget?

[8] manner
[9] everywhere
[10] separate

EVERYMAN: Why askest thou?
Wouldest thou wit?[11]
DEATH: Yea, sir; I will show you:
In great haste I am sent to thee 90
From God out of his majesty.
EVERYMAN: What, sent to me?
DEATH: Yea, certainly.
Though thou have forget him here,
He thinketh on thee in the heavenly sphere, 95
As, ere we depart, thou shalt know.
EVERYMAN: What desireth God of me?
DEATH: That shall I show thee:
A reckoning he will needs have
Without any longer respite. 100
EVERYMAN: To give a reckoning longer leisure I crave;
This blind[12] matter troubleth my wit.
DEATH: On thee thou must take a long journey;
Therefore thy book of count[13] with thee thou bring,
For turn again thou cannot by no way. 105
And look thou be sure of thy reckoning,
For before God thou shalt answer, and show
Thy many bad deeds, and good but a few;
How thou hast spent thy life, and in what wise,
Before the chief Lord of paradise. 110
Have ado[14] that we were in that way,[15]
For, wit thou well, thou shalt make none[16] attorney.
EVERYMAN: Full unready I am such reckoning to give.
I know thee not. What messenger art thou?
DEATH: I am Death, that no man dreadeth,[17] 115
For every man I rest,[18] and no man spareth;
For it is God's commandment
That all to me shall be obedient.
EVERYMAN: O Death, thou comest when I had thee least in mind!
In thy power it lieth me to save; 120
Yet of my good will I give thee, if thou will be kind:
Yea, a thousand pound shalt thou have,
And defer this matter till another day.
DEATH: Everyman, it may not be, by no way.
I set not by[19] gold, silver, nor riches, 125
Ne by pope, emperor, king, duke, ne princes;

[11] know
[12] obscure
[13] account
[14] see to it
[15] on that journey
[16] have no
[17] dreads no man
[18] arrest
[19] do not care for

For, and I would receive gifts great,
All the world I might get;
But my custom is clean contrary.
I give thee no respite. Come hence, and not tarry. 130

EVERYMAN: Alas, shall I have no longer respite?
I may say Death giveth no warning!
To think on thee, it maketh my heart sick,
For all unready is my book of reckoning.
But twelve year and I might have abiding, 135
My counting-book I would make so clear
That my reckoning I should not need to fear.
Wherefore, Death, I pray thee, for God's mercy,
Spare me till I be provided of remedy.

DEATH: Thee availeth not to cry, weep, and pray; 140
But haste thee lightly[20] that thou were gone that journey,
And prove thy friends if thou can;
For, wit thou well, the tide abideth no man,
And in the world each living creature
For Adam's sin must die of nature.[21] 145

EVERYMAN: Death, if I should this pilgrimage take,
And my reckoning surely make,
Show me, for[22] saint charity,
Should I not come again shortly?

DEATH: No, Everyman; and thou be once there, 150
Thou mayst never more come here,
Trust me verily.

EVERYMAN: O gracious God in the high seat celestial,
Have mercy on me in this most need!
Shall I have no company from this vale terrestrial 155
Of mine acquaintance, that way me to lead?

DEATH: Yea, if any be so hardy
That would go with thee and bear thee company.
Hie[23] thee that thou were gone to God's magnificence,
Thy reckoning to give before his presence. 160
What, weenest[24] thou thy life is given thee,
And thy worldly goods also?

EVERYMAN: I had wend[25] so, verily.

DEATH: Nay, nay; it was but lent thee;
For as soon as thou art go, 165
Another a while shall have it, and then go therefro,[26]
Even as thou hast done.

[20] quickly
[21] as a natural thing
[22] in the name of
[23] hurry
[24] think
[25] thought
[26] from it

Everyman, thou art mad! Thou hast thy wits five,
And here on earth will not amend thy life;
For suddenly I do come. 170

EVERYMAN: O wretched caitiff, whither shall I flee,
That I might scape this endless sorrow?
Now, gentle Death, spare me till to-morrow,
That I may amend me
With good advisement.[27] 175

DEATH: Nay, thereto I will not consent,
Nor no man will I respite;
But to the heart suddenly I shall smite
Without any advisement.
And now out of thy sight I will me hie; 180
See thou make thee ready shortly,
For thou mayst say this is the day
That no man living may scape away. (*Exit* DEATH.)

EVERYMAN: Alas, I may well weep with sighs deep!
Now have I no manner of company 185
To help me in my journey, and me to keep;
And also my writing is full unready.
How shall I do now for to excuse me?
I would to God I had never be get![28]
To my soul a full great profit it had be; 190
For now I fear pains huge and great.
The time passeth. Lord, help, that all wrought!
For though I mourn it availeth nought.
The day passeth, and is almost ago;[29]
I wot not well what for to do. 195
To whom were I best my complaint to make?
What and I to Fellowship thereof spake,
And showed him of this sudden chance?
For in him is all mine affiance;[30]
We have in the world so many a day 200
Be good friends in sport and play.
I see him yonder, certainly.
I trust that he will bear me company;
Therefore to him will I speak to ease my sorrow.
Well met, good Fellowship, and good morrow! 205

(FELLOWSHIP *speaketh:*)

FELLOWSHIP: Everyman, good morrow, by this day!
Sir, why lookest thou so piteously?

[27] reflection
[28] been born
[29] gone
[30] trust

If any thing be amiss, I pray thee me say,
That I may help to remedy.
EVERYMAN: Yea, good Fellowship, yea; 210
I am in great jeopardy.
FELLOWSHIP: My true friend, show to me your mind;
I will not forsake thee to my life's end,
In the way of good company.
EVERYMAN: That was well spoken, and lovingly. 215
FELLOWSHIP: Sir, I must needs know your heaviness;[31]
I have pity to see you in any distress.
If any have you wronged, ye shall revenged be,
Though I on the ground be slain for thee –
Though that I know before that I should die. 220
EVERYMAN: Verily, Fellowship, gramercy.
FELLOWSHIP: Tush! by thy thanks I set not a straw.
Show me your grief, and say no more.
EVERYMAN: If I my heart should to you break,[32]
And then you to turn your mind from me, 225
And would not me comfort when ye hear me speak,
Then should I ten times sorrier be.
FELLOWSHIP: Sir, I say as I will do indeed.
EVERYMAN: Then be you a good friend at need:
I have found you true herebefore. 230
FELLOWSHIP: And so ye shall evermore;
For, in faith, and thou go to hell,
I will not forsake thee by the way.
EVERYMAN: Ye speak like a good friend; I believe you well.
I shall deserve it, and I may. 235
FELLOWSHIP: I speak of no deserving, by this day!
For he that will say, and nothing do,
Is not worthy with good company to go;
Therefore show me the grief of your mind,
As to your friend most loving and kind. 240
EVERYMAN: I shall show you how it is:
Commanded I am to go a journey,
A long way, hard and dangerous,
And give a strait count, without delay,
Before the high Judge, Adonai.[33] 245
Wherefore, I pray you, bear me company,
As ye have promised, in this journey.
FELLOWSHIP: That is matter indeed. Promise is duty;
But, and I should take such a voyage on me,

[31] sorrow
[32] open
[33] Hebrew name for God

I know it well, it should be to my pain; 250
Also it maketh me afeard, certain.
But let us take counsel here as well as we can,
For your words would fear[34] a strong man.
EVERYMAN: Why, ye said if I had need
Ye would me never forsake, quick[35] ne dead, 255
Though it were to hell, truly.
FELLOWSHIP: So I said, certainly,
But such pleasures be set aside, the sooth to say;
And also, if we took such a journey,
When should we come again? 260
EVERYMAN: Nay, never again, till the day of doom.
FELLOWSHIP: In faith, then will not I come there!
Who hath you these tidings brought?
EVERYMAN: Indeed, Death was with me here.
FELLOWSHIP: Now, by God that all hath bought, 265
If Death were the messenger,
For no man that is living to-day
I will not go that loath journey —
Not for the father that begat me!
EVERYMAN: Ye promised otherwise, pardie.[36] 270
FELLOWSHIP: I wot well I said so, truly;
And yet if thou wilt eat, and drink, and make good cheer,
Or haunt to women the lusty company,[37]
I would not forsake you while the day is clear,[38]
Trust me verily. 275
EVERYMAN: Yea, thereto ye would be ready!
To go to mirth, solace, and play,
Your mind will sooner apply,
Than to bear me company in my long journey.
FELLOWSHIP: Now, in good faith, I will not that way. 280
But and thou will murder, or any man kill,
In that I will help thee with a good will.
EVERYMAN: O, that is a simple advice indeed.
Gentle fellow, help me in my necessity!
We have loved long, and now I need; 285
And now, gentle Fellowship, remember me.
FELLOWSHIP: Whether ye have loved me or no,
By Saint John, I will not with thee go.
EVERYMAN: Yet, I pray thee, take the labour, and do so much for me
To bring me forward,[39] for saint charity, 290
And comfort me till I come without the town.

[34] frighten
[35] alive
[36] by God
[37] frequent the pleasant company of women
[38] until daybreak
[39] escort me

FELLOWSHIP: Nay, and thou would give me a new gown,
I will not a foot with thee go;
But, and thou had tarried, I would not have left thee so.
And as now God speed thee in thy journey, 295
For from thee I will depart as fast as I may.
EVERYMAN: Whither away, Fellowship? Will thou forsake me?
FELLOWSHIP: Yea, by my fay![40] To God I betake[41] thee.
EVERYMAN: Farewell, good Fellowship; for thee my heart is sore.
Adieu for ever! I shall see thee no more. 300
FELLOWSHIP: In faith, Everyman, farewell now at the ending;
For you I will remember that parting is mourning.
(*Exit* FELLOWSHIP.)
EVERYMAN: Alack! shall we thus depart indeed –
Ah, Lady, help! – without any more comfort?
Lo, Fellowship forsaketh me in my most need. 305
For help in this world whither shall I resort?
Fellowship herebefore with me would merry make,
And now little sorrow for me doth he take.
It is said, 'In prosperity men friends may find,
Which in adversity be full unkind.' 310
Now whither for succour shall I flee,
Sith that[42] Fellowship hath forsaken me?
To my kinsmen I will, truly,
Praying them to help me in my necessity;
I believe that they will do so, 315
For kind[43] will creep where it may not go.
I will go say, for yonder I see them.
Where be ye now, my friends and kinsmen?

(*Enter* KINDRED *and* COUSIN.)

KINDRED: Here be we now at your commandment.
Cousin, I pray you show us your intent 320
In any wise, and do not spare.[44]
COUSIN: Yea, Everyman, and to us declare
If ye be disposed to go anywhither;
For, wit you well, we will live and die together.
KINDRED: In wealth and woe we will with you hold, 325
For over his kin a man may be bold.[45]
EVERYMAN: Gramercy, my friends and kinsmen kind.
Now shall I show you the grief of my mind:
I was commanded by a messenger,

[40] faith
[41] commend
[42] since
[43] kinship, family
[44] hold back
[45] a man may freely command the services of his family

That is a high king's chief officer; 330
He bade me go a pilgrimage, to my pain,
And I know well I shall never come again;
Also I must give a reckoning strait,
For I have a great enemy[46] that hath me in wait,
Which intendeth me for to hinder. 335

KINDRED: What account is that which ye must render?
That would I know.

EVERYMAN: Of all my works I must show
How I have lived and my days spent;
Also of ill deeds that I have used[47] 340
In my time, sith life was me lent;
And of all virtues that I have refused.
Therefore, I pray you, go thither with me
To help to make mine account, for saint charity.

COUSIN: What, to go thither? Is that the matter? 345
Nay, Everyman, I had liefer[48] fast[49] bread and water
All this five year and more.

EVERYMAN: Alas, that ever I was bore![50]
For now shall I never be merry,
If that you forsake me. 350

KINDRED: Ah, sir, what ye be a merry man!
Take good heart to you, and make no moan.
But one thing I warn you, by Saint Anne —
As for me, ye shall go alone.

EVERYMAN: My Cousin, will you not with me go? 355

COUSIN: No, by our Lady! I have the cramp in my toe.
Trust not to me, for, so God me speed,
I will deceive you in your most need.

KINDRED: It availeth not us to tice.[51]
Ye shall have my maid with all my heart; 360
She loveth to go to feasts, there to be nice,[52]
And to dance, and abroad to start:[53]
I will give her leave to help you in that journey,
If that you and she may agree.

EVERYMAN: Now show me the very effect of your mind: 365
Will you go with me, or abide behind?

KINDRED: Abide behind? Yea, that will I, and I may!
Therefore farewell till another day. (*Exit* KINDRED.)

EVERYMAN: How should I be merry or glad?
For fair promises men to me make, 370

[46] i.e., the Devil
[47] practiced
[48] rather
[49] have nothing but
[50] born
[51] entice
[52] wanton
[53] rush

But when I have most need they me forsake.
I am deceived; that maketh me sad.
COUSIN: Cousin Everyman, farewell now,
For verily I will not go with you.
Also of mine own an unready reckoning 375
I have to account; therefore I make tarrying.
Now God keep thee, for now I go. (*Exit* COUSIN.)
EVERYMAN: Ah, Jesus, is all come hereto?
Lo, fair words maketh fools fain,[54]
They promise, and nothing will do, certain. 380
My kinsmen promised me faithfully
For to abide with me steadfastly,
And now fast away do they flee:
Even so Fellowship promised me.
What friend were best me of to provide?[55] 385
I lose my time here longer to abide.
Yet in my mind a thing there is:
All my life I have loved riches;
If that my Good[56] now help me might,
He would make my heart full light. 390
I will speak to him in this distress –
Where art thou, my Goods and riches?

(GOODS *speaks from a corner:*)

GOODS: Who calleth me? Everyman? What! hast thou haste?
I lie here in corners, trussed and piled so high,
And in chests I am locked so fast, 395
Also sacked in bags. Thou mayst see with thine eye
I cannot stir; in packs low I lie.
What would ye have? Lightly me say.
EVERYMAN: Come hither, Good, in all the haste thou may,
For of counsel I must desire thee. 400
GOODS: Sir, and ye in the world have sorrow or adversity,
That can I help you to remedy shortly.
EVERYMAN: It is another disease that grieveth me;
In this world it is not, I tell thee so.
I am sent for, another way to go, 405
To give a strait count general
Before the highest Jupiter of all;
And all my life I have had joy and pleasure in thee,
Therefore, I pray thee, go with me;
For, peradventure, thou mayst before God Almighty 410

[54] glad
[55] to provide me with
[56] goods, possessions

My reckoning help to clean and purify;
For it is said ever among[57]
That money maketh all right that is wrong.
GOODS: Nay, Everyman, I sing another song.
I follow no man in such voyages; 415
For, and I went with thee,
Thou shouldst fare much the worst for me;
For because on me thou did set thy mind,
Thy reckoning I have made blotted and blind,
That thine account thou cannot make truly; 420
And that hast thou for the love of me.
EVERYMAN: That would grieve me full sore,
When I should come to that fearful answer.
Up, let us go thither together.
GOODS: Nay, not so! I am too brittle, I may not endure; 425
I will follow no man one foot, be ye sure.
EVERYMAN: Alas, I have thee loved, and had great pleasure
All my life-days on good and treasure.
GOODS: That is to thy damnation, without leasing,
For my love is contrary to the love everlasting; 430
But if thou had me loved moderately during,
As to the poor to give part of me,
Then shouldst thou not in this dolour be,
Nor in this great sorrow and care.
EVERYMAN: Lo, now was I deceived ere I was ware, 435
And all I may wite[58] misspending of time.
GOODS: What, weenest thou that I am thine?
EVERYMAN: I had wend so.
GOODS: Nay, Everyman, I say no.
As for a while I was lent thee; 440
A season thou hast had me in prosperity.
My condition is man's soul to kill;
If I save one, a thousand I do spill.
Weenest thou that I will follow thee?
Nay, not from this world, verily. 445
EVERYMAN: I had wend otherwise.
GOODS: Therefore to thy soul Good is a thief;
For when thou art dead, this is my guise[59] —
Another to deceive in this same wise
As I have done thee, and all to his soul's reprief.[60] 450
EVERYMAN: O false Good, cursed may thou be,
Thou traitor to God, that hast deceived me
And caught me in thy snare!

[57] at times
[58] blame on
[59] practice
[60] shame

GOODS: Marry, thou brought thyself in care,
Whereof I am glad; 455
I must needs laugh, I cannot be sad.
EVERYMAN: Ah, Good, thou hast had long my heartly love;
I gave thee that which should be the Lord's above.
But wilt thou not go with me indeed?
I pray thee truth to say. 460
GOODS: No, so God me speed!
Therefore farewell, and have good day. (*Exit* GOODS.)
EVERYMAN: O, to whom shall I make my moan
For to go with me in that heavy journey?
First Fellowship said he would with me gone; 465
His words were very pleasant and gay,
But afterward he left me alone.
Then spake I to my kinsmen, all in despair,
And also they gave me words fair;
They lacked no fair speaking, 470
But all forsook me in the ending.
Then went I to my Goods, that I loved best,
In hope to have comfort, but there had I least;
For my Goods sharply did me tell
That he bringeth many into hell. 475
Then of myself I was ashamed,
And so I am worthy to be blamed;
Thus may I well myself hate.
Of whom shall I now counsel take?
I think that I shall never speed. 480
Till that I go to my Good Deed.
But, alas, she is so weak
That she can neither go nor speak;
Yet will I venture on her now.
My Good Deeds, where be you? 485

(GOOD DEEDS *speaks from the ground:*)

GOOD DEEDS: Here I lie, cold in the ground;
Thy sins hath me sore bound,
That I cannot stir.
EVERYMAN: O Good Deeds, I stand in fear!
I must you pray of counsel, 490
For help now should come right well.
GOOD DEEDS: Everyman, I have understanding
That ye be summoned account to make
Before Messias, of Jerusalem King;
And you do by me,[61] that journey with you will I take. 495

[61] as I advise

EVERYMAN: Therefore I come to you, my moan to make;
I pray you that ye will go with me.
GOOD DEEDS: I would full fain, but I cannot stand, verily.
EVERYMAN: Why, is there anything on you fall?
GOOD DEEDS: Yea, sir, I may thank you of[62] all; 500
If ye had perfectly cheered me,
Your book of count full ready had be.
Look, the books of your works and deeds eke![63]
Behold how they lie under the feet,
To your soul's heaviness. 505
EVERYMAN: Our Lord Jesus help me!
For one letter here I cannot see.
GOOD DEEDS: There is a blind reckoning in time of distress.
EVERYMAN: Good Deeds, I pray you help me in this need,
Or else I am for ever damned indeed; 510
Therefore help me to make reckoning
Before the Redeemer of all thing,
That King is, and was, and ever shall.
GOOD DEEDS: Everyman, I am sorry of your fall,
And fain would I help you, and I were able. 515
EVERYMAN: Good Deeds, your counsel I pray you give me.
GOOD DEEDS: That shall I do verily;
Though that on my feet I may not go,
I have a sister that shall with you also,
Called Knowledge, which shall with you abide, 520
To help you to make that dreadful reckoning.

(*Enter* KNOWLEDGE.)

KNOWLEDGE: Everyman, I will go with thee, and be thy guide,
In thy most need to go by thy side.
EVERYMAN: In good condition I am now in every thing,
And am wholly content with this good thing, 525
Thanked be God my creator.
GOOD DEEDS: And when she hath brought you there
Where thou shalt heel thee of thy smart,[64]
Then go you with your reckoning and your Good Deeds together,
For to make you joyful at heart 530
Before the blessed Trinity.
EVERYMAN: My Good Deeds, gramercy!
I am well content, certainly,
With your words sweet.

[62] for
[63] also
[64] pain

KNOWLEDGE: Now go we together lovingly 535
To Confession, that cleansing river.
EVERYMAN: For joy I weep; I would we were there!
But, I pray you, give me cognition
Where dwelleth that holy man, Confession.
KNOWLEDGE: In the house of salvation: 540
We shall find him in that place,
That shall us comfort, by God's grace.

(KNOWLEDGE *takes* EVERYMAN *to* CONFESSION.)

Lo, this is Confession. Kneel down and ask mercy,
For he is in good conceit[65] with God Almighty.
EVERYMAN: O glorious fountain, that all uncleanness doth clarify, 545
Wash from me the spots of vice unclean,
That on me no sin may be seen.
I come with Knowledge for my redemption,
Redempt with heart and full contrition;
For I am commanded a pilgrimage to take, 550
And great accounts before God to make.
Now I pray you, Shrift,[66] mother of salvation,
Help my Good Deeds for my piteous exclamation.
CONFESSION: I know your sorrow well, Everyman.
Because with Knowledge ye come to me, 555
I will you comfort as well as I can,
And a precious jewel I will give thee,
Called penance, voider of adversity;
Therewith shall your body chastised be,
With abstinence and perseverance in God's service. 560
Here shall you receive that scourge of me,
Which is penance strong that ye must endure,
To remember thy Saviour was scourged for thee
With sharp scourges, and suffered it patiently;
So must thou, ere thou scape that painful pilgrimage. 565
Knowledge, keep him in this voyage,
And by that time Good Deeds will be with thee.
But in any wise be siker[67] of mercy,
For your time draweth fast; and ye will saved be,
Ask God mercy, and he will grant truly. 570
When with the scourge of penance man doth him[68] bind,
The oil of forgiveness then shall he find.
EVERYMAN: Thanked be God for his gracious work!
For now I will my penance begin;

[65] esteem
[66] confession
[67] sure
[68] himself

This hath rejoiced and lighted my heart, 575
Though the knots be painful and hard within.
KNOWLEDGE: Everyman, look your penance that ye fulfil,
What pain that ever it to you be;
And Knowledge shall give you counsel at will
How your account ye shall make clearly. 580
EVERYMAN: O eternal God, O heavenly figure,
O way of righteousness, O goodly vision,
Which descended down in a virgin pure
Because he would every man redeem,
Which Adam forfeited by his disobedience: 585
O blessed Godhead, elect and high divine,
Forgive my grievous offence;
Here I cry thee mercy in this presence.
O ghostly treasure, O ransomer and redeemer,
Of all the world hope and conductor,[69] 590
Mirror of joy, and founder of mercy,
Which enlumineth heaven and earth thereby,[70]
Hear my clamorous complaint, though it late be;
Receive my prayers, of thy benignity;
Though I be a sinner most abominable, 595
Yet let my name be written in Moses' table.
O Mary, pray to the Maker of all thing,
Me for to help at my ending;
And save me from the power of my enemy,
For Death assaileth me strongly. 600
And, Lady, that I may by mean of thy prayer
Of your Son's glory to be[71] partner,
By the means of his passion, I it crave;
I beseech you help my soul to save.
Knowledge, give me the scourge of penance; 605
My flesh therewith shall give acquittance:[72]
I will now begin, if God give me grace.
KNOWLEDGE: Everyman, God give you time and space!
Thus I bequeath you in the hands of our Saviour;
Now may you make your reckoning sure. 610
EVERYMAN: In the name of the Holy Trinity,
My body sore punished shall be:
Take this, body, for the sin of the flesh!

(*Scourges himself.*)

Also thou delightest to go gay and fresh,
And in the way of damnation thou did me bring, 615

[69] guide
[70] besides
[71] be
[72] atonement

Therefore suffer now strokes and punishing.
Now of penance I will wade the water clear,
To save me from purgatory, that sharp fire.

(GOOD DEEDS *rises from the ground.*)

GOOD DEEDS: I thank God, now I can walk and go,
And am delivered of my sickness and woe. 620
Therefore with Everyman I will go, and not spare;
His good works I will help him to declare.
KNOWLEDGE: Now, Everyman, be merry and glad!
Your Good Deeds cometh now; ye may not be sad.
Now is your Good Deeds whole and sound, 625
Going upright upon the ground.
EVERYMAN: My heart is light, and shall be evermore;
Now will I smite faster than I did before.
GOOD DEEDS: Everyman, pilgrim, my special friend,
Blessed be thou without end; 630
For thee is preparate the eternal glory.
Ye have me made whole and sound,
Therefore I will bide by thee in every stound.[73]
EVERYMAN: Welcome, my Good Deeds; now I hear thy voice,
I weep for very sweetness of love. 635
KNOWLEDGE: Be no more sad, but ever rejoice;
God seeth thy living in his throne above.
Put on this garment to they behoof,[74]
Which is wet with your tears,
Or else before God you may it miss, 640
When ye to your journey's end come shall.
EVERYMAN: Gentle Knowledge, what do ye it call?
KNOWLEDGE: It is a garment of sorrow:
From pain it will you borrow;[75]
Contrition it is, 645
That geteth forgiveness;
It pleaseth God passing well.
GOOD DEEDS: Everyman, will you wear it for your heal?
EVERYMAN: Now blessed be Jesu, Mary's Son,
For now have I on true contrition. 650
And let us go now without tarrying;
Good Deeds, have we clear our reckoning?
GOOD DEEDS: Yea, indeed, I have it here.
EVERYMAN: Then I trust we need not fear;
Now, friends, let us not part in twain. 655

[73] always (or: in every attack)
[74] advantage
[75] take

KNOWLEDGE: Nay, Everyman, that will we not, certain.
GOOD DEEDS: Yet must thou lead with thee
  Three persons of great might.
EVERYMAN: Who should they be?
GOOD DEEDS: Discretion and Strength they hight,[76] 660
  And thy Beauty may not abide behind.
KNOWLEDGE: Also ye must call to mind
  Your Five Wits as for your counsellors.
GOOD DEEDS: You must have them ready at all hours.
EVERYMAN: How shall I get them hither? 665
KNOWLEDGE: You must call them all together,
  And they will hear you incontinent.[77]
EVERYMAN: My friends, come hither and be present,
  Discretion, Strength, my Five Wits,[78] and Beauty.

(*Enter* BEAUTY, STRENGTH, DISCRETION, *and* FIVE WITS.)

BEAUTY: Here at your will we be all ready. 670
  What will ye that we should do?
GOOD DEEDS: That ye would with Everyman go,
  And help him in his pilgrimage.
  Advise you, will ye with him or not in that voyage?
STRENGTH: We will bring him all thither, 675
  To his help and comfort, ye may believe me.
DISCRETION: So will we go with him all together.
EVERYMAN: Almighty God, lofed[79] may thou be!
  I give thee laud that I have hither brought
  Strength, Discretion, Beauty, and Five Wits. Lack I nought. 680
  And my Good Deeds, with Knowledge clear,
  All be in my company at my will here;
  I desire no more to[80] my business.
STRENGTH: And I, Strength, will by you stand in distress,
  Though thou would in battle fight on the ground. 685
FIVE WITS: And though it were through the world round,
  We will not depart for sweet ne sour.
BEAUTY: No more will I unto death's hour,
  Whatsoever thereof befall.
DISCRETION: Everyman, advise you first of all; 690
  Go with a good advisement and deliberation.
  We all give you virtuous monition
  That all shall be well.
EVERYMAN: My friends, harken what I will tell:

[76] are called
[77] immediately
[78] senses
[79] praised
[80] for

I pray God reward you in his heavenly sphere. 695
Now harken, all that be here,
For I will make my testament
Here before you all present:
In alms half my good I will give with my hands twain
In the way of charity, with good intent, 700
And the other half still shall remain
In queth,[81] to be returned there[82] it ought to be.
This I do in despite of the fiend of hell,
To go quit out of his peril
Ever after and this day. 705

KNOWLEDGE: Everyman, harken what I say:
Go to priesthood, I you advise,
And receive of him in any wise
The holy sacrament and ointment together.
Then shortly see ye turn again hither; 710
We will all abide you here.

FIVE WITS: Yea, Everyman, hie you that ye ready were.
There is no emperor, king, duke, ne baron,
That of God hath commission
As hath the least priest in the world being; 715
For of the blessed sacraments pure and benign
He beareth the keys, and thereof hath the cure[83]
For man's redemption — it is ever sure —
Which God for our soul's medicine
Gave us out of his heart with great pine. 720
Here in this transitory life, for thee and me,
The blessed sacraments seven there be:
Baptism, confirmation, with priesthood good,
And the sacrament of God's precious flesh and blood,
Marriage, the holy extreme unction, and penance; 725
These seven be good to have in remembrance,
Gracious sacraments of high divinity.

EVERYMAN: Fain would I receive that holy body,
And meekly to my ghostly father I will go.

FIVE WITS: Everyman, that is the best that ye can do. 730
God will you to salvation bring,
For priesthood exceedeth all other thing:
To us Holy Scripture they do teach,
And converteth man from sin heaven to reach;
God hath to them more power given 735

[81] bequest
[82] where
[83] charge

Than to any angel that is in heaven.
With five words[84] he may consecrate,
God's body in flesh and blood to make,
And handleth his Maker between his hands.
The priest bindeth and unbindeth all bands, 740
Both in earth and in heaven.
Thou ministers[85] all the sacraments seven;
Though we kissed thy feet, thou were worthy;
Thou art surgeon that cureth sin deadly:
No remedy we find under God 745
But all only[86] priesthood.
Everyman, God gave priests that dignity,
And setteth them in his stead among us to be;
Thus be they above angels in degree.

(EVERYMAN *goes to the priest to receive the last sacraments.*)

KNOWLEDGE: If priests be good, it is so,[87] surely. 750
But when Jesus hanged on the cross with great smart,
There he gave out of his blessed heart
The same sacrament in great torment:
He sold them not to us, that Lord omnipotent.
Therefore Saint Peter the apostle doth say 755
That Jesu's curse hath all they
Which God their Saviour do buy or sell,
Or they for any money do take or tell.[88]
Sinful priests giveth the sinners example bad;
Their children sitteth by other men's fires, I have heard; 760
And some haunteth women's company
With unclean life, as lusts of lechery:
These be with sin made blind.
FIVE WITS: I trust to God no such may we find;
Therefore let us priesthood honour, 765
And follow their doctrine for our souls' succour.
We be their sheep, and they shepherds be
By whom we all be kept in surety.
Peace, for yonder I see Everyman come,
Which hath made true satisfaction. 770
GOOD DEEDS: Methink it is he indeed.

(*Re-enter* EVERYMAN.)

[84] i.e., *Hoc est enim corpus meum* (Lat. "For this is my body"; from the sacrament of the Eucharist)
[85] administer
[86] except
[87] i.e., "above angels in degree"
[88] count

EVERYMAN: Now Jesu be your alder speed![89]
I have received the sacrament for my redemption,
And then mine extreme unction:
Blessed be all they that counselled me to take it! 775
And now, friends, let us go without longer respite;
I thank God that ye have tarried so long.
Now set each of you on this rood[90] your hand,
And shortly follow me:
I go before there I would be; God be our guide! 780
STRENGTH: Everyman, we will not from you go
Till ye have done this voyage long.
DISCRETION: I, Discretion, will bide by you also.
KNOWLEDGE: And though this pilgrimage be never so strong,[91]
I will never part you fro. 785
STRENGTH: Everyman, I will be as sure by thee
As ever I did by Judas Maccabee.[92]

(EVERYMAN *comes to his grave.*)

EVERYMAN: Alas, I am so faint I may not stand;
My limbs under me doth fold.
Friends, let us not turn again to this land, 790
Not for all the world's gold;
For into this cave must I creep
And turn to earth, and there to sleep.
BEAUTY: What, into this grave? Alas!
EVERYMAN: Yea, there shall ye consume, more and less.[93] 795
BEAUTY: And what, should I smother here?
EVERYMAN: Yea, by my faith, and never more appear.
In this world live no more we shall,
But in heaven before the highest Lord of all.
BEAUTY: I cross out all this; adieu, by Saint John! 800
I take my cap in my lap, and am gone.
EVERYMAN: What, Beauty, whither will ye?
BEAUTY: Peace, I am deaf; I look not behind me,
Not and thou wouldest give me all the gold in thy chest.
(*Exit* BEAUTY.)
EVERYMAN: Alas, whereto may I trust? 805

[89] help to all of you
[90] cross
[91] hard, difficult
[92] Jewish religious and national leader against Syria in the 2nd century B.C. He told his men that "the success of war is not in the multitude: but strength cometh from heaven" (Apocrypha, I Maccabees, 3:19)
[93] high and low

Beauty goeth fast away from me;
She promised with me to live and die.
STRENGTH: Everyman, I will thee also forsake and deny;
Thy game liketh me not at all.
EVERYMAN: Why, then, ye will forsake me all? 810
Sweet Strength, tarry a little space.
STRENGTH: Nay, sir, by the rood of grace!
I will hie me from thee fast,
Though thou weep till thy heart to-brast.[94]
EVERYMAN: Ye would ever bide by me, ye said. 815
STRENGTH: Yea, I have you far enough conveyed.
Ye be old enough, I understand,
Your pilgrimage to take on hand;
I repent me that I hither came.
EVERYMAN: Strength, you to displease I am to blame; 820
Yet promise is debt, this ye well wot.
STRENGTH: In faith, I care not.
Thou art but a fool to complain;
You spend your speech and waste your brain.
Go thrust thee into the ground! (*Exit* STRENGTH.) 825
EVERYMAN: I had wend surer I should you have found.
He that trusteth in his Strength
She him deceiveth at the length.
Both Strength and Beauty forsaketh me;
Yet they promised me fair and lovingly. 830
DISCRETION: Everyman, I will after Strength be gone;
As for me, I will leave you alone.
EVERYMAN: Why, Discretion, will ye forsake me?
DISCRETION: Yea, in faith, I will go from thee,
For when Strength goeth before 835
I follow after evermore.
EVERYMAN: Yet, I pray thee, for the love of the Trinity,
Look in my grave once piteously.
DISCRETION: Nay, so nigh will I not come;
Farewell, every one! (*Exit* DISCRETION.) 840
EVERYMAN: O, all thing faileth, save God alone —
Beauty, Strength, and Discretion;
For when Death bloweth his blast,
They all run from me full fast.
FIVE WITS: Everyman, my leave now of thee I take; 845
I will follow the other, for here I thee forsake.
EVERYMAN: Alas, then may I wail and weep,
For I took you for my best friend.

[94] broke to pieces

FIVE WITS: I will no longer thee keep;
Now farewell, and there an end. (*Exit* FIVE WITS.) 850
EVERYMAN: O Jesu, help! All hath forsaken me.
GOOD DEEDS: Nay, Everyman; I will bide with thee.
I will not forsake thee indeed;
Thou salt find me a good friend at need.
EVERYMAN: Gramercy, Good Deeds! Now may I true friends see. 855
They have forsaken me, every one;
I loved them better than my Good Deeds alone.
Knowledge, will ye forsake me also?
KNOWLEDGE: Yea, Everyman, when ye to Death shall go;
But not yet, for no manner of danger. 860
EVERYMAN: Gramercy, Knowledge, with all my heart.
KNOWLEDGE: Nay, yet I will not from hence depart
Till I see where ye shall become.
EVERYMAN: Methink, alas, that I must be gone
To make my reckoning and my debts pay, 865
For I see my time is nigh spent away.
Take example, all ye that this do hear or see,
How they that I loved best do forsake me,
Except my Good Deeds that bideth truly.
GOOD DEEDS: All earthly things is but vanity: 870
Beauty, Strength, and Discretion do man forsake,
Foolish friends, and kinsmen, that fair spake —
All fleeth save Good Deeds, and that am I.
EVERYMAN: Have mercy on me, God most mighty;
And stand by me, thou mother and maid, holy Mary. 875
GOOD DEEDS: Fear not; I will speak for thee.
EVERYMAN: Here I cry God mercy.
GOOD DEEDS: Short[95] our end, and minish our pain;
Let us go and never come again.
EVERYMAN: Into thy hands, Lord, my soul I commend; 880
Receive it, Lord, that it be not lost.
As thou me boughtest, so me defend,
And save me from the fiend's boast,
That I may appear with that blessed host
That shall be saved at the day of doom. 885
*In manus tuas,* of mights most
For ever, *commendo spiritum meum.*[96] (*He sinks into his grave.*)
KNOWLEDGE: Now hath he suffered that we all shall endure;
The Good Deeds shall make all sure.
Now hath he made ending; 890
Methinketh that I hear angels sing,

[95] shorten
[96] into thy hands I commend my spirit (Luke, 23:46)

And make great joy and melody
Where Everyman's soul received shall be.

ANGEL: Come, excellent elect spouse, to Jesu!
Hereabove thou shalt go 895
Because of thy singular virtue.
Now the soul is taken the body fro,
Thy reckoning is crystal-clear.
Now shalt thou into the heavenly sphere,
Unto the which all ye shall come 900
That liveth well before the day of doom.

(*Enter* DOCTOR.)

DOCTOR: This moral men may have in mind.
Ye hearers, take it of worth,[97] old and young,
And forsake Pride, for he deceiveth you in the end;
And remember Beauty, Five Wits, Strength, and Discretion, 905
They all at the last do every man forsake,
Save[98] his Good Deeds there doth he take.
But beware, for and they be small
Before God, he hath no help at all;
None excuse may be there for every man. 910
Alas, how shall he do then?
For after death amends may no man make,
For then mercy and pity doth him forsake.
If his reckoning be not clear when he doth come,
God will say: *'Ite, maledicti, in ignem eternum.'* [99] 915
And he that hath his account whole and sound,
High in heaven he shall be crowned;
Unto which place God bring us all thither,
That we may live body and soul together.
Thereto help the Trinity! 920
Amen, say ye, for saint charity.

*Thus Endeth this Moral Play of* EVERYMAN.

*Everyman* is the most famous of all English morality plays, a type of allegorical drama that flourished in western Europe during the late Middle Ages. The morality derived from an older liturgical drama and contributed in turn to the development of Elizabethan drama. *Everyman* may have been based on a contemporary Dutch play, dated

[97] value it
[98] unless
[99] depart, ye cursed, into everlasting fire (Matthew, 25:41)

about 1500. The earliest extant texts of the English play were printed in the early sixteenth century. The play has had successful stagings in our time, including a famous adaptation by the German playwright Hugo von Hofmannsthal.

Medieval drama was independent of the drama of antiquity but had, like it, a religious origin. After the collapse of classical civilization, theatrical activity was largely limited to performances by strolling bands of actors and minstrels – *mimes* – heirs to the decadent traditions of the late Roman theater. The Catholic Church was against such vulgar vagabond spectacles and looked upon the remaining Roman theaters as temples of sin, but it was the Church itself that revived serious drama. As ancient drama began in ritual spectacle and song, so medieval drama began as a development of the potential drama in the celebration of Mass and in antiphonal singing. From as early as the tenth century there is a record of clerical impersonation of characters from the Bible and the acting out of brief Biblical scenes in chanted speech before the congregation. Such dramatizations of Biblical stories, with words and melodies added, are called *tropes.* The first recorded trope is known, from its opening words, as the "Quem Quaeritis" ("Whom Seek Ye?"), an enactment of the meeting of the three Mary's and the Angel at Christ's empty tomb on Easter morning. Tropes later developed into short plays in the vernacular, known (with no clear distinction) as miracles and mysteries. With the change in language the plays could serve to make Christian lore imaginatively real for illiterate audiences who knew no Latin. After the Pope instituted the Feast of Corpus Christi in 1264, mystery plays became part of the annual celebration of the Feast in early summer. As the mysteries grew more elaborate, performance moved out of the church and the church precincts to the marketplace, and departures from the Biblical script became common, including the introduction of comic characters often represented with earthy realism. After 1210 the English clergy were no longer allowed to participate in profane theatricals, and the staging of the mysteries was wholly taken over by the town guilds. Members of a guild performed one of the plays in a larger cycle. The sacred story assigned a guild to stage was often one that was felt to be appropriate to the guild's particular craft, as when the fishmongers and bakers enacted the story of Christ feeding the multitude in the wilderness and the carpenters enacted the Crucifixion. The cycle plays were usually staged on platforms on wheels (pageants), appearing in sequence before stationary audiences along a route through the town. The surviving mysteries were parts of the cycles given in the towns of Coventry, Wakefield, Chester, and York in the Midlands and northern England. *The Second Shepherd's Play,* from the Wakefield (or Towneley) cycle, is probably the mystery play most familiar to modern readers. The cycle plays were at their height from about 1300 to 1450.

Despite the strong religious content in a play like *Everyman,* the morality represents a later stage in the gradual secularization of the old liturgical plays; and its successor in the development of English drama, the sixteenth-century *interlude,* carries secularization still further in its change from religious to more purely intellectual subject matter. Rather than episodes from the Bible or from saints' lives the moralities are dramatic allegorizations of universal moral and religious concepts — usually some version of the struggle between good and evil for man's soul on its perilous journey through life to salvation or perdition. The characters are personified abstracts with names like Youth, Mankind, Everyman, Good and Bad Angel, World, Vanity, Vice, and Death.

A superficial reading of *Everyman* may leave an impression of nothing more than a quaintly pious but longwinded and simple-minded statement of venerable Christian platitudes, dotted with undigested bits of Church polemic against the selling of holy office. The sacerdotal bias may be felt to be intrusive and the insistent didacticism stifling to any genuinely dramatic treatment of character and event.

Clearly, it is the sequence of encounters between Everyman and the personified forces that the medieval mind thought of as governing a Christian life that constitutes the action of the play. Just as clearly, it is an action contrived as an *exemplum* for the good of the spectator's soul rather than from any interest in plot or psychology for their own sakes. But it is also the stark simplicity of the dramatic movement and the singlemindedness of the didactic thrust that account for the play's naive but massive strength. In the words of the Messenger-Prologue, its "matter" is "wondrous precious": Everyman's eternal life is at stake. Dramatic tension is established the moment he is given the command to set his spiritual house in order, and for all the length of some of the individual episodes that follow, the pace and the tension thereafter never slacken. The fact that he is, after all, given respite to repent is not so much inconsistent with the initial premise of imminent doom as it is a way of making the spiritual drama possible at all. Faced with the alternatives of Heaven and Hell, Everyman, it could be argued, can claim small moral merit for his deathbed repentance, but to stress that point is to miss the deeper significance of the allegory and to ignore its didactic purpose. Death's challenge becomes a means to salvation, a further token of God's mercy to sinful man. The spectacle of Everyman's response is meant to summon us to eschatological fear, not to moral judgment. Moreover, we hardly think of the action as proceeding in worldly time. *Everyman* is a specimen of dramatic expressionism in the sense that its scene is the human soul and its time the timeless moment when the guilty conscience confronts death.

With sure sense of dramatic economy the playwright gives us only a few glimpses of Everyman's earlier, self-indulgent life as Fellowship's companion in revelling and violence. What he dramatizes is the impingement of God's will on the world. The lesson of the play is that life is only a loan, for which the borower is accountable. The repeated encounters with worldly associates (extrinsic, in the form of friends, kin, and material possessions; intrinsic, in the form of properties of mind and body), who all fail the ultimate test of loyalty, have an incremental effect. The distinct point of reversal comes midway through the action as Everyman with the help of Knowledge, Confession, and Penance (the last a potential rather than an actual personification) raises his Good Deeds from the ground. It is followed by a further complication — dramatically if not theologically unexpected — when his spiritual advisers leave him on the brink of his grave. Everyman is to face God's judgment alone, accompanied only — a distinct Catholic touch — by his Good Deeds. To say why Everyman is able to bear the second desertion better than the first is to define the nature of his growing spiritual strength. His foolish complacency and sensualism collapse in despair, and rehabilitation comes through the mustering of his inner resources. The play begins with God in his Heaven and ends with Everyman sinking into his grave, but the theological corollary to this downward movement reverses its direction as the redeemed soul rises into Heaven. And both descending and ascending action are comprised in Everyman's psychological movement from worldly folly through despair to the faith manifest in the Latin phrases he intones as he submits to death.

The characters come alive in little touches of psychological realism. There is the contrast between Everyman's reluctance to tell Fellowship about his predicament and his friend's effusive and ironically unsolicited professions of loyalty. There are Death's solemn colloquialisms, the nice distinctions in tone and attitude between Cousin and Kindred, the almost human pathos in God's "I could do no more than I did, truly." Among them, the personified abstractions cover a range of wryly perceived human realities. And if it is true that the verse hobbles, it is also true that its very roughness contributes to the mood of homespun earnestness and to the anxious concern with the one thing that matters in a Christian life. Musical lilt would have worked against the purpose of the play. Nor is the prosody quite so haphazard as it may seem at first: the shorter, three-stressed line and the masculine endings have a way of turning up in passages of special momentousness.

Everyman himself is both an individual and all mankind, both the single and the collective object of God's care. His character encompasses the two sides of man's nature. He is blindly selfish, fallen, appetitive man, the thoughtless hedonist who answers Death's question if he had really thought that his worldly possessions were his to keep, "I had wend so, verily." But he is also man potentially resurrect, God's blessed pensioner:

> I hoped well that every man
> In my glory should make his mansion,
> And thereto I had them all elect.

The irregularity in grammar — "every man" is the antecedent for "them" — brings together the simultaneous singular and plural significance of the title pronoun which is the play's key figure of speech, the vehicle for its terrifying relevance. The personification is more than a stale allegorical convention. The longer one considers the play, the more one becomes conscious of how much compressed tension, psychological insight, theological sophistication, and formal beauty the naive surface conceals. Goods says:

> I lie here in corners, trussed and piled so high.
> And in chests I am locked so fast,
> Also sacked in bags.

The lines don't just visualize wealth for us, they also insinuate the truth that material possessions are spiritually inert and therefore literally incapable of accompanying Everyman on his final journey. A small, vivid fact has inobtrusively become a large symbol. There is nothing simpleminded about such artistry.

The brevity of life, the vanity of the world, the treacherous falling-off of the gifts it offers, the sense of living under sentence of death, the desire to warn us all — these are traditional motifs in Christian forensics. But even nonbelievers can understand the critic who said that after *Everyman* all other plays somehow seem to deal with inessentials.

# WILLIAM SHAKESPEARE

# The Tragedy of Hamlet Prince of Denmark

DRAMATIS PERSONAE

CLAUDIUS, King of Denmark
HAMLET, son to the late, and nephew to the present, King
POLONIUS, Lord Chamberlain
HORATIO, friend to Hamlet
LAERTES, son to Polonius
VOLTEMAND, CORNELIUS, ROSENCRANTZ, GUILDENSTERN, OSRIC, A GENTLEMAN — courtiers
A PRIEST
MARCELLUS, BARNARDO — officers
FRANCISCO, a soldier
REYNALDO, servant to Polonius
PLAYERS
TWO CLOWNS, gravediggers
FORTINBRAS, Prince of Norway
A NORWEGIAN CAPTAIN
ENGLISH AMBASSADORS
GERTRUDE, Queen of Denmark, mother to Hamlet
OPHELIA, daughter to Polonius
GHOST OF HAMLET'S FATHER
LORDS, LADIES, OFFICERS, SOLDIERS, SAILORS, MESSENGERS, ATTENDANTS

*Scene: Elsinore*

# ACT I

## SCENE 1. [A GUARD PLATFORM OF THE CASTLE.]

*Enter* BARNARDO *and* FRANCISCO, *two sentinels.*

BARNARDO: Who's there?
FRANCISCO: Nay, answer me. Stand and unfold[1]* yourself.
BARNARDO: Long live the King![2]
FRANCISCO: Barnardo?
BARNARDO: He. 5
FRANCISCO: You come most carefully upon your hour.
BARNARDO: 'Tis now struck twelve. Get thee to bed, Francisco.
FRANCISCO: For this relief much thanks. 'Tis bitter cold,
And I am sick at heart.
BARNARDO: Have you had quiet guard?
FRANCISCO: Not a mouse stirring. 10
BARNARDO: Well, good night.
If you do meet Horatio and Marcellus,
The rivals[3] of my watch, bid them make haste.

(*Enter* HORATIO *and* MARCELLUS.)

FRANCISCO: I think I hear them. Stand, ho! Who is there?
HORATIO: Friends to this ground.
MARCELLUS: And liegemen to the Dane.[4] 15
FRANCISCO: Give you[5] good night.
MARCELLUS: O, farewell, honest soldier.
Who hath relieved you?
FRANCISCO: Barnardo hath my place.
Give you good night. (*Exit* FRANCISCO.)
MARCELLUS: Holla, Barnardo!
BARNARDO: Say —
What, is Horatio there?
HORATIO: A piece of him.
BARNARDO: Welcome, Horatio. Welcome, good Marcellus. 20
MARCELLUS: What, has this thing appeared again tonight?
BARNARDO: I have seen nothing.
MARCELLUS: Horatio says 'tis but our fantasy,
And will not let belief take hold of him

* [These are Professor Edward Hubler's notes for the Signet edition of *Hamlet*.— Editor's note.]
[1] disclose
[2] (perhaps a password, perhaps a greeting)
[3] partners
[4] loyal subjects to the King of Denmark
[5] God give you

Touching this dreaded sight twice seen of us; 25
Therefore I have entreated him along
With us to watch the minutes of this night,
That, if again this apparition come,
He may approve[6] our eyes and speak to it.

HORATIO: Tush, tush, 'twill not appear.

BARNARDO: Sit down awhile, 30
And let us once again assail your ears,
That are so fortified against our story,
What we have two nights seen.

HORATIO: Well, sit we down,
And let us hear Barnardo speak of this.

BARNARDO: Last night of all, 35
When yond same star that's westward from the pole[7]
Had made his course t' illume that part of heaven
Where now it burns, Marcellus and myself.
The bell then beating one —

(*Enter* GHOST.)

MARCELLUS: Peace, break thee off. Look where it comes again. 40

BARNARDO: In the same figure like the king that's dead.

MARCELLUS: Thou art a scholar; speak to it, Horatio.

BARNARDO: Looks 'a not like the king? Mark it, Horatio.

HORATIO: Most like: it harrows me with fear and wonder.

BARNARDO: It would be spoke to.

MARCELLUS: Speak to it, Horatio. 45

HORATIO: What art thou that usurp'st this time of night,
Together with that fair and warlike form
In which the majesty of buried Denmark[8]
Did sometimes march? By heaven I charge thee, speak.

MARCELLUS: It is offended.

BARNARDO: See, it stalks away. 50

HORATIO: Stay! Speak, speak. I charge thee, speak. (*Exit* GHOST.)

MARCELLUS: 'Tis gone and will not answer.

BARNARDO: How now, Horatio? You tremble and look pale.
Is not this something more than fantasy?
What think you on't? 55

HORATIO: Before my God, I might not this believe
Without the sensible and true avouch[9]
Of mine own eyes.

MARCELLUS: Is it not like the King?

HORATIO: As thou art to thyself.
Such was the very armor he had on 60

[6] confirm
[7] polestar
[8] the buried King of Denmark
[9] sensory and true proof

When he the ambitious Norway[10] combated:
So frowned he once, when, in an angry parle,[11]
He smote the sledded Polacks[12] on the ice.
'Tis strange.

MARCELLUS: Thus twice before, and jump[13] at this dead hour, 65
With martial stalk hath he gone by our watch.

HORATIO: In what particular thought to work I know not;
But, in the gross and scope[14] of my opinion,
This bodes some strange eruption to our state.

MARCELLUS: Good now, sit down, and tell me he that knows, 70
Why this same strict and most observant watch
So nightly toils the subject[15] of the land,
And why such daily cast of brazen cannon
And foreign mart[16] for implements of war,
Why such impress[17] of shipwrights, whose sore task 75
Does not divide the Sunday from the week,
What might be toward[18] that this sweaty haste
Doth make the night joint-laborer with the day?
Who is't that can inform me?

HORATIO: That can I.
At least the whisper goes so: our last king, 80
Whose image even but now appeared to us,
Was, as you know, by Fortinbras of Norway,
Thereto pricked on by a most emulate pride,
Dared to the combat; in which our valiant Hamlet
(For so this side of our known world esteemed him) 85
Did slay this Fortinbras, who, by a sealed compact
Well ratified by law and heraldry,[19]
Did forfeit, with his life, all those his lands
Which he stood seized[20] of, to the conqueror;
Against the which a moiety competent[21] 90
Was gagèd[22] by our King, which had returned
To the inheritance of Fortinbras,
Had he been vanquisher, as, by the same comart[23]
And carriage of the article designed,[24]
His fell to Hamlet. Now, sir, young Fortinbras, 95
Of unimprovèd[25] mettle hot and full,

[10] King of Norway
[11] parley
[12] Poles in sledges
[13] just
[14] general drift
[15] makes the subjects toil
[16] trading
[17] forced service
[18] in preparation
[19] heraldic law (governing the combat)
[20] possessed
[21] equal portion
[22] engaged, pledged
[23] agreement
[24] import of the agreement drawn up
[25] untried

Hath in the skirts[26] of Norway here and there
Sharked up[27] a list of lawless resolutes,[28]
For food and diet, to some enterprise
That hath a stomach in't;[29] which is no other, 100
As it doth well appear unto our state,
But to recover of us by strong hand
And terms compulsatory, those foresaid lands
So by his father lost; and this, I take it,
Is the main motive of our preparations, 105
The source of this our watch, and the chief head[30]
Of this posthaste and romage[31] in the land.

BARNARDO: I think it be no other but e'en so;
Well may it sort[32] that this portentous figure
Comes armèd through our watch so like the King 110
That was and is the question of these wars.

HORATIO: A note it is to trouble the mind's eye:
In the most high and palmy state of Rome,
A little ere the mightiest Julius fell,
The graves stood tenantless, and the sheeted dead 115
Did squeak and gibber in the Roman streets;[33]
As stars with trains of fire and dews of blood,
Disasters[34] in the sun; and the moist star,[35]
Upon whose influence Neptune's empire stands,
Was sick almost to doomsday with eclipse. 120
And even the like precurse[36] of feared events,
As harbingers[37] preceding still[38] the fates
And prologue to the omen[39] coming on,
Have heaven and earth together demonstrated
Unto our climatures[40] and countrymen. 125

(*Enter* GHOST.)

But soft, behold, lo where it comes again!
I'll cross it,[41] though it blast me. – Stay, illusion.

(*It spreads his*[42] *arms.*)

26 borders
27 collected indiscriminately (as a shark gulps its prey)
28 desperadoes
29 i.e., requires courage
30 fountainhead, origin
31 bustle
32 befit
33 (the break in the sense which follows this line suggests that a line has dropped out)
34 threatening signs
35 moon
36 precursor, foreshadowing
37 forerunners
38 always
39 calamity
40 regions
41 (1) cross its path, confront it, (2) make the sign of the cross in front of it
42 i.e., its, the ghost's (though possibly what is meant is that Horatio spreads his own arms, making a cross of himself)

If thou hast any sound or use of voice,
Speak to me.
If there be any good thing to be done 130
That may to thee do ease and grace to me,
Speak to me.
If thou art privy to thy country's fate,
Which happily[43] foreknowing may avoid,
O, speak! 135
Or if thou hast uphoarded in thy life
Extorted[44] treasure in the womb of earth,
For which, they say, you spirits oft walk in death,

(*The cock crows.*)

Speak of it. Stay and speak. Stop it, Marcellus.
MARCELLUS: Shall I strike at it with my partisan?[45] 140
HORATIO: Do, if it will not stand.
BARNARDO: 'Tis here.
HORATIO: 'Tis here.
MARCELLUS: 'Tis gone. (*Exit* GHOST.)
We do it wrong, being so majestical,
To offer it the show of violence,
For it is as the air, invulnerable, 145
And our vain blows malicious mockery.
BARNARDO: It was about to speak when the cock crew.
HORATIO: And then it started, like a guilty thing
Upon a fearful summons. I have heard,
The cock, that is the trumpet to the morn, 150
Doth with his lofty and shrill-sounding throat
Awake the god of day, and at his warning,
Whether in sea or fire, in earth or air,
Th' extravagant and erring[46] spirit hies
To his confine; and of the truth herein 155
This present object made probation.[47]
MARCELLUS: It faded on the crowing of the cock.
Some say that ever 'gainst[48] that season comes
Wherein our Savior's birth is celebrated,
This bird of dawning singeth all night long, 160
And then, they say, no spirit dare stir abroad,
The nights are wholesome, then no planets strike,[49]
No fairy takes,[50] nor witch hath power to charm:
So hallowed and so gracious is that time.

[43] haply, perhaps
[44] ill-won
[45] pike (a long-handled weapon)
[46] out of bounds and wandering
[47] proof
[48] just before
[49] exert an evil influence
[50] bewitches

HORATIO: So have I heard and do in part believe it. 165
But look, the morn in russet mantle clad
Walks o'er the dew of yon high eastward hill.
Break we our watch up, and by my advice
Let us impart what we have seen tonight
Unto young Hamlet, for upon my life 170
This spirit, dumb to us, will speak to him.
Do you consent we shall acquaint him with it,
As needful in our loves, fitting our duty?
MARCELLUS: Let's do't, I pray, and I this morning know
Where we shall find him most convenient. *(Exeunt.)* 175

## SCENE 2. [THE CASTLE.]

*Flourish.*[1] *Enter* CLAUDIUS, *King of Denmark,* GERTRUDE *the Queen,* COUNCILORS, POLONIUS *and his son* LAERTES, HAMLET, *cum aliis*[2] [*including* VOLTEMAND *and* CORNELIUS].

KING: Though yet of Hamlet our dear brother's death
The memory be green, and that it us befitted
To bear our hearts in grief, and our whole kingdom
To be contracted in one brow of woe,
Yet so far hath discretion fought with nature 5
That we with wisest sorrow think on him
Together with remembrance of ourselves.
Therefore our sometime sister,[3] now our Queen,
Th' imperial jointress[4] to this warlike state,
Have we, as 'twere, with a defeated joy, 10
With an auspicious[5] and a dropping eye,
With mirth in funeral, and with dirge in marriage,
In equal scale weighing delight and dole,
Taken to wife. Nor have we herein barred
Your better wisdoms, which have freely gone 15
With this affair along. For all, our thanks.
Now follows that you know young Fortinbras,
Holding a weak supposal of our worth,
Or thinking by our late dear brother's death
Our state to be disjoint and out of frame,[6] 20
Colleaguèd with this dream of his advantage,[7]
He hath not failed to pester us with message,

[1] fanfare of trumpets
[2] with others (Latin)
[3] my (the royal "we") former sister-in-law
[4] joint tenant, partner
[5] joyful
[6] order
[7] superiority

Importing the surrender of those lands
Lost by his father, with all bands of law,
To our most valiant brother. So much for him. 25
Now for ourself and for this time of meeting.
Thus much the business is: we have here writ
To Norway, uncle of young Fortinbras —
Who, impotent and bedrid, scarcely hears
Of this his nephew's purpose — to suppress 30
His further gait[8] herein, in that the levies,
The lists, and full proportions[9] are all made
Out of his subject,[10] and we here dispatch
You, good Cornelius, and you, Voltemand,
For bearers of this greeting to old Norway, 35
Giving to you no further personal power
To business with the King, more than the scope
Of these delated articles[11] allow.
Farewell, and let your haste commend your duty.

CORNELIUS, VOLTEMAND: In that, and all things, will we show our duty. 40

KING: We doubt it nothing. Heartily farewell.

(*Exit* VOLTEMAND *and* CORNELIUS.)

And now, Laertes, what's the news with you?
You told us of some suit. What is't, Laertes?
You cannot speak of reason to the Dane
And lose your voice.[12] What wouldst thou beg, Laertes, 45
That shall not be my offer, not thy asking?
The head is not more native[13] to the heart,
The hand more instrumental to the mouth,
Than is the throne of Denmark to thy father.
What wouldst thou have, Laertes?

LAERTES: My dread lord, 50
Your leave and favor to return to France,
From whence, though willingly I came to Denmark
To show my duty in your coronation,
Yet now I must confess, that duty done,
My thoughts and wishes bend again toward France 55
And bow them to your gracious leave and pardon.

KING: Have you your father's leave? What says Polonius?

POLONIUS: He hath, my lord, wrung from me my slow leave
By laborsome petition, and at last

[8] proceeding
[9] supplies for war
[10] i.e., out of old Norway's subjects and realm
[11] detailed documents
[12] waste your breath
[13] related

Upon his will I sealed my hard consent.[14] 60
I do beseech you give him leave to go.
KING: Take thy fair hour, Laertes. Time be thine,
And thy best graces spend it at thy will.
But now, my cousin[15] Hamlet, and my son —
HAMLET [*aside*]: A little more than kin, and less than kind![16] 65
KING: How is it that the clouds still hang on you?
HAMLET: Not so, my lord. I am too much in the sun.[17]
QUEEN: Good Hamlet, cast thy nighted color off,
And let thine eye look like a friend on Denmark.
Do not forever with thy vailèd lids[18] 70
Seek for thy noble father in the dust.
Thou know'st 'tis common; all that lives must die,
Passing through nature to eternity.
HAMLET: Ay, madam, it is common.[19]
QUEEN: If it be,
Why seems it so particular with thee? 75
HAMLET: Seems, madam? Nay, it is. I know not "seems."
'Tis not alone my inky cloak, good mother,
Nor customary suits of solemn black,
Nor windy suspiration[20] of forced breath,
No, nor the fruitful river in the eye, 80
Nor the dejected havior of the visage,
Together with all forms, moods, shapes of grief,
That can denote me truly. These indeed seem,
For they are actions that a man might play,
But I have that within which passes show; 85
These but the trappings and the suits of woe.
KING: 'Tis sweet and commendable in your nature, Hamlet,
To give these mourning duties to your father,
But you must know your father lost a father,
That father lost, lost his, and the survivor bound 90
In filial obligation for some term
To do obsequious[21] sorrow. But to persever
In obstinate condolement[22] is a course
Of impious stubbornness. 'Tis unmanly grief.
It shows a will most incorrect to heaven, 95

14 to his desire I gave my reluctant consent
15 kinsman
16 (pun on the meanings "kindly" and "natural"; though doubly related — *more than kin* — Hamlet asserts that he neither resembles Claudius in nature nor feels kindly toward him)
17 sunshine of royal favor (with a pun on "son")
18 lowered
19 (1) universal, (2) vulgar
20 heavy sighing
21 suitable to obsequies (funerals)
22 mourning

A heart unfortified, a mind impatient,
An understanding simple and unschooled.
For what we know must be and is as common
As any the most vulgar[23] thing to sense,
Why should we in our peevish opposition 100
Take it to heart? Fie, 'tis a fault to heaven,
A fault against the dead, a fault to nature,
To reason most absurd, whose common theme
Is death of fathers, and who still hath cried,
From the first corse[24] till he that died today, 105
"This must be so." We pray you throw to earth
This unprevailing[25] woe, and think of us
As of a father, for let the world take note
You are the most immediate to our throne,
And with no less nobility of love 110
Than that which dearest father bears his son
Do I impart toward you. For your intent
In going back to school in Wittenberg,
It is most retrograde[26] to our desire,
And we beseech you, bend you[27] to remain 115
Here in the cheer and comfort of our eye,
Our chiefest courtier, cousin, and our son.

QUEEN: Let not thy mother lose her prayers, Hamlet.
I pray thee stay with us, go not to Wittenberg.

HAMLET: I shall in all my best obey you, madam. 120

KING: Why, 'tis a loving and a fair reply.
Be as ourself in Denmark. Madam, come.
This gentle and unforced accord of Hamlet
Sits smiling to my heart, in grace whereof
No jocund health that Denmark drinks today, 125
But the great cannon to the clouds shall tell,
And the King's rouse[28] the heaven shall bruit[29] again,
Respeaking earthly thunder. Come away.

(*Flourish. Exeunt all but* HAMLET.)

HAMLET: O that this too too sullied[30] flesh would melt,
Thaw, and resolve itself into a dew, 130
Or that the Everlasting had not fixed
His canon[31] 'gainst self-slaughter. O God, God,

[23] common
[24] corpse
[25] unavailing
[26] contrary
[27] incline
[28] deep drink
[29] announce noisily

[30] (Q2 [Second Quarto] has *sallied,* here modernized to *sullied,* which makes sense and is therefore given; but the Folio reading, *solid,* which fits better with *melt,* is quite possibly correct)
[31] law

How weary, stale, flat, and unprofitable
Seem to me all the uses of this world!
Fie on't, ah, fie, 'tis an unweeded garden 135
That grows to seed. Things rank and gross in nature
Possess it merely.[32] That it should come to this:
But two months dead, nay, not so much, not two,
So excellent a king, that was to this
Hyperion[33] to a satyr, so loving to my mother 140
That he might not beteem[34] the winds of heaven
Visit her face too roughly. Heaven and earth,
Must I remember? Why, she would hang on him
As if increase of appetite had grown
By what it fed on; and yet within a month — 145
Let me not think on't; frailty, thy name is woman —
A little month, or ere those shoes were old
With which she followed my poor father's body
Like Niobe,[35] all tears, why she, even she —
O God, a beast that wants discourse of reason[36] 150
Would have mourned longer — married with my uncle,
My father's brother, but no more like my father
Than I to Hercules. Within a month,
Ere yet the salt of most unrighteous tears
Had left the flushing[37] in her gallèd eyes, 155
She married. O, most wicked speed, to post[38]
With such dexterity to incestuous[39] sheets!
It is not, nor it cannot come to good.
But break my heart, for I must hold my tongue.

(*Enter* HORATIO, MARCELLUS, *and* BARNARDO.)

HORATIO: Hail to your lordship!
HAMLET: I am glad to see you well. 160
Horatio — or I do forget myself.
HORATIO: The same, my lord, and your poor servant ever.
HAMLET: Sir, my good friend, I'll change[40] that name with you.
And what make you from Wittenberg, Horatio?
Marcellus. 165
MARCELLUS: My good lord!
HAMLET: I am very glad to see you. [*To* BARNARDO.] Good even, sir.
But what, in faith, make you from Wittenberg?

[32] entirely
[33] the sun god, a model of beauty
[34] allow
[35] a mother who wept profusely at the death of her children
[36] lacks reasoning power
[37] stopped reddening
[38] hasten
[39] (canon law considered marriage with a deceased brother's widow to be incestuous)
[40] exchange

HORATIO: A truant disposition, good my lord.
HAMLET: I would not hear your enemy say so, 170
Nor shall you do my ear that violence
To make it truster[41] of your own report
Against yourself. I know you are no truant.
But what is your affair in Elsinore?
We'll teach you to drink deep ere you depart. 175
HORATIO: My lord, I came to see your father's funeral.
HAMLET: I prithee do not mock me, fellow student.
I think it was to see my mother's wedding.
HORATIO: Indeed, my lord, it followed hard upon.
HAMLET: Thrift, thrift, Horatio. The funeral baked meats 180
Did coldly furnish forth the marriage tables.
Would I had met my dearest[42] foe in heaven
Or ever I had seen that day, Horatio!
My father, methinks I see my father.
HORATIO: Where, my lord?
HAMLET: In my mind's eye, Horatio. 185
HORATIO: I saw him once. 'A[43] was a goodly king.
HAMLET: 'A was a man, take him for all in all,
I shall not look upon his like again.
HORATIO: My lord, I think I saw him yesternight.
HAMLET: Saw? Who? 190
HORATIO: My lord, the King your father.
HAMLET: The King my father?
HORATIO: Season your admiration[44] for a while
With an attent ear till I may deliver
Upon the witness of these gentlemen
This marvel to you.
HAMLET: For God's love let me hear! 195
HORATIO: Two nights together had these gentlemen,
Marcellus and Barnardo, on their watch
In the dead waste and middle of the night
Been thus encountered. A figure like your father,
Armèd at point exactly, cap-a-pe,[45] 200
Appears before them, and with solemn march
Goes slow and stately by them. Thrice he walked
By their oppressed and fear-surprisèd eyes,
Within his truncheon's length,[46] whilst they, distilled[47]
Almost to jelly with the act[48] of fear, 205
Stand dumb and speak not to him. This to me

41 believer
42 most intensely felt
43 he
44 control your wonder
45 head to foot
46 space of a short staff
47 reduced
48 action

In dreadful[49] secrecy impart they did,
And I with them the third night kept the watch,
Where, as they had delivered, both in time,
Form of the thing, each word made true and good, 210
The apparition comes. I knew your father.
These hands are not more like.

HAMLET: But where was this?

MARCELLUS: My lord, upon the platform where we watched.

HAMLET: Did you not speak to it?

HORATIO: My lord, I did;
But answer made it none. Yet once methought 215
It lifted up it[50] head and did address
Itself to motion like as it would speak:
But even then the morning cock crew loud,
And at the sound it shrunk in haste away
And vanished from our sight.

HAMLET: 'Tis very strange. 220

HORATIO: As I do live, my honored lord, 'tis true,
And we did think it writ down in our duty
To let you know of it.

HAMLET: Indeed, indeed, sirs, but this troubles me.
Hold you the watch tonight?

ALL: We do, my lord. 225

HAMLET: Armed, say you?

ALL: Armed, my lord.

HAMLET: From top to toe?

ALL: My lord, from head to foot.

HAMLET: Then saw you not his face.

HORATIO: O, yes, my lord. He wore his beaver[51] up. 230

HAMLET: What, looked he frowningly?

HORATIO: A countenance more in sorrow than in anger.

HAMLET: Pale or red?

HORATIO: Nay, very pale.

HAMLET: And fixed his eyes upon you?

HORATIO: Most constantly.

HAMLET: I would I had been there. 235

HORATIO: It would have much amazed you.

HAMLET: Very like, very like. Stayed it long?

HORATIO: While one with moderate haste might tell[52] a hundred.

BOTH: Longer, longer.

HORATIO: Not when I saw't.

HAMLET: His beard was grizzled,[53] no? 240

[49] terrified
[50] its
[51] visor, face guard
[52] count
[53] gray

HORATIO: It was as I have seen it in his life,
A sable silvered.[54]
HAMLET: I will watch tonight.
Perchance 'twill walk again.
HORATIO: I warr'nt it will.
HAMLET: If it assume my noble father's person,
I'll speak to it though hell itself should gape 245
And bid me hold my peace. I pray you all,
If you have hitherto concealed this sight,
Let it be tenable[55] in your silence still,
And whatsomever else shall hap tonight,
Give it an understanding but no tongue; 250
I will requite your loves. So fare you well.
Upon the platform 'twixt eleven and twelve
I'll visit you.
ALL: Our duty to your honor.
HAMLET: Your loves, as mine to you. Farewell.
(*Exeunt [all but* HAMLET].)
My father's spirit — in arms? All is not well. 255
I doubt[56] some foul play. Would the night were come!
Till then sit still, my soul. Foul deeds will rise,
Though all the earth o'erwhelm them, to men's eyes. (*Exit.*)

## SCENE 3. [A ROOM.]

*Enter* LAERTES *and* OPHELIA, *his sister.*

LAERTES: My necessaries are embarked. Farewell.
And, sister, as the winds give benefit
And convoy[1] is assistant, do not sleep,
But let me hear from you.
OPHELIA: Do you doubt that?
LAERTES: For Hamlet, and the trifling of his favor, 5
Hold it a fashion and a toy[2] in blood,
A violet in the youth of primy[3] nature,
Forward,[4] not permanent, sweet, not lasting,
The perfume and suppliance[5] of a minute,
No more.

[54] black mingled with white
[55] held
[56] suspect

---

[1] conveyance
[2] idle fancy
[3] springlike
[4] premature
[5] diversion

OPHELIA: No more but so?

LAERTES: Think it no more. 10

For nature crescent[6] does not grow alone
In thews[7] and bulk, but as this temple[8] waxes,
The inward service of the mind and soul
Grows wide withal. Perhaps he loves you now,
And now no soil nor cautel[9] doth besmirch 15
The virtue of his will; but you must fear,
His greatness weighed,[10] his will is not his own.
For he himself is subject to his birth.
He may not, as unvalued[11] persons do,
Carve for himself; for on his choice depends 20
The safety and health of this whole state;
And therefore must his choice be circumscribed
Unto the voice and yielding of that body
Whereof he is the head. Then if he says he loves you,
It fits your wisdom so far to believe it 25
As he in his particular act and place
May give his saying deed, which is no further
Than the main voice of Denmark goes withal.
Then weigh what loss your honor may sustain
If with too credent[12] ear you list his songs, 30
Or lose your heart, or your chaste treasure open
To his unmastered importunity.
Fear it, Ophelia, fear it, my dear sister,
And keep you in the rear of your affection,
Out of the shot and danger of desire. 35
The chariest maid is prodigal enough
If she unmask her beauty to the moon.
Virtue itself scapes not calumnious strokes.
The canker[13] galls the infants of the spring
Too oft before their buttons[14] be disclosed, 40
And in the morn and liquid dew of youth
Contagious blastments are most imminent.
Be wary then; best safety lies in fear;
Youth to itself rebels, though none else near.

OPHELIA: I shall the effect of this good lesson keep 45
As watchman to my heart, but, good my brother,
Do not, as some ungracious[15] pastors do,
Show me the steep and thorny way to heaven,

6 growing
7 muscles and sinews
8 i.e., the body
9 deceit
10 high rank considered
11 of low rank
12 credulous
13 cankerworm
14 buds
15 lacking grace

Whiles, like a puffed and reckless libertine,
Himself the primrose path of dalliance treads 50
And recks not his own rede.[16]

(*Enter* POLONIUS.)

LAERTES: O, fear me not.
I stay too long. But here my father comes.
A double blessing is a double grace;
Occasion smiles upon a second leave.
POLONIUS: Yet here, Laertes? Aboard, aboard, for shame! 55
The wind sits in the shoulder of your sail,
And you are stayed for. There – my blessing with thee,
And these few precepts in thy memory
Look thou character.[17] Give thy thoughts no tongue,
Nor any unproportioned[18] thought his act. 60
Be thou familiar, but by no means vulgar.
Those friends thou hast, and their adoption tried,
Grapple them unto thy soul with hoops of steel,
But do not dull thy palm with entertainment
Of each new-hatched, unfledged courage.[19] Beware 65
Of entrance to a quarrel; but being in,
Bear't that th' opposèd may beware of thee.
Give every man thine ear, but few thy voice;
Take each man's censure,[20] but reserve thy judgment.
Costly thy habit as thy purse can buy, 70
But not expressed in fancy; rich, not gaudy,
For the apparel oft proclaims the man,
And they in France of the best rank and station
Are of a most select and generous, chief in that.[21]
Neither a borrower nor a lender be, 75
For loan oft loses both itself and friend,
And borrowing dulleth edge of husbandry.[22]
This above all, to thine own self be true,
And it must follow, as the night the day,
Thou canst not then be false to any man. 80
Farewell. My blessing season this[23] in thee!
LAERTES: Most humbly do I take my leave, my lord.
POLONIUS: The time invites you. Go, your servants tend.[24]

[16] does not heed his own advice
[17] inscribe
[18] unbalanced
[19] gallant youth
[20] opinion
[21] show their fine taste and their gentlemanly instincts more in that than in any other point of manners (Kittredge)
[22] thrift
[23] make fruitful this (advice)
[24] attend

LAERTES: Farewell, Ophelia, and remember well
What I have said to you.
OPHELIA: 'Tis in my memory locked, 85
And you yourself shall keep the key of it.
LAERTES: Farewell. (*Exit* LAERTES.)
POLONIUS: What is't, Ophelia, he hath said to you?
OPHELIA: So please you, something touching the Lord Hamlet.
POLONIUS: Marry,[25] well bethought. 90
'Tis told me he hath very oft of late
Given private time to you, and you yourself
Have of your audience been most free and bounteous.
If it be so — as so 'tis put on me,
And that in way of caution — I must tell you 95
You do not understand yourself so clearly
As it behooves my daughter and your honor.
What is between you? Give me up the truth.
OPHELIA: He hath, my lord, of late made many tenders[26]
Of his affection to me. 100
POLONIUS: Affection pooh! You speak like a green girl,
Unsifted[27] in such perilous circumstance.
Do you believe his tenders, as you call them?
OPHELIA: I do not know, my lord, what I should think.
POLONIUS: Marry, I will teach you. Think yourself a baby 105
That you have ta'en these tenders for true pay
Which are not sterling. Tender yourself more dearly,
Or (not to crack the wind of the poor phrase)
Tend'ring it thus you'll tender me a fool.[28]
OPHELIA: My lord, he hath importuned me with love 110
In honorable fashion.
POLONIUS: Ay, fashion you may call it. Go to, go to.
OPHELIA: And hath given countenance to his speech, my lord,
With almost all the holy vows of heaven.
POLONIUS: Ay, springes to catch woodcocks.[29] I do know, 115
When the blood burns, how prodigal the soul
Lends the tongue vows. These blazes, daughter,
Giving more light than heat, extinct in both,
Even in their promise, as it is a-making,
You must not take for fire. From this time 120

[25] (a light oath, from "By the Virgin Mary")

[26] offers (in line 103 it has the same meaning, but in line 106 Polonius speaks of *tenders* in the sense of counters or chips; in line 109 *Tend'ring* means "holding," and *tender* means "give," "present")

[27] untried

[28] (1) present me with a fool, (2) present me with a baby

[29] snares to catch stupid birds

Be something scanter of your maiden presence.
Set your entreatments[30] at a higher rate
Than a command to parley. For Lord Hamlet,
Believe so much in him that he is young,
And with a larger tether may he walk 125
Than may be given you. In few, Ophelia,
Do not believe his vows, for they are brokers,[31]
Not of that dye[32] which their investments[33] show,
But mere implorators[34] of unholy suits,
Breathing like sanctified and pious bonds,[35] 130
The better to beguile. This is for all:
I would not, in plain terms, from this time forth
Have you so slander[36] any moment leisure
As to give words or talk with the Lord Hamlet.
Look to't, I charge you. Come your ways. 135

OPHELIA: I shall obey, my lord. *(Exeunt.)*

### SCENE 4. [A GUARD PLATFORM.]

*Enter* HAMLET, HORATIO, *and* MARCELLUS.

HAMLET: The air bites shrewdly;[1] it is very cold.
HORATIO: It is a nipping and an eager[2] air.
HAMLET: What hour now?
HORATIO: I think it lacks of twelve.
MARCELLUS: No, it is struck.
HORATIO: Indeed? I heard it not. It then draws near the season 5
Wherein the spirit held his wont to walk.

*(A flourish of trumpets, and two pieces go off.)*

What does this mean, my lord?
HAMLET: The King doth wake[3] tonight and takes his rouse,[4]
Keeps wassail, and the swagg'ring upspring[5] reels,
And as he drains his draughts of Rhenish[6] down 10

[30] interviews
[31] procurers
[32] i.e., kind
[33] garments
[34] solicitors
[35] pledges
[36] disgrace

---

[1] bitterly
[2] sharp
[3] hold a revel by night
[4] carouses
[5] a dance
[6] Rhine wine

The kettledrum and trumpet thus bray out
The triumph of his pledge.[7]

HORATIO: Is it a custom?

HAMLET: Ay, marry, is't,
But to my mind, though I am native here
And to the manner born, it is a custom 15
More honored in the breach than the observance.
This heavy-headed revel east and west
Makes us traduced and taxed of[8] other nations.
They clepe[9] us drunkards and with swinish phrase
Soil our addition,[10] and indeed it takes 20
From our achievements, though performed at height,
The pith and marrow of our attribute.[11]
So oft it chances in particular men
That for some vicious mole[12] of nature in them,
As in their birth, wherein they are not guilty, 25
(Since nature cannot choose his origin)
By the o'ergrowth of some complexion,[13]
Oft breaking down the pales[14] and forts of reason,
Or by some habit that too much o'erleavens[15]
The form of plausive[16] manners, that (these men, 30
Carrying, I say, the stamp of one defect,
Being nature's livery, or fortune's star[17])
Their virtues else, be they as pure as grace,
As infinite as man may undergo,
Shall in the general censure[18] take corruption 35
From that particular fault. The dram of evil
Doth all the noble substance of a doubt,
To his own scandal.[19]

(*Enter* GHOST.)

HORATIO: Look, my lord, it comes.

HAMLET: Angels and ministers of grace defend us!
Be thou a spirit of health[20] or goblin damned, 40

[7] the achievement (of drinking a wine cup in one draught) of his toast
[8] blamed by
[9] call
[10] reputation (literally, "title of honor")
[11] reputation
[12] blemish
[13] natural disposition
[14] enclosures
[15] mixes with, corrupts
[16] pleasing
[17] nature's equipment (i.e., "innate"), or a person's destiny determined by the stars
[18] popular judgment
[19] (though the drift is clear, there is no agreement as to the exact meaning of these lines)
[20] good spirit

Bring with thee airs from heaven or blasts from hell,
Be thy intents wicked or charitable,
Thou com'st in such a questionable[21] shape
That I will speak to thee. I'll call thee Hamlet,
King, father, royal Dane. O, answer me! 45
Let me not burst in ignorance, but tell
Why thy canonized[22] bones, hearsèd in death,
Have burst their cerements,[23] why the sepulcher
Wherein we saw thee quietly interred
Hath oped his ponderous and marble jaws 50
To cast thee up again. What may this mean
That thou, dead corse, again in complete steel,
Revisits thus the glimpses of the moon,
Making night hideous, and we fools of nature
So horridly to shake our disposition[24] 55
With thoughts beyond the reaches of our souls?
Say, why is this? Wherefore? What should we do?

(GHOST *beckons* HAMLET.)

HORATIO: It beckons you to go away with it,
As if it some impartment[25] did desire
To you alone.
MARCELLUS: Look with what courteous action 60
It waves you to a more removèd ground.
But do not go with it.
HORATIO: No, by no means.
HAMLET: It will not speak. Then I will follow it.
HORATIO: Do not, my lord.
HAMLET: Why, what should be the fear?
I do not set my life at a pin's fee, 65
And for my soul, what can it do to that,
Being a thing immortal as itself?
It waves me forth again. I'll follow it.
HORATIO: What if it tempt you toward the flood, my lord,
Or to the dreadful summit of the cliff 70
That beetles[26] o'er his base into the sea,
And there assume some other horrible form,
Which might deprive your sovereignty of reason[27]
And draw you into madness? Think of it.
The very place puts toys[28] of desperation, 75

[21] (1) capable of discourse, (2) dubious
[22] buried according to the canon or ordinance of the church
[23] waxed linen shroud
[24] disturb us
[25] communication
[26] juts out
[27] destroy the sovereignty of your reason
[28] whims, fancies

Without more motive, into every brain
That looks so many fathoms to the sea
And hears it roar beneath.

HAMLET: It waves me still.
Go on; I'll follow thee.

MARCELLUS: You shall not go, my lord.

HAMLET: Hold off your hands. 80

HORATIO: Be ruled. You shall not go.

HAMLET: My fate cries out
And makes each petty artere[29] in this body
As hardy as the Nemean lion's nerve.[30]
Still am I called! Unhand me, gentlemen.
By heaven, I'll make a ghost of him that lets[31] me! 85
I say, away! Go on. I'll follow thee. (*Exit* GHOST, *and* HAMLET.)

HORATIO: He waxes desperate with imagination.

MARCELLUS: Let's follow. 'Tis not fit thus to obey him.

HORATIO: Have after! To what issue will this come?

MARCELLUS: Something is rotten in the state of Denmark. 90

HORATIO: Heaven will direct it.

MARCELLUS: Nay, let's follow him. (*Exeunt.*)

## SCENE 5. [THE BATTLEMENTS.]

*Enter* GHOST *and* HAMLET.

HAMLET: Whither wilt thou lead me? Speak; I'll go no further.

GHOST: Mark me.

HAMLET: I will.

GHOST: My hour is almost come,
When I to sulf'rous and tormenting flames
Must render up myself.

HAMLET: Alas, poor ghost.

GHOST: Pity me not, but lend thy serious hearing 5
To what I shall unfold.

HAMLET: Speak. I am bound to hear.

GHOST: So art thou to revenge, when thou shalt hear.

HAMLET: What?

GHOST: I am thy father's spirit,
Doomed for a certain term to walk the night, 10
And for the day confined to fast in fires,

[29] artery
[30] sinews of the mythical lion slain by Hercules
[31] hinders

Till the foul crimes[1] done in my days of nature
Are burnt and purged away. But that I am forbid
To tell the secrets of my prison house,
I could a tale unfold whose lightest word 15
Would harrow up thy soul, freeze thy young blood,
Make thy two eyes like stars start from their spheres,[2]
Thy knotted and combinèd locks to part,
And each particular hair to stand an end
Like quills upon the fearful porpentine.[3] 20
But this eternal blazon[4] must not be
To ears of flesh and blood. List, list, O, list!
If thou didst ever they dear father love —

HAMLET: O God!

GHOST: Revenge his foul and most unnatural murder. 25

HAMLET: Murder?

GHOST: Murder most foul, as in the best it is,
But this most foul, strange, and unnatural.

HAMLET: Haste me to know't, that I, with wings as swift
As meditation[5] or the thoughts of love, 30
May sweep to my revenge.

GHOST: I find thee apt,
And duller shouldst thou be than the fat weed
That roots itself in ease on Lethe wharf,[6]
Wouldst thou not stir in this. Now, Hamlet, hear.
'Tis given out that, sleeping in my orchard, 35
A serpent stung me. So the whole ear of Denmark
Is by a forgèd process[7] of my death
Rankly abused. But know, thou noble youth,
The serpent that did sting thy father's life
Now wears his crown.

HAMLET: O my prophetic soul! 40
My uncle?

GHOST: Ay, that incestuous, that adulterate[8] beast,
With witchcraft of his wits, with traitorous gifts —
O wicked wit and gifts, that have the power
So to seduce! — won to his shameful lust 45
The will of my most seeming-virtuous queen.
O Hamlet, what a falling-off was there,
From me, whose love was of that dignity

[1] sins
[2] (in Ptolemaic astronomy, each planet was fixed in a hollow transparent shell concentric with the earth)
[3] timid porcupine
[4] revelation of eternity
[5] thought
[6] bank of the river of forgetfulness in Hades
[7] false account
[8] adulterous

That it went hand in hand even with the vow
I made to her in marriage, and to decline 50
Upon a wretch whose natural gifts were poor
To those of mine.
But virtue, as it never will be moved,
Though lewdness[9] court it in a shape of heaven,
So lust, though to a radiant angel linked, 55
Will sate itself in a celestial bed
And prey on garbage.
But soft, methinks I scent the morning air;
Brief let me be. Sleeping within my orchard,
My custom always of the afternoon, 60
Upon my secure[10] hour thy uncle stole
With juice of cursed hebona[11] in a vial,
And in the porches of my ears did pour
The leperous distillment, whose effect
Holds such an enmity with blood of man 65
That swift as quicksilver it courses through
The natural gates and alleys of the body,
And with a sudden vigor it doth posset[12]
And curd, like eager[13] droppings into milk,
The thin and wholesome blood. So did it mine, 70
And a most instant tetter[14] barked about
Most lazarlike[15] with vile and loathsome crust
All my smooth body.
Thus was I, sleeping, by a brother's hand
Of life, of crown, of queen at once dispatched, 75
Cut off even in the blossoms of my sin,
Unhouseled, disappointed, unaneled,[16]
No reck'ning made, but sent to my account
With all my imperfections on my head.
O, horrible! O, horrible! Most horrible! 80
If thou hast nature in thee, bear it not.
Let not the royal bed of Denmark be
A couch for luxury[17] and damnèd incest.
But howsomever thou pursues this act,
Taint not thy mind, nor let thy soul contrive 85
Against thy mother aught. Leave her to heaven
And to those thorns that in her bosom lodge
To prick and sting her. Fare thee well at once.

[9] lust
[10] unsuspecting
[11] a poisonous plant
[12] curdle
[13] acid
[14] scab
[15] leperlike
[16] without the sacrament of communion, unabsolved, without extreme unction
[17] lust

The glowworm shows the matin[18] to be near
And 'gins to pale his uneffectual fire. 90
Adieu, adieu, adieu. Remember me. (*Exit.*)

HAMLET: O all you host of heaven! O earth! What else?
And shall I couple hell? O fie! Hold, hold, my heart,
And you, my sinews, grow not instant old,
But bear me stiffly up. Remember thee? 95
Ay, thou poor ghost, whiles memory holds a seat
In this distracted globe.[19] Remember thee?
Yea, from the table[20] of my memory
I'll wipe away all trivial fond[21] records,
All saws[22] of books, all forms, all pressures[23] past 100
That youth and observation copied there,
And thy commandment all alone shall live
Within the book and volume of my brain,
Unmixed with baser matter. Yes, by heaven!
O most pernicious woman! 105
O villain, villain, smiling, damnèd villain!
My tables — meet it is I set it down
That one may smile, and smile, and be a villain.
At least I am sure it may be so in Denmark. [*Writes.*]
So, uncle, there you are. Now to my word: 110
It is "Adieu, adieu, remember me."
I have sworn't.

HORATIO AND MARCELLUS (*within*): My lord, my lord!

(*Enter* HORATIO *and* MARCELLUS.)

MARCELLUS: Lord Hamlet!

HORATIO: Heavens secure him!

HAMLET: So be it!

MARCELLUS: Illo, ho, ho,[24] my lord! 115

HAMLET: Hillo, ho, ho, boy! Come, bird, come.

MARCELLUS: How is't, my noble lord?

HORATIO: What news, my lord?

HAMLET: O, wonderful!

HORATIO: Good my lord, tell it.

HAMLET: No, you will reveal it.

HORATIO: Not I, my lord, by heaven.

MARCELLUS: Nor I, my lord. 120

[18] morning
[19] i.e., his head
[20] tablet, notebook
[21] foolish
[22] maxims
[23] impressions
[24] (falconer's call to his hawk)

HAMLET: How say you then? Would heart of man once think it?
But you'll be secret?
BOTH: Ay, by heaven, my lord.
HAMLET: There's never a villain dwelling in all Denmark
But he's an arrant knave.
HORATIO: There needs no ghost, my lord, come from the grave 125
To tell us this.
HAMLET: Why, right, you are in the right;
And so, without more circumstance[25] at all,
I hold it fit that we shake hands and part:
You, as your business and desire shall point you,
For every man hath business and desire 130
Such as it is, and for my own poor part,
Look you, I'll go pray.
HORATIO: These are but wild and whirling words, my lord.
HAMLET: I am sorry they offend you, heartily;
Yes, faith, heartily.
HORATIO: There's no offense, my lord. 135
HAMLET: Yes, by Saint Patrick, but there is, Horatio,
And much offense too. Touching this vision here,
It is an honest ghost,[26] that let me tell you.
For your desire to know what is between us,
O'ermaster't as you may. And now, good friends, 140
As you are friends, scholars, and soldiers,
Give me one poor request.
HORATIO: What is't, my lord? We will.
HAMLET: Never make known what you have seen tonight.
BOTH: My lord, we will not.
HAMLET: Nay, but swear't.
HORATIO: In faith, 145
My lord, not I.
MARCELLUS: Nor I, my lord – in faith.
HAMLET: Upon my sword.
MARCELLUS: We have sworn, my lord, already.
HAMLET: Indeed, upon my sword, indeed.

(GHOST *cries under the stage.*)

GHOST: Swear.
HAMLET: Ha, ha, boy, say'st thou so? Art thou there, truepenny?[27] 150

[25] details
[26] i.e., not a demon in his father's shape
[27] honest fellow

Come on. You hear this fellow in the cellarage.
Consent to swear.

HORATIO: Propose the oath, my lord.

HAMLET: Never to speak of this that you have seen.
Swear by my sword.

GHOST [*beneath*]: Swear. 155

HAMLET: *Hic et ubique?*[28] Then we'll shift our ground;
Come hither, gentlemen,
And lay your hands again upon my sword.
Swear by my sword
Never to speak of this that you have heard. 160

GHOST [*beneath*]: Swear by his sword.

HAMLET: Well said, old mole! Canst work i' th' earth so fast?
A worthy pioner![29] Once more remove, good friends.

HORATIO: O day and night, but this is wondrous strange!

HAMLET: And therefore as a stranger give it welcome. 165
There are more things in heaven and earth, Horatio,
Than are dreamt of in your philosophy.
But come:
Here as before, never, so help you mercy,
How strange or odd some'er I bear myself 170
(As I perchance hereafter shall think meet
To put an antic disposition[30] on),
That you, at such times seeing me, never shall
With arms encumb'red[31] thus, or this headshake,
Or by pronouncing of some doubtful phrase, 175
As "Well, well, we know," or "We could, an if we would,"
Or "If we list to speak," or "There be, an if they might,"
Or such ambiguous giving out, to note
That you know aught of me — this do swear,
So grace and mercy at your most need help you. 180

GHOST [*beneath*]: Swear.

[*They swear.*]

HAMLET: Rest, rest, perturbèd spirit. So, gentlemen,
With all my love I do commend me[32] to you,
And what so poor a man as Hamlet is
May do t' express his love and friending to you, 185
God willing, shall not lack. Let us go in together,

[28] here and everywhere (Latin)
[29] digger of mines
[30] fantastic behavior
[31] folded
[32] entrust myself

And still your fingers on your lips, I pray.
The time is out of joint. O cursèd spite,
That ever I was born to set it right!
Nay, come, let's go together. (*Exeunt.*) 190

## ACT II

### SCENE 1. [A ROOM.]

*Enter old* POLONIUS, *with his man* REYNALDO.

POLONIUS: Give him this money and these notes, Reynaldo.
REYNALDO: I will, my lord.
POLONIUS: You shall do marvell's[1] wisely, good Reynaldo,
Before you visit him, to make inquire
Of his behavior.
REYNALDO: My lord, I did intend it. 5
POLONIUS: Marry, well said, very well said. Look you sir,
Inquire me first what Danskers[2] are in Paris,
And how, and who, what means, and where they keep,[3]
What company, at what expense; and finding
By this encompassment[4] and drift of question 10
That they do know my son, come you more nearer
Than your particular demands[5] will touch it.
Take you as 'twere some distant knowledge of him,
As thus, "I know his father and his friends,
And in part him." Do you mark this, Reynaldo? 15
REYNALDO: Ay, very well, my lord.
POLONIUS: "And in part him, but," you may say, "not well,
But if't be he I mean, he's very wild,
Addicted so and so." And there put on him
What forgeries[6] you please; marry, none so rank 20
As may dishonor him — take heed of that —
But, sir, such wanton, wild, and usual slips
As are companions noted and most known
To youth and liberty.
REYNALDO: As gaming, my lord.
POLONIUS: Ay, or drinking, fencing, swearing, quarreling, 25
Drabbing.[7] You may go so far.

[1] marvelous(ly)
[2] Danes
[3] dwell
[4] circling
[5] questions
[6] inventions
[7] wenching

REYNALDO: My lord, that would dishonor him.

POLONIUS: Faith, no, as you may season it in the charge.
You must not put another scandal on him,
That he is open to incontinency.[8] 30
That's not my meaning. But breathe his faults so quaintly[9]
That they may seem the taints of liberty,
The flash and outbreak of a fiery mind,
A savageness in unreclaimèd blood,
Of general assault.[10]

REYNALDO: But, my good lord —— 35

POLONIUS: Wherefore should you do this?

REYNALDO: Ay, my lord,
I would know that.

POLONIUS: Marry, sir, here's my drift,
And I believe it is a fetch of warrant.[11]
You laying these slight sullies on my son
As 'twere a thing a little soiled i' th' working, 40
Mark you,
Your party in converse, him you would sound,
Having ever seen in the prenominate crimes[12]
The youth you breathe of guilty, be assured
He closes with you in this consequence:[13] 45
"Good sir," or so, or "friend," or "gentleman" –
According to the phrase or the addition[14]
Of man and country –

REYNALDO: Very good, my lord.

POLONIUS: And then, sir, does 'a[15] this – 'a does –
What was I about to say? By the mass, I was about to say something! 50
Where did I leave?

REYNALDO: At "closes in the consequence," at "friend or so," and "gentleman."

POLONIUS: At "closes in the consequence" – Ay, marry!
He closes thus: "I know the gentleman; 55
I saw him yesterday, or t'other day,
Or then, or then, with such or such, and, as you say,
There was 'a gaming, there o'ertook in's rouse,
There falling out at tennis"; or perchance,
"I saw him enter such a house of sale," 60
Videlicet,[16] a brothel, or so forth.

[8] habitual licentiousness
[9] ingeniously, delicately
[10] common to all men
[11] justifiable device
[12] if he has ever seen in the aforementioned crimes
[13] he falls in with you in this conclusion
[14] title
[15] he
[16] namely

See you now —
Your bait of falsehood take this carp of truth,
And thus do we of wisdom and of reach,[17]
With windlasses[18] and with assays of bias,[19] 65
By indirections find directions out.
So, by my former lecture and advice,
Shall you my son. You have me, have you not?

REYNALDO: My lord, I have.

POLONIUS: God bye ye, fare ye well.

REYNALDO: Good my lord. 70

POLONIUS: Observe his inclination in yourself.[20]

REYNALDO: I shall, my lord.

POLONIUS: And let him ply his music.

REYNALDO: Well, my lord.

POLONIUS: Farewell. (*Exit* REYNALDO)

(*Enter* OPHELIA.)

How now, Ophelia, what's the matter?

OPHELIA: O my lord, my lord, I have been so affrighted! 75

POLONIUS: With what, i' th' name of God?

OPHELIA: My lord, as I was sewing in my closet,[21]
Lord Hamlet, with his doublet all unbraced,[22]
No hat upon his head, his stockings fouled,
Ungartered, and down-gyvèd[23] to his ankle, 80
Pale as his shirt, his knees knocking each other,
And with a look so piteous in purport,[24]
As if he had been loosèd out of hell
To speak of horrors — he comes before me.

POLONIUS: Mad for thy love?

OPHELIA: My lord, I do not know, 85
But truly I do fear it.

POLONIUS: What said he?

OPHELIA: He took me by the wrist and held me hard;
Then goes he to the length of all his arm,
And with his other hand thus o'er his brow
He falls to such perusal of my face 90
As 'a would draw it. Long stayed he so.
At last, a little shaking of mine arm,
And thrice his head thus waving up and down,
He raised a sigh so piteous and profound

[17] far-reaching awareness(?)
[18] circuitous courses
[19] indirect attempts (metaphor from bowling; *bias* = curved course)
[20] for yourself
[21] private room
[22] jacket entirely unlaced
[23] hanging down like fetters
[24] expression

As it did seem to shatter all his bulk 95
And end his being. That done, he lets me go,
And, with his head over his shoulder turned,
He seemed to find his way without his eyes,
For out o' doors he went without their helps,
And to the last bended their light on me. 100

POLONIUS: Come, go with me. I will go seek the King.
This is the very ecstasy[25] of love,
Whose violent property fordoes[26] itself
And leads the will to desperate undertakings
As oft as any passions under heaven 105
That does afflict our natures. I am sorry.
What, have you given him any hard words of late?

OPHELIA: No, my good lord; but as you did command,
I did repel his letters and denied
His access to me.

POLONIUS: That hath made him made. 110
I am sorry that with better heed and judgment
I had not quoted[27] him. I feared he did but trifle
And meant to wrack thee; but beshrew my jealousy.[28]
By heaven, it is as proper[29] to our age
To cast beyond ourselves[30] in our opinions 115
As it is common for the younger sort
To lack discretion. Come, go we to the King.
This must be known, which, being kept close, might move
More grief to hide than hate to utter love.[31]
Come. *(Exeunt.)* 120

## Scene 2. [The Castle.]

*Flourish. Enter* KING *and* QUEEN, ROSENCRANTZ, *and* GUILDENSTERN [*with others*].

KING: Welcome, dear Rosencrantz and Guildenstern.
Moreover that[1] we much did long to see you,
The need we have to use you did provoke
Our hasty sending. Something have you heard
Of Hamlet's transformation: so call it, 5

25 madness
26 quality destroys
27 noted
28 curse on my suspicions
29 natural
30 to be overcalculating
31 (the general meaning is that while telling the King of Hamlet's love may anger the King, more grief would come from keeping it secret)

1 beside the fact that

Sith[2] nor th' exterior nor the inward man
Resembles that it was. What it should be,
More than his father's death, that thus hath put him
So much from th' understanding of himself,
I cannot dream of. I entreat you both 10
That, being of so[3] young days brought up with him,
And sith so neighbored to his youth and havior,[4]
That you vouchsafe your rest[5] here in our court
Some little time, so by your companies
To draw him on to pleasures, and to gather 15
So much as from occasion you may glean,
Whether aught to us unknown afflicts him thus,
That opened[6] lies within our remedy.

QUEEN: Good gentlemen, he hath much talked of you,
And sure I am, two men there is not living 20
To whom he more adheres. If it will please you
To show us so much gentry[7] and good will
As to expend your time with us awhile
For the supply and profit of our hope,
Your visitation shall receive such thanks 25
As fits a king's remembrance.

ROSENCRANTZ: Both your Majesties
Might, by the sovereign power you have of us,
Put your dread pleasures more into command
Than to entreaty.

GUILDENSTERN: But we both obey,
And here give up ourselves in the full bent[8] 30
To lay our service freely at your feet,
To be commanded.

KING: Thanks, Rosencrantz and gentle Guildenstern.

QUEEN: Thanks, Guildenstern and gentle Rosencrantz.
And I beseech you instantly to visit 35
My too much changèd son. Go, some of you,
And bring these gentlemen where Hamlet is.

GUILDENSTERN: Heavens make our presence and our practices
Pleasant and helpful to him!

QUEEN: Ay, amen!

(*Exeunt* ROSENCRANTZ *and* GUILDENSTERN
[*with some Attendants*].)

(*Enter* POLONIUS.)

[2] since
[3] from such
[4] behavior in his youth
[5] consent to remain
[6] revealed
[7] courtesy
[8] entirely (the figure is of a bow bent to its capacity)

POLONIUS: Th' ambassadors from Norway, my good lord, 40
Are joyfully returned.
KING: Thou still[9] hast been the father of good news.
POLONIUS: Have I, my lord? Assure you, my good liege,
I hold my duty, as I hold my soul,
Both to my God and to my gracious king; 45
And I do think, or else this brain of mine
Hunts not the trail of policy so sure[10]
As it hath used to do, that I have found
The very cause of Hamlet's lunacy.
KING: O, speak of that! That do I long to hear. 50
POLONIUS: Give first admittance to th' ambassadors.
My news shall be the fruit to that great feast.
KING: Thyself do grace to them and bring them in. [*Exit* POLONIUS.]
He tells me, my dear Gertrude, he hath found
The head and source of all your son's distemper. 55
QUEEN: I doubt[11] it is no other but the main,[12]
His father's death and our o'erhasty marriage.
KING: Well, we shall sift him.

(*Enter* POLONIUS, VOLTEMAND, *and* CORNELIUS.)

Welcome, my good friends.
Say, Voltemand, what from our brother Norway?
VOLTEMAND: Most fair return of greetings and desires. 60
Upon our first,[13] he sent out to suppress
His nephew's levies, which to him appeared
To be a preparation 'gainst the Polack;
But better looked into, he truly found
It was against your Highness, whereat grieved, 65
That so his sickness, age, and impotence
Was falsely borne in hand,[14] sends out arrests
On Fortinbras; which he, in brief, obeys,
Receives rebuke from Norway, and in fine,[15]
Makes vow before his uncle never more 70
To give th' assay[16] of arms against your Majesty.
Whereon old Norway, overcome with joy,
Gives him threescore thousand crowns in annual fee
And his commission to employ those soldiers,

[9] always
[10] does not follow clues of political doings with such sureness
[11] suspect
[12] principal point
[13] first audience
[14] deceived
[15] finally
[16] trial

So levied as before, against the Polack, 75
With an entreaty, herein further shown, [*Gives a paper.*]
That it might please you to give quiet pass
Through your dominions for this enterprise,
On such regards of safety and allowance[17]
As therein are set down.

KING: It likes us well; 80
And at our more considered time[18] we'll read,
Answer, and think upon this business.
Meantime, we thank you for your well-took labor.
Go to your rest; at night we'll feast together.
Most welcome home! (*Exeunt* AMBASSADORS.)

POLONIUS: This business is well ended. 85
My liege and madam, to expostulate[19]
What majesty should be, what duty is,
Why day is day, night night, and time is time,
Were nothing but to waste night, day, and time.
Therefore, since brevity is the soul of wit,[20] 90
And tediousness the limbs and outward flourishes,
I will be brief. Your noble son is mad.
Mad call I it, for, to define true madness,
What is't but to be nothing else but mad?
But let that go.

QUEEN: More matter, with less art. 95

POLONIUS: Madam, I swear I use no art at all.
That he's mad, 'tis true: 'tis true 'tis pity,
And pity 'tis 'tis true — a foolish figure.[21]
But farewell it, for I will use no art.
Mad let us grant him then; and now remains 100
That we find out the cause of this effect,
Or rather say, the cause of this defect,
For this effect defective comes by cause.
Thus it remains, and the remainder thus.
Perpend.[22] 105
I have a daughter: have, while she is mine,
Who in her duty and obedience, mark,
Hath given me this. Now gather, and surmise.

([*Reads*] *the letter.*)

17 i.e., conditions
18 time proper for considering
19 discuss
20 wisdom, understanding
21 figure of rhetoric
22 consider carefully

"To the celestial, and my soul's idol, the most beautified Ophelia" – 110

That's an ill phrase, a vile phrase; "beautified" is a vile phrase. But you shall hear. Thus:

"In her excellent white bosom, these, &c."

QUEEN: Came this from Hamlet to her?
POLONIUS: Good madam, stay awhile. I will be faithful. 115

"Doubt thou the stars are fire,
Doubt that the sun doth move;
Doubt[23] truth to be a liar,
But never doubt I love.

O dear Ophelia, I am ill at these numbers.[24] I have not art to reckon my groans; but that I love thee best, O most best, believe it. Adieu. 120

Thine evermore, most dear lady,
whilst this machine[25] is to him, HAMLET."

This in obedience hath my daughter shown me, 125
And more above[26] hath his solicitings,
As they fell out by time, by means, and place,
All given to mine ear.
KING: But how hath she
Received his love?
POLONIUS: What do you think of me?
KING: As of a man faithful and honorable. 130
POLONIUS: I would fain prove so. But what might you think,
When I had seen this hot love on the wing
(As I perceived it, I must tell you that,
Before my daughter told me), what might you,
Or my dear Majesty your Queen here, think, 135
If I had played the desk or table book,[27]
Or given my heart a winking,[28] mute and dumb,
Or looked upon this love with idle sight?
What might you think? No, I went round to work
And my young mistress thus I did bespeak: 140
"Lord Hamlet is a prince, out of thy star.[29]
This must not be." And then I prescripts gave her,
That she should lock herself from his resort,
Admit no messengers, receive no tokens.

23 suspect
24 unskilled in verses
25 complex device (here, his body)
26 in addition
27 i.e., been a passive recipient of secrets
28 closing of the eyes
29 sphere

Which done, she took the fruits of my advice, 145
And he, repellèd, a short tale to make,
Fell into a sadness, then into a fast,
Thence to a watch,[30] thence into a weakness,
Thence to a lightness,[31] and, by this declension,
Into the madness wherein now he raves, 150
And all we mourn for.

KING: Do you think 'tis this?

QUEEN: It may be, very like.

POLONIUS: Hath there been such a time, I would fain know that,
That I have positively said "'Tis so,"
When it proved otherwise?

KING: Not that I know. 155

POLONIUS [*pointing to his head and shoulder*]: Take this from this, if this be otherwise.
If circumstances lead me, I will find
Where truth is hid, though it were hid indeed
Within the center.[32]

KING: How may we try it further?

POLONIUS: You know sometimes he walks four hours together 160
Here in the lobby.

QUEEN: So he does indeed.

POLONIUS: At such a time I'll loose my daughter to him.
Be you and I behind an arras[33] then.
Mark the encounter. If he love her not,
And be not from his reason fall'n thereon, 165
Let me be no assistant for a state
But keep a farm and carters.

KING: We will try it.

(*Enter* HAMLET *reading on a book.*)

QUEEN: But look where sadly the poor wretch comes reading.

POLONIUS: Away, I do beseech you both, away.

(*Exit* KING *and* QUEEN.)

I'll board him presently.[34] O, give me leave. 170
How does my good Lord Hamlet?

HAMLET: Well, God-a-mercy.

POLONIUS: Do you know me, my lord?

HAMLET: Excellent well. You are a fishmonger.[35]

POLONIUS: Not I, my lord. 175

HAMLET: Then I would you were so honest a man.

30 wakefulness
31 mental derangement
32 center of the earth
33 tapestry hanging in front of a wall
34 accost him at once
35 dealer in fish (slang for a procurer)

POLONIUS: Honest, my lord?
HAMLET: Ay, sir. To be honest, as this world goes, is to be one man picked out of ten thousand.
POLONIUS: That's very true, my lord. 180
HAMLET: For if the sun breed maggots in a dead dog, being a good kissing carrion[36] —— Have you a daughter?
POLONIUS: I have, my lord.
HAMLET: Let her not walk i' th' sun. Conception[37] is a blessing, but as your daughter may conceive, friend, look to't. 185
POLONIUS [*aside*]: How say you by that? Still harping on my daughter. Yet he knew me not at first. 'A said I was a fishmonger. 'A is far gone, far gone. And truly in my youth I suffered much extremity for love, very near this. I'll speak to him again. – What do you read, my lord?
HAMLET: Words, words, words. 190
POLONIUS: What is the matter, my lord?
HAMLET: Between who?
POLONIUS: I mean the matter[38] that you read, my lord.
HAMLET: Slanders, sir; for the satirical rogue says here that old men have gray beards, that their faces are wrinkled, their eyes purging 195 thick amber and plumtree gum, and that they have a plentiful lack of wit, together with most weak hams. All which, sir, though I most powerfully and potently believe, yet I hold it not honesty[39] to have it thus set down; for you yourself, sir, should be old as I am if, like a crab, you could go backward. 200
POLONIUS [*aside*]: Though this be madness, yet there is method in't. Will you walk out of the air, my lord?
HAMLET: Into my grave.
POLONIUS: Indeed, that's out of the air. [*Aside.*] How pregnant[40] sometimes his replies are! A happiness[41] that often madness hits on, which 205 reason and sanity could not so prosperously be delivered of. I will leave him and suddenly contrive the means of meeting between him and my daughter. – My lord, I will take my leave of you.
HAMLET: You cannot take from me anything that I will more willingly part withal – except my life, except my life, except my life. 210

(*Enter* GUILDENSTERN *and* ROSENCRANTZ.)

POLONIUS: Fare you well, my lord.
HAMLET: These tedious old fools!
POLONIUS: You go to seek the Lord Hamlet? There he is.

[36] (perhaps the meaning is "a good piece of flesh to kiss," but many editors emend *good* to *god,* taking the word to refer to the sun)
[37] (1) understanding, (2) becoming pregnant
[38] (Polonius means "subject matter," but Hamlet pretends to take the word in the sense of "quarrel")
[39] decency
[40] meaningful
[41] apt turn of phrase

ROSENCRANTZ [*to* POLONIUS]: God save you, sir! [*Exit* POLONIUS.]

GUILDENSTERN: My honored lord! 215

ROSENCRANTZ: My most dear lord!

HAMLET: My excellent good friends! How dost thou, Guildenstern? Ah, Rosencrantz! Good lads, how do you both?

ROSENCRANTZ: As the indifferent[42] children of the earth.

GUILDENSTERN: Happy in that we are not overhappy. 220
On Fortune's cap we are not the very button.

HAMLET: Nor the soles of her shoe?

ROSENCRANTZ: Neither, my lord.

HAMLET: Then you live about her waist, or in the middle of her favors?

GUILDENSTERN: Faith, her privates[43] we. 225

HAMLET: In the secret parts of Fortune? O, most true! She is a strumpet. What news?

ROSENCRANTZ: None, my lord, but that the world's grown honest.

HAMLET: Then is doomsday near. But your news is not true. Let me question more in particular. What have you, my good friends, de- 230 served at the hands of Fortune that she sends you to prison hither?

GUILDENSTERN: Prison, my lord?

HAMLET: Denmark's a prison.

ROSENCRANTZ: Then is the world one.

HAMLET: A goodly one, in which there are many confines, wards,[44] and 235 dungeons, Denmark being one o' th' worst.

ROSENCRANTZ: We think not so, my lord.

HAMLET: Why, then 'tis none to you, for there is nothing either good or bad but thinking makes it so. To me it is a prison.

ROSENCRANTZ: Why then your ambition makes it one. 'Tis too narrow 240 for your mind.

HAMLET: O God, I could be bounded in a nutshell and count myself a king of infinite space, were it not that I have bad dreams.

GUILDENSTERN: Which dreams indeed are ambition, for the very substance of the ambitious is merely the shadow of a dream. 245

HAMLET: A dream itself is but a shadow.

ROSENCRANTZ: Truly, and I hold ambition of so airy and light a quality that it is but a shadow's shadow.

HAMLET: Then are our beggars bodies, and our monarchs and outstretched heroes the beggars' shadows.[45] Shall we to th' court? For, 250 by my fay,[46] I cannot reason.

BOTH: We'll wait upon you.

HAMLET: No such matter. I will not sort you with the rest of my servants, for, to speak to you like an honest man, I am most dreadfully

[42] ordinary

[43] ordinary men (with a pun on "private parts")

[44] cells

[45] i.e., by your logic, beggars (lacking ambition) are substantial, and great men are elongated shadows

[46] faith

attended. But in the beaten way of friendship, what make you at Elsinore? 255

ROSENCRANTZ: To visit you, my lord; no other occasion.

HAMLET: Beggar that I am, I am even poor in thanks, but I thank you; and sure, dear friends, my thanks are too dear a halfpenny.[47] Were you not sent for? Is it your own inclining? Is it a free visitation? 260 Come, come, deal justly with me. Come, come; nay, speak.

GUILDENSTERN: What should we say, my lord?

HAMLET: Why anything — but to th' purpose. You were sent for, and there is a kind of confession in your looks, which your modesties have not craft enough to color. I know the good King and Queen have 265 sent for you.

ROSENCRANTZ: To what end, my lord?

HAMLET: That you must teach me. But let me conjure you by the rights of our fellowship, by the consonancy of our youth, by the obligation of our ever-preserved love, and by what more dear a better proposer 270 can charge you withal, be even and direct with me, whether you were sent for or no.

ROSENCRANTZ [*aside to* GUILDENSTERN]: What say you?

HAMLET [*aside*]: Nay then, I have an eye of you. — If you love me, hold not off. 275

GUILDENSTERN: My lord, we were sent for.

HAMLET: I will tell you why; so shall my anticipation prevent your discovery,[48] and your secrecy to the King and Queen molt no feather. I have of late, but wherefore I know not, lost all my mirth, forgone all custom of exercises; and indeed, it goes so heavily with my disposi- 280 tion that this goodly frame, the earth, seems to me a sterile promontory; this most excellent canopy, the air, look you, this brave o'erhanging firmament, this majestical roof fretted[49] with golden fire: why, it appeareth nothing to me but a foul and pestilent congregation of vapors. What a piece of work is a man, how noble in reason, 285 how infinite in faculties, in form and moving how express[50] and admirable, in action how like an angel, in apprehension how like a god: the beauty of the world, the paragon of animals; and yet to me, what is this quintessence of dust? Man delights not me; nor woman neither, though by your smiling you seem to say so. 290

ROSENCRANTZ: My lord, there was no such stuff in my thoughts.

HAMLET: Why did ye laugh then, when I said "Man delights not me"?

ROSENCRANTZ: To think, my lord, if you delight not in man, what lenten[51] entertainment the players shall receive from you. We coted[52] them on the way, and hither are they coming to offer you 295 service.

[47] i.e., not worth a halfpenny
[48] forestall your disclosure
[49] adorned
[50] exact
[51] meager
[52] overtook

HAMLET: He that plays the king shall be welcome; his Majesty shall have tribute of me; the adventurous knight shall use his foil and target;[53] the lover shall not sigh gratis; the humorous man[54] shall end his part in peace; the clown shall make those laugh whose lungs are tickle o' th' sere;[55] and the lady shall say her mind freely, or[56] the blank verse shall halt[57] for't. What players are they? 300

ROSENCRANTZ: Even those you were wont to take such delight in, the tragedians of the city.

HAMLET: How chances it they travel? Their residence, both in reputation and profit, was better both ways. 305

ROSENCRANTZ: I think their inhibition[58] comes by the means of the late innovation.[59]

HAMLET: Do they hold the same estimation they did when I was in the city? Are they so followed? 310

ROSENCRANTZ: No indeed, are they not.

HAMLET: How comes it? Do they grow rusty?

ROSENCRANTZ: Nay, their endeavor keeps in the wonted pace, but there is, sir, an eyrie[60] of children, little eyases, that cry out on the top of question[61] and are most tyrannically[62] clapped for't. These are now the fashion, and so berattle the common stages[63] (so they call them) that many wearing rapiers are afraid of goosequills[64] and dare scarce come thither. 315

HAMLET: What, are they children? Who maintains 'em? How are they escoted?[65] Will they pursue the quality[66] no longer than they can sing? Will they not say afterwards, if they should grow themselves to common players (as it is most like, if their means are no better), their writers do them wrong to make them exclaim against their own succession?[67] 320

ROSENCRANTZ: Faith, there has been much to-do on both sides, and the nation holds it no sin to tarre[68] them to controversy. There was, for a while, no money bid for argument[69] unless the poet and the player went to cuffs in the question. 325

HAMLET: Is't possible?

53 shield

54 i.e., eccentric man (among stock characters in dramas were men dominated by a "humor" or odd trait)

55 on hair trigger (*sere* = part of the gunlock)

56 else

57 limp

58 hindrance

59 (probably an allusion to the companies of child actors that had become popular and were offering serious competition to the adult actors)

60 nest

61 unfledged hawks that cry shrilly above others in matters of debate

62 violently

63 cry down the public theaters (with the adult acting companies)

64 pens (of satirists who ridicule the public theaters and their audiences)

65 financially supported

66 profession of acting

67 future

68 incite

69 plot of a play

GUILDENSTERN: O, there has been much throwing about of brains. 330

HAMLET: Do the boys carry it away?

ROSENCRANTZ: Ay, that they do, my lord — Hercules and his load[70] too.

HAMLET: It is not very strange, for my uncle is King of Denmark, and those that would make mouths at him while my father lived give twenty, forty, fifty, a hundred ducats apiece for his picture in little. 335 'Sblood,[71] there is something in this more than natural, if philosophy could find it out.

(*A flourish.*)

GUILDENSTERN: There are the players.

HAMLET: Gentlemen, you are welcome to Elsinore. Your hands, come then. Th' appurtenance of welcome is fashion and ceremony. Let me 340 comply[72] with you in this garb,[73] lest my extent[74] to the players (which I tell you must show fairly outwards) should more appear like entertainment than yours. You are welcome. But my uncle-father and aunt-mother are deceived.

GUILDENSTERN: In what, my dear lord? 345

HAMLET: I am but mad north-northwest:[75] when the wind is southerly I know a hawk from a handsaw.[76]

(*Enter* POLONIUS.)

POLONIUS: Well be with you, gentlemen.

HAMLET: Hark you, Guildenstern, and you too; at each ear a hearer. That great baby you see there is not yet out of his swaddling clouts. 350

ROSENCRANTZ: Happily[77] he is the second time come to them, for they say an old man is twice a child.

HAMLET: I will prophesy he comes to tell me of the players. Mark it. — You say right, sir; a Monday morning, 'twas then indeed.

POLONIUS: My lord, I have news to tell you. 355

HAMLET: My lord, I have news to tell you. When Roscius[78] was an actor in Rome——

POLONIUS: The actors are come hither, my lord.

HAMLET: Buzz, buzz.[79]

POLONIUS: Upon my honor —— 360

HAMLET: Then came each actor on his ass ——

POLONIUS: The best actors in the world, either for tragedy, comedy, history, pastoral, pastoral-comical, historical-pastoral, tragical-his-

[70] i.e., the whole world (with a reference to the Globe Theatre, which had a sign that represented Hercules bearing the globe)

[71] by God's blood

[72] be courteous

[73] outward show

[74] behavior

[75] i.e., on one point of the compass only

[76] (*hawk* can refer not only to a bird but to a kind of pickax; *handsaw* — a carpenter's tool — may involve a similar pun on "hernshaw," a heron)

[77] perhaps

[78] a famous Roman comic actor

[79] (an interjection, perhaps indicating that the news is old)

torical, tragical-comical-historical-pastoral; scene individable,[80] or poem unlimited.[81] Seneca[82] cannot be too heavy, nor Plautus[83] too light. For the law of writ and the liberty,[84] these are the only men. 365

HAMLET: O Jeptha, judge of Israel,[85] what a treasure hadst thou!

POLONIUS: What a treasure had he, my lord?

HAMLET: Why,

"One fair daughter, and no more, 370
The which he lovèd passing well."

POLONIUS [*aside*]: Still on my daughter.

HAMLET: Am I not i' th' right, old Jeptha?

POLONIUS: If you call me Jeptha, my lord, I have a daughter that I love passing well. 375

HAMLET: Nay, that follows not.

POLONIUS: What follows then, my lord?

HAMLET: Why,

"As by lot, God wot,"

and then, you know, 380

"It came to pass, as most like it was."

The first row of the pious chanson[86] will show you more, for look where my abridgment[87] comes.

(*Enter the* PLAYERS.)

You are welcome, masters, welcome, all. I am glad to see thee well. Welcome, good friends. O, old friend, why, thy face is valanced[88] since I saw thee last. Com'st thou to beard me in Denmark? What, my young lady[89] and mistress? By'r Lady, your ladyship is nearer to heaven than when I saw you last by the altitude of a chopine.[90] Pray God your voice, like a piece of uncurrent gold, be not cracked within the ring.[91] — Masters, you are all welcome. We'll e'en to't like French falconers, fly at anything we see. We'll have a speech straight. Come, give us a taste of your quality. Come, a passionate speech. 385 390

[80] plays observing the unities of time, place, and action

[81] plays not restricted by the tenets of criticism

[82] Roman tragic dramatist

[83] Roman comic dramatist

[84] (perhaps "for sticking to the text and for improvising"; perhaps "for classical plays and for modern loosely written plays")

[85] the title of a ballad on the Hebrew judge who sacrificed his daughter (see Judges 11)

[86] stanza of the scriptural song

[87] (1) i.e., entertainers, who abridge the time, (2) interrupters

[88] fringed (with a beard)

[89] i.e., boy for female roles

[90] thick-soled shoe

[91] (a coin was unfit for legal tender if a crack extended from the edge through the ring enclosing the monarch's head. Hamlet, punning on *ring*, refers to the change of voice that the boy actor will undergo)

PLAYER: What speech, my good lord?

HAMLET: I heard thee speak me a speech once, but it was never acted, or if it was, not above once, for the play, I remember, pleased not the million; 'twas caviary to the general,[92] but it was (as I received it, and others, whose judgments in such matters cried in the top of[93] mine) an excellent play, well digested in the scenes, set down with as much modesty as cunning.[94] I remember one said there were no sallets[95] in the lines to make the matter savory; nor no matter in the phrase that might indict the author of affectation, but called it an honest method, as wholesome as sweet, and by very much more handsome than fine.[96] One speech in't I chiefly loved. 'Twas Aeneas' tale to Dido, and thereabout of it especially when he speaks of Priam's slaughter. If it live in your memory, begin at this line – let me see, let me see: 395 400 405

"The rugged Pyrrhus, like th' Hyrcanian beast[97] —"

'Tis not so; it begins with Pyrrhus:

"The rugged Pyrrhus, he whose sable[98] arms,
Black as his purpose, did the night resemble 410
When he lay couchèd in th' ominous horse,[99]
Hath now this dread and black complexion smeared
With heraldry more dismal.[100] Head to foot
Now is he total gules, horridly tricked[101]
With blood of fathers, mothers, daughters, sons, 415
Baked and impasted[102] with the parching streets,
That lend a tyrannous and a damnèd light
To their lord's murder. Roasted in wrath and fire,
And thus o'ersizèd[103] with coagulate gore,
With eyes like carbuncles, the hellish Pyrrhus 420
Old grandsire Priam seeks."

So, proceed you.

POLONIUS: Fore God, my lord, well spoken, with good accent and good discretion.

PLAYER:

"Anon he finds him, 425
Striking too short at Greeks. His antique sword,
Rebellious to his arm, lies where it falls,

[92] i.e., too choice for the multitude
[93] overtopping
[94] restraint as art
[95] salads, spicy jests
[96] well-proportioned rather than ornamented
[97] i.e., tiger (Hyrcania was in Asia)
[98] black
[99] i.e., wooden horse at the siege of Troy
[100] ill-omened
[101] all red, horridly adorned
[102] encrusted
[103] smeared over

Repugnant to command.[104] Unequal matched,
Pyrrhus at Priam drives, in rage strikes wide,
But with the whiff and wind of his fell sword 430
Th' unnervèd father falls. Then senseless Ilium,[105]
Seeming to feel this blow, with flaming top
Stoops to his base,[106] and with a hideous crash
Takes prisoner Pyrrhus' ear. For lo, his sword,
Which was declining on the milky head 435
Of reverend Priam, seemed i' th' air to stick.
So as a painted tyrant[107] Pyrrhus stood,
And like a neutral to his will and matter[108]
Did nothing.
But as we often see, against[109] some storm, 440
A silence in the heavens, the rack[110] stand still,
The bold winds speechless, and the orb below
As hush as death, anon the dreadful thunder
Doth rend the region, so after Pyrrhus' pause,
A rousèd vengeance sets him new awork, 445
And never did the Cyclops' hammers fall
On Mars's armor, forged for proof eterne,[111]
With less remorse than Pyrrhus' bleeding sword
Now falls on Priam.
Out, out, thou strumpet Fortune! All you gods, 450
In general synod[112] take away her power,
Break all the spokes and fellies[113] from her wheel,
And bowl the round nave[114] down the hill of heaven,
As low as to the fiends."

POLONIUS: This is too long. 455

HAMLET: It shall to the barber's, with your beard. — Prithee say on. He's for a jig or a tale of bawdry, or he sleeps. Say on; come to Hecuba.

PLAYER:

"But who (ah woe!) had seen the mobled[115] queen —"

HAMLET: "The mobled queen"? 460

POLONIUS: That's good. "Mobled queen" is good.

PLAYER:

"Run barefoot up and down, threat'ning the flames
With bisson rheum,[116] a clout[117] upon that head

[104] disobedient
[105] insensate Troy
[106] collapses (*his* = its)
[107] tyrant in a picture
[108] task
[109] just before
[110] clouds
[111] eternal endurance
[112] council
[113] rims
[114] hub
[115] muffled
[116] blinding tears
[117] rag

Where late the diadem stood, and for a robe,
About her lank and all o'erteemèd[118] loins, 465
A blanket in the alarm of fear caught up—
Who this had seen, with tongue in venom steeped
'Gainst Fortune's state would treason have pronounced.
But if the gods themselves did see her then,
When she saw Pyrrhus make malicious sport 470
In mincing with his sword her husband's limbs,
The instant burst of clamor that she made
(Unless things mortal move them not at all)
Would have made milch[119] the burning eyes of heaven
And passion in the gods." 475

POLONIUS: Look, whe'r[120] he has not turned his color, and has tears in's eyes. Prithee no more.

HAMLET: 'Tis well. I'll have thee speak out the rest of this soon. Good my lord, will you see the players well bestowed?[121] Do you hear? Let them be well used, for they are the abstract and brief chronicles 480 of the time. After your death you were better have a bad epitaph than their ill report while you live.

POLONIUS: My lord, I will use them according to their desert.

HAMLET: God's bodkin,[122] man, much better! Use every man after his desert, and who shall scape whipping? Use them after your own 485 honor and dignity. The less they deserve, the more merit is in your bounty. Take them in.

POLONIUS: Come, sirs.

HAMLET: Follow him, friends. We'll hear a play tomorrow. [*Aside to* PLAYER.] Dost thou hear me, old friend? Can you play *The Murder* 490 *of Gonzago*?

PLAYER: Ay, my lord.

HAMLET: We'll ha't tomorrow night. You could for a need study a speech of some dozen or sixteen lines which I would set down and insert in't, could you not? 495

PLAYER: Ay, my lord.

HAMLET: Very well. Follow that lord, and look you mock him not. My good friends, I'll leave you till night. You are welcome to Elsinore.

(*Exeunt* POLONIUS *and* PLAYERS.)

ROSENCRANTZ: Good my lord.

(*Exeunt* [ROSENCRANTZ *and* GUILDENSTERN].)

HAMLET: Ay, so, God bye to you.—Now I am alone. 500
O, what a rogue and peasant slave am I!
Is it not monstrous that this player here,

[118] exhausted with childbearing
[119] moist (literally, "milk-giving")
[120] whether
[121] housed
[122] by God's little body

But in a fiction, in a dream of passion,[123]
Could force his soul so to his own conceit[124]
That from her working all his visage wanned, 505
Tears in his eyes, distraction in his aspect,
A broken voice, and his whole function[125] suiting
With forms[126] to his conceit? And all for nothing!
For Hecuba!
What's Hecuba to him, or he to Hecuba, 510
That he should weep for her? What would he do
Had he the motive and the cue for passion
That I have? He would drown the stage with tears
And cleave the general ear with horrid speech,
Make mad the guilty and appall the free,[127] 515
Confound the ignorant, and amaze indeed
The very faculties of eyes and ears.
Yet I,
A dull and muddy-mettled[128] rascal, peak
Like John-a-dreams,[129] unpregnant of[130] my cause, 520
And can say nothing. No, not for a king,
Upon whose property and most dear life
A damned defeat was made. Am I a coward?
Who calls me villain? Breaks my pate across?
Plucks off my beard and blows it in my face? 525
Tweaks me by the nose? Gives me the lie i' th' throat
As deep as to the lungs? Who does me this?
Ha, 'swounds,[131] I should take it, for it cannot be
But I am pigeon-livered[132] and lack gall
To make oppression bitter, or ere this 530
I should ha' fatted all the region kites[133]
With this slave's offal. Bloody, bawdy villain!
Remorseless, treacherous, lecherous, kindless[134] villain!
O, vengeance!
Why, what an ass am I! This is most brave,[135] 535
That I, the son of a dear father murdered,
Prompted to my revenge by heaven and hell,
Must, like a whore, unpack my heart with words
And fall a-cursing like a very drab,[136]

123 imaginary emotion
124 imagination
125 action
126 bodily expressions
127 terrify (make pale?) the guiltless
128 weak-spirited
129 mope like a dreamer
130 unquickened by
131 by God's wounds
132 gentle as a dove
133 kites (scavenger birds) of the sky
134 unnatural
135 fine
136 prostitute

A stallion![137] Fie upon't, foh! About,[138] my brains. 540
Hum —
I have heard that guilty creatures sitting at a play
Have by the very cunning of the scene
Been struck so to the soul that presently[139]
They have proclaimed their malefactions. 545
For murder, though it have no tongue, will speak
With most miraculous organ. I'll have these players
Play something like the murder of my father
Before mine uncle. I'll observe his looks,
I'll tent[140] him to the quick. If 'a do blench,[141] 550
I know my course. The spirit that I have seen
May be a devil, and the devil hath power
T' assume a pleasing shape, yea, and perhaps
Out of my weakness and my melancholy,
As he is very potent with such spirits, 555
Abuses me to damn me. I'll have grounds
More relative[142] than this. The play's the thing
Wherein I'll catch the conscience of the king. *(Exit.)*

## ACT III

### Scene 1. [The Castle.]

*Enter* KING, QUEEN, POLONIUS, OPHELIA, ROSENCRANTZ, GUILDENSTERN, LORDS.

KING: And can you by no drift of conference[1]
Get from him why he puts on this confusion,
Grating so harshly all his days of quiet
With turbulent and dangerous lunacy?
ROSENCRANTZ: He does confess he feels himself distracted, 5
But from what cause 'a will by no means speak.
GUILDENSTERN: Nor do we find him forward to be sounded,[2]
But with a crafty madness keeps aloof
When we would bring him on to some confession
Of his true state.
QUEEN: Did he receive you well? 10

[137] male prostitute (perhaps one should adopt the Folio reading, *scullion* = kitchen wench)
[138] to work
[139] immediately
[140] probe
[141] flinch
[142] (probably "pertinent," but possibly "able to be related plausibly")

[1] management of conversation
[2] willing to be questioned

ROSENCRANTZ: Most like a gentleman.
GUILDENSTERN: But with much forcing of his disposition.[3]
ROSENCRANTZ: Niggard of question,[4] but of our demands
Most free in his reply.
QUEEN: Did you assay[5] him
To any pastime? 15
ROSENCRANTZ: Madam, it so fell out that certain players
We o'erraught[6] on the way; of these we told him,
And there did seem in him a kind of joy
To hear of it. They are here about the court,
And, as I think, they have already order 20
This night to play before him.
POLONIUS: 'Tis most true,
And he beseeched me to entreat your Majesties
To hear and see the matter.
KING: With all my heart, and it doth much content me
To hear him so inclined. 25
Good gentlemen, give him a further edge
And drive his purpose into these delights.
ROSENCRANTZ: We shall, my lord.
(*Exeunt* ROSENCRANTZ *and* GUILDENSTERN.)
KING: Sweet Gertrude, leave us too,
For we have closely[7] sent for Hamlet hither,
That he, as 'twere by accident, may here 30
Affront[8] Ophelia.
Her father and myself (lawful espials[9])
Will so bestow ourselves that, seeing unseen,
We may of their encounter frankly judge
And gather by him, as he is behaved, 35
If't be th' affliction of his love or no
That thus he suffers for.
QUEEN: I shall obey you.
And for your part, Ophelia, I do wish
That your good beauties be the happy cause
Of Hamlet's wildness. So shall I hope your virtues 40
Will bring him to his wonted way again,
To both your honors.
OPHELIA: Madam, I wish it may. [*Exit* QUEEN.]
POLONIUS: Ophelia, walk you here. – Gracious, so please you,
We will bestow ourselves. [*To* OPHELIA.] Read on this book,

3 effort
4 uninclined to talk
5 tempt
6 overtook
7 secretly
8 meet face to face
9 spies

That show of such an exercise may color[10] 45
Your loneliness. We are oft to blame in this,
'Tis too much proved, that with devotion's visage
And pious action we do sugar o'er
The devil himself.

KING [*aside*]: O, 'tis too true.
How smart a lash that speech doth give my conscience! 50
The harlot's cheek, beautied with plast'ring art,
Is not more ugly to the thing that helps it
Than is my deed to my most painted word.
O heavy burden!

POLONIUS: I hear him coming. Let's withdraw, my lord. 55

[*Exeunt* KING *and* POLONIUS.]

(*Enter* HAMLET.)

HAMLET: To be, or not to be: that is the question:
Whether 'tis nobler in the mind to suffer
The slings and arrows of outrageous fortune,
Or to take arms against a sea of troubles,
And by opposing end them. To die, to sleep – 60
No more – and by a sleep to say we end
The heartache, and the thousand natural shocks
That flesh is heir to! 'Tis a consummation
Devoutly to be wished. To die, to sleep –
To sleep – perchance to dream: ay, there's the rub,[11] 65
For in that sleep of death what dreams may come
When we have shuffled off this mortal coil,[12]
Must give us pause. There's the respect[13]
That makes calamity of so long life:[14]
For who would bear the whips and scorns of time, 70
Th' oppressor's wrong, the proud man's contumely,
The pangs of despised love, the law's delay,
The insolence of office, and the spurns
That patient merit of th' unworthy takes,
When he himself might his quietus[15] make 75
With a bare bodkin?[16] Who would fardels[17] bear,
To grunt and sweat under a weary life,
But that the dread of something after death,

[10] act of devotion may give a plausible hue to (the book is one of devotion)
[11] impediment (obstruction to a bowler's ball)
[12] (1) turmoil, (2) a ring of rope (here the flesh encircling the soul)
[13] consideration
[14] (1) makes calamity so long-lived, (2) makes living so long a calamity
[15] full discharge (a legal term)
[16] dagger
[17] burdens

The undiscovered country, from whose bourn[18]
No traveler returns, puzzles the will, 80
And makes us rather bear those ills we have,
Than fly to others that we know not of?
Thus conscience[19] does make cowards of us all,
And thus the native hue of resolution
Is sicklied o'er with the pale cast[20] of thought, 85
And enterprises of great pitch[21] and moment,
With this regard[22] their currents turn awry,
And lose the name of action. – Soft you now,
The fair Ophelia! – Nymph, in thy orisons[23]
Be all my sins remembered.

OPHELIA: Good my lord, 90
How does your honor for this many a day?

HAMLET: I humbly thank you; well, well, well.

OPHELIA: My lord, I have remembrances of yours
That I have longèd long to redeliver.
I pray you now, receive them.

HAMLET: No, not I, 95
I never gave you aught.

OPHELIA: My honored lord, you know right well you did,
And with them words of so sweet breath composed
As made these things more rich. Their perfume lost,
Take these again, for to the noble mind 100
Rich gifts wax poor when givers prove unkind.
There, my lord.

HAMLET: Ha, ha! Are you honest?[24]

OPHELIA: My lord?

HAMLET: Are you fair? 105

OPHELIA: What means your lordship?

HAMLET: That if you be honest and fair, your honesty should admit no discourse to your beauty.[25]

OPHELIA: Could beauty, my lord, have better commerce than with honesty? 110

HAMLET: Ay, truly; for the power of beauty will sooner transform honesty from what it is to a bawd[26] than the force of honesty can translate beauty into his likeness. This was sometime a paradox, but now the time gives it proof. I did love you once.

OPHELIA: Indeed, my lord, you made me believe so. 115

[18] region
[19] self-consciousness, introspection
[20] color
[21] height (a term from falconry)
[22] consideration
[23] prayers
[24] (1) are you modest, (2) are you chaste, (3) have you integrity
[25] your modesty should permit no approach to your beauty
[26] procurer

HAMLET: You should not have believed me, for virtue cannot so inoculate[27] our old stock but we shall relish of it.[28] I loved you not.

OPHELIA: I was the more deceived.

HAMLET: Get thee to a nunnery. Why wouldst thou be a breeder of sinners? I am myself indifferent honest,[29] but yet I could accuse me of such things that it were better my mother had not borne me: I am very proud, revengeful, ambitious, with more offenses at my beck[30] than I have thoughts to put them in, imagination to give them shape, or time to act them in. What should such fellows as I do crawling between earth and heaven? We are arrant knaves all; believe none of us. Go thy ways to a nunnery. Where's your father? 120 125

OPHELIA: At home, my lord.

HAMLET: Let the doors be shut upon him, that he may play the fool nowhere but in's own house. Farewell.

OPHELIA: O help him, you sweet heavens! 130

HAMLET: If thou dost marry, I'll give thee this plague for thy dowry: be thou as chaste as ice, as pure as snow, thou shalt not escape calumny. Get thee to a nunnery. Go, farewell. Or if thou wilt needs marry, marry a fool, for wise men know well enough what monsters[31] you make of them. To a nunnery, go, and quickly too. Farewell. 135

OPHELIA: Heavenly powers, restore him!

HAMLET: I have heard of your paintings, well enough. God hath given you one face, and you make yourselves another. You jig and amble, and you lisp; you nickname God's creatures and make your wantonness your ignorance.[32] Go to, I'll no more on't; it hath made me mad. I say we will have no moe[33] marriage. Those that are married already — all but one — shall live. The rest shall keep as they are. To a nunnery, go. (*Exit.*) 140

OPHELIA: O what a noble mind is here o'erthrown!
The courtier's, soldier's, scholar's, eye, tongue, sword, 145
Th' expectancy and rose[34] of the fair state,
The glass of fashion, and the mold of form,[35]
Th' observed of all observers, quite, quite down!
And I, of ladies most deject and wretched,
That sucked the honey of his musicked vows, 150
Now see that noble and most sovereign reason
Like sweet bells jangled, out of time and harsh,
That unmatched form and feature of blown[36] youth

[27] graft
[28] smack of it (our old sinful nature)
[29] moderately virtuous
[30] call
[31] horned beasts, cuckolds
[32] excuse your wanton speech by pretending ignorance
[33] more
[34] i.e., fair hope
[35] the mirror of fashion, and the pattern of excellent behavior
[36] blooming

Blasted with ecstasy.[37] O, woe is me
T' have seen what I have seen, see what I see! 155

(*Enter* KING *and* POLONIUS.)

KING: Love? His affections[38] do not that way tend,
Nor what he spake, though it lacked form a little,
Was not like madness. There's something in his soul
O'er which his melancholy sits on brood,
And I do doubt[39] the hatch and the disclose 160
Will be some danger; which for to prevent,
I have in quick determination
Thus set it down: he shall with speed to England
For the demand of our neglected tribute.
Haply the seas, and countries different, 165
With variable objects, shall expel
This something-settled[40] matter in his heart,
Whereon his brains still beating puts him thus
From fashion of himself. What think you on't?
POLONIUS: It shall do well. But yet do I believe 170
The origin and commencement of his grief
Sprung from neglected love. How now, Ophelia?
You need not tell us what Lord Hamlet said;
We heard it all. My lord, do as you please,
But if you hold it fit, after the play, 175
Let his queen mother all alone entreat him
To show his grief. Let her be round[41] with him,
And I'll be placed, so please you, in the ear
Of all their conference. If she find him not,[42]
To England send him, or confine him where 180
Your wisdom best shall think.
KING: It shall be so.
Madness in great ones must not unwatched go. (*Exeunt.*)

## SCENE 2. [THE CASTLE.]

*Enter* HAMLET *and three of the* PLAYERS.

HAMLET: Speak the speech, I pray you, as I pronounced it to you, trippingly on the tongue. But if you mouth it, as many of our players do, I had as lief the town crier spoke my lines. Nor do not

37 madness
38 inclinations
39 fear
40 somewhat settled
41 blunt
42 does not find him out

saw the air too much with your hand, thus, but use all gently, for in the very torrent, tempest, and (as I may say) whirlwind of your 5 passion, you must acquire and beget a temperance that may give it smoothness. O, it offends me to the soul to hear a robustious periwig-pated[1] fellow tear a passion to tatters, to very rags, to split the ears of the groundlings,[2] who for the most part are capable of[3] nothing but inexplicable dumb shows[4] and noise. I would have such a fellow 10 whipped for o'erdoing Termagant. It out-herods Herod.[5] Pray you avoid it.

PLAYER: I warrant your honor.

HAMLET: Be not too tame neither, but let your own discretion be your tutor. Suit the action to the word, the word to the action, with this 15 special observance, that you o'erstep not the modesty of nature. For anything so o'erdone is from[6] the purpose of playing, whose end, both at the first and now, was and is, to hold, as 'twere, the mirror up to nature; to show virtue her own feature, scorn her own image, and the very age and body of the time his form and pressure.[7] Now, 20 this overdone, or come tardy off, though it makes the unskillful laugh, cannot but make the judicious grieve, the censure of the which one must in your allowance o'erweigh a whole theater of others. O, there be players that I have seen play, and heard others praise, and that highly (not to speak it profanely), that neither 25 having th' accent of Christians, nor the gait of Christian, pagan, nor man, have so strutted and bellowed that I have thought some of Nature's journeymen[8] had made men, and not made them well, they imitated humanity so abominably.

PLAYER: I hope we have reformed that indifferently[9] with us, sir. 30

HAMLET: O, reform it altogether! And let those that play your clowns speak no more than is set down for them, for there be of them that will themselves laugh, to set on some quantity of barren spectators to laugh too, though in the meantime some necessary question of the play be then to be considered. That's villainous and shows a 35 most pitiful ambition in the fool that uses it. Go make you ready.

(*Exit* PLAYERS.)

(*Enter* POLONIUS, GUILDENSTERN, *and* ROSENCRANTZ.)

How now, my lord? Will the King hear this piece of work?

[1] boisterous wig-headed

[2] those who stood in the pit of the theater (the poorest and presumably most ignorant of the audience)

[3] are able to understand

[4] (it had been the fashion for actors to preface plays or parts of plays with silent mime)

[5] (boisterous characters in the old mystery plays)

[6] contrary to

[7] image, impress

[8] workers not yet masters of their craft

[9] tolerably

POLONIUS: And the Queen too, and that presently.
HAMLET: Bid the players make haste. (*Exit* POLONIUS.)
Will you two help to hasten them? 40
ROSENCRANTZ: Ay, my lord. (*Exeunt they two.*)
HAMLET: What, ho, Horatio!

(*Enter* HORATIO.)

HORATIO: Here, sweet lord, at your service.
HAMLET: Horatio, thou art e'en as just a man
As e'er my conversation coped withal.[10] 45
HORATIO: O, my dear lord —
HAMLET: Nay, do not think I flatter.
For what advancement[11] may I hope from thee,
That no revenue hast but thy good spirits
To feed and clothe thee? Why should the poor be flattered?
No, let the candied[12] tongue lick absurd pomp, 50
And crook the pregnant[13] hinges of the knee
Where thrift[14] may follow fawning. Dost thou hear?
Since my dear soul was mistress of her choice
And could of men distinguish her election,
S' hath sealed thee[15] for herself, for thou hast been 55
As one, in suff'ring all, that suffers nothing,
A man that Fortune's buffets and rewards
Hast ta'en with equal thanks; and blest are those
Whose blood[16] and judgment are so well commeddled[17]
That they are not a pipe for Fortune's finger 60
To sound what stop she please. Give me that man
That is not passion's slave, and I will wear him
In my heart's core, ay, in my heart of heart,
As I do thee. Something too much of this —
There is a play tonight before the King. 65
One scene of it comes near the circumstance
Which I have told thee, of my father's death.
I prithee, when thou seest that act afoot,
Even with the very comment[18] of thy soul
Observe my uncle. If his occulted[19] guilt 70
Do not itself unkennel in one speech,
It is a damnèd ghost that we have seen,
And my imaginations are as foul
As Vulcan's stithy.[20] Give him heedful note,

[10] met with
[11] promotion
[12] sugared, flattering
[13] (1) pliant, (2) full of promise of good fortune
[14] profit
[15] she (the soul) has set a mark on you
[16] passion
[17] blended
[18] deepest wisdom
[19] hidden
[20] forge, smithy

For I mine eyes will rivet to his face, 75
And after we will both our judgments join
In censure of his seeming.[21]

HORATIO: Well, my lord.
If 'a steal aught the whilst this play is playing,
And scape detecting, I will pay the theft.

(*Enter Trumpets and Kettledrums,* KING, QUEEN, POLONIUS, OPHELIA, ROSENCRANTZ, GUILDENSTERN, *and other* LORDS *attendant with his* GUARD *carrying torches. Danish March. Sound a Flourish.*)

HAMLET: They are coming to the play: I must be idle;[22] 80
Get you a place.

KING: How fares our cousin Hamlet?

HAMLET: Excellent, i' faith, of the chameleon's dish;[23] I eat the air, promise-crammed; you cannot feed capons so.

KING: I have nothing with this answer, Hamlet; these words are not 85 mine.

HAMLET: No, nor mine now. [*To* POLONIUS.] My lord, you played once i' th' university, you say?

POLONIUS: That did I, my lord, and was accounted a good actor.

HAMLET: What did you enact? 90

POLONIUS: I did enact Julius Caesar. I was killed i' th' Capitol; Brutus killed me.

HAMLET: It was a brute part of him to kill so capital a calf there. Be the players ready?

ROSENCRANTZ: Ay, my lord. They stay upon your patience. 95

QUEEN: Come hither, my dear Hamlet, sit by me.

HAMLET: No, good mother. Here's metal more attractive.[24]

POLONIUS [*to the* KING]: O ho! Do you mark that?

HAMLET: Lady, shall I lie in your lap?

[*He lies at* OPHELIA*'s feet.*]

OPHELIA: No, my lord. 100

HAMLET: I mean, my head upon your lap?

OPHELIA: Ay, my lord.

HAMLET: Do you think I meant country matters?[25]

OPHELIA: I think nothing, my lord.

HAMLET: That's a fair thought to lie between maids' legs. 105

OPHELIA: What is, my lord?

HAMLET: Nothing.

[21] judgment on his looks
[22] play the fool
[23] air (on which chameleons were thought to live)
[24] magnetic
[25] rustic doings (with a pun on the vulgar word for the pudendum)

OPHELIA: You are merry, my lord.
HAMLET: Who, I?
OPHELIA: Ay, my lord. 110
HAMLET: O God, your only jig-maker![26] What should a man do but be merry? For look you how cheerfully my mother looks, and my father died within's two hours.
OPHELIA: Nay, 'tis twice two months, my lord.
HAMLET: So long? Nay then, let the devil wear black, for I'll have a suit 115 of sables.[27] O heavens! Die two months ago, and not forgotten yet? Then there's hope a great man's memory may outlive his life half a year. But, by'r Lady, 'a must build churches then, or else shall 'a suffer not thinking on, with the hobbyhorse,[28] whose epitaph is "For O, for O, the hobbyhorse is forgot!" 120

*(The trumpets sound. Dumb show follows:*
*Enter a* KING *and a* QUEEN *very lovingly, the* QUEEN *embracing him, and he her. She kneels; and makes show of protestation unto him. He takes her up, and declines his head upon her neck. He lies him down upon a bank of flowers. She, seeing him asleep, leaves him. Anon come in another man: takes off his crown, kisses it, pours poison in the sleeper's ears, and leaves him. The* QUEEN *returns, finds the* KING *dead, makes passionate action. The* POISONER, *with some three or four, come in again, seem to condole with her. The dead body is carried away. The* POISONER *woos the* QUEEN *with gifts; she seems harsh awhile, but in the end accepts love. Exeunt.)*

OPHELIA: What means this, my lord?
HAMLET: Marry, this is miching mallecho;[29] it means mischief.
OPHELIA: Belike this show imports the argument[30] of the play.

(*Enter* PROLOGUE.)

HAMLET: We shall know by this fellow. The players cannot keep counsel; they'll tell all. 125
OPHELIA: Will 'a tell us what this show meant?
HAMLET: Ay, or any show that you will show him. Be not you ashamed to show, he'll not shame to tell you what it means.
OPHELIA: You are naught,[31] you are naught; I'll mark the play.
PROLOGUE: For us, and for our tragedy, 130
Here stooping to your clemency,
We beg your hearing patiently. [*Exit.*]

[26] composer of songs and dances (often a Fool, who performed them)
[27] (pun on "black" and "luxurious furs")
[28] mock horse worn by a performer in the morris dance
[29] sneaking mischief
[30] plot
[31] wicked, improper

HAMLET: Is this a prologue, or the posy of a ring?[32]
OPHELIA: 'Tis brief, my lord.
HAMLET: As woman's love. 135

(*Enter* [*two Players as*] KING *and* QUEEN.)

PLAYER KING: Full thirty times hath Phoebus' cart[33] gone round
Neptune's salt wash[34] and Tellus'[35] orbèd ground,
And thirty dozen moons with borrowed sheen
About the world have times twelve thirties been,
Since love our hearts, and Hymen did our hands, 140
Unite commutual in most sacred bands.
PLAYER QUEEN: So many journeys may the sun and moon
Make us again count o'er ere love be done!
But woe is me, you are so sick of late,
So far from cheer and from your former state, 145
That I distrust[36] you. Yet, though I distrust,
Discomfort you, my lord, it nothing must.
For women fear too much, even as they love,
And women's fear and love hold quantity,
In neither aught, or in extremity.[37] 150
Now what my love is, proof[38] hath made you know,
And as my love is sized, my fear is so.
Where love is great, the littlest doubts are fear,
Where little fears grow great, great love grows there.
PLAYER KING: Faith, I must leave thee, love, and shortly too; 155
My operant[39] powers their functions leave to do:
And thou shalt live in this fair world behind,
Honored, beloved, and haply one as kind
For husband shalt thou —
PLAYER QUEEN: O, confound the rest!
Such love must needs be treason in my breast. 160
In second husband let me be accurst!
None wed the second but who killed the first.
HAMLET [*aside*]: That's wormwood.[40]
PLAYER QUEEN: The instances[41] that second marriage move[42]
Are base respects of thrift,[43] but none of love. 165

[32] motto inscribed in a ring
[33] the sun's chariot
[34] the sea
[35] Roman goddess of the earth
[36] am anxious about
[37] (perhaps the idea is that women's anxiety is great or little in proportion to their love. The previous line, unrhymed, may be a false start that Shakespeare neglected to delete)
[38] experience
[39] active
[40] a bitter herb
[41] motives
[42] induce
[43] considerations of profit

A second time I kill my husband dead
When second husband kisses me in bed.

PLAYER KING: I do believe you think what now you speak,
But what we do determine oft we break.
Purpose is but the slave to memory, 170
Of violent birth, but poor validity,[44]
Which now like fruit unripe sticks on the tree,
But fall unshaken when they mellow be.
Most necessary 'tis that we forget
To pay ourselves what to ourselves is debt. 175
What to ourselves in passion we propose,
The passion ending, doth the purpose lose.
The violence of either grief or joy
Their own enactures[45] with themselves destroy:
Where joy most revels, grief doth most lament; 180
Grief joys, joy grieves, on slender accident.
This world is not for aye, nor 'tis not strange
That even our loves should with our fortunes change,
For 'tis a question left us yet to prove,
Whether love lead fortune, or else fortune love. 185
The great man down, you mark his favorite flies;
The poor advanced makes friends of enemies;
And hitherto doth love on fortune tend,
For who not needs shall never lack a friend;
And who in want a hollow friend doth try, 190
Directly seasons him[46] his enemy.
But, orderly to end where I begun,
Our wills and fates do so contrary run
That our devices still are overthrown;
Our thoughts are ours, their ends none of our own. 195
So think thou wilt no second husband wed,
But die thy thoughts when thy first lord is dead.

PLAYER QUEEN: Nor earth to me give food, nor heaven light,
Sport and repose lock from me day and night,
To desperation turn my trust and hope, 200
An anchor's[47] cheer in prison be my scope,
Each opposite that blanks[48] the face of joy
Meet what I would have well, and it destroy:
Both here and hence pursue me lasting strife,
If, once a widow, ever I be wife! 205

[44] strength
[45] acts
[46] ripens him into
[47] anchorite's, hermit's
[48] adverse thing that blanches

HAMLET: If she should break it now!
PLAYER KING: 'Tis deeply sworn. Sweet, leave me here awhile;
My spirits grow dull, and fain I would beguile
The tedious day with sleep.
PLAYER QUEEN: Sleep rock thy brain,

([*He*] *sleeps.*)

And never come mischance between us twain! (*Exit.*) 210
HAMLET: Madam, how like you this play?
QUEEN: The lady doth protest too much, methinks.
HAMLET: O, but she'll keep her word.
KING: Have you heard the argument?[49] Is there no offense in't?
HAMLET: No, no, they do but jest, poison in jest; no offense i' th' world. 215
KING: What do you call the play?
HAMLET: *The Mousetrap.* Marry, how? Tropically.[50] This play is the image of a murder done in Vienna: Gonzago is the Duke's name; his wife, Baptista. You shall see anon. 'Tis a knavish piece of work, but what of that? Your Majesty, and we that have free[51] souls, it touches 220 us not. Let the galled jade winch;[52] our withers are unwrung.

(*Enter* LUCIANUS.)

This is one Lucianus, nephew to the King.
OPHELIA: You are as good as a chorus, my lord.
HAMLET: I could interpret[53] between you and your love, if I could see the puppets dallying. 225
OPHELIA: You are keen,[54] my lord, you are keen.
HAMLET: It would cost you a groaning to take off mine edge.
OPHELIA: Still better, and worse.
HAMLET: So you mistake[55] your husbands. — Begin, murderer. Leave thy damnable faces and begin. Come, the croaking raven doth bellow 230 for revenge.
LUCIANUS: Thoughts black, hands apt, drugs fit, and time agreeing,
Confederate season,[56] else no creature seeing,
Thou mixture rank, of midnight weeds collected,
With Hecate's ban[57] thrice blasted, thrice infected, 235
Thy natural magic and dire property[58]
On wholesome life usurps immediately.

(*Pours the poison in his ears.*)

[49] plot
[50] figuratively (with a pun on "trap")
[51] innocent
[52] chafed horse wince
[53] (like a showman explaining the action of puppets)
[54] (1) sharp, (2) sexually aroused
[55] err in taking
[56] the opportunity allied with me
[57] the curse of the goddess of sorcery
[58] nature

HAMLET: 'A poisons him i' th' garden for his estate. His name's Gonzago. The story is extant, and written in very choice Italian. You shall see anon how the murderer gets the love of Gonzago's wife. 240

OPHELIA: The King rises.

HAMLET: What, frighted with false fire?[59]

QUEEN: How fares my lord?

POLONIUS: Give o'er the play.

KING: Give me some light. Away! 245

POLONIUS: Lights, lights, lights!

(*Exeunt all but* HAMLET *and* HORATIO.)

HAMLET:

Why, let the strucken deer go weep,
The hart ungallèd play:
For some must watch, while some must sleep;
Thus runs the world away. 250

Would not this, sir, and a forest of feathers[60] — if the rest of my fortunes turn Turk[61] with me — with two Provincial roses[62] on my razed[63] shoes, get me a fellowship in a cry[64] of players?

HORATIO: Half a share.

HAMLET: A whole one, I. 255

For thou dost know, O Damon dear,
This realm dismantled was
Of Jove himself; and now reigns here
A very, very — pajock.[65]

HORATIO: You might have rhymed.[66] 260

HAMLET: O good Horatio, I'll take the ghost's word for a thousand pound. Didst perceive?

HORATIO: Very well, my lord.

HAMLET: Upon the talk of poisoning?

HORATIO: I did very well note him. 265

HAMLET: Ah ha! Come, some music! Come, the recorders![67]
For if the King like not the comedy,
Why then, belike he likes it not, perdy.[68]
Come, some music!

(*Enter* ROSENCRANTZ *and* GUILDENSTERN.)

59 blank discharge of firearms

60 (plumes were sometimes part of a costume)

61 i.e., go bad, treat me badly

62 rosettes like the roses of Provence (?)

63 ornamented with slashes

64 pack, company

65 peacock

66 i.e., rhymed "was" with "ass"

67 flutelike instruments

68 by God (Fr. *par dieu*)

GUILDENSTERN: Good my lord, vouchsafe me a word with you. 270
HAMLET: Sir, a whole history.
GUILDENSTERN: The King, sir —
HAMLET: Ay, sir, what of him?
GUILDENSTERN: Is in his retirement marvelous distemp'red.
HAMLET: With drink, sir? 275
GUILDENSTERN: No, my lord, with choler.[69]
HAMLET: Your wisdom should show itself more richer to signify this to the doctor, for for me to put him to his purgation would perhaps plunge him into more choler.
GUILDENSTERN: Good my lord, put your discourse into some frame,[70] 280 and start not so wildly from my affair.
HAMLET: I am tame, sir; pronounce.
GUILDENSTERN: The Queen, your mother, in most great affliction of spirit hath sent me to you.
HAMLET: You are welcome. 285
GUILDENSTERN: Nay, good my lord, this courtesy is not of the right breed. If it shall please you to make me a wholesome answer, I will do your mother's commandment: if not, your pardon and my return shall be the end of my business.
HAMLET: Sir, I cannot. 290
ROSENCRANTZ: What, my lord?
HAMLET: Make you a wholesome[71] answer; my wit's diseased. But, sir, such answer as I can make, you shall command, or rather, as you say, my mother. Therefore no more, but to the matter. My mother, you say — 295
ROSENCRANTZ: Then thus she says: your behavior hath struck her into amazement and admiration.[72]
HAMLET: *O* wonderful son, that can so stonish a mother! But is there no sequel at the heels of this mother's admiration? Impart.
ROSENCRANTZ: She desires to speak with you in her closet ere you go to 300 bed.
HAMLET: We shall obey, were she ten times our mother. Have you any further trade with us?
ROSENCRANTZ: My lord, you once did love me.
HAMLET: And do still, by these pickers and stealers.[73] 305
ROSENCRANTZ: Good my lord, what is your cause of distemper? You do surely bar the door upon your own liberty, if you deny your griefs to your friend.

[69] anger (but Hamlet pretends to take the word in its sense of "biliousness")
[70] order, control
[71] sane
[72] wonder
[73] i.e., hands (with reference to the prayer; "Keep my hands from picking and stealing")

HAMLET: Sir, I lack advancement.[74]

ROSENCRANTZ: How can that be, when you have the voice of the King himself for your succession in Denmark? 310

(*Enter the* PLAYERS *with recorders.*)

HAMLET: Ay, sir, but "while the grass grows" – the proverb[75] is something musty. O, the recorders. Let me see one. To withdraw[76] with you – why do you go about to recover the wind[77] of me as if you would drive me into a toil?[78] 315

GUILDENSTERN: O my lord, if my duty be too bold, my love is too unmannerly.[79]

HAMLET: I do not well understand that. Will you play upon this pipe?

GUILDENSTERN: My lord, I cannot.

HAMLET: I pray you. 320

GUILDENSTERN: Believe me, I cannot.

HAMLET: I pray you.

GUILDENSTERN: Believe me, I cannot.

HAMLET: I do beseech you.

GUILDENSTERN: I know no touch of it, my lord. 325

HAMLET: It is as easy as lying. Govern these ventages[80] with your fingers and thumb, give it breath with your mouth, and it will discourse most eloquent music. Look you, these are the stops.

GUILDENSTERN: But these cannot I command to any utt'rance of harmony; I have not the skill. 330

HAMLET: Why, look you now, how unworthy a thing you make of me! You would play upon me; you would seem to know my stops; you would pluck out the heart of my mystery; you would sound me from my lowest note to the top of my compass;[81] and there is much music, excellent voice, in this little organ,[82] yet cannot you make it speak. 335 'Sblood, do you think I am easier to be played on than a pipe? Call me what instrument you will, though you can fret[83] me, you cannot play upon me.

(*Enter* POLONIUS.)

God bless you, sir!

POLONIUS: My lord, the Queen would speak with you, and presently. 340

[74] promotion

[75] ("While the grass groweth, the horse starveth")

[76] speak in private

[77] get on the windward side (as in hunting)

[78] snare

[79] i.e., if these questions seem rude, it is because my love for you leads me beyond good manners

[80] vents, stops on a recorder

[81] range of voice

[82] i.e., the recorder

[83] (with a pun alluding to the frets, or ridges, that guide the fingering on some instruments)

HAMLET: Do you see yonder cloud that's almost in shape of a camel?
POLONIUS: By th' mass and 'tis, like a camel indeed.
HAMLET: Methinks it is like a weasel.
POLONIUS: It is backed like a weasel.
HAMLET: Or like a whale. 345
POLONIUS: Very like a whale.
HAMLET: Then I will come to my mother by and by. [*Aside.*] They fool me to the top of my bent.[84] – I will come by and by.[85]
POLONIUS: I will say so. (*Exit.*)
HAMLET: "By and by" is easily said. Leave me, friends. 350
[*Exeunt all but* HAMLET.]
'Tis now the very witching time of night,
When churchyards yawn, and hell itself breathes out
Contagion to this world. Now could I drink hot blood
And do such bitter business as the day
Would quake to look on. Soft, now to my mother. 355
O heart, lose not thy nature; let not ever
The soul of Nero[86] enter this firm bosom.
Let me be cruel, not unnatural;
I will speak daggers to her, but use none.
My tongue and soul in this be hypocrites: 360
How in my words somever she be shent,[87]
To give them seals[88] never, my soul, consent! (*Exit.*)

## SCENE 3. [THE CASTLE.]

*Enter* KING, ROSENCRANTZ, *and* GUILDENSTERN.

KING: I like him not, nor stands it safe with us
To let his madness range. Therefore prepare you.
I your commission will forthwith dispatch,
And he to England shall along with you.
The terms[1] of our estate may not endure 5
Hazard so near's[2] as doth hourly grow
Out of his brows.
GUILDENSTERN: We will ourselves provide.
Most holy and religious fear it is

[84] they compel me to play the fool to the limit of my capacity
[85] very soon
[86] Roman emperor who had his mother murdered
[87] rebuked
[88] confirm them with deeds

[1] conditions
[2] near us

To keep those many many bodies safe
That live and feed upon your Majesty. 10

ROSENCRANTZ: The single and peculiar[3] life is bound
With all the strength and armor of the mind
To keep itself from noyance,[4] but much more
That spirit upon whose weal depends and rests
The lives of many. The cess of majesty[5] 15
Dies not alone, but like a gulf[6] doth draw
What's near it with it; or it is a massy wheel
Fixed on the summit of the highest mount,
To whose huge spokes ten thousand lesser things
Are mortised and adjoined, which when it falls, 20
Each small annexment, petty consequence,
Attends[7] the boist'rous ruin. Never alone
Did the King sigh, but with a general groan.

KING: Arm[8] you, I pray you, to this speedy voyage,
For we will fetters put about this fear, 25
Which now goes too free-footed.

ROSENCRANTZ: We will haste us.

(*Exeunt* GENTLEMEN.)

(*Enter* POLONIUS.)

POLONIUS: My lord, he's going to his mother's closet.
Behind the arras I'll convey myself
To hear the process.[9] I'll warrant she'll tax him home,[10]
And, as you said, and wisely was it said, 30
'Tis meet that some more audience than a mother,
Since nature makes them partial, should o'erhear
The speech of vantage.[11] Fare you well, my liege.
I'll call upon you ere you go to bed
And tell you what I know.

KING: Thanks, dear my lord. 35

(*Exit* [POLONIUS].)

O, my offense is rank, it smells to heaven;
It hath the primal eldest curse[12] upon't,
A brother's murder. Pray can I not,
Though inclination be as sharp as will.
My stronger guilt defeats my strong intent, 40
And like a man to double business bound
I stand in pause where I shall first begin,

3 individual, private
4 injury
5 cessation (death) of a king
6 whirlpool
7 waits on, participates in
8 prepare
9 proceedings
10 censure him sharply
11 from an advantageous place
12 (curse of Cain, who killed Abel)

And both neglect. What if this cursèd hand
Were thicker than itself with brother's blood,
Is there not rain enough in the sweet heavens 45
To wash it white as snow? Whereto serves mercy
But to confront[13] the visage of offense?
And what's in prayer but this twofold force,
To be forestallèd ere we come to fall,
Or pardoned being down? Then I'll look up. 50
My fault is past. But, O, what form of prayer
Can serve my turn? "Forgive me my foul murder"?
That cannot be, since I am still possessed
Of those effects[14] for which I did the murder,
My crown, mine own ambition, and my queen. 55
May one be pardoned and retain th' offense?
In the corrupted currents of this world
Offense's gilded hand may shove by justice,
And oft 'tis seen the wicked prize itself
Buys out the law. But 'tis not so above. 60
There is no shuffling;[15] there the action lies
In his true nature, and we ourselves compelled,
Even to the teeth and forehead of our faults,
To give in evidence. What then? What rests?[16]
Try what repentance can. What can it not? 65
Yet what can it when one cannot repent?
O wretched state! O bosom black as death!
O limèd[17] soul, that struggling to be free
Art more engaged![18] Help, angels! Make assay.[19]
Bow, stubborn knees, and, heart with strings of steel, 70
Be soft as sinews of the newborn babe.
All may be well. [*He kneels.*]

(*Enter* HAMLET.)

HAMLET: Now might I do it pat, now 'a is a-praying,
And now I'll do't. And so 'a goes to heaven,
And so am I revenged. That would be scanned.[20] 75
A villain kills my father, and for that
I, his sole son, do this same villain send
To heaven.
Why, this is hire and salary, not revenge.
'A took my father grossly, full of bread,[21] 80

[13] oppose
[14] things gained
[15] trickery
[16] remains
[17] caught (as with birdlime, a sticky substance spread on boughs to snare birds)
[18] ensnared
[19] an attempt
[20] ought to be looked into
[21] i.e., worldly gratification

With all his crimes broad blown,[22] as flush[23] as May;
And how his audit[24] stands, who knows save heaven?
But in our circumstance and course of thought,
'Tis heavy with him; and am I then revenged,
To take him in the purging of his soul, 85
When he is fit and seasoned for his passage?
No.
Up, sword, and know thou a more horrid hent.[25]
When he is drunk asleep, or in his rage,
Or in th' incestuous pleasure of his bed, 90
At game a-swearing, or about some act
That has no relish[26] of salvation in't —
Then trip him, that his heels may kick at heaven,
And that his soul may be as damned and black
As hell, whereto it goes. My mother stays. 95
This physic[27] but prolongs thy sickly days. (*Exit.*)

KING [*rises*]: My words fly up, my thoughts remain below.
Words without thoughts never to heaven go. (*Exit.*)

## SCENE 4. [THE QUEEN'S CLOSET.]

*Enter* [QUEEN] GERTRUDE *and* POLONIUS.

POLONIUS: 'A will come straight. Look you lay home[1] to him.
Tell him his pranks have been too broad[2] to bear with,
And that your Grace hath screened and stood between
Much heat and him. I'll silence me even here.
Pray you be round with him. 5

HAMLET (*within*): Mother, Mother, Mother!

QUEEN: I'll warrant you; fear me not. Withdraw; I hear him coming.
[POLONIUS *hides behind the arras.*]

(*Enter* HAMLET.)

HAMLET: Now, Mother, what's the matter?

QUEEN: Hamlet, thou hast thy father much offended. 10

HAMLET: Mother, you have my father much offended.

QUEEN: Come, come, you answer with an idle[3] tongue.

22 sins in full bloom
23 vigorous
24 account
25 grasp (here, occasion for seizing)
26 flavor
27 (Claudius's purgation by prayer, as Hamlet thinks in line 85)

---

1 thrust (rebuke) him sharply
2 unrestrained
3 foolish

HAMLET: Go, go, you question with a wicked tongue.
QUEEN: Why, how now, Hamlet?
HAMLET: What's the matter now?
QUEEN: Have you forgot me?
HAMLET: No, by the rood,[4] not so! 15
You are the Queen, your husband's brother's wife,
And, would it were not so, you are my mother.
QUEEN: Nay, then I'll set those to you that can speak.
HAMLET: Come, come, and sit you down. You shall not budge.
You go not till I set you up a glass[5] 20
Where you may see the inmost part of you!
QUEEN: What wilt thou do? Thou wilt not murder me?
Help, ho!
POLONIUS [*behind*]: What, ho! Help!
HAMLET [*draws*]: How now? A rat? Dead for a ducat, dead! 25

([*Makes a pass through the arras and*] *kills* POLONIUS.)

POLONIUS [*behind*]: O, I am slain!
QUEEN: O me, what hast thou done?
HAMLET: Nay, I know not. Is it the King?
QUEEN: O, what a rash and bloody deed is this!
HAMLET: A bloody deed — almost as bad, good Mother,
As kill a king, and marry with his brother. 30
QUEEN: As kill a king?
HAMLET: Ay, lady, it was my word.

[*Lifts up the arras and sees* POLONIUS.]

Thou wretched, rash, intruding fool, farewell!
I took thee for thy better. Take thy fortune.
Thou find'st to be too busy is some danger. —
Leave wringing of your hands. Peace, sit you down 35
And let me wring your heart, for so I shall
If it be made of penetrable stuff,
If damnèd custom have not brazed[6] it so
That it be proof[7] and bulwark against sense.[8]
QUEEN: What have I done that thou dar'st wag thy tongue 40
In noise so rude against me?
HAMLET: Such an act
That blurs the grace and blush of modesty,
Calls virtue hypocrite, takes off the rose
From the fair forehead of an innocent love,

[4] cross
[5] mirror
[6] hardened like brass
[7] armor
[8] feeling

And sets a blister[9] there, makes marriage vows 45
As false as dicers' oaths. O, such a deed
As from the body of contraction[10] plucks
The very soul, and sweet religion makes
A rhapsody[11] of words! Heaven's face does glow
O'er this solidity and compound mass 50
With heated visage, as against the doom
Is thoughtsick at the act.[12]

QUEEN: Ay me, what act,
That roars so loud and thunders in the index?[13]

HAMLET: Look here upon this picture, and on this,
The counterfeit presentment[14] of two brothers. 55
See what a grace was seated on this brow:
Hyperion's curls, the front[15] of Jove himself,
An eye like Mars, to threaten and command,
A station[16] like the herald Mercury
New lighted on a heaven-kissing hill — 60
A combination and a form indeed
Where every god did seem to set his seal
To give the world assurance of a man.
This was your husband. Look you now what follows.
Here is your husband, like a mildewed ear 65
Blasting his wholesome brother. Have you eyes?
Could you on this fair mountain leave to feed,
And batten[17] on this moor? Ha! Have you eyes?
You cannot call it love, for at your age
The heyday[18] in the blood is tame, it's humble, 70
And waits upon the judgment, and what judgment
Would step from this to this? Sense[19] sure you have,
Else could you not have motion, but sure that sense
Is apoplexed,[20] for madness would not err,
Nor sense to ecstasy[21] was ne'er so thralled 75
But it reserved some quantity of choice
To serve in such a difference. What devil was't
That thus hath cozened you at hoodman-blind?[22]
Eyes without feeling, feeling without sight,
Ears without hands or eyes, smelling sans[23] all, 80

[9] brands (as a harlot)
[10] marriage contract
[11] senseless string
[12] i.e., the face of heaven blushes over this earth (compounded of four elements), the face hot, as if Judgment Day were near, and it is thoughtsick at the act
[13] prologue
[14] represented image
[15] forehead
[16] bearing
[17] feed gluttonously
[18] excitement
[19] feeling
[20] paralyzed
[21] madness
[22] cheated you at blindman's buff
[23] without

Or but a sickly part of one true sense
Could not so mope.[24]
O shame, where is thy blush? Rebellious hell,
If thou canst mutine in a matron's bones,
To flaming youth let virtue be as wax 85
And melt in her own fire. Proclaim no shame
When the compulsive ardor[25] gives the charge,
Since frost itself as actively doth burn,
And reason panders will.[26]

QUEEN: O Hamlet, speak no more.
Thou turn'st mine eyes into my very soul, 90
And there I see such black and grainèd[27] spots
As will not leave their tinct.[28]

HAMLET: Nay, but to live
In the rank sweat of an enseamed[29] bed,
Stewed in corruption, honeying and making love
Over the nasty sty —

QUEEN: O, speak to me no more. 95
These words like daggers enter in my ears.
No more, sweet Hamlet.

HAMLET: A murderer and a villain,
A slave that is not twentieth part the tithe[30]
Of your precedent lord, a vice[31] of kings,
A cutpurse of the empire and the rule, 100
That from a shelf the precious diadem stole
And put it in his pocket —

QUEEN: No more.

(*Enter* GHOST.)

HAMLET: A king of shreds and patches —
Save me and hover o'er me with your wings,
You heavenly guards! What would your gracious figure? 105

QUEEN: Alas, he's mad.

HAMLET: Do you not come your tardy son to chide,
That, lapsed in time and passion, lets go by
Th' important acting of your dread command?
O, say! 110

GHOST: Do not forget. This visitation
Is but to whet thy almost blunted purpose.

[24] be stupid
[25] compelling passion
[26] reason acts as a procurer for desire
[27] dyed in grain (fast dyed)
[28] color
[29] (perhaps "soaked in grease," i.e., sweaty; perhaps "much wrinkled")
[30] tenth part
[31] (like the Vice, a fool and mischief-maker in the old morality plays)

But look, amazement on thy mother sits.
O, step between her and her fighting soul!
Conceit[32] in weakest bodies strongest works. 115
Speak to her, Hamlet.

HAMLET: How is it with you, lady?

QUEEN: Alas, how is't with you,
That you do bend your eye on vacancy,
And with th' incorporal[33] air do hold discourse?
Forth at your eyes your spirits wildly peep, 120
And as the sleeping soldiers in th' alarm
Your bedded hair[34] like life in excrements[35]
Start up and stand an end.[36] O gentle son,
Upon the heat and flame of thy distemper
Sprinkle cool patience. Whereon do you look? 125

HAMLET: On him, on him! Look you, how pale he glares!
His form and cause conjoined, preaching to stones,
Would make them capable.[37] – Do not look upon me,
Lest with this piteous action you convert
My stern effects.[38] Then what I have to do 130
Will want true color; tears perchance for blood.

QUEEN: To whom do you speak this?

HAMLET: Do you see nothing there?

QUEEN: Nothing at all; yet all that is I see.

HAMLET: Nor did you nothing hear?

QUEEN: No, nothing but ourselves.

HAMLET: Why, look you there! Look how it steals away! 135
My father, in his habit[39] as he lived!
Look where he goes even now out at the portal! (*Exit* GHOST.)

QUEEN: This is the very coinage of your brain.
This bodiless creation ecstasy
Is very cunning in.

HAMLET: Ecstasy? 140
My pulse as yours doth temperately keep time
And makes as healthful music. It is not madness
That I have uttered. Bring me to the test,
And I the matter will reword, which madness
Would gambol[40] from. Mother, for love of grace, 145
Lay not that flattering unction[41] to your soul,

[32] imagination
[33] bodiless
[34] hairs laid flat
[35] outgrowths (here, the hair)
[36] on end
[37] receptive
[38] divert my stern deeds
[39] garment (Q1, although a "bad" quarto, is probably correct in saying that at line 102 the ghost enters "in his nightgown," i.e., dressing gown)
[40] start away
[41] ointment

That not your trespass but my madness speaks.
It will but skin and film the ulcerous place
Whiles rank corruption, mining[42] all within,
Infects unseen. Confess yourself to heaven, 150
Repent what's past, avoid what is to come,
And do not spread the compost[43] on the weeds
To make them ranker. Forgive me this my virtue.
For in the fatness of these pursy[44] times
Virtue itself of vice must pardon beg, 155
Yea, curb[45] and woo for leave to do him good.

QUEEN: O Hamlet, thou hast cleft my heart in twain.

HAMLET: O, throw away the worser part of it,
And live the purer with the other half.
Good night – but go not to my uncle's bed. 160
Assume a virtue, if you have it not.
That monster custom, who all sense doth eat,
Of habits devil, is angel yet in this,
That to the use[46] of actions fair and good
He likewise gives a frock or livery[47] 165
That aptly is put on. Refrain tonight,
And that shall lend a kind of easiness
To the next abstinence; the next more easy;
For use almost can change the stamp of nature,
And either[48] the devil, or throw him out 170
With wondrous potency. Once more, good night,
And when you are desirous to be blest,
I'll blessing beg of you. – For this same lord,
I do repent; but heaven hath pleased it so,
To punish me with this, and this with me, 175
That I must be their[49] scourge and minister.
I will bestow[50] him and will answer well
The death I gave him. So again, good night.
I must be cruel only to be kind.
Thus bad begins, and worse remains behind. 180
One word more, good lady.

QUEEN: What shall I do?

HAMLET: Not this, by no means, that I bid you do:

[42] undermining
[43] fertilizing substance
[44] bloated
[45] bow low
[46] practice
[47] characteristic garment (punning on "habits" in line 163)
[48] (probably a word is missing after *either;* among suggestions are "master," "curb," and "house"; but possibly *either* is a verb meaning "make easier")
[49] i.e., the heavens'
[50] stow, lodge

Let the bloat King tempt you again to bed,
Pinch wanton on your cheek, call you his mouse,
And let him, for a pair of reechy[51] kisses, 185
Or paddling in your neck with his damned fingers,
Make you to ravel[52] all this matter out,
That I essentially am not in madness,
But mad in craft. 'Twere good you let him know,
For who that's but a queen, fair, sober, wise, 190
Would from a paddock,[53] from a bat, a gib,[54]
Such dear concernings hide? Who would do so?
No, in despite of sense and secrecy,
Unpeg the basket on the house's top,
Let the birds fly, and like the famous ape, 195
To try conclusions,[55] in the basket creep
And break your own neck down.

QUEEN: Be thou assured, if words be made of breath,
And breath of life, I have no life to breathe
What thou hast said to me. 200

HAMLET: I must to England; you know that?

QUEEN: Alack,
I had forgot. 'Tis so concluded on.

HAMLET: There's letters sealed, and my two schoolfellows,
Whom I will trust as I will adders fanged,
They bear the mandate;[56] they must sweep my way 205
And marshal me to knavery. Let it work;
For 'tis the sport to have the enginer
Hoist with his own petar,[57] and 't shall go hard
But I will delve one yard below their mines
And blow them at the moon. O, 'tis most sweet 210
When in one line two crafts[58] directly meet.
This man shall set me packing:
I'll lug the guts into the neighbor room.
Mother, good night. Indeed, this counselor
Is now most still, most secret, and most grave, 215
Who was in life a foolish prating knave.
Come, sir, to draw toward an end with you.
Good night, Mother.

([*Exit the* QUEEN. *Then*] *exit* HAMLET,
*tugging in* POLONIUS.)

51 foul (literally "smoky")
52 unravel, reveal
53 toad
54 tomcat
55 to make experiments
56 command
57 bomb
58 (1) boats, (2) acts of guile, crafty schemes

## ACT IV

### SCENE 1. [THE CASTLE.]

*Enter* KING *and* QUEEN, *with* ROSENCRANTZ *and* GUILDENSTERN.

KING: There's matter in these sighs. These profound heaves
You must translate; 'tis fit we understand them.
Where is your son?
QUEEN: Bestow this place on us a little while.
[*Exeunt* ROSENCRANTZ *and* GUILDENSTERN.]
Ah, mine own lord, what have I seen tonight! 5
KING: What, Gertrude? How does Hamlet?
QUEEN: Mad as the sea and wind when both contend
Which is the mightier. In his lawless fit,
Behind the arras hearing something stir,
Whips out his rapier, cries, "A rat, a rat!" 10
And in this brainish apprehension[1] kills
The unseen good old man.
KING: O heavy deed!
It had been so with us, had we been there.
His liberty is full of threats to all,
To you yourself, to us, to every one. 15
Alas, how shall this bloody deed be answered?
It will be laid to us, whose providence[2]
Should have kept short, restrained, and out of haunt[3]
This mad young man. But so much was our love
We would not understand what was most fit, 20
But, like the owner of a foul disease,
To keep it from divulging, let it feed
Even on the pith of life. Where is he gone?
QUEEN: To draw apart the body he hath killed;
O'er whom his very madness, like some ore 25
Among a mineral[4] of metals base,
Shows itself pure. 'A weeps for what is done.
KING: O Gertrude, come away!
The sun no sooner shall the mountains touch
But we will ship him hence, and this vile deed 30
We must with all our majesty and skill
Both countenance and excuse. Ho, Guildenstern!

(*Enter* ROSENCRANTZ *and* GUILDENSTERN.)

[1] mad imagination
[2] foresight
[3] away from association with others
[4] vein of gold in a mine

Friends both, go join you with some further aid:
Hamlet in madness hath Polonius slain,
And from his mother's closet hath he dragged him. 35
Go seek him out; speak fair, and bring the body
Into the chapel. I pray you haste in this.
[*Exeunt* ROSENCRANTZ *and* GUILDENSTERN.]
Come, Gertrude, we'll call up our wisest friends
And let them know both what we mean to do
And what's untimely done . . .[5] 40
Whose whisper o'er the world's diameter,
As level as the cannon to his blank[6]
Transports his poisoned shot, may miss our name
And hit the woundless[7] air. O, come away!
My soul is full of discord and dismay. (*Exeunt.*) 45

## SCENE 2. [THE CASTLE.]

*Enter* HAMLET.

HAMLET: Safely stowed.
GENTLEMEN (*within*): Hamlet! Lord Hamlet!
HAMLET: But soft, what noise? Who calls on Hamlet?
O, here they come.

(*Enter* ROSENCRANTZ *and* GUILDENSTERN.)

ROSENCRANTZ: What have you done, my lord, with the dead body? 5
HAMLET: Compounded it with dust, whereto 'tis kin.
ROSENCRANTZ: Tell us where 'tis, that we may take it thence
And bear it to the chapel.
HAMLET: Do not believe it.
ROSENCRANTZ: Believe what? 10
HAMLET: That I can keep your counsel and not mine own. Besides, to be demanded of[1] a sponge, what replication[2] should be made by the son of a king?
ROSENCRANTZ: Take you me for a sponge, my lord?
HAMLET: Ay, sir, that soaks up the King's countenance,[3] his rewards, 15 his authorities. But such officers do the King best service in the end. He keeps them, like an ape, in the corner of his jaw, first mouthed,

[5] (evidently something has dropped out of the text. Capell's conjecture, "So, haply slander," is usually printed)
[6] white center of a target
[7] invulnerable

[1] questioned by
[2] reply
[3] favor

to be last swallowed. When he needs what you have gleaned, it is but squeezing you and, sponge, you shall be dry again.

ROSENCRANTZ: I understand you not, my lord. 20

HAMLET: I am glad of it: a knavish speech sleeps in a foolish ear.

ROSENCRANTZ: My lord, you must tell us where the body is and go with us to the King.

HAMLET: The body is with the King, but the King is not with the body. The King is a thing — 25

GUILDENSTERN: A thing, my lord?

HAMLET: Of nothing. Bring me to him. Hide fox, and all after.[4]

(*Exeunt.*)

## Scene 3. [The Castle.]

*Enter* KING, *and two or three.*

KING: I have sent to seek him and to find the body:
How dangerous it is that this man goes loose!
Yet must not we put the strong law on him:
He's loved of the distracted[1] multitude,
Who like not in their judgment, but their eyes, 5
And where 'tis so, th' offender's scourge is weighed,
But never the offense. To bear[2] all smooth and even,
This sudden sending him away must seem
Deliberate pause.[3] Diseases desperate grown
By desperate appliance are relieved, 10
Or not at all.

(*Enter* ROSENCRANTZ, [GUILDENSTERN,] *and all the rest.*)

How now? What hath befall'n?

ROSENCRANTZ: Where the dead body is bestowed, my lord,
We cannot get from him.

KING: But where is he?

ROSENCRANTZ: Without, my lord; guarded, to know your pleasure.

KING: Bring him before us.

ROSENCRANTZ: Ho! Bring in the lord. 15

(*They enter.*)

KING: Now, Hamlet, where's Polonius?

[4] (a cry in a game such as hide-and-seek; Hamlet runs from the stage)

---

[1] bewildered, senseless
[2] carry out
[3] planning

HAMLET: At supper.

KING: At supper? Where?

HAMLET: Not where he eats, but where 'a is eaten. A certain convocation of politic[4] worms are e'en at him. Your worm is your only emperor for diet. We fat all creatures else to fat us, and we fat ourselves for maggots. Your fat king and your lean beggar is but variable service[5] — two dishes, but to one table. That's the end. 20

KING: Alas, alas!

HAMLET: A man may fish with the worm that hath eat of a king, and eat of the fish that hath fed of that worm. 25

KING: What dost thou mean by this?

HAMLET: Nothing but to show you how a king may go a progress[6] through the guts of a beggar.

KING: Where is Polonius? 30

HAMLET: In heaven. Send thither to see. If your messenger find him not there, seek him i' th' other place yourself. But if indeed you find him not within this month, you shall nose him as you go up the stairs into the lobby.

KING [*to* ATTENDANTS]: Go seek him there. 35

HAMLET: 'A will stay till you come. [*Exeunt* ATTENDANTS.]

KING: Hamlet, this deed, for thine especial safety,
Which we do tender[7] as we dearly grieve
For that which thou hast done, must send thee hence
With fiery quickness. Therefore prepare thyself. 40
The bark is ready and the wind at help,
Th' associates tend,[8] and everything is bent
For England.

HAMLET: For England?

KING: Ay, Hamlet.

HAMLET: Good.

KING: So is it, if thou knew'st our purposes.

HAMLET: I see a cherub[9] that sees them. But come, for England! Farewell, dear Mother. 45

KING: Thy loving father, Hamlet.

HAMLET: My mother — father and mother is man and wife, man and wife is one flesh, and so, my mother. Come, for England! (*Exit.*)

KING: Follow him at foot;[10] tempt him with speed aboard. 50
Delay it not; I'll have him hence tonight.
Away! For everything is sealed and done
That else leans[11] on th' affair. Pray you make haste.

[*Exeunt all but the* KING.]

[4] statesmanlike, shrewd
[5] different courses
[6] royal journey
[7] hold dear
[8] wait
[9] angel of knowledge
[10] closely
[11] depends

And, England, if my love thou hold'st at aught –
As my great power thereof may give thee sense, 55
Since yet thy cicatrice[12] looks raw and red
After the Danish sword, and thy free awe[13]
Pays homage to us – thou mayst not coldly set
Our sovereign process,[14] which imports at full
By letters congruing to that effect 60
The present[15] death of Hamlet. Do it, England,
For like the hectic[16] in my blood he rages,
And thou must cure me. Till I know 'tis done,
Howe'er my haps,[17] my joys were ne'er begun. *(Exit.)*

## SCENE 4. [A PLAIN IN DENMARK.]

*Enter* FORTINBRAS *with his* ARMY *over the stage.*

FORTINBRAS: Go, Captain, from me greet the Danish king.
Tell him that by his license Fortinbras
Craves the conveyance of[1] a promised march
Over his kingdom. You know the rendezvous.
If that his Majesty would aught with us, 5
We shall express our duty in his eye;[2]
And let him know so.
CAPTAIN: I will do't, my lord.
FORTINBRAS: Go softly[3] on. *[Exeunt all but the* CAPTAIN.*]*

*(Enter* HAMLET, ROSENCRANTZ, *&c.)*

HAMLET: Good sir, whose powers[4] are these?
CAPTAIN: They are of Norway, sir. 10
HAMLET: How purposed, sir, I pray you?
CAPTAIN: Against some part of Poland.
HAMLET: Who commands them, sir?
CAPTAIN: The nephew to old Norway, Fortinbras.
HAMLET: Goes it against the main[5] of Poland, sir, 15
Or for some frontier?
CAPTAIN: Truly to speak, and with no addition,[6]
We go to gain a little patch of ground
That hath in it no profit but the name.
To pay five ducats, five, I would not farm it, 20

[12] scar
[13] uncompelled submission
[14] regard slightly our royal command
[15] instant
[16] fever
[17] chances, fortunes

---

[1] escort for
[2] before his eyes (i.e., in his presence)
[3] slowly
[4] forces
[5] main part
[6] plainly

Nor will it yield to Norway or the Pole
A ranker[7] rate, should it be sold in fee.[8]
HAMLET: Why, then the Polack never will defend it.
CAPTAIN: Yes, it is already garrisoned.
HAMLET: Two thousand souls and twenty thousand ducats 25
Will not debate[9] the question of this straw.
This is th' imposthume[10] of much wealth and peace,
That inward breaks, and shows no cause without
Why the man dies. I humbly thank you, sir.
CAPTAIN: God bye you, sir. [*Exit.*]
ROSENCRANTZ: Will't please you go, my lord? 30
HAMLET: I'll be with you straight. Go a little before.
[*Exeunt all but* HAMLET.]
How all occasions do inform against me
And spur my dull revenge! What is a man,
If his chief good and market[11] of his time
Be but to sleep and feed? A beast, no more. 35
Sure he that made us with such large discourse,[12]
Looking before and after, gave us not
That capability and godlike reason
To fust[13] in us unused. Now, whether it be
Bestial oblivion,[14] or some craven scruple 40
O thinking too precisely on th' event[15] —
A thought which, quartered, hath but one part wisdom
And ever three parts coward — I do not know
Why yet I live to say, "This thing's to do,"
Sith I have cause, and will, and strength, and means 45
To do't. Examples gross[16] as earth exhort me.
Witness this army of such mass and charge,[17]
Led by a delicate and tender prince,
Whose spirit, with divine ambition puffed,
Makes mouths at the invisible event,[18] 50
Exposing what is mortal and unsure
To all that fortune, death, and danger dare,
Even for an eggshell. Rightly to be great
Is not[19] to stir without great argument,[20]
But greatly[21] to find quarrel in a straw 55
When honor's at the stake. How stand I then,

7 higher
8 outright
9 settle
10 abscess, ulcer
11 profit
12 understanding
13 grow moldy
14 forgetfulness
15 outcome
16 large, obvious
17 expense
18 makes scornful faces (is contemptuous of) the unseen outcome
19 (the sense seems to require "not not")
20 reason
21 i.e., nobly

That have a father killed, a mother stained,
Excitements[22] of my reason and my blood,
And let all sleep, while to my shame I see
The imminent death of twenty thousand men 60
That for a fantasy and trick of fame[23]
Go to their graves like beds, fight for a plot
Whereon the numbers cannot try the cause,
Which is not tomb enough and continent[24]
To hide the slain? O, from this time forth, 65
My thoughts be bloody, or be nothing worth! *(Exit.)*

## SCENE 5. [THE CASTLE.]

*Enter* HORATIO, [QUEEN] GERTRUDE, *and a* GENTLEMAN.

QUEEN: I will not speak with her.
GENTLEMAN: She is importunate, indeed distract.
Her mood will needs be pitied.
QUEEN: What would she have?
GENTLEMAN: She speaks much of her father, says she hears
There's tricks i' th' world, and hems, and beats her heart, 5
Spurns enviously at straws,[1] speaks things in doubt[2]
That carry but half sense. Her speech is nothing,
Yet the unshapèd use of it doth move
The hearers to collection;[3] they yawn[4] at it,
And botch the words up fit to their own thoughts, 10
Which, as her winks and nods and gestures yield them,
Indeed would make one think there might be thought,
Though nothing sure, yet much unhappily.
HORATIO: 'Twere good she were spoken with, for she may strew
Dangerous conjectures in ill-breeding minds. 15
QUEEN: Let her come in. [*Exit* GENTLEMAN.]
[*Aside.*] To my sick soul (as sin's true nature is)
Each toy seems prologue to some great amiss;[5]
So full of artless jealousy[6] is guilt
It spills[7] itself in fearing to be spilt. 20

(*Enter* OPHELIA [*distracted*].)

[22] incentives
[23] illusion and trifle of reputation
[24] receptacle, container

---

[1] objects spitefully to insignificant matters
[2] uncertainly
[3] i.e., yet the formless manner of it moves her listeners to gather up some sort of meaning
[4] gape (?)
[5] misfortune
[6] crude suspicion
[7] destroys

OPHELIA: Where is the beauteous majesty of Denmark?
QUEEN: How now, Ophelia?
OPHELIA: (*She sings.*)

How should I your truelove know
  From another one?
By his cockle hat[8] and staff 25
  And his sandal shoon.[9]

QUEEN: Alas, sweet lady, what imports this song?
OPHELIA: Say you? Nay, pray you mark.

He is dead and gone, lady, (*Song.*)
  He is dead and gone; 30
At his head a grass-green turf,
  At his heels a stone.

O, ho!
QUEEN: Nay, but Ophelia —
OPHELIA: Pray you mark. [*Sings.*] 35

White his shroud as the mountain snow —

(*Enter* KING.)

QUEEN: Alas, look here, my lord.
OPHELIA:

  Larded[10] all with sweet flowers (*Song.*)
Which bewept to the grave did not go
  With truelove showers. 40

KING: How do you, pretty lady?
OPHELIA: Well, God dild[11] you! They say the owl was a baker's daughter.[12] Lord, we know what we are, but know not what we may be. God be at your table!
KING: Conceit[13] upon her father. 45
OPHELIA: Pray let's have no words of this, but when they ask you what it means, say you this:

Tomorrow is Saint Valentine's day.[14] (*Song.*)
  All in the morning betime,
And I a maid at your window, 50
  To be your Valentine.

[8] (a cockleshell on the hat was the sign of a pilgrim who had journeyed to shrines overseas. The association of lovers and pilgrims was a common one)
[9] shoes
[10] decorated
[11] yield, i.e., reward
[12] (an allusion to a tale of a baker's daughter who begrudged bread to Christ and was turned into an owl)
[13] brooding
[14] Feb. 14 (the notion was that a bachelor would become the truelove of the first girl he saw on this day)

Then up he rose and donned his clothes
And dupped[15] the chamber door,
Let in the maid, that out a maid
Never departed more. 55

KING: Pretty Ophelia.
OPHELIA: Indeed, la, without an oath, I'll make an end on't:

[*Sings.*] By Gis[16] and by Saint Charity,
Alack, and fie for shame!
Young men will do't if they come to't, 60
By Cock,[17] they are to blame.
Quoth she, "Before you tumbled me,
You promised me to wed."

He answers:

"So would I 'a' done, by yonder sun, 65
An thou hadst not come to my bed."

KING: How long hath she been thus?
OPHELIA: I hope all will be well. We must be patient, but I cannot choose but weep to think they would lay him i' th' cold ground. My brother shall know of it; and so I thank you for your good counsel. 70
Come, my coach! Good night, ladies, good night. Sweet ladies, good night, good night. (*Exit.*)
KING: Follow her close; give her good watch, I pray you.
[*Exit* HORATIO.]
O, this is the poison of deep grief; it springs
All from her father's death – and now behold! 75
O Gertrude, Gertrude,
When sorrows come, they come not single spies,
But in battalions: first, her father slain;
Next, your son gone, and he most violent author
Of his own just remove; the people muddied,[18] 80
Thick and unwholesome in their thoughts and whispers
For good Polonius' death, and we have done but greenly[19]
In huggermugger[20] to inter him; poor Ophelia
Divided from herself and her fair judgment,
Without the which we are pictures or mere beasts; 85
Last, and as much containing as all these,
Her brother is in secret come from France,
Feeds on his wonder,[21] keeps himself in clouds,

[15] opened (did up)
[16] (contraction of "Jesus")
[17] (1) God, (2) phallus
[18] muddled
[19] foolishly
[20] secret haste
[21] suspicion

And wants not buzzers[22] to infect his ear
With pestilent speeches of his father's death, 90
Wherein necessity, of matter beggared,[23]
Will nothing stick[24] our person to arraign
In ear and ear. O my dear Gertrude, this,
Like to a murd'ring piece,[25] in many places
Gives me superfluous death. (*A noise within.*)

(*Enter a* MESSENGER.)

QUEEN: Alack, what noise is this? 95
KING: Attend, where are my Switzers?[26] Let them guard the door.
What is the matter?
MESSENGER: Save yourself, my lord.
The ocean, overpeering of his list,[27]
Eats not the flats with more impiteous haste
Than young Laertes, in a riotous head,[28] 100
O'erbears your officers. The rabble call him lord,
And, as the world were now but to begin,
Antiquity forgot, custom not known,
The ratifiers and props of every word,
They cry, "Choose we! Laertes shall be king!" 105
Caps, hands, and tongues applaud it to the clouds,
"Laertes shall be king! Laertes king!" (*A noise within.*)
QUEEN: How cheerfully on the false trail they cry!
O, this is counter,[29] you false Danish dogs!

(*Enter* LAERTES *with others.*)

KING: The doors are broke. 110
LAERTES: Where is this king? — Sirs, stand you all without.
ALL: No, let's come in.
LAERTES: I pray you give me leave.
ALL: We will, we will.
LAERTES: I thank you. Keep the door. [*Exeunt his* FOLLOWERS.]
O thou vile King,
Give me my father.
QUEEN: Calmly, good Laertes. 115
LAERTES: That drop of blood that's calm proclaims me bastard,
Cries cuckold[30] to my father, brands the harlot

[22] does not lack talebearers
[23] unprovided with facts
[24] will not hesitate
[25] (a cannon that shot a kind of shrapnel)
[26] Swiss guards
[27] shore
[28] with a rebellious force
[29] (a hound runs counter when he follows the scent backward from the prey)
[30] man whose wife is unfaithful

Even here between the chaste unsmirchèd brow
Of my true mother.

KING: What is the cause, Laertes,
That thy rebellion looks so giantlike? 120
Let him go, Gertrude. Do not fear[31] our person.
There's such divinity doth hedge a king
That treason can but peep to[32] what it would,
Acts little of his will. Tell me, Laertes,
Why thou art thus incensed. Let him go, Gertrude. 125
Speak, man.

LAERTES: Where is my father?

KING: Dead.

QUEEN: But not by him.

KING: Let him demand his fill.

LAERTES: How came he dead? I'll not be juggled with.
To hell allegiance, vows to the blackest devil, 130
Conscience and grace to the profoundest pit!
I dare damnation. To this point I stand,
That both the worlds I give to negligence,[33]
Let come what comes, only I'll be revenged
Most throughly for my father.

KING: Who shall stay you? 135

LAERTES: My will, not all the world's.
And for my means, I'll husband them[34] so well
They shall go far with little.

KING: Good Laertes,
If you desire to know the certainty
Of your dear father, is't writ in your revenge 140
That swoopstake[35] you will draw both friend and foe,
Winner and loser?

LAERTES: None but his enemies.

KING: Will you know them then?

LAERTES: To his good friends thus wide I'll ope my arms
And like the kind life-rend'ring pelican[36] 145
Repast[37] them with my blood.

KING: Why, now you speak
Like a good child and a true gentleman.
That I am guiltless of your father's death,
And am most sensibly[38] in grief for it,

[31] fear for
[32] i.e., look at from a distance
[33] i.e., I care not what may happen (to me) in this world or the next
[34] use them economically
[35] in a clean sweep
[36] (thought to feed its young with its own blood)
[37] feed
[38] acutely

It shall as level to your judgment 'pear 150
As day does to your eye.

(*A noise within:* "Let her come in.")

LAERTES: How now? What noise is that?

(*Enter* OPHELIA.)

O heat, dry up my brains; tears seven times salt
Burn out the sense and virtue[39] of mine eye!
By heaven, thy madness shall be paid with weight 155
Till our scale turn the beam.[40] O rose of May,
Dear maid, kind sister, sweet Ophelia!
O heavens, is't possible a young maid's wits
Should be as mortal as an old man's life?
Nature is fine[41] in love, and where 'tis fine, 160
It sends some precious instance[42] of itself
After the thing it loves.

OPHELIA:

They bore him barefaced on the bier (*Song.*)
Hey non nony, nony, hey nony
And in his grave rained many a tear — 165

Fare you well, my dove!

LAERTES: Hadst thou thy wits, and didst persuade revenge,
It could not move thus.

OPHELIA: You must sing "A-down a-down, and you call him a-down-a."
O, how the wheel[43] becomes it! It is the false steward, that stole 170
his master's daughter.

LAERTES: This nothing's more than matter.[44]

OPHELIA: There's rosemary, that's for remembrance. Pray you, love, remember. And there is pansies, that's for thoughts.

LAERTES: A document[45] in madness, thoughts and remembrance fitted. 175

OPHELIA: There's fennel[46] for you, and columbines. There's rue for you, and here's some for me. We may call it herb of grace o' Sundays. O, you must wear your rue with a difference. There's a daisy. I would

39 power

40 weigh down the bar (of the balance)

41 refined, delicate

42 sample

43 (of uncertain meaning, but probably a turn or dance of Ophelia's, rather than Fortune's wheel)

44 this nonsense has more meaning than matters of consequence

45 lesson

46 (the distribution of flowers in the ensuing lines has symbolic meaning, but the meaning is disputed. Perhaps *fennel,* flattery; *columbines,* cuckoldry; *rue,* sorrow for Ophelia and repentance for the Queen; *daisy,* dissembling; *violets,* faithfulness. For other interpretations, see J. W. Lever in *Review of English Studies,* New Series 3 [1952], pp. 123–29)

give you some violets, but they withered all when my father died.
They say 'a made a good end. [*Sings.*] 180

For bonny sweet Robin is all my joy.

LAERTES: Thought and affliction, passion, hell itself,
She turns to favor[47] and to prettiness.

OPHELIA:

And will 'a not come again? (*Song.*)
And will 'a not come again? 185
No, no, he is dead,
Go to thy deathbed,
He never will come again.

His beard was as white as snow,
All flaxen was his poll[48] 190
He is gone, he is gone,
And we cast away moan.
God 'a' mercy on his soul!

And of all Christian souls, I pray God. God bye you. [*Exit.*]

LAERTES: Do you see this, O God? 195

KING: Laertes, I must commune with your grief,
Or you deny me right. Go but apart,
Make choice of whom your wisest friends you will,
And they shall hear and judge 'twixt you and me.
If by direct or by collateral[49] hand 200
They find us touched,[50] we will our kingdom give,
Our crown, our life, and all that we call ours,
To you in satisfaction; but if not,
Be you content to lend your patience to us,
And we shall jointly labor with your soul 205
To give it due content.

LAERTES: Let this be so.
His means of death, his obscure funeral —
No trophy, sword, nor hatchment[51] o'er his bones,
No noble rite nor formal ostentation[52] —
Cry to be heard, as 'twere from heaven to earth, 210
That I must call't in question.

KING: So you shall;
And where th' offense is, let the great ax fall.
I pray you go with me. (*Exeunt.*)

[47] charm, beauty
[48] white as flax was his head
[49] indirect
[50] implicated
[51] tablet bearing the coat of arms of the dead
[52] ceremony

## SCENE 6. [THE CASTLE.]

(*Enter* HORATIO *and others.*)

HORATIO: What are they that would speak with me?
GENTLEMAN: Seafaring men, sir. They say they have letters for you.
HORATIO: Let them come in. [*Exit* ATTENDANT.]
I do not know from what part of the world
I should be greeted, if not from Lord Hamlet. 5

(*Enter* SAILORS.)

SAILOR: God bless you, sir.
HORATIO: Let Him bless thee too.
SAILOR: 'A shall, sir, an't please Him. There's a letter for you, sir – it came from th' ambassador that was bound for England – if your name be Horatio, as I am let to know it is. 10
HORATIO [*reads the letter*]:
"Horatio, when thou shalt have overlooked[1] this, give these fellows some means to the King. They have letters for him. Ere we were two days old at sea, a pirate of very warlike appointment[2] gave us chase. Finding ourselves too slow of sail, we put on a compelled valor, and in the grapple I boarded them. On the instant they got 15 clear of our ship; so I alone became their prisoner. They have dealt with me like thieves of mercy, but they knew what they did: I am to do a good turn for them. Let the King have the letters I have sent, and repair thou to me with as much speed as thou wouldest fly death. I have words to speak in thine ear will make thee dumb; yet 20 are they much too light for the bore[3] of the matter. These good fellows will bring thee where I am. Rosencrantz and Guildenstern hold their course for England. Of them I have much to tell thee. Farewell.
He that thou knowest thine, HAMLET." 25

Come, I will give you way for these your letters,
And do't the speedier that you may direct me
To him from whom you brought them. (*Exeunt.*)

## SCENE 7. [THE CASTLE.]

*Enter* KING *and* LAERTES.

KING: Now must your conscience my acquittance seal,
And you must put me in your heart for friend,

1 surveyed
2 equipment
3 caliber (here, "importance")

Sith you have heard, and with a knowing ear,
That he which hath your noble father slain
Pursued my life.

LAERTES: It well appears. But tell me 5
Why you proceeded not against these feats
So criminal and so capital[1] in nature,
As by your safety, greatness, wisdom, all things else,
You mainly[2] were stirred up.

KING: O, for two special reasons,
Which may to you perhaps seem much unsinewed,[3] 10
But yet to me they're strong. The Queen his mother
Lives almost by his looks, and for myself –
My virtue or my plague, be it either which –
She is so conjunctive[4] to my life and soul,
That, as the star moves not but in his sphere, 15
I could not but by her. The other motive
Why to a public count[5] I might not go
Is the great love the general gender[6] bear him,
Who, dipping all his faults in their affection,
Would, like the spring that turneth wood to stone,[7] 20
Convert his gyves[8] to graces; so that my arrows,
Too slightly timbered[9] for so loud a wind,
Would have reverted to my bow again,
And not where I had aimed them.

LAERTES: And so have I a noble father lost, 25
A sister driven into desp'rate terms,[10]
Whose worth, if praises may go back again,[11]
Stood challenger on mount of all the age
For her perfections. But my revenge will come.

KING: Break not your sleeps for that. You must not think 30
That we are made of stuff so flat and dull
That we can let our beard be shook with danger,
And think it pastime. You shortly shall hear more.
I loved your father, and we love ourself,
And that, I hope, will teach you to imagine —— 35

(*Enter a* MESSENGER *with letters.*)

How now? What news?

[1] deserving death
[2] powerfully
[3] weak
[4] closely united
[5] reckoning
[6] common people
[7] (a spring in Shakespeare's county was so charged with lime that it would petrify wood placed in it)
[8] fetters
[9] shafted
[10] conditions
[11] revert to what is past

MESSENGER: Letters, my lord, from Hamlet:
These to your Majesty; this to the Queen.
KING: From Hamlet? Who brought them?
MESSENGER: Sailors, my lord, they say; I saw them not.
They were given me by Claudio; he received them 40
Of him that brought them.
KING: Laertes, you shall hear them. —
Leave us. (*Exit* MESSENGER.)

[*Reads.*] "High and mighty, you shall know I am set naked[12] on your kingdom. Tomorrow shall I beg leave to see your kingly eyes; when I shall (first asking your pardon thereunto) recount the occasion of my sudden and more strange return. 45

HAMLET."

What should this mean? Are all the rest come back?
Or is it some abuse,[13] and no such thing?
LAERTES: Know you the hand?
KING: 'Tis Hamlet's character.[14] "Naked"! 50
And in a postscript here, he says "alone."
Can you devise[15] me?
LAERTES: I am lost in it, my lord. But let him come.
It warms the very sickness in my heart
That I shall live and tell him to his teeth, 55
"Thus did'st thou."
KING: If it be so, Laertes
(As how should it be so? How otherwise?),
Will you be ruled by me?
LAERTES: Ay, my lord,
So you will not o'errule me to a peace.
KING: To thine own peace. If he be now returned, 60
As checking at[16] his voyage, and that he means
No more to undertake it, I will work him
To an exploit now ripe in my device,
Under the which he shall not choose but fall;
And for his death no wind of blame shall breathe, 65
But even his mother shall uncharge the practice[17]
And call it accident.
LAERTES: My lord, I will be ruled;
The rather if you could devise it so
That I might be the organ.
KING: It falls right.
You have been talked of since your travel much, 70

[12] destitute
[13] deception
[14] handwriting
[15] advise
[16] turning away from (a term in falconry)
[17] not charge the device with treachery

And that in Hamlet's hearing, for a quality
Wherein they say you shine. Your sum of parts
Did not together pluck such envy from him
As did that one, and that, in my regard,
Of the unworthiest siege.[18]

LAERTES: What part is that, my lord? 75

KING: A very riband in the cap of youth,
Yet needful too, for youth no less becomes
The light and careless livery that it wears
Than settled age his sables and his weeds,[19]
Importing health and graveness. Two months since 80
Here was a gentleman of Normandy.
I have seen myself, and served against, the French,
And they can[20] well on horseback, but this gallant
Had witchcraft in't. He grew unto his seat,
And to such wondrous doing brought his horse 85
As had he been incorpsed and deminatured
With the brave beast. So far he topped my thought
That I, in forgery[21] of shapes and tricks,
Come short of what he did.

LAERTES: A Norman was't?

KING: A Norman. 90

LAERTES: Upon my life, Lamord.

KING: The very same.

LAERTES: I know him well. He is the brooch[22] indeed
And gem of all the nation.

KING: He made confession[23] of you,
And gave you such a masterly report, 95
For art and exercise in your defense,
And for your rapier most especial,
That he cried out 'twould be a sight indeed
If one could match you. The scrimers[24] of their nation
He swore had neither motion, guard, nor eye, 100
If you opposed them. Sir, this report of his
Did Hamlet so envenom with his envy
That he could nothing do but wish and beg
Your sudden coming o'er to play with you.
Now, out of this ——

LAERTES: What out of this, my lord? 105

KING: Laertes, was your father dear to you?

[18] rank
[19] i.e., sober attire
[20] do
[21] invention
[22] ornament
[23] report
[24] fencers

Or are you like the painting of a sorrow,
A face without a heart?

LAERTES: Why ask you this?

KING: Not that I think you did not love your father,
But that I know love is begun by time, 110
And that I see, in passages of proof,[25]
Time qualifies[26] the spark and fire of it.
There lives within the very flame of love
A kind of wick or snuff[27] that will abate it,
And nothing is at a like goodness still,[28] 115
For goodness, growing to a plurisy,[29]
Dies in his own too-much. That we would do
We should do when we would, for this "would" changes,
And hath abatements and delays as many
As there are tongues, are hands, are accidents, 120
And then this "should" is like a spendthrift sigh,[30]
That hurts by easing. But to the quick[31] of th' ulcer —
Hamlet comes back; what would you undertake
To show yourself in deed your father's son
More than in words?

LAERTES: To cut his throat i' th' church! 125

KING: No place indeed should murder sanctuarize;[32]
Revenge should have no bounds. But, good Laertes,
Will you do this? Keep close within your chamber.
Hamlet returned shall know you are come home.
We'll put on those[33] shall praise your excellence 130
And set a double varnish on the fame
The Frenchman gave you, bring you in fine[34] together
And wager on your heads. He, being remiss,
Most generous, and free from all contriving,
Will not peruse the foils, so that with ease, 135
Or with a little shuffling, you may choose
A sword unbated,[35] and, in a pass of practice,[36]
Requite him for your father.

LAERTES: I will do't,
And for that purpose I'll anoint my sword.
I bought an unction of a mountebank,[37] 140

[25] proved cases
[26] diminishes
[27] residue of burnt wick (which dims the light)
[28] always
[29] fullness, excess
[30] (sighing provides ease, but because it was thought to thin the blood and so shorten life it was spendthrift)
[31] sensitive flesh
[32] protect
[33] we'll incite persons who
[34] finally
[35] not blunted
[36] treacherous thrust
[37] quack

So mortal that, but dip a knife in it,
Where it draws blood, no cataplasm[38] so rare,
Collected from all simples[39] that have virtue[40]
Under the moon, can save the thing from death
That is but scratched withal. I'll touch my point 145
With this contagion, that, if I gall him slightly,
It may be death.

KING: Let's further think of this,
Weigh what convenience both of time and means
May fit us to our shape.[41] If this should fail,
And that our drift look through[42] our bad performance, 150
'Twere better not assayed. Therefore this project
Should have a back or second, that might hold
If this did blast in proof.[43] Soft, let me see.
We'll make a solemn wager on your cunnings –
I ha't! 155
When in your motion you are hot and dry –
As make your bouts more violent to that end –
And that he calls for drink, I'll have prepared him
A chalice for the nonce,[44] whereon but sipping,
If he by chance escape your venomed stuck,[45] 160
Our purpose may hold there. – But stay, what noise?

(*Enter* QUEEN.)

QUEEN: One woe doth tread upon another's heel.
So fast they follow. Your sister's drowned, Laertes.

LAERTES: Drowned! O, where?

QUEEN: There is a willow grows askant[46] the brook, 165
That shows his hoar[47] leaves in the glassy stream:
Therewith[48] fantastic garlands did she make
Of crowflowers, nettles, daisies, and long purples,
That liberal[49] shepherds give a grosser name,
But our cold maids do dead men's fingers call them. 170
There on the pendent boughs her crownet[50] weeds
Clamb'ring to hang, an envious sliver[51] broke,
When down her weedy trophies and herself
Fell in the weeping brook. Her clothes spread wide,
And mermaidlike awhile they bore her up, 175

[38] poultice
[39] medicinal herbs
[40] (to heal)
[41] role
[42] purpose show through
[43] burst (fail) in performance
[44] occasion
[45] thrust
[46] aslant
[47] silver-gray
[48] i.e., with willow twigs
[49] free-spoken, coarse-mouthed
[50] coronet
[51] malicious branch

Which time she chanted snatches of old lauds,[52]
As one incapable[53] of her own distress,
Or like a creature native and indued[54]
Unto that element. But long it could not be
Till that her garments, heavy with their drink, 180
Pulled the poor wretch from her melodious lay
To muddy death.

LAERTES: Alas, then she is drowned?

QUEEN: Drowned, drowned.

LAERTES: Too much of water hast thou, poor Ophelia,
And therefore I forbid my tears; but yet 185
It is our trick;[55] nature her custom holds,
Let shame say what it will: when these are gone,
The woman[56] will be out. Adieu, my lord.
I have a speech o' fire, that fain would blaze,
But that this folly drowns it. (*Exit.*)

KING: Let's follow, Gertrude. 190
How much I had to do to calm his rage!
Now fear I this will give it start again;
Therefore let's follow. (*Exeunt.*)

# ACT V

## SCENE 1. [A CHURCHYARD.]

*Enter two* CLOWNS.[1]

CLOWN: Is she to be buried in Christian burial when she willfully seeks her own salvation?

OTHER: I tell thee she is. Therefore make her grave straight.[2] The crowner[3] hath sate on her, and finds it Christian burial.

CLOWN: How can that be, unless she drowned herself in her own defense? 5

OTHER: Why, 'tis found so.

CLOWN: It must be *se offendendo;*[4] it cannot be else. For here lies the point: if I drown myself wittingly, it argues an act, and an act hath three branches — it is to act, to do, to perform. Argal,[5] she drowned herself wittingly. 10

52 hymns
53 unaware
54 in harmony with
55 trait, way
56 i.e., womanly part of me

1 rustics
2 straightway
3 coroner
4 (blunder for *se defendendo,* a legal term meaning "in self-defense")
5 (blunder for Latin *ergo,* "therefore")

OTHER: Nay, but hear you, Goodman Delver.

CLOWN: Give me leave. Here lies the water — good. Here stands the man — good. If the man go to this water and drown himself, it is, will he nill he,[6] he goes; mark you that. But if the water come to him and drown him, he drowns not himself. Argal, he that is not guilty of his own death, shortens not his own life. 15

OTHER: But is this law?

CLOWN: Ay marry, is't — crowner's quest[7] law.

OTHER: Will you ha' the truth on't? If this had not been a gentlewoman, she should have been buried out o' Christian burial. 20

CLOWN: Why, there thou say'st. And the more pity that great folk should have count'nance[8] in this world to drown or hang themselves more than their even-Christen.[9] Come, my spade. There is no ancient gentlemen but gard'ners, ditchers, and gravemakers. They hold up[10] Adam's profession. 25

OTHER: Was he a gentleman?

CLOWN: 'A was the first that ever bore arms.[11]

OTHER: Why, he had none.

CLOWN: What, art a heathen? How dost thou understand the Scripture? The Scripture says Adam digged. Could he dig without arms? I'll put another question to thee. If thou answerest me not to the purpose, confess thyself—— 30

OTHER: Go to.

CLOWN: What is he that builds stronger than either the mason, the shipwright, or the carpenter? 35

OTHER: The gallowsmaker, for that frame outlives a thousand tenants.

CLOWN: I like thy wit well, in good faith. The gallows does well. But how does it well? It does well to those that do ill. Now thou dost ill to say the gallows is built stronger than the church. Argal, the gallows may do well to thee. To't again, come. 40

OTHER: Who builds stronger than a mason, a shipwright, or a carpenter?

CLOWN: Ay, tell me that, and unyoke.[12]

OTHER: Marry, now I can tell.

CLOWN: To't. 45

OTHER: Mass,[13] I cannot tell.

(*Enter* HAMLET *and* HORATIO *afar off.*)

CLOWN: Cudgel thy brains no more about it, for your dull ass will not mend his pace with beating. And when you are asked this question

[6] will he or will he not (whether he will or will not)
[7] inquest
[8] privilege
[9] fellow Christian
[10] keep up
[11] had a coat of arms (the sign of a gentleman)
[12] i.e., stop work for the day
[13] by the mass

next, say "a gravemaker." The houses he makes lasts till doomsday. Go, get thee in, and fetch me a stoup[14] of liquor. 50

[*Exit Other* CLOWN.]

In youth when I did love, did love, (*Song.*)
Methought it was very sweet
To contract — O — the time for — a — my behove,[15]
O, methought there — a — was nothing — a — meet.

HAMLET: Has this fellow no feeling of his business? 'A sings in grave-making. 55

HORATIO: Custom hath made it in him a property of easiness.[16]

HAMLET: 'Tis e'en so. The hand of little employment hath the daintier sense.[17]

CLOWN:

But age with his stealing steps (*Song.*) 60
Hath clawed me in his clutch,
And hath shipped me into the land,
As if I had never been such.

[*Throws up a skull.*]

HAMLET: That skull had a tongue in it, and could sing once. How the knave jowls[18] it to the ground, as if 'twere Cain's jawbone, that did the first murder! This might be the pate of a politician, which this ass now o'erreaches,[19] one that would circumvent God, might it not? 65

HORATIO: It might, my lord.

HAMLET: Or of a courtier, which could say "Good morrow, sweet lord! How dost thou, sweet lord?" This might be my Lord Such-a-one, that praised my Lord Such-a-one's horse when 'a went to beg it, might it not? 70

HORATIO: Ay, my lord.

HAMLET: Why, e'en so, and now my Lady Worm's, chapless,[20] and knocked about the mazzard[21] with a sexton's spade. Here's fine revolution, an we had the trick to see't. Did these bones cost no more the breeding but to play at loggets[22] with them? Mine ache to think on't. 75

CLOWN:

A pickax and a spade, a spade, (*Song.*)
For and a shrouding sheet; 80

[14] tankard
[15] advantage
[16] easy for him
[17] is more sensitive (because it is not calloused)
[18] hurls
[19] (1) reaches over, (2) has the advantage over
[20] lacking the lower jaw
[21] head
[22] (a game in which small pieces of wood were thrown at an object)

O, a pit of clay for to be made
For such a guest is meet.

[*Throws up another skull.*]

HAMLET: There's another. Why may not that be the skull of a lawyer? Where be his quiddities[23] now, his quillities,[24] his cases, his tenures,[25] and his tricks( Why does he suffer this mad knave now to knock him about the sconce[26] with a dirty shovel, and will not tell him of his action of battery? Hum! This fellow might be in's time a great buyer of land, with his statutes, his recognizances, his fines,[27] his double vouchers, his recoveries. Is this the fine[28] of his fines, and the recovery of his recoveries, to have his fine pate full of fine dirt? Will his vouchers vouch him no more of his purchases, and double ones too, than the length and breadth of a pair of indentures?[29] The very conveyances[30] of his lands will scarcely lie in this box, and must th' inheritor himself have no more, ha? 85 90

HORATIO: Not a jot more, my lord. 95

HAMLET: Is not parchment made of sheepskins?

HORATIO: Ay, my lord, and of calveskins too.

HAMLET: They are sheep and calves which seek out assurance[31] in that. I will speak to this fellow. Whose grave's this, sirrah?

CLOWN: Mine, sir. [*Sings.*] 100

O, a pit of clay for to be made
For such a guest is meet.

HAMLET: I think it be thine indeed, for thou liest in't.

CLOWN: You lie out on't, sir, and therefore 'tis not yours. For my part, I do not lie in't, yet it is mine. 105

HAMLET: Thou dost lie in't, to be in't and say it is thine. 'Tis for the dead, not for the quick;[32] therefore thou liest.

CLOWN: 'Tis a quick lie, sir; 'twill away again from me to you.

HAMLET: What man dost thou dig it for?

CLOWN: For no man, sir. 110

HAMLET: What woman then?

CLOWN: For none neither.

HAMLET: Who is to be buried in't?

CLOWN: One that was a woman, sir; but, rest her soul, she's dead.

[23] subtle arguments (Lat. *quidditas,* "whatness")

[24] fine distinctions

[25] legal means of holding land

[26] head

[27] his documents giving a creditor control of a debtor's land, his bonds of surety, his documents changing an entailed estate into fee simple (unrestricted ownership)

[28] end

[29] contracts

[30] legal documents for the transference of land

[31] safety

[32] living

HAMLET: How absolute[33] the knave is! We must speak by the card,[34] or equivocation[35] will undo us. By the Lord, Horatio, this three years I have took note of it, the age is grown so picked[36] that the toe of the peasant comes so near the heel of the courtier he galls his kibe.[37] How long hast thou been a gravemaker? 115

CLOWN: Of all the days i' th' year, I came to't that day that our last king Hamlet overcame Fortinbras. 120

HAMLET: How long is that since?

CLOWN: Cannot you tell that? Every fool can tell that. It was that very day that young Hamlet was born – he that is mad, and sent into England. 125

HAMLET: Ay, marry, why was he sent into England?

CLOWN: Why, because 'a was mad. 'A shall recover his wits there; or, if 'a do not, 'tis no great matter there.

HAMLET: Why?

CLOWN: 'Twill not be seen in him there. There the men are as mad as he. 130

HAMLET: How came he mad?

CLOWN: Very strangely, they say.

HAMLET: How strangely?

CLOWN: Faith, e'en with losing his wits. 135

HAMLET: Upon what ground?

CLOWN: Why, here in Denmark. I have been sexton here, man and boy, thirty years.

HAMLET: How long will a man lie i' th' earth ere he rot?

CLOWN: Faith, if 'a be not rotten before 'a die (as we have many pocky corses[38] nowadays that will scarce hold the laying in), 'a will last you some eight year or nine year. A tanner will last you nine year. 140

HAMLET: Why he, more than another?

CLOWN: Why, sir, his hide is so tanned with his trade that 'a will keep out water a great while, and your water is a sore decayer of your whoreson dead body. Here's a skull now hath lien you i' th' earth three and twenty years. 145

HAMLET: Whose was it?

CLOWN: A whoreson mad fellow's it was. Whose do you think it was?

HAMLET: Nay, I know not. 150

CLOWN: A pestilence on him for a mad rogue! 'A poured a flagon of Rhenish on my head once. This same skull, sir, was, sir, Yorick's skull, the King's jester.

HAMLET: This?

CLOWN: E'en that. 155

[33] positive, decided
[34] by the compass card, i.e., exactly
[35] ambiguity
[36] refined
[37] sore on the back of the heel
[38] bodies of persons who had been infected with the pox (syphilis)

HAMLET: Let me see. [*Takes the skull.*] Alas, poor Yorick! I knew him, Horatio, a fellow of infinite jest, of most excellent fancy. He hath borne me on his back a thousand times. And now how abhorred in my imagination it is! My gorge rises at it. Here hung those lips that I have kissed I know not how oft. Where be your gibes now? 160 Your gambols, your songs, your flashes of merriment that were wont to set the table on a roar? Not one now to mock your own grinning? Quite chapfall'n?[39] Now get you to my lady's chamber, and tell her, let her paint an inch thick, to this favor[40] she must come. Make her laugh at that. Prithee, Horatio, tell me one thing. 165

HORATIO: What's that, my lord?

HAMLET: Dost thou think Alexander looked o' this fashion i' th' earth?

HORATIO: E'en so.

HAMLET: And smelt so? Pah! [*Puts down the skull.*]

HORATIO: E'en so, my lord. 170

HAMLET: To what base uses we may return, Horatio! Why may not imagination trace the noble dust of Alexander till 'a find it stopping a bunghole?

HORATIO: 'Twere to consider too curiously,[41] to consider so.

HAMLET: No, faith, not a jot, but to follow him thither with modesty 175 enough,[42] and likelihood to lead it; as thus: Alexander died, Alexander was buried, Alexander returneth to dust; the dust is earth; of earth we make loam; and why of that loam whereto he was converted might they not stop a beer barrel?

Imperious Caesar, dead and turned to clay, 180
Might stop a hole to keep the wind away.
O, that that earth which kept the world in awe
Should patch a wall t' expel the winter's flaw![43]
But soft, but soft awhile! Here comes the King.

(*Enter* KING, QUEEN, LAERTES, *and a coffin, with* LORDS *attendant* [*and a* DOCTOR OF DIVINITY].)

The Queen, the courtiers. Who is this they follow? 185
And with such maimèd[44] rites? This doth betoken
The corse they follow did with desp'rate hand
Fordo it[45] own life. 'Twas of some estate.[46]
Couch[47] we awhile, and mark. [*Retires with* HORATIO.]

LAERTES: What ceremony else?

HAMLET: That is Laertes, 190
A very noble youth. Mark.

[39] (1) down in the mouth, (2) jawless
[40] facial appearance
[41] minutely
[42] without exaggeration
[43] gust
[44] incomplete
[45] destroy its
[46] high rank
[47] hide

LAERTES: What ceremony else?

DOCTOR: Her obsequies have been as far enlarged
As we have warranty. Her death was doubtful,[48]
And, but that great command o'ersways the order, 195
She should in ground unsanctified been lodged
Till the last trumpet. For charitable prayers,
Shards,[49] flints, and pebbles should be thrown on her.
Yet here she is allowed her virgin crants,[50]
Her maiden strewments,[51] and the bringing home 200
Of bell and burial.

LAERTES: Must there no more be done?

DOCTOR: No more be done.
We should profane the service of the dead
To sing a requiem and such rest to her
As to peace-parted souls.

LAERTES: Lay her i' th' earth, 205
And from her fair and unpolluted flesh
May violets spring! I tell thee, churlish priest,
A minist'ring angel shall my sister be
When thou liest howling!

HAMLET: What, the fair Ophelia?

QUEEN: Sweets to the sweet! Farewell. [*Scatters flowers.*] 210
I hoped thou shouldst have been my Hamlet's wife.
I thought thy bride bed to have decked, sweet maid,
And not have strewed thy grave.

LAERTES: O, treble woe
Fall ten times treble on that cursèd head
Whose wicked deed thy most ingenious sense[52] 215
Deprived thee of! Hold off the earth awhile,
Till I have caught her once more in mine arms.

(*Leaps in the grave.*)

Now pile your dust upon the quick and dead
Till of this flat a mountain you have made
T'o'ertop old Pelion[53] or the skyish head 220
Of blue Olympus.

HAMLET (*coming forward*):
What is he whose grief
Bears such an emphasis, whose phrase of sorrow
Conjures the wand'ring stars,[54] and makes them stand

[48] suspicious
[49] broken pieces of pottery
[50] garlands
[51] i.e., of flowers
[52] finely endowed mind
[53] (according to classical legend, giants in their fight with the gods sought to reach heaven by piling Mount Pelion and Mount Ossa on Mount Olympus)
[54] planets

Like wonder-wounded hearers? This is I,
Hamlet the Dane.
LAERTES: The devil take thy soul! 225

[*Grapples with him.*][55]

HAMLET: Thou pray'st not well.
I prithee take thy fingers from my throat,
For, though I am not splenitive[56] and rash,
Yet have I in me something dangerous,
Which let thy wisdom fear. Hold off thy hand. 230
KING: Pluck them asunder.
QUEEN: Hamlet, Hamlet!
ALL: Gentlemen!
HORATIO: Good my lord, be quiet.

[*Attendants part them.*]

HAMLET: Why, I will fight with him upon this theme
Until my eyelids will no longer wag.
QUEEN: O my son, what theme? 235
HAMLET: I loved Ophelia. Forty thousand brothers
Could not with all their quantity of love
Make up my sum. What wilt thou do for her?
KING: O, he is mad, Laertes.
QUEEN: For love of God forbear him. 240
HAMLET: 'Swounds, show me what thou't do.
Woo't weep? Woo't fight? Woo't fast? Woo't tear thyself?
Woo't drink up eisel?[57] Eat a crocodile?
I'll do't. Dost thou come here to whine?
To outface me with leaping in her grave? 245
Be buried quick with her, and so will I.
And if thou prate of mountains, let them throw
Millions of acres on us, till our ground,
Singeing his pate against the burning zone,[58]
Make Ossa like a wart! Nay, an thou'lt mouth, 250
I'll rant as well as thou.
QUEEN: This is mere madness;
And thus a while the fit will work on him.
Anon, as patient as the female dove

[55] (Q1, a bad quarto, presumably reporting a version that toured, has a previous direction saying "Hamlet leaps in after Laertes." Possibly he does so, somewhat hysterically. But such a direction — absent from the two good texts, Q2 and F — makes Hamlet the aggressor, somewhat contradicting his next speech. Perhaps Laertes leaps out of the grave to attack Hamlet)
[56] fiery (the spleen was thought to be the seat of anger)
[57] vinegar
[58] sun's orbit

When that her golden couplets are disclosed,[59]
His silence will sit drooping.

HAMLET: Hear you, sir. 255
What is the reason that you use me thus?
I loved you ever. But it is no matter.
Let Hercules himself do what he may,
The cat will mew, and dog will have his day.

KING: I pray thee, good Horatio, wait upon him. 260

(*Exit* HAMLET *and* HORATIO.)

[*To* LAERTES.] Strengthen your patience in our last night's speech.
We'll put the matter to the present push.[60]
Good Gertrude, set some watch over your son.
This grave shall have a living[61] monument.
An hour of quiet shortly shall we see; 265
Till then in patience our proceeding be. (*Exeunt.*)

## SCENE 2. [THE CASTLE.]

*Enter* HAMLET *and* HORATIO.

HAMLET: So much for this, sir; now shall you see the other.
You do remember all the circumstance?

HORATIO: Remember it, my lord!

HAMLET: Sir, in my heart there was a kind of fighting
That would not let me sleep. Methought I lay 5
Worse than the mutines in the bilboes.[1] Rashly
(And praised be rashness for it) let us know,
Our indiscretion sometime serves us well
When our deep plots do pall,[2] and that should learn us
There's a divinity that shapes our ends, 10
Rough-hew them how we will.

HORATIO: That is most certain.

HAMLET: Up from my cabin,
My sea gown scarfed about me, in the dark
Groped I to find out them, had my desire,
Fingered[3] their packet, and in fine[4] withdrew 15
To mine own room again, making so bold,
My fears forgetting manners, to unseal

59 (the dove lays two eggs, and the newly hatched [*disclosed*] young are covered with golden down)

60 immediate test

61 lasting (with perhaps also a reference to the plot against Hamlet's life)

1 mutineers in fetters

2 fail

3 stole

4 finally

Their grand commission; where I found, Horatio—
Ah, royal knavery!—an exact command,
Larded[5] with many several sorts of reasons, 20
Importing Denmark's health, and England's too,
With, ho, such bugs and goblins in my life,[6]
That on the supervise,[7] no leisure bated,[8]
No, not to stay the grinding of the ax,
My head should be struck off.

HORATIO: Is't possible? 25

HAMLET: Here's the commission; read it at more leisure.
But wilt thou hear now how I did proceed?

HORATIO: I beseech you.

HAMLET: Being thus benetted round with villains,
Or[9] I could make a prologue to my brains, 30
They had begun the play. I sat me down,
Devised a new commission, wrote it fair.
I once did hold it, as our statists[10] do,
A baseness to write fair,[11] and labored much
How to forget that learning, but, sir, now 35
It did me yeoman's service. Wilt thou know
Th' effect[12] of what I wrote?

HORATIO: Ay, good my lord.

HAMLET: An earnest conjuration from the King,
As England was his faithful tributary,
As love between them like the palm might flourish, 40
As peace should still her wheaten garland wear
And stand a comma[13] 'tween their amities,
And many suchlike as's of great charge,[14]
That on the view and knowing of these contents,
Without debatement further, more or less, 45
He should those bearers put to sudden death,
Not shriving[15] time allowed.

HORATIO: How was this sealed?

HAMLET: Why, even in that was heaven ordinant.[16]
I had my father's signet in my purse,
Which was the model[17] of that Danish seal, 50
Folded the writ up in the form of th' other,

[5] enriched
[6] such bugbears and imagined terrors if I were allowed to live
[7] reading
[8] delay allowed
[9] ere
[10] statesmen
[11] clearly
[12] purport
[13] link
[14] (1) serious exhortation, (2) heavy burden (punning on *as's* and "asses")
[15] absolution
[16] ruling
[17] counterpart

Subscribed it, gave't th' impression, placed it safely,
The changeling never known. Now, the next day
Was our sea fight, and what to this was sequent
Thou knowest already. 55

HORATIO: So Guildenstern and Rosencrantz go to't.

HAMLET: Why, man, they did make love to this employment.
They are not near my conscience; their defeat
Does by their own insinuation[18] grow.
'Tis dangerous when the baser nature comes 60
Between the pass[19] and fell[20] incensèd points
Of mighty opposites.

HORATIO: Why, what a king is this!

HAMLET: Does it not, think thee, stand me now upon[21] —
He that hath killed my king, and whored my mother,
Popped in between th' election[22] and my hopes, 65
Thrown out his angle[23] for my proper life,[24]
And with such coz'nage[25] — is't not perfect conscience
To quit[26] him with this arm? And is't not to be damned
To let this canker of our nature come
In further evil? 70

HORATIO: It must be shortly known to him from England
What is the issue of the business there.

HAMLET: It will be short; the interim's mine,
And a man's life's no more than to say "one."
But I am very sorry, good Horatio, 75
That to Laertes I forgot myself,
For by the image of my cause I see
The portraiture of his. I'll court his favors.
But sure the bravery[27] of his grief did put me
Into a tow'ring passion.

HORATIO: Peace, who comes here? 80

(*Enter young* OSRIC, *a courtier.*)

OSRIC: Your lordship is right welcome back to Denmark.

HAMLET: I humbly thank you, sir. [*Aside to* HORATIO.]
Dost know this waterfly?

HORATIO [*aside to* HAMLET]: No, my good lord.

HAMLET [*aside to* HORATIO]: Thy state is the more gracious, for 'tis a 85
vice to know him. He hath much land, and fertile. Let a beast be

[18] meddling
[19] thrust
[20] cruel
[21] become incumbent upon me
[22] (the Danish monarchy was elective)
[23] fishing line
[24] my own life
[25] trickery
[26] pay back
[27] bravado

lord of beasts, and his crib shall stand at the king's mess.[28] 'Tis a chough,[29] but, as I say, spacious[30] in the possession of dirt.

OSRIC: Sweet lord, if your lordship were at leisure, I should impart a thing to you from his Majesty. 90

HAMLET: I will receive it, sir, with all diligence of spirit. Put your bonnet to his right use. 'Tis for the head.

OSRIC: I thank your lordship, it is very hot.

HAMLET: No, believe me, 'tis very cold; the wind is northerly.

OSRIC: It is indifferent cold, my lord, indeed. 95

HAMLET: But yet methinks it is very sultry and hot for my complexion.[31]

OSRIC: Exceedingly, my lord; it is very sultry, as 'twere – I cannot tell how. But, my lord, his Majesty bade me signify to you that 'a has laid a great wager on your head. Sir, this is the matter —— 100

HAMLET: I beseech you remember.

[HAMLET *moves him to put on his hat.*]

OSRIC: Nay, good my lord; for my ease, in good faith. Sir, here is newly come to court Laertes – believe me, an absolute gentleman, full of most excellent differences,[32] of very soft society and great showing. Indeed, to speak feelingly[33] of him, he is the card[34] or calendar of 105 gentry; for you shall find in him the continent[35] of what part a gentleman would see.

HAMLET: Sir, his definement[36] suffers no perdition[37] in you, though, I know, to divide him inventorially would dozy[38] th' arithmetic of memory, and yet but yaw neither in respect of his quick sail.[39] But, 110 in the verity of extolment, I take him to be a soul of great article,[40] and his infusion[41] of such dearth and rareness as, to make true diction[42] of him, his semblable[43] is his mirror, and who else would trace him, his umbrage,[44] nothing more.

OSRIC: Your lordship speaks most infallibly of him. 115

HAMLET: The concernancy,[45] sir? Why do we wrap the gentleman in our more rawer breath?

OSRIC: Sir?

[28] table
[29] jackdaw (here, chatterer)
[30] well off
[31] temperament
[32] distinguishing characteristics
[33] justly
[34] chart
[35] summary
[36] description
[37] loss
[38] dizzy
[39] i.e., and yet only stagger despite all (*yaw neither*) in trying to overtake his virtues
[40] (literally, "item," but here perhaps "traits" or "importance")
[41] essential quality
[42] description
[43] likeness
[44] shadow
[45] meaning

HORATIO: Is't not possible to understand in another tongue? You will to't,[46] sir, really. 120

HAMLET: What imports the nomination of this gentleman?

OSRIC: Of Laertes?

HORATIO [*aside to* HAMLET]: His purse is empty already. All's golden words are spent.

HAMLET: Of him, sir. 125

OSRIC: I know you are not ignorant —

HAMLET: I would you did, sir; yet, in faith, if you did, it would not much approve[47] me. Well, sir?

OSRIC: You are not ignorant of what excellence Laertes is —

HAMLET: I dare not confess that, lest I should compare with him in excellence; but to know a man well were to know himself. 130

OSRIC: I mean, sir, for his weapon; but in the imputation[48] laid on him by them, in his meed[49] he's unfellowed.

HAMLET: What's his weapon?

OSRIC: Rapier and dagger. 135

HAMLET: That's two of his weapons — but well.

OSRIC: The King, sir, hath wagered with him six Barbary horses, against the which he has impawned,[50] as I take it, six French rapiers and poniards, with their assigns,[51] as girdle, hangers,[52] and so. Three of the carriages,[53] in faith, are very dear to fancy, very responsive[54] to the hilts, most delicate carriages, and of very liberal conceit.[55] 140

HAMLET: What call you the carriages?

HORATIO [*aside to* HAMLET]: I knew you must be edified by the margent[56] ere you had done.

OSRIC: The carriages, sir, are the hangers. 145

HAMLET: The phrase would be more germane to the matter if we could carry a cannon by our sides. I would it might be hangers till then. But on! Six Barbary horses against six French swords, their assigns, and three liberal-conceited carriages — that's the French bet against the Danish. Why is this all impawned, as you call it? 150

OSRIC: The King, sir, hath laid, sir, that in a dozen passes between yourself and him he shall not exceed you three hits; he hath laid on twelve for nine, and it would come to immediate trial if your lordship would vouchsafe the answer.

HAMLET: How if I answer no? 155

OSRIC: I mean, my lord, the opposition of your person in trial.

[46] will get there
[47] commend
[48] reputation
[49] merit
[50] wagered
[51] accompaniments
[52] straps hanging the sword to the belt
[53] (an affected word for hangers)
[54] corresponding
[55] elaborate design
[56] i.e., marginal (explanatory) comment

HAMLET: Sir, I will walk here in the hall. If it please his Majesty, it is the breathing time of day with me.[57] Let the foils be brought, the gentleman willing, and the King hold his purpose, I will win for him an I can; if not, I will gain nothing but my shame and the odd hits. 160

OSRIC: Shall I deliver you e'en so?

HAMLET: To this effect, sir, after what flourish your nature will.

OSRIC: I commend my duty to your lordship.

HAMLET: Yours, yours. [*Exit* OSRIC.] 165

He does well to commend it himself; there are no tongues else for's turn.

HORATIO: This lapwing[58] runs away with the shell on his head.

HAMLET: 'A did comply, sir, with his dug[59] before 'a sucked it. Thus has he, and many more of the same breed that I know the drossy age dotes on, only got the tune of the time and, out of an habit of encounter,[60] a kind of yeasty[61] collection, which carries them through and through the most fanned and winnowed opinions; and do but blow them to their trial, the bubbles are out.[62] 170

(*Enter a* LORD.)

LORD: My lord, his Majesty commended him to you by young Osric, who brings back to him that you attend him in the hall. He sends to know if your pleasure hold to play with Laertes, or that you will take longer time. 175

HAMLET: I am constant to my purposes; they follow the King's pleasure. If his fitness speaks, mine is ready; now or whensoever, provided I be so able as now. 180

LORD: The King and Queen and all are coming down.

HAMLET: In happy time.

LORD: The Queen desires you to use some gentle entertainment[63] to Laertes before you fall to play. 185

HAMLET: She well instructs me. [*Exit* LORD.]

HORATIO: You will lose this wager, my lord.

HAMLET: I do not think so. Since he went into France I have been in continual practice. I shall win at the odds. But thou wouldst not think how ill all's here about my heart. But it is no matter. 190

HORATIO: Nay, good my lord —

[57] time when I take exercise

[58] (the new-hatched lapwing was thought to run around with half its shell on its head)

[59] he was ceremoniously polite to his mother's breast

[60] out of his own superficial way of meeting and conversing with people

[61] frothy

[62] i.e., they are blown away (the reference is to the "yeasty collection")

[63] to be courteous

HAMLET: It is but foolery, but it is such a kind of gaingiving[64] as would perhaps trouble a woman.

HORATIO: If your mind dislike anything, obey it. I will forestall their repair hither and say you are not fit. 195

HAMLET: Not a whit, we defy augury. There is special providence in the fall of a sparrow.[65] If it be now, 'tis not to come; if it be not to come, it will be now; if it be not now, yet it will come. The readiness is all. Since no man of aught he leaves knows, what is't to leave betimes?[66] Let be. 200

(*A table prepared.* [*Enter*] *Trumpets, Drums, and* OFFICERS *with cushions;* KING, QUEEN, [OSRIC,] *and all the State,* [*with*] *foils, daggers,* [*and stoups of wine borne in*]; *and* LAERTES.)

KING: Come, Hamlet, come, and take this hand from me.

[*The* KING *puts* LAERTES' *hand into* HAMLET'*s.*]

HAMLET: Give me your pardon, sir. I have done you wrong,
But pardon't, as you are a gentleman.
This presence[67] knows, and you must needs have heard,
How I am punished with a sore distraction. 205
What I have done
That might your nature, honor, and exception[68]
Roughly awake, I here proclaim was madness.
Was't Hamlet wronged Laertes? Never Hamlet.
If Hamlet from himself be ta'en away, 210
And when he's not himself does wrong Laertes,
Then Hamlet does it not, Hamlet denies it.
Who does it then? His madness. If't be so,
Hamlet is of the faction[69] that is wronged;
His madness is poor Hamlet's enemy. 215
Sir, in this audience,
Let my disclaiming from a purposed evil
Free me so far in your most generous thoughts
That I have shot my arrow o'er the house
And hurt my brother.

LAERTES: I am satisfied in nature, 220
Whose motive in this case should stir me most
To my revenge. But in my terms of honor
I stand aloof, and will no reconcilement

[64] misgiving

[65] (cf. Matthew 10:29: "Are not two sparrows sold for a farthing? and one of them shall not fall on the ground without your Father")

[66] early

[67] royal assembly

[68] disapproval

[69] party, side

Till by some elder masters of known honor
I have a voice and precedent[70] of peace 225
To keep my name ungored. But till that time
I do receive your offered love like love,
And will not wrong it.

HAMLET: I embrace it freely,
And will this brother's wager frankly play.
Give us the foils. Come on.

LAERTES: Come, one for me. 230

HAMLET: I'll be your foil,[71] Laertes. In mine ignorance
Your skill shall, like a star i' th' darkest night,
Stick fiery off[72] indeed.

LAERTES: You mock me, sir.

HAMLET: No, by this hand.

KING: Give them the foils, young Osric. Cousin Hamlet, 235
You know the wager?

HAMLET: Very well, my lord.
Your grace has laid the odds o' th' weaker side.

KING: I do not fear it, I have seen you both;
But since he is bettered,[73] we have therefore odds.

LAERTES: This is too heavy; let me see another. 240

HAMLET: This likes me well. These foils have all a length?

(*Prepare to play.*)

OSRIC: Ay, my good lord.

KING: Set me the stoups of wine upon that table.
If Hamlet give the first or second hit,
Or quit[74] in answer of the third exchange, 245
Let all the battlements their ordnance fire.
The King shall drink to Hamlet's better breath,
And in the cup an union[75] shall he throw
Richer than that which four successive kings
In Denmark's crown have worn. Give me the cups, 250
And let the kettle[76] to the trumpet speak,
The trumpet to the cannoneer without,
The cannons to the heavens, the heaven to earth,
"Now the King drinks to Hamlet." Come, begin.

(*Trumpets the while.*)

And you, the judges, bear a wary eye. 255

[70] authoritative opinion justified by precedent
[71] (1) blunt sword, (2) background (of metallic leaf) for a jewel
[72] stand out brilliantly
[73] has improved (in France)
[74] repay, hit back
[75] pearl
[76] kettledrum

HAMLET: Come on, sir.
LAERTES: Come, my lord.

(*They play.*)

HAMLET: One.
LAERTES: No.
HAMLET: Judgment?
OSRIC: A hit, a very palpable hit.

(*Drum, trumpets, and shot. Flourish; a piece goes off.*)

LAERTES: Well, again.
KING: Stay, give me drink. Hamlet, this pearl is thine.
Here's to thy health. Give him the cup.
HAMLET: I'll play this bout first; set it by awhile. 260
Come.

[*They play.*]

Another hit. What say you?
LAERTES: A touch, a touch; I do confess't.
KING: Our son shall win.
QUEEN: He's fat,[77] and scant of breath.
Here, Hamlet, take my napkin, rub thy brows.
The Queen carouses to thy fortune, Hamlet. 265
HAMLET: Good madam!
KING: Gertrude, do not drink.
QUEEN: I will, my lord; I pray you pardon me. [*Drinks.*]
KING [*aside*]: It is the poisoned cup; it is too late.
HAMLET: I dare not drink yet, madam — by and by.
QUEEN: Come, let me wipe thy face. 270
LAERTES: My lord, I'll hit him now.
KING: I do not think't.
LAERTES [*aside*]: And yet it is almost against my conscience.
HAMLET: Come for the third, Laertes. You do but dally.
I pray you pass with your best violence;
I am sure you make a wanton[78] of me. 275
LAERTES: Say you so? Come on.

([*They*] *play.*)

OSRIC: Nothing neither way.
LAERTES: Have at you now!

(*In scuffling they change rapiers,* [*and both are wounded*].)

[77] (1) sweaty, (2) out of training
[78] spoiled child

KING: Part them. They are incensed.
HAMLET: Nay, come – again!

[*The* QUEEN *falls.*]

OSRIC: Look to the Queen there, ho!
HORATIO: They bleed on both sides. How is it, my lord? 280
OSRIC: How is't, Laertes?
LAERTES: Why, as a woodcock to mine own springe,[79] Osric.
I am justly killed with mine own treachery.
HAMLET: How does the Queen?
KING: She sounds[80] to see them bleed.
QUEEN: No, no, the drink, the drink! O my dear Hamlet! 285
The drink, the drink! I am poisoned. [*Dies.*]
HAMLET: O villainy! Ho! Let the door be locked.
Treachery! Seek it out.

[LAERTES *falls.*]

LAERTES: It is here, Hamlet. Hamlet, thou art slain;
No med'cine in the world can do thee good. 290
In thee there is not half an hour's life.
The treacherous instrument is in thy hand,
Unbated and envenomed. The foul practice[81]
Hath turned itself on me. Lo, here I lie,
Never to rise again. Thy mother's poisoned. 295
I can no more. The King, the King's to blame.
HAMLET: The point envenomed too?
Then, venom, to thy work. (*Hurts the* KING.)
ALL: Treason! Treason!
KING: O, yet defend me, friends. I am but hurt. 300
HAMLET: Here, thou incestuous, murd'rous, damnèd Dane,
Drink off this potion. Is thy union here?
Follow my mother. (KING *dies.*)
LAERTES: He is justly served.
It is a poison tempered[82] by himself.
Exchange forgiveness with me, noble Hamlet. 305
Mine and my father's death come not upon thee,
Nor thine on me! (*Dies.*)
HAMLET: Heaven make thee free of it! I follow thee.
I am dead, Horatio. Wretched Queen, adieu!
You that look pale and tremble at this chance, 310
That are but mutes[83] or audience to this act,

[79] snare
[80] swoons
[81] deception
[82] mixed
[83] performers who have no words to speak

Had I but time (as this fell sergeant,[84] Death,
Is strict in his arrest) O, I could tell you –
But let it be. Horatio, I am dead;
Thou livest; report me and my cause aright 315
To the unsatisfied.[85]

HORATIO: Never believe it.
I am more an antique Roman[86] than a Dane.
Here's yet some liquor left.

HAMLET: As th' art a man,
Give me the cup. Let go. By heaven, I'll ha't!
O God, Horatio, what a wounded name, 320
Things standing thus unknown, shall live behind me!
If thou didst ever hold me in thy heart,
Absent thee from felicity[87] awhile,
And in this harsh world draw thy breath in pain,
To tell my story. (*A march afar off.* [*Exit* OSRIC.])
What warlike noise is this? 325

(*Enter* OSRIC.)

OSRIC: Young Fortinbras, with conquest come from Poland,
To th' ambassadors of England gives
This warlike volley.

HAMLET: O, I die, Horatio!
The potent poison quite o'ercrows[88] my spirit.
I cannot live to hear the news from England, 330
But I do prophesy th' election lights
On Fortinbras. He has my dying voice.
So tell him, with th' occurrents,[89] more and less,
Which have solicited[90] – the rest is silence. (*Dies.*)

HORATIO: Now cracks a noble heart. Good night, sweet Prince, 335
And flights of angels sing thee to thy rest.

[*March within.*]

Why does the drum come hither?

(*Enter* FORTINBRAS, *with the* AMBASSADORS *with Drum, Colors, and* ATTENDANTS.)

FORTINBRAS: Where is this sight?

HORATIO: What is it you would see?
If aught of woe or wonder, cease your search.

[84] dread sheriff's officers
[85] uninformed
[86] (with reference to the old Roman fashion of suicide)
[87] i.e., the felicity of death
[88] overpowers (as a triumphant cock crows over its weak opponent)
[89] occurrences
[90] incited

FORTINBRAS: This quarry[91] cries on havoc.[92] O proud Death, 340
What feast is toward[93] in thine eternal cell
That thou so many princes at a shot
So bloodily hast struck?

AMBASSADOR: The sight is dismal;
And our affairs from England come too late.
The ears are senseless that should give us hearing 345
To tell him his commandment is fulfilled,
That Rosencrantz and Guildenstern are dead.
Where should we have our thanks?

HORATIO: Not from his[94] mouth,
Had it th' ability of life to thank you.
He never gave commandment for their death. 350
But since, so jump[95] upon this bloody question,
You from the Polack wars, and you from England,
Are here arrived, give order that these bodies
High on a stage[96] be placèd to the view,
And let me speak to th' yet unknowing world 355
How these things came about. So shall you hear
Of carnal, bloody, and unnatural acts,
Of accidental judgments, casual[97] slaughters,
Of deaths put on by cunning and forced cause,
And, in this upshot, purposes mistook 360
Fall'n on th' inventors' heads. All this can I
Truly deliver.

FORTINBRAS: Let us haste to hear it,
And call the noblest to the audience.
For me, with sorrow I embrace my fortune.
I have some rights of memory[98] in this kingdom, 365
Which now to claim my vantage doth invite me.

HORATIO: Of that I shall have also cause to speak,
And from his mouth whose voice will draw on[99] more.
But let this same be presently performed,
Even while men's minds are wild, lest more mischance 370
On[100] plots and errors happen.

FORTINBRAS: Let four captains
Bear Hamlet like a soldier to the stage,
For he was likely, had he been put on,[101]
To have proved most royal; and for his passage[102]

[91] heap of slain bodies
[92] proclaims general slaughter
[93] in preparation
[94] (Claudius's)
[95] precisely
[96] platform
[97] not humanly planned, chance
[98] remembered claims
[99] vote will influence
[100] on top of
[101] advanced (to the throne)
[102] death

The soldiers' music and the rite of war 375
Speak loudly for him.
Take up the bodies. Such a sight as this
Becomes the field,[103] but here shows much amiss.
Go, bid the soldiers shoot.

(*Exeunt marching; after the which a peal of ordnance are shot off.*)

FINIS

When we think of great drama, *Hamlet* is the play likely to come to mind first. In our culture it is *the* play. That a tragedy holds this special place is not strange, for tragedy is a dialogue with the absolute, in which man wrests wisdom and dignity from the inscrutables that defeat him. Tragedy, said Milton, "hath been ever held the gravest, moralest, and most profitable of all other poems." Nor is it surprising that the tragedy is one of Shakespeare's, for no other voice speaks so closely to so many of our deepest concerns as his. What may not be so obvious is why *Hamlet* has been singled out for distinction among all Shakespeare's tragedies. *Othello* has more strength and poignancy of plot; *Antony and Cleopatra* more lyrical intensity and larger imagery of word and action; *King Lear* rawer suffering, greater moral passion, and more titanic utterance. What is the reason for *Hamlet's* unique prestige?

The answer, to judge from two hundred years of criticism, is Hamlet himself, the brightest, wittiest, and most attractive of all Shakespeare's tragic heroes and the hardest to understand. It is not that his motives are unfathomable or that his thought lies too deep for words, for though what he does may surprise us, his actions are always unmistakably his, and his soliloquies express recognizable emotions and rather commonplace thoughts of the satire-against-the-world variety. His language is vivid, precise, and imaginative, sometimes racy and violent, but not dense, and his metaphors are striking but not obscure. The mystery of Hamlet is a *gestalt* of the whole situation of a young man of exquisite sensibility and intelligence called upon to redeem a world from which he feels alienated. Between his intent and his act lies the riddle.

Hamlet is the only intellectual among Shakespeare's tragic protagonists. More than the others, he lives in a world his mind has made. Life at Elsinore, with its various statecraft, preparations for war, court ceremonial, and the comings and goings of embassies, old friends, and traveling players, is "weary, stale, flat, and unprofitable"; Denmark is

[103] battlefield

an "unweeded garden"; and after the Ghost reveals Claudius's crime, Denmark is also a "prison" ruled by a "vice of kings," the "serpent" in Old Hamlet's orchard of innocence, a Cain, whose willing consort is Hamlet's own mother. The corrupted garden-prison holds his mind: "O God, I could be bound in a nutshell and count myself a king of infinite space, were it not that I have bad dreams." His disgust extends to existence itself. The world's "goodly frame" under a "most excellent canopy, . . . this brave, o'erhanging firmament," has become a "sterile promontory" under "a foul and pestilential congregation of vapors." In the most famous of his soliloquies, human life is a catalogue of moral and physical ills. Man is a victim of the cruel paradox of his being. "Infinite in faculties," he is yet nothing but "this quintessence of dust," "crawling between earth and heaven." Because Hamlet's sentience is finer than what it perceives, he is sick with thought, and his madness is more than a ruse. In his affronted and divided imagination, he is a riddle no more to others than to himself. "You would pluck out the heart of my mystery," he cries to Guildenstern and will not and cannot unlock his secret.

The record of *Hamlet* criticism is much more, of course, than the futile record of Guildenstern's folly. Still, if more has been written about *Hamlet* than about any other play, it is because the mystery remains. There is a residue of unexpounded and unexpoundable meaning at the end of even the most searching analysis of any great tragedy. It is part, we feel, of what makes it great. If this quality of elusive enigma behind the accessible coherence of character and event seems stronger in *Hamlet* than in other plays, the reason is that Hamlet's own singular radiance leaves us more aware of tragic human waste and gives greater urgency to the questions we ask of ultimate justice. Shakespeare's other tragic heroes are all, in different ways and to different extents, complicit in the evil that causes their suffering, but Hamlet's debilitation of will and befoulment of imagination are the consequence of his mother's and his uncle's corrupted appetites. His world has failed his trust, but he accepts responsibility for its redemption and dies effecting it.

The reason why so high a price is exacted has often been said to be a flaw in Hamlet himself. A different man, like Laertes or Fortinbras, would have swept to his revenge. By "thinking too precisely on th' event" Hamlet fails to act. When he traces "the noble dust of Alexander" to the bung in a beer barrel, he is still, we may feel, a victim of that terrible reflective clairvoyance which for three long acts has disabled him for the task he is supposed to perform. What good is any human action in the face of the inevitable charnel house realities which the Gravedigger's shovel unearths? Horatio's reply to Hamlet's vision of futility, " 'Twere to consider too curiously to consider so," deepens our sense of Hamlet's tragic isolation. Even the one man whom he wears in his "heart of hearts" refuses to follow him in his pursuit of the ultimate questions. His isolation becomes neither less absolute nor less tragic when we say that common sense sides with Horatio: some queries are better left alone; things are as they are in their inexplicable oddity.

But there is a curious quality about Hamlet's mood in the graveyard scene. He no longer rages against himself for failing to take action against the King. Instead of disgust with the world and himself, there is a kind of stoical acceptance, a resignation to Providence, a realization that "the readiness is all." His absence at sea has changed him. He now confronts the visible evidence that man is the quintessence of dust in a spirit of almost playful fatalism. He has passed through suffering and — like all tragic heroes in the moment of recognition — left mere common sense behind. His mind in Act V is no less penetrating and lucid than before, and it has gained a new composure.

A successfully resolute Hamlet would of course have been the hero of a melodrama, and it is tragedy we want. And what, perhaps, finally defines our sense of what is tragic in the story of Hamlet is not pity that the "vicious mole" of too scrupulous thinking in the nature of the sweet and noble prince caused him fatally to delay his revenge, but rather terror that our existence is such that the highest and finest thought has such consequences. This is to say that the philosophical thrust of the play involves something like an anti-theodicy: rather than justifying the ways of the universe to rebellious man, *Hamlet* is the tragedy of an imagination required to impose value on a dark existence, to resurrect a fallen world. Hamlet's telling Rosencrantz and Guildenstern that "there is nothing either good or bad but thinking makes it so" does not mean that a desperate solipsism is his tragic flaw. Rather, it means that the flaw is in a condition that compels the mind to such desperate freedom.

There are tragedies from the past from which we feel we can infer certain philosophical verities shared alike by playwright and audience. With all their differences, such tragedies share an implicit belief in a hierarchy of created things, sustained by stable laws which human nature, in its difficult duality of mind and body, must come to terms with or else suffer. Such shared assumptions presumably made for a community not just of belief but of feeling and imagination which could relate life on stage meaningfully to the entire life of society beyond the stage. In *Hamlet,* too, we are aware of such assumptions, but in *Hamlet* we also feel that they are being tested in a way which is not quite the way in which they are being tested in such plays as Aeschylus's *Oresteia,* Sophocles's Theban trilogy, Shakespeare's own *King Lear,* and Racine's and Ibsen's dramatizations of the destructive conflict between reason and passion in the human soul. Those other tragedies build tragic worlds which are if anything more severe than that of *Hamlet,* and they are no less unflinching or inclusive in their vision of the human predicament. The difference is Hamlet's position of guiltlessness among evil. In no other tragedy do we get a stronger sense of the mysterious fact that man may suffer not despite but because of his virtue. And so we say that still another reason for the unique hold *Hamlet* has on us is that it is the most modern of older tragedies. We take to the element of metaphysical protest in it. We see Hamlet's dilemma as our own: to be or not to be in a world of intolerable seeming. And we like to think of ourselves as victims of that same sickness of the time that paralyzes his enterprise and nearly unbalances his superb mind.

But here a doubt arises. If we claim kinship with Hamlet as existential man deadlocked in absurdity, how did earlier ages see him? Does what we find in the play tell us why it has always seemed more challenging and absorbing than other plays – why it has become, in T. S. Eliot's words, "the Mona Lisa of literature"?

Perhaps it does, because the fashionable terminology in which we try to express our sense of life as grotesque and violent futility may obscure what our experience has in common with that of earlier times. Reviewing the main issues in *Hamlet* criticism, we discover continuity, not always of opinion but of concern, where we too readily may have been assuming discontinuity. Past responses to the play are proof that our age has no monopoly on psychological perplexity and metaphysical anxiety.

The main problem for the critic of *Hamlet* has always been how to account for Hamlet's delayed revenge, however differently critics may have phrased the problem. For Dr. Johnson in the eighteenth century, the delay was a flaw that made Hamlet himself "rather an instrument than an agent" and which rendered his feigned madness dramatically pointless. The Romantics, in a characteristic shift in critical interest, were the first to locate the problem in psychology rather than in dramaturgy, and there it remained until well into the twentieth century. For Goethe, Hamlet was a sensitive soul unfit for the great task of revenge: "There is an oak-tree planted in a precious vase, . . . the roots expand, the vase is shattered." For other Romantic critics, the play was a "tragedy of thought" (Schlegel) and Hamlet himself "the prince of speculative philosophers" (Hazlitt), nearly neurotic in his excessive meditativeness, and defeating his purpose by "continually resolving to do, yet doing nothing but resolve" (Coleridge). A. C. Bradley read *Hamlet* as a tragedy of blighted idealism. It is the play, he says, that "most brings home to us at once the sense of the soul's infinity, and the sense of doom which not only circumscribes that infinity but appears to be its offspring." Ernest Jones, Freud's collaborator and biographer, saw in Hamlet the victim of an Oedipus complex, who has transferred his ambivalent feelings about his real father to the usurper of his father's place. Because the King has achieved what Hamlet subconsciously desires, the taboo on incest and parricide keeps Hamlet from accomplishing his conscious intent. Sir Laurence Olivier's interpretation of Hamlet in his film version of the play was influenced by this Freudian view.

Psychological criticism of *Hamlet* has achieved a number of valuable insights, nowhere more than in Bradley's culminating study. But it leads to both narrowness and over-interpretation because of the fallacy of its tacit assumption that a character in literature is a real person rather than a verbal construct. Unlike people in real life Hamlet will have "life" for as long as Shakespeare's play is being read and staged, but by the same token his life is confined to the words Shakespeare wrote. That is why Bradley's query, "Where was Hamlet at the time of his father's death?" is both unanswerable and irrelevant. Hamlet's whereabouts at the time is not among the facts Shakespeare chose to make part of the imaginary world of *Hamlet.* Had he had real-life existence, it would be logical to say of Hamlet that he either was or was not at (say) Wittenberg when his father died. The conditions of physical life leave no other alternatives, and the alternatives are mutually exclusive. But because he is a creation of Shakespeare's imagination, the proposition does not apply. It isn't just that the text will not admit a definite answer; it will not admit the question. As a fiction Hamlet is not to be supposed to occupy or to have occupied a particular piece of space at a particular time unless words in the play tell us he does or did — the way we learn that Hamlet and Horatio at one time were fellow students at Wittenberg and the way we learn that at one time during the action Hamlet is on board a ship headed for England.

There is an attraction in bestowing the full concreteness of real existence on literary characters who capture our imagination. We pay tribute to the author's ability to create an illusion of life when we do so. But by taking the literary work as a record of reality we are denying it its own particular mode of existence and are violating its integrity as an image — not a copy — of reality. In reaction against Bradley's extrapolated Hamlet, modern critics have seen that "the Prince of Denmark without *Hamlet*" represents a hardly less disabling approach to the play than its proverbial reverse. The Hamlet character is a function of life at the court of Elsinore, just as that life is largely defined for us by Hamlet's attitude toward and behavior in it. When the sentinel in the opening scene is "sick at heart," when Polonius sends Reynaldo to Paris to spy on Laertes, when the Queen in adding her thanks to her husband's innocently reduces Rosencrantz and Guildenstern to the interchangeable nonentities they are by inverting the order of their names, when the dead Polonius will stink up the castle unless his body is found, and when the King speaks of Hamlet as the raging "hectic in my blood," the verbal images establish the moral climate of the Danish court no less relevantly than Hamlet's own direct comments on it. The error of the psychological critics was not their recognition of the central importance of the title character but their tendency to abstract him from his dramatic context in trying to account for his psychology and deriving from it lessons on how to live.

Twentieth-century criticism of Shakespeare is, as a body, much too rich and versatile to be adequately described in a few sentences, but a few examples of post-Bradleyan approaches may suggest its range. Historical criticism has given new perspectives on old problems. The delayed revenge was a conventional feature in Elizabethan revenge tragedy, and Shakespeare's contemporaries are less likely to have regarded Hamlet's procrastination as a psychological puzzle than as a plot device without which Shakespeare would have had no play. Shakespeare may also have sought to add topical relevance to his exploitation of a popular dramatic convention by so altering his source as to make the action reflect political hesitancy in high places — a powerful topic during the last years of Queen Elizabeth's reign, when the rebellious Earl of Essex threatened the stability of the state. T. S. Eliot refused to grant *Hamlet* a place among Shakespeare's masterpieces on the neoclassical grounds that great literature is depersonalized emotion and a son's disgust with his mother's sexual sin is an emotion that has not found, and perhaps could not find, adequate expression in the plot that came to Shakespeare's hand. For some reason, Shakespeare was unable to turn the old story into a stageable equivalent for Hamlet's feeling; he failed to find — Eliot's phrase has entered the critical vocabulary — an "objective correlative" for it, and the enigmatic quality of the play is a sign of artistic failure rather than of success. Eliot's sense of disparity between act and feeling in *Hamlet* has not been shared by those critics who, without constituting a single school of criticism, have added to our understanding of the play by treating it as a complex, multi-leveled formal structure, in which verbal and scenic imagery, rhetoric, plot patterns, and Renaissance concepts about man, the state, and the universe collaborate in an extended metaphor of human life as a system of rival ethical norms in conflict.

One of the distinctive strengths of current Shakespearean criticism — or so, at least, it appears to a contemporary — is its recognition of the value of critical pluralism. Textual criticism and history of ideas, political and social history, and scholarly findings on the Elizabethan playhouse and on its literary and theatrical conventions are requisite tools for a responsible, close study of the way in which the local verbal textures cumulatively build the inclusive meaning of the plays. Before he can argue that Hamlet is a conventional revenger figure, or the scapegoat prince of archetypal myth who must die in the process of redeeming his diseased land, or a soul divided against itself and made indecisive by a conflict between Christian conscience and the imperative of a more primitive ethos for private revenge, the critic must be sure he is working with a sound text of a play that was written for a certain kind of theater.

In addition to providing his colleagues with plays to act in, Shakespeare was an actor himself in the theatrical company of which he was a shareholding member. Before 1603 the company was known as the Chamberlain's Men, and after the succession of King James I as the King's Men. If it ever occurred to Shakespeare to label his profession, chances are that he would have thought of himself as a man of the theater rather than as an author. What little evidence there is of his acting career suggests that he took secondary parts. According to tradition, he was the original Ghost in *Hamlet* vis à vis Richard Burbage's Prince.

In 1598–99 the Chamberlain's Men removed the lumber from an older theater building north of the Thames to a site on the Bankside south of the river and used it to build the Globe Theater, which remained its exclusive home for the next ten years. In 1609 the company began to give performances in the Blackfriars Theater within the city precincts during the winter season. In 1613 the Globe was burned down during a performance of Shakespeare's *Henry VIII.* The second Globe was built the following year. It survived until 1644, when it was pulled down during the regime of the theater-hating Puritans.

We don't know the exact shape and size of the first Globe, in which presumably *Hamlet* was first performed. Reconstruction of the original Globe playhouse has been an issue of scholarly controversy in this century. The description that follows covers features which modern research fairly confidently has established as typical of the London playhouses in late Elizabethan and Jacobean times. There is no reason to believe that they were all essentially identical in structure.

The only Elizabethan theater for which a building contract has been preserved is the Fortune, built in 1600. But because it was explicitly modeled on the Globe, the contractors, unfortunately for us, did not specify other details of construction than those in which the Fortune was to differ from the Globe. From the fact that the Fortune contract calls for a square structure, we may infer that the Globe was not square. We know there were other round or polygonal theaters in Elizabethan London. An engraved panorama of London in the early 1640's designates a round building as the Globe, but the accuracy of the view is in doubt. The Globe probably had three-tiered galleries with seats for those who could afford them; the poorer of the audience ("the groundlings") watched the performance standing in the "pit," the unroofed courtyard which the galleries surrounded on all sides. On one side, the third story of the building housed the musicians and the trumpeter who announced the beginning of the play. The second story was an upper stage, or "balcony." On the ground floor was a "tiring-house," or dressingroom, for the actors. Either two or three doors connected the tiring-house with the "apron," a platform stage that was the main acting area and which extended perhaps the entire length of the tiring-house and projected half way into the open yard. (The Fortune stage was 43 feet wide and about 27 feet deep.) The platform was raised 5 to 6 feet above the ground to make room for entries and exits of ghosts and witches through a trapdoor in the stage floor. During performance the space below the apron was covered by curtains. Part of the apron was covered by a roof set on posts, "the heavens." A particularly difficult point in the reconstruction of the Elizabethan playhouse is whether an inner stage or recess back of the apron was used for action set in such places as bedrooms, studies, and caves, or whether such scenes were acted in semi-permanent booths or pavilions on the apron itself, with curtain walls that could be pulled to open the interior to the view of the audience. Such structures would represent a development of the "mansions" on the pageant stage of the medieval liturgical plays and the later moralities, which were still being performed in Stratford during Shakespeare's youth. Costumes were often sumptuous, and there was some use of props. One contemporary list of props includes a rock, "three tombs," a "Hell mouth," a cage, a bay tree, a "wooden canopy," an altar, a bed, and two "moss banks." But there was no illusionistic scene painting, and considering the facts that performances took place in daylight, that adolescent boys played women's parts, and that technical devices for creating realistic effects were limited, the whole production must have been stylized, creating a symbolic rather than a lifelike "world." The largest Elizabethan playhouses could seat about 2,000 spectators or perhaps more. For all that, they were intimate theaters, in which actor and audience were both physically and psychologically closer than in a modern, picture-frame structure, where an audience seated in darkness faces an artificially lighted peekbox stage. And the absence of elaborate sets and technical machinery and of act and scene divisions made for a fluid, uncluttered, and fast-paced dramatic form.

*Hamlet* was entered in the Stationers' Register on July 26, 1602. The Register was a list of the titles which members of the company, or guild, of booksellers intended to publish. Its main purpose was to protect the publisher-bookseller's copyright, but it also facilitated the government's control over printed matter. *Hamlet* does not appear in the list of Shakespeare's plays included in *Palladis Tamia,* a kind of miscellany or commonplace book on literary and other topics, which Francis Meres, a schoolmaster divine, wrote in 1598. Since Meres lists just about every play that we know or have good reasons for believing that Shakespeare had written by 1598 (the only exceptions are the three *Henry VI* plays and *The Taming of the Shrew*, which may be the play that Meres calls "Love labours wonne"), a reasonable inference is that Shakespeare wrote *Hamlet* after Meres compiled his list. There have been arguments for a more accurate date for the composition of the play within the 1598–1602 period, but in the absence of conclusive evidence it must suffice here to say that scholars consider 1601–02 a likely date.

The play first appeared in print in 1603 in a corrupt and almost certainly unauthorized (pirated) text, the First (or "bad") Quarto, which is only a little more than half the length of the Second Quarto, which appeared in two imprints in 1604 and 1605, respectively. ("Quarto" and "folio" are printer's terms referring to the format of the printed sheets.) The Second Quarto was probably based on Shakespeare's own unrevised manuscript. It includes some 200 lines not in the Folio edition published in 1623. The Folio was a collection of all but one of Shakespeare's plays, which was prepared by two of Shakespeare's colleagues in the King's Company, John Heminges and Henry Condell. On the other hand, the Folio includes 85 lines not in the Second Quarto. Presumably, both sets of cuts were authentic — that is, representing Shakespeare's own editing of his play. Shakespeare did not regard his plays as books to be printed but as scripts to be performed, and the discrepancies between the Second Quarto and the Folio texts are accounted for if we consider both texts acting versions used at different times during provincial tours. There are no divisions into acts and scenes in either of the two quartos, and in the Folio such divisions are restricted to the beginning of the first two acts. Modern editions of *Hamlet* are based on both the Second Quarto and the Folio.

As for all his plays (except, possibly, the first, *Love's Labor Lost*), Shakespeare found his plot in older sources. His most immediate source was an earlier *Hamlet* play, written, probably by Thomas Kyd, some time before 1590. There are references to this play in several contemporary sources, and there are good reasons why no one today believes the references to be to Shakespeare's play. The ultimate source for this *Ur-Hamlet* (or "original" *Hamlet*) is a legendary Scandinavian story first given literary form about 1200 in a *Danish History* written in Latin by the Danish historian Saxo Grammaticus. Saxo's history was first printed in 1514. In 1576 the Frenchman Belleforest wrote an adaptation of it for his *Histoires Tragiques*, from which, or possibly through an English intermediary, it came to the author of *Ur-Hamlet*. The Ghost, we know, was an important figure in *Ur-Hamlet*. Except for it and the play-within-the-play, all the major features of Shakespeare's plot are in both Saxo and Belleforest, but there are also differences. In the early narrative versions Hamlet is a teen-ager, the murder of his father by his uncle is public knowledge, Hamlet feigns madness to save his life, the King suspects the sham and tries to expose it by using a light-virtued girl as a lure, and in the end Hamlet, with aid from England, succeeds in killing his uncle by burning down the royal hall where the King sits drinking with his men.

A seventeenth-century German play, *Der Bestrafte Brudermord* (*Fratricide Punished*), apparently derives from *Ur-Hamlet* and gives us some clues to its content. But since *Ur-Hamlet* is not extant, we don't know the exact extent of Shakespeare's indebtedness to it. Very likely it was quite strong. By all indications, *Ur-Hamlet* was a typical revenge drama in the tradition of Seneca's tragedies, which had been translated into English in 1580 and almost immediately had become a vogue. One reason for attributing *Ur-Hamlet* to Thomas Kyd is his *Spanish Tragedy* (probably 1586–87), in which the ghost of a murdered son appears to his father for revenge and the father feigns madness in order to get at his enemies. With its revenge plot, midnight scenes, ghostly apparitions, brooding violence, real and dissembled madness, treachery, poison, eavesdropping, and a stage full of corpses at the end, Shakespeare's *Hamlet* obviously belongs to the same genre. Shakespeare's achievement was the transformation of his sensationalist source into what Maynard Mack calls "a paradigm of the life of man."

The plot of *Hamlet* is not a model of compact unilinearity; if it had been, it could not have served as vehicle for a view of life as a mesh of interlocking destinies in a fallen and disordered world of disguised purpose and capricious fate. Its shape is huge, its harmony of proportion is not self-evident, and its pace is irregular. But it does have shaped coherence.

Gradually, other lives are drawn into and destroyed by the clash of the "mighty opposites" of criminal and avenger: the Queen, the Polonius family, Rosencrantz and Guildenstern. The conflict spreads to involve the political relations between Denmark and England. In the background, and intermittently entering the on-stage action, Fortinbras gathers and moves his Norwegian forces. Because his effective military bustle contrasts with Hamlet's fretful inaction, it is as if Hamlet's ordeal is being given symbolic sanction as a form of heroic warfare when Fortinbras at the end orders a soldier's funeral for the dead Prince. The analogy-with-difference among Hamlet, Fortinbras, and Laertes, all young men with a father to avenge, has both a cohesive and a thematic function, with Fortinbras occupying an intermediary position between Hamlet's scrupulous reflectiveness and Laertes's fickle and febrile rashness. But the main coherence of action in the play is in Hamlet's inner movement through three phases, divided by distinct breaks in the surface continuity of plot: a lapse in time between Acts I and II, and the hero's absence both from the stage and from Denmark between IV, 5 and V, 1. In the first phase, Hamlet's world-weary melancholia finds its object and its potential relief when the Ghost reveals the King's crime (Act I). In the second, his purpose dissipates itself in procrastination interrupted by futile bursts of violence (against Ophelia, Polonius, and the Queen) and self-reproach (Acts II–IV). In the third, his new calm of mind after his return from sea leads to his acceptance of Laertes's challenge and the consequent accomplishment of his avenger's mission in catastrophe (Act V). Alternating between active and passive suffering, the reluctant righter of the disjointed world undergoes a purgatory of the spirit, until the "cursèd spite" that directs his fate is laid to rest in his tragic triumph.

If stages in Hamlet's progress of soul define the tragic action, imagery defines the kind of world in which the action takes place. The master image of the play is that of deceptive appearance — guilt masking itself as innocence, disease as health, corruption as wholesomeness. The king who rules this world sees himself as a painted harlot. It is a world in which human motives must be forever scanned, where the worth of any action is in doubt, and where justice itself becomes suspect and arbitrary. Disaster and death follow in the path of the noble avenger; he harrows the Danish court like some mortal disease. On the melodrama of the old story Shakespeare's consistent image patterns have grafted a philosophical problem play.

When the Queen in Act I tries to dispel her son's depression by reminding him that a father's death is a natural occurrence that should not "seem particular" to him, Hamlet replies that he knows not "seems." The reply is ironic, for he knows little else. He is surrounded by false or uncertain appearance. The Ghost who looks like his father may be a demon from Hell come to lure his soul to perdition. His mother, once the seeming paragon of chaste fidelity, is actually frail flesh incarnate, her lust blistering even "the fair forehead of an innocent love." Ophelia paints her face and lets herself be used as a decoy. A joyful reunion with old friends turns into an encounter with enemy spies. When Hamlet finds the King at prayer, the moment of retribution seems at hand. Then reflection intervenes: killing the villain at his prayer would be to send his soul straight to Heaven and would seem like a poor kind of revenge. But here is seeming within seeming. The appearance of prayer is false; this *was* the moment for striking. Hamlet visits his mother, who seems to be alone but isn't. He lunges at the King behind the arras, but it isn't the King. He is to be sent to England to recover his wits, but actually to be killed. After his return, Laertes and he are to seal their reconciliation in a friendly exercise of arms, but the illusion of deadly combat is reality, and the refreshing drink is poison.

Such is the nature of Hamlet's world that he who knows not "seems" himself partakes in the general deceptiveness. He begins his revenge by dissembling madness. Deadly hatred motivates his "antic disposition," not love, as Polonius thinks. He uses a troupe of professional make-believers to expose the King's pretended innocence. What looks like an evening's pleasant entertainment for the court is actually the King's confrontation with his own crime; that is the mirror the players' art holds up to the King's corrupted nature. After the mousetrap scene, the King realizes that Hamlet is a guileful and dangerous enemy and not the madcap fooler with a secret that he had seemed to be. Hamlet sends his unsuspecting companions to their execution in England. He equivocates with Laertes when he tells him it was his madness and not his true self that killed Polonius. Where, finally, is the dividing line between lunacy and sanity, guilt and innocence, illusion and reality, right and wrong? Is Hamlet simply play-acting when he rages against Ophelia, or is he relieving his mind of pained outrage at the deceptiveness that taints even his love?

The mere seemingness of all things is one main motif. Another is the image of "rank corruption," which, "mining all within, / Infects unseen" until it finally breaks out. It first appears in Horatio's early speech that the coming of the Ghost "bodes some strange eruption to our state," words that prophetically describe the entire course of events that follow. It is implicit in Marcellus's words after the second appearance of the Ghost, "Something is rotten in the state of Denmark," and in the Ghost's description of the way his brother poisoned him. It turns up in other passages as well.

The deception motif and the image of concealed corruption slowly ripening meet in King Claudius, the smiling villain who is the secret ulcer that infects the entire body politic. In Renaissance concepts of monarchy, the king embodies his nation. In Rosencrantz's words:

> The cess of majesty
> Dies not alone, but like a gulf doth draw
> What's near it with it. . . .
> Never alone
> Did the King sigh, but with a general groan.

The spreading infection that follows the evil act of murdering a king disintegrates the murderer-usurper's realm on all its levels. The state is first threatened with invasion, then with Laertes's rebellion, and is, in the end, in fact invaded. Natural family relationships turn unnatural following the initial violence done to brother by brother: wife is set against husband, mother (and "father") against son, and lovers are separated. On the level of individual life Ophelia's madness is a dissolution of the natural order in the self — chaos subverting the harmonious microcosm of man.

On the surface, all seems fair in Claudius's Denmark. He has succeeded to the throne and married his brother's wife with the approval of the whole Council. (Whether the union is to be considered incestuous or not is one of the play's many uncertainties.) He rules with wisdom, authority, and proper pomp. His first political act is a piece of successful diplomacy. But corruption "inward breaks": ruling without the grace of God, he is unable to pray; guilt-ridden, he is forever draining goblets of wine; self-loathing, he prefers to execute his designs through others.

The graveyard scene at the beginning of Act V visualizes the exhumation of the hidden corruption in anticipation of the climax at the end. Its macabre comedy — jokes among skulls — has human life itself as theme. The emperor's might, the lawyer's tricks, the jester's songs and gibes, the lady's beauty — all end in bones, mold, and stench. What the Gravedigger discloses symbolizes the reality of Claudius's rotten realm, and Clown and Prince, the two supreme realists in the play, share the same task. The deception that masks Denmark's sickness with fair appearance is the same deception that masks the ripening corruption within all life. Hamlet completes his task only when he is already dying and leaves his purged heritage politically powerless, as if the restoration of innocence were not a viable condition. His death is an escape from an existence in which he has been both an exile and a prisoner.

# MOLIÈRE

# Tartuffe

*Translated by Richard Wilbur*

CHARACTERS

MME PERNELLE, Orgon's mother
ORGON, Elmire's husband
ELMIRE, Orgon's wife
DAMIS, Orgon's son, Elmire's stepson
MARIANE, Orgon's daughter, Elmire's stepdaughter, in love with Valère
VALÈRE, in love with Mariane
CLÉANTE, Orgon's brother-in-law
TARTUFFE, a hypocrite
DORINE, Mariane's lady's-maid
M. LOYAL, a bailiff
A POLICE OFFICER
FLIPOTE, Mme Pernelle's maid

*The scene throughout:* ORGON*'s house in Paris*

# ACT I

## SCENE 1

MADAME PERNELLE and FLIPOTE, her maid
ELMIRE DORINE CLÉANTE
MARIANE DAMIS

MADAME PERNELLE: Come, come, Flipote; it's time I left this place.
ELMIRE: I can't keep up, you walk at such a pace.
MADAME PERNELLE: Don't trouble, child; no need to show me out.
It's not your manners I'm concerned about.
ELMIRE: We merely pay you the respect we owe. 5
But, Mother, why this hurry? Must you go?
MADAME PERNELLE: I must. This house appalls me. No one in it
Will pay attention for a single minute.
Children, I take my leave much vexed in spirit.
I offer good advice, but you won't hear it. 10
You all break in and chatter on and on.
It's like a madhouse with the keeper gone.
DORINE: If . . .
MADAME PERNELLE: Girl, you talk too much, and I'm afraid
You're far too saucy for a lady's-maid.
You push in everywhere and have your say. 15
DAMIS: But . . .
MADAME PERNELLE: You, boy, grow more foolish every day.
To think my grandson should be such a dunce!
I've said a hundred times, if I've said it once,
That if you keep the course on which you've started,
You'll leave your worthy father broken-hearted. 20
MARIANE: I think . . .
MADAME PERNELLE: And you, his sister, seems so pure,
So shy, so innocent, and so demure.
But you know what they say about still waters.
I pity parents with secretive daughters.
ELMIRE: Now, Mother . . .
MADAME PERNELLE: And as for you, child, let me add 25
That your behavior is extremely bad,
And a poor example for these children, too.
Their dear, dead mother did far better than you.

---

You're much too free with money, and I'm distressed
To see you so elaborately dressed. 30
When it's one's husband that one aims to please,
One has no need of costly fripperies.

CLÉANTE: Oh, Madam, really . . .

MADAME PERNELLE: You are her brother, Sir,
And I respect and love you; yet if I were
My son, this lady's good and pious spouse, 35
I wouldn't make you welcome in my house.
You're full of worldly counsels which, I fear,
Aren't suitable for decent folk to hear.
I've spoken bluntly, Sir; but it behooves us
Not to mince words when righteous fervor moves us. 40

DAMIS: Your man Tartuffe is full of holy speeches . . .

MADAME PERNELLE: And practises precisely what he preaches.
He's a fine man, and should be listened to.
I will not hear him mocked by fools like you.

DAMIS: Good God! Do you expect me to submit 45
To the tyranny of that carping hypocrite?
Must we forgo all joys and satisfactions
Because that bigot censures all our actions?

DORINE: To hear him talk – and he talks all the time –
There's nothing one can do that's not a crime. 50
He rails at everything, your dear Tartuffe.

MADAME PERNELLE: Whatever he reproves deserves reproof.
He's out to save your souls, and all of you
Must love him, as my son would have you do.

DAMIS: Ah no, Grandmother, I could never take 55
To such a rascal, even for my father's sake.
That's how I feel, and I shall not dissemble.
His every action makes me seethe and tremble
With helpless anger, and I have no doubt
That he and I will shortly have it out. 60

DORINE: Surely it is a shame and a disgrace
To see this man usurp the master's place –
To see this beggar who, when first he came,
Had not a shoe or shoestring to his name
So far forget himself that he behaves 65
As if the house were his, and we his slaves.

MADAME PERNELLE: Well, mark my words, your souls would fare far better
If you obeyed his precepts to the letter.

DORINE: You see him as a saint. I'm far less awed;
In fact, I see right through him. He's a fraud. 70

MADAME PERNELLE: Nonsense!
DORINE: His man Laurent's the same, or worse;
I'd not trust either with a penny purse.
MADAME PERNELLE: I can't say what his servant's morals may be;
His own great goodness I can guarantee.
You all regard him with distaste and fear 75
Because he tells you what you're loath to hear,
Condemns your sins, points out your moral flaws,
And humbly strives to further Heaven's cause.
DORINE: If sin is all that bothers him, why is it
He's so upset when folk drop in to visit? 80
Is Heaven so outraged by a social call
That he must prophesy against us all?
I'll tell you what I think: if you ask me,
He's jealous of my mistress' company.
MADAME PERNELLE: Rubbish! (*To* ELMIRE.) He's not alone, child, in
complaining 85
Of all your promiscuous entertaining.
Why, the whole neighborhood's upset, I know,
By all these carriages that come and go,
With crowds of guests parading in and out
And noisy servants loitering about. 90
In all of this, I'm sure there's nothing vicious;
But why give people cause to be suspicious?
CLÉANTE: They need no cause; they'll talk in any case.
Madam, this world would be a joyless place
If, fearing what malicious tongues might say, 95
We locked our doors and turned our friends away.
And even if one did so dreary a thing,
D'you think those tongues would cease their chattering?
One can't fight slander; it's a losing battle;
Let us instead ignore their tittle-tattle. 100
Let's strive to live by conscience' clear decrees,
And let the gossips gossip as they please.
DORINE: If there is talk against us, I know the source:
It's Daphne and her little husband, of course.
Those who have greatest cause for guilt and shame 105
Are quickest to besmirch a neighbor's name.
When there's a chance for libel, they never miss it;
When something can be made to seem illicit
They're off at once to spread the joyous news,
Adding to fact what fantasies they choose. 110
By talking up their neighbor's indiscretions
They seek to camouflage their own transgressions,

Hoping that others' innocent affairs
Will lend a hue of innocence to theirs,
Or that their own black guilt will come to seem 115
Part of a general shady color-scheme.

MADAME PERNELLE: All that is quite irrelevant. I doubt
That anyone's more virtuous and devout
Than dear Orante; and I'm informed that she
Condemns your mode of life most vehemently. 120

DORINE: Oh, yes, she's strict, devout, and has no taint
Of worldliness; in short, she seems a saint.
But it was time which taught her that disguise;
She's thus because she can't be otherwise.
So long as her attractions could enthrall, 125
She flounced and flirted and enjoyed it all,
But now that they're no longer what they were
She quits a world which fast is quitting her,
And wears a veil of virtue to conceal
Her bankrupt beauty and her lost appeal. 130
That's what becomes of old coquettes today:
Distressed when all their lovers fall away,
They see no recourse but to play the prude,
And so confer a style on solitude.
Thereafter, they're severe with everyone, 135
Condemning all our actions, pardoning none,
And claiming to be pure, austere, and zealous
When, if the truth were known, they're merely jealous,
And cannot bear to see another know
The pleasures time has forced them to forgo. 140

MADAME PERNELLE (*initially to* ELMIRE): That sort of talk is what you like to hear;
Therefore you'd have us all keep still, my dear,
While Madam rattles on the livelong day.
Nevertheless, I mean to have my say.
I tell you that you're blest to have Tartuffe 145
Dwelling, as my son's guest, beneath this roof;
That Heaven has sent him to forestall its wrath
By leading you, once more, to the true path;
That all he reprehends its reprehensible,
And that you'd better heed him, and be sensible. 150
These visits, balls, and parties in which you revel
Are nothing but inventions of the Devil.
One never hears a word that's edifying:
Nothing but chaff and foolishness and lying,
As well as vicious gossip in which one's neighbor 155
Is cut to bits with epee, foil, and saber.

People of sense are driven half-insane
At such affairs, where noise and folly reign
And reputations perish thick and fast.
As a wise preacher said on Sunday last, 160
Parties are Towers of Babylon, because
The guests all babble on with never a pause;
And then he told a story which, I think . . .
(*To* CLÉANTE.) I heard that laugh, Sir, and I saw that wink!
Go find your silly friends and laugh some more! 165
Enough; I'm going; don't show me to the door.
I leave this household much dismayed and vexed;
I cannot say when I shall see you next.
(*Slapping* FLIPOTE.) Wake up, don't stand there gaping into space!
I'll slap some sense into that stupid face. 170
Move, move, you slut.

## SCENE 2

CLÉANTE
DORINE

CLÉANTE: I think I'll stay behind;
I want no further pieces of her mind.
How that old lady . . .
DORINE: Oh, what wouldn't she say
If she could hear you speak of her that way!
She'd thank you for the *lady,* but I'm sure 5
She'd find the *old* a little premature.
CLÉANTE: My, what a scene she made, and what a din!
And how this man Tartuffe has taken her in!
DORINE: Yes, but her son is even worse deceived;
His folly must be seen to be believed. 10
In the late troubles, he played an able part
And served his king with wise and loyal heart,
But he's quite lost his senses since he fell
Beneath Tartuffe's infatuating spell.
He calls him brother, and loves him as his life, 15
Preferring him to mother, child, or wife.
In him and him alone will he confide;
He's made him his confessor and his guide;
He pets and pampers him with love more tender
Than any pretty mistress could engender, 20
Gives him the place of honor when they dine,
Delights to see him gorging like a swine,
Stuffs him with dainties till his guts distend,
And when he belches, cries "God bless you, friend!"

In short, he's mad; he worships him; he dotes; 25
His deeds he marvels at, his words he quotes,
Thinking each act a miracle, each word
Oracular as those that Moses heard.
Tartuffe, much pleased to find so easy a victim,
Has in a hundred ways beguiled and tricked him, 30
Milked him of money, and with his permission
Established here a sort of Inquisition.
Even Laurent, his lackey, dares to give
Us arrogant advice on how to live;
He sermonizes us in thundering tones 35
And confiscates our ribbons and colognes.
Last week he tore a kerchief into pieces
Because he found it pressed in a *Life of Jesus:*
He said it was a sin to juxtapose
Unholy vanities and holy prose. 40

## SCENE 3

ELMIRE DAMIS DORINE
MARIANE CLÉANTE

ELMIRE (*to* CLÉANTE): You did well not to follow; she stood in the door
And said *verbatim* all she'd said before.
I saw my husband coming. I think I'd best
Go upstairs now, and take a little rest.
CLÉANTE: I'll wait and greet him here; then I must go. 5
I've really only time to say hello.
DAMIS: Sound him about my sister's wedding, please.
I think Tartuffe's against it, and that he's
Been urging Father to withdraw his blessing.
As you well know, I'd find that most distressing. 10
Unless my sister and Valère can marry,
My hopes to wed *his* sister will miscarry,
And I'm determined . . .
DORINE: He's coming.

## SCENE 4

ORGON
CLÉANTE
DORINE

ORGON: Ah, Brother, good-day.
CLÉANTE: Well, welcome back. I'm sorry I can't stay.
How was the country? Blooming, I trust, and green?

ORGON: Excuse me, Brother; just one moment.
(*To* DORINE.) Dorine . . .
(*To* CLÉANTE.) To put my mind at rest, I always learn 5
The household news the moment I return.
(*To* DORINE.) Has all been well, these two days I've been gone?
How are the family? What's been going on?
DORINE: Your wife, two days ago, had a bad fever,
And a fierce headache which refused to leave her. 10
ORGON: Ah. And Tartuffe?
DORINE: Tartuffe? Why, he's round and red,
Bursting with health, and excellently fed.
ORGON: Poor fellow!
DORINE: That night, the mistress was unable
To take a single bite at the dinner-table.
Her headache-pains, she said, were simply hellish. 15
ORGON: Ah. And Tartuffe?
DORINE: He ate his meal with relish,
And zealously devoured in her presence
A leg of mutton and a brace of pheasants.
ORGON: Poor fellow!
DORINE: Well, the pains continued strong,
And so she tossed and tossed the whole night long, 20
Now icy-cold, now burning like a flame.
We sat beside her bed till morning came.
ORGON: Ah. And Tartuffe?
DORINE: Why, having eaten, he rose
And sought his room, already in a doze,
Got into his warm bed, and snored away 25
In perfect peace until the break of day.
ORGON: Poor fellow!
DORINE: After much ado, we talked her
Into dispatching someone for the doctor.
He bled her, and the fever quickly fell.
ORGON: Ah. And Tartuffe?
DORINE: He bore it very well. 30
To keep his cheerfulness at any cost,
And make up for the blood *Madame* had lost,
He drank, at lunch, four beakers full of port.
ORGON: Poor fellow!
DORINE: Both are doing well, in short.
I'll go and tell *Madame* that you've expressed 35
Keen sympathy and anxious interest.

## SCENE 5

ORGON
CLÉANTE

CLÉANTE: That girl was laughing in your face, and though
I've no wish to offend you, even so
I'm bound to say that she had some excuse.
How can you possibly be such a goose?
Are you so dazed by this man's hocus-pocus 5
That all the world, save him, is out of focus?
You've given him clothing, shelter, food, and care;
Why must you also . . .
ORGON: Brother, stop right there.
You do not know the man of whom you speak.
CLÉANTE: I grant you that. But my judgment's not so weak 10
That I can't tell, by his effect on others . . .
ORGON: Ah, when you meet him, you two will be like brothers!
There's been no loftier soul since time began.
He is a man who . . . a man who . . . an excellent man.
To keep his precepts is to be reborn, 15
And view this dunghill of a world with scorn.
Yes, thanks to him I'm a changed man indeed.
Under his tutelage my soul's been freed
From earthly loves, and every human tie:
My mother, children, brother, and wife could die, 20
And I'd not feel a single moment's pain.
CLÉANTE: That's a fine sentiment, Brother; most humane.
ORGON: Oh, had you seen Tartuffe as I first knew him,
Your heart, like mine, would have surrendered to him.
He used to come into our church each day 25
And humbly kneel nearby, and start to pray.
He'd draw the eyes of everybody there
By the deep fervor of his heartfelt prayer;
He'd sigh and weep, and sometimes with a sound
Of rapture he would bend and kiss the ground; 30
And when I rose to go, he'd run before
To offer me holy-water at the door.
His serving-man, no less devout than he,
Informed me of his master's poverty;
I gave him gifts, but in his humbleness 35
He'd beg me every time to give him less.
"Oh, that's too much," he'd cry, "too much by twice!
I don't deserve it. The half, Sir, would suffice."
And when I wouldn't take it back, he'd share

Half of it with the poor, right then and there. 40
At length, Heaven prompted me to take him in
To dwell with us, and free our souls from sin.
He guides our lives, and to protect my honor
Stays by my wife, and keeps an eye upon her;
He tells me whom she sees, and all she does, 45
And seems more jealous than I ever was!
And how austere he is! Why, he can detect
A mortal sin where you would least suspect;
In smallest trifles, he's extremely strict.
Last week, his conscience was severely pricked 50
Because, while praying, he had caught a flea
And killed it, so he felt, too wrathfully.

CLÉANTE: Good God, man! Have you lost your common sense —
Or is this all some joke at my expense?
How can you stand there and in all sobriety . . . 55

ORGON: Brother, your language savors of impiety.
Too much free-thinking's made your faith unsteady,
And as I've warned you many times already,
'Twill get you into trouble before you're through.

CLÉANTE: So I've been told before by dupes like you: 60
Being blind, you'd have all others blind as well;
The clear-eyed man you call an infidel,
And he who sees through humbug and pretense
Is charged, by you, with want of reverence.
Spare me your warnings, Brother; I have no fear 65
Of speaking out, for you and Heaven to hear,
Against affected zeal and pious knavery.
There's true and false in piety, as in bravery,
And just as those whose courage shines the most
In battle, are the least inclined to boast, 70
So those whose hearts are truly pure and lowly
Don't make a flashy show of being holy.
There's a vast difference, so it seems to me,
Between true piety and hypocrisy:
How do you fail to see it, may I ask? 75
Is not a face quite different from a mask?
Cannot sincerity and cunning art,
Reality and semblance, be told apart?
Are scarecrows just like men, and do you hold
That a false coin is just as good as gold? 80
Ah, Brother, man's a strangely fashioned creature
Who seldom is content to follow Nature,
But recklessly pursues his inclination
Beyond the narrow bounds of moderation,

And often, by transgressing Reason's laws, 85
Perverts a lofty aim or noble cause.
A passing observation, but it applies.

ORGON: I see, dear Brother, that you're profoundly wise;
You harbor all the insight of the age.
You are our one clear mind, our only sage, 90
The era's oracle, its Cato too,
And all mankind are fools compared to you.

CLÉANTE: Brother, I don't pretend to be a sage,
Nor have I all the wisdom of the age.
There's just one insight I would dare to claim: 95
I know that true and false are not the same;
And just as there is nothing I more revere
Than a soul whose faith is steadfast and sincere,
Nothing that I more cherish and admire
Than honest zeal and true religious fire, 100
So there is nothing that I find more base
Than specious piety's dishonest face —
Than these bold mountebanks, these histrios
Whose impious mummeries and hollow shows
Exploit our love of Heaven, and make a jest 105
Of all that men think holiest and best;
These calculating souls who offer prayers
Not to their Maker, but as public wares,
And seek to buy respect and reputation
With lifted eyes and sighs of exaltation; 110
These charlatans, I say, whose pilgrim souls
Proceed, by way of Heaven, toward earthly goals,
Who weep and pray and swindle and extort,
Who preach the monkish life, but haunt the court,
Who make their zeal the partner of their vice — 115
Such men are vengeful, sly, and cold as ice,
And when there is an enemy to defame
They cloak their spite in fair religion's name,
Their private spleen and malice being made
To seem a high and virtuous crusade, 120
Until, to mankind's reverent applause,
They crucify their foe in Heaven's cause.
Such knaves are all too common; yet, for the wise,
True piety isn't hard to recognize,
And, happily, these present times provide us 125
With bright examples to instruct and guide us.
Consider Ariston and Périandre;
Look at Oronte, Alcidamas, Clitandre;
Their virtue is acknowledged; who could doubt it?

But you won't hear them beat the drum about it. 130
They're never ostentatious, never vain,
And their religion's moderate and humane;
It's not their way to criticize and chide:
They think censoriousness a mark of pride,
And therefore, letting others preach and rave, 135
They show, by deeds, how Christians should behave.
They think no evil of their fellow man,
But judge of him as kindly as they can.
They don't intrigue and wangle and conspire;
To lead a good life is their one desire; 140
The sinner wakes no rancorous hate in them;
It is the sin alone which they condemn;
Nor do they try to show a fiercer zeal
For Heaven's cause than Heaven itself could feel.
These men I honor, these men I advocate 145
As models for us all to emulate.
Your man is not their sort at all, I fear:
And, while your praise of him is quite sincere,
I think that you've been dreadfully deluded.

ORGON: Now then, dear Brother, is your speech concluded? 150

CLÉANTE: Why, yes.

ORGON: Your servant, Sir. (*He turns to go.*)

CLÉANTE: No, Brother; wait.
There's one more matter. You agreed of late
That young Valère might have your daughter's hand.

ORGON: I did.

CLÉANTE: And set the date, I understand.

ORGON: Quite so.

CLÉANTE: You've now postponed it; is that true? 155

ORGON: No doubt.

CLÉANTE: The match no longer pleases you?

ORGON: Who knows?

CLÉANTE: D'you mean to go back on your word?

ORGON: I won't say that.

CLÉANTE: Has anything occurred
Which might entitle you to break your pledge?

ORGON: Perhaps.

CLÉANTE: Why must you hem, and haw, and hedge? 160
The boy asked me to sound you in this affair . . .

ORGON: It's been a pleasure.

CLÉANTE: But what shall I tell Valère?

ORGON: Whatever you like.

CLÉANTE: But what have you decided?
What are your plans?

ORGON: I plan, Sir, to be guided
By Heaven's will.
CLÉANTE: Come, Brother, don't talk rot. 165
You've given Valère your word; will you keep it, or not?
ORGON: Good day.
CLÉANTE: This looks like poor Valère's undoing;
I'll go and warn him that there's trouble brewing.

## ACT II

### SCENE 1

ORGON
MARIANE

ORGON: Mariane.
MARIANE: Yes, Father?
ORGON: A word with you; come here.
MARIANE: What are you looking for?
ORGON (*peering into a small closet*): Eavesdroppers, dear.
I'm making sure we shan't be overheard.
Someone in there could catch our every word.
Ah, good, we're safe. Now, Mariane, my child, 5
You're a sweet girl who's tractable and mild,
Whom I hold dear, and think most highly of.
MARIANE: I'm deeply grateful, Father, for your love.
ORGON: That's well said, Daughter; and you can repay me
If, in all things, you'll cheerfully obey me. 10
MARIANE: To please you, Sir, is what delights me best
ORGON: Good, good. Now, what d'you think of Tartuffe, our guest?
MARIANE: I, Sir?
ORGON: Yes. Weigh your answer; think it through.
MARIANE: Oh, dear. I'll say whatever you wish me to.
ORGON: That's wisely said, my Daughter. Say of him, then, 15
That he's the very worthiest of men,
And that you're fond of him, and would rejoice
In being his wife, if that should be my choice.
Well?
MARIANE: What?
ORGON: What's that?
MARIANE: I . . .
ORGON: Well?
MARIANE: Forgive me, pray.
ORGON: Did you not hear me?
MARIANE: Of *whom,* Sir, must I say 20

That I am fond of him, and would rejoice
In being his wife, if that should be your choice?
ORGON: Why, of Tartuffe.
MARIANE: But, Father, that's false, you know.
Why would you have me say what isn't so?
ORGON: Because I am resolved it shall be true. 25
That it's my wish should be enough for you.
MARIANE: You can't mean, Father . . .
ORGON: Yes, Tartuffe shall be
Allied by marriage to this family,
And he's to be your husband, is that clear?
It's a father's privilege . . . 30

## SCENE 2

DORINE
ORGON
MARIANE

ORGON (*to* DORINE): What are you doing in here?
Is curiosity so fierce a passion
With you, that you must eavesdrop in this fashion?
DORINE: There's lately been a rumor going about —
Based on some hunch or chance remark, no doubt — 5
That you mean Mariane to wed Tartuffe.
I've laughed it off, of course, as just a spoof.
ORGON: You find it so incredible?
DORINE: Yes, I do.
I won't accept that story, even from you.
ORGON: Well, you'll believe it when the thing is done. 10
DORINE: Yes, yes, of course. Go on and have your fun.
ORGON: I've never been more serious in my life.
DORINE: Ha!
ORGON: Daughter, I mean it; you're to be his wife.
DORINE: No, don't believe your father; it's all a hoax.
ORGON: See here, young woman . . .
DORINE: Come, Sir, no more jokes; 15
You can't fool us.
ORGON: How dare you talk that way?
DORINE: All right, then: we believe you, sad to say.
But how a man like you, who looks so wise
And wears a moustache of such splendid size,
Can be so foolish as to . . .
ORGON: Silence, please! 20
My girl, you take too many liberties.
I'm master here, as you must not forget.

DORINE: Do let's discuss this calmly; don't be upset.
You can't be serious, Sir, about this plan.
What should that bigot want with Mariane? 25
Praying and fasting ought to keep him busy.
And then, in terms of wealth and rank, what is he?
Why should a man of property like you
Pick out a beggar son-in-law?

ORGON: That will do.
Speak of his poverty with reverence. 30
His is a pure and saintly indigence
Which far transcends all worldly pride and pelf.
He lost his fortune, as he says himself,
Because he cared for Heaven alone, and so
Was careless of his interests here below. 35
I mean to get him out of his present straits
And help him to recover his estates —
Which, in his part of the world, have no small fame.
Poor though he is, he's a gentleman just the same.

DORINE: Yes, so he tells us; and, Sir, it seems to me 40
Such pride goes very ill with piety.
A man whose spirit spurns this dungy earth
Ought not to brag of lands and noble birth;
Such worldly arrogance will hardly square
With meek devotion and the life of prayer. 45
. . . But this approach, I see, has drawn a blank;
Let's speak, then, of his person, not his rank.
Doesn't it seem to you a trifle grim
To give a girl like her to a man like him?
When two are so ill-suited, can't you see 50
What the sad consequence is bound to be?
A young girl's virtue is imperilled, Sir,
When such a marriage is imposed on her;
For if one's bridegroom isn't to one's taste,
It's hardly an inducement to be chaste, 55
And many a man with horns upon his brow
Has made his wife the thing that she is now.
It's hard to be a faithful wife, in short,
To certain husbands of a certain sort,
And he who gives his daughter to a man she hates 60
Must answer for her sins at Heaven's gates.
Think, Sir, before you play so risky a role.

ORGON: This servant-girl presumes to save my soul!

DORINE: You would do well to ponder what I've said.

ORGON: Daughter, we'll disregard this dunderhead. 65
Just trust your father's judgment. Oh, I'm aware

That I once promised you to young Valère;
But now I hear he gambles, which greatly shocks me;
What's more, I've doubts about his orthodoxy.
His visits to church, I note, are very few. 70
DORINE: Would you have him go at the same hours as you,
And kneel nearby, to be sure of being seen?
ORGON: I can dispense with such remarks, Dorine.
(*To* MARIANE.) Tartuffe, however, is sure of Heaven's blessing,
And that's the only treasure worth possessing. 75
This match will bring you joys beyond all measure;
Your cup will overflow with every pleasure;
You two will interchange your faithful loves
Like two sweet cherubs, or two turtle-doves.
No harsh word shall be heard, no frown be seen, 80
And he shall make you happy as a queen.
DORINE: And she'll make him a cuckold, just wait and see.
ORGON: What language!
DORINE: Oh, he's a man of destiny;
He's *made* for horns, and what the stars demand
Your daughter's virtue surely can't withstand. 85
ORGON: Don't interrupt me further. Why can't you learn
That certain things are none of your concern?
DORINE: It's for your own sake that I interfere.

(*She repeatedly interrupts* ORGON *just as he is turning to speak to his daughter:*)

ORGON: Most kind of you. Now, hold your tongue, d'you hear?
DORINE: If I didn't love you . . .
ORGON: Spare me your affection. 90
DORINE: I love you, Sir, in spite of your objection.
ORGON: Blast!
DORINE: I can't bear, Sir, for your honor's sake,
To let you make this ludicrous mistake.
ORGON: You mean to go on talking?
DORINE: If I didn't protest
This sinful marriage, my conscience couldn't rest. 95
ORGON: If you don't hold your tongue, you little shrew . . .
DORINE: What, lost your temper? A pious man like you?
ORGON: Yes! Yes! You talk and talk. I'm maddened by it.
Once and for all, I tell you to be quiet.
DORINE: Well, I'll be quiet. But I'll be thinking hard. 100
ORGON: Think all you like, but you had better guard
That saucy tongue of yours, or I'll . . .
(*Turning back to* MARIANE.) Now, child,
I've weighed this matter fully.

DORINE (*aside*): It drives me wild
That I can't speak.

(ORGON *turns his head, and she is silent.*)

ORGON: Tartuffe is no young dandy,
But, still, his person . . .
DORINE (*aside*): Is as sweet as candy. 105
ORGON: Is such that, even if you shouldn't care
For his other merits . . .

(*He turns and stands facing* DORINE, *arms crossed.*)

DORINE (*aside*): They'll make a lovely pair.
If I were she, no man would marry me
Against my inclination, and go scot-free.
He'd learn, before the wedding-day was over, 110
How readily a wife can find a lover.
ORGON (*to* DORINE): It seems you treat my orders as a joke.
DORINE: Why, what's the matter? 'Twas not to you I spoke.
ORGON: What *were* you doing?
DORINE: Talking to myself, that's all.
ORGON: Ah! (*Aside.*) One more bit of impudence and gall, 115
And I shall give her a good slap in the face.

(*He puts himself in position to slap her;* DORINE, *whenever he glances at her, stands immobile and silent:*)

Daughter, you shall accept, and with good grace,
The husband I've selected . . . Your wedding-day . . .
(*To* DORINE.) Why don't you talk to yourself?
DORINE: I've nothing to say.
ORGON: Come, just one word.
DORINE: No thank you, Sir. I pass. 120
ORGON: Come, speak; I'm waiting.
DORINE: I'd not be such an ass.
ORGON (*turning to* MARIANE): In short, dear Daughter, I mean to be obeyed,
And you must bow to the sound choice I've made.
DORINE (*moving away*): I'd not wed such a monster, even in jest.

(ORGON *attempts to slap her, but misses.*)

ORGON: Daughter, that maid of yours is a thorough pest; 125
She makes me sinfully annoyed and nettled.
I can't speak further; my nerves are too unsettled.
She's so upset me by her insolent talk,
I'll calm myself by going for a walk.

## SCENE 3

DORINE
MARIANE

DORINE (*returning*): Well, have you lost your tongue, girl? Must I play
Your part, and say the lines you ought to say?
Faced with a fate so hideous and absurd,
Can you not utter one dissenting word?
MARIANE: What good would it do? A father's power is great. 5
DORINE: Resist him now, or it will be too late.
MARIANE: But . . .
DORINE: Tell him one cannot love at a father's whim;
That you shall marry for yourself, not him;
That since it's you who are to be the bride,
It's you, not he, who must be satisfied; 10
And that if his Tartuffe is so sublime,
He's free to marry him at any time.
MARIANNE: I've bowed so long to Father's strict control,
I couldn't oppose him now, to save my soul.
DORINE: Come, come, Mariane. Do listen to reason, won't you? 15
Valère has asked your hand. Do you love him, or don't you?
MARIANE: Oh, how unjust of you! What can you mean
By asking such a question, dear Dorine?
You know the depth of my affection for him;
I've told you a hundred times how I adore him. 20
DORINE: I don't believe in everything I hear;
Who knows if your professions were sincere?
MARIANE: They were, Dorine, and you do me wrong to doubt it;
Heaven knows that I've been all too frank about it.
DORINE: You love him, then?
MARIANE: Oh, more than I can express. 25
DORINE: And he, I take it, cares for you no less?
MARIANE: I think so.
DORINE: And you both, with equal fire,
Burn to be married?
MARIANE: That is our one desire.
DORINE: What of Tartuffe, then? What of your father's plan?
MARIANE: I'll kill myself, if I'm forced to wed that man. 30
DORINE: I hadn't thought of that recourse. How splendid!
Just die, and all your troubles will be ended!
A fine solution. Oh, it maddens me
To hear you talk in that self-pitying key.
MARIANE: Dorine, how harsh you are! It's most unfair. 35
You have no sympathy for my despair.

DORINE: I've none at all for people who talk drivel
And, faced with difficulties, whine and snivel.
MARIANE: No doubt I'm timid, but it would be wrong . . .
DORINE: True love requires a heart that's firm and strong. 40
MARIANE: I'm strong in my affection for Valère,
But coping with my father is his affair.
DORINE: But if your father's brain has grown so cracked
Over his dear Tartuffe that he can retract
His blessing, though your wedding-day was named, 45
It's surely not Valère who's to be blamed.
MARIANE: If I defied my father, as you suggest,
Would it not seem unmaidenly, at best?
Shall I defend my love at the expense
Of brazenness and disobedience? 50
Shall I parade my heart's desires, and flaunt . . .
DORINE: No, I ask nothing of you. Clearly you want
To be Madame Tartuffe, and I feel bound
Not to oppose a wish so very sound.
What right have I to criticize the match? 55
Indeed, my dear, the man's a brilliant catch.
Monsieur Tartuffe! Now, there's a man of weight!
Yes, yes, Monsieur Tartuffe, I'm bound to state,
Is quite a person; that's not to be denied;
'Twill be no little thing to be his bride. 60
The world already rings with his renown;
He's a great noble — in his native town;
His ears are red, he has a pink complexion,
And all in all, he'll suit you to perfection.
MARIANE: Dear God!
DORINE: Oh, how triumphant you will feel 65
At having caught a husband so ideal!
MARIANE: Oh, do stop teasing, and use your cleverness
To get me out of this appalling mess.
Advise me, and I'll do whatever you say.
DORINE: Ah no, a dutiful daughter must obey 70
Her father, even if he weds her to an ape.
You've a bright future; why struggle to escape?
Tartuffe will take you back where his family lives,
To a small town aswarm with relatives —
Uncles and cousins whom you'll be charmed to meet. 75
You'll be received at once by the elite,
Calling upon the bailiff's wife, no less —
Even, perhaps, upon the mayoress,
Who'll sit you down in the *best* kitchen chair.
Then, once a year, you'll dance at the village fair 80

To the drone of bagpipes – two of them, in fact –
And see a puppet-show, or an animal act.
Your husband . . .

MARIANE: Oh, you turn my blood to ice!
Stop torturing me, and give me your advice.

DORINE (*threatening to go*): Your servant, Madam.

MARIANE: Dorine, I beg of you . . . 85

DORINE: No, you deserve it; this marriage must go through.

MARIANE: Dorine!

DORINE: No.

MARIANE: Not Tartuffe! You know I think him . . .

DORINE: Tartuffe's your cup of tea, and you shall drink him.

MARIANE: I've always told you everything, and relied . . .

DORINE: No. You deserve to be tartuffified. 90

MARIANE: Well, since you mock me and refuse to care,
I'll henceforth seek my solace in despair:
Despair shall be my counsellor and friend,
And help me bring my sorrows to an end.

(*She starts to leave.*)

DORINE: There now, come back; my anger has subsided. 95
You do deserve some pity, I've decided.

MARIANE: Dorine, if Father makes me undergo
This dreadful martyrdom, I'll die, I know.

DORINE: Don't fret; it won't be difficult to discover
Some plan of action . . . But here's Valère, your lover. 100

## SCENE 4

VALÈRE
MARIANE
DORINE

VALÈRE: Madam, I've just received some wondrous news
Regarding which I'd like to hear your views.

MARIANE: What news?

VALÈRE: You're marrying Tartuffe.

MARIANE: I find
That Father does have such a match in mind.

VALÈRE: Your father, Madam . . .

MARIANE: . . . has just this minute said 5
That it's Tartuffe he wishes me to wed.

VALÈRE: Can he be serious?

MARIANE: Oh, indeed he can;
He's clearly set his heart upon the plan.

VALÈRE: And what position do you propose to take,
Madam?
MARIANE: Why — I don't know.
VALÈRE: For heaven's sake — 10
You don't know?
MARIANE: No.
VALÈRE: Well, well!
MARIANE: Advise me, do.
VALÈRE: Marry the man. That's my advice to you.
MARIANE: That's your advice?
VALÈRE: Yes.
MARIANE: Truly?
VALÈRE: Oh, absolutely.
You couldn't choose more wisely, more astutely.
MARIANE: Thanks for this counsel; I'll follow it, of course. 15
VALÈRE: Do, do; I'm sure 'twill cost you no remorse.
MARIANE: To give it didn't cause your heart to break.
VALÈRE: I gave it, Madam, only for your sake.
MARIANE: And it's for your sake that I take it, Sir.
DORINE (*withdrawing to the rear of the stage*): Let's see which fool will
prove the stubborner. 20
VALÈRE: So! I am nothing to you, and it was flat
Deception when you . . .
MARIANE: Please, enough of that.
You've told me plainly that I should agree
To wed the man my father's chosen for me,
And since you've designed to counsel me so wisely, 25
I promise, Sir, to do as you advise me.
VALÈRE: Ah, no, 'twas not by me that you were swayed.
No, your decision was already made;
Though now, to save appearances, you protest
That you're betraying me at my behest. 30
MARIANE: Just as you say.
VALÈRE: Quite so. And I now see
That you were never truly in love with me.
MARIANE: Alas, you're free to think so if you choose.
VALÈRE: I choose to think so, and here's a bit of news:
You've spurned my hand, but I know where to turn 35
For kinder treatment, as you shall quickly learn.
MARIANE: I'm sure you do. Your noble qualities
Inspire affection . . .
VALÈRE: Forget my qualities, please.
They don't inspire you overmuch, I find.
But there's another lady I have in mind 40

Whose sweet and generous nature will not scorn
To compensate me for the loss I've borne.
MARIANE: I'm no great loss, and I'm sure that you'll transfer
Your heart quite painlessly from me to her.
VALÈRE: I'll do my best to take it in my stride. 45
The pain I feel at being cast aside
Time and forgetfulness may put an end to.
Or if I can't forget, I shall pretend to.
No self-respecting person is expected
To go on loving once he's been rejected. 50
MARIANE: Now, that's a fine, high-minded sentiment.
VALÈRE: One to which any sane man would assent.
Would you prefer it if I pined away
In hopeless passion till my dying day?
Am I to yield you to a rival's arms 55
And not console myself with other charms?
MARIANE: Go then: console yourself; don't hesitate.
I wish you to; indeed, I cannot wait.
VALÈRE: You wish me to?
MARIANE: Yes.
VALÈRE: That's the final straw.
Madam, farewell. Your wish shall be my law. 60

(*He starts to leave, and then returns: this repeatedly:*)

MARIANE: Splendid.
VALÈRE (*coming back again*):
This breach, remember, is of your making;
It's you who've driven me to the step I'm taking.
MARIANE: Of course.
VALÈRE (*coming back again*):
Remember, too, that I am merely
Following your example.
MARIANE: I see that clearly.
VALÈRE: Enough. I'll go and do your bidding, then. 65
MARIANE: Good.
VALÈRE (*coming back again*):
You shall never see my face again.
MARIANE: Excellent.
VALÈRE (*walking to the door, then turning about*):
Yes?
MARIANE: What?
VALÈRE: What's that? What did you say?
MARIANE: Nothing. You're dreaming.

VALÈRE: Ah. Well, I'm on my way.
Farewell, *Madame.*

*(He moves slowly away.)*

MARIANE: Farewell.
DORINE (*to* MARIANE): If you ask me,
Both of you are as mad as mad can be. 70
Do stop this nonsense, now. I've only let you
Squabble so long to see where it would get you.
Whoa there, Monsieure Valère!

(*She goes and seizes* VALÈRE *by the arm; he makes a great show of resistance.*)

VALÈRE: What's this, Dorine?
DORINE: Come here.
VALÈRE: No, no, my heart's too full of spleen.
Don't hold me back; her wish must be obeyed. 75
DORINE: Stop!
VALÈRE: It's too late now; my decision's made.
DORINE: Oh, pooh!
MARIANE (*aside*): He hates the sight of me, that's plain.
I'll go, and so deliver him from pain.
DORINE (*leaving* VALÈRE, *running after* MARIANE):
And now *you* run away! Come back.
MARIANE: No, No.
Nothing you say will keep me here. Let go! 80
VALÈRE (*aside*): She cannot bear my presence, I perceive.
To spare her further torment, I shall leave.
DORINE (*leaving* MARIANE, *running after* VALÈRE): Again! You'll not escape, Sir; don't you try it.
Come here, you two. Stop fussing, and be quiet.

(*She takes* VALÈRE *by the hand, then* MARIANE, *and draws them together.*)

VALÈRE (*to* DORINE): What do you want of me?
MARIANE (*to* DORINE): What is the point of this? 85
DORINE: We're going to have a little armistice.
(*To* VALÈRE.) Now weren't you silly to get so overheated?
VALÈRE: Didn't you see how badly I was treated?
DORINE (*to* MARIANE): Aren't you a simpleton, to have lost your head?
MARIANE: Didn't you hear the hateful things he said? 90
DORINE (*to* VALÈRE): You're both great fools. Her sole desire, Valère,
Is to be yours in marriage. To that I'll swear.
(*To* MARIANE.) He loves you only, and he wants no wife
But you, Mariane. On that I'll stake my life.

MARIANE (*to* VALÈRE): Then why you advised me so, I cannot see. 95
VALÈRE (*to* MARIANE): On such a question, why ask advice of *me?*
DORINE: Oh, you're impossible. Give me your hands, you two.
(*To* VALÈRE.) Yours first.
VALÈRE (*giving* DORINE *his hand*): But why?
DORINE (*to* MARIANE): And now a hand from you.
MARIANE (*also giving* DORINE *her hand*):
What are you doing?
DORINE: There: a perfect fit.
You suit each other better than you'll admit. 100

(VALÈRE *and* MARIANE *hold hands for some time without looking at each other.*)

VALÈRE (*turning toward* MARIANE): Ah, come, don't be so haughty. Give a man
A look of kindness, won't you, Mariane?

(MARIANE *turns toward* VALÈRE *and smiles.*)

DORINE: I tell you, lovers are completely mad!
VALÈRE (*to* MARIANE): Now come, confess that you were very bad
To hurt my feelings as you did just now. 105
I have a just complaint, you must allow.
MARIANE: *You* must allow that you were most unpleasant . . .
DORINE: Let's table that discussion for the present;
Your father has a plan which must be stopped.
MARIANE: Advise us, then; what means must we adopt? 110
DORINE: We'll use all manner of means, and all at once.
(*To* MARIANE.) Your father's addled; he's acting like a dunce.
Therefore you'd better humor the old fossil.
Pretend to yield to him, be sweet and docile,
And then postpone, as often as necessary, 115
The day on which you have agreed to marry.
You'll thus gain time, and time will turn the trick.
Sometimes, for instance, you'll be taken sick,
And that will seem good reason for delay;
Or some bad omen will make you change the day — 120
You'll dream of muddy water, or you'll pass
A dead man's hearse, or break a looking-glass.
If all else fails, no man can marry you
Unless you take his ring and say "I do."
But now, let's separate. If they should find 125
Us talking here, our plot might be divined.
(*To* VALÈRE.) Go to your friends, and tell them what's occurred,
And have them urge her father to keep his word.
Meanwhile, we'll stir her brother into action,

And get Elmire, as well, to join our faction. 130
Good-bye.

VALÈRE (*to* MARIANE):
Though each of us will do his best,
It's your true heart on which my hopes shall rest.

MARIANE (*to* VALÈRE): Regardless of what Father may decide,
None but Valère shall claim me as his bride.

VALÈRE: Oh, how those words content me! Come what will . . . 135

DORINE: Oh, lovers, lovers! Their tongues are never still.
Be off, now.

VALÈRE (*turning to go, then turning back*):
One last word . . .

DORINE: No time to chat:
*You* leave by this door; and *you* leave by that.

(DORINE *pushes them, by the shoulders, toward opposing doors.*)

## ACT III

### Scene 1

DAMIS
DORINE

DAMIS: May lightning strike me even as I speak,
May all men call me cowardly and weak,
If any fear or scruple holds me back
From settling things, at once, with that great quack!

DORINE: Now, don't give way to violent emotion. 5
Your father's merely talked about this notion,
And words and deeds are far from being one.
Much that is talked about is left undone.

DAMIS: No, I must stop that scoundrel's machinations;
I'll go and tell him off; I'm out of patience. 10

DORINE: Do calm down and be practical. I had rather
My mistress dealt with him – and with your father.
She has some influence with Tartuffe, I've noted.
He hangs upon her words, seems most devoted,
And may, indeed, be smitten by her charm. 15
Pray Heaven it's true! 'Twould do our cause no harm.
She sent for him, just now, to sound him out
On this affair you're so incensed about;
She'll find out where he stands, and tell him, too,
What dreadful strife and trouble will ensue 20
If he lends countenance to your father's plan.
I couldn't get in to see him, but his man

Says that he's almost finished with his prayers.
Go, now. I'll catch him when he comes downstairs.
DAMIS: I want to hear this conference, and I will. 25
DORINE: No, they must be alone.
DAMIS: Oh, I'll keep still.
DORINE: Not you. I know your temper. You'd start a brawl,
And shout and stamp your foot and spoil it all.
Go on.
DAMIS: I won't; I have a perfect right . . .
DORINE: Lord, you're a nuisance! He's coming; get out of sight. 30

(DAMIS *conceals himself in a closet at the rear of the stage.*)

## SCENE 2

TARTUFFE
DORINE

TARTUFFE *(observing* DORINE, *and calling to his manservant offstage)*:
Hang up my hair-shirt, put my scourge in place,
And pray, Laurent, for Heaven's perpetual grace.
I'm going to the prison now, to share
My last few coins with the poor wretches there.
DORINE (*aside*): Dear God, what affectation! What a fake! 5
TARTUFFE: You wished to see me?
DORINE: Yes . . .
TARTUFFE (*taking a handkerchief from his pocket*):
For mercy's sake,
Please take this handkerchief, before you speak.
DORINE: What?
TARTUFFE: Cover that bosom, girl. The flesh is weak,
And unclean thoughts are difficult to control.
Such sights as that can undermine the soul. 10
DORINE: Your soul, it seems, has very poor defenses,
And flesh makes quite an impact on your senses.
It's strange that you're so easily excited;
My own desires are not so soon ignited,
And if I saw you naked as a beast, 15
Not all your hide would tempt me in the least.
TARTUFFE: Girl, speak more modestly; unless you do,
I shall be forced to take my leave of you.
DORINE: Oh, no, it's I who must be on my way;
I've just one little message to convey. 20
*Madame* is coming down, and begs you, Sir,
To wait and have a word or two with her.
TARTUFFE: Gladly.

DORINE (*aside*): *That* had a softening effect!
I think my guess about him was correct.
TARTUFFE: Will she be long?
DORINE: No: that's her step I hear. 25
Ah, here she is, and I shall disappear.

### SCENE 3

ELMIRE
TARTUFFE

TARTUFFE: May Heaven, whose infinite goodness we adore,
Preserve your body and soul forevermore,
And bless your days, and answer thus the plea
Of one who is its humblest votary.
ELMIRE: I thank you for that pious wish. But please, 5
Do take a chair and let's be more at ease.

(*They sit down.*)

TARTUFFE: I trust that you are once more well and strong?
ELMIRE: Oh, yes: the fever didn't last for long.
TARTUFFE: My prayers are too unworthy, I am sure,
To have gained from Heaven this most gracious cure; 10
But lately, Madam, my every supplication
Has had for object your recuperation.
ELMIRE: You shouldn't have troubled so. I don't deserve it.
TARTUFFE: Your health is priceless, Madam, and to preserve it
I'd gladly give my own, in all sincerity. 15
ELMIRE: Sir, you outdo us all in Christian charity.
You've been most kind. I count myself your debtor.
TARTUFFE: 'Twas nothing, Madam. I long to serve you better.
ELMIRE: There's a private matter I'm anxious to discuss.
I'm glad there's no one here to hinder us. 20
TARTUFFE: I too am glad; it floods my heart with bliss
To find myself alone with you like this.
For just this chance I've prayed with all my power —
But prayed in vain, until this happy hour.
ELMIRE: This won't take long, Sir, and I hope you'll be 25
Entirely frank and unconstrained with me.
TARTUFFE: Indeed, there's nothing I had rather do
Than bare my inmost heart and soul to you.
First, let me say that what remarks I've made
About the constant visits you are paid 30
Were prompted not by any mean emotion,
But rather by a pure and deep devotion,
A fervent zeal . . .

ELMIRE: No need for explanation.
Your sole concern, I'm sure, was my salvation.
TARTUFFE (*taking* ELMIRE'*s hand and pressing her fingertips*): Quite so; and such great fervor do I feel . . . 35
ELMIRE: Ooh! Please! You're pinching!
TARTUFFE: 'Twas from excess of zeal.
I never meant to cause you pain, I swear.
I'd rather . . .

(*He places his hand on* ELMIRE'*s knee.*)

ELMIRE: What can your hand be doing there?
TARTUFFE: Feeling your gown; what soft, fine-woven stuff! 40
ELMIRE: Please, I'm extremely ticklish. That's enough.

(*She draws her chair away;* TARTUFFE *pulls his after her.*)

TARTUFFE (*fondling the lace collar of her gown*): My, my, what lovely lacework on your dress!
The workmanship's miraculous, no less.
I've not seen anything to equal it.
ELMIRE: Yes, quite. But let's talk business for a bit.
They say my husband means to break his word 45
And give his daughter to you, Sir. Had you heard?
TARTUFFE: He did once mention it. But I confess
I dream of quite a different happiness.
It's elsewhere, Madam, that my eyes discern
The promise of that bliss for which I yearn. 50
ELMIRE: I see: you care for nothing here below.
TARTUFFE: Ah, well — my heart's not made of stone, you know.
ELMIRE: All your desires mount heavenward, I'm sure,
In scorn of all that's earthly and impure.
TARTUFFE: A love of heavenly beauty does not preclude 55
A proper love for earthly pulchritude;
Our senses are quite rightly captivated
By perfect works our Maker has created.
Some glory clings to all that Heaven has made;
In you, all Heaven's marvels are displayed. 60
On that fair face, such beauties have been lavished,
The eyes are dazzled and the heart is ravished;
How could I look on you, O flawless creature,
And not adore the Author of all Nature,
Feeling a love both passionate and pure 65
For you, his triumph of self-portraiture?
At first, I trembled lest that love should be
A subtle snare that Hell had laid for me;
I vowed to flee the sight of you, eschewing

A rapture that might prove my soul's undoing; 70
But soon, fair being, I became aware
That my deep passion could be made to square
With rectitude, and with my bounden duty.
I thereupon surrendered to your beauty.
It is, I know, presumptuous on my part 75
To bring you this poor offering of my heart,
And it is not my merit, Heaven knows,
But your compassion on which my hopes repose.
You are my peace, my solace, my salvation;
On you depends my bliss — or desolation; 80
I bide your judgment and, as you think best,
I shall be either miserable or blest.

ELMIRE: Your declaration is most gallant, Sir,
But don't you think it's out of character?
You'd have done better to restrain your passion 85
And think before you spoke in such a fashion.
It ill becomes a pious man like you . . .

TARTUFFE: I may be pious, but I'm human too:
With your celestial charms before his eyes,
A man has not the power to be wise. 90
I know such words sound strangely, coming from me,
But I'm no angel, nor was meant to be,
And if you blame my passion, you must needs
Reproach as well the charms on which it feeds.
Your loveliness I had no sooner seen 95
Than you became my soul's unrivalled queen;
Before your seraph glance, divinely sweet,
My heart's defenses crumbled in defeat,
And nothing fasting, prayer, or tears might do
Could stay my spirit from adoring you. 100
My eyes, my sighs have told you in the past
What now my lips make bold to say at last,
And if, in your great goodness, you will deign
To look upon your slave, and ease his pain, —
If, in compassion for my soul's distress, 105
You'll stoop to comfort my unworthiness,
I'll raise to you, in thanks for that sweet manna,
An endless hymn, an infinite hosanna.
With me, of course, there need be no anxiety,
No fear of scandal or of notoriety. 110
These young court gallants, whom all the ladies fancy,
Are vain in speech, in action rash and chancy;
When they succeed in love, the world soon knows it;
No favor's granted them but they disclose it

And by the looseness of their tongues profane 115
The very altar where their hearts have lain.
Men of my sort, however, love discreetly,
And one may trust our reticence completely.
My keen concern for my good name insures
The absolute security of yours; 120
In short, I offer you, my dear Elmire,
Love without scandal, pleasure without fear.

ELMIRE: I've heard your well-turned speeches to the end,
And what you urge I clearly apprehend.
Aren't you afraid that I may take a notion 125
To tell my husband of your warm devotion,
And that, supposing he were duly told,
His feelings toward you might grow rather cold?

TARTUFFE: I know, dear lady, that your exceeding charity
Will lead your heart to pardon my temerity; 130
That you'll excuse my violent affection
As human weakness, human imperfection;
And that — O fairest! — you will bear in mind
That I'm but flesh and blood, and am not blind.

ELMIRE: Some women might do otherwise, perhaps, 135
But I shall be discreet about your lapse;
I'll tell my husband nothing of what's occurred
If, in return, you'll give your solemn word
To advocate as forcefully as you can
The marriage of Valère and Mariane, 140
Renouncing all desire to dispossess
Another of his rightful happiness,
And . . .

## SCENE 4

DAMIS
ELMIRE
TARTUFFE

DAMIS (*emerging from the closet where he has been hiding*):
No! We'll not hush up this vile affair;
I heard it all inside that closet there,
Where Heaven, in order to confound the pride
Of this great rascal, prompted me to hide.
Ah, now I have my long-awaited chance 5
To punish his deceit and arrogance,
And give my father clear and shocking proof
Of the black character of his dear Tartuffe.

ELMIRE: Ah no, Damis; I'll be content if he

Will study to deserve my leniency. 10
I've promised silence — don't make me break my word;
To make a scandal would be too absurd.
Good wives laugh off such trifles, and forget them;
Why should they tell their husbands, and upset them?

DAMIS: You have your reasons for taking such a course, 15
And I have reasons, too, of equal force.
To spare him now would be insanely wrong.
I've swallowed my just wrath for far too long
And watched this insolent bigot bringing strife
And bitterness into our family life. 20
Too long he's meddled in my father's affairs,
Thwarting my marriage-hopes, and poor Valère's.
It's high time that my father was undeceived,
And now I've proof that can't be disbelieved —
Proof that was furnished me by Heaven above. 25
It's too good not to take advantage of.
This is my chance, and I deserve to lose it
If, for one moment, I hesitate to use it.

ELMIRE: Damis . . .

DAMIS: No, I must do what I think right.
Madam, my heart is bursting with delight, 30
And, say whatever you will, I'll not consent
To lose the sweet revenge on which I'm bent.
I'll settle matters without more ado;
And here, most opportunely, is my cue.

## SCENE 5

ORGON TARTUFFE
DAMIS ELMIRE

DAMIS: Father, I'm glad you've joined us. Let us advise you
Of some fresh news which doubtless will surprise you.
You've just now been repaid with interest
For all your loving-kindness to our guest.
He's proved his warm and grateful feelings toward you; 5
It's with a pair of horns he would reward you.
Yes, I surprised him with your wife, and heard
His whole adulterous offer, every word.
She, with her all too gentle disposition,
Would not have told you of his proposition; 10
But I shall not make terms with brazen lechery,
And feel that not to tell you would be treachery.

ELMIRE: And I hold that one's husband's peace of mind
Should not be spoilt by tattle of this kind.

One's honor doesn't require it: to be proficient 15
In keeping men at bay is quite sufficient.
These are my sentiments, and I wish, Damis,
That you had heeded me and held your peace.

## SCENE 6

ORGON
DAMIS
TARTUFFE

ORGON: Can it be true, this dreadful thing I hear?
TARTUFFE: Yes, Brother, I'm a wicked man, I fear:
A wretched sinner, all depraved and twisted,
The greatest villain that has ever existed.
My life's one heap of crimes, which grows each minute; 5
There's naught but foulness and corruption in it;
And I perceive that Heaven, outraged by me,
Has chosen this occasion to mortify me.
Charge me with any deed you wish to name;
I'll not defend myself, but take the blame. 10
Believe what you are told, and drive Tartuffe
Like some base criminal from beneath your roof;
Yes, drive me hence, and with a parting curse:
I shan't protest, for I deserve far worse.
ORGON (*to* DAMIS): Ah, you deceitful boy, how dare you try 15
To stain his purity with so foul a lie?
DAMIS: What! Are you taken in by such a bluff?
Did you not hear . . . ?
ORGON: Enough, you rogue, enough!
TARTUFFE: Ah, Brother, let him speak: you're being unjust.
Believe his story; the boy deserves your trust. 20
Why, after all, should you have faith in me?
How can you know what I might do, or be?
Is it on my good actions that you base
Your favor? Do you trust my pious face?
Ah, no, don't be deceived by hollow shows; 25
I'm far, alas, from being what men suppose;
Though the world takes me for a man of worth,
I'm truly the most worthless man on earth.
(*To* DAMIS.) Yes, my dear son, speak out now: call me the chief
Of sinners, a wretch, a murderer, a thief; 30
Load me with all the names men most abhor;
I'll not complain; I've earned them all, and more;
I'll kneel here while you pour them on my head
As a just punishment for the life I've led.

ORGON (*to* TARTUFFE): This is too much, dear Brother.
(*To* DAMIS.) Have you no heart? 35
DAMIS: Are you so hoodwinked by this rascal's art . . . ?
ORGON: Be still, you monster.
(*To* TARTUFFE.) Brother, I pray you, rise.
(*To* DAMIS.) Villain!
DAMIS: But . . .
ORGON: Silence!
DAMIS: Can't you realize . . . ?
ORGON: Just one word more, and I'll tear you limb from limb.
TARTUFFE: In God's name, Brother, don't be harsh with him. 40
I'd rather far be tortured at the stake
Than see him bear one scratch for my poor sake.
ORGON (*to* DAMIS): Ingrate!
TARTUFFE: If I must beg you, on bended knee,
To pardon him . . .
ORGON (*falling to his knees, addressing* TARTUFFE):
Such goodness cannot be!
(*To* DAMIS.) Now, *there's* true charity!
DAMIS: What, you . . . ?
ORGON: Villain, be still! 45
I know your motives; I know you wish him ill:
Yes, all of you — wife, children, servants, all —
Conspire against him and desire his fall,
Employing every shameful trick you can
To alienate me from this saintly man. 50
Ah, but the more you seek to drive him away,
The more I'll do to keep him. Without delay,
I'll spite this household and confound its pride
By giving him my daughter as his bride.
DAMIS: You're going to force her to accept his hand? 55
ORGON: Yes, and this very night, d'you understand?
I shall defy you all, and make it clear
That I'm the one who gives the orders here.
Come, wretch, kneel down and clasp his blessed feet,
And ask his pardon for your black deceit. 60
DAMIS: I ask that swindler's pardon? Why, I'd rather . . .
ORGON: So! You insult him, and defy your father!
A stick! A stick! (*To* TARTUFFE.) No, no — release me, do.
(*To* DAMIS.) Out of my house this minute! Be off with you,
And never dare set foot in it again. 65
DAMIS: Well, I shall go, but . . .
ORGON: Well, go quickly, then.
I disinherit you; an empty purse
Is all you'll get from me — except my curse!

## SCENE 7

ORGON
TARTUFFE

ORGON: How he blasphemed your goodness! What a son!
TARTUFFE: Forgive him, Lord, as I've already done.
(*To* ORGON.) You can't know how it hurts when someone tries
To blacken me in my dear Brother's eyes.
ORGON: Ahh!
TARTUFFE: The mere thought of such ingratitude 5
Plunges my soul into so dark a mood . . .
Such horror grips my heart . . . I gasp for breath,
And cannot speak, and feel myself near death.
ORGON: (*He runs, in tears, to the door through which he has just driven his son.*) You blackguard! Why did I spare you? Why did I not
Break you in little pieces on the spot? 10
Compose yourself, and don't be hurt, dear friend.
TARTUFFE: These scenes, these dreadful quarrels, have got to end.
I've much upset your household, and I perceive
That the best thing will be for me to leave.
ORGON: What are you saying!
TARTUFFE: They're all against me here; 15
They'd have you think me false and insincere.
ORGON: Ah, what of that? Have I ceased believing in you?
TARTUFFE: Their adverse talk will certainly continue,
And charges which you now repudiate
You may find credible at a later date. 20
ORGON: No, Brother, never.
TARTUFFE: Brother, a wife can sway
Her husband's mind in many a subtle way.
ORGON: No, no.
TARTUFFE: To leave at once is the solution;
Thus only can I end their persecution.
ORGON: No, no, I'll not allow it; you shall remain. 25
TARTUFFE: Ah, well; 'twill mean much martyrdom and pain,
But if you wish it . . .
ORGON: Ah!
TARTUFFE: Enough; so be it.
But one thing must be settled, as I see it.
For your dear honor, and for our friendship's sake,
There's one precaution I feel bound to take. 30
I shall avoid your wife, and keep away . . .
ORGON: No, you shall not, whatever they may say.
It pleases me to vex them, and for spite

I'd have them see you with her day and night.
What's more, I'm going to drive them to despair 35
By making you my only son and heir;
This very day, I'll give to you alone
Clear deed and title to everything I own.
A dear, good friend and son-in-law-to-be
Is more than wife, or child, or kin to me. 40
Will you accept my offer, dearest son?
TARTUFFE: In all things, let the will of Heaven be done.
ORGON: Poor fellow! Come, we'll go draw up the deed.
Then let them burst with disappointed greed!

## ACT IV

### SCENE 1

CLÉANTE
TARTUFFE

CLÉANTE: Yes, all the town's discussing it, and truly,
Their comments do not flatter you unduly.
I'm glad we've met, Sir, and I'll give my view
Of this sad matter in a word or two.
As for who's guilty, that I shan't discuss; 5
Let's say it was Damis who caused the fuss;
Assuming, then, that you have been ill-used
By young Damis, and groundlessly accused,
Ought not a Christian to forgive, and ought
He not to stifle every vengeful thought? 10
Should you stand by and watch a father make
His only son an exile for your sake?
Again I tell you frankly, be advised:
The whole town, high and low, is scandalized;
This quarrel must be mended, and my advice is 15
Not to push matters to a further crisis.
No, sacrifice your wrath to God above,
And help Damis regain his father's love.
TARTUFFE: Alas, for my part I should take great joy
In doing so. I've nothing against the boy. 20
I pardon all, I harbor no resentment;
To serve him would afford me much contentment.
But Heaven's interest will not have it so:
If he comes back, then I shall have to go.
After his conduct – so extreme, so vicious – 25
Our further intercourse would look suspicious.

God knows what people would think! Why, they'd describe
My goodness to him as a sort of bribe;
They'd say that out of guilt I made pretense
Of loving-kindness and benevolence — 30
That, fearing my accuser's tongue, I strove
To buy his silence with a show of love.

CLÉANTE: Your reasoning is badly warped and stretched,
And these excuses, Sir, are most far-fetched.
Why put yourself in charge of Heaven's cause? 35
Does Heaven need our help to enforce its laws?
Leave vengeance to the Lord, Sir; while we live,
Our duty's not to punish, but forgive;
And what the Lord commands, we should obey
Without regard to what the world may say. 40
What! Shall the fear of being misunderstood
Prevent our doing what is right and good?
No, no; let's simply do what Heaven ordains,
And let no other thoughts perplex our brains.

TARTUFFE: Again, Sir, let me say that I've forgiven 45
Damis, and thus obeyed the laws of Heaven;
But I am not commanded by the Bible
To live with one who smears my name with libel.

CLÉANTE: Were you commanded, Sir, to indulge the whim
Of poor Orgon, and to encourage him 50
In suddenly transferring to your name
A large estate to which you have no claim?

TARTUFFE: 'Twould never occur to those who know me best
To think I acted from self-interest.
The treasures of this world I quite despise; 55
Their specious glitter does not charm my eyes;
And if I have resigned myself to taking
The gift which my dear Brother insists on making,
I do so only, as he well understands,
Lest so much wealth fall into wicked hands, 60
Lest those to whom it might descend in time
Turn it to purposes of sin and crime,
And not, as I shall do, make use of it
For Heaven's glory and mankind's benefit.

CLÉANTE: Forget these trumped-up fears. Your argument 65
Is one the rightful heir might well resent;
It *is* a moral burden to inherit
Such wealth, but give Damis a chance to bear it.
And would it not be worse to be accused
Of swindling, than to see that wealth misused? 70
I'm shocked that you allowed Orgon to broach

This matter, and that you feel no self-reproach;
Does true religion teach that lawful heirs
May freely be deprived of what is theirs?
And if the Lord has told you in your heart 75
That you and young Damis must dwell apart,
Would it not be the decent thing to beat
A generous and honorable retreat,
Rather than let the son of the house be sent,
For your convenience, into banishment? 80
Sir, if you wish to prove the honesty
Of your intentions . . .

TARTUFFE: Sir, it is half-past three.
I've certain pious duties to attend to,
And hope my prompt departure won't offend you.

CLÉANTE (*alone*): Damn.

## Scene 2

ELMIRE CLÉANTE
MARIANE DORINE

DORINE: Stay, Sir, and help Mariane, for Heaven's sake!
She's suffering so, I fear her heart will break.
Her father's plan to marry her off tonight
Has put the poor child in a desperate plight.
I hear him coming. Let's stand together, now, 5
And see if we can't change his mind, somehow,
About this match we all deplore and fear.

## Scene 3

ORGON MARIANE DORINE
ELMIRE CLÉANTE

ORGON: Hah! Glad to find you all assembled here.
(*To* MARIANE.) This contract, child, contains your happiness,
And what it says I think your heart can guess.

MARIANE (*falling to her knees*): Sir, by that Heaven which sees me here
distressed,
And by whatever else can move your breast, 5
Do not employ a father's power, I pray you,
To crush my heart and force it to obey you,
Nor by your harsh commands oppress me so
That I'll begrudge the duty which I owe —
And do not so embitter and enslave me 10
That I shall hate the very life you gave me.
If my sweet hopes must perish, if you refuse

To give me to the one I've dared to choose,
Spare me at least — I beg you, I implore —
The pain of wedding one whom I abhor; 15
And do not, by a heartless use of force,
Drive me to contemplate some desperate course.

ORGON (*feeling himself touched by her*): Be firm, my soul. No human weakness, now.

MARIANE: I don't resent your love for him. Allow
Your heart free rein, Sir; give him your property, 20
And if that's not enough, take mine from me;
He's welcome to my money; take it, do,
But don't, I pray, include my person too.
Spare me, I beg you; and let me end the tale
Of my sad days behind a convent veil. 25

ORGON: A convent! Hah! When crossed in their amours,
All lovesick girls have the same thought as yours.
Get up! The more you loathe the man, and dread him,
The more ennobling it will be to wed him.
Marry Tartuffe, and mortify your flesh! 30
Enough; don't start that whimpering afresh.

DORINE: But why . . . ?

ORGON: Be still, there. Speak when you're spoken to.
Not one more bit of impudence out of you.

CLÉANTE: If I may offer a word of counsel here . . .

ORGON: Brother, in counseling you have no peer; 35
All your advice is forceful, sound, and clever;
I don't propose to follow it, however.

ELMIRE (*to* ORGON): I am amazed, and don't know what to say;
Your blindness simply takes my breath away.
You are indeed bewitched, to take no warning 40
From our account of what occurred this morning.

ORGON: Madam, I know a few plain facts, and one
Is that you're partial to my rascal son;
Hence, when he sought to make Tartuffe the victim
Of a base lie, you dared not contradict him. 45
Ah, but you underplayed your part, my pet;
You should have looked more angry, more upset.

ELMIRE: When men make overtures, must we reply
With righteous anger and a battle-cry?
Must we turn back their amorous advances 50
With sharp reproaches and with fiery glances?
Myself, I find such offers merely amusing,
And make no scenes and fusses in refusing;
My taste is for good-natured rectitude,
And I dislike the savage sort of prude 55

Who guards her virtue with her teeth and claws,
And tears men's eyes out for the slightest cause:
The Lord preserve me from such honor as that,
Which bites and scratches like an alley-cat!
I've found that a polite and cool rebuff 60
Discourages a lover quite enough.

ORGON: I know the facts, and I shall not be shaken.

ELMIRE: I marvel at your power to be mistaken.
Would it, I wonder, carry weight with you
If I could *show* you that our tale was true? 65

ORGON: Show me?

ELMIRE: Yes.

ORGON: Rot.

ELMIRE: Come, what if I found a way
To make you see the facts as plain as day?

ORGON: Nonsense.

ELMIRE: Do answer me; don't be absurd.
I'm not now asking you to trust our word.
Suppose that from some hiding-place in here 70
You learned the whole sad truth by eye and ear —
What would you say of your good friend, after that?

ORGON: Why, I'd say . . . nothing, by Jehoshaphat!
It can't be true.

ELMIRE: You've been too long deceived,
And I'm quite tired of being disbelieved. 75
Come now: let's put my statements to the test,
And you shall see the truth made manifest.

ORGON: I'll take that challenge. Now do your uttermost.
We'll see how you make good your empty boast.

ELMIRE (*to* DORINE): Send him to me.

DORINE: He's crafty; it may be hard 80
To catch the cunning scoundrel off his guard.

ELMIRE: No, amorous men are gullible. Their conceit
So blinds them that they're never hard to cheat.
Have him come down (*To* CLÉANTE & MARIANE.) Please leave us, for a bit.

## SCENE 4

ELMIRE
ORGON

ELMIRE: Pull up this table, and get under it.

ORGON: What?

ELMIRE: It's essential that you be well-hidden.

ORGON: Why there?

ELMIRE: Oh, Heavens! Just do as you are bidden.
I have my plans; we'll soon see how they fare.
Under the table, now; and once you're there, 5
Take care that you are neither seen nor heard.
ORGON: Well, I'll indulge you, since I gave my word
To see you through this infantile charade.
ELMIRE: Once it is over, you'll be glad we played.
(*To her husband, who is now under the table.*) I'm going to act quite strangely, now, and you 10
Must not be shocked at anything I do.
Whatever I may say, you must excuse
As part of that deceit I'm forced to use.
I shall employ sweet speeches in the task
Of making that impostor drop his mask; 15
I'll give encouragement to his bold desires,
And furnish fuel to his amorous fires.
Since it's for your sake, and for his destruction,
That I shall seem to yield to his seduction,
I'll gladly stop whenever you decide 20
That all your doubts are fully satisfied.
I'll count on you, as soon as you have seen
What sort of man he is, to intervene,
And not expose me to his odious lust
One moment longer than you feel you must. 25
Remember: you're to save me from my plight
Whenever . . . He's coming! Hush! Keep out of sight!

## SCENE 5

TARTUFFE
ELMIRE
ORGON

TARTUFFE: You wish to have a word with me, I'm told.
ELMIRE: Yes. I've a little secret to unfold.
Before I speak, however, it would be wise
To close that door, and look about for spies.

(TARTUFFE *goes to the door, closes it, and returns.*)

The very last thing that must happen now 5
Is a repetition of this morning's row.
I've never been so badly caught off guard.
Oh, how I feared for you! You saw how hard
I tried to make that troublesome Damis
Control his dreadful temper, and hold his peace. 10
In my confusion, I didn't have the sense

Simply to contradict his evidence;
But as it happened, that was for the best,
And all has worked out in our interest.
This storm has only bettered your position; 15
My husband doesn't have the least suspicion,
And now, in mockery of those who do,
He bids me be continually with you.
And that is why, quite fearless of reproof,
I now can be alone with my Tartuffe, 20
And why my heart — perhaps too quick to yield —
Feels free to let its passion be revealed.

TARTUFFE: Madam, your words confuse me. Not long ago,
You spoke in quite a different style, you know.

ELMIRE: Ah, Sir, if that refusal made you smart, 25
It's little that you know of woman's heart,
Or what that heart is trying to convey
When it resists in such a feeble way!
Always, at first, our modesty prevents
The frank avowal of tender sentiments; 30
However high the passion which inflames us,
Still, to confess its power somehow shames us.
Thus we reluct, at first, yet in a tone
Which tells you that our heart is overthrown,
That what our lips deny, our pulse confesses, 35
And that, in time, all noes will turn to yesses.
I fear my words are all too frank and free,
And a poor proof of woman's modesty;
But since I'm started, tell me, if you will —
Would I have tried to make Damis be still, 40
Would I have listened, calm and unoffended,
Until your lengthy offer of love was ended,
And been so very mild in my reaction,
Had your sweet words not given me satisfaction?
And when I tried to force you to undo 45
The marriage-plans my husband has in view,
What did my urgent pleading signify
If not that I admired you, and that I
Deplored the thought that someone else might own
Part of a heart I wished for mine alone? 50

TARTUFFE: Madam, no happiness is so complete
As when, from lips we love, come words so sweet;
Their nectar floods my every sense, and drains
In honeyed rivulets through all my veins.
To please you is my joy, my only goal; 55
Your love is the restorer of my soul;

And yet I must beg leave, now, to confess
Some lingering doubts as to my happiness.
Might this not be a trick? Might not the catch
Be that you wish me to break off the match 60
With Mariane, and so have feigned to love me?
I shan't quite trust your fond opinion of me
Until the feelings you've expressed so sweetly
Are demonstrated somewhat more concretely,
And you have shown, by certain kind concessions, 65
That I may put my faith in your professions.

ELMIRE: (*She coughs, to warn her husband.*) Why be in such a hurry?
Must my heart
Exhaust its bounty at the very start?
To make that sweet admission cost me dear,
But you'll not be content, it would appear, 70
Unless my store of favors is disbursed
To the last farthing, and at the very first.

TARTUFFE: The less we merit, the less we dare to hope,
And with our doubts, mere words can never cope.
We trust no promised bliss till we receive it; 75
Not till a joy is ours can we believe it.
I, who so little merit your esteem,
Can't credit this fulfillment of my dream,
And shan't believe it, Madam, until I savor
Some palpable assurance of your favor. 80

ELMIRE: My, how tyrannical your love can be,
And how it flusters and perplexes me!
How furiously you take one's heart in hand,
And make your every wish a fierce command!
Come, must you hound and harry me to death? 85
Will you not give me time to catch my breath?
Can it be right to press me with such force,
Give me no quarter, show me no remorse,
And take advantage, by your stern insistence,
Of the fond feelings which weaken my resistance? 90

TARTUFFE: Well, if you look with favor upon my love,
Why, then, begrudge me some clear proof thereof?

ELMIRE: But how can I consent without offense
To Heaven, toward which you feel such reverence?

TARTUFFE: If Heaven is all that holds you back, don't worry. 95
I can remove that hindrance in a hurry.
Nothing of that sort need obstruct our path.

ELMIRE: Must one not be afraid of Heaven's wrath?

TARTUFFE: Madam, forget such fears, and be my pupil,
And I shall teach you how to conquer scruple. 100

Some joys, it's true, are wrong in Heaven's eyes;
Yet Heaven is not averse to compromise;
There is a science, lately formulated,
Whereby one's conscience may be liberated,
And any wrongful act you care to mention 105
May be redeemed by purity of intention.
I'll teach you, Madam, the secrets of that science;
Meanwhile, just place on me your full reliance.
Assuage my keen desires, and feel no dread:
The sin, if any, shall be on my head. 110

(ELMIRE *coughs, this time more loudly.*)

You've a bad cough.

ELMIRE: Yes, yes. It's bad indeed.

TARTUFFE (*producing a little paper bag*): A bit of licorice may be what you need.

ELMIRE: No, I've a stubborn cold, it seems. I'm sure it
Will take much more than licorice to cure it.

TARTUFFE: How aggravating.

ELMIRE: Oh, more than I can say. 115

TARTUFFE: If you're still troubled, think of things this way:
No one shall know our joys, save us alone,
And there's no evil till the act is known;
It's scandal, Madam, which makes it an offense,
And it's no sin to sin in confidence. 120

ELMIRE (*having coughed once more*): Well, clearly I must do as you require,
And yield to your importunate desire.
It is apparent, now, that nothing less
Will satisfy you, and so I acquiesce.
To go so far is much against my will; 125
I'm vexed that it should come to this; but still,
Since you are so determined on it, since you
Will not allow mere language to convince you,
And since you ask for concrete evidence, I
See nothing for it, now, but to comply. 130
If this is sinful, if I'm wrong to do it,
So much the worse for him who drove me to it.
The fault can surely not be charged to me.

TARTUFFE: Madam, the fault is mine, if fault there be,
And . . .

ELMIRE: Open the door a little, and peek out; 135
I wouldn't want my husband poking about.

TARTUFFE: Why worry about the man? Each day he grows
More gullible; one can lead him by the nose.

To find us here would fill him with delight,
And if he saw the worst, he'd doubt his sight. 140
ELMIRE: Nevertheless, do step out for a minute
Into the hall, and see that no one's in it.

## SCENE 6

ORGON
ELMIRE

ORGON (*coming out from under the table*): That man's a perfect monster, I must admit!
I'm simply stunned. I can't get over it.
ELMIRE: What, coming out so soon? How premature!
Get back in hiding, and wait until you're sure.
Stay till the end, and be convinced completely; 5
We mustn't stop till things are proved concretely.
ORGON: Hell never harbored anything so vicious!
ELMIRE: Tut, don't be hasty. Try to be judicious.
Wait, and be certain that there's no mistake.
No jumping to conclusions, for Heaven's sake! 10

(*She places* ORGON *behind her, as* TARTUFFE *re-enters.*)

## SCENE 7

TARTUFFE
ELMIRE
ORGON

TARTUFFE (*not seeing* ORGON): Madam, all things have worked out to perfection;
I've given the neighboring rooms a full inspection;
No one's about; and now I may at last . . .
ORGON (*intercepting him*): Hold on, my passionate fellow, not so fast!
I should advise a little more restraint. 5
Well, so you thought you'd fool me, my dear saint!
How soon you wearied of the saintly life—
Wedding my daughter, and coveting my wife!
I've long suspected you, and had a feeling
That soon I'd catch you at your double-dealing. 10
Just now, you've given me evidence galore;
It's quite enough; I have no wish for more.
ELMIRE (*To* TARTUFFE): I'm sorry to have treated you so slyly,
But circumstances forced me to be wily.
TARTUFFE: Brother, you can't think . . .
ORGON: No more talk from you; 15
Just leave this household, without more ado.

TARTUFFE: What I intended . . .
ORGON: That seems fairly clear.
Spare me your falsehoods and get out of here.
TARTUFFE: No, I'm the master, and you're the one to go!
This house belongs to me, I'll have you know, 20
And I shall show you that you can't hurt *me*
By this contemptible conspiracy,
That those who cross me know not what they do,
And that I've means to expose and punish you,
Avenge offended Heaven, and make you grieve 25
That ever you dared order me to leave.

### Scene 8

ELMIRE
ORGON

ELMIRE: What was the point of all that angry chatter?
ORGON: Dear God, I'm worried. This is no laughing matter.
ELMIRE: How so?
ORGON: I fear I understood his drift.
I'm much disturbed about that deed of gift.
ELMIRE: You gave him . . . ?
ORGON: Yes, it's all been drawn and signed. 5
But one thing more is weighing on my mind.
ELMIRE: What's that?
ORGON: I'll tell you; but first let's see if there's
A certain strong-box in his room upstairs.

## ACT V

### Scene 1

ORGON
CLÉANTE

CLÉANTE: Where are you going so fast?
ORGON: God knows!
CLÉANTE: Then wait;
Let's have a conference, and deliberate
On how this situation's to be met.
ORGON: That strong-box has me utterly upset;
This is the worst of many, many shocks. 5
CLÉANTE: Is there some fearful mystery in that box?
ORGON: My poor friend Argas brought that box to me
With his own hands, in utmost secrecy;
'Twas on the very morning of his flight.

It's full of papers which, if they came to light, 10
Would ruin him — or such is my impression.
CLÉANTE: Then why did you let it out of your possession?
ORGON: Those papers vexed my conscience, and it seemed best
To ask the counsel of my pious guest.
The cunning scoundrel got me to agree 15
To leave the strong-box in his custody,
So that, in case of an investigation,
I could employ a slight equivocation
And swear I didn't have it, and thereby,
At no expense to conscience, tell a lie. 20
CLÉANTE: It looks to me as if you're out on a limb.
Trusting him with that box, and offering him
That deed of gift, were actions of a kind
Which scarcely indicate a prudent mind.
With two such weapons, he has the upper hand, 25
And since you're vulnerable, as matters stand,
You erred once more in bringing him to bay.
You should have acted in some subtler way.
ORGON: Just think of it: behind that fervent face,
A heart so wicked, and a soul so base! 30
I took him in, a hungry beggar, and then . . .
Enough, by God! I'm through with pious men:
Henceforth I'll hate the whole false brotherhood,
And persecute them worse than Satan could.
CLÉANTE: Ah, there you go — extravagant as ever! 35
Why can you not be rational? You never
Manage to take the middle course, it seems,
But jump, instead, between absurd extremes.
You've recognized your recent grave mistake
In falling victim to a pious fake; 40
Now, to correct that error, must you embrace
An even greater error in its place,
And judge our worthy neighbors as a whole
By what you've learned of one corrupted soul?
Come, just because one rascal made you swallow 45
A show of zeal which turned out to be hollow,
Shall you conclude that all men are deceivers,
And that, today, there are no true believers?
Let atheists make that foolish inference;
Learn to distinguish virtue from pretense, 50
Be cautious in bestowing admiration,
And cultivate a sober moderation.
Don't humor fraud, but also don't asperse
True piety; the latter fault is worse,

And it is best to err, if err one must, 55
As you have done, upon the side of trust.

## SCENE 2

DAMIS
ORGON
CLÉANTE

DAMIS: Father, I hear that scoundrel's uttered threats
Against you; that he pridefully forgets
How, in his need, he was befriended by you,
And means to use your gifts to crucify you.
ORGON: It's true, my boy. I'm too distressed for tears. 5
DAMIS: Leave it to me, Sir; let me trim his ears.
Faced with such insolence, we must not waver.
I shall rejoice in doing you the favor
Of cutting short his life, and your distress.
CLÉANTE: What a display of young hotheadedness! 10
Do learn to moderate your fits of rage.
In this just kingdom, this enlightened age,
One does not settle things by violence.

## SCENE 3

MADAME PERNELLE DORINE ORGON
MARIANE DAMIS CLÉANTE
ELMIRE

MADAME PERNELLE: I hear strange tales of very strange events.
ORGON: Yes, strange events which these two eyes beheld.
The man's ingratitude is unparalleled.
I save a wretched pauper from starvation,
House him, and treat him like a blood relation, 5
Shower him every day with my largesse,
Give him my daughter, and all that I possess;
And meanwhile the unconscionable knave
Tries to induce my wife to misbehave;
And not content with such extreme rascality, 10
Now threatens me with my own liberality,
And aims, by taking base advantage of
The gifts I gave him out of Christian love,
To drive me from my house, a ruined man,
And make me end a pauper, as he began. 15
DORINE: Poor fellow!
MADAME PERNELLE: No, my son, I'll never bring
Myself to think him guilty of such a thing.

ORGON: How's that?
MADAME PERNELLE: The righteous always were maligned.
ORGON: Speak clearly, Mother. Say what's on your mind.
MADAME PERNELLE: I mean that I can smell a rat, my dear. 20
You know how everybody hates him, here.
ORGON: That has no bearing on the case at all.
MADAME PERNELLE: I told you a hundred times, when you were small,
That virtue in this world is hated ever;
Malicious men may die, but malice never. 25
ORGON: No doubt that's true, but how does it apply?
MADAME PERNELLE: They've turned you against him by a clever lie.
ORGON: I've told you, I was there and saw it done.
MADAME PERNELLE: Ah, slanderers will stop at nothing, Son.
ORGON: Mother, I'll lose my temper . . . For the last time, 30
I tell you I was witness to the crime.
MADAME PERNELLE: The tongues of spite are busy night and noon,
And to their venom no man is immune.
ORGON: You're talking nonsense. Can't you realize
I saw it; saw it; saw it with my eyes? 35
Saw, do you understand me? Must I shout it
Into your ears before you'll cease to doubt it?
MADAME PERNELLE: Appearances can deceive, my son. Dear me,
We cannot always judge by what we see.
ORGON: Drat! Drat!
MADAME PERNELLE: One often interprets things awry; 40
Good can seem evil to a suspicious eye.
ORGON: Was I to see his pawing at Elmire
As an act of charity?
MADAME PERNELLE: Till his guilt is clear,
A man deserves the benefit of the doubt.
You should have waited, to see how things turned out. 45
ORGON: Great God in Heaven, what more proof did I need?
Was I to sit there, watching, until he'd . . .
You drive me to the brink of impropriety.
MADAME PERNELLE: No, no, a man of such surpassing piety
Could not do such a thing. You cannot shake me. 50
I don't believe it, and you shall not make me.
ORGON: You vex me so that, if you weren't my mother,
I'd say to you . . . some dreadful thing or other.
DORINE: It's your turn now, Sir, not to be listened to;
You'd not trust us, and now she won't trust you. 55
CLÉANTE: My friends, we're wasting time which should be spent
In facing up to our predicament.
I fear that scoundrel's threats weren't made in sport.
DAMIS: Do you think he'd have the nerve to go to court?

ELMIRE: I'm sure he won't: they'd find it all too crude 60
A case of swindling and ingratitude.
CLÉANTE: Don't be too sure. He won't be at a loss
To give his claims a high and righteous gloss;
And clever rogues with far less valid cause
Have trapped their victims in a web of laws. 65
I say again that to antagonize
A man so strongly armed was most unwise.
ORGON: I know it; but the man's appalling cheek
Outraged me so, I couldn't control my pique.
CLÉANTE: I wish to Heaven that we could devise 70
Some truce between you, or some compromise.
ELMIRE: If I had known what cards he held, I'd not
Have roused his anger by my little plot.
ORGON (*to* DORINE, *as* M. LOYAL *enters*): What is that fellow looking for? Who is he?
Go talk to him — and tell him that I'm busy. 75

## SCENE 4

MONSIEUR LOYAL, DAMIS, ELMIRE, MADAME PERNELLE, MARIANE, CLÉANTE, ORGON, DORINE

MONSIEUR LOYAL: Good day, dear sister. Kindly let me see
Your master.
DORINE: He's involved with company,
And cannot be disturbed just now, I fear.
MONSIEUR LOYAL: I hate to intrude; but what has brought me here
Will not disturb your master, in any event. 5
Indeed, my news will make him most content.
DORINE: Your name?
MONSIEUR LOYAL: Just say that I bring greetings from
Monsieur Tartuffe, on whose behalf I've come.
DORINE (*to* ORGON): Sir, he's a very gracious man, and bears
A message from Tartuffe, which, he declares, 10
Will make you most content.
CLÉANTE: Upon my word,
I think this man had best be seen, and heard.
ORGON: Perhaps he has some settlement to suggest.
How shall I treat him? What manner would be best?
CLÉANTE: Control your anger, and if he should mention 15
Some fair adjustment, give him your full attention.
MONSIEUR LOYAL: Good health to you, good Sir. May Heaven confound
Your enemies, and may your joys abound.

ORGON (*aside, to* CLÉANTE): A gentle salutation: it confirms
My guess that he is here to offer terms. 20
MONSIEUR LOYAL: I've always held your family most dear;
I served your father, Sir, for many a year.
ORGON: Sir, I must ask your pardon; to my shame,
I cannot now recall your face or name.
MONSIEUR LOYAL: Loyal's my name; I come from Normandy, 25
And I'm a bailiff, in all modesty.
For forty years, praise God, it's been my boast
To serve with honor in that vital post,
And I am here, Sir, if you will permit
The liberty, to serve you with this writ . . . 30
ORGON: To — *what?*
MONSIEUR LOYAL: Now, please, Sir, let us have no friction:
It's nothing but an order of eviction.
You are to move your goods and family out
And make way for new occupants, without
Deferment or delay, and give the keys . . . 35
ORGON: I? Leave this house?
MONSIEUR LOYAL: Why yes, Sir, if you please.
This house, Sir, from the cellar to the roof,
Belongs now to the good Monsieur Tartuffe,
And he is lord and master of your estate
By virtue of a deed of present date, 40
Drawn in due form, with clearest legal phrasing . . .
DAMIS: Your insolence is utterly amazing!
MONSIEUR LOYAL: Young man, my business here is not with you,
But with your wise and temperate father, who,
Like every worthy citizen, stands in awe 45
Of justice, and would never obstruct the law.
ORGON: But . . .
MONSIEUR LOYAL: Not for a million, Sir, would you rebel
Against authority; I know that well.
You'll not make trouble, Sir, or interfere
With the execution of my duties here. 50
DAMIS: Someone may execute a smart tattoo
On that black jacket of yours, before you're through.
MONSIEUR LOYAL: Sir, bid your son be silent. I'd much regret
Having to mention such a nasty threat
Of violence, in writing my report. 55
DORINE (*aside*): This man Loyal's a most disloyal sort!
MONSIEUR LOYAL: I love all men of upright character,
And when I agreed to serve these papers, Sir,
It was your feelings that I had in mind.
I couldn't bear to see the case assigned 60

To someone else, who might esteem you less
And so subject you to unpleasantness.
ORGON: What's more unpleasant than telling a man to leave
His house and home?
MONSIEUR LOYAL: You'd like a short reprieve?
If you desire it, Sir, I shall not press you, 65
But wait until tomorrow to dispossess you.
Splendid. I'll come and spend the night here, then,
Most quietly, with half a score of men.
For form's sake, you might bring me, just before
You go to bed, the keys to the front door. 70
My men, I promise, will be on their best
Behavior, and will not disturb your rest.
But bright and early, Sir, you must be quick
And move out all your furniture, every stick:
The men I've chosen are both young and strong, 75
And with their help it shouldn't take you long.
In short, I'll make things pleasant and convenient,
And since I'm being so extremely lenient,
Please show me, Sir, a like consideration,
And give me your entire cooperation. 80
ORGON (*aside*): I may be all but bankrupt, but I vow
I'd give a hundred louis, here and now,
Just for the pleasure of landing one good clout
Right on the end of that complacent snout.
CLÉANTE: Careful; don't make things worse.
DAMIS: My bootsole itches 85
To give that beggar a good kick in the breeches.
DORINE: Monsieur Loyal, I'd love to hear the whack
Of a stout stick across your fine broad back.
MONSIEUR LOYAL: Take care: a woman too may go to jail if
She uses threatening language to a bailiff. 90
CLÉANTE: Enough, enough, Sir. This must not go on.
Give me that paper, please, and then begone.
MONSIEUR LOYAL: Well, *au revoir*. God give you all good cheer!
ORGON: May God confound you, and him who sent you here!

## SCENE 5

ORGON, ELMIRE, DORINE, CLÉANTE, MADAME PERNELLE, DAMIS, MARIANE

ORGON: Now, Mother, was I right or not? This writ
Should change your notion of Tartuffe a bit.
Do you perceive his villainy at last?

MADAME PERNELLE: I'm thunderstruck. I'm utterly aghast.
DORINE: Oh, come, be fair. You mustn't take offense 5
At this new proof of his benevolence.
He's acting out of selfless love, I know.
Material things enslave the soul, and so
He kindly has arranged your liberation
From all that might endanger your salvation. 10
ORGON: Will you not ever hold your tongue, you dunce?
CLÉANTE: Come, you must take some action, and at once.
ELMIRE: Go tell the world of the low trick he's tried.
The deed of gift is surely nullified
By such behavior, and public rage will not 15
Permit the wretch to carry out his plot.

## SCENE 6

VALÈRE, ELMIRE, DAMIS, ORGON, MARIANE, DORINE, CLÉANTE, MADAME PERNELLE

VALÈRE: Sir, though I hate to bring you more bad news,
Such is the danger that I cannot choose.
A friend who is extremely close to me
And knows my interest in your family
Has, for my sake, presumed to violate 5
The secrecy that's due to things of state,
And sends me word that you are in a plight
From which your one salvation lies in flight.
That scoundrel who's imposed upon you so
Denounced you to the King an hour ago 10
And, as supporting evidence, displayed
The strong-box of a certain renegade
Whose secret papers, so he testified,
You had disloyally agreed to hide.
I don't know just what charges may be pressed, 15
But there's a warrant out for your arrest;
Tartuffe has been instructed, furthermore,
To guide the arresting officer to your door.
CLÉANTE: He's clearly done this to facilitate
His seizure of your house and your estate. 20
ORGON: That man, I must say, is a vicious beast!
VALÈRE: Quick, Sir; you mustn't tarry in the least.
My carriage is outside, to take you hence;
This thousand louis should cover all expense.
Let's lose no time, or you shall be undone; 25
The sole defense, in this case, is to run.

I shall go with you all the way, and place you
In a safe refuge to which they'll never trace you.
ORGON: Alas, dear boy, I wish that I could show you
My gratitude for everything I owe you. 30
But now is not the time; I pray the Lord
That I may live to give you your reward.
Farewell, my dears; be careful . . .
CLÉANTE: Brother, hurry.
We shall take care of things; you needn't worry.

## SCENE 7

| THE OFFICER | ELMIRE | DORINE |
|---|---|---|
| TARTUFFE | MARIANE | CLÉANTE |
| VALÈRE | MADAME PERNELLE | DAMIS |
| ORGON | | |

TARTUFFE: Gently, Sir, gently; stay right where you are.
No need for haste; your lodging isn't far.
You're off to prison, by order of the Prince.
ORGON: This is the crowning blow, you wretch; and since
It means my total ruin and defeat, 5
Your villainy is now at last complete.
TARTUFFE: You needn't try to provoke me; it's no use.
Those who serve Heaven must expect abuse.
CLÉANTE: You are indeed most patient, sweet, and blameless.
DORINE: How he exploits the name of Heaven! It's shameless. 10
TARTUFFE: Your taunts and mockeries are all for naught;
To do my duty is my only thought.
MARIANE: Your love of duty is most meritorious,
And what you've done is little short of glorious.
TARTUFFE: All deeds are glorious, Madam, which obey 15
The sovereign prince who sent me here today.
ORGON: I rescued you when you were destitute;
Have you forgotten that, you thankless brute?
TARTUFFE: No, no, I well remember everything;
But my first duty is to serve my King. 20
That obligation is so paramount
That other claims, beside it, do not count;
And for it I would sacrifice my wife,
My family, my friend, or my own life.
ELMIRE: Hypocrite!
DORINE: All that we most revere, he uses 25
To cloak his plots and camouflage his ruses.
CLÉANTE: If it is true that you are animated
By pure and loyal zeal, as you have stated,

Why was this zeal not roused until you'd sought
To make Orgon a cuckold, and been caught? 30
Why weren't you moved to give your evidence
Until your outraged host had driven you hence?
I shan't say that the gift of all his treasure
Ought to have damped your zeal in any measure;
But if he is a traitor, as you declare, 35
How could you condescend to be his heir?

TARTUFFE (*to the* OFFICER): Sir, spare me all this clamor; it's growing shrill.
Please carry out your orders, if you will.

OFFICER: Yes, I've delayed too long, Sir. Thank you kindly.
You're just the proper person to remind me. 40
Come, you are off to join the other boarders
In the King's prison, according to his orders.

TARTUFFE: Who? I, Sir?

OFFICER: Yes.

TARTUFFE: To prison? This can't be true!

OFFICER: I owe an explanation, but not to you.
(*To* ORGON.) Sir, all is well; rest easy, and be grateful. 45
We serve a Prince to whom all sham is hateful,
A Prince who sees into our inmost hearts,
And can't be fooled by any trickster's arts.
His royal soul, though generous and human,
Views all things with discernment and acumen; 50
His sovereign reason is not lightly swayed,
And all his judgments are discreetly weighed.
He honors righteous men of every kind,
And yet his zeal for virtue is not blind,
Nor does his love of piety numb his wits 55
And make him tolerant of hypocrites.
'Twas hardly likely that this man could cozen
A King who's foiled such liars by the dozen.
With one keen glance, the King perceived the whole
Perverseness and corruption of his soul, 60
And thus high Heaven's justice was displayed:
Betraying you, the rogue stood self-betrayed.
The King soon recognized Tartuffe as one
Notorious by another name, who'd done
So many vicious crimes that one could fill 65
Ten volumes with them, and be writing still.
But to be brief: our sovereign was appalled
By this man's treachery toward you, which he called
The last, worst villainy of a vile career,
And bade me follow the impostor here 70

To see how gross his impudence could be,
And force him to restore your property.
Your private papers, by the King's command,
I hereby seize and give into your hand.
The King, by royal order, invalidates 75
The deed which gave this rascal your estates,
And pardons, furthermore, your grave offense
In harboring an exile's documents.
By these decrees, our Prince rewards you for
Your loyal deeds in the late civil war, 80
And shows how heartfelt is his satisfaction
In recompensing any worthy action,
How much he prizes merit, and how he makes
More of men's virtues than of their mistakes.

DORINE: Heaven be praised!

MADAME PERNELLE: I breathe again, at last. 85

ELMIRE: We're safe.

MARIANE: I can't believe the danger's past.

ORGON (*to* TARTUFFE): Well, traitor, now you see . . .

CLÉANTE: Ah, Brother, please,
Let's not descend to such indignities.
Leave the poor wretch to his unhappy fate,
And don't say anything to aggravate 90
His present woes; but rather hope that he
Will soon embrace an honest piety,
And mend his ways, and by a true repentance
Move our just King to moderate his sentence.
Meanwhile, go kneel before your sovereign's throne 95
And thank him for the mercies he has shown.

ORGON: Well said: let's go at once and, gladly kneeling,
Express the gratitude which all are feeling.
Then, when that first great duty has been done,
We'll turn with pleasure to a second one, 100
And give Valère, whose love has proven so true,
The wedded happiness which is his due.

*Tartuffe* represents the neoclassical drama of seventeenth-century France. From Italian stagecraft of the Renaissance, the French theater during the reign of Louis XIV developed most of the features of the conventional modern theater: a deep box stage framed by a proscenium arch, with the audience seated in front; a curtain; wings for movable sets; artificial light; elaborate painted scenery and backstage mechanical devices for special effects; actresses in female roles. It also took over some of the dramatic conventions of the Italian theater, particularly the three unities and — in comedy — the characters of the *commedia dell'arte,* semi-farces in which characters and plot were given but the dialogue improvised during performance. In *Tartuffe,* we recognize Orgon, the foolish and tyrannical father, Valère and Mariane, the nice if somewhat bland young lovers, and Dorine, the pert and clever maid, as descendants from their stock Italian prototypes.

*Tartuffe* had a complicated birth. An early version of its present first three acts made up the whole play when it was first given at Versailles in 1664. King Louis himself was amused, but the religious bigots at court took offense and prevailed upon him to ban the play. "The King," says a contemporary, "could not in his delicate carefulness for the things that concern religion suffer vice to be made so like virtue, that one might be taken for the other." The play was, however, given private readings and even performances during the next few years, probably in a five-act version. For a public performance of the play (in five acts) in 1667 Molière had changed his title to *The Impostor,* to leave no one in doubt that he was attacking only false piety, and dressed Tartuffe as a fop rather than in priest-like black, but again he drew the ire of the religious authorities. Only in 1669 did the King permit the play, with its original title restored and in its present form, to be freely performed.

For us, living in a more liberal — or indifferent — age, the implications of Tartuffe's hypocrisy are likely to be less controversial, though hardly less meaningful. Tartuffe threatens a family with ruin, almost disrupts the basic social unit, breaks natural bonds. He is himself a solitary outsider, familyless, friendless, loveless, without any social context. But the fact that he is not related to anybody or anything before Orgon picks him up is not, somehow, a cause for pity. Rather, it makes him a sinister, antisocial figure, lone evil against the vital group.

Behind the deliberate artifice of the whole play, behind the farcical intrigue, the stylization of character, and the fluent and funny couplet verse, is a dark moral fable for which the comic conventions of the neoclassical theater shockingly serve as an almost perfect vehicle. Tartuffe's mask of devoutness conceals a monster of greed, lechery, and ingratitude; but the human grotesque is an actual menace; the caricature has the power to destroy. The bourgeois society reflected in the play is a fallen world, in which evil deception is both plausible and resourceful because its main victim fails to temper religious zeal with worldly wisdom. Piety becomes monomania.

This is only one of the play's many ironies. Shared fear almost separates the lovers when their romance is threatened. Honesty provokes self-righteous wrath in Orgon. Orgon's folly forces the faithful Elmire to play the role of adulterous coquette — and forces Orgon to listen to her performance. M. Loyal is a model of politeness while he dispossesses Orgon of his house; the public bailiff is "loyal" only to hypocritical villainy. Where plain speaking has been forbidden, sarcasm — the rhetoric for devious meaning — becomes the voice of wise virtue, like Dorine's. The most richly ironic scene in the whole play is Scene 6 in Act III, but the richness is largely a matter of implications that carry us beyond the realm of high comedy to which the scene ostensibly and brilliantly belongs. When Damis denounces Tartuffe to his father as Elmire's would-be seducer, Tartuffe readily admits his sinfulness in such sweeping terms of self-abasement that Orgon becomes only further convinced of his Christian humility and turns Damis out of the house. The villain uses truth as a means to deception. This is the sort of thing that places *Tartuffe,* like *The Misanthrope* (though for different reasons), among Molière's problem comedies. Our laughter may well be uncomfortable. Somehow it implicates us in the vice and folly on stage.

Formally, what is most striking about the play is the delay of Tartuffe's appearance for more than two acts. The delay represents a daring piece of dramaturgy, for though the gain in audience suspense is obvious, there is also the risk of anticlimax when the title character *does* appear. But his first speech, "Hang up my hair-shirt, put my scourge in place,/And pray, Laurent, for Heaven's perpetual grace," brilliantly justifies the device. False unction is on display forever in this penitent ascetic with a valet.

The little scene reveals a major characteristic of Molière's comic art. What his characters are they are with an intensity and thoroughness and sharpness of outline that establish their identity once and for all. We are dealing in blacks and whites. There are no complexities or ambiguities or subtle depths. Virtue and wisdom exist less for their own sake than as antitheses to vice and folly, and if the gulls appear as stereotypes that is no more than their own doing. They are diminishers of their own humanity. The opening dialogue between old Madame Pernelle and the various members of the household, in which they all take turns trying to interrupt the old lady's harangue but only succeed in drawing her fire, represents a patterning of speech that is obviously unnatural but which nevertheless justifies itself not only as a certain rhythm of dialogue but also as a method by which human attitudes are clearly defined and contrasted. Molière is not interested in photographic realism or in doing justice to the infinite complexities of the human soul, in discovering the good that surely must reside somewhere even in a bigot. He is interested in providing us with a memorable spectacle of hypocrisy, gullibility, and obstinacy in action. The long, stilted speeches, the alternating passages of fast, cut-and-thrust dialogue, the exaggerations and oversimplifications and contrivances of situation and character, these are all deliberate formalizations of the dramatist's art, devices that both heighten the comedy – or farce, if one likes – and extend the anatomy of basic human attitudes. Take a famous scene that presents some characteristic difficulties in the way of enjoying Molière – Scene 4 in Act I. Orgon has just returned from a trip to the country and asks the maid Dorine how everyone has been during his absence. Dorine tells him his wife has had an attack of fever, to which he replies, "Ah! And Tartuffe?" Dorine says he is comfortable and in excellent health, and Orgon exclaims, "Poor fellow!" This sequence of four speeches is repeated three times. Again a pattern is established, and we gather an impression of Orgon's perversion of values.

But is it funny? Does it reflect actual human behavior, even allowing the playwright the privilege of exaggeration for heightened effect? What does it *mean* to say "Poor fellow" about someone you have just been told is perfectly well and content? Why is the speech repeated?

The exchange is, obviously, a shortcut to characterization as well as a piece of verbal slapstick. But if it were only that, we would not be dealing with great comedy. We are, though, and the reason is that we can feel the unnaturalness and idiocy of Orgon's replies to be functional to Molière's theme. Orgon's affection for Tartuffe, to the point of ignoring and even injuring his own family, *is* a form of lunacy. His response to the news of his wife's illness is no more insane than his later decision to give his daughter in marriage to a man who is hateful to her or to disinherit his son in favor of that man and to entrust him with a friend's secrets. While Dorine's speeches in the scene are full and flavorful, vivid with concrete detail, Orgon's are limited to five words, two set phrases, the expression of a small and frozen attitude. He listens and yet does not listen. What Dorine tells him about Tartuffe does not reach him as meaning; it only triggers a piece of pious cant; he answers automatically, totally inadequate to the human situation. He speaks like a man hypnotized, or under a spell. There is poetic justice (as Dorine points out) in the scene in which Madame Pernelle obstinately refuses to believe that Tartuffe could have designs on Elmire, even after her son has been convinced by the evidence of his own eyes. If, after the spell has been broken, Orgon is frustrated by his equally stubborn mother into contemplating the absurdity of his own previous behavior, this is precisely Molière's point. Orgon has only himself to blame for his troubles and for his flatness of character. In a sense, the play is about inflexibility of spirit as much as it is about hypocrisy.

Against Orgon's obstinate stupidity and unnaturalness of feeling and against the increasingly sinister presence of Tartuffe (consider the function and effect of M. Loyal in this connection), the play asserts the primary value of sane moderation in human relationships. Three characters represent these values: Cléante, the voice of wisdom and restraint, whose most significant speech is the one in which he objects to Orgon's vow never again to trust a pious man; Dorine, who constantly deflates stuffiness and pretension and who saves Valère and Mariane from their own foolish pride; and Elmire, who refuses to become hysterical over Tartuffe's advances and succeeds in opening Orgon's eyes by using herself as bait to lure Tartuffe into giving himself away. These three combine goodness with intelligence and strength. In contrast, there are the good characters who suffer because of some excess of feeling: Damis's rash anger, like his father's later, ends in his discomfiture and the temporary strengthening of Tartuffe's hand; and Mariane has to be rescued from her own despair. Valère's character is ambivalent in this respect. He and Mariane are too stubbornly proud to manage their own romance, but at the very end of the play he passes from folly to a kind of heroism and becomes Tartuffe's contrast (*foil,* in the technical term): Tartuffe repays Orgon's kindness with ingratitude; Valère repays Orgon's injustice with kindness.

If Cléante is Molière's spokesman (*raisonneur*), it becomes significant that he and his allies are rendered helpless against the efficacy of evil at the end. The best they can hope for is some way of coming to terms with Tartuffe. To recover what Orgon's error has cost them appears impossible. For a moment in Act V, the play seems about to turn into a kind of tragedy — the family to be destroyed by the evil intruder. At this point Molière does something that courses in writing drama warn against; he introduces a *deus ex machina,* a person (or fact) who has not entered the action before and who steps in to resolve a deadlocked situation. In this case, the god from the wings is King Louis XIV, represented by the officer who arrests Tartuffe. Nothing earlier in the play has led us to expect this development. Is it, therefore, more than fulsome flattery of Molière's royal patron as the earthly representative of divine providence and an awkward way out of a plot that threatened to master the supposed writer of comedy? It is certainly not playing the game according to the rules of detective fiction.

Again one must keep in mind Molière's artistic end — not plausibility but communication of wisdom in effective drama. The fact that outside help is needed, that the all-powerful hand of the king must interfere to keep evil from succeeding against innocence, becomes a plot metaphor for the simple truth that discovery of one's error and sincere remorse for it do not necessarily rectify its consequences. We are moving here on the very edge of comedy, where the forces of stupidity and evil somehow seem more substantial than those of reason and goodness. The comedy turns serious. Innocent, gullible, well-meaning man is unable to cope with evil alone. He needs kingly help.

# SIR GEORGE ETHEREGE

# The Man of Mode; or, Sir Fopling Flutter

*A Comedy*

## PROLOGUE

BY SIR CAR SCROOPE,[1] BARONET

Like dancers on the ropes poor poets fare,
Most perish young, the rest in danger are;
This (one would think) should make our authors wary,
But, gamester-like, the giddy fools miscarry.
A lucky hand or two so tempts 'em on,
They cannot leave off play till they're undone.
With modest fears a Muse does first begin,
Like a young wench newly entice'd to sin;
But tickl'd once with praise, by her good will,
The wanton fool would never more lie still.
'Tis an old mistress you'll meet here to-night,

From *Restoration Plays,* edited by Brice Harris, 1953. Reprinted by permission of Random House, Inc.

1 (1649–80) courtier and minor poet

Whose charms you once have look'd on with delight.
But now of late such dirty drabs[2] have known ye,
A Muse o'th' better sort's ashamed to own ye.
Nature well drawn, and wit, must now give place
To gaudy nonsense and to dull grimace;
Nor is it strange that you should like so much
That kind of wit, for most of yours is such.
But I'm afraid that while to France we go,
To bring you home fine dresses, dance, and show,
The stage, like you, will but more foppish[3] grow.
Of foreign wares, why should we fetch the scum,
When we can be so richly serv'd at home?
For heav'n be thank'd, 'tis not so wise an age
But your own follies may supply the stage.
Tho' often plough'd, there's no great fear the soil
Should barren grow by the too frequent toil;
While at your doors are to be daily found
Such loads of dunghill to manure the ground.
'Tis by your follies that we players thrive,
As the physicians by diseases live;
And as each year some new distemper reigns,
Whose friendly poison helps to increase their gains,
So, among you, there starts up every day
Some new, unheard-of fool for us to play.
Then, for your own sakes be not too severe,
Nor what you all admire at home, damn here;
Since each is fond of his own ugly face,
Why should you, when we hold it, break the glass?

## THE ACTORS' NAMES

GENTLEMEN:

- MR. DORIMANT
- MR. MEDLEY
- OLD HARRY BELLAIR
- YOUNG HARRY BELLAIR
- SIR FOPLING FLUTTER

GENTLEWOMEN:

- LADY TOWNLEY
- EMILIA
- MRS. LOVEIT
- BELLINDA
- LADY WOODVILL, and
- HARRIET, her daughter

WAITING WOMEN:

- PERT and
- BUSY

TOM, a Shoemaker
NAN, an Orange-Woman
THREE SLOVENLY BULLIES
TWO CHAIRMEN
MR. SMIRK, a Parson
HANDY, a *Valet-de-chambre*
PAGES, FOOTMEN, &c.

[2] whores
[3] silly and affected (particularly in dress and speech)

## ACT I

*Scene: A dressing-room; a table covered with a toilet, clothes laid ready.*

*Enter* DORIMANT *in his gown and slippers, with a note in his hand, made up;*[1] *repeating verses.*

DORIMANT:

Now for some ages had the pride of Spain
Made the sun shine on half the world in vain.[2]

(*Then looking on the note.*)

"For Mrs. Loveit." What a dull, insipid thing is a billet-doux written in cold blood, after the heat of the business is over! It is a tax upon good nature which I have here been labouring to pay, and have done it, but with as much regret as ever fanatic[3] paid the Royal Aid or church duties. 'Twill have the same fate, I know, that all my notes to her have had of late: 'twill not be thought kind enough. 'Faith, women are i'the right when they jealously examine our letters, for in them we always first discover our decay of passion. – Hey! who waits?[4]

(*Enter* HANDY.)

HANDY: Sir ——.

DORIMANT: Call a footman.

HANDY: None of 'em are come yet.

DORIMANT: Dogs! Will they ever lie snoring abed till noon?

HANDY: 'Tis all one, Sir; if they're up, you indulge 'em so they're ever poaching after whores all the morning.

DORIMANT: Take notice henceforward who's wanting in his duty; the next clap he gets, he shall rot for an example. What vermin are those chattering without?

HANDY: Foggy[5] Nan, the orange-woman, and Swearing Tom, the shoemaker.

DORIMANT: Go, call in that overgrown jade with the flasket[6] of guts before her; fruit is refreshing in a morning. (*Exit* HANDY.)

[1] completed and ready to be sent

[2] (from a poem by the Cavalier poet Edmund Waller [1606–87]. Dorimant quotes Waller's "smooth" couplets throughout the play. These notes will identify the author of a quotation only when he is *not* Waller)

[3] Puritan (the Puritans were opposed to both the monarchy and the Church of England)

[4] is in attendance

[5] flabby

[6] basket

It is not that I love you less
Than when before your feet I lay —

(*Enter* ORANGE-WOMAN *and* HANDY.)

— How now, double tripe,[7] what news do you bring?

ORANGE-WOMAN: News! Here's the best fruit has come to town t'year; gad, I was up before four o'clock this morning and bought all the choice i'the market.

DORIMANT: The nasty refuse of your shop.

ORANGE-WOMAN: You need not make mouths at it; I assure you, 'tis all culled ware.

DORIMANT: The citizens[8] buy better on a holiday in their walk to Tottenham.[9]

ORANGE-WOMAN: Good or bad, 'tis all one; I never knew you commend anything. Lord! would the ladies had heard you talk of 'em as I have done! (*Sets down the fruit.*) Here, bid your man give me an angel.[10]

DORIMANT: Give the bawd[11] her fruit again.

ORANGE-WOMAN: Well, on my conscience, there never was the like of you! God's my life, I had almost forgot to tell you there is a young gentlewoman lately come to town with her mother, that is so taken with you.

DORIMANT: Is she handsome?

ORANGE-WOMAN: Nay, gad, there are few finer women, I tell you but so, and a hugeous fortune, they say. Here, eat this peach. It comes from the stone; 'tis better than any Newington[12] y'have tasted.

DORIMANT (*taking the peach*): This fine woman, I'll lay my life, is some awkward, ill-fashioned country toad who, not having above four dozen of black hairs on her head, has adorned her baldness with a large, white fruz,[13] that she may look sparkishly in the forefront of the King's box at an old play.

ORANGE-WOMAN: Gad, you'd change your note quickly if you did but see her.

DORIMANT: How came she to know me?

ORANGE-WOMAN: She saw you yesterday at the Change;[14] she told me you came and fooled with the woman at the next shop.

DORIMANT: I remember there was a mask[15] observed me, indeed. Fooled, did she say?

ORANGE-WOMAN: Ay; I vow she told me twenty things you said, too, and acted with head and with her body so like you —

(*Enter* MEDLEY.)

[7] (1) paunch, (2) trash

[8] tradespeople

[9] lower middle-class suburb north of London

[10] gold coin worth about ten shillings

[11] (young orange-women were often prostitutes, and old ones often procured girls for their male customers)

[12] town in Kent, famous for its orchards

[13] wig of short, curled hair

[14] the New Exchange, a fashionable shopping area near the Strand

[15] i.e., a masked woman (cf. "vizard," note 25, this act)

MEDLEY: Dorimant, my life, my joy, my darling sin! how dost thou?

ORANGE-WOMAN: Lord, what a filthy trick these men have got of kissing one another! (*She spits.*)

MEDLEY: Why do you suffer this cartload of scandal to come near you and make your neighbors think you so improvident to need a bawd?

ORANGE-WOMAN: Good, now! we shall have it you did but want[16] him to help you! Come, pay me for my fruit.

MEDLEY: Make us thankful for it, huswife, bawds are as much out of fashion as gentlemen-ushers; none but old formal ladies use the one, and none but foppish old stagers[17] employ the other. Go! You are an insignificant brandy bottle.

DORIMANT: Nay, there you wrong her; three quarts of Canary is her business.

ORANGE-WOMAN: What you please, gentlemen.

DORIMANT: To him! give him as good as he brings.

ORANGE-WOMAN: Hang him, there is not such another heathen in the town again, except it be the shoemaker without.

MEDLEY: I shall see you hold up your hand at the bar next sessions for murder, huswife; that shoemaker can take his oath you are in fee with the doctors to sell green fruit to the gentry that the crudities may breed diseases.

ORANGE-WOMAN: Pray, give me my money.

DORIMANT: Not a penny! When you bring the gentlewoman hither you spoke of, you shall be paid.

ORANGE-WOMAN: The gentlewoman! the gentlewoman may be as honest[18] as your sisters for aught as I know. Pray, pay me, Mr. Dorimant, and do not abuse me so; I have an honester way[19] of living – you know it.

MEDLEY: Was there ever such a resty[20] bawd?

DORIMANT: Some jade's tricks she has, but she makes amends when she's in good humour. —— Come, tell me the lady's name and Handy shall pay you.

ORANGE-WOMAN: I must not; she forbid me.

DORIMANT: That's a sure sign she would have you.

MEDLEY: Where does she live?

ORANGE-WOMAN: They lodge at my house.

MEDLEY: Nay, then she's in a hopeful way.

ORANGE-WOMAN: Good Mr. Medley, say your pleasure of me, but take heed how you affront my house! God's my life! – "in a hopeful way"!

DORIMANT: Prithee, peace! What kind of woman's the mother?

ORANGE-WOMAN: A goodly grave gentlewoman. Lord, how she talks against the wild young men o' the town! As for your part, she thinks you an arrant devil; should she see you, on my conscience she would look if you had not a cloven foot.

[16] need
[17] veterans, old hands
[18] chaste
[19] i.e., than being a bawd
[20] lazy, sluggish

DORIMANT: Does she know me?

ORANGE-WOMAN: Only by hearsay; a thousand horrid stories have been told her of you, and she believes 'em all.

MEDLEY: By the character this should be the famous Lady Woodvill and her daughter Harriet.

ORANGE-WOMAN: The devil's in him for guessing, I think.

DORIMANT: Do you know 'em?

MEDLEY: Both very well; the mother's a great admirer of the forms and civility of the last age.

DORIMANT: An antiquated beauty may be allowed to be out of humour at the freedoms of the present. This is a good account of the mother; pray, what is the daughter?

MEDLEY: Why, first, she's an heiress — vastly rich.

DORIMANT: And handsome?

MEDLEY: What alteration a twelvemonth may have bred in her I know not, but a year ago she was the beautifullest creature I ever saw: a fine, easy, clean shape; light brown hair in abundance; her features regular; her complexion clear and lively; large, wanton eyes; but above all, a mouth that has made me kiss it a thousand times in imagination; teeth white and even, and pretty, pouting lips, with a little moisture ever hanging on them, that look like the Provins rose fresh on the bush, ere the morning sun has quite drawn up the dew.

DORIMANT: Rapture! mere[21] rapture!

ORANGE-WOMAN: Nay, gad, he tells you true; she's a delicate creature.

DORIMANT: Has she wit?

MEDLEY: More than is usual in her sex, and as much malice. Then, she's as wild as you would wish her, and has a demureness in her looks that makes it so surprising.

DORIMANT: Flesh and blood cannot hear this and not long to know her.

MEDLEY: I wonder what makes her mother bring her up to town; an old doting keeper cannot be more jealous of his mistress.

ORANGE-WOMAN: She made me laugh yesterday; there was a judge came to visit 'em, and the old man, she told me, did so stare upon her, and when he saluted[22] her smacked so heartily. Who would think it of 'em?

MEDLEY: God-a-mercy, judge!

DORIMANT: Do 'em right; the gentlemen of the long robe have not been wanting by their good examples to countenance the crying sin o' the nation.

MEDLEY: Come, on with your trappings; 'tis later than you imagine.

DORIMANT: Call in the shoemaker, Handy.

ORANGE-WOMAN: Good Mr. Dorimant, pay me. Gad, I had rather give you my fruit than stay to be abused by that foul-mouthed rogue; what you

[21] sheer
[22] kissed

gentlemen say, it matters not much, but such a dirty fellow does one more disgrace.

DORIMANT: Give her ten shillings, and be sure you tell the young gentlewoman I must be acquainted with her.

ORANGE-WOMAN: Now do you long to be tempting this pretty creature. Well, heavens mend you!

MEDLEY: Farewell, bog![23] (*Exit* ORANGE-WOMAN *and* HANDY.) Dorimant, when did you see your *pisaller*,[24] as you call her, Mrs. Loveit?

DORIMANT: Not these two days.

MEDLEY: And how stand affairs between you?

DORIMANT: There has been great patching of late, much ado; we make a shift to hang together.

MEDLEY: I wonder how her mighty spirit bears it.

DORIMANT: Ill enough, on all conscience; I never knew so violent a creature.

MEDLEY: She's the most passionate in her love and the most extravagant in her jealousy of any woman I ever heard of. What note is that?

DORIMANT: An excuse I am going to send her for the neglect I am guilty of.

MEDLEY: Prithee, read it.

DORIMANT: No; but if you will take the pains, you may.

MEDLEY (*reads*):

I never was a lover of business, but now I have a just reason to hate it, since it has kept me these two days from seeing you. I intend to wait upon you in the afternoon, and in the pleasure of your conversation forget all I have suffered during this tedious absence.

This business of yours, Dorimant, has been with a vizard[25] at the playhouse; I have had an eye on you. If some malicious body should betray you, this kind note would hardly make your peace with her.

DORIMANT: I desire no better.

MEDLEY: Why, would her knowledge of it oblige you?

DORIMANT: Most infinitely; next to the coming to a good understanding with a new mistress, I love a quarrel with an old one. But the devil's in't, there has been such a calm in my affairs of late, I have not had the pleasure of making a woman so much as break her fan, to be sullen, or forswear herself, these three days.

MEDLEY: A very great misfortune. Let me see; I love mischief well enough to forward this business myself. I'll about it presently, and though I know the truth of what y'ave done will set her a-raving, I'll heighten it a little with invention, leave her in a fit o' the mother,[26] and be here again before y'are ready.

DORIMANT: Pray, stay; you may spare yourself the labour. The business is

[23] soggy person

[24] (Fr. "to go worst") a substitute for someone better

[25] a masked woman, usually a prostitute

[26] hysteria

undertaken already by one who will manage it with as much address, and I think with a little more malice, than you can.

MEDLEY: Who i'the devil's name can this be!

DORIMANT: Why, the vizard – that very vizard you saw me with.

MEDLEY: Does she love mischief so well as to betray herself to spite another?

DORIMANT: Not so neither, Medley. I will make you comprehend the mystery: this mask, for a farther confirmation of what I have been these two days swearing to her, made me yesterday at the playhouse make her a promise before her face utterly to break off with Loveit, and, because she tenders[27] my reputation and would not have me do a barbarous thing, has contrived a way to give me a handsome occasion.

MEDLEY: Very good.

DORIMANT: She intends about an hour before me, this afternoon, to make Loveit a visit, and, having the privilege, by reason of a professed friendship between 'em, to talk of her concerns ——

MEDLEY: Is she a friend?

DORIMANT: Oh, an intimate friend!

MEDLEY: Better and better; pray, proceed.

DORIMANT: She means insensibly[28] to insinuate[29] a discourse of me and artificially[30] raise her jealousy to such a height that, transported with the first motions of her passion, she shall fly upon me with all the fury imaginable as soon as ever I enter; the quarrel being thus happily begun, I am to play my part, confess and justify all my roguery, swear her impertinence and ill-humour makes her intolerable, tax her with the next fop that comes into my head, and in a huff march away, slight her, and leave her to be taken by whosoever thinks it worth his time to lie down before her.

MEDLEY: This vizard is a spark and has a genius that makes her worthy of yourself, Dorimant.

(*Enter* HANDY, SHOEMAKER, *and* FOOTMAN.)

DORIMANT: You rogue there who sneak like a dog that has flung down a dish, if you do not mend your waiting, I'll uncase[31] you and turn you loose to the wheel of fortune. Handy, seal this and let him run with it presently. (*Exit* FOOTMAN.)

MEDLEY: Since y'are resolved on a quarrel, why do you send her this kind note?

DORIMANT: To keep her at home in order to the business. – (*To the* SHOEMAKER.) How now, you drunken sot?

SHOEMAKER: 'Zbud,[32] you have no reason to talk; I have not had a bottle of sack[33] of yours in my belly this fortnight.

27 is solicitous about
28 slyly
29 introduce in a devious way
30 artfully
31 strip (of his livery; i.e., dismiss from service)
32 by God's blood
33 dry white wine

MEDLEY: The orange-woman says your neighbours take notice what a heathen you are, and design to inform the bishop and have you burned for an atheist.

SHOEMAKER: Damn her, dunghill, if her husband does not remove her, she stinks so, the parish intend to indict him for a nuisance.

MEDLEY: I advise you like a friend; reform your life. You have brought the envy of the world upon you by living above yourself. Whoring and swearing are vices too genteel for a shoemaker.

SHOEMAKER: 'Zbud, I think you men of quality will grow as unreasonable as the women. You would ingross[34] the sins of the nation; poor folks can no sooner be wicked but th'are railed at by their betters.

DORIMANT: Sirrah,[35] I'll have you stand i'the pillory for this libel!

SHOEMAKER: Some of you deserve it, I'm sure; there are so many of 'em, that our journeymen nowadays, instead of harmless ballads, sing nothing but your damned lampoons.

DORIMANT: Our lampoons, you rogue!

SHOEMAKER: Nay, good Master, why should not you write your own commentaries as well as Cæsar?

MEDLEY: The rascal's read, I perceive.

SHOEMAKER: You know the old proverb – ale and history.[36]

DORIMANT: Draw on my shoes, Sirrah.

SHOEMAKER: Here's a shoe —— !

DORIMANT: Sits with more wrinkles than there are in an angry bully's forehead!

SHOEMAKER: 'Zbud, as smooth as your mistress's skin does upon her! So; strike your foot in home. 'Zbud, if e'er a monsieur of 'em all[37] make more fashionable ware, I'll be content to have my ears whipped off with my own paring knife.

MEDLEY: And served up in a ragout instead of coxcombs to a company of French shoemakers for a collation.

SHOEMAKER: Hold, hold! Damn 'em, caterpillars![38] let 'em feed upon cabbage. Come Master, your health this morning next my heart now!

DORIMANT: Go, get you home and govern your family better! Do not let your wife follow you to the ale-house, beat your whore, and lead you home in triumph.

SHOEMAKER: 'Zbud, there's never a man i'the town lives more like a gentleman with his wife than I do. I never mind her motions,[39] she never inquires into mine; we speak to one another civilly, hate one another heartily, and because 'tis vulgar to lie and soak[40] together, we have each of us our several[41] settle-bed.[42]

[34] monopolize
[35] a term of address used to one's inferiors
[36] ("Truth is in ale as in history")
[37] any Frenchman
[38] ravagers, extortioners
[39] doings
[40] drink
[41] separate
[42] daybed

DORIMANT: Give him half a crown.

MEDLEY: Not without[43] he will promise to be bloody drunk.

SHOEMAKER: "Tope"[44] 's the word i'the eye of the world, for my master's honor, Robin!

DORIMANT: Do not debauch my servants, Sirrah.

SHOEMAKER: I only tip him the wink;[45] he knows an ale-house from a hovel. (*Exit* SHOEMAKER.)

DORIMANT: My clothes, quickly.

MEDLEY: Where shall we dine today?

(*Enter* YOUNG BELLAIR.)

DORIMANT: Where you will; here comes a good third man.

YOUNG BELLAIR: Your servant, gentlemen.

MEDLEY: Gentle Sir, how will you answer this visit to your honourable mistress? 'Tis not her interest you should keep company with men of sense who will be talking reason.

YOUNG BELLAIR: I do not fear[46] her pardon; do you but grant me yours for my neglect of late.

MEDLEY: Though y'ave made us miserable by the want of your good company, to show you I am free from all resentment, may the beautiful cause of our misfortune give you all the joys happy lovers have shared ever since the world began.

YOUNG BELLAIR: You wish me in heaven, but you believe me on my journey to hell.

MEDLEY: You have a good strong faith, and that may contribute much towards your salvation. I confess I am but of an untoward[47] constitution, apt to have doubts and scruples, and in love they are no less distracting than in religion. Were I so near marriage, I should cry out by fits as I ride in my coach, "Cuckold, cuckold!" with no less fury than the mad fanatic does "glory!" in Bethlem.[48]

YOUNG BELLAIR: Because religion makes some run mad must I live an atheist?

MEDLEY: Is it not great indiscretion for a man of credit, who may have money enough on his word, to go and deal with Jews, who for little sums make men enter into bonds and give judgments?

YOUNG BELLAIR: Preach no more on this text. I am determined, and there is no hope of my conversion.

DORIMANT (*to* HANDY, *who is fiddling about him*): Leave your unnecessary fiddling; a wasp that's buzzing about a man's nose at dinner is not more troublesome than thou art.

[43] unless

[44] (1) to drink heavily, (2) to pledge (the Shoemaker is either improving upon Medley's vulgar language or accepting his condition that he spend the money on drink; or he intends both meanings)

[45] give him a hint

[46] worry about

[47] disinclined (to believe in the religion of marriage)

[48] Bethlehem Hospital for the insane (often "Bedlam")

HANDY: You love to have your clothes hang just, Sir.

DORIMANT: I love to be well dressed, Sir, and think it no scandal to my understanding.

HANDY: Will you use the essence[49] or orange flower water?

DORIMANT: I will smell as I do to-day, no offence to the ladies' noses.

HANDY: Your pleasure, Sir. (*Exit* HANDY.)

DORIMANT: That a man's excellency should lie in neatly tying of a ribband or a cravat![50] How careful's nature in furnishing the world with necessary coxcombs![51]

YOUNG BELLAIR: That's a mighty pretty suit of yours, Dorimant.

DORIMANT: I am glad't has your approbation.

YOUNG BELLAIR: No man in town has a better fancy in his clothes than you have.

DORIMANT: You will make me have an opinion of my genius.

MEDLEY: There is a great critic, I hear, in these matters, lately arrived piping hot from Paris.

YOUNG BELLAIR: Sir Fopling Flutter, you mean.

MEDLEY: The same.

YOUNG BELLAIR: He thinks himself the pattern of modern gallantry.

DORIMANT: He is indeed the pattern of modern foppery.

MEDLEY: He was yesterday at the play, with a pair of gloves up to his elbows, and a periwig[52] more exactly curled than a lady's head newly dressed for a ball.

YOUNG BELLAIR: What a pretty lisp he has!

DORIMANT: Ho! that he affects in imitation of the people of quality of France.

MEDLEY: His head stands, for the most part, on one side, and his looks are more languishing than a lady's when she lolls at stretch in her coach or leans her head carelessly against the side of a box i'the playhouse.

DORIMANT: He is a person indeed of great acquired follies.

MEDLEY: He is like many others, beholding to his education for making him so eminent a coxcomb; many a fool had been lost to the world had their indulgent parents wisely bestowed neither learning nor good breeding on 'em.

YOUNG BELLAIR: He has been, as the sparkish[53] word is, "brisk[54] upon the ladies" already. He was yesterday at my Aunt Townley's and gave Mrs. Loveit a catalogue of his good qualities under the character of a complete gentleman, who, according to Sir Fopling, ought to dress well, dance well, fence well, have a genius for love letters, and agreeable voice

[49] perfume
[50] silk scarf worn around the neck
[51] conceited fools, fops
[52] wig
[53] fashionable (with derogatory overtones: foppish)
[54] lively, forward

for a chamber, be very amorous, something[55] discreet, but not over-constant.

MEDLEY: Pretty ingredients to make an accomplished person!

DORIMANT: I am glad he pitched upon Loveit.

YOUNG BELLAIR: How so?

DORIMANT: I wanted a fop to lay to her charge, and this is as pat as may be.

YOUNG BELLAIR: I am confident she loves no man but you.

DORIMANT: The good fortune were enough to make me vain, but that I am in my nature modest.

YOUNG BELLAIR: Hark you, Dorimant. — With your leave, Mr. Medley; 'tis only a secret concerning a fair lady.

MEDLEY: Your good breeding, Sir, gives you too much trouble; you might have whispered without all this ceremony.

YOUNG BELLAIR (*to* DORIMANT): How stand your affairs with Bellinda of late?

DORIMANT: She's a little jilting baggage.

YOUNG BELLAIR: Nay, I believe her false enough, but she's ne'er the worse for your purpose; she was with you yesterday in a disguise at the play.

DORIMANT: There we fell out and resolved never to speak to one another more.

YOUNG BELLAIR: The occasion?

DORIMANT: Want of courage to meet me at the place appointed. These young women apprehend[56] loving as much as the young men do fighting, at first; but, once entered, like them too, they all turn bullies straight.

(*Enter* HANDY.)

HANDY (*to* YOUNG BELLAIR): Sir, your man without[57] desires to speak with you.

YOUNG BELLAIR: Gentlemen, I'll return immediately. (*Exit* YOUNG BELLAIR.)

MEDLEY: A very pretty fellow this.

DORIMANT: He's handsome, well-bred, and by much the most tolerable of all the young men that do not abound in wit.

MEDLEY: Ever well dressed, always complaisant,[58] and seldom impertinent. You and he are grown very intimate, I see.

DORIMANT: It is our mutual interest to be so: it makes the women think the better of his understanding, and judge more favourably of my reputation; it makes him pass upon some for a man of very good sense, and I upon others for a very civil person.

MEDLEY: What was that whisper?

[55] somewhat
[56] are apprehensive about
[57] outside
[58] pleasant, obliging

DORIMANT: A thing which he would fain have known, but I did not think it fit to tell him; it might have frighted him from his honourable intentions of marrying.

MEDLEY: Emilia, give her her due, has the best reputation of any young woman about the town who has beauty enough to provoke detraction; her carriage[59] is unaffected, her discourse modest, not at all censorious nor pretending, like the counterfeits of the age.

DORIMANT: She's a discreet maid, and I believe nothing can corrupt her but a husband.

MEDLEY: A husband?

DORIMANT: Yes, a husband: I have known many women make a difficulty of losing a maidenhead, who have afterwards made none of making a cuckold.

MEDLEY: This prudent consideration, I am apt to think, has made you confirm poor Bellair in the desperate resolution he has taken.

DORIMANT: Indeed, the little hope I found there was of her, in the state she was in, has made me by my advice contribute something towards the changing of her condition.

(*Enter* YOUNG BELLAIR.)

Dear Bellair, by heavens, I thought we had lost thee; men in love are never to be reckoned on when we would form a company.

YOUNG BELLAIR: Dorimant, I am undone. My man has brought the most surprising news i'the world.

DORIMANT: Some strange misfortune is befallen your love.

YOUNG BELLAIR: My father came to town last night and lodges i'the very house where Emilia lies.

MEDLEY: Does he know it is with her you are in love?

YOUNG BELLAIR: He knows I love, but knows not whom, without some officious sot has betrayed me.

DORIMANT: Your Aunt Townley is your confidante and favours the business.

YOUNG BELLAIR: I do not apprehend any ill office from her. I have received a letter in which I am commanded by my father to meet him at my aunt's this afternoon. He tells me farther he has made a match for me and bids me resolve to be obedient to his will or expect to be disinherited.

MEDLEY: Now's your time, Bellair; never had lover such an opportunity of giving a generous proof of his passion.

YOUNG BELLAIR: As how, I pray?

MEDLEY: Why, hang[60] an estate, marry Emilia out of hand, and provoke your father to do what he threatens; 'tis but despising a coach, humbling

[59] conduct, deportment
[60] never mind, "damn!"

yourself to a pair of goloshes,[61] being out of countenance when you meet your friends, pointed at and pitied wherever you go by all the amorous fops that know you, and your fame will be immortal.

YOUNG BELLAIR: I could find in my heart to resolve not to marry at all.

DORIMANT: Fie, fie! That would spoil a good jest and disappoint the well-natured town of an occasion of laughing at you.

YOUNG BELLAIR: The storm I have so long expected hangs o'er my head and begins to pour down upon me; I am on the rack and can have no rest till I'm satisfied in what I fear. Where do you dine?

DORIMANT: At Long's or Locket's.[62]

MEDLEY: At Long's let it be.

YOUNG BELLAIR: I'll run and see Emilia and inform myself how matters stand. If my misfortunes are not so great as to make me unfit for company, I'll be with you. (*Exit* YOUNG BELLAIR.)

(*Enter a* FOOTMAN *with a letter.*)

FOOTMAN (*to* DORIMANT): Here's a letter, Sir.

DORIMANT: The superscription's right: "For Mr. Dorimant."

MEDLEY: Let's see; the very scrawl and spelling of a true-bred whore.

DORIMANT: I know the hand; the style is admirable, I assure you.

MEDLEY: Prithee, read it.

DORIMANT (*reads*):

I told you you dud not love me, if you dud, you would have seen me again ere now. I have no money and am very mallicolly; pray send me a guynie to see the operies.

Your servant to command,
MOLLY.

MEDLEY: Pray, let the whore have a favourable answer, that she may spark it in a box and do honour to her profession.

DORIMANT: She shall, and perk up[63] i'the face of quality. Is the coach at door?

HANDY: You did not bid me send for it.

DORIMANT: Eternal blockhead! (HANDY *offers to go out.*) Hey, sot —

HANDY: Did you call me, Sir?

DORIMANT: I hope you have no just exception to the name, Sir?

HANDY: I have sense, Sir.

DORIMANT: Not so much as a fly in winter. — How did you come, Medley?

MEDLEY: In a chair.

FOOTMAN: You may have a hackney coach if you please, Sir.

[61] wooden shoes
[62] fashionable London taverns
[63] show off

DORIMANT: I may ride the elephant if I please, Sir. Call another chair and let my coach follow to Long's.

Be calm, ye great parents, etc.

(*Exeunt, singing.*)

## ACT II

### SCENE 1

*Enter my* LADY TOWNLEY *and* EMILIA.

LADY TOWNLEY: I was afraid, Emilia, all had been discovered.

EMILIA: I tremble with the apprehension still.

LADY TOWNLEY: That my brother should take lodgings i'the very house where you lie!

EMILIA: 'Twas lucky we had timely notice to warn the people to be secret. He seems to be a mighty good-humoured old man.

LADY TOWNLEY: He ever had a notable smirking way with him.

EMILIA: He calls me rogue, tells me he can't abide me, and does so bepat me.

LADY TOWNLEY: On my word, you are much in his favour then.

EMILIA: He has been very inquisitive, I am told, about my family, my reputation, and my fortune.

LADY TOWNLEY: I am confident he does not i'the least suspect you are the woman his son's in love with.

EMILIA: What should make him, then, inform himself so particularly of me?

LADY TOWNLEY: He was always of a very loving temper himself; it may be he has a doting fit upon him – who knows?

EMILIA: It cannot be.

(*Enter* YOUNG BELLAIR.)

LADY TOWNLEY: Here comes my nephew. — Where did you leave your father?

YOUNG BELLAIR: Writing a note within. Emilia, this early visit looks as if some kind jealousy would not let you rest at home.

EMILIA: The knowledge I have of my rival gives me a little cause to fear your constancy.

YOUNG BELLAIR: My constancy! I vow —

EMILIA: Do not vow. Our love is frail as is our life and full as little in our power; and are you sure you shall outlive this day?

YOUNG BELLAIR: I am not; but when we are in perfect health, 'twere an idle thing to fright ourselves with the thoughts of sudden death.

LADY TOWNLEY: Pray, what has passed between you and your father i'the garden?

YOUNG BELLAIR: He's firm in his resolution, tells me I must marry Mrs.

Harriet, or swears he'll marry himself and disinherit me. When I saw I could not prevail with him to be more indulgent, I dissembled an obedience to his will, which has composed his passion and will give us time, and, I hope, opportunity, to deceive him.

(*Enter* OLD BELLAIR *with a note in his hand.*)

LADY TOWNLEY: Peace, here he comes!

OLD BELLAIR: Harry, take this and let your man carry it for me to Mr. Fourbe's[1] chamber, my lawyer i'the Temple.[2]

(*Exit* YOUNG BELLAIR.)

(*To* EMILIA.) Neighbour, a dod![3] I am glad to see thee here. Make much of her, Sister; she's one of the best of your acquaintance. I like her countenance and her behaviour well; she has a modesty that is not common i'this age, a dod, she has!

LADY TOWNLEY: I know her value, Brother, and esteem her accordingly.

OLD BELLAIR: Advise her to wear a little more mirth in her face; a dod, she's too serious.

LADY TOWNLEY: The fault is very excusable in a young woman.

OLD BELLAIR: Nay, a dod, I like her ne'er the worse. A melancholy beauty has her charms. I love a pretty sadness in a face, which varies now and then, like changeable colours, into a smile.

LADY TOWNLEY: Methinks you speak very feelingly, Brother.

OLD BELLAIR: I am but five and fifty, Sister, you know, an age not altogether unsensible. – (*To* EMILIA.) Cheer up, sweetheart! I have a secret to tell thee may chance to make thee merry. We three will make collation together anon; i'the meantime, mum,[4] I can't abide you! go, I can't abide you!

(*Enter* YOUNG BELLAIR.)

Harry, come! you must along with me to my Lady Woodvill's. I am going to slip the boy at a mistress.

YOUNG BELLAIR: At a wife, Sir, you would say.

OLD BELLAIR: You need not look so glum, Sir; a wife is no curse when she brings the blessing of a good estate with her; but an idle town flirt, with a painted face, a rotten reputation, and a crazy fortune, a dod! is the devil and all, and such a one I hear you are in league with.

YOUNG BELLAIR: I cannot help detraction, Sir.

OLD BELLAIR: Out! A pise[5] o' their breeches, there are keeping[6] fools enough for such flaunting baggages, and they are e'en too good for 'em. – (*To* EMILIA.) Remember 'night. Go, y'are a rogue, y'are a rogue! Fare you well, fare you well! —— Come, come, come along, Sir!

(*Exeunt* OLD *and* YOUNG BELLAIR.)

[1] i.e., Mr. Cheat (Fr.)
[2] the lawyers' quarter in London
[3] Ah, God! (cf. "egad!")
[4] not a word!
[5] pox (?)
[6] i.e., mistress-keeping

LADY TOWNLEY: On my word, the old man comes on apace; I'll lay my life he's smitten.

EMILIA: This is nothing but the pleasantness of his humour.

LADY TOWNLEY: I know him better than you. Let it work; it may prove lucky.

(*Enter a* PAGE.)

PAGE: Madam, Mr. Medley has sent to know whether a visit will not be troublesome this afternoon.

LADY TOWNLEY: Send him word his visits never are so. (*Exit* PAGE.)

EMILIA: He's a very pleasant man.

LADY TOWNLEY: He's a very necessary man among us women; he's not scandalous i'the least, perpetually contriving to bring good company together, and always ready to stop up a gap at ombre;[7] then, he knows all the little news o'the town.

EMILIA: I love to hear him talk o'the intrigues; let 'em be never so dull in themselves, he'll make 'em pleasant i'the relation.

LADY TOWNLEY: But he improves things so much one can take no measure of the truth from him. Mr. Dorimant swears a flea or a maggot is not made more monstrous by a magnifying glass than a story is by his telling it.

(*Enter* MEDLEY.)

EMILIA: Hold, here he comes.

LADY TOWNLEY: Mr. Medley.

MEDLEY: Your servant, Madam.

LADY TOWNLEY: You have made yourself a stranger of late.

EMILIA: I believe you took a surfeit of ombre last time you were here.

MEDLEY: Indeed, I had my bellyful of that termagant, Lady Dealer. There never was so unsatiable a carder;[8] an old gleeker[9] never loved to sit to't like her. I have played with her now at least a dozen times till she's worn out all her fine complexion and her tour[10] would keep in curl no longer.

LADY TOWNLEY: Blame her not, poor woman; she loves nothing so well as a black ace.[11]

MEDLEY: The pleasure I have seen her in when she has had hope in drawing for a matadore!

EMILIA: 'Tis as pretty sport to her as persuading masks off is to you, to make discoveries.

[7] a card game with forty cards played by 3 persons (cf. Alexander Pope's *Rape of the Lock,* Canto III)

[8] card-player

[9] one of the players in a three-handed card game

[10] crescent-shaped front of false hair

[11] (the black aces were two of the three highest trumps, or matadors, in ombre)

LADY TOWNLEY: Pray, where's your friend Mr. Dorimant?

MEDLEY: Soliciting his affairs; he's a man of great employment, has more mistresses now depending than the most eminent lawyer in England has causes.

EMILIA: Here has been Mrs. Loveit so uneasy and out of humour these two days.

LADY TOWNLEY: How strangely love and jealousy rage in that poor woman!

MEDLEY: She could not have picked out a devil upon earth so proper to torment her; he's made her break a dozen or two of fans already, tear half a score points[12] in pieces, and destroy hoods and knots[13] without number.

LADY TOWNLEY: We heard of a pleasant serenade he gave her t'other night.

MEDLEY: A Danish serenade with kettle-drums and trumpets.

EMILIA: Oh, barbarous!

MEDLEY: What! You are of the number of the ladies whose ears are grown so delicate since our operas you can be charmed with nothing but *flûtes douces*[14] and French hautboys?[15]

EMILIA: Leave your raillery, and tell us, is there any new wit come forth, songs or novels?

MEDLEY: A very pretty piece of gallantry, by an eminent author, called *The Diversions of Bruxelles,* very necessary to be read by all old ladies who are desirous to improve themselves at questions and commands,[16] blindman's bluff, and the like fashionable recreations.

EMILIA: Oh, ridiculous!

MEDLEY: Then there is *The Art of Affectation,* written by a late beauty of quality, teaching you how to draw up your breasts, stretch up your neck, to thrust out your breech, to play with your head, to toss up your nose, to bite your lips, to turn up your eyes, to speak in a silly, soft tone of a voice, and use all the foolish French words that will infallibly make your person and conversation charming; with a short apology at the latter end in the behalf of young ladies who notoriously wash[17] and paint though they have naturally good complexions.

EMILIA: What a deal of stuff you tell us!

MEDLEY: Such as the town affords, Madam. The Russians, hearing the great respect we have for foreign dancing, have lately sent over some of their best balladines,[18] who are now practising a famous ballet which will be suddenly danced at the Bear Garden.

LADY TOWNLEY: Pray, forbear your idle stories, and give us an account of the state of love as it now stands.

[12] pieces of lace
[13] bows of ribbon
[14] (Fr.) soft flutes
[15] oboes
[16] a parlor game
[17] use cosmetic washes
[18] ballet dancers

MEDLEY: Truly, there has been some revolutions in those affairs, great chopping and changing[19] among the old, and some new lovers whom malice, indiscretion, and misfortune have luckily brought into play.

LADY TOWNLEY: What think you of walking into the next room and sitting down before you engage in this business?

MEDLEY: I wait upon you, and I hope (though women are commonly unreasonable) by the plenty of scandal I shall discover, to give you very good content, ladies. (*Exeunt.*)

## SCENE 2

*Enter* MRS. LOVEIT *and* PERT. MRS. LOVEIT *putting up*[1] *a letter, then pulling out her pocket-glass and looking in it.*

MRS. LOVEIT: Pert.

PERT: Madam?

MRS. LOVEIT: I hate myself, I look so ill today.

PERT: Hate the wicked cause on't, that base man Mr. Dorimant, who makes you torment and vex yourself continually.

MRS. LOVEIT: He is to blame, indeed.

PERT: To blame to be two days without sending, writing, or coming near you, contrary to his oath and covenant! 'Twas to much purpose to make him swear! I'll lay my life there's not an article but he has broken — talked to the vizards i'the pit, waited upon the ladies from the boxes to their coaches, gone behind the scenes, and fawned upon those little insignificant creatures, the players. 'Tis impossible for a man of his inconstant temper to forbear, I'm sure.

MRS. LOVEIT: I know he is a devil, but he has something of the angel yet undefaced in him, which makes him so charming and agreeable that I must love him, be he never so wicked.

PERT: I little thought, Madam, to see your spirit tamed to this degree, who banished poor Mr. Lackwit but for taking up another lady's fan in your presence.

MRS. LOVEIT: My knowing of such odious fools contributes to the making of me love Dorimant the better.

PERT: Your knowing of Mr. Dorimant, in my mind, should rather make you hate all mankind.

MRS. LOVEIT: So it does, besides himself.

PERT: Pray, what excuse does he make in his letter?

MRS. LOVEIT: He has had business.

PERT: Business in general terms would not have been a current[2] excuse for

[19] (1) buying and selling, (2) changing frequently

---

[1] putting away
[2] valid

another. A modish man is always very busy when he is in pursuit of a new mistress.

MRS. LOVEIT: Some fop has bribed you to rail at him. He had business; I will believe it, and will forgive him.

PERT: You may forgive him anything, but I shall never forgive him his turning me into ridicule, as I hear he does.

MRS. LOVEIT: I perceive you are of the number of those fools his wit has made his enemies.

PERT: I am of the number of those he's pleased to rally, Madam, and if we may believe Mr. Wagfan and Mr. Caperwell, he sometimes makes merry with yourself too, among his laughing companions.

MRS. LOVEIT: Blockheads are as malicious to witty men as ugly women are to the handsome; 'tis their interest, and they make it their business to defame 'em.

PERT: I wish Mr. Dorimant would not make it his business to defame you.

MRS. LOVEIT: Should he, I had rather be made infamous by him than owe my reputation to the dull discretion of those fops you talk of.

(*Enter* BELLINDA.)

Bellinda! (*Running to her.*)

BELLINDA: My dear!

MRS. LOVEIT: You have been unkind of late.

BELLINDA: Do not say unkind – say unhappy.

MRS. LOVEIT: I could chide you. Where have you been these two days?

BELLINDA: Pity me rather, my dear, where I have been – so tired with two or three country gentlewomen, whose conversation has been more unsufferable than a country fiddle.

MRS. LOVEIT: Are they relations?

BELLINDA: No, Welsh acquaintance I made when I was last year at St. Winifred's. They have asked me a thousand questions of the modes and intrigues of the town, and I have told 'em almost as many things for news that hardly were so when their gowns were in fashion.

MRS. LOVEIT: Provoking creatures! How could you endure 'em?

BELLINDA (*aside*): Now to carry on my plot. Nothing but love could make me capable of so much falsehood. 'Tis time to begin, lest Dorimant should come before her jealousy has stung her. – (*Laughs, and then speaks on.*) I was yesterday at a play with 'em, where I was fain to show 'em the living as the man at Westminster does the dead: "That is Mrs. Such-a-one, admired for her beauty; that is Mr. Such-a-one, cried up for a wit; That is sparkish Mr. Such-a-one, who keeps reverend Mrs. Such-a-one; and there sits fine Mrs. Such-a-one who was lately cast off by my Lord Such-a-one."

MRS. LOVEIT: Did you see Dorimant there?

BELLINDA: I did, and imagine you were there with him and have no mind to own it.

MRS. LOVEIT: What should make you think so?

BELLINDA: A lady masked in a pretty *déshabillé*,[3] whom Dorimant entertained with more respect than the gallants do a common vizard.

MRS. LOVEIT (*aside*): Dorimant at the play entertaining a mask! Oh, heavens!

BELLINDA (*aside*): Good!

MRS. LOVEIT: Did he stay all the while?

BELLINDA: Till the play was done, and then led her out, which confirms me it was you.

MRS. LOVEIT: Traitor!

PERT: Now you may believe he had business, and you may forgive him too.

MRS. LOVEIT: Ingrateful, perjured man!

BELLINDA: You seem so much concerned, my dear, I fear I have told you unawares what I had better have concealed for your quiet.

MRS. LOVEIT: What manner of shape had she?

BELLINDA: Tall and slender. Her motions were very genteel; certainly she must be some person of condition.

MRS. LOVEIT: Shame and confusion be ever in her face when she shows it!

BELLINDA: I should blame your discretion for loving that wild man, my dear, but they say he has a way so bewitching that few can defend their hearts who know him.

MRS. LOVEIT: I will tear him from mine or die i'the attempt.

BELLINDA: Be more moderate.

MRS. LOVEIT: Would I had daggers, darts, or poisoned arrows in my breast, so I could but remove the thoughts of him from thence!

BELLINDA: Fie, fie! your transports are too violent, my dear; this may be but an accidental gallantry, and 'tis likely ended at her coach.

PERT: Should it proceed farther, let your comfort be, the conduct Mr. Dorimant affects will quickly make you know your rival, ten to one let you see her ruined, her reputation exposed to the town – a happiness none will envy her but yourself, Madam.

MRS. LOVEIT: Whoe'er she be, all the harm I wish her is, may she love him as well as I do and may he give her as much cause to hate him.

PERT: Never doubt the latter end of your curse, Madam.

MRS. LOVEIT: May all the passions that are raised by neglected love – jealousy, indignation, spite, and thirst of revenge – eternally rage in her soul, as they do now in mine. (*Walks up and down with a distracted air.*)

(*Enter a* PAGE.)

PAGE: Madam, Mr. Dorimant ——

MRS. LOVEIT: I will not see him.

PAGE: I told him you were within, Madam.

MRS. LOVEIT: Say you lied – say I'm busy – shut the door – say anything!

[3] (Fr.) loose, low-cut, sometimes "see-through" dress

PAGE: He's here, Madam.

(*Enter* DORIMANT.)

DORIMANT:

> They taste of death who do at heaven arrive;
> But we this paradise approach alive.

(*To* MISTRESS LOVEIT.) What, dancing *The Galloping Nag* without a fiddle? (*Offers to catch her by the hand; she flings away and walks on, he pursuing her.*) I fear this restlessness of the body, Madam, proceeds from an unquietness of the mind. What unlucky accident puts you out of humour? A point ill washed, knots spoiled i'the making up, hair shaded awry, or some other little mistake in setting you in order?

PERT: A trifle, in my opinion, Sir, more inconsiderable than any you mention.

DORIMANT: O Mrs. Pert! I never knew you sullen enough to be silent; come, let me know the business.

PERT: The business, Sir, is the business that has taken you up these two days. How have I seen you laugh at men of business, and now to become a man of business yourself!

DORIMANT: We are not masters of our own affections; our inclinations daily alter: now we love pleasure, and anon we shall dote on business. Human frailty will have it so, and who can help it?

MRS. LOVEIT: Faithless, inhuman, barbarous man ——

DORIMANT (*aside*): Good! Now the alarm strikes.

MRS. LOVEIT: Without sense of love, of honour, or of gratitude, tell me, for I will know, what devil masked she was you were with at the play yesterday?

DORIMANT: Faith, I resolved as much as you, but the devil was obstinate and would not tell me.

MRS. LOVEIT: False in this as in your vows to me! — you do know.

DORIMANT: The truth is, I did all I could to know.

MRS. LOVEIT: And dare you own it to my face? Hell and furies! (*Tears her fan in pieces.*)

DORIMANT: Spare your fan, Madam; you are growing hot and will want it to cool you.

MRS. LOVEIT: Horror and distraction seize you! Sorrow and remorse gnaw your soul, and punish all your perjuries to me! (*Weeps.*)

DORIMANT (*turning to* BELLINDA):

> So thunder breaks the cloud in twain
> And makes a passage for the rain.[4]

(*To* BELLINDA.) Bellinda, you are the devil that have raised this storm;

[4] (from a poem by Matthew Roydon, a minor Elizabethan poet)

you were at the play yesterday and have been making discoveries to your dear.

BELLINDA: Y'are the most mistaken man i'the world.

DORIMANT: It must be so, and here I vow revenge – resolve to pursue and persecute you more impertinently than ever any loving fop did his mistress, hunt you i'the Park, trace you i'the Mail,[5] dog you in every visit you make, haunt you at the plays and i'the drawing-room, hang my nose in your neck and talk to you whether you will or no, and ever look upon you with such dying[6] eyes till your friends grow jealous of me, send you out of town, and the world suspect your reputation. – (*In a lower voice.*) At my Lady Townley's when we go from hence. (*He looks kindly on* BELLINDA.)

BELLINDA: I'll meet you there.

DORIMANT: Enough.

MRS. LOVEIT (*pushing* DORIMANT *away*): Stand off! You sha' not stare upon her so.

DORIMANT: Good; there's one made jealous already.

MRS. LOVEIT: Is this the constancy you vowed?

DORIMANT: Constancy at my years! 'Tis not a virtue in season; you might as well expect the fruit the autumn ripens i'the spring.

MRS. LOVEIT: Monstrous principle!

DORIMANT: Youth has a long journey to go, Madam; should I have set up my rest at the first inn I lodged at, I should never have arrived at the happiness I now enjoy.

MRS. LOVEIT: Dissembler, damned dissembler!

DORIMANT: I am so, I confess: good nature and good manners corrupt me. I am honest in my inclinations, and would not, wer't not to avoid offence, make a lady a little in years believe I think her young, willfully mistake art for nature, and seem as fond of a thing I am weary of as when I doted on't in earnest.

MRS. LOVEIT: False man!

DORIMANT: True woman!

MRS. LOVEIT: Now you begin to show yourself.

DORIMANT: Love gilds us over and makes us show fine things to one another for a time, but soon the gold wears off and then again the native brass appears.

MRS. LOVEIT: Think on your oaths, your vows and protestations, perjured man!

DORIMANT: I made 'em when I was in love.

MRS. LOVEIT: And therefore ought they not to bind? Oh, impious!

DORIMANT: What we swear at such a time may be a certain proof of a present passion, but, to say truth, in love there is no security to be given for the future.

[5] the Mall, a walk bordering St. James's Park
[6] swooning

MRS. LOVEIT: Horrid and ingrateful, begone, and never see me more!

DORIMANT: I am not one of those troublesome coxcombs who, because they were once well received, take the privilege to plague a woman with their love ever after. I shall obey you, Madam, though I do myself some violence.

(*He offers to go and* MRS. LOVEIT *pulls him back.*)

MRS. LOVEIT: Come back! You sha' not go! Could you have the ill-nature to offer it?

DORIMANT: When love grows diseased, the best thing we can do is to put it to a violent death. I cannot endure the torture of a lingering and consumptive passion.

MRS. LOVEIT: Can you think mine sickly?

DORIMANT: Oh, 'tis desperately ill. What worse symptoms are there than your being always uneasy when I visit you, your picking quarrels with me on slight occasions, and in my absence kindly listening to the impertinences of every fashionable fool that talks to you?

MRS. LOVEIT: What fashionable fool can you lay to my charge?

DORIMANT: Why, the very cock-fool of all those fools – Sir Fopling Flutter.

MRS. LOVEIT: I never saw him in my life but once.

DORIMANT: The worse woman you, at first sight to put on all your charms, to entertain him with that softness in your voice, and all that wanton kindness in your eyes you so notoriously affect when you design a conquest.

MRS. LOVEIT: So damned a lie did never malice yet invent. Who told you this?

DORIMANT: No matter. That ever I should love a woman that can dote on a senseless caper, a tawdry French ribband, and a formal cravat!

MRS. LOVEIT: You make me mad.

DORIMANT: A guilty conscience may do much. Go on, be the game-mistress o' the town, and enter[7] all our young fops as fast as they come from travel.

MRS. LOVEIT: Base and scurrilous!

DORIMANT: A fine mortifying reputation 'twill be for a woman of your pride, wit, and quality!

MRS. LOVEIT: This jealousy's a mere pretence, a cursed trick of your own devising. I know you.

DORIMANT: Believe it and all the ill of me you can: I would not have a woman have the least good thought of me that can think well of Fopling. Farewell! Fall to, and much good may do[8] you with your coxcomb.

MRS. LOVEIT: Stay, oh stay! and I will tell you all.

DORIMANT: I have been told too much already. (*Exit* DORIMANT.)

MRS. LOVEIT: Call him again!

[7] initiate
[8] may it do

PERT: E'en[9] let him go – a fair riddance.

MRS. LOVEIT: Run, I say! call him again! I will have him called!

PERT: The devil should carry him away first were it my concern. (*Exit* PERT.)

BELLINDA: He's frighted me from the very thoughts of loving men. For heaven's sake, my dear, do not discover what I told you! I dread his tongue as much as you ought to have done his friendship.

(*Enter* PERT.)

PERT: He's gone, Madam.

MRS. LOVEIT: Lightning blast him!

PERT: When I told him you desired him to come back, he smiled, made a mouth at me, flung into his coach, and said ––

MRS. LOVEIT: What did he say?

PERT: "Drive away!" and then repeated verses.

MRS. LOVEIT: Would I had made a contract to be a witch when first I entertained this greater devil, monster, barbarian! I could tear myself in pieces. Revenge – nothing but revenge can ease me. Plague, war, famine, fire – all that can bring universal ruin and misery on mankind – with joy I'd perish to have you in my power but this moment.

(*Exit* MRS. LOVEIT.)

PERT: Follow, Madam; leave her not in this outrageous passion!

(PERT *gathers up the things.*)

BELLINDA (*aside*): He's given me the proof which I desired of his love,

But 'tis a proof of his ill-nature too.
I wish I had not seen him use her so.
I sigh to think that Dorimant may be
One day as faithless and unkind to me. (*Exeunt.*)

## ACT III

### Scene 1

*Scene*: LADY WOODVILL*'s lodgings.*

*Enter* HARRIET *and* BUSY, *her woman.*

BUSY: Dear Madam, let me set that curl in order.

HARRIET: Let me alone; I will shake 'em all out of order.

BUSY: Will you never leave this wildness?

HARRIET: Torment me not.

BUSY: Look! There's a knot falling off.

HARRIET: Let it drop.

[9] just

BUSY: But one pin, dear Madam.

HARRIET: How do I daily suffer under thy officious fingers!

BUSY: Ah, the difference that is between you and my Lady Dapper! how uneasy she is if the least thing be amiss about her!

HARRIET: She is indeed most exact; nothing is ever wanting to make her ugliness remarkable.

BUSY: Jeering people say so.

HARRIET: Her powdering, painting, and her patching[1] never fail in public to draw the tongues and eyes of all the men upon her.

BUSY: She is, indeed, a little too pretending.

HARRIET: That women should set up for beauty as much in spite of nature as some men have done for wit!

BUSY: I hope without offence one may endeavour to make one's self agreeable.

HARRIET: Not when 'tis impossible. Women then ought to be no more fond of dressing than fools should be of talking; hoods and modesty, masks and silence, things that shadow and conceal — they should think of nothing else.

BUSY: Jesu! Madam, what will your mother think is become of you? For heaven's sake go in again!

HARRIET: I won't.

BUSY: This is the extravagantest thing that ever you did in your life, to leave her and a gentleman who is to be your husband.

HARRIET: My husband! Hast thou so little wit to think I spoke what I meant when I overjoyed her in the country with a low curtsey and "What you please, Madam; I shall ever be obedient"?

BUSY: Nay, I know not, you have so many fetches.[2]

HARRIET: And this was one, to get her up to London! Nothing else, I assure thee.

BUSY: Well, the man, in my mind, is a fine man.

HARRIET: The man indeed wears his clothes fashionably and has a pretty, negligent way with him, very courtly and much affected; he bows, and talks, and smiles so agreeably, as he thinks.

BUSY: I never saw anything so genteel.

HARRIET: Varnished over with good breeding, many a blockhead makes a tolerable show.

BUSY: I wonder you do not like him.

HARRIET: I think I might be brought to endure him, and that is all a reasonable woman should expect in a husband; but there is duty i'the case, and like the haughty Merab,[3] I

Find much aversion in my stubborn mind,

[1] sticking small pieces of black silk on the face as beauty spots

[2] dodges, tricks

[3] Saul's daughter, promised to David but married to someone else (I Sam. 18:17–19)

Which
Is bred by being promis'd and design'd.[4]

BUSY: I wish you do not design your own ruin. I partly guess your inclinations, Madam — that Mr. Dorimant ——

HARRIET: Leave your prating and sing some foolish song or other.

BUSY: I will — the song you love so well ever since you saw Mr. Dorimant.

*Song*

When first Amintas charm'd my heart,
My heedless sheep began to stray;
The wolves soon stole the greatest part,
And all will now be made a prey.

Ah, let not love your thoughts possess,
'Tis fatal to a shepherdess;
The dang'rous passion you must shun,
Or else like me be quite undone.

HARRIET: Shall I be paid down by a covetous parent for a purchase? I need no land; no, I'll lay myself out[5] all in love. It is decreed —

(*Enter* YOUNG BELLAIR.)

YOUNG BELLAIR: What generous resolution are you making, Madam?

HARRIET: Only to be disobedient, Sir.

YOUNG BELLAIR: Let me join hands with you in that.

HARRIET: With all my heart; I never thought I should have given you mine so willingly. Here I, Harriet ——

YOUNG BELLAIR: And I, Harry ——

HARRIET: Do solemnly protest ——

YOUNG BELLAIR: And vow ——

HARRIET: That I with you ——

YOUNG BELLAIR: And I with you ——

BOTH: Will never marry.

HARRIET: A match!

YOUNG BELLAIR: And no match! How do you like this indifference now?

HARRIET: You expect I should take it ill, I see.

YOUNG BELLAIR: 'Tis not unnatural for you women to be a little angry: you miss a conquest, though you would slight the poor man were he in your power.

HARRIET: There are some, it may be, have an eye like Bart'lomew[6] — big enough for the whole fair; but I am not of the number, and you may

[4] (from *The Davideis,* an unfinished epic poem by Abraham Cowley [1618–67].)

[5] spend myself

[6] Bartholomew Cokes, a glutton and curiosity-seeker in Ben Jonson's comedy *Bartholomew Fair* (1614) (the title of the play refers to the fair held annually about the time of St. Bartholomew's Day, August 24, in Smithfield, north of London)

keep your gingerbread. 'Twill be more acceptable to the lady whose dear image it wears, Sir.

YOUNG BELLAIR: I must confess, Madam, you came a day after the fair.[7]

HARRIET: You own then you are in love?

YOUNG BELLAIR: I do.

HARRIET: The confidence is generous, and in return I could almost find in my heart to let you know my inclinations.

YOUNG BELLAIR: Are you in love?

HARRIET: Yes, with this dear town, to that degree I can scarce endure the country in landscapes and in hangings.

YOUNG BELLAIR: What a dreadful thing 'twould be to be hurried back to Hampshire!

HARRIET: Ah, name it not!

YOUNG BELLAIR: As for us, I find we shall agree well enough. Would we could do something to deceive the grave people!

HARRIET: Could we delay their quick proceeding, 'twere well. A reprieve is a good step towards the getting of a pardon.

YOUNG BELLAIR: If we give over the game, we are undone. What think you of playing it on booty?[8]

HARRIET: What do you mean?

YOUNG BELLAIR: Pretend to be in love with one another; 'twill make some dilatory excuses we may feign pass the better.

HARRIET: Let us do't, if it be but for the dear pleasure of dissembling.

YOUNG BELLAIR: Can you play your part?

HARRIET: I know not what it is to love, but I have made pretty remarks[9] by being now and then where lovers meet. Where did you leave their gravities?[10]

YOUNG BELLAIR: I'th' next room. Your mother was censuring our modern gallant.

(*Enter* OLD BELLAIR *and* LADY WOODVILL.)

HARRIET: Peace! here they come. I will lean against this wall and look bashfully down upon my fan, while you, like an amorous spark, modishly entertain me.

LADY WOODVILL: Never go about to excuse 'em; come, come, it was not so when I was a young woman.

OLD BELLAIR: A dod, they're something disrespectful —

LADY WOODVILL: Quality was then considered, and not rallied by every fleering[11] fellow.

OLD BELLAIR: Youth will have its jest, a dod, it will.

LADY WOODVILL: 'Tis good breeding now to be civil to none but players

[7] (proverbial)
[8] two players conspiring to cheat a third
[9] observations
[10] i.e., their parents
[11] jeering, snickering

and Exchange women; they are treated by 'em as much above their condition as others are below theirs.

OLD BELLAIR: Out! a pise on 'em! talk no more. The rogues ha' got an ill habit of preferring beauty no matter where they find it.

LADY WOODVILL: See your son and my daughter; they have improved their acquaintance since they were within.

OLD BELLAIR: A dod, methinks they have! Let's keep back and observe.

YOUNG BELLAIR: Now for a look and gestures that may persuade 'em I am saying all the passionate things imaginable.

HARRIET: Your head a little more on one side. Ease yourself on your left leg and play with your right hand.

YOUNG BELLAIR: Thus, is it not?

HARRIET: Now set your right leg firm on the ground, adjust your belt, then look about you.

YOUNG BELLAIR: A little exercising will make me perfect.

HARRIET: Smile, and turn to me again very sparkish.

YOUNG BELLAIR: Will you take your turn and be instructed?

HARRIET: With all my heart!

YOUNG BELLAIR: At one motion play your fan, roll your eyes, and then settle a kind look upon me.

HARRIET: So!

YOUNG BELLAIR: Now spread your fan, look down upon it, and tell the sticks with a finger.

HARRIET: Very modish!

YOUNG BELLAIR: Clap your hand up to your bosom, hold down your gown. Shrug a little, draw up your breasts, and let 'em fall again gently, with a sigh or two, etc.

HARRIET: By the good instructions you give, I suspect you for one of those malicious observers who watch people's eyes, and from innocent looks make scandalous conclusions.

YOUNG BELLAIR: I know some, indeed, who out of mere love to mischief are as vigilant as jealousy itself, and will give you an account of every glance that passes at a play and i'th' Circle.[12]

HARRIET: 'Twill not be amiss now to seem a little pleasant.

YOUNG BELLAIR: Clap your fan, then, in both your hands, snatch it to your mouth, smile, and with a lively motion fling your body a little forwards. So! Now spread it, fall back on the sudden, cover your face with it and break out into a loud laughter – take up, look grave, and fall a-fanning of yourself. – Admirably well acted!

HARRIET: I think I am pretty apt at these matters.

OLD BELLAIR: A dod, I like this well!

LADY WOODVILL: This promises something.

[12] (1) a circular path in Hyde Park, (2) a small social set, coterie

OLD BELLAIR: Come! there is love i'th' case, a dod there is, or will be. What say you, young lady?

HARRIET: All in good time, Sir; you expect we should fall to and love as game-cocks fight, as soon as we are set together. A dod, y'are unreasonable!

OLD BELLAIR: A dod, Sirrah, I like thy wit well.

(*Enter a* SERVANT.)

SERVANT: The coach is at the door, Madam.

OLD BELLAIR: Go, get you and take the air together.

LADY WOODVILL: Will not you go with us?

OLD BELLAIR: Out! a pise! A dod, I ha' business and cannot. We shall meet at night at my sister Townley's.

YOUNG BELLAIR (*aside*): He's going to Emilia. I overheard him talk of a collation.

(*Exeunt.*)

## SCENE 2

*Enter* LADY TOWNLEY, EMILIA, *and* MR. MEDLEY.

LADY TOWNLEY: I pity the young lovers we last talked of, though to say truth their conduct has been so indiscreet they deserve to be unfortunate.

MEDLEY: Y'have had an exact account, from the great lady i'th' box down to the little orange wench.

EMILIA: Y'are a living libel, a breathing lampoon. I wonder you are not torn in pieces.

MEDLEY: What think you of setting up an office of intelligence for these matters? The project may get money.

LADY TOWNLEY: You would have great dealings with country ladies.

MEDLEY: More than Muddiman[1] has with their husbands.

(*Enter* BELLINDA.)

LADY TOWNLEY: Bellinda, what has become of you? We have not seen you here of late with your friend Mrs. Loveit.

BELLINDA: Dear creature, I left her but now so sadly afflicted!

LADY TOWNLEY: With her old distemper, jealousy!

MEDLEY: Dorimant has played her some new prank.

BELLINDA: Well, that Dorimant is certainly the worst man breathing.

EMILIA: I once thought so.

BELLINDA: And do you not think so still?

EMILIA: No, indeed!

[1](1629–92) editor of a popular scandal sheet and newsletter

BELLINDA: Oh, Jesu!

EMILIA: The town does him a great deal of injury, and I will never believe what it says of a man I do not know, again, for his sake.

BELLINDA: You make me wonder.

LADY TOWNLEY: He's a very well-bred man.

BELLINDA: But strangely ill-natured.

EMILIA: Then he's a very witty man.

BELLINDA: But a man of no principles.

MEDLEY: Your man of principles is a very fine thing, indeed.

BELLINDA: To be preferred to men of parts by women who have regard to their reputation and quiet. Well, were I minded to play the fool, he should be the last man I'd think of.

MEDLEY: He has been the first in many ladies' favours, though you are so severe, Madam.

LADY TOWNLEY: What he may be for a lover, I know not; but he's a very pleasant acquaintance, I am sure.

BELLINDA: Had you seen him use Mrs. Loveit as I have done, you would never endure him more.

EMILIA: What, he has quarreled with her again!

BELLINDA: Upon the slightest occasion; he's jealous of Sir Fopling.

LADY TOWNLEY: She never saw him in her life but yesterday, and that was here.

EMILIA: On my conscience, he's the only man in town that's her aversion! How horribly out of humour she was all the while he talked to her!

BELLINDA: And somebody has wickedly told him ——

EMILIA: Here he comes.

(*Enter* DORIMANT.)

MEDLEY: Dorimant! you are luckily come to justify yourself: here's a lady ——

BELLINDA: Has a word or two to say to you from a disconsolate person.

DORIMANT: You tender your reputation too much, I know, Madam, to whisper with me before this good company.

BELLINDA: To serve Mrs. Loveit I'll make a bold venture.

DORIMANT: Here's Medley, the very spirit of scandal.

BELLINDA: No matter!

EMILIA: 'Tis something you are unwilling to hear, Mr. Dorimant.

LADY TOWNLEY: Tell him, Bellinda, whether he will or no.

BELLINDA (*aloud*): Mrs. Loveit ——

DORIMANT: Softly! these are laughers; you do not know 'em.

BELLINDA (*to* DORIMANT *apart*): In a word, y'ave made me hate you, which I thought you never could have done.

DORIMANT: In obeying your commands.

BELLINDA: 'Twas a cruel part you played. How could you act it?

DORIMANT: Nothing is cruel to a man who could kill himself to please you. Remember five o'clock to-morrow morning!

BELLINDA: I tremble when you name it.

DORIMANT: Be sure you come!

BELLINDA: I sha'not.

DORIMANT: Swear you will!

BELLINDA: I dare not.

DORIMANT: Swear, I say!

BELLINDA: By my life – by all the happiness I hope for ——

DORIMANT: You will.

BELLINDA: I will!

DORIMANT: Kind!

BELLINDA: I am glad I've sworn. I vow I think I should ha' failed you else!

DORIMANT: Surprisingly kind! In what temper did you leave Loveit?

BELLINDA: Her raving was prettily[2] over, and she began to be in a brave[3] way of defying you and all your works. Where have you been since you went from thence?

DORIMANT: I looked in at the play.

BELLINDA: I have promised, and must return to her again.

DORIMANT: Persuade her to walk in the Mail this evening.

BELLINDA: She hates the place and will not come.

DORIMANT: Do all you can to prevail with her.

BELLINDA: For what purpose?

DORIMANT: Sir Fopling will be here anon; I'll prepare him to set upon her there before me.

BELLINDA: You persecute her too much, but I'll do all you'll ha' me.

DORIMANT (*aloud*): Tell her plainly 'tis grown so dull a business I can drudge on no longer.

EMILIA: There are afflictions in love, Mr. Dorimant.

DORIMANT: You women make 'em, who are commonly as unreasonable in that as you are at play – without the advantage be on your side, a man can never quietly give over when he's weary.

MEDLEY: If you would play[4] without being obliged to complaisance, Dorimant, you should play in public places.

DORIMANT: Ordinaries[5] were a very good thing for that, but gentlemen do not of late frequent 'em. The deep play is now in private houses.

(BELLINDA *offering to steal away.*)

LADY TOWNLEY: Bellinda, are you leaving us so soon?

[2] fairly well

[3] fine

[4] (both Medley here and Dorimant in his reply use "play" as a double entendre, meaning both gambling and sex. Medley means that if Dorimant wants to feel free to quit the game when he feels like it he should not involve either his partner or himself too deeply)

[5] taverns

BELLINDA: I am to go to the Park with Mrs. Loveit, Madam.

(*Exit* BELLINDA.)

LADY TOWNLEY: This confidence will go nigh to spoil this young creature.

MEDLEY: 'Twill do her good, Madam. Young men who are brought up under practising lawyers prove the abler counsel when they come to be called to the bar themselves.

DORIMANT: The town has been very favourable to you this afternoon, my Lady Townley; you use to have an *embarras*[6] of chairs and coaches at your door, an uproar of footmen in your hall, and a noise of fools above here.

LADY TOWNLEY: Indeed, my house is the general rendezvous, and next to the playhouse is the common refuge of all the young idle people.

EMILIA: Company is a very good thing, Madam, but I wonder you do not love it a little more chosen.

LADY TOWNLEY: 'Tis good to have an universal taste; we should love wit, but for variety be able to divert ourselves with the extravagancies of those who want[7] it.

MEDLEY: Fools will make you laugh.

EMILIA: For once or twice, but the repetition of their folly after a visit or two grows tedious and unsufferable.

LADY TOWNLEY: You are a little too delicate, Emilia.

(*Enter a* PAGE.)

PAGE: Sir Fopling Flutter, Madam, desires to know if you are to be seen.

LADY TOWNLEY: Here's the freshest fool in town, and one who has not cloyed you yet. —— Page!

PAGE: Madam!

LADY TOWNLEY: Desire him to walk up. (*Exit* PAGE.)

DORIMANT: Do not you fall on him, Medley, and snub him. Soothe him up in his extravagance; he will show the better.

MEDLEY: You know I have a natural indulgence for fools and need not this caution, Sir.

(*Enter* SIR FOPLING FLUTTER *with his* PAGE *after him.*)

SIR FOPLING: Page, wait without. (*Exit* PAGE.)
(*To* LADY TOWNLEY.) Madam, I kiss your hands. I see yesterday was nothing of chance; the *belles assemblées*[8] form themselves here every day. (*To* EMILIA.) Lady, your servant. —— Dorimant, let me embrace thee! Without lying, I have not met with any of my acquaintance who retain so much of Paris as thou dost — the very air thou hadst when the marquise

[6] (Fr.) bothersome excess
[7] lack
[8] (Fr.) elegant gatherings

mistook thee i'th' Tuileries and cried, "Hey, Chevalier!" and then begged thy pardon.

DORIMANT: I would fain wear in fashion as long as I can, Sir; 'tis a thing to be valued in men as well as baubles.[9]

SIR FOPLING: Thou art a man of wit and understands the town. Prithee, let thee and I be intimate; there is no living without making some good man the confidant of our pleasures.

DORIMANT: 'Tis true! but there is no man so improper for such a business as I am.

SIR FOPLING: Prithee, why hast thou so modest an opinion of thyself?

DORIMANT: Why, first, I could never keep a secret in my life; and then, there is no charm so infallibly makes me fall in love with a woman as my knowing a friend loves her. I deal honestly with you.

SIR FOPLING: Thy humour's very gallant, or let me perish! I knew a French count so like thee!

LADY TOWNLEY: Wit, I perceive, has more power over you than beauty, Sir Fopling, else you would not have let this lady stand so long neglected.

SIR FOPLING (*to* EMILIA): A thousand pardons, Madam; some civility's due of course upon the meeting a long absent friend. The *éclat*[10] of so much beauty, I confess, ought to have charmed me sooner.

EMILIA: The *brillant*[11] of so much good language, Sir, has much more power than the little beauty I can boast.

SIR FOPLING: I never saw anything prettier than this high work on your *point d'Espagne*.[12]

EMILIA: 'Tis not so rich as *point de Venise*.[13]

SIR FOPLING: Not altogether, but looks cooler and is more proper for the season. — Dorimant, is not that Medley?

DORIMANT: The same, Sir.

SIR FOPLING: Forgive me, Sir; in this *embarras* of civilities I could not come to have you in my arms sooner. You understand an equipage[14] the best of any man in town, I hear.

MEDLEY: By my own you would not guess it.

SIR FOPLING: There are critics who do not write, Sir.

MEDLEY: Our peevish poets will scarce allow it.

SIR FOPLING: Damn 'em, they'll allow no man wit who does not play the fool like themselves and show it! Have you taken notice of the gallesh[15] I brought over?

MEDLEY: Oh, yes! 't has quite another air than th' English makes.

[9] trinkets
[10] (Fr.) splendor
[11] (Fr.) sparkle
[12] (Fr.) Spanish lace
[13] (Fr.) Venetian lace
[14] (1) carriage (with or without horses and attendant servants), (2) retinue
[15] calèche, light carriage with a folding hood, buggy

SIR FOPLING: 'Tis as easily known from an English tumbril[16] as an Inns of Court man[17] is from one of us.

DORIMANT: Truly; there is a *bel air*[18] in galleshes as well as men.

MEDLEY: But there are few so delicate to observe it.

SIR FOPLING: The world is generally very *grossier*[19] here, indeed.

LADY TOWNLEY: He's very fine.

EMILIA: Extreme proper.

SIR FOPLING: A slight suit I made to appear in at my first arrival – not worthy your consideration, ladies.

DORIMANT: The pantaloon[20] is very well mounted.

SIR FOPLING: The tassels are new and pretty.

MEDLEY: I never saw a coat better cut.

SIR FOPLING: It makes me show long-waisted, and, I think, slender.

DORIMANT: That's the shape our ladies dote on.

MEDLEY: Your breech, though, is a handful too high, in my eye, Sir Fopling.

SIR FOPLING: Peace, Medley! I have wished it lower a thousand times, but a pox on't! 'twill not be.

LADY TOWNLEY: His gloves are well fringed, large and graceful.

SIR FOPLING: I was always eminent for being *bien ganté*.[21]

EMILIA: He wears nothing but what are originals of the most famous hands in Paris.

SIR FOPLING: You are in the right, Madam.

LADY TOWNLEY: The suit!

SIR FOPLING: Barroy.[22]

EMILIA: The garniture![23]

SIR FOPLING: Le Gras.

MEDLEY: The shoes!

SIR FOPLING: Piccar.

DORIMANT: The periwig!

SIR FOPLING: Chedreux.

LADY TOWNLEY:<br>EMILIA: } The gloves!

SIR FOPLING: Orangerie[24] – you know the smell, ladies. —— Dorimant, I could find in my heart for an amusement to have a gallantry with some of our English ladies.

DORIMANT: 'Tis a thing no less necessary to confirm the reputation of your wit than a duel will be to satisfy the town of your courage.

SIR FOPLING: Here was a woman yesterday ——

DORIMANT: Mistress Loveit.

16 dung-cart
17 i.e., lawyer
18 (Fr.) graceful style
19 (Fr.) coarse
20 trousers
21 (Fr.) well-gloved
22 (Barroy, LeGras, Piccar, and Chedreux were the proprietors of fashionable shops in Paris)
23 ornament
24 (Fr.) "Orange House" (perhaps the name of a perfume shop)

SIR FOPLING: You have named her.

DORIMANT: You cannot pitch on a better for your purpose.

SIR FOPLING: Prithee, what is she?

DORIMANT: A person of quality, and one who has a rest of reputation enough to make the conquest considerable; besides, I hear she likes you too.

SIR FOPLING: Methoughts she seemed, though, very reserved and uneasy all the time I entertained her.

DORIMANT: Grimace and affectation! You will see her i' th' Mail to-night.

SIR FOPLING: Prithee, let thee and I take the air together.

DORIMANT: I am engaged to Medley, but I'll meet you at St. James's and give you some information upon the which you may regulate your proceedings.

SIR FOPLING: All the world will be in the Park to-night. Ladies, 'twere pity to keep so much beauty longer within doors and rob the Ring[25] of all those charms that should adorn it. —— Hey, Page!

(*Enter* PAGE.)

See that all my people be ready. (PAGE *goes out again.*)
—Dorimant, *au revoir.* (*Exit.*)

MEDLEY: A fine mettled coxcomb.

DORIMANT: Brisk and insipid.

MEDLEY: Pert and dull.

EMILIA: However you despise him, gentlemen, I'll lay my life he passes for a wit with many.

DORIMANT: That may very well be; Nature has her cheats, stums[26] a brain, and puts sophisticate[27] dulness often on the tasteless multitude for true wit and good humour. Medley, come!

MEDLEY: I must go a little way; I will meet you i'the Mail.

DORIMANT: I'll walk through the garden thither. — (*To the women.*) We shall meet anon and bow.

LADY TOWNLEY: Not to-night. We are engaged about a business the knowledge of which may make you laugh hereafter.

MEDLEY: Your servant, ladies.

DORIMANT: *Au revoir,* as Sir Fopling says.

(*Exeunt* MEDLEY *and* DORIMANT.)

LADY TOWNLEY: The old man will be here immediately.

EMILIA: Let's expect[28] him i'th' garden.

LADY TOWNLEY: Go! you are a rogue.

EMILIA: I can't abide you. (*Exeunt.*)

[25] (cf. note 12, Scene 1 in this act)
[26] re-ferments (as with wine that has grown vapid)
[27] adulterated, artificial
[28] wait for

### SCENE 3

*Scene: The Mail.*

*Enter* HARRIET *and* YOUNG BELLAIR, *she pulling him.*

HARRIET: Come along.
YOUNG BELLAIR: And leave your mother!
HARRIET: Busy will be sent with a hue and cry after us, but that's no matter.
YOUNG BELLAIR: 'Twill look strangely in me.
HARRIET: She'll believe it a freak of mine and never blame your manners.
YOUNG BELLAIR: What reverend acquaintance is that she has met?
HARRIET: A fellow-beauty of the last king's time,[1] though by the ruins you would hardly guess it. (*Exeunt.*)

(*Enter* DORIMANT *and crosses the stage.*
*Enter* YOUNG BELLAIR *and* HARRIET.)

YOUNG BELLAIR: By this time your mother is in a fine taking.
HARRIET: If your friend Mr. Dorimant were but here now, that she might find me talking with him!
YOUNG BELLAIR: She does not know him, but dreads him, I hear, of all mankind.
HARRIET: She concludes if he does but speak to a woman, she's undone – is on her knees every day to pray heaven defend me from him.
YOUNG BELLAIR: You do not apprehend him so much as she does?
HARRIET: I never saw anything in him that was frightful.
YOUNG BELLAIR: On the contrary, have you not observed something extreme delightful in his wit and person?
HARRIET: He's agreeable and pleasant, I must own, but he does so much affect being so, he displeases me.
YOUNG BELLAIR: Lord, Madam! all he does and says is so easy and so natural.
HARRIET: Some men's verses seem so to the unskillful, but labour i'the one and affectation in the other to the judicious plainly appear.
YOUNG BELLAIR: I never heard him accused of affectation before.

(*Enter* DORIMANT *and stares upon her.*)

HARRIET: It passes on the easy town, who are favourably pleased in him to call it humour. (*Exeunt* YOUNG BELLAIR *and* HARRIET.)
DORIMANT: 'Tis she! it must be she – that lovely hair, that easy shape, those wanton eyes, and all those melting charms about her mouth which

[1] i.e., the reign of Charles I (1625–49)

Medley spoke of! I'll follow the lottery and put in for a prize with my friend Bellair. (*Exeunt* DORIMANT *repeating:*

In love the victors from the vanquish'd fly;
They fly that wound, and they pursue that die.)

(*Enter* YOUNG BELLAIR *and* HARRIET *and after them* DORIMANT *standing at a distance.*)

YOUNG BELLAIR: Most people prefer High Park[2] to this place.

HARRIET: It has the better reputation, I confess; but I abominate the dull diversions there — the formal bows, the affected smiles, the silly by-words and amorous tweers[3] in passing. Here one meets with a little conversation now and then.

YOUNG BELLAIR: These conversations have been fatal to some of your sex, Madam.

HARRIET: It may be so; because some who want temper[4] have been undone by gaming, must others who have it wholly deny themselves the pleasure of play?

DORIMANT (*coming up gently and bowing to her*): Trust me, it were unreasonable, Madam.

HARRIET: (*She starts and looks grave.*) Lord, who's this?

YOUNG BELLAIR: Dorimant!

DORIMANT: Is this the woman your father would have you marry?

YOUNG BELLAIR: It is.

DORIMANT: Her name?

YOUNG BELLAIR: Harriet.

DORIMANT: I am not mistaken; she's handsome.

YOUNG BELLAIR: Talk to her; her wit is better than her face. We were wishing for you but now.

DORIMANT (*to* HARRIET): Overcast with seriousness o'the sudden! A thousand smiles were shining in that face but now; I never saw so quick a change of weather.

HARRIET (*aside*): I feel as great a change within, but he shall never know it.

DORIMANT: You were talking of play, Madam. Pray, what may be your stint?[5]

HARRIET: A little harmless discourse in public walks, or at most an appointment in a box, barefaced,[6] at the playhouse: you are for masks and private meetings, where women engage for all they are worth, I hear.

DORIMANT: I have been used to deep play, but I can make one at small game when I like my gamester well.

HARRIET: And be so unconcerned you'll ha' no pleasure in't.

[2] Hyde Park
[3] leers
[4] lack self-control
[5] limit
[6] i.e., without a mask

DORIMANT: Where there is a considerable sum to be won, the hope of drawing people in makes every trifle considerable.

HARRIET: The sordidness of men's natures, I know, makes 'em willing to flatter and comply with the rich, though they are sure never to be the better for 'em.

DORIMANT: 'Tis in their power to do us good, and we despair not but at some time or other they may be willing.

HARRIET: To men who have fared in this town like you, 'twould be a great mortification to live on hope. Could you keep a Lent for a mistress?

DORIMANT: In expectation of a happy Easter and, though time be very precious, think forty days well lost to gain your favour.

HARRIET: Mr. Bellair, let us walk; 'tis time to leave him. Men grow dull when they begin to be particular.

DORIMANT: Y'are mistaken; flattery will not ensue, though I know y'are greedy of the praises of the whole Mail.

HARRIET: You do me wrong.

DORIMANT: I do not. As I followed you, I observed how you were pleased when the fops cried, "She's handsome, very handsome! by God she is!" and whispered aloud your name; the thousand several forms[7] you put your face into; then, to make yourself more agreeable, how wantonly you played with your head, flung back your locks, and looked smilingly over your shoulder at 'em!

HARRIET: I do not go begging the men's, as you do the ladies', good liking, with a sly softness in your looks and a gentle slowness in your bows as you pass by 'em – as thus, Sir. (*Acts him.*) Is not this like you?

(*Enter* LADY WOODVILL *and* BUSY.)

YOUNG BELLAIR: Your mother, Madam. (*Pulls* HARRIET; *she composes herself.*)

LADY WOODVILL: Ah, my dear child Harriet!

BUSY: Now is she so pleased with finding her again she cannot chide her.

LADY WOODVILL: Come away!

DORIMANT: 'Tis now but high Mail,[8] Madam, the most entertaining time of all the evening.

HARRIET: I would fain see that Dorimant, Mother, you so cry out of for a monster; he's in the Mail, I hear.

LADY WOODVILL: Come away then! The plague is here and you should dread the infection.

YOUNG BELLAIR: You may be misinformed of the gentleman.

LADY WOODVILL: Oh, no! I hope you do not know him. He is the prince of all the devils in the town – delights in nothing but in rapes and riots!

DORIMANT: If you did but hear him speak, Madam!

[7] expressions
[8] the most popular hour in the Mall

LADY WOODVILL: Oh, he has a tongue, they say, would tempt the angels to a second fall.

(*Enter* SIR FOPLING *with his equipage, six* FOOTMEN *and a* PAGE.)

SIR FOPLING: Hey! Champagne, Norman, La Rose, La Fleur, La Tour, La Verdure! — Dorimant —

LADY WOODVILL: Here, here he is among this rout! He names him! Come away, Harriet; come away!

(*Exeunt* LADY WOODVILL, HARRIET, BUSY, *and* YOUNG BELLAIR.)

DORIMANT: This fool's coming has spoiled all. She's gone, but she has left a pleasing image of herself behind that wanders in my soul – it must not settle there.

SIR FOPLING: What reverie is this? Speak, man!

DORIMANT:

Snatcht from myself, how far behind
Already I behold the shore!

(*Enter* MEDLEY.)

MEDLEY: Dorimant, a discovery! I met with Bellair.

DORIMANT: You can tell me no news, Sir; I know all.

MEDLEY: How do you like the daughter?

DORIMANT: You never came so near truth in your life as you did in her description.

MEDLEY: What think you of the mother?

DORIMANT: Whatever I think of her, she thinks very well of me, I find.

MEDLEY: Did she know you?

DORIMANT: She did not; whether she does now or no, I know not. Here was a pleasant scene towards,[9] when in came Sir Fopling, mustering up his equipage, and at the latter end named me and frighted her away.

MEDLEY: Loveit and Bellinda are not far off; I saw 'em alight at St. James's.

DORIMANT: Sir Fopling! Hark you, a word or two. (*Whispers.*) Look you do not want assurance.[10]

SIR FOPLING: I never do on these occasions.

DORIMANT: Walk on; we must not be seen together. Make your advantage of what I have told you. The next turn you will meet the lady.

SIR FOPLING: Hey! Follow me all!

(*Exeunt* SIR FOPLING *and his equipage.*)

DORIMANT: Medley, you shall see good sport anon between Loveit and this Fopling.

MEDLEY: I thought there was something toward, by that whisper.

[9] in progress
[10] an air of confidence

DORIMANT: You know a worthy principle of hers?

MEDLEY: Not to be so much as civil to a man who speaks to her in the presence of him she professes to love.

DORIMANT: I have encouraged Fopling to talk to her to-night.

MEDLEY: Now you are here, she will go nigh to beat him.

DORIMANT: In the humour she's in, her love will make her do some very extravagant thing doubtless.

MEDLEY: What was Bellinda's business with you at my Lady Townley's?

DORIMANT: To get me to meet Loveit here in order to an *éclaircissement*.[11] I made some difficulty of it and have prepared this rencounter to make good my jealousy.

MEDLEY: Here they come.

(*Enter* MRS. LOVEIT, BELLINDA, *and* PERT.)

DORIMANT: I'll meet her and provoke her with a deal of dumb civility in passing by, then turn short and be behind her when Sir Fopling sets upon her —

See how unregarded now
That piece of beauty passes.[12]

(*Exeunt* DORIMANT *and* MEDLEY.)

BELLINDA: How wonderful respectfully he bowed!

PERT: He's always over-mannerly when he has done a mischief.

BELLINDA: Methoughts, indeed, at the same time he had a strange, despising countenance.

PERT: The unlucky[13] look he thinks becomes him.

BELLINDA: I was afraid you would have spoke to him, my dear.

MRS. LOVEIT: I would have died first; he shall no more find me the loving fool he has done.

BELLINDA: You love him still?

MRS. LOVEIT: No!

PERT: I wish you did not.

MRS. LOVEIT: I do not, and I will have you think so. — What made you hale me to this odious place, Bellinda?

BELLINDA: I hate to be hulched up[14] in a coach; walking is much better.

MRS. LOVEIT: Would we could meet Sir Fopling now!

BELLINDA: Lord, would you not avoid him?

MRS. LOVEIT: I would make him all the advances that may be.

BELLINDA: That would confirm Dorimant's suspicion, my dear.

MRS. LOVEIT: He is not jealous; but I will make him so, and be revenged a way he little thinks on.

[11] (Fr.) clarification

[12] (opening lines of Sonnet I by Sir John Suckling [1609–42], like Waller a Cavalier poet)

[13] mischievous

[14] hunched up

BELLINDA (*aside*): If she should make him jealous, that may make him fond of her again. I must dissuade her from it. — Lord, my dear, this will certainly make him hate you.

MRS. LOVEIT: 'Twill make him uneasy, though he does not care for me. I know the effects of jealousy on men of his proud temper.

BELLINDA: 'Tis a fantastic remedy; its operations are dangerous and uncertain.

MRS. LOVEIT: 'Tis the strongest cordial we can give to dying love: it often brings it back when there's no sign of life remaining. But I design not so much the reviving of his, as my revenge.

(*Enter* SIR FOPLING *and his equipage.*)

SIR FOPLING: Hey! Bid the coachman send home four of his horses and bring the coach to Whitehall; I'll walk over the Park. — Madam, the honour of kissing your fair hands is a happiness I missed this afternoon at my Lady Townley's.

MRS. LOVEIT: You were very obliging, Sir Fopling, the last time I saw you there.

SIR FOPLING: The preference was due to your wit and beauty. — Madam, your servant; there never was so sweet an evening.

BELLINDA: 'T has drawn all the rabble of the town hither.

SIR FOPLING: 'Tis pity there's not an order made that none but the *beau monde*[15] should walk here.

MRS. LOVEIT: 'Twould add much to the beauty of the place. See what a sort of nasty fellows are coming!

(*Enter four ill-fashioned* FELLOWS, *singing:*)

'Tis not for kisses alone,[16] etc.

MRS. LOVEIT: Fo! Their periwigs are scented with tobacco so strong —

SIR FOPLING: It overcomes our pulvillio.[17] Methinks I smell the coffee-house they come from.

1 MAN: Dorimant's convenient,[18] Madam Loveit.

2 MAN: I like the oily buttock[19] with her.

3 MAN: What spruce prig[20] is that?

1 MAN: A caravan[21] lately come from Paris.

2 MAN: Peace! they smoke.[22] (*All of them coughing; exeunt singing:*

There's something else to be done,[23] etc.)

(*Enter* DORIMANT *and* MEDLEY.)

15 (Fr.) the fashionable world, society
16 (the first line of an anonymous bawdy song)
17 scented powder
18 i.e., mistress
19 "lush lay"
20 fop
21 traveling company
22 observe, take notice of (us)
23 (another line from the same song)

DORIMANT: They're engaged.

MEDLEY: She entertains him as if she liked him!

DORIMANT: Let us go forward – seem earnest in discourse and show ourselves; then you shall see how she'll use him.

BELLINDA: Yonder's Dorimant, my dear.

MRS. LOVEIT (*aside*): I see him. He comes insulting, but I will disappoint him in his expectation. (*To* SIR FOPLING.) I like this pretty, nice humour of yours, Sir Fopling. — With what a loathing eye he looked upon those fellows!

SIR FOPLING: I sat near one of 'em at a play to-day and was almost poisoned with a pair of cordovan[24] gloves he wears.

MRS. LOVEIT: Oh, filthy cordovan! How I hate the smell! (*Laughs in a loud, affected way.*)

SIR FOPLING: Did you observe, Madam, how their cravats hung loose an inch from their neck and what a frightful air it gave 'em?

MRS. LOVEIT: Oh, I took particular notice of one that is always spruced up with a deal of dirty sky-coloured ribband.

BELLINDA: That's one of the walking flageolets[25] who haunt the Mail o'nights.

MRS. LOVEIT: Oh, I remember him; h'has a hollow tooth enough to spoil the sweetness of an evening.

SIR FOPLING: I have seen the tallest walk the streets with a dainty pair of boxes[26] neatly buckled on.

MRS. LOVEIT: And a little foot-boy at his heels, pocket-high, with a flat cap, a dirty face —

SIR FOPLING: And a snotty nose.

MRS. LOVEIT: Oh, odious! – There's many of my own sex with that Holborn equipage trig to Gray's Inn Walks and now and then travel hither on a Sunday.

MEDLEY: She takes no notice of you.

DORIMANT: Damn her! I am jealous of a counterplot.

MRS. LOVEIT: Your liveries are the finest, Sir Fopling – oh, that page! that page is the prettily'st dressed – they are all Frenchmen.

SIR FOPLING: There's one damned English blockhead among 'em; you may know him by his mien.

MRS. LOVEIT: Oh, that's he – that's he! What do you call him?

SIR FOPLING: Hey – I know not what to call him —

MRS. LOVEIT: What's your name?

FOOTMAN: John Trott, Madam.

SIR FOPLING: Oh, unsufferable! Trott, Trott, Trott! There's nothing so barbarous as the names of our English servants. — What countryman are you, Sirrah?

[24] horse leather from Cordova, Spain

[25] small wind instrument

[26] wooden shoes

FOOTMAN: Hampshire, Sir.

SIR FOPLING: Then Hampshire be your name. Hey, Hampshire!

MRS. LOVEIT: Oh, that sound – that sound becomes the mouth of a man of quality!

MEDLEY: Dorimant, you look a little bashful on the matter.

DORIMANT: She dissembles better than I thought she could have done.

MEDLEY: You have tempted her with too luscious a bait. She bites at the coxcomb.

DORIMANT: She cannot fall from loving me to that.

MEDLEY: You begin to be jealous in earnest.

DORIMANT: Of one I do not love —

MEDLEY: You did love her.

DORIMANT: The fit has long been over.

MEDLEY: But I have known men fall into dangerous relapses when they have found a woman inclining to another.

DORIMANT (*to himself*): He guesses the secret of my heart. I am concerned, but dare not show it, lest Bellinda should mistrust all I have done to gain her.

BELLINDA (*aside*): I have watched his look and find no alteration there. Did he love her, some signs of jealousy would have appeared.

DORIMANT: I hope this happy evening, Madam, has reconciled you to the scandalous Mail. We shall have you now hankering[27] here again —

MRS. LOVEIT: Sir Fopling, will you walk?

SIR FOPLING: I am all obedience, Madam.

MRS. LOVEIT: Come along then, and let's agree to be malicious on all the ill-fashioned things we meet.

SIR FOPLING: We'll make a critique on the whole Mail, Madam.

MRS. LOVEIT: Bellinda, you shall engage[28] —

BELLINDA: To the reserve of[29] our friends, my dear.

MRS. LOVEIT: No! no exceptions!

SIR FOPLING: We'll sacrifice all to our diversion.

MRS. LOVEIT: All – all.

SIR FOPLING: All.

BELLINDA: All? Then let it be.

(*Exeunt* SIR FOPLING, MRS. LOVEIT, BELLINDA, *and* PERT, *laughing.*)

MEDLEY: Would you had brought some more of your friends, Dorimant, to have been witnesses of Sir Fopling's disgrace and your triumph.

DORIMANT: 'Twere unreasonable to desire you not to laugh at me; but pray do not expose me to the town this day or two.

MEDLEY: By that time you hope to have regained your credit.

DORIMANT: I know she hates Fopling and only makes use of him in hope to work me on again; had it not been for some powerful considerations

[27] hanging about expectantly and longingly

[28] i.e., be one of us, participate

[29] excluding

which will be removed to-morrow morning, I had made her pluck off this mask and show the passion that lies panting under.

(*Enter a* FOOTMAN.)

MEDLEY: Here comes a man from Bellair with news of your last adventure.

DORIMANT: I am glad he sent him; I long to know the consequence of our parting.

FOOTMAN: Sir, my master desires you to come to my Lady Townley's presently and bring Mr. Medley with you. My Lady Woodvill and her daughter are there.

MEDLEY: Then all's well, Dorimant.

FOOTMAN: They have sent for the fiddles and mean to dance. He bid me tell you, Sir, the old lady does not know you, and would have you own yourself to be Mr. Courtage. They are all prepared to receive you by that name.

DORIMANT: That foppish admirer of quality, who flatters the very meat at honourable tables and never offers love to a woman below a lady-grandmother.

MEDLEY: You know the character you are to act, I see.

DORIMANT: This is Harriet's contrivance – wild, witty, lovesome, beautiful, and young! —— Come along, Medley.

MEDLEY: This new woman would well supply the loss of Loveit.

DORIMANT: That business must not end so; before to-morrow sun is set I will revenge and clear it.
And you and Loveit, to her cost, shall find,
I fathom all the depths of womankind. (*Exeunt.*)

## ACT IV

### SCENE 1

*The Scene opens with the Fiddles playing a Country Dance.*

*Enter* DORIMANT *and* LADY WOODVILL, YOUNG BELLAIR *and* MRS. HARRIET, OLD BELLAIR *and* EMILIA, MR. MEDLEY *and* LADY TOWNLEY, *as having just ended the Dance.*

OLD BELLAIR: So, so, so! – a smart bout, a very smart bout, a dod!

LADY TOWNLEY: How do you like Emilia's dancing, Brother?

OLD BELLAIR: Not at all – not at all!

LADY TOWNLEY: You speak not what you think, I am sure.

OLD BELLAIR: No matter for that; go, bid her dance no more. It don't become her – it don't become her. Tell her I say so. (*Aside.*) A dod, I love her!

DORIMANT (*to* LADY WOODVILL): All people mingle nowadays, Madam. And in public places women of quality have the least respect showed 'em.

LADY WOODVILL: I protest you say the truth, Mr. Courtage.

DORIMANT: Forms and ceremonies, the only things that uphold quality and greatness, are now shamefully laid aside and neglected.

LADY WOODVILL: Well, this is not the women's age, let 'em think what they will. Lewdness is the business now; love was the business in my time.

DORIMANT: The women, indeed, are little beholding to the young men of this age; they're generally only dull admirers of themselves, and make their court to nothing but their periwigs and their cravats, and would be more concerned for the disordering of 'em, though on a good occasion, than a young maid would be for the tumbling of her head or handkercher.[1]

LADY WOODVILL: I protest you hit 'em.

DORIMANT: They are very assiduous to show themselves at court, well dressed, to the women of quality, but their business is with the stale mistresses of the town, who are prepared to receive their lazy addresses by industrious old lovers who have cast 'em off and made 'em easy.

HARRIET: He fits my mother's humour so well, a little more and she'll dance a kissing dance with him anon.

MEDLEY: Dutifully observed, Madam.

DORIMANT: They pretend to be great critics in beauty. By their talk you would think they liked no face, and yet can dote on an ill one if it belong to a laundress or a tailor's daughter. They cry, "A woman's past her prime at twenty, decayed at four-and-twenty, old and unsufferable at thirty."

LADY WOODVILL: Unsufferable at thirty! That they are in the wrong, Mr. Courtage, at five-and-thirty, there are living proofs enough to convince 'em.

DORIMANT: Ay, Madam. There's Mrs. Setlooks, Mrs. Droplip, and my Lady Lowd; show me among all our opening buds a face that promises so much beauty as the remains of theirs.

LADY WOODVILL: The depraved appetite of this vicious age tastes nothing but green fruit, and loathes it when 'tis kindly[2] ripened.

DORIMANT: Else so many deserving women, Madam, would not be so untimely neglected.

LADY WOODVILL: I protest, Mr. Courtage, a dozen such good men as you would be enough to atone for that wicked Dorimant and all the under debauchees of the town.

(HARRIET, EMILIA, YOUNG BELLAIR, MEDLEY, LADY TOWNLEY *break out into a laughter.*)

—What's the matter there?

[1] a small scarf worn around the neck
[2] naturally, seasonably

MEDLEY: A pleasant mistake, Madam, that a lady has made, occasions a little laughter.

OLD BELLAIR: Come, come, you keep 'em idle! They are impatient till the fiddles play again.

DORIMANT: You are not weary, Madam?

LADY WOODVILL: One dance more; I cannot refuse you, Mr. Courtage.

(*They dance. After the dance,* OLD BELLAIR, *singing and dancing up to* EMILIA.)

EMILIA: You are very active, Sir.

OLD BELLAIR: A dod, Sirrah! when I was a young fellow I could ha' capered up to my woman's gorget.[3]

DORIMANT: You are willing to rest yourself, Madam ——

LADY TOWNLEY: We'll walk into my chamber and sit down.

MEDLEY: Leave us Mr. Courtage; he's a dancer, and the young ladies are not weary yet.

LADY WOODVILL: We'll send him out again.

HARRIET: If you do not quickly, I know where to send for Mr. Dorimant.

LADY WOODVILL: This girl's head, Mr. Courtage, is ever running on that wild fellow.

DORIMANT: 'Tis well you have got her a good husband, Madam; that will settle it.

(*Exeunt* LADY TOWNLEY, LADY WOODVILL, *and* DORIMANT.)

OLD BELLAIR (*to* EMILIA): A dod, sweetheart, be advised and do not throw thyself away on a young, idle fellow.

EMILIA: I have no such intention, Sir.

OLD BELLAIR: Have a little patience! Thou shalt have the man I spake of. A dod, he loves thee and will make a good husband – but no words!

EMILIA: But, Sir ——

OLD BELLAIR: No answer – out a pise! peace! and think on't.

(*Enter* DORIMANT.)

DORIMANT: Your company is desired within, Sir.

OLD BELLAIR: I go, I go! Good Mr. Courtage, fare you well! – (*To* EMILIA.) Go, I'll see you no more!

EMILIA: What have I done, Sir?

OLD BELLAIR: You are ugly, you are ugly! – Is she not, Mr. Courtage?

EMILIA: Better words or I shan't abide you.

OLD BELLAIR: Out a pise; a dod, what does she say? Hit her a pat for me there. (*Exit* OLD BELLAIR.)

MEDLEY: You have charms for the whole family.

DORIMANT: You'll spoil all with some unseasonable jest, Medley.

[3] a woman's ornamental collar or neckpiece

MEDLEY: You see I confine my tongue and am content to be a bare spectator, much contrary to my nature.

EMILIA: Methinks, Mr. Dorimant, my Lady Woodvill is a little fond of you.

DORIMANT: Would her daughter were!

MEDLEY: It may be you may find her so. Try her – you have an opportunity.

DORIMANT: And I will not lose it. —— Bellair, here's a lady has something to say to you.

YOUNG BELLAIR: I wait upon her. —— Mr. Medley, we have both business with you.

DORIMANT: Get you all together then. (*To* HARRIET.) That demure curtsey is not amiss in jest, but do not think in earnest it becomes you.

HARRIET: Affectation is catching, I find; from your grave bow I got it.

DORIMANT: Where had you all that scorn and coldness in your look?

HARRIET: From nature, Sir; pardon my want of art. I have not learnt those softnesses and languishings which now in faces are so much in fashion.

DORIMANT: You need 'em not; you have a sweetness of your own, if you would but calm your frowns and let it settle.

HARRIET: My eyes are wild and wandering like my passions, and cannot yet be tied to rules of charming.

DORIMANT: Women, indeed, have commonly a method of managing those messengers of love. Now they will look as if they would kill, and anon they will look as if they were dying. They point and rebate[4] their glances, the better to invite us.

HARRIET: I like this variety well enough, but hate the set face that always looks as it would say, "Come love me!" – a woman who at plays makes the *doux yeux*[5] to a whole audience and at home cannot forbear 'em to her monkey.

DORIMANT: Put on a gentle smile and let me see how well it will become you.

HARRIET: I am sorry my face does not please you as it is, but I shall not be complaisant and change it.

DORIMANT: Though you are obstinate, I know 'tis capable of improvement, and shall do you justice, Madam, if I chance to be at Court when the critics of the Circle pass their judgment; for thither you must come.

HARRIET: And expect to be taken in pieces, have all my features examined, every motion censured, and on the whole be condemned to be but pretty, or a beauty of the lowest rate. What think you?

DORIMANT: The women – nay, the very lovers who belong to the drawing-room – will maliciously allow you more than that: they always grant what is apparent, that they may the better be believed when they name concealed faults they cannot easily be disproved in.

HARRIET: Beauty runs as great a risk exposed at Court as wit does on the stage, where the ugly and the foolish all are free to censure.

[4] blunt
[5] (Fr.) soft eyes

DORIMANT (*aside*): I love her and dare not let her know it; I fear sh'as an ascendant o'er me and may revenge the wrongs I have done her sex. (*To her.*) Think of making a party,[6] Madam; love will engage.

HARRIET: You make me start! I did not think to have heard of love from you.

DORIMANT: I never knew what 'twas to have a settled ague[7] yet, but now and then have had irregular fits.

HARRIET: Take heed! sickness after long health is commonly more violent and dangerous.

DORIMANT (*aside*): I have took the infection from her, and feel the disease now spreading in me. (*To her.*) Is the name of love so frightful that you dare not stand it?

HARRIET: 'Twill do little execution out of your mouth on me, I am sure.

DORIMANT: It has been fatal ——

HARRIET: To some easy women, but we are not all born to one destiny. I was informed you use to laugh at love and not make it.

DORIMANT: The time has been, but now I must speak ——

HARRIET: If it be on that idle subject, I will put on my serious look, turn my head carelessly from you, drop my lip, let my eyelids fall and hang half o'er my eyes – thus – while you buzz a speech of an hour long in my ear, and I answer never a word. Why do you not begin?

DORIMANT: That the company may take notice how passionately I make advances of love, and how disdainfully you receive 'em!

HARRIET: When your love's grown strong enough to make you bear being laughed at, I'll give you leave to trouble me with it. Till when pray forbear, Sir.

(*Enter* SIR FOPLING *and others in masks.*)

DORIMANT: What's here – masquerades?

HARRIET: I thought that foppery had been left off, and people might have been in private with a fiddle.

DORIMANT: 'Tis endeavoured to be kept on foot still by some who find themselves the more acceptable the less they are known.

YOUNG BELLAIR: This must be Sir Fopling.

MEDLEY: That extraordinary habit shows it.

YOUNG BELLAIR: What are the rest?

MEDLEY: A company of French rascals whom he picked up in Paris and has brought over to be his dancing equipage on these occasions. Make him own himself; a fool is very troublesome when he presumes he is incognito.

SIR FOPLING (*to* HARRIET): Do you know me?

HARRIET: Ten to one but I guess at you?

SIR FOPLING: Are you women as fond of a vizard as we men are?

HARRIET: I am very fond of a vizard that covers a face I do not like, Sir.

[6] joining the social circle
[7] fever

YOUNG BELLAIR: Here are no masks, you see, Sir, but those which came with you. This was intended a private meeting; but because you look like a gentleman, if you will discover yourself and we know you to be such, you shall be welcome.

SIR FOPLING (*pulling off his mask*): Dear Bellair!

MEDLEY: Sir Fopling! How came you hither?

SIR FOPLING: Faith, as I was coming late from Whitehall, after the King's *couchée*,[8] one of my people told me he had heard fiddles at my Lady Townley's, and ——

DORIMANT: You need not say any more, Sir.

SIR FOPLING: Dorimant, let me kiss thee.

DORIMANT: Hark you, Sir Fopling —— (*Whispers.*)

SIR FOPLING: Enough, enough, Courtage. —— A pretty kind of young woman that, Medley. I observed her in the Mail – more *éveillée*[9] than our English women commonly are. Prithee, what is she?

MEDLEY: The most noted coquette in town. Beware of her.

SIR FOPLING: Let her be what she will, I know how to take my measures. In Paris the mode is to flatter the *prude,* laugh at the *faux-prude,*[10] make serious love to the *demi-prude,*[11] and only rally with the *coquette.*[12] Medley, what think you?

MEDLEY: That for all this smattering of the mathematics, you may be out in your judgment at tennis.

SIR FOPLING: What a *coq-à-l'âne*[13] is this? I talk of women and thou answer'st tennis.

MEDLEY: Mistakes will be for want of apprehension.

SIR FOPLING: I am very glad of the acquaintance I have with this family.

MEDLEY: My lady truly is a good woman.

SIR FOPLING: Ah, Dorimant – Courtage, I would say – would thou hadst spent the last winter in Paris with me! When thou wert there, La Corneus and Sallyes were the only habitudes[14] we had: a comedian would have been a *bonne fortune.*[15] No stranger ever passed his time so well as I did some months before I came over. I was well received in a dozen families where all the women of quality used to visit; I have intrigues to tell thee more pleasant than ever thou read'st in a novel.

HARRIET: Write 'em Sir, and oblige us women. Our language wants such little stories.

SIR FOPLING: Writing, Madam, 's a mechanic part of wit. A gentleman should never go beyond a song or a *billet.*

HARRIET: Bussy was a gentleman.

[8] (Fr.) evening reception
[9] (Fr.) lively
[10] (Fr.) sham-prude
[11] (Fr.) half-prude
[12] (Fr.) flirt
[13] (Fr. "from rooster to donkey") string of nonsense
[14] familiar relations
[15] (Fr.) piece of good luck

SIR FOPLING: Who, d'Ambois?[16]

MEDLEY: Was there ever such a brisk blockhead?

HARRIET: Not d'Ambois, Sir, but Rabutin[17] — he who writ the loves of France.

SIR FOPLING: That may be, Madam; many gentlemen do things that are below 'em. Damn your authors, Courtage; women are the prettiest things we can fool away our time with.

HARRIET: I hope ye have wearied yourself to-night at Court, Sir, and will not think of fooling with anybody here.

SIR FOPLING: I cannot complain of my fortune there, Madam. —— Dorimant ——

DORIMANT: Again!

SIR FOPLING: Courtage — a pox on't! — I have something to tell thee. When I had made my court within, I came out and flung myself upon the mat under the state[18] i'th' outward room, i'th' midst of half a dozen beauties who were withdrawn to jeer among themselves, as they called it.

DORIMANT: Did you know 'em?

SIR FOPLING: Not one of 'em, by heavens! — not I. But they were all your friends.

DORIMANT: How are you sure of that?

SIR FOPLING: Why, we laughed at all the town — spared nobody but yourself. They found me a man for their purpose.

DORIMANT: I know you are malicious, to your power.[19]

SIR FOPLING: And faith, I had occasion to show it, for I never saw more gaping fools at a ball or on a birthday.

DORIMANT: You learned who the women were?

SIR FOPLING: No matter; they frequent the drawing-room.[20]

DORIMANT: And entertain themselves pleasantly at the expense of all the fops who come there.

SIR FOPLING: That's their business. Faith, I sifted 'em,[21] and find they have a sort of wit among them. —— Ah, filthy! (*Pinches a tallow candle.*)

DORIMANT: Look, he has been pinching the tallow candle.

SIR FOPLING: How can you breathe in a room where there's grease frying? —— Dorimant, thou art intimate with my lady; advise her, for her own sake and the good company that comes hither, to burn wax lights.

HARRIET: What are these masquerades who stand so obsequiously at a distance?

SIR FOPLING: A set of balladines whom I picked out of the best in France and brought over with a *flûte-douce* or two — my servants. They shall entertain you.

[16] Bussy d'Ambois, the title hero of a play by George Chapman (1607)

[17] Roger de Rabutin (1618–93), Comte de Bussy, wrote the *Histoire Amoreuse des Gaules*

[18] canopy

[19] as malicious as you know how to be

[20] i.e., court assembly

[21] tried them out

HARRIET: I had rather see you dance yourself, Sir Fopling.

SIR FOPLING: And I had rather do it – all the company knows it – but, Madam ——

MEDLEY: Come, come, no excuses, Sir Fopling!

SIR FOPLING: By heavens, Medley ——

MEDLEY: Like a woman I find you must be struggled with before one brings you to what you desire.

HARRIET (*aside*): Can he dance?

EMILIA: And fence and sing too, if you'll believe him.

DORIMANT: He has no more excellence in his heels than in his head. He went to Paris a plain, bashful English blockhead, and is returned a fine undertaking[22] French fop.

MEDLEY: I cannot prevail.

SIR FOPLING: Do not think it want of complaisance, Madam.

HARRIET: You are too well bred to want that, Sir Fopling. I believe it want of power.

SIR FOPLING: By heavens, and so it is! I have sat up so damned late and drunk so cursed hard since I came to this lewd town, that I am fit for nothing but low dancing now – a *courante,* a *bourrée,* or a *menuet.*[23] But St. André tells me, if I will but be regular, in one month I shall rise again. Pox on this debauchery! (*Endeavours at a caper.*)

EMILIA: I have heard your dancing much commended.

SIR FOPLING: It had the good fortune to please in Paris. I was judged to rise within an inch as high as the Basque in an entry I danced there.

HARRIET: I am mightily taken with this fool; let us sit. —— Here's a seat, Sir Fopling.

SIR FOPLING: At your feet, Madam; I can be nowhere so much at ease. —— By your leave, gown.

HARRIET:<br>EMILIA: } Ah, you'll spoil it!

SIR FOPLING: No matter; my clothes are my creatures. I make 'em to make my court to you ladies. —— Hey! *Qu'on commence!*[24] (*Dance.*) —— To an English dancer, English motions. I was forced to entertain[25] this fellow, one of my set miscarrying.[26] —— Oh, horrid! Leave your damned manner of dancing and put on the French air: have you not a pattern before you? —— Pretty well! imitation in time may bring him to something.

(*After the dance, enter* OLD BELLAIR, LADY WOODVILL, *and* LADY TOWNLEY.)

OLD BELLAIR: Hey, a dod, what have we here – a mumming?[27]

LADY WOODVILL: Where's my daughter? Harriet!

22 enterprising

23 (all "low" dances because they are slow and stately)

24 (Fr.) begin!

25 employ

26 having an accident

27 costumed play-acting

DORIMANT: Here, here, Madam! I know not but under these disguises there may be dangerous sparks; I gave the young lady warning.

LADY WOODVILL: Lord! I am so obliged to you, Mr. Courtage.

HARRIET: Lord, how you admire this man!

LADY WOODVILL: What have you to except against him?

HARRIET: He's a fop.

LADY WOODVILL: He's not a Dorimant, a wild extravagant fellow of the times.

HARRIET: He's a man made up of forms and commonplaces sucked out of the remaining lees of the last age.

LADY WOODVILL: He's so good a man that, were you not engaged ——

LADY TOWNLEY: You'll have but little night to sleep in.

LADY WOODVILL: Lord, 'tis perfect day.[28]

DORIMANT (*aside*): The hour is almost come I appointed Bellinda, and I am not so foppishly in love here to forget. I am flesh and blood yet.

LADY TOWNLEY: I am very sensible,[29] Madam.

LADY WOODVILL: Lord, Madam!

HARRIET: Look! in what a struggle is my poor mother yonder!

YOUNG BELLAIR: She has much ado to bring out the compliment.

DORIMANT: She strains hard for it.

HARRIET: See, see! her head tottering, her eyes staring, and her under lip trembling ——

DORIMANT: Now — now she's in the very convulsions of her civility. (*Aside.*) 'Sdeath, I shall lose Bellinda! I must fright her hence; she'll be an hour in this fit of good manners else. (*To* LADY WOODVILL.) Do you not know Sir Fopling, Madam?

LADY WOODVILL: I have seen that face — oh, heaven! 'tis the same we met in the Mail. How came he here?

DORIMANT: A fiddle, in this town, is a kind of fop-call; no sooner it strikes up but the house is besieged with an army of masquerades straight.

LADY WOODVILL: Lord! I tremble, Mr. Courtage. For certain, Dorimant is in the company.

DORIMANT: I cannot confidently say he is not. You had best be gone. I will wait upon you; your daughter is in the hands of Mr. Bellair.

LADY WOODVILL: I'll see her before me. —— Harriet, come away.

YOUNG BELLAIR: Lights! lights!

LADY TOWNLEY: Light, down there!

OLD BELLAIR: A dod, it needs not ——

DORIMANT: Call my Lady Woodvill's coach to the door quickly.

(*Exeunt* YOUNG BELLAIR, HARRIET, LADY TOWNLEY, DORIMANT, *and* LADY WOODVILL.)

OLD BELLAIR: Stay, Mr. Medley: let the young fellows do that duty; we will

[28] broad daylight
[29] i.e., of the honor you have done me by being my guest

drink a glass of wine together. 'Tis good after dancing. What mumming spark is that?

MEDLEY: He is not to be comprehended in few words.

SIR FOPLING: Hey, La Tour!

MEDLEY: Whither away, Sir Fopling?

SIR FOPLING: I have business with Courtage.

MEDLEY: He'll but put the ladies into their coach and come up again.

OLD BELLAIR: In the meantime I'll call for a bottle. (*Exit* OLD BELLAIR.)

(*Enter* YOUNG BELLAIR.)

MEDLEY: Where's Dorimant?

YOUNG BELLAIR: Stolen home. He has had business waiting for him there all this night, I believe, by an impatience I observed in him.

MEDLEY: Very likely; 'tis but dissembling drunkenness, railing at his friends, and the kind soul will embrace the blessing and forget the tedious expectation.

SIR FOPLING: I must speak with him before I sleep.

YOUNG BELLAIR: Emilia and I are resolved on that business.

MEDLEY: Peace! here's your father.

(*Enter* OLD BELLAIR *and* BUTLER *with a bottle of wine.*)

OLD BELLAIR: The women are all gone to bed. — Fill, boy! — Mr. Medley, begin a health.

MEDLEY (*whispers*): To Emilia!

OLD BELLAIR: Out a pise! she's a rogue, and I'll not pledge you.

MEDLEY: I know you will.

OLD BELLAIR: A dod, drink it, then!

SIR FOPLING: Let us have the new bacchic.

OLD BELLAIR: A dod, that is a hard word. What does it mean, Sir?

MEDLEY: A catch or drinking-song.

OLD BELLAIR: Let us have it then.

SIR FOPLING: Fill the glasses round and draw up in a body. — Hey, music!

(*They sing.*)

The pleasures of love and the joys of good wine
To perfect our happiness wisely we join.
We to beauty all day
Give the sovereign sway
And her favourite nymphs devoutly obey.
At the plays we are constantly making our court,
And when they are ended we follow the sport
To the Mall and the Park,
Where we love till 'tis dark;
Then sparkling champagne
Puts an end to their reign;

It quickly recovers
Poor languishing lovers;
Makes us frolic and gay, and drowns all our sorrow.
But alas! we relapse again on the morrow.
Let every man stand
With his glass in his hand,
And briskly discharge at the word of command:
Here's a health to all those
Whom to-night we depose!
Wine and beauty by turns great souls should inspire;
Present all together! and now, boys, give fire!

OLD BELLAIR: A dod, a pretty business and very merry!

SIR FOPLING: Hark you, Medley, let you and I take the fiddles and go waken Dorimant.

MEDLEY: We shall do him a courtesy, if it be as I guess. For after the fatigue of this night he'll quickly have his belly full and be glad of an occasion to cry, "Take away, Handy!"

YOUNG BELLAIR: I'll go with you, and there we'll consult about affairs, Medley.

OLD BELLAIR (*looks on his watch*): A dod, 'tis six o'clock!

SIR FOPLING: Let's away, then.

OLD BELLAIR: Mr. Medley, my sister tells me you are an honest man — and a dod, I love you. Few words and hearty — that's the way with old Harry, old Harry.

SIR FOPLING: Light your flambeaux.[30] Hey!

OLD BELLAIR: What does the man mean?

MEDLEY: 'Tis day, Sir Fopling.

SIR FOPLING: No matter; our serenade will look the greater.

(*Exeunt omnes.*)

## Scene 2

*Scene:* DORIMANT'*s lodging. A table, a candle, a toilet, etc.* HANDY, *tying up linen.*

*Enter* DORIMANT *in his gown, and* BELLINDA.

DORIMANT: Why will you be gone so soon?

BELLINDA: Why did you stay out so late?

DORIMANT: Call a chair, Handy. — What makes you tremble so?

BELLINDA: I have a thousand fears about me. Have I not been seen, think you?

DORIMANT: By nobody but myself and trusty Handy.

[30] torches

BELLINDA: Where are all your people?

DORIMANT: I have dispersed 'em on sleeveless[1] errands. What does that sigh mean?

BELLINDA: Can you be so unkind to ask me? Well – (*sighs*) – were it to do again ——

DORIMANT: We should do it, should we not?

BELLINDA: I think we should – the wickeder man you to make me love so well. Will you be discreet now?

DORIMANT: I will.

BELLINDA: You cannot.

DORIMANT: Never doubt it.

BELLINDA: I will not expect it.

DORIMANT: You do me wrong.

BELLINDA: You have no more power to keep the secret than I had not to trust you with it.

DORIMANT: By all the joys I have had and those you keep in store ——

BELLINDA: You'll do for my sake what you never did before.

DORIMANT: By that truth thou hast spoken, a wife shall sooner betray herself to her husband.

BELLINDA: Yet I had rather you should be false in this than in another thing you promised me.

DORIMANT: What's that?

BELLINDA: That you would never see Loveit more but in public places – in the Park, at Court and plays.

DORIMANT: 'Tis not likely a man should be fond of seeing a damned old play when there is a new one acted.

BELLINDA: I dare not trust your promise.

DORIMANT: You may ——

BELLINDA: This does not satisfy me. You shall swear you never will see her more.

DORIMANT: I will, a thousand oaths. By all ——

BELLINDA: Hold! You shall not, now I think on't better.

DORIMANT: I will swear!

BELLINDA: I shall grow jealous of the oath and think I owe your truth to that, not to your love.

DORIMANT: Then, by my love; no other oath I'll swear.

(*Enter* HANDY.)

HANDY: Here's a chair.

BELLINDA: Let me go.

DORIMANT: I cannot.

BELLINDA: Too willingly, I fear.

DORIMANT: Too unkindly feared. When will you promise me again?

1 useless (Dorimant has made sure that all his servants are out of the way)

BELLINDA: Not this fortnight.

DORIMANT: You will be better than your word.

BELLINDA: I think I shall. Will it not make you love me less? (*Starting.*) Hark! what fiddles are these? (*Fiddles without.*)

DORIMANT: Look out, Handy. (*Exit* HANDY *and returns.*)

HANDY: Mr. Medley, Mr. Bellair, and Sir Fopling; they are coming up.

DORIMANT: How got they in?

HANDY: The door was open for the chair.

BELLINDA: Lord, let me fly!

DORIMANT: Here, here, down the back stairs! I'll see you into your chair.

BELLINDA: No, no! Stay and receive 'em. And be sure you keep your word and never see Loveit more. Let it be a proof of your kindness.

DORIMANT: It shall. — Handy, direct her. (*Kissing her hand.*) Everlasting love go along with thee. (*Exeunt* BELLINDA *and* HANDY.)

(*Enter* YOUNG BELLAIR, MEDLEY, *and* SIR FOPLING.)

YOUNG BELLAIR: Not abed yet?

MEDLEY: You have had an irregular fit, Dorimant.

DORIMANT: I have.

YOUNG BELLAIR: And is it off already?

DORIMANT: Nature has done her part, gentlemen; when she falls kindly to work, great cures are effected in little time, you know.

SIR FOPLING: We thought there was a wench in the case, by the chair that waited. Prithee, make us a *confidence.*[2]

DORIMANT: Excuse me.

SIR FOPLING: *Le sage*[3] Dorimant! Was she pretty?

DORIMANT: So pretty she may come to keep her coach and pay parish duties[4] if the good humour of the age continue.

MEDLEY: And be of the number of the ladies kept by public-spirited men for the good of the whole town.

SIR FOPLING (*dancing by himself*): Well said, Medley.

YOUNG BELLAIR: See Sir Fopling dancing!

DORIMANT: You are practising and have a mind to recover, I see.

SIR FOPLING: Prithee, Dorimant, why hast not thou a glass hung up here? A room is the dullest thing without one.

YOUNG BELLAIR: Here is company to entertain you.

SIR FOPLING: But I mean in case of being alone. In a glass a man may entertain himself —

DORIMANT: The shadow of himself, indeed.

SIR FOPLING: Correct the errors of his motions and his dress.

MEDLEY: I find, Sir Fopling, in your solitude you remember the saying of the wise man, and study yourself.

[2] take us into your confidence
[3] (Fr.) prudent, discreet
[4] i.e., become rich and respectable

SIR FOPLING: 'Tis the best diversion in our retirements. Dorimant, thou art a pretty fellow and wear'st thy clothes well, but I never saw thee have a handsome cravat. Were they made up like mine, they'd give another air to thy face. Prithee, let me send my man to dress thee but one day; by heavens, an Englishman cannot tie a ribbon.

DORIMANT: They are something clumsy fisted ——

SIR FOPLING: I have brought over the prettiest fellow that ever spread a toilet. He served some time under Merille, the greatest *genie* in the world for a *valet-de-chambre*.

DORIMANT: What! he who formerly belonged to the Duke of Candale?

SIR FOPLING: The same, and got him his immortal reputation.

DORIMANT: Y'have a very fine brandenburgh[5] on, Sir Fopling.

SIR FOPLING: It serves to wrap me up after the fatigue of a ball.

MEDLEY: I see you often in it, with your periwig tied up.

SIR FOPLING: We should not always be in a set dress; 'tis more *en cavalier*[6] to appear now and then in a *déshabillé*.

MEDLEY: Pray, how goes your business with Loveit?

SIR FOPLING: You might have answered yourself in the Mail last night. Dorimant, did you not see the advances she made me? I have been endeavouring at a song.

DORIMANT: Already!

SIR FOPLING: 'Tis my *coup d'essai*[7] in English: I would fain have thy opinion of it.

DORIMANT: Let's see it.

SIR FOPLING: Hey, page, give me my song. —— Bellair, here; thou hast a pretty voice – sing it.

YOUNG BELLAIR: Sing it yourself, Sir Fopling.

SIR FOPLING: Excuse me.

YOUNG BELLAIR: You learnt to sing in Paris.

SIR FOPLING: I did – of Lambert, the greatest master in the world. But I have his own fault, a weak voice, and care not to sing out of a *ruelle*.[8]

DORIMANT (*aside*): A *ruelle* is a pretty cage for a singing fop, indeed.

YOUNG BELLAIR (*reads the song*):

> How charming Phillis is, how fair!
>   Ah, that she were as willing
> To ease my wounded heart of care,
>   And make her eyes less killing.
> I sigh, I sigh, I languish now,
>   And love will not let me rest;
> I drive about the Park and bow,
>   Still as[9] I meet my dearest.

[5] morning gown

[6] (Fr.) stylish, fitting for a man-about-town

[7] (Fr.) first effort

[8] (Fr.) lady's select circle

[9] whenever

SIR FOPLING: Sing it! sing it, man; it goes to a pretty new tune which I am confident was made by Baptiste.[10]

MEDLEY: Sing it yourself, Sir Fopling; he does not know the tune.

SIR FOPLING: I'll venture.

(SIR FOPLING *sings.*)

DORIMANT: Ay, marry! now 'tis something. I shall not flatter you, Sir Fopling; there is not much thought in't, but 'tis passionate and well turned.

MEDLEY: After the French way.

SIR FOPLING: That I aimed at. Does it not give you a lively image of the thing? Slap! down goes the glass, and thus we are at it.

DORIMANT: It does, indeed, I perceive, Sir Fopling. You'll be the very head of the sparks who are lucky in compositions of this nature.

(*Enter* SIR FOPLING'S FOOTMAN.)

SIR FOPLING: La Tour, is the bath ready?

FOOTMAN: Yes, Sir.

SIR FOPLING: *Adieu donc, mes chers.*[11] (*Exit* SIR FOPLING.)

MEDLEY: When have you your revenge on Loveit, Dorimant?

DORIMANT: I will but change my linen and about it.

MEDLEY: The powerful considerations which hindered have been removed then?

DORIMANT: Most luckily this morning. You must along with me; my reputation lies at stake there.

MEDLEY: I am engaged to Bellair.

DORIMANT: What's your business?

MEDLEY: Ma-tri-mony, an't[12] like you.

DORIMANT: It does not, Sir.

YOUNG BELLAIR: It may in time, Dorimant: what think you of Mrs. Harriet?

DORIMANT: What does she think of me?

YOUNG BELLAIR: I am confident she loves you.

DORIMANT: How does it appear?

YOUNG BELLAIR: Why, she's never well but when she's talking of you — but then, she finds all the faults in you she can. She laughs at all who commend you — but then, she speaks ill of all who do not.

DORIMANT: Women of her temper betray themselves by their over-cunning. I had once a growing love with a lady who would always quarrel with me when I came to see her, and yet was never quiet if I stayed a day from her.

YOUNG BELLAIR: My father is in love with Emilia.

DORIMANT: That is a good warrant for your proceedings. Go on and prosper; I must to Loveit. Medley, I am sorry you cannot be a witness.

[10] Jean Baptiste Lully (1633–87), composer and master of music at Louis XIV's court

[11] (Fr.) goodbye then, dear fellows

[12] if it

MEDLEY: Make her meet Sir Fopling again in the same place and use him ill before me.

DORIMANT: That may be brought about, I think. I'll be at your aunt's anon and give you joy, Mr. Bellair.

YOUNG BELLAIR: You had not best think of Mrs. Harriet too much; without church security there's no taking up there.

DORIMANT: I may fall into the snare too. But —
The wise will find a difference in our fate;
You wed a woman, I a good estate. *(Exeunt.)*

## SCENE 3

*Enter the chair with* BELLINDA; *the men set it down and open it.* BELLINDA *starting.*

BELLINDA (*surprised*): Lord, where am I? – in the Mail! Whither have you brought me?

1 CHAIRMAN: You gave us no directions, Madam.

BELLINDA (*aside*): The fright I was in made me forget it.

1 CHAIRMAN: We use to carry a lady from the Squire's hither.

BELLINDA (*aside*): This is Loveit: I am undone if she sees me. – Quickly, carry me away!

1 CHAIRMAN: Whither, an't like your honour?

BELLINDA: Ask no questions —

(*Enter* MRS. LOVEIT'S FOOTMAN.)

FOOTMAN: Have you seen my lady, Madam?

BELLINDA: I am just come to wait upon her.

FOOTMAN: She will be glad to see you, Madam. She sent me to you this morning to desire your company, and I was told you went out by five o'clock.

BELLINDA (*aside*): More and more unlucky!

FOOTMAN: Will you walk in, Madam?

BELLINDA: I'll discharge my chair and follow. Tell your mistress I am here. (*Exit* FOOTMAN.)
(*Gives the* CHAIRMAN *money.*) Take this, and if ever you should be examined, be sure you say you took me up in the Strand over against the Exchange, as you will answer it[1] to Mr. Dorimant.

CHAIRMAN: We will, an't like your honor. (*Exeunt* CHAIRMEN.)

BELLINDA: Now to come off, I must on —
In confidence and lies some hope is left;
'Twere hard to be found out in the first theft. (*Exit.*)

[1] be held accountable for it

## ACT V

### SCENE 1

*Enter* MRS. LOVEIT *and* PERT, *her woman.*

PERT: Well! in my eyes Sir Fopling is no such despicable person.
MRS. LOVEIT: You are an excellent judge!
PERT: He's as handsome a man as Mr. Dorimant, and as great a gallant.
MRS. LOVEIT: Intolerable! Is't not enough I submit to his impertinences, but must I be plagued with yours too?
PERT: Indeed, Madam —
MRS. LOVEIT: 'Tis false, mercenary malice —

(*Enter her* FOOTMAN.)

FOOTMAN: Mrs. Bellinda, Madam.
MRS. LOVEIT: What of her?
FOOTMAN: She's below.
MRS. LOVEIT: How came she?
FOOTMAN: In a chair; Ambling Harry brought her.
MRS. LOVEIT: He bring her! His chair stands near Dorimant's door and always brings me from thence. — Run and ask him where he took her up. (*Exit* FOOTMAN.)
Go! there is no truth in friendship neither. Women, as well as men, all are false — or all are so to me, at least.
PERT: You are jealous of her too?
MRS. LOVEIT: You had best tell her I am. 'Twill become the liberty you take of late. This fellow's bringing of her, her going out by five o'clock – I know not what to think.

(*Enter* BELLINDA.)

Bellinda, you are grown an early riser, I hear.
BELLINDA: Do you not wonder, my dear, what made me abroad so soon?
MRS. LOVEIT: You do not use to be so.
BELLINDA: The country gentlewomen I told you of (Lord, they have the oddest diversions!) would never let me rest till I promised to go with them to the markets this morning to eat fruit and buy nosegays.
MRS. LOVEIT: Are they so fond of a filthy nosegay?
BELLINDA: They complain of the stinks of the town, and are never well but when they have their noses in one.
MRS. LOVEIT: There are essences and sweet waters.
BELLINDA: Oh, they cry out upon perfumes, they are unwholesome; one of 'em was falling into a fit with the smell of these *nerolii*.[1]

[1] essence of orange flowers

MRS. LOVEIT: Methinks in complaisance you should have had a nosegay too.

BELLINDA: Do you think, my dear, I could be so loathsome to trick myself up with carnations and stock-gillyflowers? I begged their pardon and told them I never wore anything but orange flowers and tuberose. That which made me willing to go was a strange desire I had to eat some fresh nectarines.

MRS. LOVEIT: And had you any?

BELLINDA: The best I ever tasted.

MRS. LOVEIT: Whence came you now?

BELLINDA: From their lodgings, where I crowded out of a coach and took a chair to come and see you, my dear.

MRS. LOVEIT: Whither did you send for that chair?

BELLINDA: 'Twas going by empty.

MRS. LOVEIT: Where do these country gentlewomen lodge, I pray?

BELLINDA: In the Strand over against the Exchange.

PERT: That place is never without a nest of 'em. They are always, as one goes by, fleering in balconies or staring out of windows.

(*Enter* FOOTMAN.)

MRS. LOVEIT (*to the* FOOTMAN): Come hither! (*Whispers.*)

BELLINDA (*aside*): This fellow by her order has been questioning the chairmen. I threatened 'em with the name of Dorimant; if they should have told truth, I am lost forever.

MRS. LOVEIT: In the Strand, said you?

FOOTMAN: Yes, Madam; over against the Exchange. (*Exit* FOOTMAN.)

MRS. LOVEIT (*aside*): She's innocent, and I am much to blame.

BELLINDA (*aside*): I am so frighted, my countenance will betray me.

MRS. LOVEIT: Bellinda, what makes you look so pale?

BELLINDA: Want of my usual rest and jolting up and down so long in an odious hackney.

(FOOTMAN *returns.*)

FOOTMAN: Madam, Mr. Dorimant.

MRS. LOVEIT: What makes him here?

BELLINDA (*aside*): Then I am betrayed, indeed. He's broke his word, and I love a man that does not care for me!

MRS. LOVEIT: Lord, you faint, Bellinda!

BELLINDA: I think I shall — such an oppression here on the sudden.

PERT: She has eaten too much fruit, I warrant you.

MRS. LOVEIT: Not unlikely.

PERT: 'Tis that lies heavy on her stomach.

MRS. LOVEIT: Have her into my chamber, give her some surfeit water,[2] and let her lie down a little.

[2] remedy for indigestion

PERT: Come, Madam! I was a strange devourer of fruit when I was young — so ravenous —— (*Exeunt* BELLINDA, *and* PERT, *leading her off.*)

MRS. LOVEIT: Oh, that my love would be but calm awhile, that I might receive this man with all the scorn and indignation he deserves!

(*Enter* DORIMANT.)

DORIMANT: Now for a touch of Sir Fopling to begin with. Hey, page, give positive order that none of my people stir. Let the *canaille*[3] wait as they should do. Since noise and nonsense have such powerful charms,

I, that I may successful prove,
Transform myself to what you love.

MRS. LOVEIT: If that would do, you need not change from what you are: you can be vain and loud enough.

DORIMANT: But not with so good a grace as Sir Fopling. Hey, Hampshire! Oh, that sound, that sound becomes the mouth of a man of quality![4]

MRS. LOVEIT: Is there a thing so hateful as a senseless mimic?

DORIMANT: He's a great grievance indeed to all who, like yourself, Madam, love to play the fool in quiet.

MRS. LOVEIT: A ridiculous animal, who has more of the ape than the ape has of the man in him!

DORIMANT: I have as mean an opinion of a sheer mimic as yourself; yet were he all ape, I should prefer him to the gay, the giddy, brisk, insipid noisy fool you dote on.

MRS. LOVEIT: Those noisy fools, however you despise 'em, have good qualities which weigh more (or ought at least) with us women than all the pernicious wit you have to boast of.

DORIMANT: That I may hereafter have a just value for their merit, pray do me the favour to name 'em.

MRS. LOVEIT: You'll despise 'em as the dull effects of ignorance and vanity; yet I care not if I mention some. First, they really admire us, while you at best but flatter us well.

DORIMANT: Take heed! Fools can dissemble too.

MRS. LOVEIT: They may, but not so artificially as you. There is no fear they should deceive us. Then, they are assiduous, Sir; they are ever offering us their service, and always waiting on our will.

DORIMANT: You owe that to their excessive idleness. They know not how to entertain themselves at home, and find so little welcome abroad they are fain to fly to you who countenance 'em, as a refuge against the solitude they would be otherwise condemned to.

MRS. LOVEIT: Their conversation, too, diverts us better.

[3] (Fr.) rabble
[4] (cf. III, 3, p. 303)

DORIMANT: Playing with your fan, smelling to your gloves, commending your hair, and taking notice how 'tis cut and shaded after the new way —

MRS. LOVEIT: Were it sillier than you can make it, you must allow 'tis pleasanter to laugh at others than to be laughed at ourselves, though never so wittily. Then, though they want skill to flatter us, they flatter themselves so well they save us the labour. We need not take that care and pains to satisfy 'em of our love, which we so often lose on you.

DORIMANT: They commonly, indeed, believe too well of themselves, and always better of you than you deserve.

MRS. LOVEIT: You are in the right. They have an implicit faith in us which keeps 'em from prying narrowly into our secrets and saves us the vexatious trouble of clearing doubts which your subtle and causeless jealousies every moment raise.

DORIMANT: There is an inbred falsehood in women which inclines 'em still to them whom they may most easily deceive.

MRS. LOVEIT: The man who loves above his quality does not suffer more from the insolent impertinence of his mistress than the woman who loves above her understanding does from the arrogant presumptions of her friend.

DORIMANT: You mistake the use of fools; they are designed for properties,[5] and not for friends. You have an indifferent[6] stock of reputation left yet. Lose it all like a frank gamester on the square; 'twill then be time enough to turn rook[7] and cheat it up again on a good, substantial bubble.[8]

MRS. LOVEIT: The old and the ill-favoured are only fit for properties, indeed, but young and handsome fools have met with kinder fortunes.

DORIMANT: They have, to the shame of your sex be it spoken! 'Twas this, the thought of this, made me by a timely jealousy endeavour to prevent the good fortune you are providing for Sir Fopling. But against a woman's frailty all our care is vain.

MRS. LOVEIT: Had I not with a dear experience bought the knowledge of your falsehood, you might have fooled me yet. This is not the first jealousy you have feigned, to make a quarrel with me and get a week to throw away on some such unknown, inconsiderable slut as you have been lately lurking with at plays.

DORIMANT: Women, when they would break off with a man, never want th' address to turn the fault on him.

MRS. LOVEIT: You take a pride of late in using of me ill, that the town may know the power you have over me, which now (as unreasonably as yourself) expects that I (do me all the injuries you can) must love you still.

[5] "things" to be used
[6] moderate
[7] sharper
[8] dupe

DORIMANT: I am so far from expecting that you should, I begin to think you never did love me.

MRS. LOVEIT: Would the memory of it were so wholly worn out in me, that I did doubt it too! What made you come to disturb my growing quiet?

DORIMANT: To give you joy of your growing infamy.

MRS. LOVEIT: Insupportable! Insulting devil! – this from you, the only author of my shame! This from another had been but justice, but from you 'tis a hellish and inhumane outrage. What have I done?

DORIMANT: A thing that puts you below my scorn, and makes my anger as ridiculous as you have made my love.

MRS. LOVEIT: I walked last night with Sir Fopling.

DORIMANT: You did, Madam, and you talked and laughed aloud, "Ha, ha, ha!" – Oh, that laugh! that laugh becomes the confidence of a woman of quality.

MRS. LOVEIT: You who have more pleasure in the ruin of a woman's reputation than in the endearments of her love, reproach me not with yourself – and I defy you to name the man can lay a blemish on my fame.

DORIMANT: To be seen publicly so transported with the vain follies of that notorious fop, to me is an infamy below the sin of prostitution with another man.

MRS. LOVEIT: Rail on! I am satisfied in the justice of what I did; you had provoked me to't.

DORIMANT: What I did was the effect of a passion whose extravagancies you have been willing to forgive.

MRS. LOVEIT: And what I did was the effect of a passion you may forgive if you think fit.

DORIMANT: Are you so indifferent grown?

MRS. LOVEIT: I am.

DORIMANT: Nay, then 'tis time to part. I'll send you back your letters you have so often asked for. I have two or three of 'em about me.

MRS. LOVEIT: Give 'em me.

DORIMANT: You snatch as if you thought I would not. There! and may the perjuries in 'em be mine if e'er I see you more! (*Offers to go; she catches him.*)

MRS. LOVEIT: Stay!

DORIMANT: I will not.

MRS. LOVEIT: You shall.

DORIMANT: What have you to say?

MRS. LOVEIT: I cannot speak it yet.

DORIMANT: Something more in commendation of the fool. —— Death, I want patience; let me go!

MRS. LOVEIT: I cannot. (*Aside.*) I can sooner part with the limbs that hold him. —— I hate that nauseous fool; you know I do.

DORIMANT: Was it the scandal you were fond of then?

MRS. LOVEIT: Y'had raised my anger equal to my love – a thing you ne'er could do before, and in revenge I did – I know not what I did. Would you would not think on't any more!

DORIMANT: Should I be willing to forget it, I shall be daily minded of it; 'twill be a commonplace for all the town to laugh at me, and Medley, when he is rhetorically drunk, will ever be declaiming on it in my ears.

MRS. LOVEIT: 'Twill be believed a jealous spite. Come, forget it.

DORIMANT: Let me consult my reputation; you are too careless of it. (*Pauses.*) You shall meet Sir Fopling in the Mail again to-night.

MRS. LOVEIT: What mean you?

DORIMANT: I have thought on it, and you must. 'Tis necessary to justify my love to the world. You can handle a coxcomb as he deserves when you are not out of humour, Madam.

MRS. LOVEIT: Public satisfaction for the wrong I have done you! This is some new device to make me more ridiculous.

DORIMANT: Hear me!

MRS. LOVEIT: I will not.

DORIMANT: You will be persuaded.

MRS. LOVEIT: Never!

DORIMANT: Are you so obstinate?

MRS. LOVEIT: Are you so base?

DORIMANT: You will not satisfy my love?

MRS. LOVEIT: I would die to satisfy that; but I will not, to save you from a thousand racks, do a shameless thing to please your vanity.

DORIMANT: Farewell, false woman!

MRS. LOVEIT: Do! go!

DORIMANT: You will call me back again.

MRS. LOVEIT: Exquisite fiend, I knew you came but to torment me!

(*Enter* BELLINDA *and* PERT.)

DORIMANT (*surprised*): Bellinda here!

BELLINDA (*aside*): He starts and looks pale! The sight of me has touched his guilty soul.

PERT: 'Twas but a qualm, as I said – a little indigestion; the surfeit water did it, Madam, mixed with a little mirabilis.[9]

DORIMANT (*aside*): I am confounded, and cannot guess how she came hither!

MRS. LOVEIT: 'Tis your fortune, Bellinda, ever to be here when I am abused by this prodigy of ill-nature.

BELLINDA: I am amazed to find him here. How has he the face to come near you?

DORIMANT (*aside*): Here is fine work towards! I never was at such a loss before.

[9] *aqua mirabilis* (Lat. "wonder water"), another remedy for indigestion

BELLINDA: One who makes a public profession of breach of faith and ingratitude – I loathe the sight of him.

DORIMANT (*aside*): There is no remedy: I must submit to their tongues now, and some other time bring myself off as well as I can.

BELLINDA: Other men are wicked, but then, they have some sense of shame. He is never well but when he triumphs – nay, glories to a woman's face in his villainies.

MRS. LOVEIT: You are in the right, Bellinda, but methinks your kindness for me makes you concern yourself too much with him.

BELLINDA: It does indeed, my dear. His barbarous carriage to you yesterday made me hope you ne'er would see him more, and the very next day to find him here again, provokes me strangely. But because I know you love him, I have done.

DORIMANT: You have reproached me handsomely, and I deserve it for coming hither; but ——

PERT: You must expect it, Sir. All women will hate you for my lady's sake.

DORIMANT (*aside to* BELLINDA): Nay, if she begins too, 'tis time to fly; I shall be scolded to death else. —— I am to blame in some circumstances, I confess; but as to the main, I am not so guilty as you imagine. I shall seek a more convenient time to clear myself.

MRS. LOVEIT: Do it now. What impediments are here?

DORIMANT: I want time, and you want temper.

MRS. LOVEIT: These are weak pretences.

DORIMANT: You were never more mistaken in your life; and so farewell. (DORIMANT *flings off*.)

MRS. LOVEIT: Call a footman, Pert, quickly; I will have him dogged.

PERT: I wish you would not, for my quiet and your own.

MRS. LOVEIT: I'll find out the infamous cause of all our quarrels, pluck her mask off, and expose her barefaced to the world! (*Exit* PERT.)

BELLINDA (*aside*): Let me but escape this time, I'll never venture more.

MRS. LOVEIT: Bellinda, you shall go with me.

BELLINDA: I have such a heaviness hangs on me with what I did this morning, I would fain go home and sleep, my dear.

MRS. LOVEIT: Death and eternal darkness! I shall never sleep again. Raging fevers seize the world and make mankind as restless all as I am! (*Exit* MRS. LOVEIT.)

BELLINDA: I knew him false and helped to make him so. Was not her ruin enough to fright me from the danger? It should have been, but love can take no warning. (*Exit* BELLINDA.)

## SCENE 2

*Scene:* LADY TOWNLEY'*s house.*

*Enter* MEDLEY, YOUNG BELLAIR, LADY TOWNLEY, EMILIA, *and* CHAPLAIN.

MEDLEY: Bear up, Bellair, and do not let us see that repentance in thine we daily do in married faces.

LADY TOWNLEY: This wedding will strangely surprise my brother when he knows it.

MEDLEY: Your nephew ought to conceal it for a time, Madam; since marriage has lost its good name, prudent men seldom expose their own reputations till 'tis convenient to justify their wives.

OLD BELLAIR (*without*): Where are you all there? Out, a dod! will nobody hear?

LADY TOWNLEY: My brother! Quickly, Mr. Smirk, into this closet! you must not be seen yet. (SMIRK *goes into the closet.*[1])

(*Enter* OLD BELLAIR *and* LADY TOWNLEY'*s* PAGE.)

OLD BELLAIR: Desire Mr. Fourbe to walk into the lower parlour; I will be with him presently. (*To* YOUNG BELLAIR.) Where have you been, Sir, you could not wait on me to-day?

YOUNG BELLAIR: About a business.

OLD BELLAIR: Are you so good at business? A dod, I have a business, too, you shall dispatch out of hand, Sir. — Send for a parson, Sister; my Lady Woodvill and her daughter are coming.

LADY TOWNLEY: What need you huddle up[2] things thus?

OLD BELLAIR: Out a pise! youth is apt to play the fool, and 'tis not good it should be in their power.

LADY TOWNLEY: You need not fear your son.

OLD BELLAIR: He's been idling this morning, and a dod, I do not like him. (*To* EMILIA.) How dost thou do, sweetheart?

EMILIA: You are very severe, Sir — married in such haste.

OLD BELLAIR: Go to, thou'rt a rogue, and I will talk with thee anon. Here's my Lady Woodvill come.

(*Enter* LADY WOODVILL, HARRIET, *and* BUSY.)

Welcome, Madam; Mr. Fourbe's below with the writings.

LADY WOODVILL: Let us down and make an end then.

OLD BELLAIR: Sister, show the way. (*To* YOUNG BELLAIR, *who is talking to* HARRIET.) Harry, your business lies not there yet. — Excuse him till we

[1] small, private room
[2] hurry

have done, lady, and then, a dod, he shall be for thee. Mr. Medley, we must trouble you to be a witness.

MEDLEY: I luckily came for that purpose, Sir.

(*Exeunt* OLD BELLAIR, MEDLEY, YOUNG BELLAIR, LADY TOWNLEY, *and* LADY WOODVILL.)

BUSY: What will you do, Madam?

HARRIET: Be carried back and mewed[3] up in the country again – run away here – anything rather than be married to a man I do not care for! Dear Emilia, dō thou advise me.

EMILIA: Mr. Bellair is engaged, you know.

HARRIET: I do, but know not what the fear of losing an estate may fright him to.

EMILIA: In the desperate condition you are in, you should consult with some judicious man. What think you of Mr. Dorimant?

HARRIET: I do not think of him at all.

BUSY (*aside*): She thinks of nothing else, I am sure.

EMILIA: How fond your mother was of Mr. Courtage!

HARRIET: Because I contrived the mistake to make a little mirth, you believe I like the man.

EMILIA: Mr. Bellair believes you love him.

HARRIET: Men are seldom in the right when they guess at a woman's mind. Would she whom he loves loved him no better!

BUSY (*aside*): That's e'en well enough, on all conscience.

EMILIA: Mr. Dorimant has a great deal of wit.

HARRIET: And takes a great deal of pains to show it.

EMILIA: He's extremely well fashioned.

HARRIET: Affectedly grave, or ridiculously wild and apish.

BUSY: You defend him still against your mother!

HARRIET: I would not were he justly rallied, but I cannot hear anyone undeservedly railed at.

EMILIA: Has your woman learnt the song you were so taken with?

HARRIET: I was fond of a new thing; 'tis dull at second hearing.

EMILIA: Mr. Dorimant made it.

BUSY: She knows it, Madam, and has made me sing it at least a dozen times this morning.

HARRIET: Thy tongue is as impertinent as thy fingers.

EMILIA: You have provoked her.

BUSY: 'Tis but singing the song and I shall appease her.

EMILIA: Prithee, do.

HARRIET: She has a voice will grate your ears worse than a cat-call, and dresses so ill she's scarce fit to trick up a yeoman's daughter on a holiday.

(BUSY *sings*.)

[3] cooped

*Song*

BY SIR C. S.

As Amoret with Phillis sat,
One evening on the plain,
And saw the charming Strephon wait
To tell the nymph his pain;

The threat'ning danger to remove,
She whisper'd in her ear,
"Ah, Phillis, if you would not love,
This shepherd do not hear!

"None ever had so strange an art,
His passion to convey
Into a list'ning virgin's heart,
And steal her soul away.

"Fly, fly betimes,[4] for fear you give
Occasion for your fate."
"In vain," she said; "in vain I strive!
Alas, 'tis now too late."

(*Enter* DORIMANT.)

DORIMANT:

Music so softens and disarms the mind —

HARRIET:

That not one arrow does resistance find.

DORIMANT: Let us make use of the lucky minute, then.

HARRIET (*aside, turning from* DORIMANT): My love springs with my blood into my face; I dare not look upon him yet.

DORIMANT: What have we here? the picture of celebrated beauty giving audience in public to a declared lover?

HARRIET: Play the dying fop and make the piece complete, Sir.

DORIMANT: What think you if the hint were well improved — the whole mystery of making love pleasantly designed and wrought in a suit of hangings?[5]

HARRIET: 'Twere needless to execute fools in effigy who suffer daily in their own persons.

DORIMANT (*to* EMILIA, *aside*): Mrs. Bride, for such I know this happy day has made you —

EMILIA (*aside*): Defer the formal joy you are to give me, and mind your business with her. (*Aloud.*) Here are dreadful preparations, Mr. Dorimant — writings, sealing, and a parson sent for.

[4] in time
[5] set of draperies or tapestries

DORIMANT: To marry this lady —

BUSY: Condemned she is, and what will become of her I know not, without you generously engage in a rescue.

DORIMANT: In this sad condition, Madam, I can do no less than offer you my service.

HARRIET: The obligation is not great; you are the common sanctuary for all young women who run from their relations.

DORIMANT: I have always my arms open to receive the distressed. But I will open my heart and receive you, where none yet did ever enter. You have filled it with a secret, might I but let you know it —

HARRIET: Do not speak it if you would have me believe it; your tongue is so famed for falsehood, 'twill do the truth an injury. (*Turns away her head.*)

DORIMANT: Turn not away, then, but look on me and guess it.

HARRIET: Did you not tell me there was no credit to be given to faces? that women nowadays have their passions as much at will as they have their complexions, and put on joy and sadness, scorn and kindness, with the same ease they do their paint and patches? Are they the only counterfeits?

DORIMANT: You wrong your own while you suspect my eyes. By all the hope I have in you, the inimitable colour in your cheeks is not more free from art than are the sighs I offer.

HARRIET: In men who have been long hardened in sin we have reason to mistrust the first signs of repentance.

DORIMANT: The prospect of such a heaven will make me persevere and give you marks that are infallible.

HARRIET: What are those?

DORIMANT: I will renounce all the joys I have in friendship and in wine, sacrifice to you all the interest I have in other women —

HARRIET: Hold! Though I wish you devout, I would not have you turn fanatic. Could you neglect these a while and make a journey into the country?

DORIMANT: To be with you, I could live there and never send one thought to London.

HARRIET: Whate'er you say, I know all beyond High Park's a desert to you, and that no gallantry can draw you farther.

DORIMANT: That has been the utmost limit of my love; but now my passion knows no bounds, and there's no measure to be taken of what I'll do for you from anything I ever did before.

HARRIET: When I hear you talk thus in Hampshire I shall begin to think there may be some truth enlarged upon.

DORIMANT: Is this all? Will you not promise me —

HARRIET: I hate to promise; what we do then is expected from us and wants much of the welcome it finds when it surprises.

DORIMANT: May I not hope?

HARRIET: That depends on you and not on me, and 'tis to no purpose to forbid it. (*Turns to* BUSY.)

BUSY: Faith, Madam, now I perceive the gentleman loves you too, e'en let him know your mind, and torment yourselves no longer.

HARRIET: Dost think I have no sense of modesty?

BUSY: Think, if you lose this you may never have another opportunity.

HARRIET: May he hate me (a curse that frights me when I speak it), if ever I do a thing against the rules of decency and honour.

DORIMANT (*to* EMILIA): I am beholding to you for your good intentions, Madam.

EMILIA: I thought the concealing of our marriage from her might have done you better service.

DORIMANT: Try her again.

EMILIA: What have you resolved, Madam? The time draws near.

HARRIET: To be obstinate and protest against this marriage.

(*Enter* LADY TOWNLEY *in haste.*)

LADY TOWNLEY (*to* EMILIA): Quickly, quickly! let Mr. Smirk out of the closet.

(SMIRK *comes out of the closet.*)

HARRIET: A parson! Had you laid him in here?

DORIMANT: I knew nothing of him.

HARRIET: Should it appear you did, your opinion of my easiness may cost you dear.

(*Enter* OLD BELLAIR, YOUNG BELLAIR, MEDLEY, *and* LADY WOODVILL.)

OLD BELLAIR: Out a pise! the canonical hour[6] is almost past. Sister, is the man of God come?

LADY TOWNLEY: He waits your leisure.

OLD BELLAIR: By your favour, Sir. —— A dod, a pretty spruce[7] fellow. What may we call him?

LADY TOWNLEY: Mr. Smirk – my Lady Biggot's chaplain.

OLD BELLAIR: A wise woman! a dod, she is. The man will serve for the flesh as well as the spirit. Please you, Sir, to commission a young couple to go to bed together a God's name? —— Harry!

YOUNG BELLAIR: Here, Sir.

OLD BELLAIR: Out a pise! Without your mistress in your hand!

SMIRK: Is this the gentleman?

OLD BELLAIR: Yes, Sir.

[6] (the hours from 8 A.M. to 3 P.M. were the legal marriage hours in English parish churches)

[7] neat, dapper

SMIRK: Are you not mistaken, Sir?
OLD BELLAIR: A dod, I think not, Sir.
SMIRK: Sure, you are, Sir!
OLD BELLAIR: You look as if you would forbid the banns, Mr. Smirk. I hope you have no pretension to the lady.
SMIRK: Wish him joy, Sir; I have done him the good office to-day already.
OLD BELLAIR: Out a pise! What do I hear?
LADY TOWNLEY: Never storm, Brother; the truth is out.
OLD BELLAIR: How say you, Sir? Is this your wedding day?
YOUNG BELLAIR: It is, Sir.
OLD BELLAIR: And a dod, it shall be mine too. (*To* EMILIA.) Give me thy hand, sweetheart. What dost thou mean? Give me thy hand, I say.

(EMILIA *kneels and* YOUNG BELLAIR.)

LADY TOWNLEY: Come, come! give her your blessing; this is the woman your son loved and is married to.
OLD BELLAIR: Ha! cheated! cozened! and by your contrivance, Sister!
LADY TOWNLEY: What would you do with her? She's a rogue and you can't abide her.
MEDLEY: Shall I hit her a pat for you, Sir?
OLD BELLAIR: A dod, you are all rogues, and I never will forgive you.
LADY TOWNLEY: Whither? Whither away?
MEDLEY: Let him go and cool awhile.
LADY WOODVILL (*to* DORIMANT): Here's a business broke out now, Mr. Courtage; I am made a fine fool of.
DORIMANT: You see the old gentleman knew nothing of it.
LADY WOODVILL: I find he did not. I shall have some trick put upon me if I stay in this wicked town any longer. — Harriet, dear child, where art thou? I'll into the country straight.
OLD BELLAIR: A dod, Madam, you shall hear me first.

(*Enter* MRS. LOVEIT *and* BELLINDA.)

MRS. LOVEIT: Hither my man dogged him.
BELLINDA: Yonder he stands, my dear.
MRS. LOVEIT: I see him (*Aside.*) and with him the face that has undone me. Oh, that I were but where I might throw out the anguish of my heart! Here it must rage within and break it.
LADY TOWNLEY: Mrs. Loveit! Are you afraid to come forward?
MRS. LOVEIT: I was amazed to see so much company here in a morning. The occasion sure is extraordinary.
DORIMANT (*aside*): Loveit and Bellinda! The devil owes me a shame to-day and I think never will have done paying it.
MRS. LOVEIT: Married! dear Emilia! How am I transported with the news!
HARRIET (*to* DORIMANT): I little thought Emilia was the woman Mr. Bellair was in love with. I'll chide her for not trusting me with the secret.

DORIMANT: How do you like Mrs. Loveit?

HARRIET: She's a famed mistress of yours, I hear.

DORIMANT: She has been, on occasion.

OLD BELLAIR (*to* LADY WOODVILL): A dod, Madam, I cannot help it.

LADY WOODVILL: You need make no more apologies, Sir.

EMILIA (*to* MRS. LOVEIT): The old gentleman's excusing himself to my Lady Woodvill.

MRS. LOVEIT: Ha, ha, ha! I never heard of anything so pleasant!

HARRIET (*to* DORIMANT): She's extremely overjoyed at something.

DORIMANT: At nothing. She is one of those hoyting[8] ladies who gaily fling themselves about and force a laugh when their aching hearts are full of discontent and malice.

MRS. LOVEIT: O heaven! I was never so near killing myself with laughing. — Mr. Dorimant, are you a brideman?

LADY WOODVILL: Mr. Dorimant! — Is this Mr. Dorimant, Madam?

MRS. LOVEIT: If you doubt it, your daughter can resolve you, I suppose.

LADY WOODVILL: I am cheated too — basely cheated!

OLD BELLAIR: Out a pise! what's here? More knavery yet?

LADY WOODVILL: Harriet, on my blessing come away, I charge you!

HARRIET: Dear Mother, do but stay and hear me.

LADY WOODVILL: I am betrayed and thou art undone, I fear.

HARRIET: Do not fear it; I have not, nor never will, do anything against my duty — believe me, dear Mother, do!

DORIMANT (*to* MRS. LOVEIT): I had trusted you with this secret but that I knew the violence of your nature would ruin my fortune, as now unluckily it has. I thank you, Madam.

MRS. LOVEIT: She's an heiress, I know, and very rich.

DORIMANT: To satisfy you, I must give up my interest[9] wholly to my love. Had you been a reasonable woman, I might have secured 'em both and been happy.

MRS. LOVEIT: You might have trusted me with anything of this kind — you know you might. Why did you go under a wrong name?

DORIMANT: The story is too long to tell you now. Be satisfied, this is the business; this is the mask has kept me from you.

BELLINDA (*aside*): He's tender of my honour though he's cruel to my love.

MRS. LOVEIT: Was it no idle mistress, then?

DORIMANT: Believe me, a wife to repair the ruins of my estate, that needs it.

MRS. LOVEIT: The knowledge of this makes my grief hang lighter on my soul, but I shall never more be happy.

DORIMANT: Bellinda!

BELLINDA: Do not think of clearing yourself with me; it is impossible. Do all men break their words thus?

[8] loud and restless
[9] material advantage

DORIMANT: Th'extravagant words they speak in love. 'Tis as unreasonable to expect we should perform all we promise then, as do all we threaten when we are angry. When I see you next —

BELLINDA: Take no notice of me, and I shall not hate you.

DORIMANT: How came you to Mrs. Loveit?

BELLINDA: By a mistake the chairmen made for want of my giving them directions.

DORIMANT: 'Twas a pleasant one. We must meet again.

BELLINDA: Never.

DORIMANT: Never!

BELLINDA: When we do, may I be as infamous as you are false.

LADY TOWNLEY: Men of Mr. Dorimant's character always suffer in the general opinion of the world.

MEDLEY: You can make no judgment of a witty man from common fame, considering the prevailing faction, Madam.

OLD BELLAIR: A dod, he's in the right.

MEDLEY: Besides, 'tis a common error among women to believe too well of them they know, and too ill of them they don't.

OLD BELLAIR: A dod, he observes well.

LADY TOWNLEY: Believe me, Madam, you will find Mr. Dorimant as civil a gentleman as you thought Mr. Courtage.

HARRIET: If you would but know him better —

LADY WOODVILL: You have a mind to know him better! Come away! You shall never see him more.

HARRIET: Dear Mother, stay!

LADY WOODVILL: I wo'not[10] be consenting to your ruin.

HARRIET: Were my fortune in your power —

LADY WOODVILL: Your person is.

HARRIET: Could I be disobedient, I might take it out of yours and put it into his.

LADY WOODVILL: 'Tis that you would be at; you would marry this Dorimant.

HARRIET: I cannot deny it; I would, and never will marry any other man.

LADY WOODVILL: Is this the duty that you promised?

HARRIET: But I will never marry him against your will.

LADY WOODVILL (*aside*): She knows the way to melt my heart. – (*To* HARRIET.) Upon yourself light your undoing!

MEDLEY (*to* OLD BELLAIR): Come, Sir, you have not the heart any longer to refuse your blessing.

OLD BELLAIR: A dod, I ha' not. — Rise, and God bless you both! Make much of her, Harry; she deserves thy kindness. (*To* EMILIA.) A dod, Sirrah, I did not think it had been in thee.

(*Enter* SIR FOPLING *and's* PAGE.)

[10] will not

SIR FOPLING: 'Tis a damned windy day. — Hey, page, is my periwig right?

PAGE: A little out of order, Sir.

SIR FOPLING: Pox o' this apartment! It wants an antechamber to adjust oneself in. (*To* MRS. LOVEIT.) Madam, I came from your house, and your servants directed me hither.

MRS. LOVEIT: I will give order hereafter they shall direct you better.

SIR FOPLING: The great satisfaction I had in the Mail last night has given me much disquiet since.

MRS. LOVEIT: 'Tis likely to give me more than I desire.

SIR FOPLING (*aside*): What the devil makes her so reserved? — Am I guilty of an indiscretion, Madam?

MRS. LOVEIT: You will be of a great one if you continue your mistake, Sir.

SIR FOPLING: Something puts you out of humour.

MRS. LOVEIT: The most foolish, inconsiderable thing that ever did.

SIR FOPLING: Is it in my power?

MRS. LOVEIT: To hang or drown it. Do one of 'em and trouble me no more.

SIR FOPLING: So *fière?*[11] *Serviteur,*[12] Madam! — Medley, where's Dorimant?

MEDLEY: Methinks the lady has not made you those advances to-day she did last night, Sir Fopling.

SIR FOPLING: Prithee, do not talk of her!

MEDLEY: She would be a *bonne fortune.*

SIR FOPLING: Not to me at present.

MEDLEY: How so?

SIR FOPLING: An intrigue now would be but a temptation to me to throw away that vigour on one which I mean shall shortly make my court to the whole sex in a ballet.

MEDLEY: Wisely considered, Sir Fopling.

SIR FOPLING: No one woman is worth the loss of a cut in a caper.

MEDLEY: Not when 'tis so universally designed.

LADY WOODVILL: Mr. Dorimant, everyone has spoke so much in your behalf that I can no longer doubt but I was in the wrong.

MRS. LOVEIT: There's nothing but falsehood and impertinence in this world; all men are villains or fools. Take example from my misfortunes. Bellinda, if thou wouldst be happy, give thyself wholly up to goodness.

HARRIET (*to* MRS. LOVEIT): Mr. Dorimant has been your God Almighty long enough; 'tis time to think of another.

MRS. LOVEIT: Jeered by her! I will lock myself up in my house and never see the world again.

HARRIET: A nunnery is the more fashionable place for such a retreat, and has been the fatal consequence of many a *belle passion.*[13]

[11] (Fr.) haughty
[12] (Fr.) servant
[13] (Fr.) strong passion

MRS. LOVEIT (*aside*): Hold, heart, till I get home! Should I answer, 'twould make her triumph greater. (*Is going out.*)

DORIMANT: Your hand, Sir Fopling —

SIR FOPLING: Shall I wait upon you, Madam?

MRS. LOVEIT: Legion of fools, as many devils take thee! (*Exit* MRS. LOVEIT.)

MEDLEY: Dorimant, I pronounce thy reputation clear; and henceforward when I would know anything of woman, I will consult no other oracle.

SIR FOPLING: Stark mad, by all that's handsome! — Dorimant, thou hast engaged me in a pretty business.

DORIMANT: I have not leisure now to talk about it.

OLD BELLAIR: Out a pise! What does this man of mode do here again?

LADY TOWNLEY: He'll be an excellent entertainment within, Brother, and is luckily come to raise the mirth of the company.

LADY WOODVILL: Madam, I take my leave of you.

LADY TOWNLEY: What do you mean, Madam?

LADY WOODVILL: To go this afternoon part of my way to Hartly.

OLD BELLAIR: A dod, you shall stay and dine first! Come, we will all be good friends, and you shall give Mr. Dorimant leave to wait upon you and your daughter in the country.

LADY WOODVILL: If his occasions bring him that way, I have now so good an opinion of him, he shall be welcome.

HARRIET: To a great rambling, lone house that looks as it were not inhabited, the family's so small. There you'll find my mother, an old lame aunt, and myself, Sir, perched up on chairs at a distance in a large parlour, sitting moping like three or four melancholy birds in a spacious volary.[14] Does not this stagger your resolution?

DORIMANT: Not at all, Madam. The first time I saw you you left me with the pangs of love upon me, and this day my soul has quite given up her liberty.

HARRIET: This is more dismal than the country! Emilia, pity me, who am going to that sad place. Methinks I hear the hateful noise of rooks already – kaw, kaw, kaw! There's music in the worst cry[15] in London – My dill and cowcumbers to pickle!

OLD BELLAIR: Sister, knowing of this matter, I hope you have provided us some good cheer.

LADY TOWNLEY: I have, Brother, and the fiddles too.

OLD BELLAIR: Let 'em strike up, then; the young lady shall have a dance before she departs.

(*Dance.*)

(*After the dance.*) — So! now we'll in and make this an arrant[16] wedding-day. (*To the pit.*)

[14] large birdcage
[15] i.e., of the street-vendors
[16] downright, regular

And if these honest gentlemen rejoice,
A dod, the boy has made a happy choice.

(*Exeunt omnes.*)

## EPILOGUE

BY MR. DRYDEN

Most modern wits such monstrous fools have shown,[1]
They seem'd not of heav'n's making, but their own.
Those nauseous harlequins[2] in farce may pass,
But there goes more to a substantial ass.
Something of man must be expos'd to view
That, gallants, they may more resemble you.
Sir Fopling is a fool so nicely writ,
The ladies would mistake him for a wit;
And when he sings, talks loud, and cocks,[3] would cry,
"I vow, methinks he's pretty company!
So brisk, so gay, so travell'd, so refin'd,
As[4] he took pains to graff[5] upon his kind."
True fops help nature's work and go to school,
To file[6] and finish God A'mighty's fool.
Yet none Sir Fopling him, or him, can call;
He's knight o'th' shire,[7] and represents ye all.
From each he meets, he culls whate'er he can;
Legion's his name, a people in a man.
His bulky folly gathers as it goes
And, rolling o'er you, like a snowball grows.
His various modes from various fathers follow;
One taught the toss, and one the new French wallow.[8]
His sword-knot,[9] this; his cravat, this design'd;
And this, the yard-long snake[10] he twirls behind.
From one the sacred periwig he gain'd,
Which wind ne'er blew, nor touch of hat profan'd.
Another's diving bow he did adore,
Which with a shog[11] casts all the hair before[12]
Till he with full decorum brings it back,

[1] shown themselves
[2] stock comic characters in Italian commedia dell'arte, part lovers and part clowns, wearing multicolored dress
[3] struts
[4] as if
[5] graft
[6] polish
[7] parliamentary representative
[8] rolling gait
[9] ribbon or tassel tied to the hilt of a sword
[10] i.e., the pigtail of his wig
[11] shake
[12] forward, in front

And rises with a water spaniel shake.
As for his songs (the ladies' dear delight),
Those sure he took from most of you who write.
Yet every man is safe from what he feared,
For no one fool is hunted from the herd.

In 1660, eleven years after King Charles I had been executed by the Puritan Parliament, his son returned from exile in France and, as most of the nation cheered, assumed the throne of his father. The whole period from 1660 until about 1700 takes its name from this restoration of the House of Stuart, but actually the Restoration restored very little else. In literary history, particularly, 1660 is one of those dates that definitely divide one age from another. For the ordinary Englishman in 1660 the painful memories of the Civil War and of Cromwell's military dictatorship were overlaid with relief that the Puritans' repression of delight in things of this world had come to an end. He now took his models for behavior and his tastes in art from the Stuart court, which had learned its sophisticated and easygoing ways in the country where most of the Cavaliers had waited out the fall of the Commonwealth. In the prevailing tone of Restoration literature such few voices of Puritanism as remained — Milton's, Bunyan's — sound strangely alien.

But the Puritan interlude was not easily dismissed, as witnessed by the stridency with which the new literary fashions presumed that it could be. In 1660, pre–Civil War times were still less than a generation past, but already the image of the Elizabethans was receding into semi-nostalgic memory as that of "the Giant Race before the Flood." As if in quest of a continuum that had been broken, Restoration authors like John Dryden were given to comparing their own accomplishment with those of the authors of what they referred to as "the last age." A cliché of such comparisons was the Restoration writers' pride in their greater refinement of language and in their more scrupulous observation of the decorum of the classical genres. But together with their public air of condescension toward Spenser's quaintly archaic allegory, Shakespeare's "wildness," and Donne's harshness and obscurity went an awareness that their predecessors had been graced with a robust vitality departed from their own lesser age. This ambivalence of self-assessment is one of the recurrent themes of Restoration literary criticism. The times themselves fostered it.

Charles II was a man of charm and intelligence, and he was personally popular, but it did not take many years of the restored monarchy to make it clear that his reign was no golden age. In retrospect, a series of public catastrophes in the middle years of his first decade as king seemed like ill omens borne out by future events: the Plague in 1665, the Great Fire of London in 1666, the burning of English ships by a Dutch flotilla in the Thames estuary in 1667. Charles was a good-natured, unprincipled, and pragmatic libertine who considered it his main task as king to hang on to the throne he had regained. His finances were in such a mess that he had to sacrifice British and Protestant interests as the price for getting funds from Louis XIV of France, and only his manipulation of men and money preserved the legitimate succession to the throne and kept religious and political factionalism — these were the years of the rise of political parties — from breaking out in a renewal of civil war. His brother, who succeeded him in 1685, was a less adroit politician as well as a rigid Roman Catholic and lost his throne in the Revolution of 1688. But long before, the glorious promise of the Restoration had turned into a shabby and violent reality. It was an age in which public events and the private actions of public men easily could breed cynical disillusionment in the sensible and the sensitive, and very often they did. Some of the best Restoration plays are evidence.

Restoration comedy denotes a large and varied body of plays, but what users of the term most commonly have in mind are the prose plays of witty dialogue and sexual intrigue among Londoners of high fashion, written by George Etherege, William Wycherley, and William Congreve. Less pure (the adjective refers to genre, not to morals) contributions to this kind of comedy were made by Dryden and other, lesser, playwrights. Thomas Shadwell tried to adapt the older comedy of humors by Ben Jonson to the new taste for stage naughtiness in sprawling plays of naive social gusto, and a little later John Vanbrugh and George Farquhar modified their models in comedies whose provincial settings, spacious structures, and incipient sentimentalizations of marriage place them only on the fringes of the comedy of sex as it is more narrowly defined by plays like *The Man of Mode* and Wycherley's *The Country Wife*. Even in Congreve's last plays, including *The Way of the World*, which is sometimes considered the epitome of Restoration comedy of sex but really is not, the earlier treatment of sex as a gay and cruel game for social control is beginning to give way to more conventionally decent attitudes.

Dryden's praise of Shakespeare's "large and comprehensive" soul in the *Essay of Dramatic Poesy* (1668) is a recognition of that inclusiveness of a disinterested imagination that makes one world of the whole of Shakespearean drama. The same gathering vision is not evident in the drama of Dryden's own age, which may be why so many critics have been reluctant to call it "great." Dryden himself was an extraordinarily versatile playwright, who wrote superior plays in almost every genre he attempted. Too much of a pragmatist and skeptic to lock his creative impulse in a single form, his versatility was that of a gifted professional who had to please his fickle audiences or starve and who was lucky enough to take delight in the forced exercise of his craft in a variety of dramatic and theatrical styles, rather than that of a genius so large of soul that nothing less than a universe of human situations, values, and voices was commensurate with his sense of life. In Dryden's drama in particular and in Restoration drama in general our impression of variety comes from sets of separate, smaller grasps of experience, fragmented and ambiguously felt, products of an anxious and sometimes meretricious search for expressive form. It is not by accident that Restoration drama has never elicited more critical interest than it does at the present.

A main reason for this impression of uncertain and scattering dramatic energies is the fact that Restoration drama seems (in the words of a modern critic) "positively schizophrenic" in its pursuit of two kinds of plays that seem completely at odds with one another. The same audiences that flocked to see rakes and their gamesome ladies elegantly seduce one another and exchange witty repartee in fashionable London parks and drawing rooms among cuckolds, fops, amorous harridans, country boors, tyrannical parents, and mercenary clergymen apparently took equal pleasure in plays in rhymed couplets declaimed by royal characters of absolute virtue or villainy in exotic lands who were engaged in a bewildering, turbulent succession of martial and romantic intrigue. What the spectator was supposed to get from these plays was the equivalent in drama of Homer's and Virgil's epics, "imitations of the highest patterns of human life" and with "love and valor" therefore as their proper subjects. That is why they are called *heroic* plays and why their verse is *heroic* couplets. What the spectator actually did get was frenetic melodrama, in which the skillful interweaving of military and erotic plots, the splendid costumes and the shifting spectacle, and the passional couplet eloquence achieved a kind of preposterous but spellbinding integrity. The very exclusiveness of their consistent extravagance of sentiment and event turns the best of these plays into superb theatricals of color, movement, and fine words. But this is not the highest kind of dramatic merit, and, paradoxically, the cynical frivolities of the comedies of bad sexual manners somehow seem more serious and more relevant to deeper concerns in human life than the larger-than-life feelings and the resounding platitudes of the heroic plays. The immediate problem, however, is to account for the coexistence of both types of drama in Restoration London. Rather remarkably, both attained their clearest form and their greatest popular success in the mid-1670's.

Perhaps the best explanation is the simplest one. The sex comedies and the heroic plays appealed respectively to the two sides of the Restoration playgoer's divided feelings about his society, as if illustrating Aristotle's point that human reality lies between its polarized extremes in the two genres of drama, tragedy showing men as "better" than they are in real life and comedy as "worse." The comedies enjoyed the patronage of licentious aristocrats so secure in their station and so casual about propriety that they did not mind having their outrageous manners mimicked on the public stage. The commoners in the audience were still on the rebound from years of Puritan censorship; for a long time after 1660 going to the theater was a way of repudiating the Commonwealth, which (not altogether successfully) had closed the theaters and banned all shows in 1642. Now, with a mixture, perhaps, of envy and titillated glee, they enjoyed the spectacle of the loose living of their social betters. The satiric implications of the scene with the Shoemaker in Act I of *The Man of Mode* can hardly have been lost on the social levellers and the thoughtful cynics in the audience: when man is reduced to a bundle of physical appetites fine gentlemen must protect their status by monopolizing sin, lest class distinctions disappear in a democracy of vice.

But the libertine image, in the comedies, of man as a scheming sensualist gratifying his passions in a social world whose glitter only covers the brutalities of the primeval Hobbesian jungle was balanced in the heroic plays by the spectacle of heroes and heroines of surpassing bravery, fidelity, and chaste love, embodiments of pure Platonic essences of virtue. In their triumphs, moral or factual or both at the same time, the playgoer could feel his soul purified and ennobled by vicariously sharing in a life more just and heroic than that presided over by a lazy and corrupt king who indiscriminately paraded blue-blooded duchesses and an ex–orange-woman and actress like Nell Gwyn as his royal mistresses. Both kinds of plays presented a limited view of life; they were successful precisely to the extent that their particular ethos could be felt to be simple and severely "closed" and exclusive. And, again, to the extent that it really was so the drama missed true excellence.

In this view, the sex comedies and the heroic plays appear much less as opposites inexplicably flourishing together than as complementary reductives for audiences of divided and troubled moral and social, political and religious, allegiancies. And the view allows us to discover similarities behind the obvious differences. For example, the furious bombast of the frustrated villains, male and female, in the heroic play sounds very much like the outbursts of the jealous cuckolds and the abandoned mistresses in the sex comedies. And the rake-hero's intrigues for sexual conquest and mastery of his social group in the comedies bespeak the same fierce desire for conquest of both empire and beauteous queen that motivates the heroic hero. Dryden's ten-act *Conquest of Granada* (1670–71) is perhaps the most perfect example of heroic drama, and its hero Almanzor has more than a little – not everything, but something—in common with Etherege's Dorimant. Almanzor's grand rhetoric of simile and antithesis shares with Dorimant's flip cadences of perfectly polished prose the function of expressing the hero's uncompromising pride and single-minded drive of selfhood. The concepts underlying both characters owe a debt to Hobbes's view of natural man as a creature of aggressive egoism moved by the impulses of his body. Thus, on closer inspection, the apparent schizophrenia of Restoration drama reveals significant signs of a complex and unified sensibility. In the small number of dramatic masterpieces from the age this unity-in-complexity is achieved within the conventions of a single dramatic form.

The history of the Restoration theater is mainly the story of the shifting fortunes of the two theatrical companies which, by royal patents issued shortly after the Restoration in 1660, held a monopoly on public productions of plays and operas throughout the period. In 1682 the King's Company, weakened by internal dissension and the loss of its theater by fire, was forced to merge with the Duke's Company; actually, the merger amounted to the absorption of the weaker company by the stronger. The United Company remained the only licensed company acting in London till 1695, when a dissident group of actors led by Thomas Betterton, the leading actor of his generation, broke out and re-established theatrical rivalry. The scarcity and smallness of Restoration theaters compared with those of Elizabethan London are the most striking evidence we have that the new age drew a much more narrow audience than the old.

Unlike the Elizabethan playhouse, such as Shakespeare's Globe, the Restoration playhouse was an enclosed structure where performance took place by artificial light. The largest of them, the Theatre Royal in Drury Lane, could hold perhaps close to 1,000 spectators. The Duke's house in Dorset Garden was only a little smaller but much more elaborate. A modified version of the apron, the main acting area projecting into the audience, was a feature taken over from the Elizabethan playhouse. There was no upper stage. The deep, raked inner stage was separated from the apron by a proscenium arch with a curtain which was drawn when the performance began and which remained open until it ended. Costumes were elaborate, and the stage design attempted at least a degree of realistic illusion in the use of props and painted "flats" or "shutters." The latter were wings that moved in grooves before the fixed, painted backdrop. The use of "machines" for special, spectacular effects was frequent and popular. Boxes ran around the theater room on three sides, the most expensive seats being those in the side boxes opening directly on the apron. The Restoration equivalents of the Elizabethan groundlings sat on benches on the floor in front of the stage. Below the apron was a pit for the orchestra, which played before the curtain opened and between acts.

An immensely popular innovation was the introduction of actresses within a year or two of the reopening of the theaters. It is said that this was done on Charles II's personal initiative. Several Restoration actors and actresses gained reputations for brilliant acting, but their social standing remained low and even perilous; they were held answerable for roles which the royal Master of Revels considered seditious or otherwise offensive, and actresses were considered fair game for the rakes. Because of the short run of even successful new plays, the companies had to operate on a repertory system, which put a considerable strain on the actors. A play that ran for twelve consecutive nights was considered a hit. The playwright's sole income from his play came from the box office take on the third night. A performance was usually a pretty rowdy affair: orange-women vended their wares, footmen boisterously held seats for their masters, people came and went and moved about – the fops to be seen, the rakes to pick up girls, friends to talk, all of them intentionally or not disturbing the actors on stage and those spectators who had come to see and hear the play. Criticism of play and performance was immediate and uninhibited and sometimes took physical form. There were occasional brawls. Playwrights and actors had to strive for strong effects in order to hold the attention of the spectators, many of whom were there not just for theatrical amusement. In general, the physical features of the Restoration playhouse were those of the baroque theater of contemporary France, with certain native features retained from the pre-Commonwealth theater. In physical structure and in manner of staging it may be said that the London Restoration theater represented something like a midpoint between the Elizabethan and the conventional modern playhouse.

Etherege's *Man of Mode* opened at the Duke's theater in Dorset Garden on April 11, 1676. Betterton played Dorimant in a manner which, it was widely believed, Etherege and he intended as a representation of John Wilmot, Earl of Rochester, courtier, poet, and the most notorious of Charles II's playboy friends.

The play offers an admirable test case for the critical status of Restoration sex comedy in general. If it, commonly regarded as one of the two or three finest specimens of its kind, fails to survive critical scrutiny, the whole case for the sex comedies as something more than salacious frivolity collapses.

One of the axioms of neoclassical criticism was that the function of literature is to teach morality delightfully, "to please and instruct," as the Horatian dictum had it – not necessarily by direct didacticism but at least by implicit example. In 1698, in a long pamphlet entitled *A Short View of the Immorality and Profaneness of the English Stage,* Jeremy Collier, a blunt-spoken clergyman of strong moral convictions and no critical subtlety, attacked a number of Restoration playwrights and plays for their corrupting influence on good Christians. He charged them with indecency and profanity of language and for slandering the clergy and the nobility; but what really fired his indignation was their violation of poetic justice, a moralistic concept of criticism which obliged the playwright to improve upon the sadly arbitrary state of things in a fallen world by rigorously rewarding virtue and punishing vice. But in a play like *The Man of Mode* not only is whoring held up as the model behavior of a complete gentleman, it is also shown to be the way to social and sexual success. After getting rid of one mistress and acquiring another the hero is rewarded with the love and quite possibly the hand of a bright and beautiful heiress. What wholesome lesson can an audience bring away from watching such unblushing exploits? As it happens, Etherege escaped Collier's censure, presumably because he was dead by the time Collier wrote and the clergyman was generous enough to attack only living authors. But had Etherege been around to defend himself (Congreve was and was chastised for plays no bawdier than Etherege's), *The Man of Mode* would almost certainly have been one of Collier's exhibits of stage immorality. It is hard to say whether Collier was cause or effect in the change in popular taste in comedy that followed the Collier controversy — whether, that is, he initiated the change or at least hastened its accomplishment or just seized the opportunity for fame by speaking up on behalf of a new trend that would have been just as successful had he never written. Probably he did a bit of both. At any rate, the fact is that after about 1700 comedy turned benevolent and sentimental, reforming its rakes in firm endorsements of pre-marital chastity and marital fidelity.

Collier's polemical method was to cite passages out of context as examples of behavior and language that every right-thinking, God-fearing person would abominate in real life. In equating art with life Collier absurdly overstated his case, but the issues he raised are real and those which subsequent generations of critics, particularly in the nineteenth century, have focused on. A pleasant but ultimately self-defeating argument in defense of the comedies is that of Charles Lamb in one of the *Essays of Elia* (1822). There is, says Lamb, really no moral issue involved at all, since the world of the comedies is a "Utopia of gallantry, where pleasure is duty, and the manners perfect freedom, . . . altogether a speculative scene of things, which has no reference whatever to the world that is." But in claiming the immunity of the amoral for the comedies, this kind of argument makes them trivial or even meaningless; one cannot take seriously — in fact, it is difficult to conceive of — plays that have "no reference whatever" to the world of real men and women. Far more destructively than Collier's angry bluster, Lamb's smiling acceptance of them as delightful romps in a fairyland of fornication reduces them to escape literature, to the self-indulgent irresponsibilities of pornography. Thomas Macaulay would have none of Lamb's argument. The trouble with the morality of a play like *The Country Wife,* he says in a review in 1841, is that it reflects a world "which is a great deal too real." And a playwright of genius "makes an ill use of his powers" when he glamorizes sexual profligacy "by uniting it with beauty, grace, dignity, spirit, a high social position, popularity, literature, wit, taste, knowledge of the world, brilliant success in every undertaking." This is almost straight Collier; the playwright is still being faulted for ignoring poetic justice.

Modern critics have generally felt that judging a work of literature in terms of its presumed effects on its audience inevitably leads to arguments over the intrinsic merits and the pragmatic value of whatever ideology the work is supposed to propound and that this is a futile exercise as far as understanding *literature* is concerned. They prefer to deal with the values implicit in the structures of the work itself. As a result, opposition to Restoration sex comedy today does not take the form of Collier's and the Victorians' disapproval of its looseness of manners but develops the implications of Lamb's dangerous apology and turns them against the plays. The comedies of wit and intrigue, says L. C. Knights in an influential essay, have "no significant relation to the best thought of the time." Their dialogue isn't really *about* anything; there is only a general air of cynicism "without the tough strength of disillusion." Their language, compared with that of Elizabethan comedy, which also could be both witty and racy (racier, in fact; there are few dirty words in the Restoration comedies), betrays their intellectual thinness in the monotony of the mechanical see-saw pattern of balanced antithesis.* "The criticism that defenders of Restoration comedy need to answer," Knights concludes, "is not that the comedies are 'immoral,' but that they are trivial, gross and dull."

Some linked, general observations bearing upon the argument over the what and why of content in the comedies are called for at this point. First, the critic who feels that at least a few of them are serious and superior drama is not obliged to argue that they have no pornographic appeal at all — that is, that they never or nowhere stimulate the sexual imagination as an end in itself. Second, he does not have to believe that the playwrights were innocent of any intent to provide

* The quality Knights has in mind is much more prominent in Congreve's style than in Etherege's, but there are at least two illustrations of it in *The Man of Mode.* In Act III, Dorimant tells Sir Fopling Flutter that an affair with a lady is "a thing no less necessary to confirm the reputation of your wit than a duel will be to satisfy the town of your courage." And in Act V, Mrs. Loveit tells Dorimant that "the man who loves above his quality does not suffer more from the impertinence of his mistress than the woman who loves above her understanding does from the arrogant presumptions of her friend."

stage pornography or, if he decides that they were not, to deny that they had any thought of exploiting it for money or popularity. He can make these concessions and still feel that the plays have something of more importance to say. Third, such concessions do not force him to argue that the only redeeming value of the plays is the way they document the manners of their debauched age, or expose the depravity of their upper-class audiences under cover of amusing them with smut, or both at the same time. Though it is difficult today to determine how accurately the comedies reflected actual behavior in the fast, young set among the idle rich in Charles II's London, there is evidence that they probably were as truthful to the social facts of their time as successful comedies of manners in any age generally are. And there certainly is satire in *The Man of Mode,* not just in such obvious figures of fun as Sir Fopling and Old Bellair but also in the insinuated image of the life of selfish hedonism as a fretful, futile round of alternating anxiety and ennui. But pornography and social history and realistic satire do not exhaust the play's meaning, and there are other possible responses to the notion that Dorimant is the play's model of a perfect gentleman than either moral outrage or cynical scorn.

Elizabethan comedy had sought to romanticize the sexual urge and Jacobean tragic melodrama to criminalize it as lust. Restoration sex comedy, developing the conventions in such earlier city comedies as those of James Shirley, a late Jacobean playwright, sought not so much to reconcile romance and lust as to use the tensions between them to delineate the behavior of people forced to accommodate their desires to the rules of society. In *The Man of Mode,* the main plot about Dorimant and the subplot about Emilia and Young Bellair are partly analogous, because both use dissembling as plot motif, and partly in counterpoint, because one is libidinal and the other romantic in motivation. The play roughly observes the unity of time not because the playwright is mechanically obeying a rule of neoclassical playmaking or because Dorimant's erotic escapades are so many and complicated that crowding them all together within the space of some twenty-four hours amounts to a triumph of ingenious plotting, but because Etherege wants to sharpen our sense of the energy behind Dorimant's egoistical enterprise. Everything in the play goes to turning an essentially simple story of the tentative taming of a rake into a comprehensive and ambivalent image of man as social animal. A scheme of values is being wryly anatomized in which man's highest achievement is the gratification of his ego and his senses in a manner acceptable to his elegant and sophisticated but jealously censorious peers. Human relationships are largely determined by the requirement that people conceal their selfishly appetitive "nature" by the "art" of good manners. As in any age in which the nature-art dichotomy is felt to be a central problem of social ethics, English neoclassical comedy tends to be comedy of manners: plays in which mastery of or submission to, conformity with or deviation from, a group code distinguishes between social success and failure, between an "in" group of gentlemen of true wit and young ladies wise and attractive enough to win the game of love and the "outs" of foppish would-be-wits and cast-off mistresses. Because the delicate game is *social,* the emphasis in such comedies is on dialogue and behavior – on gossip, argument, repartee, epigram, innuendo, dress, deportment, and food – rather than on fullness of characterization and elaborate intrigue.

Sex is a major concern in these plays because success in sex depends both on the expression of the appetitive self and on graceful social control. That is why sex in a play like *The Man of Mode* stands for more than itself. Its many metaphorical disguises include business, gambling, play-acting, religion, warfare, and the eating of fruit. The range and frequency of the sexual innuendo in the dialogue suggest, two centuries before Freud, the libidinal nature of man's psychic force in all its manifestations. The most serious challenge to Dorimant's glamorous position in his circle is how he can manage to end his affair with Loveit in such a way that Medley, the suave and detached arbiter in matters of "reputation" in the play, will acquit him of the imputation that Loveit dropped him rather than he her. And when Loveit breaks her fan in a fit of jealousy, she disarms herself of an object that is both a cooling device and an instrument for subtle coquetry, woman's weapon in the duel of flirtation. Her act symbolizes a fatal loss of rational control of her passions.

Such episodes have philosophical implications. The play assumes one of the psychological commonplaces of classical and Christian humanism. Man is a creature of both reason and passion, suspended somewhere between the stations of angels and beasts in the great scheme of things, "created half to rise, and half to fall," as Alexander Pope was to put it in the *Essay on Man,* the most concise poetic compendium of neoclassical concepts of human nature. His passions move his soul; it is his moral obligation to use his reason to guide the movement. As a social being, he wins the good life when he achieves a maximum of personal freedom within the limits set by necessary social restraint.

Dorimant is charming, witty, educated, intelligent, graceful, and romantic, but he is also arrogant, heartless, ambitious, lecherous, mercenary, and inconstant – a "devil" with "something of the angel yet undefaced in him." It is this duality in human nature that *The Man of Mode* is all about. In the game of sex, the two sides of human nature interpenetrate: wit, a faculty of reason, the angelic element, is a major sexual attraction; sexual conquest, an act of passion, the animal element, is part of the conqueror's mastery of his social group.

Because his business is pleasure, pleasure becomes his business — that is, an occupation of serious social and economic consequences, in which, inevitably, there are losses as well as gains. Marriage links sex and money. Though wealth, or at least a sufficiency, is taken for granted — no one has to work for a living in Restoration comedy — an estate is an important consideration in choosing a wife for both Dorimant and Young Bellair. The conventionally ambivalent treatment of marriage in the sex comedies is involved in this business-pleasure dichotomy/equation. The fashionable attitude is that marriage breeds boredom, cuckolds, and neglected wives. Stylish couples politely hate and ignore one another. And yet, marriage is a goal sought after by most of the heroes and heroines, and most of them end up romantically married. Those who don't, like Horner in Wycherley's *Country Wife,* seem, for that reason, only qualified social successes. Marriage both is and is not romantic bliss, both is and is not a matter of pecuniary interest.

One reason why marriage is a calculated risk is man's desire for sexual variety. His inconstancy of affection is a function of his awareness of mortality; by variety he can sustain an illusion of richness of life within his limited span. There is irony affecting both the Emilia–Young Bellair marriage and the possible match between Harriet and Dorimant in the fact that the play leaves open the question of whether Dorimant's love will survive the trial of a stay among the rooks in Hampshire with old Lady Woodvill and "an old lame aunt" or whether he will return to his customary haunts, the boudoirs in London, and attempt a discreet affair with Emilia, who now, as a married woman, may, by the theory Dorimant expounds to Medley in Act I, be available for seduction. This would not be out of either his or her character. On the very verge of his provisional engagement to Harriet, Dorimant tells Bellinda they "must meet again," and Emilia tells her lover, "Do not vow. Our love is frail as is our life and full as little in our power." The losers in the game of sex are those who presume on the permanence of passion. "Constancy at my years!" Dorimant protests to Loveit. " 'Tis not a virtue in season; . . . Youth has a long journey to go, Madam." The fools in the play are, in one way or another, "humor" characters, whose fixity of emotion limits their social agility and testifies to their paucity of soul and sense. Lady Woodvill and Old Bellair are harmless and gullible blocking characters near the end of their journey, one a superannuate, the other a silly pretender to a young girl's love. More pathetic are the two characters who are too shallow and rigid for the code they affect: Sir Fopling, who is nothing but a fop, and Loveit, trapped in her jealous passion. The only concession the play makes to those whom age or character disqualifies for the perils and pleasures of the love game is Lady Townley, Young Bellair's worldly-wise aunt, a spectator-adviser figure who opens her house to the frolics of youth. Bellinda, sensuous, sentimental, and resourceful, worried about her reputation and troubled by her falseness to Loveit, in love with Dorimant but unable to keep him, belongs neither with the wits nor with the fools. The most complex of Dorimant's three conquests, she elicits sympathy and interest of a kind which the brittle decorum of the play can barely contain.

When Dorimant at the end of Act III turns from a rhapsody on Harriet's charms to plans for revenge on Loveit, and when at Lady Townley's party in Act IV he breaks off his courtship of Harriet to keep his early morning assignation with Bellinda, it seems almost pointless to be shocked by his fickleness and insincerity. He is sincerely living his libertine philosophy: "I am flesh and blood yet." A little earlier a group of maskers has arrived at Lady Townley's and has been asked to remove their masks because the occasion is not a masquerade. But it is: Dorimant is there as "Mr. Courtage," assiduous in his attentions to Lady Woodvill but about to pretend "business." Libertinism requires dissembling: Loveit acts infatuation with Sir Fopling in the park; Bellinda pretends friendship with Loveit; Emilia conceals her marriage; Harriet "acts" Dorimant when they first meet; less innocently, she is the author of Dorimant's deception of her mother; and she and Young Bellair, another of the less equivocally "nice" young people in the play, deliberately fool their parents in a charade of wooing.

To maintain his reputation as masterful seducer Dorimant must turn his public self as a sober and courteous "Mr. Courtage" into a vindictive and promiscuous Machiavel; his chosen role leaves him no other choice. The "foppery" he despises includes, by his own definition, being deeply in love, and it may be that he is so committed to the brilliant part he has cast himself in that he has lost the freedom to love strongly enough to "bear," as Harriet puts it to him in Act IV, "being laughed at." If he has, he may yet fail her test. Her comment is the most probing comment in the whole play on the code it dramatizes. That both Dorimant and Sir Fopling could qualify for the part of title hero says something about the constrictive quality of the former's performance. When the "four ill-fashioned fellows" in Act III vulgarly comment on Sir Fopling's appearance before exiting as suddenly as they entered, we catch a glimpse of what a man of mode looks like in the perspective of a broader social scene. There is a difference in style and intelligence of performance, certainly, but in a deeper sense is Dorimant's dissembling really so very different from Sir Fopling's foolish pretense to sexual irresistibility and fine manners? Dorimant's success as exemplary gentleman depends on his walking a narrow line between foppery and the crude sensualism of his social inferiors, like the whore who writes to him in Act I, asking for money for the "operies" to cure her "mallicolly." Between Sir Fopling and the Shoemaker, Dorimant has not much room to move. Sir Fopling is a caricature of a fine gentleman, and yet in the eyes of the world which Dorimant both commands and obeys he is his plausible rival for Loveit's affections. "She cannot fall from loving me to that" is his own incredulous but worried comment on her performance with Sir Fopling in the Mall. The Shoemaker is the brute inside every fine gentleman, aping the ways of his betters in practicing the vices natural to all men, provoking his genteel customer to a rudeness of manner rather below his own.

The ambivalence of Dorimant's personality and situation is at the center of the social exhibit which Etherege's play asks us to contemplate — neither to censure nor to admire but to contemplate. To say that it simply discloses — intentionally or not — the grossness, the triviality, the cruelty, and the hypocrisy of Dorimant and his set is to miss the ironic poise of its view of social man. If Dorimant is as "wicked" as he is "charming," he is also as "charming" as he is "wicked"; the two epithets demand equal rights. No tidy hierarchy of moral absolutes that we may want to erect will fit a plot in which a virtuous young woman falls in love at first sight with an accomplished rake, is brought to his knowledge by a woman who is probably a bawd, causes him to remove from the fashionable "town" to the unfashionable "country" because he wants to marry her, and may tame him by her "wildness." Harriet's and Dorimant's romance is as tentative and inconclusive as the balance between his sexual anarchy and her sexual order — between the self's instinctive predatoriness and its disciplined sociality. *The Man of Mode* is a play that uses the artifices of manners in a small and exclusive social class to pose the problem of how the jungle of society can become a genuine civilization, and it does so without suggesting that this can ever be anything other than a fragile and uncertain achievement. Such a play has a "significant relation to the best thought" of an age that habitually thought in antitheses and whose uneasy civic peace was the result of compromises. Its relevance to our own age could be similarly argued.

HENRIK IBSEN

# The Wild Duck

*Translated by Otto Reinert*

CHARACTERS

WERLE, a manufacturer and merchant
GREGERS WERLE, his son
OLD EKDAL
HJALMAR EKDAL, his son, a photographer
GINA EKDAL, Hjalmar's wife
HEDVIG, their daughter, fourteen years old
MRS. SØRBY, Werle's housekeeper
RELLING, a physician
MOLVIK, a former student of theology
GRÅBERG, a bookkeeper in Werle's office
PETTERSEN, Werle's servant
JENSEN, a hired waiter
A FLABBY GENTLEMAN
A THIN-HAIRED GENTLEMAN
A NEARSIGHTED GENTLEMAN
SIX OTHER GENTLEMEN, Werle's dinner guests
OTHER HIRED WAITERS

*Scene: The first act takes place at* WERLE'*s; the other four, in* HJALMAR EKDAL'*s studio.*

## ACT I

*An expensive-looking and comfortable study in* WERLE'S *house; bookcases and upholstered furniture; in the middle of the room a desk with papers and ledgers; lamps with green shades give the room a soft, subdued light. In the rear, open double doors with portieres pulled apart reveal a large, elegant drawing room, brightly illuminated by lamps and candles. Front right, a small door to the office wing. Front left, a fireplace with glowing coals in it. Farther back on the left wall, double doors to the dining room.*

PETTERSEN, WERLE'S *servant, in livery, and the hired waiter* JENSEN, *in black, are setting the study in order for the guests. In the drawing room, two or three other hired waiters are lighting candles, moving chairs, etc. Sounds of conversation and laughter of many people come from the dining room. Someone signals he wishes to make a speech by touching his glass with his knife. Silence follows, a short speech is made, there are noises of approval, then again conversation.*

PETTERSEN (*lights a lamp by the fireplace and puts a shade on it*): Just listen to that, Jensen. There's the old man now, proposing a long toast to Mrs. Sørby.

JENSEN (*moving an armchair*): Do you think it's true what people say, that the two of 'em – y'know – ?

PETTERSEN: Couldn't say.

JENSEN: I bet he used to be quite a goat in the old days.

PETTERSEN: Maybe so.

JENSEN: They say this dinner is for his son.

PETTERSEN: That's right. He came home yesterday.

JENSEN: It's the first I've heard Werle has a son.

PETTERSEN: He has a son, all right. But he's up at the works at Høydal all the time. He hasn't been home as long as I've been here.

A HIRED WAITER (*in the drawing room doorway*): Pst, Pettersen, there's an old fellow here, says he –

PETTERSEN (*under his breath*): Dammit! Can't have anybody in here now!

(OLD EKDAL *appears from the right in the drawing room. He is dressed in a shabby old coat with a high collar. Wool mittens. He carries a walking stick and a fur cap in his hand. Under his arm a parcel in thick paper. Dirty, reddish brown wig. Small, gray mustache.*)

PETTERSEN (*going towards him*): Good Lord! What are *you* doing here?

EKDAL (*in the doorway*): Got to get into the office, Pettersen.

PETTERSEN: The office closed an hour ago, and –

EKDAL: They told me that downstairs. But Gråberg is still in there. Be a good boy, Pettersen; let me in this way. (*Points to the small office door.*) Been through here before.

PETTERSEN: Oh well, all right. (*Opens the door.*) But see you go out the other way. We're having guests tonight.

EKDAL: I know, I know — h'm! Thanks a lot, Pettersen, old boy. Good old friend. Thanks. (*Mutters.*) Ass!

(*He enters the office.* PETTERSEN *closes the door behind him.*)

JENSEN: Is he one of them office people, too?

PETTERSEN: Oh no. He just does some extra copying for them, when they need it. But he's been a fine enough fellow in his day, old Ekdal has.

JENSEN: You know, he sort of looked like that.

PETTERSEN: Oh yes. He used to be a lieutenant.

JENSEN: I'll be damned! A lieutenant!

PETTERSEN: Yessir. Then he got mixed up in some forest deal or something. They say he pretty near ruined Werle once. The two of 'em were partners — owned the Høydal works together. Oh yes, Ekdal and I are good friends. We've had many a drink together at Madam Eriksen's, we have.

JENSEN: Didn't look to me like he'd have that kind of money.

PETTERSEN: Good Lord, Jensen. It's my treat, of course. I always say one should be nice to people who've seen better days.

JENSEN: So he went bankrupt?

PETTERSEN: Worse than that. He went to prison.

JENSEN: Prison!

PETTERSEN: Or something. — (*Listens.*) Shhh. They are getting up from the table.

(*Servants open the doors to the dining room.* MRS. SØRBY *appears, in conversation with a couple of the dinner guests. The rest of the company follows in small groups.* WERLE *is among them. The last to appear are* HJALMAR EKDAL *and* GREGERS WERLE.)

MRS. SØRBY (*to the servant, in passing*): Pettersen, tell them to serve the coffee in the music room, will you?

PETTERSEN: Very well, Mrs. Sørby.

(*She and the two guests go into the drawing room and disappear, right.* PETTERSEN *and* JENSEN *follow them out.*)

A FLABBY GENTLEMAN (*to* A THIN-HAIRED *one*): Phew! That dinner — It was almost too much for me.

THE THIN-HAIRED GENTLEMAN: Oh, I don't know. With a little bit of good will, it's amazing what one can accomplish in three hours.

THE FLABBY GENTLEMAN: Yes, but afterwards, afterwards, my dear chamberlain!

A THIRD GENTLEMAN: I am told the coffee and liqueurs will be served in the music room.

THE FLABBY GENTLEMAN: Wonderful! Then maybe Mrs. Sørby will play something for us.

THE THIN-HAIRED GENTLEMAN (*in a low voice*): If only she doesn't play us a different tune one of these days.

THE FLABBY GENTLEMAN: Don't worry. Bertha isn't one to let old friends down.

(*They laugh and enter the drawing room.*)

WERLE (*in a low and troubled voice*): I don't think anybody noticed, Gregers.

GREGERS (*looks at him*): Noticed what?

WERLE: You didn't either?

GREGERS: What?

WERLE: We were thirteen at the table.

GREGERS: Really? Were we thirteen?

WERLE (*with a glance at* HJALMAR EKDAL): Usually we are only twelve. (*To the other guests.*) Gentlemen!

(*He and the remaining guests, except* HJALMAR *and* GREGERS, *leave through the drawing room, rear right.*)

HJALMAR (*who has overheard the conversation*): You shouldn't have invited me, Gregers.

GREGERS: Nonsense! This is supposed to be a party for *me*. Shouldn't I invite my one and only friend?

HJALMAR: But I don't think your father approves. I never come to this house.

GREGERS: So I hear. But I wanted to see you and talk to you. – Well, well, we two old school fellows have certainly drifted apart. It must be sixteen – seventeen years since we saw each other.

HJALMAR: Is it really that long?

GREGERS: It is indeed. And how are you? You look fine. You've gained weight.

HJALMAR: Hardly that, but I suppose I look a little more manly than I used to.

GREGERS: Yes, you do. You look very well after all these years.

HJALMAR (*gloomily*): But the inner man – ! Believe me, that's a different story. You know, of course, how utterly everything has collapsed for me and mine since we last met.

GREGERS (*in a lower voice*): How is your father these days?

HJALMAR: I'd just as soon not talk about him. My poor, unfortunate father lives with me, of course. He has no one else in the whole world to turn to. But it's so terribly difficult for me to talk about these things. Tell me rather how you have been – up there at the works.

GREGERS: Lonely — blissfully lonely. I've had all the time in the world to think over all sorts of things. — Here. Let's make ourselves comfortable.

*(He sits down in an armchair near the fireplace and gets* HJALMAR *to take another chair beside him.)*

HJALMAR (*softly*): All the same, I do want to thank you, Gregers, for inviting me to your father's table. It proves to me you no longer bear me a grudge.

GREGERS (*surprised*): Grudge? What makes you think I ever did?

HJALMAR: You did at first, you know.

GREGERS: When?

HJALMAR: Right after the tragedy. Of course, that was only natural. After all, your own father only escaped by the skin of his teeth. Oh, that terrible old business!

GREGERS: And so I bore you a grudge? Who told you that?

HJALMAR: I know you did, Gregers. Your father said so himself.

GREGERS (*startled*): Father! Really? H'm. So that's why you've never written — not a single word.

HJALMAR: Yes.

GREGERS: Not even when you decided to become a photographer?

HJALMAR: Your father thought it would be better if I didn't write about anything at all.

GREGERS (*looking straight ahead*): Oh well, maybe he was right, at that. — But tell me, Hjalmar — do you feel you have adjusted pretty well to your situation?

HJALMAR (*with a small sigh*): Oh yes, I think I have. Can't say I haven't, anyway. At first, of course, things seemed very strange. My circumstances were so completely different. But then, everything had changed. Father's great, ruinous tragedy — The shame — The disgrace —

GREGERS (*feelingly*): Yes, yes. I understand.

HJALMAR: Of course there was no way in which I could pursue my studies. There wasn't a penny left. Rather the opposite; there was debt. Mainly to your father, I think.

GREGERS: H'm —

HJALMAR: Well — then I thought it best to take the bull by the horns and make a clean break with the past — you know, all at once. Your father thought so, too, and since he had been so helpful, and —

GREGERS: Father helped you?

HJALMAR: Yes, surely you know that? Where do you think I got the money to learn photography and to set up my own studio? Things like that are expensive, I can tell you.

GREGERS: And father paid for all that?

HJALMAR: Yes, didn't you know? I understood him to say he had written to you about it.

GREGERS: Not a word that it was *he*. He must have forgotten. We only write business letters. So it was father — !

HJALMAR: It certainly was. But he has never wanted people to know that. It was he who made it possible for me to get married, too. Or maybe — maybe you didn't know that, either?

GREGERS: No! How could I? (*Shakes* HJALMAR'*s arm.*) My dear Hjalmar, I can't tell you how happy all this makes me — and pains me, too. Perhaps I have been unfair to father. In some respects, anyway. For this shows he has a heart, you know. A kind of conscience —

HJALMAR: Conscience?

GREGERS: Or whatever you want to call it. No, really, I can't tell you how glad I am to hear this about father. — So you are married, Hjalmar. That's more than I ever will be. I trust you find yourself happy as a married man?

HJALMAR: Yes, I certainly do. She is as good and competent a wife as any man could ask for. And she is by no means without culture.

GREGERS (*a little taken aback*): No, of course not.

HJALMAR: Life itself is an education, you see. Being with me every day — And then there are a couple of remarkable men we see quite a lot of. I assure you, you'd hardly recognize Gina.

GREGERS: Gina?

HJALMAR: Yes. Surely you remember her name was Gina?

GREGERS: Whose name? I haven't the slightest idea —

HJALMAR: But don't you remember she was here in the house for a while?

GREGERS (*looks at him*): Is it Gina Hansen — ?

HJALMAR: Of course it is Gina Hansen.

GREGERS: — who kept house for us the last year of mother's illness?

HJALMAR: That's it. But my dear friend, I know for a fact that your father wrote you about my marriage.

GREGERS (*who has risen*): Yes, so he did, that's true, but not that — (*Paces the floor.*) Wait a minute — Yes, he did — now when I think back. But father always writes such short letters. (*Sits down on the arm of the chair.*) Listen, Hjalmar — this interests me — how did you make Gina's acquaintance — your wife, I mean?

HJALMAR: Quite simply. You remember she didn't stay here very long. Everything was so unsettled during your mother's illness. Gina couldn't take that, so she gave notice and moved out. That was the year before your mother died. Or maybe it was the same year.

GREGERS: It was the same year. I was up at Høydal at the time. Then what happened?

HJALMAR: Well, Gina moved in with her mother, Madam Hansen, an excellent, hardworking woman, who ran a small eating place. And she had a room for rent, too. A nice, comfortable room.

GREGERS: Which you were lucky enough to get?

HJALMAR: Yes. Through your father, in fact. And it was there I really learned to know Gina.

GREGERS: And then you got engaged?

HJALMAR: Yes. It's easy for young people to fall in love, you know. H'm —

GREGERS (*gets up, walks up and down*): Tell me — after you'd become engaged, was that when father — I mean, was that when you took up photography?

HJALMAR: That's right. Naturally, I wanted to get married and have a place of my own, the sooner the better. And both your father and I agreed that photography was the best thing I could get into. Gina thought so, too. Oh yes, that was another reason. It so happened that Gina had learned how to retouch.

GREGERS: What a wonderful coincidence.

HJALMAR (*smiling contentedly*): Yes, wasn't it? Don't you think it worked out very well?

GREGERS: Remarkably well, I should say. So father has really been a kind of Providence for you, Hjalmar; hasn't he?

HJALMAR (*moved*): He did not abandon his old friend's son in his days of need. That's one thing about your father: he does have a heart.

MRS. SØRBY (*enters on* WERLE'*s arm*): I don't want to hear another word, my dear sir. You are not to stay in there staring at all those bright lights. It isn't good for you.

WERLE (*letting go of her arm and moving his hand across his eyes*): I almost think you are right.

(PETTERSEN *and* JENSEN *enter carrying trays with glasses of punch.*)

MRS. SØRBY (*to the guests in the drawing room*): Gentlemen, if you want a glass of punch, you'll have to take the trouble to come in here.

THE FLABBY GENTLEMAN (*to* MRS. SØRBY): Dear Mrs. Sørby, please tell me it isn't so. You have not withdrawn your cherished permission to smoke?

MRS. SØRBY: Yes, Chamberlain. No smoking here in Mr. Werle's own sanctum.

THE THIN-HAIRED GENTLEMAN: And when did you append these harsh paragraphs to the tobacco regulations, Mrs. Sørby?

MRS. SØRBY: After the last dinner, Chamberlain, when certain persons abused their liberties.

THE THIN-HAIRED GENTLEMAN: And will not even the smallest infraction be tolerated, Mrs. Sørby? Really none at all?

MRS. SØRBY: None whatsoever, Chamberlain.

(*Most of the guests are gathered in the study. The servants are serving punch.*)

WERLE (*to* HJALMAR, *over by a table*): Well, Ekdal, what is that you are looking at?

HJALMAR: Oh, just an album, sir.

THE THIN-HAIRED GENTLEMAN (*moving about*): Ah yes! Photographs! That's your line, of course.

THE FLABBY GENTLEMAN (*seated*): Haven't you brought some of your own along?

HJALMAR: No, I haven't.

THE FLABBY GENTLEMAN: Too bad. Looking at pictures is good for the digestion, you know.

THE THIN-HAIRED GENTLEMAN: And then it would have contributed a mite to the general entertainment.

A NEARSIGHTED GENTLEMAN: And all contributions are gratefully received.

MRS. SØRBY: The chamberlains think that when one has been invited to dinner, one ought to work for one's food, Mr. Ekdal.

THE FLABBY GENTLEMAN: With a cuisine like this that's only a pleasure.

THE THIN-HAIRED GENTLEMAN: Oh well, if it's a question of the struggle for existence —

MRS. SØRBY: You are so right!

(*They continue their conversation, laughing and joking.*)

GREGERS (*in a low voice*): You must join in, Hjalmar.

HJALMAR (*with a twist of his body*): What am I to say?

THE FLABBY GENTLEMAN: Don't you believe, sir, that Tokay may be considered relatively beneficial to the stomach?

WERLE (*by the fireplace*): I'll guarantee the Tokay you were served tonight, at any rate. It is one of the very best years. I am sure you noticed that yourself.

THE FLABBY GENTLEMAN: Yes, it really was unusually delicate-tasting.

HJALMAR (*hesitantly*): Do the years differ?

THE FLABBY GENTLEMAN (*laughs*): Ah, Mr. Ekdal! Splendid!

WERLE (*with a smile*): I see it is hardly worth while to serve you fine wine.

THE THIN-HAIRED GENTLEMAN: Tokay is like photographs, Mr. Ekdal. Both need sunshine. Or isn't that so?

HJALMAR: Yes, sunshine has something to do with it.

MRS. SØRBY: Just the same with chamberlains. They need sunshine, too — royal sunshine, as the saying goes.

THE THIN-HAIRED GENTLEMAN: Ouch! That's a tired old joke, Mrs. Sørby.

THE NEARSIGHTED GENTLEMAN: The lady will have her fun —

THE FLABBY GENTLEMAN: — and at our expense. (*Wagging his finger.*) Madam Bertha! Madam Bertha!

MRS. SØRBY: But it is true that vintages differ widely sometimes. The older the better.

THE NEARSIGHTED GENTLEMAN: Do you count me among the older vintages?

MRS. SØRBY: Far from it.

THE THIN-HAIRED GENTLEMAN: Well, well! But what about me, Mrs. Sørby?

THE FLABBY GENTLEMAN: And me? What vintages do we belong to?
MRS. SØRBY: I reckon you among the sweet vintages, gentlemen.

(*She sips a glass of punch. The chamberlains laugh and flirt with her.*)

WERLE: Mrs. Sørby always finds a way out — when she wants to. But gentlemen, you aren't drinking! Pettersen, please see to it that — ! Gregers, let's have a glass together.

(GREGERS *does not move.*)

Won't you join us, Ekdal? I had no opportunity at the table —

(GRÅBERG *comes in through the office door.*)

GRÅBERG: Beg your pardon, Mr. Werle, but I can't get out.
WERLE: They've locked you in again, eh?
GRÅBERG: Yes, they have, sir. And Flakstad has left with the keys.
WERLE: That's all right. You just come through here.
GRÅBERG: But there is somebody else —
WERLE: Doesn't matter. Come on, both of you.

(GRÅBERG *and* OLD EKDAL *enter from the office.*)

WERLE (*involuntarily*): Damn!

(*Laughter and talk among the guests cease.* HJALMAR *gives a start when he sees his father, puts down his glass, and turns away toward the fireplace.*)

EKDAL (*does not look up but makes quick little bows to both sides, as he mutters*): Beg pardon. Came the wrong way. Gate's locked. Gate's locked. Beg pardon. (*He and* GRÅBERG *go out, rear right.*)
WERLE (*between his teeth*): That idiot Gråberg!
GREGERS (*staring, his mouth hanging open, to* HJALMAR): Don't tell me that was — !
THE FLABBY GENTLEMAN: What is it? Who was that?
GREGERS: Nothing. Just the bookkeeper and somebody else.
THE NEARSIGHTED GENTLEMAN (*to* HJALMAR): Did *you* know that man?
HJALMAR: I don't know — I didn't notice —
THE FLABBY GENTLEMAN (*getting up*): What the devil has gotten into everybody? (*He walks over to some other guests, who are talking in low voices.*)
MRS. SØRBY (*whispers to the servant*): Give him something from the kitchen to take home. Something good.
PETTERSEN (*nods his head*): I'll do that, ma'am. (*Goes out.*)
GREGERS (*shocked, in a low voice to* HJALMAR): Then it really was he?
HJALMAR: Yes.
GREGERS: And you stood there and denied him!
HJALMAR (*in a fierce whisper*): But how *could* I — ?

GREGERS: — acknowledge your own father?

HJALMAR (*pained*): Oh, if you had been in my place, maybe —

(*The low conversation among the guests changes to forced gaiety.*)

THE THIN-HAIRED GENTLEMAN (*approaching* HJALMAR *and* GREGERS, *in a friendly mood*): Aha! Reminiscing about university days, gentlemen? — Don't you smoke, Mr. Ekdal? Can I give you a light? Oh that's right. We are not allowed —

HJALMAR: Thanks, I don't smoke.

THE FLABBY GENTLEMAN: Don't you have a nice little poem you could recite for us, Mr. Ekdal? You used to do that so beautifully.

HJALMAR: I am sorry. I don't remember any.

THE FLABBY GENTLEMAN: That's a shame. Well, in that case, Balle, what do we do?

(*They both walk into the drawing room.*)

HJALMAR (*gloomily*): Gregers — I am leaving! You see, when a man has felt Fate's crushing blow — Say goodbye to your father for me.

GREGERS: Yes, of course. Are you going straight home?

HJALMAR: Yes. Why?

GREGERS: I thought I might come up and see you a little later.

HJALMAR: No, don't do that. Not to my home. My home is a gloomy one, Gregers, particularly after a brilliant banquet such as this. We can meet somewhere in town.

MRS. SØRBY (*has come up to them; in a low voice*): Are you leaving, Ekdal?

HJALMAR: Yes.

MRS. SØRBY: Say hello to Gina for me.

HJALMAR: Thank you. I'll do that.

MRS. SØRBY: Tell her I'll be up to see her one of these days.

HJALMAR: Fine. (*To* GREGERS.) You stay here. I'll slip out without anybody noticing. (*Drifts off. A little later he goes into the drawing room and out right.*)

MRS. SØRBY (*in a low voice to the servant who has returned*): Well, did you give the old man something?

PETTERSEN: Oh yes. A bottle of brandy.

MRS. SØRBY: Oh dear. Couldn't you have found something better?

PETTERSEN: But Mrs. Sørby, there's nothing he likes better than brandy.

THE FLABBY GENTLEMAN (*in the doorway to the drawing room, with a sheet of music in his hand*): Will you play a duet, Mrs. Sørby?

MRS. SØRBY: Yes, gladly.

THE GUESTS: Good! Good!

(*She and all the guests go out rear right.* GREGERS *remains standing by the fireplace.* WERLE *is looking for something on the desk and appears to wish to be left alone. Since* GREGERS *does not leave,* WERLE *walks towards the drawing room door.*)

GREGERS: Father, do you have a moment?
WERLE (*stops*): What is it?
GREGERS: I'd like a word with you.
WERLE: Couldn't it wait till we're alone?
GREGERS: No, it can't, for maybe we'll never be alone again.
WERLE (*coming closer*): What's that supposed to mean?

(*During the following scene, the sound of a piano is faintly heard from the music room.*)

GREGERS: How is it that that family has been allowed to go to ruin so miserably?
WERLE: I suppose you refer to the Ekdals?
GREGERS: Yes, I do mean the Ekdals. Lieutenant Ekdal was once your close friend.
WERLE: Yes, unfortunately. Too close. I have felt that keenly enough for many years. It was his fault that my good name and reputation, too, were — somewhat tarnished.
GREGERS (*in a low voice*): Was he the only one who was guilty?
WERLE: Who else, do you mean?
GREGERS: The two of you were together on that big purchase of forest land, weren't you?
WERLE: But it was Ekdal who surveyed the area — surveyed it fraudulently. It was he who felled all that timber on state property. He was responsible for everything that went on up there. I didn't know what he was doing.
GREGERS: I doubt that Lieutenant Ekdal himself knew what he was doing.
WERLE: That may well be. The fact remains that he was convicted and I was not.
GREGERS: Yes, I know there were no proofs.
WERLE: Acquittal is acquittal. Why do you want to bring back that miserable old business that gave me gray hairs before my time? Is that what has been on your mind all these years up there? I can assure you, Gregers, here in town that whole story has been forgotten long ago, as far as *I* am concerned.
GREGERS: But what about that unfortunate family?
WERLE: Well, now, exactly what do you want me to do for those people? When Ekdal got out, he was a broken man, beyond help altogether. Some people go to the bottom as soon as they've got some buckshot in them and never come up again. Believe me, Gregers, I've done all I possibly could do, if I didn't want to put myself in a false light and give people occasion for all sorts of talk and suspicion —

GREGERS: Suspicion? I see.

WERLE: I have given Ekdal copying work to do for the office, and I pay him far, far more than he is worth.

GREGERS (*without looking at him*): H'm. I don't doubt that.

WERLE: You are laughing? Don't you think I am telling you the truth? Oh, to be sure, you won't find it in my books. I never enter expenses like that.

GREGERS (*with a cold smile*): No, I suppose there are certain expenses that are better not entered.

WERLE (*puzzled*): What do you mean?

GREGERS (*being brave*): Have you entered what it cost you to let Hjalmar Ekdal learn photography?

WERLE: I? What do you mean – entered?

GREGERS: I know now it was you who paid for it. And I also know it was you who set him up in business – quite comfortably, too.

WERLE: All right! And you still say I have done nothing for the Ekdals! I assure you, Gregers, those people have cost me a pretty penny!

GREGERS: Have you entered those expenses?

WERLE: Why do you ask?

GREGERS: I have my reasons. Listen – at the time you were providing so kindly for your old friend's son, wasn't that just when he was getting married?

WERLE: Damn it, Gregers! How can I remember – ! After so many years – !

GREGERS: You wrote me a letter at the time. A business letter, of course. And in a postscript you mentioned very briefly that Hjalmar Ekdal had married one Miss Hansen.

WERLE: That's right. That was her name.

GREGERS: But you did not say anything about Miss Hansen being Gina Hansen, our ex-housekeeper.

WERLE (*with scornful but forced laughter*): No, to tell the truth, it didn't occur to me that you were particularly interested in our ex-housekeeper.

GREGERS: I wasn't. But – (*lowers his voice*) somebody else in this house was.

WERLE: What do you mean? (*Flaring up.*) Don't tell me you're referring to me!

GREGERS (*in a low but firm voice*): Yes, I am referring to you.

WERLE: And you dare – ! You have the audacity – ! How can that ingrate, that – that photographer fellow – how dare he make accusations like that!

GREGERS: Hjalmar hasn't said a word. I don't think he has the faintest suspicion of anything like this.

WERLE: Then where do you get it from? Who could have said a thing like that?

GREGERS: My poor, unfortunate mother. The last time I saw her.

WERLE: Your mother! I might have thought so! You and she – you always stood together. It was she who first turned you against me.

GREGERS: No, it was all she had to go through, till things became too much for her and she died in sheer misery.

WERLE: Oh, nonsense! She didn't have to go through anything! No more than what others have had to, anyway. There's just no way of getting on with morbid, hysterical people — that's something *I* have had to learn! And here you are, with a suspicion like that — dabbling in old rumors and gossip against your own father. Listen here, Gregers. It really seems to me that at your age you might find something more useful to do.

GREGERS: Yes, it's about time.

WERLE: Then maybe your mind would be more at ease than it seems to be now. What is the point of working away, year in and year out, as just an ordinary clerk up there at Høydal, with not so much as a penny beyond regular wages? It's plain silly!

GREGERS: I wish I could believe that.

WERLE: Not that I don't understand, mind you. You want to be independent, don't want to be obliged to me for anything. But right now there is a chance for you to become independent, to be on your own in everything.

GREGERS: Oh? How so?

WERLE: When I wrote you that I needed you here in town right away — h'm —

GREGERS: Yes, what is it you want of me? I've been waiting to hear all day.

WERLE: I am offering you a partnership in the firm.

GREGERS: I! In your firm? As a partner?

WERLE: Yes. That doesn't mean we have to be together all the time. You could take over the business here in town and I could go up to Høydal.

GREGERS: You would want to do that?

WERLE: Well, you see, Gregers. I can't work as well as I used to. I'll have to save my eyes. They are getting weaker.

GREGERS: You have always had weak eyes.

WERLE: Not as bad as now. Besides — there are other things, too, that may make it advisable for me to live up there — for a while, anyway.

GREGERS: Nothing like this has ever even occurred to me.

WERLE: Look here, Gregers. I know there are many things that stand between us. But after all, we are father and son. It seems to me we ought to be able to come to some sort of understanding.

GREGERS: For appearance's sake, I suppose you mean.

WERLE: Well, that would be something, anyway. Think it over, Gregers. Wouldn't that be possible? What do you say?

GREGERS (*looks at him coldly*): There is something behind this.

WERLE: I don't understand.

GREGERS: You want to use me for something.

WERLE: In a relationship as close as ours I suppose one person can always be of use to the other.

GREGERS: Yes. So they say.

WERLE: I want to have you at home with me for a while. I am a lonely man, Gregers. I have always been lonely, but mostly now, when I am getting older. I need somebody around me.

GREGERS: You have Mrs. Sørby.

WERLE: So I do, and she has become almost indispensable to me. She is bright, she has an even temper, she brings life into the house – and I badly need that.

GREGERS: Well, then, everything is just as you want it.

WERLE: Yes, but I am afraid it won't last. A woman in her circumstances can easily have her position misconstrued in the eyes of the world. I'll almost go so far as to say it does a man no good either.

GREGERS: Oh, I don't know. When a man gives the kind of dinner parties you do he can take quite a few liberties.

WERLE: Yes, but what about *her*, Gregers? I am afraid she will not put up with it much longer. And even if she did, even if she ignored what people are saying and all that sort of thing, out of devotion to me – Do you really think, Gregers, you with your strong sense of justice, do you feel it would be –

GREGERS (*interrupting*): Just tell me this: are you going to marry her?

WERLE: What if I did? What then?

GREGERS: That's what I am asking. What then?

WERLE: Would it displease you very much?

GREGERS: No, not at all.

WERLE: Well, you see, I didn't know – I thought perhaps out of regard for your mother –

GREGERS: I am not given to melodramatics.

WERLE: Well, whether you are or not, you have lifted a stone from my heart. I can't tell you how pleased I am that I can count on your support in this matter.

GREGERS (*looks intently at him*): Now I see what you want to use me for.

WERLE: Use you for? What an expression!

GREGERS: Let's not be particular in our choice of words – not as long as we're by ourselves, at any rate. (*Laughs.*) So that's it. That's why I had to come to town at all costs. Because of Mrs. Sørby, there are arrangements being made for family life in this house. Touching scene between father and son! That would indeed be something new!

WERLE: I won't have you use that tone!

GREGERS: When were we ever a family here? Never in my memory. But now, of course, there is need for a display of domestic affection. It will look very well to have the son hastening home on wings of filial feeling to attend the aging father's marriage feast. What happens then to all the talk of what the poor, deceased mother had to suffer? It evaporates. Her son takes care of that.

WERLE: Gregers, I don't believe there is anyone you detest as much as me.

GREGERS (*in a low voice*): I have seen too much of you.

WERLE: You've seen me with your mother's eyes. (*Lowers his voice a little.*) But don't forget that those eyes were – clouded at times.

GREGERS (*his voice trembles*): I know what you have in mind. But who's to blame for mother's tragic weakness? You and all those – ! The last one was that female you palmed off on Hjalmar Ekdal, when you yourself no longer – !

WERLE (*shrugs his shoulders*): Word for word as if I were hearing your mother.

GREGERS (*paying no attention*): – and there he is now, with his great, trusting child's soul in the middle of all this deceit – sharing his roof with a woman like that, unaware that what he calls his home is based on a lie! (*Steps closer to* WERLE.) When I look back upon all you have done, I seem to see a battlefield strewn with mangled human destinies.

WERLE: I almost think the gap between us is too wide.

GREGERS (*with a formal bow*): So I have observed. That is why I take my hat and leave.

WERLE: You're leaving? The house?

GREGERS: Yes. For now at last I see a mission to live for.

WERLE: What mission is that?

GREGERS: You'd only laugh if I told you.

WERLE: A lonely man doesn't laugh so easily, Gregers.

GREGERS (*pointing to the rear*): Look, father. The chamberlains are playing blindman's buff with Mrs. Sørby. – Goodnight and goodbye.

(*He goes out rear right. The sound of people talking, laughing, and playing games can be heard from the drawing room, where the guests are now coming into view.*)

WERLE (*mutters scornfully*): Hah – ! The fool! And he says he is not melodramatic!

## ACT II

HJALMAR EKDAL'*s studio, a large attic room. To the right, a slanting roof with skylights, half covered by blue cloth. The entrance door from the hallway is in the far right corner; the door to the living room farther forward on the same wall. There are two doors to the left, as well, with an iron stove between them. In the rear, wide, sliding, double doors. The studio is unpretentious but cozy. Between the two doors on the right and a little out from the wall is a sofa with a table and some chairs in front of it. On the table is a lighted lamp with a shade. Near the wall by the stove is an old armchair. Various pieces of photographic equipment here and there in the room. In the rear, to the left of the sliding doors, a shelf with a few books, bottles with chemical solutions, tools, and some other objects. Photographs, brushes, paper, etc., are lying on the table.*

GINA EKDAL *sits by the table, sewing.* HEDVIG *sits on the sofa, reading, her hands shading her eyes, her thumbs in her ears.*

GINA (*glances at* HEDVIG *a few times, as if secretly anxious*): Hedvig!

HEDVIG (*does not hear.*)

GINA (*louder*): Hedvig!

HEDVIG (*takes away her hands and looks up*): Yes, mother?

GINA: Hedvig, be a good girl. Don't read any more tonight.

HEDVIG: Please, mother, just a little bit longer? Can't I?

GINA: No. I want you to put that book away. Your father doesn't like you to read so much. He never reads at night.

HEDVIG (*closing her book*): Well, father doesn't care much for reading, anyway.

GINA (*puts her sewing aside and picks up a pencil and a small notebook from the table*): Do you remember how much we spent for the butter today?

HEDVIG: One crown and sixty-five øre.

GINA: That's right. (*Writes it down.*) We're using an awful lot of butter in this family. Then there was the sausage and the cheese – let me see – (*writing*) – and the ham – (*Mumbles figures while adding up.*) Goodness! it does add up –

HEDVIG: And the beer.

GINA: Right. (*Writes.*) It gets terrible expensive, but it can't be helped.

HEDVIG: And you and I didn't need anything hot for supper since father was out.

GINA: No, that's right. That helps some. And I did get eight crowns and fifty øre for the pictures.

HEDVIG: Was it that much?

GINA: Eight-fifty, exactly.

(*Silence.* GINA *picks up her sewing.* HEDVIG *takes paper and pencil and starts drawing, her left hand shading her eyes.*)

HEDVIG: Isn't it nice to think that father is at that big dinner party at Mr. Werle's?

GINA: Can't rightly say he's *his* guest. It was the son who invited him. (*After a pause.*) We have nothing to do with the old man.

HEDVIG: I can't wait till father comes home. He promised to ask Mrs. Sørby if he could take home something good for me.

GINA: Why yes, you can be sure there are plenty of good things in *that* house.

HEDVIG (*still drawing*): Besides, I think I am a little bit hungry, too.

(OLD EKDAL *enters right rear, the brown paper parcel under his arm, another parcel in his coat pocket.*)

GINA: So late you are today, Grandpa.

EKDAL: They'd locked the office. Had to wait for Gråberg. And then I had to go through — h'm —

HEDVIG: Did they give you any more copying to do, Grandpa?

EKDAL: This whole parcel. Look.

GINA: That's nice.

HEDVIG: And you've got another one in your pocket.

EKDAL: What? Oh never mind. That's nothing. (*Puts his walking stick away in the corner.*) This will keep me busy a long time, Gina. (*Slides one of the double doors half open.*) Shhh! (*Peeks into the attic for a while, then he cautiously slides the door shut. Chuckling.*) They're sound asleep, the whole lot of 'em. And she herself's in the basket.

HEDVIG: Are you sure she won't be cold in that basket, Grandpa?

EKDAL: Cold? With all that straw? Don't you worry about *that.* (*Goes towards the door left rear.*) There are matches, aren't there?

GINA: On the dresser.

(EKDAL *goes into his room.*)

HEDVIG: It's nice that he got all that new work to do.

GINA: Yes, poor old thing. It will give him a little spending money.

HEDVIG: And he won't be able to stay down at that awful Madam Eriksen's all morning.

GINA: No; there's that, too.

HEDVIG: Do you think they're still at the table?

GINA: Lord knows. Could be.

HEDVIG: Just think of all that delicious food. I'm sure he'll be in a good mood when he comes home. Don't you think so, mother?

GINA: Yes, but what if we could tell him we'd rented the room. Wouldn't that be nice?

HEDVIG: But we don't need that tonight.

GINA: Oh yes we do. We could always use the money. The room is no good to us as it is.

HEDVIG: No, I mean that father will be in a good mood tonight, anyway. It's better to have the room for some other time.

GINA (*looking at her*): You like it when you have something nice to tell father when he comes home nights, don't you?

HEDVIG: It makes things more pleasant.

GINA (*reflectively*): Yes, I guess you're right about that.

(OLD EKDAL *enters from his room, heads for the kitchen door, left front.*)

GINA (*turning half around in her chair*): Do you need anything in the kitchen, Grandpa?

EKDAL: Yes. But don't you get up. (*Goes out.*)

GINA: I hope he isn't fooling around with the fire out there. (*After a while.*) Hedvig, go out and see what he's doing.

(OLD EKDAL *enters with a pitcher of hot water.*)

HEDVIG: Getting hot water, Grandpa?

EKDAL: That's right. Got some writing to do, but the ink's as thick as gruel. H'm –

GINA: But hadn't you better have supper first? It's all ready for you in your room.

EKDAL: Never mind supper, Gina, I tell you I'm busy. I don't want anybody coming in to me. Not anybody. H'm.

(*He goes into his room.* GINA *and* HEDVIG *look at each other.*)

GINA (*in a low voice*): I can't think where he got the money from. Can you?

HEDVIG: From Gråberg, maybe.

GINA: No, it wouldn't be that. Gråberg always gives me the money.

HEDVIG: Maybe he got a bottle on credit.

GINA: Him! Who'd give him credit?

(HJALMAR EKDAL, *in overcoat and gray hat, enters right.*)

GINA (*throws down her sewing, gets up*): Heavens, Ekdal! Home already?

HEDVIG (*getting up at the same time*): Father? So soon!

HJALMAR (*puts down his hat*): Most of them seemed to be leaving now.

HEDVIG: Already?

HJALMAR: Well, it was a dinner party, you know. (*Takes his coat off.*)

GINA: Let me help you.

HEDVIG: Me too. (*They help him off with his coat.* GINA *hangs it up in the rear.*) Were there many there, father?

HJALMAR: Not too many. About twelve or fourteen at the table.

GINA: Did you get to talk to all of them?

HJALMAR: Oh yes, a little. Though Gregers kept me engaged most of the evening.

GINA: Is he as ugly as he used to be?

HJALMAR: Well – I suppose nobody would call him handsome. Is father back?

HEDVIG: Yes, he is in there writing.

HJALMAR: Did he say anything?

GINA: No. About what?

HJALMAR: He didn't mention – ? I thought I heard he'd been with Gråberg. I think I'll go in to him for a moment.

GINA: No, you'd better not.

HJALMAR: Why not? Did he say he didn't want to see me?

GINA: He doesn't want to see anybody.

HEDVIG (*making signs to her*): Ahem!

GINA (*doesn't notice*): He's gotten himself some hot water.
HJALMAR: Ah! So he is —
GINA: Looks that way.
HJALMAR: Ah yes — my poor old white-haired father. Let him enjoy his little pleasures as best he can.

(OLD EKDAL, *a lighted pipe in his mouth, enters in an old smoking jacket.*)

EKDAL: Home again? Thought it was you I heard talking.
HJALMAR: Yes. I just came back.
EKDAL: Guess you didn't see me, did you?
HJALMAR: No, but they told me you'd gone through, so I thought I'd catch up with you.
EKDAL: H'm. That's good of you, Hjalmar. Who were they — all those people?
HJALMAR: Oh — all sorts. Chamberlain Flor and Chamberlain Balle and Chamberlain Kaspersen and chamberlain this and that. I don't know —
EKDAL (*nodding his head*): Hear that, Gina? He's been with nothing but chamberlains all evening.
GINA: Yes, I hear as they've become quite fancy in that house now.
HEDVIG: Did the chamberlains sing, father? Or recite poetry?
HJALMAR: No. They just talked nonsense. They wanted *me* to recite, though, but I didn't want to.
EKDAL: They couldn't get you to, eh?
GINA: Seems to me you might have done that.
HJALMAR: No. I don't see any reason why one has to oblige every Tom, Dick, and Harry all the time. (*Walks up and down.*) At any rate, I won't.
EKDAL: No point in being too obliging, you know. That's Hjalmar for you.
HJALMAR: I don't see why *I* always have to be the one who provides entertainment on the rare occasions when I am out for dinner. Let the others exert themselves for a change. Those fellows go from one big meal to the next, stuffing themselves day in and day out. Let *them* do something for all the food they are getting!
GINA: You didn't tell them that though, did you?
HJALMAR (*humming a little*): Well, I don't know about that. They were told a thing or two.
EKDAL: The chamberlains?
HJALMAR: Mmm — (*Casually.*) Then we had a little controversy over Tokay wine.
EKDAL: Tokay, no less! Say, that's a fine wine!
HJALMAR (*stops his walking*): It *may* be a fine wine. But let me tell you: not all the vintages are equally fine. It depends on how much sunshine the grapes get.
GINA: If you don't know everything — !
EKDAL: And they quarreled with that?

HJALMAR: They tried to, but then it was pointed out to them that it was the same way with chamberlains. Not all vintages are equally fine among chamberlains, either — so they were told.

GINA: Goodness! What you don't think of!

EKDAL: Heh-heh! So they got that to put in their pipe.

HJALMAR: Right to their face. That's how they got it.

EKDAL: Gina, d'ye hear that? He gave it to them right to their face!

GINA: Right to their face! Imagine!

HJALMAR: Yes, but I don't want you to talk about it. One doesn't talk about such things. Of course, the whole thing was done in the friendliest possible way. They are all of them pleasant, easy-going people. Why should I hurt them? No point in that.

EKDAL: Right to their face, though —

HEDVIG (*ingratiatingly*): It's so nice to see you all dressed up, father. You look very well in tails.

HJALMAR: Yes, don't you think so? And it really fits me perfectly. Practically tailor-made. Possibly a trifle tight in the armpits, that's all. Help me, Hedvig. (*Takes his dinner jacket off.*) I'd rather wear my own coat. Where is it, Gina?

GINA: Here it is. (*Helps him on with it.*)

HJALMAR: There now! Be sure to have Molvik get his suit back first thing in the morning.

GINA (*putting the clothes away*): I'll take care of it.

HJALMAR (*stretching*): Aaahh. This feels nicer after all. And this kind of loose-fitting, casual wear is really more in keeping with my whole appearance; don't you think so, Hedvig?

HEDVIG: Oh yes, father!

HJALMAR: Especially when I tie my neckcloth with loose, flying ends — like this? What do you think?

HEDVIG: Yes, it goes extremely well with your mustache. And with your curls, too.

HJALMAR: I'd hardly call my hair curly. Wavy, rather.

HEDVIG: Yes, for the curls are so large.

HJALMAR: Waves, really.

HEDVIG (*after a moment, pulling his sleeve*): Father?

HJALMAR: What is it?

HEDVIG: Oh, you know very well what it is!

HJALMAR: I certainly don't.

HEDVIG (*laughing and pleading*): Oh come on, father! Don't tease me!

HJALMAR: But what is it?

HEDVIG (*shaking him*): Father! Give it to me! You know, you promised me. Something good to eat.

HJALMAR: Oh, dear! I completely forgot!

HEDVIG: You are only teasing, father. Shame on you! Where is it?

HJALMAR: No, honest, I really did forget. But wait a moment. I have something else for you, Hedvig. (*Goes and searches his coat pockets.*)

HEDVIG (*jumps up and down, clapping her hands*): Oh mother, mother!

GINA: See what I mean? If you just give him time –

HJALMAR (*with a piece of paper*): Here it is.

HEDVIG: That? But that's just a piece of paper.

HJALMAR: It's the menu, Hedvig, the entire menu. Look here. It says "Menu." That means what you get to eat.

HEDVIG: Haven't you anything else for me?

HJALMAR: I tell you, I forgot all about it. But take my word for it: it's not such a great treat, all that rich food. You just sit down and read the menu, now, and I'll tell you later what the things taste like. Here you are, Hedvig.

HEDVIG (*swallowing her tears*): Thank you.

(*She sits down but doesn't read.* GINA *signals to her.* HJALMAR *notices.*)

HJALMAR (*pacing the floor*): It is really unbelievable all the things a father is supposed to keep in mind. And if he forgets the smallest item – ! Long faces right away. Oh well. One gets used to that, too. (*Stops by the stove where* OLD EKDAL *is sitting.*) Have you looked at them tonight, father?

EKDAL: I certainly have! She's in the basket!

HJALMAR: No! Really? In the basket? She is getting used to it then, I guess.

EKDAL: Didn't I tell you she would? But look, Hjalmar, there are still a few things –

HJALMAR: – improvements; yes, I know.

EKDAL: They've got to be done.

HJALMAR: Right. Let's talk about it now, father. Come over here to the sofa.

EKDAL: All right. H'm. Guess I want to fill my pipe first, though. Need to clean it, too – h'm – (*Goes into his room.*)

GINA (*with a smile, to* HJALMAR): Cleaning his pipe –

HJALMAR: Oh well, Gina – let him. The poor shipwrecked old man. – About those improvements – We'd better get to them tomorrow.

GINA: You won't have time tomorrow, Ekdal.

HEDVIG (*interrupting*): Oh, yes, mother.

GINA: For remember those prints you were going to retouch? They came for 'em again today.

HJALMAR: I see. It's those prints again, is it? Well, they'll get done. You can be sure of that. Perhaps there are some new orders come in, too?

GINA: Not a thing, worse luck. Tomorrow I've got only those two portraits I told you about.

HJALMAR: Is that all? Well, if one doesn't exert oneself, what can you expect?

GINA: But what can I do? I advertise in the papers all I can, seems to me.

HJALMAR: The papers, the papers — you see yourself how far that gets us. I suppose there hasn't been anyone to look at the room, either?

GINA: No, not yet.

HJALMAR: Just as I thought. Well, no — if one doesn't *do* anything — One has to make a real effort, Gina!

HEDVIG (*going to him*): Shall I get your flute, father?

HJALMAR: No, not the flute. *I* need no pleasures. (*Paces up and down.*) You'll see if I don't work tomorrow! You don't need to worry about *that!* You can be sure I shall work as long as my strength holds out —

GINA: But Ekdal, dear — I didn't mean it that way.

HEDVIG: How about a bottle of beer, father?

HJALMAR: Not at all. I don't need anything — (*Stops.*) Beer? Did you say beer?

HEDVIG (*brightly*): Yes, father; lovely, cool beer.

HJALMAR: Oh well — all right — since you insist, I suppose you may bring me a bottle.

GINA: Yes, do that. That'll be nice and cozy.

(HEDVIG *runs towards the kitchen door.*)

HJALMAR (*by the stove, stops her, looks at her, takes her by the head and presses her to him*): Hedvig! Hedvig!

HEDVIG (*happy, in tears*): Oh father! You are so sweet and good!

HJALMAR: No, no, don't say that. There I was — seated at the rich man's table — gorging myself on his ample fare — and I couldn't even remember —

GINA (*seated by the table*): Nonsense, Ekdal.

HJALMAR: It is not nonsense. But you must not count too strictly. You know I love you, regardless.

HEDVIG (*throwing her arms around him*): And we love you, father, so much, so much!

HJALMAR: And if I am unreasonable at times, remember — God forgive me — remember I am a man beset by a host of sorrows. Well, well! (*Drying his eyes.*) No beer at such a moment. Give me my flute.

(HEDVIG *runs to the shelf and fetches it.*)

HJALMAR: Thank you. There now. With my flute in my hand and you two around me — ah!

(HEDVIG *sits down by the table next to* GINA. HJALMAR *walks back and forth, playing a Bohemian folk dance. He plays loudly but in slow tempo and with pronounced sentiment.*)

HJALMAR (*interrupts his playing, gives his left hand to* GINA, *and says with strong emotion*): Our home may be mean and humble, Gina. But it is our home. And I say to you both: here dwells contentment!

(*He resumes his playing. Presently there is a knock on the door.*)

GINA (*getting up*): Shh, Ekdal. I think somebody's coming.
HJALMAR (*putting the flute back on the shelf*): Yes, yes of course. Somebody would —

(GINA *goes to open the door.*)

GREGERS WERLE (*out in the hall*): I beg your pardon —
GINA (*taking a step back*): Oh!
GREGERS: — isn't this where Mr. Ekdal lives, the photographer?
GINA: Yes, it is.
HJALMAR (*going to the door*): Gregers! So you did come, after all. Come in.
GREGERS (*entering*): I told you I wanted to see you.
HJALMAR: But tonight — ? Have you left the party?
GREGERS: Both party and home. Good evening, Mrs. Ekdal. I don't know if you recognize me.
GINA: Oh yes. Young Mr. Werle isn't hard to recognize.
GREGERS: No, for I look like my mother, and you remember her, I am sure.
HJALMAR: You have left your home?
GREGERS: Yes. I have taken a room at a hotel.
HJALMAR: Really? — Well, since you're here, take off your coat and sit down.
GREGERS: Thanks. (*Removes his overcoat. He has changed clothes and is now dressed in a plain, gray suit, of somewhat unfashionable cut.*)
HJALMAR: Here on the sofa. Make yourself comfortable.

(GREGERS *sits down on the sofa,* HJALMAR *on a chair by the table.*)

GREGERS (*looking around*): So this is where you live, Hjalmar. This is your home.
HJALMAR: This is the studio, as you can see.
GINA: It's roomier in here, so we mostly stay out here.
HJALMAR: The apartment we had before was really nicer than this, but there is one big advantage here: we have plenty of space.
GINA: And we have a room across the hallway that we're renting out.
GREGERS (*to* HJALMAR): You have lodgers, too?
HJALMAR: No, not yet. These things take time, you see. One has to be on the lookout. (*To* HEDVIG.) What about that beer?

(HEDVIG *nods her head and goes out into the kitchen.*)

GREGERS: So that's your daughter.
HJALMAR: Yes, that's Hedvig.

GREGERS: Your only child, isn't she?

HJALMAR: Our only one. Our greatest joy in the world, and (*lowers his voice*) our greatest sorrow, as well.

GREGERS: What are you saying!

HJALMAR: Yes, Gregers, for there is every probability that she'll lose her sight.

GREGERS: Becoming blind!

HJALMAR: Yes. So far, there are only early symptoms, and things may be well with her for some time yet. But the doctor has warned us. It is coming, irresistibly.

GREGERS: But this is nothing less than a tragedy! How do you account for it?

HJALMAR (*with a sigh*): Heredity, most likely.

GREGERS (*struck*): Heredity?

GINA: Ekdal's mother had weak eyes.

HJALMAR: That's what father says. I, of course, don't remember her.

GREGERS: Poor child. How does she take it?

HJALMAR: Oh, we can't bring ourselves to tell her – I'm sure you can understand that. She suspects nothing. Joyous and carefree, chirping like a little bird, she'll flutter into life's endless night. (*Overcome by emotion.*) Oh Gregers, this is such a terrible burden for me.

(HEDVIG *enters with a tray with beer and glasses. She puts it down on the table.*)

HJALMAR (*stroking her hair*): Thanks. Thank you, Hedvig.

HEDVIG (*puts her arms around his neck and whispers something in his ear.*)

HJALMAR: No. No sandwiches now. (*Looks off.*) That is – unless Gregers wants some?

GREGERS (*with a gesture of refusal*): No. No thanks.

HJALMAR (*still in a melancholy mood*): Oh well, you might as well bring in some, all the same. A crust, if you have one. And plenty of butter, please.

GREGERS (*who has followed her with his eyes*): Otherwise she seems healthy enough.

HJALMAR: Yes, thank God, there is nothing else wrong with her.

GREGERS: I think she is going to look like you, Mrs. Ekdal. How old is she?

GINA: Hedvig is just about fourteen. Her birthday is day after tomorrow.

GREGERS: Quite big for her age, isn't she?

GINA: Yes, she has grown a lot lately.

GREGERS: It's by the children we tell we're growing older ourselves. How long have you two been married now?

GINA: We've been married for – let's see – fifteen years, pretty near.

GREGERS: Just imagine! Has it really been that long?

GINA (*taking notice, looks at him*): It certainly has.

HJALMAR: That's right. Fifteen years, less a few months. (*Changing topic.*) Those must have been long years for you up there at the works, Gregers.

GREGERS: They were long while they lasted. Now afterwards I hardly know where they went.

(OLD EKDAL *enters from his room, without his pipe, but with his old-fashioned lieutenant's cap on his head. His walk is a trifle unsteady.*)

EKDAL: I'm ready for you now, Hjalmar. Let's talk about this – h'm – What was it again?

HJALMAR (*going towards him*): Father, there's someone here. Gregers Werle. I don't know if you remember him?

EKDAL (*looks at* GREGERS, *who has stood up*): Werle? That's the son, isn't it? What does he want from me?

HJALMAR: Nothing. He has come to see me.

EKDAL: Then there's nothing wrong?

HJALMAR: Of course not.

EKDAL (*swinging one arm back and forth*): Not that I am scared, mind you, but –

GREGERS (*goes up to him*): I just wanted to bring you greetings from your old hunting grounds, Lieutenant Ekdal.

EKDAL: Hunting grounds?

GREGERS: Yes, the woods up around the Høydal works.

EKDAL: Oh yes, up there. Yes, I used to know that country quite well in the old days.

GREGERS: You were quite a hunter then, weren't you?

EKDAL: Could be. Maybe I was. You're looking at my get-up. I don't ask anybody's permission to wear it in the house. Just as long as I don't go outside –

(HEDVIG *brings a plate with open-faced sandwiches, which she puts down on the table.*)

HJALMAR: You sit down, father, and have a glass of beer. Help yourself, Gregers.

(EKDAL *mutters something and shuffles over to the sofa.* GREGERS *sits down on a chair next to him;* HJALMAR *is on the other side of* GREGERS. GINA *sits some distance from the table, sewing.* HEDVIG *is standing by her father.*)

GREGERS: Do you remember, Lieutenant Ekdal, when Hjalmar and I used to come up and visit you summers and Christmas?

EKDAL: You did? No; can't say as I do. But it's true I used to be a good hunter, if I do say so myself. I've killed bears, too. Nine of 'em.

GREGERS (*looks at him with compassion*): And now your hunting days are over.

EKDAL: Oh — I wouldn't say that. I still go hunting once in a while. Well, yes, not in the old way, of course. For you see, the woods — the woods — the woods — ! (*Drinks.*) Nice-looking woods up there now?

GREGERS: Not as in your time. They have cut a great deal.

EKDAL: Cut? (*In a lower voice and as if afraid.*) That's risky business, that is. It has consequences. The woods are vengeful.

HJALMAR (*filling his glass*): Here, father. Have some more.

GREGERS: How can a man like you — such an outdoors man as you used to be — how can you stand living here in the middle of a musty city, within four walls?

EKDAL (*chuckles, glancing at* HJALMAR): Oh, it's not so bad here. Not bad at all.

GREGERS: But surely — all the things your soul grew used to up there — ? The cool, invigorating breezes? The free life in woods and mountains, among beasts and birds — ?

EKDAL (*smiling*): Hjalmar, shall we show it to him?

HJALMAR (*quickly, a little embarrassed*): Oh no, father. Not tonight.

GREGERS: What is it he wants to show me?

HJALMAR: Oh, it's just — something. You can see it some other time.

GREGERS (*continues addressing* OLD EKDAL): You see, this is what I had in mind, Lieutenant. Why don't you come up to Høydal with me? I'll probably be going back shortly. I'm sure you could get some copying work to do up there as well. For down here you can't have a thing to cheer you up and keep you occupied.

EKDAL (*looks at him in astonishment*): Don't *I* have — !

GREGERS: Yes, of course, you have Hjalmar. But then he has his own family. And a man like you, who have always loved the outdoors —

EKDAL (*striking the table*): Hjalmar, he *shall* see it!

HJALMAR: But father, do you really think so? It's dark and —

EKDAL: Nonsense. There's a moon. (*Getting up.*) I say he's got to see it. Let me out. Come and help me, Hjalmar!

HEDVIG: Oh yes, father! Do!

HJALMAR (*getting up*): Oh well, all right.

GREGERS (*to* GINA): What is it?

GINA: Oh, don't expect anything much.

(EKDAL *and* HJALMAR *have gone to the rear of the room. Each of them slides one of the double doors back.* HEDVIG *is helping the old man.* GREGERS *remains standing by the sofa.* GINA *keeps on sewing, paying no attention. Through the opened doors can be seen a big, elongated, irregular-shaped attic, with nooks and corners and a couple of chimneys standing free from the wall. Moonlight falls through several skylights, illuminating some parts of the room, while others are in deep shadow.*)

EKDAL (*to* GREGERS): You are welcome to come closer, sir.

GREGERS (*goes up to them*): What is this really?

EKDAL: See for yourself. H'm.

HJALMAR (*somewhat embarrassed*): This is all father's, you understand.

GREGERS (*at the door, peering into the attic*): Do you keep chickens, Lieutenant?

EKDAL: Should say we do. They're roosting now. But you ought to see those chickens in daylight!

HEDVIG: And there is –

EKDAL: Hush, don't say anything yet.

GREGERS: And I see you've got pigeons, too.

EKDAL: Could be we have. We've got pigeons, all right! The roosts are up on the rafters, for pigeons like to be up high, you know.

HJALMAR: They aren't all of them just ordinary pigeons.

EKDAL: Ordinary! I should say not! We've got tumblers and even a couple of pouters. But come over here. Do you see that pen over by the wall?

GREGERS: Yes. What do you use that for?

EKDAL: That's where the rabbits are at night.

GREGERS: Oh? You have rabbits, too, do you?

EKDAL: Damn right we have rabbits! He asks if we have rabbits, Hjalmar! H'm. But now we're coming to the *real* thing. Here we are. Move, Hedvig. You stand here and look down – there; that's right. Now, do you see a basket with straw in it?

GREGERS: Yes, I do. And I see a bird.

EKDAL: H'm – A "bird."

GREGERS: Isn't it a duck?

EKDAL (*offended*): I'd say it's a duck!

HJALMAR: But what kind of duck, do you think?

HEDVIG: It's not just an ordinary duck.

EKDAL: Hush!

GREGERS: And it's not a muscovy duck, either.

EKDAL: No, Mr. – Werle; it's not a muscovy, for it's a wild duck!

GREGERS: Is it really? A wild duck?

EKDAL: That's what it is. The – "bird," as you called it. A wild duck. It's our wild duck.

HEDVIG: *My* wild duck. For it belongs to me.

GREGERS: And it lives here in the attic? It's thriving?

EKDAL: What's so odd about that? She's got a big pail of water to splash around in.

HJALMAR: Fresh water every other day.

GINA (*turning to* HJALMAR): Ekdal, please. I'm freezing.

EKDAL: H'm. All right; let's close up. Just as well not to disturb their night's rest, anyway. Help me Hedvig.

(HJALMAR *and* HEDVIG *slide the double doors shut.*)

EKDAL: You can have a good look at her some other time. (*Sits down in the armchair by the stove.*) I'm telling you, they are strange birds, those wild ducks.

GREGERS: But how did you ever catch it, Lieutenant?

EKDAL: I didn't. There's a certain man in this town we can thank for her.

GREGERS: (*struck by a thought*): Would that man be my father?

EKDAL: Indeed it is. It's your father, sure enough. H'm.

HJALMAR: Funny you'd guess that, Gregers.

GREGERS: You told me before that you owed a great deal to my father, so I thought that perhaps –

GINA: But we didn't get the duck from Werle himself.

EKDAL: It's Håkon Werle we have to thank for her all the same, Gina. (*To* GREGERS.) He was out in a boat, see, and took a shot at her. But he doesn't see so well, your father doesn't. H'm. Anyway, she was only wounded.

GREGERS: I see. She got some buckshot in her.

HJALMAR: Yes. A little.

HEDVIG: Right under the wing, so she couldn't fly.

GREGERS: Then she went to the bottom, I suppose.

EKDAL (*sleepily, his voice muffled*): So it did. Always do that, wild ducks. Dive straight to the bottom – far as they can, sir. Bite themselves fast in the grasses and roots and weeds and all the other damn stuff down there. And never come up again.

GREGERS: But, Lieutenant, *your* wild duck did.

EKDAL: He had such a wonderfully clever dog, your father. And that dog – it went down and got the duck up.

GREGERS (*to* HJALMAR): And so it came to you?

HJALMAR: Not right away. First your father took it home with him, but it didn't seem to get on too well there, and then he told Pettersen to get rid of it.

EKDAL (*half asleep*): H'm – Pettersen – Ass –

HJALMAR: That's how we got it, for father knows Pettersen a little, and when he heard about the wild duck, he asked Pettersen to give it to him.

GREGERS: And now it seems perfectly contented in there in the attic.

HJALMAR: Yes, you would hardly believe how well it gets on. It's becoming fat. I think perhaps it's been in there so long that it has forgotten what wild life is like. And that makes all the difference.

GREGERS: I am sure you are right, Hjalmar. The thing to do is never to let it look at sea and sky again. – But I don't think I should stay any longer. I believe your father is asleep.

HJALMAR: Oh, as far as that is concerned –

GREGERS: Oh yes, one thing more. You said you had a room for rent? A vacant room?

HJALMAR: We do. What of it? Do you know anyone who – ?

GREGERS: Could I get it?

HJALMAR: You?

GINA: Oh, Mr. Werle, I'm sure *you* don't want to –

GREGERS: Couldn't I have it? If I can, I'll move in first thing in the morning.

HJALMAR: Yes, indeed, with the greatest pleasure.

GINA: No, but Mr. Werle, that's not a room for you.

HJALMAR: Gina! How can you say that?

GINA: It's not large enough or light enough, and –

GREGERS: That doesn't matter, Mrs. Ekdal.

HJALMAR: I think it's quite a nice room myself, and decently furnished, too.

GINA: But remember those two downstairs.

GREGERS: Who are they?

GINA: There's one who used to be a private tutor.

HJALMAR: Molvik is his name. He studied to be a minister once.

GINA: And then there's a doctor, name of Relling.

GREGERS: Relling? I know him slightly. He used to practice up at Høydal.

GINA: They are a couple of real wild characters those two. Out all hours of the night, and when they come home they aren't always – y'know –

GREGERS: One gets used to that sort of thing. I hope I'll be like the wild duck.

GINA: H'm. Well, *I* think you ought to sleep on it first.

GREGERS: I take it you don't really want me in the house, Mrs. Ekdal.

GINA: Good Lord! How can you say a thing like that?

HJALMAR: Yes, Gina. It really does seem very odd of you. (*To* GREGERS.) Does this mean you'll be staying in town for a while?

GREGERS (*putting on his overcoat*): Yes, I think I'll stay.

HJALMAR: But not with your father? What do you intend to do?

GREGERS: If I knew that, Hjalmar, I'd be much better off. But when you're cursed with a name like "Gregers" – and then "Werle" after that – Did you ever hear of an uglier name?

HJALMAR: I don't think it's ugly at all.

GREGERS: Ugh! I feel like spitting in the face of anybody with a name like that. But since it's my cross in life to be Gregers Werle, such as I am –

HJALMAR: Ha-ha! If you weren't Gregers Werle, what would you like to be?

GREGERS: If I could choose, I'd like to be a really clever dog.

GINA: A dog!

HEDVIG (*involuntarily*): Oh no!

GREGERS: Yes, an exceptionally skillful dog – the kind that goes down to the bottom after wild ducks when they've dived down among the weeds and the grass down there in the mud.

HJALMAR: Honestly, Gregers. This makes no sense whatever.

GREGERS: I suppose it doesn't. But tomorrow morning, then, I'll be moving in. (*To* GINA.) You won't have any trouble with me; I'll do everything myself. (*To* HJALMAR.) The other things we can talk about tomorrow. – Goodnight, Mrs. Ekdal. (*Nods to* HEDVIG.) Goodnight!

GINA: Goodnight, Mr. Werle.

HEDVIG: Goodnight.

HJALMAR (*who has lighted a candle*): Wait a moment. I'll see you down. I'm sure it's all dark on the stairs.

(GREGERS *and* HJALMAR *go out through the entrance door, right rear.*)

GINA (*staring ahead, her sewing lowered in her lap*): Wasn't it funny all that talk about wanting to be a dog?

HEDVIG: Do you know, mother – I think he really meant something else.

GINA: What would that be?

HEDVIG: No, I couldn't say, but it was just like he had something else in mind all the time.

GINA: You think so? It sure was funny, though.

HJALMAR (*returning*): The lamp was still burning. (*Blows out the candle and sits down.*) Ah, at last it's possible to get a bite to eat. (*Starts on the sandwiches.*) Now do you see what I mean, Gina – about seizing the opportunity?

GINA: What opportunity?

HJALMAR: Well – it was lucky, wasn't it, that we got the room rented? And then to somebody like Gregers, a dear old friend.

GINA: Well, I don't know what to say to that.

HEDVIG: Oh mother, you'll see it will be fun.

HJALMAR: I must say you are strange. First you wanted nothing more than to get a lodger; then when we do, you don't like it.

GINA: I know, Ekdal. If only it had been somebody else. What do you think old Werle will say?

HJALMAR: He? It's none of his business.

GINA: But don't you see that something's bound to be wrong between the two of 'em, since the young one is moving out. Sure you know how those two are.

HJALMAR: That may be so, but –

GINA: And maybe Werle will think you are behind it!

HJALMAR: All right! Let him think that. Oh, by all means, Werle has done a great deal for me – I'm the first to admit it. But that doesn't mean I everlastingly have to let him run my life.

GINA: But Ekdal, dear, it could hurt Grandpa. Perhaps he'll lose what little he's making from working for Gråberg.

HJALMAR: I almost wish he would! Is it not humiliating for a man like me to see his gray-haired father treated like dirt? Ah, but soon now the time will be ripe. I feel it. (*Takes another sandwich.*) As sure as I have a mission in life, it shall be accomplished!

HEDVIG: Oh yes, father!

GINA: Shhh! Don't wake him up.

HJALMAR (*in a lower voice*): I say it again: I *will* accomplish it! The day will come, when – That's why it's such a good thing we got the room rented out, for that makes me more independent. And that's necessary for a man with a mission in life. (*Over by the armchair, with feeling.*) Poor old white-haired father. Trust your Hjalmar. He has broad enough shoulders – powerful shoulders, at any rate. Some day you'll wake up, and – (*To* GINA.) Or don't you believe that?

GINA (*getting up*): Sure I do, but let's first get him to bed.

HJALMAR: Yes, let's.

(*They tenderly lift the old man.*)

## ACT III

*The studio. It is morning. Daylight comes in through the skylight, the blue cloth having been pulled aside.*

HJALMAR *sits at the table, retouching a photograph. Several other photographs are lying in front of him. After a while,* GINA, *in coat and hat, enters from outside. She is carrying a covered basket.*

HJALMAR: Back already, Gina?

GINA: Yes. I'm in a hurry. (*Puts the basket down on a chair and takes off her coat and hat.*)

HJALMAR: Did you look in at Gregers's?

GINA: I did. It looks real nice in there. He fixed up the place real pretty, soon as he moved in.

HJALMAR: Oh?

GINA: Remember, he was to take care of everything himself? Well, he built a fire in the stove, but he hadn't opened the flue, so the whole room got filled with smoke. Phew! It smelled like –

HJALMAR: Oh dear –

GINA: Then do you know what he does? This really beats everything. He wanted to put out the fire, so he pours the water from the wash basin into the stove. The whole floor is sloppy with filth!

HJALMAR: I am sorry.

GINA: I've got the janitor's wife to clean up after him, pig as he is, but the room can't be lived in till this afternoon.

HJALMAR: Where is he now?

GINA: He said he was going out for a while.

HJALMAR: I went in there for a moment, too – right after you'd left.

GINA: He told me. You've asked him for breakfast.

HJALMAR: Just a bit of a late morning meal. It's the first day and all. We can hardly do less. I am sure you have something.

GINA: I'll have to find something, at any rate.

HJALMAR: Be sure it's plenty, though. I think Relling and Molvik are coming, too. I ran into Relling on the stairs just now, and so of course I had to –

GINA: So we are to have those two as well.

HJALMAR: Good heavens, one or two more or less – can that make any difference?

EKDAL (*opens his door and looks in*): Listen, Hjalmar – (*Sees* GINA.) Well, never mind.

GINA: Do you want something, Grandpa?

EKDAL: No. It doesn't matter. H'm! (*Goes back inside his room.*)

GINA (*picking up her basket*): Make sure he doesn't go out.

HJALMAR: Yes, I will. – Say, Gina – how about some herring salad? I believe Relling and Molvik made a night of it again last night.

GINA: If only they don't get here too soon.

HJALMAR: I'm sure they won't. Just take your time.

GINA: Well, all right. Then you can work some in the meantime.

HJALMAR: I *am* working! I'm working as hard as I can!

GINA: All I mean is you'd have it out of the way for later. (*Goes into the kitchen.*)

(HJALMAR *picks up the photograph and the brush and works for a while – slowly and with evident distaste.*)

EKDAL (*peeks in, looks around, says in a low voice*): Pst! Are you busy?

HJALMAR: Yes. I am struggling with these everlasting pictures –

EKDAL: All right, all right. If you're busy, then you're busy. H'm! (*Goes back inside his room. The door remains open.*)

HJALMAR (*works in silence for a while, puts his brush down, walks over to* EKDAL*'s door*): Are *you* busy, father?

EKDAL (*grumbling inside his room*): When *you* are busy, *I* am busy! H'm!

HJALMAR: Oh all right. (*Returns to his work.*)

EKDAL (*appears in his door again after a while*): H'm, Hjalmar, listen – I'm not so *terribly* busy, you know.

HJALMAR: I thought you were writing.

EKDAL: Dammit all! Can't that Gråberg wait a day or two? Didn't think it was a matter of life and death.

HJALMAR: Of course not. And you aren't a slave, after all.

EKDAL: And there is this other job in there –

HJALMAR: Just what I was thinking. Do you want to go in there now? Shall I open the door for you?

EKDAL: Good idea.

HJALMAR (*getting up*): Then we'd have that job out of the way.

EKDAL: Exactly. It has to be ready for tomorrow, anyway. It *is* tomorrow, isn't it?

HJALMAR: Sure it's tomorrow.

*(They slide the double doors open. The morning sun is shining through the skylight. Some pigeons are flying around; others are cooing on their perches. From farther inside the room the chickens are heard clucking once in a while.)*

HJALMAR: All right, father. Guess you can go ahead.

EKDAL (*entering the attic*): Aren't you coming?

HJALMAR: Yes, do you know – I almost think I will. (*Notices* GINA *in the kitchen door.*) I? No, I don't have the time. I have to work. But there is this thing –

*(He pulls a cord. A curtain comes down from within the attic. Its lower part is made out of a strip of old sailcloth; its upper part is a piece of stretched-out fish net. The attic floor is now no longer visible.)*

HJALMAR (*returns to the table*): Now! Maybe I can have peace for a few minutes.

GINA: Is he fooling around in there again?

HJALMAR: Would you rather he went down to Madam Eriksen? (*Sitting down.*) Do you want anything? I thought you said –

GINA: I just wanted to ask you if you think we can set the table in here?

HJALMAR: Yes. There aren't any appointments this early, are there?

GINA: No – only those two sweethearts who want their picture taken.

HJALMAR: Damn! Couldn't they come some other time!

GINA: Goodness, Ekdal, they'll be here after dinner, when you're asleep.

HJALMAR: Oh, in that case it's all right. Yes, let's eat in here.

GINA: Fine. But there's no hurry with the table. You're welcome to use it some more.

HJALMAR: Can't you see I *am* using it?

GINA: Then you'll be all done for afterwards, you know. (*Goes into the kitchen.*)

*(Brief silence.)*

EKDAL (*in the door to the attic, inside the fish net*): Hjalmar!

HJALMAR: What?

EKDAL: Afraid we'll have to move the pail, after all.

HJALMAR: What else have I been saying all along?

EKDAL: H'm – h'm – h'm! (*Disappears inside again.*)

HJALMAR (*keeps on working for a moment, glances over towards the attic, half rises, as* HEDVIG *enters from the kitchen. He quickly sits down again*): What do you want?

HEDVIG: Just to be with you, father.

HJALMAR (*after a short while*): Seems to me like you're snooping around. Have you been told to watch me, perhaps?

HEDVIG: No, of course not.

HJALMAR: What is mother doing?

HEDVIG: Mother is in the middle of the herring salad. (*Comes over to the table.*) Isn't there any little thing I can help you with, father?

HJALMAR: Oh no. It is better I do it all alone — as long as my strength lasts. There is no need for you to worry about anything, Hedvig, as long as your father is allowed to keep his health.

HEDVIG: Oh father. I won't have you talk that horrid way. (*She walks around a bit, stops by the opening to the inner room and looks in.*)

HJALMAR: What is he doing in there?

HEDVIG: Looks like a new ladder up to the water pail.

HJALMAR: He'll never manage that by himself! And here I am condemned to sit — !

HEDVIG (*goes to him*): Give me the brush, father. I can do it.

HJALMAR: I won't hear of it. You'll just be ruining your eyes.

HEDVIG: No, I won't. Give me the brush.

HJALMAR (*getting up*): It would only be for a minute or two —

HEDVIG: What possible harm could that do? (*Takes the brush.*) There now. (*Sits down.*) And here is one I can use as model.

HJALMAR: But don't ruin your eyes! Do you hear me? I will not take the responsibility. It's all yours. I'm just telling you.

HEDVIG (*working*): Yes, of course.

HJALMAR: You are really very good at it, Hedvig. It will only be for a few minutes, you understand.

(*He slips into the attic by the edge of the curtain.* HEDVIG *keeps on working.* HJALMAR *and* EKDAL *can be heard talking behind the curtain.*)

HJALMAR (*appearing inside the net*): Hedvig, please give me the pliers on the shelf. And the chisel. (*Turns around.*) See here, father. Just let me show you what I have in mind first.

(HEDVIG *fetches the tools from the shelf and gives them to him.*)

HJALMAR: Thank you. It was a good thing I went in.

(*He leaves the doorway. Sounds of carpentering and conversation are heard from inside.* HEDVIG *remains watching them. After a while there is a knock on the entrance door. She does not notice.*)

GREGERS (*bareheaded and coatless, enters, stops near the door*): H'm!

HEDVIG (*turns around and walks towards him*): Good morning! Won't you please come in?

GREGERS: Thank you. (*Looks towards the attic.*) You seem to have workmen in the house.

HEDVIG: Oh no. It's just father and Grandpa. I'll tell them you're here.

GREGERS: Please don't. I'd rather wait a while. (*Sits down on the sofa.*)

HEDVIG: It's such a mess in here — (*Begins removing the photographs.*)

GREGERS: Never mind. Are they pictures you are retouching?
HEDVIG: Yes. It is something I'm helping father with.
GREGERS: Please don't let me disturb you.
HEDVIG: I won't.

(*She moves the things more within her reach and resumes work.* GREGERS *watches her in silence.*)

GREGERS: Did the wild duck sleep well last night?
HEDVIG: Yes, thank you. I think so.
GREGERS (*turning towards the attic*): In daylight it looks quite different from last night when there was a moon.
HEDVIG: Yes, it varies so. In the morning it looks different than in the afternoon, and when it rains it looks different than when the sun is shining.
GREGERS: You have noticed that?
HEDVIG: Yes, of course.
GREGERS: Do you too spend much time with the wild duck?
HEDVIG: Yes, when I can.
GREGERS: I suppose you don't have much spare time, though. You are going to school, of course?
HEDVIG: Not any more. Father is afraid I'll ruin my eyes.
GREGERS: Then he reads with you himself?
HEDVIG: He has promised to, but he hasn't had the time yet.
GREGERS: But isn't there anyone else who can help you?
HEDVIG: Well, yes, there is Mr. Molvik, but he isn't always – you know – quite –
GREGERS: You mean he is drunk sometimes.
HEDVIG: I think so.
GREGERS: Well, in that case you have time for many things. And in there, I suppose, it's like a world all its own?
HEDVIG: Yes, quite. And there are so many strange things in there.
GREGERS: There are?
HEDVIG: Yes, there are big closets with books in them, and in many of the books there are pictures.
GREGERS: I see.
HEDVIG: And there is an old desk with drawers and drop-down leaves and a big clock with figures that come out. But the clock doesn't run any more.
GREGERS: So time has stopped in there where the wild duck lives?
HEDVIG: Yes. And there are old coloring sets and that sort of thing, and then all the books.
GREGERS: I expect you read the books.
HEDVIG: Yes, whenever I have a chance. But most of them are in English and I can't read that. But I look at the pictures. There is a great, big book that's called "Harrison's History of London." I think it is a hun-

dred years old. There are ever so many pictures in it. In front it shows a picture of Death with an hourglass and a girl. I think that is horrible. But then there are all the pictures of churches and castles and streets and big ships that sail the seas.

GREGERS: Tell me — where do all those strange things come from?

HEDVIG: There was an old sea captain who used to live here. He brought them home. They called him The Flying Dutchman. And that's odd, I think, for he wasn't a Dutchman at all.

GREGERS: No?

HEDVIG: No. But finally he disappeared at sea, and all the things were left here.

GREGERS: Listen — when you sit in there looking at the pictures, don't you ever want to travel and see the real, big world for yourself?

HEDVIG: Oh no. I want to stay here at home always and help father and mother.

GREGERS: With the photographs?

HEDVIG: Not just with that. Best of all I'd like to learn how to engrave pictures like those in the English books.

GREGERS: H'm. And what does your father say to that?

HEDVIG: I don't think father likes the idea very much. He is funny about things like that. You know, he says I ought to learn basket-weaving and straw-plaiting. But I don't think that sounds like much of anything at all.

GREGERS: No, I don't think it does either.

HEDVIG: Though of course father is quite right in saying that if I had learned basket-weaving I could have made the new basket for the wild duck.

GREGERS: That's true. And that really ought to have been your job, you know.

HEDVIG: Yes. Because it is my wild duck.

GREGERS: So I hear.

HEDVIG: Oh yes. I own it. But father and Grandpa get to borrow it as often as they like.

GREGERS: So? And what do they do with it?

HEDVIG: Oh — they take care of it and build things for it and that sort of thing.

GREGERS: I see. For of course the wild duck is the noblest of all the animals in there.

HEDVIG: Yes, she is, for she is a real, wild bird. And then I feel sorrier for her than for any of the others, because she's all alone, poor thing.

GREGERS: No family, like the rabbits.

HEDVIG: No. And the chickens, they have so many they were little chicks together with. But she is all alone, with none of her own near by. And there is the strange thing about the wild duck. Nobody knows her and nobody knows where she is from.

GREGERS: And she has been down to the depths of the sea.

HEDVIG (*glances quickly at him, suppresses a smile, asks*): Why do you say "the depths of the sea"?

GREGERS: What should I say?

HEDVIG: You could say "the sea bottom" or "the bottom of the sea."

GREGERS: Can't I just as well say "the depths of the sea"?

HEDVIG: Yes, but I think it sounds so strange when other people say "the depths of the sea."

GREGERS: Why is that? Tell me.

HEDVIG: No, I won't, for it is so silly.

GREGERS: I don't think so. Please tell me why you smiled.

HEDVIG: It's because every time I think of what's in there – when it comes into my head all of a sudden, I mean – I always feel that the whole room and everything that's in it are the depths of the sea. But that's silly.

GREGERS: Don't say that.

HEDVIG: Yes, for it's just an old attic, you know.

GREGERS (*looking intently at her*): Are you sure?

HEDVIG (*surprised*): That it's an attic?

GREGERS: Yes. Are you sure it is?

(HEDVIG *stares at him in silence, her mouth open in astonishment.* GINA *enters from the kitchen with linen, silverware, etc., to set the table.*)

GREGERS (*getting up*): I am afraid I am too early for you.

GINA: Oh well. You have to be somewhere. Things are almost ready now, anyway. Clear the table, Hedvig.

(*During the next scene* HEDVIG *clears the table and* GINA *sets it.* GREGERS *seats himself in the armchair and starts leafing through an album of photographs.*)

GREGERS: I understand you know how to retouch, Mrs. Ekdal.

GINA (*looks at him out of the corner of her eye*): That's right.

GREGERS: That was fortunate.

GINA: How – fortunate?

GREGERS: I mean since Ekdal is a photographer.

HEDVIG: Mother knows how to take pictures, too.

GINA: Oh yes, I've had to learn *that* business, all right.

GREGERS: Perhaps it is you who are responsible for the daily routine?

GINA: Yes, when Ekdal himself doesn't have the time –

GREGERS: I suppose he busies himself a great deal with his old father?

GINA: Yes, and then it's not for a man like Ekdal to waste his time taking pictures of everybody and his grandmother.

GREGERS: I quite agree, but since he did choose this as his profession, shouldn't he – ?

GINA: You know just as well as I do, Mr. Werle, that Ekdal isn't just one of your common, ordinary photographers.

GREGERS: Of course not, but — nevertheless —

(*A shot is heard from the attic.*)

GREGERS (*jumps up*): What was that?

GINA: Ugh! There they go, firing away again!

GREGERS: They shoot, too?

HEDVIG: They go hunting.

GREGERS: What? (*Over by the door to the attic.*) Do you go hunting, Hjalmar?

HJALMAR (*inside the curtain*): Have you arrived? I didn't know — I've been so busy — (*To* HEDVIG.) And you — not letting us know — ! (*Comes into the studio.*)

GREGERS: Do you go shooting in the attic?

HJALMAR (*showing him a double-barreled pistol*): Oh, it's only this old thing.

GINA: You and Grandpa are going to have an accident with that pestol of yours one of these days.

HJALMAR (*irritated*): I believe I have told you that this kind of firearm is called a pistol.

GINA: I don't see that that makes it any better.

GREGERS: So you have taken up hunting, too, Hjalmar?

HJALMAR: Only a little rabbit hunting now and then. It's mostly for father's sake, you understand.

GINA: Menfolks are strange. They always need something to diverge themselves with.

HJALMAR (*grimly*): That's right. We always need something to divert ourselves with.

GINA: That's exactly what I'm saying.

HJALMAR: Oh well — ! H'm! (*To* GREGERS.) Well, you see, we're fortunate in that the attic is situated so that nobody can hear the shots. (*Puts the pistol on the top shelf.*) Don't touch the pistol, Hedvig! Remember, one barrel is loaded!

GREGERS (*peering through the net*): You have a hunting rifle, too, I see.

HJALMAR: That's father's old gun. It doesn't work any more. There's something wrong with the lock. But it's rather fun to have it around all the same, for we take it apart and clean it once in a while and grease it and put it back together again. It's mostly father, of course, who amuses himself with things like that.

HEDVIG (*standing next to* GREGERS): Now you can get a good look at the wild duck.

GREGERS: I was just looking at it. One wing is drooping a bit, isn't it?

HJALMAR: Well that's not so strange. She was hit, you know.

GREGERS: And she drags her foot a little. Or doesn't she?

HJALMAR: Perhaps a little bit.

HEDVIG: Yes, for that is the foot the dog seized her by.

HJALMAR: But aside from that she has no other hurt or defect, and that's really quite remarkable when you consider that she has a charge of buckshot in her and has been between the teeth of a dog.

GREGERS (*with a glance at* HEDVIG): Yes, and been down to the depths of the sea – for so long.

HEDVIG (*smiles*): Yes.

GINA (*busy at the table*): Oh yes, that precious wild duck. There sure is enough circumstance made over it.

HJALMAR: H'm. Will you be done setting the table soon?

GINA: In a minute. Hedvig, I need your help. (GINA *and* HEDVIG *go into the kitchen.*)

HJALMAR (*in a low voice*): You had better not watch father. He doesn't like it.

GREGERS (*leaves the attic door.*)

HJALMAR: And I ought to close this before the others arrive. (*Shoos the birds away with his hands.*) Shoo! Shoo – you! (*Raising the curtain and sliding the doors back.*) This arrangement is my own invention. It is really quite amusing to fool around with these things and to fix them when they get broken. And it's absolutely necessary to have something like it, for Gina won't stand for rabbits and chickens in the studio.

GREGERS: No, I suppose not. And perhaps the studio is your wife's department?

HJALMAR: I generally leave the daily run of the business to her. That gives me a chance to retire into the living room and give my thoughts to more important things.

GREGERS: What things, Hjalmar?

HJALMAR: I have been wondering why you haven't asked me that before. Or maybe you haven't heard about the invention?

GREGERS: Invention? No.

HJALMAR: Really? You haven't? Oh well – up there in the woods and wilderness –

GREGERS: So you have invented something!

HJALMAR: Not quite yet, but I am working on it. As you can well imagine, when I decided to devote myself to photography it was not my intent to do nothing but take portraits of all sorts of ordinary people.

GREGERS: I suppose not. Your wife just said the same thing.

HJALMAR: I made a pledge to myself that if I were to give my powers to this profession, I would raise it so high that it would become both an art and a science. That is how I decided to make some remarkable invention.

GREGERS: What is it? What does it do?

HJALMAR: Well, Gregers, you must not ask for details just yet. You see, it takes time. And don't think I am driven by vanity. I can truthfully say I am not working for my own sake. Far from it. It is my life's mission that is in my thoughts night and day.

GREGERS: What mission?

HJALMAR: The old man with the silver hair – can you forget him?

GREGERS: Yes, your poor father. But what exactly do you think you can do for him?

HJALMAR: I can resurrect his respect for himself by once again raising the name of Ekdal to fame and honor.

GREGERS: So that is your life's mission.

HJALMAR: Yes. I will rescue that shipwrecked man. For he was shipwrecked the moment the storm broke. During those terrible inquiries he was not himself. The pistol over yonder – the one we use to shoot rabbits with – it has played its part in the tragedy of the Ekdal family.

GREGERS: The pistol? Really?

HJALMAR: When sentence had been pronounced and he was to be confined – he had that pistol in his hand –

GREGERS: He tried to – !

HJALMAR: Yes, but didn't dare. He was a coward. So much of a wreck, so spiritually ruined was he already then. Can you understand it? He, an officer, the killer of nine bears, descended from two lieutenant colonels – I mean one after the other, of course – Can you understand it, Gregers?

GREGERS: I can indeed.

HJALMAR: Not I. – But the pistol came to figure in our family chronicle a second time. When he had begun to wear the garb of gray and sat there behind bolt and bar – oh, those were terrible days for me, believe me. I kept the shades down on both windows. When I looked out, I saw the sun shining as usual. I saw people in the street laughing and talking about nothing. I could not understand it. It seemed to me that all of existence ought to come to a standstill, as during an eclipse of the sun.

GREGERS: I felt that way when mother died.

HJALMAR: In such an hour Hjalmar Ekdal turned the pistol against himself –

GREGERS: You too were thinking of – ?

HJALMAR: Yes.

GREGERS: But you did not pull the trigger?

HJALMAR: No. In the decisive moment I won a victory over myself. I remained alive. Take my word for it: it requires courage to go on living in a situation like that.

GREGERS: That depends on how you look at it.

HJALMAR: No, it doesn't. At any rate, it all turned out to be for the best. For soon now I will finish my invention, and when I do, Doctor Relling thinks, as I do myself, that father will be allowed to wear his uniform again. I shall claim that as my only reward.

GREGERS: So it is this business with the uniform that mostly –

HJALMAR: Yes, to be able to wear it again is what he dreams of and longs for. You have no idea how it cuts me to the quick to see him. Whenever we have a little family celebration here, like Gina's and my wedding anniversary or whatever it may be, then the old man appears in his lieutenant's uniform from happier days. But no sooner is there a knock on the door than he scuttles back to his own little room as fast as his old legs will carry him. He doesn't dare to show himself to strangers, you know. A sight like that lacerates a son's heart, Gregers!

GREGERS: About when do you think the invention will be ready?

HJALMAR: Heavens, you must not ask for details like that. An invention, you see, is something you don't altogether control yourself. It is very largely a matter of inspiration – a sudden idea – and it is next to impossible to tell beforehand when that may come.

GREGERS: But it is progressing?

HJALMAR: Certainly, it is progressing. It occupies my thoughts every day. It fills me. Every afternoon, after dinner, I shut myself up in the living room to ponder in peace. I just can't be hurried; it won't do any good. That is what Relling says, too.

GREGERS: And you don't think that all this business in the attic interferes too much, distracts you from your work?

HJALMAR: No, no, no. Quite the contrary. You must not say a thing like that. After all, I cannot everlastingly be pursuing the same exhausting train of thought. I need something else, something to occupy me during the waiting period. The inspiration, the sudden flash of insight, don't you see? – when it comes, it comes.

GREGERS: My dear Hjalmar, I almost think there is something of the wild duck in you.

HJALMAR: The wild duck? How do you mean?

GREGERS: You have plunged down through the sea and got yourself entangled in the grasses on the bottom.

HJALMAR: Are you perhaps referring to the well-nigh fatal shot that lodged in father's wing and hit me, too?

GREGERS: Not to that so much. I won't say you are crippled. But you are in a poisonous marsh, Hjalmar. You have contracted an insidious disease and gone to the bottom to die in the dark.

HJALMAR: I? Die in the dark? Honestly, Gregers. You really shouldn't say such things.

GREGERS: Don't you worry. I'll get you up again. For I, too, have got a mission in life. I found it yesterday.

HJALMAR: That may well be, but I shall ask you kindly to leave me out of it. I assure you that – aside from my easily explainable melancholia, of course – I am as contented a man as anybody could wish to be.

GREGERS: The fact that you are – that is one of the symptoms of the poisoning.

HJALMAR: No, really, Gregers. Please don't talk to me any more about disease and poison. I am not used to that sort of talk. In my house we never discuss unpleasant topics.

GREGERS: That I can well believe.

HJALMAR: No, for it isn't good for me. And there is no marshy air here, as you call it. The roof may be low in the poor photographer's home — I know very well it is — and my lot is lowly. But I am an inventor, and a provider as well. That is what raises me above my humble circumstances. — Ah! Here's lunch!

(GINA *and* HEDVIG *enter with bottles of beer, a decanter of brandy, glasses, and other appurtenances. At the same moment,* RELLING *and* MOLVIK *come through the entrance door. Neither one wears a hat or coat.* MOLVIK *is dressed in black.*)

GINA (*putting the things down on the table*): Well, you two arrive just in time.

RELLING: Molvik thought he could smell herring salad, and then there was no holding him. — Good morning again, Ekdal.

HJALMAR: Gregers, may I introduce you to Mr. Molvik — And Doctor — that's right, you two already know each other, don't you.

GREGERS: Slightly.

RELLING: Oh yes, young Mr. Werle. We used to do some skirmishing up at the Høydal works. I take it you have just moved in?

GREGERS: This morning.

RELLING: Well, Molvik and I live downstairs, so you don't have far to go for doctor and minister if you need them.

GREGERS: Thank you; maybe I shall. We were thirteen at the table yesterday.

HJALMAR: Come now! Please don't start any of that unpleasantness again!

RELLING: Calm down, Ekdal. You are immune.

HJALMAR: I hope so, for my family's sake. — Sit down. Let's eat, drink, and be merry.

GREGERS: Aren't we going to wait for your father?

HJALMAR: No, he'll eat later in his own room. Do sit down!

(*The men seat themselves and begin eating and drinking.* GINA *and* HEDVIG *wait on them.*)

RELLING: Molvik got pretty high last night, Mrs. Ekdal.

GINA: Again?

RELLING: Didn't you hear me bring him home?

GINA: Can't say I did.

RELLING: That's good, for Molvik was awful last night.

GINA: Is that true, Molvik?

MOLVIK: Let us consign last night's events to oblivion. They do not represent my better self.

RELLING (*to* GREGERS): It comes over him like an irresistible impulse. Then he has to go out and get drunk. You see, Molvik is demonic.

GREGERS: Demonic?

RELLING: That's right. Molvik is demonic.

GREGERS: H'm.

RELLING: And demonic natures aren't made to follow the straight and narrow path. They have to take off for the fields once in a while. — So you still stick it out up at that filthy old place?

GREGERS: So far.

RELLING: Did you ever collect on that claim you went around presenting?

GREGERS: Claim? (*Looks at him and understands.*) Oh I see.

HJALMAR: Have you been a bill collector, Gregers?

GREGERS: Oh nonsense.

RELLING: Oh yes, he has. He went around to all the cottages up there, trying to collect on something he called "the claim of the ideal."

GREGERS: I was young.

RELLING: You're right. You were very young. And the claim of the ideal — you never collected as long as I was up there.

GREGERS: Not since then, either.

RELLING: In that case, I suppose you have been wise enough to reduce the amount somewhat.

GREGERS: Never when I have to do with a real and genuine human being.

HJALMAR: I think that is reasonable enough. — Some butter, Gina.

RELLING: And a piece of bacon for Molvik.

MOLVIK: Ugh! Not bacon!

(*There is a knock from inside the door to the attic.*)

HJALMAR: Go and open, Hedvig. Father wants to get out.

(HEDVIG *opens the door a little.* OLD EKDAL *enters with the skin of a freshly flayed rabbit.* HEDVIG *closes the door after him.*)

EKDAL: Good morning, gentlemen! Good hunting today. Got me a big one.

HJALMAR: And you skinned it yourself, I see.

EKDAL: Salted it, too. It's nice, tender meat, rabbit is. It's sweet, y'know. Tastes like sugar. Good appetite, gentlemen! (*Goes into his room.*)

MOLVIK (*getting up*): Excuse me — I can't — Got to get downstairs —

RELLING: Drink soda water, you idiot!

MOLVIK: Uh — Uh — (*Hurries out, right rear.*)

RELLING (*to* HJALMAR): Let us drink to the old hunter.

HJALMAR (*touching* RELLING'*s glass with his own*): For the sportsman on the brink of the grave — yes.

RELLING: For the gray-haired — (*Drinks.*) Tell me, is his hair gray or is it white?

HJALMAR: In between, I think. Though I don't think there are many hairs left on his head at all.

RELLING: Oh well. One can live happily with a wig, too. Ah, yes, Ekdal. You are really a very happy man. You have this beautiful ambition of yours to strive for —

HJALMAR: Believe me, I am striving.

RELLING: Then you have your excellent wife, shuffling about in slippered feet with that comfortable waddle of hers, making things nice and pleasant for you.

HJALMAR: Yes, Gina — (*nods to her*) — you are a good companion on life's journey.

GINA: Aw, you don't need to sit there and dissectate me!

RELLING: And your Hedvig, Ekdal.

HJALMAR (*moved*): Ah yes, the child! The child above all. Hedvig, come to me. (*Stroking her hair.*) What day is tomorrow?

HEDVIG (*playfully shaking him*): Oh, stop it, father!

HJALMAR: It's like a knife through my heart, when I consider how little we can do. Just a small celebration here in the attic.

HEDVIG: But that's just the way I like it!

RELLING: You wait till the invention is all done, Hedvig.

HJALMAR: Yes! Then you'll see, Hedvig. I have decided to secure your future. You shall be made comfortable for as long as you live. I will ask for something for you, something or other. That will be the impecunious inventor's sole reward.

HEDVIG (*whispers, her arms around his neck*): Oh you good, sweet father!

RELLING (*to* GREGERS): Well, now, don't you think it's nice for a change to sit down to a good table in a happy family circle?

HJALMAR: Yes, I really relish these hours at the table.

GREGERS: I, for one, don't like to breathe marsh air.

RELLING: Marsh air?

HJALMAR: Oh, don't start all that again!

GINA: I'll have you know there is no marsh air here, Mr. Werle. The place is aired every single day.

GREGERS (*leaving the table*): The stench I have in mind you don't get rid of by opening windows.

HJALMAR: Stench!

GINA: Yes, how do you like that, Ekdal!

RELLING: Begging your pardon — it wouldn't by any chance be you yourself who brings the stench with you from the Høydal mines?

GREGERS: It's just like you to call stench what I bring to this house.

RELLING (*walks over to* GREGERS): Listen here, Mr. Werle junior. I strongly suspect that you still carry the claim of the ideal around in your rear pocket.

GREGERS: I carry it in my heart.

RELLING: I don't care where the hell you carry it as long as you don't go bill collecting here while *I* am around.

GREGERS: And if I do so, nevertheless?

RELLING: Then you'll go head first down the stairs. Now you know!

HJALMAR: No, really, Relling — !

GREGERS: Go ahead! Throw me out!

GINA (*interposing*): No, we won't have any of that, Relling. But I will say this to you, Mr. Werle, that it seems like you are not the right person to come here and talk about stench after what you did to the stove in your room this morning.

(*There is a knock on the door.*)

HEDVIG: Mother, someone's knocking.

HJALMAR: Oh yes, let's have customers on top of everything else — !

GINA: I'll handle it. (*Opens the door, gives a start, steps back*): Oh dear!

(WERLE, *in a fur coat, steps inside.*)

WERLE: I beg your pardon, but I am told my son is here.

GINA (*swallowing hard*): Yes sir.

HJALMAR (*closer*): Sir, wouldn't you like to — ?

WERLE: Thanks. I just want a word with my son.

GREGERS: Well. Here I am.

WERLE: I want to talk with you in your room.

GREGERS: In my room — ? Oh, all right. (*Is about to leave.*)

GINA: Good Lord, no! That's not a fit place!

WERLE: All right; out here in the hall, then. I want to see you alone.

HJALMAR: You may do that right here, Mr. Werle. Relling, come into the living room with me.

(HJALMAR *and* RELLING *go out, right front.* GINA *takes* HEDVIG *with her into the kitchen, left front.*)

GREGERS (*after a brief silence*): Well. We are alone.

WERLE: You dropped some hints last night. And since you have moved in with the Ekdals, I can only assume that you are planning something or other against me.

GREGERS: I plan to open Hjalmar Ekdal's eyes. He is to see his position as it really is. That's all.

WERLE: Is that the life mission you mentioned yesterday?

GREGERS: Yes. You have left me no other.

WERLE: So you feel it is I who have twisted your mind, Gregers?

GREGERS: You have twisted my whole life. I am not thinking of all that with mother. But it is you I can thank for the fact that I am being haunted and driven by a guilty conscience.

WERLE: Ah, I see. So your conscience is ailing.

GREGERS: I should have opposed you the time you were laying traps for Lieutenant Ekdal. I should have warned him, for I suspected how things were going.

WERLE: Yes, in that case you certainly ought to have said something.

GREGERS: I didn't have the courage. I was a coward – frightened. I felt an unspeakable fear of you – both then and for a long, long time afterwards.

WERLE: That fear appears to have left you now.

GREGERS: Yes, fortunately. What has been done to Old Ekdal, both by me and by – others, for that there is no remedy. But Hjalmar I can rescue from the web of lies and deceit in which he is suffocating.

WERLE: Do you think that is a good thing to do?

GREGERS: I am sure it is.

WERLE: I take it you think Mr. Photographer Ekdal is the kind of man who will be grateful for your friendly services?

GREGERS: Yes! He is that kind of man.

WERLE: H'm. We'll see.

GREGERS: Besides, if I am to continue living, I have to find a way to heal my sick conscience.

WERLE: It will never get well. Your conscience has been sickly from the time you were a child. It's hereditary, Gregers. You have it from your mother. The only inheritance she left you.

GREGERS (*with a contemptuous half smile*): I see you still haven't forgotten your disappointment when you found out mother wasn't rich.

WERLE: Let's not change the subject. Am I to think, then, that you are firmly resolved to guide Hjalmar Ekdal into the path you consider the right one?

GREGERS: Yes. That is my firm intent.

WERLE: In that case I could have saved myself coming all the way up here. For then I suppose there is no point in my asking you to move back home again?

GREGERS: No.

WERLE: And you don't want to join the firm?

GREGERS: No.

WERLE: Very well. But since I am to marry again, your part of the estate will have to be paid you.

GREGERS (*quickly*): No, I don't want that.

WERLE: You don't want it?

GREGERS: I dare not, for my conscience's sake.

WERLE (*after a brief pause*): Are you going back up to Høydal?

GREGERS: No. I consider myself released from your service.

WERLE: But what do you want to do with yourself?

GREGERS: Accomplish my mission. Nothing else.

WERLE: But afterwards? What are you going to live on?

GREGERS: I have saved some of my salary.

WERLE: How long do you think that will last?

GREGERS: I think it will do for the time I have left.

WERLE: What is that supposed to mean?
GREGERS: I won't answer any more questions.
WERLE: Well, goodbye, Gregers.
GREGERS: Goodbye.

(WERLE *leaves.*)

HJALMAR (*looks in*): Did he leave?
GREGERS: Yes.

(HJALMAR *and* RELLING *enter from the living room,* GINA *and* HEDVIG *from the kitchen.*)

RELLING: Now that was a very successful breakfast.
GREGERS: Put on your coat, Hjalmar. I want you to take a long walk with me.
HJALMAR: Gladly. What did your father want? Did it have to do with me?
GREGERS: Just come. We'll talk. I'll go and get my coat. (*Goes out.*)
GINA: You shouldn't go with him, Ekdal.
RELLING: No, don't. Stay here.
HJALMAR (*taking his hat and coat*): What! When an old friend feels the need to open his heart for me in private — !
RELLING: But goddamit! Can't you see that the fellow is mad, cracked, out of his head!
GINA: Yes, listen to Relling. His mother used to have physicological fits, too.
HJALMAR: All the more reason why he needs a friend's alert eyes. (*To* GINA.) Be sure to have dinner ready at the usual time. Goodbye. (*Goes out.*)
RELLING: It's nothing less than a disaster that that man didn't go straight to hell down one of the shafts up at Høydal.
GINA: Heavens — ! Why do you say that?
RELLING (*mutters*): I have my reasons.
GINA: Do you really think young Werle is crazy?
RELLING: No, unfortunately. He is no madder than most people. He is sick, though.
GINA: What do you think is wrong with him?
RELLING: That I can tell you, Mrs. Ekdal. He suffers from an acute attack of moral integrity.
GINA: Moral integrity?
HEDVIG: Is that a disease?
RELLING: Yes, it is a national disease, but it occurs only sporadically. (*Nods to* GINA.) That was a good meal, thank you. (*Goes out.*)
GINA (*troubled, walks up and down*): Ugh! That Gregers Werle — he's always been a weird fish.
HEDVIG (*by the table, looks at her searchingly*): I think all this is very strange.

## ACT IV

*The studio. Photographs have just been taken. A cloth-covered camera on a tripod, a couple of chairs, and a small table are standing about in the middle of the floor. Afternoon light. The sun is about to disappear. After a while darkness begins to fall.*

GINA *stands in the open entrance door with a small box and a wet glass plate in her hand. She is talking to someone not in sight.*

GINA: Absolutely. When I promise something, I keep it. I'll have the first dozen ready for you on Monday. – Goodbye.

(*Sounds of someone descending the stairs.* GINA *closes the door, puts the plate inside the box and the box into the camera.*)

HEDVIG (*enters from the kitchen*): Did they leave?
GINA (*putting things in order*): Yes, thank goodness. I finally got rid of them.
HEDVIG: Can you understand why father isn't back yet?
GINA: You're sure he is not down at Relling's?
HEDVIG: No, he is not there. I just went down the kitchen stairs to ask.
GINA: His food is getting cold and everything.
HEDVIG: Yes. And father who is always so particular about having dinner on time.
GINA: Oh well. You'll see he'll be back soon.
HEDVIG: I wish he'd come. Everything seems so strange.

(HJALMAR *enters from outside.*)

HEDVIG (*towards him*): Father! If you knew how we've been waiting for you!
GINA (*glancing at him*): You've been gone quite some time.
HJALMAR (*without looking at her*): Yes, I suppose I have.

(*He starts taking his coat off.* GINA *and* HEDVIG *both go to help him. He turns them away.*)

GINA: Maybe you and Werle had something to eat some place?
HJALMAR (*hanging up his coat*): No.
GINA (*towards the kitchen door*): I'll get your dinner.
HJALMAR: Never mind. I don't feel like eating now.
HEDVIG (*coming closer*): Are you sick, father?
HJALMAR: Sick? No, I'm not sick – exactly. We had a strenuous walk, Gregers and I.
GINA: You shouldn't do that, Ekdal. You aren't used to it.

HJALMAR: H'm. There are many things in life a man has to get used to. (*Paces up and down.*) Anybody here while I've been gone?

GINA: Only that engaged couple.

HJALMAR: No new appointments?

GINA: No, not today.

HEDVIG: There will be some tomorrow, father, I am sure.

HJALMAR: I hope you are right, for tomorrow I plan to go to work in earnest.

HEDVIG: Tomorrow! But don't you remember what day is tomorrow?

HJALMAR: That's right. Well, then, the day after tomorrow. From now on I'll do everything myself. I want to assume the entire work load.

GINA: Whatever for, Ekdal? That's only making yourself miserable. I'll manage the pictures. You just go on with the invention.

HEDVIG: And the wild duck, father. And the chickens and the rabbits and –

HJALMAR: Don't ever mention all that junk to me again! Starting tomorrow, I'll never more set foot in the attic.

HEDVIG: But father, you promised that tomorrow we're having a celebration –

HJALMAR: H'm. That's right. Day after tomorrow then. That damn wild duck. I'd like to wring its neck!

HEDVIG (*with a cry*): The wild duck!

GINA: Now I've heard everything!

HEDVIG (*shaking him*): But father – it's *my* wild duck!

HJALMAR: That's why I won't do it. I don't have the heart – for your sake, Hedvig. But deep down I feel I ought to do it. I shouldn't harbor under my roof a creature that has been in those hands.

GINA: For heaven's sake! Even if Grandpa *did* get it from that awful Pettersen.

HJALMAR (*walking up and down*): There are certain demands – what shall I call them? Let me say ideal demands – certain claims, that a man disregards only at the peril of his soul.

HEDVIG (*following after him*): But think – the wild duck! That poor wild duck!

HJALMAR (*halts*): Didn't I tell you I'll spare it – for your sake? Not a hair on its head will be – h'm. Well, as I said, I'll spare it. After all, there are bigger tasks awaiting me. But you ought to go out for a little walk, Hedvig. The twilight is just right for you.

HEDVIG: I don't care to go out now.

HJALMAR: Yes, do. Seems to me you are squinting. The fumes in here aren't good for you. The air is close under this roof.

HEDVIG: All right. I'll run down the kitchen stairs and walk around a bit. Where are my things? Oh yes, in my room. Father, please – don't do anything bad to the wild duck while I'm gone!

HJALMAR: Not a feather shall be plucked from its head. (*Clutches her to him.*) You and I, Hedvig – we two! Be on your way now.

(HEDVIG *nods goodbye to her parents and goes out through the kitchen door.*)

HJALMAR (*pacing back and forth*): Gina.

GINA: Yes?

HJALMAR: Starting tomorrow – or let's say the day after tomorrow – I'd like to keep account of the housekeeping expenses myself.

GINA: So you want to keep the accounts too?

HJALMAR: Keep track of what we take in, at any rate.

GINA: Lord knows, that's easily done!

HJALMAR: One wouldn't think so. It seems to me you make the money go incredibly far. (*Stops and looks at her.*) How do you do it?

GINA: It's because Hedvig and I need so little.

HJALMAR: Is it true that father is overpaid for the copying work he does for Werle?

GINA: I couldn't say about that. I don't know the rates.

HJALMAR: Well, what *does* he get? In round figures. – I want to know.

GINA: It differs. I guess it comes to about what he costs us, plus a little extra in spending money.

HJALMAR: What he costs us! And you haven't told me that!

GINA: No, I couldn't, for you were so happy because he got everything from you.

HJALMAR: And it has really been Werle all the time!

GINA: Oh well. He can afford it.

HJALMAR: Light the lamp!

GINA (*lighting the lamp*): And as far as that is concerned, how do we know it is Werle himself? It may be Gråberg –

HJALMAR: Really, Gina. You know that isn't so. Why do you say a thing like that?

GINA: I don't know. I just thought –

HJALMAR: H'm!

GINA: It wasn't me who got Grandpa all that copying to do. It was Bertha, when she took service there.

HJALMAR: It sounds to me like your voice is trembling.

GINA (*putting the shade on the lamp*): Does it?

HJALMAR: And your hands are shaking. Aren't they?

GINA (*firmly*): You might as well tell me straight, Ekdal. What has he been saying about me?

HJALMAR: Is it true – *can* it be true – that there was some kind of affair between you and Werle while you were in his house?

GINA: That's not so. Not then. He was after me, though. And Mrs. Werle thought there was something going on, and she made a fuss and a big hullaballoo about it, and she beat me and pulled me around – and so I quit.

HJALMAR: But afterwards – !

GINA: Well, then I went to live with mother. And you see – mother – she wasn't all the woman you thought she was, Ekdal. She talked to me about this, that, and the other. For Werle was a widower by that time –

HJALMAR: And then – ?

GINA: You might as well know it, I guess. He didn't give up till he had his way.

HJALMAR (*striking his hands together*): And this is the mother of my child! How could you keep a thing like this from me?

GINA: Yes, I know it was wrong. I should have told you long ago, I suppose.

HJALMAR: You should have told me right away; that's what you should have. Then I would have known what sort of woman you were.

GINA: But would you have married me, irregardless?

HJALMAR: Of course, I wouldn't!

GINA: I didn't think so, and that's why I didn't dare to tell you. I had come to care for you, you know – a whole lot I cared for you. And I just couldn't see making myself as unhappy as all that –

HJALMAR (*walking about*): And this is my Hedvig's mother! And to know that everything I lay my eyes on here (*kicks a chair*) – my whole home – I owe to a favored predecessor! Oh, that seducer, that damn Werle!

GINA: Do you regret the fourteen-fifteen years we've had together?

HJALMAR (*fronting her*): Tell me if you haven't felt every day and every hour to be one long agony of repentance for that web of deceitful silence you have woven around me, like a spider? Answer me! Haven't you lived here in perpetual torture of guilt and remorse?

GINA: Bless you, Ekdal! I've been plenty busy with the house and the pictures –

HJALMAR: So you never cast a probing glance at your past?

GINA: No, to tell the truth, I had almost forgotten all those old stories.

HJALMAR: Oh, this dull, apathetic calm! There is something shocking about it. Not even repentant – !

GINA: Just tell me this, Ekdal. What do you think would have become of you if you hadn't got yourself a wife like me?

HJALMAR: Like you – !

GINA: Yes, for you know I have always been more practical and able to cope with things than you. Of course, I am a couple of years older –

HJALMAR: What would have become of me!

GINA: For you've got to admit you weren't living exactly right when you first met me.

HJALMAR: So you call that living wrong! Oh, what do you know about a man's feelings when he sorrows and despairs – especially a man of my fiery temperament.

GINA: No, I guess I don't know. And I don't mean to execrete you for it, either, for you turned into as decent a man as they come as soon as you got a house and a family of your own to take care of. And now we were getting on so nicely here, and Hedvig and I were just thinking that pretty soon we might spend some money on clothes for ourselves.

HJALMAR: Yes, in the swamp of deceit!

GINA: That that fellow ever poked his nose inside here!

HJALMAR: I, too, thought our home a pleasant one. That was a mistake. Where now do I gather the necessary inner resilience to bring my invention into the world of reality? Perhaps it will die with me. If it does, it will be your past, Gina, that has killed it.

GINA (*on the verge of tears*): Please, Ekdal — don't be saying such things! I that have all my days only tried to make things nice and pleasant for you!

HJALMAR: I ask — what happens now to the breadwinner's dream? As I reclined in there on the sofa, pondering the invention, it came to me that it was going to drain me of my last drop of vitality. I knew that the day the patent was issued and in my hands — that day would be my — my day of farewell. And then it was my dream that you were to live on as the late inventor's well-to-do widow.

GINA (*wiping her tears*): I won't have you talk that way, Ekdal. May the good Lord never let me live the day when I'm your widow!

HJALMAR: Oh what difference does it all make! It is all over now, anyway. Everything!

(GREGERS *cautiously opens the entrance door and peers in.*)

GREGERS: May I come in?

HJALMAR: Yes, do.

GREGERS (*goes up to them with a beaming, happy face, reaches out his hands to them*): Now, then — you dear people — ! (*Looks from one to the other, whispers to* HJALMAR.) It hasn't happened yet?

HJALMAR (*loud*): It has happened.

GREGERS: It has?

HJALMAR: I have lived through the bitterest moment of my life.

GREGERS: But also, I trust, its most exalted one.

HJALMAR: Anyway, it's done and over with.

GINA: May God forgive you, Mr. Werle.

GREGERS (*greatly bewildered*): But I don't understand — !

HJALMAR: What don't you understand?

GREGERS: As crucial a conversation as this — a conversation that is to be the foundation for a whole new way of life — a life, a partnership, in truth and frankness —

HJALMAR: I know. I know it very well.

GREGERS: I was so sure that when I came in here now I would be met with a splendor of revelation shining from both husband and wife. But all I see is this dull, heavy gloom –

GINA: So that's it. (*Removes the lamp shade.*)

GREGERS: You refuse to understand me, Mrs. Ekdal. Well, I suppose you need time. But you, Hjalmar? Surely, you must have felt a higher consecration in this great crisis.

HJALMAR: Of course I did. That is, in a way.

GREGERS: For surely nothing in the world can be compared to finding forgiveness in your heart for one who has erred and lovingly lifting her up to your own heights.

HJALMAR: Do you think a man so easily forgets the draught of wormwood I just drained?

GREGERS: An ordinary man, maybe not. But a man like you – !

HJALMAR: Oh, I know. But you must not rush me, Gregers. It takes time.

GREGERS: There is much of the wild duck in you, Hjalmar.

(RELLING *has entered.*)

RELLING: Ah! Here we go with the wild duck again!

HJALMAR: Mr. Werle's crippled prey – yes.

RELLING: Werle? Is it him you're talking about?

HJALMAR: About him – and about ourselves.

RELLING (*in a low voice, to* GREGERS): Damn you to hell!

HJALMAR: What are you saying?

RELLING: I am just expressing an ardent wish that this quack here would betake himself home. If he stays around he is likely to ruin both of you.

GREGERS: Those two cannot be ruined, Mr. Relling. Of Hjalmar I need say nothing. Him we know. But she, too, has surely in the depths of her being something reliable, something of integrity –

GINA (*almost crying*): Why didn't you leave me alone then?

RELLING (*to* GREGERS): Is it impertinent to ask exactly what you want in this house?

GREGERS: I want to lay the foundation for a true marriage.

RELLING: So you don't think the Ekdals' marriage is good enough as it is?

GREGERS: I daresay it is as good a marriage as most, unfortunately. But a true marriage it has yet to become.

HJALMAR: You have never had an eye for the claim of the ideal, Relling!

RELLING: Nonsense, boy! – Begging your pardon, Mr. Werle – how many – roughly – how many true marriages have you observed in your life?

GREGERS: Hardly a single one.

RELLING: Nor have I.

GREGERS: But I have seen a number of the other kind. And I have had occasion to witness what havoc a marriage like that can work in a pair of human beings.

HJALMAR: A man's whole moral foundation may crumble under his feet; that's the terrible thing.

RELLING: Well, I can't say I've ever been exactly married, so I can't judge about that. But I do know this, that the child belongs to marriage too. And you had better leave the child alone.

HJALMAR: Oh, Hedvig! My poor Hedvig!

RELLING: Yes — keep Hedvig out of it, you two! You are grown-ups. In God's name, do whatever fool things you like to your marriage. But I am warning you: be careful what you do to Hedvig. If you're not, there is no telling what may happen to her.

HJALMAR: Happen to her!

RELLING: Yes, she may bring a disaster upon herself — and perhaps on others, too.

GINA: But how can you tell about that, Relling?

HJALMAR: Are you saying there is some immediate danger to her eyes?

RELLING: This has nothing whatever to do with her eyes. Hedvig is in a difficult age. She may do all sorts of crazy things.

GINA: I know — she does already. She's taken to fooling around with the woodstove in the kitchen. Playing fire, she calls it. Sometimes I'm scared she'll burn the whole house down.

RELLING: There you are. I knew it.

GREGERS (*to* RELLING): But how do you explain a thing like that?

RELLING (*sullenly*): Her voice is changing, sir.

HJALMAR: As long as the child has *me* — ! As long as *my* head is above the ground!

(*There is a knock on the door.*)

GINA: Shhh, Ekdal. There are people outside.

(MRS. SØRBY *enters, wearing hat and coat.*)

MRS. SØRBY: Good evening!

GINA (*going to her*): Goodness! Is it you, Bertha!

MRS. SØRBY: So it is. Maybe it's inconvenient — ?

HJALMAR: Oh by no means! A messenger from *that* house — !

MRS. SØRBY (*to* GINA): Frankly, I had hoped you'd be without your menfolks this time of day. I've just dropped in to have a word with you about something and say goodbye.

GINA: You're going away?

MRS. SØRBY: Tomorrow morning — to Høydal. Mr. Werle left this afternoon. (*Casually, to* GREGERS.) He asked me to say hello.

GINA: Imagine — !

HJALMAR: So Mr. Werle has left? And you are going after him?

MRS. SØRBY: Yes. What do you say to that, Ekdal?

HJALMAR: Look out, is all I say.

GREGERS: I can explain. Father and Mrs. Sørby are getting married.

GINA: Oh Bertha! At long last!

RELLING (*his voice trembling a little*): Surely, this cannot be true?

MRS. SØRBY: Yes, my dear Relling, true it is.

RELLING: You want to get married again?

MRS. SØRBY: That's what it amounts to. Werle has got the license. We'll have a quiet little party up at the works.

GREGERS: I suppose I should tender my felicitations like a good stepson.

MRS. SØRBY: Thank you, if you really mean it. I hope this will be for the best for both Werle and myself.

RELLING: I am sure you have every reason to think it will. Mr. Werle never gets drunk – at least not to my knowledge. Nor do I believe he is in the habit of beating up his wife, like the late lamented horse doctor.

MRS. SØRBY: Let Sørby rest quietly in his grave. He had his good sides, too.

RELLING: Mr. Industrialist Werle has better ones, I am sure.

MRS. SØRBY: At least he has not thrown away what is best in himself. The man who does that must take the consequences.

RELLING: Tonight I'll go out with Molvik.

MRS. SØRBY: Don't do that, Relling. Don't – for my sake.

RELLING: There's nothing else to do. (*To* HJALMAR.) Want to come along?

GINA: No, thank you. Ekdal doesn't go in for excapades like that.

HJALMAR (*angrily, in a half whisper*): For heaven's sake! Keep your mouth shut!

RELLING: Goodbye – Mrs. Werle! (*Goes out.*)

GREGERS (*to* MRS. SØRBY): It appears that you and Doctor Relling know each other quite well?

MRS. SØRBY: Yes, we've known each other for a good many years. At one time it looked as if we might have made a match of it.

GREGERS: I'm sure it was lucky for you that you didn't.

MRS. SØRBY: You may well say that. But I've always been wary of acting on impulse. A woman can't just throw herself away, you know.

GREGERS: Aren't you afraid I'll let my father know about this old acquaintanceship?

MRS. SØRBY: Do you really believe I haven't told him myself?

GREGERS: Oh?

MRS. SØRBY: Your father knows every little thing people might say about me with any show of truth at all. I have told him everything. That was the first thing I did when I realized what his intentions were.

GREGERS: It seems to me you are more than usually frank.

MRS. SØRBY: I have always been frank. For us women that's the best policy.

HJALMAR: What do you say to that, Gina?

GINA: Oh, women differ. Some do it one way, others do it different.

MRS. SØRBY: Well, Gina, in my opinion my way is best. And Werle hasn't kept back anything either. You see, that's what mainly brought us together. Now he can sit and talk to me as openly as a child. He has never been able to do that before. A healthy, vigorous man like him – all through his youth and all the best years of his life he had his ears drummed full with angry sermons. And very often sermons about sins he hadn't even committed – according to what I have been told.

GINA: That's the truth.

GREGERS: If you ladies want to pursue that topic any further, I had better absent myself.

MRS. SØRBY: You may just as well stay as far as that's concerned. I won't say another word. I just wanted you to know I haven't kept anything back or played him false in any way. Maybe people will say I am a very fortunate woman, and in a way of course that's true. But I don't think I am getting any more than I am giving. I'll certainly never desert him. And I can be of more service and use to him than anybody else, now that he'll soon be helpless.

HJALMAR: Will he be helpless?

GREGERS (*to* MRS. SØRBY): Don't say anything about that here.

MRS. SØRBY: It can't be kept secret any longer, much as he'd like to. He is going blind.

HJALMAR (*struck*): Blind? That's strange. He, too?

GINA: Lots of people go blind.

MRS. SØRBY: And I'm sure you can tell yourself what that must mean to a businessman. Well, I'll try to be his eyes, the best I know how. – But I can't stay any longer. There's such a lot of things I've got to do. – Oh yes, what I wanted to tell you, Ekdal, is that if Werle can be of any service to you, all you need to do is to get in touch with Gråberg.

GREGERS: That is an offer I am sure Hjalmar Ekdal will decline.

MRS. SØRBY: Really? It seems to me he hasn't always been so –

GINA: Yes, Bertha. Ekdal won't need any more help from Mr. Werle.

HJALMAR (*slowly, with weight*): Tell your husband-to-be from me, that in the very near future I intend to go to Mr. Gråberg –

GREGERS: What! You can't mean that!

HJALMAR: – I say, go to Mr. Gråberg, and demand an account of the sum I owe his employer. I desire to pay this debt of honor – ha-ha-ha! – let us call it a debt of honor! Enough! I shall pay it all, with five per cent interest.

GINA: But Ekdal – goodness! We don't have that kind of money!

HJALMAR: Be so good as to inform your fiancé that I am working incessantly on my invention. Please tell him that what sustains my mind during this exhausting enterprise is my ambition to free myself from a painful burden of debt. This is why I am an inventor. The entire proceeds from my invention are to be devoted to liberating myself from the obligation to remunerate your husband-to-be for his expenses on behalf of my family.

MRS. SØRBY: Something has happened here.

HJALMAR: Indeed, something has.

MRS. SØRBY: Well, goodbye. I had something else I wanted to talk to you about, Gina, but that will have to wait till some other time. Goodbye.

(HJALMAR *and* GREGERS *return her greeting silently.* GINA *sees her to the door.*)

HJALMAR: Not beyond the threshold, Gina!

(MRS. SØRBY *leaves.* GINA *closes the door.*)

HJALMAR: There, now, Gregers. I have that burdensome debt off my chest.
GREGERS: You soon will, at any rate.
HJALMAR: I believe my attitude must be deemed the proper one.
GREGERS: You are the man I have always taken you to be.
HJALMAR: In certain cases it is impossible to disregard the claims of the ideal. As provider for my family, I am bound, of course, to find my course of action difficult and painful. Believe me, it is no joke for a man situated as I am, without means, to assume a debt of many years' standing — a debt, you might say, covered by the sands of oblivion. But never mind. The man in me demands his rights.
GREGERS (*placing his hand on his shoulder*): Dear Hjalmar — wasn't it a good thing that I came?
HJALMAR: Yes.
GREGERS: That your whole situation was made clear to you — wasn't that a good thing?
HJALMAR (*a bit impatiently*): Of course it was. But there is one thing that shocks my sense of justice.
GREGERS: What is that?
HJALMAR: It is this that — But I don't know that I ought to speak so freely about your father —
GREGERS: Don't let that worry you. Say what you want.
HJALMAR: All right. Well, you see, there is something shocking in the notion that now it's he and not I who realizes the true marriage.
GREGERS: How can you say a thing like that!
HJALMAR: Well, it is. For your father and Mrs. Sørby are about to solemnify a union built on full mutual confidence, on complete, unconditional frankness on both sides. They conceal nothing from each other, there are no deceitful silences, there has been declared, if I may put it so, mutual absolution between them.
GREGERS: Well, what of it?
HJALMAR: Well, then — it's all there! All the difficult conditions you yourself said are prerequisites for the building of a true marriage.
GREGERS: But that's in quite a different way, Hjalmar. Surely, you won't compare either yourself or Gina with those two — ? Oh I am sure you know what I mean.

HJALMAR: Yet I can't get away from the thought that in all this there is something that offends my sense of justice. It looks exactly as if there were no just order in the universe.

GINA: Ekdal, for God's sake, don't talk like that!

GREGERS: H'm. Let's not get involved in those issues.

HJALMAR: Though, on the other hand, I do in a way discern fate's ruling finger, too. He is going blind.

GINA: We don't know that yet.

HJALMAR: There is no doubt about it. At least, we ought not to doubt it, for in that very fact lies the proof of just retribution. He did once hoodwink a trusting fellow being.

GREGERS: I am afraid he has hoodwinked many.

HJALMAR: And here comes the inexorable, the inscrutable, claiming Werle's own eyes.

GINA: How you talk! I think it's scary.

HJALMAR: It is salutary at times to contemplate the night side of existence.

(HEDVIG, *dressed for the outside, enters. She is happy, breathless.*)

GINA: Back so soon?

HEDVIG: Yes. I didn't feel like walking any farther. It was a good thing, too, for I met somebody as I was coming in.

HJALMAR: Mrs. Sørby, I suppose.

HEDVIG: Yes.

HJALMAR (*pacing the floor*): I hope you have seen her for the last time.

(*Silence.* HEDVIG, *troubled, looks from one to the other in order to gauge their mood.*)

HEDVIG (*approaching* HJALMAR, *ingratiatingly*): Father?

HJALMAR: All right – what is it, Hedvig?

HEDVIG: Mrs. Sørby had something for me.

HJALMAR (*halts*): For you?

HEDVIG: Yes. Something for tomorrow.

GINA: Bertha always brings you a little something for your birthday.

HJALMAR: What is it?

HEDVIG: No, you're not to find out now. Mother is to give it to me in the morning, when she brings me breakfast in bed.

HJALMAR: What is all this mystification? Why am I to be kept in the dark?

HEDVIG (*quickly*): I'll be glad to let you see it, father. It's a big letter. (*Takes the letter out of her coat pocket.*)

HJALMAR: A letter too?

HEDVIG: The letter is all there is. I suppose the other thing will come later. Just think – a letter! I never got a letter before. And it says "Miss" on the envelope. (*Reads.*) "Miss Hedvig Ekdal." Just think – that's me!

HJALMAR: Let me see that letter.

HEDVIG: Here you are. (*Hands it to him.*)

HJALMAR: It's Werle's handwriting.

GINA: Are you sure, Ekdal?

HJALMAR: See for yourself.

GINA: How would I know?

HJALMAR: Hedvig, may I open the letter? Read it?

HEDVIG: If you like.

GINA: Not tonight, Ekdal. It's supposed to be for tomorrow.

HEDVIG (*in a low voice*): Please let him read it! It's bound to be something good, and then father will be in a good mood, and everything will be nice again.

HJALMAR: You say I may open it?

HEDVIG: Yes, please, father. I'd like to know what it is about, too.

HJALMAR: Good. (*Opens the envelope, reads the letter inside. Appears confused.*) What *is* this — ?

GINA: What does it say?

HEDVIG: Please, father — tell us!

HJALMAR: Be quiet. (*Reads the letter again. He is pale, but his voice is controlled.*) It is a gift letter, Hedvig.

HEDVIG: Imagine! What is it I get?

HJALMAR: Read for yourself.

(HEDVIG *goes over to the lamp and reads.*)

HJALMAR (*in a low voice, clenches his fists*): The eyes, the eyes! And now that letter!

HEDVIG (*interrupting her reading*): Seems to me like it's Grandpa who gets it.

HJALMAR (*taking the letter away from her*): You, Gina — can you make any sense out of this?

GINA: I don't know a blessed thing about it. Why don't you just tell me?

HJALMAR: Werle writes to Hedvig that her old grandfather no longer needs to trouble himself with the copying work he has been doing, but that he may go to the office every month and draw one hundred crowns —

GREGERS: Aha!

HEDVIG: One hundred crowns, mother! I read that.

GINA: That will be nice for Grandpa.

HJALMAR: — one hundred crowns for as long as he needs it. That means, of course, till he closes his eyes.

GINA: So *he* is all taken care of, poor soul.

HJALMAR: Then it comes. You can't have read that far, Hedvig. After his death, that money will be yours.

HEDVIG: Mine? All of it?

HJALMAR: He writes that the same amount has been set aside for you for the rest of your life. Are you listening, Gina?

GINA: Yes, I hear.

HEDVIG: Just think — all the money I'll be getting! (*Shaking* HJALMAR'*s arm.*) Father! Father! But aren't you glad?

HJALMAR (*going away from her*): Glad! (*Walking about.*) Oh what vistas, what perspectives, open up before me! It is Hedvig he is so generous to!

GINA: Well, she's the one with the birthday.

HEDVIG: And of course you will get it anyway, father! Don't you know I'll give it all to you and mother?

HJALMAR: To mother, yes! That's just it!

GREGERS: Hjalmar, this is a trap being prepared for you.

HJALMAR: You think this may be another trap?

GREGERS: When he was here this morning, he said, "Hjalmar Ekdal is not the man you think he is."

HJALMAR: Not the man — !

GREGERS: "You just wait and see," he said.

HJALMAR: You were to see me selling myself for money — !

HEDVIG: Mother, what *is* all this?

GINA: Go out and take your wraps off.

(HEDVIG, *almost crying, goes out into the kitchen.*)

GREGERS: Well, Hjalmar — now we shall see who is right — he or I.

HJALMAR (*slowly tearing the letter in two, putting the pieces down on the table*): Here is my answer.

GREGERS: Just as I thought.

HJALMAR (*to* GINA, *who is standing near the stove; in a low voice*): No more concealment now. If everything was over between you and him when you — came to care for me, as you call it, then why did he make it possible for us to get married?

GINA: I guess he thought he'd make free of the house.

HJALMAR: Just that? He wasn't worried about a certain possibility?

GINA: I don't know what you're talking about.

HJALMAR: I want to know — if your child has the right to live under my roof.

GINA (*drawing herself up, her eyes flashing*): You ask me that!

HJALMAR: Just tell me one thing. Is Hedvig mine or — ? — Well?

GINA (*looks at him with cold defiance*): I don't know.

HJALMAR (*with a slight tremble*): You don't know!

GINA: How can I? A woman like me!

HJALMAR (*quietly, turning away from her*): In that case I have nothing more to do in this house.

GREGERS: Think it over, Hjalmar!

HJALMAR (*putting his overcoat on*): For a man like me there is nothing to think over.

GREGERS: Yes, there is ever so much to think over. You three must stay together if you are to attain to the sacrificial spirit of sublime forgivingness.

HJALMAR: I don't want that! Never! Never! My hat! (*Takes his hat.*) My house is in ruins about me! (*Bursts out crying.*) Gregers! I have no child!

HEDVIG (*who has opened the kitchen door*): Father! What are you saying!

GINA: Oh dear!

HJALMAR: Don't come near me, Hedvig! Go far away from me. I can't stand looking at you. Oh those eyes — ! Goodbye. (*Is about to go out.*)

HEDVIG (*clings to him, cries*): No! No! Don't leave me!

GINA: Look at the child, Ekdal! Look at the child!

HJALMAR: I will not! I cannot! I must get out — away from all this! (*He tears himself loose from* HEDVIG *and exits.*)

HEDVIG (*her eyes desperate*): He's leaving us, mother! He's leaving us! He'll never come back!

GINA: Just don't cry, Hedvig. Father will be back. You wait.

HEDVIG (*throws herself sobbing down on the sofa*): No! No! He'll never come back to us any more!

GREGERS: Do you believe I meant all for the best, Mrs. Ekdal?

GINA: Yes, I suppose you did, but God forgive you all the same.

HEDVIG (*on the sofa*): I want to die! What have I done to him, mother? You just have to get him back again!

GINA: Yes, yes, yes; only be quiet. I'll go out and look for him. (*Putting on her coat.*) Perhaps he's gone down to Relling's. But you're not to lie there, bawling like that. Promise?

HEDVIG (*sobbing convulsively*): All right, I'll stop, if only father comes home again.

GREGERS (*to* GINA, *who is leaving*): But would it not be better to let him fight his agony through by himself?

GINA: He can do that afterwards. First we've got to get the child quieted down. (*Goes out.*)

HEDVIG (*sitting up, drying her eyes*): Now you have to tell me what this is all about. Why doesn't father want me any more?

GREGERS: You must not ask that till you're big and grown-up.

HEDVIG (*sobbing*): But I just can't stay as miserable as this all the time till I'm grown up. — But I know what it is. Maybe I'm not really father's child.

GREGERS (*uneasily*): How could that be?

HEDVIG: Mother might have found me. And now perhaps father has found out about it. I have read about things like that.

GREGERS: Well, if it really were so —

HEDVIG: I think he could love me just as much, regardless. More, almost. The wild duck is a gift, too, and I love her very, very much.

GREGERS (*glad to turn the conversation*): Oh yes, the wild duck. Let's talk about the wild duck, Hedvig.

HEDVIG: That poor wild duck. He can't stand the sight of her, either. Just think, he wants to wring her neck!

GREGERS: Oh, I don't think he'll do that.

HEDVIG: No, but he said it. And I think that was horrid of father, for I pray for the wild duck every night, that she may be kept safe from death and all that's evil.

GREGERS (*looks at her*): Do you usually say prayers at night?

HEDVIG: Yes, I do.

GREGERS: Who taught you that?

HEDVIG: Myself, for father was terribly sick once and had leeches on his neck, and then he said that death was his dread companion.

GREGERS: And — ?

HEDVIG: So I prayed for him when I went to bed. And I have done so ever since.

GREGERS: And now you pray for the wild duck, too?

HEDVIG: I thought it was best to mention her as well, for she was so sickly when we first got her.

GREGERS: Do you say morning prayers, too?

HEDVIG: Of course not.

GREGERS: Why is that so of course?

HEDVIG: Because it's light in the morning. There's not so much to be afraid of then.

GREGERS: And the wild duck you love so much — your father said he'd like to wring her neck?

HEDVIG: No, he said it would be better for him if he did, but he was going to spare her for my sake. And that was good of him.

GREGERS (*closer to her*): How would it be if you decided to sacrifice the wild duck for *his* sake?

HEDVIG (*getting up*): The wild duck!

GREGERS: What if you willingly gave up the dearest thing in the whole world for him?

HEDVIG: Do you think that would help?

GREGERS: Try it, Hedvig.

HEDVIG (*softly, with shining eyes*): Yes. I want to.

GREGERS: Do you think you have the right kind of strength?

HEDVIG: I shall ask Grandpa to shoot the wild duck for me.

GREGERS: Yes, do that. But not a word to your mother about this!

HEDVIG: Why not?

GREGERS: She doesn't understand us.

HEDVIG: The wild duck? I'll try it in the morning!

(GINA *enters from the hall.*)

HEDVIG (*towards her*): Did you find him, mother?

GINA: No, but I found out he's got Relling with him.

GREGERS: Are you sure?

GINA: Yes, the janitor's wife said so. Molvik's with them also.

GREGERS: Just now, when his soul so sorely needs to struggle in solitude — !

GINA (*taking off her coat*): Yes, men are funny. God knows where Relling is taking him! I ran over to Madam Eriksen's, but they aren't there.

HEDVIG (*struggling with her tears*): What if he never comes back!

GREGERS: He'll come back. I'll get word to him tomorrow, and then you'll see *how* he comes back. You count on that, Hedvig, and get a good night's sleep. Goodnight. (*Goes out.*)

HEDVIG (*throws herself sobbing on* GINA'*s neck*): Mother! Mother!

GINA (*patting her back, sighing*): Yes, Relling was right. This is what happens when crazy people come around pestering us with the claim of the ordeal.

## ACT V

*The studio. Cold, gray morning light. There is wet snow on the big panes of the skylight.*

GINA, *aproned, with broom and dust cloth in her hand, enters from the kitchen and goes towards the living room door.* HEDVIG *hurries in from the outside at the same moment.*

GINA (*stops*): Well?

HEDVIG: Yes, mother, I almost think he's down at Relling's —

GINA: What did I tell you!

HEDVIG: — for the janitor's wife said she heard Relling bring two others home with him last night.

GINA: I knew it.

HEDVIG: But what good does it do, if he doesn't come up here to us?

GINA: I want to go down and have a talk with him, anyway.

(OLD EKDAL, *in dressing gown and slippers and with his lighted pipe, appears in the door to his room.*)

EKDAL: Eh — Hjalmar — ? Isn't Hjalmar here?

GINA: No, he is out, Grandpa.

EKDAL: So early? In this blizzard? Well, I can walk by myself in the morning, I can, if it comes to that.

(*He slides the attic door open.* HEDVIG *helps him. He enters. She closes the door behind him.*)

HEDVIG (*in a low voice*): Mother, what do you think will happen when poor Grandpa hears that father has left us?

GINA: Silly! Grandpa mustn't hear anything about it, of course. It was a good thing he wasn't home last night, during all that hullaballoo.

HEDVIG: Yes, but —

(GREGERS *enters.*)

GREGERS: Well? Have you traced him yet?
GINA: They say he's down at Relling's.
GREGERS: At Relling's! Has he really been out with those two?
GINA: It looks like it.
GREGERS: But he is so badly in need of solitude — to find himself in earnest —
GINA: Yes. I should think so, too.

(RELLING *enters.*)

HEDVIG (*goes towards him*): Is father with you?
GINA (*at the same time*): Is he down there?
RELLING: He certainly is.
HEDVIG: And you haven't told us!
RELLING: I know. I'm a big, bad beast. But I had this other big, bad beast to take care of, too — I mean the demonic one. And after that, I just fell asleep — sound asleep —
GINA: What does Ekdal say today?
RELLING: Not a thing.
HEDVIG: Doesn't he say anything at all?
RELLING: Not a blessed word.
GREGERS: I think I understand that.
GINA: But what's he doing?
RELLING: He is on the sofa, snoring.
GINA: Oh? Yes, Ekdal sure snores a lot.
HEDVIG: He's asleep? Can he sleep now?
RELLING: It certainly looks that way.
GREGERS: That's reasonable enough, after the spiritual turmoil he's just been through —
GINA: And he isn't used to be out revelling nights, either.
HEDVIG: It may be a good thing that he's sleeping, mother.
GINA: That's what I am thinking. Anyway, we'd better not wake him up too soon. Thank you, Relling. First of all I've got to clean things up a bit and make the place look nice. Come and help me, Hedvig. (*They go into the living room.*)
GREGERS (*turning to* RELLING): Can you account for the present spiritual unrest in Hjalmar Ekdal?
RELLING: To tell you the truth, I haven't noticed any spiritual unrest in him.
GREGERS: What? At such a turning point — When his whole life is acquiring a new basis? How can you think that a personality like Hjalmar Ekdal — ?

RELLING: Personality? He? If he ever had any tendency to sprout the kind of abnormal growth you call personality, I can assure you that all roots and tendrils were thoroughly extirpated in his boyhood.

GREGERS: That would indeed be strange, considering the loving upbringing he enjoyed.

RELLING: By those two crackpot, hysterical spinster aunts of his, you mean?

GREGERS: Let me tell you that they were women who never forgot the claim of the ideal – though I suppose you'll just be making fun of me again.

RELLING: No, I'm not in the mood. I do know about them, though. He has often enough held forth about "his soul's two mothers." Personally, I don't think he has much to be grateful to them for. Ekdal's misfortune is that he has always been looked upon as a shining light in his own circle.

GREGERS: And you don't think he is that? I mean, when it comes to depth of soul?

RELLING: I have never noticed it. That his father thought so is one thing. The old lieutenant has been an idiot all his days.

GREGERS: He has all his days been a man with a childlike mind. That is what you don't understand.

RELLING: All right. But after our dear, sweet Hjalmar had taken up studying – after a fashion – right away he was the light of the future among his friends, too. He was handsome enough, the rascal – red and white, just the way little shop-girls like the fellows. And he had this sentimental temperament and this warm-hearted voice, and he could give such pretty declamations of other people's poetry and other people's thoughts –

GREGERS (*indignantly*): Is this Hjalmar Ekdal you are describing?

RELLING: Yes, if you please. For this is what he looks like on the inside, the idol you are prostrating yourself for.

GREGERS: I didn't know I was as blind as all that.

RELLING: Well – not far from it. For you are sick, too, you see.

GREGERS: That is true.

RELLING: Yes it is. And yours is a complicated case. First, there is this pesky integrity fever you're suffering from, and then something worse – you are forever walking around in a delirium of adoration, always looking for something to admire outside of yourself.

GREGERS: Yes, there certainly wouldn't be much point in looking for it within myself.

RELLING: But you are always so hideously wrong about all those big, wonderful flies you see and hear buzzing around you. Once again you have entered a cottage with your claim of the ideal. People here just can't pay.

GREGERS: If this is the way you think of Hjalmar Ekdal, what sort of pleasure can you derive from your constant association with him?

RELLING: Oh well. I am supposed to be a kind of doctor, believe it or not, so the least I can do is to look after the poor patients I share quarters with.

GREGERS: Ah, I see. Hjalmar Ekdal is sick, too?

RELLING: Most people are, worse luck.

GREGERS: And what treatment do you apply in Hjalmar's case?

RELLING: My usual one. I see to it that his vital lie is kept up.

GREGERS: Vital – lie? I'm not sure I heard what you said.

RELLING: That's right. I said the vital lie. You see, that's the stimulating principle.

GREGERS: May I ask with what vital lie you have infected Hjalmar?

RELLING: You may not. I never reveal professional secrets to quacks. You are capable of messing him up for me even more than you have. But the method is proven. I have used it with Molvik, too. I have made him demonic. That's the suppurative I have applied to *his* neck.

GREGERS: But *isn't* he demonic?

RELLING: What the hell does it mean – being demonic? It's just some nonsense I thought of to save his life. If I hadn't, the poor, pitiful swine would have succumbed to self-hatred and despair many a year ago. Not to mention the old lieutenant! Though he has found his own cure.

GREGERS: Lieutenant Ekdal? What about him?

RELLING: What do you think? There he is, the old slayer of bears, chasing rabbits in a dark attic. And yet, there isn't a happier hunter alive than that old man when he is playing with all that junk. The four or five dried-out Christmas trees he has saved are the whole big, wild Høydal forest to him. The rooster and the chickens are wild fowl in the tree tops, and the rabbits bouncing about on the floor are bears he's grappling with – the frisky old sportsman.

GREGERS: Ah, yes – that unfortunate old Lieutenant Ekdal. He has certainly had to compromise the ideals of his youth.

RELLING: While I think of it, Mr. Werle – don't use the foreign word "ideals." We have available a good native one: "lies."

GREGERS: You think the two things are related?

RELLING: About as closely as typhus and putrid fever.

GREGERS: Doctor Relling! I won't give up till I have rescued Hjalmar from your clutches!

RELLING: That might be his bad luck. Take his vital lie away from the average person, and you take his happiness, too. (*To* HEDVIG, *who enters from the living room.*) Well, now, little duck mother. I am going down to see if papa is still in bed pondering that wonderful invention of his. (*Goes out.*)

GREGERS (*approaching* HEDVIG): I can tell from looking at you that it has not yet been accomplished.

HEDVIG: What? Oh, that about the wild duck? No.

GREGERS: Your strength of purpose deserted you, I suppose, when the time for action had come.

HEDVIG: No, it wasn't that. But when I woke up this morning and remembered what we had talked about, it all seemed so strange.

GREGERS: Strange?

HEDVIG: Yes, I don't know — Last night, just at the time — I thought there was something very wonderful about it, but when I had slept and I thought about it again, it didn't seem like anything much.

GREGERS: I see. I could hardly expect you to grow up in this environment without injury to your soul.

HEDVIG: I don't care about that, if only father would come home again.

GREGERS: If only your eyes were opened to what gives life its worth — if only you possessed the true, joyful, brave, sacrificial spirit, then you'd see he'll return. But I still have faith in you, Hedvig. (*Goes out.*)

(HEDVIG *walks around aimlessly. She is about to enter the kitchen, when there is a knock on the inside of the door to the attic.* HEDVIG *opens the doors wide enough for* OLD EKDAL *to come out. She shuts them again.*)

EKDAL: H'm. Not much fun taking a walk by yourself, y'know.

HEDVIG: Wouldn't you like to go hunting, Grandpa?

EKDAL: It isn't hunting weather today. Too dark. Can hardly see a thing.

HEDVIG: Don't you ever want to shoot something besides rabbits?

EKDAL: Aren't the rabbits good enough, perhaps?

HEDVIG: Yes, but what about the wild duck?

EKDAL: Haw! So you're scared I'll shoot your wild duck? I'll never do that, Hedvig. Never.

HEDVIG: No, for I bet you don't know how. I've heard it's difficult to shoot wild ducks.

EKDAL: Don't know how! Should say I do!

HEDVIG: How would you do it, Grandpa? — I don't mean *my* wild duck, but another one.

EKDAL: Would try to get a shot in just below the breast; that's the best place. And try to shoot *against* the feathers, not *with*.

HEDVIG: Then they die?

EKDAL: Damn right they do — if you shoot right. — Well, better go in and dress up. H'm. Y'know. H'm — (*Goes into his own room.*)

(HEDVIG *waits a moment, glances towards the living room door, stands on tiptoe, takes the double-barreled pistol down from the shelf, looks at it.* GINA, *with broom and dust cloth, enters from the living room.* HEDVIG *quickly puts the pistol back, without* GINA'*s noticing.*)

GINA: Don't fool with father's things, Hedvig.

HEDVIG (*leaving the shelf*): I just wanted to straighten up some.

GINA: Why don't you go into the kitchen and see if the coffee is keeping hot? I am taking a tray with me when I go down.

(HEDVIG *goes into the kitchen.* GINA *starts putting the studio in order.*

*After a short while, the door to the outside is hesitantly opened and* HJALMAR *looks in. He is wearing a coat but no hat. He looks unkempt and unwashed. His eyes are dull and lusterless.*)

GINA (*stands staring at him, still with the broom in her hand*): Bless you, Ekdal — so you did come back, after all!

HJALMAR (*enters, answers in a dull voice*): I return — only to leave.

GINA: Yes, yes, I suppose. But good Lord! how you look!

HJALMAR: Look?

GINA: And your nice winter coat? I'd say that's done for.

HEDVIG (*in the kitchen door*): Mother, don't you want me to — (*Sees* HJALMAR, *gives a shout of joy and runs towards him.*) Father! Father!

HJALMAR (*turning away, with a gesture*): Go away! Go away! (*To* GINA.) Get her away from me, I say!

GINA (*in a low voice*): Go into the living room, Hedvig.

(HEDVIG *leaves silently.*)

HJALMAR (*busy, pulling out the table drawer*): I need my books with me. Where are my books?

GINA: Which books?

HJALMAR: My scientific works, of course — the technical journals I need for my invention.

GINA (*looking on the shelf*): Do you mean these over here, with no covers on them?

HJALMAR: Yes, yes, of course.

GINA (*puts a pile of journals down on the table*): Don't you want me to get Hedvig to cut them open for you?

HJALMAR: No. Nobody needs to cut any pages for me.

(*Brief silence.*)

GINA: So you *are* going to leave us, Ekdal?

HJALMAR (*rummaging among the books*): That goes without saying, I should think.

GINA: All right.

HJALMAR (*violently*): For you can hardly expect me to want to stay where my heart is pierced every single hour of the day!

GINA: God forgive you for thinking so bad of me!

HJALMAR: Proof — !

GINA: Seems to me, you're the one who should bring proof.

HJALMAR: After a past like yours? There are certain claims — I might call them the claims of the ideal —

GINA: What about Grandpa? What is *he* going to do, poor old man?

HJALMAR: I know my duty. The helpless one goes with me. I'll go out and make arrangements — H'm (*Hesitantly.*) Has anybody found my hat on the stairs?

GINA: No. Have you lost your hat?

HJALMAR: I most certainly had it on when I came home last night; there isn't the slightest doubt about that. But now I can't find it.

GINA: Good Lord! Where did you go with those two drunks?

HJALMAR: Oh, don't ask about inessentials. Do you think I'm in a mood for remembering details?

GINA: I only hope you haven't got a cold, Ekdal (*Goes into the kitchen.*)

HJALMAR (*speaking to himself, in a low voice, angrily, as he empties the drawer*): You're a scoundrel, Relling! — A villain is what you are! — Miserable traitor! — I'd gladly see you assassinated — !

(*He puts aside some old letters, discovers the torn gift letter from the day before, picks it up and looks at the two pieces, puts them down quickly as* GINA *enters.*)

GINA (*putting a tray with food down on the table*): Here's a drop of coffee, if you want it. And some salt meat sandwiches.

HJALMAR (*glancing at the tray*): Salt meat? Never under this roof! True it is, I haven't taken solid nourishment for almost twenty-four hours, but that can't be helped. — My notes! My incipient memoirs! Where is my diary — all my important papers! (*Opens the door to the living room, but steps back.*) If she isn't there, too!

GINA: Heavens, Ekdal. She's got to be somewhere.

HJALMAR: Leave! (*He makes room.* HEDVIG, *scared, enters the studio. With his hand on the door knob; to* GINA.) During the last moments I spend in my former home I wish to be spared the sight of intruders — (*Enters the living room.*)

HEDVIG (*starts, asks her mother in a low and trembling voice*): Does that mean me?

GINA: Stay in the kitchen, Hedvig, or no — go to your own room. (*To* HJALMAR, *as she enters the living room.*) Wait a minute, Ekdal. Don't make such a mess in the dresser. I know where everything is.

HEDVIG (*remains motionless for a moment, in helpless fright, presses her lips together not to cry, clenches her hands, whispers*): The wild duck!

(*She tiptoes over to the shelf and takes the pistol down, opens the doors to the inner attic, goes inside, closes behind her.* HJALMAR *and* GINA *are heard talking in the living room.*)

HJALMAR (*appears with some notebooks and a pile of old papers, which he puts down on the table*): The bag obviously won't be big enough. There are thousands of things I need to take with me!

GINA (*entering with the bag*): Can't you leave most of it behind for now and just pick up a clean shirt and some underwear?

HJALMAR: Phew — ! These exhausting preparations — ! (*Takes off his overcoat and throws it on the sofa.*)

GINA: And there's the coffee getting cold too.

HJALMAR: H'm. (*Without thinking, he takes a sip, and then another one.*)

GINA (*dusting off the back of chairs*): How are you ever going to find a large enough attic for the rabbits?

HJALMAR: You mean I have to drag all those rabbits along, too?

GINA: Grandpa can't do without his rabbits — you know that as well as I do.

HJALMAR: He'll have to get used to that. I shall have to give up higher values in life than a bunch of rabbits.

GINA (*dusting off the shelf*): Shall I put the flute in for you?

HJALMAR: No. No flute for me. But give me my pistol.

GINA: You want that old pestol?

HJALMAR: Yes. My loaded pistol.

GINA (*looking for it*): It's gone. He must have taken it inside with him.

HJALMAR: Is he in the attic?

GINA: Sure, he's in the attic.

HJALMAR: H'm. The lonely grayhead — (*He eats a sandwich, empties his cup of coffee.*)

GINA: If only we hadn't rented that room, you could have moved in there.

HJALMAR: And stay under the same roof as — ! Never! Never again!

GINA: But couldn't you stay in the living room for a day or two? There you'd have everything to yourself.

HJALMAR: Not within these walls!

GINA: How about down at Relling's and Molvik's, then?

HJALMAR: Don't mention their names to me! I get sick just thinking about them. Oh no — it's out into the wind and the snowdrifts for me — to walk from house to house seeking shelter for father and myself.

GINA: But you have no hat, Ekdal! You've lost your hat, remember?

HJALMAR: Oh, those two abominations! Rich in nothing but every vice! A hat must be procured. (*Takes another sandwich.*) Arrangements must be made. After all, I don't intend to catch my death. (*Looks for something on the tray.*)

GINA: What are you looking for?

HJALMAR: Butter.

GINA: Just a moment. (*Goes out into the kitchen.*)

HJALMAR (*shouting after her*): Oh never mind. Dry bread is good enough for me.

GINA (*bringing a plate with butter*): Here. This is supposed to be freshly churned.

(*She pours him another cup of coffee. He sits down on the sofa, puts more butter on his bread, eats and drinks in silence.*)

HJALMAR (*after a pause*): Could I, without being disturbed by anyone — and I mean *anyone* — stay in the living room for a day or two?

GINA: You certainly can, if you want to.

HJALMAR: You see, I don't know how to get all of father's things moved out on such short notice.

GINA: And there is this, too, that first you'd have to tell him that you don't want to live together with the rest of us any more.

HJALMAR (*pushing his cup away*): Yes, yes, yes. I shall have to go into all those intricate relationships once again, to explain — I must think, I must have air to breathe, I can't bear all the burdens in one single day.

GINA: Of course not. And in such awful weather too —

HJALMAR (*moving* WERLE'*s letter*): I notice this piece of paper still lying around.

GINA: Well, *I* haven't touched it.

HJALMAR: Not that it concerns *me* —

GINA: I'm sure *I* don't expect to make use of it —

HJALMAR: Nevertheless, I suppose we shouldn't let it get completely lost. In all the fuss of moving, something might easily —

GINA: I'll take care of it, Ekdal.

HJALMAR: For the gift letter belongs to father, first of all. It's his affair whether he wants to make use of it or not.

GINA (*with a sigh*): Yes, poor old Grandpa —

HJALMAR: Just to make sure — Is there any glue?

GINA (*walks over to the shelf*): Here's a bottle.

HJALMAR: And a brush?

GINA: Here. (*Brings him both.*)

HJALMAR (*picks up a pair of scissors*): Just a strip of paper on the back — (*Cuts and glues.*) Far be it from me to lay hand on somebody else's property — least of all the property of a poverty-stricken old man. — Well — not on — that other one's, either. — There, now! Leave it to dry for a while. And when it's dry, remove it. I don't want to lay eyes on that document again — ever!

(GREGERS *enters.*)

GREGERS (*a little surprised*): What? So this is where you are, Hjalmar!

HJALMAR (*quickly gets up*): Sheer exhaustion drove me to sit down.

GREGERS: And I see you've had breakfast.

HJALMAR: The body, too, makes demands at times.

GREGERS: Well, what have you decided to do?

HJALMAR: For a man like me, there is only one way open. I am in the process of gathering up my most important possessions. Obviously, that takes time.

GINA (*a trifle impatient*): Do you want me to make the living room ready for you, or do you want me to pack the bag?

HJALMAR (*after an irritated glance at* GREGERS): Pack — and make the room ready.

GINA (*picking up the bag*): All right. I'll just put in the shirts and those other things. (*She goes into the living room, closing the door behind her.*)

GREGERS (*after a short silence*): I had no idea this would be the end of it. Is it really necessary for you to leave house and home?

HJALMAR (*paces restlessly up and down*): What do you want me to do? I am not made to be unhappy, Gregers. I require peace and security and comfort around me.

GREGERS: But you can have all that, Hjalmar. Just try. It seems to me there is a firm foundation to build upon now. Start all over again. And remember, you still have your invention to live for.

HJALMAR: Oh don't talk about that invention. It may take a long time yet.

GREGERS: So?

HJALMAR: Well, yes, for heaven's sake, what do you expect me to invent, anyway? The others have invented most of it already. It's getting more difficult every day.

GREGERS: But all the labor you've put into it — ?

HJALMAR: It was that dissipated Relling who got me started on it.

GREGERS: Relling?

HJALMAR: Yes, it was he who first called attention to my talent for making some fabulous invention or other in photography.

GREGERS: I see. It was Relling — !

HJALMAR: Ah — I have been so wonderfully happy about it. Not so much about the invention itself, but because Hedvig believed in it — believed with all the strength and power of a child's soul. — That is, I *thought* she did — fool as I was.

GREGERS: Can you really think that Hedvig would be false to you?

HJALMAR: I can believe anything now. It is Hedvig who's in the way. She it is who is shutting the sun out of my entire life.

GREGERS: Hedvig? You mean Hedvig? How in the world is she going to be an obstacle?

HJALMAR (*without answering*): I have loved that child more than I can ever say. You have no idea how happy I was whenever I came back to my humble dwelling and she rushed towards me with her sweet, squinting eyes. Ha, credulous fool that I was! She was so unspeakably dear to me — and so I lulled myself into the dream that I was equally dear to her.

GREGERS: You call that a dream?

HJALMAR: How can I tell? I can't get anything out of Gina. Besides, she completely lacks any sense of the ideal aspects of the issue. But to you I can open up, Gregers. It is this terrible doubt — perhaps Hedvig has never really loved me.

GREGERS: Maybe you'll receive proof — (*Listens.*) Shh! What's that? The wild duck?

HJALMAR: It's just quacking. Father's in the attic.

GREGERS: He is! (*Joy lights his face.*) I tell you again, Hjalmar — maybe you will find proof that your poor, misunderstood Hedvig has always loved you!

HJALMAR: Pah! What proof could she give? I dare not trust to mere asseverations.

GREGERS: Surely, Hedvig doesn't know what deceit is.

HJALMAR: Ah, Gregers – that is just what I cannot be certain of. Who knows what Gina and this Mrs. Sørby may have been whispering and scheming? And Hedvig's ears are big enough, believe you me. Maybe that gift letter didn't come as such a surprise to her. It seemed to me I noticed something like that.

GREGERS: For heaven's sake, Hjalmar! What kind of spirit is this that's taken possession of you!

HJALMAR: I have had my eyes opened. You just wait. It may turn out that the gift letter was just the beginning. Mrs. Sørby has always been very fond of Hedvig, and now, of course, it's in her power to do anything she likes for the child. They can take her away from me what day and hour they choose.

GREGERS: Hedvig will never leave you, Hjalmar. Never.

HJALMAR: Don't be too sure. If they beckon her with their arms full – ? And I who have loved her so infinitely much! I, whose greatest joy it was to take her tenderly by the hand and lead her, as one leads a frightened child through a dark and deserted room! Now I feel this painful certainty that the poor photographer in his attic has never really meant very much to her. She has only cleverly managed to keep on good terms with him while she bided her time.

GREGERS: You don't believe this yourself, Hjalmar.

HJALMAR: That's just what's so terrible – I don't know what to believe – I'll never be able to find out! But do you really doubt that I am right? Ah, Gregers, you put too much trust in the claim of the ideal! If those others were to come now, with their ample offerings, and called to the child: Leave him; life awaits you here with us –

GREGERS (*quickly*): Yes, what then – ?

HJALMAR: If then I were to ask her: Hedvig, are you willing to give your life for me? (*Laughs scornfully.*) Oh yes – you'd find out soon enough what answer I'd get!

(*A pistol shot is heard from within the attic.*)

GREGERS (*with a shout of joy*): Hjalmar!

HJALMAR: Must he go shooting today – !

GINA (*enters*): Can't say I like this, Ekdal – Grandpa in there all by himself, banging away.

HJALMAR: I'll take a look –

GREGERS (*agitated, feelingly*): Wait! Do you know what that was?

HJALMAR: Yes, of course I do.

GREGERS: No, you don't. But *I* know. It was the proof!

HJALMAR: What proof?

GREGERS: It was a child's sacrifice. She has got your father to shoot the wild duck.

HJALMAR: Shoot the wild duck!

GINA: Heavens – !

HJALMAR: Whatever for?

GREGERS: She wanted to sacrifice to you what she held dearest in the whole world. For then she thought you'd love her again.

HJALMAR (*softly, moved*): Oh that child!

GINA: What she thinks of!

GREGERS: All she wanted was your love, Hjalmar. Without it, life didn't seem possible to her.

GINA (*struggling with tears*): *Now,* do you see, Ekdal?

HJALMAR: Gina, where is she?

GINA (*sniffling*): Poor thing. She is sitting out in the kitchen, I guess.

HJALMAR (*walks to the kitchen door, flings it open, says*): Hedvig – come! Come to me! (*Looks around.*) No. She isn't here.

GINA: Then she must be in her own room.

HJALMAR (*offstage*): No, she isn't there, either. (*Re-entering the studio.*) She must have gone out.

GINA: Yes, for you know you didn't want to see hide nor hair of her in the house.

HJALMAR: If only she'd come back soon – so I can tell her – Now I feel that everything will be all right, Gregers. Now I think we can start life over again.

GREGERS (*quietly*): I knew it. Restitution would come through the child.

(OLD EKDAL *appears in the door to his room. He is in full uniform and is buckling on his sabre.*)

HJALMAR (*surprised*): Father! You're in there!

GINA: Do you go shooting in your room, now, Grandpa?

EKDAL (*approaches indignantly*): So you're off hunting by yourself, are you Hjalmar?

HJALMAR (*tense, confused*): You mean it wasn't you who fired that shot in the attic just now?

EKDAL: I? Fired? H'm.

GREGERS (*shouts to* HJALMAR): She has shot the wild duck herself?

HJALMAR: What's going on? (*He hurriedly slides the attic doors open, looks in, gives a loud cry.*) Hedvig!

GINA (*runs to the door*): Oh God! What is it?

HJALMAR (*going inside*): She is lying on the floor!

GREGERS: Lying – ! (*Follows* HJALMAR *inside.*)

GINA (*at the same time*): Hedvig! (*Enters the attic.*) No! No! No!

EKDAL: Ho-ho! So *she* has taken to hunting too, now!

(HJALMAR, GINA, *and* GREGERS *drag* HEDVIG *into the studio. Her trailing right hand clasps the pistol tightly.*)

HJALMAR (*beside himself*): The pistol went off! She's hit! Call for help! Help!

GINA (*running out into the hallway, shouts down*): Relling! Relling! Doctor Relling! Hurry up here, fast as you can!

(HJALMAR *and* GREGERS *put* HEDVIG *down on the sofa.*)

EKDAL (*quietly*): The woods avenge themselves.

HJALMAR (*on his knees beside* HEDVIG): She's coming to now. She is coming to. Oh yes, yes, yes –

GINA (*having returned*): Where's she hit? I can't see a thing.

(RELLING *enters hurriedly, followed by* MOLVIK. *The latter is without vest and tie, his tailcoat thrown open.*)

RELLING: What's the matter?

GINA: They say Hedvig has shot herself.

HJALMAR: Come and help us!

RELLING: Shot herself! (*He pulls the table back and begins to examine her.*)

HJALMAR (*still on his knees, looking anxiously at* RELLING): It can't be dangerous, can it, Relling? What, Relling? She hardly bleeds at all. It can't possibly be dangerous?

RELLING: How did this happen?

HJALMAR: Oh, I don't know –

GINA: She was going to shoot the wild duck.

RELLING: The wild duck?

HJALMAR: The pistol must have gone off.

RELLING: H'm. I see.

EKDAL: The woods avenge themselves. But I'm not afraid. (*Enters the attic and closes the doors behind him.*)

HJALMAR: Relling – why don't you say anything?

RELLING: The bullet has entered her chest.

HJALMAR: Yes, but she's coming to!

RELLING: Can't you see that Hedvig is dead?

GINA (*bursts into tears*): Oh, the child, the child – !

GREGERS (*hoarsely*): In the depths of the sea –

HJALMAR (*jumps to his feet*): She must live! I want her to live! For God's sake, Relling – just for a moment – just so I can tell her how unspeakably much I have loved her all the time!

RELLING: Her heart has been pierced. Internal hemorrhage. She died instantly.

HJALMAR: And I who chased her away from me like an animal! Frightened and lonely she crawled into the attic and died for love of me. (*Sobbing.*) Never to be able to make up for it! Never to tell her – ! (*Shakes his fists upwards.*) You! You above! If thou art at all – ! Why hast thou done this unto me?

GINA: Shhh, shhh. You mustn't make such a fuss. We had no right to keep her, I suppose.

MOLVIK: The child is not dead. It sleepeth.

RELLING: Rubbish!

HJALMAR (*quieting down, walks over to the sofa, looks at* HEDVIG, *his arms crossed*): There she lies, so stiff and still.

RELLING (*trying to release the pistol*): She holds on so tightly, I can't —

GINA: No, no, Relling. Don't break her fingers. Let the pestol be.

HJALMAR: Let her have it with her.

GINA: Yes, let her. But the child isn't going to lie out here for a show. She is going into her own little room, right now. Give me a hand, Ekdal.

(HJALMAR *and* GINA *carry* HEDVIG *between them.*)

HJALMAR (*carrying*): Gina, Gina — do you think you can bear this?

GINA: The one has to help the other. Seems to me like now we both have a share in her.

MOLVIK (*raising his arms, muttering*): Praise be the Lord, to dust thou returnest, to dust thou returnest —

RELLING (*whispers*): Shut up, man! You're drunk.

(HJALMAR *and* GINA *carry* HEDVIG *through the kitchen door.* RELLING *closes the door behind them.* MOLVIK *slinks quietly out into the hall.*)

RELLING (*goes up to* GREGERS): Nobody is going to tell me this was an accident.

GREGERS (*who has remained stunned, moving convulsively*): Who is to say how this terrible thing happened?

RELLING: There were powder burns on her dress. She must have placed the muzzle against her chest and pulled the trigger.

GREGERS: Hedvig has not died in vain. Did you notice how grief released what is great in him?

RELLING: There is a touch of greatness in most of us when we stand in sorrow by a corpse. How long do you think that will last with him?

GREGERS: As if it won't last and grow throughout the rest of his days!

RELLING: Within a year little Hedvig won't be anything to him but an occasion for spouting pretty sentiments.

GREGERS: And you dare say that about Hjalmar Ekdal!

RELLING: Let's talk about this again when the first grass has withered on her grave. You'll hear all about "the child so early taken from the father's heart." You'll see him wallow in sentimentality and self-admiration and self-pity. You just wait!

GREGERS: If you are right and I am wrong, life isn't worth living.

RELLING: Oh, life would be fairly tolerable if only we'd be spared these blasted bill collectors who come around pestering us paupers with the claim of the ideal.

GREGERS (*staring ahead*): In that case I am glad my destiny is what it is.
RELLING: Beg your pardon – what *is* your destiny?
GREGERS (*about to leave*): To be the thirteenth man at the table.
RELLING: The hell it is.

"To be an author," said Ibsen, "is to see." He meant an author of imaginative literature, *ein Dichter*. Yet in his later years he rarely went to the theater and always referred to his plays as "books" and to his audience as his "readers." If there is a contradiction here it disappears in the concept of drama as visualized dialogue. *The Wild Duck,* which, like all of Ibsen's later plays, appeared in book form before it was staged, *can* be successfully staged because it was first of all conceived and realized in a poet's imagination.

In a dramatic canon that Ibsen himself urged should be read as one continuous, unbroken whole, *The Wild Duck* (1884) marks a transition. The canon is continuous in the sense that all Ibsen's plays deal with the problem of self-realization, but it can be divided into separate sequences, the most important of which consists of the twelve realistic plays in prose he wrote between 1877 and 1899. In the early plays within this sequence, the conflict is between the individual and the pressures of social institutions that corrupt and inhibit the self. In the later plays the struggle is internalized, the issues are revealed rather than debated, and the realistic surface is charged with multiple symbolic meaning. The change is from implicitly engaged polemics on social problems to disinterested exhibits of the psychology of the subconscious. *The Wild Duck* deals with domestic morals in a carefully delineated milieu, but its inner movement is on submerged levels of the psyche.

Its earliest readers and audiences found it obscure and morbid ("a facetious genre picture with a meaningless and uninteresting splotch of blood away in one corner"), and even today, when it is generally considered one of Ibsen's greatest plays, there are critics who accept the judgment but insist that it does not say very much. They object to the Scribean machinery of the too-logical action, to the disingenuousness of the carefully casual disclosures of the past in innuendo, to the unrelieved mediocrity of language, to the inelegant and perfunctory opening expository scene between the two servants, to the shift in setting between Acts I and II that tends to reduce the former to mere prologue, to the note of pseudo-poetic profundity and melodrama in Old Ekdal's vengeful woods, to the way discussions issue in slogans ("Take his vital lie away from the average man, and you take his happiness, too"), and to the stereotypes of naturalistic characterization: the old roué, the drunken lodger, the broken father, the drab but loyal wife, the innocent and suffering child. Hjalmar, they say, may be fine enough with beer and chamberlains, but the total figure is a caricature. This would not matter in some kinds of plays, but it matters here, for Ibsen writes in a convention that puts a premium on plausibility of character and incident. It is hard to accept as basic plot premise Gregers Werle's continuing faith in the greatness of a man who shows himself to be an obvious phony every time he opens his mouth. Gregers may be sick, but he is not supposed to be stupid.

For others, however, the play survives its imperfections, real or alleged, and it may illuminate the nature of the strength of naturalistic drama to try to answer why and how it does so.

It stays close to Ibsen's usual pattern. A member or a friend of a middle-class family returns after long absence and by his return triggers disastrous revelations. The action is nearly all exposition — the gradual discovery of the painful truth about the past concealed in the family's decorous and complacent present. We recognize the pattern from *Oedipus Rex,* and *The Wild Duck* does, in fact, share with Sophocles's play a tightness of structure and a concentration of events in small compass of time and space that have been made possible by the playwrights' seizure of their stories near their climax. The plot is a looking-back on the past responsible for the present crisis. It is a "fifth act play" compared with the panoramic, expansive, chronologically developed Shakespearean drama.

But aside from its retrospective structure, *The Wild Duck* has little enough in common with classical tragedy. No kingdom trembles when Hjalmar Ekdal is in agony. His suffering is not ceremonial. He is too small a man to be the concern of gods, too meanly petty to be even wicked. His case is too random to appear archetypal. Beside the language of traditional tragedy, dialogue here is small talk indeed and Hjalmar's eloquence merely absurd. Hedvig innocently exposes him when she asks whether the chamberlains sang and recited poetry at Werle's party; that, in her experience, is what admirable men do when they function socially. Compared with the public settings of tragedy, focuses for the life of an entire society, the Ekdal studio is a small and shrunken world — banal, pathetic, ridiculous. But can it not be argued that the inapplicability of the yardstick of great tragedy to *The Wild Duck* is less a comment on the play than on modern man and his disoriented values? Every age gets the drama it deserves.

And if *The Wild Duck* is not in the tragic tradition, neither does it belong with those pat, once shocking, now commonplace, social messages that date such a large part of naturalistic drama of the last and this century: exposés of skeletons, today more dead than fearful, in Victorian closets. Ibsen has been unfairly blamed for the dreary successes of what Shaw with a misnomer called "Ibsenism." The battles won, their champions have become bores, holding forth apropos of nothing. People had resented what they took to be Ibsen's attack on the entrenched sanctities of religion, married life, and democracy in the plays immediately preceding *The Wild Duck* and had been scandalized by his reference (in *Ghosts*) to incest and venereal disease. *The Wild Duck* records, with deceptive blandness, the meaning of the public's reaction to the playwright's anatomies of bourgeois values: most people not only do not want the truth about themselves, they are actually much better off with comfortable lies. Its mood is delicately balanced between two statements, opposite in tone, of the same single fact about man: Swift's virulent irony in *A Tale of a Tub* in defining "the sublime and refined point of felicity" as "the possession of being well deceived"; and the compassionate excuse for the grieving women of Canterbury that T. S. Eliot puts into the mouth of Saint Thomas à Becket in *Murder in the Cathedral:* "Human kind cannot bear very much reality." In conjunction with *An Enemy of the People, The Wild Duck* demonstrates Ibsen's nearly compulsive habit — the genuine dramatist's — of seeing every issue from opposite sides. In the earlier play he had put much of himself into Dr. Stockmann, the hearty, indomitable fighter for truth. Here he seems to parody his own reforming self in the character of the gloomy Gregers Werle, whose officious mania for truth ends in a child's death.

But the play never surrenders the ambiguities of its poise between tragedy and farce, pathos and cynicism, pity and ridicule. It is skeptical and relativistic, not doctrinaire. If its whole point is to tell us that the ordinary person's happiness depends on a protective illusion against brutal fact, its spokesman appears oddly chosen. As in so many realistic plays of the late nineteenth century (including some of Ibsen's own), the voice of the common-sensical *raisonneur* in *The Wild Duck* is that of a man of science, but Dr. Relling is pretty much a human wreck. Mrs. Sørby, who should know and who is the play's most sensible character, calls him a man who has "thrown away what is best in himself." At the news of her marriage to Werle he promptly takes his own medicine and runs off to a saloon — just like Old Ekdal scuttling off to his room at the advent of reality. His much-quoted formula for happy adjustment can be regarded as the play's thesis only if we ignore his flawed personality and his inferior plot position as commentator rather than main actor and, for that matter, the shoddiness of his tolerant and cynical psychological wisdom. Nor is the principle of the "vital lie" a major plot issue, for only incidentally does Hedvig kill herself in order to restore Hjalmar's faith in his "invention."

The action of the play may be defined as the conflict between Relling and Gregers for control of Hjalmar. They are rival social workers, or amateur psychologists, on the Ekdal case. Hjalmar's character renders the *agon* ridiculous rather than heroic. He is a photographer who is blind even to his own reality and whose only professional activity, significantly, is retouching. Self-indulgent, confused, borrowing his image of himself from his worshiping friend, acted upon rather than acting, he seems like an early version of the contemporary anti-hero. Gregers initiates the action but is its antagonist rather than its protagonist. His mission of truth succeeds only ironically when it leads to the death of the one lovable and wholly innocent member of the entire household. There is no real recognition. Hedvig dies because her sight fails spiritually as well as physically: she never sees through Hjalmar. Gregers's belief in Hjalmar's greatness of soul remains unshaken at the end. And there is no reason to doubt the accuracy of Relling's prediction that Hedvig's death soon will be nothing to Hjalmar but an occasion for mawkish sentimentality. And, as if to keep us from extracting any larger significance from these sordid events, Ibsen ends his play by having Relling's profanity explode the pretentious melodramatics of Gregers's belief — *his* vital lie — that he is "the thirteenth man at the table" — superfluous, tragically chosen by destiny to bring bad luck to others. Neither the cynic's realism nor the neurotic's idealism receives ultimate sanction. They balance inconclusively on Hjalmar's rhetoric of grief. We don't even know with absolute certainty that he is *not* Hedvig's real father. Gina herself says she doesn't know, and there is no proof she is lying. Certainty, the play suggests, is a luxury that paupers cannot afford.

By convention, naturalism admits only symbols whose credentials as naturalism are in order — that is, they must first be facts or concretes in the surface life-likeness. The unseen wild duck is the symbolic center of the play, from which "meanings" radiate. But before it is anything else it is part of the Ekdal establishment, an object as real as the photographs and the flute and the herring salad. It presides in the attic world of fantasy and escape, a denizen of the depths of the sea, content among the shipwrecked skipper's assorted belongings. It is one of Ibsen's triumphs that the whole unlikely contrivance of the barnyard attic is both believable as solid fact and rich and beautiful in its symbolic suggestiveness. It convinces because it is comical and pitiful, haunting and bizarre, all at the same time.

Seeing the wild duck as a symbol is a part of the plot. The idea is Gregers's, not that of critics bent on "reading things into" the play. As the messiah figure he aspires to be, Gregers, in fact, is addicted to symbol-mongering, insisting that things are not just what they seem to be but something else. Reality to him is a metaphor: the attic is not just an attic, Hjalmar and Gina live in a poisonous marsh, Old Werle is a callous and wanton and inexpert hunter, Hjalmar is a wounded wild duck, Gregers himself is a clever retriever, his "mission" collecting outstanding bills on behalf of some moral or metaphysical absolute.

But the wild duck is a more versatile symbol than Gregers's monomania can recognize. It offers — and has offered — irresistible and endless game for interpretive ingenuity. What does it stand for? Escape from reality? Wounded innocence? The guilty past? Whom does it represent — and *for* whom? Gregers thinks Hjalmar is a wild duck, but aren't there ways in which the duck could be said to symbolize as well not only Molvik and Old Ekdal, but Hedvig and Relling and Old Werle and Gregers himself? May we ignore Relling's reference to Gina's "comfortable waddle" or the fact that she, like the duck, has passed from Werle's hands into Hjalmar's, somewhat the worse for wear? To make choices here seems wrong. Rather, by defining the attitudes of the different members of the household to the wild duck and to the attic where it lives one grasps the play's main unifying image and goes a long way toward understanding the characters and their relationships and their position vis à vis the general issue of reality versus illusion. Like all successful symbols, the wild duck is not elaboration but concentration, does not obscure but clarifies, is not a poetic device but what the poetry is about.

All this further suggests that "meaning" in *The Wild Duck* is not to be sought in a thesis or a concept but in such realities as Old Ekdal's reluctance to use the pronoun "I," in Hjalmar's uncut technical journals, in Gina's infinitely patient and competent housekeeping. The stage language — both scenic and verbal — of naturalism did not banish poetry from the theater. There is in *The Wild Duck* careful organization of words for esthetic purposes. In addition to its utilitarian value in establishing social milieu and setting off Hjalmar's excursions into oratory, the drab, colloquial dialogue also reveals deeper levels of imagery that bear upon theme and character. The allusions to sight and blindness, darkness and light, that weave in and out of Hjalmar's and Gregers's speeches reinforce the blindness motif in the plot and achieve effects of telling irony with reference to "blindness" as a spiritual quality: Gregers rejects Relling's estimate of Hjalmar's character with the words, "I didn't know I was as blind as all that"; Hjalmar is forced by circumstance to admit to weaker eyesight than "the Nearsighted Gentleman" and refuses to "look at the child" after "he has had his eyes opened." The subdued green light in Werle's study in Act I is a relevant scenic image in preparing us visually for "the depths of the sea" that are, figuratively, the setting for the four acts that follow.

What Ibsen "saw" in the world of *The Wild Duck* was something more than the trivialities of middle-class life, the pointless thrill of adultery and uncertain parentage, or the proof of a social tract. His vision takes in neither tragedy's sublime affirmation of man's significance in a dark world nor the scrupulous factuality of a documentary but, compassionately and unsentimentally, the lives af small people suffering under the high cost of truth.

# BERNARD SHAW

# Cæsar and Cleopatra

*A History*

## PROLOGUE

*In the doorway of the temple of Ra in Memphis. Deep gloom. An august personage with a hawk's head is mysteriously visible by his own light in the darkness within the temple. He surveys the modern audience with great contempt; and finally speaks the following words to them:*

Peace! Be silent and hearken unto me, ye quaint little islanders. Give ear, ye men with white paper on your breasts and nothing written thereon (to signify the innocence of your minds). Hear me, ye women who adorn yourselves alluringly and conceal your thoughts from your men, leading them to believe that ye deem them wondrous strong and masterful whilst in truth ye hold them in your hearts as children without judgment. Look upon my hawk's head; and know that I am Ra, who was once in Egypt a mighty god. Ye cannot kneel nor prostrate yourselves; for ye are packed in rows without freedom to move, obstructing one another's vision; neither do any of ye regard it as seemly to do ought until ye see all the rest do so too; wherefore it commonly happens that in great emergencies ye do nothing though each telleth his fellow that something must be done. I ask you not for worship, but for silence. Let not your men speak nor your women cough; for I am come to draw you back two thousand years over the graves of sixty generations. Ye poor posterity, think not that ye are the first. Other fools before ye have seen the sun rise and set, and the moon change her shape and her hour. As they were so ye are; and yet not so great; for the pyramids my people built stand to this day; whilst the dust-heaps on which ye slave, and which ye call empires, scatter in the wind even as ye pile your dead sons' bodies on them to make yet more dust.

Hearken to me then, oh ye compulsorily educated ones. Know that even as there is an old England and a new, and ye stand perplexed between the twain; so in the days when I was worshipped was there an old Rome and a new, and men standing perplexed between them. And the old Rome was poor and little, and greedy and fierce, and evil in many ways; but because its mind was little and its work was simple, it knew its own mind and did its own work; and the gods pitied it and helped it and strengthened it and shielded it; for the gods are patient with littleness. Then the old Rome, like the beggar on horseback, presumed on the favor of the gods, and said, "Lo! there is neither riches nor greatness in our littleness: the road to riches and greatness is through robbery of the poor and slaughter of the weak." So they robbed their own poor until they became great masters of that art, and knew by what laws it could be made to appear seemly and honest. And when they had squeezed their own poor dry, they robbed the poor of other lands, and added those lands to Rome until there came a new Rome, rich and huge. And I, Ra, laughed; for the minds of the Romans remained the same size whilst their dominion spread over the earth.

Now mark me, that ye may understand what ye are presently to see. Whilst the Romans still stood between the old Rome and the new, there arose among them a mighty soldier: Pompey the Great. And the way of the soldier is the way of death; but the way of the gods is the way of life; and so it comes that a god at the end of his way is wise and a soldier at the end of his way is a fool. So Pompey held by the old Rome, in which only soldiers could become great; but the gods turned to the new Rome, in which any man with wit enough could become what he would. And Pompey's friend Julius Cæsar was on the side of the gods; for he saw that Rome had passed beyond the control of the little old Romans. This Cæsar was a great talker and a politician: he bought men with words and with gold, even as ye are bought. And when they would not be satisfied with words and gold, and demanded also the glories of war, Cæsar in his middle age turned his hand to that trade; and they that were against him when he sought their welfare, bowed down before him when he became a slayer and a conqueror; for such is the nature of you mortals. And as for Pompey, the gods grew tired of his triumphs and his airs of being himself a god; for he talked of law and duty and other matters that concerned not a mere human worm. And the gods smiled on Cæsar; for he lived the life they had given him boldly, and was not forever rebuking us for our indecent ways of creation, and hiding our handiwork as a shameful thing. Ye know well what I mean; for this is one of your own sins.

And thus it fell out between the old Rome and the new, that Cæsar said, "Unless I break the law of old Rome, I cannot take my share in ruling her; and the gift of ruling that the gods gave me will perish without fruit." But Pompey said, "The law is above all; and if thou break it thou shalt die." Then said Cæsar, "I will break it: kill me who can." And he broke it. And Pompey went for him, as ye say, with a great army to slay him and uphold the old Rome. So Cæsar fled across the Adriatic sea; for the high gods had a lesson to teach him, which lesson they shall also teach you in due time if ye continue to forget them and to worship that cad among gods, Mammon. Therefore before they raised Cæsar to be master of the world, they were minded to throw him down into the dust, even beneath the feet of Pompey, and blacken his face before the nations. And Pompey they raised higher than ever, he and his laws and his high mind that aped the gods, so that his fall might be the more terrible. And Pompey followed Cæsar, and overcame him with all the majesty of old Rome, and stood over him and over the whole world even as ye stand over it with your fleet that covers thirty miles of the sea. And when Cæsar was brought down to utter nothingness, he made a last stand to die honorably, and did not despair; for he said, "Against me there is Pompey, and the old Rome, and the law and the legions: all against me; but high above these are the gods; and Pompey is a fool." And the gods laughed and approved; and on the field of Pharsalia the impossible came to pass; the blood and iron ye pin your faith on fell before the spirit of man; for the spirit of man is the will of the gods; and Pompey's power crumbled in his hand, even as the power of imperial Spain crumbled when it was set against your fathers in the days when England was little, and knew her own mind, and had a mind to know instead of a circulation of newspapers. Wherefore look to it, lest some little people whom ye would enslave rise up and become in the hand of God the scourge of your boastings and your injustices and your lusts and stupidities.

And now, would ye know the end of Pompey, or will ye sleep while a god speaks? Heed my words well; for Pompey went where ye have gone, even to Egypt, where there was a Roman occupation even as there was but now a British one. And Cæsar pursued Pompey to Egypt; a Roman fleeing, and a Roman pursuing: dog eating dog. And the Egyptians said, "Lo: those Romans which have lent money to our kings and levied a distraint upon us with their arms, call for ever upon us to be loyal to them by betraying our own country to them. But now behold two Romes! Pompey's Rome and Cæsar's Rome! To which of the twain shall we pretend to be loyal?" So they turned in their perplexity to a soldier that had once served Pompey, and that knew the ways of Rome and was full of her lusts. And they said to him, "Lo: in thy country dog eats dog; and both dogs are coming to eat us: what counsel hast thou to give us?" And this soldier, whose name was Lucius Septimius, and whom ye shall presently see before ye, replied, "Ye shall diligently consider which is the bigger dog of the two; and ye shall kill the other dog for his sake and thereby earn his favor." And the Egyptians said, "Thy counsel is expedient; but if we kill a man outside the law we set ourselves in the place of the gods; and this we dare not do. But thou, being a Roman, art accustomed to this kind of killing; for thou hast imperial instincts. Wilt thou therefore kill the lesser dog for us?" And he said, "I will; for I have made my home in Egypt; and I desire consideration and influence among you." And they said, "We knew well thou wouldst not do it for nothing: thou shalt have thy reward." Now when Pompey came, he came alone in a little galley, putting his trust in the law and the constitution. And it was plain to the people of Egypt that Pompey was now but a very small dog. So when he set his foot on the shore he was greeted by his old comrade Lucius Septimius, who welcomed him with one hand and with the other smote off his head, and kept it as it were a pickled cabbage to make a present to Cæsar. And mankind shuddered; but the gods laughed; for Septimius was but a knife that Pompey had sharpened; and when it turned against his own throat they said that Pompey had better have made Septimius a ploughman than so brave and ready-handed a slayer. Therefore again I bid you beware, ye who would all be Pompeys if ye dared; for war is a wolf that may come to your own door.

Are ye impatient with me? Do ye crave for a story of an unchaste woman? Hath the name of Cleopatra tempted ye hither? Ye foolish ones; Cleopatra is as yet but a child that is whipped by her nurse. And what I am about to shew you for the good of your souls is how Cæsar, seeking Pompey in Egypt, found Cleopatra; and how he received that present of a pickled cabbage that was once the head of Pompey; and what things happened between the old Cæsar and the child queen before he left Egypt and battled his way back to Rome to be slain there as Pompey was slain, by men in whom the spirit of Pompey still lived. All this ye shall see; and ye shall marvel, after your ignorant manner, that men twenty centuries ago were already just such as you, and spoke and lived as ye speak and live, no worse and no better, no wiser and no sillier. And the two thousand years that have past are to me, the god Ra, but a moment; nor is this day any other than the day in which Cæsar set foot in the land of my people. And now I leave you; for ye are a dull folk, and instruction is wasted on you; and I had not spoken so much but that it is in the nature of a god to struggle for ever with the dust and the darkness, and to drag from them, by the force of his longing for the divine, more life and more light. Settle ye therefore in your seats and keep silent; for ye are about to hear a man speak, and a great man he was, as ye count greatness. And fear not that I shall speak to you again: the rest of the story must ye learn from them that lived it. Farewell; and do not presume to applaud me.

(*The temple vanishes in utter darkness.*)

## AN ALTERNATIVE TO THE PROLOGUE

*An October night on the Syrian border of Egypt towards the end of the XXXIII Dynasty, in the year 706 by Roman computation, afterwards reckoned by Christian computation at 48* B.C. *A great radiance of silver fire, the dawn of a moonlit night, is rising in the east. The stars and the cloudless sky are our own contemporaries, nineteen and a half centuries younger than we know them; but you would not guess that from their appearance. Below them are two notable drawbacks of civilization: a palace, and soldiers. The palace, an old, low, Syrian building of whitened mud, is not so ugly as Buckingham Palace; and the officers in the courtyard are more highly civilized than modern English officers: for example, they do not dig up the corpses of their dead enemies and mutilate them, as we dug up Cromwell and the Mahdi. They are in two groups: one intent on the gambling of their captain* BELZANOR, *a warrior of fifty, who, with his spear on the ground beside his knee, is stooping to throw dice with a sly-looking young* PERSIAN *recruit; the other gathered about a guardsman who has just finished telling a naughty story (still current in English barracks) at which they are laughing uproariously. They are about a dozen in number, all highly aristocratic young Egyptian* GUARDSMEN, *handsomely equipped with weapons and armor, very unEnglish in point of not being ashamed of and uncomfortable in their professional dress; on the contrary, rather ostentatiously and arrogantly warlike, as valuing themselves on their military caste.*

BELZANOR *is a typical veteran, tough and wilful; prompt, capable and crafty where brute force will serve; helpless and boyish when it will not: an effective sergeant, an incompetent general, a deplorable dictator. Would, if influentially connected, be employed in the two last capacities by a modern European State on the strength of his success in the first. Is rather to be pitied just now in view of the fact that that* JULIUS CÆSAR *is invading his country. Not knowing this, is intent on his game with the* PERSIAN, *whom, as a foreigner, he considers quite capable of cheating him.*

*His subalterns are mostly handsome young fellows whose interest in the game and the story symbolize with tolerable completeness the main interests in life of which they are conscious. Their spears are leaning against the walls, or lying on the ground ready to their hands. The corner of the courtyard forms a triangle of which one side is the front of the palace, with a doorway, the other a wall with a gateway. The storytellers are on the palace side: the gamblers, on the gateway side. Close to the gateway, against the wall, is a stone block high enough to enable a Nubian* SENTINEL, *standing on it, to look over the wall. The yard is lighted by a torch stuck in the wall. As the laughter from the group round the storyteller dies away, the kneeling* PERSIAN, *winning the throw, snatches up the stake from the ground.*

BELZANOR: By Apis, Persian, thy gods are good to thee.
PERSIAN: Try yet again, O captain. Double or quits!
BELZANOR: No more. I am not in the vein.
SENTINEL (*poising his javelin as he peers over the wall*): Stand. Who goes there?

(*They all start, listening. A strange* VOICE *replies from without.*)

VOICE: The bearer of evil tidings.
BELZANOR (*calling to the sentry*): Pass him.
SENTINEL (*grounding his javelin*): Draw near, O bearer of evil tidings.
BELZANOR (*pocketing the dice and picking up his spear*): Let us receive this man with honor. He bears evil tidings.

(*The* GUARDSMEN *seize their spears and gather about the gate, leaving a way through for the* NEW COMER.)

PERSIAN (*rising from his knee*): Are evil tidings, then, so honorable?
BELZANOR: O barbarous Persian, hear my instruction. In Egypt the bearer of good tidings is sacrificed to the gods as a thank offering; but no god will accept the blood of the messenger of evil. When we have good tidings, we are careful to send them in the mouth of the cheapest slave we can find. Evil tidings are borne by young noblemen who desire to bring themselves into notice. (*They join the rest at the gate.*)
SENTINEL: Pass, O young captain; and bow the head in the House of the Queen.
VOICE: Go anoint thy javelin with fat of swine, O Blackamoor; for before morning the Romans will make thee eat it to the very butt.

(*The owner of the* VOICE, *a fairhaired dandy, dressed in a different fashion from that affected by the* GUARDSMEN, *but no less extravagantly, comes through the gateway laughing. He is somewhat battlestained; and his left forearm, bandaged, comes through a torn sleeve. In his right hand he carries a Roman sword in its sheath. He swaggers down the courtyard, the* PERSIAN *on his right,* BELZANOR *on his left, and the* GUARDSMEN *crowding down behind him.*)

BELZANOR: Who are thou that laughest in the House of Cleopatra the Queen, and in the teeth of Belzanor, the captain of her guard?
NEW COMER: I am Bel Affris, descended from the gods.
BELZANOR (*ceremoniously*): Hail, cousin!
ALL (*except the* PERSIAN): Hail, cousin!

PERSIAN: All the Queen's guards are descended from the gods, O stranger, save myself. I am Persian, and descended from many kings.

BEL AFFRIS (*to the* GUARDSMEN): Hail, cousins! (*To the* PERSIAN, *condescendingly.*) Hail, mortal!

BELZANOR: You have been in battle, Bel Affris; and you are a soldier among soldiers. You will not let the Queen's women have the first of your tidings.

BEL AFFRIS: I have no tidings, except that we shall have our throats cut presently, women, soldiers, and all.

PERSIAN (*to* BELZANOR): I told you so.

SENTINEL (*who has been listening*): Woe, alas!

BEL AFFRIS (*calling to him*): Peace, peace, poor Ethiop: destiny is with the gods who painted thee black. (*To* BELZANOR.) What has this mortal (*indicating the* PERSIAN) told you?

BELZANOR: He says that the Roman Julius Cæsar, who has landed on our shores with a handful of followers, will make himself master of Egypt. He is afraid of the Roman soldiers. (*The* GUARDSMEN *laugh with boisterous scorn.*) Peasants, brought up to scare crows and follow the plough! Sons of smiths and millers and tanners! And we nobles, consecrated to arms, descended from the gods!

PERSIAN: Belzanor: the gods are not always good to their poor relations.

BELZANOR (*hotly, to the* PERSIAN): Man to man, are we worse than the slaves of Cæsar?

BEL AFFRIS (*stepping between them*): Listen, cousin. Man to man, we Egyptians are as gods above the Romans.

GUARDSMEN (*exultantly*): Aha!

BEL AFFRIS: But this Cæsar does not pit man against man: he throws a legion at you where you are weakest as he throws a stone from a catapult; and that legion is as a man with one head, a thousand arms, and no religion. I have fought against them; and I know.

BELZANOR (*derisively*): Were you frightened, cousin?

(*The* GUARDSMEN *roar with laughter, their eyes sparkling at the wit of their captain.*)

BEL AFFRIS: No, cousin; but I was beaten. They were frightened (perhaps); but they scattered us like chaff.

(*The* GUARDSMEN, *much damped, utter a growl of contemptuous disgust.*)

BELZANOR: Could you not die?

BEL AFFRIS: No: that was too easy to be worthy of a descendant of the gods. Besides, there was no time: all was over in a moment. The attack came just where we least expected it.

BELZANOR: That shews that the Romans are cowards.

BEL AFFRIS: They care nothing about cowardice, these Romans: they fight to win. The pride and honor of war are nothing to them.

PERSIAN: Tell us the tale of the battle. What befell?

GUARDSMEN (*gathering eagerly round* BEL AFFRIS): Ay: the tale of the battle.

BEL AFFRIS: Know then, that I am a novice in the guard of the temple of Ra in Memphis, serving neither Cleopatra nor her brother Ptolemy, but only the high gods. We went a journey to inquire of Ptolemy why he had driven Cleopatra into Syria, and how we of Egypt should deal with the Roman Pompey, newly come to our shores after his defeat by Cæsar at Pharsalia. What, think ye, did we learn? Even that Cæsar is coming also in hot pursuit of his foe, and that Ptolemy has slain Pompey, whose severed head he holds in readiness to present to the conqueror. (*Sensation among the* GUARDSMEN.) Nay, more: we found that Cæsar is already come; for we had not made half a day's journey on our way back when we came upon a city rabble flying from his legions, whose landing they had gone out to withstand.

BELZANOR: And ye, the temple guard! did ye not withstand these legions?

BEL AFFRIS: What a man could that we did. But there came the sound of a trumpet whose voice was as the cursing of a black mountain. Then saw we a moving wall of shields coming towards us. You know how the heart burns when you charge a fortified wall; but how if the fortified wall were to charge *you?*

PERSIAN (*exulting in having told them so*): Did I not say it?

BEL AFFRIS: When the wall came nigh, it changed into a line of men — common fellows enough, with helmets, leather tunics, and breastplates. Every man of them flung his javelin: the one that came my way drove through my shield as through a papyrus — lo there! (*he points to the bandage on his left arm*) and would have gone through my neck had I not stooped. They were charging at the double then, and were upon us with short swords almost as soon as their javelins. When a man is close to you with such a sword, you can do nothing with our weapons: they are all too long.

PERSIAN: What did you do?

BEL AFFRIS: Doubled my fist and smote my Roman on the sharpness of his jaw. He was but mortal after all: he lay down in a stupor; and I took his sword and laid it on. (*Drawing the sword.*) Lo! a Roman sword with Roman blood on it!

GUARDSMEN (*approvingly*): Good! (*They take the sword and hand it round, examining it curiously.*)

PERSIAN: And your men?

BEL AFFRIS: Fled. Scattered like sheep.

BELZANOR (*furiously*): The cowardly slaves! Leaving the descendants of the gods to be butchered!

BEL AFFRIS (*with acid coolness*): The descendants of the gods did not stay to be butchered, cousin. The battle was not to the strong; but the race was to the swift. The Romans, who have no chariots, sent a cloud of horsemen in pursuit, and slew multitudes. Then our high priest's captain rallied a dozen descendants of the gods and exhorted us to die fighting. I said to myself: surely it is safer to stand than to lose my breath and be stabbed in the back; so I joined our captain and stood. Then the Romans treated us with respect; for no man attacks a lion when the field is full of sheep, except for the pride and honor of war, of which these Romans know nothing. So we escaped with our lives; and I am come to warn you that you must open your gates to Cæsar; for his advance guard is scarce an hour behind me; and not an Egyptian warrior is left standing between you and his legions.

SENTINEL: Woe, alas! (*He throws down his javelin and flies into the palace.*)

BELZANOR: Nail him to the door, quick! (*The* GUARDSMEN *rush for him with their spears; but he is too quick for them.*) Now this news will run through the palace like fire through stubble.

BEL AFFRIS: What shall we do to save the women from the Romans?

BELZANOR: Why not kill them?

PERSIAN: Because we should have to pay blood money for some of them. Better let the Romans kill them: it is cheaper.

BELZANOR (*awestruck at his brain power*): O subtle one! O serpent!

BEL AFFRIS: But your Queen?

BELZANOR: True: we must carry off Cleopatra.

BEL AFFRIS: Will ye not await her command?

BELZANOR: Command! a girl of sixteen! Not we. At Memphis ye deem her a Queen: here we know better. I will take her on the crupper of my horse. When we soldiers have carried her out of Cæsar's reach, then the priests and the nurses and the rest of them can pretend she is a Queen again, and put their commands into her mouth.

PERSIAN: Listen to me, Belzanor.

BELZANOR: Speak, O subtle beyond thy years.

PERSIAN: Cleopatra's brother Ptolemy is at war with her. Let us sell her to him.

GUARDSMEN: O subtle one! O serpent!

BELZANOR: We dare not. We are descended from the gods; but Cleopatra is descended from the river Nile; and the lands of our fathers will grow no grain if the Nile rises not to water them. Without our father's gifts we should live the lives of dogs.

PERSIAN: It is true: the Queen's guard cannot live on its pay. But hear me further, O ye kinsmen of Osiris.

GUARDSMEN: Speak, O subtle one. Hear the serpent-begotten!

PERSIAN: Have I heretofore spoken truly to you of Cæsar, when you thought I mocked you?

GUARDSMEN: Truly, truly.

BELZANOR (*reluctantly admitting it*): So Bel Affris says.

PERSIAN: Hear more of him, then. This Cæsar is a great lover of women: he makes them his friends and counsellors.

BELZANOR: Faugh! This rule of women will be the ruin of Egypt!

PERSIAN: Let it rather be the ruin of Rome! Cæsar grows old now: he is past fifty and full of labors and battles. He is too old for the young women; and the old women are too wise to worship him.

BEL AFFRIS: Take heed, Persian. Cæsar is by this time almost within earshot.

PERSIAN: Cleopatra is not yet a woman: neither is she wise. But she already troubles men's wisdom.

BELZANOR: Ay: that is because she is descended from the river Nile and a black kitten of the sacred White Cat. What then?

PERSIAN: Why, sell her secretly to Ptolemy, and then offer ourselves to Cæsar as volunteers to fight for the overthrow of her brother and the rescue of our Queen, the Great Granddaughter of the Nile.

GUARDSMEN: O serpent!

PERSIAN: He will listen to us if we come with her picture in our mouths. He will conquer and kill her brother, and reign in Egypt with Cleopatra for his Queen. And we shall be her guard.

GUARDSMEN: O subtlest of all the serpents! O admiration! O wisdom!

BEL AFFRIS: He will also have arrived before you have done talking, O word spinner.

BELZANOR: That is true. (*An affrighted uproar in the palace interrupts him.*) Quick: the flight has begun: guard the door. (*They rush to the door and form a cordon before it with their spears. A mob of women-servants and nurses surges out. Those in front recoil from the spears, screaming to those behind to keep back.* BELZANOR*'s voice dominates the disturbance as he shouts.*) Back there. In again, unprofitable cattle.

GUARDSMEN: Back, unprofitable cattle.

BELZANOR: Send us out Ftatateeta, the Queen's chief nurse.

THE WOMEN (*calling into the palace*): Ftatateeta, Ftatateeta. Come, come. Speak to Belzanor.

A WOMAN: Oh, keep back. You are thrusting me on the spearheads.

(*A huge grim woman, her face covered with a network of tiny wrinkles, and her eyes old, large, and wise; sinewy handed, very tall, very strong; with the mouth of a bloodhound and the jaws of a bulldog, appears on the threshold. She is dressed like a person of consequence in the palace, and confronts the* GUARDSMEN *insolently.*)

FTATATEETA: Make way for the Queen's chief nurse.

BELZANOR (*with solemn arrogance*): Ftatateeta: I am Belzanor, the captain of the Queen's guard, descended from the gods.

FTATATEETA (*retorting his arrogance with interest*): Belzanor: I am Ftatateeta, the Queen's chief nurse; and your divine ancestors were proud to be painted on the wall in the pyramids of the kings whom my fathers served.

(*The* WOMEN *laugh triumphantly.*)

BELZANOR (*with grim humor*): Ftatateeta: daughter of a long-tongued, swivel-eyed chameleon, the Romans are at hand. (*A cry of terror from the* WOMEN: *they would fly but for the spears.*) Not even the descendants of the gods can resist them; for they have each man seven arms, each carrying seven spears. The blood in their veins is boiling quicksilver; and their wives become mothers in three hours, and are slain and eaten the next day.

(*A shudder of horror from the* WOMEN. FTATATEETA, *despising them and scorning the soldiers, pushes her way through the crowd and confronts the spear points undismayed.*)

FTATATEETA: Then fly and save yourselves, O cowardly sons of the cheap clay gods that are sold to fish porters; and leave us to shift for ourselves.

BELZANOR: Not until you have first done our bidding, O terror of manhood. Bring out Cleopatra the Queen to us; and then go whither you will.

FTATATEETA (*with a derisive laugh*): Now I know why the gods have taken her out of our hands. (*The* GUARDSMEN *start and look at one another.*) Know, thou foolish soldier, that the Queen has been missing since an hour past sundown.

BELZANOR (*furious*): Hag: you have hidden her to sell to Cæsar or her brother. (*He grasps her by the left wrist, and drags her, helped by a few of the* GUARD, *to the middle of the courtyard, where, as they fling her on her knees, he draws a murderous looking knife.*) Where is she? Where is she? or — (*He threatens to cut her throat.*)

FTATATEETA (*savagely*): Touch me, dog; and the Nile will not rise on your fields for seven times seven years of famine.

BELZANOR (*frightened, but desperate*): I will sacrifice: I will pay. Or stay. (*To the* PERSIAN.) You, O subtle one: your father's lands lie far from the Nile. Slay her.

PERSIAN (*threatening her with his knife*): Persia has but one god; yet he loves the blood of old women. Where is Cleopatra?

FTATATEETA: Persian: as Osiris lives, I do not know. I chid her for bringing evil days upon us by talking to the sacred cats of the priests, and carrying them in her arms. I told her she would be left alone here when the Romans came as a punishment for her disobedience. And now she is gone — run away — hidden. I speak the truth. I call Osiris to witness —

THE WOMEN (*protesting officiously*): She speaks the truth, Belzanor.

BELZANOR: You have frightened the child: she is hiding. Search — quick — into the palace — search every corner.

(*The* GUARDS, *led by* BELZANOR, *shoulder their way into the palace through the flying crowd of* WOMEN, *who escape through the courtyard gate.*)

FTATATEETA (*screaming*): Sacrilege! Men in the Queen's chambers! Sa — (*Her voice dies away as the* PERSIAN *puts his knife to her throat.*)

BEL AFFRIS (*laying a hand on* FTATATEETA'*s left shoulder*): Forbear her yet a moment, Persian. (*To* FTATATEETA, *very significantly.*) Mother: your gods are asleep or away hunting; and the sword is at your throat. Bring us to where the Queen is hid, and you shall live.

FTATATEETA (*contemptuously*): Who shall stay the sword in the hand of a fool, if the high gods put it there? Listen to me, ye young men without understanding. Cleopatra fears me; but she fears the Romans more. There is but one power greater in her eyes than the wrath of the Queen's nurse and the cruelty of Cæsar; and that is the power of the Sphinx that sits in the desert watching the way to the sea. What she would have it know, she tells into the ears of the sacred cats; and on her birthday she sacrifices to it and decks it with poppies. Go ye therefore into the desert and seek Cleopatra in the shadow of the Sphinx; and on your heads see to it that no harm comes to her.

BEL AFFRIS (*to the* PERSIAN): May we believe this, O subtle one?

PERSIAN: Which way come the Romans?

BEL AFFRIS: Over the desert, from the sea, by this very Sphinx.

PERSIAN (*to* FTATATEETA): O mother of guile! O aspic's tongue! You have made up this tale so that we two may go into the desert and perish on the spears of the Romans. (*Lifting his knife.*) Taste death.

FTATATEETA: Not from thee, baby. (*She snatches his ankle from under him and flies stooping along the palace wall, vanishing in the darkness within its precinct.* BEL AFFRIS *roars with laughter as the* PERSIAN *tumbles. The* GUARDSMEN *rush out of the palace with* BELZANOR *and a mob of fugitives, mostly carrying bundles.*)

PERSIAN: Have you found Cleopatra?

BELZANOR: She is gone. We have searched every corner.

SENTINEL (*appearing at the door of the palace*): Woe! Alas! Fly, fly!

BELZANOR: What is the matter now?

SENTINEL: The sacred white cat has been stolen.

ALL: Woe! woe! (*General panic. They all fly with cries of consternation. The torch is thrown down and extinguished in the rush. The noise of the fugitives dies away. Darkness and dead silence.*)

## ACT I

*The same darkness into which the temple of Ra and the Syrian palace vanished. The same silence. Suspense. Then the blackness and stillness break softly into silver mist and strange airs as the windswept harp of Memnon plays at the dawning of the moon. It rises full over the desert; and a vast horizon comes into relief, broken by a huge shape which soon reveals itself in the spreading radiance as a Sphinx pedestalled on the sands. The light still clears, until the upraised eyes of the image are distinguished looking straight forward and upward in infinite fearless vigil, and a mass of color between its great paws defines itself as a heap of red poppies on which a girl lies motionless, her silken vest heaving gently and regularly with the breathing of a dreamless sleeper, and her braided hair glittering in a shaft of moonlight like a bird's wing.*

*Suddenly there comes from afar a vaguely fearful sound (it might be the bellow of a Minotaur softened by great distance) and Memnon's music stops. Silence: then a few faint high-ringing trumpet notes. Then silence again. Then a man comes from the south with stealing steps, ravished by the mystery of the night, all wonder, and halts, lost in contemplation, opposite the left flank of the Sphinx, whose bosom, with its burden, is hidden from him by its massive shoulder.*

THE MAN: Hail, Sphinx: salutation from Julius Cæsar! I have wandered in many lands, seeking the lost regions from which my birth into this world exiled me, and the company of creatures such as I myself. I have found flocks and pastures, men and cities, but no other Cæsar, no air native to me, no man kindred to me, none who can do my day's deed, and think my night's thought. In the little world yonder, Sphinx, my place is as high as yours in this great desert; only I wander, and you sit still; I conquer, and you endure; I work and wonder, you watch and wait; I look up and am dazzled, look down and am darkened, look round and am puzzled, whilst your eyes never turn from looking out – out of the world – to the lost region – the home from which we have strayed. Sphinx, you and I, strangers to the race of men, are no strangers to one another: have I not been conscious of you and of this place since I was born? Rome is a madman's dream: this is my Reality. These starry lamps of yours I have seen from afar in Gaul, in Britain, in Spain, in Thessaly, signalling great secrets to some eternal sentinel below, whose post I never could find. And here at last is their sentinel – an image of the constant and immortal part of my life, silent, full of thoughts, alone in the silver desert. Sphinx, Sphinx: I have climbed mountains at night to hear in the distance the stealthy footfall of the winds that chase your sands in forbidden play – our invisible children, O Sphinx, laughing in whispers. My way hither was the way of destiny; for I am he of whose genius you are the symbol: part brute, part woman, and part god – nothing of man in me at all. Have I read your riddle, Sphinx?

THE GIRL (*who has wakened, and peeped cautiously from her nest to see who is speaking*): Old gentleman.

CÆSAR (*staring violently, and clutching his sword*): Immortal gods!

THE GIRL: Old gentleman: dont run away.

CÆSAR (*stupefied*): "Old gentleman: dont run away"!!! This! to Julius Cæsar!

THE GIRL (*urgently*): Old gentleman.

CÆSAR: Sphinx: you presume on your centuries. I am younger than you, though your voice is but a girl's voice as yet.

THE GIRL: Climb up here, quickly; or the Romans will come and eat you.

CÆSAR (*running forward past the Sphinx's shoulder, and seeing her*): A child at its breast! a divine child!

THE GIRL: Come up quickly. You must get up at its side and creep round.

CÆSAR (*amazed*): Who are you?

THE GIRL: Cleopatra, Queen of Egypt.

CÆSAR: Queen of the Gypsies, you mean.

CLEOPATRA: You must not be disrespectful to me, or the Sphinx will let the Romans eat you. Come up. It is quite cosy here.

CÆSAR (*to himself*): What a dream! What a magnificent dream! Only let me not wake, and I will conquer ten continents to pay for dreaming it out to the end. (*He climbs to the Sphinx's flank, and presently reappears to her on the pedestal, stepping round its right shoulder.*)

CLEOPATRA: Take care. Thats right. Now sit down: you may have its other paw. (*She seats herself comfortably on its left paw.*) It is very powerful and will protect us; but (*shivering, and with plaintive loneliness*) it would not take any notice of me or keep me company. I am glad you have come: I was very lonely. Did you happen to see a white cat anywhere?

CÆSAR (*sitting slowly down on the right paw in extreme wonderment*): Have you lost one?

CLEOPATRA: Yes: the sacred white cat: is it not dreadful? I brought him here to sacrifice him to the Sphinx; but when we got a little way from the city a black cat called him, and he jumped out of my arms and ran away to it. Do you think that the black cat can have been my great-great-great-grandmother?

CÆSAR (*staring at her*): Your great-great-great-grandmother! Well, why not? Nothing would surprise me on this night of nights.

CLEOPATRA: I think it must have been. My great-grandmother's great-grandmother was a black kitten of the sacred white cat; and the river Nile made her his seventh wife. That is why my hair is so wavy. And I always want to be let do as I like, no matter whether it is the will of the gods or not: that is because my blood is made with Nile water.

CÆSAR: What are you doing here at this time of night? Do you live here?

CLEOPATRA: Of course not: I am the Queen; and I shall live in the palace at Alexandria when I have killed my brother, who drove me out of it. When I am old enough I shall do just what I like. I shall be able to poison the slaves and see them wriggle, and pretend to Ftatateeta that she is going to be put into the fiery furnace.

CÆSAR: Hm! Meanwhile why are you not at home and in bed?

CLEOPATRA: Because the Romans are coming to eat us all. You are not at home and in bed either.

CÆSAR (*with conviction*): Yes I am. I live in a tent; and I am now in that tent, fast asleep and dreaming. Do you suppose that I believe you are real, you impossible little dream witch?

CLEOPATRA (*giggling and leaning trustfully towards him*): You are a funny old gentleman. I like you.

CÆSAR: Ah, that spoils the dream. Why dont you dream that I am young?

CLEOPATRA: I wish you were; only I think I should be more afraid of you. I like men, especially young men with round strong arms; but I am afraid of them. You are old and rather thin and stringy; but you have a nice voice; and I like to have somebody to talk to, though I think you are a little mad. It is the moon that makes you talk to yourself in that silly way.

CÆSAR: What! you heard that, did you? I was saying my prayers to the great Sphinx.

CLEOPATRA: But this isn't the great Sphinx.

CÆSAR (*much disappointed, looking up at the statue*): What!

CLEOPATRA: This is only a dear little kitten of a Sphinx. Why, the great Sphinx is so big that it has a temple between its paws. This is my pet Sphinx. Tell me: do you think the Romans have any sorcerers who could take us away from the Sphinx by magic?

CÆSAR: Why? Are you afraid of the Romans?

CLEOPATRA (*very seriously*): Oh, they would eat us if they caught us. They are barbarians. Their chief is called Julius Cæsar. His father was a tiger and his mother a burning mountain; and his nose is like an elephant's trunk. (CÆSAR *involuntarily rubs his nose.*) They all have long noses, and ivory tusks, and little tails, and seven arms with a hundred arrows in each; and they live on human flesh.

CÆSAR: Would you like me to shew you a real Roman?

CLEOPATRA (*terrified*): No. You are frightening me.

CÆSAR: No matter: this is only a dream —

CLEOPATRA (*excitedly*): It is not a dream: it is not a dream. See, see. (*She plucks a pin from her hair and jabs it repeatedly into his arm.*)

CÆSAR: Ffff — Stop. (*Wrathfully.*) How dare you?

CLEOPATRA (*abashed*): You said you were dreaming. (*Whimpering.*) I only wanted to shew you —

CÆSAR (*gently*): Come, come: dont cry. A queen mustnt cry. (*He rubs his arm, wondering at the reality of the smart.*) Am I awake? (*He strikes his hand against the Sphinx to test its solidity. It feels so real that he begins to be alarmed, and says perplexedly.*) Yes, I — (*quite panic-stricken*) no: impossible: madness, madness! (*Desperately.*) Back to camp — to camp. (*He rises to spring down from the pedestal.*)

CLEOPATRA (*flinging her arms in terror round him*): No: you shant leave me. No, no, no: dont go. I'm afraid — afraid of the Romans.

CÆSAR (*as the conviction that he is really awake forces itself on him*): Cleopatra: can you see my face well?

CLEOPATRA: Yes. It is so white in the moonlight.

CÆSAR: Are you sure it is the moonlight that makes me look whiter than an Egyptian? (*Grimly.*) Do you notice that I have a rather long nose?

CLEOPATRA (*recoiling, paralysed by a terrible suspicion*): Oh!

CÆSAR: It is a Roman nose, Cleopatra.

CLEOPATRA: Ah! (*With a piercing scream she springs up; darts round the left shoulder of the Sphinx; scrambles down to the sand; and falls on her knees in frantic supplication, shrieking.*) Bite him in two, Sphinx: bite him in two. I meant to sacrifice the white cat – I did indeed – I (CÆSAR, *who has slipped down from the pedestal, touches her on the shoulder.*) – Ah! (*She buries her head in her arms.*)

CÆSAR: Cleopatra: Shall I teach you a way to prevent Cæsar from eating you?

CLEOPATRA (*clinging to him piteously*): Oh do, do, do. I will steal Ftatateeta's jewels and give them to you. I will make the river Nile water your lands twice a year.

CÆSAR: Peace, peace, my child. Your gods are afraid of the Romans: you see the Sphinx dare not bite me, nor prevent me carrying you off to Julius Cæsar.

CLEOPATRA (*in pleading murmurings*): You wont, you wont. You said you wouldnt.

CÆSAR: Cæsar never eats women.

CLEOPATRA (*springing up full of hope*): What!

CÆSAR (*impressively*): But he eats girls (*she relapses*) and cats. Now you are a silly little girl; and you are descended from the black kitten. You are both a girl and a cat.

CLEOPATRA (*trembling*): And will he eat *me?*

CÆSAR: Yes; unless you make him believe that you are a woman.

CLEOPATRA: Oh, you must get a sorcerer to make a woman of me. Are you a sorcerer?

CÆSAR: Perhaps. But it will take a long time; and this very night you must stand face to face with Cæsar in the palace of your fathers.

CLEOPATRA: No, no. I darent.

CÆSAR: Whatever dread may be in your soul – however terrible Cæsar may be to you – you must confront him as a brave woman and a great queen; and you must feel no fear. If your hand shakes: if your voice quavers; then – night and death! (*She moans.*) But if he thinks you worthy to rule, he will set you on the throne by his side and make you the real ruler of Egypt.

CLEOPATRA (*despairingly*): No: he will find me out: he will find me out.

CÆSAR (*rather mournfully*): He is easily deceived by women. Their eyes dazzle him; and he sees them not as they are, but as he wishes them to appear to him.

CLEOPATRA (*hopefully*): Then we will cheat him. I will put on Ftatateeta's head-dress; and he will think me quite an old woman.

CÆSAR: If you do that he will eat you at one mouthful.

CLEOPATRA: But I will give him a cake with my magic opal and seven hairs of the white cat baked in it; and –

CÆSAR (*abruptly*): Pah! you are a little fool. He will eat your cake and you too. (*He turns contemptuously from her.*)

CLEOPATRA (*running after him and clinging to him*): Oh please, *please!* I will do whatever you tell me. I will be good. I will be your slave. (*Again the terrible bellowing note sounds across the desert, now closer at hand. It is the bucina, the Roman war trumpet.*)

CÆSAR: Hark!

CLEOPATRA (*trembling*): What was that?

CÆSAR: Cæsar's voice.

CLEOPATRA (*pulling at his hand*): Let us run away. Come. Oh, come.

CÆSAR: You are safe with me until you stand on your throne to receive Cæsar. Now lead me thither.

CLEOPATRA (*only too glad to get away*): I will, I will. (*Again the bucina.*) Oh come, come, come: the gods are angry. Do you feel the earth shaking?

CÆSAR: It is the tread of Cæsar's legions.

CLEOPATRA (*drawing him away*): This way, quickly. And let us look for the white cat as we go. It is he that has turned you into a Roman.

CÆSAR: Incorrigible, oh, incorrigible! Away! (*He follows her, the bucina sounding louder as they steal across the desert. The moonlight wanes: the horizon again shows black against the sky, broken only by the fantastic silhouette of the Sphinx. The sky itself vanishes in darkness, from which there is no relief until the gleam of a distant torch falls on great Egyptian pillars supporting the roof of a majestic corridor. At the further end of this corridor a Nubian slave appears carrying the torch.* CÆSAR, *still led by* CLEOPATRA, *follows him. They come down the corridor,* CÆSAR *peering keenly about at the strange architecture, and at the pillar shadows between which, as the passing torch makes them hurry noiselessly backwards, figures of men with wings and hawks' heads, and vast black marble cats, seem to flit in and out of ambush. Further along, the wall turns a corner and makes a spacious transept in which* CÆSAR *sees, on his right, a throne, and behind the throne a door. On each side of the throne is a slender pillar with a lamp on it.*)

CÆSAR: What place is this?

CLEOPATRA: This is where I sit on the throne when I am allowed to wear my crown and robes. (*The slave holds his torch to shew the throne.*)

CÆSAR: Order the slave to light the lamps.

CLEOPATRA (*shyly*): Do you think I may?

CÆSAR: Of course. You are the Queen. (*She hesitates.*) Go on.

CLEOPATRA (*timidly, to the slave*): Light all the lamps.

FTATATEETA (*suddenly coming from behind the throne*): Stop. (*The slave stops. She turns sternly to* CLEOPATRA, *who quails like a naughty child.*) Who is this you have with you; and how dare you order the lamps to be lighted without my permission? (CLEOPATRA *is dumb with apprehension.*)

CÆSAR: Who is she?

CLEOPATRA: Ftatateeta.

FTATATEETA (*arrogantly*): Chief nurse to –

CÆSAR (*cutting her short*): I speak to the Queen. Be silent. (*To* CLEOPATRA.) Is this how your servants know their places? Send her away; and do you (*to the slave*) do as the Queen has bidden. (*The slave lights the lamps. Meanwhile* CLEOPATRA *stands hesitating, afraid of* FTATATEETA.) You are the Queen: send her away.

CLEOPATRA (*cajoling*): Ftatateeta, dear: you must go away – just for a little.

CÆSAR: You are not commanding her to go away: you are begging her. You are no Queen. You will be eaten. Farewell. (*He turns to go.*)

CLEOPATRA (*clutching him*): No, no, no. Dont leave me.

CÆSAR: A Roman does not stay with queens who are afraid of their slaves.

CLEOPATRA: I am not afraid. Indeed I am not afraid.

FTATATEETA: We shall see who is afraid here. (*Menacingly.*) Cleopatra –

CÆSAR: On your knees, woman: am I also a child that you dare trifle with me? (*He points to the floor at* CLEOPATRA'*s feet.* FTATATEETA, *half cowed, half savage, hesitates.* CÆSAR *calls to the* NUBIAN.) Slave. (*The* NUBIAN *comes to him.*) Can you cut off a head? (*The* NUBIAN *nods and grins ecstatically, showing all his teeth. Cæsar takes his sword by the scabbard, ready to offer the hilt to the* NUBIAN, *and turns again to* FTATATEETA, *repeating his gesture.*) Have you remembered yourself, mistress?

(FTATATEETA, *crushed, kneels before* CLEOPATRA, *who can hardly believe her eyes.*)

FTATATEETA (*hoarsely*): O Queen, forget not thy servant in the days of thy greatness.

CLEOPATRA (*blazing with excitement*): Go. Begone. Go away. (FTATATEETA *rises with stooped head, and moves backwards towards the door.* CLEOPATRA *watches her submission eagerly, almost clapping her hands, which are trembling. Suddenly she cries.*) Give me something to beat her with. (*She snatches a snake-skin from the throne and dashes after* FTATATEETA, *whirling it like a scourge in the air.* CÆSAR *makes a bound and manages to catch her and hold her while* FTATATEETA *escapes.*)

CÆSAR: You scratch, kitten, do you?

CLEOPATRA (*breaking from him*): I *will* beat somebody. I will beat *him.* (*She attacks the slave.*) There, there, there! (*The slave flies for his life up the corridor and vanishes. She throws the snake-skin away and jumps on the step of the throne with her arms waving, crying.*) I am a real Queen at last – a real, real Queen! Cleopatra the Queen! (CÆSAR *shakes his head dubiously, the advantage of the change seeming open to question from the point of view of the general welfare of Egypt. She turns and looks at him exultantly. Then she jumps down from the steps, runs to him, and flings her arms round him rapturously, crying.*) Oh, I love you for making me a Queen.

CÆSAR: But queens love only kings.

CLEOPATRA: I will make all the men I love kings. I will make you a king. I will have many young kings, with round strong arms; and when I am tired of them I will whip them to death; but you shall always be my king: my nice, kind, wise, good old king.

CÆSAR: Oh, my wrinkles, my wrinkles! And my child's heart! You will be the most dangerous of all Cæsar's conquests.

CLEOPATRA (*appalled*): Cæsar! I forgot Cæsar. (*Anxiously.*) You will tell him that I am a Queen, will you not? – a real Queen. Listen! (*stealthily coaxing him*) let us run away and hide until Cæsar is gone.

CÆSAR: If you fear Cæsar, you are no true queen; and though you were to hide beneath a pyramid, he would go straight to it and lift it with one hand. And then – ! (*He chops his teeth together.*)

CLEOPATRA (*trembling*): Oh!

CÆSAR: Be afraid if you dare. (*The note of the bucina resounds again in the distance. She moans with fear.* CÆSAR *exults in it, exclaiming.*) Aha! Cæsar approaches the throne of Cleopatra. Come: take your place. (*He takes her hand and leads her to the throne. She is too downcast to speak.*) Ho, there, Teetatota. How do you call your slaves?

CLEOPATRA (*spiritlessly, as she sinks on the throne and cowers there, shaking*): Clap your hands.

(*He claps his hands.* FTATATEETA *returns.*)

CÆSAR: Bring the Queen's robes, and her crown, and her women; and prepare her.

CLEOPATRA (*eagerly – recovering herself a little*): Yes, the crown, Ftatateeta: I shall wear the crown.

FTATATEETA: For whom must the Queen put on her state?

CÆSAR: For a citizen of Rome. A king of kings, Totateeta.

CLEOPATRA (*stamping at her*): How dare you ask questions? Go and do as you are told. (FTATATEETA *goes out with a grim smile.* CLEOPATRA *goes on eagerly, to* CÆSAR.) Cæsar will know that I am a Queen when he sees my crown and robes, will he not?

CÆSAR: No. How shall he know that you are not a slave dressed up in the Queen's ornaments?

CLEOPATRA: You must tell him.

CÆSAR: He will not ask me. He will know Cleopatra by her pride, her courage, her majesty, and her beauty. (*She looks very doubtful.*) Are you trembling?

CLEOPATRA (*shivering with dread*): No, I – I – (*In a very sickly voice.*) No.

(FTATATEETA *and three* WOMEN *come in with the regalia.*)

FTATATEETA: Of all the Queen's women, these three alone are left. The rest are fled. (*They begin to deck* CLEOPATRA, *who submits, pale and motionless.*)

CÆSAR: Good, good. Three are enough. Poor Cæsar generally has to dress himself.

FTATATEETA (*contemptuously*): The Queen of Egypt is not a Roman barbarian. (*To* CLEOPATRA.) Be brave, my nursling. Hold up your head before this stranger.

CÆSAR (*admiring* CLEOPATRA, *and placing the crown on her head*): Is it sweet or bitter to be a Queen, Cleopatra?

CLEOPATRA: Bitter.

CÆSAR: Cast out fear; and you will conquer Cæsar. Tota: are the Romans at hand?

FTATATEETA: They are at hand; and the guard has fled.

THE WOMEN (*wailing subduedly*): Woe to us!

(*The* NUBIAN *comes running down the hall.*)

NUBIAN: The Romans are in the courtyard. (*He bolts through the door. With a shriek, the* WOMEN *fly after him.* FTATATEETA*'s jaw expresses savage resolution: she does not budge.* CLEOPATRA *can hardly restrain herself from following them.* CÆSAR *grips her wrist, and looks steadfastly at her. She stands like a martyr.*)

CÆSAR: The Queen must face Cæsar alone. Answer "So be it."

CLEOPATRA (*white*): So be it.

CÆSAR (*releasing her*): Good.

(*A tramp and tumult of armed men is heard.* CLEOPATRA*'s terror increases. The bucina sounds close at hand, followed by a formidable clangor of trumpets. This is too much for* CLEOPATRA: *she utters a cry and darts towards the door.* FTATATEETA *stops her ruthlessly.*)

FTATATEETA: You are my nursling. You have said "So be it"; and if you die for it, you must make the Queen's word good. (*She hands* CLEOPATRA *to* CÆSAR, *who takes her back, almost beside herself with apprehension, to the throne.*)

CÆSAR: Now, if you quail — ! (*He seats himself on the throne.*)

(*She stands on the step, all but unconscious, waiting for death. The Roman soldiers troop in tumultuously through the corridor, headed by their ensign with his eagle, and their bucinator, a burly fellow with his instrument coiled round his body, its brazen bell shaped like the head of a howling wolf. When they reach the transept, they stare in amazement at the throne; dress into ordered rank opposite it; draw their swords and lift them in the air with a shout of* Hail, Cæsar. CLEOPATRA *turns and stares wildly at* CÆSAR; *grasps the situation; and, with a great sob of relief, falls into his arms.*)

# ACT II

*Alexandria. A hall on the first floor of the Palace, ending in a loggia approached by two steps. Through the arches of the loggia the Mediterranean can be seen, bright in the morning sun. The clean lofty walls, painted with a procession of the Egyptian theocracy, presented in profile as flat ornament, and the absence of mirrors, sham perspectives, stuffy upholstery and textiles, make the place handsome, wholesome, simple and cool, or, as a rich English manufacturer would express it, poor, bare, ridiculous and unhomely. For Tottenham Court Road civilization is to this Egyptian civilization as glass bead and tattoo civilization is to Tottenham Court Road.*

*The young king* PTOLEMY DIONYSUS *(aged ten) is at the top of the steps, on his way in through the loggia, led by his guardian* POTHINUS, *who has him by the hand. The court is assembled to receive him. It is made up of men and women (some of the women being officials) of various complexions and races, mostly Egyptian; some of them, comparatively fair, from lower Egypt, some, much darker, from upper Egypt; with a few Greeks and Jews. Prominent in a group on* PTOLEMY*'s right hand is* THEODOTUS, PTOLEMY*'s tutor. Another group, on* PTOLEMY*'s left, is headed by* ACHILLAS, *the general of* PTOLEMY*'s troops.* THEODOTUS *is a little old man, whose features are as cramped and wizened as his limbs, except his tall straight forehead, which occupies more space than all the rest of his face. He maintains an air of magpie keenness and profundity, listening to what the others say with the sarcastic vigilance of a philosopher listening to the exercises of his disciples.* ACHILLAS *is a tall handsome man of thirty-five, with a fine black beard curled like the coat of a poodle. Apparently not a clever man, but distinguished and dignified.* POTHINUS *is a vigorous man of fifty, a eunuch, passionate, energetic and quick witted, but of common mind and character; impatient and unable to control his temper. He has fine tawny hair, like fur.* PTOLEMY, *the King, looks much older than an English boy of ten; but he has the childish air, the habit of being in leading strings, the mixture of impotence and petulance, the appearance of being excessively washed, combed and dressed by other hands, which is exhibited by court-bred princes of all ages.*

*All receive the King with reverences. He comes down the steps to a chair of state which stands a little to his right, the only seat in the hall. Taking his place before it, he looks nervously for instructions to* POTHINUS, *who places himself at his left hand.*

POTHINUS: The King of Egypt has a word to speak.

THEODOTUS (*in a squeak which he makes impressive by sheer self-opinionativeness*): Peace for the King's word!

PTOLEMY (*without any vocal inflexions: he is evidently repeating a lesson*): Take notice of this all of you. I am the first-born son of Auletes the Flute Blower who was your King. My sister Berenice drove him from his throne and reigned in his stead but — but — (*he hesitates*) —

POTHINUS (*stealthily prompting*): — but the gods would not suffer —

PTOLEMY: Yes — the gods would not suffer — not suffer — (*He stops; then, crestfallen.*) I forget what the gods would not suffer.

THEODOTUS: Let Pothinus, the King's guardian, speak for the King.

POTHINUS (*suppressing his impatience with difficulty*): The King wished to say that the gods would not suffer the impiety of his sister to go unpunished.

PTOLEMY (*hastily*): Yes: I remember the rest of it. (*He resumes his monotone.*) Therefore the gods sent a stranger one Mark Antony a Roman captain of horsemen across the sands of the desert and he set my father again upon the throne. And my father took Berenice my sister and struck her head off. And now that my father is dead yet another of his daughters my sister Cleopatra would snatch the kingdom from me and reign in my place. But the gods would not suffer — (POTHINUS *coughs admonitorily*) — the gods — the gods would not suffer —

POTHINUS (*prompting*): — will not maintain —

PTOLEMY: Oh yes — will not maintain such iniquity they will give her head to the axe even as her sister's. But with the help of the witch Ftatateeta she hath cast a spell on the Roman Julius Cæsar to make him uphold her false pretence to rule in Egypt. Take notice then that I will not suffer — that I will not suffer — (*Pettishly, to* POTHINUS.) What is it that I will not suffer?

POTHINUS (*suddenly exploding with all the force and emphasis of political passion*): The King will not suffer a foreigner to take from him the throne of our Egypt. (*A shout of applause.*) Tell the King, Achillas, how many soldiers and horsemen follow the Roman?

THEODOTUS: Let the King's general speak!

ACHILLAS: But two Roman legions, O King. Three thousand soldiers and scarce a thousand horsemen.

(*The court breaks into derisive laughter; and a great chattering begins, amid which* RUFIO, *a Roman officer, appears in the loggia. He is a burly, black-bearded man of middle age, very blunt, prompt and rough, with small clear eyes, and plump nose and cheeks, which, however, like the rest of his flesh, are in iron-hard condition.*)

RUFIO (*from the steps*): Peace, ho! (*The laughter and chatter cease abruptly.*) Cæsar approaches.

THEODOTUS (*with much presence of mind*): The King permits the Roman commander to enter!

(CÆSAR, *plainly dressed, but wearing an oak wreath to conceal his bald-*

*ness, enters from the loggia, attended by* BRITANNUS, *his secretary, a Briton, about forty, tall, solemn, and already slightly bald, with a heavy, drooping, hazel-coloured moustache trained so as to lose its ends in a pair of trim whiskers. He is carefully dressed in blue, with portfolio, inkhorn, and reed pen at his girdle. His serious air and sense of the importance of the business in hand is in marked contrast to the kindly interest of* CÆSAR, *who looks at the scene, which is new to him, with the frank curiosity of a child, and then turns to the King's chair:* BRITANNUS *and* RUFIO *posting themselves near the steps at the other side.*)

CÆSAR (*looking at* POTHINUS *and* PTOLEMY): Which is the King? the man or the boy?

POTHINUS: I am Pothinus, the guardian of my lord the King.

CÆSAR (*patting* PTOLEMY *kindly on the shoulder*): So you are the King. Dull work at your age, eh? (*To* POTHINUS.) Your servant, Pothinus. (*He turns away unconcernedly and comes slowly along the middle of the hall, looking from side to side at the courtiers until he reaches* ACHILLAS.) And this gentleman?

THEODOTUS: Achillas, the King's general.

CÆSAR (*to* ACHILLAS, *very friendly*): A general, eh? I am a general myself. But I began too old, too old. Health and many victories, Achillas!

ACHILLAS: As the gods will, Cæsar.

CÆSAR (*turning to* THEODOTUS): And you, sir, are — ?

THEODOTUS: Theodotus, the King's tutor.

CÆSAR: You teach men how to be kings, Theodotus. That is very clever of you. (*Looking at the gods on the walls as he turns away from* THEODOTUS *and goes up again to* POTHINUS.) And this place?

POTHINUS: The council chamber of the chancellors of the King's treasury, Cæsar.

CÆSAR: Ah! that reminds me. I want some money.

POTHINUS: The King's treasury is poor, Cæsar.

CÆSAR: Yes: I notice that there is but one chair in it.

RUFIO (*shouting gruffly*): Bring a chair there, some of you, for Cæsar.

PTOLEMY (*rising shyly to offer his chair*): Cæsar —

CÆSAR (*kindly*): No, no, my boy: that is your chair of state. Sit down.

(*He makes* PTOLEMY *sit down again. Meanwhile* RUFIO, *looking about him, sees in the nearest corner an image of the god Ra, represented as a seated man with the head of a hawk. Before the image is a bronze tripod, about as large as a three-legged stool, with a stick of incense burning on it.* RUFIO, *with Roman resourcefulness and indifference to foreign superstitions, promptly seizes the tripod; shakes off the incense; blows away the ash; and dumps it down behind* CÆSAR, *nearly in the middle of the hall.*)

RUFIO: Sit on that, Cæsar.

(*A shiver runs through the court, followed by a hissing whisper of* Sacrilege!)

CÆSAR (*seating himself*): Now, Pothinus, to business. I am badly in want of money.

BRITANNUS (*disapproving of these informal expressions*): My master would say that there is a lawful debt due to Rome by Egypt, contracted by the King's deceased father to the Triumvirate; and that it is Cæsar's duty to his country to require immediate payment.

CÆSAR (*blandly*): Ah, I forgot. I have not made my companions known here. Pothinus: this is Britannus, my secretary. He is an islander from the western end of the world, a day's voyage from Gaul. (BRITANNUS *bows stiffly.*) This gentleman is Rufio, my comrade in arms. (RUFIO *nods.*) Pothinus: I want 1,600 talents.

(*The courtiers, appalled, murmur loudly, and* THEODOTUS *and* ACHILLAS *appeal mutely to one another against so monstrous a demand.*)

POTHINUS (*aghast*): Forty million sesterces! Impossible. There is not so much money in the King's treasury.

CÆSAR (*encouragingly*): *Only* 1,600 talents, Pothinus. Why count it in sesterces? A sestertius is only worth a loaf of bread.

POTHINUS: And a talent is worth a racehorse. I say it is impossible. We have been at strife here, because the King's sister Cleopatra falsely claims his throne. The King's taxes have not been collected for a whole year.

CÆSAR: Yes they have, Pothinus. My officers have been collecting them all morning. (*Renewed whisper and sensation, not without some stifled laughter, among the courtiers.*)

RUFIO (*bluntly*): You must pay, Pothinus. Why waste words? You are getting off cheaply enough.

POTHINUS (*bitterly*): Is it possible that Cæsar, the conqueror of the world, has time to occupy himself with such a trifle as our taxes?

CÆSAR: My friend: taxes are the chief business of a conqueror of the world.

POTHINUS: Then take warning, Cæsar. This day, the treasures of the temple and the gold of the King's treasury shall be sent to the mint to be melted down for our ransom in the sight of the people. They shall see us sitting under bare walls and drinking from wooden cups. And their wrath be on your head, Cæsar, if you force us to this sacrilege!

CÆSAR: Do not fear, Pothinus: the people know how well wine tastes in wooden cups. In return for your bounty, I will settle this dispute about the throne for you, if you will. What say you?

POTHINUS: If I say no, will that hinder you?

RUFIO (*defiantly*): No.

CÆSAR: You say the matter has been at issue for a year, Pothinus. May I have ten minutes at it?

POTHINUS: You will do your pleasure, doubtless.

CÆSAR: Good! But first, let us have Cleopatra here.

THEODOTUS: She is not in Alexandria: she is fled into Syria.

CÆSAR: I think not. (*To* RUFIO.) Call Totateeta.

RUFIO (*calling*): Ho there, Teetatota.

(FTATATEETA *enters the loggia, and stands arrogantly at the top of the steps.*)

FTATATEETA: Who pronounces the name of Ftatateeta, the Queen's chief nurse?

CÆSAR: Nobody can pronounce it, Tota, except yourself. Where is your mistress?

(CLEOPATRA, *who is hiding behind* FTATATEETA, *peeps out at them laughing.* CÆSAR *rises.*)

CÆSAR: Will the Queen favor us with her presence for a moment?

CLEOPATRA (*pushing* FTATATEETA *aside and standing haughtily on the brink of the steps*): Am I to behave like a Queen?

CÆSAR: Yes.

(CLEOPATRA *immediately comes down to the chair of state; seizes* PTOLEMY; *drags him out of his seat; then takes his place in the chair.* FTATATEETA *seats herself on the steps of the loggia, and sits there, watching the scene with sibylline intensity.*)

PTOLEMY (*mortified, and struggling with his tears*): Cæsar: this is how she treats me always. If I am a king why is she allowed to take everything from me?

CLEOPATRA: You are not to be King, you little cry-baby. You are to be eaten by the Romans.

CÆSAR (*touched by* PTOLEMY'*s distress*): Come here, my boy, and stand by me.

(PTOLEMY *goes over to* CÆSAR, *who, resuming his seat on the tripod, takes the boy's hand to encourage him.* CLEOPATRA, *furiously jealous, rises and glares at them.*)

CLEOPATRA (*with flaming cheeks*): Take your throne: I don't want it. (*She flings away from the chair, and approaches* PTOLEMY, *who shrinks from her.*) Go this instant and sit down in your place.

CÆSAR: Go, Ptolemy. Always take a throne when it is offered to you.

RUFIO: I hope you will have the good sense to follow your own advice when we return to Rome, Cæsar.

(PTOLEMY *slowly goes back to the throne, giving* CLEOPATRA *a wide berth, in evident fear of her hands. She takes his place beside* CÆSAR.)

CÆSAR: Pothinus —

CLEOPATRA (*interrupting him*): Are you not going to speak to me?

CÆSAR: Be quiet. Open your mouth again before I give you leave and you shall be eaten.

CLEOPATRA: I am not afraid. A queen must not be afraid. Eat my husband there, if you like: *he* is afraid.

CÆSAR (*starting*): Your husband! What do you mean?

CLEOPATRA (*pointing to* PTOLEMY): That little thing.

(*The two Romans and the Briton stare at one another in amazement.*)

THEODOTUS: Cæsar: you are a stranger here, and not conversant with our laws. The kings and queens of Egypt may not marry except with their own royal blood. Ptolemy and Cleopatra are born king and consort just as they are born brother and sister.

BRITANNUS (*shocked*): Cæsar: this is not proper.

THEODOTUS (*outraged*): How!

CÆSAR (*recovering his self-possession*): Pardon him, Theodotus: he is a barbarian, and thinks that the customs of his tribe and island are the laws of nature.

BRITANNUS: On the contrary, Cæsar, it is these Egyptians who are barbarians; and you do wrong to encourage them. I say it is a scandal.

CÆSAR: Scandal or not, my friend, it opens the gate of peace. (*He addresses* POTHINUS *seriously.*) Pothinus: hear what I propose.

RUFIO: Hear Cæsar there.

CÆSAR: Ptolemy and Cleopatra shall reign jointly in Egypt.

ACHILLAS: What of the King's younger brother and Cleopatra's younger sister?

RUFIO (*explaining*): There is another little Ptolemy, Cæsar: so they tell me.

CÆSAR: Well, the little Ptolemy can marry the other sister; and we will make them both a present of Cyprus.

POTHINUS (*impatiently*): Cyprus is of no use to anybody.

CÆSAR: No matter: you shall have it for the sake of peace.

BRITANNUS (*unconsciously anticipating a later statesman*): Peace with honor, Pothinus.

POTHINUS (*mutinously*): Cæsar: be honest. The money you demand is the price of our freedom. Take it; and leave us to settle our own affairs.

THE BOLDER COURTIERS (*encouraged by* POTHINUS'*s tone and* CÆSAR'*s quietness*): Yes, yes. Egypt for the Egyptians!

(*The conference now becomes an altercation, the Egyptians becoming more and more heated.* CÆSAR *remains unruffled; but* RUFIO *grows fiercer and doggeder, and* BRITANNUS *haughtily indignant.*)

RUFIO (*contemptuously*): Egypt for the Egyptians! Do you forget that there is a Roman army of occupation here, left by Aulus Gabinius when he set up your toy king for you?

ACHILLAS (*suddenly asserting himself*): And now under *my* command. *I* am the Roman general here, Cæsar.

CÆSAR (*tickled by the humor of the situation*): And also the Egyptian general, eh?

POTHINUS (*triumphantly*): That is so, Cæsar.

CÆSAR (*to* ACHILLAS): So you can make war on the Egyptians in the name of Rome, and on the Romans – on me, if necessary – in the name of Egypt?

ACHILLAS: That is so, Cæsar.

CÆSAR: And which side are you on at present, if I may presume to ask, general?

ACHILLAS: On the side of the right and of the gods.

CÆSAR: Hm! How many men have you?

ACHILLAS: That will appear when I take the field.

RUFIO (*truculently*): Are your men Romans? If not, it matters not how many there are, provided you are no stronger than 500 to ten.

POTHINUS: It is useless to try to bluff us, Rufio. Cæsar has been defeated before and may be defeated again. A few weeks ago Cæsar was flying for his life before Pompey: a few months hence he may be flying for his life before Cato and Juba of Numidia, the African King.

ACHILLAS (*following up* POTHINUS'*s speech menacingly*): What can you do with 4,000 men?

THEODOTUS (*following up* ACHILLAS'*s speech with a raucous squeak*): And without money? Away with you.

ALL THE COURTIERS (*shouting fiercely and crowding towards* CÆSAR): Away with you. Egypt for the Egyptians! Begone!

(RUFIO *bites his beard, too angry to speak.* CÆSAR *sits as comfortably as if he were at breakfast, and the cat were clamoring for a piece of Finnan-haddie.*)

CLEOPATRA: Why do you let them talk to you like that, Cæsar? Are you afraid?

CÆSAR: Why, my dear, what they say is quite true.

CLEOPATRA: But if you go away, I shall not be Queen.

CÆSAR: I shall not go away until you are Queen.

POTHINUS: Achillas: if you are not a fool, you will take that girl whilst she is under your hand.

RUFIO (*daring them*): Why not take Cæsar as well, Achillas?

POTHINUS (*retorting the defiance with interest*): Well said, Rufio. Why not?

RUFIO: Try, Achillas. (*Calling.*) Guard there.

(*The loggia immediately fills with* CÆSAR'*s soldiers, who stand, sword in hand, at the top of the steps, waiting the word to charge from their centurion, who carries a cudgel. For a moment the Egyptians face them proudly: then they retire sullenly to their former places.*)

BRITANNUS: You are Cæsar's prisoners, all of you.
CÆSAR (*benevolently*): Oh no, no, no. By no means. Cæsar's guests, gentlemen.
CLEOPATRA: Won't you cut their heads off?
CÆSAR: What! Cut off your brother's head?
CLEOPATRA: Why not? He would cut off mine, if he got the chance. Wouldn't you, Ptolemy?
PTOLEMY (*pale and obstinate*): I would. I will, too, when I grow up.

(CLEOPATRA *is rent by a struggle between her newly-acquired dignity as a queen, and a strong impulse to put out her tongue at him. She takes no part in the scene which follows, but watches it with curiosity and wonder, fidgeting with the restlessness of a child, and sitting down on* CÆSAR'*s tripod when he rises.*)

POTHINUS: Cæsar: if you attempt to detain us —
RUFIO: He will succeed, Egyptian: make up your mind to that. We hold the palace, the beach, and the eastern harbor. The road to Rome is open; and you shall travel it if Cæsar chooses.
CÆSAR (*courteously*): I could do no less, Pothinus, to secure the retreat of my own soldiers. I am accountable for every life among them. But you are free to go. So are all here, and in the palace.
RUFIO (*aghast at this clemency*): What! Renegades and all?
CÆSAR (*softening the expression*): Roman army of occupation and all, Rufio.
POTHINUS (*bewildered*): But — but — but —
CÆSAR: Well, my friend?
POTHINUS: You are turning us out of our own palace into the streets; and you tell us with a grand air that we are free to go! It is for you to go.
CÆSAR: Your friends are in the street, Pothinus. You will be safer there.
POTHINUS: This is a trick. I am the King's guardian: I refuse to stir. I stand on my right here. Where is your right?
CÆSAR: It is in Rufio's scabbard, Pothinus. I may not be able to keep it there if you wait too long.

(*Sensation.*)

POTHINUS (*bitterly*): And this is Roman justice!
THEODOTUS: But not Roman gratitude, I hope.
CÆSAR: Gratitude! Am I in your debt for any service, gentlemen?
THEODOTUS: Is Cæsar's life of so little account to him that he forgets that we have saved it?
CÆSAR: My life! Is that all?
THEODOTUS: Your life. Your laurels. Your future.
POTHINUS: It is true. I can call a witness to prove that but for us, the Roman army of occupation, led by the greatest soldier in the world, would now have Cæsar at its mercy. (*Calling through the loggia.*) Ho, there, Lucius

Septimius (CÆSAR *starts, deeply moved*): if my voice can reach you, come forth and testify before Cæsar.

CÆSAR (*shrinking*): No, no.

THEODOTUS: Yes, I say. Let the military tribune bear witness.

(LUCIUS SEPTIMIUS, *a clean-shaven, trim athlete of about 40, with symmetrical features, resolute mouth, and handsome, thin Roman nose, in the dress of a Roman officer, comes in through the loggia and confronts* CÆSAR, *who hides his face with his robe for a moment; then, mastering himself, drops it, and confronts the tribune with dignity.*)

POTHINUS: Bear witness, Lucius Septimius. Cæsar came hither in pursuit of his foe. Did we shelter his foe?

LUCIUS: As Pompey's foot touched the Egyptian shore, his head fell by the stroke of my sword.

THEODOTUS (*with viperish relish*): Under the eyes of his wife and child! Remember that, Cæsar! They saw it from the ship he had just left. We have given you a full and sweet measure of vengeance.

CÆSAR (*with horror*): Vengeance!

POTHINUS: Our first gift to you, as your galley came into the roadstead, was the head of your rival for the empire of the world. Bear witness, Lucius Septimius: is it not so?

LUCIUS: It is so. With this hand, that slew Pompey, I placed his head at the feet of Cæsar.

CÆSAR: Murderer! So would you have slain Cæsar, had Pompey been victorious at Pharsalia.

LUCIUS: Woe to the vanquished, Cæsar! When I served Pompey, I slew as good men as he, only because he conquered them. His turn came at last.

THEODOTUS (*flatteringly*): The deed was not yours, Cæsar, but ours — nay, mine; for it was done by my counsel. Thanks to us, you keep your reputation for clemency, and have your vengeance too.

CÆSAR: Vengeance! Vengeance!! Oh, if I could stoop to vengeance, what would I not exact from you as the price of this murdered man's blood? (*They shrink back, appalled and disconcerted.*) Was he not my son-in-law, my ancient friend, for 20 years the master of great Rome, for 30 years the compeller of victory? Did not I, as a Roman, share his glory? Was the Fate that forced us to fight for the mastery of the world, of our making? Am I Julius Cæsar, or am I a wolf, that you fling to me the grey head of the old soldier, the laurelled conqueror, the mighty Roman, treacherously struck down by this callous ruffian, and then claim my gratitude for it! (*To* LUCIUS SEPTIMIUS.) Begone: you fill me with horror.

LUCIUS (*cold and undaunted*): Pshaw! You have seen severed heads before, Cæsar, and severed right hands too, I think; some thousands of them, in Gaul, after you vanquished Vercingetorix. Did you spare him, with all your clemency? Was that vengeance?

CÆSAR: No, by the gods! would that it had been! Vengeance at least is human. No, I say: those severed right hands, and the brave Vercingetorix basely strangled in a vault beneath the Capitol, were (*with shuddering satire*) a wise severity, a necessary protection to the commonwealth, a duty of statesmanship — follies and fictions ten times bloodier than honest vengeance! What a fool was I then! To think that men's lives should be at the mercy of such fools! (*Humbly.*) Lucius Septimius, pardon me: why should the slayer of Vercingetorix rebuke the slayer of Pompey? You are free to go with the rest. Or stay if you will: I will find a place for you in my service.

LUCIUS: The odds are against you, Cæsar. I go. (*He turns to go out through the loggia.*)

RUFIO (*full of wrath at seeing his prey escaping*): That means that he is a Republican.

LUCIUS (*turning defiantly on the loggia steps*): And what are you?

RUFIO: A Cæsarian, like all Cæsar's soldiers.

CÆSAR (*courteously*): Lucius: believe me, Cæsar is no Cæsarian. Were Rome a true republic, then were Cæsar the first of Republicans. But you have made your choice. Farewell.

LUCIUS: Farewell. Come, Achillas, whilst there is yet time.

(CÆSAR, *seeing that* RUFIO*'s temper threatens to get the worse of him, puts his hand on his shoulder and brings him down the hall out of harm's way,* BRITANNUS *accompanying them and posting himself on* CÆSAR*'s right hand. This movement brings the three in a little group to the place occupied by* ACHILLAS, *who moves haughtily away and joins* THEODOTUS *on the other side.* LUCIUS SEPTIMIUS *goes out through the soldiers in the loggia.* POTHINUS, THEODOTUS *and* ACHILLAS *follow him with the courtiers, very mistrustful of the soldiers, who close up in their rear and go out after them, keeping them moving without much ceremony. The King is left in his chair, piteous, obstinate, with twitching face and fingers. During these movements* RUFIO *maintains an energetic grumbling, as follows: —* )

RUFIO (*as* LUCIUS *departs*): Do you suppose he would let us go if he had our heads in his hands?

CÆSAR: I have no right to suppose that his ways are any baser than mine.

RUFIO: Pshaw!

CÆSAR: Rufio: if I take Lucius Septimius for my model, and become exactly like him, ceasing to be Cæsar, will you serve me still?

BRITANNUS: Cæsar: this is not good sense. Your duty to Rome demands that her enemies should be prevented from doing further mischief. (CÆSAR, *whose delight in the moral eye-to-business of his British secretary is inexhaustible, smiles indulgently.*)

RUFIO: It is no use talking to him, Britannus: you may save your breath to cool your porridge. But mark this, Cæsar. Clemency is very well for you; but what is it for your soldiers, who have to fight to-morrow the men you spared yesterday? You may give what orders you please; but I tell you that your next victory will be a massacre, thanks to your clemency. *I*, for one, will take no prisoners. I will kill my enemies in the field; and then you can preach as much clemency as you please: I shall never have to fight them again. And now, with your leave, I will see these gentry off the premises. (*He turns to go.*)

CÆSAR (*turning also and seeing* PTOLEMY): What! have they left the boy alone! Oh shame, shame!

RUFIO (*taking* PTOLEMY*'s hand and making him rise*): Come, your majesty!

PTOLEMY (*to* CÆSAR, *drawing away his hand from* RUFIO): Is he turning me out of my palace?

RUFIO (*grimly*): You are welcome to stay if you wish.

CÆSAR (*kindly*): Go, my boy. I will not harm you but you will be safer away, among your friends. Here you are in the lion's mouth.

PTOLEMY (*turning to go*): It is not the lion I fear, but (*looking at* RUFIO) the jackal. (*He goes out through the loggia.*)

CÆSAR (*laughing approvingly*): Brave boy!

CLEOPATRA (*jealous of* CÆSAR*'s approbation, calling after* PTOLEMY): Little silly. You think that very clever.

CÆSAR: Britannus: attend the King. Give him in charge to that Pothinus fellow. (BRITANNUS *goes out after* PTOLEMY.)

RUFIO (*pointing to* CLEOPATRA): And this piece of goods? What is to be done with *her?* However, I suppose I may leave that to you. (*He goes out through the loggia.*)

CLEOPATRA (*flushing suddenly and turning on* CÆSAR): Did you mean me to go with the rest?

CÆSAR (*a little preoccupied, goes with a sigh to* PTOLEMY*'s chair, whilst she waits for his answer with red cheeks and clenched fist*): You are free to do just as you please, Cleopatra.

CLEOPATRA: Then you do not care whether I stay or not?

CÆSAR (*smiling*): Of course I had rather you stayed.

CLEOPATRA: Much, *much* rather?

CÆSAR (*nodding*): Much, much rather.

CLEOPATRA: Then I consent to stay, because I am asked. But I do not want to, mind.

CÆSAR: That is quite understood. (*Calling.*) Totateeta.

(FTATATEETA, *still seated, turns her eyes on him with a sinister expression, but does not move.*)

CLEOPATRA (*with a splutter of laughter*): Her name is not Totateeta: it is Ftatateeta. (*Calling.*) Ftatateeta. (FTATATEETA *instantly rises and comes to* CLEOPATRA.)

CÆSAR (*stumbling over the name*): Tfatafeeta will forgive the erring tongue of a Roman. Tota: the Queen will hold her state here in Alexandria. Engage women to attend upon her; and do all that is needful.

FTATATEETA: Am I then the mistress of the Queen's household?

CLEOPATRA (*sharply*): No: *I* am the mistress of the Queen's household. Go and do as you are told, or I will have you thrown into the Nile this very afternoon, to poison the poor crocodiles.

CÆSAR (*shocked*): Oh no, no.

CLEOPATRA: Oh yes, yes. You are very sentimental, Cæsar; but you are clever; and if you do as I tell you, you will soon learn to govern.

(CÆSAR, *quite dumbfounded by this impertinence, turns in his chair and stares at her.* FTATATEETA, *smiling grimly, and showing a splendid set of teeth, goes, leaving them alone together.*)

CÆSAR: Cleopatra: I really think I must eat you, after all.

CLEOPATRA (*kneeling beside him and looking at him with eager interest, half real, half affected to shew how intelligent she is*): You must not talk to me now as if I were a child.

CÆSAR: You have been growing up since the Sphinx introduced us the other night; and you think you know more than I do already.

CLEOPATRA (*taken down, and anxious to justify herself*): No: that would be very silly of me: of course I know that. But – (*suddenly*) are you angry with me?

CÆSAR: No.

CLEOPATRA (*only half believing him*): Then why are you so thoughtful?

CÆSAR (*rising*): I have work to do, Cleopatra.

CLEOPATRA (*drawing back*): Work! (*Offended.*) You are tired of talking to me; and that is your excuse to get away from me.

CÆSAR (*sitting down again to appease her*): Well, well: another minute. But then – work!

CLEOPATRA: Work! what nonsense! You must remember that you are a king now: I have made you one. Kings dont work.

CÆSAR: Oh! Who told you that, little kitten? Eh.

CLEOPATRA: My father was King of Egypt; and he never worked. But he was a great king, and cut off my sister's head because she rebelled against him and took the throne from him.

CÆSAR: Well; and how did he get his throne back again?

CLEOPATRA (*eagerly, her eyes lighting up*): I will tell you. A beautiful young man, with strong round arms, came over the desert with many horsemen, and slew my sister's husband and gave my father back his throne. (*Wistfully.*) I was only twelve then. Oh, I wish he would come again, now that I am a queen, I would make him my husband.

CÆSAR: It might be managed, perhaps; for it was I who sent that beautiful young man to help your father.

CLEOPATRA (*enraptured*): You know him!

CÆSAR (*nodding*): I do.

CLEOPATRA: Has he come with you? (CÆSAR *shakes his head: she is cruelly disappointed.*) Oh, I wish he had, I wish he had. If only I were a little older; so that he might not think me a mere kitten, as you do! But perhaps that is because *you* are old. He is many, *many* years younger than you, is he not?

CÆSAR (*as if swallowing a pill*): He is somewhat younger.

CLEOPATRA: Would he be my husband, do you think, if I asked him?

CÆSAR: Very likely.

CLEOPATRA: But I should not like to ask him. Could you not persuade him to ask me — without knowing that I wanted him to?

CÆSAR (*touched by her innocence of the beautiful young man's character*): My poor child!

CLEOPATRA: Why do you say that as if you were sorry for me? Does he love anyone else?

CÆSAR: I am afraid so.

CLEOPATRA (*tearfully*): Then I shall not be his first love.

CÆSAR: Not quite the first. He is greatly admired by women.

CLEOPATRA: I wish I could be the first. But if he loves me, I will make him kill all the rest. Tell me: is he still beautiful? Do his strong round arms shine in the sun like marble?

CÆSAR: He is in excellent condition — considering how much he eats and drinks.

CLEOPATRA: Oh, you must not say common, earthly things about him; for I love him. He is a god.

CÆSAR: He is a great captain of horsemen, and swifter of foot than any other Roman.

CLEOPATRA: What is his real name?

CÆSAR (*puzzled*): His *real* name?

CLEOPATRA: Yes. I always call him Horus, because Horus is the most beautiful of our gods. But I want to know his real name.

CÆSAR: His name is Mark Antony.

CLEOPATRA (*musically*): Mark Antony, Mark Antony, Mark Antony! What a beautiful name! (*She throws her arms round* CÆSAR'*s neck.*) Oh, how I love you for sending him to help my father! Did you love my father very much?

CÆSAR: No, my child; but your father, as you say, never worked. I always work. So when he lost his crown he had to promise me 16,000 talents to get it back for him.

CLEOPATRA: Did he ever pay you?

CÆSAR: Not in full.

CLEOPATRA: He was quite right: it was too dear. The whole world is not worth 16,000 talents.

CÆSAR: That is perhaps true, Cleopatra. Those Egyptians who work paid as much of it as he could drag from them. The rest is still due. But as I most likely shall not get it, I must go back to my work. So you must run away for a little and send my secretary to me.

CLEOPATRA (*coaxing*): No: I want to stay and hear you talk about Mark Antony.

CÆSAR: But if I do not get to work, Pothinus and the rest of them will cut us off from the harbor; and then the way from Rome will be blocked.

CLEOPATRA: No matter: I dont want you to go back to Rome.

CÆSAR: But you want Mark Antony to come from it.

CLEOPATRA (*springing up*): Oh yes, yes, yes: I forgot. Go quickly and work, Cæsar; and keep the way over the sea open for my Mark Antony. (*She runs out through the loggia, kissing her hand to Mark Antony across the sea.*)

CÆSAR (*going briskly up the middle of the hall to the loggia steps*): Ho, Britannus. (*He is startled by the entry of a wounded Roman* SOLDIER, *who confronts him from the upper step.*) What now?

SOLDIER (*pointing to his bandaged head*): This, Cæsar; and two of my comrades killed in the market place.

CÆSAR (*quiet, but attending*): Ay. Why?

SOLDIER: There is an army come to Alexandria, calling itself the Roman army.

CÆSAR: The Roman army of occupation. Ay?

SOLDIER: Commanded by one Achillas.

CÆSAR: Well?

SOLDIER: The citizens rose against us when the army entered the gates. I was with two others in the market place when the news came. They set upon us. I cut my way out; and here I am.

CÆSAR: Good. I am glad to see you alive. (RUFIO *enters the loggia hastily, passing behind the soldier to look out through one of the arches at the quay beneath.*) Rufio: we are besieged.

RUFIO: What! Already?

CÆSAR: Now or to-morrow: what does it matter? We *shall* be besieged.

(BRITANNUS *runs in.*)

BRITANNUS: Cæsar —

CÆSAR (*anticipating him*): Yes: I know. (RUFIO *and* BRITANNUS *come down the hall from the loggia at opposite sides, past* CÆSAR, *who waits for a moment near the step to say to the soldier:*) Comrade: give the word to turn out on the beach and stand by the boats. Get your wounded attended to. Go. (*The* SOLDIER *hurries out.* CÆSAR *comes down the hall between* RUFIO *and* BRITANNUS.) Rufio: we have some ships in the west harbor. Burn them.

RUFIO (*staring*): Burn them!!

CÆSAR: Take every boat we have in the east harbor, and seize the Pharos — that island with the lighthouse. Leave half our men behind to hold the beach and the quay outside this palace: that is the way home.

RUFIO (*disapproving strongly*): Are we to give up the city?

CÆSAR: We have not got it, Rufio. This palace we have; and – what is that building next door?

RUFIO: The theatre.

CÆSAR: We will have that too: it commands the strand. For the rest, Egypt for the Egyptians!

RUFIO: Well, you know best, I suppose. Is that all?

CÆSAR: That is all. Are those ships burnt yet?

RUFIO: Be easy: I shall waste no more time. (*He runs out.*)

BRITANNUS: Cæsar: Pothinus demands speech of you. In my opinion he needs a lesson. His manner is most insolent.

CÆSAR: Where is he?

BRITANNUS: He waits without.

CÆSAR: Ho there! admit Pothinus.

(POTHINUS *appears in the loggia, and comes down the hall very haughtily to* CÆSAR'*s left hand.*)

CÆSAR: Well, Pothinus?

POTHINUS: I have brought you our ultimatum, Cæsar.

CÆSAR: Ultimatum! The door was open: you should have gone out through it before you declared war. You are my prisoner now. (*He goes to the chair and loosens his toga.*)

POTHINUS (*scornfully*): I *your* prisoner! Do you know that you are in Alexandria, and that King Ptolemy, with an army outnumbering your little troop a hundred to one, is in possession of Alexandria?

CÆSAR (*unconcernedly taking off his toga and throwing it on the chair*): Well, my friend, get out if you can. And tell your friends not to kill any more Romans in the market place. Otherwise my soldiers, who do not share my celebrated clemency, will probably kill you. Britannus: pass the word to the guard; and fetch my armor. (BRITANNUS *runs out,* RUFIO *returns.*) Well?

RUFIO (*pointing from the loggia to a cloud of smoke drifting over the harbor*): See there! (POTHINUS *runs eagerly up the steps to look out.*)

CÆSAR: What, ablaze already! Impossible!

RUFIO: Yes, five good ships, and a barge laden with oil grappled to each. But it is not my doing: the Egyptians have saved me the trouble. They have captured the west harbor.

CÆSAR (*anxiously*): And the east harbor? The lighthouse, Rufio?

RUFIO (*with a sudden splutter of raging ill usage, coming down to* CÆSAR *and scolding him*): Can I embark a legion in five minutes? The first cohort is already on the beach. We can do no more. If you want faster work, come and do it yourself.

CÆSAR (*soothing him*): Good, good. Patience, Rufio, patience.

RUFIO: Patience! Who is impatient here, you or I? Would I be here, if I could not oversee them from that balcony?

CÆSAR: Forgive me, Rufio; and (*anxiously*) hurry them as much as—

(*He is interrupted by an outcry as of an old man in the extremity of misfortune. It draws near rapidly; and* THEODOTUS *rushes in, tearing his hair, and squeaking the most lamentable exclamations.* RUFIO *steps back to stare at him, amazed at his frantic condition.* POTHINUS *turns to listen.*)

THEODOTUS (*on the steps, with uplifted arms*): Horror unspeakable! Woe, alas! Help!

RUFIO: What now?

CÆSAR (*frowning*): Who is slain?

THEODOTUS: Slain! Oh, worse than the death of ten thousand men! Loss irreparable to mankind!

RUFIO: What has happened, man?

THEODOTUS (*rushing down the hall between them*): The fire has spread from your ships. The first of the seven wonders of the world perishes. The library of Alexandria is in flames.

RUFIO: Pshaw! (*Quite relieved, he goes up to the loggia and watches the preparations of the troops on the beach.*)

CÆSAR: Is that all?

THEODOTUS (*unable to believe his senses*): All! Cæsar: will you go down to posterity as a barbarous soldier too ignorant to know the value of books?

CÆSAR: Theodotus: I am an author myself; and I tell you it is better that the Egyptians should live their lives than dream them away with the help of books.

THEODOTUS (*kneeling, with genuine literary emotion: the passion of the pedant*): Cæsar: once in ten generations of men, the world gains an immortal book.

CÆSAR (*inflexible*): If it did not flatter mankind, the common executioner would burn it.

THEODOTUS: Without history, death will lay you beside your meanest soldier.

CÆSAR: Death will do that in any case. I ask no better grave.

THEODOTUS: What is burning there is the memory of mankind.

CÆSAR: A shameful memory. Let it burn.

THEODOTUS (*wildly*): Will you destroy the past?

CÆSAR: Ay, and build the future with its ruins. (THEODOTUS, *in despair, strikes himself on the temples with his fists.*) But hearken, Theodotus, teacher of kings: you who valued Pompey's head no more than a shepherd values an onion, and who now kneel to me, with tears in your old eyes, to plead for a few sheepskins scrawled with errors. I cannot spare you a man or a bucket of water just now; but you shall pass freely out of the palace. Now, away with you to Achillas; and borrow his legions to put out the fire. (*He hurries him to the steps.*)

POTHINUS (*significantly*): You understand. Theodotus: I remain a prisoner.

THEODOTUS: A prisoner!

CÆSAR: Will you stay to talk whilst the memory of mankind is burning? (*Calling through the loggia.*) Ho there! Pass Theodotus out. (*To* THEODOTUS.) Away with you.

THEODOTUS (*to* POTHINUS): I must go to save the library. (*He hurries out.*)

CÆSAR: Follow him to the gate, Pothinus. Bid him urge your people to kill no more of my soldiers, for your sake.

POTHINUS: My life will cost you dear if you take it, Cæsar. (*He goes out after* THEODOTUS.)

(RUFIO, *absorbed in watching the embarkation, does not notice the departure of the two Egyptians.*)

RUFIO (*shouting from the loggia to the beach*): All ready, there?

CENTURION (*from below*): All ready. We wait for Cæsar.

CÆSAR: Tell them Cæsar is coming – the rogues! (*Calling.*) Britannicus. (*This magniloquent version of his secretary's name is one of* CÆSAR'*s jokes. In later years it would have meant, quite seriously and officially, Conqueror of Britain.*)

RUFIO (*calling down*): Push off, all except the longboat. Stand by it to embark, Cæsar's guard there. (*He leaves the balcony and comes down into the hall.*) Where are those Egyptians? Is this more clemency? Have you let them go?

CÆSAR (*chuckling*): I have let Theodotus go to save the library. We must respect literature, Rufio.

RUFIO (*raging*): Folly on folly's head! I believe if you could bring back all the dead of Spain, Gaul, and Thessaly to life, you would do it that we might have the trouble of fighting them over again.

CÆSAR: Might not the gods destroy the world if their only thought were to be at peace next year? (RUFIO, *out of all patience, turns away in anger.* CÆSAR *suddenly grips his sleeve, and adds slyly in his ear.*) Besides, my friend: every Egyptian we imprison means imprisoning two Roman soldiers to guard him. Eh?

RUFIO: Agh! I might have known there was some fox's trick behind your fine talking. (*He gets away from* CÆSAR *with an ill-humored shrug, and goes to the balcony for another look at the preparations; finally goes out.*)

CÆSAR: Is Britannus asleep? I sent him for my armor an hour ago. (*Calling.*) Britannicus, thou British islander. Britannicus!

(CLEOPATRA *runs in through the loggia with* CÆSAR'*s helmet and sword, snatched from* BRITANNUS, *who follows her with a cuirass and greaves. They come down to* CÆSAR, *she to his left hand,* BRITANNUS *to his right.*)

CLEOPATRA: I am going to dress you, Cæsar. Sit down. (*He obeys.*) These

Roman helmets are so becoming! (*She takes off his wreath.*) Oh! (*She bursts out laughing at him.*)

CÆSAR: What are you laughing at?

CLEOPATRA: Youre bald (*beginning with a big B, and ending with a splutter*).

CÆSAR (*almost annoyed*): Cleopatra! (*He rises, for the convenience of* BRITANNUS, *who puts the cuirass on him.*)

CLEOPATRA: So that is why you wear the wreath – to hide it.

BRITANNUS: Peace, Egyptian: they are the bays of the conqueror. (*He buckles the cuirass.*)

CLEOPATRA: Peace, thou: islander! (*To* CÆSAR.) You should rub your head with strong spirits of sugar, Cæsar. That will make it grow.

CÆSAR (*with a wry face*): Cleopatra: do you like to be reminded that you are very young?

CLEOPATRA (*pouting*): No.

CÆSAR (*sitting down again, and setting out his leg for* BRITANNUS, *who kneels to put on his greaves*): Neither do I like to be reminded that I am – middle aged. Let me give you ten of my superfluous years. That will make you 26, and leave me only – no matter. Is it a bargain?

CLEOPATRA: Agreed. 26, mind. (*She puts the helmet on him.*) Oh! How nice! You look only about 50 in it!

BRITANNUS (*looking up severely at* CLEOPATRA): You must not speak in this manner to Cæsar.

CLEOPATRA: Is it true that when Cæsar caught you on that island, you were painted all over blue?

BRITANNUS: Blue is the colour worn by all Britons of good standing. In war we stain our bodies blue; so that though our enemies may strip us of our clothes and our lives, they cannot strip us of our respectability. (*He rises.*)

CLEOPATRA (*with* CÆSAR'*s sword*): Let me hang this on. Now you look splendid. Have they made any statues of you in Rome?

CÆSAR: Yes, many statues.

CLEOPATRA: You must send for one and give it to me.

RUFIO (*coming back into the loggia, more impatient than ever*): Now Cæsar: have you done talking? The moment your foot is aboard there will be no holding our men back: the boats will race one another for the lighthouse.

CÆSAR (*drawing his sword and trying the edge*): Is this well set today, Britannicus? At Pharsalia it was as blunt as a barrel-hoop.

BRITANNUS: It will split one of the Egyptian's hairs today, Cæsar. I have set it myself.

CLEOPATRA (*suddenly throwing her arms in terror round* CÆSAR): Oh, you are not really going into battle to be killed?

CÆSAR: No, Cleopatra. No man goes to battle to be killed.

CLEOPATRA: But they do get killed. My sister's husband was killed in battle. You must not go. Let *him* go. (*Pointing to* RUFIO. *They all laugh at her.*) Oh please, *please* dont go. What will happen to me if you never come back?

CÆSAR (*gravely*): Are you afraid?

CLEOPATRA (*shrinking*): No.

CÆSAR (*with quiet authority*): Go to the balcony; and you shall see us take the Pharos. You must learn to look on battles. Go. (*She goes, downcast, and looks out from the balcony.*) That is well. Now, Rufio. March.

CLEOPATRA (*suddenly clapping her hands*): Oh, you will not be able to go!

CÆSAR: Why? What now?

CLEOPATRA: They are drying up the harbor with buckets – a multitude of soldiers – over there (*pointing out across the sea to her left*) – they are dipping up the water.

RUFIO (*hastening to look*): It is true. The Egyptian army! Crawling over the edge of the west harbor like locusts. (*With sudden anger he strides down to* CÆSAR.) This is your accursed clemency, Cæsar. Theodotus has brought them.

CÆSAR (*delighted at his own cleverness*): I meant him to, Rufio. They have come to put out the fire. The library will keep them busy whilst we seize the lighthouse. Eh? (*He rushes out buoyantly through the loggia, followed by* BRITANNUS.)

RUFIO (*disgustedly*): More foxing! Agh! (*He rushes off. A shout from the soldiers announces the appearance of* CÆSAR *below.*)

CENTURION (*below*): All aboard. Give way there. (*Another shout.*)

CLEOPATRA (*waving her scarf through the loggia arch*): Goodbye, goodbye, dear Cæsar. Come back safe. Goodbye!

## ACT III

*The edge of the quay in front of the palace, looking out west over the east harbor of Alexandria to Pharos island, just off the end of which, and connected with it by a narrow mole, is the famous lighthouse, a gigantic square tower of white marble diminishing in size storey by storey to the top, on which stands a cresset beacon. The island is joined to the main land by the Heptastadium, a great mole or causeway five miles long bounding the harbor on the south.*

*In the middle of the quay a Roman* SENTINEL *stands on guard pilum in hand, looking out to the lighthouse with strained attention, his left hand shading his eyes. The pilum is a stout wooden shaft 4½ feet long, with an iron spit about three feet long fixed in it. The* SENTINEL *is so absorbed that he does not notice the approach from the north end of the quay of four Egyptian market* PORTERS *carrying rolls of carpet, preceded by* FTATATEETA *and* APOLLODORUS *the Sicilian.* APOL-

LODORUS *is a dashing young man of about 24, handsome and debonair, dressed with deliberate æstheticism in the most delicate purples and dove greys, with ornaments of bronze, oxidized silver, and stones of jade and agate. His sword, designed as carefully as a medieval cross, has a blue blade showing through an openwork scabbard of purple leather and filigree. The* PORTERS, *conducted by* FTATATEETA, *pass along the quay behind the* SENTINEL *to the steps of the palace, where they put down their bales and squat on the ground.* APOLLODORUS *does not pass along with them: he halts, amused by the preoccupation of the* SENTINEL.

APOLLODORUS (*calling to the* SENTINEL): Who goes there, eh?

SENTINEL (*starting violently and turning with his pilum at the charge, revealing himself as a small, wiry, sandy-haired, conscientious young man with an elderly face*): Whats this? Stand. Who are you?

APOLLODORUS: I am Apollodorus the Sicilian. Why, man, what are you dreaming of? Since I came through the lines beyond the theatre there, I have brought my caravan past three sentinels, all so busy staring at the lighthouse that not one of them challenged me. Is this Roman discipline?

SENTINEL: We are not here to watch the land but the sea. Cæsar has just landed on the Pharos. (*Looking at* FTATATEETA.) What have you here? Who is this piece of Egyptian crockery?

FTATATEETA: Apollodorus: rebuke this Roman dog; and bid him bridle his tongue to the presence of Ftatateeta, the mistress of the Queen's household.

APOLLODORUS: My friend: this is a great lady, who stands high with Cæsar.

SENTINEL (*not at all impressed, pointing to the carpets*): And what is all this truck?

APOLLODORUS: Carpets for the furnishing of the Queen's apartments in the palace. I have picked them from the best carpets in the world; and the Queen shall choose the best of my choosing.

SENTINEL: So you are the carpet merchant?

APOLLODORUS (*hurt*): My friend: I am a patrician.

SENTINEL: A patrician! A patrician keeping a shop instead of following arms!

APOLLODORUS: I do not keep a shop. Mine is a temple of the arts. I am a worshipper of beauty. My calling is to choose beautiful things for beautiful queens. My motto is Art for Art's sake.

SENTINEL: That is not the password.

APOLLODORUS: It is a universal password.

SENTINEL: I know nothing about universal passwords. Either give me the password for the day or get back to your shop.

(FTATATEETA, *roused by his hostile tone, steals towards the edge of the quay with the step of a panther, and gets behind him.*)

APOLLODORUS: How if I do neither?

SENTINEL: Then I will drive this pilum through you.

APOLLODORUS: At your service, my friend. (*He draws his sword, and springs to his guard with unruffled grace.*)

FTATATEETA (*suddenly seizing the* SENTINEL'S *arms from behind*): Thrust your knife into the dog's throat, Apollodorus. (*The chivalrous* APOLLODORUS *laughingly shakes his head; breaks ground away from the* SENTINEL *towards the palace; and lowers his point.*)

SENTINEL (*struggling vainly*): Curse on you! Let me go. Help ho!

FTATATEETA (*lifting him from the ground*): Stab the little Roman reptile. Spit him on your sword.

(*A couple of Roman soldiers, with a* CENTURION, *come running along the edge of the quay from the north end. They rescue their comrade, and throw off* FTATATEETA, *who is sent reeling away on the left hand of the* SENTINEL.)

CENTURION (*an unattractive man of fifty, short in his speech and manners, with a vinewood cudgel in his hand*): How now? What is all this?

FTATATEETA (*to* APOLLODORUS): Why did you not stab him? There was time!

APOLLODORUS: Centurion: I am here by order of the Queen to —

CENTURION (*interrupting him*): The Queen! Yes, yes: (*to the* SENTINEL) pass him in. Pass all these bazaar people in to the Queen, with their goods. But mind you pass no one out that you have not passed in — not even the Queen herself.

SENTINEL: This old woman is dangerous: she is as strong as three men. She wanted the merchant to stab me.

APOLLODORUS: Centurion: I am not a merchant. I am a patrician and a votary of art.

CENTURION: Is the woman your wife?

APOLLODORUS (*horrified*): No, no! (*Correcting himself politely.*) Not that the lady is not a striking figure in her own way. But (*emphatically*) she is *not* my wife.

FTATATEETA (*to the* CENTURION): Roman: I am Ftatateeta, the mistress of the Queen's household.

CENTURION: Keep your hands off our men, mistress; or I will have you pitched into the harbor, though you were as strong as ten men. (*To his men.*) To your posts: march! (*He returns with his men the way they came.*)

FTATATEETA (*looking malignantly after him*): We shall see whom Isis loves best: her servant Ftatateeta or a dog of a Roman.

SENTINEL (*to* APOLLODORUS, *with a wave of his pilum towards the palace*): Pass in there; and keep your distance. (*Turning to* FTATATEETA.) Come within a yard of me, you old crocodile; and I will give you this (*the pilum*) in your jaws.

CLEOPATRA (*calling from the palace*): Ftatateeta, Ftatateeta.

FTATATEETA (*looking up, scandalized*): Go from the window, go from the window. There are men here.

CLEOPATRA: I am coming down.

FTATATEETA (*distracted*): No, no. What are you dreaming of? O ye gods, ye gods! Apollodorus: bid your men pick up your bales; and in with me quickly.

APOLLODORUS: Obey the mistress of the Queen's household.

FTATATEETA (*impatiently, as the* PORTERS *stoop to lift the bales*): Quick, quick: she will be out upon us. (CLEOPATRA *comes from the palace and across the quay to* FTATATEETA.) Oh that ever I was born!

CLEOPATRA (*eagerly*): Ftatateeta: I have thought of something. I want a boat — at once.

FTATATEETA: A boat! No, no: you cannot. Apollodorus: speak to the Queen.

APOLLODORUS (*gallantly*): Beautiful queen: I am Apollodorus the Sicilian, your servant, from the bazaar. I have brought you the three most beautiful Persian carpets in the world to choose from.

CLEOPATRA: I have no time for carpets to-day. Get me a boat.

FTATATEETA: What whim is this? You cannot go on the water except in the royal barge.

APOLLODORUS: Royalty, Ftatateeta lies not in the barge but in the Queen. (*To* CLEOPATRA.) The touch of your majesty's foot on the gunwale of the meanest boat in the harbor will make it royal. (*He turns to the harbor and calls seaward.*) Ho there, boatman! Pull in to the steps.

CLEOPATRA: Apollodorus: you are my perfect knight; and I will always buy my carpets through you. (APOLLODORUS *bows joyously. An oar appears above the quay; and the* BOATMAN, *a bullet-headed, vivacious, grinning fellow, burnt almost black by the sun, comes up a flight of steps from the water on the* SENTINEL*'s right, oar in hand, and waits at the top.*) Can you row, Apollodorus?

APOLLODORUS: My oars shall be your majesty's wings. Whither shall I row my Queen?

CLEOPATRA: To the lighthouse. Come. (*She makes for the steps.*)

SENTINEL (*opposing her with his pilum at the charge*): Stand. You cannot pass.

CLEOPATRA (*flushing angrily*): How dare you? Do you know that I am the Queen?

SENTINEL: I have my orders. You cannot pass.

CLEOPATRA: I will make Cæsar have you killed if you do not obey me.

SENTINEL: He will do worse to me if I disobey my officer. Stand back.

CLEOPATRA: Ftatateeta: strangle him.

SENTINEL (*alarmed — looking apprehensively at* FTATATEETA, *and brandishing his pilum*): Keep off, there.

CLEOPATRA (*running to* APOLLODORUS): Apollodorus: make your slaves help us.

APOLLODORUS: I shall not need their help, lady. (*He draws his sword.*) Now, soldier: choose which weapon you will defend yourself with. Shall it be sword against pilum, or sword against sword?

SENTINEL: Roman against Sicilian, curse you. Take that. (*He hurls his pilum at* APOLLODORUS, *who drops expertly on one knee. The pilum passes whizzing over his head and falls harmless.* APOLLODORUS, *with a cry of triumph, springs up and attacks the* SENTINEL, *who draws his sword and defends himself, crying*:) Ho there, guard. Help!

(CLEOPATRA, *half frightened, half delighted, takes refuge near the palace, where the* PORTERS *are squatting among the bales. The* BOATMAN, *alarmed, hurries down the steps out of harm's way, but stops, with his head just visible above the edge of the quay, to watch the fight. The* SENTINEL *is handicapped by his fear of an attack in the rear from* FTATATEETA. *His swordsmanship, which is of a rough and ready sort, is heavily taxed, as he has occasionally to strike at her to keep her off between a blow and a guard with* APOLLODORUS. *The* CENTURION *returns with several soldiers.* APOLLODORUS *springs back towards* CLEOPATRA *as this reinforcement confronts him.*)

CENTURION (*coming to the* SENTINEL*'s right hand*): What is this? What now?

SENTINEL (*panting*): I could do well enough by myself if it werent for the old woman. Keep her off me: this is all the help I need.

CENTURION: Make your report, soldier. What has happened?

FTATATEETA: Centurion: he would have slain the Queen.

SENTINEL (*bluntly*): I would, sooner than let her pass. She wanted to take a boat, and go — so she said — to the lighthouse. I stopped her, as I was ordered to; and she set this fellow on me. (*He goes to pick up his pilum and returns to his place with it.*)

CENTURION (*turning to* CLEOPATRA): Cleopatra: I am loth to offend you; but without Cæsar's express order we dare not let you pass beyond the Roman lines.

APOLLODORUS: Well, Centurion; and has not the lighthouse been within the Roman lines since Cæsar landed there?

CLEOPATRA: Yes, yes. Answer that, if you can.

CENTURION (*to* APOLLODORUS): As for you, Apollodorus, you may thank the gods that you are not nailed to the palace door with a pilum for your meddling.

APOLLODORUS (*urbanely*): My military friend, I was not born to be slain by so ugly a weapon. When I fall, it will be (*holding up his sword*) by this white queen of arms, the only weapon fit for an artist. And now that you are convinced that we do not want to go beyond the lines, let me finish killing your sentinel and depart with the Queen.

CENTURION (*as the* SENTINEL *makes an angry demonstration*): Peace there, Cleopatra: I must abide by my orders, and not by the subtleties of this

Sicilian. You must withdraw into the palace and examine your carpets there.

CLEOPATRA (*pouting*): I will not: I am the Queen. Cæsar does not speak to me as you do. Have Cæsar's centurions changed manners with his scullions?

CENTURION (*sulkily*): I do my duty. That is enough for me.

APOLLODORUS: Majesty: when a stupid man is doing something he is ashamed of, he always declares that it is his duty.

CENTURION (*angry*): Apollodorus –

APOLLODORUS (*interrupting him with defiant elegance*): I will make amends for that insult with my sword at fitting time and place. Who says artist, says duellist. (*To* CLEOPATRA.) Hear my counsel, star of the east. Until word comes to these soldiers from Cæsar himself, you are a prisoner. Let me go to him with a message from you, and a present; and before the sun has stooped half way to the arms of the sea, I will bring you back Cæsar's order of release.

CENTURION (*sneering at him*): And you will sell the Queen the present, no doubt.

APOLLODORUS: Centurion: the Queen shall have from me, without payment, as the unforced tribute of Sicilian taste to Egyptian beauty, the richest of these carpets for her present to Cæsar.

CLEOPATRA (*exultantly, to the* CENTURION): Now you see what an ignorant common creature you are!

CENTURION (*curtly*): Well, a fool and his wares are soon parted. (*He turns to his men.*) Two more men to this post here; and see that no one leaves the palace but this man and his merchandise. If he draws his sword again inside the lines, kill him. To your posts. March.

(*He goes out, leaving two* AUXILIARY SENTINELS *with the other.*)

APOLLODORUS (*with polite goodfellowship*): My friends: will you not enter the palace and bury our quarrel in a bowl of wine? (*He takes out his purse, jingling the coins in it.*) The Queen has presents for you all.

SENTINEL (*very sulkily*): You heard our orders. Get about your business.

FIRST AUXILIARY: Yes: you ought to know better. Off with you.

SECOND AUXILIARY (*looking longingly at the purse – this sentinel is a hook-nosed man, unlike his comrade, who is squab faced*): Do not tantalize a poor man.

APOLLODORUS (*to* CLEOPATRA): Pearl of Queens: the centurion is at hand; and the Roman soldier is incorruptible when his officer is looking. I must carry your word to Cæsar.

CLEOPATRA (*who has been meditating among the carpets*): Are these carpets very heavy?

APOLLODORUS: It matters not how heavy. There are plenty of porters.

CLEOPATRA: How do they put the carpets into boats? Do they throw them down?

APOLLODORUS: Not into small boats, majesty. It would sink them.

CLEOPATRA: Not into that man's boat, for instance? (*Pointing to the* BOATMAN.)

APOLLODORUS: No. Too small.

CLEOPATRA: But you can take a carpet to Cæsar in it if I send one?

APOLLODORUS: Assuredly.

CLEOPATRA: And you will have it carried gently down the steps and take great care of it?

APOLLODORUS: Depend on me.

CLEOPATRA: Great, *great* care?

APOLLODORUS: More than of my own body.

CLEOPATRA: You will promise me not to let the porters drop it or throw it about?

APOLLODORUS: Place the most delicate glass goblet in the palace in the heart of the roll, Queen; and if it be broken, my head shall pay for it.

CLEOPATRA: Good. Come, Ftatateeta. (FTATATEETA *comes to her.* APOLLODORUS *offers to squire them into the palace.*) No, Apollodorus, you must not come. I will choose a carpet for myself. You must wait here. (*She runs into the palace.*)

APOLLODORUS (*to the* PORTERS): Follow this lady (*indicating* FTATATEETA); and obey her.

(*The* PORTERS *rise and take up their bales.*)

FTATATEETA (*addressing the* PORTERS *as if they were vermin*): This way. And take your shoes off before you put your feet on those stairs.

(*She goes in, followed by the* PORTERS *with the carpets. Meanwhile* APOLLODORUS *goes to the edge of the quay and looks out over the harbor. The* SENTINELS *keep their eyes on him malignantly.*)

APOLLODORUS (*addressing the* SENTINEL): My friend —

SENTINEL (*rudely*): Silence there.

FIRST AUXILIARY: Shut your muzzle, you.

SECOND AUXILIARY (*in a half whisper, glancing apprehensively towards the north end of the quay*): Cant you wait a bit?

APOLLODORUS: Patience, worthy three-headed donkey. (*They mutter ferociously; but he is not at all intimidated.*) Listen: were you set here to watch me, or to watch the Egyptians?

SENTINEL: We know our duty.

APOLLODORUS: Then why dont you do it? There is something going on over there. (*Pointing southwestward to the mole.*)

SENTINEL (*sulkily*): I do not need to be told what to do by the like of you.

APOLLODORUS: Blockhead. (*He begins shouting.*) Ho there, Centurion. Hoiho!

SENTINEL: Curse your meddling. (*Shouting.*) Hoiho! Alarm! Alarm!

FIRST AND SECOND AUXILIARIES: Alarm! Alarm! Hoiho!

(*The* CENTURION *comes running in with his guard.*)

CENTURION: What now? Has the old woman attacked you again? (*Seeing* APOLLODORUS.) Are *you* here still?

APOLLODORUS (*pointing as before*): See there. The Egyptians are moving. They are going to recapture the Pharos. They will attack by sea and land: by land along the great mole; by sea from the west harbor. Stir yourselves, my military friends: the hunt is up. (*A clangor of trumpets from several points along the quay.*) Aha! I told you so.

CENTURION (*quickly*): The two extra men pass the alarm to the south posts. One man keep guard here. The rest with me – quick.

(*The two* AUXILIARY SENTINELS *run off to the south. The* CENTURION *and his guard run off northward; and immediately afterwards the bucina sounds. The four* PORTERS *come from the palace carrying a carpet, followed by* FTATATEETA.)

SENTINEL (*handling his pilum apprehensively*): You again! (*The* PORTERS *stop.*)

FTATATEETA: Peace, Roman fellow: you are now singlehanded. Apollodorus: this carpet is Cleopatra's present to Cæsar. It has rolled up in it ten precious goblets of the thinnest Iberian crystal, and a hundred eggs of the sacred blue pigeon. On your honor, let not one of them be broken.

APOLLODORUS: On my head be it! (*To the* PORTERS.) Into the boat with them carefully.

(*The* PORTERS *carry the carpet to the steps.*)

FIRST PORTER (*looking down at the boat*): Beware what you do, sir. Those eggs of which the lady speaks must weigh more than a pound apiece. This boat is too small for such a load.

BOATMAN (*excitedly rushing up the steps*): Oh thou injurious porter! Oh thou unnatural son of a she-camel! (*To* APOLLODORUS.) My boat, sir, hath often carried five men. Shall it not carry your lordship and a bale of pigeon's eggs? (*To the* PORTER.) Thou mangy dromedary, the gods shall punish thee for this envious wickedness.

FIRST PORTER (*stolidly*): I cannot quit this bale now to beat thee; but another day I will lie in wait for thee.

APOLLODORUS (*going between them*): Peace there. If the boat were but a single plank, I would get to Cæsar on it.

FTATATEETA (*anxiously*): In the name of the gods, Apollodorus, run no risks with that bale.

APOLLODORUS: Fear not, thou venerable grotesque: I guess its great worth.

(*To the* PORTERS.) Down with it, I say; and gently; or ye shall eat nothing but stick for ten days.

(*The* BOATMAN *goes down the steps, followed by the* PORTERS *with the bale:* FTATATEETA *and* APOLLODORUS *watching from the edge.*)

APOLLODORUS: Gently, my sons, my children — (*with sudden alarm*) gently, ye dogs. Lay it level in the stern — so — tis well.

FTATATEETA (*screaming down at one of the* PORTERS): Do not step on it, do not step on it. Oh thou brute beast!

FIRST PORTER (*ascending*): Be not excited, mistress: all is well.

FTATATEETA (*panting*): All well! Oh, thou hast given my heart a turn! (*She clutches her side, gasping.*)

(*The four* PORTERS *have now come up and are waiting at the stairhead to be paid.*)

APOLLODORUS: Here, ye hungry ones. (*He gives money to the* FIRST PORTER, *who holds it in his hand to shew to the others. They crowd greedily to see how much it is, quite prepared, after the Eastern fashion, to protest to heaven against their patron's stinginess. But his liberality overpowers them.*)

FIRST PORTER: O bounteous prince!

SECOND PORTER: O lord of the bazaar!

THIRD PORTER: O favored of the gods!

FOURTH PORTER: O father to all the porters of the market!

SENTINEL (*enviously, threatening them fiercely with his pilum*): Hence, dogs: off. Out of this. (*They fly before him northward along the quay.*)

APOLLODORUS: Farewell, Ftatateeta. I shall be at the lighthouse before the Egyptians. (*He descends the steps.*)

FTATATEETA: The gods speed thee and protect my nursling!

(*The* SENTRY *returns from chasing the* PORTERS *and looks down at the boat, standing near the stairhead lest* FTATATEETA *should attempt to escape.*)

APOLLODORUS (*from beneath, as the boat moves off*): Farewell, valiant pilum pitcher.

SENTINEL: Farewell, shopkeeper.

APOLLODORUS: Ha, ha! Pull, thou brave boatman, pull. Soho-o-o-o-o! (*He begins to sing in barcarolle measure to the rhythm of the oars.*)

My heart, my heart, spread out thy wings:
Shake off thy heavy load of love —

Give me the oars, O son of a snail.

SENTINEL (*threatening* FTATATEETA): Now mistress: back to your henhouse. In with you.

FTATATEETA (*falling on her knees and stretching her hands over the waters*): Gods of the seas, bear her safely to the shore!

SENTINEL: Bear *who* safely? What do you mean?

FTATATEETA (*looking darkly at him*): Gods of Egypt and of Vengeance, let this Roman fool be beaten like a dog by his captain for suffering her to be taken over the waters.

SENTINEL: Accursed one: is she then in the boat? (*He calls over the sea.*) Hoiho, there, boatman! Hoiho!

APOLLODORUS (*singing in the distance*):

My heart, my heart, be whole and free:
Love is thine only enemy.

(*Meanwhile* RUFIO, *the morning's fighting done, sits munching dates on a faggot of brushwood outside the door of the lighthouse, which towers gigantic to the clouds on his left. His helmet, full of dates, is between his knees; and a leathern bottle of wine is by his side. Behind him the great stone pedestal of the lighthouse is shut in from the open sea by a low stone parapet, with a couple of steps in the middle of the broad coping. A huge chain with a hook hangs down from the lighthouse crane above his head. Faggots like the one he sits on lie beneath it ready to be drawn up to feed the beacon.* CÆSAR *is standing on the step at the parapet looking out anxiously, evidently ill at ease.* BRITANNUS *comes out of the lighthouse door.*)

RUFIO: Well, my British islander. Have you been up to the top?

BRITANNUS: I have. I reckon it at 200 feet high.

RUFIO: Anybody up there?

BRITANNUS: One elderly Tyrian to work the crane; and his son, a well conducted youth of 14.

RUFIO (*looking at the chain*): What! An old man and a boy work that! Twenty men, you mean.

BRITANNUS: Two only, I assure you. They have counterweights, and a machine with boiling water in it which I do not understand: it is not of British design. They use it to haul up barrels of oil and faggots to burn in the brazier on the roof.

RUFIO: But –

BRITANNUS: Excuse me: I came down because there are messengers coming along the mole to us from the island. I must see what their business is.

(*He hurries out past the lighthouse.*)

CÆSAR (*coming away from the parapet, shivering and out of sorts*): Rufio: this has been a mad expedition. We shall be beaten. I wish I knew how our men are getting on with that barricade across the great mole.

RUFIO (*angrily*): Must I leave my food and go starving to bring you a report?

CÆSAR (*soothing him nervously*): No, Rufio, no. Eat, my son, eat. (*He takes another turn,* RUFIO *chewing dates meanwhile.*) The Egyptians cannot be such fools as not to storm the barricade and swoop down on us here before it is finished. It is the first time I have ever run an avoidable risk. I should not have come to Egypt.

RUFIO: An hour ago you were all for victory.

CÆSAR (*apologetically*): Yes: I was a fool – rash, Rufio – boyish.

RUFIO: Boyish! Not a bit of it. Here (*offering him a handful of dates*).

CÆSAR: What are these for?

RUFIO: To eat. Thats whats the matter with you. When a man comes to your age, he runs down before his midday meal. Eat and drink; and then have another look at our chances.

CÆSAR (*taking the dates*): My age! (*He shakes his head and bites a date.*) Yes, Rufio: I am an old man – worn out now – true, quite true. (*He gives way to melancholy contemplation, and eats another date.*) Achillas is still in his prime: Ptolemy is a boy. (*He eats another date, and plucks up a little.*) Well, every dog has his day; and I have had mine: I cannot complain. (*With sudden cheerfulness.*) These dates are not bad, Rufio. (BRITANNUS *returns, greatly excited, with a leathern bag.* CÆSAR *is himself again in a moment.*) What now?

BRITANNUS (*triumphantly*): Our brave Rhodian mariners have captured a treasure. There! (*He throws the bag down at* CÆSAR'*s feet.*) Our enemies are delivered into our hands.

CÆSAR: In that bag?

BRITANNUS: Wait till you hear, Cæsar. This bag contains all the letters which have passed between Pompey's party and the army of occupation here.

CÆSAR: Well?

BRITANNUS (*impatient of* CÆSAR'*s slowness to grasp the situation*): Well, we shall now know who your foes are. The name of every man who has plotted against you since you crossed the Rubicon may be in these papers, for all we know.

CÆSAR: Put them in the fire.

BRITANNUS: Put them – (*he gasps*)!!!!

CÆSAR: In the fire. Would you have me waste the next three years of my life in proscribing and condemning men who will be my friends when I have proved that my friendship is worth more than Pompey's was – than Cato's is. O incorrigible British islander: am I a bull dog, to seek quarrels merely to shew how stubborn my jaws are?

BRITANNUS: But your honor – the honor of Rome –

CÆSAR: I do not make human sacrifices to my honor, as your Druids do. Since you will not burn these, at least I can drown them. (*He picks up the bag and throws it over the parapet into the sea.*)

BRITANNUS: Cæsar: this is mere eccentricity. Are traitors to be allowed to go free for the sake of a paradox?

RUFIO (*rising*): Cæsar: when the islander has finished preaching, call me again. I am going to have a look at the boiling water machine.

(*He goes into the lighthouse.*)

BRITANNUS (*with genuine feeling*): O Cæsar, my great master, if I could but persuade you to regard life seriously, as men do in my country!

CÆSAR: Do they truly do so, Britannus?

BRITANNUS: Have you not been there? Have you not seen them? What Briton speaks as you do in your moments of levity? What Briton neglects to attend the services at the sacred grove? What Briton wears clothes of many colors as you do, instead of plain blue, as all solid, well esteemed men should? These are moral questions with us.

CÆSAR: Well, well, my friend: some day I shall settle down and have a blue toga, perhaps. Meanwhile, I must get on as best I can in my flippant Roman way. (APOLLODORUS *comes past the lighthouse.*) What now?

BRITANNUS (*turning quickly, and challenging the stranger with official haughtiness*): What is this? Who are you? How did you come here?

APOLLODORUS: Calm yourself, my friend: I am not going to eat you. I have come by boat, from Alexandria, with precious gifts for Cæsar.

CÆSAR: From Alexandria!

BRITANNUS (*severely*): That is Cæsar, sir.

RUFIO (*appearing at the lighthouse door*): Whats the matter now?

APOLLODORUS: Hail, great Cæsar! I am Apollodorus the Sicilian, an artist.

BRITANNUS: An artist! Why have they admitted this vagabond?

CÆSAR: Peace, man. Apollodorus is a famous patrician amateur.

BRITANNUS (*disconcerted*): I crave the gentleman's pardon. (*To* CÆSAR.) I understood him to say that he was a professional. (*Somewhat out of countenance, he allows* APOLLODORUS *to approach* CÆSAR, *changing places with him.* RUFIO, *after looking* APOLLODORUS *up and down with marked disparagement, goes to the other side of the platform.*)

CÆSAR: You are welcome, Apollodorus. What is your business?

APOLLODORUS: First, to deliver to you a present from the Queen of Queens.

CÆSAR: Who is that?

APOLLODORUS: Cleopatra of Egypt.

CÆSAR (*taking him into his confidence in his most winning manner*): Apollodorus: this is no time for playing with presents. Pray you, go back to the Queen, and tell her that if all goes well I shall return to the palace this evening.

APOLLODORUS: Cæsar: I cannot return. As I approached the lighthouse, some fool threw a great leathern bag into the sea. It broke the nose of my boat; and I had hardly time to get myself and my charge to the shore before the poor little cockleshell sank.

CÆSAR: I am sorry, Apollodorus. The fool shall be rebuked. Well, well: what have you brought me? The Queen will be hurt if I do not look at it.

RUFIO: Have we time to waste on this trumpery? The Queen is only a child.

CÆSAR: Just so: that is why we must not disappoint her. What is the present, Apollodorus?

APOLLODORUS: Cæsar: it is a Persian carpet – a beauty! And in it are – so I am told – pigeons' eggs and crystal goblets and fragile precious things. I dare not for my head have it carried up that narrow ladder from the causeway.

RUFIO: Swing it up by the crane, then. We will send the eggs to the cook, drink our wine from the goblets; and the carpet will make a bed for Cæsar.

APOLLODORUS: The crane! Cæsar: I have sworn to tender this bale of carpets as I tender my own life.

CÆSAR (*cheerfully*): Then let them swing you up at the same time; and if the chain breaks, you and the pigeons' eggs will perish together. (*He goes to the chain and looks up along it, examining it curiously.*)

APOLLODORUS (*to* BRITANNUS): Is Cæsar serious?

BRITANNUS: His manner is frivolous because he is an Italian; but he means what he says.

APOLLODORUS: Serious or not, he spake well. Give me a squad of soldiers to work the crane.

BRITANNUS: Leave the crane to me. Go and await the descent of the chain.

APOLLODORUS: Good. You will presently see me there (*turning to them all and pointing with an eloquent gesture to the sky above the parapet*) rising like the sun with my treasure.

(*He goes back the way he came.* BRITANNUS *goes into the lighthouse.*)

RUFIO (*ill-humoredly*): Are you really going to wait here for this foolery, Cæsar?

CÆSAR (*backing away from the crane as it gives signs of working*): Why not?

RUFIO: The Egyptians will let you know why not if they have the sense to make a rush from the shore end of the mole before our barricade is finished. And here we are waiting like children to see a carpet full of pigeons' eggs.

(*The chain rattles, and is drawn up high enough to clear the parapet. It then swings round out of sight behind the lighthouse.*)

CÆSAR: Fear not, my son Rufio. When the first Egyptian takes his first step along the mole, the alarm will sound; and we two will reach the barricade from our end before the Egyptians reach it from their end – we two, Rufio: I, the old man, and you, his biggest boy. And the old man will be there first. So peace; and give me some more dates.

APOLLODORUS (*from the causeway below*): Soho, haul away. So-ho-o-o-o! (*The chain is drawn up and comes round again from behind the lighthouse.* APOLLODORUS *is swinging in the air with his bale of carpet at the end of it. He breaks into song as he soars above the parapet.*)

Aloft, aloft, behold the blue
That never shone in woman's eyes—

Easy there: stop her. (*He ceases to rise.*) Further round! (*The chain comes forward above the platform.*)

RUFIO (*calling up*): Lower away there. (*The chain and its load begin to descend.*)

APOLLODORUS (*calling up*): Gently—slowly—mind the eggs.

RUFIO (*calling up*): Easy there—slowly—slowly.

(APOLLODORUS *and the bale are deposited safely on the flags in the middle of the platform.* RUFIO *and* CÆSAR *help* APOLLODORUS *to cast off the chain from the bale.*)

RUFIO: Haul up.

(*The chain rises clear of their heads with a rattle.* BRITANNUS *comes from the lighthouse and helps them to uncord the carpet.*)

APOLLODORUS (*when the cords are loose*): Stand off, my friends: let Cæsar see. (*He throws the carpet open.*)

RUFIO: Nothing but a heap of shawls. Where are the pigeons' eggs?

APOLLODORUS: Approach, Cæsar; and search for them among the shawls.

RUFIO (*drawing his sword*): Ha, treachery. Keep back, Cæsar: I saw the shawl move: there is something alive in there.

BRITANNUS (*drawing his sword*): It is a serpent.

APOLLODORUS: Dares *Cæsar* thrust his hand into the sack where the serpent moves?

RUFIO (*turning on him*): Treacherous dog—

CÆSAR: Peace. Put up your swords. Apollodorus: your serpent seems to breathe very regularly. (*He thrusts his hand under the shawls and draws out a bare arm.*) This is a pretty little snake.

RUFIO (*drawing out the other arm*): Let us have the rest of you.

(*They pull* CLEOPATRA *up by the wrists into a sitting position.* BRITANNUS, *scandalized, sheathes his sword with a drive of protest.*)

CLEOPATRA (*gasping*): Oh, I'm smothered. Oh, Cæsar, a man stood on me in the boat; and a great sack of something fell upon me out of the sky; and then the boat sank; and then I was swung up into the air and bumped down.

CÆSAR (*petting her as she rises and takes refuge on his breast*): Well, never mind: here you are safe and sound at last.

RUFIO: Ay, and now that she *is* here, what are we to do with her?

BRITANNUS: She cannot stay here, Cæsar, without the companionship of some matron.

CLEOPATRA (*jealously, to* CÆSAR, *who is obviously perplexed*): Arent you glad to see me?

CÆSAR: Yes, yes; *I* am very glad. But Rufio is very angry; and Britannus is shocked.

CLEOPATRA (*contemptuously*): You can have their heads cut off, can you not?

CÆSAR: They would not be so useful with their heads cut off as they are now, my sea bird.

RUFIO (*to* CLEOPATRA): We shall have to go away presently and cut some of your Egyptians' heads off. How will you like being left here with the chance of being captured by that little brother of yours if we are beaten?

CLEOPATRA: But you mustnt leave me alone. Cæsar: you will not leave me alone, will you?

RUFIO: What! not when the trumpet sounds and all our lives depend on Cæsar's being at the barricade before the Egyptians reach it? Eh?

CLEOPATRA: Let them lose their lives: they are only soldiers.

CÆSAR (*gravely*): Cleopatra: when that trumpet sounds, we must take every man his life in his hand, and throw it in the face of Death. And of my soldiers who have trusted me there is not one whose hand I shall not hold more sacred than your head. (CLEOPATRA *is overwhelmed. Her eyes fill with tears.*) Apollodorus: you must take her back to the palace.

APOLLODORUS: Am I a dolphin, Cæsar, to cross the seas with young ladies on my back? My boat is sunk: all yours are either at the barricade or have returned to the city. I will hail one if I can: that is all I can do. (*He goes back to the causeway.*)

CLEOPATRA (*struggling with her tears*): It does not matter. I will not go back. Nobody cares for me.

CÆSAR: Cleopatra —

CLEOPATRA: You want me to be killed.

CÆSAR (*still more gravely*): My poor child: your life matters little here to anyone but yourself. (*She gives way altogether at this, casting herself down on the faggots weeping. Suddenly a great tumult is heard in the distance, bucinas and trumpets sounding through a storm of shouting.* BRITANNUS *rushes to the parapet and looks along the mole.* CÆSAR *and* RUFIO *turn to one another with quick intelligence.*)

CÆSAR: Come, Rufio.

CLEOPATRA (*scrambling to her knees and clinging to him*): No, no. Do not leave me, Cæsar. (*He snatches his skirt from her clutch.*) Oh!

BRITANNUS (*from the parapet*): Cæsar: we are cut off. The Egyptians have landed from the west harbor between us and the barricade!!!

RUFIO (*running to see*): Curses! It is true. We are caught like rats in a trap.

CÆSAR (*ruthfully*): Rufio, Rufio: my men at the barricade are between the sea party and the shore party. I have murdered them.

RUFIO (*coming back from the parapet to* CÆSAR'*s right hand*): Ay: that comes of fooling with this girl here.

APOLLODORUS (*coming up quickly from the causeway*): Look over the parapet, Cæsar.

CÆSAR: We have looked, my friend. We must defend ourselves here.

APOLLODORUS: I have thrown the ladder into the sea. They cannot get in without it.

RUFIO: Ay; and we cannot get out. Have you thought of that?

APOLLODORUS: Not get out! Why not? You have ships in the east harbor.

BRITANNUS (*hopefully, at the parapet*): The Rhodian galleys are standing in towards us already. (CÆSAR *quickly joins* BRITANNUS *at the parapet.*)

RUFIO (*to* APOLLODORUS, *impatiently*): And by what road are we to walk to the galleys, pray?

APOLLODORUS (*with gay, defiant rhetoric*): By the road that leads everywhere — the diamond path of the sun and moon. Have you never seen the child's shadow play of The Broken Bridge? "Ducks and geese with ease get over" — eh? (*He throws away his cloak and cap, and binds his sword on his back.*)

RUFIO: What are you talking about?

APOLLODORUS: I will shew you. (*Calling to* BRITANNUS.) How far off is the nearest galley?

BRITANNUS: Fifty fathom.

CÆSAR: No, no: they are further off than they seem in this clear air to your British eyes. Nearly quarter of a mile, Apollodorus.

APOLLODORUS: Good. Defend yourselves here until I send you a boat from that galley.

RUFIO: Have you wings, perhaps?

APOLLODORUS: Water wings, soldier. Behold!

(*He runs up the steps between* CÆSAR *and* BRITANNUS *to the coping of the parapet; springs into the air; and plunges head foremost into the sea.*)

CÆSAR (*like a schoolboy — wildly excited*): Bravo, bravo! (*Throwing off his cloak.*) By Jupiter, I will do that too.

RUFIO (*seizing him*): You are mad. You shall not.

CÆSAR: Why not? Can I not swim as well as he?

RUFIO (*frantic*): Can an old fool dive and swim like a young one? He is twenty-five and you are fifty.

CÆSAR (*breaking loose from* RUFIO): Old!!!

BRITANNUS (*shocked*): Rufio: you forget yourself.

CÆSAR: I will race you to the galley for a week's pay, father Rufio.

CLEOPATRA: But me! me!!! me!!! what is to become of me?

CÆSAR: I will carry you on my back to the galley like a dolphin. Rufio: when you see me rise to the surface, throw her in: I will answer for her. And then in with you after her, both of you.

CLEOPATRA: No, no, NO. I shall be drowned.

BRITANNUS: Cæsar: I am a man and a Briton, not a fish. I must have a boat. I cannot swim.

CLEOPATRA: Neither can I.

CÆSAR (*to* BRITANNUS): Stay here, then, alone, until I recapture the lighthouse: I will not forget you. Now, Rufio.

RUFIO: You have made up your mind to this folly?

CÆSAR: The Egyptians have made it up for me. What else is there to do? And mind where you jump: I do not want to get your fourteen stone in the small of my back as I come up. (*He runs up the steps and stands on the coping.*)

BRITANNUS (*anxiously*): One last word, Cæsar. Do not let yourself be seen in the fashionable part of Alexandria until you have changed your clothes.

CÆSAR (*calling over the sea*): Ho, Apollodorus. (*He points skyward and quotes the barcarolle.*)

The white upon the blue above –

APOLLODORUS (*swimming in the distance*):

Is purple on the green below –

CÆSAR (*exultantly*): Aha! (*He plunges into the sea.*)

CLEOPATRA (*running excitedly to the steps*): Oh, let me see. He will be drowned. (RUFIO *seizes her.*) – Ah – ah – ah – ah! (*He pitches her screaming into the sea.* RUFIO *and* BRITANNUS *roar with laughter.*)

RUFIO (*looking down after her*): He has got her. (*To* BRITANNUS.) Hold the fort, Briton. Cæsar will not forget you. (*He springs off.*)

BRITANNUS (*running to the steps to watch them as they swim*): All safe, Rufio?

RUFIO (*swimming*): All safe.

CÆSAR (*swimming further off*): Take refuge up there by the beacon; and pile the fuel on the trap door, Britannus.

BRITANNUS (*calling in reply*): I will first do so, and then commend myself to my country's gods. (*A sound of cheering from the sea.* BRITANNUS *gives full vent to his excitement.*) The boat has reached him: Hip, hip, hip, hurrah!

## ACT IV

CLEOPATRA*'s sousing in the east harbor of Alexandria was in October 48* B.C. *In March 47 she is passing the afternoon in her boudoir in the palace, among a bevy of her ladies, listening to a slave girl who is playing the harp in the middle of the room. The harpist's master, an old* MUSICIAN, *with a lined face, prominent brows, white beard, moustache and eyebrows twisted and horned at the ends, and a consciously keen and pretentious expression, is squatting on the floor close to her on her right, watching her performance.* FTATATEETA *is in attendance near* *the door, in front of a group of female slaves. Except the harp player all are seated:* CLEOPATRA *in a chair opposite the door on the other side of the room; the rest on the ground.* CLEOPATRA*'s ladies are all young, the most conspicuous being* CHARMIAN *and* IRAS, *her favorites.* CHARMIAN *is a hatchet faced, terra cotta colored little goblin, swift in her movements, and neatly finished at the hands and feet.* IRAS *is a plump, goodnatured creature, rather fatuous, with a profusion of red hair, and a tendency to giggle on the slightest provocation.*

CLEOPATRA: Can I —

FTATATEETA (*insolently, to the player*): Peace, thou! The Queen speaks. (*The player stops.*)

CLEOPATRA (*to the old* MUSICIAN): I want to learn to play the harp with my own hands. Cæsar loves music. Can you teach me?

MUSICIAN: Assuredly I and no one else can teach the Queen. Have I not discovered the lost method of the ancient Egyptians, who could make a pyramid tremble by touching a bass string? All the other teachers are quacks: I have exposed them repeatedly.

CLEOPATRA: Good: you shall teach me. How long will it take?

MUSICIAN: Not very long: only four years. Your Majesty must first become proficient in the philosophy of Pythagoras.

CLEOPATRA: Has she (*indicating the slave*) become proficient in the philosophy of Pythagoras?

MUSICIAN: Oh, she is but a slave. She learns as a dog learns.

CLEOPATRA: Well, then, I will learn as a dog learns; for she plays better than you. You shall give me a lesson every day for a fortnight. (*The* MUSICIAN *hastily scrambles to his feet and bows profoundly.*) After that, whenever I strike a false note you shall be flogged; and if I strike so many that there is not time to flog you, you shall be thrown into the Nile to feed the crocodiles. Give the girl a piece of gold; and send them away.

MUSICIAN (*much taken aback*): But true art will not be thus forced.

FTATATEETA (*pushing him out*): What is this? Answering the Queen, forsooth. Out with you.

(*He is pushed out by* FTATATEETA, *the girl following with her harp, amid the laughter of the ladies and slaves.*)

CLEOPATRA: Now, can any of you amuse me? Have you any stories or any news?

IRAS: Ftatateeta —

CLEOPATRA: Oh. Ftatateeta, Ftatateeta, always Ftatateeta. Some new tale to set me against her.

IRAS: No: this time Ftatateeta has been virtuous. (*All the ladies laugh — not the slaves.*) Pothinus has been trying to bribe her to let him speak with you.

CLEOPATRA (*wrathfully*): Ha! you all sell audiences with me, as if I saw whom you please, and not whom I please. I should like to know how much of her gold piece that harp girl will have to give up before she leaves the palace.

IRAS: We can easily find that out for you.

(*The ladies laugh.*)

CLEOPATRA (*frowning*): You laugh; but take care, take care. I will find out some day how to make myself served as Cæsar is served.

CHARMIAN: Old hooknose! (*They laugh again.*)

CLEOPATRA (*revolted*): Silence. Charmain: do not you be a silly little Egyptian fool. Do you know why I allow you all to chatter impertinently just as you please, instead of treating you as Ftatateeta would treat you if she were Queen?

CHARMIAN: Because you try to imitate Cæsar in everything; and he lets everybody say what they please to him.

CLEOPATRA: No; but because I asked him one day why he did so; and he said "Let your women talk; and you will learn something from them." What have I to learn from them? I said. "What they are," said he; and oh! you should have seen his eye as he said it. You would have curled up, you shallow things. (*They laugh. She turns fiercely on* IRAS.) At whom are you laughing – at me or at Cæsar?

IRAS: At Cæsar.

CLEOPATRA: If you were not a fool, you would laugh at me; and if you were not a coward you would not be afraid to tell me so. (FTATATEETA *returns.*) Ftatateeta: they tell me that Pothinus has offered you a bribe to admit him to my presence.

FTATATEETA (*protesting*): Now by my father's gods –

CLEOPATRA (*cutting her short despotically*): Have I not told you not to deny things? You would spend the day calling your father's gods to witness to your virtues if I let you. Go take the bribe; and bring in Pothinus. (FTATATEETA *is about to reply.*) Dont answer me. Go.

(FTATATEETA *goes out; and* CLEOPATRA *rises and begins to prowl to and fro between her chair and the door, meditating. All rise and stand.*)

IRAS (*as she reluctantly rises*): Heigho! I wish Cæsar were back in Rome.

CLEOPATRA (*threateningly*): It will be a bad day for you all when he goes. Oh, if I were not ashamed to let him see that I am as cruel at heart as my father, I would make you repent that speech! Why do you wish him away?

CHARMIAN: He makes you so terribly prosy and serious and learned and philosophical. It is worse than being religious, at *our* ages. (*The ladies laugh.*)

CLEOPATRA: Cease that endless cackling, will you. Hold your tongues.

CHARMIAN (*with mock resignation*): Well, well: we must try to live up to Cæsar.

(*They laugh again.* CLEOPATRA *rages silently as she continues to prowl to and fro.* FTATATEETA *comes back with* POTHINUS, *who halts on the threshold.*)

FTATATEETA (*at the door*): Pothinus craves the ear of the –

CLEOPATRA: There, there: that will do: let him come in. (*She resumes her seat. All sit down except* POTHINUS, *who advances to the middle of the room.* FTATATEETA *takes her former place.*) Well, Pothinus: what is the latest news from your rebel friends?

POTHINUS (*haughtily*): I am no friend of rebellion. And a prisoner does not receive news.

CLEOPATRA: You are no more a prisoner than I am – than Cæsar is. These six months we have been besieged in this palace by my subjects. You are allowed to walk on the beach among the soldiers. Can I go further myself, or can Cæsar?

POTHINUS: You are but a child, Cleopatra, and do not understand these matters.

(*The ladies laugh.* CLEOPATRA *looks inscrutably at him.*)

CHARMIAN: I see you do not know the latest news, Pothinus.

POTHINUS: What is that?

CHARMIAN: That Cleopatra is no longer a child. Shall I tell you how to grow much older, and much, *much* wiser in one day?

POTHINUS: I should prefer to grow wiser without growing older.

CHARMIAN: Well, go up to the top of the lighthouse; and get somebody to take you by the hair and throw you into the sea. (*The ladies laugh.*)

CLEOPATRA: She is right, Pothinus: you will come to the shore with much conceit washed out of you. (*The ladies laugh.* CLEOPATRA *rises impatiently.*) Begone, all of you. I will speak with Pothinus alone. Drive them out, Ftatateeta. (*They run out laughing.* FTATATEETA *shuts the door on them.*) What are *you* waiting for?

FTATATEETA: It is not meet that the Queen remain alone with –

CLEOPATRA (*interrupting her*): Ftatateeta: must I sacrifice you to your father's gods to teach you that *I* am Queen of Egypt, and not you?

FTATATEETA (*indignantly*): You are like the rest of them. You want to be what these Romans call a New Woman. (*She goes out, banging the door.*)

CLEOPATRA (*sitting down again*): Now, Pothinus: why did you bribe Ftatateeta to bring you hither?

POTHINUS (*studying her gravely*): Cleopatra: what they tell me is true. You are changed.

CLEOPATRA: Do you speak with Cæsar every day for six months: and *you* will be changed.

POTHINUS: It is the common talk that you are infatuated with this old man.

CLEOPATRA: Infatuated? What does that mean? Made foolish, is it not? Oh no: I wish I were.

POTHINUS: You wish you were made foolish! How so?

CLEOPATRA: When I was foolish, I did what I liked, except when Ftatateeta beat me; and even then I cheated her and did it by stealth. Now that Cæsar has made me wise, it is no use my liking or disliking: I do what must be done, and have no time to attend to myself. That is not happiness; but it is greatness. If Cæsar were gone, I think I could govern the Egyptians; for what Cæsar is to me, I am to the fools around me.

POTHINUS (*looking hard at her*): Cleopatra: this may be the vanity of youth.

CLEOPATRA: No, no: it is not that I am so clever, but that the others are so stupid.

POTHINUS (*musingly*): Truly, that is the great secret.

CLEOPATRA: Well, now tell me what you came to say?

POTHINUS (*embarrassed*): I! Nothing.

CLEOPATRA: Nothing!

POTHINUS: At least – to beg for my liberty: that is all.

CLEOPATRA: For that you would have knelt to Cæsar. No, Pothinus: you came with some plan that depended on Cleopatra being a little nursery kitten. Now that Cleopatra is a Queen, the plan is upset.

POTHINUS (*bowing his head submissively*): It is so.

CLEOPATRA (*exultant*): Aha!

POTHINUS (*raising his eyes keenly to hers*): Is Cleopatra then indeed a Queen, and no longer Cæsar's prisoner and slave?

CLEOPATRA: Pothinus: we are all Cæsar's slaves – all we in this land of Egypt – whether we will or no. And she who is wise enough to know this will reign when Cæsar departs.

POTHINUS: You harp on Cæsar's departure.

CLEOPATRA: What if I do?

POTHINUS: Does he not love you?

CLEOPATRA: Love me! Pothinus: Cæsar loves no one. Who are those we love. Only those whom we do not hate: all people are strangers and enemies to us except those we love. But it is not so with Cæsar. He has no hatred in him: he makes friends with everyone as he does with dogs and children. His kindness to me is a wonder; neither mother, father, nor nurse have ever taken so much care for me, or thrown open their thoughts to me so freely.

POTHINUS: Well: is not this love?

CLEOPATRA: What! when he will do as much for the first girl he meets on his way back to Rome? Ask his slave, Britannus: he has been just as good to him. Nay, ask his very horse! His kindness is not for anything in me: it is in his own nature.

POTHINUS: But how can you be sure that he does not love you as men love women?

CLEOPATRA: Because I cannot make him jealous. I have tried.

POTHINUS: Hm! Perhaps I should have asked, then, do *you* love *him?*

CLEOPATRA: Can one love a god? Besides, I love another Roman: one whom I saw long before Cæsar – no god, but a man – one who can love and hate – one whom I can hurt and who would hurt me.

POTHINUS: Does Cæsar know this?

CLEOPATRA: Yes.

POTHINUS: And he is not angry?

CLEOPATRA: He promises to send him to Egypt to please me!

POTHINUS: I do not understand this man.

CLEOPATRA (*with superb contempt*): *You* understand Cæsar! How could you? (*Proudly.*) I do – by instinct.

POTHINUS (*deferentially, after a moment's thought*): Your Majesty caused me to be admitted to-day. What message has the Queen for me?

CLEOPATRA: This. You think that by making my brother king, you will rule in Egypt, because you are his guardian and he is a little silly.

POTHINUS: The Queen is pleased to say so.

CLEOPATRA: The Queen is pleased to say this also. That Cæsar will eat up you, and Achillas, and my brother, as a cat eats up mice; and that he will put on this land of Egypt as a shepherd puts on his garment. And when he has done that, he will return to Rome, and leave Cleopatra here as his viceroy.

POTHINUS (*breaking out wrathfully*): That he shall never do. We have a thousand men to his ten; and we will drive him and his beggarly legions into the sea.

CLEOPATRA (*with scorn, getting up to go*): You rant like any common fellow. Go, then, and marshal your thousands; and make haste; for Mithridates of Pergamos is at hand with reinforcements for Cæsar. Cæsar has held you at bay with two legions: we shall see what he will do with twenty.

POTHINUS: Cleopatra –

CLEOPATRA: Enough, enough: Cæsar has spoiled me for talking to weak things like you. (*She goes out.* POTHINUS, *with a gesture of rage, is following, when* FTATATEETA *enters and stops him.*)

POTHINUS: Let me go forth from this hateful place.

FTATATEETA: What angers you?

POTHINUS: The curse of all the gods of Egypt be upon her! She has sold her country to the Roman, that she may buy it back from him with her kisses.

FTATATEETA: Fool: did she not tell you that she would have Cæsar gone?

POTHINUS: You listened?

FTATATEETA: I took care that some honest woman should be at hand whilst you were with her.

POTHINUS: Now by the gods –

FTATATEETA: Enough of your gods! Cæsar's gods are all powerful here. It is no use *you* coming to Cleopatra: you are only an Egyptian. She will not listen to any of her own race: she treats us all as children.

POTHINUS: May she perish for it!

FTATATEETA (*balefully*): May your tongue wither for that wish! Go! send for Lucius Septimius, the slayer of Pompey. He is a Roman: may be she will listen to him. Begone!

POTHINUS (*darkly*): I know to whom I must go now.

FTATATEETA (*suspiciously*): To whom, then?

POTHINUS: To a greater Roman than Lucius. And mark this, mistress. You thought, before Cæsar came, that Egypt should presently be ruled by you and your crew in the name of Cleopatra. I set myself against it –

FTATATEETA (*interrupting him – wrangling*): Ay; that it might be ruled by you and *your* crew in the name of Ptolemy.

POTHINUS: Better me, or even you, than a woman with a Roman heart; and that is what Cleopatra is now become. Whilst I live, she shall never rule. So guide yourself accordingly. (*He goes out.*)

(*It is by this time drawing on to dinner time. The table is laid on the roof of the palace; and thither* RUFIO *is now climbing, ushered by a majestic palace* OFFICIAL, *wand of office in hand, and followed by a* SLAVE *carrying an inlaid stool. After many stairs they emerge at last into a massive colonnade on the roof. Light curtains are drawn between the columns on the north and east to soften the westering sun. The* OFFICIAL *leads* RUFIO *to one of these shaded sections. A cord for pulling the curtains apart hangs down between the pillars.*)

OFFICIAL (*bowing*): The Roman commander will await Cæsar here.

(*The* SLAVE *sets down the stool near the southernmost column, and slips out through the curtains.*)

RUFIO (*sitting down, a little blown*): Pouf! That was a climb. How high have we come?

OFFICIAL: We are on the palace roof, O Beloved of Victory!

RUFIO: Good! the Beloved of Victory has no more stairs to get up.

(*A* SECOND OFFICIAL *enters from the opposite end, walking backwards.*)

SECOND OFFICIAL: Cæsar approaches.

(CÆSAR, *fresh from the bath, clad in a new tunic of purple silk, comes in, beaming and festive, followed by two* SLAVES *carrying a light couch, which is hardly more than an elaborately designed bench. They place it near the northmost of the two curtained columns. When this is done they slip out through the curtains; and the two* OFFICIALS, *formally bowing, follow them.* RUFIO *rises to receive* CÆSAR.)

CÆSAR (*coming over to him*): Why, Rufio! (*Surveying his dress with an air of admiring astonishment.*) A new baldrick! A new golden pommel to your sword! And you have had your hair cut. But not your beard – ?

impossible! (*He sniffs at* RUFIO's *beard.*) Yes, perfumed, by Jupiter Olympus!

RUFIO (*growling*): Well: is it to please myself?

CÆSAR (*affectionately*): No, my son Rufio, but to please me – to celebrate my birthday.

RUFIO (*contemptuously*): Your birthday! You always have a birthday when there is a pretty girl to be flattered or an ambassador to be conciliated. We had seven of them in ten months last year.

CÆSAR (*contritely*): It is true, Rufio! I shall never break myself of these petty deceits.

RUFIO: Who is to dine with us – besides Cleopatra?

CÆSAR: Apollodorus the Sicilian.

RUFIO: That popinjay!

CÆSAR: Come! the popinjay is an amusing dog – tells a story; sings a song; and saves us the trouble of flattering the Queen. What does she care for old politicians and camp-fed bears like us? No: Apollodorus is good company, Rufio, good company.

RUFIO: Well, he can swim a bit and fence a bit: he might be worse, if he only knew how to hold his tongue.

CÆSAR: The gods forbid he should ever learn! Oh, this military life! this tedious, brutal life of action! That is the worst of us Romans: we are mere doers and drudgers: a swarm of bees turned into men. Give me a good talker – one with wit and imagination enough to live without continually doing something!

RUFIO: Ay! a nice time he would have of it with you when dinner was over! Have you noticed that I am before my time?

CÆSAR: Aha! I thought that meant something. What is it?

RUFIO: Can we be overheard here?

CÆSAR: Our privacy invites eavesdropping. I can remedy that. (*He claps his hands twice. The curtains are drawn, revealing the roof garden with a banqueting table set across in the middle for four persons, one at each end, and two side by side. The side next* CÆSAR *and* RUFIO *is blocked with golden wine vessels and basins. A gorgeous* MAJOR-DOMO *is superintending the laying of the table by a staff of* SLAVES. *The colonnade goes round the garden at both sides to the further end, where a gap in it, like a great gateway, leaves the view open to the sky beyond the western edge of the roof, except in the middle, where a life size image of Ra, seated on a huge plinth, towers up, with hawk head and crown of asp and disk. His altar, which stands at his feet, is a single white stone.*) Now everybody can see us, nobody will think of listening to us. (*He sits down on the bench left by the two* SLAVES.)

RUFIO (*sitting down on his stool*): Pothinus wants to speak to you. I advise you to see him: there is some plotting going on here among the women.

CÆSAR: Who is Pothinus?

RUFIO: The fellow with hair like squirrel's fur — the little King's bear leader, whom you kept prisoner.

CÆSAR (*annoyed*): And has he not escaped?

RUFIO: No.

CÆSAR (*rising imperiously*): Why not? You have been guarding this man instead of watching the enemy. Have I not told you always to let prisoners escape unless there are special orders to the contrary? Are there not enough mouths to be fed without him?

RUFIO: Yes; and if you would have a little sense and let me cut his throat, you would save his rations. Anyhow, he *wont* escape. Three sentries have told him they would put a pilum through him if they saw him again. What more can they do? He prefers to stay and spy on us. So would I if I had to do with generals subject to fits of clemency.

CÆSAR (*resuming his seat, argued down*): Hm! And so he wants to see me.

RUFIO: Ay. I have brought him with me. He is waiting there (*jerking his thumb over his shoulder*) under guard.

CÆSAR: And you want me to see him?

RUFIO (*obstinately*): I dont want anything. I daresay you will do what you like. Dont put it on to me.

CÆSAR (*with an air of doing it expressly to indulge* RUFIO): Well, well: let us have him.

RUFIO (*calling*): Ho there, guard! Release your man and send him up. (*Beckoning.*) Come along!

(POTHINUS *enters and stops mistrustfully between the two, looking from one to the other.*)

CÆSAR (*graciously*): Ah, Pothinus! You are welcome. And what is the news this afternoon?

POTHINUS: Cæsar: I come to warn you of a danger, and to make you an offer.

CÆSAR: Never mind the danger. Make the offer.

RUFIO: Never mind the offer. Whats the danger?

POTHINUS: Cæsar: you think that Cleopatra is devoted to you.

CÆSAR (*gravely*): My friend: I already know what I think. Come to your offer.

POTHINUS: I will deal plainly. I know not by what strange gods you have been enabled to defend a palace and a few yards of beach against a city and an army. Since we cut you off from Lake Mareotis, and you dug wells in the salt sea sand and brought up buckets of fresh water from them, we have known that your gods are irresistible, and that you are a worker of miracles. I no longer threaten you —

RUFIO (*sarcastically*): Very handsome of you, indeed.

POTHINUS: So be it: you are the master. Our gods sent the north west winds to keep you in our hands; but you have been too strong for them.

CÆSAR (*gently urging him to come to the point*): Yes, yes, my friend. But what then?

RUFIO: Spit it out, man. What have you to say?

POTHINUS: I have to say that you have a traitress in your camp. Cleopatra –

MAJOR-DOMO (*at the table, announcing*): The Queen! (CÆSAR *and* RUFIO *rise.*)

RUFIO (*aside to* POTHINUS): You should have spat it out sooner, you fool. Now it is too late.

(CLEOPATRA, *in gorgeous raiment, enters in state through the gap in the colonnade, and comes down past the image of Ra and past the table to* CÆSAR. *Her retinue, headed by* FTATATEETA, *joins the staff at the table,* CÆSAR *gives* CLEOPATRA *his seat, which she takes.*)

CLEOPATRA (*quickly, seeing* POTHINUS): What is *he* doing here?

CÆSAR (*seating himself beside her, in the most amiable of tempers*): Just going to tell me something about you. You shall hear it. Proceed, Pothinus.

POTHINUS (*disconcerted*): Cæsar – (*He stammers.*)

CÆSAR: Well, out with it.

POTHINUS: What I have to say is for your ear, not for the Queen's.

CLEOPATRA (*with subdued ferocity*): There are means of making you speak. Take care.

POTHINUS (*defiantly*): Cæsar does not employ those means.

CÆSAR: My friend: when a man has anything to tell in this world, the difficulty is not to make him tell it, but to prevent him from telling it too often. Let me celebrate my birthday by setting you free. Farewell: we shall not meet again.

CLEOPATRA (*angrily*): Cæsar: this mercy is foolish.

POTHINUS (*to* CÆSAR): Will you not give me a private audience? Your life may depend on it. (CÆSAR *rises loftily.*)

RUFIO (*aside to* POTHINUS): Ass! Now we shall have some heroics.

CÆSAR (*oratorically*): Pothinus –

RUFIO (*interrupting him*): Cæsar: the dinner will spoil if you begin preaching your favorite sermon about life and death.

CLEOPATRA (*priggishly*): Peace, Rufio. I desire to hear Cæsar.

RUFIO (*bluntly*): Your Majesty has heard it before. You repeated it to Apollodorus last week; and he thought it was all your own. (CÆSAR'*s dignity collapses. Much tickled, he sits down again and looks roguishly at* CLEOPATRA, *who is furious.* RUFIO *calls as before.*) Ho there, guard! Pass the prisoner out. He is released. (*To* POTHINUS.) Now off with you. You have lost your chance.

POTHINUS (*his temper overcoming his prudence*): I *will* speak.

CÆSAR (*to* CLEOPATRA): You see. Torture would not have wrung a word from him.

POTHINUS: Cæsar: you have taught Cleopatra the arts by which the Romans govern the world.

CÆSAR: Alas! they cannot even govern themselves. What then?

POTHINUS: What then? Are you so besotted with her beauty that you do not see that she is impatient to reign in Egypt alone, and that her heart is set on your departure?

CLEOPATRA (*rising*): Liar!

CÆSAR (*shocked*): What! Protestations! Contradictions!

CLEOPATRA (*ashamed, but trembling with suppressed rage*): No. I do not deign to contradict. Let him talk. (*She sits down again.*)

POTHINUS: From her own lips I have heard it. You are to be her catspaw: you are to tear the crown from her brother's head and set it on her own, delivering us all into her hand – delivering yourself also. And when Cæsar can return to Rome, or depart through the gate of death, which is nearer and surer.

CÆSAR (*calmly*): Well, my friend; and is not this very natural?

POTHINUS (*astonished*): Natural! Then you do not resent treachery?

CÆSAR: Resent! O thou foolish Egyptian, what have I to do with resentment? Do I resent the wind when it chills me, or the night when it makes me stumble in the darkness? Shall I resent youth when it turns from age, and ambition when it turns from servitude? To tell me such a story as this is but to tell me that the sun will rise to-morrow.

CLEOPATRA (*unable to contain herself*): But it is false – false. I swear it.

CÆSAR: It is true, though you swore it a thousand times, and believed all you swore. (*She is convulsed with emotion. To screen her, he rises and takes* POTHINUS *to* RUFIO, *saying:*) Come, Rufio: let us see Pothinus past the guard. I have a word to say to him. (*Aside to them.*) We must give the Queen a moment to recover herself. (*Aloud.*) Come. (*He takes* POTHINUS *and* RUFIO *out with him, conversing with them meanwhile.*) Tell your friends, Pothinus, that they must not think I am opposed to a reasonable settlement of the country's affairs – (*They pass out of hearing.*)

CLEOPATRA (*in a stifled whisper*): Ftatateeta, Ftatateeta.

FTATATEETA (*hurrying to her from the table and petting her*): Peace, child: be comforted –

CLEOPATRA (*interrupting her*): Can they hear us?

FTATATEETA: No, dear heart, no.

CLEOPATRA: Listen to me. If he leaves the Palace alive, never see my face again.

FTATATEETA: He? Poth –

CLEOPATRA (*striking her on the mouth*): Strike his life out as I strike his name from your lips. Dash him down from the wall. Break him on the stones. Kill, kill, *kill* him.

FTATATEETA (*shewing all her teeth*): The dog shall perish.

CLEOPATRA: Fail in this, and you go out from before me for ever.

FTATATEETA (*resolutely*): So be it. You shall not see my face until his eyes are darkened.

(CÆSAR *comes back, with* APOLLODORUS, *exquisitely dressed, and* RUFIO.)

CLEOPATRA (*to* FTATATEETA): Come soon — soon. (FTATATEETA *turns her meaning eyes for a moment on her mistress; then goes grimly away past Ra and out.* CLEOPATRA *runs like a gazelle to* CÆSAR.) So you have come back to me, Cæsar. (*Caressingly.*) I thought you were angry. Welcome, Apollodorus. (*She gives him her hand to kiss, with her other arm about* CÆSAR.)

APOLLODORUS: Cleopatra grows more womanly beautiful from week to week.

CLEOPATRA: Truth, Apollodorus?

APOLLODORUS: Far, far short of the truth! Friend Rufio threw a pearl into the sea: Cæsar fished up a diamond.

CÆSAR: Cæsar fished up a touch of rheumatism, my friend. Come: to dinner! to dinner! (*They move towards the table.*)

CLEOPATRA (*skipping like a young fawn*): Yes, to dinner. I have ordered *such* a dinner for you, Cæsar!

CÆSAR: Ay? What are we to have?

CLEOPATRA: Peacocks' brains.

CÆSAR (*as if his mouth watered*): Peacocks' brains, Apollodorus!

APOLLODORUS: Not for me. I prefer nightingales' tongues. (*He goes to one of the two covers set side by side.*)

CLEOPATRA: Roast boar, Rufio!

RUFIO (*gluttonously*): Good! (*He goes to the seat next* APOLLODORUS, *on his left.*)

CÆSAR (*looking at his seat, which is at the end of the table, to Ra's left hand*): What has become of my leathern cushion?

CLEOPATRA (*at the opposite end*): I have got new ones for you.

MAJOR-DOMO: These cushions, Cæsar, are of Maltese gauze, stuffed with rose leaves.

CÆSAR: Rose leaves! Am I a caterpillar? (*He throws the cushions away and seats himself on the leather mattress underneath.*)

CLEOPATRA: What a shame! My new cushions!

MAJOR-DOMO (*at* CÆSAR'*s elbow*): What shall we serve to whet Cæsar's appetite?

CÆSAR: What have you got?

MAJOR-DOMO: Sea hedgehogs, black and white sea acorns, sea nettles, beccaficoes, purple shellfish —

CÆSAR: Any oysters?

MAJOR-DOMO: Assuredly.

CÆSAR: *British* oysters?

MAJOR-DOMO (*assenting*): British oysters, Cæsar.

CÆSAR: Oysters, then. (*The* MAJOR-DOMO *signs to a* SLAVE *at each order; and the* SLAVE *goes out to execute it.*) I have been in Britain — that western land of romance — the last piece of earth on the edge of the ocean that surrounds the world. I went there in search of its famous pearls. The British pearl was a fable; but in searching for it I found the British oyster.

APOLLODORUS: All posterity will bless you for it. (*To the* MAJOR-DOMO.) Sea hedgehogs for me.

RUFIO: Is there nothing solid to begin with?

MAJOR-DOMO: Fieldfares with asparagus —

CLEOPATRA (*interrupting*): Fattened fowls! have some fattened fowls, Rufio.

RUFIO: Ay, that will do.

CLEOPATRA (*greedily*): Fieldfares for me.

MAJOR-DOMO: Cæsar will deign to choose his wine? Sicilian, Lesbian, Chian —

RUFIO (*contemptuously*): All Greek.

APOLLODORUS: Who would drink Roman wine when he could get Greek. Try the Lesbian, Cæsar.

CÆSAR: Bring me my barley water.

RUFIO (*with intense disgust*): Ugh! Bring *me* my Falernian. (*The Falernian is presently brought to him.*)

CLEOPATRA (*pouting*): It is waste of time giving you dinners, Cæsar. My scullions would not condescend to your diet.

CÆSAR (*relenting*): Well, well: let us try the Lesbian. (*The* MAJOR-DOMO *fills* CÆSAR'*s goblet; then* CLEOPATRA'*s and* APOLLODORUS'*s.*) But when I return to Rome, I will make laws against these extravagances. I will even get the laws carried out.

CLEOPATRA (*coaxing*): Never mind. To-day you are to be like other people: idle, luxurious, and kind. (*She stretches her hand to him along the table.*)

CÆSAR: Well, for once I will sacrifice my comfort — (*kissing her hand*) there! (*He takes a draught of wine.*) Now are you satisfied?

CLEOPATRA: And you no longer believe that I long for your departure for Rome?

CÆSAR: I no longer believe anything. My brains are asleep. Besides, who knows whether I shall return to Rome?

RUFIO (*alarmed*): How? Eh? What?

CÆSAR: What has Rome to shew me that I have not seen already? One year of Rome is like another, except that I grow older, whilst the crowd in the Appian Way is always the same age.

APOLLODORUS: It is no better here in Egypt. The old men, when they are tired of life, say "We have seen everything except the source of the Nile."

CÆSAR (*his imagination catching fire*): And why not see that? Cleopatra: will you come with me and track the flood to its cradle in the heart of the regions of mystery? Shall we leave Rome behind us — Rome, that has achieved greatness only to learn how greatness destroys nations of men who are not great! Shall I make you a new kingdom, and build you a holy city there in the great unknown?

CLEOPATRA (*rapturously*): Yes, yes. You shall.

RUFIO: Ay: now he will conquer Africa with two legions before we come to the roast boar.

APOLLODORUS: Come: no scoffing. This is a noble scheme: in it Cæsar is no longer merely the conquering soldier, but the creative poet-artist. Let us name the holy city, and consecrate it with Lesbian wine.

CÆSAR: Cleopatra shall name it herself.

CLEOPATRA: It shall be called Cæsar's Gift to his Beloved.

APOLLODORUS: No, no. Something vaster than that – something universal, like the starry firmament.

CÆSAR (*prosaically*): Why not simply The Cradle of the Nile?

CLEOPATRA: No: the Nile is my ancestor; and he is a god. Oh! I have thought of something. The Nile shall name it himself. Let us call upon him. (*To the* MAJOR-DOMO.) Send for him. (*The three men stare at one another; but the* MAJOR-DOMO *goes out as if he had received the most matter-of-fact order.*) And (*to the retinue*) away with you all.

(*The retinue withdraws, making obeisance. A* PRIEST *enters, carrying a miniature Sphinx with a tiny tripod before it. A morsel of incense is smoking in the tripod. The* PRIEST *comes to the table and places the image in the middle of it. The light begins to change to the magenta purple of the Egyptian sunset, as if the god had brought a strange colored shadow with him. The three men are determined not to be impressed; but they feel curious in spite of themselves.*)

CÆSAR: What hocus-pocus is this?

CLEOPATRA: You shall see. And it is *not* hocus-pocus. To do it properly, we should kill something to please him; but perhaps he will answer Cæsar without that if we spill some wine to him.

APOLLODORUS (*turning his head to look up over his shoulder at Ra*): Why not appeal to our hawkheaded friend here?

CLEOPATRA (*nervously*): Sh! He will hear you and be angry.

RUFIO (*phlegmatically*): The source of the Nile is out of his district, I expect.

CLEOPATRA: No: I will have my city named by nobody but my dear little Sphinx, because it was in its arms that Cæsar found me asleep. (*She languishes at* CÆSAR *then turns curtly to the* PRIEST.) Go. I am a priestess, and have power to take your charge from you. (*The* PRIEST *makes a reverence and goes out.*) Now let us call on the Nile altogether. Perhaps he will rap on the table.

CÆSAR: What! table rapping! Are such superstitions still believed in this year 707 of the Republic?

CLEOPATRA: It is no superstition: our priests learn lots of things from the tables. Is it not so, Apollodorus?

APOLLODORUS: Yes: I profess myself a converted man. When Cleopatra is priestess, Apollodorus is devotee. Propose the conjuration.

CLEOPATRA: You must say with me "Send us thy voice, Father Nile."

ALL FOUR (*holding their glasses together before the idol*): Send us thy voice, Father Nile.

(*The death cry of a man in mortal terror and agony answers them. Appalled, the men set down their glasses, and listen. Silence. The purple deepens in the sky.* CÆSAR, *glancing at* CLEOPATRA, *catches her pouring out her wine before the god, with gleaming eyes, and mute assurances of gratitude and worship.* APOLLODORUS *springs up and runs to the edge of the roof to peer down and listen.*)

CÆSAR (*looking piercingly at* CLEOPATRA): What was that?

CLEOPATRA (*petulantly*): Nothing. They are beating some slave.

CÆSAR: Nothing.

RUFIO: A man with a knife in him, I'll swear.

CÆSAR (*rising*): A murder.

APOLLODORUS (*at the back, waving his hand for silence*): S-sh! Silence. Did you hear that?

CÆSAR: Another cry?

APOLLODORUS (*returning to the table*): No, a thud. Something fell on the beach, I think.

RUFIO (*grimly, as he rises*): Something with bones in it, eh?

CÆSAR (*shuddering*): Hush, hush, Rufio. (*He leaves the table and returns to the colonnade:* RUFIO *following at his left elbow, and* APOLLODORUS *at the other side.*)

CLEOPATRA (*still in her place at the table*): Will you leave me, Cæsar? Apollodorus: are you going?

APOLLODORUS: Faith, dearest Queen, my appetite is gone.

CÆSAR: Go down to the courtyard, Apollodorus; and find out what has happened.

(APOLLODORUS *nods and goes out, making for the staircase by which* RUFIO *ascended.*)

CLEOPATRA: Your soldiers have killed somebody, perhaps. What does it matter?

(*The murmur of a crowd rises from the beach below.* CÆSAR *and* RUFIO *look at one another.*)

CÆSAR: This must be seen to. (*He is about to follow* APOLLODORUS *when* RUFIO *stops him with a hand on his arm as* FTATATEETA *comes back by the far end of the roof, with dragging steps, a drowsy satiety in her eyes and in the corners of the bloodhound lips. For a moment* CÆSAR *suspects that she is drunk with wine. Not so* RUFIO: *he knows well the red vintage that has inebriated her.*)

RUFIO (*in a low tone*): There is some mischief between those two.

FTATATEETA: The Queen looks again on the face of her servant.

(CLEOPATRA *looks at her for a moment with an exultant reflection of her murderous expression. Then she flings her arms round her; kisses her repeatedly and savagely; and tears off her jewels and heaps them on her. The two men turn from the spectacle to look at one another.* FTATATEETA *drags herself sleepily to the altar; kneels before Ra; and remains there in prayer.* CÆSAR *goes to* CLEOPATRA, *leaving* RUFIO *in the colonnade.*)

CÆSAR (*with searching earnestness*): Cleopatra: what has happened?

CLEOPATRA (*in mortal dread of him, but with her utmost cajolery*): Nothing, dearest Cæsar. (*With sickly sweetness, her voice almost failing.*) Nothing. I am innocent. (*She approaches him affectionately.*) Dear Cæsar: are you angry with me? Why do you look at me so? I have been here with you all the time. How can I know what has happened?

CÆSAR (*reflectively*): That is true.

CLEOPATRA (*greatly relieved, trying to caress him*): Of course it is true. (*He does not respond to the caress.*) *You* know it is true, Rufio.

(*The murmur without suddenly swells to a roar and subsides.*)

RUFIO: I shall know presently. (*He makes for the altar in the burly trot that serves him for a stride, and touches* FTATATEETA *on the shoulder.*) Now, mistress: I shall want you. (*He orders her, with a gesture, to go before him.*)

FTATATEETA (*rising and glowering at him*): My place is with the Queen.

CLEOPATRA: She has done no harm, Rufio.

CÆSAR (*to* RUFIO): Let her stay.

RUFIO (*sitting down on the altar*): Very well. Then my place is here too; and you can see what is the matter for yourself. The city is in a pretty uproar, it seems.

CÆSAR (*with grave displeasure*): Rufio: there is a time for obedience.

RUFIO: And there is a time for obstinacy. (*He folds his arms doggedly.*)

CÆSAR (*to* CLEOPATRA): Send her away.

CLEOPATRA (*whining in her eagerness to propitiate him*): Yes, I will. I will do whatever you ask me, Cæsar, always, because I love you. Ftatateeta: go away.

FTATATEETA: The Queen's word is my will. I shall be at hand for the Queen's call. (*She goes out past Ra, as she came.*)

RUFIO (*following her*): Remember, Cæsar, *your* bodyguard also is within call. (*He follows her out.*)

(CLEOPATRA, *presuming upon* CÆSAR'S *submission to* RUFIO, *leaves the table and sits down on the bench in the colonnade.*)

CLEOPATRA: Why do you allow Rufio to treat you so? You should teach him his place.

CÆSAR: Teach him to be my enemy, and to hide his thoughts from me as you are now hiding yours.

CLEOPATRA (*her fears returning*): Why do you say that, Cæsar? Indeed, indeed, I am not hiding anything. You are wrong to treat me like this. (*She stifles a sob.*) I am only a child; and you turn into stone because you think some one has been killed. I cannot bear it. (*She purposely breaks down and weeps. He looks at her with profound sadness and complete coldness. She looks up to see what effect she is producing. Seeing that he is unmoved, she sits up, pretending to struggle with her emotion and to put it bravely away.*) But there: I know you hate tears: you shall not be troubled with them. I know you are not angry, but only sad; only I am so silly, I cannot help being hurt when you speak coldly. Of course you are quite right: it is dreadful to think of anyone being killed or even hurt; and I hope nothing really serious has — (*Her voice dies away under his contemptuous penetration.*)

CÆSAR: What has frightened you into this? What have you done? (*A trumpet sounds on the beach below.*) Aha! that sounds like the answer.

CLEOPATRA (*sinking back trembling on the bench and covering her face with her hands*): I have not betrayed you, Cæsar: I swear it.

CÆSAR: I know that. I have not trusted you. (*He turns from her, and is about to go out when* APOLLODORUS *and* BRITANNUS *drag in* LUCIUS SEPTIMIUS *to him.* RUFIO *follows.* CÆSAR *shudders.*) Again, Pompey's murderer!

RUFIO: The town has gone mad, I think. They are for tearing the palace down and driving us into the sea straight away. We laid hold of this renegade in clearing them out of the courtyard.

CÆSAR: Release him. (*They let go his arms.*) What has offended the citizens, Lucius Septimius?

LUCIUS: What did you expect, Cæsar? Pothinus was a favorite of theirs.

CÆSAR: What has happened to Pothinus? I set him free, here, not half an hour ago. Did they not pass him out?

LUCIUS: Ay, through the gallery arch sixty feet above ground, with three inches of steel in his ribs. He is as dead as Pompey. We are quits now, as to killing — you and I.

CÆSAR (*shocked*): Assassinated! — our prisoner, our guest! (*He turns reproachfully on* RUFIO.) Rufio —

RUFIO (*emphatically — anticipating the question*): Whoever did it was a wise man and a friend of yours (CLEOPATRA *is greatly emboldened*); but none of us had a hand in it. So it is no use to frown at me. (CÆSAR *turns and looks at* CLEOPATRA.)

CLEOPATRA (*violently — rising*): He was slain by order of the Queen of Egypt. I am not Julius Cæsar the dreamer, who allows every slave to insult him. Rufio has said I did well: now the others shall judge me too.

(*She turns to the others.*) This Pothinus sought to make me conspire with him to betray Cæsar to Achillas and Ptolemy. I refused; and he cursed me and came privily to Cæsar to accuse me of his own treachery. I caught him in the act; and he insulted me — *me,* the Queen! to my face. Cæsar would not avenge me: he spoke him fair and set him free. Was I right to avenge myself? Speak, Lucius.

LUCIUS: I do not gainsay it. But you will get little thanks from Cæsar for it.

CLEOPATRA: Speak, Apollodorus. Was I wrong?

APOLLODORUS: I have only one word of blame, most beautiful. You should have called upon me, your knight; and in fair duel I should have slain the slanderer.

CLEOPATRA (*passionately*): I will be judged by your very slave, Cæsar. Britannus: speak. Was I wrong?

BRITANNUS: Were treachery, falsehood, and disloyalty left unpunished, society must become like an arena full of wild beasts, tearing one another to pieces. Cæsar is in the wrong.

CÆSAR (*with quiet bitterness*): And so the verdict is against me, it seems.

CLEOPATRA (*vehemently*): Listen to me, Cæsar. If one man in all Alexandria can be found to say that I did wrong, I swear to have myself crucified on the door of the palace by my own slaves.

CÆSAR: If one man in all the world can be found, now or forever, to *know* that you did wrong, that man will have either to conquer the world as I have, or be crucified by it. (*The uproar in the streets again reaches them.*) Do you hear? These knockers at your gate are also believers in vengeance and in stabbing. You have slain their leader: it is right that they shall slay you. If you doubt it, ask your four counsellors here. And then in the name of that *right* (*he emphasizes the word with great scorn*) shall I not slay them for murdering their Queen, and be slain in my turn by their countrymen as the invader of their fatherland? Can Rome do less then than slay these slayers, too, to shew the world how Rome avenges her sons and her honor. And so, to the end of history, murder shall breed murder, always in the name of right and honor and peace, until the gods are tired of blood and create a race that can understand. (*Fierce uproar.* CLEOPATRA *becomes white with terror.*) Hearken, you who must not be insulted. Go near enough to catch their words: you will find them bitterer than the tongue of Pothinus. (*Loftily, wrapping himself up in an impenetrable dignity.*) Let the Queen of Egypt now give her orders for vengeance, and take her measures for defence; for she has renounced Cæsar. (*He turns to go.*)

CLEOPATRA (*terrified, running to him and falling on her knees*): You will not desert me, Cæsar. You will defend the palace.

CÆSAR: You have taken the powers of life and death upon you. I am only a dreamer.

CLEOPATRA: But they will kill me.

CÆSAR: And why not?

CLEOPATRA: In pity —

CÆSAR: Pity! What! has it come to this so suddenly, that nothing can save you now but pity? Did it save Pothinus?

*(She rises, wringing her hands, and goes back to the bench in despair.* APOLLODORUS *shews his sympathy with her by quietly posting himself behind the bench. The sky has by this time become the most vivid purple, and soon begins to change to a glowing pale orange, against which the colonnade and the great image shew darklier and darklier.)*

RUFIO: Cæsar: enough of preaching. The enemy is at the gate.

CÆSAR: (*turning on him and giving way to his wrath*): Ay; and what has held him baffled at the gate all these months? Was it my folly, as you deem it, or your wisdom? In this Egyptian Red Sea of blood, whose hand has held all your heads above the waves? (*Turning on* CLEOPATRA.) And yet, when Cæsar says to such an one, "Friend, go free," you, clinging for your little life to my sword, dare steal out and stab him in the back? And you, soldiers and gentlemen, and honest servants as you forget that you are, applaud this assassination, and say "Cæsar is in the wrong." By the gods, I am tempted to open my hand and let you all sink into the flood.

CLEOPATRA (*with a ray of cunning hope*): But, Cæsar, if you do, you will perish yourself.

(CÆSAR*'s eyes blaze.*)

RUFIO (*greatly alarmed*): Now, by great Jove, you filthy little Egyptian rat, that is the very word to make him walk out alone into the city and leave us here to be cut to pieces. (*Desperately, to* CÆSAR.) Will you desert us because we are a parcel of fools? I mean no harm by killing: I do it as a dog kills a cat, by instinct. We are all dogs at your heels; but we have served you faithfully.

CÆSAR (*relenting*): Alas, Rufio, my son, my son: as dogs we are like to perish now in the streets.

APOLLODORUS (*at his post behind* CLEOPATRA*'s seat*): Cæsar: what you say has an Olympian ring in it: it must be right; for it is fine art. But I am still on the side of Cleopatra. If we must die, she shall not want the devotion of a man's heart nor the strength of a man's arm.

CLEOPATRA (*sobbing*): But I dont want to die.

CÆSAR (*sadly*): Oh, ignoble, ignoble!

LUCIUS (*coming forward between* CÆSAR *and* CLEOPATRA): Hearken to me, Cæsar. It may be ignoble; but I also mean to live as long as I can.

CÆSAR: Well, my friend, you are likely to outlive Cæsar. Is it any magic of mine, think you, that has kept your army and this whole city at bay for so long? Yesterday, what quarrel had they with me that they should risk their lives against me? But today we have flung them down their hero, murdered; and now every man of them is set upon clearing out this nest of assassins — for such we are and no more. Take courage then; and sharpen your sword. Pompey's head has fallen; and Cæsar's head is ripe.

APOLLODORUS: Does Cæsar despair?

CÆSAR (*with infinite pride*): He who has never hoped can never despair. Cæsar, in good or bad fortune, looks his fate in the face.

LUCIUS: Look it in the face, then; and it will smile as it always has on Cæsar.

CÆSAR (*with involuntary haughtiness*): Do you presume to encourage me?

LUCIUS: I offer you my services. I will change sides if you will have me.

CÆSAR (*suddenly coming down to earth again, and looking sharply at him, divining that there is something behind the offer*): What! At this point?

LUCIUS (*firmly*): At this point.

RUFIO: Do you suppose Cæsar is mad, to trust you?

LUCIUS: I do not ask him to trust me until he is victorious. I ask for my life, and for a command in Cæsar's army. And since Cæsar is a fair dealer, I will pay in advance.

CÆSAR: Pay! How?

LUCIUS: With a piece of good news for you.

(CÆSAR *divines the news in a flash.*)

RUFIO: What news?

CÆSAR (*with an elated and buoyant energy which makes* CLEOPATRA *sit up and stare*): What news! What news, did you say, my son Rufio? The relief has arrived: what other news remains for us? Is it not so, Lucius Septimius? Mithridates of Pergamos is on the march.

LUCIUS: He has taken Pelusium.

CÆSAR (*delighted*): Lucius Septimius: you are henceforth my officer. Rufio: the Egyptians must have sent every soldier from the city to prevent Mithridates crossing the Nile. There is nothing in the streets now but mob — mob!

LUCIUS: It is so. Mithridates is marching by the great road to Memphis to cross above the Delta. Achillas will fight him there.

CÆSAR (*all audacity*): Achillas shall fight Cæsar there. See, Rufio. (*He runs to the table; snatches a napkin; and draws a plan on it with his finger dipped in wine, whilst* RUFIO *and* LUCIUS SEPTIMIUS *crowd about him to watch, all looking closely, for the light is now almost gone.*) Here is the palace (*pointing to his plan*): here is the theatre. You (*to* RUFIO) take twenty men and pretend to go by *that* street (*pointing it out*); and whilst they are stoning you, out go the cohorts by this and this. My streets are right, are they, Lucius?

LUCIUS: Ay, that is the fig market —

CÆSAR (*too much excited to listen to him*): I saw them the day we arrived. Good! (*He throws the napkin on the table, and comes down again into the colonnade.*) Away, Britannus: tell Petronius that within an hour half our forces must take ship for the western lake. See to my horse and armor. (BRITANNUS *runs out.*) With the rest, *I* shall march round the lake and up the Nile to meet Mithridates. Away, Lucius; and give the word. (LUCIUS *hurries out after* BRITANNUS.) Apollodorus: lend me your sword and your right arm for this campaign.

APOLLODORUS: Ay, and my heart and life to boot.

CÆSAR (*grasping his hand*): I accept both. (*Mighty handshake.*) Are you ready for work?

APOLLODORUS: Ready for Art — the Art of War. (*He rushes out after* LUCIUS, *totally forgetting* CLEOPATRA.)

RUFIO: Come! this is something like business.

CÆSAR (*buoyantly*): Is it not, my only son? (*He claps his hands. The* SLAVES *hurry in to the table.*) No more of this mawkish revelling: away with all this stuff: shut it out of my sight and be off with you. (*The* SLAVES *begin to remove the table; and the curtains are drawn, shutting in the colonnade.*) You understand about the streets, Rufio?

RUFIO: Ay, I think I do. I will get through them, at all events.

(*The bucina sounds busily in the courtyard beneath.*)

CÆSAR: Come, then: we must talk to the troops and hearten them. You down to the beach: I to the courtyard. (*He makes for the staircase.*)

CLEOPATRA (*rising from her seat, where she has been quite neglected all this time, and stretching out her hands timidly to him*): Cæsar.

CÆSAR (*turning*): Eh?

CLEOPATRA: Have you forgotten me?

CÆSAR (*indulgently*): I am busy now, my child, busy. When I return your affairs shall be settled. Farewell; and be good and patient.

(*He goes, preoccupied and quite indifferent. She stands with clenched fists, in speechless rage and humiliation.*)

RUFIO: That game is played and lost, Cleopatra. The woman always gets the worst of it.

CLEOPATRA (*haughtily*): Go. Follow your master.

RUFIO (*in her ear, with rough familiarity*): A word first. Tell your executioner that if Pothinus had been properly killed — in the *throat* — he would not have called out. Your man bungled his work.

CLEOPATRA (*enigmatically*): How do you know it was a man?

RUFIO (*startled, and puzzled*): It was not you: you were with us when it happened. (*She turns her back scornfully on him. He shakes his head, and draws the curtains to go out. It is now a magnificent moonlit night. The table has been removed.* FTATATEETA *is seen in the light of the moon and stars, again in prayer before the white altarstone of Ra.* RUFIO *starts; closes the curtains again softly; and says in a low voice to* CLEOPATRA.) Was it she? with her own hand?

CLEOPATRA (*threateningly*): Whoever it was, let my enemies beware of her.

Look to it, Rufio, you who dare make the Queen of Egypt a fool before Cæsar.

RUFIO (*looking grimly at her*): I will look to it, Cleopatra. (*He nods in confirmation of the promise, and slips out through the curtains, loosening his sword in its sheath as he goes.*)

ROMAN SOLDIERS (*in the courtyard below*): Hail, Cæsar! Hail, hail!

(CLEOPATRA *listens. The bucina sounds again, followed by several trumpets.*)

CLEOPATRA (*wringing her hands and calling*): Ftatateeta. Ftatateeta. It is dark; and I am alone. Come to me. (*Silence.*) Ftatateeta. (*Louder.*) Ftatateeta. (*Silence. In a panic she snatches the cord and pulls the curtains apart.* FTATATEETA *is lying dead on the altar of Ra, with her throat cut. Her blood deluges the white stone.*)

## ACT V

*High noon. Festival and military pageant on the esplanade before the palace. In the east harbor* CÆSAR'*s galley, so gorgeously decorated that it seems to be rigged with flowers, is alongside the quay, close to the steps* APOLLODORUS *descended when he embarked with the carpet. A Roman* GUARD *is posted there in charge of a gangway, whence a red floorcloth is laid down the middle of the esplanade, turning off to the north opposite the central gate in the palace front, which shuts in the esplanade on the south side. The broad steps of the gate, crowded with* CLEOPATRA'*s ladies, all in their gayest attire, are like a flower garden. The façade is lined by her guard, officered by the same gallants to whom* BEL AFFRIS *announced the coming of* CÆSAR *six months before in the old palace on the Syrian border. The north side is lined by Roman* SOLDIERS, *with the townsfolk on tiptoe behind them, peering over their heads at the cleared esplanade, in which the* OFFICERS *stroll about, chatting. Among these are* BELZANOR *and the* PERSIAN; *also the* CENTURION, *vinewood cudgel in hand, battle worn, thick-booted and much outshone, both socially and decoratively, by the Egyptian officers.*

APOLLODORUS *makes his way through the townsfolk and calls to the officers from behind the Roman line.*

APOLLODORUS: Hullo! May I pass?

CENTURION: Pass Apollodorus the Sicilian there! (*The* SOLDIERS *let him through.*)

BELZANOR: Is Cæsar at hand?

APOLLODORUS: Not yet. He is still in the market place. I could not stand any more of the roaring of the soldiers! After half an hour of the enthusiasm of an army, one feels the need of a little sea air.

PERSIAN: Tell us the news. Hath he slain the priests?

APOLLODORUS: Not he. They met him in the market place with ashes on their heads and their gods in their hands. They placed the gods at his feet. The only one that was worth looking at was Apis: a miracle of gold and ivory work. By my advice he offered the chief priest two talents for it.

BELZANOR (*appalled*): Apis the all-knowing for two talents! What said the Priest?

APOLLODORUS: He invoked the mercy of Apis, and asked for five.

BELZANOR: There will be famine and tempest in the land for this.

PERSIAN: Pooh! Why did not Apis cause Cæsar to be vanquished by Achillas? Any fresh news from the war, Apollodorus?

APOLLODORUS: The little King Ptolemy was drowned.

BELZANOR: Drowned! How?

APOLLODORUS: With the rest of them. Cæsar attacked them from three sides at once and swept them into the Nile. Ptolemy's barge sank.

BELZANOR: A marvellous man, this Cæsar! Will he come soon, think you?

APOLLODORUS: He was settling the Jewish question when I left.

(*A flourish of trumpets from the north, and commotion among the townsfolk, announces the approach of* CÆSAR.)

PERSIAN: He has made short work of them. Here he comes. (*He hurries to his post in front of the Egyptian lines.*)

BELZANOR (*following him*): Ho there! Cæsar comes.

(*The* SOLDIERS *stand at attention, and dress their lines.* APOLLODORUS *goes to the Egyptian line.*)

CENTURION (*hurrying to the gangway* GUARD): Attention there! Cæsar comes.

(CÆSAR *arrives in state with* RUFIO: BRITANNUS *following. The* SOLDIERS *receive him with enthusiastic shouting.*)

CÆSAR: I see my ship awaits me. The hour of Cæsar's farewell to Egypt has arrived. And now, Rufio, what remains to be done before I go?

RUFIO (*at his left hand*): You have not yet appointed a Roman governor for this province.

CÆSAR (*looking whimsically at him, but speaking with perfect gravity*): What say you to Mithridates of Pergamos, my reliever and rescuer, the great son of Eupator?

RUFIO: Why, that you will want him elsewhere. Do you forget that you have some three or four armies to conquer on your way home?

CÆSAR: Indeed! Well, what say you to yourself?

RUFIO (*incredulously*): I! I a governor! What are you dreaming of? Do you not know that I am only the son of a freedman?

CÆSAR (*affectionately*): Has not Cæsar called you his son? (*Calling to the whole assembly.*) Peace awhile there; and hear me.

ROMAN SOLDIERS: Hear Cæsar.

CÆSAR: Hear the service, quality, rank and name of the Roman governor. By service, Cæsar's shield; by quality, Cæsar's friend; by rank, a Roman soldier. (*The Roman* SOLDIERS *give a triumphant shout.*) By name, Rufio. (*They shout again.*)

RUFIO (*kissing* CÆSAR'*s hand*): Ay: I am Cæsar's shield; but of what use shall I be when I am no longer on Cæsar's arm? Well, no matter – (*He becomes husky, and turns away to recover himself.*)

CÆSAR: Where is that British Islander of mine?

BRITANNUS (*coming forward on* CÆSAR'*s right hand*): Here, Cæsar.

CÆSAR: Who bade you, pray, thrust yourself into the battle of the Delta, uttering the barbarous cries of your native land, and affirming yourself a match for any four of the Egyptians, to whom you applied unseemly epithets?

BRITANNUS: Cæsar: I ask you to excuse the language that escaped me in the heat of the moment.

CÆSAR: And how did you, who cannot swim, cross the canal with us when we stormed the camp?

BRITANNUS: Cæsar: I clung to the tail of your horse.

CÆSAR: These are not the deeds of a slave, Britannicus, but of a free man.

BRITANNUS: Cæsar: I was born free.

CÆSAR: But they call you Cæsar's slave.

BRITANNUS: Only as Cæsar's slave have I found real freedom.

CÆSAR (*moved*): Well said. Ungrateful that I am, I was about to set you free; but now I will not part from you for a million talents. (*He claps him friendly on the shoulder.* BRITANNUS, *gratified, but a trifle shamefaced, takes his hand and kisses it sheepishly.*)

BELZANOR (*to the* PERSIAN): This Roman knows how to make men serve him.

PERSIAN: Ay: men too humble to become dangerous rivals to him.

BELZANOR: O subtle one! O cynic!

CÆSAR (*seeing* APOLLODORUS *in the Egyptian corner, and calling to him*): Apollodorus: I leave the art of Egypt in your charge. Remember: Rome loves art and will encourage it ungrudgingly.

APOLLODORUS: I understand, Cæsar. Rome will produce no art itself; but it will buy up and take away whatever the other nations produce.

CÆSAR: What! Rome produce no art! Is peace not an art? is war not an art? is government not an art? is civilization not an art? All these we give you in exchange for a few ornaments. You will have the best of the bargain. (*Turning to* RUFIO.) And now, what else have I to do before I embark? (*Trying to recollect.*) There is something I cannot remember: what *can* it be? Well, well: it must remain undone: we must not waste this favorable wind. Farewell, Rufio.

RUFIO: Cæsar: I am loth to let you go to Rome without your shield. There are too many daggers there.

CÆSAR: It matters not: I shall finish my life's work on my way back; and then I shall have lived long enough. Besides: I have always disliked the idea of dying: I had rather be killed. Farewell.

RUFIO (*with a sigh, raising his hands and giving* CÆSAR *up as incorrigible.*) Farewell. (*They shake hands.*)

CÆSAR (*waving his hand to* APOLLODORUS): Farewell, Apollodorus, and my friends, all of you. Aboard!

(*The gangway is run out from the quay to the ship. As* CÆSAR *moves towards it,* CLEOPATRA, *cold and tragic, cunningly dressed in black, without ornaments or decoration of any kind, and thus making a striking figure among the brilliantly dressed bevy of ladies as she passes through it, comes from the palace and stands on the steps.* CÆSAR *does not see her until she speaks.*)

CLEOPATRA: Has Cleopatra no part in this leavetaking?

CÆSAR (*enlightened*): Ah, I *knew* there was something. (*To* RUFIO.) How could you let me forget her, Rufio? (*Hastening to her.*) Had I gone without seeing you, I should never have forgiven myself. (*He takes her hands, and brings her into the middle of the esplanade. She submits stonily.*) Is this mourning for me?

CLEOPATRA: No.

CÆSAR (*remorsefully*): Ah, that was thoughtless of me! It is for your brother.

CLEOPATRA: No.

CÆSAR: For whom, then?

CLEOPATRA: Ask the Roman governor whom you have left us.

CÆSAR: Rufio?

CLEOPATRA: Yes: Rufio. (*She points at him with deadly scorn.*) He who is to rule here in Cæsar's name, in Cæsar's way, according to Cæsar's boasted laws of life.

CÆSAR (*dubiously*): He is to rule as he can, Cleopatra. He has taken the work upon him, and will do it in his own way.

CLEOPATRA: Not in your way, then?

CÆSAR (*puzzled*): What do you mean by my way?

CLEOPATRA: Without punishment. Without revenge. Without judgment.

CÆSAR (*approvingly*): Ay: that is the right way, the great way, the only possible way in the end. (*To* RUFIO.) Believe it Rufio, if you can.

RUFIO: Why, I believe it, Cæsar. You have convinced me of it long ago. But look you. You are sailing for Numidia today. Now tell me: if you meet a hungry lion there, you will not punish it for wanting to eat you?

CÆSAR (*wondering what he is driving at*): No.

RUFIO: Nor revenge upon it the blood of those it has already eaten.

CÆSAR: No.

RUFIO: Nor judge it for its guiltiness.

CÆSAR: No.

RUFIO: What, then, will you do to save your life from it?

CÆSAR (*promptly*): Kill it, man, without malice, just as it would kill me. What does this parable of the lion mean?

RUFIO: Why, Cleopatra had a tigress that killed men at her bidding. I thought she might bid it kill you some day. Well, had I not been Cæsar's pupil, what pious things might I not have done to that tigress! I might have punished it. I might have revenged Pothinus on it.

CÆSAR (*interjects*): Pothinus!

RUFIO (*continuing*): I might have judged it. But I put all these follies behind me; and, without malice, only cut its throat. And that is why Cleopatra comes to you in mourning.

CLEOPATRA (*vehemently*): He has shed the blood of my servant Ftatateeta. On your head be it as upon his, Cæsar, if you hold him free of it.

CÆSAR (*energetically*): On my head be it, then; for it was well done. Rufio: had you set yourself in the seat of the judge, and with hateful ceremonies and appeals to the gods handed that woman over to some hired executioner to be slain before the people in the name of justice, never again would I have touched your hand without a shudder. But this was natural slaying: I feel no horror at it.

(RUFIO, *satisfied, nods at* CLEOPATRA, *mutely inviting her to mark that.*)

CLEOPATRA (*pettish and childish in her impotence*): No: not when a Roman slays an Egyptian. All the world will now see how unjust and corrupt Cæsar is.

CÆSAR (*taking her hands coaxingly*): Come: do not be angry with me. I am sorry for that poor Totateeta. (*She laughs in spite of herself.*) Aha! you are laughing. Does that mean reconciliation?

CLEOPATRA (*angry with herself for laughing*): No, *no,* NO!! But it is so ridiculous to hear you call her Totateeta.

CÆSAR: What! As much a child as ever, Cleopatra! Have I not made a woman of you after all?

CLEOPATRA: Oh, it is you who are a great baby: you make me seem silly because you will not behave seriously. But you have treated me badly; and I do not forgive you.

CÆSAR: Bid me farewell.

CLEOPATRA: I will not.

CÆSAR (*coaxing*): I will send you a beautiful present from Rome.

CLEOPATRA (*proudly*): Beauty from Rome to Egypt indeed! What can Rome give *me* that Egypt cannot give me?

APOLLODORUS: That is true, Cæsar. If the present is to be really beautiful, I shall have to buy it for you in Alexandria.

CÆSAR: You are forgetting the treasures for which Rome is most famous, my friend. You cannot buy *them* in Alexandria.

APOLLODORUS: What are they, Cæsar?

CÆSAR: Her sons. Come, Cleopatra: forgive me and bid me farewell; and I will send you a man, Roman from head to heel and Roman of the noblest; not old and ripe for the knife; not lean in the arms and cold in the heart; not hiding a bald head under his conqueror's laurels; not stooped with the weight of the world on his shoulders; but brisk and fresh, strong and young, hoping in the morning, fighting in the day, and revelling in the evening. Will you take such an one in exchange for Cæsar?

CLEOPATRA (*palpitating*): His name, his name?

CÆSAR: Shall it be Mark Antony? (*She throws herself into his arms.*)

RUFIO: You are a bad hand at a bargain, mistress, if you will swop Cæsar for Antony.

CÆSAR: So now you are satisfied.

CLEOPATRA: You will not forget.

CÆSAR: I will not forget. Farewell: I do not think we shall meet again. Farewell. (*He kisses her on the forehead. She is much affected and begins to sniff. He embarks.*)

ROMAN SOLDIERS (*as he sets his foot on the gangway*): Hail, Cæsar; and farewell!

(*He reaches the ship and returns* RUFIO'*s wave of the hand.*)

APOLLODORUS (*to* CLEOPATRA): No tears, dearest Queen: they stab your servant to the heart. He will return some day.

CLEOPATRA: I hope not. But I cant help crying, all the same.

(*She waves her handkerchief to* CÆSAR; *and the ship begins to move.*)

ROMAN SOLDIERS (*drawing their swords and raising them in the air*): Hail, Cæsar!

*Cæsar and Cleopatra* was written in 1898. Shaw was sick with an infected foot during much of the time he worked on the play, but there is hardly evidence of sickness in it – unless the mellow resignation of Cæsar's wit be so considered. It was first performed in Chicago in 1901. The first London production, in 1907, was not a success, but later productions were. In 1913 Shaw added Ra's prologue. Today *Cæsar and Cleopatra* ranks among the dozen or so plays that by general consent make up Shaw's major canon. It was first published in 1901 in a collection entitled *Three Plays for Puritans.*

As Puritans notoriously abominated plays, the title is a paradox, though not a difficult one. *Cæsar and Cleopatra,* according to Shaw's preface to the volume, is "for Puritans," first, because it ignores the conventional premise of the popular theater that since romance is mankind's main business the function of plays is to titillate the sensual imagination (but decorously, since this is a polite age), and, second, because it does not smother dialogue in expensive pageantry in the manner of contemporary productions of historical plays. But, as is commonly the case with Shaw, the explanation of one paradox only raises a larger one: here, a play about Cæsar and Cleopatra that is unheroic and unromantic. *This* paradox is the heart of the play. We may approach it by way of Shaw's prefatory objection to pageantry.

The objection may seem strange, since *Cæsar and Cleopatra* itself is excellent pageantry. Any one of Shaw's stage directions introducing the several acts will reveal his unfailing sense for scenic architecture, the fineness of his artist's eye, and his relish for tasteful and appropriate color and texture in dress and sets. Once one has enjoyed the glorious athleticism of the theatrically superb (though dramatically thin) Act III, or has seen, actually or imaginatively, the moonlit desert scene in Act I, with Cleopatra asleep between the paws of the Sphinx on "a heap of red poppies," while the conqueror of the world apostrophizes the silvery stillness, the popular notion that Shaw is a purely cerebral writer vanishes forever. Shaw was intelligent, witty, argumentative, didactic, and paradoxical, but his greatness as playright is at least as much a matter of his masterful command of theater space as of the lucid, speakable stage prose by which he communicates pointed meaning with graceful ease.

His objection is simply that when pageantry becomes an end in itself drama dies. In the London theater of late Victorian times Shakespeare's dialogue was cut to make room for what producers and audiences thought of as genuine Shakespearean spectacle: processions and battles and tiny stage business for the sake of authentic atmosphere — the products of painstaking research into medieval and Elizabethan costuming, heraldry, armor, choreography, furniture, architecture, and domestic details. Such showy historicity enraged Shaw. He admitted pageantry only as an appropriate setting for the play of ideas which to him was always the drama's sole reason for being. "New ideas," he wrote in the Preface, "make their technique as water makes its channel; and the technician without ideas is as useless as the canal constructor without water, though he may do very skillfully what the Mississippi does very rudely."

In *Cæsar and Cleopatra* the Shavian ideas amount to a refutation of the kind of activity which the exotic splendors of the historical setting and the glamorous aura surrounding the famous names invite and seem proper to. The action keeps failing to deliver the high drama of passion and conquest which title and locale and even the facts of history promise. After all, Cæsar and Cleopatra *were* lovers; they even had a child together. Then why won't Shaw give us the romance we expect to see? Not just because paradox is his manner and he aims to disoblige by deglamorizing history and debunking golden legend. *Why* is it his manner? The reason is not flippant. He wants to show us the unheroic, unromantic contemporaneity of the past. Idea is ironically played off against spectacle, and in our disappointed expectation of seeing staged for us the rich associations that encrust fact and legend, the moral fable we *do* get seems all the more sardonically telling. Pageantry, in short, helps to convey the history lesson which is Shaw's theme.

In general, literature uses history in one of two ways. Fictitious main characters may be placed in a setting of fact, in which the principals and circumstance of true history function as parts of the authenticating backdrop. This is Thackeray's method in *Henry Esmond* and Tolstoy's in *War and Peace* (except in the Napoleon and Kutuzov scenes). Or historical figures may be made protagonists in a more or less imaginative treatment of the facts. This is Shakespeare's method in his history plays and Shaw's in *The Man of Destiny, Cæsar and Cleopatra,* and *Saint Joan.*

Neither one wrote an antiquarian's kind of historical play, disengaged and meticulous, respectfully and learnedly observing chronology and authentic language. Museum pieces don't come alive by being made to move on a stage. By Shakespeare's and Shaw's example, a history play is an evocation of an image of the past for useful contemplation by the present. We see reflected in Shakespeare's dramatizations of royal English history in (roughly) the fifteenth century the political ideals of an enlightened Elizabethan. The plays are about the responsibilities of kingship, the blessings of a strong and sanctified monarchy, and the horrors of usurpation and civil war. Perhaps Shakespeare's conscious aim was simply to supply attractive entertainment for London audiences from the storehouse of Hall's and Holinshed's chronicles. Nevertheless, the plays, singly and in sequence, express what scholars call "the Tudor myth." They amount to a loyal patriot's concerned comment on past national anarchy that might return. Shakespeare's Henry V may seem more Tudor than Lancaster and his environment more late sixteenth century than early fifteenth century. But what else could he be?

One section of Shaw's Preface to *Three Plays for Puritans* is headed, "Better Than Shakespeare?" (hostile critics have ignored the question mark). The comparison is inevitable, since Shaw's title characters in *Cæsar and Cleopatra* are title characters in Shakespeare, too (though not together). Drama for Shaw was not art if it was not didactic, and his alleged arrogance is his suggestion that his Victorian view of Cæsar and Cleopatra may be better for – that is, more relevant to the particular problems of – the Victorian age than Shakespeare's Elizabethan view. To deny that there is an issue here at all, says Shaw, is to be a victim of bardolatry; i.e., the conviction that as a dramatist Shakespeare was not subject to human limitations. Bardolatry is bad for the worshipper, bad for drama, and bad even for Shakespeare, since it feeds on invincible ignorance. Doing Cæsar better than Shakespeare did is not to disparage Shakespeare, and it is not just a matter of making use of the discoveries and insights of historical scholarship (though Shaw acknowledges his debt to the German historian Theodor Mommsen for his conception of Cæsar). It is, like Shakespeare, to search the past for political allegory of present relevance. Shaw turns Shakespeare's practice into critical tenet and holds that every age must reinterpret the past by its own lights. The question that has prompted his play is: What, for us, is the truth about the historical Julius Cæsar?

Shaw's truth about Cæsar-in-Egypt is a twofold lesson of history: that the record of the past is nothing but a record of our own current errors (it is because he knows this that Cæsar so calmly can receive the news that the library of Alexandria is burning); and that moral progress — the only kind that matters — in public affairs must await the world's conversion to Cæsar's system of political ethics.

As only an anachronistic King Henry V could serve Shakespeare's political fable, so Shaw, too, writes anachronistically. In fact, he capitalizes on anachronisms; they are his chief dramatic metaphor. The dialogue is full of them: "Double or quits," "Egypt for the Egyptians," "Peace with honor," "Art for Art's sake." And so is the characterization. Britannus is probably the most striking example. Shaw's solemn declaration in the Notes to the contrary, Britannus is only a likeness of the decent, insularly bigoted Englishman of some 2,000 years after Cæsar's time. But no more than the deglamorization of the legend are the anachronisms mere irreverence. By definition, an anachronism is a confusion of past and present. In *Cæsar and Cleopatra* they are recurrent symptoms in the characters' speech and manners of what the whole play argues, viz., that progress is a myth. If past and present are alike, if, as the god Ra says in the Prologue, "men twenty centuries ago were already just such as you, and spoke and lived as ye speak and live, no worse and no better, no wiser and no sillier," then even the pedant's objections fall to the ground. How can there be anachronism where there has been no change?

The main conflict in *Cæsar and Cleopatra* is not between Rome and Egypt. The siege, the politics, the military moves are nothing but events on which Shaw hangs his lesson of history. Nor is the conflict the more sophisticated one between the imperial love story we might have had and the quaint father-daughter, teacher-pupil relationship we actually get. The main conflict is not in a romantic but in a pedagogic situation. It ends in the separation, literal and figurative, of tutor and tutored. The separating issue is the murder of Pothinus. Cleopatra calls Cæsar a dreamer because he refuses to take revenge on his enemies. Pothinus and Britannus have at different times been equally astonished at his strange clemency. But events show him to be more practical and efficient than anyone else in the play. He outfights, out-talks, and out-foxes the Egyptians whenever he wants. He approves of necessary killing. But he does not believe in murderous passion parading as justice, virtue, and honor. When Cleopatra seeks to vindicate the murder of Pothinus, she is supported by Cæsar's own men. Inasmuch as the honest soldier Rufio, the brave moralist Britannus, and the gay artist Apollodorus collectively represent a sampling of the world's vital values, their support darkens the moral issue between Cleopatra and Cæsar and is one of the reasons why the play is felt to transcend the ideological simplemindedness and dogmatism that limit most thesis plays to a kind of dramatic journalism. Encouraged, and still heated with her righteous vengeance, Cleopatra shifts from defense to attack:

> CLEOPATRA (*vehemently*): Listen to me, Cæsar. If one man in all Alexandria can be found to say that I did wrong, I swear to have myself crucified on the door of the palace by my own slaves.
>
> CÆSAR: If one man in all the world can be found, now or forever, to know that you did wrong, that man will have either to conquer the world as I have or be crucified by it.

The allusion to Christ is probably the most discreet anachronism in the play, but it is also its most important one. It enriches the earlier associations of Cæsar with divinity: in Ra's Prologue, in Cæsar's claiming kinship with the immortal Sphinx, in the boy-king Ptolemy's assumption that it was the gods who sent Mark Antony to Egypt, and in Cleopatra's identification of Cæsar with a god in her talk with Pothinus early in Act IV. It is noteworthy that except for an occasional pompous phrase by the Egyptian leaders the only examples of noncolloquial language in the play are the god Ra's Prologue and Cæsar's apostrophe to the Sphinx. Both speakers represent eternal values, and the Cæsar-Cleopatra conflict could also be defined as one between divine permanence of reason and of universal love and the impermanence of man's exclusive passions. One of the paradoxes of Shaw's theme is that Cæsar, who seeks change, represents timelessness, whereas the world, which refuses to change, is in continuous flux. If the play's middle (Acts II–IV) seems disorderly and diffuse, there is a good reason for it. It translates into stage action the irony of the moral inertia of melodramatic busyness.

Ironic, too, is the failure of even the apparently more successful of the two alternative saviors of the world that Cæsar mentions and the fact that his failure is due to the changes time brings. His mortality betrays his divinity. Balding and wrinkled, he is no lover for Cleopatra. Their first scene together obliquely anticipates his failure. It is not a scene of a god-conqueror solving the Sphinx's riddle but only of an "old gentleman" pointlessly addressing "a little kitten of a Sphinx," a "pet" Sphinx. When Pothinus asks Cleopatra in Act IV whether she is in love with Cæsar, she counters with another question: "Can one love a god?" She is wise enough to wish she *were* in love with him, but not wise enough to realize that her rejoinder is an inadequate answer. To the question of why one cannot love a godlike Cæsar, a Cleopatra answers, "Because he is not a beautiful young man with strong, round arms" — and at that moment the world slips from grace. Cleopatra's education toward ideal queenship has gone far, as her words to Pothinus early in Act IV show. Already by the end of Act I Cæsar has taught her to make herself obeyed, and when Rufio pitches her into the sea at the end of Act III it is as if she were being baptized into a new maturity. But the murder of Pothinus shows that it has not gone far enough. The kitten has only grown claws. She founders on passion. And the sulking, giggle-prone Cleopatra of Act V is closer to the silly, charming girl of Act I than to the wise and humble queen she seemed to have become by Act IV. Time present is still time past.

As the play has a Prologue (and an "Alternative to the Prologue") to the action of Cleopatra's truncated education, so it also has an epilogue: Act V. Soon after Cæsar's disillusionment with his pupil the stage once more becomes busy with military and political affairs, and the moral drama ends. When he is about to embark for Rome he almost forgets to say goodbye to Cleopatra. But the light, almost burlesque, tone of the departure scene is made ominous with hints of the daggers waiting in Rome. Cæsar, we know, falls, and the world reverts to its Pompeian and Antonian ways after the Cæsarian interlude, to "the way of the soldier . . . the way of death," as Ra calls it, after Cæsar's "way of the gods . . . the way of life." And so, Rome remains "a madman's dream." As the doomed Cæsar resigns Cleopatra to her young lover-soldier and to her deathless fate as siren, history's old, passionate melodrama resumes. Two thousand years have done nothing to disprove Cæsar's prophecy:

> . . . And so, to the end of history, murder shall breed murder, always in the name of right and honor and peace, until the gods are tired of blood and create a race that can understand.

Here is Shaw's earliest reference in drama to the Superman whom he later celebrated as John Tanner in *Man and Superman* (1903) and as the wise Ancients in *Back to Methuselah* (1921), the two plays which have been called the trunk of his dramatic canon, on which all the other plays are branches. Joan of Arc in *Saint Joan* (1924) is, like Cæsar, a historical example of the Superman race. Superman's (or -woman's) superiority over ordinary men is his commitment, conscious or unconscious, to the service of the Life Force, the vital principle in what Shaw called Creative Evolution toward ever higher forms of contemplative intelligence. Cæsar, says Shaw in his Notes, "is greater off the battle field than on it." This seems like a paradox in the eyes of the world and will remain so until the world learns from its violent past not to reject its Superman saviors — its Cæsars, its Christs, and its saints. "He will return some day," says Apollodorus as Cæsar leaves. "I hope not," replies Cleopatra. "But I cant help crying, all the same." Between her hope and her tears is the world's impasse.

*Cæsar and Cleopatra* is a thesis play, if by a thesis play is meant a play in which the playwright tells us something which he hopes will change our ways. Nevertheless, it is not irrelevant to ask whether it ends as a kind of comedy or as a kind of tragedy. It is a difficult question.

# ANTON CHEKHOV

# The Three Sisters

*Translated by Stark Young*

CHARACTERS

PROZOROFF, ANDREI SERGEEVICH
NATALIA IVANOVNA, his fiancée, later his wife
OLGA, MASHA, IRINA — his sisters
KULYGIN, FYODOR ILYICH, a high-school teacher, husband of Masha
VERSHININ, ALEXANDER IGNATIEVICH, Lieutenant Colonel, a battery Commander
TUSENBACH, NIKOLAI LVOVICH, Baron, Lieutenant
SOLYONY, VASILI VASILIEVICH, Staff Captain
TCHEBUTYKIN, IVAN ROMANOVICH, an Army Doctor
FEDOTIK, ALEXEI PETROVICH, Second Lieutenant
RODAY, VLADIMIR KARLOVICH, Second Lieutenant
FERAPONT, porter of the District Board, an old man
ANFISA, the nurse, an old woman of eighty

*The action takes place in a provincial town in Russia.*

## ACT I

*In the* PROZOROFFS' *house. A drawing room with columns, beyond which a large room is seen. Midday: outside it is sunny and bright. The table in the dining room is being set for lunch.* OLGA, *in the blue uniform of a girls' high-school teacher, is busy correcting school papers, standing and walking to and fro;* MASHA, *in a black dress with her hat on her knees, sits and reads a book;* IRINA, *in a white dress, stands lost in thought.*

OLGA: Father died just a year ago today, on the fifth of May – your saint's day, Irina. It was very cold then and snowing. I thought I could never live through it; you were lying in a dead faint. But now a year has passed and we can talk of it freely; you've a white dress on, your face is beaming. (*The clock strikes twelve.*) And the clock was striking then too. (*A pause.*) I remember as they carried Father along, the band was playing, and at the cemetery they fired a volley. He was a brigadier general; but at that there were very few people walking behind his coffin. It was raining, though, then. Heavy rain and snow.

IRINA: Why think of it?

(*Behind the columns in the dining room near the table,* BARON TUSENBACH, TCHEBUTYKIN *and* SOLYONY *appear.*)

OLGA: It's warm today. We can keep the windows wide open, but the birches haven't any leaves yet. Father was given his brigade and left Moscow with us eleven years ago, and I remember distinctly that early in May, at this very time, in Moscow everything is in bloom, it's warm, everything is bathed in sunshine. That's eleven years ago, but I remember it all as if we'd left there yesterday. Oh, God! I woke up this morning, saw a flood of light, saw the spring, and my heart leapt with joy. And I did long passionately to go home again.

TCHEBUTYKIN: The devil!

TUSENBACH: Of course, it's all rot.

(MASHA, *brooding over a book, softly whistles a song.*)

OLGA: Don't whistle, Masha. How can you do that! (*A pause.*) I'm at the high school every day giving lessons till evening, that's why my head aches all the time and what thoughts I have might just as well belong to an old woman and be done with it. These four years I've been teaching in high school, I have felt my strength and youth going out of me day by day, drop by drop. And just one dream grows stronger and stronger. . . .

IRINA: To go to Moscow. Sell the house, wind up everything here and to Moscow.

OLGA: Yes! Soon to Moscow.

(TCHEBUTYKIN *and* TUSENBACH *laugh.*)

IRINA: Brother will be a professor very likely, but all the same he won't live here. The one thing that stops us is poor Masha.

OLGA: Masha will be coming to Moscow for the whole summer every year.

(MASHA *is softly whistling a song.*)

IRINA: God grant it all works out! (*Looking out of the window.*) The weather is beautiful today. I don't know why my heart's so light! This morning I remembered it was my saint's day and suddenly felt happy, and remembered when I was a child and Mother was still alive. And such wonderful thoughts thrilled me; such thoughts!

OLGA: You look radiant today, lovelier than ever. And Masha is lovely too. Andrei would be good-looking if he hadn't got so heavy, it's not becoming to him. And I've grown older, a lot thinner; it must be because I get cross with the girls. Now that I'm free today and am here at home and my head's not aching, I feel younger than yesterday. I'm only twenty-eight. . . . It's all good, all God's will, but it seems to me if I had married and stayed at home the whole day long, it would have been better. (*A pause.*) I'd have loved my husband.

TUSENBACH (*to* SOLYONY): You talk such nonsense that I'm tired of listening to you. (*Entering the drawing room.*) Forgot to tell you. Today you'll receive a call from our new Battery Commander Vershinin. (*Sitting down at the piano.*)

OLGA: Well, I'll be very glad of it.

IRINA: Is he old?

TUSENBACH: No, not very. Forty or forty-five at most. (*Playing softly.*) He seems a nice chap. Not stupid, that's certain. Except that he talks a lot.

IRINA: Is he an interesting person?

TUSENBACH: Yes, quite, only there is a wife, a mother-in-law and two girls. What's more he's married for the second time. He pays calls and says everywhere that he has a wife and two girls. And he'll say so here. The wife is sort of half-crazy, wears long girlish braids, speaks only of lofty matters, philosophizes, and often tries to commit suicide, obviously to plague the husband. I'd have left such a woman long ago myself, but he puts up with her and merely complains.

SOLYONY (*entering the drawing room from the dining room with* TCHEBUTYKIN): With one hand I can lift only fifty pounds, but with both, one hundred eighty, or even two hundred pounds. From this I conclude that two men are not twice as strong as one, but three times, even more. . . .

TCHEBUTYKIN (*reading a newspaper as he comes in*): For falling hair . . . two ounces of naphthalene to half a bottle of spirits. . . . Dissolve and use daily. . . . (*Writing it down in his notebook.*) Let's write it down! (*To* SOLYONY.) And so, I tell you, a little cork is put in a bottle and through the cork there's a glass tube. . . . Then you take a pinch of plain ordinary alum . . .

IRINA: Ivan Romanovich, dear Ivan Romanovich!

TCHEBUTYKIN: What is it, my child, my sweet?

IRINA: Tell me, why am I so happy today? It's just as if I were going full sail, with the wide blue sky above me and great white birds floating there. Why is that? Why?

TCHEBUTYKIN (*kissing both her hands tenderly*): My white bird . . .

IRINA: This morning when I awoke and got up and bathed, it seemed all at once that everything in this world was clear to me and I knew how one must live. Dear Ivan Romanovich, I know everything. A man must do something, he must toil by the sweat of his brow, no matter who he is; and all the meaning and aim of his life, his happiness, his ecstasies must lie in this only. How good it is to be a workman who gets up at dawn and breaks stones in the street, or a shepherd, or a schoolmaster who teaches children, or an engineer on a railroad. My God! Next to being a man, it's better to be an ox, it's better to be a common horse, if only you do some work, than be a young woman who wakes up at twelve o'clock, has coffee in bed, and then dresses for two hours. . . . Oh, but that's dreadful! Just as on hot days one may have a craving for water, I have a craving for work. And if I don't get up early and go to work, give me up as a friend, Ivan Romanovich.

TCHEBUTYKIN (*tenderly*): I'll give you up, I'll give you up —

OLGA: Father trained us to get up at seven. Now Irina wakes at seven and lies there till at least nine thinking. And looking so serious! (*Laughing.*)

IRINA: You are used to thinking of me as a little girl, so it seems strange to you when I look serious. I'm twenty years old.

TUSENBACH: Longing for work. Oh my God, how I understand that! I have never worked in my life. I was born in Petersburg, cold, idle Petersburg, in a family that never knew any sort of work or worry. I remember when I came home from military school the footman pulled off my boots while I fidgeted and my mother looked adoringly at me, and was surprised when the others didn't look at me the same way. I was shielded from work. Though I doubt if they succeeded in shielding me, I doubt it! The time has come, something tremendous is hovering over us all, a vast, healing storm is gathering; it's coming, it's near already, and will soon clear our society of the laziness, the indifference, the prejudice against work, the rotten boredom. I'll work and in another twenty-five or thirty years, every man will be working. Every one!

TCHEBUTYKIN: I shan't work.

TUSENBACH: You don't count.

SOLYONY: Twenty-five years from now you won't even be on earth, thank God! In two or three years you'll die of distemper, or I'll forget myself and put a bullet in your forehead, my angel. (*Taking a phial of perfume from his pocket and sprinkling his chest and hands.*)

TCHEBUTYKIN (*laughing*): And I really never did anything. Since I left the University, I haven't lifted a finger, I've not read a single book even, but just read the newspapers. . . . (*Taking another newspaper out of his pocket.*) Listen – I know from the newspapers that there was, let's say, a Dobrolyubov, but what he wrote about I don't know. God only knows. (*A knock is heard on the floor from the floor below.*) Listen. . . . They are calling me from downstairs, somebody has come to see me. I'll be back right away. . . . Wait. . . . (*He leaves hurriedly, combing out his beard as he goes.*)

IRINA: He's up to something.

TUSENBACH: Yes. He left with a triumphant face, obviously he will now bring you a present.

IRINA: That's too bad.

OLGA: Yes, it's awful. He always does something childish.

MASHA: By the curved seashore a green oak, a golden chain upon that oak . . . a golden chain upon that oak. (*Getting up and singing softly.*)

OLGA: You are not very merry today, Masha.

(MASHA *sings as she puts on her hat.*)

OLGA: Where to?

MASHA: Home.

IRINA: That's strange. . . .

TUSENBACH: To leave a saint's day party!

MASHA: It's all the same. . . . I'll come this evening. Good-by, my pretty . . . (*Kissing* IRINA.) I wish you once again good health and happiness. When father was alive, thirty or forty officers used to come to our birthday parties, it was good and noisy; but nowadays there's only a man and a half, and it's quiet as the desert. . . . I'm going. . . . I've got the blues today, I feel depressed, so don't listen to me. (*Laughing through her tears.*) We'll talk later on, so good-by now, my dear, I'll go somewhere or other.

IRINA (*vexed*): Oh, you are such a . . .

OLGA (*tearfully*): I understand you, Masha.

SOLYONY: If a man philosophizes, it will be philosophy or sophistry; but if a woman philosophizes, or two women, it will be – like cracking your fingers.

MASHA: What are you trying to say, you terribly dreadful man?

SOLYONY: Nothing. Quick as a flash, the bear made a dash. . . . (*A pause.*)

MASHA (*to* OLGA, *crossly*): Don't howl.

(ANFISA *enters, and after her,* FERAPONT *with a cake.*)

ANFISA: Here, little Father. Come in, your feet are clean. (*To* IRINA.) From the District Board, from Mikhail Ivanovich Protopopov . . . a cake.

IRINA: Thank you. Thank him for me. (*Taking the cake.*)

FERAPONT: How's that?

IRINA (*louder*): Thank him for me.

OLGA: Nursey, give him some pie. Go on, Ferapont. They'll give you some pie.

FERAPONT: How's that?

ANFISA: Come on, little Father, Ferapont Spiridonich. Come on. . . . (*Goes out with* FERAPONT.)

MASHA: I don't like Protopopov, that Mikhail Potopich or Ivanovich. He should not be invited.

IRINA: I didn't do the inviting.

MASHA: That's fine!

(TCHEBUTYKIN *enters, behind him an* ORDERLY *with a silver samovar; there is a hum of astonishment and displeasure.*)

OLGA (*covering her face with her hands*): A samovar! This is terrible. (*Going to the table in the dining room.*)

IRINA: Darling Ivan Romanovich, what are you doing?

TUSENBACH (*laughing*): I told you so.

MASHA: Ivan Romanovich, you're simply shameless.

TCHEBUTYKIN: My darlings, my good littles ones, you are all I have, to me you are everything that's most precious in the world. I'll soon be sixty, I'm an old man, a lonely worthless old man. . . . There is nothing good about me but this love for you, and if it weren't for you I'd long ago have stopped living in this world. . . . (*To* IRINA.) My dear, my little child, I have known you since the day you were born. . . . I carried you in my arms. . . . I loved your dear mother. . . .

IRINA: But why such expensive presents!

TCHEBUTYKIN (*through his tears, angrily*): Expensive presents! . . . Why, you're completely . . . (*To the* ORDERLY.) Carry the samovar in there. . . . (*Mimicking.*) Expensive presents . . .

(*The* ORDERLY *carries the samovar into the dining room.*)

ANFISA (*passing through the drawing room*): My dears, there's a colonel, a stranger. He's already taken off his overcoat, children, and is coming in here. Irinushka, now be a nice, polite girl. (*As she goes out.*) And it was time for lunch long ago. . . . Lord have mercy! . . .

TUSENBACH: It must be Vershinin.

(VERSHININ *enters.*)

TUSENBACH: Lieutenant Colonel Vershinin!

VERSHININ (*to* MASHA *and* IRINA): I have the honor to introduce myself: Vershinin. I'm very, very glad that at last I am in your house. How you've grown! Ay! Ay!

IRINA: Please sit down. We are delighted.

VERSHININ (*gaily*): How glad I am! How glad I am! But you are three sisters. I remember – three girls. Your faces I don't remember now, but your father, Colonel Prozoroff, had three little girls, I remember that perfectly, I saw them with my own eyes. How time does pass! Oh, oh, how time does pass!

TUSENBACH: Alexander Ignatievich is from Moscow.

IRINA: From Moscow. You are from Moscow?

VERSHININ: Yes, from there. Your father was a battery commander there, and I was an officer in the same brigade. (*To* MASHA.) It seems to me now I do remember your face rather.

MASHA: And you I — No!

IRINA: Olya! Olya! (*Calling into the dining room.*) Olya! Come here. (OLGA *comes in from the dining room.*) Lieutenant Colonel Vershinin, it turns out, is from Moscow.

VERSHININ: You must be Olga Sergeevna, the eldest. . . . And you Maria. . . . And you Irina — the youngest. . . .

OLGA: You are from Moscow?

VERSHININ: Yes. I was at school in Moscow and began my service in Moscow, served there a long time, was finally assigned a battery here — moved here, as you see. I don't remember you, as a matter of fact, but only that you were three sisters. Your father is fresh in my memory; I can close my eyes now and see him as plain as life. I used to pay you calls in Moscow. . . .

OLGA: I thought I remembered everybody, and look, all of a sudden . . .

VERSHININ: My name is Alexander Ignatievich.

IRINA: Alexander Ignatievich, you are from Moscow. What a surprise!

OLGA: We are going to move there, you know.

IRINA: We think by autumn we'll be there. It's our native town, we were born there. . . . In Old Basmanny Street.

(*They both laugh delightedly.*)

MASHA: Unexpectedly we see a fellow countryman. (*Vivaciously.*) Now I remember! Do you remember, Olya, at our house they used to say, "The lovesick major." You were a lieutenant then and in love with someone, and they all teased you for some reason as the lovesick major.

VERSHININ (*laughing*): That's right! That's right! The lovesick major. That was it!

MASHA: But you had only a mustache then. . . . Oh, how much older you look! (*Tearfully.*) How much older you look!

VERSHININ: Yes, when they called me the lovesick major, I was still young, I was in love. Not so now.

OLGA: But you still haven't a single gray hair. You look older, but you are still not old.

VERSHININ: For all that, I'm in my forty-third year. Is it long since you left Moscow?

IRINA: Eleven years. But why are you crying, Masha, you little fool? (*Through her tears.*) I'm starting to cry, too. . . .

MASHA: I'm all right. And in what street did you live?

VERSHININ: In Old Basmanny.

OLGA: And we lived there, too. . . .

VERSHININ: At one time I lived in Nemetzky Street. I used to walk from Nemetzky Street to the Red Barracks. There's a sullen-looking bridge on the way, and under the bridge you hear the water roaring. A lonely man feels sick at heart there. (*A pause.*) But here, what a broad, what a superb river! A wonderful river!

OLGA: Yes, except that it's cold. It's cold here and there are mosquitoes. . . .

VERSHININ: How can you! You have such a fine, healthy Russian climate here. Woods, river . . . and birches too. Sweet, modest birches, of all trees I love them best. It's good to live here. And yet, strangely enough, the railway station is thirteen miles away. . . . And nobody knows why that is.

SOLYONY: But I know why it is. (*Everyone looks at him.*) Because if the station were right here then 'twere not off there, and if it is off there, then it's not right here.

(*An awkward silence.*)

TUSENBACH: You're a joker, Vasili Vasilievich.

OLGA: Now I remember you too. I remember.

VERSHININ: I knew your mother.

TCHEBUTYKIN: She was a lovely woman . . . bless her soul!

IRINA: Mother is buried in Moscow.

OLGA: In the Novo Devichy. . . .

MASHA: Imagine, I'm already beginning to forget her face. Just as we won't be remembered either. They'll forget us.

VERSHININ: Yes. They'll forget us. Such is our fate, it can't be helped. What seems to us serious, significant, highly important — the time will come when it will be forgotten or seem unimportant. (*A pause.*) And it's an interesting thing, we can't possibly tell now just what will be considered great, or important, and what pitiful, ridiculous. Didn't the discoveries of Copernicus or, let's say, Columbus, seem at first unnecessary, ridiculous, and some shallow nonsense written by a fool seem to be the truth? And it may be that our present life, to which we are so reconciled, will seem very strange some day, uncomfortable, stupid, not pure enough, perhaps even sinful. . . .

TUSENBACH: Who knows? Perhaps our life will be called superior and remembered with respect. Nowadays there are no tortures, no executions, no invasions, though, for all that, there's so much unhappiness!

SOLYONY (*in a high-pitched voice*): Chick, chick, chick. . . . Don't feed the Baron grain, just let him philosophize.

TUSENBACH: Vasili Vasilievich, I beg you leave me alone. (*Sits at another place.*) After all, it's tiresome.

SOLYONY (*in a high-pitched voice*): Chick, chick, chick . . .

TUSENBACH (*to* VERSHININ): The unhappiness we see now, however, though there is still so much of it even now — bespeaks a certain moral regeneration that has already reached society. . . .

VERSHININ: Yes, yes, of course.

TCHEBUTYKIN: You just said, Baron, that they will call our present life superior; but, all the same, people are small. . . . (*Standing up.*) Look how small I am. It would only be to console me if anybody called my life a superior, understandable thing.

(*Behind the scenes a violin plays.*)

MASHA: It's Andrei playing, our brother.

IRINA: He is the learned member of the family. It looks as if he'd be a professor. Father was a military man, but his son chose for himself a learned career.

MASHA: According to Father's wish.

OLGA: Today we teased him to death. It seems he's a bit in love.

IRINA: With a local girl. She'll be with us today, there's every chance of it.

MASHA: Oh, how she dresses! Not merely ugly and out of style but simply pitiful. Some sort of strange, loud, yellowish skirt with a vulgar fringe and a red blouse. And her cheeks are so scrubbed, scrubbed! Andrei isn't in love — I won't admit it, after all he has taste, he's simply teasing us, he's fooling. I heard yesterday that she is marrying Protopopov, the Chairman of the Board. And that's fine — (*At the side door.*) Andrei, come here! Darling, just for a minute!

(ANDREI *enters.*)

OLGA: This is my brother, Andrei Sergeevich.

VERSHININ: Vershinin.

ANDREI: Prozoroff. (*He wipes his perspiring face.*) You are our new Battery Commander?

OLGA: Can you imagine, Alexander Ignatievich is from Moscow.

ANDREI: Yes? Well, I congratulate you, now my little sisters won't give you any peace.

VERSHININ: I have already had time to tire your sisters out.

IRINA: Look at the frame Andrei gave me today! (*Showing the frame.*) He made it himself.

VERSHININ (*looking at the frame and not knowing what to say*): Yes. . . . A thing . . .

IRINA: And the frame that's over the piano there, he made that, too.

(ANDREI *waves his hand as if disparagingly and moves away.*)

OLGA: He is not only our learned one, he also plays the violin and he saws various things out of wood. In sum he has a hand for anything. Andrei, don't go away! That's the way he does — he's always leaving us. Come here!

(MASHA *and* IRINA, *laughing, take him by the arms and lead him back.*)

MASHA: Come! Come!

ANDREI: Let me alone, please.

MASHA: How funny he is! Alexander Ignatievich used to be called the lovesick major and he didn't get a bit angry.

VERSHININ: Not a bit.

MASHA: And I want to call you the lovesick violinist!

IRINA: Or the lovesick professor! . . .

OLGA: He's in love! Andrusha's in love!

IRINA (*applauding*): Bravo, bravo! *Bis!* Andrushka is in love!

TCHEBUTYKIN (*comes up behind* ANDREI *and puts both arms around his waist*): For love alone did Nature put us in this world. (*Laughing. All the while he is holding a newspaper.*)

ANDREI: Well, that's enough, that's enough. . . . (*Wiping his face.*) I haven't slept all night and now I'm not myself, as they say. Till four o'clock I read, then lay down, but nothing happened. I thought of this and of that, and then, of course, at the crack of dawn here the sun swarms into my bedroom. During the summer while I am here, I want to translate a certain book from English.

VERSHININ: And do you read English?

ANDREI: Yes. Our father — bless his soul! — loaded us down with education. It's ridiculous and stupid, but all the same I must admit that in a year after his death, I began to fill out and get fat like this, as if my body were freed from the load. Thanks to Father, my sisters and I know the French, German and English languages and Irina knows Italian too. But at what a cost!

MASHA: In this town, to know three languages is an unnecessary luxury. It isn't even a luxury, it's a sort of unnecessary appendage like a sixth finger. We know a lot that's useless.

VERSHININ: There we have it! (*Laughing.*) You know a lot that is useless! It seems to me there's not and can't be a town so boring and dull that a clever, educated person would be unnecessary in it. Let's suppose that among the hundred thousand inhabitants of this town, which evidently is backward and crude, there are only three such people as you. It is obvious that you cannot triumph over the dark masses that surround you; in the course of your life you'll have to yield little by little and be lost in the crowd of a hundred thousand; life will stifle you, but just the same you'll still be there and not without influence; your kind, after you, will begin to appear, six, perhaps, then twelve, and so on, until finally your kind will get to be the majority. After two or three hundred years, life on earth will be unimaginably beautiful, wonderful. Man needs such a life, and if it is not here yet, he must anticipate it, wait, dream of it, be prepared for it, for it he must see and know more than his grandfather and father saw and knew. (*Laughing.*) And you complain of knowing a lot that's useless.

MASHA (*taking off her hat*): I am staying for lunch.

IRINA (*with a sigh*): Really all that should be written down. . . .

(ANDREI *is not to be seen, he has gone out unobserved.*)

TUSENBACH: After many years, you say, life on earth will be beautiful, wonderful. That's true. But to share it now, even from afar, we must prepare ourselves for it, must be doing something. . . .

VERSHININ (*getting up*): Yes. How many flowers you have! (*Looking around.*) And a beautiful apartment. I envy you! And all my life I have hung around little apartments with two chairs, a sofa and a stove that always smokes. In my life I have lacked just such flowers . . . (*Rubbing his hands.*) Well, nothing can be done about it!

TUSENBACH: Yes, one must work. You probably think the German is getting sentimental. But on my word of honor, I am Russian and don't even speak German. My father was Orthodox. . . .

(*A pause.*)

VERSHININ (*walking about the stage*): I often think; what might happen if we began life anew, and did it consciously? If one life, already lived through, had been, as it were the first draft, the other, the final copy! Then each of us, I think, would try above all things not to repeat himself, at least he would create for himself a different setting for his life, would arrange for himself an apartment such as this, with flowers, with a flood of light. . . . I have a wife and two girls; and, at that, the wife is a delicate lady, and so forth and so on, well, and if I were to begin life anew, I would never marry. . . . No, no!

(KULYGIN *enters, in a schoolteacher's uniform.*)

KULYGIN (*going up to* IRINA): My dear sister, allow me to congratulate you on your saint's day and wish you sincerely, from my heart, health and all that could be wished for a girl of your age. And then to present this book to you as a gift. (*Giving her the book.*) A history of our high school covering fifty years, written by me. A trifle of a book, written out of nothing else to do, but all the same you must read it. Good morning, gentlemen! (*To* VERSHININ.) Kulygin, teacher in the local high school, County Councilor. (*To* IRINA.) In this book you will find a list of all the graduates of our high school for the last fifty years. *Feci, quod potui, faciant meliora potentes.*[1] (*He kisses* MASHA.)

IRINA: But you've already given me a book like that at Easter.

KULYGIN (*laughing*): It couldn't be! In that case give it back, or better still,

[1] (Lat.) I have done what I could, let those do better who can

give it to the Colonel. Take it, Colonel. Read it sometime when you are bored.

VERSHININ: Thank you. (*He is about to leave.*) I am extremely glad I made your acquaintance. . . .

OLGA: You are leaving? No, no!

IRINA: Stay and lunch with us. Please.

OLGA: I beg you!

VERSHININ (*bowing*): It seems I've stumbled on to a saint's day party. Forgive me, I didn't know, didn't congratulate you. (*Goes with* OLGA *to the dining room.*)

KULYGIN: Today is Sunday, gentlemen, a day of rest, let us rest, let us be gay, each one according to his age and position. The rugs should be taken up for the summer and stored till winter. . . . Persian powder or naphthalene. . . . The Romans were healthy because they knew how to work, knew how to rest, they had *mens sana in corpore sano.*[2] Their life flowed on according to fixed forms. Our director says: the principal thing in every life is its form. . . . That which loses its form ends itself—and it's the same with our everyday existence. (*Takes* MASHA *by the waist, laughing.*) Masha loves me. My wife loves me. And the window curtains, too, together with the rugs. . . . Today, I am gay, in a splendid mood. Masha, at four o'clock today we are to be at the director's. There's a walk being arranged for the teachers and their families.

MASHA: I am not going.

KULYGIN (*aggrieved*): Dear Masha, why?

MASHA: Later on about that. . . . (*Angrily.*) Oh, very well, I'll go, but just leave me alone, please. . . . (*Walks away.*)

KULYGIN: And then we'll spend the evening at the director's. In spite of his sickly state of health, this man tries above all else to be sociable. A superior, bright personality. A magnificent man. Yesterday, after the teachers' conference, he says to me: "I am tired, Fyodor Ilyich: I am tired!" (*Looks at the clock on the wall, then at his watch.*) Your clock is seven minutes fast. Yes, he says, I am tired!

(*Behind the scene a violin is playing.*)

OLGA: Ladies and gentlemen, come to lunch, please! There's a meat-pie.

KULYGIN: Ah, my dear Olga, my dear! Yesterday, I worked from early morning till eleven o'clock in the evening, got tired and today I feel happy. (*Goes into the dining room and up to the table.*)

TCHEBUTYKIN (*puts the newspaper in his pocket, combs his beard*): A meat-pie? Splendid!

MASHA (*to* TCHEBUTYKIN, *sternly*): Only, look out: nothing to drink today. Do you hear? Drinking's bad for you.

[2] (Lat.) a healthy mind in a healthy body

TCHEBUTYKIN: Oh, go on! I'm past all that. It is two years I've not been on a drunk. (*Impatiently.*) Ah, old girl, isn't it all the same?

MASHA: All the same, don't you dare drink. Don't you dare. (*Angrily, but so that her husband doesn't hear.*) The Devil take it, to be bored again all evening long at the director's.

TUSENBACH: I wouldn't go if I were in your place. It's very simple.

TCHEBUTYKIN: Don't go, dearie.

MASHA: Yes, don't go. . . . This curst, unbearable life . . . (*Going to the dining room.*)

TCHEBUTYKIN (*going with her*): Now!

SOLYONY (*going to the dining room*): Chick, chick, chick. . . .

TUSENBACH: That's enough, Vasili Vasilievich. Drop it!

SOLYONY: Chick, chick, chick. . . .

KULYGIN (*gaily*): Your health, Colonel! I am a pedagogue and here in this house I'm one of the family, Masha's husband. . . . She is kind, very kind. . . .

VERSHININ: I'll have some of that dark vodka. . . . (*Drinking.*) Your health! (*To* OLGA.) I feel so good in your house! . . .

(*In the drawing room only* IRINA *and* TUSENBACH *are left.*)

IRINA: Masha is in a bad humor today. She got married at eighteen, when he seemed to her the most intelligent of men. But now it's not the same. He's the kindest but not the most intelligent.

OLGA (*impatiently*): Andrei, do come, after all!

ANDREI (*behind the scenes*): This minute. (*Enters and goes to the table.*)

TUSENBACH: What are you thinking about?

IRINA: This: I dislike and I'm afraid of that Solyony of yours. He talks nothing but nonsense. . . .

TUSENBACH: He is a strange person. I am both sorry for him and annoyed, but more sorry. It seems to me he's shy. . . . When the two of us are alone, he's very clever and gentle sometimes; but in company he is a crude fellow, a bully. Don't go away, let them get settled at the table. Let me be near you awhile. What are you thinking about? (*A pause.*) You are twenty, I am not yet thirty. How many years there are left for us ahead, a long, long row of days, full of my love for you. . . .

IRINA: Nikolai Lvovich, don't talk to me of love.

TUSENBACH (*not listening*): I have a passionate thirst for life, struggle, work, and that thirst is mingled in my soul with love for you, Irina. And it's as though it were by some design that you are beautiful and life seems beautiful to me because of you. What are you thinking about?

IRINA: You say life is beautiful. Yes, but what if it only seems so! With us three sisters, life hasn't yet been beautiful, it has stifled us as weeds do grass. . . . I'm letting my tears fall. I shouldn't do that. . . . (*Quickly wiping her face, smiling.*) We must do something, must work. That's why we are not happy and look at life so gloomily — we don't know anything about working. We come of people who despised work.

(NATALIA IVANOVNA *enters; she has a pink dress with a green belt.*)

NATASHA: Look, they are already sitting down to lunch. . . . I'm late. . . . (*She steals a glance at herself in the mirror and tidies herself up.*) My hair seems to be all right. . . . (*Seeing* IRINA.) Dear Irina Sergeevna, I congratulate you! (*Kissing her vigorously and long.*) You have lots of guests, I really feel shy. . . . How do you do, Baron!

OLGA (*entering the living room*): Well, and here is Natalia Ivanovna. Good day, my dear. (*They kiss.*)

NATASHA: Congratulations on the saint's day. You have so much company, I feel awfully that . . .

OLGA: Never mind, it's just the family. (*In an undertone, alarmed.*) You have on a green belt! My dear, that's not right!

NATASHA: Is it a sign of something?

OLGA: No, it just doesn't match . . . and somehow it looks odd —

NATASHA (*in a tearful voice*): Yes? But it's not really green, it's more of a neutral color. (*Follows* OLGA *into the dining room.*)

(*In the dining room they are sitting down to lunch; there is not a soul in the living room.*)

KULYGIN: I wish you, Irina, a good fiancé! It's time you married.

TCHEBUTYKIN: Natalia Ivanovna, I wish you a fiancé too.

KULYGIN: Natalia Ivanovna already has a fiancé.

MASHA (*strikes her plate with her fork*): I'll take a little drink! What the . . . life is all roses, I'll risk it. . . .

KULYGIN: Your conduct gets C minus.

VERSHININ: And the liqueur tastes good. What's it made of?

SOLYONY: Cockroaches.

IRINA (*in a tearful voice*): Phew! How disgusting! . . .

OLGA: For supper there will be roast turkey and apple pie. Thank the Lord, I'll be at home all day, and in the evening — at home. . . . Everybody must come this evening. . . .

VERSHININ: Allow me, too, to come this evening!

IRINA: Please do.

NATASHA: They are very informal.

TCHEBUTYKIN: For love alone did Nature put us in this world. (*Laughing.*)

ANDREI (*angrily*): Stop it, everybody! Aren't you tired of it?

(FEDOTIK *and* RODAY *enter with a big basket of flowers.*)

FEDOTIK: But say, they are already lunching.

RODAY (*talking loud and affectedly*): Lunching? Yes, already lunching. . . .

FEDOTIK: Wait a minute! (*Taking a snapshot.*) One! Wait, just one more.

. . . (*Taking another snapshot.*) Two! Now, ready! (*They pick up the basket and go to the dining room, where they are greeted noisily.*)

RODAY (*in a loud voice*): Congratulations, I wish you everything, everything! The weather today is charming, perfectly magnificent. Today, all morning long, I was walking with the high school boys. I teach gymnastics at the high school. . . .

FEDOTIK: You may move, Irina Sergeevna, you may! (*Taking a snapshot.*) You look well today. (*Getting a top out of his pocket.*) By the way, see this top. . . . It has an amazing sound. . . .

IRINA: How delightful!

MASHA: By the curved seashore a green oak, a golden chain upon that oak. . . . A golden chain upon that oak. . . . (*Tearfully.*) Now, why do I say that? This phrase has stuck in my mind ever since morning. . . .

KULYGIN: Thirteen at the table!

RODAY (*in a loud voice*): Could it really be, ladies and gentlemen, that you attach importance to these superstitions?

(*Laughing.*)

KULYGIN: Thirteen at the table shows that there are lovers here. It's not you, Ivan Romanovich by any chance? (*Laughter.*)

TCHEBUTYKIN: I am an old sinner, but why Natalia Ivanovna should be embarrassed I simply can't understand.

(*Loud laughter;* NATASHA *runs out from the dining room into the living room,* ANDREI *following her.*)

ANDREI: Come on, don't pay any attention to them! Wait. . . . Stop. . . . I beg you. . . .

NATASHA: I'm ashamed. . . . I don't know what it's all about and they are making fun of me. It was bad manners for me to leave the table just now, but I can't . . . I can't . . . (*Covers her face with her hands.*)

ANDREI: My dear, I beg you, I entreat you, don't be upset. I assure you they are only joking, they have kind hearts. My darling, my beautiful, they all are gentle, kind-hearted people and they love me and you. Come over here to the window, they can't see us here. . . . (*He glances around.*)

NATASHA: I am so unused to being in society! . . .

ANDREI: Ah, youth, wonderful, beautiful youth! My dear, my darling, don't be so upset! . . . Believe me, believe . . . I feel so happy, my soul is full of love, ecstasy. . . . Oh, they can't see us! They can't see! Why, why I fell in love with you; when I fell in love. My dear, darling, pure one, be my wife! I love you, love . . . as nobody ever. . . . (*A kiss.*)

(*The* TWO OFFICERS *enter and seeing the pair kissing, stop in astonishment.*)

CURTAIN

## ACT II

*The setting is the same as in Act I. It is eight o'clock in the evening. Offstage faintly we hear an accordion, playing in the street. There are no lights.*

NATALIA IVANOVNA *enters in a dressing gown, with a candle; she comes in and stops at the door that leads into* ANDREI*'s room.*

NATASHA: Andrusha, what are you doing? Reading? It's nothing, I just . . . (*Goes and opens another door and after looking in, closes it.*) If there's a light . . .

ANDREI (*enters with a book in his hand*): You what, Natasha?

NATASHA: Looking to see if there's a light. . . . Now it's Carnival week the servants are beside themselves, we have to look and look, so that nothing goes wrong. Last night at midnight, I passed through the dining room, and a candle was burning there. Who lighted it I couldn't find out. (*Putting down her candle.*) What time is it?

ANDREI (*looking at his watch*): It's a quarter past eight.

NATASHA: And Olga and Irina not in yet. They haven't come in. Always working, poor girls! Olga at the Teachers' Council, Irina at the telegraph office. . . . (*Sighing.*) This morning I say to your sister: "Spare yourself, I say, Irina darling." But she won't listen. Quarter past eight, you say? I am anxious for fear, our Bobik is not at all well. Why is he so cold? Yesterday he had fever, and today he is cold all over. . . . I am so anxious!

ANDREI: It's nothing, Natasha. The boy is all right.

NATASHA: Still it's better to put him on a diet. I'm anxious. And tonight, around ten o'clock, they said, the maskers will be here, it would be better if they didn't come, Andrusha.

ANDREI: Really, I don't know. But they were invited.

NATASHA: This morning the little fellow wakes up and looks at me and all at once he smiles; so he knew me. "Bobik," I say, "good morning! Good morning, dear!" And he laughs. Children understand, they understand perfectly. So, Andrusha, I'll tell them not to let the maskers in.

ANDREI (*indecisively*): But that's for my sisters to say, they are mistresses here.

NATASHA: And they too, I'll tell them. They are kind. . . . (*Going.*) For supper I ordered some buttermilk. The doctor says, you're to have nothing but buttermilk or you'll never get any thinner. (*Stopping.*) Bobik is cold. I'm afraid he may be cold in that room of his. We ought to – at least till warm weather comes – put him in a different room. For instance, Irina's room is just right for a child; it's dry and sunny too all day long. I must tell her that. For a while at least she could be in the same room with Olga. . . . She's not at home during the day anyhow, she only spends the night. . . . (*A pause.*) Andrushanchik, why don't you say something?

ANDREI: I was just thinking — Besides there's nothing to talk about. . . .

NATASHA: Yes. . . . There's something I wanted to tell you. . . . Oh, yes. Ferapont has just come from the District Board, he's asking for you.

ANDREI (*yawning*): Call him in.

(NATASHA *goes out.* ANDREI, *bending over to the candle, which she has forgotten to take along, reads his book.* FERAPONT *enters; he is in a shabby old coat, with the collar turned up, a scarf over his ears.*)

ANDREI: Good evening, my good soul. What have you got to say?

FERAPONT: The Chairman has sent you a book and a paper of some kind. Here. . . . (*He gives the book and an envelope to* ANDREI.)

ANDREI: Thanks. Good! But why did you come so late? It's after eight now?

FERAPONT: How's that?

ANDREI (*louder*): I say you came late, it's now after eight.

FERAPONT: Exactly. I got here when it was still light, but they all wouldn't let me in. The master, they said, is busy. Well, it's like this. You're busy, very busy. I have nowhere to hurry to. (*Thinking that* ANDREI *is asking him something.*) How's that?

ANDREI: Nothing. (*Examining the book.*) Tomorrow is Friday, we haven't any school, but all the same I'll come, just to be doing something. It's tiresome at home. . . . (*A pause.*) Dear Grandpa, how strangely it changes, how life deceives one! Today, out of boredom, out of nothing else to do, I picked up this book here — old university lectures, and I felt like laughing. . . . My God! I'm the secretary of the District Board, that board where Protopopov presides, I am the secretary and the very most I can hope for — is to be a member of the District Board! Me, a member of the local district board, I who dream every night that I'm a professor in Moscow University, a famous scholar whom this Russian land is proud of!

FERAPONT: I wouldn't know. Don't hear well. . . .

ANDREI: If you could hear well, I might not have talked to you. I must talk to somebody, but my wife doesn't understand me, and I am afraid of my sisters somehow, I'm afraid they will laugh at me, make me ashamed. . . . I don't drink, don't like bars; but with what pleasure I could be sitting right now in Moscow at Testoff's or in the Bolshoy Moscoffsky, my dear fellow.

FERAPONT: And in Moscow, so a contractor was saying the other day at the District Board, some merchants were eating bliny; one of them, it seems, ate forty blinies and died. It was either forty or fifty. I wouldn't remember.

ANDREI: You sit in Moscow in a huge room at a restaurant, you don't know anybody, and nobody knows you, but at the same time you don't feel like a stranger. . . . And here you know everybody and everybody knows you, but you are a stranger, a stranger. . . . A stranger and lonely.

FERAPONT: How's that? (*A pause.*) And the same contractor was saying — maybe he was just lying — that a rope is stretched all the way across Moscow.

ANDREI: What for?

FERAPONT: I wouldn't know. The contractor said so.

ANDREI: Fiddlesticks. (*Reading.*) Were you ever in Moscow?

FERAPONT (*after a pause*): Never was. God didn't grant me that. (*A pause.*) Shall I go?

ANDREI: You may go. Good-by. (FERAPONT *goes out.*) Good-by. (*Reading.*) Come tomorrow morning and get these papers. . . . Go. . . . (*A pause.*) He's gone. (*A bell rings.*) Yes, it's a business — (*Stretching and going slowly into his room.*)

(*Behind the scenes a nurse is singing, rocking a child.* MASHA *and* VERSHININ *enter conversing. In the dining room one of the maids is lighting a lamp and the candles.*)

MASHA: I don't know. (*A pause.*) I don't know. Of course habit means a lot. For example, after Father's death it took us a long time to get used to not having orderlies in the house. But even apart from habit, I think, common justice makes me say it — in other places it may not be so, but in our town the most decent, the most honorable and well-brought-up people — are the military.

VERSHININ: I'm thirsty. I'd drink some tea.

MASHA (*glancing at the clock*): It will soon be here. They married me off when I was eighteen years old, and I was afraid of my husband because he was a teacher, and that was when I had barely finished my courses. He seemed to me terribly learned then, clever, and important. But now it's not the same, unfortunately.

VERSHININ: So — yes.

MASHA: I am not talking about my husband. I'm used to him, but among the civilians generally there are so many people who are crude and unfriendly and haven't any manners. Rudeness upsets me and offends me, I suffer when I see that a man is not fine enough, gentle enough, polite. When I happen to be among the teachers, my husband's colleagues, I'm simply miserable.

VERSHININ: Yes. . . . But it seems to me it's all the same whether they are civilian or military, they are equally uninteresting, at any rate in this town they are. It's all the same! If you listen to one of the local intelligentsia — civilian or military — what you hear is that he's worn out with his wife, worn out with his home, worn out with his estate, worn out with his horses. . . . A Russian is quite supremely given to lofty ways in thought, but will you tell me why it is that in life he strikes so low? Why?

MASHA: Why?

VERSHININ: Why is he worn out with his children, worn out with his wife? And why are the wife and the children worn out with him?

MASHA: You are not in a very good humor today.

VERSHININ: Perhaps. I haven't had any dinner today, nothing to eat since morning. One of my daughters is not very well, and when my girls are ailing, I am seized with anxiety, and my conscience torments me for their having such a mother. Oh, if you'd seen her today! What a miserable wretch! We began to quarrel at seven o'clock in the morning, and at nine I slammed the door and went out. (*A pause.*) I never speak of it, and strangely enough I complain just to you. (*Kissing her hand.*) Don't be angry with me. But for you alone, I'd not have anybody — nobody. . . .

(*A pause.*)

MASHA: What a noise in the stove! At home, just before Father died, it was howling in the chimney. There, just like that!

VERSHININ: Are you superstitious?

MASHA: Yes.

VERSHININ: That's strange. (*Kissing her hand.*) You are a magnificent, wonderful woman. Magnificent, wonderful! It is dark here, but I see the sparkle of your eyes.

MASHA (*moving to another chair*): It's lighter here.

VERSHININ: I love, love, love. . . . Love your eyes, your gestures, I see them in my dreams. . . . Magnificent, wonderful woman!

MASHA (*laughing quietly*): When you talk to me like that, for some reason or other, I laugh, though I'm frightened. Don't do it again, I beg you. . . . (*In a low voice.*) But talk, though, it's all the same to me. (*Covering her face with her hands.*) It's all the same to me. They're coming here — talk about something else. . . .

(IRINA *and* TUSENBACH *enter from the dining room.*)

TUSENBACH: I have a triple name. I am called Tusenbach — Krone — Altschauer — but I am Russian, Orthodox, like you. There's very little German left in me, perhaps only this patience and stubbornness that I bore you with. I see you home every evening.

IRINA: I'm so tired!

TUSENBACH: And every day I'll come to the telegraph office and see you home, I'll do that for ten, twenty, years, for as long as you don't drive me away. . . . (*Seeing* MASHA *and* VERSHININ, *delightedly.*) It's you? Good evening.

IRINA: Here I am home at last. (*To* MASHA.) Just now a lady came, telegraphed her brother in Saratov that her son died today, and couldn't remember the address at all. So she sent it without the address, simply to Saratov. She was crying. And I was rude to her for no reason whatever. "I haven't got time," I said. 'Twas so silly! Are the maskers coming tonight?

MASHA: Yes.

IRINA (*she sits down in an armchair*): I must rest. I'm tired.

TUSENBACH (*smiling*): When you come back from your office, you seem so young, unhappy. . . .

(*A pause.*)

IRINA: I'm tired. No, I don't like the telegraphing, I don't like it.

MASHA: You are thinner. . . . (*She begins to whistle.*) And look younger and your face begins to look like a little boy's.

TUSENBACH: That's from her hair.

IRINA: I must try and find another position, this one is not for me. What I wanted so, what I dreamed of, that's exactly what's not there. Work without poetry, without thoughts. . . . (*A knock on the floor.*) The doctor is knocking. . . . (*To* TUSENBACH.) Knock back, dear. . . . I can't. . . . I'm tired. . . .

(TUSENBACH *knocks on the floor.*)

IRINA: He'll come this minute. Something or other will have to be done about it. The doctor and our Andrei were at the club yesterday and lost again. They say Andrei lost two hundred roubles.

MASHA (*indifferently*): So what's there to do now?

IRINA: Two weeks ago he lost, in December he lost. If he'd lose everything soon, perhaps we'd go away from this town. Oh my Lord God, I dream of Moscow every night, I am like someone completely possessed. (*Laughing.*) We are moving there in June and from now to June leaves still . . . February, March, April, May. . . . Almost half a year!

MASHA: The only thing is Natasha mustn't some way or other hear of his losses.

IRINA: It's all one to her, I imagine.

(TCHEBUTYKIN, *who has just got out of bed — he has been resting after dinner — enters the dining room combing his beard, then sits down at the table and takes a newspaper from his pocket.*)

MASHA: There he comes. . . . Has he paid anything on his apartment?

IRINA (*laughing*): No. Not a kopeck for eight months. He's forgotten it evidently.

MASHA (*laughing*): How importantly he sits!

(*Everybody laughs; a pause.*)

IRINA: Why are you so quiet, Alexander Ignatievich?

VERSHININ: I don't know. What I'd like is some tea. Half my life for a glass of tea! I've eaten nothing since morning. . . .

TCHEBUTYKIN: Irina Sergeevna!

IRINA: What do you want?

TCHEBUTYKIN: Please come here. *Venez ici!* (IRINA *goes and sits down at the table.*) I can't do without you.

(IRINA *lays out the cards for patience.*)

VERSHININ: Well? If they are not giving us any tea, let's at least philosophize.

TUSENBACH: Yes, let's. What about?

VERSHININ: What about? Let's dream . . . for example, of the life that will come after us in two or three hundred years.

TUSENBACH: Well? After us they will fly in balloons, the style of coats will change, they will discover the sixth sense perhaps, and develop it; but life will remain quite the same, a difficult life, mysterious and happy. And after a thousand years, man will be sighing the same: "Ah, how hard it is to live!" and meanwhile, exactly the same as now, he will be afraid of death and not want to die.

VERSHININ (*after a moment's thought*): How shall I put it? It seems to me everything on earth must change little by little and is already changing before our very eyes. In two or three hundred, eventually a thousand, years — it's not a matter of time — a new, happy life will come. We won't share in that life of course, but we are living for it now, working, well — suffering; we are creating it — and in that alone lies the purpose of our being and, if you like, our happiness.

(MASHA *laughs softly.*)

TUSENBACH: What are you laughing at?

MASHA: I don't know. All day today I've been laughing, ever since morning.

VERSHININ: I was graduated from the same school you were, but was not at the academy; I read a great deal, but don't know how to choose books, and read, perhaps, not at all what I should; and meanwhile the longer I live the more I want to know. My hair is turning gray, I'm almost an old man now, but I know very little, oh, how very little! And yet it does seem to me that what's most important and real I do know, know solidly. And I'd so like to prove to you that there's no happiness, there should not be, and there won't be, for us. . . . We should only work and work, and happiness — that's the lot of our remote descendants. (*A pause.*) Not I, but at least the descendants of my descendants.

(FEDOTIK *and* RODAY *appear in the dining room; they sit down and sing softly, strumming a guitar.*)

TUSENBACH: According to you, we are not even to dream of happiness! But what if I'm happy?

VERSHININ: No.

TUSENBACH (*throwing up his hands and laughing*): Obviously we don't understand each other. Well, how can I convince you?

(MASHA *laughs softly.*)

TUSENBACH (*holding up a finger to her*): Laugh! (*To* VERSHININ.) Not only in two or three hundred but in a million years, even, life will be just the same as it was; it doesn't change, it stays constant, following its own laws, which are none of our affair, or which, at least you will never know. Birds of passage, cranes, for example, fly and fly, and no matter what thoughts, great or small, stray through their heads, they will fly just the same and not know why and where. They fly and will fly, no matter what philosophers spring up among them; and they may philosophize as much as they like so long as they fly. . . .

MASHA: Just the same, has it meaning?

TUSENBACH: Meaning. . . . Look, it's snowing. What meaning has that?

(*A pause.*)

MASHA: It seems to me a man must be a believer or must seek some belief, otherwise his life is empty, empty. . . . To live and not know why the cranes fly, why children are born, why there are stars in the sky. . . . Either he knows what he's living for, or it's all nonsense, waste.

VERSHININ: Yet it's a shame youth is gone. . . .

MASHA: Gogol says: It is boring to live in this world, gentlemen.

TUSENBACH: And I say: it is difficult to argue with you, gentlemen! Why you completely. . . .

TCHEBUTYKIN (*reading a newspaper*): Balzac was married in Berdichev. (IRINA *sings softly.*) Really I'll put that in my book. (*Writing.*) Balzac was married in Berdichev. (*Reading his newspaper.*)

IRINA (*as she lays out cards for patience, musing*): Balzac was married in Berdichev.

TUSENBACH: The die is cast. You know, Maria Sergeevna, I have tendered my resignation.

MASHA: So I heard. And I don't see anything good about that. I don't like civilians.

TUSENBACH: Just the same . . . (*Getting up.*) I'm not handsome, what sort of military man am I? Well, well, but all the same, however. . . . I shall work. For just one day in my life, work so that I come home in the evening, drop exhausted into bed and fall asleep right off. (*Going into the dining room.*) Workmen must sleep soundly!

FEDOTIK (*to* IRINA): I bought you some crayons on Moscoffsky Street, at Pyjokoff's, and this penknife.

IRINA: You are used to treating me as if I were little, but I'm grown up now. . . . (*She takes the crayons and the penknife, gaily.*) How delightful!

FEDOTIK: And I bought a knife for myself. . . . Look here . . . a blade, and another blade, a third, this to pick the ears, these small scissors, this to clean the nails. . . .

RODAY (*talking very loud*): Doctor, what's your age?
TCHEBUTYKIN: Me? Thirty-two.

(*Laughter.*)

FEDOTIK: I'll now show you another game of patience. . . . (*Laying out cards for patience.*)

(*The samovar is brought:* ANFISA *is at the samovar; a little later* NATASHA *also comes in and hovers near the table;* SOLYONY *enters and after greetings, sits down at the table.*)

VERSHININ: But what a wind!
MASHA: Yes. I'm tired of winter. I've already forgotten what summer is like.
IRINA: It's coming out right, the patience, I see. We shall be in Moscow.
FEDOTIK: No, it's not coming out right. Look, the eight falls on the two of spades. (*Laughing.*) So you will not be in Moscow.
TCHEBUTYKIN (*reading his newspaper*): Tsitsikar. Smallpox is raging here.
ANFISA (*approaching* MASHA): Masha, have some tea, little one. (*To* VERSHININ.) If you please, Your Excellency. . . . Excuse me, dear sir, your name, your family name, I've forgotten. . . .
MASHA: Bring it here, Nurse. I'm not going there.
IRINA: Nurse!
ANFISA: I'm coming!
NATASHA (*to* SOLYONY): Bobik understands beautifully. "Good morning," I say, "Bobik. Good morning, dear!" He gave me a special look somehow. You think I'm only a mother talking, but no, no, I assure you! That's an unusual child.
SOLYONY: If this child were mine, I would have fried him in a skillet and eaten him. (*He goes with his glass into the living room and sits down in the corner.*)
NATASHA (*covering her face with her hands*): Rude, ill-bred man!
MASHA: Happy is he who does not notice whether it's summer now or winter. If I were in Moscow, I think I should scorn the weather. . . .
VERSHININ: The other day I read the diary of a certain French Minister, written in prison. The Minister was convicted of fraud. With what rapture and delight, he mentions the birds he saw through the prison window and had never noticed before when he was a Minister. And now, of course, that he's released, it's the same as it was before, he doesn't notice the birds. Just as you won't notice Moscow when you live there. Happiness we have not and it does not exist, we only long for it.
TUSENBACH (*taking a box from the table*): But where's the candy?
IRINA: Solyony ate it all.
TUSENBACH: All of it?
ANFISA (*serving tea*): A letter for you, dear sir.
VERSHININ: For me? (*Taking the letter.*) From my daughter. (*Reading.*)

Yes, of course . . . Forgive me, Maria Sergeevna, I'll just slip out. Not any tea for me — (*Getting up very much disturbed.*) These eternal messes. . . .

MASHA: What is it? Not a secret?

VERSHININ (*in a low voice*): The wife has taken poison again. Got to go. I'll slip out, won't be seen. Terribly unpleasant, all this. (*Kissing* MASHA'*s hand.*) My dear, kind, good woman. . . . I'll slip out of here quietly. . . . (*He goes out.*)

ANFISA: Where is he going now? And I have poured his tea. . . . Such a . . .

MASHA (*losing her temper*): Let it be! Plaguing us around here, there's no rest from you. . . . (*Going to the table with her cup.*) I am tired of you, old woman!

ANFISA: Why are you offended? Darling!

ANDREI'S VOICE: Anfisa!

ANFISA (*mocking him*): Anfisa! Sitting there. . . . (*She goes out.*)

MASHA (*in the dining room at the table, angrily*): Do let me sit down! (*Musses up the cards on the table.*) Lounging here with the cards. Drink your tea!

IRINA: You are spiteful, Masha.

MASHA: If I'm spiteful, don't talk to me. Don't touch me!

TCHEBUTYKIN (*laughing*): Don't touch her, don't touch. . . .

MASHA: You are sixty years old, and you are like a little boy, always prattling the devil knows what.

NATASHA (*sighing*): Dear Masha, why use such expressions in your conversation? With your beautiful looks you'd be, I'll tell you candidly, simply charming in a decent, well-bred society, if it weren't for these words of yours. *Je vous prie, pardonnez-moi, Marie, mais vous avez des manières un peu grossières.*[3]

TUSENBACH (*suppressing a laugh*): Give me. . . . Give me. . . . Seems there's some cognac.

NATASHA: *Il parait que mon Bobik déjà ne dort pas,*[4] he's waked up. He doesn't seem to me very well today. I'm going to him, excuse me. . . . (*She goes out.*)

IRINA: And where's Alexander Ignatievich gone?

MASHA: Home. There's something extraordinary the matter with his wife again.

TUSENBACH (*going to* SOLYONY, *with a decanter of cognac*): You sit by yourself all the time, you are thinking of something — and there's no grasping what it is. Well, let's make peace. Let's drink some cognac. (*Drinking.*) I'll have to play the piano all night tonight probably, play all kinds of trash. . . . Come what may!

SOLYONY: Why make peace? I have not quarreled with you.

[3] (Fr.) Please forgive me, Masha, but your manners are a little rude

[4] (Fr.) It seems as if my Bobik is awake already (Natasha's French is not very good. The proper idiom is ". . . *que mon Bobik ne dort plus*")

TUSENBACH: You always give me a sort of feeling that something has happened between us. You are a strange character, we must admit.

SOLYONY (*declaiming*): I am strange, who isn't strange! Don't be angry, Aleko!

TUSENBACH: But why this Aleko. . . .

(*A pause.*)

SOLYONY: When I am alone with someone I'm all right, I am like everybody else, but in company I am gloomy, shy and . . . talk all kinds of rot. Nevertheless, I am more honest and nobler than many, many others are. And I can prove it.

TUSENBACH: I often get sore at you, you are forever plaguing me when we are in company, but just the same you attract me somehow. Come what may, I'll get drunk today. Let's drink!

SOLYONY: Let's do. (*Drinking.*) I've never had anything against you, Baron. But I have the disposition of Lermontov. (*In a low voice.*) I even resemble Lermontov a little. . . . So they say. . . . (*Getting a bottle of perfume out of his pocket and pouring some of it over his hands.*)

TUSENBACH: I am sending in my resignation. *Basta!* For five years I kept pondering it and finally decided. I'm going to work.

SOLYONY (*declaiming*): Don't be angry, Aleko. . . . Forget, forget those dreams of yours. . . .

(*While they are talking,* ANDREI *comes in quietly with a book and sits down near a candle.*)

TUSENBACH: I'm going to work.

TCHEBUTYKIN (*going into the living room with* IRINA): And the refreshments were real Caucasian too: onion soup, and for the roast — tchehartma, meat.

SOLYONY: Tcheremsha is not meat at all, but a plant something like our onion.

TCHEBUTYKIN: No, my angel . . . Tchehartma is not onion but a mutton roast.

SOLYONY: And I tell you, tcheremsha — onion.

TCHEBUTYKIN: And I tell you, tchehartma — mutton.

SOLYONY: And I tell you, tcheremsha — onion.

TCHEBUTYKIN: But why should I argue with you, you never were in the Caucasus, and never ate tchehartma.

SOLYONY: I haven't eaten it because I can't bear it. Tcheremsha smells exactly like garlic.

ANDREI (*imploringly*): That's enough, gentlemen! I beg you!

TUSENBACH: When are the maskers coming?

IRINA: They promised toward nine; which means, this minute.

TUSENBACH (*embracing* ANDREI, *singing*): Oh, you porch, my porch, new porch of mine. . . .

ANDREI (*dancing and singing*): New porch of maple. . . .
TCHEBUTYKIN (*dancing*): Made of lattice!

(*Laughter.*)

TUSENBACH (*kissing* ANDREI): The Devil take it, let's have a drink! Andrusha, let us drink with you. And I'll go with you, Andrusha, to Moscow, to the university.
SOLYONY: To which one? In Moscow there are two universities.
ANDREI: In Moscow, there's one university.
SOLYONY: And I tell you — two.
ANDREI: Let there be three even. So much the better!
SOLYONY: In Moscow there are two universities! (*Disapproval and hisses.*) In Moscow there are two universities: the old and the new. And if you don't want to listen, if my words irritate you, I can stop talking. I can even go to another room. . . . (*He goes out through one of the doors.*)
TUSENBACH: Bravo, bravo! (*Laughing.*) Ladies and gentlemen, begin, I am sitting down to play! Funny this Solyony. . . . (*Sitting down at the piano and playing a waltz.*)
MASHA (*waltzing by herself*): The Baron is drunk, the Baron is drunk, the Baron is drunk. (NATASHA *enters.*)
NATASHA (*to* TCHEBUTYKIN): Ivan Romanovich!

(*She says something to* TCHEBUTYKIN, *then goes out quietly.* TCHEBUTYKIN *touches* TUSENBACH *on the shoulder and whispers something to him.*)

IRINA: What is it?
TCHEBUTYKIN: It's time for us to go.
TUSENBACH: Good night. It's time to go.
IRINA: But look here — what about the maskers?
ANDREI (*embarrassed*): There won't be any maskers. Don't you see, my dear, Natasha says that Bobik isn't quite well, and therefore . . . In sum, I don't know, it's all the same to me, absolutely.
IRINA (*shrugging her shoulders*): Bobik not well!
MASHA: What of it! If they run us out, we must go. (*To* IRINA.) It is not Bobik that's sick, but she herself is. . . . Here! (*Tapping her forehead.*) Common creature!

(ANDREI *goes through the right door into his room.* TCHEBUTYKIN *follows him: in the dining room good-bys are being said.*)

FEDOTIK: What a pity! I counted on spending the evening, but if the child is sick, of course . . . Tomorrow I'll bring him some toys. . . .
RODAY (*in a loud voice*): I purposely took a nap after dinner today, thought I would dance all night. Why, it's only nine o'clock now.
MASHA: Let's go out in the street: we'll talk things over there. We'll decide what's what.

(*Sounds of:* "Good-by! . . . Farewell!" *You can hear* TUSENBACH's *gay laughter. Everyone is gone.* ANFISA *and a maid clear the table, put out the lights. A nurse can be heard singing.* ANDREI *in his coat and hat and* TCHEBUTYKIN *enter quietly.*)

TCHEBUTYKIN: I've had no time to marry because life has flashed by me like lightning, and also because I was madly in love with your mother, who was married. . . .

ANDREI: One shouldn't marry. One shouldn't, it's boring.

TCHEBUTYKIN: That may be so, but the loneliness! You may philosophize as much as you please, but loneliness is a frightful thing, my boy. . . . Though as a matter of fact . . . of course it's absolutely all the same.

ANDREI: Let's go quick.

TCHEBUTYKIN: Why hurry? We have time.

ANDREI: I am afraid the wife might stop us.

TCHEBUTYKIN: Ah!

ANDREI: Today I shan't play, but just sit. I don't feel well. . . . What shall I do, Ivan Romanovich, for shortness of breath?

TCHEBUTYKIN: Why ask me? Don't remember, my boy. Don't know.

ANDREI: Let's go through the kitchen.

(*They go out. A ring, then another ring; voices are heard, laughter.* IRINA *enters.*)

IRINA: What is it?

ANFISA (*in a whisper*): The maskers!

(*A ring.*)

IRINA: Tell them, Nursey, nobody's at home. They must excuse us.

(ANFISA *goes out.* IRINA *paces the room, thinking things over, she is perturbed.* SOLYONY *enters.*)

SOLYONY (*in a quandary*): Nobody here. . . . But where are they all?

IRINA: Gone home.

SOLYONY: That's odd. Are you alone here?

IRINA: Alone. (*A pause.*) Good-by.

SOLYONY: I behaved without enough restraint just now, tactlessly. But you are not like the rest of them, you are superior and pure, you can see the truth. . . . Only you alone can understand me. I love you, deeply, love you without end. . . .

IRINA: Good-by! Go away.

SOLYONY: I can't live without you. (*Following her.*) Oh, my delight! (*Through his tears.*) Oh, happiness! Such glorious, wonderful, marvelous eyes as I have never seen in any other woman. . . .

IRINA (*coldly*): Stop it, Vasili Vasilievich!

SOLYONY: I'm speaking of love to you for the first time and it's as if I were not on earth but on another planet. (*Rubbing his forehead.*) Well, it's all the same. Love is not to be forced, certainly. . . . But lucky rivals I cannot have. . . . Cannot. . . . I swear to you by all that's holy, I'll kill any rival. . . . Oh, wonderful creature!

(NATASHA *passes by with a candle.*)

NATASHA (*looks in at one door, then at another and passes by the door leading into her husband's room*): Andrei is there. Let him read. Excuse me, Vasili Vasilievich, I didn't know you were here. I'm in my dressing gown.

SOLYONY: It's all the same to me. Good-by! (*He goes out.*)

NATASHA: And you are tired, my dear, poor girl! (*Kissing* IRINA.) You should go to bed a little earlier.

IRINA: Is Bobik asleep?

NATASHA: Asleep. But not sound asleep. By the way, dear, I wanted to tell you, but you are never here, or else I haven't time. . . . In the nursery Bobik has now, seems to me it's cold and damp. And your room is so good for a child. My dear, my own, move in with Olya for a while!

IRINA (*not understanding*): Where?

(*A troika with bells is heard driving up to the house.*)

NATASHA: You and Olya will be in one room, for this little while, and your room will be for Bobik. He's such a darling, today I say to him: "Bobik, you are mine! Mine!" And he looks at me with his little eyes. (*A ring.*) It must be Olga. How late she is!

(*A* MAID *comes and whispers in* NATASHA'*s ear.*)

NATASHA: Protopopov? What a queer man! Protopopov has come, he's asking me to go for a ride with him in a troika. (*Laughing.*) How strange these men are . . . ! (*A ring.*) Somebody's come out there. I might go ride for a quarter of an hour. . . . (*To the* MAID.) Tell him right away — (*A ring.*) There's a ring. . . . Olga must be here. (*She goes out.*)

(*The* MAID *runs out;* IRINA *sits there thinking.* KULYGIN, OLGA *enter, behind them* VERSHININ.)

KULYGIN: There you are! And they said there would be a party.

VERSHININ: Strange, I went away a while ago, half an hour ago, and they were expecting the maskers. . . .

IRINA: They have all gone.

KULYGIN: And Masha's gone? Where did she go? And why is Protopopov downstairs waiting in the troika? Who's he waiting for?

IRINA: Don't ask questions. . . . I'm tired.

KULYGIN: Well, Miss Caprice . . .

OLGA: The council has just finished. I'm exhausted. Our headmistress is ill, and I'm taking her place. My head, my head aches, my head . . .

(*Sitting down.*) Andrei lost two hundred roubles yesterday at cards. . . . The whole town is talking about it. . . .

KULYGIN: Yes, and I got tired at the council. (*He sits down.*)

VERSHININ: My wife decided just now to scare me, she almost poisoned herself. It all passed over and I'm happy, I'm easy now. . . . The order is we must leave here. So — let me wish you all well. Fyodor Ilyich, go somewhere with me. I can't stay at home, absolutely cannot. . . . Let's go!

KULYGIN: I'm tried. I'm not going. (*Rising.*) I'm tired. Has the wife come home?

IRINA: She must have.

KULYGIN (*kissing* IRINA*'s hand*): Good-by. Tomorrow and the day after I'll rest all day long. I wish you well. (*Going.*) I'd like some tea very much. I counted on spending the evening in pleasant company and — *o, fallacem hominum spem!*[5] Accusative case exclamatory. . . .

VERSHININ: Which means I'm going by myself. (*He goes out with* KULYGIN, *whistling.*)

OLGA: My head aches, my head . . . Andrei has lost . . . the whole town is talking. . . . I'll go lie down. . . . (*Starting out of the room.*) Tomorrow I am free. . . . O Lord, how pleasant it is! Tomorrow is free, day after tomorrow is free. . . . My head aches, my head . . . (*She goes out.*)

IRINA (*alone*): They've all gone. There's nobody here.

(*In the street an accordion is heard, the* NURSE *sings a song.*)

NATASHA (*with a fur coat and cap, passes through the dining room; behind her a* MAID): I'll be home in half an hour. I'll take just a little ride. (*She goes out.*)

IRINA (*left alone, dejected*): To Moscow! To Moscow! To Moscow!

CURTAIN

## ACT III

OLGA*'s and* IRINA*'s room. To the left and to the right are beds, with screens around them. It is going on three o'clock in the morning. Offstage they are ringing the firebell for a fire that began a long time back. Plainly no one in the house has gone to bed yet.* MASHA *lies on the sofa, she wears, as usual, a black dress.* OLGA *and* ANFISA *enter.*

ANFISA: Sitting down there now under the staircase . . . I say — "If you please, come upstairs, as if," I say, "you could sit there like that!" — they are crying, "Daddy," they say, "we don't know where Daddy is. God forbid," they say, "he's burned!" They thought that up! And in the courtyard there are some people. . . . They are undressed too.

[5] (Lat.) O, the folly of human hopes!

OLGA (*taking some dresses out of the closet*): Here, this gray one — take it. . . . And this one here. . . . The blouse too . . . And take the skirt, Nursey. . . . All Kirsanoffsky Street seems to be burned down. . . . Take this. . . . Take this. . . . (*Throws the dresses for her to catch.*) The poor Vershinins were frightened. . . . Their house nearly burned up. They must spend the night here. . . . We can't let them go home. . . . At poor Fedotik's everything got burned, there's nothing left. . . .

ANFISA: You'll have to call Ferapont, Olyushka, or I can't carry . . .

OLGA: (*She rings.*) Nobody answers. . . . (*Through the door.*) Come here, whoever it is! (*Through the open door she sees a window glowing red with the fire; a fire brigade is heard passing the house.*) How frightful! And how sickening! (FERAPONT *enters.*) Here, take this and carry it downstairs. . . . Down there under the staircase are the young Kolotilin girls. . . . Give it to them. And give this. . . .

FERAPONT: Yes, miss. In the year '12, Moscow also burned. Oh my Lord God! The French were astonished.

OLGA: Go on, step along. . . .

FERAPONT: Yes, miss. (*He goes out.*)

OLGA: Nursey, dear, give everything away. We don't need anything. Give everything away! Nursey . . . I'm tired, I can barely stand on my feet. . . . The Vershinins shouldn't be allowed to go home. . . . The girls can sleep in the drawing room, and Alexander Ignatievich downstairs at the Baron's . . . Fedotik too at the Baron's, or let him stay with us in the dining room. . . . The doctor, as if he'd done it on purpose, is drunk, terribly drunk, and we mustn't send anyone to him. And Vershinin's wife too in the drawing room.

ANFISA (*wearily*): Olyushka, dear, don't you drive me away! Don't drive me away!

OLGA: You are talking nonsense, Nurse. Nobody's driving you away.

ANFISA (*laying her head on* OLGA'*s breast*): My own, my treasure, I do try, I work. . . . I'll get feeble and everybody will say: get out! And where will I go? Eighty years old. My eighty-second year. . . .

OLGA: You sit down a while, Nursey. . . . You are tired, poor thing. . . . (*Making her sit down.*) Rest, my dear good old Nurse. You look so pale!

(NATASHA *enters.*)

NATASHA: They are saying it around that we must form right off a relief society for those who have been burnt out. Why not! It's a fine idea. We must be quick to help poor people, that's the duty of the rich. Bobik and Sofotchka have just gone to sleep, they sleep as if nothing had happened. There are so many people everywhere here that anywhere you go the house is full. There's influenza in town now, I'm afraid the children may catch it.

OLGA (*not listening to her*): In this room you don't see the fire, it's peaceful here. . . .

NATASHA: Yes. . . . I must be very much disheveled. (*In front of the mirror.*) They say I have filled out. . . . And it isn't true! Not at all! And Masha's sleeping, exhausted . . . poor thing. . . . (*To* ANFISA, *coldly.*) In my presence, don't you dare sit down! Get up! Get out of here! (ANFISA *goes out; a pause.*) Why you keep this old woman I don't understand!

OLGA (*taken aback*): Excuse me, I don't understand either. . . .

NATASHA: For no reason at all she's here. She is a peasant, she should live in the country. . . . What a lot of pampering! I like in a house to have order. Useless people shouldn't be in a house. (*Stroking* OLGA*'s cheek.*) Poor dear, you are tired! Our headmistress is tired. And when my Sofotchka grows up and enters high school, I shall be afraid of you.

OLGA: I shan't be the headmistress.

NATASHA: You will be elected, Olitchka, that's decided.

OLGA: I'll decline it. I can't, I've not the strength for it. (*Drinking some water.*) You were so rude just now to Nurse. . . . Forgive me, I'm not in any condition to bear . . . It's getting all black before my eyes. . . .

NATASHA (*disturbed*): Forgive me, Olya, forgive me. . . . I didn't mean to distress you.

(MASHA *gets up, takes a pillow and goes out, angrily.*)

OLGA: Understand, my dear . . . perhaps we were brought up strangely, but I can't bear it. That kind of attitude depresses me, I get sick. . . . I'm just sick at heart!

NATASHA: Forgive me, forgive me. . . . (*Kissing her.*)

OLGA: Every rudeness, even the slightest, even a word indelicately spoken, upsets me. . . .

NATASHA: I often talk too much, it's true, but you must agree, my dear, she might very well have lived in the country.

OLGA: She's been these thirty years with us.

NATASHA: But now, though, she can't do anything. It's either that I don't understand or else you don't want to understand me. She is not up to doing any sort of work, she just sleeps and sits.

OLGA: But let her sit.

NATASHA (*surprised*): How let her sit? She's a servant nevertheless. (*Tearfully.*) I don't understand you, Olya. I have a nurse, have a wet nurse, we have a maid, a cook. . . . What do we have that old woman too for? What for?

(*Behind the scene the fire-alarm rings.*)

OLGA: I have aged ten years in this one night!

NATASHA: We must come to some sort of understanding, Olya. You are at high school, I'm at home; you have the teaching, I have the housekeeping. And if I say anything about the servants, I know what I'm saying. I know what I'm saying. . . . And by tomorrow there won't be this old thief here, this old hag. (*Stamping her foot.*) This witch . . . Don't dare cross me! Don't you dare! (*Catching herself.*) Really, if you don't move downstairs, we'll always be quarreling. It's terrible.

(KULYGIN *enters.*)

KULYGIN: Where is Masha? It's quite time to go home. The fire, they say, is subsiding. (*Stretching.*) Burnt just one section of the town, in spite of the fact that there was a wind; at first it looked as if the whole town was on fire. (*Sitting down.*) I'm tired out, Olitchka, my dear. . . . I often think if there hadn't been Masha, I'd have married you, Olitchka. You are so good. . . . I'm exhausted. (*Listening for something.*)

OLGA: What is it?

KULYGIN: As if on purpose, the doctor is drunk, he's terribly drunk. As if on purpose! (*Getting up.*) There he is coming here, I imagine . . . Do you hear? Yes, coming . . . (*Laughing.*) What a fellow, really . . . I'll hide. (*Going to the cupboard and standing in the corner.*) Such a rascal!

OLGA: For two years he hasn't been drinking and here all of a sudden he's gone and got drunk. (*Following* NATASHA *to the back of the room.*)

(TCHEBUTYKIN *enters; without staggering, is if he were sober, he walks across the room, stops, looks around, then goes to the washstand and begins to wash his hands.*)

TCHEBUTYKIN (*crossly*): The Devil take all of 'em, take — They think I'm a doctor, know how to cure any sickness, but I know absolutely nothing, I've forgotten everything I ever knew, remember nothing, absolutely nothing. (OLGA *and* NATASHA *go out, unnoticed by him.*) The Devil take it! Last Wednesday, I treated a woman at Zasip — she died, and I'm to blame for her dying. Yes . . . I knew a little something twenty-five years ago, but now I don't remember anything. Nothing. Perhaps I'm not even a man, but only give the appearance here of having hands and legs and a head; perhaps I don't even exist, and it only seems to me that I walk and eat and sleep. (*Crying.*) Oh, that I didn't exist! (*No longer crying, crossly.*) The Devil knows . . . ! Three days ago there was a conversation at the club, they were talking about Shakespeare, Voltaire . . . I hadn't read them, hadn't read them at all, but I looked as if I had read them. And the others did too, just as I did. The banality of it! The meanness! And that woman I killed Wednesday came back to me . . . And everything came back to me, and it weighed on my soul, crooked, foul, disgusting . . . I went and got drunk. . . .

(IRINA, VERSHININ *and* TUSENBACH *enter;* TUSENBACH *wears civilian clothes, new and stylish.*)

IRINA: Let's sit here. Nobody's coming here.

VERSHININ: If it were not for the soldiers, the whole town would be burnt up. Brave boys! (*Rubbing his hands with pleasure.*) Salt of the earth! Ah, what brave boys!

KULYGIN: What's the time, gentlemen?

TUSENBACH: Going on four by now. It's getting light.

IRINA: Everybody is sitting in the dining room, nobody is going out. And that Solyony of yours is sitting . . . (*To* TCHEBUTYKIN.) Doctor, you should have gone to sleep.

TCHEBUTYKIN: Not at all . . . Thank you . . . (*Combing his beard.*)

KULYGIN (*laughing*): You got a little tipsy, Ivan Romanovich! (*Slapping him on the shoulder.*) Bravo! *In vino veritas,* said the ancients.

TUSENBACH: They keep asking me to arrange a concert for the benefit of the refugees.

IRINA: Well, who is there to . . . ?

TUSENBACH: It could be arranged if we wanted to do it. Maria Sergeevna, in my opinion, plays the piano wonderfully.

KULYGIN: She does play wonderfully!

IRINA: She has forgotten how by now. It's three years since she's played. . . . Or four.

TUSENBACH: Here in this town absolutely nobody understands music, not one soul; but I, I do understand it, and on my word of honor, I assure you that Maria Sergeevna plays magnificently, almost with genius.

KULYGIN: You are right, Baron. I love her very much, I love my Masha. She's sweet.

TUSENBACH: Think of being able to play so splendidly and at the same time know quite well that nobody, nobody, understands you!

KULYGIN (*sighing*): Yes. . . . But is it proper for her to take part in a concert? (*A pause.*) Really, gentlemen, I don't know anything about that. Perhaps it would be a good thing. I must admit our director is a fine man, in fact, very fine, of the brainiest; but he has such views that . . . Of course, it's not his affair, but just the same, if you like, I might talk with him.

(TCHEBUTYKIN *is taking up a china clock in both hands and examining it.*)

VERSHININ: I got all covered with dirt at the fire — I'm not presentable. (*A pause.*) Yesterday I heard in passing that they might transfer our brigade somewhere far away. Some say to the Kingdom of Poland, others — that it looks like Chita.

TUSENBACH: I heard that too. And so what? The town will be completely empty then.

IRINA: And we shall go away!

TCHEBUTYKIN: (*He drops the clock, shattering it.*) All to pieces!

(*A pause; everyone is distressed and embarrassed.*)

KULYGIN (*picks up the pieces*): To break such a precious thing — Oh, Ivan Romanovich, Ivan Romanovich! Minus zero to you for conduct.

IRINA: That clock was our dear mother's.

TCHEBUTYKIN: Perhaps . . . Mother's, then, mother's. Perhaps I didn't break it but only seemed to break it. Perhaps it only seems to us that we exist, and we don't really. I don't know anything, nobody knows anything. (*By the door.*) What are you looking at? Natasha has an affair with Protopopov, and you don't see it. . . . There you sit and see nothing, and Natasha has an affair with Protopopov. . . . (*Singing.*) How do you like swallowing that dose . . . ?[6] (*He goes out.*)

VERSHININ: Yes. . . . (*Laughing.*) How strange all this is at bottom! (*A pause.*) When the fire began, I ran home fast; got there, looked . . . our house was unharmed and out of danger, but my two girls stood at the door in nothing but their underclothes, the mother wasn't there, people were scurrying about, horses running around, and dogs, and on my girls' faces was all that anxiety, terror, entreaty, who knows what; my heart was wrung when I saw those faces. My God, I thought, what more will these girls have to go through, in a long life! I grabbed them, ran and kept thinking one thing: What more will they have to live through in this world! (*Fire-alarm; a pause.*) I came this way and the mother was here, shouting, angry.

(MASHA *enters with a pillow and sits down on the sofa.*)

VERSHININ: And while my girls were standing at the door in nothing but their underclothes and the street was red with the fire, the noise was terrible, I reflected that something like that used to happen when the enemy made a sudden raid, plundering and burning as they went. Meanwhile what a difference there is essentially between what is and what was! And a little more time will pass, some two or three hundred years, and they will look on this life of ours now with fear and derision, everything now will seem then to be all angles and heavy and most inconvenient and strange. Oh, what a life that will be, what a life! (*Laughing.*) Forgive me, I'm philosophizing again. Allow me to continue, ladies and gentlemen. I'd like awfully to philosophize, now that I'm in such a mood for it. (*A pause.*) It's as if everybody were asleep. And so I say: What a life it will be! You can just imagine. . . . Here in town there are only three of your kind now, but in coming generations there will be more, always more and more; a time will come when everything will veer to you, they will live like you, and then, too, later on you'll get antiquated, there'll be people springing up who are better than you. . . . (*Laughing.*) I am in a most singular mood today. I want like the devil to live. . . . (*Singing.*) Unto love all ages bow, its pangs are blest. . . .

MASHA: Tram-tum-tum. . . .

VERSHININ: Tum-tum . . .

MASHA: Tra-ra-ra?

[6] (a mistranslation of the Russian *finik,* meaning "date" [the fruit], perhaps from mistaking it for *fizik,* "physicist," and assuming the latter to be cognate with the English "physic." Tchebutykin is asking, "Would you like a date?")

VERSHININ: Tra-ta-ta. (*Laughing.*)

(FEDOTIK *enters.*)

FEDOTIK (*dancing*): Burnt out, burnt out! Absolutely everything!

(*Laughter.*)

IRINA: What sort of a joke is that? Is it all gone?

FEDOTIK (*laughing*): Absolutely everything. There's nothing left. And the guitar burned, and the photography outfit burned, and all my letters. . . . And I wanted to present you with a notebook . . . it burned up too.

(SOLYONY *enters.*)

IRINA: No. Please go away, Vasili Vasilievich. You can't come in here.

SOLYONY: But why is it the Baron can and I can't?

VERSHININ: We must go, really. How's the fire?

SOLYONY: They say it's subsiding. No, it's decidedly strange to me, why is it the Baron can and I can't? (*Taking out the perfume bottle and sprinkling himself.*)

VERSHININ: Tram-tum-tum.

MASHA: Tram-tum.

VERSHININ (*laughing, to* SOLYONY): Let's go to the dining room.

SOLYONY: Very well, I'll make a note of it so. This thought could be made more clear, but 'twould annoy the geese, I fear. . . . (*Looking at* TUSENBACH.) Chick, chick, chick. . . . (*He goes out with* VERSHININ *and* FEDOTIK.)

IRINA: How that Solyony has smoked things up. (*With surprise.*) The Baron is asleep! Baron! Baron!

TUSENBACH (*waking up*): I'm tired, however. . . . The brickyard. . . . I'm not saying this in my sleep, for it's a fact that I'll soon be going to the brickyard to start work. . . . It's already been discussed. (*To* IRINA, *tenderly.*) You are so pale, beautiful, bewitching. . . . It seems to me your paleness brightens the dark air like light. . . . You are sad, you are not satisfied with life. . . . Oh, come along with me, let's go to work together!

MASHA: Nikolai Lvovich, do go on out of here!

TUSENBACH (*laughing*): You here? I didn't see you. (*Kissing* IRINA*'s hand.*) Good-by, I'm going. . . . I'm looking at you now and am reminded of how long ago once on your saint's day you were all so gay and happy, talking of the joy of work. . . . And what a happy life I dreamed of then! Where is it? (*Kissing her hand.*) You have tears in your eyes. Go to bed. . . . It's getting light now . . . morning has begun. . . . If only it were granted me to give my life for you!

MASHA: Nikolai Lvovich, go on! Why, really, what . . .

TUSENBACH: I'm going. . . . (*He goes out.*)

MASHA (*lying down*): Are you asleep, Fyodor?

KULYGIN: Eh?

MASHA: You ought to go home.

KULYGIN: My darling Masha, my dear Masha. . . .

IRINA: She's tired. . . . You ought to let her rest, Fedya.

KULYGIN: I'm going right away. . . . My good wife, darling . . . I love you, my one and only. . . .

MASHA (*bored and cross*): *Amo, amas, amat, amamus, amatis, amant.*[7]

KULYGIN (*laughing*): No, really, she's amazing. I've been married to you for seven years; but it seems as if we'd married only yesterday. Word of honor! No, really, you are an amazing woman. I am content, I am content, I am content!

MASHA: Bored, bored, bored. . . . (*She sits up, and speaks sitting.*) It just won't go out of my head. . . . It's simply shocking. It's there like a nail in my head. I can't stay silent. I mean about Andrei. . . . He's mortgaged this house to the bank and his wife grabbed all the money, but the house belongs not just to him, but to the four of us! He ought to know that if he's a decent man.

KULYGIN: What do you care, Masha! Why should you? Andrusha is in debt all round, well, God reward him!

MASHA: Anyhow it's shocking. (*She lies back down.*)

KULYGIN: You and I are not poor. I work, I go to the high school, and then give private lessons. . . . I'm an honest man. Simple. . . . *Omnia mea mecum porto,*[8] as they say.

MASHA: I don't need anything. But injustice makes me furious. (*A pause.*) Go on, Fyodor!

KULYGIN (*kissing her*): You are tired, rest about half an hour, and I'll sit and wait out there. Sleep. . . . (*Going.*) I am content, I am content, I am content. (*He goes out.*)

IRINA: How small our Andrei has grown, how he has dried up and aged beside that woman! There was a time when he was preparing for a professorship, and yesterday he was bragging that at last he could become a member of the District Board. He a member of the board and Protopopov chairman. . . . The whole town's talking, is laughing, and he's the only one who knows nothing and sees nothing. And now, everybody has rushed off to the fire, but he sits there in his room and pays not the least attention to it. He just plays the violin. (*Nervously.*) Oh, it's awful, awful, awful! (*Crying.*) I can't, I can't bear any more! . . . I can't – I can't!

(OLGA *enters. She tidies up her dressing table.*)

IRINA (*sobbing aloud*): Cast me out, cast me out, I can't stand any more! . . .

OLGA (*alarmed*): What is it, what is it? Darling!

IRINA (*sobbing*): Where? Where is it all gone? Where is it? Oh, my God, my God! I've forgotten everything, I've forgotten . . . it's muddled in my

[7] (conjugation of the present indicative tense of the Latin verb "to love": I love, you love, he loves, etc.)

[8] (Lat.) All I have I carry with me

head. . . . I don't remember what in Italian *window* is, or the ceiling there. . . . I'm forgetting everything, every day forgetting, and life slips away and will never return, never, we'll never go to Moscow. . . . I can see we'll never go.

OLGA: Darling, darling. . . .

IRINA (*restraining herself*): Oh, I'm miserable. . . . I can't work and won't work. I'm sick of it, sick of it! I was a telegraph operator, and now have a place with the Town Board, and hate and despise everything they give me to do. . . . I'm going on twenty-four and have already been working a long time, and my brain's drying up, I'm getting thin, losing my looks, getting old, and there's nothing, nothing — no satisfaction of any kind — and time is passing, and it all seems to be moving away from any real, beautiful life, all moving away farther and farther into some abyss. . . . I'm in despair, and how I'm alive, how it is I haven't killed myself, I can't understand. . . .

OLGA: Don't cry, my own little girl, don't cry. . . .

IRINA: I am not crying, not crying. . . . I'm sick of it. . . . Now look — I am not crying any more. I'm sick of it. . . . I'm sick of it!

OLGA: Darling, I'm telling you as a sister, as a friend, if you want my advice, marry the Baron!

(IRINA *weeps silently.*)

OLGA: Why, you respect him, you value him highly. It's true he's not good-looking, but he's so decent and clean. . . . Why, one doesn't marry for love but to do one's duty. At least, I think so, and I would marry without being in love. At any rate I'd marry anyone who proposed to me so long as he was an honorable man. I'd marry even an old man. . . .

IRINA: I kept expecting us to move to Moscow; there I'd meet my real beloved, I dreamed of him, loved him. But it turned out just foolishness, just foolishness! . . .

OLGA (*embracing her sister*): My dear, lovely sister, I understand it all; when Baron Nikolai Lvovich left the military service and came to see us in civilian clothes, he seemed to me so homely that I even cried. He asked, "Why are you crying?" How could I tell him! But if God should grant he married you, I'd be happy. Now, that's different, quite different!

(NATASHA *crosses the stage from the right door to the left, without speaking, a candle in her hand.*)

MASHA (*sitting up*): She walks as if she had been the one to start the fire.

OLGA: Masha, you are silly! The silliest one in our family is you. Forgive me, please.

(*A pause.*)

MASHA: I want to confess, my dear sisters. I'm tired in my soul. I'll confess to you and then to nobody else, never. . . . I'll say it this minute. (*Quietly.*) It's my secret, but you must know everything. . . . I can't be silent. . . . (*A pause.*) I love, love . . . I love that man. . . . You just saw him. . . . Well, there it is. In one word, I love Vershinin. . . .

OLGA (*going behind her screen*): Stop that. At any rate I'm not hearing.

MASHA: What is there to do about it? (*Clutching her head.*) At first he seemed to me strange, then I felt sorry for him. . . . Then I began to love him . . . began to love him with his voice, his words, his misfortunes, his two girls. . . .

OLGA (*behind the screen*): I'm not hearing you at any rate. Whatever silly things you say, at any rate I'm not hearing you!

MASHA: Oh, Olya, you are silly. I love – such, that is to say, is my fate. That is to say my lot is such. . . . And he loves me. . . . All that is frightening. Yes? Is it wrong? (*Taking* IRINA *by the hand and drawing her to her.*) Oh, my darling . . . how are we going to live our life, what's to become of us? . . . When one reads some novel, all this seems old and all of it so understandable, but when you fall in love yourself, you begin to see that nobody knows anything and everybody must decide for himself. . . . My darlings, my sisters. . . . I confessed to you, now I'll be silent. . . . I'll be now like Gogol's madman . . . silence . . . silence. . . .

(ANDREI *enters, followed by* FERAPONT.)

ANDREI (*annoyed*): What do you want? I don't understand.

FERAPONT (*standing in the door, impatiently*): Andrei Sergeevich, I have already told you ten times.

ANDREI: First, I am not Andrei Sergeevich to you but Your Excellency!

FERAPONT: The firemen, Your Excellentness, ask your permission to go to the river through your garden. As it is, they are driving round and round – it's pure punishment.

ANDREI: Very well. Tell them, very well. (FERAPONT *goes out.*) That's enough of them. Where's Olga? (OLGA *comes out from behind the screen.*) I've come to ask you to give me the key to the cupboard. I've lost mine. You have one of the little keys. (OLGA *gives him the key without speaking.* IRINA *goes behind her screen; a pause.*) And what a tremendous fire! It's starting to die down now. The devil take it, that Ferapont's made me lose my temper. I said a stupid thing to him. . . . Your Excellency. . . . (*A pause.*) But why are you silent, Olya? (*A pause.*) It's high time to stop this silliness and stop pouting for no reason at all. . . . You are here, Masha, Irina's here, well, that's fine – let's have it out once and for all. What have you got against me? Now what?

OLGA: Let it rest, Andrusha. Tomorrow we'll have it out. (*Anxiously.*) What a night of torment!

ANDREI (*he is very much confused*): Don't be upset. I ask you absolutely in cold blood: what have you got against me? Speak right out.

VERSHININ'S VOICE: Tram-tum-tum!

MASHA (*rising, in a loud voice*): Tra-ta-ta! (*To* OLGA.) Good-by, Olya, God be with you! (*She goes behind the screen, kisses* IRINA.) Sleep well. . . . Good-by, Andrei. Go on away, they are tired. . . . Tomorrow you will have it out. (*She goes out.*)

OLGA: Indeed, Andrusha, let's put it off till tomorrow. . . . (*She goes behind her screen.*) It's time to go to sleep.

ANDREI: I'll just say it and go. Right away. . . . In the first place, you have something against Natasha, my wife, and that I have noticed from the very day of my wedding. Natasha is a splendid, honest person, straightforward, and honorable – in my opinion. I love and respect my wife, understand, I respect her and demand that others respect her too. I repeat, she is an honest, honorable person, and all your dissatisfactions, excuse me, are simply caprices. . . . (*A pause.*) In the second place, you seem to be angry because of the fact that I am not a professor, don't occupy myself with learning. But I serve in the Zemstvo, I am a member of the District Board, and this service of mine I consider just as sacred and lofty as service to learning. I'm a member of the District Board and I'm proud of it, if you want to know. . . . (*A pause.*) In the third place, I have something else to say . . . : I mortgaged the house without asking your permission. . . . Of that I am guilty, yes, and ask you to forgive me. I was forced to it by debts. . . . Thirty-five thousand. . . . I don't play cards any more, gave it up long ago, but the chief thing I can say in my own justification, is that you – girls, as of the privileged sex, you receive a pension, while I didn't have . . . my earnings, so to speak. . . . (*A pause.*)

KULYGIN (*at the door*): Masha not here? (*Perturbed.*) But where is she? That's strange. . . . (*He goes out.*)

ANDREI: They don't listen. Natasha is a superior, honest person. (*Walks up and down the stage in silence, then stops.*) When I married, I thought we should be happy . . . everybody happy . . . but, my God . . . ! (*Crying.*) My dear sisters, darling sisters, don't believe me, don't believe . . . (*He goes out.*)

KULYGIN (*at the door, anxiously*): Where is Masha? Masha's not here? What an astonishing business! (*He goes out.*)

(*Fire-alarm; the stage is empty.*)

IRINA (*behind the screen*): Olya! Who is that knocking on the floor?

OLGA: It's the doctor, Ivan Romanovich. He's drunk.

IRINA: What a torn-up night! (*A pause.*) Olya! (*Looking out from behind the screen.*) Did you hear? They are taking the brigade from us, transferring it somewhere far away.

OLGA: That's only a rumor.

IRINA: We'll be left alone then. . . . Olya!

OLGA: Well?

IRINA: Darling, precious, I respect, I value the Baron, he's a marvelous person, I'll marry him, I consent, only let's go to Moscow! I beg you, let's go! There's nothing in the world better than Moscow! Let's go, Olya! Let's go!

CURTAIN

## ACT IV

*An old garden in front of the* PROZOROFFS' *house. A long alley of fir trees, at the end of which a river is seen. On the other side of the river, a wood. To the right a terrace of the house and on it a table with bottles and glasses; you can see they have just been drinking champagne. Twelve o'clock noon. Now and then on their way from the street to the river, people cross the garden; four or five soldiers pass that way, walking fast.* TCHEBUTYKIN, *in an amiable mood, which does not leave him during the entire Act, sits in an easy chair, in the garden, waiting to be called; he wears a military cap and carries a stick.* IRINA, KULYGIN *with a decoration around his neck, with no mustache, and* TUSENBACH, *are standing on the terrace, saying good-by to* FEDOTIK *and* RODAY, *who are going down the steps; both officers are in campaign uniform.*

TUSENBACH (*exchanging kisses with* FEDOTIK): You are a good fellow, we lived like good friends. (*Exchanging kisses with* RODAY.) Once again. . . . Good-by, my dear boy. . . .

IRINA: Till we meet again.

FEDOTIK: It's not meet again, but good-by, we shall never meet again.

KULYGIN: Who knows! (*Wiping his eyes, smiling.*) There, I'm beginning to cry too.

IRINA: Some day we'll run across each other.

FEDOTIK: In ten or fifteen years maybe? But by then we'll scarcely know each other, we'll greet each other coldly. . . . (*Taking a snapshot.*) Stand still. . . . Once more, for the last time.

RODAY (*embracing* TUSENBACH): We won't meet again. . . . (*Kissing* IRINA'*s hand.*) Thank you for everything, for everything!

FEDOTIK (*vexed*): Oh, wait a little!

TUSENBACH: God grant we meet. Write us though. Without fail write.

RODAY (*casting a glance around the garden*): Good-by, trees! (*Shouting.*) Yoo hoo! (*A pause.*) Good-by, echo!

KULYGIN: I am afraid you'll marry there in Poland. . . . The Polish wife will embrace you and say: "*Kochany!*" (*Laughing.*)

FEDOTIK (*looking at his watch*): There's less than an hour left. Out of our battery only Solyony is going on the barge, we are with the rank and file.

Three battery divisions are going today, tomorrow three more — and quiet and peace will reign in the town. . . .

TUSENBACH: And terrible boredom.

RODAY: And where is Maria Sergeevna?

KULYGIN: Masha is in the garden.

FEDOTIK: We must say good-by to her.

RODAY: Good-by, I must go or I'll be crying. . . . (*He hurriedly embraces* TUSENBACH *and* KULYGIN, *kisses* IRINA*'s hand.*) It was fine living here.

FEDOTIK (*to* KULYGIN): This is a memento for you. . . . A notebook with a pencil. . . . We'll go this way to the river. . . . (*They move off, both look back.*)

RODAY (*shouts*): Yoo hoo!

KULYGIN (*shouts*): Good-by!

(*At the rear of the stage* FEDOTIK *and* RODAY *meet* MASHA *and bid her good-by. She walks away with them.*)

IRINA: They are gone. . . . (*Sitting down on the bottom step of the terrace.*)

TCHEBUTYKIN: And forgot to say good-by to me.

IRINA: And what about you?

TCHEBUTYKIN: And I forgot too somehow. Anyway I'll soon see them, I'm leaving tomorrow. Yes. . . . One more short day is left. In a year they will retire me, I'll come back here and live out my little span near you. Just one short year is left before my pension. (*He puts one newspaper in his pocket and takes out another.*) I'll come here to you and change my life from the very roots. I'll become so quiet, right — right-minded, respectable.

IRINA: And you really should change your life, dovey. You should somehow.

TCHEBUTYKIN: Yes, I feel so. (*Singing softly.*) Ta-ra-ra-boom-de-aye. . . . Sit on a curb I may. . . .

KULYGIN: You're incorrigible, Ivan Romanovich! You're incorrigible!

TCHEBUTYKIN: Now then, if you'd only teach me! Then I'd be reformed.

IRINA: Fyodor has shaved off his mustache. I can't bear to look at him.

KULYGIN: Why not?

TCHEBUTYKIN: I could say what your physiognomy looks like now, but I can't.

KULYGIN: Well! It's the accepted thing, it is *modus vivendi.* Our director shaved off his mustache, and as soon as I became inspector, I shaved clean too. Nobody likes it, but that's all the same to me. I am content. I may be with a mustache, or without a mustache, but I'm equally content. . . . (*Sitting down.*)

(*At the rear of the stage* ANDREI *passes, wheeling a baby-carriage with a child asleep in it.*)

IRINA: Ivan Romanovich, my own darling, I am terribly disturbed. You were on the boulevard yesterday, tell me what happened there?

TCHEBUTYKIN: What happened? Nothing. Fiddlesticks. (*Reading the newspaper.*) All the same!

KULYGIN: What they are saying is that Solyony and the Baron met yesterday on the boulevard near the theatre. . . .

TUSENBACH: Stop it! Well, what really. . . . (*With a wave of his hand he goes into the house.*)

KULYGIN: Near the theatre . . . Solyony began picking on the Baron, and he wouldn't tolerate it, he said something insulting. . . .

TCHEBUTYKIN: I don't know. It's all nonsense.

KULYGIN: In a certain theological seminary a teacher wrote on a composition paper, "Nonsense" and the pupil read "consensus" – thought it was written in Latin. (*Laughing.*) Amazingly funny. It's said that Solyony is in love with Irina, and that he's begun to hate the Baron. . . . That's understandable. Irina is a very nice girl. She even resembles Masha, just as thoughtful. It's merely that you have a gentle character, Irina. Though Masha, too, has a very fine character. I love her, my Masha.

(*At the rear of the garden offstage:* "Yoo, hoo!")

IRINA (*shivering*): Somehow everything frightens me today. (*A pause.*) I have everything all ready, after dinner I'm sending off my things. The Baron and I are getting married tomorrow, and tomorrow we are leaving for the brickyard, and day after tomorrow I'll be at the school, a new life is beginning. Somehow God will help me! When I passed my teacher's examination I cried for pure joy . . . so happy. (*A pause.*) The cart will soon be here for my things. . . .

KULYGIN: That's all very well, only somehow it's not serious. Just ideas – and very little seriousness. However, I wish you luck with all my heart.

TCHEBUTYKIN (*tenderly*): My darling, my dear child. . . . My treasure. . . . You have gone far away. I can't catch up with you. I'm left behind, like a bird of passage that has grown old, that can't fly. Fly on, my dears, fly on and God be with you! (*A pause.*) It's too bad, Fyodor Ilyich, you shaved off your mustache.

KULYGIN: That'll do from you! (*Sighing.*) Well, today the officers are leaving and everything will go on again as of old. Whatever they may say, Masha is a good, honest woman and I love her very much and I am thankful for my fate. People's fate differs. . . . In the excise office here a certain Kozyroff works. He went to school with me, was expelled from the fifth class at high school because he just couldn't understand *ut consecutivum.*[9] Now he is terribly poor, ill, and when we meet I say to him: "Greetings, *ut consecutivum!*" Yes, he says, that's it, *consecutivum* . . . and then coughs. . . . And here I am, all my life I've been successful, I am happy, I have the Order of Stanislav, Second Degree, and am teaching

[9] (a grammatical term for a certain syntactical construction in Latin)

others myself now that *ut consecutivum.* Of course, I am a clever man, cleverer than many others, but happiness doesn't consist in that. . . .

(*In the house they are playing "The Maiden's Prayer" on the piano.*)

IRINA: And tomorrow evening I won't be hearing that "Maiden's Prayer" any more, and won't be meeting Protopopov. . . . (*A pause.*) And Protopopov is sitting there in the drawing room now; he came again today. . . .

KULYGIN: The headmistress has not come yet?

IRINA: No. They have sent for her. If only you knew how hard it is for me to live here alone, without Olya. . . . She lives at the high school; she's the headmistress, busy all day long with her duties, and I'm alone, I am bored with nothing to do, and the very room I live in is hateful. . . . So I have made up my mind: If it isn't my lot to be in Moscow, then let it be so. That's my lot. There's nothing to be done. All is God's will, that's the truth. Nikolai Lvovich proposed to me. . . . Well, then? I thought it over and made up my mind. He is a good man, it is really amazing how good. . . . And suddenly as if wings had grown on my soul, I grew happier, relieved, and felt once more the desire for work, work. . . . Except that something happened yesterday, there's something hidden that's hanging over me. . . .

TCHEBUTYKIN: Consensus. Nonsense.

NATASHA (*at the window*): The headmistress!

KULYGIN: The headmistress has arrived. Let's go. (*He goes with* IRINA *into the house.*)

TCHEBUTYKIN (*reading the newspaper, softly singing to himself*): Ta-ra-ra-boom-de-aye. . . . Sit on the curb I may. . . .

(MASHA *approaches; in the background* ANDREI *is seen pushing the baby-carriage.*)

MASHA: There he sits, all settled. . . .

TCHEBUTYKIN: And what?

MASHA (*sitting down*): Nothing. . . . (*A pause.*) Did you love my mother?

TCHEBUTYKIN: Very much.

MASHA: And did she love you?

TCHEBUTYKIN (*after a pause*): That I no longer remember.

MASHA: Is "mine" here? Our cook Marfa used to talk about her policeman like that: mine. Is "mine" here?

TCHEBUTYKIN: Not yet.

MASHA: When you get happiness in snatches, in bits, and you lose it, like me, then little by little you harden, you grow bitter. (*Pointing to her breast.*) Right here I'm boiling. . . . (*Looking at her brother* ANDREI *pushing the baby-carriage.*) There's Andrei, our little brother. . . . All our hopes gone. . . . Once upon a time thousands of people were hoisting a bell, a lot of effort and money were spent, and then suddenly it fell and broke. Suddenly for neither one reason nor another. The same with Andrei.

ANDREI: And when will they finally quiet down in the house? Such noise!

TCHEBUTYKIN: Soon. (*Looking at his watch.*) I have a very old watch, with chimes. . . . (*Winding the watch; it chimes.*) The first, second, and fifth batteries are going at one o'clock sharp. (*A pause.*) And I tomorrow.

ANDREI: For good?

TCHEBUTYKIN: I don't know. I might return in a year. Though the devil knows . . . it's all the same. . . .

(*Somewhere far off a harp and violin are playing.*)

ANDREI: The town will be dead. As if they had covered it with a cowl. (*A pause.*) Something happened yesterday near the theatre; everybody is talking about it, but I don't know what it was.

TCHEBUTYKIN: Nothing. Nonsense. Solyony began to pick on the Baron and he lost his temper and insulted him, and it got finally to the point where Solyony had to challenge him to a duel. (*Looks at his watch.*) It's time now, I believe. At half-past twelve, in the State forest there, the one we see from here, beyond the river. . . . Piff — paff. (*Laughing.*) Solyony imagines he is Lermontov and even writes verses. Now jokes are jokes, but it is the third duel for him.

MASHA: For whom?

TCHEBUTYKIN: For Solyony.

MASHA: And for the Baron?

TCHEBUTYKIN: What for the Baron?

(*A pause.*)

MASHA: I'm all confused in the head. All the same, I say it shouldn't be allowed. He might wound the Baron or even kill him.

TCHEBUTYKIN: The Baron is a good man but one baron more, one less — isn't it all the same? Let them! All the same! (*Beyond the garden there are shouts:* "Yoo hoo." *Answering the shout.*) You can wait. (*To* MASHA.) That's Skvortzoff shouting, the second. He's sitting in a boat.

(*A pause.*)

ANDREI: To my mind either to engage in a duel or to be present at one even in the capacity of doctor, is simply immoral.

TCHEBUTYKIN: That only seems so. We are not here, there is nothing in the world, we don't exist, but it only seems that we exist. . . . And isn't it all the same!

MASHA: Just like that . . . all day long they talk, talk. . . . (*Going.*) To live in such a climate, be afraid it will snow any minute, and still to have these conversations — (*Stopping.*) I'm not going into the house, I can't. . . . When Vershinin comes let me know — (*She goes down the alley.*)

And the birds of passage are flying already. . . . (*Looking up.*) Swans or geese. . . . My dear ones, my happy ones — ! (*She goes out.*)

ANDREI: Our house will be empty. The officers will go, you will go, my sister will be married, and I'll be left alone in the house.

TCHEBUTYKIN: And your wife?

(FERAPONT *enters with some papers.*)

ANDREI: A wife is a wife. She is honest, decent, well — kind, but along with all that there's something in her that reduces her to the level of some sort of petty, blind, coarse animal. In any case, she's not a human being. I say this to you as to a friend, the only man I can open my soul to. I love Natasha, it's true, but at times she seems to me amazingly vulgar, and then I lose my wits, I don't understand, what for or why, I love her so or, at least, did love. . . .

TCHEBUTYKIN (*getting up*): Brother, I'm going away tomorrow, we may never see each other again, so here is my advice to you. You know, put on your hat, take a walking-stick in your hands and be off — Be off, and go, go without looking back. And the farther you get the better.

(SOLYONY *walks by at the rear of the stage with two officers; seeing* TCHEBUTYKIN *he turns toward him; the officers walk on.)*

SOLYONY: Doctor, it's time! Half-past twelve. (*Greeting* ANDREI.)

TCHEBUTYKIN: Directly. I've had enough of you all. (*To* ANDREI.) If anybody asks for me, Andrusha, say that I — directly . . . (*Sighing.*) Oho-ho-ho —

SOLYONY (*starting off with* TCHEBUTYKIN): Quick as a flash the bear made a dash — Why are you grunting, old man?

TCHEBUTYKIN: Get out!

SOLYONY: How's your health?

TCHEBUTYKIN (*angrily*): Smooth as butter.

SOLYONY: The old man is needlessly upset. I'll indulge myself a little, I'll only wing him like a snipe. (*Takes out the perfume and sprinkles it on his hands.*) There, I've poured a whole bottle out today and they still smell. My hands smell of a corpse. (*A pause.*) So . . . Do you remember the poem? "And, rebellious, he seeks the storm, as if in storms were peace." . . .

TCHEBUTYKIN: Yes. Quick as a flash, the bear made a dash! (*He goes out with* SOLYONY.)

(*Shouts are heard:* "Yoo hoo!" ANDREI *and* FERAPONT *enter.*)

FERAPONT: The papers to sign. . . .

ANDREI (*nervously*): Leave me alone! Leave me! I beg of you! (*He walks away with the baby-carriage.*)

FERAPONT: But that's what papers are for, so they can be signed. (*He goes to the rear of the stage.*)

(*Enter* IRINA *and* TUSENBACH, TUSENBACH *in a straw hat,* KULYGIN *crosses the stage, calling* "Ah-oo, Masha, Ah-oo.")

TUSENBACH: That seems to be the only man in town who's glad the officers are leaving.

IRINA: That's understandable. (*A pause.*) Our town will be empty now.

TUSENBACH: Dear, I'll come right back.

IRINA: Where are you going?

TUSENBACH: I have to go to town, then . . . to see my comrades off.

IRINA: It's not true. . . . Nikolai, why are you so distraught today? (*A pause.*) What happened yesterday near the theatre?

TUSENBACH (*with an impatient gesture*): In an hour I'll be back and will be with you again. (*Kissing her hand.*) My beloved. . . . (*Looking into her face.*) It's five years now I've loved you, and somehow I can't get used to it, and you seem always more beautiful to me. What lovely, wonderful hair! What eyes! I'll take you away tomorrow, we will work, we'll be rich, my dreams will come true. You shall be happy. Only there is one thing, one thing: You don't love me.

IRINA: That's not in my power! I'll be your wife, faithful and obedient, but it's not love, what is there to do! (*Crying.*) I have never been in love — not once in my life. Oh, I've dreamed so of love, I've dreamed of it a long time now, day and night, but my soul is like some fine piano that's locked and the key is lost. (*A pause.*) You have a restless look.

TUSENBACH: I haven't slept all night. There is nothing in my life so terrible that it could frighten me, and only that lost key tortures my soul — won't let me sleep. Say something to me. (*A pause.*) Say something to me. . . .

IRINA: What? What shall I say? What?

TUSENBACH: Something.

IRINA: That's enough! That's enough!

(*A pause.*)

TUSENBACH: What nothings sometimes in life, what foolish trifles will take on meaning suddenly, for no reason at all. You laugh at them as you've always done, you consider them nothings, and yet you go on and feel that you haven't the strength to stop. Oh, let's not talk about that! I feel gay. I see these firs, maples, birches now as if I were seeing them for the first time and they are all looking at me curiously and waiting. What beautiful trees and what a beautiful life there should be under them! (*A shout:* "Yoo hoo!") I must go. It's time. . . . There's a tree that's dead, but it still waves with the others in the wind. So it seems to me even if I die, I'll still share in life somehow or other. Good-by, my dearest. . . . (*Kissing her hands.*) The papers you gave me are lying on my table, under the calendar.

IRINA: But I'm going with you.

TUSENBACH (*alarmed*): No, no! (*Going quickly, stopping in the alley.*) Irina!

IRINA: What?

TUSENBACH (*not knowing what to say*): I didn't drink any coffee today. Tell them, so that they'll make me some. . . . (*He goes quickly out.*)

(IRINA *stands thinking, then goes to the rear of the stage and sits down in the swing.* ANDREI *comes in with the baby-carriage;* FERAPONT *appears.*)

FERAPONT: But Andrei Sergeevich, the papers aren't mine, they are official. I didn't think them up.

ANDREI: Oh, where is it, where is gone my past, when I was young and gay and clever, when my dreams and thoughts were full of grace, and the present and future bright with hope? Why is it that when we have barely begun to live we grow dull, gray, uninteresting, lazy, indifferent, useless, unhappy. . . . Our town has been in existence now for two hundred years, a hundred thousand people living in it, and there's not one who's not just like the others, not one that's outstanding either in the past or in the present, not one scholar, not one artist, not one who's even faintly remarkable, and would arouse envy or any passionate desire to imitate him. They just eat, drink, sleep, and then die. . . . Others are born and they, too, eat, drink, sleep and to keep from sinking into the torpor of boredom, vary their lives with foul gossip, vodka, cards, chicanery, and the wives deceive the husbands, while the husbands lie, pretend not to see anything, hear anything, and an unavoidably banal influence weighs on the children, and the divine spark dies in them and they become just as pitiful, identical corpses as their fathers and mothers were. . . . (*To* FERAPONT, *crossly.*) What do you want?

FERAPONT: Hey? Papers to sign.

ANDREI: I've had enough of you.

FERAPONT (*handing over the paper*): Just now the doorman from the State Chamber was saying . . . It appears he says, this winter in Petersburg there was a frost of two hundred degrees.

ANDREI: The present is hateful, but on the other hand, when I think of the future — Oh, how good it is! I begin to feel so easy, so free; and in the distance a light dawns, I see freedom, I see how my children and I are freed from idleness, from kvass, from goose with cabbage, from naps after dinner, from despicable sloth. . . .

FERAPONT: Two thousand people were frozen, it appears. The people, they say, were horrified. It was either in Petersburg, or it was in Moscow — I can't remember.

ANDREI (*seized with a tender feeling*): My dear sisters, my wonderful sisters (*Tearfully.*) Masha, my sister. . . .

NATASHA (*in the window*): Who is it talking so loud out here? Is is you, Andrusha? You will wake up Sofie. *Il ne faut pas faire du bruit, la Sofie est dormie déjà. Vous êtes un ours.*[10] (*Getting angry.*) If you want to talk,

[10] (Fr.) You mustn't make so much noise, Sophie is already asleep. You are a bear.

give the carriage and child to somebody else. Ferapont, take the carriage from your master.

FERAPONT: Yes, ma'am. (*He takes the carriage.*)

ANDREI (*embarrassed*): I'm speaking low.

NATASHA (*behind the window, caressing her child*): Bobik! Mischievous Bobik! Naughty Bobik!

ANDREI (*glancing through the papers*): Very well, I'll look through them and sign what's necessary, and you can take them back to the Board. . . . (*He goes into the house, reading the papers;* FERAPONT *pushes the baby-carriage toward the rear of the garden.*)

NATASHA (*behind the window*): Bobik, what is your Mama's name? Darling, darling! And who is this? This is Aunt Olya. Say to Auntie: "How do you do, Olya!"

(*Some wandering musicians, a man and a girl, begin to play a violin and a harp;* VERSHININ, OLGA *and* ANFISA *emerge from the house, and listen quietly for a moment.* IRINA *joins them.*)

OLGA: Our garden's like a lot opening into several streets, they walk and drive through it. Nurse, give these musicians something!

ANFISA (*giving money to the musicians*): Good-by, my dear souls! (*The musicians bow and go away.*) Hard lives they have! When you're full you don't play. (*To* IRINA.) Good morning, Irisha! (*Kissing her.*) M-m-m-m, child, how I live! How I live! At the high school in a Government apartment, with Olyushka – God has granted me that for my old age. Not since I was born, sinner that I am, have I lived so. . . . A large apartment, the Government's, and a whole room for me and a little bed. All the Government's. I wake up in the night and – Oh Lord, Mother of God, there's nobody happier than I am.

VERSHININ (*looking at his watch*): We are going now, Olga Sergeevna. It's time. (*A pause.*) I wish you everything, everything. . . . Where's Maria Sergeevna?

IRINA: She's somewhere in the garden. I'll go look for her.

VERSHININ: Kindly, I'm in a hurry.

ANFISA: I'll go, too, and look for her. (*Calling.*) Mashenka. Ah, oo-oo! (*Going away with* IRINA *to the rear of the garden.*) Ah, oo-oo! Ah, oo-oo!

VERSHININ: Everything has its end. And here we are parting. (*Looking at his watch.*) The town gave our company a sort of lunch, we drank champagne, the Mayor made a speech, I ate and listened, but in my heart I was here with you all – (*Looking around the garden.*) I've grown used to you. . . .

OLGA: Are we ever to see each other again?

VERSHININ: Most likely not. (*A pause.*) My wife and my two girls are leaving here in about two months; please, if anything happens, if anything is needed. . . .

OLGA: Yes, yes, of course. Be sure of that. (*A pause.*) By tomorrow there won't be an officer in town; it will all be a memory and for us, of course, a new life will begin. . . . (*A pause.*) Everything turns out not as we'd like to have it. I didn't want to be a headmistress and yet I became one. Which means we are not to be in Moscow.

VERSHININ: Well. . . . Thank you for everything. Forgive me, if anything was not quite. . . . Much, much too much, I've talked – forgive me for that, too, don't bear me any grudge.

OLGA (*wiping her eyes*): Now why doesn't Masha come. . . .

VERSHININ: What else can I say to you as we part? What shall I philosophize about? . . . (*Laughing.*) Life is difficult. It presents itself to many of us as blank and hopeless, and yet, one must admit, it gets always clearer and easier, and the day is not far off, apparently, when it will be wholly bright. (*Looking at his watch.*) It's time for me to go, it's time! Once humanity was occupied with wars, filling its whole existence with marches, invasions, conquests, whereas now all of that is outlived, leaving behind it an enormous empty space which so far there is nothing to fill; humanity is searching passionately and, of course, will find it. Ah, if only it were quicker! (*A pause.*) You know, if culture were added to industry and industry to culture. . . . (*Looking at his watch.*) However, it's time for me. . . .

OLGA: There she comes.

(MASHA *enters.*)

VERSHININ: I came to say good-by. . . .

(OLGA *moves a little away so as not to disturb their farewell.*)

MASHA (*looking into his face*): Good-by. . . . (*A long kiss.*)

OLGA: Now, now. . . .

(MASHA *sobs violently.*)

VERSHININ: Write to me. . . . Don't forget me! Let me go . . . it's time. . . . Olga Sergeevna, take her, I'm all ready – it's time . . . late – (*Deeply moved, he kisses* OLGA'S *hand, then embraces* MASHA *again and goes quickly out.*)

OLGA: There, Masha! Stop, darling! . . .

(KULYGIN *enters.*)

KULYGIN (*embarrassed*): No matter, let her cry, let her. . . . My good Masha, my kind Masha. . . . You are my wife and I am happy whatever happens. . . . I don't complain. . . . I don't make you a single reproach. And here's Olga to witness. . . . We'll begin to live again as we used to, and I won't say one word to you, not a breath. . . .

MASHA (*stifling her sobs*): By the curved seashore a green oak, a golden chain upon that oak. . . . A golden chain upon that oak. . . . I'm going out of my mind. . . . By the curved seashore . . . a green oak. . . .

OLGA: Be calm, Masha. . . . Be calm. . . . Give her some water.

MASHA: I am not crying any more.

KULYGIN: She is not crying now. . . . She's good. . . .

(*A shot is heard, faintly, from a distance.*)

MASHA: By the curved seashore a green oak, a golden chain upon that oak. . . . The cat's green . . . the oak's green. . . . I am mixing it up. . . . (*Taking a drink of water.*) My life is a failure. I don't want anything now. I'll soon be calm. It's all the same. . . . What does it mean: "By the curved seashore"? Why does this word keep running through my head? My thoughts are all mixed up.

(IRINA *enters.*)

OLGA: Be calm, Masha. Now, that's a good girl. . . . Let's go in. . . .

MASHA (*angrily*): I'm not going in there. (*Sobbing, but checking herself at once.*) I don't go in the house any more, so I won't do it now.

IRINA: Let's sit down together just quietly. Well, tomorrow I'm going away. . . .

(*A pause.*)

KULYGIN: In the third grade yesterday I took this mustache and beard from a boy, see — (*Putting on the mustache and beard.*) I look like the German teacher. . . . (*Laughing.*) Isn't that so? Funny, these boys. . . .

MASHA: Really you do look like your German.

OLGA (*laughing*): Yes.

(MASHA *weeps.*)

IRINA: There, Masha!

KULYGIN: A lot like. . . .

(NATASHA *enters.*)

NATASHA (*to the maid*): What? Protopopov will sit with Sofotchka, Mikhail Ivanovich, and let Andrei Sergeevich wheel Bobik. There's so much bother with children. . . . (*To* IRINA.) Irina, you are going away tomorrow — it's such a pity! Stay at least another week. (*Seeing* KULYGIN *she gives a shriek; he laughs and takes off the mustache and beard.*) Why, look at you, you scared me! (*To* IRINA.) I am used to you and do you think parting with you will be easy for me? I'll give orders to put Andrei in your room, with his violin — let him saw away there! — and in his room we'll put Sofotchka. Marvelous, wonderful child! What a girl! Today she looked at me with such eyes, and — "Mama!"

KULYGIN: Beautiful child, that's true.

NATASHA: And so tomorrow I'll be all alone here. (*Sighing.*) First of all,

I'll give orders to chop down this alley of fir trees, then this maple here. . . . In the evening it looks so ugly. . . . (*To* IRINA.) Dear, that belt doesn't suit you at all. . . . It's in very poor taste. You need something light. . . . And I'll order flowers planted, everywhere, flowers, and there'll be a fragrance . . . (*Severely.*) What's a fork doing here on the bench? (*She goes into the house, to the maid.*) What's a fork doing here on the bench, I'd like to know? (*Shouting.*) Shut up!

KULYGIN: She's off again!

(*Behind the scenes a band is playing a march; everybody listens.*)

OLGA: They are leaving.

(TCHEBUTYKIN *enters.*)

MASHA: Our friends are going. Well, then. . . . A pleasant journey to them! (*To her husband.*) We must go home. . . . Where are my hat and cape?

KULYGIN: I carried them in the house . . . I'll get them right away.

OLGA: Yes, now we can all go home. It's time.

TCHEBUTYKIN: Olga Sergeevna!

OLGA: What? (*A pause.*) What?

TCHEBUTYKIN: Nothing. . . . Don't know how to tell you. . . . (*Whispering in her ear.*)

OLGA (*Alarmed*): It's not possible!

TCHEBUTYKIN: Yes. . . . What a story. . . . I'm tired, completely exhausted, don't want to talk any more. (*Irritably.*) However, it's all the same!

MASHA: What happened?

OLGA (*embracing* IRINA): It's a terrible day today. . . . I don't know how to tell you, my darling. . . .

IRINA: What? Say it quick. . . . What? for God's sake! (*Crying.*)

TCHEBUTYKIN: The Baron was killed just now in a duel.

IRINA (*weeping quietly*): I knew, I knew. . . .

TCHEBUTYKIN (*sitting down on a bench to the rear of the stage*): I'm tired. . . . (*Taking a newspaper out of his pocket.*) Let them cry a little. . . . (*Singing softly.*) Ta-ra-ra-boom-de-aye. . . . Sit on a curb I may. . . . As if it weren't all the same!

(*The three sisters stand with their arms around one another.*)

MASHA: Oh, how the music is playing! They are leaving us, one has gone entirely, entirely, forever. We'll be left alone to begin our life over again. We must live. . . . We must live. . . .

IRINA (*putting her head on* OLGA'*s breast*): The time will come when all will know why all this is, what these sufferings are for, there will be no secrets – but meanwhile we must live – must work, only work! Tomorrow I'm going away alone, I'll teach in the school and give my whole life to those who need it perhaps. It's autumn now; winter will soon come and cover everything with snow, and I'll work, work. . . .

OLGA (*embracing both her sisters*): The music plays so gaily, bravely, and one wants to live. Oh, Lord! Time will pass and we shall be gone forever, they will forget us, they will forget our faces, voices, and how many of us there were, but our sufferings will turn into joy for those who will be living after us, happiness and peace will come on earth, and they will remember with some gentle word those who live now and will bless them. Oh, dear sisters, our life isn't over yet. We shall live! The music plays so gaily, so joyously, and it looks as if a little more and we shall know why we live, why we suffer. . . . If we only knew, if we only knew!

(*The music plays always softer and softer;* KULYGIN, *smiling and gay, brings the hat and cape,* ANDREI *is pushing the baby-carriage with Bobik in it.*)

TCHEBUTYKIN (*singing softly*): Ta-ra-ra-boom-de-aye. . . . Sit on a curb I may. . . . (*Reading the newspaper.*) It's all the same! It's all the same!

OLGA: If we only knew, if we only knew!

CURTAIN

Chekhov has become a classic of the modern theater for reasons that may not be clear to those who have never seen good productions of his plays. It takes histrionic imagination to perceive the shaped substance within their surface of small social rounds, with provincials forever fretting about the frustrating monotony of their lives but too feckless to do anything to change it. Even in the theater there are still sensible people to whom *The Three Sisters* is a big bore: "four acts about not going to Moscow." Since his imitators have been better at reproducing the surface than the substance, Chekhov has been blamed for a whole tradition of unstructured insignificance in modern drama. If strong plot – so the argument goes – has informed plays as far apart in time and convention as *Oedipus Rex, Hamlet, Tartuffe,* and *The Wild Duck,* it is because the human mind is held by the spectacle of coherent events building toward a significant resolution. The Chekhovian manner produces rambling mood pictures, poignant, perhaps, but of wan and meaningless verisimilitude and spasmodic, inconclusive dialogue. Its plotless diffusion defeats the purpose of drama. The apathy on stage seeps across the footlights and settles on the audience.

Chekhov's own attempt to vindicate his art against such criticism does not seem persuasive. Irritated with critics who found *The Three Sisters* a dull and depressing play when it was first performed by the Stanislavsky company at the Moscow Art Theater in 1901, Chekhov wrote to a friend: "All I wanted was to say to people, 'Have a look at yourselves and see how bad and dreary your lives are!' The important thing is that they should realize that, for when they do they will certainly create a better life for themselves." But Vershinin's belief in human progress and Irina's and Tusenbach's gospel of work do not cover the whole play, and Chekhov's assumption that if properly understood his drama will lift indolent incompetents out of their rut sounds only naive if taken at face value, and, if not, like an effort to justify a new dramatic form in terms comprehensible to an age committed to useful literature. As social propaganda *The Three Sisters* carries a muted message. Even Soviet critics have found it difficult to fit it into their view of Chekhov as a pre-revolutionary anti-bourgeois. His self-defense seems irrelevant.

There are two better and more obvious retorts to people who find *The Three Sisters* difficult and dull because it is a play in which "nothing happens." First, there are plenty of happenings in the Prozoroff household. Gifts are given, lunches eaten, clocks dropped, false beards put on, pictures taken, papers signed, babies wheeled. Characters arrive and depart, are quarrelsome and adulterous, gay and gloomy. They drink, dance, gamble, sing, read, play patience, and die. Second, the play has an action even in the larger, traditional sense — not the manipulated intrigue of the well-made play, but unilinear and progressive coherence nonetheless. What happens in *The Three Sisters* is the wearing down of the sisters' youth and hopes as their house is being usurped by their sister-in-law Natasha. Their tolerant gentility yields to her coarse and grasping selfishness. It is a story of the displacement of good life by mean. Olga's rise to the headmistress-ship she doesn't want, the frustration of Masha's and Irina's love affairs, and Andrei's corruption are corollaries to this main line of action.

What is new in Chekhov is that he doesn't tell his story as a tight chain of causally linked events. In his plays as in his short stories he catches life not in intricate and pointed plotting but in a carefully crafted succession of little individual epiphanies and moments of social discord, some pathetic, some funny. Because there is no plot that continuously has to be furthered, scenes and speeches can play themselves out in the varying tempos and intensities and the little banalities and irrelevancies by which life proceeds in the ordinary living room. The difference between Ibsen's kind of social realism and Chekhov's is that Ibsen stages only the final moments of crisis in a long, causal development, most of which is revealed retrospectively, while Chekhov moves his action obliquely and over a longer time through odd, off moments of reflection and social trivia that sample the destinies that are slowly being shaped by events and decisions (and non-decisions) occurring off-stage or between the acts. Ibsen's compressed form achieves taut tension, a rush of events toward a relentlessly determined climax, but it is a moot question which of the two is the superior realist. Compared with Chekhov's, many of Ibsen's domestic scenes may seem crude and contrived.

In Chekhov, situations and images, scenic and verbal, form analogues and contrasts of effects more lyrical than narrative. Romance ends in futility with the transfer of Masha's lover, the death of Irina's fiancé, and Natasha employing both husband and lover as babysitters. Masha is a romantic adulteress, Irina is engaged but not in love, Kulygin suspects he should have married Olga rather than Masha. Olga is and Irina intends to become a schoolteacher; Olga stays and Irina will go away. In Act III, Tchebutykin breaks a china clock that used to belong to the General's wife. In Act IV, Masha describes her own and her sisters' and brother's disappointment with their lives by the image of the fall of a huge bell from a tower: "A lot of effort and money were spent, and then suddenly it fell and broke." The point of the repeated motif is not so much the associative process in Masha's mind as the transformation of a small household calamity into symbol. In Act IV, Natasha takes revenge on Irina for Olga's remark on her tasteless dress in Act I. When there are thirteen people at lunch in Act I Kulygin makes a kindly joke about Natasha's love for Andrei; later, as Natasha, the intruding outsider, takes over control of the house, the old superstition assumes another and sinister meaning. Masha sees a connection between Natasha's lighted candle and the town fire. The red glow from the fire in Act III contrasts with the unlit stage in Act II and both contrast with the sunny brightness in Act I. Sometimes spectacle by itself establishes human relationships. The stage picture in Act III tells us that Irina has given up her room to little Bobik, and near the end of the act she and Olga remain invisible behind their bed screens and Masha leaves the room just as Andrei starts having it out with his sisters in an awkward speech of self-justification. In Act IV, Kulygin, in what is surely his noblest moment in the play, mimics the German teacher for Olga's and Masha's amusement just after Vershinin has kissed Masha goodbye for the last time.

The end of Act II illustrates Chekhov's achievement in a single, extended passage of dramatic coherence through lyrical organization of an apparent miscellany of episode, off-stage sound, spectacle, topic, and tonality. A pleasant scene of song and dance is interrupted first by Andrei's and Solyony's silly argument about the number of universities in Moscow and then by Natasha's demand that everyone leave so Bobik can have quiet. On the emptied stage, off-stage goodbyes and Tusenbach's laughter die away in the sound of a lullaby. Anfisa and a maid enter to clear the table and turn off the lights. In the dark Andrei and Tchebutykin dispiritedly discuss marriage. We hear the carnival party arrive and be turned away. Solyony tries to make love to Irina. He leaves, lovelorn and ominous. Natasha, carrying a candle, tries to get Irina to give up her room to Bobik. Then she goes for a sleigh ride with her lover. Vershinin returns, disappointed not to find a party in progress. There is some desultory talk between Olga and Kulygin about a teachers' meeting and Andrei's gambling. Irina is left alone. Someone plays an accordion in the street, and the nurse sings her lullaby in the next room. Irina cries out for Moscow.

The initial cut-off point for this sample passage is arbitrary. The sequence of scenes marks no distinct phase in a larger plot dynamic and neither opens nor concludes any dramatic issue. But the very shapelessness of these fleeting encounters of separate minds and moods that break and rejoin produces an authentic impression of unarranged leisure with its own kind of inevitability. And the shifts from ensemble scene to soliloquy, from crowded to empty and from lighted to darkened stage, and from chatter to silence, dance to listlessness, argument to lullaby, and farce to pathos say something about the vanity of human wishes, the fragility of social pleasure, the loneliness of the individual, and the aimlessness of a random fragment of large and chaotic domesticity. This is the inclusive poetry of Chekhov's theater, and there is nothing slipshod or fortuitous about it. "Chekhov," says the English director Peter Brook,

> never just made a slice of life—he was a doctor who with infinite gentleness and care took thousands of fine layers off life. These he cultured, and then arranged them in an exquisitely cunning, completely artificial and meaningful order, in which part of the cunning lay in so disguising the artifice that the result looked like the keyhole view it never had been.
>
> *The Empty Space* (London, 1968), p. 79

Speech in *The Three Sisters* is constantly punctuated by pauses that leave remarks hanging on the air. Self-musing tirades dissipate in silence or embarrassed changes of topic. There are squabbles about nothing. Philosophical discussions end nowhere, are taken up again, and again dropped. Solyony makes literary allusions that no one understands. Neither Masha nor anyone else can tell why a certain line of romantic poetry keeps running in her head. No one listens when Tchebutykin reads newspaper fillers aloud. No one laughs at Solyony's jokes or at Kulygin's school anecdotes and Latin tags. Masha and Vershinin communicate in snatches of hummed song. Solyony and Tchebutykin quarrel about the ingredients in a Caucasian dish without realizing that they are talking about two different dishes. Only the antagonist Natasha's speeches seem purposeful, imposing her practical will on others. After a while language seems less an effective means to social interaction than a way of registering the pressure exercised by characters who never appear: the dead General Prozoroff and his wife; Natasha's children; Protopopov, Natasha's lover and Andrei's superior on the City Council; Vershinin's wife and two little girls; the director of Olga's and Kulygin's school. The social life of the play extends beyond the stage, and language is only one of its media.

But this ruptured, rambling speech does more than just suggest the futility of efforts at human contact; it also creates counterpoint effects of subtle scenic semantics. Mutually modulating speeches, of effects more readily felt than explicated, are main units of meaning in Chekhov's dialogue. Near the beginning of the play Olga's passionate outburst of longing for Moscow is interrupted by Tchebutykin's and Tusenbach's voices from the next room:

> The devil!
> Of course, it's all rot.

We never learn what they have been talking about, but the inappropriateness of the interruption and the fact that it doesn't serve any plot interest send our minds in search of a covert connection before the play ripples on — and longing for Moscow is no longer an unambivalent emotion in the play. One could do worse than guess that Chekhov introduces Masha's thoughtless whistling here both to turn the dialogue and to allow time for the inadvertent intrusion into Olga's revery to take effect. In Act I, just as Vershinin is saying he would like a chance to change the rough draft of his life into a fair copy, Kulygin enters and gives Irina a book he has written on the history of the local school and which he has given her once before. His fatuous felicitations are such an incongruous response to Vershinin's sad pensiveness that they assume a farcical relevance in the larger scene of social discord that Chekhov is making. But doesn't the twice-given gift of a dull book on a dull subject on an occasion which is the Russian equivalent of a western birthday also comment on Vershinin's wish for a second chance at life? This is the sort of implication that tends to evaporate in the spelling out, but it is there, if only for a moment and on the edge of our consciousness. In Act II, Vershinin tells a story about a French cabinet minister who delighted in watching little birds through his prison window but forgot all about them when he was released. For Vershinin the moral of the story is our perverse inability to have enjoyment without pain: "Happiness we have not and it does not exist, we only long for it." At that point Tusenbach asks where all the candy has gone. Do we say simply that Vershinin's observation, already vulnerable from a touch of self-pitying pomposity, is annihilated by the banality of Tusenbach's question? Or do we say that Tusenbach's vexation is a small, unexpected illustration of Vershinin's general truth? Because human happiness does not depend on candy, the juxtaposition is a piece of bathos, but without the bathos would Vershinin's statement have seemed fairly tested or Tusenbach's disappointment have seemed representative of man's dubious lot?

It is probably easier today than in 1901 to do justice to Chekhov's achievement. Artistic form can be many things as it responds to changing perceptions of reality. In a world drained of meaning the philosophical and psychological assumptions behind the Aristotelian dramaturgy seem a litte less certain than they used to, and Aristotelian plays seem a little rigid and simpleminded in their confident teleology and their definiteness of event. Successful contemporary plays are being written about alienated and inarticulate anti-heroes, and phenomenological playwrights are substituting naked moments of existence and the integrity of the uninterpreted fact for plot structure and character analysis. Ever since Strindberg and Pirandello, character itself, as a unique psychic continuum, has been a suspect concept. From one of the most seminal of recent plays we have learned that passive waiting can be an exciting and moving action.

Chekhov's use of smalltalk as a symptom of non-communication has become a fashionable convention of our theater. His ironic detachment from his characters appeals to the strain of ambiguity in the modern consciousness. *The Three Sisters* is about more than the wasting of good and sensitive lives in ineffectuality. We sense a rationalistic impertinence in those who seek the hidden causes of Solyony's aggressiveness or the precise depth of Vershinin's feelings for Masha. We deliberately do not demand singleminded interpretation of symbols. The military uniforms, Irina's game of patience, Solyony's bottle of scent, and Fedotik's photography are the stuff of reality: acts, facts, and objects that *are* before they signify and which signify at all only because they so unmistakably *are*. Is stasis or transience Chekhov's main image for human experience in *The Three Sisters*? There is much in circumstance and event to suggest the former; the human analogues to the birds of passage so many of the characters keep mentioning suggest the latter. The suspended ambiguity seems preferable to the choice of one image over the other. It taps our own sense of life in compelling the thought that man is both transient and trapped. And we respond to the slow intermittence of Chekhov's dramatic momentum not as to artistic disorder but as to a questioning of the convenient convention that life runs in plots and as to an image of life as a tragicomedy of attrition. The four Prozoroffs don't get to Moscow, but Moscow is such an indeterminate place that their frustrated longing for it becomes, perhaps, only a foolish illusion. To them it is the city where all dreams of love and ambition come true, but to Vershinin it is a place of gloomy bridges and no birch trees where he lived as a sad and lonely "lovesick major," and to old Ferapont it is a fabled town where merchants eat themselves dead on pancakes and a mysterious rope is stretched all across. In the best tragicomedies the tragic and the comic elements do not just clash; they re-enforce one another. Man is tragic partly because his limitations mock his pretensions to noble agony, and he is comic partly because of the seriousness with which he takes his suffering and because of the vanity of his tragic aspirations. It is comic that he thinks he is tragic and tragic that he is actually comic. With this interlocking double vision of man, tragicomedy is a distinctly modern genre, and Chekhov's attitude to his characters — a poise somewhere between pitying respect for sensitive endurance and an ironist's ridicule of self-absorbed lassitude — makes him one of its supreme practitioners. His plays simply will not surrender their subleties to the kind of critical inquiry that worked for the drama of psychological naturalism and social polemics that was popular when they were written.

It is useful to recognize in Chekhov techniques and sensibilities that he shares with certain forms of modern drama. It is not by accident that his high reputation at the present coincides with a vogue for dramatic absurdism. But the similarities can be overemphasized. His domestic interiors are as plausibly cluttered with things — samovars, cameras, forks in the garden — as Pinter's and Albee's, but they are not weird or enigmatic, and they will not serve as settings for Beckett's and Ionesco's fantastic allegories. His characters talk beside one another, but his stage is not an eventless void with no one to listen to the persistent human monologue. Most important, his objectivity is too absolute to be violated by any particular philosophical stance.

The character closest to having a choric function in the play is Tchebutykin, the old drunken doctor, whose only remaining emotion is his half-forgotten love for Irina's mother. To him nothing matters, for "there is nothing in the world, we don't exist, but it only seems that we exist. . . ." His muttering voice of total negation is heard in the middle background of several scenes, and he has all but the last word in the play. Is the play therefore philosophically nihilistic? A little scene in Act II may illustrate Chekhov's use of such ideas.

Tusenbach is saying that life never changes, that its laws are undiscoverable and don't concern us, that our thoughts make no difference to the vast, mindless process.

MASHA: Just the same, has it meaning?

TUSENBACH: Meaning. . . . Look, it's snowing. What meaning has that? (*A pause.*)

MASHA: It seems to me a man must be a believer or must seek some belief, otherwise his life is empty, empty. . . .

She goes on like this a little longer. When she stops, the argument stops.

TCHEBUTYKIN (*reading a newspaper*): Balzac was married in Berdichev. (IRINA *sings softly.*) Really I'll put that in my book. (*Writing.*) Balzac was married in Berdichev. (*Reading his newspaper.*)

IRINA (*as she lays out cards for patience, musing*): Balzac was married in Berdichev.

By the third time it is mentioned, Balzac's marriage seems to have no more human significance than the snow falling outside, but it is hard to say whether the sequence does or does not validate Masha's opinion that, if she is wrong and Tusenbach right, "it's all nonsense, waste." Life (one supposes) may or may not make sense, and it may or may not be necessary to believe it does, but Chekhov isn't telling us what to think about the ultimate issues or even what *he* thinks. He is giving stage life to a casual group of people, some of whom take the problem seriously while the rest are indifferent semi-listeners to their discussion. The argument is important for what it reveals about human reality, not for its rights and wrongs. Not all literary meaning is cognitive.

What "meaning" *The Three Sisters* has is not propounded in argument or insinuated in fable but accumulated in the moment-to-moment life on stage. Because no single scene in the successive minutiae of daily life is quite decisive enough to disrupt the uncertain flow of sociality, the action of Natasha taking control of the house away from the sisters develops indirectly through the inner momentum of character and circumstance interacting in time — the disingenuous patterning of limp remark and petty act. Time in Chekhov is more than the dimension in which we necessarily apprehend any literary work; it is a primary fact of consciousness, the alterer of looks, the agent of frustration, the measure of failure. Indications of time link the four discontinuous acts in a single symbolic form of near symmetry. The first act takes place in the spring, the last in the fall five years later. The first and the last take place at midday, the second at eight in the evening, the third at three in the morning. Throughout there are references to clocks and watches. By its main events each act represents a separate stage in one parabolic curve of experience: a family celebration and a new arrival; the disappointed hope for an evening of frolic; a town disaster; and separation, death, and uncertainty. The changes in the sisters' dream of returning to Moscow are similarly ordered: in Act I it is an announced intention; at the end of Acts II and III it is Irina's desperate hope; in Act IV it is referred to as an abandoned plan. Between beginning and end Masha meets, loves, and loses Vershinin; Irina rejects, accepts, and loses Tusenbach; Olga turns into an old maid; Andrei grows dull and fat; and Natasha changes from an awkward young girl in love to a formidable and unfaithful matron, whose progress is marked by the birth and growth of her children, the demoralization of her husband, her ascendancy over her lover, and the growing frequency of her French phrases — all events of duration. Both ends of the play are open, its present linked both with the past and the future. The litany of Olga's nostalgia as the play begins is followed by Irina's, Tusenbach's, and Vershinin's monologues of reminiscence. In Act I Olga has already begun her unfulfilling career, Masha is already disillusioned with her marriage, and even the "happy" Irina already thinks of their life as a stifling of garden flowers by weeds. As the opening scene points back to the sisters' girlhood in Moscow, so does their final embrace leave unanswered the question of what life will be like for them from now on. Ironically, at the end of the play only the ancient Anfisa is happily settled. As later in *The Cherry Orchard,* the mention in the last act of cutting down old trees signifies the passing of an old and the coming of a new order, as gentility cedes to vulgarity. And the most intense moments in the play are those in which life's lonely losers introspect their entrapment, conscious of their inertia as they move through time. In *The Three Sisters,* as in human affairs generally, time is the enemy, and one measure of the greatness of Chekhov's art is the way in which he turns that fact into matter of moral relevance.

# JOHN MILLINGTON SYNGE

# Riders to the Sea

CHARACTERS

MAURYA, an old woman
BARTLEY, her son
CATHLEEN, her daughter
NORA, a younger daughter
MEN and WOMEN

*Scene: An Island off the West of Ireland.*

*Cottage kitchen, with nets, oilskins, spinning-wheel, some new boards standing by the wall, etc.* CATHLEEN, *a girl of about twenty, finishes kneading cake, and puts it down in the pot-oven by the fire; then wipes her hands, and begins to spin at the wheel.* NORA, *a young girl, puts her head in at the door.*

NORA (*in a low voice*): Where is she?

CATHLEEN: She's lying down, God help her, and maybe sleeping, if she's able.

(NORA *comes in softly, and takes a bundle from under her shawl.*)

CATHLEEN (*spinning the wheel rapidly*): What is it you have?

NORA: The young priest is after bringing[1] them. It's a shirt and a plain stocking were got off a drowned man in Donegal.

(CATHLEEN *stops her wheel with a sudden movement, and leans out to listen.*)

NORA: We're to find out if it's Michael's they are, some time herself[2] will be down looking by the sea.

CATHLEEN: How would they be Michael's, Nora? How would he go the length of that way to the far north?

NORA: The young priest says he's known the like of it. "If it's Michael's they are," says he, "you can tell herself he's got a clean burial by the grace of God, and if they're not his, let no one say a word about them, for she'll be getting her death," says he, "with crying and lamenting."

(*The door which* NORA *half closed is blown open by a gust of wind.*)

CATHLEEN (*looking out anxiously*): Did you ask him would he stop Bartley going this day with the horses to the Galway fair?

NORA: "I won't stop him," says he, "but let you not be afraid. Herself does be saying prayers half through the night, and the Almighty God won't leave her destitute," says he, "with no son living."

CATHLEEN: Is the sea bad by the white rocks, Nora?

NORA: Middling bad, God help us. There's a great roaring in the west, and it's worse it'll be getting when the tide's turned to the wind. (*She goes over to the table with the bundle.*) Shall I open it now?

CATHLEEN: Maybe she'd wake up on us, and come in before we'd done. (*Coming to the table.*) It's a long time we'll be, and the two of us crying.

NORA (*goes to the inner door and listens*): She's moving about on the bed. She'll be coming in a minute.

CATHLEEN: Give me the ladder, and I'll put them up in the turf-loft, the way[3] she won't know of them at all, and maybe when the tide turns she'll be going down to see would he be floating from the east.

(*They put the ladder against the gable of the chimney;* CATHLEEN *goes up a few steps and hides the bundle in the turf-loft.* MAURYA *comes from the inner room.*)

MAURYA (*looking up at* CATHLEEN *and speaking querulously*): Isn't it turf enough you have for this day and evening?

CATHLEEN: There's a cake baking at the fire for a short space (*throwing down the turf*), and Bartley will want it when the tide turns if he goes to Connemara.

(NORA *picks up the turf and puts it round the pot-oven.*)

[1] has just brought
[2] i.e., Maurya, the head of the household
[3] so that

MAURYA (*sitting down on a stool at the fire*): He won't go this day with the wind rising from the south and west. He won't go this day, for the young priest will stop him surely.

NORA: He'll not stop him, mother, and I heard Eamon Simon and Stephen Pheety and Colum Shawn saying he would go.

MAURYA: Where is he itself?

NORA: He went down to see would there be another boat sailing in the week, and I'm thinking it won't be long till he's here now, for the tide's turning at the green head, and the hooker's[4] tacking from the east.

CATHLEEN: I hear some one passing the big stones.

NORA (*looking out*): He's coming now, and he in a hurry.

BARTLEY (*comes in and looks round the room. Speaking sadly and quietly*): Where is the bit of new rope, Cathleen, was bought in Connemara?

CATHLEEN (*coming down*): Give it to him, Nora; it's on a nail by the white boards. I hung it up this morning, for the pig with the black feet was eating it.

NORA (*giving him a rope*): Is that it, Bartley?

MAURYA: You'd do right to leave that rope, Bartley, hanging by the boards. (*Bartley takes the rope.*) It will be wanting in this place, I'm telling you, if Michael is washed up to-morrow morning, or the next morning, or any morning in the week, for it's a deep grave we'll make him by the grace of God.

BARTLEY (*beginning to work with the rope*): I've no halter the way I can ride down on the mare, and I must go now quickly. This is the one boat going for two weeks or beyond it, and the fair will be a good fair for horses I heard them saying below.

MAURYA: It's a hard thing they'll be saying below if the body is washed up and there's no man in it[5] to make the coffin, and I after giving a big price for the finest white boards you'd find in Connemara.

(*She looks round at the boards.*)

BARTLEY: How would it be washed up, and we after looking[6] each day for nine days, and a strong wind blowing a while back from the west and south?

MAURYA: If it isn't found itself,[7] that wind is raising the sea, and there was a star up against the moon, and it rising in the night. If it was a hundred horses, or a thousand horses you had itself, what is the price of a thousand horses against a son where there is one son only?

BARTLEY (*working at the halter, to* CATHLEEN): Let you go down each day, and see the sheep aren't jumping in on the rye, and if the jobber comes you can sell the pig with the black feet if there is a good price going.

[4] a one-masted fishing vessel
[5] i.e., the house
[6] when we have been looking
[7] even if it isn't found

MAURYA: How would the like of her get a good price for a pig?

BARTLEY (*to* CATHLEEN): If the west wind holds with the last bit of the moon let you and Nora get up weed[8] enough for another cock[9] for the kelp.[10] It's hard set we'll be from this day with no one in it but one man to work.

MAURYA: It's hard set we'll be surely the day you're drownd'd with the rest. What way will I live and the girls with me, and I an old woman looking for the grave?

(BARTLEY *lays down the halter, takes off his old coat, and puts on a newer one of the same flannel.*)

BARTLEY (*to* NORA): Is she coming to the pier?

NORA (*looking out*): She's passing the green head and letting fall her sails.

BARTLEY (*getting his purse and tobacco*): I'll have half an hour to go down, and you'll see me coming again in two days, or in three days, or maybe in four days if the wind is bad.

MAURYA (*turning round to the fire, and putting her shawl over her head*): Isn't it a hard and cruel man won't hear a word from an old woman, and she holding him from the sea?

CATHLEEN: It's the life of a young man to be going on the sea, and who would listen to an old woman with one thing and she saying it over?

BARTLEY (*taking the halter*): I must go now quickly. I'll ride down on the red mare, and the gray pony'll run behind me. . . . The blessing of God on you.

(*He goes out.*)

MAURYA (*crying out as he is in the door*): He's gone now, God spare us, and we'll not see him again. He's gone now, and when the black night is falling I'll have no son left me in the world.

CATHLEEN: Why wouldn't you give him your blessing and he looking round in the door? Isn't it sorrow enough is on every one in this house without your sending him out with an unlucky word behind him, and a hard word in his ear?

(MAURYA *takes up the tongs and begins raking the fire aimlessly without looking round.*)

NORA (*turning towards her*): You're taking away the turf from the cake.

CATHLEEN (*crying out*): The Son of God forgive us, Nora, we're after forgetting his bit of bread.

(*She comes over to the fire.*)

NORA: And it's destroyed[11] he'll be going till dark night, and he after eating nothing since the sun went up.

[8] seaweed
[9] conical rick
[10] ashes of seaweed, from which iodine is obtained
[11] i.e., with hunger and fatigue

CATHLEEN (*turning the cake out of the oven*): It's destroyed he'll be, surely. There's no sense left on any person in a house where an old woman will be talking for ever.

(MAURYA *sways herself on her stool.*)

CATHLEEN (*cutting off some of the bread and rolling it in a cloth; to* MAURYA): Let you go down now to the spring well and give him this and he passing. You'll see him then and the dark word will be broken, and you can say "God speed you," the way he'll be easy in his mind.

MAURYA (*taking the bread*): Will I be in it[12] as soon as himself?

CATHLEEN: If you go now quickly.

MAURYA (*standing up unsteadily*): It's hard set I am to walk.

CATHLEEN (*looking at her anxiously*): Give her the stick, Nora, or maybe she'll slip on the big stones.

NORA: What stick?

CATHLEEN: The stick Michael brought from Connemara.

MAURYA (*taking a stick* NORA *gives her*): In the big world the old people do be leaving things after them for their sons and children, but in this place it is the young men do be leaving things behind for them that do be old.

(*She goes out slowly.* NORA *goes over to the ladder.*)

CATHLEEN: Wait, Nora, maybe she'd turn back quickly. She's that sorry, God help her, you wouldn't know the thing she'd do.

NORA: Is she gone round by the bush?

CATHLEEN (*looking out*): She's gone now. Throw it down quickly, for the Lord knows when she'll be out of it again.

NORA (*getting the bundle from the loft*): The young priest said he'd be passing to-morrow, and we might go down and speak to him below if it's Michael's they are surely.

CATHLEEN (*taking the bundle*): Did he say what way they were found?

NORA (*coming down*): "There were two men," says he, "and they rowing round with poteen[13] before the cocks crowed, and the oar of one of them caught the body, and they passing the black cliffs of the north."

CATHLEEN (*trying to open the bundle*): Give me a knife, Nora, the string's perished with the salt water, and there's a black knot on it you wouldn't loosen in a week.

NORA (*giving her a knife*): I've heard tell it was a long way to Donegal.

CATHLEEN (*cutting the string*): It is surely. There was a man here a while ago — the man sold us that knife — and he said if you set off walking from the rocks beyond, it would be in seven days you'd be in Donegal.

NORA: And what time would a man take, and he floating?

[12] there
[13] moonshine whiskey

(CATHLEEN *opens the bundle and takes out a bit of a stocking. They look at them eagerly.*)

CATHLEEN (*in a low voice*): The Lord spare us, Nora! isn't it a queer hard thing to say if it's his they are surely?

NORA: I'll get his shirt off the hook the way we can put the one flannel on the other. (*She looks through some clothes hanging in the corner.*) It's not with them, Cathleen, and where will it be?

CATHLEEN: I'm thinking Bartley put it on him in the morning, for his own shirt was heavy with the salt in it. (*Pointing to the corner.*) There's a bit of a sleeve was of the same stuff. Give me that and it will do.

(NORA *brings it to her and they compare the flannel.*)

CATHLEEN: It's the same stuff, Nora; but if it is itself aren't there great rolls of it in the shops of Galway, and isn't it many another man may have a shirt of it as well as Michael himself?

NORA (*who has taken up the stocking and counted the stitches, crying out*): It's Michael, Cathleen, it's Michael; God spare his soul, and what will herself say when she hears this story, and Bartley on the sea?

CATHLEEN (*taking the stocking*): It's a plain stocking.

NORA: It's the second one of the third pair I knitted, and I put up three score stitches, and I dropped four of them.

CATHLEEN (*counts the stitches*): It's that number is in it. (*Crying out.*) Ah, Nora, isn't it a bitter thing to think of him floating that way to the far north, and no one to keen him but the black hags that do be flying on the sea?

NORA (*swinging herself half round, and throwing out her arms on the clothes*): And isn't it a pitiful thing when there is nothing left of a man who was a great rower and fisher, but a bit of an old shirt and a plain stocking?

CATHLEEN (*after an instant*): Tell me is herself coming, Nora? I hear a little sound on the path.

NORA (*looking out*): She is, Cathleen. She's coming up to the door.

CATHLEEN: Put these things away before she'll come in. Maybe it's easier she'll be after giving her blessing to Bartley, and we won't let on we've heard anything the time he's on the sea.

NORA (*helping* CATHLEEN *to close the bundle*): We'll put them here in the corner.

(*They put them into a hole in the chimney corner.* CATHLEEN *goes back to the spinning-wheel.*)

NORA: Will she see it was crying I was?

CATHLEEN: Keep your back to the door the way the light'll not be on you.

(NORA *sits down at the chimney corner, with her back to the door.* MAURYA *comes in very slowly, without looking at the girls, and goes over to her stool at the other side of the fire. The cloth with the bread is still in her hand. The girls look at each other, and* NORA *points to the bundle of bread.*)

CATHLEEN (*after spinning for a moment*): You didn't give him his bit of bread?

(MAURYA *begins to keen softly, without turning round.*)

CATHLEEN: Did you see him riding down?

(MAURYA *goes on keening.*)

CATHLEEN (*a little impatiently*): God forgive you; isn't it a better thing to raise your voice and tell what you seen, than to be making lamentation for a thing that's done? Did you see Bartley, I'm saying to you.

MAURYA (*with a weak voice*): My heart's broken from this day.

CATHLEEN (*as before*): Did you see Bartley?

MAURYA: I seen the fearfulest thing.

CATHLEEN (*leaves her wheel and looks out*): God forgive you; he's riding the mare now over the green head, and the gray pony behind him.

MAURYA (*starts, so that her shawl falls back from her head and shows her white tossed hair. With a frightened voice*): The gray pony behind him. . . .

CATHLEEN (*coming to the fire*): What is it ails you, at all?

MAURYA (*speaking very slowly*): I've seen the fearfulest thing any person has seen, since the day Bride Dara seen the dead man with the child in his arms.

CATHLEEN AND NORA: Uah.

(*They crouch down in front of the old woman at the fire.*)

NORA: Tell us what it is you seen.

MAURYA: I went down to the spring well, and I stood there saying a prayer to myself. Then Bartley came along, and he riding on the red mare with the gray pony behind him. (*She puts up her hands, as if to hide something from her eyes.*) The Son of God spare us, Nora!

CATHLEEN: What is it you seen?

MAURYA: I seen Michael himself.

CATHLEEN (*speaking softly*): You did not, mother. It wasn't Michael you seen, for his body is after being found in the far north, and he's got a clean burial by the grace of God.

MAURYA (*a little defiantly*): I'm after seeing him this day, and he riding and galloping. Bartley came first on the red mare; and I tried to say "God speed you," but something choked the words in my throat. He went by quickly; and "the blessing of God on you," says he, and I could say nothing. I looked up then, and I crying, at the gray pony, and there was Michael upon it — with fine clothes on him, and new shoes on his feet.

CATHLEEN (*begins to keen*): It's destroyed we are from this day. It's destroyed, surely.

NORA: Didn't the young priest say the Almighty God won't leave her destitute with no son living?

MAURYA (*in a low voice, but clearly*): It's little the like of him knows of the sea. . . . Bartley will be lost now, and let you call in Eamon and make me a good coffin out of the white boards, for I won't live after them. I've had a husband, and a husband's father, and six sons in this house – six fine men, though it was a hard birth I had with every one of them and they coming to the world – and some of them were found and some of them were not found, but they're gone now the lot of them. . . . There were Stephen, and Shawn, were lost in the great wind, and found after in the Bay of Gregory of the Golden Mouth, and carried up the two of them on one plank, and in by that door.

(*She pauses for a moment, the girls start as if they heard something through the door that is half open behind them.*)

NORA (*in a whisper*): Did you hear that, Cathleen? Did you hear a noise in the north-east?

CATHLEEN (*in a whisper*): There's some one after crying out by the seashore.

MAURYA (*continues without hearing anything*): There was Sheamus and his father, and his own father again, were lost in a dark night, and not a stick or sign was seen of them when the sun went up. There was Patch after was drowned out of a curagh[14] that turned over. I was sitting here with Bartley, and he a baby, lying on my two knees, and I seen two women, and three women, and four women coming in, and they crossing themselves, and not saying a word. I looked out then, and there were men coming after them, and they holding a thing in the half of a red sail, and water dripping out of it – it was a dry day, Nora – and leaving a track to the door.

(*She pauses again with her hand stretched out towards the door. It opens softly and old women begin to come in, crossing themselves on the threshold, and kneeling down in front of the stage with their backs to the people, and the white waist-bands of the red petticoats they wear over their heads just seen from behind.*)

MAURYA (*half in a dream, to* CATHLEEN): Is it Patch, or Michael, or what is it at all?

CATHLEEN: Michael is after being found in the far north, and when he is found there how could he be here in this place?

MAURYA: There does be a power of young men floating round in the sea, and what way would they know if it was Michael they had, or another

[14] a light, open boat

man like him, for when a man is nine days in the sea, and the wind blowing, it's hard set his own mother would be to say what man was in it.

CATHLEEN: It's Michael, God spare him, for they're after sending us a bit of his clothes from the far north.

(*She reaches out and hands* MAURYA *the clothes that belonged to Michael.* MAURYA *stands up slowly, and takes them in her hands.* NORA *looks out.*)

NORA: They're carrying a thing among them and there's water dripping out of it and leaving a track by the big stones.

CATHLEEN (*in a whisper to the women who have come in*): Is it Bartley it is?

ONE OF THE WOMEN: It is surely, God rest his soul.

(*Two younger women come in and pull out the table. Then men carry in the body of* BARTLEY, *laid on a plank, with a bit of a sail over it, and lay it on the table.*)

CATHLEEN (*to the women, as they are doing so*): What way was he drowned?

ONE OF THE WOMEN: The gray pony knocked him over into the sea, and he was washed out where there is a great surf on the white rocks.

(MAURYA *has gone over and knelt down at the head of the table. The women are keening softly and swaying themselves with a slow movement.* CATHLEEN *and* NORA *kneel at the other end of the table. The men kneel near the door.*)

MAURYA (*raising her head and speaking as if she did not see the people around her*): They're all gone now, and there isn't anything more the sea can do to me. . . . I'll have no call now to be up crying and praying when the wind breaks from the south, and you can hear the surf is in the east, and the surf is in the west, making a great stir with the two noises, and they hitting one on the other. I'll have no call now to be going down and getting Holy Water in the dark nights after Samhain,[15] and I won't care what way the sea is when the other women will be keening. (*To* NORA.) Give me the Holy Water, Nora, there's a small cup still on the dresser.

(NORA *gives it to her.*)

MAURYA (*drops Michael's clothes across* BARTLEY'*s feet, and sprinkles the Holy Water over him*): It isn't that I haven't prayed for you, Bartley, to the Almighty God. It isn't that I haven't said prayers in the dark night till you wouldn't know what I'd be saying; but it's a great rest I'll have now, and it's time surely. It's a great rest I'll have now, and great

[15] All Souls' Day, November 1

sleeping in the long nights after Samhain, if it's only a bit of wet flour we do have to eat, and maybe a fish that would be stinking.

(*She kneels down again, crossing herself, and saying prayers under her breath.*)

CATHLEEN (*to an old man*): Maybe yourself and Eamon would make a coffin when the sun rises. We have fine white boards herself bought, God help her, thinking Michael would be found, and I have a new cake you can eat while you'll be working.

THE OLD MAN (*looking at the boards*): Are there nails with them?

CATHLEEN: There are not, Colum; we didn't think of the nails.

ANOTHER MAN: It's a great wonder she wouldn't think of the nails, and all the coffins she's seen made already.

CATHLEEN: It's getting old she is, and broken.

(MAURYA *stands up again very slowly and spreads out the pieces of Michael's clothes beside the body, sprinkling them with the last of the Holy Water.*)

NORA (*in a whisper to* CATHLEEN): She's quiet now and easy; but the day Michael was drowned you could hear her crying out from this to the spring well. It's fonder she was of Michael, and would any one have thought that?

CATHLEEN (*slowly and clearly*): An old woman will be soon tired with anything she will do, and isn't it nine days herself is after crying and keening, and making great sorrow in the house?

MAUYRA (*puts the empty cup mouth downwards on the table, and lays her hands together on* BARTLEY'*s feet*): They're all together this time, and the end is come. May the Almighty God have mercy on Bartley's soul, and on Michael's soul, and on the souls of Sheamus and Patch, and Stephen and Shawn (*bending her head*); and may He have mercy on my soul, Nora, and on the soul of every one is left living in the world.

(*She pauses, and the keen rises a little more loudly from the women, then sinks away.*)

MAURYA (*continuing*): Michael has a clean burial in the far north, by the grace of the Almighty God. Bartley will have a fine coffin out of the white boards, and a deep grave surely. What more can we want than that? No man at all can be living for ever, and we must be satisfied.

(*She kneels down again and the curtain falls slowly.*)

By 1896 Synge had abandoned his plan to become a professional musician and was living in Paris, studying language and literature at the Sorbonne, and trying, without much success, to be a poet. There, in December, he met W. B. Yeats. Yeats, six years older than Synge and already actively promoting a national Irish literature, urged him to give up both his studies and his conventional poetry and to find his own matter and voice in the unspoiled folk life of his native country. "Go to the Aran Islands," he told him. "Live there as if you were one of the people themselves; express a life that has never found expression."

Their meeting set Synge on the course that was to take him to his brief literary fulfillment. Beginning in 1898 and for five successive years he spent a total of almost five months on the Arans, three small limestone islands, windswept, seaweed-ringed, and fog-bound, lying at the mouth of Galway Bay on the Irish west coast. The first year, he was there in May and June; his later visits were all in early fall. He spent most of his time on Inishmaan, the middle island, among a few hundred people making their living by fishing, burning kelp, turf-cutting, and growing a few, sparse crops. The daily struggle with sea and soil within the larger seasonal cycle gave a natural rhythm to a life that was harsh and simple but not joyless or without beauty and sturdy dignity. In this small community on a bleak Atlantic island Synge found what had eluded him in the cultural capital of Europe. He discovered a way to reconcile his commitment to social fact with escape from the "pallid words" which were all he heard in the middle-class living rooms on the Ibsenite stage. The elemental quality of island life became the pastoral mode of his plays.

Synge had little interest in reworking the traditional stock of native Irish folklore and myth, which Yeats and many others in the national movement considered a main aspect of the Irish literary revival. What fascinated him were actual people and the poetic resources in peasant speech, not the romantic patriotism of the nationalist writers. His literary sensibility delighted in the lilting rhythms of the islanders' spoken English and in its quaint blend of formality and directness — a product, perhaps, of their bilingualism — but it was offended by what he called "the incoherent twaddle that is passed off as Irish by the Gaelic League." He regarded the League's effort to establish the ancient Gaelic tongue as the national language of Ireland as vulgar and sentimental archaism that would either prove abortive or else serve only further to isolate the Irish from the rest of Europe. The distinctive language of Synge's own plays is in no strict sense a dialect. Their Irishness and rural flavor are intense and pervasive, but they go the errand of no social or political or cultural cause. If some of them caused controversy – most notably in the case of the riots at the opening run of *The Playboy of the Western World* in 1907 – it was because chauvinists and moralists were scandalized by his unsentimental presentation of Irish peasantry and mistook his artistic disinterestedness for callous condescension to primitives.

Yeats's prediction that the Aran Islands would make a poet of Synge first came true in the summer of 1902 when Synge wrote *In the Shadow of the Glen* and *Riders to the Sea,* the first two of his six plays. Both are set in western Ireland, but only *Riders to the Sea* is based directly on Synge's island experience. Its language is the Aran idiom carefully cadenced and its subject matter the stern physical and emotional facts of Aran life. The play was first performed by the Irish National Theater Society on February 25, 1904, in Molesworth Hall in Dublin. The audience seems to have received it with indifference. In December of that year the company moved into its new permanent home in Abbey Street.

In *The Aran Islands,* an autobiographical account of his first four visits, which he published in 1907, Synge notes "the reverence for life and the sea that is inevitable in this place" – a good description of the sustaining emotion of *Riders to the Sea.* Synge's book shows that his play is an authentic picture of Aran life in its specifics as well. Landscape and weather and the bitter island economics, food and dress and implements, the circumstances of Michael's and Bartley's deaths, even some actual speeches, have their counterparts in *The Aran Islands.* "Isn't it great danger and sorrow is on everyone on this island?" an old woman asks Synge when the body of a young man is recovered after three weeks in the sea. "On these islands," writes Synge, "the women live only for their childern. . . . The maternal feeling is so powerful . . . that it gives a life of torment to the women." When they bewail their dead in the traditional keen, half spontaneous, half ritual, he thinks he hears "the plaintive intonation of an old race that is worn with sorrow." There is no better gloss on *Riders to the Sea* than the following:

> This grief of the keen is no personal complaint . . . but seems to contain the whole passionate rage that lurks somewhere in every native of the island. In this cry of pain the inner consciousness of the people seems to lay itself bare for an instant, and to reveal the mood of beings who feel their isolation in the face of a universe that wars on them with winds and seas.

To the people of Aran, the educated and cosmopolitan Synge can hardly have been more than a likable outsider, but this was not a handicap to his writing about them. His detachment kept his intuitive sympathy with those who lost friends and kin at sea from subverting the objectivity of his perceptions, and he had the philosophical sophistication and the right words to express the timeless, placeless quality of their grief. In *Riders to the Sea,* art has invested the realistic particulars of local conditions with larger significance without burying them in generalization. The setting of the play on "an island off the west of Ireland" rather than on "the Aran Islands" strikes just the right balance between the specific and the archetypal, between the allegorist's universal "anywhere" and the sociologist's documented "there." It is the same kind of artistic tact that spares us the details of what happens to a body that floats in rough seas for nine days. What is acceptable as a bit of gruesome hearsay in the corresponding incident in *The Aran Islands* would in the play have been a ghoulish intrusion into the self-absorbed lyricism of Maurya's lament. The grim fact remains only as a hint of strange but not ugly sea-change in one of Maurya's speeches after she knows the sea has done its worst and can hurt her no more.

To say that *Riders to the Sea* transcends the limitations of its particulars because the particulars have been so intensely realized sounds like a paradox, but it is only an illustration of the old truism that it takes an individual to be a type, a story to be an allegory, and something concrete to be a symbol. The girls' knitting and the black knot that has to be cut are facts of life in Maurya's cottage, immediate and plausible, but they also resonate with the old mythology of female figures of fate who weave and cut the web of men's lives. The black pig eating the white rope and Bartley's wearing Michael's shirt because his own is water-soaked are portents of death. Basic colors suggest a vivid, unchanging world of primal values: white rocks, gray sea, black hags, black pig, black knot, gray pony, red mare, red sail, red petticoats, green head of land — life against death, land against sea. The stinking fish that Maurya and her daughters will be eating now that all their men are dead, the neighbor's grumble over Maurya's failure to get nails for the coffin boards, and Cathleen's attributing her mother's final calm to physical and emotional exhaustion keep the mythic image of man's frailty in a hostile environment and his spiritual nobility in physical defeat embedded in small, sad actuality. The play achieves its transcendent meaning because island life is life stripped to its essentials and because it is rendered through an accumulation of honest detail. Maurya's fate speaks to us of primal fears, hard necessity, suffering, hope, courage, and endurance, and her cottage represents all the shelters that man vainly erects between himself and the destructive forces of nature. All we see on the stage is the human world; the antagonist remains ironically invisible, except when Bartley's dripping corpse brings the sea into the cottage in a climactic symbolic action. In *The Aran Islands,* Synge says after talking with some fishermen, "I could not help feeling that I was talking to men under judgment of death." So, of course, are we all, and it is because in *Riders to the Sea* sudden death is such a continuously imminent actuality that the whole play is a symbol of all of human life as a brief, embattled stay on a small island in the midst of an implacable sea. We are all, as one critic puts it, riders to the sea.

That so short a play can achieve such large meaning is all the more astonishing in view of its small range of feeling. Its main event is the death of men at sea, but it is about the surviving women. There are only three male characters, and two of them are part of the choric group at the end and have only one speech each. Bartley's part is larger, but he is less a character with an inner life — almost all he says concerns small, practical matters — than the occasion for Maurya's long years of grief and anxiety to come to a climax and an end. His sole function in the play is to be her last son who goes out and dies. Moreover, the womanly feeling on which the play concentrates is almost exclusively maternal feeling. Maurya is more mother than wife or widow, and her daughters worry more about her feelings than about their own. As a result, she is the main character even before she appears. But small focus gives depth and sharpness of vision. Within half an hour on stage Synge's play compresses a lifetime of bereavement, a story of a mother's grief finally set free.

The economy of the play is also the result of the way a number of key speeches seem to reach out for the kind of general folk wisdom that is distilled in proverbs: "What is the price of a thousand horses against a son where there is one son only?" "There's no sense left on any person in a house where an old woman will be talking forever." "In the big world the old people do be leaving things after them for their sons and children, but in this place it is the young men do be leaving things behind for them that do be old." "Isn't it a pitiful thing when there is nothing left of a man who was a great rower and fisher, but a bit of an old shirt and a plain stocking?" "There does be a power of young men floating round in the sea." "An old woman will soon be tired with anything she will do." Because the momentum of feeling in such speeches is away from the individual toward the communal, a kind of inertia of psychic dynamics begins to operate in the reader or spectator, pushing the communal feeling in the direction of the universal: "It's the life of a young man to be going on the sea, and who would listen to an old woman with one thing and she saying it over?"

James Joyce said of *Riders to the Sea* that it was "un-Aristotelian" and meant by that to call attention to a shortcoming.* What exactly he found wanting in the play by the norms of the Aristotelian poetic of tragedy he didn't say, but we can guess. The play deals with a situation rather than with an action, and it is therefore possible to argue that it has no distinct beginning, middle, and end. Since local conditions of climate and topography determine events and since a particular way of island life determines responses to the events, the real protagonist could be said to be the communal ethos rather than an individual. The proverbial thrust of so many speeches contributes to this impression. In this sense, the play is both a naturalistic and a folk or group play, and Maurya has archetypal dimensions largely because she represents feelings and attitudes common to all island mothers. It is not a play of ideas; there is in it no open or hidden theme of social or metaphysical protest. Events prove the young priest wrong when he reassures Nora that God surely will spare Maurya's last son, but the point of his misplaced faith is not anti-clerical satire, atheism, or human indictment of divine severity. Maurya's comment, "It's little the like of him knows of the sea," is only a stoic recognition of the cruel indifference of a power alien to a tidy theological scheme. There is no character whose soul is divided by clashing imperatives. Bartley does not resent the necessity that sends him out to sea when "there's a great roaring in the west, and it's worse it'll be getting when the tide's turned to the wind"; Maurya's states of mind and feeling are successive, not conflicting; and Nora and Cathleen control their grief by busying themselves with practical concerns — the level of their feelings hardly ever changes. Most important, what happens has no moral significance since the human sufferer is necessarily passive under the catastrophe and the destructive agent is an amoral, mindless force built into the physical universe. The world of the play is ruthless but not evil. These are good reasons for challenging not just the usual view that *Riders to the Sea* is one of the greatest one-act tragedies in the language but that it is a tragedy at all.

Labeling literary works is pointless pedantry unless the labels help us better understand what they label. The point in raising the issue of whether or not *Riders to the Sea* is a tragedy is neither to grant it nor to withhold from it the ultimate critical tribute ("tragedy," unfortunately, having become an honorific rather than simply a descriptive term), but to try to account for a common response to the play which is akin to our response to traditional tragedies but one for which there may seem to be no assignable cause in Synge's play.

Joyce cannot have meant that the play is without its moment of

* Joyce later admired the play, though this does not necessarily mean that he found it a true tragedy by Aristotelian criteria.

Aristotelian peripety. It comes in Maurya's vision of the dead Michael "with fine clothes on him, and new shoes on his feet," riding the gray pony behind his still living brother on the red mare. Her vision brings about a change in her, which, if it does not constitute an Aristotelian plot, does represent a significant human action; the main character is not static. Before her vision Maurya is a fretful old woman, petulantly and — in terms of the circumstances — unreasonably trying to keep Bartley from doing what he must do. After her vision, she accepts Bartley's death as a certainty, even before it has actually occurred. In commenting in *The Aran Islands* on the actual incident on which he based this detail in his play, Synge writes, "These people make no distinction between the natural and the supernatural." This is clearly Maurya's case, but Synge has transmuted island superstition into a dramatic image that achieves an effect of catharsis, Aristotle's term for the final release of the spectator's feelings of pity and fear at the end of the tragic action. Bartley's body is carried in just as Maurya is telling Cathleen and Nora how the men brought Patch in many years ago, wrapped in "the half of a red sail." The room in which she is lost in memory is the same as it was then, and the distinction between naturalism and the supernatural disappears, as reality and imagination, past and present, become one in the spectacle that stages the past she is narrating. In the crowding scene, Maurya's maternal sorrow is lifted to some timeless dimension of resignation and acceptance, beyond the immediate realism of drowned man and keening women. The scene ritualizes her last loss, and the ritual releases the coiled spring of an anguish that has been gathering through a life of human losses. The dead brothers are together, wearing fine clothes and new shoes. The sea has taken her last son, and she triumphs in the invulnerability of her ultimate bereavement:

> . . . there isn't anything more the sea can do to me. . . . I'll have no call now to be up crying and praying when the wind breaks from the south, and you can hear the surf in the east. . . . It's a great rest I'll have now, and it's time surely. It's a great rest I'll have now, and great sleeping in the long nights after Samhain. . . .

If there is no *moral* victory in Maurya's final serenity and peace, if she is only a woman to whom things have happened, she speaks from an awareness for which mere exhaustion is an inadequate as well as an irrelevant explanation. She has gained recognition and she accepts her destiny: "No man at all can be living for ever, and we must be satisfied." There is nothing in her final calm that does not meet the Aristotelian requirements of character (*ethos*) and thought (*dianoia*) proper to tragedy.

AUGUST STRINDBERG

# The Ghost Sonata

*Translated by Elizabeth Sprigge*

CHARACTERS

THE OLD MAN, Hummel, a Company Director
THE STUDENT, Arkenholtz
THE MILKMAID, an apparition
THE CARETAKER'S WIFE
THE CARETAKER
THE LADY IN BLACK, the daughter of the Caretaker's Wife and the Dead Man. Also referred to as the Dark Lady
THE COLONEL
THE MUMMY, the Colonel's wife
THE GIRL, the Colonel's daughter, actually the daughter of the Old Man
THE ARISTOCRAT, Baron Skanskorg. Engaged to the Lady in Black
JOHANSSON, the Old Man's servant
BENGTSSON, the Colonel's servant
THE FIANCÉE, a white-haired old woman, once betrothed to the Old Man
THE COOK
A MAIDSERVANT
BEGGARS

## SCENE I

*Outside the house. The corner of the façade of a modern house, showing the ground floor above, and the street in front. The ground floor terminates on the right in the Round Room, above which, on the first floor, is a balcony with a flagstaff. The windows of the Round*

*Room face the street in front of the house, and at the corner look on to the suggestion of a side-street running toward the back. At the beginning of the scene the blinds of the Round Room are down. When, later, they are raised, the white marble statue of a young woman can be seen, surrounded with palms and brightly lighted by rays of sunshine.*

*To the left of the Round Room is the Hyacinth Room; its window filled with pots of hyacinths, blue, white and pink. Further left, at the back, is an imposing double front door with laurels in tubs on either side of it. The doors are wide open, showing a staircase of white marble with a banister of mahogany and brass. To the left of the front door is another ground-floor window, with a window-mirror.*[1] *On the balcony rail in the corner above the Round Room are a blue silk quilt and two white pillows. The windows to the left of this are hung with white sheets.*[2]

*In the foreground, in front of the house, is a green bench; to the right a street drinking-fountain, to the left an advertisement column.*

*It is a bright Sunday morning, and as the curtain rises the bells of several churches, some near, some far away, are ringing.*

*On the staircase the* LADY IN BLACK *stands motionless.*

*The* CARETAKER'S WIFE *sweeps the doorstep, then polishes the brass on the door and waters the laurels.*

*In a wheelchair by the advertisement column sits the* OLD MAN, *reading a newspaper. His hair and beard are white and he wears spectacles.*

*The* MILKMAID *comes round the corner on the right, carrying milk bottles in a wire basket. She is wearing a summer dress with brown shoes, black stockings and a white cap. She takes off her cap and hangs it on the fountain, wipes the perspiration from her forehead, washes her hands and arranges her hair, using the water as a mirror.*

*A steamship bell is heard, and now and then the silence is broken by the deep notes of an organ in a nearby church.*

*After a few moments, when all is silent and the* MILKMAID *has finished her toilet, the* STUDENT *enters from the left. He has had a sleepless night and is unshaven. He goes straight up to the fountain. There is a pause before he speaks.*

STUDENT: May I have the cup?

(*The* MILKMAID *clutches the cup to her.*)

Haven't you finished yet?

(*The* MILKMAID *looks at him with horror.*)

[1] "Set at an angle inside the window, so as to show what is going on in the street." [Sprigge's note.]

[2] "Sign of mourning." [Sprigge's note.]

OLD MAN (*to himself*): Who's he talking to? I don't see anybody. Is he crazy? (*He goes on watching them in great astonishment.*)

STUDENT (*to the* MILKMAID): What are you staring at? Do I look so terrible? Well, I've had no sleep, and of course you think I've been making a night of it . . .

(*The* MILKMAID *stays just as she is.*)

You think I've been drinking, eh? Do I smell of liquor?

(*The* MILKMAID *does not change.*)

I haven't shaved, I know. Give me a drink of water, girl. I've earned it. (*Pause.*) Oh well, I suppose I'll have to tell you. I spent the whole night dressing wounds and looking after the injured. You see, I was there when that house collapsed last night. Now you know.

(*The* MILKMAID *rinses the cup and gives him a drink.*)

Thanks.

(*The* MILKMAID *stands motionless. Slowly.*)

Will you do me a great favor? (*Pause.*) The thing is, my eyes, as you can see, are inflamed, but my hands have been touching wounds and corpses, so it would be dangerous to put them near my eyes. Will you take my handkerchief – it's quite clean – and dip it in the fresh water and bathe my eyes? Will you do this? Will you play the good Samaritan?

(*The* MILKMAID *hesitates, but does as he bids.*)

Thank you, my dear. (*He takes out his purse. She makes a gesture of refusal.*) Forgive my stupidity, but I'm only half-awake. . . .

(*The* MILKMAID *disappears.*)

OLD MAN (*to the* STUDENT): Excuse me speaking to you, but I heard you say you were at the scene of the accident last night. I was just reading about it in the paper.

STUDENT: Is it in the paper already?

OLD MAN: The whole thing, including your portrait. But they regret that they have been unable to find out the name of the splendid young student. . . .

STUDENT: Really? (*Glances at the paper.*) Yes, that's me. Well I never!

OLD MAN: Who was it you were talking to just now?

STUDENT: Didn't you see? (*Pause.*)

OLD MAN: Would it be impertinent to inquire – what in fact your name is?

STUDENT: What would be the point? I don't care for publicity. If you get any praise, there's always disapproval too. The art of running people down has been developed to such a pitch. . . . Besides, I don't want any reward.

OLD MAN: You're well off, perhaps.

STUDENT: No, indeed. On the contrary, I'm very poor.

OLD MAN: Do you know, it seems to me I've heard your voice before. When I was young I had a friend who pronounced certain words just as you do. I've never met anyone else with quite that pronunciation. Only him — and you. Are you by any chance related to Mr. Arkenholtz, the merchant?

STUDENT: He was my father.

OLD MAN: Strange are the paths of fate. I saw you when you were an infant, under very painful circumstances.

STUDENT: Yes, I understand I came into the world in the middle of a bankruptcy.

OLD MAN: Just that.

STUDENT: Perhaps I might ask your name.

OLD MAN: I am Mr. Hummel.

STUDENT: Are you the? . . . I remember that . . .

OLD MAN: Have you often heard my name mentioned in your family?

STUDENT: Yes.

OLD MAN: And mentioned perhaps with a certain aversion?

(*The* STUDENT *is silent.*)

Yes, I can imagine it. You were told, I suppose, that I was the man who ruined your father? All who ruin themselves through foolish speculations consider they were ruined by those they couldn't fool. (*Pause.*) Now these are the facts. Your father robbed me of seventeen thousand crowns — the whole of my savings at that time.

STUDENT: It's queer that the same story can be told in two such different ways.

OLD MAN: You surely don't believe I'm telling you what isn't true?

STUDENT: What am I to believe? My father didn't lie.

OLD MAN: That is so true. A father never lies. But I too am a father, and so it follows . . .

STUDENT: What are you driving at?

OLD MAN: I saved your father from disaster, and he repaid me with all the frightful hatred that is born of an obligation to be grateful. He taught his family to speak ill of me.

STUDENT: Perhaps you made him ungrateful by poisoning your help with unnecessary humiliation.

OLD MAN: All help is humiliating, sir.

STUDENT: What do you want from me?

OLD MAN: I'm not asking for the money, but if you will render me a few small services, I shall consider myself well paid. You see that I am a cripple. Some say it is my own fault; others lay the blame on my parents. I prefer to blame life itself, with its pitfalls. For if you escape one snare, you fall headlong into another. In any case, I am unable to climb stairs or ring doorbells, and that is why I am asking you to help me.

STUDENT: What can I do?

OLD MAN: To begin with, push my chair so that I can read those playbills. I want to see what is on tonight.

STUDENT (*pushing the chair*): Haven't you got an attendant?

OLD MAN: Yes, but he has gone on an errand. He'll be back soon. Are you a medical student?

STUDENT: No, I am studying languages, but I don't know at all what I'm going to do.

OLD MAN: Aha! Are you good at mathematics?

STUDENT: Yes, fairly.

OLD MAN: Good. Perhaps you would like a job.

STUDENT: Yes, why not?

OLD MAN: Splendid. (*He studies the playbills.*) They are doing *The Valkyrie* for the matinée. That means the Colonel will be there with his daughter, and as he always sits at the end of the sixth row, I'll put you next to him. Go to that telephone kiosk please and order a ticket for seat eighty-two in the sixth row.

STUDENT: Am I to go to the Opera in the middle of the day?

OLD MAN: Yes. Do as I tell you and things will go well with you. I want to see you happy, rich and honored. Your début last night as the brave rescuer will make you famous by tomorrow and then your name will be worth something.

STUDENT (*going to the telephone kiosk*): What an odd adventure!

OLD MAN: Are you a gambler?

STUDENT: Yes, unfortunately.

OLD MAN: We'll make it fortunately. Go on now, telephone.

(*The* STUDENT *goes. The* OLD MAN *reads his paper. The* LADY IN BLACK *comes out on to the pavement and talks to the* CARETAKER'S WIFE. *The* OLD MAN *listens, but the audience hears nothing. The* STUDENT *returns.*)

Did you fix it up?

STUDENT: It's done.

OLD MAN: You see that house?

STUDENT: Yes, I've been looking at it a lot. I passed it yesterday when the sun was shining on the windowpanes, and I imagined all the beauty and elegance there must be inside. I said to my companion: "Think of living up there in the top flat, with a beautiful young wife, two pretty little children and an income of twenty thousand crowns a year."

OLD MAN: So that's what you said. That's what you said. Well, well! I too am very fond of this house.

STUDENT: Do you speculate in houses?

OLD MAN: Mm — yes. But not in the way you mean.

STUDENT: Do you know the people who live here?

OLD MAN: Every one of them. At my age one knows everybody, and their parents and grandparents too, and one's always related to them in some way or other. I am just eighty, but no one knows me — not really. I take an interest in human destiny.

(*The blinds of the Round Room are drawn up. The* COLONEL *is seen, wearing mufti. He looks at the thermometer outside one of the windows, then turns back into the room and stands in front of the marble statue.*)

Look, that's the Colonel, whom you will sit next to this afternoon.

STUDENT: Is he — the Colonel? I don't understand any of this, but it's like a fairy story.

OLD MAN: My whole life's like a book of fairy stories, sir. And although the stories are different, they are held together by one thread, and the main theme constantly recurs.

STUDENT: Who is that marble statue of?

OLD MAN: That, naturally, is his wife.

STUDENT: Was she such a wonderful person?

OLD MAN: Er . . . yes.

STUDENT: Tell me.

OLD MAN: We can't judge people, young man. If I were to tell you that she left him, that he beat her, that she returned to him and married him a second time, and that now she is sitting inside there like a mummy, worshipping her own statue — then you would think me crazy.

STUDENT: I don't understand.

OLD MAN: I didn't think you would. Well, then we have the window with the hyacinths. His daughter lives there. She has gone out for a ride, but she will be home soon.

STUDENT: And who is the dark lady talking to the caretaker?

OLD MAN: Well, that's a bit complicated, but it is connected with the dead man, up there where you see the white sheets.

STUDENT: Why, who was he?

OLD MAN: A human being like you or me, but the most conspicuous thing about him was his vanity. If you were a Sunday child, you would see him presently come out of that door to look at the Consulate flag flying at half-mast. He was, you understand, a Consul, and he reveled in coronets and lions and plumed hats and colored ribbons.

STUDENT: Sunday child, you say? I'm told I was born on a Sunday.

OLD MAN: No, were you really? I might have known it. I saw it from the color of your eyes. Then you can see what others can't. Have you noticed that?

STUDENT: I don't know what others do see, but at times. . . . Oh, but one doesn't talk of such things!

OLD MAN: I was almost sure of it. But you can talk to me, because I understand such things.

STUDENT: Yesterday, for instance . . . I was drawn to that obscure little street where later on the house collapsed. I went there and stopped in front of that building which I had never seen before. Then I noticed a crack in the wall. . . . I heard the floor boards snapping. . . . I dashed over and picked up a child that was passing under the wall. . . . The next moment the house collapsed. I was saved, but in my arms, which I thought held the child, was nothing at all.

OLD MAN: Yes, yes, just as I thought. Tell me something. Why were you gesticulating that way just now by the fountain? And why were you talking to yourself?

STUDENT: Didn't you see the milkmaid I was talking to?

OLD MAN (*in horror*): Milkmaid?

STUDENT: Surely. The girl who handed me the cup.

OLD MAN: Really? So that's what was going on. Ah well, I haven't second sight, but there are things I can do.

(THE FIANCÉE *is now seen to sit down by the window which has the window-mirror.*)

Look at that old woman in the window. Do you see her? Well, she was my fiancée once, sixty years ago. I was twenty. Don't be alarmed. She doesn't recognize me. We see one another every day, and it makes no impression on me, although once we vowed to love one another eternally. Eternally!

STUDENT: How foolish you were in those days! We never talk to our girls like that.

OLD MAN: Forgive us, young man. We didn't know any better. But can you see that that old woman was once young and beautiful?

STUDENT: It doesn't show. And yet there's some charm in her looks. I can't see her eyes.

(*The* CARETAKER'S WIFE *comes out with a basket of chopped fir branches.*[3])

OLD MAN: Ah, the caretaker's wife! That dark lady is her daughter by the dead man. That's why her husband was given the job of caretaker. But the dark lady has a suitor, who is an aristocrat with great expectations. He is in the process of getting a divorce — from his present wife, you understand. She's presenting him with a stone mansion in order to be rid of him. This aristocratic suitor is the son-in-law of the dead man, and you can see his bedclothes being aired on the balcony upstairs. It is complicated, I must say.

[3] "It was customary in Sweden to strew the ground with these for a funeral." [Sprigge's note.]

STUDENT: It's fearfully complicated.

OLD MAN: Yes, that it is, internally and externally, although it looks quite simple.

STUDENT: But then who was the dead man?

OLD MAN: You asked me that just now, and I answered. If you were to look round the corner, where the tradesmen's entrance is, you would see a lot of poor people whom he used to help — when it suited him.

STUDENT: He was a kind man then.

OLD MAN: Yes — sometimes.

STUDENT: Not always?

OLD MAN: No-o. That's the way of people. Now, sir, will you push my chair a little, so that it gets into the sun. I'm horribly cold. When you're never able to move about, the blood congeals. I'm going to die soon, I know that, but I have a few things to do first. Take my hand and feel how cold I am.

STUDENT (*taking it*): Yes, inconceivably. (*He shrinks back, trying in vain to free his hand.*)

OLD MAN: Don't leave me. I am tired now and lonely, but I haven't always been like this, you know. I have an enormously long life behind me, enormously long. I have made people unhappy and people have made me unhappy — the one cancels out the other — but before I die I want to see you happy. Our fates are entwined through your father — and other things.

STUDENT: Let go of my hand. You are taking all my strength. You are freezing me. What do you want with me?

OLD MAN (*letting go*): Be patient and you shall see and understand. Here comes the young lady.

(*They watch the* GIRL *approaching, though the audience cannot yet see her.*)

STUDENT: The Colonel's daughter?

OLD MAN: His daughter — yes. Look at her. Have you ever seen such a masterpiece?

STUDENT: She is like the marble statue in there.

OLD MAN: That's her mother, you know.

STUDENT: You are right. Never have I seen such a woman of woman born. Happy the man who may lead her to the altar and his home.

OLD MAN: You can see it. Not everyone recognizes her beauty. So, then, it is written.

(*The* GIRL *enters, wearing an English riding habit. Without noticing anyone she walks slowly to the door, where she stops to say a few words to the* CARETAKER'S WIFE. *Then she goes into the house. The* STUDENT *covers his eyes with his hand.*)

OLD MAN: Are you weeping?

STUDENT: In the face of what's hopeless there can be nothing but despair.

OLD MAN: I can open doors and hearts, if only I find an arm to do my will. Serve me and you shall have power.

STUDENT: Is it a bargain? Am I to sell my soul?

OLD MAN: Sell nothing. Listen. All my life I have *taken*. Now I have a craving to give – give. But no one will accept. I am rich, very rich, but I have no heirs, except for a good-for-nothing who torments the life out of me. Become my son. Inherit me while I am still alive. Enjoy life so that I can watch, at least from a distance.

STUDENT: What am I to do?

OLD MAN: First go to *The Valkyrie*.

STUDENT: That's settled. What else?

OLD MAN: This evening you must be in there – in the Round Room.

STUDENT: How am I to get there?

OLD MAN: By way of *The Valkyrie*.

STUDENT: Why have you chosen me as your medium? Did you know me before?

OLD MAN: Yes, of course. I have had my eye on you for a long time. But now look up there at the balcony. The maid is hoisting the flag to half-mast for the Consul. And now she is turning the bedclothes. Do you see that blue quilt? It was made for two to sleep under, but now it covers only one.

(*The* GIRL, *having changed her dress, appears in the window and waters the hyacinths.*)

There is my little girl. Look at her, look! She is talking to the flowers. Is she not like that blue hyacinth herself? She gives them drink – nothing but pure water, and they transform the water into color and fragrance. Now here comes the Colonel with the newspaper. He is showing her the bit about the house that collapsed. Now he's pointing to your portrait. She's not indifferent. She's reading of your brave deed. . . .

I believe it's clouding over. If it turns to rain I shall be in a pretty fix, unless Johansson comes back soon.

(*It grows cloudy and dark. The* FIANCÉE *at the window-mirror closes her window.*)

Now my fiancée is closing the window. Seventy-nine years old. The window-mirror is the only mirror she uses, because in it she sees not herself, but the world outside – in two directions. But the world can see her; she hasn't thought of that. Anyhow she's a handsome old woman.

(*Now the* DEAD MAN, *wrapped in a winding sheet, comes out of the door.*)

STUDENT: Good God, what do I see?

OLD MAN: What do you see?

STUDENT: Don't *you* see? There, in the doorway, the dead man?

OLD MAN: I see nothing, but I expected this. Tell me.

STUDENT: He is coming out into the street. (*Pause.*) Now he is turning his head and looking up at the flag.

OLD MAN: What did I tell you? You may be sure he'll count the wreaths and read the visiting cards. Woe to him who's missing.

STUDENT: Now he's turning the corner.

OLD MAN: He's gone to count the poor at the back door. The poor are in the nature of a decoration, you see. "Followed by the blessings of many." Well, he's not going to have my blessing. Between ourselves he was a great scoundrel.

STUDENT: But charitable.

OLD MAN: A charitable scoundrel, always thinking of his grand funeral. When he knew his end was near, he cheated the State out of fifty thousand crowns. Now his daughter has relations with another woman's husband and is wondering about the Will. Yes, the scoundrel can hear every word we're saying, and he's welcome to it. Ah, here comes Johansson!

(JOHANSSON *enters.*)

Report!

(JOHANSSON *speaks, but the audience does not hear.*)

Not at home, eh? You are an ass. And the telegram? Nothing? Go on. . . . At six this evening? That's good. Special edition, you say? With his name in full. Arkenholtz, a student, born . . . parents . . . That's splendid. . . . I think it's beginning to rain. . . . What did he say about it? So — so. He wouldn't? Well, he must. Here comes the aristocrat. Push me round the corner, Johansson, so I can hear what the poor are saying. And, Arkenholtz, you wait for me here. Understand? (*To* JOHANSSON.) Hurry up now, hurry up.

(JOHANSSON *wheels the chair round the corner. The* STUDENT *remains watching the* GIRL, *who is now loosening the earth round the hyacinths. The* ARISTOCRAT, *wearing mourning, comes in and speaks to the* DARK LADY, *who has been walking to and fro on the pavement.*)

ARISTOCRAT: But what can we do about it? We shall have to wait.

LADY: I can't wait.

ARISTOCRAT: You can't? Well then, go into the country.

LADY: I don't want to do that.

ARISTOCRAT: Come over here or they will hear what we are saying.

(*They move toward the advertisement column and continue their conversation inaudibly.* JOHANSSON *returns.*)

JOHANSSON (*to the* STUDENT): My master asks you not to forget that other thing, sir.

STUDENT (*hesitating*): Look here . . . first of all tell me . . . who is your master?

JOHANSSON: Well, he's so many things, and he has been everything.

STUDENT: Is he a wise man?

JOHANSSON: Depends what that is. He says all his life he's been looking for a Sunday child, but that may not be true.

STUDENT: What does he want? He's grasping, isn't he?

JOHANSSON: It's power he wants. The whole day long he rides round in his chariot like the god Thor himself. He looks at houses, pulls them down, opens up new streets, builds squares. . . . But he breaks into houses too, sneaks through windows, plays havoc with human destinies, kills his enemies — and never forgives. Can you imagine it, sir? This miserable cripple was once a Don Juan — although he always lost his women.

STUDENT: How do you account for that?

JOHANSSON: You see he's so cunning he makes the women leave him when he's tired of them. But what he's most like now is a horse thief in the human market. He steals human beings in all sorts of different ways. He literally stole me out of the hands of the law. Well, as a matter of fact I'd made a slip — hm, yes — and only he knew about it. Instead of getting me put in gaol, he turned me into a slave. I slave — for my food alone, and that's none of the best.

STUDENT: Then what is it he means to do in this house?

JOHANSSON: I'm not going to talk about that. It's too complicated.

STUDENT: I think I'd better get away from it all.

(*The* GIRL *drops a bracelet out the window.*)

JOHANSSON: Look! The young lady has dropped her bracelet out of the window.

(*The* STUDENT *goes slowly over, picks up the bracelet and returns it to the* GIRL, *who thanks him stiffly. The* STUDENT *goes back to* JOHANSSON.)

So you mean to get away. That's not so easy as you think, once he's got you in his net. And he's afraid of nothing between heaven and earth — yes, of one thing he is — of one person rather. . . .

STUDENT: Don't tell me. I think perhaps I know.

JOHANSSON: How can you know?

STUDENT: I'm guessing. Is it a little milkmaid he's afraid of?

JOHANSSON: He turns his head the other way whenever he meets a milk cart. Besides, he talks in his sleep. It seems he was once in Hamburg. . . .

STUDENT: Can one trust this man?

JOHANSSON: You can trust him — to do anything.

STUDENT: What's he doing now round the corner?

JOHANSSON: Listening to the poor. Sowing a little word, loosening one stone at a time, till the house falls down — metaphorically speaking. You see I'm an educated man. I was once a book-seller. . . . Do you still mean to go away?

STUDENT: I don't like to be ungrateful. He saved my father once, and now he only asks a small service in return.

JOHANSSON: What is that?

STUDENT: I am to go to *The Valkyrie.*

JOHANSSON: That's beyond me. But he's always up to new tricks. Look at him now, talking to that policeman. He is always thick with the police. He uses them, gets them involved in his interests, holds them with false promises and expectations, while all the time he's pumping them. You'll see that before the day is over he'll be received in the Round Room.

STUDENT: What does he want there? What connection has he with the Colonel?

JOHANSSON: I think I can guess, but I'm not sure. You'll see for yourself once you're in there.

STUDENT: I shall never be in there.

JOHANSSON: That depends on yourself. Go to *The Valkyrie.*

STUDENT: Is that the way?

JOHANSSON: Yes, if he said so. Look. Look at him in his war chariot, drawn in triumph by the beggars, who get nothing for their pains but the hint of a treat at his funeral.

(*The* OLD MAN *appears standing up in his wheel-chair, drawn by one of the beggars and followed by the rest.*)

OLD MAN: Hail the noble youth who, at the risk of his own life, saved so many others in yesterday's accident. Three cheers for Arkenholtz!

(*The* BEGGARS *bare their heads but do not cheer. The* GIRL *at the window waves her handkerchief. The* COLONEL *gazes from the window of the Round Room. The* OLD WOMAN *rises at her window. The* MAID *on the balcony hoists the flag to the top.*)

Clap your hands, citizens. True, it is Sunday, but the ass in the pit and the ear in the corn field will absolve us. And although I am not a Sunday child, I have the gift of prophecy and also that of healing. Once I brought a drowned person back to life. That was in Hamburg on a Sunday morning just like this. . . .

(*The* MILKMAID *enters, seen only by the* STUDENT *and the* OLD MAN. *She raises her arms like one who is drowning and gazes fixedly at the* OLD MAN. *He sits down, then crumples up, stricken with horror.*)

Johansson! Take me away! Quick! . . . Arkenholtz, don't forget *The Valkyrie.*

STUDENT: What is all this?

JOHANSSON: We shall see. We shall see.

## SCENE II

*Inside the Round Room. At the back is a white porcelain stove. On either side of it are a mirror, a pendulum clock and candelabra. On the right of the stove is the entrance to the hall beyond which is a glimpse of a room furnished in green and mahogany. On the left of the stove is the door to a cupboard, papered like the wall. The statue, shaded by palms, has a curtain which can be drawn to conceal it.*

*A door on the left leads into the Hyacinth Room, where the* GIRL *sits reading.*

*The back of the* COLONEL *can be seen, as he sits in the Green Room, writing.*

BENGTSSON, *the Colonel's servant, comes in from the hall. He is wearing livery, and is followed by* JOHANSSON, *dressed as a waiter.*

BENGTSSON: Now you'll have to serve the tea, Johansson, while I take the coats. Have you ever done it before?

JOHANSSON: It's true I push a war chariot in the daytime, as you know, but in the evenings I go as a waiter to receptions and so forth. It's always been my dream to get into this house. They're queer people here, aren't they?

BENGTSSON: Ye-es. A bit out of the ordinary anyhow.

JOHANSSON: Is it to be a musical party or what?

BENGTSSON: The usual ghost supper, as we call it. They drink tea and don't say a word — or else the Colonel does all the talking. And they crunch their biscuits, all at the same time. It sounds like rats in an attic.

JOHANSSON: Why do you call it the ghost supper?

BENGTSSON: They look like ghosts. And they've kept this up for twenty years, always the same people saying the same things or saying nothing at all for fear of being found out.

JOHANSSON: Isn't there a mistress of the house?

BENGTSSON: Oh yes, but she's crazy. She sits in a cupboard because her eyes can't bear the light. (*He points to the papered door.*) She sits in there.

JOHANSSON: In there?

BENGTSSON: Well, I told you they were a bit out of the ordinary.

JOHANSSON: But then — what does she look like?

BENGTSSON: Like a mummy. Do you want to have a look at her? (*He opens the door.*) There she is.

(*The figure of the* COLONEL'S WIFE *is seen, white and shrivelled into a* MUMMY.)

JOHANSSON: Oh my God!

MUMMY (*babbling*): Why do you open the door? Haven't I told you to keep it closed?

BENGTSSON (*in a wheedling tone*): Ta, ta, ta, ta. Be a good girl now, then you'll get something nice. Pretty Polly.

MUMMY (*parrot-like*): Pretty Polly. Are you there, Jacob? Currrrr!

BENGTSSON: She thinks she's a parrot, and maybe she's right. (*To the* MUMMY.) Whistle for us, Polly.

(*The* MUMMY *whistles.*)

JOHANSSON: Well, I've seen a few things in my day, but this beats everything.

BENGTSSON: You see, when a house gets old, it grows moldy, and when people stay a long time together and torment each other they go mad. The mistress of the house– shut up, Polly! – that mummy there, has been living here for forty years – same husband, same furniture, same relatives, same friends. (*He closes the papered door.*) And the goings-on in this house – well, they're beyond me. Look at that statue – that's her when she was young.

JOHANSSON: Good Lord! Is that the mummy?

BENGTSSON: Yes. It's enough to make you weep. And somehow, carried away by her own imagination or something, she's got to be a bit like a parrot – the way she talks and the way she can't stand cripples or sick people. She can't stand the sight of her own daughter, because she's sick.

JOHANSSON: Is the young lady sick?

BENGTSSON: Didn't you know that?

JOHANSSON: No. And the Colonel, who is he?

BENGTSSON: You'll see.

JOHANSSON (*looking at the statue*): It's horrible to think that . . . How old is she now?

BENGTSSON: Nobody knows. But it's said that when she was thirty-five she looked nineteen, and that's what she made the Colonel believe she was – here in this very house. Do you know what that black Japanese screen by the couch is for? They call it the death-screen, and when someone's going to die, they put it round – same as in a hospital.

JOHANSSON: What a horrible house! And the student was longing to get in, as if it were paradise.

BENGTSSON: What student? Oh, I know. The one who's coming here this evening. The Colonel and the young lady happened to meet him at the Opera, and both of them took a fancy to him. Hm. Now it's my turn to ask questions. Who is your master – the man in the wheelchair?

JOHANSSON: Well, he . . . er . . . Is he coming here too?

BENGTSSON: He hasn't been invited.

JOHANSSON: He'll come uninvited – if need be.

(*The* OLD MAN *appears in the hall on crutches, wearing a frock-coat and top-hat. He steals forward and listens.*)

BENGTSSON: He's a regular old devil, isn't he?
JOHANSSON: Up to the ears.
BENGTSSON: He looks like old Nick himself.
JOHANSSON: And he must be a wizard too, for he goes through locked doors.

(*The* OLD MAN *comes forward and takes hold of* JOHANSSON *by the ear.*)

OLD MAN: Rascal — take care! (*To* BENGTSSON.) Tell the Colonel I am here.
BENGTSSON: But we are expecting guests.
OLD MAN: I know. But my visit is as good as expected, if not exactly looked forward to.
BENGTSSON: I see. What name shall I say? Mr. Hummel?
OLD MAN: Exactly. Yes.

(BENGTSSON *crosses the hall to the Green Room, the door of which he closes behind him.*)

(*To* JOHANSSON.) Get out!

(JOHANSSON *hesitates.*)

Get out!

(JOHANSSON *disappears into the hall. The* OLD MAN *inspects the room and stops in front of the statue in much astonishment.*)

Amelia! It is she — she!
MUMMY (*from the cupboard*): Prrr-etty Polly.

(*The* OLD MAN *starts.*)

OLD MAN: What was that? Is there a parrot in the room? I don't see it.
MUMMY: Are you there, Jacob?
OLD MAN: The house is haunted.
MUMMY: Jacob!
OLD MAN: I'm scared. So these are the kind of secrets they guard in this house. (*With his back turned to the cupboard he stands looking at a portrait.*) There he is — he!

(*The* MUMMY *comes out behind the* OLD MAN *and gives a pull at his wig.*)

MUMMY: Currrrr! Is it . . . ? Currrrr!
OLD MAN (*jumping out of his skin*): God in heaven! Who is it?
MUMMY (*in a natural voice*): Is it Jacob?
OLD MAN: Yes, my name is Jacob.
MUMMY (*with emotion*): And my name is Amelia.
OLD MAN: No, no, no . . . Oh my God!
MUMMY: That's how I look. Yes. (*Pointing to the statue.*) And that's how I *did* look. Life opens one's eyes, does it not? I live mostly in the cupboard to avoid seeing and being seen. . . . But, Jacob, what do you want here?

OLD MAN: My child. Our child.

MUMMY: There she is.

OLD MAN: Where?

MUMMY: There – in the Hyacinth Room.

OLD MAN (*looking at the* GIRL): Yes, that is she. (*Pause.*) And what about her father – the Colonel, I mean – your husband?

MUMMY: Once, when I was angry with him, I told him everything.

OLD MAN: Well . . . ?

MUMMY: He didn't believe me. He just said: "That's what all wives say when they want to murder their husbands." It was a terrible crime none the less. It has falsified his whole life – his family tree too. Sometimes I take a look in the Peerage, and then I say to myself: Here she is, going about with a false birth certificate like some servant girl, and for such things people are sent to the reformatory.

OLD MAN: Many do it. I seem to remember your own date of birth was given incorrectly.

MUMMY: My mother made me do that. I was not to blame. And in our crime, *you* played the biggest part.

OLD MAN: No. Your husband caused that crime, when he took my fiancée from me. I was born one who cannot forgive until he has punished. That was to me an imperative duty – and is so still.

MUMMY: What are you expecting to find in this house? What do you want? How did you get in? Is it to do with my daughter? If you touch her, you shall die.

OLD MAN: I mean well by her.

MUMMY: Then you must spare her father.

OLD MAN: No.

MUMMY: Then you shall die. In this room, behind that screen.

OLD MAN: That may be. But I can't let go once I've got my teeth into a thing.

MUMMY: You want to marry her to that student. Why? He is nothing and has nothing.

OLD MAN: He will be rich, through me.

MUMMY: Have you been invited here tonight?

OLD MAN: No, but I propose to get myself an invitation to this ghost supper.

MUMMY: Do you know who is coming?

OLD MAN: Not exactly.

MUMMY: The Baron. The man who lives up above – whose father-in-law was buried this afternoon.

OLD MAN: The man who is getting a divorce in order to marry the daughter of the Caretaker's wife . . . The man who used to be – your lover.

MUMMY: Another guest will be your former fiancée, who was seduced by my husband.

OLD MAN: A select gathering.

MUMMY: Oh God, if only we might die, might die!

OLD MAN: Then why have you stayed together?

MUMMY: Crime and secrets and guilt bind us together. We have broken our bonds and gone our own ways, times without number, but we are always drawn together again.

OLD MAN: I think the Colonel is coming.

MUMMY: Then I will go in to Adèle. (*Pause.*) Jacob, mind what you do. Spare him. (*Pause. She goes into the Hyacinth Room and disappears.*)

(*The* COLONEL *enters, cold and reserved, with a letter in his hand.*)

COLONEL: Be seated, please.

(*Slowly the* OLD MAN *sits down. Pause. The* COLONEL *stares at him.*)

You wrote this letter, sir?

OLD MAN: I did.

COLONEL: Your name is Hummel?

OLD MAN: It is. (*Pause.*)

COLONEL: As I understand, you have bought in all my unpaid promissory notes. I can only conclude that I am in your hands. What do you want?

OLD MAN: I want payment, in one way or another.

COLONEL: In what way?

OLD MAN: A very simple one. Let us not mention the money. Just bear with me in your house as a guest.

COLONEL: If so little will satisfy you . . .

OLD MAN: Thank you.

COLONEL: What else?

OLD MAN: Dismiss Bengtsson.

COLONEL: Why should I do that? My devoted servant, who has been with me a lifetime, who has the national medal for long and faithful service – why should I do that?

OLD MAN: That's how you see him – full of excellent qualities. He is not the man he appears to be.

COLONEL: Who is?

OLD MAN (*taken aback*): True. But Bengtsson must go.

COLONEL: Are you going to run my house?

OLD MAN: Yes. Since everything here belongs to me – furniture, curtains, dinner service, linen . . . and more too.

COLONEL: How do you mean – more?

OLD MAN: Everything. I own everything here. It is mine.

COLONEL: Very well, it is yours. But my family escutcheon and my good name remain my own.

OLD MAN: No, not even those. (*Pause.*) You are not a nobleman.

COLONEL: How dare you!

OLD MAN (*producing a document*): If you read this extract from *The*

*Armorial Gazette*, you will see that the family whose name you are using has been extinct for a hundred years.

COLONEL: I have heard rumors to this effect, but I inherited the name from my father. (*Reads.*) It is true. You are right. I am not a nobleman. Then I must take off my signet ring. It is true, it belongs to you. (*Gives it to him.*) There you are.

OLD MAN (*pocketing the ring*): Now we will continue. You are not a Colonel either.

COLONEL: I am not . . . ?

OLD MAN: No. You once held the temporary rank of Colonel in the American Volunteer Force, but after the war in Cuba and the reorganization of the Army, all such titles were abolished.

COLONEL: Is this true?

OLD MAN (*indicating his pocket*): Do you want to read it?

COLONEL: No, that's not necessary. Who are you, and what right have you to sit there stripping me in this fashion?

OLD MAN: You will see. But as far as stripping you goes . . . do you know who you are?

COLONEL: How dare you?

OLD MAN: Take off that wig and have a look at yourself in the mirror. But take your teeth out at the same time and shave off your moustache. Let Bengtsson unlace your metal stays and perhaps a certain X.Y.Z., a lackey, will recognize himself. The fellow who was a cupboard lover in a certain kitchen . . .

(*The* COLONEL *reaches for the bell on the table, but* HUMMEL *checks him.*)

Don't touch that bell, and don't call Bengtsson. If you do, I'll have him arrested. (*Pause.*) And now the guests are beginning to arrive. Keep your composure and we will continue to play our old parts for a while.

COLONEL: Who are you? I recognize your voice and eyes.

OLD MAN: Don't try to find out. Keep silent and obey.

(*The* STUDENT *enters and bows to the* COLONEL.)

STUDENT: How do you do, sir.

COLONEL: Welcome to my house, young man. Your splendid behavior at that great disaster has brought your name to everybody's lips, and I count it an honor to receive you in my home.

STUDENT: My humble descent, sir . . . Your illustrious name and noble birth. . . .

COLONEL: May I introduce Mr. Arkenholtz — Mr. Hummel. If you will join the ladies in here, Mr. Arkenholtz — I must conclude my conversation with Mr. Hummel.

(*He shows the* STUDENT *into the Hyacinth Room, where he remains visible, talking shyly to the* GIRL.)

A splendid young man, musical, sings, writes poetry. If he only had blue blood in him, if he were of the same station, I don't think I should object . . .

OLD MAN: To what?

COLONEL: To my daughter . . .

OLD MAN: *Your* daughter! But apropos of that, why does she spend all her time in there?

COLONEL: She insists on being in the Hyacinth Room except when she is out-of-doors. It's a peculiarity of hers. Ah, here comes Miss Beatrice von Holsteinkrona — a charming woman, a pillar of the Church, with just enough money of her own to suit her birth and position.

OLD MAN (*to himself*): My fiancée.

(*The* FIANCÉE *enters, looking a little crazy.*)

COLONEL: Miss Holsteinkrona — Mr. Hummel.

(*The* FIANCÉE *curtseys and takes a seat. The* ARISTOCRAT *enters and seats himself. He wears mourning and looks mysterious.*)

Baron Skanskorg . . .

OLD MAN (*aside, without rising*): That's the jewel-thief, I think. (*To the* COLONEL.) If you bring in the Mummy, the party will be complete.

COLONEL (*at the door of the Hyacinth Room*): Polly!

MUMMY (*entering*): Currrrr . . . !

COLONEL: Are the young people to come in too?

OLD MAN: No, not the young people. They shall be spared.

(*They all sit silent in a circle.*)

COLONEL: Shall we have the tea brought in?

OLD MAN: What's the use? No one wants tea. Why should we pretend about it?

COLONEL: Then shall we talk?

OLD MAN: Talk of the weather, which we know? Inquire about each other's health, which we know just as well? I prefer silence — then one can hear thoughts and see the past. Silence cannot hide anything — but words can. I read the other day that differences of language originated among savages for the purpose of keeping one tribe's secrets hidden from another. Every language therefore is a code, and he who finds the key can understand every language in the world. But this does not prevent secrets from being exposed without a key, specially when there is a question of paternity to be proved. Proof in a Court of Law is another matter. Two false witnesses suffice to prove anything about which they are agreed, but one does not take witnesses along on the kind of explorations I have in mind. Nature herself has instilled in human beings a sense of modesty which tries to hide what should be hidden, but we slip into situations unintentionally, and by chance sometimes the deepest secret is divulged – the mask torn from the impostor, the villain exposed. . . .

(*Pause. All look at each other in silence.*)

What a silence there is now!

(*Long silence.*)

Here, for instance, in this honorable house, in this elegant home, where beauty, wealth and culture are united. . . .

(*Long silence.*)

All of us now sitting here know who we are – do we not? There's no need for me to tell you. And you know me, although you pretend ignorance. (*He indicates the Hyacinth Room.*) In there is my daughter. *Mine* – you know that too. She had lost the desire to live, without knowing why. The fact is she was withering away in this air charged with crime and deceit and falseness of every kind. That is why I looked for a friend for her in whose company she might enjoy the light and warmth of noble deeds.

(*Long silence.*)

That was my mission in this house: to pull up the weeds, to expose the crimes, to settle all accounts, so that those young people might start afresh in this home, which is my gift to them.

(*Long silence.*)

Now I am going to grant safe-conduct, to each of you in his and her proper time and turn. Whoever stays I shall have arrested.

(*Long silence.*)

Do you hear the clock ticking like a death-watch beetle in the wall? Do you hear what it says? "It's time, it's time, it's time." When it strikes, in a few moments, your time will be up. Then you can go, but not before. It's raising its arm against you before it strikes. Listen! It is warning you. "The clock can strike." And I can strike too. (*He strikes the table with one of his crutches.*) Do you hear?

(*Silence. The* MUMMY *goes up to the clock and stops it, then speaks in a normal and serious voice.*)

MUMMY: But I can stop time in its course. I can wipe out the past and undo what is done. But not with bribes, not with threats – only through suffering and repentance. (*She goes up to the* OLD MAN.) We are miserable human beings, that we know. We have erred and we have sinned, we like all the rest. We are not what we seem, because at bottom we are better than ourselves, since we detest our sins. But when you, Jacob Hummel, with your false name, choose to sit in judgment over us, you prove yourself worse than us miserable sinners. For you are not the one you appear to be. You are a thief of human souls. You stole me once with false promises. You murdered the Consul who was buried today; you strangled him with debts. You have stolen the student, binding him by the pretence of a claim on his father, who never owed you a farthing.

(*Having tried to rise and speak, the* OLD MAN *sinks back in his chair and crumples up more and more as she goes on.*)

But there is one dark spot in your life which I am not quite sure about, although I have my suspicions. I think Bengtsson knows. (*She rings the bell on the table.*)

OLD MAN: No, not Bengtsson, not him.

MUMMY: So he does know. (*She rings again.*)

(*The* MILKMAID *appears in the hallway door, unseen by all but the* OLD MAN, *who shrinks back in horror. The* MILKMAID *vanishes as* BENGTSSON *enters.*)

Do you know this man, Bengtsson?

BENGTSSON: Yes, I know him and he knows me. Life, as you are aware, has its ups and downs. I have been in his service; another time he was in mine. For two whole years he was a sponger in my kitchen. As he had to be away by three, the dinner was got ready at two, and the family had to eat the warmed-up leavings of that brute. He drank the soup stock, which the cook then filled up with water. He sat out there like a vampire, sucking the marrow out of the house, so that we became like skeletons. And he nearly got us put in prison when we called the cook a thief. Later I met this man in Hamburg under another name. He was a usurer then, a blood-sucker. But while he was there he was charged with having lured a young girl out on to the ice so as to drown her, because she had seen him commit a crime he was afraid would be discovered. . . .

(*The* MUMMY *passes her hand over the* OLD MAN's *face.*)

MUMMY: *This* is you. Now give up the notes and the Will.

(JOHANSSON *appears in the hallway door and watches the scene with great interest, knowing he is now to be freed from slavery. The* OLD MAN *produces a bundle of papers and throws it on the table. The* MUMMY *goes over and strokes his back.*)

Parrot. Are you there, Jacob?

OLD MAN (*like a parrot*): Jacob is here. Pretty Polly. Currrrr!

MUMMY: May the clock strike?

OLD MAN (*with a clucking sound*): The clock may strike. (*Imitating a cuckoo clock.*) Cuckoo, cuckoo, cuckoo. . . .

(*The* MUMMY *opens the cupboard door.*)

MUMMY: Now the clock has struck. Rise, and enter the cupboard where I have spent twenty years repenting our crime. A rope is hanging there, which you can take as the one with which you strangled the Consul, and with which you meant to strangle your benefactor. . . . Go!

(*The* OLD MAN *goes in to the cupboard. The* MUMMY *closes the door.*)

Bengtsson! Put up the screen — the death-screen.

(BENGTSSON *places the screen in front of the door.*)

It is finished. God have mercy on his soul.

ALL: Amen. (*Long silence.*)

(*The* GIRL *and the* STUDENT *appear in the Hyacinth Room. She has a harp, on which she plays a prelude, and then accompanies the* STUDENT*'s recitation.*)

STUDENT: *I saw the sun. To me it seemed*
*that I beheld the Hidden.*
*Men must reap what they have sown;*
*blest is he whose deeds are good.*
*Deeds which you have wrought in fury,*
*cannot in evil find redress.*
*Comfort him you have distressed*
*with loving-kindness — this will heal.*
*No fear has he who does no ill.*
*Sweet is innocence.*

## SCENE III

*Inside the Hyacinth Room. The general effect of the room is exotic and oriental. There are hyacinths everywhere, of every color, some in pots, some with the bulbs in glass vases and the roots going down into the water.*

*On top of the tiled stove is a large seated Buddha, in whose lap rests a bulb from which rises the stem of a shallot (Allium ascalonicum), bearing its globular cluster of white, starlike flowers.*

*On the right is an open door, leading into the Round Room, where the* COLONEL *and the* MUMMY *are seated, inactive and silent. A part of the death-screen is also visible.*

*On the left is a door to the pantry and kitchen.*

*The* STUDENT *and the* GIRL (Adèle) *are beside the table; he standing, she seated with her harp.*

GIRL: Now sing to my flowers.

STUDENT: Is this the flower of your soul?

GIRL: The one and only. Do you too love the hyacinth?

STUDENT: I love it above all other flowers — its virginal shape rising straight and slender out of the bulb, resting on the water and sending its pure white roots down into the colorless fluid. I love its colors: the snow-white, pure as innocence, the yellow honey-sweet, the youthful pink, the ripe red, but best of all the blue — the dewy blue, deep-eyed and full of faith. I love them all, more than gold or pearls. I have loved them ever since I was a child, have worshipped them because they have all the fine qualities I lack. . . . And yet . . .

GIRL: Go on.

STUDENT: My love is not returned, for these beautiful blossoms hate me.

GIRL: How do you mean?

STUDENT: Their fragrance, strong and pure as the early winds of spring which have passed over melting snows, confuses my senses, deafens me, blinds me, thrusts me out of the room, bombards me with poisoned arrows that wound my heart and set my head on fire. Do you know the legend of that flower?

GIRL: Tell it to me.

STUDENT: First its meaning. The bulb is the earth, resting on the water or buried in the soil. Then the stalk rises, straight as the axis of the world, and at the top are the six-pointed star-flowers.

GIRL: Above the earth — the stars. Oh, that is wonderful! Where did you learn this? How did you find it out?

STUDENT: Let me think . . . In your eyes. And so, you see, it is an image of the Cosmos. This is why Buddha sits holding the earth-bulb, his eyes brooding as he watches it grow, outward and upward, transforming itself into a heaven. This poor earth will become a heaven. It is for this that Buddha waits.

GIRL: I see it now. Is not the snowflake six-pointed too like the hyacinth flower?

STUDENT: You are right. The snowflakes must be falling stars.

GIRL: And the snowdrop is a snow-star, grown out of snow.

STUDENT: But the largest and most beautiful of all the stars in the firmament, the golden-red Sirius, is the narcissus with its gold and red chalice and its six white rays.

GIRL: Have you seen the shallot in bloom?

STUDENT: Indeed I have. It bears its blossoms within a ball, a globe like the celestial one, strewn with white stars.

GIRL: Oh how glorious! Whose thought was that?

STUDENT: Yours.

GIRL: Yours.

STUDENT: Ours. We have given birth to it together. We are wedded.

GIRL: Not yet.

STUDENT: What's still to do?

GIRL: Waiting, ordeals, patience.

STUDENT: Very well. Put me to the test. (*Pause.*) Tell me. Why do your parents sit in there so silently, not saying a single word?

GIRL: Because they have nothing to say to each other, and because neither believes what the other says. This is how my father puts it: What's the point of talking, when neither of us can fool the other?

STUDENT: What a horrible thing to hear!

GIRL: Here comes the Cook. Look at her, how big and fat she is.

(*They watch the* COOK, *although the audience cannot yet see her.*)

STUDENT: What does she want?

GIRL: To ask me about the dinner. I have to do the housekeeping as my mother's ill.

STUDENT: What have we to do with the kitchen?

GIRL: We must eat. Look at the Cook. I can't bear the sight of her.

STUDENT: Who is that ogress?

GIRL: She belongs to the Hummel family of vampires. She is eating us.

STUDENT: Why don't you dismiss her?

GIRL: She won't go. We have no control over her. We've got her for our sins. Can't you see that we are pining and wasting away?

STUDENT: Don't you get enough to eat?

GIRL: Yes, we get many dishes, but all the strength has gone. She boils the nourishment out of the meat and gives us the fibre and water, while she drinks the stock herself. And when there's a roast, she first boils out the marrow, eats the gravy and drinks the juices herself. Everything she touches loses its savor. It's as if she sucked with her eyes. We get the grounds when she has drunk the coffee. She drinks the wine and fills the bottles up with water.

STUDENT: Send her packing.

GIRL: We can't.

STUDENT: Why not?

GIRL: We don't know. She won't go. No one has any control over her. She has taken all our strength from us.

STUDENT: May I get rid of her?

GIRL: No. It must be as it is. Here she is. She will ask me what is to be for dinner. I shall tell her. She will make objections and get her own way.

STUDENT: Let her do the ordering herself then.

GIRL: She won't do that.

STUDENT: What an extraordinary house! It is bewitched.

GIRL: Yes. But now she is turning back, because she has seen you.

THE COOK (*in the doorway*): No, that wasn't the reason. (*She grins, showing all her teeth.*)

STUDENT: Get out!

COOK: When it suits me. (*Pause.*) It does suit me now. (*She disappears.*)

GIRL: Don't lose your temper. Practice patience. She is one of the ordeals we have to go through in this house. You see, we have a housemaid too, whom we have to clean up after.

STUDENT: I am done for. *Cor in æthere.* Music!

GIRL: Wait.

STUDENT: Music!

GIRL: Patience. This room is called the room of ordeals. It looks beautiful, but it is full of defects.

STUDENT: Really? Well, such things must be seen to. It is very beautiful, but a little cold. Why don't you have a fire?

GIRL: Because it smokes.

STUDENT: Can't you have the chimney swept?

GIRL: It doesn't help. You see that writing-desk there?

STUDENT: An unusually fine piece.

GIRL: But it wobbles. Every day I put a piece of cork under that leg, and every day the housemaid takes it away when she sweeps and I have to cut a new piece. The penholder is covered with ink every morning and so is the inkstand. I have to clean them up every morning after that woman, as sure as the sun rises. (*Pause.*) What's the worst job you can think of?

STUDENT: To count the washing. Ugh!

GIRL: That I have to do. Ugh!

STUDENT: What else?

GIRL: To be waked in the middle of the night and have to get up and see to the window, which the housemaid has left banging.

STUDENT: What else?

GIRL: To get up on a ladder and tie the cord on the damper[4] which the housemaid has torn off.

STUDENT: What else?

GIRL: To sweep after her, to dust after her, to light the fire in the stove when all she's done is throw in some wood. To see to the damper, to wipe the glasses, to lay the table over again, to open the bottles, to see that the rooms are aired, to remake my bed, to rinse the water-bottle when it's green with sediment, to buy matches and soap which are always lacking, to wipe the chimneys and trim the wicks to keep the lamps from smoking — and so that they don't go out when we have company, I have to fill them myself. . . .

[4] "Damper to the big stove." [Sprigge's note.]

STUDENT: Music!

GIRL: Wait. The labor comes first. The labor of keeping the dirt of life at a distance.

STUDENT: But you are wealthy and have two servants.

GIRL: It doesn't help. Even if we had three. Living is hard work, and sometimes I grow tired. (*Pause.*) Think then if there were a nursery as well.

STUDENT: The greatest of joys.

GIRL: And the costliest. Is life worth so much hardship?

STUDENT: That must depend on the reward you expect for your labors. I would not shrink from anything to win your hand.

GIRL. Don't say that. You can never have me.

STUDENT: Why not?

GIRL: You mustn't ask. (*Pause.*)

STUDENT: You dropped your bracelet out of the window. . . .

GIRL: Because my hand has grown so thin. (*Pause.*)

(*The* COOK *appears with a Japanese bottle in her hand.*)

There she is — the one who devours me and all of us.

STUDENT: What has she in her hand?

GIRL: It is the bottle of coloring matter that has letters like scorpions on it. It is the soy which turns water into soup and takes the place of gravy. She makes cabbage soup with it — and mock-turtle soup too.

STUDENT (*to* COOK): Get out!

COOK: You drain us of sap, and we drain you. We take the blood and leave you the water, but colored . . . colored. I am going now, but all the same I shall stay, as long as I please. (*She goes out.*)

STUDENT: Why did Bengtsson get a medal?

GIRL: For his great merits.

STUDENT: Has he no defects?

GIRL: Yes, great ones. But you don't get a medal for them.

(*They smile.*)

STUDENT: You have many secrets in this house.

GIRL: As in all others. Permit us to keep ours.

STUDENT: Don't you approve of candor?

GIRL: Yes — within reason.

STUDENT: Sometimes I'm seized with a raging desire to say all I think. But I know the world would go to pieces if one were completely candid. (*Pause.*) I went to a funeral the other day . . . in church. It was very solemn and beautiful.

GIRL: Was it Mr. Hummel's?

STUDENT: My false benefactor's — yes. At the head of the coffin stood an old friend of the deceased. He carried the mace. I was deeply impressed by the dignified manner and moving words of the clergyman. I cried.

We all cried. Afterwards we went to a tavern, and there I learned that the man with the mace had been in love with the dead man's son. . . .

(*The* GIRL *stares at him, trying to understand.*)

And that the dead man had borrowed money from his son's admirer. (*Pause.*) Next day the clergyman was arrested for embezzling the church funds. A pretty story.

GIRL: Oh . . . ! (*Pause.*)

STUDENT: Do you know how I am thinking about you now?

GIRL: Don't tell me, or I shall die.

STUDENT: I must, or I shall die.

GIRL: It is in asylums that people say everything they think.

STUDENT: Exactly. My father finished up in an asylum.

GIRL: Was he ill?

STUDENT: No, he was well, but he was mad. You see, he broke out once — in these circumstances. Like all of us, he was surrounded with a circle of acquaintances; he called them friends for short. They were a lot of rotters, of course, as most people are, but he had to have some society — he couldn't get on all alone. Well, as you know, in everyday life no one tells people what he thinks of them, and he didn't either. He knew perfectly well what frauds they were — he'd sounded the depths of their deceit — but as he was a wise and well-bred man, he was always courteous to them. Then one day he gave a big party. It was in the evening and he was tired by the day's work and by the strain of holding his tongue and at the same time talking rubbish with his guests. . . .

(*The* GIRL *is frightened.*)

Well, at the dinner table he rapped for silence, raised his glass, and began to speak. Then something loosed the trigger. He made an enormous speech in which he stripped the whole company naked, one after the other, and told them of all their treachery. Then, tired out, he sat down on the table and told them all to go to hell.

GIRL: Oh!

STUDENT: I was there, and I shall never forget what happened then. Father and Mother came to blows, the guests rushed for the door . . . and my father was taken to a madhouse, where he died. (*Pause.*) Water that is still too long stagnates, and so it is in this house too. There is something stagnating here. And yet I thought it was paradise itself that first time I saw you coming in here. There I stood that Sunday morning, gazing in. I saw a Colonel who was no Colonel. I had a benefactor who was a thief and had to hang himself. I saw a mummy who was not a mummy and an old maid — what of the maidenhood, by the way? Where is beauty to be found? In nature, and in my own mind, when it is in its Sunday clothes. Where are honor and faith? In fairy-tales and children's fancies. Where is anything that fulfills its promise? In my imagination. Now your flowers have poisoned me and I have given the poison back to you. I asked you to become my wife in a home full of poetry and song and music. Then the Cook came. . . . *Sursum Corda!* Try once more to strike fire and glory out of the golden harp. Try, I beg you, I implore you on my knees. (*Pause.*) Then I will do it myself. (*He picks up the harp, but the strings give no sound.*) It is dumb and deaf. To think that the most beautiful flowers are so poisonous, are the most poisonous. The curse lies over the whole of creation, over life itself. Why will you not be my bride? Because the very life-spring within you is sick . . . now I can feel that vampire in the kitchen beginning to suck me. I believe she is a Lamia, one of those that suck the blood of children. It is always in the kitchen quarters that the seed-leaves of the children are nipped, if it has not already happened in the bedroom. There are poisons that destroy the sight and poisons that open the eyes. I seem to have been born with the latter kind, for I cannot see what is ugly as beautiful, nor call evil good. I cannot. Jesus Christ descended into hell. That was His pilgrimage on earth — to this madhouse, this prison, this charnel-house, this earth. And the madmen killed Him when He wanted to set them free; but the robber they let go. The robber always gets the sympathy. Woe! Woe to us all. Saviour of the world, save us! We perish.

(*And now the* GIRL *has drooped, and it is seen that she is dying. She rings.* BENGTSSON *enters.*)

GIRL: Bring the screen. Quick. I am dying.

(BENGTSSON *comes back with the screen, opens it and arranges it in front of the* GIRL.)

STUDENT: The Liberator is coming. Welcome, pale and gentle one. Sleep, you lovely, innocent, doomed creature, suffering for no fault of your own. Sleep without dreaming, and when you wake again . . . may you be greeted by a sun that does not burn, in a home without dust, by friends without stain, by a love without flaw. You wise and gentle Buddha, sitting there waiting for a Heaven to sprout from the earth, grant us patience in our ordeal and purity of will, so that this hope may not be confounded.

(*The strings of the harp hum softly and a white light fills the room.*)

*I saw the sun. To me it seemed*
*that I beheld the Hidden.*
*Men must reap what they have sown;*
*blest is he whose deeds are good.*
*Deeds which you have wrought in fury,*
*cannot in evil find redress.*
*Comfort him you have distressed*

*with loving-kindness — this will heal.*
*No fear has he who does no ill.*
*Sweet is innocence.*

(*A faint moaning is heard behind the screen.*)

You poor little child, child of this world of illusion, guilt, suffering, and death, this world of endless change, disappointment, and pain. May the Lord of Heaven be merciful to you upon your journey.

(*The room disappears. Böcklin's picture* The Island of the Dead *is seen in the distance, and from the island comes music, soft, sweet, and melancholy.*)

When Strindberg wrote *The Ghost Sonata* (in 1907) his Intimate Theater in Stockholm had just opened and he was worried about its success, his domestic arrangements were made trying by problems with servants (one reason, perhaps, for the prominent and rather obtusely ridiculed "kitchen imagery" in the play), and he suffered from a severe attack of psoriasis (a painful skin disease) of the hands. *The Ghost Sonata,* he wrote to his German translator, had been written "with bleeding hands."

The difficulties one experiences with *The Ghost Sonata* could be due to something we might call the inertia of literary taste. Perhaps the play baffles because it seems so unlike the kind of plays with which we are familiar, plays like *The Wild Duck* and *The Three Sisters,* in which people much like ourselves suffer and triumph, are good and evil, sick and sane, noble and ignoble, act or fail to act, in a world much like our own. If we get past our initial sense of being lost among incoherent and inexplicable events, we may begin to recognize familiar themes. Strindberg, too, looks behind the façade of middle-class life and uncovers its moral iniquities. Like Ibsen's, his characters are guilt-haunted captives of their past. And his picture of life stagnating and rotting in a petty and sordid everyday — where people torture one another with silences and where "the labor of keeping the dirt of life at a distance" saps the good and the young — is close to Chekhov's.

Still, the differences between *The Ghost Sonata* and naturalistic plays are obvious. Strindberg's play is not an authentic image of what actual life appears to be. It deals with the irrational, the mystical, in human life; it is scarcely a coincidence that it is roughly contemporary with the birth of psychoanalysis. Strindberg's stage is more than a setting for the action. It is plastic and fluid, responsive to the playwright's shifting phantasmagoria, an integral part of the play. To move from *The Three Sisters* to *The Ghost Sonata* is to leave the familiar living room, drab, perhaps, and stifling, but safely *real,* and to enter a nightmare where ordinary realities appear in new and changing shapes and grotesque combinations, all the more disturbing for being recognizable as their ordinary selves behind the distortions. Clocks and screens and a bottle of soya sauce loom larger than life in Strindberg's ghostly dream. And yet, they are not symbols. They are nothing but themselves, only, somehow, more frighteningly so than in real life; they are solidly there, as things, but imbued with more than thing-like power. And *as* things they will not allow us to think the nightmare unreal. Here horror is a commonplace, normality a dread beyond comprehension and remedy. It is of the essence of Strindberg's art that his ultimate "ghost" is a lazy and impudent cook. The ordinary is both ordinary and supernatural, both tiresome and terrifying.

The reader who still feels that the play "doesn't make sense" may take the dream metaphor a step further. If in Ibsen and Chekhov our position as audience is that of unobserved observer, fly on the living room wall, in *The Ghost Sonata* it may be thought of as that of troubled dreamer. And dreams are not required to make sense. That they do not is often what makes them most compelling.

*The Ghost Sonata* has come to be regarded as a pioneer specimen of a kind of drama that has been given the name *expressionistic.* The term is not Strindberg's — it is unlikely that he ever heard it applied to his plays — but it is as meaningful as such labels ever are. Expressionists do not try to copy nature, don't care to make a cow look like a cow. They express themselves, turn reality inside out, fragmentize it, bring its meaning (to them) to the surface, record the feel of experience in bone and nerve. They claim for their subjectivity as much reality as does the scientist for his objectivity. Suppose you don't like liver or colonial furniture (the expressionist may say). What is for you the truer statement about these things: that liver has a certain color, texture, chemical composition, nutritional value, price per pound? Or that it makes you sick? That American colonial is characterized by certain lines and shapes and finishes, a certain use of maple wood? Or that it is ugly? Isn't the second statement in each case as true as the first? Isn't it as important, since it takes account of your feelings? Isn't it at any rate worth expressing?

The distortions of objective reality in this art — sometimes to the point of the unrecognizability of pure abstractionism — serve to universalize it. The emphasis is on the feeling rather than on the real-life object that happens to occasion the feeling. "Abstractionism," says a modern practitioner, "can touch many springs in the human spirit, whereas reality can touch only one." The same premise underlies expressionism — though it is surrealistic rather than non-realistic, like abstractionism. In expressing himself the artist expresses every man's subjectivity, articulates the inarticulate, helps us for the moment exercise our human potential. His work is evocative rather than representational; it intimates experience and does not try to recreate it or account for it or argue about it. "We don't live in reality," says Strindberg, "but in what we take reality to be." Perhaps the theory of expressionism is best summed up in the answer a painter acquaintance of Strindberg's gave to a technology-minded friend's suggestion that in an age of photography paint and brush were old-fashioned and inaccurate tools for recording truth: "As long as the camera can't enter heaven and hell," said Edvard Munch, "people will keep on painting and other people keep on looking at what they paint." In *The Ghost Sonata* Strindberg enters hell.

Hell (in this connection) is a state of mind, a climate of the soul, something experienced rather than understood. The musical term "sonata" in the title suggests a work that calls for a sensory and emotional response to its evocation of evil, not for explanation; and Strindberg's use of fairy-tale archetypes (the Old Man is a male equivalent of the fairy godmother, the Student the poor but good and plucky young man with supernatural helpers, and the Girl the beautiful princess in the enchanted castle) contributes to the quality of timeless fable in the play and re-enforces its dark meaning by inverting the happy ending of the romantic folk tale. The play's theme is the universality of evil, the suffering of the innocent, the ambiguity of human motives. The Old Man seems to be a satanic figure — the Mummy calls him "a thief of human souls" — but we cannot really be sure that he is not also the would-be redeemer of his natural daughter and the benefactor of the young man whose father he once wronged (or did he?). The anguish of sin and shame that constitutes the human condition in this most mercilessly dark of all Strindberg's plays is expressed in personal relationships seen as a vast and complicated network of mutual guilt and recrimination.* This is the master image of the play, and it explains why some of the structurally most important characters

* It may be as well to clarify those relationships here. To do so is not to "get" the play; it is not even a necessary step toward adequate response. But the relationships are so involved and so implausible (as realism) that they are likely to be obstacles to enjoyment if left unclarified.

There are two sets of relationships, both adulterous and both involving an illegitimate daughter. (1) The Caretaker's Wife is the mother of the Dark Lady by the Dead Man (the Consul). The Dark Lady is engaged to be married to Baron Skanskorg (the Aristocrat) and is apparently pregnant with his child. The Baron is getting a divorce from another daughter (presumably legitimate) of the Dead Man. (2) The Mummy is the wife of the Colonel and the mother of the Girl by the Old Man (Hummel). The Old Man seduced the Mummy in revenge for the Colonel's seduction of the Old Man's Fiancée. The two sets of relationships are linked by still another illicit affair: that between the Mummy and the Baron. (The Old Man's relationships with the Student and the Student's father, with Johansson and Bengtsson, and with the Milkmaid, while part of the general mesh of past and hidden crimes, do not concern these love entanglements.)

are little more than names. Their function is to be strands in the web of universal sin. Their anonymity furthers that function.

The play's world is a world of deceptions. Scene I begins in hope and promise as a penniless young hero is befriended by a wealthy old man on a bright Sunday morning. But the sun disappears, the kindly benefactor appears as a stricken Thor, the blustering heathen god of wrath and war, and the blessing of being a Sunday child amounts only to seeing ghosts from the Old Man's evil past. The second "movement" of the sonata marks the seeming fulfillment of the Student's hopes. He enters the elegant apartment house and meets his beloved. But the remainder of the scene disillusions hope in a sequence of disclosure and counter-disclosure. The Old Man's exposure of his victims and the purgation of his sinful past are frustrated at their moment of apparent fruition in a dramatization of something close to Christ's "Judge not, that ye be not judged." Acting outside of time, the insane Mummy suddenly turns sane savior, and the wise benefactor hangs himself – the unmasker unmasked. But the company stands revealed: a seduced virgin; a jewel thief turned baron about to enter a mésalliance; a host who is fake father, fake officer, fake nobleman, whose very appearance is faked by means of wig, false teeth, and iron corset; an adulterous wife; a master who once was servant and a servant who once was master.

In the third movement, the house of promised happiness has shrunk to a room of desperate but passive suffering, the Hyacinth room of ordeals, beautiful but fatal, where the mysterious poetry of love decays to complaints about servants and housekeeping, where flowers sicken and the Girl dies. Here rules the same vampire evil that had seemed to die with the Old Man, and the suffering of the beautiful and the innocent is presided over by a statue of Buddha, incarnating that infinite patience with which weary mankind must await the miraculous liberation from the curse of life.

Anticipation, disillusionment, suffering – these are the phases of life. Existence, poisoned at the roots, is paralysis in the contemplation of one's own damnation or slow dystrophy in the endless execution of small and distasteful domestic tasks. The kitchen is in charge of a giant, undismissible slattern, whose actions contradict her calling: she grows fat on the food she should serve others. There is no restoration of the ruined house, no atonement for the Old Man, the Mummy, or the Colonel. Salvation is hardly more than a pious hope and a prayer set to soft music before a sentimental picture. The action does not include the Christian redemption the ending hints at. The burden of life is too heavy to bear; blessed are those who, like the Girl, find release in death. "Oh God, if only we might die, might die!" cries the Mummy. But the sleep of death is denied these tormented souls. They are ghosts, miserably, hopelessly, immortal.

Philosophically, the pervasive gloom of *The Ghost Sonata* may not survive scrutiny. The play is not, as far as reader or spectator can discover, based on any rational, coherent system of thought. It asserts, or, rather, it shows — it does not prove. On the other hand, that Strindberg has not philosophized his vision renders it immune to rational criticism. It does not presume to conform to its tenets and can refuse to be judged on its terms. That may be its strength. Its sense-defying manipulation of fragments of reality weaves a spell for those who once have shared, if only in a dream, the awareness of evil at the very core of human existence. It haunts our imagination long after our daylight minds have granted or refused to grant assent to its ghastly judgment.

# EUGENE O'NEILL

# The Emperor Jones

CHARACTERS

BRUTUS JONES, Emperor
HENRY SMITHERS, A Cockney Trader
AN OLD NATIVE WOMAN
LEM, A Native Chief
SOLDIERS, Adherents of Lem
THE LITTLE FORMLESS FEARS
JEFF
THE NEGRO CONVICTS
THE PRISON GUARD
THE PLANTERS
THE AUCTIONEER
THE SLAVES
THE CONGO WITCH-DOCTOR
THE CROCODILE GOD

*The action of the play takes place on an island in the West Indies as yet not self-determined by white Marines. The form of native government is, for the time being, an empire.*

## SCENE I

*Scene — The audience chamber in the palace of the Emperor — a spacious, high-ceilinged room with bare, white-washed walls. The floor is of white tiles. In the rear, to the left of center, a wide archway giving out on a portico with white pillars. The palace is evidently situated on high ground for beyond the portico nothing can be seen but a vista of distant hills, their summits crowned with thick groves of palm trees. In the right wall, center, a smaller arched doorway leading to the living quarters of the palace. The room is bare of furniture with the exception of one huge chair made of uncut wood which stands at center, its back to rear. This is very apparently the Emperor's throne. It is painted a dazzling, eye-smiting scarlet. There is a brilliant orange cushion on the seat and another smaller one is placed on the floor to serve as a footstool. Strips of matting, dyed scarlet, lead from the foot of the throne to the two entrances.*

*It is late afternoon but the sunlight still blazes yellowly beyond the portico and there is an oppressive burden of exhausting heat in the air.*

*As the curtain rises, a native Negro woman sneaks in cautiously from the entrance on the right. She is very old, dressed in cheap calico, bare-footed, a red bandana handkerchief covering all but a few stray wisps of white hair. A bundle bound in colored cloth is carried over her shoulder on the end of a stick. She hesitates beside the doorway, peering back as if in extreme dread of being discovered. Then she begins to glide noiselessly, a step at a time, toward the doorway in the rear. At this moment,* SMITHERS *appears beneath the portico.*

SMITHERS *is a tall, stoop-shouldered man about forty. His bald head, perched on a long neck with an enormous Adam's apple, looks like an egg. The tropics have tanned his naturally pasty face with its small, sharp features to a sickly yellow, and native rum has painted his pointed nose to a startling red. His little, washy-blue eyes are red-rimmed and dart about him like a ferret's. His expression is one of unscrupulous meanness, cowardly and dangerous. He is dressed in a worn riding suit of dirty white drill, puttees, spurs, and wears a white cork helmet. A cartridge belt with an automatic revolver is around his waist. He carries a riding whip in his hand. He sees the woman and stops to watch her suspiciously. Then, making up his mind, he steps quickly on tiptoe into the room. The woman, looking back over her shoulder continually, does not see him until it is too late. When she does* SMITHERS *springs forward and grabs her firmly by the shoulder. She struggles to get away, fiercely but silently.*

SMITHERS (*tightening his grasp – roughly*): Easy! None o' that, me birdie. You can't wriggle out now. I got me 'ooks on yer.

WOMAN (*seeing the uselessness of struggling, gives way to frantic terror, and sinks to the ground, embracing his knees supplicatingly*): No tell him! No tell him, Mister!

SMITHERS (*with great curiosity*): Tell 'im? (*Then scornfully.*) Oh, you mean 'is bloomin' Majesty. What's the gaime, any 'ow? What are you sneakin' away for? Been stealin' a bit, I s'pose. (*He taps her bundle with his riding whip significantly.*)

WOMAN (*shaking her head vehemently*): No, me no steal.

SMITHERS: Bloody liar! But tell me what's up. There's somethin' funny goin' on. I smelled it in the air first thing I got up this mornin'. You blacks are up to some devilment. This palace of 'is is like a bleedin' tomb. Where's all the 'ands?

(*The woman keeps sullenly silent.* SMITHERS *raises his whip threateningly.*)

Ow, yer won't, won't yer? I'll show yer what's what.

WOMAN (*coweringly*): I tell, Mister. You no hit. They go – all go. (*She makes a sweeping gesture toward the hills in the distance.*)

SMITHERS: Run away – to the 'ills?

WOMAN: Yes, Mister. Him Emperor – Great Father. (*She touches her forehead to the floor with a quick mechanical jerk.*) Him sleep after eat. Then they go – all go. Me old woman. Me left only. Now me go too.

SMITHERS (*his astonishment giving way to an immense, mean satisfaction*): Ow! So that's the ticket! Well, I know bloody well wot's in the air – when they runs orf to the 'ills. The tom-tom 'll be thumping out there bloomin' soon. (*With extreme vindictiveness.*) And I'm bloody glad of it, for one! Serve 'im right! Puttin' on airs, the stinkin' nigger! 'Is Majesty! Gawd blimey! I only 'opes I'm there when they takes 'im out to shoot 'im. (*Suddenly.*) 'E's still 'ere all right, ain't 'e?

WOMAN: Yes. Him sleep.

SMITHERS: 'E's bound to find out soon as 'e wakes up. 'E's cunnin' enough to know when 'is time's come.

(*He goes to the doorway on right and whistles shrilly with his fingers in his mouth. The old woman springs to her feet and runs out of the doorway, rear.* SMITHERS *goes after her, reaching for his revolver.*)

Stop or I'll shoot! (*Then stopping – indifferently.*) Pop orf then, if yer like, yer black cow. (*He stands in the doorway, looking after her.*)

(JONES *enters from the right. He is a tall, powerfully-built, full-blooded Negro of middle age. His features are typically negroid, yet there is something decidedly distinctive about his face – an underlying strength of will, a hardy, self-reliant confidence in himself that inspires respect. His eyes are alive with a keen, cunning intelligence. In manner he is shrewd, suspicious, evasive. He wears a light blue uniform coat, sprayed with brass buttons, heavy gold chevrons on his shoulders, gold braid on the collar, cuffs, etc. His pants are bright red with a light blue stripe down the side. Patent-leather laced boots with brass spurs, and a belt with a long-barreled, pearl-handled revolver in a holster complete his make up. Yet there is something not altogether ridiculous about his grandeur. He has a way of carrying it off.*)

JONES (*not seeing anyone — greatly irritated and blinking sleepily — shouts*): Who dare whistle dat way in my palace? Who dare wake up de Emperor? I'll git de hide fravled off some o' you niggers sho'!

SMITHERS (*showing himself — in a manner half-afraid and half-defiant*): It was me whistled to yer. (*As* JONES *frowns angrily.*) I got news for yer.

JONES (*putting on his suavest manner, which fails to cover up his contempt for the white man*): Oh, it's you, Mister Smithers. (*He sits down on his throne with easy dignity.*) What news you got to tell me?

SMITHERS (*coming close to enjoy his discomfiture*): Don't yer notice nothin' funny today?

JONES (*coldly*): Funny? No. I ain't perceived nothin' of de kind!

SMITHERS: Then yer ain't so foxy as I thought yer was. Where's all your court? (*Sarcastically.*) The Generals and the Cabinet Ministers and all?

JONES (*imperturbably*): Where dey mostly runs de minute I closes my eyes — drinkin' rum and talkin' big down in de town. (*Sarcastically.*) How come you don't know dat? Ain't you sousin' with 'em most every day?

SMITHERS (*stung but pretending indifference — with a wink*): That's part of the day's work. I got ter — ain't I — in my business?

JONES (*contemptuously*): Yo' business!

SMITHERS (*imprudently enraged*): Gawd blimey, you was glad enough for me ter take yer in on it when you landed here first. You didn' 'ave no 'igh and mighty airs in them days!

JONES (*his hand going to his revolver like a flash — menacingly*): Talk polite, white man! Talk polite, you heah me! I'm boss heah now, is you fergettin'? (*The Cockney seems about to challenge this last statement with the facts but something in the other's eyes holds and cows him.*)

SMITHERS (*in a cowardly whine*): No 'arm meant, old top.

JONES (*condescendingly*): I accepts yo' apology. (*Lets his hand fall from his revolver.*) No use'n you rakin' up ole times. What I was den is one thing. What I is now 's another. You didn't let me in on yo' crooked work out o' no kind feelin's dat time. I done de dirty work fo' you — and most o' de brain work, too, fo' dat matter — and I was wu'th money to you, dat's de reason.

SMITHERS: Well, blimey, I give yer a start, didn't I — when no one else would.

I wasn't afraid to 'ire yer like the rest was — 'count of the story about your breakin' jail back in the States.

JONES: No, you didn't have no s'cuse to look down on me fo' dat. You been in jail you'self more'n once.

SMITHERS (*furiously*): It's a lie! (*Then trying to pass it off by an attempt at scorn.*) Garn! Who told yer that fairy tale?

JONES: Dey's some tings I ain't got to be tole. I kin see 'em in folk's eyes. (*Then after a pause — meditatively.*) Yes, you sho' give me a start. And it didn't take long from dat time to git dese fool, woods' niggers right where I wanted dem. (*With pride.*) From stowaway to Emperor in two years! Dat's goin' some!

SMITHERS (*with curiosity*): And I bet you got yer pile o' money 'id safe some place.

JONES (*with satisfaction*): I sho' has! And it's in a foreign bank where no pusson don't ever git it out but me no matter what come. You didn't s'pose I was holdin' down dis Emperor job for de glory in it, did you? Sho'! De fuss and glory part of it, dat's only to turn de heads o' de low-flung, bush niggers dat's here. Dey wants de big circus show for deir money. I gives it to 'em an' I gits de money. (*With a grin.*) De long green, dat's me every time! (*Then rebukingly.*) But you ain't got no kick agin me, Smithers. I'se paid you back all you done for me many times. Ain't I pertected you and winked at all de crooked tradin' you been doin' right out in de broad day? Sho' I has — and me makin' laws to stop it at de same time! (*He chuckles.*)

SMITHERS (*grinning*): But, meanin' no 'arm, you been grabbin' right and left yourself, ain't yer? Look at the taxes you've put on 'em! Blimey! You've squeezed 'em dry!

JONES (*chuckling*): No, dey ain't *all* dry yet. I'se still heah, ain't I?

SMITHERS (*smiling at his secret thought*): They're dry right now, you'll find out. (*Changing the subject abruptly.*) And as for me breakin' laws, you've broke 'em all yerself just as fast as yer made 'em.

JONES: Ain't I de Emperor? De laws don't go for him. (*Judicially.*) You heah what I tells you, Smithers. Dere's little stealin' like you does, and dere's big stealin' like I does. For de little stealin' dey gits you in jail soon or late. For de big stealin' dey makes you Emperor and puts you in de Hall o' Fame when you croaks. (*Reminiscently.*) If dey's one thing I learns in ten years on de Pullman ca's listenin' to de white quality talk, it's dat same fact. And when I gits a chance to use it I winds up Emperor in two years.

SMITHERS (*unable to repress the genuine admiration of the small fry for the large*): Yes, yer turned the bleedin' trick, all right. Blimey, I never seen a bloke 'as 'ad the bloomin' luck you 'as.

JONES (*severely*): Luck? What you mean — luck?

SMITHERS: I suppose you'll say as that swank about the silver bullet ain't luck – and that was what first got the fool blacks on yer side the time of the revolution, wasn't it?

JONES (*with a laugh*): Oh, dat silver bullet! Sho' was luck! But I makes dat luck, you heah? I loads de dice! Yessuh! When dat murderin' nigger ole Lem hired to kill me takes aim ten feet away and his gun misses fire and I shoots him dead, what you heah me say?

SMITHERS: You said yer'd got a charm so's no lead bullet'd kill yer. You was so strong only a silver bullet could kill yer, you told 'em. Blimey, wasn't that swank for yer – and plain, fat-'eaded luck?

JONES (*proudly*): I got brains and I uses 'em quick. Dat ain't luck.

SMITHERS: Yer know they wasn't 'ardly liable to get no silver bullets. And it was luck 'e didn't 'it you that time.

JONES (*laughing*): And dere all dem fool, bush niggers was kneelin' down and bumpin' deir heads on de ground like I was a miracle out o' de Bible. Oh Lawd, from dat time on I has dem all eatin' out of my hand. I cracks de whip and dey jumps through.

SMITHERS (*with a sniff*): Yankee bluff done it.

JONES: Ain't a man's talkin' big what makes him big – long as he makes folks believe it? Sho', I talks large when I ain't got nothin' to back it up, but I ain't talkin' wild just de same. I knows I kin fool 'em – I *knows* it – and dat's backin' enough fo' my game. And ain't I got to learn deir lingo and teach some of dem English befo' I kin talk to 'em? Ain't dat wuk? You ain't never learned ary word er it, Smithers, in de ten years you been heah, dough yo' knows it's money in yo' pocket tradin' wid 'em if you does. But you'se too shiftless to take de trouble.

SMITHERS (*flushing*): Never mind about me. What's this I've 'eard about yer really 'avin' a silver bullet moulded for yourself?

JONES: It's playin' out my bluff. I has de silver bullet moulded and I tells 'em when de time comes I kills myself wid it. I tells 'em dat's 'cause I'm de on'y man in de world big enuff to git me. No use'n deir tryin'. And dey falls down and bumps deir heads. (*He laughs.*) I does dat so's I kin take a walk in peace widout no jealous nigger gunnin' at me from behind de trees.

SMITHERS (*astonished*): Then you 'ad it made – 'onest?

JONES: Sho' did. Heah she be. (*He takes out his revolver, breaks it, and takes the silver bullet out of one chamber.*) Five lead an' dis silver baby at de last. Don't she shine pretty? (*He holds it in his hand, looking at it admiringly, as if strangely fascinated.*)

SMITHERS: Let me see. (*Reaches out his hand for it.*)

JONES (*harshly*): Keep yo' hands whar dey b'long, white man. (*He replaces it in the chamber and puts the revolver back on his hip.*)

SMITHERS (*snarling*): Gawd blimey! Think I'm a bleedin' thief, you would.

JONES: No, 'tain't dat. I knows you'se scared to steal from me. On'y I ain't 'lowin' nary body to touch dis baby. She's my rabbit's foot.

SMITHERS (*sneering*): A bloomin' charm, wot? (*Venomously.*) Well, you'll need all the bloody charms you 'as before long, s' 'elp me!

JONES (*judicially*): Oh, I'se good for six months yit 'fore dey gits sick o' my game. Den, when I sees trouble comin', I makes my getaway.

SMITHERS: Ho! You got it all planned, ain't yer?

JONES: I ain't no fool. I knows dis Emperor's time is sho't. Dat why I make hay when de sun shine. Was you thinkin' I'se aimin' to hold down dis job for life? No, suh! What good is gittin' money if you stays back in dis raggedy country? I wants action when I spends. And when I sees dese niggers gittin' up deir nerve to tu'n me out, and I'se got all de money in sight, I resigns on de spot and beats it quick.

SMITHERS: Where to?

JONES: None o' yo' business.

SMITHERS: Not back to the bloody States, I'll lay my oath.

JONES (*suspiciously*): Why don't I? (*Then with an easy laugh.*) You mean 'count of dat story 'bout me breakin' from jail back dere? Dat's all talk.

SMITHERS (*skeptically*): Ho, yes!

JONES (*sharply*): You ain't 'sinuatin' I'se a liar, is you?

SMITHERS (*hastily*): No, Gawd strike me! I was only thinkin' o' the bloody lies you told the blacks 'ere about killin' white men in the States.

JONES (*angered*): How come dey're lies?

SMITHERS: You'd 'ave been in jail if you 'ad, wouldn't yer then? (*With venom.*) And from what I've 'eard, it ain't 'ealthy for a black to kill a white man in the States. They burns 'em in oil, don't they?

JONES (*with cool deadliness*): You mean lynchin' 'd scare me? Well, I tells you, Smithers, maybe I does kill one white man back dere. Maybe I does. And maybe I kills another right heah 'fore long if he don't look out.

SMITHERS (*trying to force a laugh*): I was on'y spoofin' yer. Can't yer take a joke? And you was just sayin' you'd never been in jail.

JONES (*in the same tone — slightly boastful*): Maybe I goes to jail dere for gettin' in an argument wid razors ovah a crap game. Maybe I gits twenty years when dat colored man die. Maybe I gits in 'nother argument wid de prison guard was overseer ovah us when we're wukin' de roads. Maybe he hits me wid a whip and I splits his head wid a shovel and runs away and files de chain off my leg and gits away safe. Maybe I does all dat an' maybe I don't. It's a story I tells you so's you knows I'se de kind of man dat if you evah repeats one word of it, I ends yo' stealin' on dis yearth mighty damn quick!

SMITHERS (*terrified*): Think I'd peach on yer? Not me! Ain't I always been yer friend?

JONES (*suddenly relaxing*): Sho' you has — and you better be.

SMITHERS (*recovering his composure — and with it his malice*): And just to show yer I'm yer friend, I'll tell yer that bit o' news I was goin' to.

JONES: Go ahead! Shoot de piece. Must be bad news from de happy way you look.

SMITHERS (*warningly*): Maybe it's gettin' time for you to resign — with that bloomin' silver bullet, wot? (*He finishes with a mocking grin.*)

JONES (*puzzled*): What's dat you say? Talk plain.

SMITHERS: Ain't noticed any of the guards or servants about the place today, I 'aven't.

JONES (*carelessly*): Dey're all out in de garden sleepin' under de trees. When I sleeps, dey sneaks a sleep, too, and I pretends I never suspicions it. All I got to do is to ring de bell and dey come flyin', makin' a bluff dey was wukin' all de time.

SMITHERS (*in the same mocking tone*): Ring the bell now an' you'll bloody well see what I means.

JONES (*startled to alertness, but preserving the same careless tone*): Sho' I rings. (*He reaches below the throne and pulls out a big, common dinner bell which is painted the same vivid scarlet as the throne. He rings this vigorously — then stops to listen. Then he goes to both doors, rings again, and looks out.*)

SMITHERS (*watching him with malicious satisfaction, after a pause — mockingly*): The bloody ship is sinkin' an' the bleedin' rats 'as slung their 'ooks.

JONES (*in a sudden fit of anger flings the bell clattering into a corner*): Low-flung, woods' niggers! (*Then catching* SMITHERS' *eye on him, he controls himself and suddenly bursts into a low chuckling laugh.*) Reckon I overplays my hand dis once! A man can't take de pot on a bob-tailed flush all de time. Was I sayin' I'd sit in six months mo'? Well, I'se changed my mind den. I cashes in and resigns de job of Emperor right dis minute.

SMITHERS (*with real admiration*): Blimey, but you're a cool bird, and no mistake.

JONES: No use'n fussin'. When I knows de game's up I kisses it good-bye widout no long waits. Dey've all run off to de hills, ain't dey?

SMITHERS: Yes — every bleedin' man jack of 'em.

JONES: Den de revolution is at de post. And de Emperor better git his feet smokin' up de trail. (*He starts for the door in rear.*)

SMITHERS: Goin' out to look for your 'orse? Yer won't find any. They steals the 'orses first thing. Mine was gone when I went for 'im this mornin'. That's wot first give me a suspicion of wot was up.

JONES (*alarmed for a second, scratches his head, then philosophically*): Well, den I hoofs it. Feet, do yo' duty! (*He pulls out a gold watch and looks at it.*) Three-thuty. Sundown's at six-thuty or dereabouts. (*Puts his watch back — with cool confidence.*) I got plenty o' time to make it easy.

SMITHERS: Don't be so bloomin' sure of it. They'll be after you 'ot and 'eavy. Ole Lem is at the bottom o' this business an' 'e 'ates you like 'ell. 'E'd rather do for you than eat 'is dinner, 'e would!

JONES (*scornfully*): Dat fool no-count nigger! Does you think I'se scared o' him? I stands him on his thick head more'n once befo' dis, and I does it again if he come in my way . . . (*Fiercely.*) And dis time I leave him a dead nigger fo' sho'!

SMITHERS: You'll 'ave to cut through the big forest — an' these blacks 'ere can sniff and follow a trail in the dark like 'ounds. You'd 'ave to 'ustle to get through that forest in twelve hours even if you knew all the bloomin' trails like a native.

JONES (*with indignant scorn*): Look-a-heah, white man! Does you think I'se a natural bo'n fool? Give me credit fo' havin' some sense, fo' Lawd's sake! Don't you s'pose I'se looked ahead and made sho' of all de chances? I'se gone out in dat big forest, pretendin' to hunt, so many times dat I knows it high an' low like a book. I could go through on dem trails wid my eyes shut. (*With great contempt.*) Think dese ign'rent bush niggers dat ain't got brains enuff to know deir own names even can catch Brutus Jones? Huh, I s'pects not! Not on yo' life! Why, man, de white men went after me wid bloodhounds where I come from an' I jes' laughs at 'em. It's a shame to fool dese black trash around heah, dey're so easy. You watch me, man! I'll make dem look sick, I will. I'll be 'cross de plain to de edge of de forest by time dark comes. Once in de woods in de night, dey got a swell chance o' findin' dis baby! Dawn tomorrow I'll be out at de oder side and on de coast whar dat French gunboat is stayin'. She picks me up, take me to Martinique when she go dar, and dere I is safe wid a mighty big bankroll in my jeans. It's easy as rollin' off a log.

SMITHERS (*maliciously*): But s'posin' somethin' 'appens wrong an' they do nab yer?

JONES (*decisively*): Dey don't — dat's de answer.

SMITHERS: But, just for argyment's sake — what'd you do?

JONES (*frowning*): I'se got five lead bullets in dis gun good enuff fo' common bush niggers — and after dat I got de silver bullet left to cheat 'em out o' gittin' me.

SMITHERS (*jeeringly*): Ho, I was fergettin' that silver bullet. You'll bump yourself orf in style, won't yer? Blimey!

JONES (*gloomily*): You kin bet yo' whole roll on one thing, white man. Dis baby plays out his string to de end and when he quits, he quits wid a bang de way he ought. Silver bullet ain't none too good for him when he go, dat's a fac'! (*Then shaking off his nervousness — with a confident laugh.*) Sho'! What is I talkin' about? Ain't come to dat yit and I never will — not wid trash niggers like dese yere. (*Boastfully.*) Silver bullet bring me luck anyway. I kin outguess, outrun, outfight, an' outplay de whole lot o' dem all ovah de board any time o' de day er night! You watch me!

(*From the distant hills comes the faint, steady thump of a tom-tom, low and vibrating. It starts at a rate exactly corresponding to normal pulse beat — 72 to the minute — and continues at a gradually ac-*

*celerating rate from this point uninterruptedly to the very end of the play.*

JONES *starts at the sound. A strange look of apprehension creeps into his face for a moment as he listens. Then he asks, with an attempt to regain his most casual manner.*)

What's dat drum beatin' fo'?

SMITHERS (*with a mean grin*): For you. That means the bleedin' ceremony 'as started. I've 'eard it before and I knows.

JONES: Cer'mony? What cer'mony?

SMITHERS: The blacks is 'oldin' a bloody meetin', 'avin' a war dance, gettin' their courage worked up b'fore they starts after you.

JONES: Let dem! Dey'll sho' need it!

SMITHERS: And they're there 'oldin' their 'eathen religious service — makin' no end of devil spells and charms to 'elp 'em against your silver bullet. (*He guffaws loudly.*) Blimey, but they're balmy as 'ell!

JONES (*a tiny bit awed and shaken in spite of himself*): Huh! Takes more'n dat to scare dis chicken!

SMITHERS (*scenting the other's feeling — maliciously*): Ternight when it's pitch black in the forest, they'll 'ave their pet devils and ghosts 'oundin' after you. You'll find yer bloody 'air 'll be standin' on end before termorrow mornin'. (*Seriously.*) It's a bleedin' queer place, that stinkin' forest, even in daylight. Yer don't know what might 'appen in there, it's that rotten still. Always sends the cold shivers down my back minute I gets in it.

JONES (*with a contemptuous sniff*): I an't no chicken-liver like you is. Trees an' me, we'se friends, and dar's a full moon comin' bring me light. And let dem po' niggers make all de fool spells dey'se a min' to. Does yo' s'pect I'se silly enuff to b'lieve in ghosts an' ha'nts an' all dat ole woman's talk? G'long, white man! You ain't talkin' to me. (*With a chuckle.*) Doesn't you know dey's got to do wid a man was member in good standin' o' de Baptist Church? Sho' I was dat when I was porter on de Pullmans, befo' I gits into my little trouble. Let dem try deir heathen tricks. De Baptist Church done pertect me and land dem all in hell. (*Then with more confident satisfaction.*) And I'se got little silver bullet o' my own, don't forgit.

SMITHERS: Ho! You 'aven't give much 'eed to your Baptist Church since you been down 'ere. I've 'eard myself you 'ad turned yer coat an' was takin' up with their blarsted witch-doctors, or whatever the 'ell yer calls the swine.

JONES (*vehemently*): I pretends to! Sho' I pretends! Dat's part o' my game from de fust. If I finds out dem niggers believes dat black is white, den I yells it out louder 'n deir loudest. It don't git me nothin' to do missionary work for de Baptist Church. I'se after de coin, an' I lays my Jesus on de shelf for de time bein'. (*Stops abruptly to look at his watch — alertly.*) But I ain't got de time to waste no more fool talk wid you. I'se gwine away from heah dis secon'. (*He reaches in under the throne and pulls out an expensive Panama hat with a bright multi-colored band and sets it jauntily on his head.*) So long, white man! (*With a grin.*) See you in jail sometime, maybe!

SMITHERS: Not me, you won't. Well, I wouldn't be in yer bloody boots for no bloomin' money, but 'ere's wishin' yer luck just the same.

JONES (*contemptuously*): Yo're de frightenedest man evah I see! I tells you I'se safe's 'f I was in New York City. It takes dem niggers from now to dark to git up de nerve to start somethin'. By dat time, I'se got a head start dey never kotch up wid.

SMITHERS (*maliciously*): Give my regards to any ghosts yer meets up with.

JONES (*grinning*): If dat ghost got money, I'll tell him never ha'nt you less'n he wants to lose it.

SMITHERS (*flattered*): Garn! (*Then curiously.*) Ain't yer takin' no luggage with yer?

JONES: I travels light when I wants to move fast. And I got tinned grub buried on de edge o' de forest. (*Boastfully.*) Now say dat I don't look ahead an' use my brains! (*With a wide, liberal gesture.*) I will all dat's left in de palace to you — and you better grab all you kin sneak away wid befo' dey gits here.

SMITHERS (*gratefully*): Righto — and thanks ter yer. (*As* JONES *walks toward the door in rear — cautioningly.*) Say! Look 'ere, you ain't goin' out that way, are yer?

JONES: Does you think I'd slink out de back door like a common nigger? I'se Emperor yit, ain't I? And de Emperor Jones leaves de way he comes, and dat black trash don't dare stop him — not yit, leastways. (*He stops for a moment in the doorway, listening to the far-off but insistent beat of the tom-tom.*) Listen to dat roll-call, will you? Must be mighty big drum carry dat far. (*Then with a laugh.*) Well, if dey ain't no whole brass band to see me off, I sho' got de drum part of it. So long, white man. (*He puts his hands in his pockets and with studied carelessness, whistling a tune, he saunters out of the doorway and off to the left.*)

SMITHERS (*looks after him with a puzzled admiration*): 'E's got 'is bloomin' nerve with 'im, s'elp me! (*Then angrily.*) Ho — the bleedin' nigger — puttin' on 'is bloody airs! I 'opes they nabs 'im an' gives 'im what's what! (*Then putting business before the pleasure of this thought, looking around him with cupidity.*) A bloke ought to find a 'ole lot in this palace that'd go for a bit of cash. Let's take a look, 'Arry, me lad. (*He starts for the doorway on right as*

THE CURTAIN FALLS

## SCENE II

*Scene — Nightfall. The end of the plain where the Great Forest begins. The foreground is sandy, level ground dotted by a few stones and clumps of stunted bushes covering close against the earth to escape the buffeting of the trade wind. In the rear the forest is a wall of darkness dividing the world. Only when the eye becomes accustomed to the gloom can the outlines of separate trunks of the nearest trees be made out, enormous pillars of deeper blackness. A somber monotone of wind lost in the leaves moans in the air. Yet this sound serves but to intensify the impression of the forest's relentless immobility, to form a background throwing into relief its brooding, implacable silence.*

JONES *enters from the left, walking rapidly. He stops as he nears the edge of the forest, looks around him quickly, peering into the dark as if searching for some familiar landmark. Then, apparently, satisfied that he is where he ought to be, he throws himself on the ground, dog-tired.*

Well, heah I is. In de nick o' time, too! Little mo' an' it'd be blacker'n de ace of spades heahabouts. (*He pulls a bandana handkerchief from his hip pocket and mops off his perspiring face.*) Sho'! Gimme air! I'se tuckered out sho' nuff. Dat soft Emperor job ain't no trainin' fo' a long hike ovah dat plain in de brilin' sun. (*Then with a chuckle.*) Cheah up, nigger, de worst is yet to come. (*He lifts his head and stares at the forest. His chuckle peters out abruptly. In a tone of awe.*) My goodness, look at dem woods, will you? Dat no-count Smithers said dey'd be black an' he sho' called de turn. (*Turning away from them quickly and looking down at his feet, he snatches at a chance to change the subject — solicitously.*) Feet, you is holdin' up yo' end fine an' I sutinly hopes you ain't blisterin' none. It's time you git a rest. (*He takes off his shoes, his eyes studiously avoiding the forest. He feels of the soles of his feet gingerly.*) You is still in de pink — on'y a little mite feverish. Cool yo'selfs. Remember you done got a long journey yit befo' you. (*He sits in a weary attitude, listening to the rhythmic beating of the tom-tom. He grumbles in a loud tone to cover up a growing uneasiness.*) Bush niggers! Wonder dey wouldn' get sick o' beatin' dat drum. Sound louder, seem like. I wonder if dey's startin' after me? (*He scrambles to his feet, looking back across the plain.*) Couldn't see dem now, nohow, if dey was hundred feet away. (*Then shaking himself like a wet dog to get rid of these depressing thoughts.*) Sho', dey's miles an' miles behind. What you gittin' fidgety about? (*But he sits down and begins to lace up his shoes in great haste, all the time muttering reassuringly.*) You know what? Yo' belly is empty, dat's what's de matter wid you. Come time to eat! Wid nothin' but wind on yo' stumach, o' course you feels jiggedy. Well, we eats right heah an' now soon's I gits dese pesky shoes laced up! (*He finishes lacing up his shoes.*) Dere! Now le's see. (*Gets on his hands and knees and searches the ground around him with his eyes.*) White stone, white stone, where is you? (*He sees the first white stone and crawls to it — with satisfaction.*) Heah you is! I knowed dis was de right place. Box of grub, come to me. (*He turns over the stone and feels in under it — in a tone of dismay.*) Ain't heah! Gorry, is I in de right place or isn't I? Dere's 'nother stone. Guess dat's it. (*He scrambles to the next stone and turns it over.*) Ain't heah, neither! Grub, whar is you? Ain't heah. Gorry, has I got to go hungry into dem woods — all de night? (*While he is talking he scrambles from one stone to another, turning them over in frantic haste. Finally, he jumps to his feet excitedly.*) Is I lost de place? Must have! But how dat happen when I was followin' de trail across de plain in broad daylight? (*Almost plaintively.*) I'se hungry, I is! I gotta git my feed. Whar's my strength gonna come from if I doesn't? Gorry, I gotta find dat grub high an' low somehow! Why it come dark so quick like dat? Can't see nothin'. (*He scratches a match on his trousers and peers about him. The rate of the beat of the far-off tom-tom increases perceptibly as he does so. He mutters in a bewildered voice.*) How come all dese white stones come heah when I only remembers one? (*Suddenly, with a frightened gasp, he flings the match on the ground and stamps on it.*) Nigger, is you gone crazy mad? Is you lightin' matches to show dem whar you is? Fo' Lawd's sake, use yo' haid. Gorry, I'se got to be careful! (*He stares at the plain behind him apprehensively, his hand on his revolver.*) But how come all dese white stones? And whar's dat tin box o' grub I had all wrapped up in oil cloth?

(*While his back is turned, the* LITTLE FORMLESS FEARS *creep out from the deeper blackness of the forest. They are black, shapeless, only their glittering little eyes can be seen. If they have any describable form at all it is that of a grubworm about the size of a creeping child. They move noiselessly, but with deliberate, painful effort, striving to raise themselves on end, failing and sinking prone again.* JONES *turns about to face the forest. He stares up at the tops of the trees, seeking vainly to discover his whereabouts by their conformation.*)

Can't tell nothin' from dem trees! Gorry, nothin' 'round heah look like I evah seed it befo'. I'se done lost de place sho' 'nuff! (*With mournful foreboding.*) It's mighty queer! It's mighty queer! (*With sudden forced defiance — in an angry tone.*) Woods, is you tryin' to put somethin' ovah on me?

(*From the formless creatures on the ground in front of him comes a tiny gale of low mocking laughter like a rustling of leaves. They squirm *upward toward him in twisted attitudes.* JONES *looks down, leaps backward with a yell of terror, yanking out his revolver as he does so — in a quavering voice.*)

What's dat? Who's dar? What is you? Git away from me befo' I shoots you up! You don't? . . .

(*He fires. There is a flash, a loud report, then silence broken only by the far-off, quickened throb of the tom-tom. The formless creatures have scurried back into the forest.* JONES *remains fixed in his position, listening intently. The sound of the shot, the reassuring feel of the revolver in his hand, have somewhat restored his shaken nerve. He addresses himself with renewed confidence.*)

Dey're gone. Dat shot fix 'em. Dey was only little animals — little wild pigs, I reckon. Dey've maybe rooted out yo' grub an' eat it. Sho', you fool nigger, what you think dey is — ha'nts? (*Excitedly.*) Gorry, you give de game away when you fire dat shot. Dem niggers heah dat fo' su'tin! Time you beat it in de woods widout no long waits. (*He starts for the forest — hesitates before the plunge — then urging himself in with manful resolution.*) Git in, nigger! What you skeered at? Ain't nothin' dere but de trees! Git in! (*He plunges boldly into the forest.*)

## SCENE III

*Scene — Nine o'clock. In the forest. The moon has just risen. Its beams, drifting through the canopy of leaves, make a barely perceptible, suffused, eerie glow. A dense low wall of underbrush and creepers is in the nearer foreground, fencing in a small triangular clearing. Beyond this is the massed blackness of the forest like an encompassing barrier. A path is dimly discerned leading down to the clearing from left, rear, and winding away from it again toward the right. As the scene opens nothing can be distinctly made out. Except for the beating of the tom-tom, which is a trifle louder and quicker than in the previous scene, there is silence, broken every few seconds by a queer, clicking sound. Then gradually the figure of the Negro,* JEFF, *can be discerned crouching on his haunches at the rear of the triangle. He is middle-aged, thin, brown in color, is dressed in a Pullman porter's uniform, cap, etc. He is throwing a pair of dice on the ground before him, picking them up, shaking them, casting them out with the regular, rigid, mechanical movements of an automaton. The heavy, plodding footsteps of someone approaching along the trail from the left are heard and* JONES' *voice, pitched in a slightly higher key and strained in a cheering effort to overcome its own tremors.*

De moon's rizen. Does you heah dat, nigger? You gits more light from dis out. No mo' buttin' yo' fool head agin' de trunks an' scratchin' de hide off yo' legs in de bushes. Now you sees whar yo'se gwine. So cheer up! From now on you has a snap. (*He steps just to the rear of the triangular clearing and mops off his face on his sleeve. He has lost his Panama hat. His face is scratched, his brilliant uniform shows several large rents.*) What time's it gittin' to be, I wonder? I dassent light no match to find out. Phoo'. It's wa'm an' dat's a fac'! (*Wearily.*) How long I been makin' tracks in dese woods? Must be hours an' hours. Seems like fo'evah! Yit can't be, when de moon's jes' riz. Dis am a long night fo' yo', yo' Majesty! (*With a mournful chuckle.*) Majesty! Der ain't much majesty 'bout dis baby now. (*With attempted cheerfulness.*) Never min'. It's all part o' de game. Dis night come to an end like everything else. And when you gits dar safe and has dat bankroll in yo' hands you laughs at all dis. (*He starts to whistle but checks himself abruptly.*) What yo' whistlin' for, you po' dope! Want all de worl' to heah you? (*He stops talking to listen.*) Heah dat ole drum! Sho' gits nearer from de sound. Dey're packin' it along wid 'em. Time fo' me to move. (*He takes a step forward, then stops — worriedly.*) What's dat odder queer clickety sound I heah? Dere it is! Sound close! Sound like — sound like — Fo' God sake, sound like some nigger was shootin' crap! (*Frightenedly.*) I better beat it quick when I gits dem notions. (*He walks quickly into the clear space — then stands transfixed as he sees* JEFF *— in a terrified gasp.*) Who dar? Who dat? Is dat you, Jeff? (*Starting toward the other, forgetful for a moment of his surroundings and really believing it is a living man that he sees — in a tone of happy relief.*) Jeff! I'se sho' mighty glad to see you! Dey tol' me you done died from dat razor cut I gives you. (*Stopping suddenly, bewilderedly.*) But how you come to be heah, nigger? (*He stares fascinatedly at the other who continues his mechanical play with the dice.* JONES' *eyes begin to roll wildly. He stutters.*) Ain't you gwine — look up — can't you speak to me? Is you — is you — a ha'nt? (*He jerks out his revolver in a frenzy of terrified rage.*) Nigger, I kills you dead once. Has I got to kill you again? You take it den. (*He fires. When the smoke clears away* JEFF *has disappeared.* JONES *stands trembling — then with a certain reassurance.*) He's gone, anyway. Ha'nt or no ha'nt, dat shot fix him. (*The beat of the far-off tom-tom is perceptibly louder and more rapid.* JONES *becomes conscious of it — with a start, looking back over his shoulder.*) Dey's gittin' near! Dey's comin' fast! And heah I is shootin' shots to let 'em know jes' whar I is. Oh, Gorry, I'se got to run. (*Forgetting the path he plunges wildly into the underbrush in the rear and disappears in the shadow.*)

## SCENE IV

*Scene — Eleven o'clock. In the forest. A wide dirt road runs diagonally from right, front, to left, rear. Rising sheer on both sides the forest walls it in. The moon is now up. Under its light the road glimmers ghastly and unreal. It is as if the forest had stood aside momentarily to let the road pass through and accomplish its veiled purpose. This done, the forest will fold in upon itself again and the road will be no more.* JONES *stumbles in from the forest on the right. His uniform is ragged and torn. He looks about him with numbed surprise when he sees the road, his eyes blinking in the bright moonlight. He flops down exhaustedly and pants heavily for a while. Then with sudden anger.*

I'm meltin' wid heat! Runnin' an' runnin' an' runnin'! Damn dis heah coat! Like a strait-jacket! (*He tears off his coat and flings it away from him, revealing himself stripped to the waist.*) Dere! Dat's better! Now I kin breathe! (*Looking down at his feet, the spurs catch his eye.*) And to hell wid dese high-fangled spurs. Dey're what's been a-trippin' me up an' breakin' my neck. (*He unstraps them and flings them away disgustedly.*) Dere! I gits rid o' dem frippety Emperor trappin's an' I travels lighter. Lawd! I'se tired! (*After a pause, listening to the insistent beat of the tom-tom in the distance.*) I must 'a put some distance between myself an' dem — runnin' like dat — and yit — dat damn drum sound jes' de same — nearer, even. Well, I guess I a'most holds my lead anyhow. Dey won't never catch up. (*With a sigh.*) If on'y my fool legs stands up. Oh, I'se sorry I evah went in for dis. Dat Emperor job is sho' hard to shake. (*He looks around him suspiciously.*) How'd dis road evah git heah? Good level road, too. I never remembers seein' it befo'. (*Shaking his head apprehensively.*) Dese woods is sho' full o' de queerest things at night. (*With a sudden terror.*) Lawd God, don't let me see no more o' dem ha'nts! Dey gits my goat! (*Then trying to talk himself into confidence.*) Ha'nts! You fool nigger, dey ain't no such things! Don't de Baptist parson tell you dat many time? Is you civilized, or is you like dese ign'rent black niggers heah? Sho'! Dat was all in yo' own head. Wasn't nothin' dere. Wasn't no Jeff! Know what? You jus' get seein' dem things 'cause yo' belly's empty and you's sick wid hunger inside. Hunger 'fects yo' head and yo' eyes. Any fool know dat. (*Then pleading fervently.*) But bless God, I don't come across no more o' dem, whatever dey is! (*Then cautiously.*) Rest! Don't talk! Rest! You needs it. Den you gits on yo' way again. (*Looking at the moon.*) Night's half gone a'most. You hits de coast in de mawning! Den you'se all safe.

(*From the right forward a small gang of Negroes enter. They are dressed in striped convict suits, their heads are shaven, one leg drags limpingly, shackled to a heavy ball and chain. Some carry picks, the others shovels. They are followed by a white man dressed in the uniform of a prison guard. A Winchester rifle is slung across his shoulders and he carries a heavy whip. At a signal from the* GUARD *they stop on the road opposite where* JONES *is sitting.* JONES, *who has been staring up at the sky, unmindful of their noiseless approach, suddenly looks down and sees them. His eyes pop out, he tries to get to his feet and fly, but sinks back, too numbed by fright to move. His voice catches in a choking prayer.*)

Lawd Jesus!

(*The* PRISON GUARD *cracks his whip — noiselessly — and at that signal all the convicts start to work on the road. They swing their picks, they shovel, but not a sound comes from their labor. Their movements, like those of* JEFF *in the preceding scene, are those of automatons, — rigid, slow, and mechanical. The* PRISON GUARD *points sternly at* JONES *with his whip, motions him to take his place among the other shovelers.* JONES *gets to his feet in a hypnotized stupor. He mumbles subserviently.*)

Yes, suh! Yes, suh! I'se comin'.

(*As he shuffles, dragging one foot, over to his place, he curses under his breath with rage and hatred.*)

God damn yo' soul, I gits even wid you yit, sometime.

(*As if there were a shovel in his hands he goes through weary, mechanical gestures of digging up dirt, and throwing it to the roadside. Suddenly the* GUARD *approaches him angrily, threateningly. He raises his whip and lashes* JONES *viciously across the shoulders with it.* JONES *winces with pain and cowers abjectly. The* GUARD *turns his back on him and walks away contemptuously. Instantly* JONES *straightens up. With arms upraised as if his shovel were a club in his hands he springs murderously at the unsuspecting* GUARD. *In the act of crashing down his shovel on the white man's skull,* JONES *suddenly becomes aware that his hands are empty. He cries despairingly.*)

Whar's my shovel? Gimme my shovel till I splits his damn head! (*Appealing to his fellow convicts.*) Gimme a shovel, one o' you, fo' God's sake!

(*They stand fixed in motionless attitudes, their eyes on the ground. The* GUARD *seems to wait expectantly, his back turned to the attacker.* JONES *bellows with baffled, terrified rage, tugging frantically at his revolver.*)

I kills you, you white debil, if it's de last thing I evah does! Ghost or debil, I kill you again!

*(He frees the revolver and fires point blank at the* GUARD'S *back. Instantly the walls of the forest close in from both sides, the road and the figures of the convict gang are blotted out in an enshrouding darkness. The only sounds are a crashing in the underbrush as* JONES *leaps away in mad flight and the throbbing of the tom-tom, still far distant, but increased in volume of sound and rapidity of beat.)*

## SCENE V

*Scene—One o'clock. A large circular clearing, enclosed by the serried ranks of gigantic trunks of tall trees whose tops are lost to view. In the center is a big dead stump worn by time into a curious resemblance to an auction block. The moon floods the clearing with a clear light.* JONES *forces his way in through the forest on the left. He looks wildly about the clearing with hunted, fearful glances. His pants are in tatters, his shoes cut and misshapen, flapping about his feet. He slinks cautiously to the stump in the center and sits down in a tense position, ready for instant flight. Then he holds his head in his hands and rocks back and forth, moaning to himself miserably.*

Oh Lawd, Lawd! Oh Lawd, Lawd! (*Suddenly he throws himself on his knees and raises his clasped hands to the sky — in a voice of agonized pleading.*) Lawd Jesus, heah my prayer! I'se a po' sinner, a po' sinner! I knows I done wrong, I knows it! When I cotches Jeff cheatin' wid loaded dice my anger overcomes me and I kills him dead! Lawd, I done wrong! When dat guard hits me wid de whip, my anger overcomes me, and I kills him dead. Lawd, I done wrong! And down heah whar dese fool bush niggers raises me up to the seat o' de mighty, I steals all I could grab. Lawd, I done wrong! I knows it! I'se sorry! Forgive me, Lawd! Forgive dis po' sinner! (*Then beseeching terrifiedly.*) And keep dem away, Lawd! Keep dem away from me! And stop dat drum soundin' in my ears! Dat begin to sound ha'nted, too. (*He gets to his feet, evidently slightly reassured by his prayer — with attempted confidence.*) De Lawd'll preserve me from dem ha'nts after dis. (*Sits down on the stump again.*) I ain't skeered o' real men. Let dem come. But dem odders . . . (*He shudders — then looks down at his feet, working his toes inside the shoes — with a groan.*) Oh, my po' feet! Dem shoes ain't no use no more 'ceptin' to hurt. I'se better off widout dem. (*He unlaces them and pulls them off — holds the wrecks of the shoes in his hands and regards them mournfully.*) You was real, A-one patin' leather, too. Look at you now. Emperor, you'se gittin' mighty low!

*(He sits dejectedly and remains with bowed shoulders, staring down at the shoes in his hands as if reluctant to throw them away. While*

*his attention is thus occupied, a crowd of figures silently enter the clearing from all sides. All are dressed in Southern costumes of the period of the fifties of the last century. There are middle-aged men who are evidently well-to-do planters. There is one spruce, authoritative individual — the* AUCTIONEER. *There is a crowd of curious spectators, chiefly young belles and dandies who have come to the slave-market for diversion. All exchange courtly greetings in dumb show and chat silently together. There is something stiff, rigid, unreal, marionettish about their movements. They group themselves about the stump. Finally a batch of slaves are led in from the left by an attendant — three men of different ages, two women, one with a baby in her arms, nursing. They are placed to the left of the stump, beside* JONES.

*The white planters look them over appraisingly as if they were cattle, and exchange judgments on each. The dandies point with their fingers and make witty remarks. The belles titter bewitchingly. All this in silence save for the ominous throb of the tom-tom. The* AUCTIONEER *holds up his hand, taking his place at the stump. The group strain forward attentively. He touches* JONES *on the shoulder peremptorily, motioning for him to stand on the stump — the auction block.*

JONES *looks up, sees the figures on all sides, looks wildly for some opening to escape, sees none, screams and leaps madly to the top of the stump to get as far away from them as possible. He stands there, cowering, paralyzed with horror. The* AUCTIONEER *begins his silent spiel. He points to* JONES, *appeals to the planters to see for themselves. Here is a good field hand, sound in wind and limb as they can see. Very strong still in spite of his being middle-aged. Look at that back. Look at those shoulders. Look at the muscles in his arms and his sturdy legs. Capable of any amount of hard labor. Moreover, of a good disposition, intelligent and tractable. Will any gentleman start the bidding? The* PLANTERS *raise their fingers, make their bids. They are apparently all eager to possess* JONES. *The bidding is lively, the crowd interested. While this has been going on,* JONES *has been seized by the courage of desperation. He dares to look down and around him. Over his face abject terror gives way to mystification, to gradual realization — stutteringly.*)

What you all doin', white folks? What's all dis? What you all lookin' at me fo'? What you doin' wid me, anyhow? (*Suddenly convulsed with raging hatred and fear.*) Is dis a auction? Is you sellin' me like dey uster befo' de war? (*Jerking out his revolver just as the* AUCTIONEER *knocks him down to one of the planters — glaring from him to the purchaser.*) And *you* sells me? And *you* buys me? I shows you I'se a free nigger, damn yo' souls!

*(He fires at the* AUCTIONEER *and at the* PLANTER *with such rapidity that the two shots are almost simultaneous. As if this were a signal the walls of the forest fold in. Only blackness remains and silence broken by* JONES *as he rushes off, crying with fear — and by the quickened, ever louder beat of the tom-tom.)*

## SCENE VI

*Scene — Three o'clock. A cleared space in the forest. The limbs of the trees meet over it forming a low ceiling about five feet from the ground. The interlocked ropes of creepers reaching upward to entwine the tree trunks give an arched appearance to the sides. The space thus enclosed is like the dark, noisome hold of some ancient vessel. The moonlight is almost completely shut out and only a vague, wan light filters through. There is the noise of someone approaching from the left, stumbling and crawling through the undergrowth.* JONES' *voice is heard between chattering moans.*

Oh, Lawd, what I gwine do now? Ain't got no bullet left on'y de silver one. If mo' o' dem ha'nts come after me, how I gwine skeer dem away? Oh, Lawd, on'y de silver one left — an' I gotta save dat fo' luck. If I shoots dat one I'm a goner sho'! Lawd, it's black heah! Whar's de moon? Oh, Lawd, don't dis night evah come to an end? (*By the sounds, he is feeling his way cautiously forward.*) Dere! Dis feels like a clear space. I gotta lie down an' rest. I don't care if dem niggers does cotch me. I gotta rest.

*(He is well forward now where his figure can be dimly made out. His pants have been so torn away that what is left of them is no better than a breech cloth. He flings himself full length, face downward on the ground, panting with exhaustion. Gradually it seems to grow lighter in the enclosed space and two rows of seated figures can be seen behind* JONES. *They are sitting in crumpled, despairing attitudes, hunched, facing one another with their backs touching the forest walls as if they were shackled to them. All are Negroes, naked save for loin cloths. At first they are silent and motionless. Then they begin to sway slowly forward toward each other and back again in unison, as if they were laxly letting themselves follow the long roll of a ship at sea. At the same time, a low, melancholy murmur rises among them, increasing gradually by rhythmic degrees which seem to be directed and controlled by the throb of the tom-tom in the distance, to a long, tremulous wail of despair that reaches a certain pitch, unbearably acute, then falls by slow gradations of tone into silence and is taken up again.* JONES

*starts, looks up, sees the figures, and throws himself down again to shut out the sight. A shudder of terror shakes his whole body as the wail rises up about him again. But the next time, his voice, as if under some uncanny compulsion, starts with the others. As their chorus lifts he rises to a sitting posture similar to the others, swaying back and forth. His voice reaches the highest pitch of sorrow, of desolation. The light fades out, the other voices cease, and only darkness is left.* JONES *can be heard scrambling to his feet and running off, his voice sinking down the scale and receding as he moves farther and farther away in the forest. The tom-tom beats louder, quicker, with a more insistent, triumphant pulsation.*)

## SCENE VII

*Scene — Five o'clock. The foot of a gigantic tree by the edge of a great river. A rough structure of boulders, like an altar, is by the tree. The raised river bank is in the nearer background. Beyond this the surface of the river spreads out, brilliant and unruffled in the moonlight, blotted out and merged into a veil of bluish mist in the distance.* JONES' *voice is heard from the left rising and falling in the long, despairing wail of the chained slaves, to the rhythmic beat of the tom-tom. As his voice sinks into silence, he enters the open space. The expression of his face is fixed and stony, his eyes have an obsessed glare, he moves with a strange deliberation like a sleepwalker or one in a trance. He looks around at the tree, the rough stone altar, the moonlit surface of the river beyond, and passes his hand over his head with a vague gesture of puzzled bewilderment. Then, as if in obedience to some obscure impulse, he sinks into a kneeling, devotional posture before the altar. Then he seems to come to himself partly, to have an uncertain realization of what he is doing, for he straightens up and stares about him horrifiedly — in an incoherent mumble.*

What — what is I doin'? What is — dis place? Seems like — seems like I know dat tree — an' dem stones — an' de river. I remember — seems like I been heah befo'. (*Tremblingly.*) Oh, Gorry, I'se skeered in dis place! I'se skeered! Oh, Lawd, pertect dis sinner!

(*Crawling away from the altar, he cowers close to the ground, his face hidden, his shoulders heaving with sobs of hysterical fright. From behind the trunk of the tree, as if he had sprung out of it, the figure of the* CONGO WITCH-DOCTOR *appears. He is wizened and old, naked except for the fur of some small animal tied about his waist, its bushy tail hanging down in front. His body is stained all over a bright red. Antelope horns are on each side of his head, branching upward. In one hand he carries a bone rattle, in the other a charm stick with a bunch of white cockatoo feathers tied to the end. A great number of glass beads and bone ornaments are about his neck, ears, wrists, and ankles. He struts noiselessly with a queer prancing step to a position in the clear ground between* JONES *and the altar. Then with a preliminary, summoning stamp of his foot on the earth, he begins to dance and to chant. As if in response to his summons the beating of the tom-tom grows to a fierce, exultant boom whose throbs seem to fill the air with vibrating rhythm.* JONES *looks up, starts to spring to his feet, reaches a half-kneeling, half-squatting position and remains rigidly fixed there, paralyzed with awed fascination by this new apparition. The* WITCH-DOCTOR *sways, stamping with his foot, his bone rattle clicking the time. His voice rises and falls in a weird, monotonous croon, without articulate word divisions. Gradually his dance becomes clearly one of a narrative in pantomime, his croon is an incantation, a charm to allay the fierceness of some implacable deity demanding sacrifice. He flees, he is pursued by devils, he hides, he flees again. Ever wilder and wilder becomes his flight, nearer and nearer draws the pursuing evil, more and more the spirit of terror gains possession of him. His croon, rising to intensity, is punctuated by shrill cries.* JONES *has become completely hypnotized. His voice joins in the incantation, in the cries, he beats time with his hands and sways his body to and fro from the waist. The whole spirit and meaning of the dance has entered into him, has become his spirit. Finally the theme of the pantomime halts on a howl of despair, and is taken up again in a note of savage hope. There is a salvation. The forces of evil demand sacrifice. They must be appeased. The* WITCH-DOCTOR *points with his wand to the sacred tree, to the river beyond, to the altar, and finally to* JONES *with a ferocious command.* JONES *seems to sense the meaning of this. It is he who must offer himself for sacrifice. He beats his forehead abjectly to the ground, moaning hysterically.*)

Mercy, Oh Lawd! Mercy! Mercy on dis po' sinner.

(*The* WITCH-DOCTOR *springs to the river bank. He stretches out his arms and calls to some god within its depths. Then he starts backward slowly, his arms remaining out. A huge head of a crocodile appears over the bank and its eyes, glittering greenly, fasten upon* JONES. *He stares into them fascinatedly. The* WITCH-DOCTOR *prances up to him, touches him with his wand, motions with hideous command toward the waiting monster.* JONES *squirms on his belly nearer and nearer, moaning continually.*)

Mercy, Lawd! Mercy!

(*The crocodile heaves more of his enormous bulk onto the land.* JONES *squirms toward him. The* WITCH-DOCTOR*'s voice shrills out in furious* *exultation, the tom-tom beats madly.* JONES *cries out in a fierce, exhausted spasm of anguished pleading.*)

Lawd, save me! Lawd Jesus, heah my prayer!

(*Immediately, in answer to his prayer, comes the thought of the one bullet left him. He snatches at his hip, shouting defiantly.*)

De silver bullet! You don't git me yit!

(*He fires at the green eyes in front of him. The head of the crocodile sinks back behind the river bank, the* WITCH-DOCTOR *springs behind the sacred tree and disappears.* JONES *lies with his face to the ground, his arms outstretched, whimpering with fear as the throb of the tom-tom fills the silence about him with a somber pulsation, a baffled but revengeful power.*)

## SCENE VIII

*Scene — Dawn. Same as Scene II, the dividing line of forest and plain. The nearest tree trunks are dimly revealed but the forest behind them is still a mass of glooming shadows. The tom-tom seems on the very spot, so loud and continuously vibrating are its beats.* LEM *enters from the left, followed by a small squad of his soldiers, and by the Cockney trader,* SMITHERS. LEM *is a heavy-set, ape-faced old savage of the extreme African type, dressed only in a loin cloth. A revolver and cartridge belt are about his waist. His soldiers are in different degrees of rag-concealed nakedness. All wear broad palm-leaf hats. Each one carries a rifle.* SMITHERS *is the same as in Scene I. One of the soldiers, evidently a tracker, is peering about keenly on the ground. He grunts and points to the spot where* JONES *entered the forest.* LEM *and* SMITHERS *come to look.*

SMITHERS (*after a glance, turns away in disgust*): That's where 'e went in right enough. Much good it'll do yer. 'E's miles orf by this an' safe to the Coast, damn 'is 'ide! I tole yer yer'd lose 'im, didn't I? — wastin' the 'ole bloomin' night beatin' yer bloody drum and castin' yer silly spells! Gawd blimey, wot a pack!

LEM (*gutturally*): We cotch him. You see. (*He makes a motion to his soldiers who squat down on their haunches in a semicircle.*)

SMITHERS (*exasperatedly*): Well, ain't yer goin' in an' 'unt 'im in the woods? What the 'ell's the good of waitin'?

LEM (*imperturbably — squatting down himself*): We cotch him.

SMITHERS (*turning away from him contemptuously*): Aw! Garn! 'E's a better man than the lot o' you put together. I 'ates the sight o' 'im but I'll say that for 'im.

*(A sound of snapping twigs comes from the forest. The soldiers jump to their feet, cocking their rifles alertly.* LEM *remains sitting with an imperturbable expression, but listening intently. The sound from the woods is repeated.* LEM *makes a quick signal with his hand. His followers creep quickly but noiselessly into the forest, scattering so that each enters at a different spot.)*

SMITHERS *(in the silence that follows — in a contemptuous whisper)*: You ain't thinkin' that would be 'im, I 'ope?

LEM *(calmly)*: We cotch him.

SMITHERS: Blarsted fat 'eads! *(Then after a second's thought — wonderingly.)* Still an' all, it might 'appen. If 'e lost 'is bloody way in these stinkin' woods 'e'd likely turn in a circle without 'is knowin' it. They all does.

LEM *(peremptorily)*: Sssh!

*(The reports of several rifles sound from the forest, followed a second later by savage, exultant yells. The beating of the tom-tom abruptly ceases.* LEM *looks up at the white man with a grin of satisfaction.)*

We cotch him. Him dead.

SMITHERS *(with a snarl)*: 'Ow d'yer know it's 'im an' 'ow d'yer know 'e's dead?

LEM: My mens dey got 'um silver bullets. Dey kill him shore.

SMITHERS *(astonished)*: They got silver bullets?

LEM: Lead bullet no kill him. He got um strong charm. I cook um money, make um silver bullet, make um strong charm, too.

SMITHERS *(light breaking upon him)*: So that's wot you was up to all night, wot? You was scared to put after 'im till you'd moulded silver bullets, eh?

LEM *(simply stating a fact)*: Yes. Him got strong charm. Lead no good.

SMITHERS *(slapping his thigh and guffawing)*: Haw-haw! If yer don't beat all 'ell! *(Then recovering himself — scornfully.)* I'll bet yer it ain't 'im they shot at all, yer bleedin' looney!

LEM *(calmly)*: Dey come bring him now.

*(The soldiers come out of the forest, carrying* JONES' *limp body. There is a little reddish-purple hole under his left breast. He is dead. They carry him to* LEM, *who examines his body with great satisfaction.* SMITHERS *leans over his shoulder — in a tone of frightened awe.)*

Well, they did for yer right enough, Jonsey, me lad! Dead as a 'erring! *(Mockingly.)* Where's yer 'igh an' mighty airs now, yer bloomin' Majesty? *(Then with a grin.)* Silver bullets! Gawd blimey, but yer died in the 'eighth o' style, any'ow!

*(*LEM *makes a motion to the soldiers to carry the body out left.* SMITHERS *speaks to him sneeringly.)*

SMITHERS: And I s'pose you think it's yer bleedin' charms and yer silly beatin' the drum that made 'im run in a circle when 'e'd lost 'imself, don't yer?

(*But* LEM *makes no reply, does not seem to hear the question, walks out left after his men.* SMITHERS *looks after him with contemptuous scorn.*)

Stupid as 'ogs, the lot of 'em! Blarsted niggers!

CURTAIN FALLS

The Provincetown Players' original production of *The Emperor Jones* opened on November 1, 1920, in a small theater on McDougall Street in New York's Greenwich Village. It was greeted by both audiences and critics as a major play by a major playwright—a judgment that has worn surprisingly well, considering that we no longer find O'Neill's expressionistic dramatization of depth psychology particularly avant-garde or the implications of the play's exotic island happenings particularly relevant or even true to current black experience.

The success of *The Emperor Jones,* following that of *Beyond the Horizon* earlier the same year, established O'Neill's reputation, but the play is not his best. As a popular theater version of an elusive and controversial concept, it strikes us as simple-minded and heavy-handed. Some of the long stage directions, including authorial comments more novelistic than dramatic in manner, are, as in O'Neill's other plays, intrusive and melodramatic. A spectator in the theater doesn't miss them. A reader may also find himself distracted by O'Neill's efforts to render Jones's Southern speech, Smithers's cockney, and the half-learned English of Lem and the old native woman in phonetically faithful orthography. He may understand that the spellings are realistic notations complementary to the expressionism in the play and a device authenticating Jones's jungle fantasies — and still find them irritating.

But it is difficult to think of another play by O'Neill that equals *The Emperor Jones* in swift sharpness of dramatic power. Perhaps the expository palace prologue is a little longer than its substance calls for, but once Jones's flight begins the pace and the growing tension never falter. We soon perceive the pattern the forest scenes are making and where it is taking Jones, but anticipation of the outcome does not lessen our excitement as the quickening tom-tom rhythm beats the pulse of Jones's accelerating panic. If intellectually the play has no great subtlety or range, dramatically its simplicity is its strength. It is well-built and uses the resources of the theater imaginatively, economically, and still effectively. And if we think of it today first of all as one of the small handful of plays by which American drama finally came of age, there are other reasons for our interest as well.

The title (if not the play itself) has become so familiar that it may require a conscious effort to take in its momentary shock effect: emperors don't have names like Jones. The incongruity suggests what the play is about: an identity divided against itself. It is a theme that has continued to preoccupy American playwrights. As a man who doesn't know who he really is, Brutus Jones is an early kinsman of Williams's Blanche DuBois in *Streetcar Named Desire,* Miller's Willy Loman in *Death of a Salesman,* Albee's Peter in *The Zoo Story,* and LeRoi Jones's Clay in *Dutchman.* That some unique quality in American life accounts for the way the problem of identity keeps turning up in our major plays is neither an original nor a profound suggestion, but it may be a fact. Both his biography and his plays witness to the significance the problem held for O'Neill himself. In the case of *The Emperor Jones* that significance was reinforced by a personal adventure, by contemporary political events, and by the facts of America's racist past and present.

O'Neill had first-hand experience of a Caribbean jungle from his gold-prospecting trip to Honduras in 1909. In a very general way the action of the play is based on the careers of three black emperors of Haiti. In 1915, the last of them, Guillaume Sam, was butchered by a rebel mob tired of his dictatorship. The event brought in the United States Marines, who stayed until 1934. Since O'Neill is obviously dramatizing neither his own adventures nor Haitian history, the only reasons for mentioning these "sources" at all are to place *The Emperor Jones* with the other early plays of O'Neill's that reflect the travel years of his youth and to note the nature of his creative response to news of political violence in an area he had visited.

The Negro Charles Gilpin played Brutus Jones during the original run, making theatrical history as the first successful black performer of a major role in a serious American play. But there was a painful sequel to his success. The strain of celebrity started him drinking (sometimes just before going on stage), and he also began to change some of O'Neill's words that offended his black sensibilities. He would say, for example, "black baby" where O'Neill had written "nigger." O'Neill objected, and there were quarrels with rather ugly overtones. When the company revived its production in a later season, Gilpin was not asked to reappear (the part was given to the then unknown Paul Robeson), and he was, understandably, bitter. "I created Brutus Jones," he would say. "All O'Neill did was write the play."

*The Emperor Jones,* of course, is not about race relationships in the urgent sense of today. It is, essentially, a framed dramatic monologue set to images of a deep psychological process in the Negro speaker. It is a sustained exercise in dramatic irony, not in sociology or polemics. The cockney trader Smithers is a racist, but the fact only contributes to the characterization of him as Jones's hyena; it doesn't raise a thematic issue. As a murderous exploiter of backward natives Jones himself is hardly an admirable character, but he does have a certain stature. He is not a liberator, like the noble Brutuses in Roman history, or a founder of a new Troy, like the Brutus of British royal legend, but neither is he a mean-minded coward like Smithers. He is a man with a grand scheme, shrewd and intelligent, a practical planner who changes his plans when he has to. Even in flight he remains loyal to his self-assumed rank. His exits from the palace in Scene I and from both the jungle and life in Scene VIII are done, as Smithers, the ironic chorus-figure in the play, reluctantly admits, "in the 'eighth o' style." He doesn't slink off.

But it is difficult to feel comfortable with a play about a modern American Negro's regression to jungle atavism. O'Neill's fable could presumably apply to any man, but that doesn't alter the fact that he chose to apply it to a black. It can be argued that his legitimate use of the jungle as a conventional symbol for the dark maze of human subconsciousness made the choice of a black protagonist not just natural but imperative, but inevitably it seems to carry the implication that blacks are peculiarly susceptible to lapsing back into primitive superstition because their cultural sophistication is thin and fragile. The heavy irony of Smithers's final sneer at the pursuers' "bleedin' charms" and "silly beatin' the drum" rather enforces than cancels the implication. It is one that turns the play into a hopeless anachronism for contemporary readers. We find O'Neill here scientifically wrong, sociologically naive, and humanly offensive.

Nothing we can say about the plot as a dramatization of Jungian archetypes — of "racial memory" and "collective subconscious" — can dispel the sense we have of prejudice, however unintentional, lurking at the root of O'Neill's concept of his hero's fate. But if we can be objective enough to admit that the play can still be of value in a study of dramatic form because its major sequence of scenes is a specimen of almost pure expressionism, the Jungian concepts are clearly to the point in a critical analysis. In the jungle Jones travels in a circle. He dies at dawn at the same spot at which he entered the jungle at twilight. In the course of the night he returns, both literally and symbolically, to his origins. As he sheds or loses all his imperial finery until at the end he wears nothing but a ragged loin cloth, so he is gradually stripped of all personal identity as he travels backward in time through layers first of individual, then of social, and finally of racial memory. In a sequence of tableaus that amounts to a cavalcade history of the American Negro in reverse, the swaggering emperor becomes, successively, Pullman porter, convict, Southern slave, a piece of human cargo at sea, and finally a whimpering savage about to be sacrificed to some fierce animal god.* The spectacle of the regressive divestment of both culture and clothing is in ironic counterpoint to his remark in Scene IV that "Dat Emperor job is sho' hard to shake." In the sense that the job is the reason for his entrapment in the jungle past, it *is* hard to shake; in the sense that it is only a recent and temporary role, it is not. His deeper identities as a murderer and as a descendant of slaves and of African primitives keep him from reaching the coast and the gunboat that will take him to Martinique and the freedom that will allow him to enjoy his imperial loot. His death is an ultimate return. Headed for the future, his past holds him, his rational purpose defeated. O'Neill has not made it clear whether it is guilt or superstition that counts more heavily in Jones's psychological disintegration, or what the relationship between the two factors is, but the vagueness does not matter, for he is not diagnosing but presenting Jones's case.

The jungle sequence, the heart of the play, is expressionistic in the extreme sense that it doesn't just present objective reality through the distorting prism of a subjective consciousness (*The Ghost Sonata* is an example of this) but actually stages what goes on in such a consciousness. We see and in some cases hear the phantoms in Jones's mind. But the forest scenes are framed by a prologue and an epilogue that stage events in the real world, so that the total structure of the play is analogous to Jones's circular journey. Daylight scenes frame night scenes, and dialogue scenes in open and spacious settings frame scenes of interior monologue in the dark, dense prison of the jungle. Jones's apparent mobility in the prologue turns into growing claustrophobia in the forest scenes and ends in the stillness of death, marked by the cessation of the tom-tom beats, in the epilogue; but the basic shape of the whole play is that of realism (light, objectivity, reason) enclosing expressionism (dark, subjectivity, irrationality). The transitional Scene II takes place in some uncertain border region between reality and imagination. In setting, the transition is symbolized by the failing light of nightfall

* There is an inconsistency in the general pattern of reversed chronological order in the five scenes inside the jungle. In Scene I (the prologue), Jones tells Smithers he went to prison in the States for killing a black man with a razor in a crap game. He escaped from prison after killing a white guard with a shovel. By the pattern of regressive memory, the chain gang scene (IV) should therefore precede the scene with Jeff (III). It is a small flaw and not likely to be noticed by a theater audience, but it *is* a flaw in the careful craftsmanship of the play as a whole.

in a place where plain and forest meet; and in action, by Jones's looking for his cache of food in a place he first thinks he recognizes but soon realizes he doesn't, and by the Little Formless Fears, his growing *Angst,* creeping out from the jungle. Scene VIII (the epilogue) stages no hallucination, but because the place is the same as in Scene II and the time once again the break between night and day, there is an effect of transition here, too.

The effect is strengthened by the silver bullet motif, linking the last of the forest scenes with the epilogue with Smithers, Lem, and Lem's followers. Primarily, the motif builds a cluster of dramatic ironies. The silver bullet is both a good luck charm ("my rabbit's foot") and a means of suicide in case of capture. Frightened by what he thinks is his imminent sacrifice to a heathen forest god, Jones prays to Christ, and Christ's "answer" to his prayer is to make him think of his silver bullet, a piece of un-Christian magic. He dies from bullets that are duplicates of his own protective amulet, and his killers succeed because, for all his contempt for them as ignorant "bush niggers," he proves to be as superstitious as they. Beyond such ironies, the motif establishes equivalences between the actual world and Jones's jungle imaginings, enriching the dramatic climax with larger complexities of meaning. Because of his intended use of the silver bullet, and because both he and the crocodile god are targets for silver bullets, Jones's final shot amounts to symbolic suicide — as if his consciousness breaks because it has finally *become* its fantasies and his death is a release from bondage. And because his use of the silver bullet against the river god renders him defenseless against his real pursuers, his death at their hands becomes the symbolic equivalent of the jungle sacrifice, and Lem and his men take over the Congo Witch-Doctor's function of executing the jungle god's vengeance. Expressionism and realism are not simply juxtaposed in these passages. Interpenetrating, they gather up the imagery by which Jones's total, multiple identity is defined: his individual present and his ancestral past, his rational purpose and his irrational fears, his moral guilt and his pre-moral superstition, the "Baptist in good standin' " and the defiant murderer-convict and rapacious emperor, the modern Christian and the primitive animist, the escaping criminal and the sacrificial victim. Finally, as a structural device, the volley of gunshots that kills Jones extends and brings to a climax the incremental series of shots which Jones fires at the jungle phantoms and which both separate and tie together the individual scenes in the jungle sequence. With the more obvious device of the tom-toms, the shots make for continuity through sound. O'Neill's use of non-verbal devices, such as shots, drum beats, clothing, light, and the circular structure, is so integral to what the whole play means that criticism that concentrates exclusively on O'Neill's technical skill does the play an injustice by leaving the impression that it is nothing but a succession of brilliant *coups de théâtre.*

In *The Emperor Jones,* as in most of his important plays, O'Neill sought to capture man's tragic sense of dividedness of soul. His heroes seek a spiritual home in existence; like Yank, the stoker-hero in *The Hairy Ape,* they want to, but cannot, "belong." Jones moves psychically from the false belief that he belongs to a white world of economic exploitation of cultural inferiors to a loss of self in an actual and symbolic jungle of atavistic emotions. He is less aware than Yank of what is happening to him, but he, too, turns out not to be what he thought he was. His jungle death is a homecoming that refutes his words to Smithers in the prologue. "What I was den is one thing," he says (with reference to the time of his first arrival on the island). "What I is now 's another." Only after his death does he re-emerge into the white trader's world of rational greed, which he thought he had mastered. There is obvious irony in this, but the irony cuts two ways.

Tragic irony is the traditional attendant on poetic justice, and a kind of poetic justice rules Jones's fate. He chose a role he thought he could leave at will, but the role becomes reality and kills him. "Ain't I de Emperor?" he asks once rhetorically during his hubristic phase in the prologue. "De laws don't go for him." As anticipatory irony his words clang with almost painful obviousness. The spectacle of Jones in the jungle shows us a man suffering under some very old and fundamental laws. Dark forces in his own mind and in the minds of his vengeful subjects take the false emperor at his word, but they also, as it were, legitimize the imposture. Smithers's words on the dead Jones recognize a kind of imperial grandeur in him, and until the end Lem and his men believe that Jones is a ruler who is supernaturally protected. They think they can "cotch him," and they do, only because their own rival magic is stronger than his. Jones's fate proves that Lem possesses a wisdom beyond the comprehension of the contemptible Smithers: that man's inmost reality is his irrationality.

# BERTOLT BRECHT

# The Caucasian Chalk Circle

*Translated by Eric Bentley*

CHARACTERS

OLD MAN on the right
PEASANT WOMAN on the right
YOUNG PEASANT
A VERY YOUNG WORKER
OLD MAN on the left
PEASANT WOMAN on the left
AGRICULTURIST KATO
GIRL TRACTORIST
WOUNDED SOLDIER
THE DELEGATE from the capital
THE SINGER
GEORGI ABASHWILI, the Governor
NATELLA, the Governor's wife
MICHAEL, their son
SHALVA, an adjutant
ARSEN KAZBEKI, a fat prince
MESSENGER from the capital
NIKO MIKADZE and MIKA LOLADZE, doctors
SIMON SHASHAVA, a soldier
GRUSHA VASHNADZE, a kitchen maid
OLD PEASANT with the milk
CORPORAL and PRIVATE
PEASANT and his wife
LAVRENTI VASHNADZE, Grusha's brother
ANIKO, his wife
PEASANT WOMAN, for a while Grusha's mother-in-law
JUSSUP, her son
MONK
AZDAK, village recorder
SHAUWA, a policeman
GRAND DUKE
DOCTOR
INVALID
LIMPING MAN
BLACKMAILER
LUDOVICA

INNKEEPER, her father-in-law
STABLEBOY
POOR OLD PEASANT WOMAN
IRAKLI, her brother-in-law, a bandit
THREE WEALTHY FARMERS
ILLO SHUBOLADZE and SANDRO OBOLADZE, lawyers
OLD MARRIED COUPLE

SOLDIERS, SERVANTS, PEASANTS, BEGGARS, MUSICIANS, MERCHANTS, NOBLES, ARCHITECTS

*The time and the place: After a prologue, set in 1945, we move back perhaps 1000 years.*

*The action of* The Caucasian Chalk Circle *centers on Nuka (or Nukha), a town in Azerbaijan. However, the capital referred to in the prologue is not Baku (capital of Soviet Azerbaijan) but Tiflis (or Tbilisi), capital of Georgia. When Azdak, later, refers to "the capital" he means Nuka itself, though whether Nuka was ever capital of* Georgia *I do not know: in what reading I have done on the subject I have only found Nuka to be the capital of a Nuka Khanate.*

*The word "Georgia" has not been used in this English version because of its American associations; instead, the alternative name "Grusinia" (in Russian, Gruziya) has been used.*

*The reasons for resettling the old Chinese story in Transcaucasia are not far to seek. The play was written when the Soviet chief of state, Joseph Stalin, was a Georgian, as was his favorite poet, cited in the Prologue, Mayakovsky. And surely there is a point in having this story acted out at the place where Europe and Asia meet, a place incomparably rich in legend and history. Here Jason found the Golden Fleece. Here Noah's Ark touched ground. Here the armies of both Genghis Khan and Tamerlane wrought havoc.*

*— E.B.*

## PROLOGUE

*Summer, 1945.*

*Among the ruins of a war-ravaged Caucasian village the members of two Kolkhoz villages, mostly* WOMEN *and* OLDER MEN, *are sitting in a circle, smoking and drinking wine. With them is a* DELEGATE *of the State Reconstruction Commission from Nuka.*

PEASANT WOMAN (*left, pointing*): In those hills over there we stopped three Nazi tanks, but the apple orchard was already destroyed.

OLD MAN (*right*): Our beautiful dairy farm: a ruin.

GIRL TRACTORIST: I laid the fire, Comrade.

(*Pause.*)

DELEGATE: Nuka, Azerbaijan S.S.R. Delegation received from the goat-breeding Kolkhoz "Rosa Luxemburg." This is a collective farm which moved eastwards on orders from the authorities at the approach of Hitler's armies. They are now planning to return. Their delegates have looked at the village and the land and found a lot of destruction. (DELEGATES *on the right nod.*) But the neighboring fruit farm – Kolkhoz (*to the left*) "Galinsk" – proposes to use the former grazing land of Kolkhoz "Rosa Luxemburg" for orchards and vineyards. This land lies in a valley where grass doesn't grow very well. As a delegate of the Reconstruction Commission in Nuka I request that the two Kolkhoz villages decide between themselves whether Kolkhoz "Rosa Luxemburg" shall return or not.

OLD MAN (*right*): First of all, I want to protest against the time limit on discussion. We of Kolkhoz "Rosa Luxemburg" have spent three days and three nights getting here. And now discussion is limited to half a day.

WOUNDED SOLDIER (*left*): Comrade, we haven't as many villages as we used to have. We haven't as many hands. We haven't as much time.

GIRL TRACTORIST: All pleasures have to be rationed. Tobacco is rationed, and wine. Discussion should be rationed.

OLD MAN (*right, sighing*): Death to the fascists! But I will come to the point and explain why we want our valley back. There are a great many reasons, but I'll begin with one of the simplest. Makinä Abakidze, unpack the goat cheese. (*A* PEASANT WOMAN *from right takes from a basket an enormous cheese wrapped in a cloth. Applause and laughter.*) Help yourselves, Comrades, start in!

OLD MAN (*left, suspiciously*): Is this a way of influencing us?

OLD MAN (*right, amid laughter*): How could it be a way of influencing you, Surab, you valley-thief? Everyone knows you'll take the cheese and the valley, too. (*Laughter.*) All I expect from you is an honest answer. Do you like the cheese?

OLD MAN (*left*): The answer is: yes.

OLD MAN (*right*): Really. (*Bitterly.*) I ought to have known you know nothing about cheese.

OLD MAN (*left*): Why not? When I tell you I like it?

OLD MAN (*right*): Because you can't like it. Because it's not what it was in the old days. And why not? Because our goats don't like the new grass as they did the old. Cheese is not cheese because grass is not grass, that's the thing. Please put that in your report.

OLD MAN (*left*): But your cheese is excellent.

OLD MAN (*right*): It isn't excellent. It's just passable. The new grazing land is no good, whatever the young people may say. One can't live there. It doesn't even smell of morning in the morning. (*Several people laugh.*)

DELEGATE: Don't mind their laughing: they understand you. Comrades, why does one love one's country? Because the bread tastes better there, the air smells better, voices sound stronger, the sky is higher, the ground is easier to walk on. Isn't that so?

OLD MAN (*right*): The valley has belonged to us from all eternity.

SOLDIER (*left*): What does *that* mean — from all eternity? Nothing belongs to anyone from all eternity. When you were young you didn't even belong to yourself. You belonged to the Kazbeki princes.

OLD MAN (*right*): Doesn't it make a difference, though, what kind of trees stand next to the house you are born in? Or what kind of neighbors you have? Doesn't that make a difference? We want to go back just to have you as our neighbors, valley-thieves! Now you can all laugh again.

OLD MAN (*left, laughing*): Then why don't you listen to what your neighbor, Kato Wachtang, our agriculturist, has to say about the valley?

PEASANT WOMAN (*right*): We've not said all we have to say about our valley. By no means. Not all the houses are destroyed. As for the dairy farm, at the least the foundation wall is still standing.

DELEGATE: You can claim State support — here and there — you know that. I have suggestions here in my pocket.

PEASANT WOMAN (*right*): Comrade Specialist, we haven't come here to haggle. I can't take your cap and hand you another, and say "This one's better." The other one might *be* better, but you *like* yours better.

GIRL TRACTORIST: A piece of land is not a cap — not in our country, Comrade.

DELEGATE: Don't get mad. It's true we have to consider a piece of land as a tool to produce something useful, but it's also true that we must recognize love for a particular piece of land. As far as I'm concerned, I'd like to find out more exactly what you (*to those on the left*) want to do with the valley.

OTHERS: Yes, let Kato speak.

KATO (*rising; she's in military uniform*): Comrades, last winter, while we were fighting in these hills here as Partisans, we discussed how, once the Germans were expelled, we could build up our fruit culture to ten times its original size. I've prepared a plan for an irrigation project. By means of a cofferdam on our mountain lake, 300 hectares of unfertile land can be irrigated. Our Kolkhoz could not only cultivate more fruit, but also have vineyards. The project, however, would pay only if the disputed valley of Kolkhoz "Rosa Luxemburg" were also included. Here are the calculations. (*She hands* DELEGATE *a briefcase.*)

OLD MAN (*right*): Write into the report that our Kolkhoz plans to start a new stud farm.

GIRL TRACTORIST: Comrades, the project was conceived during days and nights when we had to take cover in the mountains. We were often without ammunition for our half-dozen rifles. Even finding a pencil was difficult. (*Applause from both sides.*)

OLD MAN (*right*): Our thanks to the Comrades of Kolkhoz "Galinsk" and all those who've defended our country!

(*They shake hands and embrace.*)

PEASANT WOMAN (*left*): In doing this our thought was that our soldiers — both your men and our men —should return to a still more productive homeland.

GIRL TRACTORIST: As the poet Mayakovsky said: "The home of the Soviet people shall also be the home of Reason"!

(*The* DELEGATES *excluding the* OLD MAN *have got up, and with the* DELEGATE *specified proceed to study the Agriculturist's drawings. Exclamations such as:*)

"Why is the altitude of fall 22 meters?" —"This rock will have to be blown up" — "Actually, all they need is cement and dynamite" — "They force the water to come down here, that's clever!"

A VERY YOUNG WORKER (*right, to* OLD MAN, *right*): They're going to irrigate all the fields between the hills, look at that, Aleko!

OLD MAN (*right*): I'm not going to look. I knew the project would be good. I won't have a pistol pointed at me!

DELEGATE: But they only want to point a pencil at you!

(*Laughter.*)

OLD MAN (*right, gets up gloomily, and walks over to look at the drawings*): These valley-thieves know only too well that we in this country are suckers for machines and projects.

PEASANT WOMAN (*right*): Aleko Bereshwili, you have a weakness for new projects. That's well known.

DELEGATE: What about my report? May I write that you will all support the cession of your old valley in the interests of this project when you get back to your Kolkhoz?

PEASANT WOMAN (*right*): I will. What about you, Aleko?

OLD MAN (*right, bent over drawings*): I suggest that you give us copies of the drawings to take along.

PEASANT WOMAN (*right*): Then we can sit down and eat. Once he has the drawings and he's ready to discuss them, the matter is settled. I know him. And it will be the same with the rest of us.

(DELEGATES *laughingly embrace again.*)

OLD MAN (*left*): Long live the Kolkhoz "Rosa Luxemburg" and much luck to your horse-breeding project!

PEASANT WOMAN (*left*): In honor of the visit of the delegates from Kolkhoz "Rosa Luxemburg" and of the Specialist, the plan is that we all hear a presentation of the Singer Arkadi Tscheidse.

(*Applause.* GIRL TRACTORIST *has gone off to bring the* SINGER.)

PEASANT WOMAN (*right*): Comrades, your entertainment had better be good. It's going to cost us a valley.

PEASANT WOMAN (*left*): Arkadi Tscheidse knows about our discussion. He's promised to perform something that has a bearing on the problem.

KATO: We wired Tiflis three times. The whole thing nearly fell through at the last minute because his driver had a cold.

PEASANT WOMAN (left): Arkadi Tscheidse knows 21,000 lines of verse.

OLD MAN (*left*): He's hard to get. You and the Planning Commission should persuade him to come north more often, Comrade.

DELEGATE: We are more interested in economics, I'm afraid.

OLD MAN (*left, smiling*): You arrange the redistribution of vines and tractors, why not songs?

(*Enter the* SINGER *Arkadi Tscheidse, led by* GIRL TRACTORIST. *He is a well-built man of simple manners, accompanied by* FOUR MUSICIANS *with their instruments. The artists are greeted with applause.*)

GIRL TRACTORIST: This is the Comrade Specialist, Arkadi.

(*The* SINGER *greets them all.*)

DELEGATE: Honored to make your acquaintance. I heard about your songs when I was a boy at school. Will it be one of the old legends?

SINGER: A very old one. It's called "The Chalk Circle" and comes from the Chinese. But we'll do it, of course, in a changed version. Comrades, it's an honor for me to entertain you after a difficult debate. We hope you will find that the voice of the old poet also sounds well in the shadow of Soviet tractors. It may be a mistake to mix different wines, but old and new wisdom mix admirably. Now I hope we'll get something to eat before the performance begins – it would certainly help.

VOICES: Surely. Everyone into the Club House!

(*While everyone begins to move,* DELEGATE *turns to* GIRL TRACTORIST.)

DELEGATE: I hope it won't take long. I've got to get back tonight.

GIRL TRACTORIST: How long will it last, Arkadi? The Comrade Specialist must get back to Tiflis tonight.

SINGER (*casually*): It's actually two stories. An hour or two.

GIRL TRACTORIST (*confidentially*): Couldn't you make it shorter?

SINGER: No.

VOICE: Arkadi Tscheidse's performance will take place here in the square after the meal.

(*And they all go happily to eat.*)

## I. THE NOBLE CHILD

*As the lights go up, the* SINGER *is seen sitting on the floor, a black sheepskin cloak round his shoulders, and a little, well-thumbed notebook in his hand. A small group of listeners – the* CHORUS *– sits with him. The manner of his recitation makes it clear that he has told his story over and over again. He mechanically fingers the pages, seldom looking at them. With appropriate gestures, he gives the signal for each scene to begin.*

SINGER: In olden times, in a bloody time,
There ruled in a Caucasian city –
Men called it City of the Damned –
A Governor.
His name was Georgi Abashwili.
He was rich as Croesus
He had a beautiful wife
He had a healthy baby.
No other governor in Grusinia
Had so many horses in his stable
So many beggars on his doorstep
So many soldiers in his service
So many petitioners in his courtyard.
Georgi Abashwili – how shall I describe him to you?
He enjoyed his life.
On the morning of Easter Sunday
The Governor and his family went to church.

(*At the left a large doorway, at the right an even larger gateway.* BEGGARS *and* PETITIONERS *pour from the gateway, holding up thin* CHILDREN, *crutches, and petitions. They are followed by* IRONSHIRTS, *and then, expensively dressed, the* GOVERNOR'S FAMILY.)

BEGGARS AND PETITIONERS: – Mercy! Mercy, Your Grace! The taxes are too high.
– I lost my leg in the Persian War, where can I get . . .
– My brother is innocent, Your Grace, a misunderstanding . . .
– The child is starving in my arms!
– Our petition is for our son's discharge from the army, our last remaining son!
– Please, Your Grace, the water inspector takes bribes.

(*One* SERVANT *collects the petitions. Another distributes coins from a purse.* SOLDIERS *push the crowd back, lashing at them with thick leather whips.*)

SOLDIER: Get back! Clear the church door!

*(Behind the* GOVERNOR, *his* WIFE, *and the* ADJUTANT, *the* GOVERNOR'S CHILD *is brought through the gateway in an ornate carriage.)*

CROWD: — The baby!
— I can't see it, don't shove so hard!
— God bless the child, Your Grace!

SINGER *(while the* CROWD *is driven back with whips)*: For the first time on that Easter Sunday, the people saw the Governor's heir.
Two doctors never moved from the noble child, apple of the Governor's eye.
Even the mighty Prince Kazbeki bows before him at the church door.

*(The* FAT PRINCE *steps forwards and greets the* FAMILY.)

FAT PRINCE: Happy Easter, Natella Abashwili! What a day! When it was raining last night, I thought to myself, gloomy holidays! But this morning the sky was gay. I love a gay sky, a simple heart, Natella Abashwili. And little Michael is a governor from head to foot! Tititi! *(He tickles the* CHILD.)

GOVERNOR'S WIFE: What do you think, Arsen, at last Georgi has decided to start building the east wing. All those wretched slums are to be torn down to make room for the garden.

FAT PRINCE: Good news after so much bad! What's the latest on the war, Brother Georgi? *(The* GOVERNOR *indicates a lack of interest.)* Strategical retreat, I hear. Well, minor reverses are to be expected. Sometimes things go well, sometimes not. Such is war. Doesn't mean a thing, does it?

GOVERNOR'S WIFE: He's coughing. Georgi, did you hear? *(She speaks sharply to the* DOCTORS, *two dignified men standing close to the little carriage.)* He's coughing!

FIRST DOCTOR *(to the* SECOND): May I remind you, Niko Mikadze, that I was against the lukewarm bath? *(To the* GOVERNOR'S WIFE.) There's been a little error over warming the bath water, Your Grace.

SECOND DOCTOR *(equally polite)*: Mika Loladze, I'm afraid I can't agree with you. The temperature of the bath water was exactly what our great, beloved Mishiko Oboladze prescribed. More likely a slight draft during the night, Your Grace.

GOVERNOR'S WIFE: But do pay more attention to him. He looks feverish, Georgi.

FIRST DOCTOR *(bending over the* CHILD): No cause for alarm, Your Grace. The bath water will be warmer. It won't occur again.

SECOND DOCTOR *(with a venomous glance at the* FIRST): I won't forget that, my dear Mika Loladze. No cause for concern, Your Grace.

FAT PRINCE: Well, well, well! I always say: "A pain in my liver? Then the doctor gets fifty strokes on the soles of his feet." We live in a decadent age. In the old days one said: "Off with his head!"

GOVERNOR'S WIFE: Let's go into church. Very likely it's the draft here.

(*The procession of* FAMILY *and* SERVANTS *turns into the doorway. The* FAT PRINCE *follows, but the* GOVERNOR *is kept back by the* AJUTANT, *a handsome young man. When the crowd of* PETITIONERS *has been driven off, a young dust-stained* RIDER, *his arm in a sling, remains behind.*)

ADJUTANT (*pointing at the* RIDER, *who steps forward*): Won't you hear the messenger from the capital, Your Excellency? He arrived this morning. With confidential papers.

GOVERNOR: Not before Service, Shalva. But did you hear Brother Kazbeki wish me a happy Easter? Which is all very well, but I don't believe it did rain last night.

ADJUTANT (*nodding*): We must investigate.

GOVERNOR: Yes, at once. Tomorrow.

(*They pass through the doorway. The* RIDER, *who has waited in vain for an audience, turns sharply round and, muttering a curse, goes off. Only one of the palace guards* — SIMON SHASHAVA — *remains at the door.*)

SINGER: The city is still.
Pigeons strut in the church square.
A soldier of the Palace Guard
Is joking with a kitchen maid
As she comes up from the river with a bundle.

(*A girl* — GRUSHA VASHNADZE — *comes through the gateway with a bundle made of large green leaves under her arm.*)

SIMON: What, the young lady is not in church? Shirking?

GRUSHA: I was dressed to go. But they needed another goose for the banquet. And they asked me to get it. I know about geese.

SIMON: A goose? (*He feigns suspicion.*) I'd like to see that goose. (GRUSHA *does not understand.*) One must be on one's guard with women. "I only went for a fish," they tell you, but it turns out to be something else.

GRUSHA (*walking resolutely toward him and showing him the goose*): There! If it isn't a fifteen-pound goose stuffed full of corn, I'll eat the feathers.

SIMON: A queen of a goose! The Governor himself will eat it. So the young lady has been down to the river again?

GRUSHA: Yes, at the poultry farm.

SIMON: Really? At the poultry farm, down by the river . . . not higher up maybe? Near those willows?

GRUSHA: I only go to the willows to wash the linen.

SIMON (*insinuatingly*): Exactly.

GRUSHA: Exactly what?

SIMON (*winking*): Exactly that.

GRUSHA: Why shouldn't I wash the linen by the willows?

SIMON (*with exaggerated laughter*): "Why shouldn't I wash the linen by the willows!" That's good, really good!

GRUSHA: I don't understand the soldier. What's so good about it?

SIMON (*slyly*): "If something I know someone learns, she'll grow hot and cold by turns!"

GRUSHA: I don't know what I could learn about those willows.

SIMON: Not even if there was a bush opposite? That one could see everything from? Everything that goes on there when a certain person is – "washing linen"?

GRUSHA: What does go on? Won't the soldier say what he means and have done?

SIMON: Something goes on. Something can be seen.

GRUSHA: Could the soldier mean I dip my toes in the water when it's hot? There's nothing else.

SIMON: There's more. Your toes. And more.

GRUSHA: More what? At most my foot?

SIMON: Your foot. And a little more. (*He laughs heartily.*)

GRUSHA (*angrily*): Simon Shashava, you ought to be ashamed of yourself! To sit in a bush on a hot day and wait till a girl comes and dips her legs in the river! And I bet you bring a friend along too! (*She runs off.*)

SIMON (*shouting after her*): I didn't bring any friend along!

(*As the* SINGER *resumes his tale, the* SOLDIER *steps into the doorway as though to listen to the service.*)

SINGER: The city lies still
But why are there armed men?
The Governor's palace is at peace
But why is it a fortress?
And the Governor returned to his palace
And the fortress was a trap
And the goose was plucked and roasted
But the goose was not eaten this time
And noon was no longer the hour to eat:
Noon was the hour to die.

(*From the doorway at the left the* FAT PRINCE *quickly appears, stands still, looks around. Before the gateway at the right two* IRONSHIRTS *are squatting and playing dice. The* FAT PRINCE *sees them, walks slowly past, making a sign to them. They rise: one goes through the gateway, the other goes off at the right. Muffled voices are heard from various directions in the rear:* "To your posts!" *The palace is surrounded.*

*The* FAT PRINCE *quickly goes off. Church bells in the distance. Enter, through the doorway, the* GOVERNOR'S FAMILY *and procession, returning from church.*)

GOVERNOR'S WIFE (*passing the* ADJUTANT): It's impossible to live in such a slum. But Georgi, of course, will only build for his little Michael. Never for me! Michael is all! All for Michael!

(*The procession turns into the gateway. Again the* ADJUTANT *lingers behind. He waits. Enter the wounded* RIDER *from the doorway. Two* IRONSHIRTS *of the Palace Guard have taken up positions by the gateway.*)

ADJUTANT (*to the* RIDER): The Governor does not wish to receive military news before dinner — especially if it's depressing, as I assume. In the afternoon His Excellency will confer with prominent architects. They're coming to dinner too. And here they are! (*Enter three* GENTLEMEN *through the doorway.*) Go to the kitchen and eat, my friend. (*As the* RIDER *goes, the* ADJUTANT *greets the* ARCHITECTS.) Gentlemen, His Excellency expects you at dinner. He will devote all his time to you and your great new plans. Come!

ONE OF THE ARCHITECTS: We marvel that His Excellency intends to build. There are disquieting rumors that the war in Persia has taken a turn for the worse.

ADJUTANT: All the more reason to build! There's nothing to those rumors anyway. Persia is a long way off, and the garrison here would let itself be hacked to bits for its Governor. (*Noise from the palace. The shrill scream of a woman. Someone is shouting orders. Dumbfounded, the* ADJUTANT *moves toward the gateway. An* IRONSHIRT *steps out, points his lance at him.*) What's this? Put down that lance, you dog.

ONE OF THE ARCHITECTS: It's the Princes! Don't you know the Princes met last night in the capital? And they're against the Grand Duke and his Governors? Gentlemen, we'd better make ourselves scarce. (*They rush off. The* ADJUTANT *remains helplessly behind.*)

ADJUTANT (*furiously to the Palace Guard*): Down with those lances! Don't you see the Governor's life is threatened?

(*The* IRONSHIRTS *of the Palace Guard refuse to obey. They stare coldly and indifferently at the* ADJUTANT *and follow the next events without interest.*)

SINGER: O blindness of the great!
They go their way like gods,
Great over bent backs,
Sure of hired fists,
Trusting in the power

Which has lasted so long.
But long is not forever.
O change from age to age!
Thou hope of the people!

(*Enter the* GOVERNOR, *through the gateway, between two* SOLDIERS *armed to the teeth. He is in chains. His face is gray.*)

Up, great sir, deign to walk upright!
From your palace the eyes of many foes follow you!
And now you don't need an architect, a carpenter will do.
You won't be moving into a new palace
But into a little hole in the ground.
Look about you once more, blind man!

(*The arrested man looks round.*)

Does all you had please you?
Between the Easter Mass and the Easter meal
You are walking to a place whence no one returns.

(*The* GOVERNOR *is led off. A horn sounds an alarm. Noise behind the gateway.*)

When the house of a great one collapses
Many little ones are slain.
Those who had no share in the *good* fortunes of the mighty
Often have a share in their *mis*fortunes.
The plunging wagon
Drags the sweating oxen down with it
Into the abyss.

(*The* SERVANTS *come rushing through the gateway in panic.*)

SERVANTS (*among themselves*): – The baskets!
– Take them all into the third courtyard! Food for five days!
– The mistress has fainted! Someone must carry her down.
– She must get away.
– What about us? We'll be slaughtered like chickens, as always.
– Goodness, what'll happen? There's bloodshed already in the city, they say.
– Nonsense, the Governor has just been asked to appear at a Princes' meeting. All very correct. Everything'll be ironed out. I heard this on the best authority . . .

(*The two* DOCTORS *rush into the courtyard.*)

FIRST DOCTOR (*trying to restrain the other*): Niko Mikadze, it is your duty as a doctor to attend Natella Abashwili.

SECOND DOCTOR: My duty! It's yours!

FIRST DOCTOR: Whose turn is it to look after the child today, Niko Mikadze, yours or mine?

SECOND DOCTOR: Do you really think, Mika Loladze, I'm going to stay a minute longer in this accursed house on that little brat's account? (*They start fighting. All one hears is:* "You neglect your duty!" *and* "Duty, my foot!" *Then the* SECOND DOCTOR *knocks the* FIRST *down.*) Go to hell! (*Exit.*)

(*Enter the soldier,* SIMON SHASHAVA. *He searches in the crowd for* GRUSHA.)

SIMON: Grusha! There you are at last! What are you going to do?

GRUSHA: Nothing. If worst comes to worst, I've a brother in the mountains. How about you?

SIMON: Forget about me. (*Formally again.*) Grusha Vashnadze, your wish to know my plans fills me with satisfaction. I've been ordered to accompany Madam Abashwili as her guard.

GRUSHA: But hasn't the Palace Guard mutinied?

SIMON (*seriously*): That's a fact.

GRUSHA: Isn't it dangerous to go with her?

SIMON: In Tiflis, they say: Isn't the stabbing dangerous for the knife?

GRUSHA: You're not a knife, you're a man, Simon Shashava, what has that woman to do with you?

SIMON: That woman has nothing to do with me. I have my orders, and I go.

GRUSHA: The soldier is pigheaded: he is running into danger for nothing – nothing at all. I must get into the third courtyard, I'm in a hurry.

SIMON: Since we're both in a hurry we shouldn't quarrel. You need time for a good quarrel. May I ask if the young lady still has parents?

GRUSHA: No, just a brother.

SIMON: As time is short – my second question is this: Is the young lady as healthy as a fish in water?

GRUSHA: I may have a pain in the right shoulder once in a while. Otherwise I'm strong enough for my job. No one has complained. So far.

SIMON: That's well known. When it's Easter Sunday, and the question arises who'll run for the goose all the same, she'll be the one. My third question is this: Is the young lady impatient? Does she want apples in winter?

GRUSHA: Impatient? No. But if a man goes to war without any reason and then no message comes – that's bad.

SIMON: A message will come. And now my final question . . .

GRUSHA: Simon Shashava, I must get to the third courtyard at once. My answer is yes.

SIMON (*very embarrased*): Haste, they say, is the wind that blows down the scaffolding. But they also say: The rich don't know what haste is. I'm from . . .

GRUSHA: Kutsk . . .

SIMON: The young lady has been inquiring about me? I'm healthy, I have no dependents, I make ten piasters a month, as paymaster twenty piasters, and I'm asking — very sincerely — for your hand.

GRUSHA: Simon Shashava, it suits me well.

SIMON (*taking from his neck a thin chain with a little cross on it*): My mother gave me this cross, Grusha Vashnadze. The chain is silver. Please wear it.

GRUSHA: Many thanks, Simon.

SIMON (*hangs it round her neck*): It would be better to go to the third courtyard now. Or there'll be difficulties. Anyway, I must harness the horses. The young lady will understand?

GRUSHA: Yes, Simon.

(*They stand undecided.*)

SIMON: I'll just take the mistress to the troops that have stayed loyal. When the war's over, I'll be back. In two weeks. Or three. I hope my intended won't get tired, awaiting my return.

GRUSHA: Simon Shashava, I shall wait for you.

Go calmly into battle, soldier
The bloody battle, the bitter battle
From which not everyone returns:
When you return I shall be there.
I shall be waiting for you under the green elm
I shall be waiting for you under the bare elm
I shall wait until the last soldier has returned
And longer
When you come back from the battle
No boots will stand at my door
The pillow beside mine will be empty
And my mouth will be unkissed.
When you return, when you return
You will be able to say: It is just as it was.

SIMON: I thank you, Grusha Vashnadze. And good-bye!

(*He bows low before her. She does the same before him. Then she runs quickly off without looking round. Enter the* ADJUTANT *from the gateway.*)

ADJUTANT (*harshly*): Harness the horses to the carriage! Don't stand there doing nothing, scum!

(SIMON SHASHAVA *stands to attention and goes off. Two* SERVANTS *crowd from the gateway, bent low under huge trunks. Behind them, supported by her women, stumbles* NATELLA ABASHWILI. *She is followed by a* WOMAN *carrying the* CHILD.)

GOVERNOR'S WIFE: I hardly know if my head's still on. Where's Michael?

Don't hold him so clumsily. Pile the trunks onto the carriage. No news from the city, Shalva?

ADJUTANT: None. All's quiet so far, but there's not a minute to lose. No room for all those trunks in the carriage. Pick out what you need. (*Exit quickly.*)

GOVERNOR'S WIFE: Only essentials! Quick, open the trunks! I'll tell you what I need. (*The trunks are lowered and opened. She points at some brocade dresses.*) The green one! And, of course, the one with the fur trimming. Where are Niko Mikadze and Mika Loladze? I've suddenly got the most terrible migraine again. It always starts in the temples. (*Enter* GRUSHA.) Taking your time, eh? Go and get the hot water bottles this minute! (GRUSHA *runs off, returns later with hot water bottles; the* GOVERNOR'S WIFE *orders her about by signs.*) Don't tear the sleeves.

A YOUNG WOMAN: Pardon, madam, no harm has come to the dress.

GOVERNOR'S WIFE: Because I stopped you. I've been watching you for a long time. Nothing in your head but making eyes at Shalva Tzereteli. I'll kill you, you bitch! (*She beats the* YOUNG WOMAN.)

ADJUTANT (*appearing in the gateway*): Please make haste, Natella Abashwili. Firing has broken out in the city. (*Exit.*)

GOVERNOR'S WIFE (*letting go of the* YOUNG WOMAN): Oh dear, do you think they'll lay hands on us? Why should they? Why? (*She herself begins to rummage in the trunks.*) How's Michael? Asleep?

WOMAN WITH THE CHILD: Yes, madam.

GOVERNOR'S WIFE: Then put him down a moment and get my little saffron-colored boots from the bedroom. I need them for the green dress. (*The* WOMAN *puts down the* CHILD *and goes off.*) Just look how these things have been packed! No love! No understanding! If you don't give them every order yourself . . . At such moments you realize what kind of servants you have! They gorge themselves at your expense, and never a word of gratitude! I'll remember this.

ADJUTANT (*entering, very excited*): Natella, you must leave at once!

GOVERNOR'S WIFE: Why? I've got to take this silver dress — it cost a thousand piasters. And that one there, and where's the wine-colored one?

ADJUTANT (*trying to pull her away*): Riots have broken out! We must leave at once. Where's the baby?

GOVERNOR'S WIFE (*calling to the* YOUNG WOMAN *who was holding the baby*): Maro, get the baby ready! Where on earth are you?

ADJUTANT (*leaving*): We'll probably have to leave the carriage behind and go ahead on horseback.

(*The* GOVERNOR'S WIFE *rummages again among her dresses, throws some onto the heap of chosen clothes, then takes them off again. Noises, drums are heard. The* YOUNG WOMAN *who was beaten creeps away. The sky begins to grow red.*)

GOVERNOR'S WIFE (*rummaging desperately*): I simply cannot find the wine-colored dress. Take the whole pile to the carriage. Where's Asja? And why hasn't Maro come back? Have you all gone crazy?

ADJUTANT (*returning*): Quick! Quick!

GOVERNOR'S WIFE (*to the* FIRST WOMAN): Run! Just throw them into the carriage!

ADJUTANT: We're not taking the carriage. And if you don't come now, I'll ride off on my own.

GOVERNOR'S WIFE (*as the* FIRST WOMAN *can't carry everything*): Where's that bitch Asja? (*The* ADJUTANT *pulls her away.*) Maro, bring the baby! (*To the* FIRST WOMAN.) Go and look for Masha. No, first take the dresses to the carriage. Such nonsense! I wouldn't dream of going on horseback!

(*Turning round, she sees the red sky, and starts back rigid. The fire burns. She is pulled out by the* ADJUTANT. *Shaking, the* FIRST WOMAN *follows with the dresses.*)

MARO (*from the doorway with the boots*): Madam! (*She sees the trunks and dresses and runs toward the* CHILD, *picks it up, and holds it a moment.*) They left it behind, the beasts. (*She hands it to* GRUSHA.) Hold it a moment. (*She runs off, following the* GOVERNOR'S WIFE.)

(*Enter* SERVANTS *from the gateway.*)

COOK: Well, so they've actually gone. Without the food wagons, and not a minute too early. It's time for us to clear out.

GROOM: This'll be an unhealthy neighborhood for quite a while. (*To one of the* WOMEN.) Suliko, take a few blankets and wait for me in the foal stables.

GRUSHA: What have they done with the Governor?

GROOM (*gesturing throat cutting*): Ffffft.

A FAT WOMAN (*seeing the gesture and becoming hysterical*): Oh dear, oh dear, oh dear, oh dear! Our master Georgi Abashwili! A picture of health he was, at the morning Mass — and now! Oh, take me away, we're all lost, we must die in sin like our master, Georgi Abashwili!

OTHER WOMAN (*soothing her*): Calm down, Nina! You'll be taken to safety. You've never hurt a fly.

FAT WOMAN (*being led out*): Oh dear, oh dear, oh dear! Quick! Let's all get out before they come, before they come!

A YOUNG WOMAN: Nina takes it more to heart than the mistress, that's a fact. They even have to have their weeping done for them.

COOK: We'd better get out, all of us.

ANOTHER WOMAN (*glancing back*): That must be the East Gate burning.

YOUNG WOMAN (*seeing the* CHILD *in* GRUSHA'*s arms*): The baby! What are you doing with it?

GRUSHA: It got left behind.

YOUNG WOMAN: She simply left it there. Michael, who was kept out of all the drafts!

(*The* SERVANTS *gather round the* CHILD.)

GRUSHA: He's waking up.

GROOM: Better put him down, I tell you. I'd rather not think what'd happen to anybody who was found with that baby.

COOK: That's right. Once they get started, they'll kill each other off, whole families at a time. Let's go.

(*Exeunt all but* GRUSHA, *with the* CHILD *on her arm, and* TWO WOMEN.)

TWO WOMEN: Didn't you hear? Better put him down.

GRUSHA: The nurse asked me to hold him a moment.

OLDER WOMAN: She's not coming back, you simpleton.

YOUNGER WOMAN: Keep your hands off it.

OLDER WOMAN (*amiably*): Grusha, you're a good soul, but you're not very bright, and you know it. I tell you, if he had the plague he couldn't be more dangerous.

GRUSHA (*stubbornly*): He hasn't got the plague. He looks at me! He's human!

OLDER WOMAN: Don't look at *him*. You're a fool – the kind that always gets put upon. A person need only say, "Run for the salad, you have the longest legs," and you run. My husband has an ox cart – you can come with us if you hurry! Lord, by now the whole neighborhood must be in flames.

(*Both* WOMEN *leave, sighing. After some hesitation,* GRUSHA *puts the sleeping* CHILD *down, looks at it for a moment, then takes a brocade blanket from the heap of clothes and covers it. Then both* WOMEN *return, dragging bundles.* GRUSHA *starts guiltily away from the* CHILD *and walks a few steps to one side.*)

YOUNGER WOMAN: Haven't you packed anything yet? There isn't much time, you know. The Ironshirts will be here from the barracks.

GRUSHA: Coming!

(*She runs through the doorway. Both* WOMEN *go to the gateway and wait. The sound of horses is heard. They flee, screaming. Enter the* FAT PRINCE *with drunken* IRONSHIRTS. *One of them carries the* GOVERNOR'S *head on a lance.*)

FAT PRINCE: Here! In the middle! (*One* SOLDIER *climbs onto the other's back, takes the head, holds it tentatively over the door.*) That's not the middle. Farther to the right. That's it. What I do, my friends, I do well. (*While with hammer and nail, the* SOLDIER *fastens the head to the wall by its hair:*) This morning at the church door I said to Georgi Abashwili: "I love a gay sky." Actually, I prefer the lightning that comes out of a gay sky. Yes, indeed. It's a pity they took the brat along, though, I need him, urgently.

(*Exit with* IRONSHIRTS *through the gateway. Trampling of horses again. Enter* GRUSHA *through the doorway looking cautiously about her. Clearly she has waited for the* IRONSHIRTS *to go. Carrying a bundle, she walks toward the gateway. At the last moment, she turns to see if the* CHILD *is still there. Catching sight of the head over the doorway, she screams. Horrified, she picks up her bundle again, and is about to leave when the* SINGER *starts to speak. She stands rooted to the spot.*)

SINGER: As she was standing between courtyard and gate,
She heard or she thought she heard a low voice calling.
The child called to her,
Not whining, but calling quite sensibly,
Or so it seemed to her.
"Woman," it said, "help me."
And it went on, not whining, but saying quite sensibly:
"Know, woman, he who hears not a cry for help
But passes by with troubled ears will never hear
The gentle call of a lover nor the blackbird at dawn
Nor the happy sigh of the tired grape-picker as the Angelus rings."

(*She walks a few steps toward the* CHILD *and bends over it.*)

Hearing this she went back for one more look at the child:
Only to sit with him for a moment or two,
Only till someone should come,
His mother, or anyone.

(*Leaning on a trunk, she sits facing the* CHILD.)

Only till she would have to leave, for the danger was too great,
The city was full of flame and crying.

(*The light grows dimmer, as though evening and night were coming on.*)

Fearful is the seductive power of goodness!

(GRUSHA *now settles down to watch over the* CHILD *through the night. Once, she lights a small lamp to look at it. Once, she tucks it in with a coat. From time to time she listens and looks to see whether someone is coming.*)

And she sat with the child a long time,
Till evening came, till night came, till dawn came.
She sat too long, too long she saw
The soft breathing, the small clenched fists,
Till toward morning the seduction was complete

And she rose, and bent down and, sighing, took the child
And carried it away.

(*She does what the* SINGER *says as he describes it.*)

As if it was stolen goods she picked it up.
As if she was a thief she crept away.

## II. THE FLIGHT INTO THE NORTHERN MOUNTAINS

SINGER: When Grusha Vashnadze left the city
On the Grusinian highway
On the way to the Northern Mountains
She sang a song, she bought some milk.
CHORUS: How will this human child escape
The bloodhounds, the trap-setters?
Into the deserted mountains she journeyed
Along the Grusinian highway she journeyed
She sang a song, she bought some milk.

(GRUSHA VASHNADZE *walks on. On her back she carries the* CHILD *in a sack, in one hand is a large stick, in the other a bundle. She sings.*)

*The Song of the Four Generals*

Four generals
Set out for Iran.
With the first one, war did not agree.
The second never won a victory.
For the third the weather never was right.
For the fourth the men would never fight.
Four generals
And not a single man!

Sosso Robakidse
Went march to Iran
With him the war did so agree
He soon had won a victory.
For him the weather was always right.
For him the men would always fight.
Sosso Robakidse,
He is our man!

(*A peasant's cottage appears.*)

GRUSHA (*to the* CHILD): Noontime is meal time. Now we'll sit hopefully in the grass, while the good Grusha goes and buys a little pitcher of milk.

(*She lays the* CHILD *down and knocks at the cottage door. An* OLD MAN *opens it.*) Grandfather, could I have a little pitcher of milk? And a corn cake, maybe?

OLD MAN: Milk? We have no milk. The soldiers from the city have our goats. Go to the soldiers if you want milk.

GRUSHA: But grandfather, you must have a little pitcher of milk for a baby?

OLD MAN: And for a God-bless-you, eh?

GRUSHA: Who said anything about a God-bless-you? (*She shows her purse.*) We'll pay like princes. "Head in the clouds, backside in the water." (*The* PEASANT *goes off, grumbling, for milk.*) How much for the milk?

OLD MAN: Three piasters. Milk has gone up.

GRUSHA: Three piasters for this little drop? (*Without a word the* OLD MAN *shuts the door in her face.*) Michael, did you hear that? Three piasters! We can't afford it! (*She goes back, sits down again, and gives the* CHILD *her breast.*) Suck. Think of the three piasters. There's nothing there, but you *think* you're drinking, and that's something. (*Shaking her head, she sees that the* CHILD *isn't sucking any more. She gets up, walks back to the door, and knocks again.*) Open, grandfather, we'll pay. (*Softly.*) May lightning strike you! (*When the* OLD MAN *appears.*) I thought it would be half a piaster. But the baby must be fed. How about one piaster for that little drop?

OLD MAN: Two.

GRUSHA: Don't shut the door again. (*She fishes a long time in her bag.*) Here are two piasters. The milk better be good. I still have two days' journey ahead of me. It's a murderous business you have here – and sinful, too!

OLD MAN: Kill the soldiers if you want milk.

GRUSHA (*giving the* CHILD *some milk*): This is an expensive joke. Take a sip, Michael, it's a week's pay. Around here they think we earned our money just sitting on our behinds. Oh, Michael, Michael, you're a nice little load for a girl to take on! (*Uneasy, she gets up, puts the* CHILD *on her back, and walks on. The* OLD MAN, *grumbling, picks up the pitcher and looks after her unmoved.*)

SINGER: As Grusha Vashnadze went northward
The Princes' Ironshirts went after her.

CHORUS: How will the barefoot girl escape the Ironshirts,
The bloodhounds, the trap-setters?
They hunt even by night.
Pursuers never tire.
Butchers sleep little.

(*Two* IRONSHIRTS *are trudging along the highway.*)

CORPORAL: You'll never amount to anything, blockhead, your heart's not in it. Your senior officer sees this in little things. Yesterday, when I made the fat gal, yes, you grabbed her husband as I commanded, and you did kick him in the belly, at my request, but did you *enjoy* it, like a loyal Private, or were you just doing your duty? I've kept an eye on you, blockhead, you're a hollow reed and a tinkling cymbal, you won't get promoted. (*They walk a while in silence.*) Don't think I've forgotten how insubordinate you are, either. Stop limping! I forbid you to limp! You limp because I sold the horses, and I sold the horses because I'd never have got that price again. You limp to show me you don't like marching. I know you. It won't help. You wait. Sing!

TWO IRONSHIRTS (*singing*): Sadly to war I went my way
Leaving my loved one at her door.
My friends will keep her honor safe
Till from the war I'm back once more.

CORPORAL: Louder!

TWO IRONSHIRTS (*singing*): When 'neath a headstone I shall be
My love a little earth will bring:
"Here rest the feet that oft would run to me
And here the arms that oft to me would cling."

(*They begin to walk again in silence.*)

CORPORAL: A good soldier has his heart and soul in it. When he receives an order, he gets a hard-on, and when he drives his lance into the enemy's guts, he comes. (*He shouts for joy.*) He lets himself be torn to bits for his superior officer, and as he lies dying he takes note that his corporal is nodding approval, and that is reward enough, it's his dearest wish. *You* won't get any nod of approval, but you'll croak all right. Christ, how'm I to get my hands on the Governor's bastard with the help of a fool like you! (*They stay on stage behind.*)

SINGER: When Grusha Vashnadze came to the River Sirra
Flight grew too much for her, the helpless child too heavy.
In the cornfields the rosy dawn
Is cold to the sleepless one, only cold.
The gay clatter of the milk cans in the farmyard where the smoke rises
Is only a threat to the fugitive.
She who carries the child feels its weight and little more.

(GRUSHA *stops in front of a farm. A fat* PEASANT WOMAN *is carrying a milk can through the door.* GRUSHA *waits until she has gone in, then approaches the house cautiously.*)

GRUSHA (*to the* CHILD): Now you've wet yourself again, and you know I've no linen. Michael, this is where we part company. It's far enough from the city. They wouldn't want you *so* much that they'd follow you all *this* way, little good-for-nothing. The peasant woman is kind, and can't you just smell the milk? (*She bends down to lay the* CHILD *on the threshold.*)

So farewell, Michael, I'll forget how you kicked me in the back all night to make me walk faster. And you can forget the meager fare — it was meant well. I'd like to have kept you — your nose is so tiny — but it can't be. I'd have shown you your first rabbit, I'd have trained you to keep dry, but now I must turn around. My sweetheart the soldier might be back soon, and suppose he didn't find me? You can't ask that, can you? (*She creeps up to the door and lays the* CHILD *on the threshold. Then, hiding behind a tree, she waits until the* PEASANT WOMAN *opens the door and sees the bundle.*)

PEASANT WOMAN: Good heavens, what's this? Husband!

PEASANT: What is it? Let me finish my soup.

PEASANT WOMAN (*to the* CHILD): Where's your mother then? Haven't you got one? It's a boy. Fine linen. He's from a good family, you can see that. And they just leave him on our doorstep. Oh, these are times!

PEASANT: If they think we're going to feed it, they're wrong. You can take it to the priest in the village. That's the best we can do.

PEASANT WOMAN: What'll the priest do with him? He needs a mother. There, he's waking up. Don't you think we could keep him, though?

PEASANT (*shouting*): No!

PEASANT WOMAN: I could lay him in the corner by the armchair. All I need is a crib. I can take him into the fields with me. See him laughing? Husband, we have a roof over our heads. We can do it. Not another word out of you!

(*She carries the* CHILD *into the house. The* PEASANT *follows protesting.* GRUSHA *steps out from behind the tree, laughs, and hurries off in the opposite direction.*)

SINGER: Why so cheerful, making for home?

CHORUS: Because the child has won new parents with a laugh,
Because I'm rid of the little one, I'm cheerful.

SINGER: And why so sad?

CHORUS: Because I'm single and free, I'm sad
Like someone who's been robbed
Someone who's newly poor.

(*She walks for a short while, then meets the two* IRONSHIRTS *who point their lances at her.*)

CORPORAL: Lady, you are running straight into the arms of the Armed Forces. Where are you coming from? And when? Are you having illicit relations with the enemy? Where is he hiding? What movements is he making in your rear? How about the hills? How about the valleys? How are your stockings held in position? (GRUSHA *stands there frightened.*) Don't be scared, we always withdraw, if necessary . . . what, blockhead? I always withdraw. In that respect at least, I can be relied on. Why are you staring like that at my lance? In the field no soldier drops his lance, that's a rule. Learn it by heart, blockhead. Now, lady, where are you headed?

GRUSHA: To meet my intended, one Simon Shashava, of the Palace Guard in Nuka.

CORPORAL: Simon Shashava? Sure, I know him. He gave me the key so I could look you up once in a while. Blockhead, we are getting to be unpopular. We must make her realize we have honorable intentions. Lady, behind apparent frivolity I conceal a serious nature, so let me tell you officially: I want a child from you. (GRUSHA *utters a little scream.*) Blockhead, she understands me. Uh-huh, isn't it a sweet shock? "Then first I must take the noodles out of the oven, Officer. Then first I must change my torn shirt, Colonel." But away with jokes, away with my lance! We are looking for a baby. A baby from a good family. Have you heard of such a baby, from the city, dressed in fine linen, and suddenly turning up here?

GRUSHA: No, I haven't heard a thing. (*Suddenly she turns around and runs back, panic-stricken. The* IRONSHIRTS *glance at each other, then follow her, cursing.*)

SINGER: Run, kind girl! The killers are coming!
Help the helpless babe, helpless girl!
And so she runs!

CHORUS: In the bloodiest times
There are kind people.

(*As* GRUSHA *rushes into the cottage, the* PEASANT WOMAN *is bending over the* CHILD'S *crib.*)

GRUSHA: Hide him. Quick! The Ironshirts are coming! I laid him on your doorstep. But he isn't mine. He's from a good family.

PEASANT WOMAN: Who's coming? What Ironshirts?

GRUSHA: Don't ask questions. The Ironshirts that are looking for it.

PEASANT WOMAN: They've no business in my house. But I must have a little talk with you, it seems.

GRUSHA: Take off the fine linen. It'll give us away.

PEASANT WOMAN: Linen, my foot! In this house I make the decisions! "*You* can't vomit in *my* room!" Why did you abandon it? It's a sin.

GRUSHA (*looking out of the window*): Look, they're coming out from behind those trees! I shouldn't have run away, it made them angry. Oh, what shall I do?

PEASANT WOMAN (*looking out of the window and suddenly starting with fear*): Gracious! Ironshirts!

GRUSHA: They're after the baby.

PEASANT WOMAN: Suppose they come in!

GRUSHA: You mustn't give him to them. Say he's yours.

PEASANT WOMAN: Yes.

GRUSHA: They'll run him through if you hand him over.

PEASANT WOMAN: But suppose they ask for it? The silver for the harvest is in the house.

GRUSHA: If you let them have him, they'll run him through, right here in this room! You've got to say he's yours!

PEASANT WOMAN: Yes. But what if they don't believe me?

GRUSHA: You must be firm.

PEASANT WOMAN: They'll burn the roof over our heads.

GRUSHA: That's why you must say he's yours. His name's Michael. But I shouldn't have told you. (*The* PEASANT WOMAN *nods.*) Don't nod like that. And don't tremble – they'll notice.

PEASANT WOMAN: Yes.

GRUSHA: And stop saying yes, I can't stand it. (*She shakes the* WOMAN.) Don't you have any children?

PEASANT WOMAN (*muttering*): He's in the war.

GRUSHA: Then maybe *he's* an Ironshirt? Do you want *him* to run children through with a lance? You'd bawl him out. "No fooling with lances in my house!" you'd shout, "is that what I've reared you for? Wash your neck before you speak to your mother!"

PEASANT WOMAN: That's true, he couldn't get away with anything around here!

GRUSHA: So you'll say he's yours?

PEASANT WOMAN: Yes.

GRUSHA: Look! They're coming!

(*There is a knocking at the door. The* WOMEN *don't answer. Enter* IRONSHIRTS. *The* PEASANT WOMAN *bows low.*)

CORPORAL: Well, here she is. What did I tell you? What a nose I have! I *smelt* her. Lady, I have a question for you. Why did you run away? What did you think I would do to you? I'll bet it was something unchaste. Confess!

GRUSHA (*while the* PEASANT WOMAN *bows again and again*): I'd left some milk on the stove, and I suddenly remembered it.

CORPORAL: Or maybe you imagined I looked at you unchastely? Like there could be something between us? A carnal glance, know what I mean?

GRUSHA: I didn't see it.

CORPORAL: But it's possible, huh? You admit that much. After all, I might be a pig. I'll be frank with you: I could think of all sorts of things if we were alone. (*To the* PEASANT WOMAN.) Shouldn't you be busy in the yard? Feeding the hens?

PEASANT WOMAN (*falling suddenly to her knees*): Soldier, I didn't know a thing about it. Please don't burn the roof over our heads.

CORPORAL: What are you talking about?

PEASANT WOMAN: I had nothing to do with it. She left it on my doorstep, I swear it!

CORPORAL (*suddenly seeing the* CHILD *and whistling*): Ah, so there's a little something in the crib! Blockhead, I smell a thousand piasters. Take the old girl outside and hold on to her. It looks like I have a little cross-examining to do. (*The* PEASANT WOMAN *lets herself be led out by the* PRIVATE, *without a word.*) So, you've *got* the child I wanted from you! (*He walks toward the crib.*)

GRUSHA: Officer, he's mine. He's not the one you're after.

CORPORAL: I'll just take a look. (*He bends over the crib.*)

(GRUSHA *looks round in despair.*)

GRUSHA: He's mine! He's mine!

CORPORAL: Fine linen!

(GRUSHA *dashes at him to pull him away. He throws her off and again bends over the crib. Again looking round in despair, she sees a log of wood, seizes it, and hits the* CORPORAL *over the head from behind. The* CORPORAL *collapses. She quickly picks up the* CHILD *and rushes off.*)

SINGER: And in her flight from the Ironshirts
After twenty-two days of journeying
At the foot of the Janga-Tu Glacier
Grusha Vashnadze decided to adopt the child.

CHORUS: The helpless girl adopted the helpless child.

(GRUSHA *squats over a half-frozen stream to get the* CHILD *water in the hollow of her hand.*)

GRUSHA: Since no one else will take you, son,
I must take you.
Since no one else will take you, son,
You must take me.
O black day in a lean, lean year,
The trip was long, the milk was dear,
My legs are tired, my feet are sore:
But I wouldn't be without you any more.
I'll throw your silken shirt away
And wrap you in rags and tatters.
I'll wash you, son, and christen you in glacier water.
We'll see it through together.

(*She has taken off the* CHILD'*s fine linen and wrapped it in a rag.*)

SINGER: When Grusha Vashnadze
Pursued by the Ironshirts
Came to the bridge on the glacier
Leading to the villages of the Eastern Slope
She sang the Song of the Rotten Bridge
And risked two lives.

(*A wind has risen. The bridge on the glacier is visible in the dark. One rope is broken and half the bridge is hanging down the abyss.* MERCHANTS, *two men and a woman, stand undecided before the bridge as* GRUSHA *and the* CHILD *arrive. One man is trying to catch the hanging rope with a stick.*)

FIRST MAN: Take your time, young woman. You won't get across here anyway.

GRUSHA: But I *have* to get the baby to the east side. To my brother's place.

MERCHANT WOMAN: Have to? How d'you mean, "have to"? I have to get there, too — because I have to buy carpets in Atum — carpets a woman had to sell because her husband had to die. But can *I* do what I have to? Can she? Andrei's been fishing for that rope for hours. And I ask you, how are we going to fasten it, even if he gets it up?

FIRST MAN (*listening*): Hush, I think I hear something.

GRUSHA: The bridge isn't quite rotted through. I think I'll try it.

MERCHANT WOMAN: *I* wouldn't — if the devil himself were after me. It's suicide.

FIRST MAN (*shouting*): Hi!

GRUSHA: Don't shout! (*To the* MERCHANT WOMAN.) Tell him not to shout.

FIRST MAN: But there's someone down there calling. Maybe they've lost their way.

MERCHANT WOMAN: Why shouldn't he shout? Is there something funny about you? Are they after you?

GRUSHA: All right, I'll tell. The Ironshirts are after me. I knocked one down.

SECOND MAN: Hide our merchandise!

(*The* WOMAN *hides a sack behind a rock.*)

FIRST MAN: Why didn't you say so right away? (*To the others.*) If they catch her they'll make mincemeat out of her!

GRUSHA: Get out of my way. I've got to cross that bridge.

SECOND MAN: You can't. The precipice is two thousand feet deep.

FIRST MAN: Even with the rope it'd be no use. We could hold it up with our hands. But then we'd have to do the same for the Ironshirts.

GRUSHA: Go away.

(*There are calls from the distance:* "Hi, up there!")

MERCHANT WOMAN: They're getting near. But you can't take the child on that bridge. It's sure to break. And look!

(GRUSHA *looks down into the abyss. The* IRONSHIRTS *are heard calling again from below.*)

SECOND MAN: Two thousand feet!

GRUSHA: But those men are worse.

FIRST MAN: You can't do it. Think of the baby. Risk your life but not a child's.

SECOND MAN: With the child she's that much heavier!

MERCHANT WOMAN: Maybe she's *really* got to get across. Give *me* the baby. I'll hide it. Cross the bridge alone!

GRUSHA: I won't. We belong together. (*To the* CHILD.) "Live together, die together." (*She sings.*)

*The Song of the Rotten Bridge*

Deep is the abyss, son,
I see the weak bridge sway
But it's not for us, son,
To choose the way.

The way I know
Is the one you must tread,
And all you will eat
Is my bit of bread.

Of every four pieces
You shall have three.
Would that I knew
How big they will be!

Get out of my way, I'll try it without the rope.

MERCHANT WOMAN: You are tempting God!

(*There are shouts from below.*)

GRUSHA: Please, throw that stick away, or they'll get the rope and follow me. (*Pressing the* CHILD *to her, she steps onto the swaying bridge. The* MERCHANT WOMAN *screams when it looks as though the bridge is about to collapse. But* GRUSHA *walks on and reaches the far side.*)

FIRST MAN: She made it!

MERCHANT WOMAN (*who has fallen on her knees and begun to pray, angrily*): I still think it was a sin.

(*The* IRONSHIRTS *appear; the* CORPORAL*'s head is bandaged.*)

CORPORAL: Seen a woman with a child?

FIRST MAN (*while the* SECOND MAN *throws the stick into the abyss*): Yes, there! But the bridge won't carry you!

CORPORAL: You'll pay for this, blockhead!

(GRUSHA, *from the far bank, laughs and shows the* CHILD *to the* IRONSHIRTS. *She walks on. The wind blows.*)

GRUSHA (*turning to the* CHILD): You mustn't be afraid of the wind. He's a poor thing too. He has to push the clouds along and he gets quite cold doing it. (*Snow starts falling.*) And the snow isn't so bad, either, Michael. It covers the little fir trees so they won't die in winter. Let me sing you a little song. (*She sings.*)

*The Song of the Child*

Your father is a bandit
A harlot the mother who bore you.
Yet honorable men
Shall kneel down before you.
Food to the baby horses
The tiger's son will take.
The mothers will get milk
From the son of the snake.

## III. IN THE NORTHERN MOUNTAINS

SINGER: Seven days the sister, Grusha Vashnadze,
Journeyed across the glacier
And down the slopes she journeyed.
"When I enter my brother's house," she thought,
"He will rise and embrace me."
"Is that you, sister?" he will say,
"I have long expected you.
This is my dear wife,
And this is my farm, come to me by marriage,
With eleven horses and thirty-one cows. Sit down.
Sit down with your child at our table and eat."
The brother's house was in a lovely valley.
When the sister came to the brother,
She was ill from walking.
The brother rose from the table.

(*A fat peasant couple rise from the table.* LAVRENTI VASHNADZE *still has a napkin round his neck, as* GRUSHA, *pale and supported by a* SERVANT, *enters with the* CHILD.)

LAVRENTI: Where've *you* come from, Grusha?
GRUSHA (*feebly*): Across the Janga-Tu Pass, Lavrenti.
SERVANT: I found her in front of the hay barn. She has a baby with her.
SISTER-IN-LAW: Go and groom the mare.

(*Exit the* SERVANT.)

LAVRENTI: This is my wife Aniko.

SISTER-IN-LAW: I thought you were in service in Nuka.

GRUSHA (*barely able to stand*): Yes, I was.

SISTER-IN-LAW: Wasn't it a good job? We were told it was.

GRUSHA: The Governor got killed.

LAVRENTI: Yes, we heard there were riots. Your aunt told us. Remember, Aniko?

SISTER-IN-LAW: Here with us, it's very quiet. City people always want something going on. (*She walks toward the door, calling.*) Sosso, Sosso, don't take the cake out of the oven yet, d'you hear? Where on earth are you? (*Exit, calling.*)

LAVRENTI (*quietly, quickly*): Is there a father? (*As she shakes her head.*) I thought not. We must think up something. She's religious.

SISTER-IN-LAW (*returning*): Those servants! (*To* GRUSHA.) You have a child.

GRUSHA: It's mine. (*She collapses.* LAVRENTI *rushes to her assistance.*)

SISTER-IN-LAW: Heavens, she's ill — what are we going to do?

LAVRENTI (*escorting her to a bench near the stove*): Sit down, sit. I think it's just weakness, Aniko.

SISTER-IN-LAW: As long as it's not scarlet fever!

LAVRENTI: She'd have spots if it was. It's only weakness. Don't worry, Aniko. (*To* GRUSHA.) Better, sitting down?

SISTER-IN-LAW: Is the child hers?

GRUSHA: Yes, mine.

LAVRENTI: She's on her way to her husband.

SISTER-IN-LAW: I see. Your meat's getting cold. (LAVRENTI *sits down and begins to eat.*) Cold food's not good for you, the fat mustn't get cold, you know your stomach's your weak spot. (*To* GRUSHA.) If your husband's not in the city, where is he?

LAVRENTI: She got married on the other side of the mountain, she says.

SISTER-IN-LAW: On the other side of the mountain. I see. (*She also sits down to eat.*)

GRUSHA: I think I should lie down somewhere, Lavrenti.

SISTER-IN-LAW: If it's consumption we'll all get it. (*She goes on cross-examining her.*) Has your husband got a farm?

GRUSHA: He's a soldier.

LAVRENTI: But he's coming into a farm — a small one — from his father.

SISTER-IN-LAW: Isn't he in the war? Why not?

GRUSHA (*with effort*): Yes, he's in the war.

SISTER-IN-LAW: Then why d'you want to go to the farm?

LAVRENTI: When he comes back from the war, he'll return to his farm.

SISTER-IN-LAW: But you're going there now?

LAVRENTI: Yes, to wait for him.

SISTER-IN-LAW (*calling shrilly*): Sosso, the cake!

GRUSHA (*murmuring feverishly*): A farm — a soldier — waiting — sit down, eat.

SISTER-IN-LAW: It's scarlet fever.

GRUSHA (*starting up*): Yes, he's got a farm!

LAVRENTI: I think it's just weakness, Aniko. Would you look after the cake yourself, dear?

SISTER-IN-LAW: But when will he come back if war's broken out again as people say? (*She waddles off, shouting.*) Sosso! Where on earth are you? Sosso!

LAVRENTI (*getting up quickly and going to* GRUSHA): You'll get a bed in a minute. She has a good heart. But wait till after supper.

GRUSHA (*holding out the* CHILD *to him*): Take him.

LAVRENTI (*taking it and looking around*): But you can't stay here long with the child. She's religious, you see.

(GRUSHA *collapses.* LAVRENTI *catches her.*)

SINGER: The sister was so ill,
The cowardly brother had to give her shelter.
Summer departed, winter came.
The winter was long, the winter was short.
People mustn't know anything.
Rats mustn't bite.
Spring mustn't come.

(GRUSHA *sits over the weaving loom in a workroom. She and the* CHILD, *who is squatting on the floor, are wrapped in blankets. She sings.*)

*The Song of the Center*

And the lover started to leave
And his betrothed ran pleading after him
Pleading and weeping, weeping and teaching:
"Dearest mine, dearest mine
When you go to war as now you do
When you fight the foe as soon you will
Don't lead with the front line
And don't push with the rear line
At the front is red fire
In the rear is red smoke
Stay in the war's center
Stay near the standard bearer
The first always die
The last are also hit
Those in the center come home."

Michael, we must be clever. If we make ourselves as small as cockroaches, the sister-in-law will forget we're in the house, and then we can stay till the snow melts.

(*Enter* LAVRENTI. *He sits down beside his sister.*)

LAVRENTI: Why are you sitting there muffled up like coachmen, you two? Is it too cold in the room?

GRUSHA (*hastily removing one shawl*): It's not too cold, Lavrenti.

LAVRENTI: If it's too cold, you shouldn't be sitting here with the child. Aniko would never forgive herself! (*Pause.*) I hope our priest didn't question you about the child?

GRUSHA: He did, but I didn't tell him anything.

LAVRENTI: That's good. I wanted to speak to you about Aniko. She has a good heart but she's very, very sensitive. People need only mention our farm and she's worried. She takes everything hard, you see. One time our milkmaid went to church with a hole in her stocking. Ever since, Aniko has worn two pairs of stockings in church. It's the old family in her. (*He listens.*) Are you sure there are no rats around? If there are rats, you couldn't live here. (*There are sounds as of dripping from the roof.*) What's that, dripping?

GRUSHA: It must be a barrel leaking.

LAVRENTI: Yes, it must be a barrel. You've been here six months, haven't you? Was I talking about Aniko? (*They listen again to the snow melting.*) You can't imagine how worried she gets about your soldier-husband. "Suppose he comes back and can't find her!" she says and lies awake. "He can't come before the spring," I tell her. The dear woman! (*The drops begin to fall faster.*) When d'you think he'll come? What do *you* think? (GRUSHA *is silent.*) Not before the spring, you agree? (GRUSHA *is silent.*) You don't believe he'll come at all? (GRUSHA *is silent.*) But when the spring comes and the snow melts here and on the passes, you can't stay on. They may come and look for you. There's already talk of an illegitimate child. (*The "glockenspiel" of the falling drops has grown faster and steadier.*) Grusha, the snow is melting on the roof. Spring is here.

GRUSHA: Yes.

LAVRENTI (*eagerly*): I'll tell you what we'll do. You need a place to go, and, because of the child (*he sighs*), you have to have a husband, so people won't talk. Now I've made cautious inquiries to see if we can find you a husband. Grusha, I *have* one. I talked to a peasant woman who has a son. Just the other side of the mountain. A small farm. And she's willing.

GRUSHA: But I *can't* marry! I must wait for Simon Shashava.

LAVRENTI: Of course. That's all been taken care of. You don't need a man in bed – you need a man on paper. And I've found you one. The son of this peasant woman is going to die. Isn't that wonderful? He's at his last gasp. And all in line with our story – a husband from the other side of the mountain! And when you met him he was at the last gasp. So you're a widow. What do you say?

GRUSHA: It's true I could use a document with stamps on it for Michael.

LAVRENTI: Stamps make all the difference. Without something in writing the Shah couldn't prove he's a Shah. And you'll have a place to live.

GRUSHA: How much does the peasant woman want?
LAVRENTI: Four hundred piasters.
GRUSHA: Where will you find it?
LAVRENTI (*guiltily*): Aniko's milk money.
GRUSHA: No one would know us there. I'll do it.
LAVRENTI (*getting up*): I'll let the peasant woman know. (*Quick exit.*)
GRUSHA: Michael, you make a lot of work. I came by you as the pear tree comes by sparrows. And because a Christian bends down and picks up a crust of bread so nothing will go to waste. Michael, it would have been better had I walked quickly away on that Easter Sunday in Nuka in the second courtyard. Now I *am* a fool.

SINGER: The bridegroom was on his deathbed when the bride arrived.
The bridegroom's mother was waiting at the door, telling her to hurry.
The bride brought a child along.
The witness hid it during the wedding.

(*On one side the bed. Under the mosquito net lies a very* SICK MAN. GRUSHA *is pulled in at a run by her future mother-in-law. They are followed by* LAVRENTI *and the* CHILD.)

MOTHER-IN-LAW: Quick! Quick! Or he'll die on us before the wedding. (*To* LAVRENTI.) I was never told she had a child already.
LAVRENTI: What difference does it make? (*Pointing toward the* DYING MAN.) It can't matter to him — in his condition.
MOTHER-IN-LAW: To him? But I'll never survive the shame! We are honest people. (*She begins to weep.*) My Jussup doesn't have to marry a girl with a child!
LAVRENTI: All right, make it another two hundred piasters. You'll have it in writing that the farm will go to you: but she'll have the right to live here for two years.
MOTHER-IN-LAW (*drying her tears*): It'll hardly cover the funeral expenses. I hope she'll really lend a hand with the work. And what's happened to the monk? He must have slipped out through the kitchen window. We'll have the whole village on our necks when they hear Jussup's end is come! Oh dear! I'll go get the monk. But he mustn't see the child!
LAVRENTI: I'll take care he doesn't. But why only a monk? Why not a priest?
MOTHER-IN-LAW: Oh, he's just as good. I only made one mistake: I paid half his fee in advance. Enough to send him to the tavern. I only hope . . . (*She runs off.*)
LAVRENTI: She saved on the priest, the wretch! Hired a cheap monk.
GRUSHA: You *will* send Simon Shashava to see me if he turns up after all?
LAVRENTI: Yes. (*Pointing at the* SICK PEASANT.) Won't you take a look at him? (GRUSHA, *taking* MICHAEL *to her, shakes her head.*) He's not moving an eyelid. I hope we aren't too late.

(*They listen. On the opposite side enter* NEIGHBORS *who look around and take up positions against the walls, thus forming another wall near the bed, yet leaving an opening so that the bed can be seen. They start murmuring prayers. Enter the* MOTHER-IN-LAW *with a* MONK. *Showing some annoyance and surprise, she bows to the guests.*)

MOTHER-IN-LAW: I hope you won't mind waiting a few moments? My son's bride has just arrived from the city. An emergency wedding is about to be celebrated. (*To the* MONK *in the bedroom.*) I might have known you couldn't keep your trap shut. (*To* GRUSHA.) The wedding can take place at once. Here's the license. Me and the bride's brother (LAVRENTI *tries to hide in the background, after having quietly taken* MICHAEL *back from* GRUSHA. *The* MOTHER-IN-LAW *waves him away.*) are the witnesses.

(GRUSHA *has bowed to the* MONK. *They go to the bed. The* MOTHER-IN-LAW *lifts the mosquito net. The* MONK *starts reeling off the marriage ceremony in Latin. Meanwhile the* MOTHER-IN-LAW *beckons to* LAVRENTI *to get rid of the* CHILD, *but fearing that it will cry he draws its attention to the ceremony,* GRUSHA *glances once at the* CHILD, *and* LAVRENTI *waves the* CHILD'*s hand in a greeting.*)

MONK: Are you prepared to be a faithful, obedient, and good wife to this man, and to cleave to him until death you do part?

GRUSHA (*looking at the* CHILD): I am.

MONK (*to the* SICK PEASANT): Are you prepared to be a good and loving husband to your wife until death you do part? (*As the* SICK PEASANT *does not answer, the* MONK *looks inquiringly around.*)

MOTHER-IN-LAW: Of course he is! Didn't you hear him say yes?

MONK: All right. We declare the marriage contracted! How about extreme unction?

MOTHER-IN-LAW: Nothing doing! The wedding cost quite enough. Now I must take care of the mourners. (*To* LAVRENTI.) Did we say seven hundred?

LAVRENTI: Six hundred. (*He pays.*) Now I don't want to sit with the guests and get to know people. So farewell, Grusha, and if my widowed sister comes to visit me, she'll get a welcome from my wife, or I'll show my teeth. (*Nods, gives the* CHILD *to* GRUSHA, *and leaves. The* MOURNERS *glance after him without interest.*)

MONK: May one ask where this child comes from?

MOTHER-IN-LAW: Is there a child? I don't see a child. And you don't see a child either — you understand? Or it may turn out I saw all sorts of things in the tavern! Now come on.

(*After* GRUSHA *has put the* CHILD *down and told him to be quiet, they move over left,* GRUSHA *is introduced to the neighbors.*)

This is my daughter-in-law. She arrived just in time to find dear Jussup still alive.

ONE WOMAN: He's been ill now a whole year, hasn't he? When our Vassili was drafted he was there to say good-bye.

ANOTHER WOMAN: Such things are terrible for a farm. The corn all ripe and the farmer in bed! It'll really be a blessing if he doesn't suffer too long, I say.

FIRST WOMAN (*confidentially*): You know why we thought he'd taken to his bed? Because of the draft! And now his end is come!

MOTHER-IN-LAW: Sit yourselves down, please! And have some cakes!

(*She beckons to* GRUSHA *and both women go into the bedroom, where they pick up the cake pans off the floor. The* GUESTS, *among them the* MONK, *sit on the floor and begin conversing in subdued voices.*)

ONE PEASANT (*to whom the* MONK *has handed the bottle which he has taken from his soutane*): There's a child, you say! How can that have happened to Jussup?

A WOMAN: She was certainly lucky to get herself married, with him so sick!

MOTHER-IN-LAW: They're gossiping already. And wolfing down the funeral cakes at the same time! If he doesn't die today, I'll have to bake some more tomorrow!

GRUSHA: I'll bake them for you.

MOTHER-IN-LAW: Yesterday some horsemen rode by, and I went out to see who it was. When I came in again he was lying there like a corpse! So I sent for you. It can't take much longer. (*She listens.*)

MONK: Dear wedding and funeral guests! Deeply touched, we stand before a bed of death and marriage. The bride gets a veil; the groom, a shroud: how varied, my children, are the fates of men! Alas! One man dies and has a roof over his head, and the other is married and the flesh turns to dust from which it was made. Amen.

MOTHER-IN-LAW: He's getting his own back. I shouldn't have hired such a cheap one. It's what you'd expect. A more expensive monk would behave himself. In Sura there's one with a real air of sanctity about him, but of course he charges a fortune. A fifty piaster monk like that has no dignity, and as for piety, just fifty piasters' worth and no more! When I came to get him in the tavern he'd just made a speech, and he was shouting: "The war is over, beware of the peace!" We must go in.

GRUSHA (*giving* MICHAEL *a cake*): Eat this cake, and keep nice and still, Michael.

(*The two women offer cakes to the guests. The* DYING MAN *sits up in bed. He puts his head out from under the mosquito net, stares at the two women, then sinks back again. The* MONK *takes two bottles from his soutane and offers them to the* PEASANT *beside him. Enter three* MUSICIANS *who are greeted with a sly wink by the* MONK.)

MOTHER-IN-LAW (*to the* MUSICIANS): What are you doing here? With instruments?

ONE MUSICIAN: Brother Anastasius here (*pointing at the* MONK) told us there was a wedding on.

MOTHER-IN-LAW: What? You brought them? Three more on my neck! Don't you know there's a dying man in the next room?

MONK: A very tempting assignment for a musician: something that could be either a subdued Wedding March or a spirited Funeral Dance.

MOTHER-IN-LAW: Well, you might as well play. Nobody can stop you eating in any case.

(*The* MUSICIANS *play a potpourri. The women serve cakes.*)

MONK: The trumpet sounds like a whining baby. And you, little drum, what have you got to tell the world?

DRUNKEN PEASANT (*beside the* MONK, *sings*): There was a young woman who said:

I thought I'd be happier, wed.
But my husband is old
And remarkably cold
So I sleep with a candle instead.

(*The* MOTHER-IN-LAW *throws the* DRUNKEN PEASANT *out. The music stops. The* GUESTS *are embarrassed.*)

GUESTS (*loudly*): — Have you heard? The Grand Duke is back! But the Princes are against him.

— They say the Shah of Persia has lent him a great army to restore order in Grusinia.

— But how is that possible? The Shah of Persia is the enemy . . .

— The enemy of Grusinia, you donkey, not the enemy of the Grand Duke!

— In any case, the war's over, so our soldiers are coming back.

(GRUSHA *drops a cake pan.* GUESTS *help her pick up the cake.*)

AN OLD WOMAN (*to* GRUSHA): Are you feeling bad? It's just excitement about dear Jussup. Sit down and rest a while, my dear. (GRUSHA *staggers.*)

GUESTS: Now everything'll be the way it was. Only the taxes'll go up because now we'll have to pay for the war.

GRUSHA (*weakly*): Did someone say the soldiers are back?

A MAN: I did.

GRUSHA: It can't be true.

FIRST MAN (*to a* WOMAN): Show her the shawl. We bought it from a soldier. It's from Persia.

GRUSHA (*looking at the shawl*): They are here. (*She gets up, takes a step, kneels down in prayer, takes the silver cross and chain out of her blouse, and kisses it.*)

MOTHER-IN-LAW (*while the guests silently watch* GRUSHA): What's the matter with you? Aren't you going to look after our guests? What's all this city nonsense got to do with us?

GUESTS (*resuming conversation while* GRUSHA *remains in prayer*): – You can buy Persian saddles from the soldiers too. Though many want crutches in exchange for them.

– The leaders on one side can win a war, the soldiers on both sides lose it.

– Anyway, the war's over. It's something they can't draft you any more.

(*The* DYING MAN *sits bolt upright in bed. He listens.*)

– What we need is two weeks of good weather.

– Our pear trees are hardly bearing a thing this year.

MOTHER-IN-LAW (*offering cakes*): Have some more cakes and welcome! There are more!

(*The* MOTHER-IN-LAW *goes to the bedroom with the empty cake pans. Unaware of the* DYING MAN, *she is bending down to pick up another tray when he begins to talk in a hoarse voice.*)

PEASANT: How many more cakes are you going to stuff down their throats? D'you think I can shit money?

(*The* MOTHER-IN-LAW *starts, stares at him aghast, while he climbs out from behind the mosquito net.*)

FIRST WOMAN (*talking kindly to* GRUSHA *in the next room*): Has the young wife got someone at the front?

A MAN: It's good news that they're on their way home, huh?

PEASANT: Don't stare at me like that! Where's this wife you've saddled me with?

(*Receiving no answer, he climbs out of bed and in his nightshirt staggers into the other room. Trembling, she follows him with the cake pan.*)

GUESTS (*seeing him and shrieking*): Good God! Jussup!

(*Everyone leaps up in alarm. The* WOMEN *rush to the door.* GRUSHA, *still on her knees, turns round and stares at the* MAN.)

PEASANT: A funeral supper! You'd enjoy that, wouldn't you? Get out before I throw you out! (*As the* GUESTS *stampede from the house, gloomily to* GRUSHA.) I've upset the apple cart, huh? (*Receiving no answer, he turns round and takes a cake from the pan which his mother is holding.*)

SINGER: O confusion! The wife discovers she has a husband.
By day there's the child, by night there's the husband.
The lover is on his way both day and night.
Husband and wife look at each other.
The bedroom is small.

*(Near the bed the* PEASANT *is sitting in a high wooden bathtub, naked, the* MOTHER-IN-LAW *is pouring water from a pitcher. Opposite* GRUSHA *cowers with* MICHAEL, *who is playing at mending straw mats.)*

PEASANT (*to his* MOTHER): That's her work, not yours. Where's she hiding out now?

MOTHER-IN-LAW (*calling*): Grusha! The peasant wants you!

GRUSHA (*to* MICHAEL): There are still two holes to mend.

PEASANT (*when* GRUSHA *approaches*): Scrub my back!

GRUSHA: Can't the peasant do it himself?

PEASANT: "Can't the peasant do it himself?" Get the brush! To hell with you! Are you the wife here? Or are you a visitor? (*To the* MOTHER-IN-LAW.) It's too cold!

MOTHER-IN-LAW: I'll run for hot water.

GRUSHA: Let me go.

PEASANT: You stay here. (*The* MOTHER-IN-LAW *exits.*) Rub harder. And no shirking. You've seen a naked fellow before. That child didn't come out of thin air.

GRUSHA: The child was not conceived in joy, if that's what the peasant means.

PEASANT (*turning and grinning*): You don't look the type. (GRUSHA *stops scrubbing him, starts back. Enter the* MOTHER-IN-LAW.)

PEASANT: A nice thing you've saddled me with! A simpleton for a wife!

MOTHER-IN-LAW: She just isn't cooperative.

PEASANT: Pour — but go easy! Ow! Go easy, I said. (*To* GRUSHA.) Maybe you did something wrong in the city . . . I wouldn't be surprised. Why else should you be here? But I won't talk about that. I've not said a word about the illegitimate object you brought into my house either. But my patience has limits! It's against nature. (*To the* MOTHER-IN-LAW.) More! (*To* GRUSHA.) And even if your soldier does come back, you're married.

GRUSHA: Yes.

PEASANT: But your soldier won't come back. Don't you believe it.

GRUSHA: No.

PEASANT: You're cheating me. You're my wife and you're not my wife. Where you lie, nothing lies, and yet no other woman can lie there. When I go to work in the morning I'm tired — when I lie down at night I'm awake as the devil. God has given you sex — and what d'you do? I don't have ten piasters to buy myself a woman in the city. Besides, it's a long way. Woman weeds the fields and opens up her legs, that's what our calendar says. D'you hear?

GRUSHA (*quietly*): Yes. I didn't mean to cheat you out of it.

PEASANT: She didn't mean to cheat me out of it! Pour some more water! (*The* MOTHER-IN-LAW *pours.*) Ow!

SINGER: As she sat by the stream to wash the linen
She saw his image in the water

And his face grew dimmer with the passing moons.
As she raised herself to wring the linen
She heard his voice from the murmuring maple
And his voice grew fainter with the passing moons.
Evasions and sighs grew more numerous,
Tears and sweat flowed.
With the passing moons the child grew up.

(GRUSHA *sits by a stream, dipping linen into the water. In the rear, a few* CHILDREN *are standing.*)

GRUSHA (*to* MICHAEL): You can play with them, Michael, but don't let them boss you around just because you're the littlest. (MICHAEL *nods and joins the* CHILDREN. *They start playing.*)

BIGGEST BOY: Today it's the Heads-Off Game. (*To a* FAT BOY.) You're the Prince and you laugh. (*To* MICHAEL.) You're the Governor. (*To a* GIRL.) You're the Governor's wife and you cry when his head's cut off. And I do the cutting. (*He shows his wooden sword.*) With this. First, they lead the Governor into the yard. The Prince walks in front. The Governor's wife comes last.

(*They form a procession. The* FAT BOY *is first and laughs. Then comes* MICHAEL, *then the* BIGGEST BOY, *and then the* GIRL, *who weeps.*)

MICHAEL (*standing still*): Me cut off head!

BIGGEST BOY: That's my job. You're the littlest. The Governor's the easy part. All you do is kneel down and get your head cut off – simple.

MICHAEL: Me want sword!

BIGGEST BOY: It's mine! (*He gives* MICHAEL *a kick.*)

GIRL (*shouting to* GRUSHA): He won't play his part!

GRUSHA (*laughing*): Even the little duck is a swimmer, they say.

BIGGEST BOY: You can be the Prince if you can laugh. (MICHAEL *shakes his head.*)

FAT BOY: I laugh best. Let him cut off the head just once. Then you do it, then me.

(*Reluctantly, the* BIGGEST BOY *hands* MICHAEL *the wooden sword and kneels down. The* FAT BOY *sits down, slaps his thigh, and laughs with all his might. The* GIRL *weeps loudly.* MICHAEL *swings the big sword and "cuts off" the head. In doing so, he topples over.*)

BIGGEST BOY: Hey! I'll show you how to cut heads off!

(MICHAEL *runs away. The* CHILDREN *run after him.* GRUSHA *laughs, following them with her eyes. On looking back, she sees* SIMON SHASHAVA *standing on the opposite bank. He wears a shabby uniform.*)

GRUSHA: Simon!

SIMON: Is that Grusha Vashnadze?

GRUSHA: Simon!

SIMON (*formally*): A good morning to the young lady. I hope she is well.

GRUSHA (*getting up gaily and bowing low*): A good morning to the soldier. God be thanked he has returned in good health.

SIMON: They found better fish, so they didn't eat me, said the haddock.

GRUSHA: Courage, said the kitchen boy. Good luck, said the hero.

SIMON: How are things here? Was the winter bearable? The neighbor considerate?

GRUSHA: The winter was a trifle rough, the neighbor as usual, Simon.

SIMON: May one ask if a certain person still dips her toes in the water when rinsing the linen?

GRUSHA: The answer is no. Because of the eyes in the bushes.

SIMON: The young lady is speaking of soldiers. Here stands a paymaster.

GRUSHA: A job worth twenty piasters?

SIMON: And lodgings.

GRUSHA (*with tears in her eyes*): Behind the barracks under the date trees.

SIMON: Yes, there. A certain person has kept her eyes open.

GRUSHA: She has, Simon.

SIMON: And has not forgotten? (GRUSHA *shakes her head.*) So the door is still on its hinges as they say? (GRUSHA *looks at him in silence and shakes her head again.*) What's this? Is anything not as it should be?

GRUSHA: Simon Shashava, I can never return to Nuka. Something has happened.

SIMON: What can have happened?

GRUSHA: For one thing, I knocked an Ironshirt down.

SIMON: Grusha Vashnadze must have had her reasons for that.

GRUSHA: Simon Shashava, I am no longer called what I used to be called.

SIMON (*after a pause*): I do not understand.

GRUSHA: When do women change their names, Simon? Let me explain. Nothing stands between us. Everything is just as it was. You must believe that.

SIMON: Nothing stands between us and yet there's something?

GRUSHA: How can I explain it so fast and with the stream between us? Couldn't you cross the bridge there?

SIMON: Maybe it's no longer necessary.

GRUSHA: It is very necessary. Come over on this side, Simon. Quick!

SIMON: Does the young lady wish to say someone has come too late?

(GRUSHA *looks up at him in despair, her face streaming with tears.* SIMON *stares before him. He picks up a piece of wood and starts cutting it.*)

SINGER: So many words are said, so many left unsaid.
The soldier has come.
Where he comes from, he does not say.

Hear what he thought and did not say:
"The battle began, gray at dawn, grew bloody at noon.
The first man fell in front of me, the second behind me, the third at my side.
I trod on the first, left the second behind, the third was run through by the captain.
One of my brothers died by steel, the other by smoke.
My neck caught fire, my hands froze in my gloves, my toes in my socks.
I fed on aspen buds, I drank maple juice, I slept on stone, in water."

SIMON: I see a cap in the grass. Is there a little one already?
GRUSHA: There is, Simon. There's no keeping *that* from you. But please don't worry, it is not mine.
SIMON: When the wind once starts to blow, they say, it blows through every cranny. The wife need say no more. (GRUSHA *looks into her lap and is silent.*)

SINGER: There was yearning but there was no waiting.
The oath is broken. Neither could say why.
Hear what she thought but did not say:
"While you fought in the battle, soldier,
The bloody battle, the bitter battle
I found a helpless infant
I had not the heart to destroy him
I had to care for a creature that was lost
I had to stoop for breadcrumbs on the floor
I had to break myself for that which was not mine
That which was other people's.
Someone must help!
For the little tree needs water
The lamb loses its way when the shepherd is asleep
And its cry is unheard!"

SIMON: Give me back the cross I gave you. Better still, throw it in the stream. (*He turns to go.*)
GRUSHA (*getting up*): Simon Shashava, don't go away! He isn't mine! He isn't mine! (*She hears the children calling.*) What's the matter, children?
VOICES: Soldiers! And they're taking Michael away!

(GRUSHA *stands aghast as two* IRONSHIRTS, *with* MICHAEL *between them, come toward her.*)

ONE OF THE IRONSHIRTS: Are you Grusha? (*She nods.*) Is this your child?
GRUSHA: Yes. (SIMON *goes.*) Simon!
IRONSHIRT: We have orders, in the name of the law, to take this child, found in your custody, back to the city. It is suspected that the child is

Michael Abashwili, son and heir of the late Governor Georgi Abashwili, and his wife, Natella Abashwili. Here is the document and the seal. (*They lead the* CHILD *away.*)

GRUSHA (*running after them, shouting*): Leave him here. Please! He's mine!

SINGER: The Ironshirts took the child, the beloved child.
The unhappy girl followed them to the city, the dreaded city.
She who had borne him demanded the child.
She who had raised him faced trial.
Who will decide the case?
To whom will the child be assigned?
Who will the judge be? A good judge? A bad?
The city was in flames.
In the judge's seat sat Azdak.[1]

## IV. THE STORY OF THE JUDGE

SINGER: Hear the story of the judge
How he turned judge, how he passed judgment, what kind of judge he was.
On that Easter Sunday of the great revolt, when the Grand Duke was overthrown
And his Governor Abashwili, father of our child, lost his head
The Village Scrivener Azdak found a fugitive in the woods and hid him in his hut.

(AZDAK, *in rags and slightly drunk, is helping an* OLD BEGGAR *into his cottage.*)

AZDAK: Stop snorting, you're not a horse. And it won't do you any good with the police to run like a snotty nose in April. Stand still, I say. (*He catches the* OLD MAN, *who has marched into the cottage as if he'd like to go through the walls.*) Sit down. Feed. Here's a hunk of cheese. (*From under some rags, in a chest, he fishes out some cheese, and the* OLD MAN *greedily begins to eat.*) Haven't eaten in a long time, huh? (*The* OLD MAN *growls.*) Why were you running like that, asshole? The cop wouldn't even have seen you.

OLD MAN: Had to! Had to!

AZDAK: Blue funk? (*The* OLD MAN *stares, uncomprehending.*) Cold feet? Panic? Don't lick your chops like a Grand Duke. Or an old sow. I can't stand it. We have to accept respectable stinkers as God made them, but not you! I once heard of a senior judge who farted at a public dinner to show an independent spirit! Watching you eat like that gives me the

[1] "The name Azdak should be accented on the second syllable." [Bentley's note.]

most awful ideas. Why don't you say something? (*Sharply.*) Show me your hand. Can't you hear? (*The* OLD MAN *slowly puts out his hand.*) White! So you're not a beggar at all! A fraud, a walking swindle! And I'm hiding you from the cops like you were an honest man! Why were you running like that if you're a landowner? For that's what you are. Don't deny it! I see it in your guilty face! (*He gets up.*) Get out! (*The* OLD MAN *looks at him uncertainly.*) What are you waiting for, peasant-flogger?

OLD MAN: Pursued. Need undivided attention. Make proposition . . .

AZDAK: Make what? A proposition? Well, if that isn't the height of insolence. He's making me a proposition! The bitten man scratches his fingers bloody, and the leech that's biting him makes him a proposition! Get out, I tell you!

OLD MAN: Understand point of view! Persuasion! Pay hundred thousand piasters one night! Yes?

AZDAK: What, you think you can buy me? For a hundred thousand piasters? Let's say a hundred and fifty thousand. Where are they?

OLD MAN: Have not them here. Of course. Will be sent. Hope do not doubt.

AZDAK: Doubt very much. Get out!

(*The* OLD MAN *gets up, waddles to the door. A* VOICE *is heard offstage.*)

VOICE: Azdak!

(*The* OLD MAN *turns, waddles to the opposite corner, stands still.*)

AZDAK (*calling out*): I'm not in! (*He walks to door.*) So *you're* sniffing around here again, Shauwa?

SHAUWA (*reproachfully*): You caught another rabbit, Azdak. And you'd promised me it wouldn't happen again!

AZDAK (*severely*): Shauwa, don't talk about things you don't understand. The rabbit is a dangerous and destructive beast. It feeds on plants, especially on the species of plants known as weeds. It must therefore be exterminated.

SHAUWA: Azdak, don't be so hard on me. I'll lose my job if I don't arrest you. I know you have a good heart.

AZDAK: I do not have a good heart! How often must I tell you I'm a man of intellect?

SHAUWA (*slyly*): I know, Azdak. You're a superior person. You say so yourself. I'm just a Christian and an ignoramus. So I ask you: When one of the Prince's rabbits is stolen, and I'm a policeman, what should I do with the offending party?

AZDAK: Shauwa, Shauwa, shame on you. You stand and ask me a question, than which nothing could be more seductive. It's like you were a woman — let's say that bad girl Nunowna, and you showed me your thigh — Nunowna's thigh, that would be — and asked me: "What shall I do with my thigh, it itches?" Is she as innocent as she pretends? Of course not.

I catch a rabbit, but you catch a man. Man is made in God's image. Not so a rabbit, you know that. I'm a rabbit-eater, but you're a man-eater, Shauwa. And God will pass judgment on you. Shauwa, go home and repent. No, stop, there's something . . . (*He looks at the* OLD MAN *who stands trembling in the corner.*) No, it's nothing. Go home and repent. (*He slams the door behind* SHAUWA.) Now you're surprised, huh? Surprised I didn't hand you over? I couldn't hand over a bedbug to that animal. It goes against the grain. Now don't tremble because of a cop! So old and still so scared? Finish your cheese, but eat it like a poor man, or else they'll still catch you. Must I even explain how a poor man behaves? (*He pushes him down, and then gives him back the cheese.*) That box is the table. Lay your elbows on the table. Now, encircle the cheese on the plate like it might be snatched from you at any moment — what right have you to be safe, huh? — now, hold your knife like an undersized sickle, and give your cheese a troubled look because, like all beautiful things, it's already fading away. (AZDAK *watches him.*) They're after you, which speaks in your favor, but how can we be sure they're not mistaken about you? In Tiflis one time they hanged a landowner, a Turk, who could prove he quartered his peasants instead of merely cutting them in half, as is the custom, and he squeezed twice the usual amount of taxes out of them, his zeal was above suspicion. And yet they hanged him like a common criminal — because he was a Turk — a thing he couldn't do much about. What injustice! He got onto the gallows by a sheer fluke. In short, I don't trust you.

SINGER: Thus Azdak gave the old beggar a bed,
And learned that old beggar was the old butcher, the Grand Duke himself,
And was ashamed.
He denounced himself and ordered the policeman to take him to Nuka, to court, to be judged.

(*In the court of justice three* IRONSHIRTS *sit drinking. From a beam hangs a man in judge's robes. Enter* AZDAK, *in chains, dragging* SHAUWA *behind him.*)

AZDAK (*shouting*): I've helped the Grand Duke, the Grand Thief, the Grand Butcher, to escape! In the name of justice I ask to be severely judged in public trial!

FIRST IRONSHIRT: Who's this queer bird?

SHAUWA: That's our Village Scrivener, Azdak.

AZDAK: I am contemptible! I am a traitor! A branded criminal! Tell them, flatfoot, how I insisted on being tied up and brought to the capital. Because I sheltered the Grand Duke, the Grand Swindler, by mistake. And how I found out afterwards. See the marked man denounce himself! Tell them how I forced you to walk half the night with me to clear the whole thing up.

SHAUWA: And all by threats. That wasn't nice of you, Azdak.

AZDAK: Shut your mouth, Shauwa. You don't understand. A new age is upon us! It'll go thundering over you. You're finished. The police will be wiped out — poof! Everything will be gone into, everything will be brought into the open. The guilty will give themselves up. Why? They couldn't escape the people in any case. (*To* SHAUWA.) Tell them how I shouted all along Shoemaker Street (*with big gestures, looking at the* IRONSHIRTS) "In my ignorance I let the Grand Swindler escape! So tear me to pieces, brothers!" I wanted to get it in first.

FIRST IRONSHIRT: And what did your brothers answer?

SHAUWA: They comforted him in Butcher Street, and they laughed themselves sick in Shoemaker Street. That's all.

AZDAK: But with you it's different. I can see you're men of iron. Brothers, where's the judge? I must be tried.

FIRST IRONSHIRT (*pointing at the hanged man*): There's the judge. And please stop "brothering" us. It's rather a sore spot this evening.

AZDAK: "There's the judge." An answer never heard in Grusinia before. Townsman, where's His Excellency the Governor? (*Pointing to the ground.*) There's His Excellency, stranger. Where's the Chief Tax Collector? Where's the official Recruiting Officer? The Patriarch? The Chief of Police? There, there, there — all there. Brothers, I expected no less of you.

SECOND IRONSHIRT: What? *What* was it you expected, funny man?

AZDAK: What happened in Persia, brother, what happened in Persia?

SECOND IRONSHIRT: What did happen in Persia?

AZDAK: Everybody was hanged. Viziers, tax collectors. Everybody. Forty years ago now. My grandfather, a remarkable man by the way, saw it all. For three whole days. Everywhere.

SECOND IRONSHIRT: And who ruled when the Vizier was hanged?

AZDAK: A peasant ruled when the Vizier was hanged.

SECOND IRONSHIRT: And who commanded the army?

AZDAK: A soldier, a soldier.

SECOND IRONSHIRT: And who paid the wages?

AZDAK: A dyer. A dyer paid the wages.

SECOND IRONSHIRT: Wasn't it a weaver, maybe?

FIRST IRONSHIRT: And why did all this happen, Persian?

AZDAK: Why did all this happen? Must there be a special reason? Why do you scratch yourself, brother? War! Too long a war! And no justice! My grandfather brought back a song that tells how it was. I will sing it for you. With my friend the policeman. (*To* SHAUWA.) And hold the rope tight. It's very suitable. (*He sings, with* SHAUWA *holding the rope tight around him.*)

*The Song of Injustice in Persia*

Why don't our sons bleed any more? Why don't our daughters weep?
Why do only the slaughterhouse cattle have blood in their veins?
Why do only the willows shed tears on Lake Urmia?
The king must have a new province, the peasant must give up his savings.
That the roof of the world might be conquered, the roof of the cottage is torn down.
Our men are carried to the ends of the earth, so that great ones can eat at home.
The soldiers kill each other, the marshals salute each other.
They bite the widow's tax money to see if it's good, their swords break
The battle was lost, the helmets were paid for.
*Refrain*: Is it so? Is it so?

SHAUWA (*refrain*):
Yes, yes, yes, yes, yes it's so.

AZDAK: Want to hear the rest of it? (*The* FIRST IRONSHIRT *nods.*)
SECOND IRONSHIRT (*to* SHAUWA): Did he teach you that song?
SHAUWA: Yes, only my voice isn't very good.
SECOND IRONSHIRT: No. (*To* AZDAK.) Go on singing.
AZDAK: The second verse is about the peace. (*He sings.*)

The offices are packed, the streets overflow with officials.
The rivers jump their banks and ravage the fields.
Those who cannot let down their own trousers rule countries.
They can't count up to four, but they devour eight courses.
The corn farmers, looking round for buyers, see only the starving.
The weavers go home from their looms in rags.
*Refrain*: Is it so? Is it so?

SHAUWA (*refrain*):
Yes, yes, yes, yes, yes it's so.

AZDAK:
That's why our sons don't bleed any more, that's why our daughters don't weep,
That's why only the slaughterhouse cattle have blood in their veins,
And only the willows shed tears by Lake Urmia toward morning.

FIRST IRONSHIRT: Are you going to sing that song here in town?
AZDAK: Sure. What's wrong with it?
FIRST IRONSHIRT: Have you noticed that the sky's getting red? (*Turning round,* AZDAK *sees the sky red with fire.*) It's the people's quarters on the outskirts of town. The carpet weavers have caught the "Persian Sickness," too. And they've been asking if Prince Kazbeki isn't eating too many courses. This morning they strung up the city judge. As for us

we beat them to pulp. We were paid one hundred piasters per man, you understand?

AZDAK (*after a pause*): I understand. (*He glances shyly round and, creeping away, sits down in a corner, his head in his hands.*)

IRONSHIRTS (*to each other*): If there ever was a troublemaker it's him. — He must've come to the capital to fish in the troubled waters.

SHAUWA: Oh, I don't think he's a really bad character, gentlemen. Steals a few chickens here and there. And maybe a rabbit.

SECOND IRONSHIRT (*approaching* AZDAK): Came to fish in the troubled waters, huh?

AZDAK (*looking up*): I don't know why I came.

SECOND IRONSHIRT: Are you in with the carpet weavers maybe? (AZDAK *shakes his head.*) How about that song?

AZDAK: From my grandfather. A silly and ignorant man.

SECOND IRONSHIRT: Right. And how about the dyer who paid the wages?

AZDAK (*muttering*): That was in Persia.

FIRST IRONSHIRT: And this denouncing of yourself? Because you didn't hang the Grand Duke with your own hands?

AZDAK: Didn't I tell you I let him run? (*He creeps farther away and sits on the floor.*)

SHAUWA: I can swear to that: he let him run.

(*The* IRONSHIRTS *burst out laughing and slap* SHAUWA *on the back.* AZDAK *laughs loudest. They slap* AZDAK *too, and unchain him. They all start drinking as the* FAT PRINCE *enters with a* YOUNG MAN.)

FIRST IRONSHIRT (*to* AZDAK, *pointing at the* FAT PRINCE): There's your "new age" for you! (*More laughter.*)

FAT PRINCE: Well, my friends, what is there to laugh about? Permit me a serious word. Yesterday morning the Princes of Grusinia overthrew the warmongering government of the Grand Duke and did away with his Governors. Unfortunately the Grand Duke himself escaped. In this fateful hour our carpet weavers, those eternal troublemakers, had the effrontery to stir up a rebellion and hang the universally loved city judge, our dear Illo Orbeliani. Ts — ts — ts. My friends, we need peace, peace, peace in Grusinia! And justice! So I've brought along my dear nephew Bizergan Kazbeki. He'll be the new judge, hm? A very gifted fellow. What do you say? I want your opinion. Let the people decide!

SECOND IRONSHIRT: Does this mean *we* elect the judge?

FAT PRINCE: Precisely. Let the people propose some very gifted fellow! Confer among yourselves, my friends. (*The* IRONSHIRTS *confer.*) Don't worry, my little fox. The job's yours. And when we catch the Grand Duke we won't have to kiss this rabble's ass any longer.

IRONSHIRTS (*among themselves*): — Very funny: they're wetting their pants because they haven't caught the Grand Duke.

– When the outlook isn't so bright, they say: "My friends!" and "Let the people decide!"

– Now he even wants justice for Grusinia! But fun is fun as long as it lasts! (*Pointing at* AZDAK.) *He* knows all about justice. Hey, rascal, would you like this nephew fellow to be the judge?

AZDAK: Are you asking me? You're not asking *me?!*

FIRST IRONSHIRT: Why not? Anything for a laugh!

AZDAK: You'd like to test him to the marrow, correct? Have you a criminal on hand? An experienced one? So the candidate can show what he knows?

SECOND IRONSHIRT: Let's see. We do have a couple of doctors downstairs. Let's use them.

AZDAK: Oh, no, that's no good, we can't take real criminals till we're sure the judge will be appointed. He may be dumb, but he must be appointed, or the law is violated. And the law is a sensitive organ. It's like the spleen, you mustn't hit it – that would be fatal. Of course you can hang those two without violating the law, because there was no judge in the vicinity. But judgment, when pronounced, must be pronounced with absolute gravity – it's all such nonsense. Suppose, for instance, a judge jails a woman – let's say she's stolen a corn cake to feed her child – and this judge isn't wearing his robes – or maybe he's scratching himself while passing sentence and half his body is uncovered – a man's thigh *will* itch once in a while – the sentence this judge passes is a disgrace and the law is violated. In short it would be easier for a judge's robe and a judge's hat to pass judgment than for a man with no robe and no hat. If you don't treat it with respect, the law just disappears on you. Now you don't try out a bottle of wine by offering it to a dog; you'd only lose your wine.

FIRST IRONSHIRT: Then what do you suggest, hairsplitter?

AZDAK: I'll be the defendant.

FIRST IRONSHIRT: You? (*He bursts out laughing.*)

FAT PRINCE: What have you decided?

FIRST IRONSHIRT: We've decided to stage a rehearsal. Our friend here will be the defendant. Let the candidate be the judge and sit there.

FAT PRINCE: It isn't customary, but why not? (*To the* NEPHEW.) A mere formality, my little fox. What have I taught you? Who got there first – the slow runner or the fast?

NEPHEW: The silent runner, Uncle Arsen.

(*The* NEPHEW *takes the chair. The* IRONSHIRTS *and the* FAT PRINCE *sit on the steps. Enter* AZDAK, *mimicking the gait of the Grand Duke.*)

AZDAK (*in the Grand Duke's accent*): Is any here knows me? Am Grand Duke.

IRONSHIRTS: – *What* is he?

– The Grand Duke. He knows him, too.

– Fine. So get on with the trial.

AZDAK: Listen! Am accused instigating war? Ridiculous! Am saying ridiculous! That enough? If not, have brought lawyers. Believe five hundred. (*He points behind him, pretending to be surrounded by lawyers.*) Requisition all available seats for lawyers! (*The* IRONSHIRTS *laugh; the* FAT PRINCE *joins in.*)

NEPHEW (*to the* IRONSHIRTS): You really wish me to try this case? I find it rather unusual. From the taste angle, I mean.

FIRST IRONSHIRT: Let's go!

FAT PRINCE (*smiling*): Let him have it, my little fox!

NEPHEW: All right. People of Grusinia versus Grand Duke. Defendant, what have you got to say for yourself?

AZDAK: Plenty. Naturally, have read war lost. Only started on the advice of patriots. Like Uncle Arsen Kazbeki. Call Uncle Arsen as witness.

FAT PRINCE (*to the* IRONSHIRTS, *delightedly*): What a madcap!

NEPHEW: Motion rejected. One cannot be arraigned for declaring a war, which every ruler has to do once in a while, but only for running a war badly.

AZDAK: Rubbish! Did not run it at all! Had it run! Had it run by Princes! Naturally, they messed it up.

NEPHEW: Do you by any chance deny having been commander-in-chief?

AZDAK: Not at all! Always *was* commander-in-chief. At birth shouted at wet nurse. Was trained drop turds in toilet, grew accustomed to command. Always commanded officials rob my cash box. Officers flog soldiers only on command. Landowners sleep with peasants' wives only on strictest command. Uncle Arsen here grew his belly at *my* command!

IRONSHIRTS (*clapping*): He's good! Long live the Grand Duke!

FAT PRINCE: Answer him, my little fox: I'm with you.

NEPHEW: I shall answer him according to the dignity of the law. Defendant, preserve the dignity of the law!

AZDAK: Agreed. Command you proceed with trial!

NEPHEW: It is not your place to command me. You claim that the Princes forced you to declare war. How can you claim, then, that they — er — "messed it up"?

AZDAK: Did not send enough people. Embezzled funds. Sent sick horses. During attack, drinking in whorehouse. Call Uncle Arsen as witness.

NEPHEW: Are you making the outrageous suggestion that the Princes of this country did not fight?

AZDAK: No. Princes fought. Fought for war contracts.

FAT PRINCE (*jumping up*): That's too much! This man talks like a carpet weaver!

AZDAK: Really? Told nothing but truth.

FAT PRINCE: Hang him! Hang him!

FIRST IRONSHIRT (*pulling the* PRINCE *down*): Keep quiet! Go on, Excellency!

NEPHEW: Quiet! I now render a verdict: You must be hanged! By the neck! Having lost war!

AZDAK: Young man, seriously advise not fall publicly into jerky clipped speech. Cannot be watchdog if howl like wolf. Got it? If people realize Princes speak same language as Grand Duke, may hang Grand Duke *and Princes,* huh? By the way, must overrule verdict. Reason? War lost, but not for Princes. Princes won their war. Got 3,863,000 piasters for horses not delivered, 8,240,000 piasters for food supplies not produced. Are therefore victors. War lost only for Grusinia, which is not present in this court.

FAT PRINCE: I think that will do, my friends. (*To* AZDAK.) You can withdraw, funny man. (*To the* IRONSHIRTS.) You may now ratify the new judge's appointment, my friends.

FIRST IRONSHIRT: Yes, we can. Take down the judge's gown. (*One* IRONSHIRT *climbs on the back of the other, pulls the gown off the hanged man.*) (*To the* NEPHEW.) Now you run away so the right ass can get on the right chair. (*To* AZDAK.) Step forward! Go to the judge's seat! Now sit in it! (AZDAK *steps up, bows, and sits down.*) The judge was always a rascal! Now the rascal shall be a judge! (*The judge's gown is placed round his shoulders, the hat on his head.*) And what a judge!

SINGER: And there was civil war in the land.
The mighty were not safe.
And Azdak was made a judge by the Ironshirts.
And Azdak remained a judge for two years.

SINGER AND CHORUS: When the towns were set afire
And rivers of blood rose higher and higher,
Cockroaches crawled out of every crack.
And the court was full of schemers
And the church of foul blasphemers.
In the judge's cassock sat Azdak.

(AZDAK *sits in the judge's chair, peeling an apple.* SHAUWA *is sweeping out the hall. On one side an* INVALID *in a wheelchair. Opposite, a* YOUNG MAN *accused of blackmail. An* IRONSHIRT *stands guard, holding the Ironshirts' banner.*)

AZDAK: In consideration of the large number of cases, the Court today will hear two cases at a time. Before I open the proceedings, a short announcement — I accept. (*He stretches out his hand. The* BLACKMAILER *is the only one to produce any money. He hands it to* AZDAK.) I reserve the right to punish one of the parties for contempt of court. (*He glances at the* INVALID.) You (*to the* DOCTOR) are a doctor, and you (*to the* INVALID) are bringing a complaint against him. Is the doctor responsible for your condition?

INVALID: Yes. I had a stroke on his account.

AZDAK: That would be professional negligence.

INVALID: Worse than negligence. I gave this man money for his studies. So far, he hasn't paid me back a cent. It was when I heard he was treating a patient free that I had my stroke.

AZDAK: Rightly. (*To a* LIMPING MAN.) And what are *you* doing here?

LIMPING MAN: I'm the patient, Your Honor.

AZDAK: He treated your leg for nothing?

LIMPING MAN: The wrong leg! My rheumatism was in the left leg, he operated on the right. That's why I limp.

AZDAK: And you were treated free?

INVALID: A five-hundred-piaster operation free! For nothing! For a God-bless-you! And I paid for this man's studies! (*To the* DOCTOR.) Did they teach you to operate free?

DOCTOR: Your Honor, it is the custom to demand the fee before the operation, as the patient is more willing to pay before an operation than after. Which is only human. In the case in question I was convinced, when I started the operation, that my servant had already received the fee. In this I was mistaken.

INVALID: He was mistaken! A good doctor doesn't make mistakes! He examines before he operates!

AZDAK: That's right. (*To* SHAUWA.) Public Prosecutor, what's the other case about?

SHAUWA (*busily sweeping*): Blackmail.

BLACKMAILER: High Court of Justice, I'm innocent. I only wanted to find out from the landowner concerned if he really *had* raped his niece. He informed me very politely that this was not the case, and gave me the money only so I could pay for my uncle's studies.

AZDAK: Hm. (*To the* DOCTOR.) You, on the other hand, can cite no extenuating circumstances for your offense, huh?

DOCTOR: Except that to err is human.

AZDAK: And you are aware that in money matters a good doctor is a highly responsible person? I once heard of a doctor who got a thousand piasters for a sprained finger by remarking that sprains have something to do with blood circulation, which after all a less good doctor might have overlooked, and who, on another occasion made a real gold mine out of a somewhat disordered gall bladder, he treated it with such loving care. You have no excuse, Doctor. The corn merchant Uxu had his son study medicine to get some knowledge of trade, our medical schools are so good. (*To the* BLACKMAILER.) What's the landowner's name?

SHAUWA: He doesn't want it mentioned.

AZDAK: In that case I will pass judgment. The Court considers the blackmail proved. And you (*to the* INVALID) are sentenced to a fine of one thousand piasters. If you have a second stroke, the doctor will have to treat you free. Even if he has to amputate. (*To the* LIMPING MAN.) As compensation, you will receive a bottle of rubbing alcohol. (*To the* BLACKMAILER.) You are sentenced to hand over half the proceeds of your deal to the Public

Prosecutor to keep the landowner's name secret. You are advised, moreover, to study medicine – you seem well suited to that calling. (*To the* DOCTOR.) You have perpetrated an unpardonable error in the practice of your profession: you are acquitted. Next cases!

SINGER AND CHORUS: Men won't do much for a shilling.
For a pound they may be willing.
For twenty pounds the verdict's in the sack.
As for the many, all too many,
Those who've only got a penny –
They've one single, sole recourse: Azdak.

(*Enter* AZDAK *from the caravansary on the highroad, followed by an old bearded* INNKEEPER. *The judge's chair is carried by a stableman and* SHAUWA. *An* IRONSHIRT, *with a banner, takes up his position.*)

AZDAK: Put me down. Then we'll get some air, maybe even a good stiff breeze from the lemon grove there. It does justice good to be done in the open: the wind blows her skirts up and you can see what she's got. Shauwa, we've been eating too much. These official journeys are exhausting. (*To the* INNKEEPER.) It's a question of your daughter-in-law?
INNKEEPER: Your Worship, it's a question of the family honor. I wish to bring an action on behalf of my son, who's away on business on the other side of the mountain. This is the offending stableman, and here's my daughter-in-law.

(*Enter the* DAUGHTER-IN-LAW, *a voluptuous wench. She is veiled.*)

AZDAK (*sitting down*): I accept. (*Sighing, the* INNKEEPER *hands him some money.*) Good. Now the formalities are disposed of. This is a case of rape?
INNKEEPER: Your Honor, I caught the fellow in the act. Ludovica was in the straw on the stable floor.
AZDAK: Quite right, the stable. Lovely horses! I specially liked the little roan.
INNKEEPER: The first thing I did, of course, was to question Ludovica. On my son's behalf.
AZDAK (*seriously*): I said I specially liked the little roan.
INNKEEPER (*coldly*): Really? Ludovica confessed the stableman took her against her will.
AZDAK: Take your veil off, Ludovica. (*She does so.*) Ludovica, you please the Court. Tell us how it happened.
LUDOVICA (*well schooled*): When I entered the stable to see the new foal the stableman said to me on his own accord: "It's hot today!" and laid his hand on my left breast. I said to him: "Don't do that!" But he continued to handle me indecently, which provoked my anger. Before I realized his sinful intentions, he got much closer. It was all over when my father-in-law entered and accidentally trod on me.
INNKEEPER (*explaining*): On my son's behalf.

AZDAK (*to the* STABLEMAN): You admit you started it?
STABLEMAN: Yes.
AZDAK: Ludovica, you like to eat sweet things?
LUDOVICA: Yes, sunflower seeds!
AZDAK: You like to lie a long time in the bathtub?
LUDOVICA: Half an hour or so.
AZDAK: Public Prosecutor, drop your knife — there on the ground. (SHAUWA *does so.*) Ludovica, pick up that knife. (LUDOVICA, *swaying her hips, does so.*) See that? (*He points at her.*) The way it moves? The rape is now proven. By eating too much — sweet things, especially — by lying too long in warm water, by laziness and too soft a skin, you have raped that unfortunate man. Think you can run around with a behind like that and get away with it in court? This is a case of intentional assault with a dangerous weapon! You are sentenced to hand over to the Court the little roan which your father liked to ride "on his son's behalf." And now, come with me to the stables, so the Court can inspect the scene of the crime, Ludovica.

SINGER AND CHORUS: When the sharks the sharks devour
Little fishes have their hour.
For a while the load is off their back.
On Grusinia's highways faring
Fixed-up scales of justice bearing
Strode the poor man's magistrate: Azdak.

And he gave to the forsaken
All that from the rich he'd taken.
And a bodyguard of roughnecks was Azdak's.
And our good and evil man, he
Smiled upon Grusinia's Granny.
His emblem was a tear in sealing wax.

All mankind should love each other
But when visiting your brother
Take an ax along and hold it fast.
Not in theory but in practice
Miracles are wrought with axes
And the age of miracles is not past.

(AZDAK'*s judge's chair is in a tavern. Three rich* FARMERS *stand before* AZDAK. SHAUWA *brings him wine. In a corner stands an* OLD PEASANT WOMAN. *In the open doorway, and outside, stand villagers looking on. An* IRONSHIRT *stands guard with a banner.*)

AZDAK: The Public Prosecutor has the floor.
SHAUWA: It concerns a cow. For five weeks, the defendant has had a cow in her stable, the property of the farmer Suru. She was also found to be

in possession of a stolen ham, and a number of cows belonging to Shutoff were killed after he asked the defendant to pay the rent on a piece of land.

FARMERS: — It's a matter of my ham, Your Honor.
— It's a matter of my cow, Your Honor.
— It's a matter of my land, Your Honor.

AZDAK: Well, Granny, what have *you* got to say to all this?

OLD WOMAN: Your Honor, one night toward morning, five weeks ago, there was a knock at my door, and outside stood a bearded man with a cow. "My dear woman," he said, "I am the miracle-working Saint Banditus and because your son has been killed in the war, I bring you this cow as a souvenir. Take good care of it."

FARMERS: — The robber, Irakli, Your Honor!
— Her brother-in-law, Your Honor!
— The cow-thief!
— The incendiary!
— He must be beheaded!

(*Outside, a woman screams. The crowd grows restless, retreats. Enter the* BANDIT *Irakli with a huge ax.*)

BANDIT: A very good evening, dear friends! A glass of vodka!

FARMERS (*crossing themselves*): Irakli!

AZDAK: Public Prosecutor, a glass of vodka for our guest. And who are you?

BANDIT: I'm a wandering hermit, Your Honor. Thanks for the gracious gift. (*He empties the glass which* SHAUWA *has brought.*) Another!

AZDAK: I am Azdak. (*He gets up and bows. The* BANDIT *also bows.*) The Court welcomes the foreign hermit. Go on with your story, Granny.

OLD WOMAN: Your Honor, that first night I didn't yet know Saint Banditus could work miracles, it was only the cow. But one night, a few days later, the farmer's servants came to take the cow away again. Then they turned round in front of my door and went off without the cow. And bumps as big as a fist sprouted on their heads. So I knew that Saint Banditus had changed their hearts and turned them into friendly people.

(*The* BANDIT *roars with laughter.*)

FIRST FARMER: I know what changed them.

AZDAK: That's fine. You can tell us later. Continue.

OLD WOMAN: Your Honor, the next one to become a good man was the farmer Shutoff — a devil, as everyone knows. But Saint Banditus arranged it so he let me off the rent on the little piece of land.

SECOND FARMER: Because my cows were killed in the field.

(*The* BANDIT *laughs.*)

OLD WOMAN (*answering* AZDAK'*s sign to continue*): Then one morning the ham came flying in at my window. It hit me in the small of the back. I'm still lame, Your Honor, look. (*She limps a few steps. The* BANDIT *laughs.*) Your Honor, was there ever a time when a poor old woman could get a ham *without* a miracle?

(*The* BANDIT *starts sobbing.*)

AZDAK (*rising from his chair*): Granny, that's a question that strikes straight at the Court's heart. Be so kind as to sit here. (*The* OLD WOMAN, *hesitating, sits in the judge's chair.*)

AZDAK (*sits on the floor, glass in hand, reciting*): Granny
We could almost call you Granny Grusinia
The Woebegone
The Bereaved Mother
Whose sons have gone to war.
Receiving the present of a cow
She bursts out crying.
When she is beaten
She remains hopeful.
When she's not beaten
She's surprised.
On us
Who are already damned
May you render a merciful verdict
Granny Grusinia!

(*Bellowing at the* FARMERS.) Admit you don't believe in miracles, you atheists! Each of you is sentenced to pay five hundred piasters! For godlessness! Get out! (*The* FARMERS *slink out.*) And you Granny, and you (*to the* BANDIT) pious man, empty a pitcher of wine with the Public Prosecutor and Azdak!

SINGER AND CHORUS: And he broke the rules to save them.
Broken law like bread he gave them,
Brought them to shore upon his crooked back.
At long last the poor and lowly
Had someone who was not too holy
To be bribed by empty hands: Azdak.

For two years it was his pleasure
To give the beasts of prey short measure:
He became a wolf to fight the pack.
From All Hallows to All Hallows
On his chair beside the gallows
Dispensing justice in his fashion sat Azdak.

SINGER: But the era of disorder came to an end.
The Grand Duke returned.

The Governor's wife returned.
A trial was held.
Many died.
The people's quarters burned anew.
And fear seized Azdak.

(AZDAK'*s judge's chair stands again in the court of justice.* AZDAK *sits on the floor, shaving and talking to* SHAUWA. *Noises outside. In the rear the* FAT PRINCE'*s head is carried by on a lance.*)

AZDAK: Shauwa, the days of your slavery are numbered, maybe even the minutes. For a long time now I have held you in the iron curb of reason, and it has torn your mouth till it bleeds. I have lashed you with reasonable arguments, I have manhandled you with logic. You are by nature a weak man, and if one slyly throws an argument in your path, you *have* to snap it up, you can't resist. It is your nature to lick the hand of some superior being. But superior beings can be of very different kinds. And now, with your liberation, you will soon be able to follow your natural inclinations, which are low. You will be able to follow your infallible instinct, which teaches you to plant your fat heel on the faces of men. Gone is the era of confusion and disorder, which I find described in the Song of Chaos. Let us now sing that song together in memory of those terrible days. Sit down and don't do violence to the music. Don't be afraid. It sounds all right. And it has a fine refrain. (*He sings.*)

*The Song of Chaos*

Sister, hide your face! Brother, take your knife!
The times are out of joint!
Big men are full of complaint
And small men full of joy.
The city says:
"Let us drive the mighty from our midst!"
Offices are raided. Lists of serfs are destroyed.
They have set Master's nose to the grindstone.
They who lived in the dark have seen the light.
The ebony poor box is broken.
Sesnem[2] wood is sawed up for beds.
Who had no bread have full barns.
Who begged for alms of corn now mete it out.

[2] "I do not know what kind of wood this is, so I have left the word exactly as it stands in the German original. The song is based on an Egyptian papyrus which Brecht cites as such in his essay, "Five Difficulties in the Writing of the Truth." I should think he must have come across it in Adolf Erman's *Die Literatur der Aegypter,* 1923, pp. 130 ff. Erman too gives the word as Sesnem. The same papyrus is quoted in Karl Jaspers' *Man in the Modern Age* (Anchor edition, pp. 18–19) but without the sentence about the Sesnem wood." [Bentley's note.]

SHAUWA (*refrain*):
Oh, oh, oh, oh.

AZDAK (*refrain*):
Where are you, General, where are you?
Please, please, please, restore order!

The nobleman's son can no longer be recognized;
The lady's child becomes the son of her slave-girl
The councilors meet in a shed.
Once, this man was barely allowed to sleep on the wall;
Now, he stretches his limbs in a bed.
Once, this man rowed a boat; now, he owns ships.
Their owner looks for them, but they're his no longer.
Five men are sent on a journey by their master.
"Go yourself," they say, "we have arrived."

SHAUWA (*refrain*):
Oh, oh, oh, oh.

AZDAK (*refrain*):
Where are you, General, where are you?
Please, please, please, restore order!

Yes, so it might have been, had order been neglected much longer. But now the Grand Duke has returned to the capital, and the Persians have lent him an army to restore order with. The people's quarters are already aflame. Go and get me the big book I always sit on. (SHAUWA *brings the big book from the judge's chair.* AZDAK *opens it.*) This is the Statute Book and I've always used it, as you can testify. Now I'd better look in this book and see what they can do to me. I've let the down-and-outs get away with murder, and I'll have to pay for it. I helped poverty onto its skinny legs, so they'll hang me for drunkenness. I peeped into the rich man's pocket, which is bad taste. And I can't hide anywhere — everybody knows me because I've helped everybody.

SHAUWA: Someone's coming!

AZDAK (*in panic, he walks trembling to the chair*): It's the end. And now they'd enjoy seeing what a Great Man I am. I'll deprive them of that pleasure. I'll beg on my knees for mercy. Spittle will slobber down my chin. The fear of death is in me.

(*Enter* NATELLA ABASHWILI, *the* GOVERNOR'S WIFE, *followed by the* ADJUTANT *and an* IRONSHIRT.)

GOVERNOR'S WIFE: What sort of a creature is that, Shalva?

AZDAK: A willing one, Your Highness, a man ready to oblige.

ADJUTANT: Natella Abashwili, wife of the late Governor, has just returned. She is looking for her two-year-old son, Michael. She has been informed that the child was carried off to the mountains by a former servant.

AZDAK: The child will be brought back, Your Highness, at your service.
ADJUTANT: They say that the person in question is passing it off as her own.
AZDAK: She will be beheaded, Your Highness, at your service.
ADJUTANT: That is all.
GOVERNOR'S WIFE (*leaving*): I don't like that man.
AZDAK (*following her to door, bowing*): At your service, Your Highness, it will all be arranged.

## V. THE CHALK CIRCLE

SINGER: Hear now the story of the trial
Concerning Governor Abashwili's child
And the determination of the true mother
By the famous test of the Chalk Circle.

(*Law court in Nuka.* IRONSHIRTS *lead* MICHAEL *across stage and out at the back.* IRONSHIRTS *hold* GRUSHA *back with their lances under the gateway until the* CHILD *has been led through. Then she is admitted. She is accompanied by the former* GOVERNOR'S COOK. *Distant noises and a fire-red sky.*)

GRUSHA (*trying to hide*): He's brave, he can wash himself now.
COOK: You're lucky. It's not a real judge. It's Azdak, a drunk who doesn't know what he's doing. The biggest thieves have got by through him. Because he gets everything mixed up and the rich never offer him big enough bribes, the like of us sometimes do pretty well.
GRUSHA: I *need* luck right now.
COOK: Touch wood. (*She crosses herself.*) I'd better offer up another prayer that the judge may be drunk. (*She prays with motionless lips, while* GRUSHA *looks around, in vain, for the* CHILD.) Why must you hold on to it at any price if it isn't yours? In days like these?
GRUSHA: He's mine. I brought him up.
COOK: Have you never thought what'd happen when she came back?
GRUSHA: At first I thought I'd give him to her. Then I thought she wouldn't come back.
COOK: And even a borrowed coat keeps a man warm, hm? (GRUSHA *nods.*) I'll swear to anything for you. You're a decent girl. (*She sees the soldier* SIMON SHASHAVA *approaching.*) You've done wrong by Simon, though. I've been talking with him. He just can't understand.
GRUSHA (*unaware of* SIMON'S *presence*): Right now I can't be bothered whether he understands or not!
COOK: He knows the child isn't yours, but you married and not free "till death you do part" — he can't understand *that.*

(GRUSHA *sees* SIMON *and greets him.*)

SIMON (*gloomily*): I wish the lady to know I will swear I am the father of the child.

GRUSHA (*low*): Thank you, Simon.

SIMON: At the same time I wish the lady to know my hands are not tied — nor are hers.

COOK: You needn't have said that. You know she's married.

SIMON: And it needs no rubbing in.

(*Enter an* IRONSHIRT.)

IRONSHIRT: Where's the judge? Has anyone seen the judge?

ANOTHER IRONSHIRT (*stepping forward*): The judge isn't here yet. Nothing but a bed and a pitcher in the whole house!

(*Exeunt* IRONSHIRTS.)

COOK: I hope nothing has happened to him. With any other judge you'd have as much chance as a chicken has teeth.

GRUSHA (*who has turned away and covered her face*): Stand in front of me. I shouldn't have come to Nuka. If I run into the Ironshirt, the one I hit over the head . . .

(*She screams. An* IRONSHIRT *had stopped and, turning his back, had been listening to her. He now wheels around. It is the* CORPORAL, *and he has a huge scar across his face.*)

IRONSHIRT (*in the gateway*): What's the matter, Shotta? Do you know her?

CORPORAL (*after staring for some time*): No.

IRONSHIRT: She's the one who stole the Abashwili child, or so they say. If you know anything about it you can make some money, Shotta.

(*Exit the* CORPORAL, *cursing.*)

COOK: Was it him? (GRUSHA *nods.*) I think he'll keep his mouth shut, or he'd be admitting he was after the child.

GRUSHA: I'd almost forgotten him.

(*Enter the* GOVERNOR'S WIFE, *followed by the* ADJUTANT *and two* LAWYERS.)

GOVERNOR'S WIFE: At least there are no common people here, thank God. I can't stand their smell. It always gives me migraine.

FIRST LAWYER: Madam, I must ask you to be careful what you say until we have another judge.

GOVERNOR'S WIFE: But I didn't say anything, Illo Shuboladze. I love the people with their simple straightforward minds. It's only that their smell brings on my migraine.

SECOND LAWYER: There won't be many spectators. The whole population is sitting at home behind locked doors because of the riots in the people's quarters.

GOVERNOR'S WIFE (*looking at* GRUSHA): Is that the creature?

FIRST LAWYER: Please, most gracious Natella Abashwili, abstain from invective until it is certain the Grand Duke has appointed a new judge and we're rid of the present one, who's about the lowest fellow ever seen in judge's gown. Things are all set to move, you see.

(*Enter* IRONSHIRTS *from the courtyard.*)

COOK: Her Grace would pull your hair out on the spot if she didn't know Azdak is for the poor. He goes by the face.

(IRONSHIRTS *begin fastening a rope to a beam.* AZDAK, *in chains, is led in, followed by* SHAUWA, *also in chains. The three* FARMERS *bring up the rear.*)

AN IRONSHIRT: Trying to run away, were you? (*He strikes* AZDAK.)

ONE FARMER: Off with his judge's gown before we string him up!

(IRONSHIRTS *and* FARMERS *tear off* AZDAK'*s gown. His torn underwear is visible. Then someone kicks him.*)

AN IRONSHIRT (*pushing him into someone else*): Want a load of justice? Here it is!

(*Accompanied by shouts of* "You take it!" *and* "Let me have him, Brother!" *they throw* AZDAK *back and forth until he collapses. Then he is lifted up and dragged under the noose.*)

GOVERNOR'S WIFE (*who, during this "ballgame," has clapped her hands hysterically*): I disliked that man from the moment I first saw him.

AZDAK (*covered with blood, panting*): I can't see. Give me a rag.

AN IRONSHIRT: What is it you want to see?

AZDAK: You, you dogs! (*He wipes the blood out of his eyes with his shirt.*) Good morning, dogs! How goes it, dogs! How's the dog world? Does it smell good? Got another boot for me to lick? Are you back at each other's throats, dogs?

(*Accompanied by a* CORPORAL, *a dust-covered* RIDER *enters. He takes some documents from a leather case, looks at them, then interrupts.*)

RIDER: Stop! I bring a dispatch from the Grand Duke, containing the latest appointments.

CORPORAL (*bellowing*): Atten – shun!

RIDER: Of the new judge it says: "We appoint a man whom we have to thank for saving a life indispensable to the country's welfare – a certain Azdak of Nuka." Which is he?

SHAUWA (*pointing*): That's him, Your Excellency.

CORPORAL (*bellowing*): What's going on here?

AN IRONSHIRT: I beg to report that His Honor Azdak was already His Honor

Azdak, but on these farmers' denunciation was pronounced the Grand Duke's enemy.

CORPORAL (*pointing at the* FARMERS): March them off! (*They are marched off. They bow all the time.*) See to it that His Honor Azdak is exposed to no more violence.

(*Exeunt* RIDER *and* CORPORAL.)

COOK (*to* SHAUWA): She clapped her hands! I hope he saw it!

FIRST LAWYER: It's a catastrophe.

(AZDAK *has fainted. Coming to, he is dressed again in judge's robes. He walks, swaying, toward the* IRONSHIRTS.)

AN IRONSHIRT: What does Your Honor desire?

AZDAK: Nothing, fellow dogs, or just an occasional boot to lick. (*To* SHAUWA.) I pardon you. (*He is unchained.*) Get me some red wine, the sweet kind. (SHAUWA *stumbles off.*) Get out of here, I've got to judge a case. (*Exeunt* IRONSHIRTS. SHAUWA *returns with a pitcher of wine.* AZDAK *gulps it down.*) Something for my backside. (SHAUWA *brings the Statute Book, puts it on the judge's chair.* AZDAK *sits on it.*) I accept.

(*The* PROSECUTORS, *among whom a worried council has been held, smile with relief. They whisper.*)

COOK: Oh dear!

SIMON: A well can't be filled with dew, they say.

LAWYERS (*approaching* AZDAK, *who stands up, expectantly*): A quite ridiculous case, Your Honor. The accused has abducted a child and refuses to hand it over.

AZDAK (*stretching out his hand, glancing at* GRUSHA): A most attractive person. (*He fingers the money, then sits down, satisfied.*) I declare the proceedings open and demand the whole truth. (*To* GRUSHA.) Especially from you.

FIRST LAWYER: High Court of Justice! Blood, as the popular saying goes, is thicker than water. This old adage . . .

AZDAK (*interrupting*): The Court wants to know the lawyers' fee.

FIRST LAWYER (*surprised*): I beg your pardon? (AZDAK, *smiling, rubs his thumb and index finger.*) Oh, I see. Five hundred piasters, Your Honor, to answer the Court's somewhat unusual question.

AZDAK: Did you hear? The question is unusual. I ask it because I listen in quite a different way when I know you're good.

FIRST LAWYER (*bowing*): Thank you, Your Honor. High Court of Justice, of all ties the ties of blood are strongest. Mother and child – is there a more intimate relationship? Can one tear a child from its mother? High Court of Justice, she has conceived it in the holy ecstasies of love. She has carried it in her womb. She has fed it with her blood. She has borne it with pain. High Court of Justice, it has been observed that the wild tigress, robbed of her young, roams restless through the mountains, shrunk to a shadow. Nature herself . . .

AZDAK (*interrupting, to* GRUSHA): What's your answer to all this and anything else that lawyer might have to say?

GRUSHA: He's mine.

AZDAK: Is that all? I hope you can prove it. Why should I assign the child to you in any case?

GRUSHA: I brought him up like the priest says "according to my best knowledge and conscience." I always found him something to eat. Most of the time he had a roof over his head. And I went to such trouble for him. I had expenses too. I didn't look out for my own comfort. I brought the child up to be friendly with everyone, and from the beginning taught him to work. As well as he could, that is. He's still very little.

FIRST LAWYER: Your Honor, it is significant that the girl herself doesn't claim any tie of blood between her and the child.

AZDAK: The Court takes note of that.

FIRST LAWYER: Thank you, Your Honor. And now permit a woman bowed in sorrow — who has already lost her husband and now has also to fear the loss of her child — to address a few words to you. The gracious Natella Abashwili is . . .

GOVERNOR'S WIFE (*quietly*): A most cruel fate, sir, forces me to describe to you the tortures of a bereaved mother's soul, the anxiety, the sleepless nights, the . . .

SECOND LAWYER (*bursting out*): It's outrageous the way this woman is being treated! Her husband's palace is closed to her! The revenue of her estates is blocked, and she is cold-bloodedly told that it's tied to the heir. She can't do a thing without that child. She can't even pay her lawyers! ! (*To the* FIRST LAWYER, *who, desperate about this outburst, makes frantic gestures to keep him from speaking.*) Dear Illo Shuboladze, surely it can be divulged now that the Abashwili estates are at stake?

FIRST LAWYER: Please, Honored Sandro Oboladze! We agreed . . . (*To* AZDAK.) Of course it is correct that the trial will also decide if our noble client can take over the Abashwili estates, which are rather extensive. I say "also" advisedly, for in the foreground stands the human tragedy of a mother, as Natella Abashwili very properly explained in the first words of her moving statement. Even if Michael Abashwili were not heir to the estates, he would still be the dearly beloved child of my client.

AZDAK: Stop! The Court is touched by the mention of estates. It's a proof of human feeling.

SECOND LAWYER: Thanks, Your Honor. Dear Illo Shuboladze, we can prove in any case that the woman who took the child is not the child's mother. Permit me to lay before the Court the bare facts. High Court of Justice, by an unfortunate chain of circumstances, Michael Abashwili was left behind on that Easter Sunday while his mother was making her escape. Grusha, a palace kitchen maid, was seen with the baby . . .

COOK: All her mistress was thinking of was what dresses she'd take along!

SECOND LAWYER (*unmoved*): Nearly a year later Grusha turned up in a mountain village with a baby and there entered into the state of matrimony with . . .

AZDAK: How'd you get to that mountain village?

GRUSHA: On foot, Your Honor. And he was mine.

SIMON: I'm the father, Your Honor.

COOK: I used to look after it for them, Your Honor. For five piasters.

SECOND LAWYER: This man is engaged to Grusha, High Court of Justice: his testimony is suspect.

AZDAK: Are you the man she married in the mountain village?

AZDAK (*to* GRUSHA): Why? (*Pointing at* SIMON.) Is he no good in bed? Tell the truth.

GRUSHA: We didn't get that far. I married because of the baby. So he'd have a roof over his head. (*Pointing at* SIMON.) He was in the war, Your Honor.

AZDAK: And now he wants you back again, huh?

SIMON: I wish to state in evidence . . .

GRUSHA (*angrily*): I am no longer free, Your Honor.

AZDAK: And the child, you claim, comes from whoring? (GRUSHA *doesn't answer.*) I'm going to ask you a question: What kind of child is he? A ragged little bastard? Or from a good family?

GRUSHA (*angrily*): He's an ordinary child.

AZDAK: I mean — did he have refined features from the beginning?

GRUSHA: He had a nose on his face.

AZDAK: A very significant comment! It has been said of me that I went out one time and sniffed at a rosebush before rendering a verdict — tricks like that are needed nowadays. Well, I'll make it short, and not listen to any more lies. (*To* GRUSHA.) Especially not yours. (*To all the accused.*) I can imagine what you've cooked up to cheat me! I know you people. You're swindlers.

GRUSHA (*suddenly*): I can understand your wanting to cut it short, now I've seen what you accepted!

AZDAK: Shut up! Did I accept anything from you?

GRUSHA (*while the* COOK *tries to restrain her*): I haven't got anything.

AZDAK: True. Quite true. From starvelings I never get a thing. I might just as well starve, myself. You want justice, but do you want to pay for it, hm? When you go to a butcher you know you have to pay, but you people go to a judge as if you were off to a funeral supper.

SIMON (*loudly*): When the horse was shod, the horsefly held out its leg, as the saying is.

AZDAK (*eagerly accepting the challenge*): Better a treasure in manure than a stone in a mountain stream.

SIMON: A fine day. Let's go fishing, said the angler to the worm.

AZDAK: I'm my own master, said the servant, and cut off his foot.

SIMON: I love you as a father, said the Czar to the peasants, and had the Czarevitch's head chopped off.

AZDAK: A fool's worst enemy is himself.

SIMON: However, a fart has no nose.

AZDAK: Fined ten piasters for indecent language in court! That'll teach you what justice is.

GRUSHA (*furiously*): A fine kind of justice! You play fast and loose with us because we don't talk as refined as that crowd with their lawyers.

AZDAK: That's true. You people are too dumb. It's only right you should get it in the neck.

GRUSHA: You want to hand the child over to her, and she wouldn't even know how to keep it dry, she's so "refined"! You know about as much about justice as I do!

AZDAK: There's something in that. I'm an ignorant man. Haven't even a decent pair of pants on under this gown. Look! With me, everything goes on food and drink — I was educated in a convent. Incidentally, I'll fine you ten piasters for contempt of court. And you're a very silly girl, to turn me against you, instead of making eyes at me and wiggling your backside a little to keep me in a good temper. Twenty piasters!

GRUSHA: Even if it was thirty, I'd tell you what I think of your justice, you drunken onion! (*Incoherently.*) How dare you talk to me like the cracked Isaiah on the church window? As if you were somebody? For you weren't born to this. You weren't born to rap your own mother on the knuckles if she swipes a little bowl of salt someplace. Aren't you ashamed of yourself when you see how I tremble before you? You've made yourself their servant so no one will take their houses from them — houses they had stolen! Since when have houses belonged to the bedbugs? But you're on the watch, or they couldn't drag our men into their wars! You bribetaker!

(AZDAK *half gets up, starts beaming. With his little hammer he half-heartedly knocks on the table as if to get silence. As* GRUSHA'*s scolding continues, he only beats time with his hammer.*)

I've no respect for you. No more than for a thief or a bandit with a knife! You can do what you want. You can take the child away from me, a hundred against one, but I tell you one thing: only extortioners should be chosen for a profession like yours, and men who rape children! As punishment! Yes, let *them* sit in judgment on their fellow creatures. It is worse than to hang from the gallows.

AZDAK (*sitting down*): Now it'll be thirty! And I won't go on squabbling with you — we're not in a tavern. What'd happen to my dignity as a judge? Anyway, I've lost interest in your case. Where's the couple who wanted a divorce? (*To* SHAUWA.) Bring 'em in. This case is adjourned for fifteen minutes.

FIRST LAWYER (*to the* GOVERNOR'S WIFE): Even without using the rest of the evidence, Madam, we have the verdict in the bag.

COOK (*to* GRUSHA): You've gone and spoiled your chances with him. You won't get the child now.

GOVERNOR'S WIFE: Shalva, my smelling salts!

(*Enter a very* OLD COUPLE.)

AZDAK: I accept. (*The* OLD COUPLE *don't understand.*) I hear you want to be divorced. How long have you been together?

OLD WOMAN: Forty years, Your Honor.

AZDAK: And why do you want a divorce?

OLD MAN: We don't like each other, Your Honor.

AZDAK: Since when?

OLD WOMAN: Oh, from the very beginning, Your Honor.

AZDAK: I'll think about your request and render my verdict when I'm through with the other case. (SHAUWA *leads them back.*) I need the child. (*He beckons* GRUSHA *to him and bends not unkindly toward her.*) I've noticed you have a soft spot for justice. I don't believe he's your child, but if he *were* yours, woman, wouldn't you want him to be rich? You'd only have to say he wasn't yours, and he'd have a palace and many horses in his stable and many beggars on his doorstep and many soldiers in his service and many petitioners in his courtyard, wouldn't he? What do you say — don't you want him to be rich?

(GRUSHA *is silent.*)

SINGER: Hear now what the angry girl thought but did not say:

Had he golden shoes to wear
He'd be cruel as a bear
Evil would his life disgrace.
He'd laugh in my face.

Carrying a heart of flint
Is too troublesome a stint.
Being powerful and bad
Is hard on a lad.

Then let hunger be his foe!
Hungry men and women, no.
Let him fear the darksome night
But not daylight!

AZDAK: I think I understand you, woman.

GRUSHA (*suddenly and loudly*): I won't give him up. I've raised him, and he knows me.

(*Enter* SHAUWA *with the* CHILD.)

GOVERNOR'S WIFE: He's in rags!

GRUSHA: That's not true. But I wasn't given time to put his good shirt on.

GOVERNOR'S WIFE: He must have been in a pigsty.

GRUSHA (*furiously*): I'm not a pig, but there are some who are! Where did you leave your baby?

GOVERNOR'S WIFE: I'll show you, you vulgar creature! (*She is about to throw herself on* GRUSHA, *but is restrained by her lawyers.*) She's a criminal, she must be whipped. Immediately!

SECOND LAWYER (*holding his hand over her mouth*): Natella Abashwili, you promised . . . Your Honor, the plaintiff's nerves . . .

AZDAK: Plaintiff and defendant! The Court has listened to your case, and has come to no decision as to who the real mother is; therefore, I, the judge, am obliged to *choose* a mother for the child. I'll make a test. Shauwa, get a piece of chalk and draw a circle on the floor. (SHAUWA *does so.*) Now place the child in the center. (SHAUWA *puts* MICHAEL, *who smiles at* GRUSHA, *in the center of the circle.*) Stand near the circle, both of you. (*The* GOVERNOR'S WIFE *and* GRUSHA *step up to the circle.*) Now each of you take the child by one hand. (*They do so.*) The true mother is she who can pull the child out of the circle.

SECOND LAWYER (*quickly*): High Court of Justice, I object! The fate of the great Abashwili estates, which are tied to the child, as the heir, should not be made dependent on such a doubtful duel. In addition, my client does not command the strength of this person, who is accustomed to physical work.

AZDAK: She looks pretty well fed to me. Pull! (*The* GOVERNOR'S WIFE *pulls the* CHILD *out of the circle on her side;* GRUSHA *has let go and stands aghast.*) What's the matter with you? You didn't pull.

GRUSHA: I didn't hold on to him.

FIRST LAWYER (*congratulating the* GOVERNOR'S WIFE): What did I say! The ties of blood!

GRUSHA (*running to* AZDAK): Your Honor, I take back everything I said against you. I ask your forgiveness. But could I keep him till he can speak all the words? He knows a few.

AZDAK: Don't influence the Court. I bet you only know about twenty words yourself. All right, I'll make the test once more, just to be certain. (*The two women take up their positions again.*) Pull! (*Again* GRUSHA *lets go of the* CHILD.)

GRUSHA (*in despair*): I brought him up! Shall I also tear him to bits? I can't!

AZDAK (*rising*): And in this manner the Court has determined the true mother. (*To* GRUSHA.) Take your child and be off. I advise you not to stay in the city with him. (*To the* GOVERNOR'S WIFE.) And you disappear before I fine you for fraud. Your estates fall to the city. They'll be converted into a playground for the children. They need one, and I've decided it'll be called after me: Azdak's Garden.

*(The* GOVERNOR'S WIFE *has fainted and is carried out by the* LAWYERS *and the* ADJUTANT. GRUSHA *stands motionless.* SHAUWA *leads the* CHILD *toward her.)*

Now I'll take off this judge's gown — it's got too hot for me. I'm not cut out for a hero. In token of farewell I invite you all to a little dance in the meadow outside. Oh, I'd almost forgotten something in my excitement . . . to sign the divorce decree. *(Using the judge's chair as a table, he writes something on a piece of paper, and prepares to leave. Dance music has started.)*

SHAUWA *(having read what is on the paper)*: But that's not right. You've not divorced the old people. You've divorced Grusha!

AZDAK: Divorced the wrong couple? What a pity! And I never retract! If I did, how could we keep order in the land? *(To the* OLD COUPLE.*)* I'll invite you to my party instead. You don't mind dancing with each other, do you? *(To* GRUSHA *and* SIMON.*)* I've got forty piasters coming from you.

SIMON *(pulling out his purse)*: Cheap at the price, Your Honor. And many thanks.

AZDAK *(pocketing the cash)*: I'll be needing this.

GRUSHA *(to* MICHAEL*)*: So we'd better leave the city tonight, Michael? *(To* SIMON.*)* You like him?

SIMON: With my respects, I like him.

GRUSHA: Now I can tell you: I took him because on that Easter Sunday I got engaged to you. So he's a child of love. Michael, let's dance.

*(She dances with* MICHAEL, SIMON *dances with the* COOK, *the* OLD COUPLE *with each other.* AZDAK *stands lost in thought. The* DANCERS *soon hide him from view. Occasionally he is seen, but less and less as more couples join the dance.)*

SINGER: And after that evening Azdak vanished and was never seen again.
The people of Grusinia did not forget him but long remembered
The period of his judging as a brief golden age,
Almost an age of justice.

*(All the* COUPLES *dance off.* AZDAK *has disappeared.)*

But you, you who have listened to the Story of the Chalk Circle,
Take note what men of old concluded:
That what there is shall go to those who are good for it,
Children to the motherly, that they prosper,
Carts to good drivers, that they be driven well,
The valley to the waterers, that it yield fruit.

Simplicity in art, says Eric Bentley in his Introduction to *Seven Plays by Bertolt Brecht,* may be an achievement on the far side of complexity. It is an apt comment. In Brecht, we sense the design not as something innocent of or defiant of disorder but as immanent in it and the artistic process as revelatory rather than creative. The parable — the term is Brecht's own — emerges from the crowded bustle on the stage with the clarity and strength of a folk tale. His art is at the opposite end from the classics of modern realism. Whereas Ibsen's stage has the stability of a room, Brecht's is open and like Shakespeare's momently capable of becoming any place the imagination calls for. The inclusive dramatic form, fluid rather than unrealistic, embeds the moral scheme of the fable in the promiscuous flux of actuality, but the scheme disciplines the flux to directed movement. Parable, almost but never quite becoming abstract scheme, balanced against stage activity, almost but never quite becoming chaos, provides inner tension. The surface naiveté masks a technique that orders a vast and subtle content.

If Brecht is a difficult playwright, he has been made even more difficult by the labels of "Marxism" and "epic theater" (also his own term) with which his plays are commonly tagged. The tags would do less harm if they were simply wrong; then they could be removed. They are not wrong, however, but intrusive and misleading. They stop thought and trigger stock responses. We react, not to drama, but to political system and esthetic theory. Like all fables, Brecht's are concentrates of large and various experience. But the narrative that embodies the general pattern is not abstract. "Marxist" points to certain consistent value orientations evident in the plays and "epic" to certain distinctive ways of using the theater. But the labels say nothing about the particulars of plot and scenic reality which the Marxist outlook and the epic form shape into the pattern of fable. The journey motif in Grusha's story is a version of epic, but it is the particulars of the human and physical obstacles she encounters and the rhythm and direction of her progress, rather than the mere fact of narrative, that turn her journey into a superb theatrical demonstration of the "terribleness" of "the seductive power of goodness." The Azdak figure, the proletarian scamp-judge, whose moral superiority is that of the rabbit-eater over the man-eater, challenges propertied stuffiness and arrogance, legalism and feudal tyranny. There is revolutionary sentiment in the muted anger of his "Song of Injustice in Persia" and in the triumphant sarcasm of his "Song of Chaos." The old legend could be called proto-Marxist. But as a general concept Marxism is more of a hindrance than a help in a critical account of Azdak. His cowardice, vulgarity, and greed, his old cheese, bloody rags, and dirty, drunken jokes, the tragicomical implications of his futile self-condemnation for helping the Grand Duke to escape, the ironic fickleness of fortune by which he becomes first a mock, then a real, judge, then almost loses his neck, and then is reinstated as judge — are these, as scenic facts, "Marxist"?

The point, of course, is that a literary work does not contain ideology the way a pudding contains plums or even the way a cake contains butter. As a theoretical materialist Brecht wanted a more equitable distribution of economic goods and potential, and he believed in man's duty to try to improve his physical environment, and hence his conditioning, to the limit of his ability and control. Having tried Hollywood, he settled in East Berlin. But the problem of Marxism-in-Brecht is not solved by biography or by anxious search for pellets of subversive doctrine. Is property good or evil in *The Caucasian Chalk Circle* (1944–45)? Almost everyone in the play who owns anything is hard-hearted, not just the feudal masters, but the peasants as well: the farmer who sells Grusha milk, Lavrenti's wife, the mother-in-law, the Invalid, the three farmers charging the old woman with theft. But then we come upon Azdak taking bribes as a matter of course and Simon Shashava being able to marry Grusha because he has been promoted to paymaster at double his earlier pay and with a house of his own. Does the play say that riches corrupt? It is less presumptuous. It says that Grusha thinks that little Michael would be corrupted if he were brought up by Natella Abashwili — a much smaller and dramatically more serviceable proposition. Is there political dynamite in Azdak's epigram, "That the roof of the world may be conquered, the roof of the cottage is torn down"? A cold-war attitude? If Azdak's awarding the child to Grusha is taken to imply an attack on property rights, doesn't "Capitalism" come to seem incompatible with kindness and common sense? Brecht gives a new twist to the old story of the Solomonic test of mother's love. The comfortable assumption used to be that none but the child's real mother would sooner give up her right to the child than cause it pain. But here the natural mother is unnatural, the foster mother truly motherly. The new version (a verse Prologue Bentley has written for the play says) naggingly involves the larger question of who owns anything, "and by what right." Is this Marxism? — or political disillusionment? The whole inquiry breaks down.

We are aware, rather, of what Brecht perhaps had in mind when he once referred to Azdak's "tragic side." There is in the crude farce of his magistracy the truth that all even *his* shrewd folk wisdom achieved was "*almost* an age of justice." Does the fault lie with his justice or with the "dog's world" in which he is a judge? Isn't he a bit of a brute himself? And even if we assume that the lesson which the two kolkhozes learn from the story of Azdak is an absolute, the modern valley setting, with evidence of Nazi ravage all around, is on-stage proof that events rarely follow the rule "That what there is shall go to those who are good for it." The legend of the good judge is, after all, only an old legend.

The fact that "epic theater," unlike "Marxism," raises *literary* issues only increases the risk of hiding the play behind a label. "Epic" is misleading if it is taken to imply that Brecht's plays are undramatic ("epic" denoting a genre distinct from "drama" and "lyric"). Their solidly dimensional world can be staged in its entirety, unlike the world of novels, and by the same token is not an introspected world, like that of lyrics. "Epic" is misleading also if it suggests the slow and stately pace, the richness of reference, the elevated diction, the formulas of image and rhetoric, the mythological machinery, and the magnitude of theme, of classical or Miltonic epics.

What the term *should* denote is a drama that breaks the old five- or three-act structure and proceeds by something resembling the "stations" of the guild performances of medieval mystery and miracle plays: staged episodes in discontinuous but progressive narrative sequence. The filmic elements of large and changing cast, variety of setting, brevity of scene, and use of flashback (in the early Azdak scenes) also give a kind of epic effect.

But the main reason for calling Brecht's drama epic is that it is narrated. Like the kolkhoz farmers we are in the hands of Arkadi Tscheidse, the professional Singer from Tiflis. What we see of Grusha's and Azdak's stories are episodes selected for dramatization from a larger entertainment-with-a-purpose, which also includes choric comment and the narrator's linking synopses. The episodes are, literally, *shown*. The audience understands that it does not see the characters of the legend themselves, but their twentieth-century impersonators.

Clearly, we are dealing here with a play convention quite different from that of the realist theater. By realist convention, we are unobserved observers of real life in the process of being lived — peepers and eavesdroppers. We are invited to believe, or to pretend to believe, that the actors are not actors but businessmen and housewives, that their talk is not rehearsed but spontaneous, that they are not on a stage but in an apartment. The realist convention paradoxically denies the fact of theater. As audience we get our money's worth only if we are willing to share the denial. A realist play production, we say, is successful in direct ratio to the success with which it entices us into the make-believe and keeps us here till the curtain comes down, the lights go on, and the illusion ends.

Brecht openly violates the realist convention. For him, the stage is space inside, not outside, the theater. The devices he employs to prevent illusionism ensure theatricality.

In *The Caucasian Chalk Circle* both the most obvious and the most important of these devices is the framing of the main action in a play-within-a-play form. The device is not new. Shakespeare (for example) used it in *The Taming of the Shrew* and Beaumont in *The Knight of the Burning Pestle.* In modern drama, after Pirandello's *Six Characters in Search of an Author* (1921), it has become something of a cliché in plays that seek to insinuate a philosophy of relativism. However dissimilar such plays may be, they all have in common the effect they give of the theater being conscious of itself — an effect ambiguous, paradoxical, and elusive. Does the spectacle of art mocking art *as* art hint at a reaffirmation of the seriousness of art as true to life? Theatricalism, at any rate, produces a much subtler stage-audience relationship than does dramatic realism. In *The Chalk Circle* an audience in the theater watches an audience on stage, and both then watch — not a play of present life but a dramatization-narration of past legend.* The familiar but profound pun on the two meanings of the verb "to act" comes alive as the characters in the play-within "live" their theatrical existence.

*Verfremdung* (literally, "alienation" or "estrangement" but most often rendered as "distancing" or "esthetic distancing") is Brecht's own term for the effect on the audience of this insistent theatricality. Its function is to keep the spectator's rational faculties alert during the performance. Brecht seeks from his audience not a spellbinding imaginative projection into the life illusion on stage, but thoughtful attention to a meaningful dramatization of fable. He wants to reach minds, not to submerge them in a wash of stage-generated empathy. "I am not," he said, "greatly interested in anyone making an emotional investment in my plays." This does not mean that he fails whenever an audience gives Grusha and Azdak its sympathies or finds the play charming. It means that he uses emotional appeal as a strategy of persuasion — as a means to a rational end, not as an end in itself.

And yet, the ultimate effect of *Verfremdung* is perhaps more complex than Brecht's deliberate aim would indicate. The ambivalent status of the stage audience tends to obscure the distinction between stage and audience. From the viewpoint of the theater audience the stage audience are characters in the outer (framing) action. From the viewpoint of the performers in the inner (framed) action they are audience. Because the theater audience recognizes its own status in one of the two functions of the stage audience, it tends to identify with it in its other function as well. At the end, outer and inner action

* In Bentley's 1961 version of his adaptation of the play, members of the fruit-growing "Galinsk" kolkhoz participate in the performance, thus further blurring the stage-audience distinction.

(and present and past, theater actuality and theater imagination) merge, as the dancing couples of actors and stage audience* gradually hide Azdak from view. Then the dancers, too, disappear, and the Singer is left alone on the stage to address the epilogue-moral directly to the audience in the theater. To what extent, by now, has the latter become implicated? *Verfremdung* eliminates the possibility of mistaking the theater for reality, but it does not, like the realist theater of illusion, draw a safe line of division between them.

Sets and the use of time also add to the theatricalist effect. The outdoor scene in the distant, war-torn valley plausibly limits the Singer's use of props and scenery. The sets are crude and improvised, suggestive-symbolic rather than lifelike. In the opening scene of the inner play, a doorway marks the palace side of the stage, a gateway the town side. Place is evoked rather than represented. The whole production is stylized. The "voice" of the play shifts freely back and forth between drama, narrative, and choric comment and would only be impeded by elaborate verisimilitude.

There are shifts in time as well:

> CROWD: — The baby! — I can't see it, don't shove so hard! — God bless the child, Your Grace!
>
> SINGER (*while the* CROWD *is driven back with whips*): For the first time on that Easter Sunday, the people saw the Governor's heir.

The Singer's comment cuts off the gathering immediacy of the crowd scene. His viewpoint is the retrospective, generalizing one of a historian. His "saw" pulls us back sharply from the crowd's "I can't see." No sooner have we begun to suspend disbelief, accepting what we see as happening *here* and *now,* than the Singer steps in to remind us that the present tense applies only to the theater situation. He is presenting a show, but it is a show of what *happened — then* and *there.* Time is not always rendered realistically even within the single episode. When Lavrenti tells Grusha that she and the child must leave his farm as soon as spring comes, the accelerating drip-drip from the roof marks the passing of winter and the coming of spring even as brother and sister talk. On-stage action and dialogue proceed at normal speed, while the simultaneous off-stage sound of snow melting compresses days or weeks into the span of a few minutes.

The theatricalist fable subordinates character, too, to meaningful pattern. As the kolkhoz Prologue and the Singer's Epilogue frame the legend of Grusha and Azdak, so Grusha's scenes with Simon give a

* It has not been made explicitly clear whether or not members of the kolkhoz audience join in the final dance, but that seems to be the implication of the stage directions of the last scene. It would, at any rate, be a scenically effective conclusion, in keeping with the play-within-the-play decorum.

framework of romance to the hardships of her journey. We get a Chinese box effect, frame within frame. The mock-formal restraint of language in the lovers' dialogues suggests the blend of passion, liking, respect, and sheer sense of fun in their feelings for one another. But the point is their attractiveness as moral types rather than, simply, delightful romance or psychological complexity.

The most striking fact of structure in the play is the two-part division. The answer to the question of whose play it is, Grusha's or Azdak's, is that it belongs to both, that the two stories are complementary halves in a dramatic whole, premises in a kind of syllogism. Parallelism prepares for their final fusion. Both Grusha and Azdak perform impulsive deeds of imprudent kindness: Grusha saves Michael, Azdak the Grand Duke. Both are rewarded for their kindness (though the reward is ironic in Azdak's case, as he regrets his kindness when he learns the old man's identity). The syllogism concludes in Grusha's and Azdak's confrontation in the chalk-circle scene. The conclusion represents a multiple climax.

It releases the suspense concerning Grusha's fate, which has been accumulating while Azdak's manner of justice has been illustrated in racy anecdote. It achieves the overt meaning of the fable. Without Azdak, Grusha's story would only have proved that in violent social upheaval there are other bitter battles fought than those on the battlefield. Without Grusha, Azdak's natural justice would have lacked a morally significant context and emotive force. Only together do the two stories have what a character in the dramatic prologue calls "a bearing on the problem" of what to do with the valley. By the test of Azdak's criterion of superior yield, as applicable to use of land as to motherliness, the settlement in favor of the fruit-growing irrigators is validated.

Finally, the chalk-circle scene completes the dramatic structure. This might have been described as two converging lines, if only Grusha's movement had not been over before Azdak's even begins, and if the flashback story of Azdak ("flashback" relative to Grusha's poignant situation at the end of Section III of the play) had moved at all after he becomes judge. Dramatically, the near-hanging is an abortive episode, and the preceding collection of law-case anecdotes, though establishing Azdak's quality as an administrator of justice, is shapeless and static. A more accurate definition of the structural function of the chalk-circle scene is that it brings the dynamics of the brave and resourceful virgin mother's odyssey to rest in the stasis of Azdak's verdict and Simon Shashava's love, concluding the legend of how goodness once received justice in a Caucasian valley.

## EDWARD ALBEE

# Who's Afraid of Virginia Woolf?

THE PLAYERS

MARTHA, a large, boisterous woman, 52, looking somewhat younger. Ample, but not fleshy.

GEORGE, her husband, 46. Thin; hair going gray.

HONEY, 26, a petite blond girl, rather plain.

NICK, 30, her husband. Blond, well put-together, good looking.

*The Scene: The living room of a house on the campus of a small New England college.*

## ACT I. FUN AND GAMES

*Set in darkness. Crash against front door.* MARTHA'*s laughter heard. Front door opens, lights are switched on.* MARTHA *enters, followed by* GEORGE.

MARTHA: Je*sus*. . . .
GEORGE: . . . Shhhhhhh. . . .
MARTHA: . . . H. Christ. . . .
GEORGE: For God's sake, Martha, it's two o'clock in the. . . .
MARTHA: Oh, George!
GEORGE: Well, I'm *sorry,* but. . . .
MARTHA: What a cluck! What a cluck you are.
GEORGE: It's late, you know? Late.
MARTHA (*looks about the room. Imitates Bette Davis*): What a dump. Hey, what's that from? "What a dump!"
GEORGE: How would I know what. . . .
MARTHA: Aw, come on! What's it from? *You* know. . . .
GEORGE: . . . Martha. . . .
MARTHA: WHAT'S IT FROM, FOR CHRIST'S SAKE?
GEORGE (*wearily*): What's what from?
MARTHA: I just told you; I just did it. "What a dump!" Hunh? What's that from?
GEORGE: I haven't the faintest idea what. . . .
MARTHA: Dumbbell! It's from some goddamn Bette Davis picture . . . some goddamn Warner Brothers epic. . . .
GEORGE: *I* can't remember all the pictures that. . . .
MARTHA: Nobody's asking you to remember every single goddamn Warner Brothers epic . . . just one! One single little epic! Bette Davis gets peritonitis in the end . . . she's got this big black fright wig she wears all through the picture and she gets peritonitis, and she's married to Joseph Cotten or something. . . .
GEORGE: . . . Some*body*. . . .
MARTHA: . . . some*body* . . . and she wants to go to Chicago all the time, 'cause she's in love with that actor with the scar. . . . But she gets sick, and she sits down in front of her dressing table. . . .
GEORGE: What actor? What scar?
MARTHA: *I* can't remember his name, for God's sake. What's the name of the *picture?* I want to know what the name of the *picture* is. She sits down in front of her dressing table . . . and she's got this peritonitis . . . and she tries to put her lipstick on, but she can't . . . and she gets it all over her face . . . but she decides to go to Chicago anyway, and. . . .
GEORGE: *Chicago!* It's called *Chicago.*
MARTHA: Hunh? What . . . what is?
GEORGE: The picture . . . it's called *Chicago*. . . .
MARTHA: Good grief! Don't you know *anything? Chicago* was a 'thirties musical, starring little Miss Alice *Faye*. Don't you know *anything?*
GEORGE: Well, that was probably before my *time,* but. . . .
MARTHA: Can it! Just cut that out! This picture . . . Bette Davis comes home from a hard day at the grocery store. . . .
GEORGE: She works in a grocery store?

MARTHA: She's a housewife; she buys things . . . and she comes home with the groceries, and she walks into the modest living room of the modest cottage modest Joseph Cotten has set her up in. . . .

GEORGE: Are they married?

MARTHA (*impatiently*): Yes. They're married. To each other. Cluck! And she comes in, and she looks around, and she puts her groceries down, and she says, "What a dump!"

GEORGE: (*Pause.*) Oh.

MARTHA: (*Pause.*) She's discontent.

GEORGE: (*Pause.*) Oh.

MARTHA: (*Pause.*) Well, what's the name of the picture?

GEORGE: I really don't know, Martha. . . .

MARTHA: Well, think!

GEORGE: I'm tired, dear . . . it's late . . . and besides. . . .

MARTHA: I don't know what you're so tired about . . . you haven't *done* anything all day; you didn't have any classes, or anything. . . .

GEORGE: Well, I'm tired. . . . If your father didn't set up these goddamn Saturday night orgies all the time. . . .

MARTHA: Well, that's too bad about you, George. . . .

GEORGE (*grumbling*): Well, that's how it is, anyway.

MARTHA: You didn't *do* anything; you never *do* anything; you never *mix*. You just sit around and *talk*.

GEORGE: What do you want me to do? Do you want me to act like you? Do you want me to go around all night *braying* at everybody, the way you do?

MARTHA (*braying*): I DON'T BRAY!

GEORGE (*softly*): All right . . . you don't bray.

MARTHA (*hurt*): I do not *bray*.

GEORGE: All right. I said you didn't bray.

MARTHA (*pouting*): Make me a drink.

GEORGE: What?

MARTHA (*still softly*): I said, make me a drink.

GEORGE (*moving to the portable bar*): Well, I don't suppose a nightcap'd kill either one of us. . . .

MARTHA: A nightcap! Are you kidding? We've got guests.

GEORGE (*disbelieving*): We've got what?

MARTHA: Guests. GUESTS.

GEORGE: GUESTS!

MARTHA: Yes . . . guests . . . people. . . . We've got guests coming over.

GEORGE: When?

MARTHA: NOW!

GEORGE: Good Lord, Martha . . . do you know what time it. . . . *Who's* coming over?

MARTHA: What's-their-name.

GEORGE: Who?

MARTHA: WHAT'S-THEIR-NAME!

GEORGE: Who what's-their-name?

MARTHA: I don't know what their name is, George. . . . You met them tonight . . . they're new . . . he's in the math department, or something. . . .

GEORGE: Who . . . who are these people?

MARTHA: You met them tonight, George.

GEORGE: I don't remember meeting anyone tonight. . . .

MARTHA: Well you did . . . Will you give me my drink, please. . . . He's in the math department . . . about thirty, blond, and. . . .

GEORGE: . . . and good-looking. . . .

MARTHA: Yes . . . and good-looking. . . .

GEORGE: It figures.

MARTHA: . . . and his wife's a mousey little type, without any hips, or anything.

GEORGE (*vaguely*): Oh.

MARTHA: You remember them now?

GEORGE: Yes, I guess so, Martha. . . . But why in God's name are they coming over here now?

MARTHA (*in a so-there voice*): Because Daddy said we should be nice to them, that's why.

GEORGE (*defeated*): Oh, Lord.

MARTHA: May I have my drink, please? Daddy said we should be nice to them. Thank you.

GEORGE: But why now? It's after two o'clock in the morning, and. . . .

MARTHA: Because Daddy said we should be nice to them!

GEORGE: Yes. But I'm sure your father didn't mean we were supposed to stay up all *night* with these people. I mean, we could have them over some Sunday or something. . . .

MARTHA: Well, never mind. . . . Besides, it *is* Sunday. Very early Sunday.

GEORGE: I mean . . . it's ridiculous. . . .

MARTHA: Well, it's *done!*

GEORGE (*resigned and exasperated*): All right. Well . . . where are they? If we've got guests, where are they?

MARTHA: They'll be here soon.

GEORGE: What did they do . . . go home and get some sleep first, or something?

MARTHA: They'll *be* here!

GEORGE: I wish you'd *tell* me about something sometime. . . . I wish you'd stop *springing* things on me all the time.

MARTHA: I don't *spring* things on you all the time.

GEORGE: Yes, you do . . . you really do . . . you're always *springing* things on me.

MARTHA (*friendly-patronizing*): Oh, George!

GEORGE: Always.

MARTHA: Poor Georgie-Porgie, put-upon pie (*As he sulks.*) Awwwwww . . . what are you doing? Are you sulking? Hunh? Let me see . . . are you sulking? Is that what you're doing?

GEORGE (*very quietly*): Never mind, Martha. . . .

MARTHA: AWWWWWWWWWW!

GEORGE: Just don't bother yourself. . . .

MARTHA: AWWWWWWWWWW! (*No reaction.*) Hey! (*No reaction.*) HEY!

(GEORGE *looks at her, put-upon.*)

Hey. (*She sings.*) Who's afraid of Virginia Woolf,
Virginia Woolf,
Virginia Woolf. . . .

Ha, ha, ha, HA! (*No reaction.*) What's the matter . . . didn't you think that was funny? Hunh? (*Defiantly.*) I thought it was a scream . . . a real scream. You didn't like it, hunh?

GEORGE: It was all right, Martha. . . .

MARTHA: You laughed your head off when you heard it at the party.

GEORGE: I smiled. I didn't laugh my head off . . . I smiled, you know? . . . it was all right.

MARTHA (*gazing into her drink*): You laughed your goddamn head off.

GEORGE: It was all right. . . .

MARTHA (*ugly*): It was a scream!

GEORGE (*patiently*): It was very funny; yes.

MARTHA (*after a moment's consideration*): You make me puke!

GEORGE: What?

MARTHA: Uh . . . you make me puke!

GEORGE (*thinks about it . . . then . . .*): That wasn't a very nice thing to say, Martha.

MARTHA: That wasn't *what?*

GEORGE: . . . a very nice thing to say.

MARTHA: I like your anger. I think that's what I like about you most . . . your anger. You're such a . . . such a simp! You don't even have the . . . the what? . . .

GEORGE: . . . guts? . . .

MARTHA: PHRASEMAKER! (*Pause . . . then they both laugh.*) Hey, put some more ice in my drink, will you? You never put any ice in my drink. Why is that, hunh?

GEORGE (*takes her drink*): I always put ice in your drink. You eat it, that's all. It's that habit you have . . . chewing your ice cubes . . . like a cocker spaniel. You'll crack your big teeth.

MARTHA: THEY'RE MY BIG TEETH!

GEORGE: Some of them . . . some of them.

MARTHA: I've got more teeth than you've got.

GEORGE: Two more.

MARTHA: Well, two more's a lot more.

GEORGE: I suppose it is. I suppose it's pretty remarkable . . . considering how old you are.

MARTHA: YOU CUT THAT OUT! (*Pause.*) You're not so young yourself.

GEORGE (*with boyish pleasure . . . a chant*): I'm six years younger than you are. . . . I always have been and I always will be.

MARTHA (*glumly*): Well . . . you're going bald.

GEORGE: So are you. (*Pause . . . they both laugh.*) Hello, honey.

MARTHA: Hello. C'mon over here and give your Mommy a big sloppy kiss.

GEORGE: . . . oh, now. . . .

MARTHA: I WANT A BIG SLOPPY KISS!

GEORGE (*preoccupied*): I don't *want* to kiss you, Martha. Where *are* these people? Where are these *people* you invited over?

MARTHA: They stayed on to talk to Daddy. . . . They'll be here. . . . *Why* don't you want to kiss me?

GEORGE (*too matter-of-fact*): Well, dear, if I kissed you I'd get all excited . . . I'd get beside myself, and I'd take you, by force, right here on the living room rug, and then our little guests would walk in, and . . . well, just think what your father would say about *that.*

MARTHA: You pig!

GEORGE (*haughtily*): Oink! Oink!

MARTHA: Ha, ha, ha, HA! Make me another drink . . . lover.

GEORGE (*taking her glass*): My God, you can swill it down, can't you?

MARTHA (*imitating a tiny child*): I'm firsty.

GEORGE: Jesus!

MARTHA (*swinging around*): Look, sweetheart, I can drink you under any goddamn table you want . . . so don't worry about me!

GEORGE: Martha, I gave you the prize years ago. . . . There isn't an abomination award going that you. . . .

MARTHA: I swear . . . if you existed I'd divorce you. . . .

GEORGE: Well, just stay on your feet, that's all. . . . These people are your guests, you know, and. . . .

MARTHA: I can't even see you . . . I haven't been able to see you for years. . . .

GEORGE: . . . if you pass out, or throw up, or something . . .

MARTHA: . . . I mean, you're a blank, a cipher. . . .

GEORGE: . . . and try to keep your clothes on, too. There aren't many more sickening sights than you with a couple of drinks in you and your skirt up over your head, you know. . . .

MARTHA: . . . a zero. . . .

GEORGE: . . . your *heads,* I should say. . . .

(*The front doorbell chimes.*)

MARTHA: Party! Party!

GEORGE (*murderously*): I'm really looking forward to this, Martha. . . .

MARTHA (*same*): Go answer the door.
GEORGE (*not moving*): You answer it.
MARTHA: Get to that door, you. (*He does not move.*) I'll fix you, you. . . .
GEORGE (*fake-spits*): . . . to you. . . .

(*Door chime again.*)

MARTHA (*shouting . . . to the door*): C'MON IN! (*To* GEORGE, *between her teeth.*) I said, get over there!
GEORGE (*moves a little toward the door, smiling slightly*): All right, love . . . whatever love wants. (*Stops.*) Just don't start on the bit, that's all.
MARTHA: The bit? The bit? What kind of language is that? What are you talking about?
GEORGE: The bit. Just don't start in on the bit.
MARTHA: You imitating one of your students, for God's sake? What are you trying to do? WHAT BIT?
GEORGE: Just don't start in on the bit about the kid, that's all.
MARTHA: What do you take me for?
GEORGE: Much too much.
MARTHA (*really angered*): Yeah? Well, I'll start in on the kid if I want to.
GEORGE: Just leave the kid out of this.
MARTHA (*threatening*): He's mine as much as he is yours. I'll talk about him if I want to.
GEORGE: I'd advise against it, Martha.
MARTHA: Well, good for you. (*Knock.*) C'mon in. Get over there and open the door!
GEORGE: You've been advised.
MARTHA: Yeah . . . sure. Get over there!
GEORGE (*moving toward the door*): All right, love . . . whatever love wants. Isn't it nice the way some people have manners, though, even in this day and age? Isn't it nice that some people won't just come breaking into other people's houses even if they *do* hear some sub-human monster yowling at 'em from inside . . . ?
MARTHA: SCREW YOU!

(*Simultaneously with* MARTHA*'s last remark,* GEORGE *flings open the front door.* HONEY *and* NICK *are framed in the entrance. There is a brief silence, then. . . .*)

GEORGE (*ostensibly a pleased recognition of* HONEY *and* NICK, *but really satisfaction at having* MARTHA*'s explosion overheard*): Ahhhhhhhhh!
MARTHA (*a little too loud . . . to cover*): HI! Hi, there . . . c'mon in!
HONEY *and* NICK (*ad lib*): Hello, here we are . . . hi . . . *etc.*
GEORGE (*very matter-of-factly*): You must be our little guests.
MARTHA: Ha, ha, ha, HA! Just ignore old sour-puss over there. C'mon in, kids . . . give your coats and stuff to sour-puss.

NICK (*without expression*): Well, now, perhaps we shouldn't have come....

HONEY: Yes . . . it *is* late, and....

MARTHA: Late! Are you kidding? Throw your stuff down anywhere and c'mon in.

GEORGE (*vaguely . . . walking away*): Anywhere . . . furniture, floor . . . doesn't make any difference around this place.

NICK (*to* HONEY): I told you we shouldn't have come.

MARTHA (*stentorian*): I said c'mon in! Now c'mon!

HONEY (*giggling a little as she and* NICK *advance*): Oh, dear.

GEORGE (*imitating* HONEY'*s giggle*): Hee, hee, hee, hee.

MARTHA (*swinging on* GEORGE): Look, muckmouth . . . you cut that out!

GEORGE (*innocence and hurt*): Martha! (*To* HONEY *and* NICK.) Martha's a devil with language; she really is.

MARTHA: Hey, *kids*... sit down.

HONEY (*as she sits*): Oh, isn't this lovely!

NICK (*perfunctorily*): Yes indeed . . . very handsome.

MARTHA: Well, thanks.

NICK (*indicating the abstract painting*): Who . . . who did the . . . ?

MARTHA: That? Oh, that's by....

GEORGE: . . . some Greek with a mustache Martha attacked one night in....

HONEY (*to save the situation*): Oh, ho, ho, ho, HO.

NICK: It's got a . . . a....

GEORGE: A quiet intensity?

NICK: Well, no . . . a....

GEORGE: Oh. (*Pause.*) Well, then, a certain noisy relaxed quality, maybe?

NICK (*knows what* GEORGE *is doing, but stays grimly, cooly polite*): No. What I meant was....

GEORGE: How about . . . uh . . . a quietly noisy relaxed intensity.

HONEY: Dear! You're being joshed.

NICK (*cold*): I'm aware of that.

(*A brief, awkward silence.*)

GEORGE (*truly*): I *am* sorry.

(NICK *nods condescending forgiveness.*)

GEORGE: What it is, actually, is it's a pictorial representation of the order of Martha's mind.

MARTHA: Ha, ha, ha, HA! Make the kids a drink, George. What do you want, kids? What do you want to drink, hunh?

NICK: Honey? What would you like?

HONEY: I don't know, dear . . . A little brandy, maybe. "Never mix – never worry." (*She giggles.*)

GEORGE: Brandy? Just brandy? Simple; simple. (*Moves to the portable bar.*) What about you . . . uh....

NICK: Bourbon on the rocks, if you don't mind.

GEORGE (*as he makes drinks*): Mind? No, I don't mind. I don't think I mind. Martha? Rubbing alcohol for you?

MARTHA: Sure. "Never mix — never worry."

GEORGE: Martha's tastes in liquor have come down . . . simplified over the years . . . crystallized. Back when I was courting Martha — well, I don't know if that's exactly the right word for it — but back when I was courting Martha. . . .

MARTHA (*cheerfully*): Screw, sweetie!

GEORGE (*returning with* HONEY *and* NICK*'s drinks*): At any rate, back when I was courting Martha, she'd order the damnedest things! You wouldn't believe it! We'd go into a bar . . . you know, a *bar* . . . a whiskey, beer, and bourbon *bar* . . . and what she'd do would be, she'd screw up her face, think real hard, and come up with . . . brandy Alexanders, crème de cacao frappés, gimlets, flaming punch bowls . . . seven-layer liqueur things.

MARTHA: They were good . . . I liked them.

GEORGE: Real lady-like little drinkies.

MARTHA: Hey, where's my rubbing alcohol?

GEORGE (*returning to the portable bar*): But the years have brought to Martha a sense of essentials . . . the knowledge that cream is for coffee, lime juice for pies . . . and alcohol (*brings* MARTHA *her drink*) pure and simple . . . here you are, angel . . . for the pure and simple. (*Raises his glass.*) For the mind's blind eye, the heart's ease, and the liver's craw. Down the hatch, all.

MARTHA (*to them all*): Cheers, dears. (*They all drink.*) You have a poetic nature, George . . . a Dylan Thomas-y quality that gets me right where I live.

GEORGE: Vulgar girl! With guests here!

MARTHA: Ha, ha, ha, HA! (*To* HONEY *and* NICK.) Hey; hey!

(*Sings, conducts with her drink in her hand.* HONEY *joins in toward the end.*)

Who's afraid of Virginia Woolf,
Virginia Woolf,
Virginia Woolf,
Who's afraid of Virginia Woolf. . . .

(MARTHA *and* HONEY *laugh;* NICK *smiles.*)

HONEY: Oh, wasn't that funny? That was so funny. . . .

NICK (*snapping to*): Yes . . . yes, it was.

MARTHA: I thought I'd bust a gut; I really did. . . . I really thought I'd bust a gut laughing. George didn't like it. . . . George didn't think it was funny at all.

GEORGE: Lord, Martha, do we have to go through this again?

MARTHA: I'm trying to shame you into a sense of humor, angel, that's all.

GEORGE (*over-patiently, to* HONEY *and* NICK): Martha didn't think I laughed loud enough. Martha thinks that unless . . . as she demurely puts it . . . that unless you "bust a gut" you aren't amused. You know? Unless you carry on like a hyena you aren't having any fun.

HONEY: Well, I certainly had fun . . . it was a *wonderful* party.

NICK (*attempting enthusiasm*): Yes . . . it certainly was.

HONEY (*to* MARTHA): And your father! Oh! He is so marvelous!

NICK (*as above*): Yes . . . yes, he is.

HONEY: Oh, I tell you.

MARTHA (*genuinely proud*): He's quite a guy, isn't he? Quite a guy.

GEORGE (*at* NICK): And you'd better believe it!

HONEY (*admonishing* GEORGE): Ohhhhhhhhh! He's a wonderful man.

GEORGE: I'm not trying to tear him down. He's a God, we all know that.

MARTHA: You lay off my father!

GEORGE: Yes, love. (*To* NICK.) All I mean is . . . when you've had as many of these faculty parties as I have. . . .

NICK (*killing the attempted rapport*): I rather appreciated it. I mean, aside from enjoying it, I appreciated it. You know, when you're new at a place. . . .

(GEORGE *eyes him suspiciously.*)

Meeting everyone, getting introduced around . . . getting to know some of the men. . . . When I was teaching in Kansas. . . .

HONEY: You won't believe it, but we had to make our way all by *ourselves* . . . isn't that right, dear?

NICK: Yes, it is. . . . We. . . .

HONEY: . . . We had to make our own way. . . . I had to go up to wives . . . in the library, or at the supermarket . . . and say, "Hello, I'm new here . . . you must be Mrs. So-and-so, Doctor So-and-so's wife." It really wasn't very nice at all.

MARTHA: Well, *Daddy* knows how to run things.

NICK (*not enough enthusiasm*): He's a remarkable man.

MARTHA: You bet your sweet life.

GEORGE (*to* NICK . . . *a confidence, but not whispered*): Let me tell you a secret, baby. There are easier things in the world, if you happen to be teaching at a university, there are easier things than being married to the daughter of the president of that university. There are easier things in this world.

MARTHA (*loud . . . to no one in particular*): It *should* be an extraordinary opportunity . . . for *some* men it would be the chance of a lifetime!

GEORGE (*to* NICK . . . *a solemn wink*): There are, believe me, easier things in this world.

NICK: Well, I can understand how it might make for some . . . awkwardness, perhaps . . . conceivably, but. . . .

MARTHA: *Some* men would give their right arm for the chance!
GEORGE (*quietly*): Alas, Martha, in reality it works out that the sacrifice is usually of a somewhat more private portion of the anatomy.
MARTHA (*a snarl of dismissal and contempt*): NYYYYAAAAHHHHH!
HONEY (*rising quickly*): I wonder if you could show me where the . . . (*Her voice trails off.*)
GEORGE (*to* MARTHA, *indicating* HONEY): Martha. . . .
NICK (*to* HONEY): Are you all right?
HONEY: Of course, dear. I want to . . . put some powder on my nose.
GEORGE (*as* MARTHA *is not getting up*): Martha, won't you show her where we keep the . . . euphemism?
MARTHA: Hm? What? Oh! Sure! (*Rises.*) I'm sorry, c'mon. I want to show you the house.
HONEY: I think I'd like to. . . .
MARTHA: . . . wash up? Sure . . . c'mon with me. (*Takes* HONEY *by the arm. To the men.*) You two do some men talk for a while.
HONEY (*to* NICK): We'll be back, dear.
MARTHA (*to* GEORGE): Honestly, George, you burn me up!
GEORGE (*happily*): All right.
MARTHA: You really do, George.
GEORGE: O.K. Martha . . . O.K. Just . . . trot along.
MARTHA: You really do.
GEORGE: Just don't shoot your mouth off . . . about . . . you-know-what.
MARTHA (*surprisingly vehement*): I'll talk about any goddamn thing I want to, George!
GEORGE: O.K. O.K. Vanish.
MARTHA: Any goddamn thing I want to! (*Practically dragging* HONEY *out with her.*) C'mon. . . .
GEORGE: Vanish. (*The women have gone.*) So? What'll it be?
NICK: Oh, I don't know . . . I'll stick to bourbon, I guess.
GEORGE (*takes* NICK'*s glass, goes to portable bar*): That what you were drinking over at Parnassus?
NICK: Over at . . . ?
GEORGE: Parnassus.
NICK: I don't understand. . . .
GEORGE: Skip it. (*Hands him his drink.*) One bourbon.
NICK: Thanks.
GEORGE: It's just a private joke between li'l ol' Martha and me. (*They sit.*) So? (*Pause.*) So . . . you're in the math department, eh?
NICK: No . . . uh, no.
GEORGE: Martha said you were. I think that's what she said. (*Not too friendly.*) What made you decide to be a teacher?
NICK: Oh . . . well, the same things that . . . uh . . . motivated you, I imagine.
GEORGE: What were they?
NICK (*formal*): Pardon?

GEORGE: I said, what were they? What were the things that motivated me?

NICK (*laughing uneasily*): Well . . . I'm sure I don't know.

GEORGE: You just finished saying that the things that motivated you were the same things that motivated me.

NICK (*with a little pique*): I said I *imagined* they were.

GEORGE: Oh. (*Off-hand.*) Did you? (*Pause.*) Well . . . (*Pause.*) You like it here?

NICK (*looking about the room*): Yes . . . it's . . . it's fine.

GEORGE: I mean the University.

NICK: Oh. . . . I thought you meant. . . .

GEORGE: Yes . . . I can see you did. (*Pause.*) I meant the University.

NICK: Well, I . . . I like it . . . fine (*As George just stares at him.*) Just fine. (*Same.*) You . . . you've been here quite a long time, haven't you?

GEORGE (*absently, as if he had not heard*): What? Oh . . . yes. Ever since I married . . . uh, What's-her-name . . . uh, Martha. Even before that. (*Pause.*) Forever. (*To himself.*) Dashed hopes, and good intentions. Good, better, best, bested. (*Back to* NICK.) How do you like that for a declension, young man? Eh?

NICK: Sir, I'm sorry if we. . . .

GEORGE (*with an edge in his voice*): You didn't answer my question.

NICK: Sir?

GEORGE: Don't you condescend to me! (*Toying with him.*) I asked how you liked that for a declension: Good; better; best; bested. Hm? Well?

NICK (*with some distaste*): I really don't know what to say.

GEORGE (*feigned incredulousness*): You really don't know what to *say?*

NICK (*snapping it out*): All right . . . what do you want me to say? Do you want me to say it's funny, so you can contradict me and say it's sad? or do you want me to say it's sad so you can turn around and say no, it's funny. You can play that damn little game any way you want to, you know!

GEORGE (*feigned awe*): Very good! Very good!

NICK (*even angrier than before*): And when my wife comes back, I think we'll just. . . .

GEORGE (*sincere*): Now, now . . . calm down, my boy. Just . . . calm . . . down. (*Pause.*) All right? (*Pause.*) You want another drink? Here, give me your glass.

NICK: I still have one. I *do* think that when my wife comes downstairs. . . .

GEORGE: Here . . . I'll freshen it. Give me your glass. (*Takes it.*)

NICK: What I mean is . . . you two . . . you and your wife . . . seem to be having *some* sort of a. . . .

GEORGE: Martha and I are having . . . nothing. Martha and I are merely . . . exercising . . . that's all . . . we're merely walking what's left of our wits. Don't pay any attention to it.

NICK (*undecided*): Still. . . .

GEORGE (*an abrupt change of pace*): Well, now . . . let's sit down and talk, hunh?

NICK (*cool again*): It's just that I don't like to . . . become involved . . . (*an afterthought*) uh . . . in other people's affairs.

GEORGE (*comforting a child*): Well, you'll get over that . . . small college and all. Musical beds is the faculty sport around here.

NICK: Sir?

GEORGE: I said, musical beds is the faculty. . . . Never mind. I wish you wouldn't go "Sir" like that . . . not with the question mark at the end of it. You know? Sir? I know it's meant to be a sign of respect for your (*winces*) elders . . . but . . . uh . . . the way you do it. . . . Uh . . . Sir? . . . Madam?

NICK (*with a small, noncommittal smile*): No disrespect intended.

GEORGE: How old *are* you?

NICK: Twenty-eight.

GEORGE: I'm forty something. (*Waits for reaction . . . gets none.*) Aren't you surprised? I mean . . . don't I look older? Doesn't this . . . *gray* quality suggest the fifties? Don't I sort of fade into backgrounds . . . get lost in the cigarette smoke? Hunh?

NICK (*looking around for an ash tray*): I think you look . . . fine.

GEORGE: I've always been lean . . . I haven't put on five pounds since I was your age. I don't have a paunch, either. . . . What I've got . . . I've got this little distension just below the belt . . . but it's hard . . . It's not soft flesh. I use the handball courts. How much do *you* weigh?

NICK: I. . . .

GEORGE: Hundred and fifty-five, sixty . . . something like that? Do you play handball?

NICK: Well, yes . . . no . . . I mean, not very well.

GEORGE: Well, then . . . we shall play some time. Martha is a hundred and eight . . . years *old*. She weighs somewhat more than that. How old is *your* wife?

NICK (*a little bewildered*): She's twenty-six.

GEORGE: Martha is a remarkable woman. I would imagine she weighs around a hundred and ten.

NICK: Your . . . wife . . . weighs . . . ?

GEORGE: No, no, my boy. Yours! *Your* wife. My wife is Martha.

NICK: Yes . . . I know.

GEORGE: If you were married to Martha you would know what it means. (*Pause.*) But then, if I were married to your wife I would know what that means, too . . . wouldn't I?

NICK (*after a pause*): Yes.

GEORGE: Martha says you're in the Math Department, or something.

NICK (*as if for the hundredth time*): No . . . I'm not.

GEORGE: Martha is seldom mistaken . . . maybe you *should* be in the Math Department, or something.

NICK: I'm a biologist. I'm in the Biology Department.

GEORGE (*after a pause*): Oh. (*Then, as if remembering something.*) OH!

NICK: Sir?

GEORGE: You're the one! You're the one's going to make all that trouble . . . making everyone the same, rearranging the chromozones, or whatever it it. Isn't that right?

NICK (*with that small smile*): Not exactly: chromo*somes.*

GEORGE: I'm very mistrustful. Do you believe . . . (*shifting in his chair*) . . . do you believe that people learn nothing from history? Not that there is nothing to learn, mind you, but that people learn nothing? I am in the History Department.

NICK: Well. . . .

GEORGE: I am a Doctor. A.B. . . . M.A. . . . PH.D. . . . ABMAPHID! Abmaphid has been variously described as a wasting disease of the frontal lobes, and as a wonder drug. It is actually both. I'm really very mistrustful. Biology, hunh?

(NICK *does not answer . . . nods . . . looks.*)

I read somewhere that science fiction is really not fiction at all . . . that you people are rearranging my genes, so that everyone will be like everyone else. Now, I won't have that! It would be a . . . shame. I mean . . . look at me! Is it really such a good idea . . . if everyone was forty something and looked fifty-five? You didn't answer my question about history.

NICK: This genetic business you're talking about . . .

GEORGE: Oh, that. (*Dismisses it with a wave of his hand.*) That's very upsetting . . . very . . . disappointing. But history is a great deal more . . . disappointing. I am in the History Department.

NICK: Yes . . . you told me.

GEORGE: I know I told you. . . . I shall probably tell you several more times. Martha tells me often, that I am *in* the History Department . . . as opposed to *being* the History Department . . . in the sense of *running* the History Department. I do not run the History Department.

NICK: Well, I don't run the Biology Department.

GEORGE: You're twenty-one!

NICK: Twenty-eight.

GEORGE: Twenty-eight! Perhaps when you're forty something and look fifty-five, you will run the History Department. . . .

NICK: . . . Biology. . . .

GEORGE: . . . the Biology Department. I *did* run the History Department, for four years, during the war, but that was because everybody was away. Then . . . everybody came back . . . because nobody got killed. That's New England for you. Isn't that amazing? Not one single man in this whole place got his head shot off. That's pretty irrational. (*Broods.*) Your wife *doesn't* have any hips . . . has she . . . does she?

NICK: What?

GEORGE: I don't mean to suggest that I'm hip-happy. . . . I'm not one of those thirty-six, twenty-two, seventy-eight men. Nosiree . . . not me. Everything in proportion. I was implying that your wife is . . . slim-hipped.

NICK: Yes . . . she is.

GEORGE (*looking at the ceiling*): What are they *doing* up there? I assume that's where they are.

NICK (*false heartiness*): You know women.

GEORGE (*gives* NICK *a long stare, of feigned incredulity . . . then his attention moves*): Not one son-of-a-bitch got killed. Of course, nobody bombed Washington. No . . . that's not fair. You have any kids?

NICK: Uh . . . no . . . not yet. (*Pause.*) You?

GEORGE (*a kind of challenge*): That's for me to know and you to find out.

NICK: Indeed?

GEORGE: No kids, hunh?

NICK: Not yet.

GEORGE: People do . . . uh . . . have kids. That's what I meant about history. You people are going to make them in test tubes, aren't you? You biologists. Babies. Then the rest of us . . . them as wants to . . . can screw to their heart's content. What will happen to the tax deduction? Has anyone figured that out yet?

(NICK, *who can think of nothing better to do, laughs mildly.*)

But you *are* going to have kids . . . anyway. In spite of history.

NICK (*hedging*): *Yes* . . . certainly. We . . . want to wait . . . a little . . . until we're settled.

GEORGE: And this . . . (*with a handsweep taking in not only the room, the house, but the whole countryside*) . . . this is your heart's content — Illyria . . . Penguin Island . . . Gomorrah. . . . You think you're going to be happy here in New Carthage, eh?

NICK (*a little defensively*): I hope we'll stay here.

GEORGE: And every definition has its boundaries, eh? Well, it isn't a bad college, I guess. I mean . . . it'll do. It isn't M.I.T. . . . it isn't U.C.L.A. . . . it isn't the Sorbonne . . . or Moscow U. either, for that matter.

NICK: I don't mean . . . forever.

GEORGE: Well, don't you let that get bandied about. The old man wouldn't like it. Martha's father expects loyalty and devotion out of his . . . staff. I was going to use another word. Martha's father expects his . . . staff . . . to cling to the walls of this place, like the ivy . . . to come here and grow old . . . to fall in the line of service. One man, a professor of Latin and Elocution, actually fell in the cafeteria line, one lunch. He was buried, as many of us have been, and as many more of us will be, under the shrubbery around the chapel. It is said . . . and I have no reason to doubt it . . . that we make excellent fertilizer. But the old man is not going to be buried under the shrubbery . . . the old man is not going to die. Martha's father has the staying power of one of those Micronesian tortoises. There are rumors . . . which you must not breathe in front of Martha, for she foams at the mouth . . . that the old man, her father, is over two hundred years old. There is probably an irony involved in this, but I am not drunk enough to figure out what it is. How many kids you going to have?

NICK: I . . . I don't know. . . . My wife is. . . .

GEORGE: Slim-hipped. (*Rises.*) Have a drink.

NICK: Yes:

GEORGE: MARTHA! (*No answer.*) DAMN IT! (*To* NICK.) You asked me if I knew women. . . . Well, one of the things I do *not* know about them is what they talk about while the men are talking. (*Vaguely.*) I must find out some time.

MARTHA'S VOICE: WHADD'YA WANT?

GEORGE (*to* NICK): Isn't that a wonderful sound? What I mean is . . . what do you think they really *talk* about . . . or don't you care?

NICK: Themselves, I would imagine.

MARTHA'S VOICE: GEORGE?

GEORGE (*to* NICK): Do you find women . . . puzzling?

NICK: Well . . . yes and no.

GEORGE (*with a knowing nod*): Unh-hunh. (*Moves toward the hall, almost bumps into* HONEY, *re-entering.*) Oh! Well, here's one of you, at least.

(HONEY *moves toward* NICK. GEORGE *goes to the hall.*)

HONEY (*to* GEORGE): She'll be right down. (*To* NICK.) You must see this house, dear . . . this is such a wonderful old house.

NICK: Yes, I. . . .

GEORGE: MARTHA!

MARTHA'S VOICE: FOR CHRIST'S SAKE, HANG ON A MINUTE, WILL YOU?

HONEY (*to* GEORGE): She'll be right down . . . she's changing.

GEORGE (*incredulous*): She's *what?* She's changing?

HONEY: Yes.

GEORGE: Her clothes?

HONEY: Her dress.

GEORGE (*suspicious*): Why?

HONEY (*with a nervous little laugh*): Why, I imagine she wants to be . . . comfortable.

GEORGE (*with a threatening look toward the hall*): Oh she does, does she?

HONEY: Well, heavens, I should think. . . .

GEORGE: YOU DON'T KNOW!

NICK (*as* HONEY *starts*): You feel all right?

HONEY (*reassuring, but with the echo of a whine. A long-practiced tone*): Oh, yes, dear . . . perfectly fine.

GEORGE (*fuming . . . to himself*): So she wants to be comfortable, does she? Well, we'll see about that.

HONEY (*to* GEORGE, *brightly*): I didn't know until just a minute ago that you had a *son*.

GEORGE (*wheeling, as if struck from behind*): WHAT?

HONEY: A son! I hadn't known.

NICK: You to know and me to find out. Well, he must be quite a big. . . .

HONEY: Twenty-one . . . twenty-one tomorrow . . . tomorrow's his birthday.

NICK (*a victorious smile*): Well!

GEORGE (*to* HONEY): She told you about him?

HONEY (*flustered*): Well, *yes*. Well, I mean. . . .

GEORGE (*nailing it down*): She told you about him.

HONEY (*a nervous giggle*): Yes.

GEORGE (*strangely*): You say she's changing?

HONEY: Yes. . . .

GEORGE: And she mentioned . . . ?

HONEY (*cheerful, but a little puzzled*): . . . your son's birthday . . . yes.

GEORGE (*more or less to himself*): O.K., Martha . . . O.K.

NICK: You look pale, Honey. Do you want a . . . ?

HONEY: Yes, dear . . . a little more brandy, maybe. Just a drop.

GEORGE: O.K., Martha.

NICK: May I use the . . . uh . . . bar?

GEORGE: Hm? Oh, yes . . . yes . . . by all means. Drink away . . . you'll need it as the years go on. (*For* MARTHA, *as if she were in the room.*) You goddamn destructive. . . .

HONEY (*to cover*): What time is it, dear?

NICK: Two-thirty.

HONEY: Oh, it's so late . . . we *should* be getting home.

GEORGE (*nastily, but he is so preoccupied he hardly notices his own tone*): For what? You keeping the babysitter up, or something?

NICK (*almost a warning*): I told you we didn't have children.

GEORGE: Hm? (*Realizing.*) Oh, I'm sorry. I wasn't even listening . . . or thinking . . . (*With a flick of his hand.*) . . . whichever one applies.

NICK (*softly, to* HONEY): We'll go in a little while.

GEORGE (*driving*): Oh no, now . . . you mustn't. Martha is changing . . . and Martha is not changing for *me*. Martha hasn't changed for *me* in years. If Martha is changing, it means we'll be here for . . . days. You are being accorded an honor, and you must not forget that Martha is the daughter of our beloved boss. She is his . . . right ball, you might say.

NICK: You might not understand this . . . but I wish you wouldn't talk that way in front of my wife.

HONEY: Oh, now. . . .

GEORGE (*incredulous*): Really? Well, you're quite right. . . . We'll leave that sort of talk to Martha.

MARTHA (*entering*): What sort of talk?

(MARTHA *has changed her clothes, and she looks, now, more comfortable and . . . and this is most important . . . most voluptuous.*)

GEORGE: There you are, my pet.
NICK (*impressed; rising*): Well, now. . . .
GEORGE: Why, Martha . . . your Sunday chapel dress!
HONEY (*slightly disapproving*): Oh, that's most attractive.
MARTHA (*showing off*): You like it? Good! (*To* GEORGE.) What the hell do you mean screaming up the stairs at me like that?
GEORGE: We got lonely, darling . . . we got lonely for the soft purr of your little voice.
MARTHA (*deciding not to rise to it*): Oh. Well, then, you just trot over to the barie-poo. . . .
GEORGE (*taking the tone from her*): . . . and make your little mommy a gweat big dwink.
MARTHA (*giggles*): That's right. (*To* NICK.) Well, did you two have a nice little talk? You men solve the problems of the world, as usual?
NICK: Well, no, we . . .
GEORGE (*quickly*): What we did, actually, if you really want to know, what we did actually is try to figure out what you two were talking about.

(HONEY *giggles,* MARTHA *laughs.*)

MARTHA (*to* HONEY): Aren't they something? Aren't these . . . (*cheerfully disdainful*) . . . *men* the absolute end? (*To* GEORGE.) Why didn't you sneak upstairs and listen in?
GEORGE: Oh, I wouldn't have *listened,* Martha. . . . I would have *peeked.*

(HONEY *giggles,* MARTHA *laughs.*)

NICK (*to* GEORGE, *with false heartiness*): It's a conspiracy.
GEORGE: And now we'll never know. Shucks!
MARTHA (*to* NICK, *as* HONEY *beams*): Hey, you must be quite a boy, getting your Masters when you were . . . what? . . . twelve? You hear that, George?
NICK: Twelve-and-a-half, actually. No, nineteen really. (*To* HONEY.) Honey, you needn't have mentioned that. It. . . .
HONEY: Ohhhh . . . I'm *proud* of you. . . .
GEORGE (*seriously, if sadly*): That's very . . . impressive.
MARTHA (*aggressively*): You're damned right!
GEORGE (*between his teeth*): I said I was impressed, Martha. I'm beside myself with jealousy. What do you want me to do, throw up? (*To* NICK.) That really is very impressive. (*To* HONEY.) You should be right proud.
HONEY (*coy*): Oh, he's a pretty nice fella.
GEORGE (*to* NICK): I wouldn't be surprised if you *did* take over the History Department one of these days.

NICK: The Biology Department.

GEORGE: The *Biology* Department . . . of course. I seem preoccupied with history. Oh! What a remark. (*He strikes a pose, his hand over his heart, his head raised, his voice stentorian.*) "I am preoccupied with history."

MARTHA (*as* HONEY *and* NICK *chuckle*): Ha, ha, ha, HA!

GEORGE (*with some disgust*): I think I'll make *myself* a drink.

MARTHA: George is not preoccupied with *history*. . . . George is preoccupied with the *History Department*. George is preoccupied with the History Department because. . . .

GEORGE: . . . because he is *not* the History Department, but is only *in* the History Department. We know, Martha . . . we went all through it while you were upstairs . . . getting up. There's no need to go through it again.

MARTHA: That's right, baby . . . keep it clean. (*To the others.*) George is bogged down in the History Department. He's an old bog in the History Department, that's what George is. A bog. . . . A fen. . . . A G.D. swamp. Ha, ha, ha, HA! A SWAMP! Hey, swamp! Hey SWAMPY!

GEORGE (*with a great effort controls himself . . . then, as if she had said nothing more than "George, dear". . . .* ): Yes, Martha? Can I get you something?

MARTHA (*amused at his game*): Well . . . uh . . . sure, you can light my cigarette, if you're of a mind to.

GEORGE (*considers, then moves off*): No . . . there are limits. I mean, man can put up with only so much without he descends a rung or two on the old evolutionary ladder . . . (*Now a quick aside to* NICK.) . . . which is up your line . . . (*Then back to* MARTHA.) . . . sinks, Martha, and it's a funny ladder . . . you can't reverse yourself . . . start back up once you're descending.

(MARTHA *blows him an arrogant kiss.*)

Now . . . I'll hold your hand when it's dark and you're afraid of the bogey man, and I'll tote your gin bottles out after midnight, so no one'll see . . . but I will not light your cigarette. And that, as they say, is that.

(*Brief silence.*)

MARTHA (*under her breath*): Jesus! (*Then, immediately, to* NICK.) Hey, you played football, hunh?

HONEY (*as* NICK *seems sunk in thought*): Dear. . . .

NICK: Oh! Oh, yes . . . I was a . . . quarterback . . . but I was much more . . . adept . . . at boxing, really.

MARTHA (*with great enthusiasm*): BOXING! You hear that, George?

GEORGE (*resignedly*): Yes, Martha.

MARTHA (*to* NICK, *with peculiar intensity and enthusiasm*): You musta been pretty good at it . . . I mean, you don't look like you got hit in the face at all.

HONEY (*proudly*): He was intercollegiate state middleweight champion.

NICK (*embarrassed*): Honey. . . .

HONEY: Well, you were.

MARTHA: You look like you still got a pretty good body *now*, too . . . is that right? Have you?

GEORGE (*intensely*): Martha . . . decency forbids. . . .

MARTHA (*to* GEORGE . . . *still staring at* NICK, *though*): SHUT UP! (*Now, back to* NICK.) Well, have you? Have you kept your body?

NICK (*unselfconscious . . . almost encouraging her*): It's still pretty good. I work out.

MARTHA (*with a half-smile*): Do you!

NICK: Yeah.

HONEY: Oh, yes . . . he has a very . . . firm body.

MARTHA (*still with that smile . . . a private communication with* NICK): Have you! Oh, I think that's very nice.

NICK (*narcissistic, but not directly for* MARTHA): Well, you never know . . . (*shrugs*) . . . you know . . . once you have it. . . .

MARTHA: . . . you never know when it's going to come in handy.

NICK: I was going to say . . . why give it up until you have to.

MARTHA: I couldn't agree with you more.

(*They both smile, and there is a rapport of some unformed sort established.*)

I couldn't agree with you more.

GEORGE: Martha, your obscenity is more than. . . .

MARTHA: George, here, doesn't cotton much to body talk . . . do you sweetheart? (*No reply.*) George isn't too happy when we get to muscle. You know . . . flat bellies, pectorals. . . .

GEORGE (*to* HONEY): Would you like to take a walk around the garden?

HONEY (*chiding*): Oh, now. . . .

GEORGE (*incredulous*): You're amused? (*Shrugs.*) All right.

MARTHA: Paunchy over there isn't too happy when the conversation moves to muscle. How much do you weigh?

NICK: A hundred and fifty-five, a hundred and. . . .

MARTHA: Still at the old middleweight limit, eh? That's pretty good. (*Swings around.*) Hey George, tell 'em about the boxing match *we* had.

GEORGE (*slamming his drink down, moving toward the hall*): Christ!

MARTHA: George! Tell 'em about it!

GEORGE (*with a sick look on his face*): You tell them, Martha. You're good at it. (*Exits.*)

HONEY: Is he . . . all right?

MARTHA (*laughs*): Him? Oh sure. George and I had this boxing match . . . Oh, Lord, twenty years ago . . . a couple of years after we were married.

NICK: A boxing match? The two of you?

HONEY: Really?

MARTHA: Yup . . . the two of us . . . really.

HONEY (*with a little shivery giggle of anticipation*): I can't imagine it.

MARTHA: Well, like I say, it was twenty years ago, and it wasn't in a ring, or anything like that, you know what I mean. It was wartime, and Daddy was on this physical fitness kick . . . Daddy's always admired physical fitness . . . says a man is only part brain . . . he has a body, too, and it's his responsibility to keep both of them up . . . you know?

NICK: Unh-hunh.

MARTHA: Says the brain can't work unless the body's working, too.

NICK: Well, that's not exactly so. . . .

MARTHA: Well, maybe that *isn't* what he says . . . something like it. *But* . . . it was wartime, and Daddy got the idea all the men should learn how to box . . . self-defense. I suppose the idea was if the Germans landed on the coast, or something, the whole faculty'd go out and punch 'em to death. . . . I don't know.

NICK: It was probably more the principle of the thing.

MARTHA: No kidding. Anyway, so Daddy had a couple of us over one Sunday and we went out in the back, and Daddy put on the gloves himself. Daddy's a strong man. . . . Well, *you* know.

NICK: Yes . . . Yes.

MARTHA: And he asked George to box with him. Aaaaannnnd . . . George didn't *want* to . . . probably something about not wanting to bloody-up his meal ticket. . . .

NICK: Unh-hunh.

MARTHA: . . . Anyway, George said he didn't want to, and Daddy was saying, "Come on, young man . . . what sort of son-in-law *are* you?" . . . and stuff like that.

NICK: Yeah.

MARTHA: So, while this was going on . . . I don't know why I *did* it . . . I got into a pair of gloves myself . . . you know, I didn't lace 'em up, or anything . . . and I snuck up behind George, just kidding, and I yelled "Hey George!" and at the same time I let go sort of a roundhouse right . . . just kidding, you know?

NICK: Unh-hunh.

MARTHA: . . . and George wheeled around real quick, and he caught it right in the jaw . . . POW! (NICK *laughs.*) I hadn't meant it . . . honestly. Anyway . . . POW! Right in the jaw . . . and he was off balance . . . he must have been . . . and he stumbled back a few steps, and then, CRASH, he landed . . . flat . . . in a huckleberry bush!

(NICK *laughs.* HONEY *goes tsk, tsk, tsk, tsk, and shakes her head.*)

It was awful, really. It was funny, but it was awful. (*She thinks, gives a muffled laugh in rueful contemplation of the incident.*) I think it's colored our whole life. Really I do! It's an excuse, anyway.

(GEORGE *enters now, his hands behind his back. No one sees him.*)

It's what he uses for being bogged down, anyway . . . why he hasn't *gone* anywhere.

(GEORGE *advances.* HONEY *sees him.*)

MARTHA: And it was an *accident* . . . a real, goddamn accident!

(GEORGE *takes from behind his back a short-barreled shotgun, and calmly aims it at the back of* MARTHA'*s head.* HONEY *screams . . . rises.* NICK *rises, and, simultaneously,* MARTHA *turns her head to face* GEORGE. GEORGE *pulls the trigger.*)

GEORGE: POW!!!

(*Pop! From the barrel of the gun blossoms a large red and yellow Chinese parasol.* HONEY *screams again, this time less, and mostly from relief and confusion.*)

You're dead! Pow! You're dead!
NICK (*laughing*): Good Lord.

(HONEY *is beside herself.* MARTHA *laughs too . . . almost breaks down, her great laugh booming.* GEORGE *joins in the general laughter and confusion. It dies, eventually.*)

HONEY: Oh! My goodness!
MARTHA (*joyously*): Where'd you get that, you bastard?
NICK (*his hand out for the gun*): Let me see that, will you?

(GEORGE *hands him the gun.*)

HONEY: I've never been so frightened in my life! Never!
GEORGE (*a trifle abstracted*): Oh, I've had it awhile. Did you like that?
MARTHA (*giggling*): You bastard.
HONEY (*wanting attention*): I've *never* been so frightened . . . never.
NICK: This is quite a gadget.
GEORGE (*leaning over* MARTHA): You liked that, did you?
MARTHA: Yeah . . . that was pretty good. (*Softer.*) C'mon . . . give me a kiss.
GEORGE (*indicating* NICK *and* HONEY): Later, sweetie.

(*But* MARTHA *will not be dissuaded. They kiss,* GEORGE *standing, leaning over* MARTHA'*s chair. She takes his hand, places it on her stage-side breast. He breaks away.*)

Oh-ho! That's what you're after, is it? What are we going to have . . . blue games for the guests? Hunh? Hunh?
MARTHA (*angry-hurt*): You . . . prick!
GEORGE (*a Pyrrhic victory*): Everything in its place, Martha . . . everything in its own good time.
MARTHA (*an unspoken epithet*): You. . . .

GEORGE (*over to* NICK, *who still has the gun*): Here, let me show you . . . it goes back in, like this. (*Closes the parasol, reinserts it in the gun.*)

NICK: That's damn clever.

GEORGE (*puts the gun down*): Drinks now! Drinks for all! (*Takes* NICK*'s glass without question . . . goes to* MARTHA.)

MARTHA (*still angry-hurt*): I'm not finished.

HONEY (*as* GEORGE *puts out his hand for her glass*): Oh, I think I need *some*thing.

(*He takes her glass, moves back to the portable bar.*)

NICK: Is that Japanese?

GEORGE: Probably.

HONEY (*to* MARTHA): I was never so frightened in my life. Weren't you frightened? Just for a second?

MARTHA (*smothering her rage at* GEORGE): I don't remember.

HONEY: Ohhhh, now . . . I bet you were.

GEORGE: Did you really think I was going to kill you, Martha?

MARTHA (*dripping contempt*): You? . . . Kill me? . . . That's a laugh.

GEORGE: Well, now, I might . . . some day.

MARTHA: Fat chance.

NICK (*as* GEORGE *hands him his drink*): Where's the john?

GEORGE: Through the hall there . . . and down to your left.

HONEY: Don't you come back with any guns, or anything, now.

NICK (*laughs*): Oh, no.

MARTHA: You don't need any props, do you, baby?

NICK: Unh-unh.

MARTHA (*suggestive*): I'll bet not. No fake Jap gun for you, eh?

NICK (*smiles at* MARTHA. *Then, to* GEORGE, *indicating a side table near the hall*): May I leave my drink here?

GEORGE (*as* NICK *exits without waiting for a reply*): Yeah . . . sure . . . why not? We've got half-filled glasses everywhere in the house, wherever Martha forgets she's left them . . . in the linen closet, on the edge of the bathtub. . . . I even found one in the freezer, once.

MARTHA (*amused in spite of herself*): You did not!

GEORGE: *Yes* I did.

MARTHA (*ibid*): You did *not!*

GEORGE (*giving* HONEY *her brandy*): Yes I *did.* (*To* HONEY.) Brandy doesn't give you a hangover?

HONEY: I never mix. And then, I don't drink very much, either.

GEORGE (*grimaces behind her back*): Oh . . . that's good. Your . . . your husband was telling me all about the . . . chromosomes.

MARTHA (*ugly*): The what?

GEORGE: The chromosomes, Martha . . . the genes, or whatever they are. (*To* HONEY.) You've got quite a . . . terrifying husband.

HONEY (*as if she's being joshed*): Ohhhhhhhhh. . . .

GEORGE: No, really. He's quite terrifying, with his chromosomes, and all.
MARTHA: He's in the Math Department.
GEORGE: No, Martha . . . he's a biologist.
MARTHA (*her voice rising*): He's in the *Math* Department!
HONEY (*timidly*): Uh . . . biology.
MARTHA (*unconvinced*): Are *you sure?*
HONEY (*with a little giggle*): Well, I ought to. (*Then as an afterthought.*) Be.
MARTHA (*grumpy*): I suppose *so.* I don't know who said he was in the Math Department.
GEORGE: You did, Martha.
MARTHA (*by way of irritable explanation*): Well, I can't be expected to remember *everything.* I meet fifteen new teachers and their goddamn wives . . . present company outlawed, of course . . . (HONEY *nods, smiles sillily.*) . . . and I'm supposed to remember *everything.* (*Pause.*) So? He's a biologist. Good for him. Biology's even better. It's less . . . abstruse.
GEORGE: Abstract.
MARTHA: ABSTRUSE! In the sense of recondite. (*Sticks her tongue out at* GEORGE.) Don't you tell me words. Biology's even better. It's . . . right at the *meat* of things.

NICK (*re-enters.*)

You're right at the meat of things, baby.
NICK (*taking his drink from the side table*): Oh?
HONEY (*with that giggle*): They thought you were in the Math Department.
NICK: Well, maybe I ought to be.
MARTHA: You stay right where you are . . . you stay right at the . . . *meat* of things.
GEORGE: You're obsessed with that phrase, Martha. . . . It's ugly.
MARTHA (*ignoring* GEORGE . . . *to* NICK): You stay right there. (*Laughs.*) Hell, you can take over the History Department just as easy from there as anywhere else. God knows, *some*body's going to take over the History Department, *some* day, and it ain't going to be Georgie-boy, there . . . that's for sure. Are ya, swampy . . . are ya, hunh?
GEORGE: In my mind, Martha, you are buried in cement, right up to your neck. (MARTHA *giggles.*) No . . . right up to your nose . . . that's much quieter.
MARTHA (*to* NICK): Georgie-boy, here, says you're terrifying. Why are you terrifying?
NICK (*with a small smile*): I didn't know I was.
HONEY (*a little thickly*): It's because of your chromosomes, dear.
NICK: Oh, the chromosome business. . . .
MARTHA (*to* NICK): What's all this about chromosomes?
NICK: Well, chromosomes are. . . .
MARTHA: I know what chromosomes are, sweetie, I love 'em.
NICK: Oh. . . . Well, then.

GEORGE: Martha eats them . . . for breakfast . . . she sprinkles them on her cereal. (*To* MARTHA, *now*.) It's very simple, Martha, this young man is working on a system whereby chromosomes can be altered . . . well not all by himself – he probably has one or two co-conspirators – the genetic makeup of a sperm cell changed, reordered . . . *to* order, actually . . . for hair and eye color, stature, potency . . . I imagine . . . hairiness, features, health . . . and *mind*. Most important . . . Mind. All imbalances will be corrected, sifted out . . . propensity for various diseases will be gone, longevity assured. We will have a race of men . . . test-tube-bred . . . incubator-born . . . superb and sublime.

MARTHA (*impressed*): Hunh!

HONEY: How exciting!

GEORGE: *But!* Everyone will tend to be rather the same. . . . Alike. Everyone . . . and I'm sure I'm not wrong here . . . will tend to look like this young man *here*.

MARTHA: *That's* not a bad idea.

NICK (*impatient*): All right, now. . . .

GEORGE: It will, on the surface of it, be all rather pretty . . . quite jolly. But of course there will be a dank side to it, too. A certain amount of regulation will be necessary . . . uh . . . for the experiment to succeed. A certain number of sperm tubes will have to be cut.

MARTHA: Hunh! . . .

GEORGE: Millions upon millions of them . . . millions of tiny little slicing operations that will leave just the smallest scar, on the underside of the scrotum (MARTHA *laughs*.) but which will assure the sterility of the imperfect . . . the ugly, the stupid . . . the . . . unfit.

NICK (*grimly*): Now look . . . !

GEORGE: . . . with this, we will have, in time, a race of glorious men.

MARTHA: Hunh!

GEORGE: I suspect we will not have much music, much painting, but we will have a civilization of men, smooth, blond, and right at the middleweight limit.

MARTHA: Awww. . . .

GEORGE: . . . a race of scientists and mathematicians, each dedicated to and working for the greater glory of the supercivilization.

MARTHA: Goody.

GEORGE: There will be a certain . . . loss of liberty, I imagine, as a result of this experiment . . . but diversity will no longer be the goal. Cultures and races will eventually vanish . . . the ants will take over the world.

NICK: Are you finished?

GEORGE (*ignoring him*): And I, naturally, am rather opposed to all this. History, which is my field . . . history, of which I am one of the most famous bogs. . . .

MARTHA: Ha, ha, HA!

GEORGE: . . . will lose its glorious variety and unpredictability. I, and with me the . . . the surprise, the multiplexity, the sea-changing rhythm of . . . history, will be eliminated. There will be order and constancy . . . and I am unalterably opposed to it. I will not give up Berlin!

MARTHA: You'll give up Berlin, sweetheart. You going to defend it with your paunch?

HONEY: I don't see what Berlin has to *do* with anything.

GEORGE: There is a saloon in West Berlin where the barstools are five feet high. And the earth . . . the floor . . . is so . . . far . . . below you. I will not give up things like that. No . . . I won't. I will fight you, young man . . . one hand on my scrotum, to be sure . . . but with my free hand I will battle you to the death.

MARTHA (*mocking, laughing*): Bravo!

NICK (*to* GEORGE): That's right. And I am going to be the wave of the future.

MARTHA: You bet you are, baby.

HONEY (*quite drunk — to* NICK): I don't see why you want to do all those things, dear. You never told me.

NICK (*angry*): Oh for God's sake!

HONEY (*shocked*): OH!

GEORGE: The most profound indication of a social malignancy . . . no sense of humor. None of the monoliths could take a joke. Read history. I know something about history.

NICK (*to* GEORGE, *trying to make light of it all*): You . . . you don't know much about science, do you?

GEORGE: I know something about history. I know when I'm being threatened.

MARTHA (*salaciously — to* NICK): So, everyone's going to look like you, eh?

NICK: Oh, sure. I'm going to be a personal screwing machine!

MARTHA: Isn't that nice.

HONEY (*her hands over her ears*): Dear, you mustn't . . . you mustn't . . . you mustn't.

NICK (*impatiently*): I'm sorry, Honey.

HONEY: Such language. It's. . . .

NICK: I'm *sorry*. All right?

HONEY (*pouting*): Well . . . all right. (*Suddenly she giggles insanely, subsides. To* GEORGE.) . . . When is your son? (*Giggles again.*)

GEORGE: What?

NICK (*distastefully*): Something about your son.

GEORGE: SON!

HONEY: When is . . . where is your son . . . coming home? (*Giggles.*)

GEORGE: Ohhhh. (*Too formal.*) Martha? When is our son coming home?

MARTHA: Never mind.

GEORGE: No, no . . . I want to know . . . you brought it out into the open. When is he coming home, Martha?

MARTHA: I said never mind. I'm sorry I brought it up.

GEORGE: Him up . . . not it. You brought *him* up. Well, more or less. When's the little bugger going to appear, hunh? I mean isn't tomorrow meant to be his birthday, or something?

MARTHA: I don't want to talk about it!

GEORGE (*falsely innocent*): But Martha. . . .

MARTHA: I DON'T WANT TO TALK ABOUT IT!

GEORGE: I'll bet you don't. (*To* HONEY *and* NICK.) Martha does not want to talk about it . . . him. Martha is sorry she brought it up . . . him.

HONEY (*idiotically*): When's the little bugger coming home? (*Giggles.*)

GEORGE: Yes, Martha . . . since you had the bad taste to bring the matter up in the first place . . . when *is* the little bugger coming home?

NICK: Honey, do you think you . . . ?

MARTHA: George talks disparagingly about the little bugger because . . . well, because he has problems.

GEORGE: The little bugger has problems? What problems has the little bugger got?

MARTHA: Not the little bugger . . . stop calling him that! You! You've got problems.

GEORGE (*feigned disdain*): I've never heard of anything more ridiculous in my life.

HONEY: Neither have I!

NICK: Honey. . . .

MARTHA: George's biggest problem about the little . . . ha, ha, ha, HA! . . . about our son, about our great big son, is that deep down in the private-most pit of his gut, he's not completely sure it's his own kid.

GEORGE (*deeply serious*): My God, you're a wicked woman.

MARTHA: And I've told you a million times, baby . . . I wouldn't conceive with anyone but you . . . you know that, baby.

GEORGE: A deeply wicked person.

HONEY (*deep in drunken grief*): My, my, my, my. Oh, my.

NICK: I'm not sure that this is a subject for. . . .

GEORGE: Martha's lying. I want you to know that, right now. Martha's lying. (MARTHA *laughs.*) There are very few things in this world that I *am* sure of . . . national boundaries, the level of the ocean, political allegiances, practical morality . . . none of these would I stake my stick on any more . . . but the one thing in this whole sinking world that I am sure of is my partnership, my chromosomological partnership in the . . . creation of our . . . blond-eyed, blue-haired . . . son.

HONEY: Oh, I'm so glad!

MARTHA: That was a very pretty speech, George.

GEORGE: Thank you, Martha.

MARTHA: You rose to the occasion . . . good. Real good.

HONEY: Well . . . real well.

NICK: Honey. . . .

GEORGE: Martha knows . . . she knows better.

MARTHA (*proudly*): I know better. I been to college like everybody else.

GEORGE: Martha been to college. Martha been to a convent when she were a little twig of a thing, too.

MARTHA: And I was an atheist. (*Uncertainly.*) I still am.

GEORGE: Not an atheist, Martha . . . a pagan. (*To* HONEY *and* NICK.) Martha is the only true pagan on the eastern seaboard. (MARTHA *laughs.*)

HONEY: Oh, that's nice. Isn't that nice, dear?

NICK (*humoring her*): Yes . . . wonderful.

GEORGE: And Martha paints blue circles around her things.

NICK: You do?

MARTHA (*defensively, for the joke's sake*): Sometimes. (*Beckoning.*) You wanna see?

GEORGE (*admonishing*): Tut, tut, tut.

MARTHA: Tut, tut yourself . . . you old floozie!

HONEY: He's not a floozie . . . he can't be a floozie . . . you're a floozie. (*Giggles.*)

MARTHA (*shaking a finger at* HONEY): Now you watch yourself!

HONEY (*cheerfully*): All right. I'd like a nipper of brandy, please.

NICK: Honey, I think you've had enough, now. . . .

GEORGE: Nonsense! Everybody's ready, I think. (*Takes glasses, etc.*)

HONEY (*echoing* GEORGE): Nonsense.

NICK (*shrugging*): O.K.

MARTHA (*to* GEORGE): Our son does *not* have blue hair . . . or blue eyes, for that matter. He has green eyes . . . like me.

GEORGE: He has blue eyes, Martha.

MARTHA (*determined*): Green.

GEORGE (*patronizing*): Blue, Martha.

MARTHA (*ugly*): GREEN! (*To* HONEY *and* NICK.) He has the loveliest green eyes . . . they aren't all flaked with brown and gray, you know . . . hazel . . . they're real green . . . deep, pure green eyes . . . like mine.

NICK (*peers*): Your eyes are . . . brown, aren't they?

MARTHA: Green! (*A little too fast.*) Well, in some lights they *look* brown, but they're green. Not green like his . . . more hazel. George has watery blue eyes . . . milky blue.

GEORGE: Make up your mind, Martha.

MARTHA: I was giving you the benefit of the doubt. (*Now back to the others.*) Daddy has green eyes, too.

GEORGE: He does not! Your father has tiny red eyes . . . like a white mouse. In fact, he *is* a white mouse.

MARTHA: You wouldn't dare say a thing like that if he was here! You're a coward!

GEORGE (*to* HONEY *and* NICK): You know . . . that great shock of white hair, and those little beady red eyes . . . a great big white mouse.

MARTHA: George hates Daddy . . . not for anything Daddy's done to him, but for his own. . . .

GEORGE (*nodding . . . finishing it for her*): . . . inadequacies.

MARTHA (*cheerfully*): That's right. You hit it . . . right on the snout. (*Seeing* GEORGE *exiting*.) Where do you think *you're* going?

GEORGE: We need some more booze, angel.

MARTHA: Oh. (*Pause*.) So, go.

GEORGE (*exiting*): Thank you.

MARTHA (*seeing that* GEORGE *has gone*): He's a good bartender . . . a good bar nurse. The S.O.B., he hates my father. You know that?

NICK (*trying to make light of it*): Oh, come on.

MARTHA (*offended*): You think I'm kidding? You think I'm joking? I never joke . . . I don't have a sense of humor. (*Almost pouting*.) I have a fine sense of the ridiculous, but no sense of humor. (*Affirmatively*.) I have no sense of humor!

HONEY (*happily*): I haven't, either.

NICK (*half-heartedly*): Yes, you have, Honey . . . a quiet one.

HONEY (*proudly*): Thank you.

MARTHA: You want to know *why* the S.O.B. hates my father? You want me to tell you? All right. . . . I will now tell you why the S.O.B. hates my father.

HONEY (*swinging to some sort of attention*): Oh, good!

MARTHA (*sternly, to* HONEY): *Some* people feed on the calamities of others.

HONEY (*offended*): They do not!

NICK: Honey. . . .

MARTHA: All right! Shut up! Both of you! (*Pause*.) All right, now. Mommy died early, see, and I sort of grew up with Daddy. (*Pause – thinks*.) . . . I went away to school, and stuff, but I more or less grew up with him. Jesus, I admired that guy! I worshipped him . . . I absolutely worshipped him. I still do. And he was pretty fond of me, too . . . you know? We had a real . . . rapport going . . . a real rapport.

NICK: Yeah, yeah.

MARTHA: And Daddy built this college . . . I mean, he built it up from what it was . . . it's his whole life. He *is* the college.

NICK: Unh-hunh.

MARTHA: The college is him. You know what the endowment was when he took over, and what it is *now?* You look it up some time.

NICK: I know . . . I read about it. . . .

MARTHA: Shut up and listen . . . (*as an afterthought*) . . . cutie. So after I got done with college and stuff, I came back here and sort of . . . sat around, for a while. I wasn't married, or anything. Wellllll, I'd *been* married . . . sort of . . . for a week, my sophomore year at Miss Muff's Academy for Young Ladies . . . college. A kind of junior Lady Chatterley arrangement, as it turned out . . . the marriage. (NICK *laughs*.) He mowed the lawn at Miss Muff's, sitting up there, all naked, on a big power mower, mowing away. But Daddy and Miss Muff got together and put an end to that . . . real quick . . . annulled . . . which is a laugh . . .

because theoretically you can't get an annulment if there's entrance. Ha! Anyway, so I was revirginized, finished at Miss Muff's . . . where they had one less gardener's boy, and a real shame, that was . . . and I came back here and sort of sat around for a while. I was hostess for Daddy and I took care of him . . . and it was . . . nice. It was very nice.

NICK: Yes . . . yes.

MARTHA: What do you mean, yes, yes? How would you know?

(NICK *shrugs helplessly.*)

Lover.

(NICK *smiles a little.*)

And I got the idea, about then, that I'd marry into the college . . . which didn't seem to be quite as stupid as it turned out. I mean, Daddy had a sense of history . . . of continuation. . . . Why don't you come over here and sit by me?

NICK (*indicating* HONEY, *who is barely with it*): I . . . don't think I . . . should. . . . I. . . .

MARTHA: Suit yourself. A sense of continuation . . . history . . . and he'd always had it in the back of his mind to . . . *groom* someone to take over . . . some time, when he quit. A succession . . . you know what I mean?

NICK: Yes, I do.

MARTHA: Which is natural enough. When you've made something, you want to pass it on, to somebody. So, I was sort of on the lookout, for . . . prospects with the new men. An heir-apparent. (*Laughs.*) It wasn't *Daddy's* idea that I had to necessarily marry the guy. I mean, I wasn't the albatross . . . you didn't have to take me to get the prize, or anything like that. It was something *I* had in the back of *my* mind. And a lot of the new men were married . . . naturally.

NICK: Sure.

MARTHA (*with a strange smile*): Like you, baby.

HONEY (*a mindless echo*): Like you, baby.

MARTHA (*ironically*): But then George came along . . . along come George.

GEORGE (*re-entering, with liquor*): And along came George, bearing hooch. What are you doing now, Martha?

MARTHA (*unfazed*): I'm telling a story. Sit down . . . you'll learn something.

GEORGE (*stays standing. Puts the liquor on the portable bar*): All rightie.

HONEY: You've come back!

GEORGE: That's right.

HONEY: Dear! He's come back!

NICK: Yes, I see . . . I see.

MARTHA: Where was I?

HONEY: I'm *so* glad.

NICK: Shhhhh.

HONEY (*imitating him*): Shhhhh.

MARTHA: Oh yeah. And along came George. That's right. Who was young . . . intelligent . . . and . . . bushy-tailed, and . . . sort of cute . . . if you can imagine it. . . .

GEORGE: . . . and younger than you. . . .

MARTHA: . . . and younger than me. . . .

GEORGE: . . . by six years. . . .

MARTHA: . . . by six years. . . . It doesn't bother me, George. . . . And along he came, bright-eyed, into the History Department. And you know what I did, dumb cluck that I am? You know what I did? I fell for him.

HONEY (*dreamy*): Oh, that's nice.

GEORGE: Yes, she did. You should have seen it. She'd sit outside of my room, on the lawn, at night, and she'd howl and claw at the turf . . . I couldn't work.

MARTHA (*laughs, really amused*): I actually fell for him . . . it . . . that, there.

GEORGE: Martha's a Romantic at heart.

MARTHA: That I am. So, I actually fell for him. And the match seemed . . . practical, too. You know, Daddy was looking for someone to. . . .

GEORGE: Just a minute, Martha. . . .

MARTHA: . . . take over, some time, when he was ready to. . . .

GEORGE (*stony*): Just a minute, Martha.

MARTHA: . . . retire, and so I thought. . . .

GEORGE: STOP IT, MARTHA!

MARTHA (*irritated*): Whadda you want?

GEORGE (*too patiently*): I'd thought you were telling the story of our courtship, Martha . . . I didn't know you were going to start in on the other business.

MARTHA (*so-thereish*): Well, I am!

GEORGE: I wouldn't, if I were you.

MARTHA: Oh . . . you wouldn't? Well, you're not!

GEORGE: Now, you've already sprung a leak about you-know-what. . . .

MARTHA (*a duck*): What? What?

GEORGE: . . . about the apple of our eye . . . the sprout . . . the little bugger . . . (*spits it out*) . . . our *son* . . . and if you start in on this other business, I warn you, Martha, it's going to make me angry.

MARTHA (*laughing at him*): Oh, it is, is it?

GEORGE: I warn you.

MARTHA (*incredulous*): You *what?*

GEORGE (*very quietly*): I warn you.

NICK: Do you really think we have to go through . . . ?

MARTHA: I stand warned! (*Pause . . . then, to* HONEY *and* NICK.) So, anyway, I married the S.O.B., and I had it all planned out. . . . He was the groom . . . he was going to be groomed. He'd take over some day . . . first, he'd take over the History Department, and then, when Daddy retired, he'd take over the college . . . you know? That's the way it was supposed to be.

(*To* GEORGE, *who is at the portable bar with his back to her.*)

You getting angry, baby? Hunh? (*Now back.*) That's the way it was *supposed* to be. Very simple. And Daddy seemed to think it was a pretty good idea, too. For a while. Until he watched for a couple of years! (*To* GEORGE *again.*) You getting angrier? (*Now back.*) Until he watched for a couple of years and started thinking maybe it wasn't such a good idea after all . . . that maybe Georgie-boy didn't have the *stuff* . . . that he didn't have it in him!

GEORGE (*still with his back to them all*): Stop it, Martha.

MARTHA (*viciously triumphant*): The hell I will! You see, George didn't have much . . . push . . . he wasn't particularly . . . aggressive. In fact he was sort of a . . . (*spits the word at* GEORGE'*s back*) . . . a FLOP! A great . . . big . . . fat . . . FLOP!

(CRASH! *Immediately after* FLOP! GEORGE *breaks a bottle against the portable bar and stands there, still with his back to them all, holding the remains of the bottle by the neck. There is a silence, with everyone frozen. Then. . . .*)

GEORGE (*almost crying*): I said stop, Martha.

MARTHA (*after considering what course to take*): I hope that was an empty bottle, George. You don't want to waste good liquor . . . not on your salary.

(GEORGE *drops the broken bottle on the floor, not moving.*)

Not on an Associate Professor's salary. (*To* NICK *and* HONEY.) I mean, he'd be . . . no good . . . at trustees' dinners, fund raising. He didn't have any . . . personality, you know what I mean? Which was disappointing to Daddy, as you can imagine. So, here I am, stuck with this flop. . . .

GEORGE (*turning around*): . . . don't go on, Martha. . . .

MARTHA: . . . this BOG in the History Department. . . .

GEORGE: . . . don't, Martha, don't. . . .

MARTHA (*her voice rising to match his*): . . . who's married to the President's daughter, who's expected to *be* somebody, not just some nobody, some bookworm, somebody who's so damn . . . contemplative, he can't make anything out of himself, somebody without the *guts* to make anybody proud of him . . . ALL RIGHT, GEORGE!

GEORGE (*under her, then covering, to drown her*): I said, don't. All right . . . all right: (*sings*)
Who's afraid of Virginia Woolf,
Virginia Woolf,
Virginia Woolf,
Who's afraid of Virginia Woolf,
early in the morning.

GEORGE *and* HONEY (*who joins him drunkenly*):
Who's afraid of Virginia Woolf,
Virginia Woolf,
Virginia Woolf . . . (*etc.*)

MARTHA: STOP IT!

(*A brief silence.*)

HONEY (*rising, moving toward the hall*): I'm going to be sick . . . I'm going to be sick . . . I'm going to vomit. (*Exits.*)

NICK (*going after her*): Oh, for God's sake! (*Exits.*)

MARTHA (*going after them, looks back at* GEORGE, *contemptuously*): Jesus! (*Exits.* GEORGE *is alone on stage.*)

CURTAIN

## ACT II. WALPURGISNACHT

GEORGE, *by himself;* NICK *re-enters.*

NICK (*after a silence*): I . . . guess . . . she's all right. (*No answer.*) She . . . really shouldn't drink. (*No answer.*) She's . . . frail. (*No answer.*) Uh . . . slim-hipped, as you'd have it. (GEORGE *smiles vaguely.*) I'm really very sorry.

GEORGE (*quietly*): Where's my little yum yum? Where's Martha?

NICK: She's making coffee . . . in the kitchen. She . . . gets sick quite easily.

GEORGE (*preoccupied*): Martha? Oh no, Martha hasn't been sick a day in her life, unless you count the time she spends in the rest home. . . .

NICK (*he, too, quietly*): No, no; *my* wife . . . *my* wife gets sick quite easily. Your wife is Martha.

GEORGE (*with some rue*): Oh, yes . . . I know.

NICK (*a statement of fact*): She doesn't really spend any time in a rest home.

GEORGE: Your wife?

NICK: No. Yours.

GEORGE: Oh! Mine. (*Pause.*) No, no, she doesn't . . . *I* would; I mean if I were . . . her . . . she . . . *I* would. But I'm not . . . and so I don't. (*Pause.*) I'd like to, though. It gets pretty bouncy around here sometimes.

NICK (*coolly*): Yes . . . I'm sure.

GEORGE: Well, you saw an example of it.

NICK: I try not to. . . .

GEORGE: Get involved. Um? Isn't that right?

NICK: Yes . . . that's right.

GEORGE: I'd imagine not.

NICK: I find it . . . embarrassing.

GEORGE (*sarcastic*): Oh, you do, hunh?

NICK: Yes. Really. Quite.

GEORGE (*mimicking him*): Yes. Really. Quite. (*Then aloud, but to himself.*) IT'S DISGUSTING!

NICK: Now look! I didn't have anything. . . .

GEORGE: DISGUSTING! (*Quietly, but with great intensity.*) Do you think I like having that . . . whatever-it-is . . . ridiculing me, tearing me down, in front of . . . (*waves his hand in a gesture of contemptuous dismissal*) YOU? Do you think I *care* for it?

NICK (*cold — unfriendly*): Well, no . . . I don't imagine you care for it at all.

GEORGE: Oh, you don't imagine it, hunh?

NICK (*antagonistic*): No . . . I don't. I don't imagine you do!

GEORGE (*withering*): Your sympathy disarms me . . . your . . . your compassion makes me weep! Large, salty, unscientific tears!

NICK (*with great disdain*): I just don't see why you feel you have to subject *other* people to it.

GEORGE: *I?*

NICK: If you and your . . . wife . . . want to go at each other, like a couple of. . . .

GEORGE: *I!* Why *I* want to!

NICK: . . . animals, I don't see why you don't do it when there aren't any. . . .

GEORGE (*laughing through his anger*): Why, you smug, self-righteous little. . . .

NICK (*a genuine threat*): CAN . . . IT . . . MISTER!

(*Silence.*)

Just . . . watch it!

GEORGE: . . . scientist.

NICK: I've never hit an older man.

GEORGE (*considers it*): Oh. (*Pause.*) You just hit younger men . . . and children . . . women . . . birds. (*Sees that* NICK *is not amused.*) Well, you're quite right, of course. It isn't the prettiest spectacle . . . seeing a couple of middle-age types hacking away at each other, all red in the face and winded, missing half the time.

NICK: Oh, you two don't miss . . . you two are pretty good. Impressive.

GEORGE: And impressive things impress you, don't they? You're . . . easily impressed . . . sort of a . . . pragmatic idealism.

NICK (*a tight smile*): No, it's that sometimes I can admire things that I don't admire. Now, flagellation isn't my idea of good times, but. . . .

GEORGE: . . . but you can admire a good flagellator . . . a real pro.

NICK: Unh-hunh . . . yeah.

GEORGE: Your wife throws up a lot, eh?

NICK: I didn't say that. . . . I said she gets sick quite easily.

GEORGE: Oh. I thought by sick you meant. . . .

NICK: Well, it's true. . . . She . . . she does throw up a lot. Once she starts . . .

there's practically no stopping her. . . . I mean, she'll go right on . . . for hours. Not all the time, but . . . regularly.

GEORGE: You can tell time by her, hunh?

NICK: Just about.

GEORGE: Drink?

NICK: Sure. (*With no emotion, except the faintest distaste, as* GEORGE *takes his glass to the bar.*) I married her because she was pregnant.

GEORGE: (*Pause.*) Oh? (*Pause.*) But you said you didn't have any children. . . . When I asked you, you said. . . .

NICK: She wasn't . . . really. It was a hysterical pregnancy. She blew up, and then she went down.

GEORGE: And while she was up, you married her.

NICK: And then she went down.

(*They both laugh, and are a little surprised that they do.*)

GEORGE: Uh . . . Bourbon *is* right.

NICK: Uh . . . yes, Bourbon.

GEORGE (*at the bar, still*): When I was sixteen and going to prep school, during the Punic Wars, a bunch of us used to go into New York on the first day of vacations, before we fanned out to our homes, and in the evening this bunch of us used to go to this gin mill owned by the gangster-father of one of us — for this was during the Great Experiment, or Prohibition, as it is more frequently called, and it was a bad time for the liquor lobby, but a fine time for the crooks and the cops — and we would go to this gin mill, and we would drink with the grown-ups and listen to the jazz. And one time, in the bunch of us, there was this boy who was fifteen, and he had killed his mother with a shotgun some years before — accidentally, completely accidentally, without even an unconscious motivation, I have no doubt, no doubt at all — and this one evening this boy went with us, and we ordered our drinks, and when it came his turn he said, I'll have bergin . . . give me some bergin, please . . . bergin and water. Well, we all laughed . . . he was blond and he had the face of a cherub, and we all laughed, and his cheeks went red and the color rose in his neck, and the assistant crook who had taken our order told people at the next table what the boy had said, and then they laughed, and then more people were told and the laughter grew, and more people and more laughter, and no one was laughing more than us, and none of us more than the boy who had shot his mother. And soon, everyone in the gin mill knew what the laughter was about, and everyone started ordering bergin, and laughing when they ordered it. And soon, of course, the laughter became less general, but it did not subside, entirely, for a very long time, for always at this table or that someone would order bergin and a new area of laughter would rise. We drank free that night, and we were bought champagne by the management, by the gangster-father of one of us. And, of course, we suffered the next day, each of us, alone, on his train, away from New York, each of us with a grown-up's hangover . . . but it was the grandest day of my . . . youth. (*Hands* NICK *a drink on the word.*)

NICK (*very quietly*): Thank you. What . . . what happened to the boy . . . the boy who had shot his mother?

GEORGE: I won't tell you.

NICK: All right.

GEORGE: The following summer, on a country road, with his learner's permit in his pocket and his father on the front seat to his right, he swerved the car, to avoid a porcupine, and drove straight into a large tree.

NICK (*faintly pleading*): No.

GEORGE: He was not killed, of course. And in the hospital, when he was conscious and out of danger, and when they told him that his father *was* dead, he began to laugh, I have been told, and his laughter grew and he would not stop, and it was not until after they jammed a needle in his arm, not until after that, until his consciousness slipped away from him, that his laughter subsided . . . stopped. And when he was recovered from his injuries enough so that he could be moved without damage should he struggle, he was put in an asylum. That was thirty years ago.

NICK: Is he . . . still there?

GEORGE: Oh, yes. And I'm told that for these thirty years he has . . . not . . . uttered . . . one . . . sound.

(*A rather long silence: five seconds, please.*)

MARTHA! (*Pause.*) MARTHA!

NICK: I told you . . . she's making coffee.

GEORGE: For your hysterical wife, who goes up and down.

NICK: Went. Up and down.

GEORGE: Went. No more?

NICK: No more. Nothing.

GEORGE (*after a sympathetic pause*): The saddest thing about men. . . . Well, no, one of the saddest things about men is the way they age . . . some of them. Do you know what it is with insane people? Do you? . . . the quiet ones?

NICK: No.

GEORGE: They don't change . . . they don't grow old.

NICK: They must.

GEORGE: Well, eventually, probably, yes. But they don't . . . in the usual sense. They maintain a . . . a firm-skinned serenity . . . the . . . the underuse of everything leaves them . . . quite whole.

NICK: Are you recommending it?

GEORGE: No. Some things are sad, though. (*Imitates a pep-talker.*) But ya jest gotta buck up an' face 'em, 'at's all. Buck up! (*Pause.*) Martha doesn't have hysterical pregnancies.

NICK: My wife had *one.*

GEORGE: Yes. Martha doesn't have pregnancies at all.

NICK: Well, no . . . I don't imagine so . . . now. Do you have any other kids? Do you have any daughters, or anything?

GEORGE (*as if it's a great joke*): Do we have any *what?*

NICK: Do you have any . . . I mean, do you have only one . . . kid . . . uh . . . your son?

GEORGE (*with a private knowledge*): Oh no . . . just one . . . one boy . . . our son.

NICK: Well . . . (*shrugs*) . . . that's nice.

GEORGE: Oh ho, ho. Yes, well, he's a . . . comfort, a bean bag.

NICK: A what?

GEORGE: A bean bag. Bean bag. You wouldn't understand. (*Over-distinct.*) Bean . . . bag.

NICK: I *heard* you . . . I didn't say I was deaf . . . I said I didn't understand.

GEORGE: You didn't say that at all.

NICK: I meant I was *implying* I didn't understand. (*Under his breath.*) For Christ's sake!

GEORGE: You're getting testy.

NICK (*testy*): I'm sorry.

GEORGE: All I said was, our son . . . the apple of our three eyes, Martha being a Cyclops . . . our son is a bean bag, and you get testy.

NICK: I'm sorry! It's late, I'm tired, I've been drinking since nine o'clock, my wife is vomiting, there's been a lot of screaming going on around here. . . .

GEORGE: And so you're testy. Naturally. Don't . . . worry about it. Anybody who comes here ends up getting . . . testy. It's expected . . . don't be upset.

NICK (*testy*): I'm not upset!

GEORGE: You're testy.

NICK: Yes.

GEORGE: I'd like to set you straight about something . . . while the little ladies are out of the room . . . I'd like to set you straight about what Martha said.

NICK: I don't . . . make judgments, so there's no need, really, unless you. . . .

GEORGE: Well, I want to. I know you don't like to become involved . . . I know you like to . . . preserve your scientific detachment in the face of — for lack of a better word — Life . . . and all . . . but still, I want to tell you.

NICK (*a tight, formal smile*): I'm a . . . guest. You go right ahead.

GEORGE (*mocking appreciation*): Oh . . . well, thanks. Now! That makes me feel all warm and runny inside.

NICK: Well, if you're going to . . .

MARTHA'S VOICE: HEY!

NICK: . . . if you're going to start that kind of stuff again. . . .

GEORGE: Hark! Forest sounds.

NICK: Hm?

GEORGE: Animal noises.

MARTHA (*sticking her head in*): Hey!

NICK: Oh!

GEORGE: Well, here's nursie.

MARTHA (*to* NICK): We're sitting up . . . we're having coffee, and we'll be back in.

NICK (*not rising*): Oh . . . is there anything I should do?

MARTHA: Nayh. You just stay here and listen to George's side of things. Bore yourself to death.

GEORGE: Monstre!

MARTHA: Cochon!

GEORGE: Bête!

MARTHA: Canaille!

GEORGE: Putain!

MARTHA (*with a gesture of contemptuous dismissal*): Yaaaahhhh! You two types amuse yourselves . . . we'll be in. (*As she goes.*) You clean up the mess you made, George?

GEORGE (MARTHA *goes.* GEORGE *speaks to the empty hallway*): No, Martha, I did not clean up the mess I made. I've been trying for years to clean up the mess I made.

NICK: Have you?

GEORGE: Hm?

NICK: *Have* you been trying for years?

GEORGE (*after a long pause . . . looking at him*): Accommodation, malleability, adjustment . . . those do seem to be in the order of things, don't they?

NICK: Don't try to put me in the same class with you!

GEORGE: (*Pause.*) Oh. (*Pause.*) No, of course not. Things are simpler with you . . . you marry a woman because she's all blown up . . . while I, in my clumsy, old-fashioned way. . . .

NICK: There was more to it than that!

GEORGE: Sure! I'll bet she has money, too!

NICK (*Looks hurt. Then, determined, after a pause*): Yes.

GEORGE: Yes? (*Joyfully.*) YES! You mean I was right? I hit it?

NICK: Well, you see. . . .

GEORGE: My God, what archery! First try, too. How about that!

NICK: You see. . . .

GEORGE: There were other things.

NICK: Yes.

GEORGE: To compensate.

NICK: Yes.

GEORGE: There always are. (*Sees that* NICK *is reacting badly.*) No, I'm sure there are. I didn't mean to be . . . flip. There are *always* compensating factors . . . as in the case of Martha and myself. . . . Now, on the surface of it. . . .

NICK: We sort of grew up together, you know. . . .

GEORGE: . . . it looks to be a kind of knock-about, drag-out affair, on the *surface* of it. . . .

NICK: We knew each other from, oh God, I don't know, when we were *six,* or something. . . .

GEORGE: . . . but somewhere back there, at the beginning of it, right when I first came to New Carthage, back then. . . .

NICK (*with some irritation*): I'm *sorry.*

GEORGE: Hm? Oh. No, no . . . *I'm* sorry.

NICK: No . . . it's . . . it's all right.

GEORGE: No . . . you go ahead.

NICK: No . . . please.

GEORGE: I insist. . . . You're a guest. You go first.

NICK: Well, it seems a little silly . . . now.

GEORGE: Nonsense! (*Pause.*) But if you were six, she must have been four, or something.

NICK: Maybe I was eight . . . she was six. We . . . we used to play . . . doctor.

GEORGE: That's a good healthy heterosexual beginning.

NICK (*laughing*): Yup.

GEORGE: The scientist even then, eh?

NICK (*laughs*): Yeah. And it was . . . always taken for granted . . . you know . . . by our families, and by us, too, I guess. And . . . so, we did.

GEORGE: (*Pause.*) Did what?

NICK: We got married.

GEORGE: When you were eight?

NICK: No. No, of course not. Much later.

GEORGE: I wondered.

NICK: I wouldn't say there was any . . . particular *passion* between us, even at the beginning . . . of our marriage, I mean.

GEORGE: Well, certainly no surprise, no earth-shaking discoveries, after doctor, and all.

NICK (*uncertainly*): No. . . .

GEORGE: Everything's all pretty much the same, anyway . . . in *spite* of what they say about Chinese women.

NICK: What is that?

GEORGE: Let me freshen you up. (*Takes* NICK'*s glass.*)

NICK: Oh, thanks. After a while you don't get any drunker, do you?

GEORGE: Well, you *do* . . . but it's different . . . everything slows down . . . you get sodden . . . unless you can up-chuck . . . like your wife . . . then you can sort of start all over again.

NICK: Everybody drinks a lot here in the East. (*Thinks about it.*) Everybody drinks a lot in the Middle West, too.

GEORGE: We drink a great deal in this country, and I suspect we'll be drinking a great deal more, too . . . if we survive. We should be Arabs or Italians . . . the Arabs don't drink, and the Italians don't get drunk much, except on religious holidays. We should live on Crete, or something.

NICK (*sarcastically . . . as if killing a joke*): And that, of course, would make us cretins.

GEORGE (*mild surprise*): So it would. (*Hands* NICK *his drink.*) Tell me about your wife's money.

NICK (*suddenly suspicious*): Why?

GEORGE: Well . . . don't, then.

NICK: What do you want to know about my wife's money for? (*Ugly.*) Hunh?

GEORGE: Well, I thought it would be nice.

NICK: No you didn't.

GEORGE (*still deceptively bland*): All right. . . . I want to know about your wife's money because . . . well, because I'm fascinated by the methodology . . . by the pragmatic accommodation by which you wave-of-the-future boys are going to take over.

NICK: You're starting in again.

GEORGE: Am I? No I'm not. Look . . . Martha has money too. I mean, her father's been robbing this place blind for years, and. . . .

NICK: No, he hasn't. He has not.

GEORGE: He hasn't?

NICK: No.

GEORGE (*shrugs*): Very well. . . . Martha's father has *not* been robbing this place blind for years, and Martha does not have any money. O.K.?

NICK: We were talking about *my* wife's money . . . not yours.

GEORGE: O.K. . . . talk.

NICK: No. (*Pause.*) My father-in-law . . . was a man of the Lord, and he was very rich.

GEORGE: What faith?

NICK: He . . . my father-in-law . . . was called by God when he was six, or something, and he started preaching, and he baptized people, and he saved them, and he travelled around a lot, and he became pretty famous . . . not like some of them, but he became pretty famous . . . and when he died he had a lot of money.

GEORGE: God's money.

NICK: No . . . his own.

GEORGE: What happened to God's money?

NICK: He spent God's money . . . and he saved his own. He built hospitals, and he sent off Mercy ships, and he brought the outhouses indoors, and he brought the people outdoors, into the sun, and he built three churches, or whatever they were, and two of them burned down . . . and he ended up pretty rich.

GEORGE (*after considering it*): Well, I think that's very nice.
NICK: Yes. (*Pause. Giggles a little.*) And so, my wife's got some money.
GEORGE: But not God's money.
NICK: No. Her own.
GEORGE: Well, I think that's very nice.

(NICK *giggles a little.*)

*Martha's* got money because Martha's father's second wife . . . not Martha's mother, but after Martha's mother died . . . was a very old lady with warts who was very rich.
NICK: She was a witch.
GEORGE: She was a *good* witch, and she married the white mouse . . .

(NICK *begins to giggle.*)

. . . with the tiny red eyes . . . and he must have nibbled her warts, or something like that, because she went up in a puff of smoke almost immediately. POUF!
NICK: POUF!
GEORGE: POUF! And all that was left, aside from some wart medicine, was a big fat will. . . . A peach pie, with some for the township of New Carthage, some for the college, some for Martha's daddy, and just this much for Martha.
NICK (*quite beside himself*): Maybe . . . maybe my father-in-law and the witch with the warts should have gotten together, because he was a mouse, too.
GEORGE (*urging* NICK *on*): He was?
NICK (*breaking down*): Sure . . . he was a church mouse! (*They both laugh a great deal, but it is sad laughter . . . eventually they subside, fall silent.*) Your wife never mentioned a stepmother.
GEORGE (*considers it*): Well . . . maybe it isn't true.
NICK (*narrowing his eyes*): And maybe it is.
GEORGE: Might be . . . might not. Well, I think your story's a lot nicer . . . about your pumped-up little wife, and your father-in-law who was a priest. . . .
NICK: He was not a priest . . . he was a man of God.
GEORGE: Yes.
NICK: And my wife wasn't pumped up . . . she blew up.
GEORGE: Yes, yes.
NICK (*giggling*): Get things straight.
GEORGE: I'm sorry . . . I will. I'm sorry.
NICK: O.K.
GEORGE: You realize, of course, that I've been drawing you out on this stuff, not because I'm interested in your terrible lifehood, but only because you represent a direct and pertinent threat to my lifehood, and I want to get the goods on you.

NICK (*still amused*): Sure . . . sure.

GEORGE: I mean . . . I've warned you . . . you stand warned.

NICK: I stand warned. (*Laughs.*) It's you sneaky types worry me the most, you know. You ineffectual sons of bitches . . . you're the worst.

GEORGE: Yes . . . we are. Sneaky. An elbow in your steely-blue eye . . . a knee in your solid gold groin . . . we're the worst.

NICK: Yup.

GEORGE: Well, I'm glad you don't believe me. . . . I know you've got history on your side, and all. . . .

NICK: Unh-unh. *You've* got history on *your* side. . . . I've got biology on mine. History, biology.

GEORGE: I know the difference.

NICK: You don't act it.

GEORGE: No? I thought we'd decided that you'd take over the History Department first, before you took over the whole works. You know . . . a step at a time.

NICK (*stretching . . . luxuriating . . . playing the game*): Nyaah . . . what I thought I'd do is . . . I'd sort of insinuate myself generally, play around for a while, find all the weak spots, shore 'em up, but with my own name plate on 'em . . . become sort of a fact, and then turn into a . . . a what . . . ?

GEORGE: An inevitability.

NICK: Exactly. . . . An inevitability. You know. . . . Take over a few courses from the older men, start some special groups for myself . . . plow a few pertinent wives. . . .

GEORGE: Now that's it! You can take over all the courses you want to, and get as much of the young elite together in the gymnasium as you like, but until you start plowing pertinent wives, you really aren't working. The way to a man's heart is through his wife's belly, and don't you forget it.

NICK (*playing along*): Yeah. . . . I know.

GEORGE: And the women around here are no better than puntas — you know, South American ladies of the night. You know what they do in South America . . . in Rio? The puntas? Do you know? They hiss . . . like geese. . . . They stand around in the street and they hiss at you . . . like a bunch of geese.

NICK: Gangle.

GEORGE: Hm?

NICK: Gangle . . . gangle of geese . . . not bunch . . . gangle.

GEORGE: Well, if you're going to get all cute about it, all ornithological, it's gaggle . . . not gangle, *gaggle*.

NICK: Gaggle? Not gangle?

GEORGE: Yes, gaggle.

NICK (*crestfallen*): Oh.

GEORGE: Oh. Yes. . . . Well they stand around on the street and they hiss at you, like a bunch of geese. All the faculty wives, downtown in New

Carthage, in front of the A&P, hissing away like a bunch of geese. That's the way to power – plow 'em all!

NICK (*still playing along*): I'll bet you're right.

GEORGE: Well, I am.

NICK: And I'll bet your wife's the biggest goose in the gangle, isn't she . . . ? Her father president, and all.

GEORGE: You bet your historical inevitability she is!

NICK: Yessirree. (*Rubs his hands together.*) Well now, I'd just better get her off in a corner and mount her like a goddam dog, eh?

GEORGE: Why, you'd certainly better.

NICK (*looks at* GEORGE *a minute, his expression a little sick*): You know, I almost think you're serious.

GEORGE (*toasting him*): No, baby . . . *you* almost think you're serious, and it scares the hell out of you.

NICK (*exploding in disbelief*): ME!

GEORGE (*quietly*): Yes . . . you.

NICK: You're kidding!

GEORGE (*like a father*): I wish I were. . . . I'll give you some good advice if you want me to. . . .

NICK: Good advice! From you? Oh boy! (*Starts to laugh.*)

GEORGE: You haven't learned yet. . . . Take it wherever you can get it. . . . Listen to me, now.

NICK: Come off it!

GEORGE: I'm giving you good advice, now.

NICK: Good God . . . !

GEORGE: There's quicksand here, and you'll be dragged down, just as. . . .

NICK: Oh boy . . . !

GEORGE: . . . before you know it . . . sucked down. . . .

(NICK *laughs derisively.*)

You disgust me on principle, and you're a smug son of a bitch personally, but I'm trying to give you a survival kit. DO YOU HEAR ME?

NICK (*still laughing*): I hear you. You come in loud.

GEORGE: ALL RIGHT!

NICK: Hey, Honey.

GEORGE (*silence. Then quietly*): All right . . . O.K. You want to play it by ear, right? Everything's going to work out anyway, because the time-table's history, right?

NICK: Right . . . right. You just tend to your knitting, grandma. . . . I'll be O.K.

GEORGE (*after a silence*): I've tried to . . . tried to reach you . . . to. . . .

NICK (*contemptuously*): . . . make contact?

GEORGE: Yes.

NICK (*still*): . . . communicate?

GEORGE: Yes. Exactly.

NICK: Aw . . . that *is* touching . . . that is . . . downright moving . . . that's what it is. (*With sudden vehemence.*) UP YOURS!

GEORGE (*brief pause*): Hm?

NICK (*threatening*): You heard me!

GEORGE (*at Nick, not to him*): You take the trouble to construct a civilization . . . to . . . to build a society, based on the principles of . . . of principle . . . you endeavor to make communicable sense out of natural order, morality out of the unnatural disorder of man's mind . . . you make government and art, and realize that they are, must be, both the same . . . you bring things to the saddest of all points . . . to the point where there *is* something to lose . . . then all at once, through all the music, through all the sensible sounds of men building, attempting, comes the *Dies Irae.* And what is it? What does the trumpet sound? Up yours. I suppose there's justice to it, after all the years. . . . Up yours.

NICK (*brief pause . . . then applauding*): Ha, ha! Bravo! Ha, ha! (*Laughs on.*)

(*And* MARTHA *re-enters, leading* HONEY, *who is wan but smiling bravely.*)

HONEY (*grandly*): Thank you . . . thank you.

MARTHA: Here we are, a little shaky, but on our feet.

GEORGE: Goodie.

NICK: What? Oh . . . OH! Hi, Honey . . . you better?

HONEY: A little bit, dear. . . . I'd better sit down, though.

NICK: Sure . . . c'mon . . . you sit by me.

HONEY: Thank you, dear.

GEORGE (*beneath his breath*): Touching . . . touching.

MARTHA (*to* GEORGE): Well? Aren't you going to apologize?

GEORGE (*squinting*): For what, Martha?

MARTHA: For making the little lady throw up, what else?

GEORGE: I did not make her throw up.

MARTHA: You most certainly did!

GEORGE: I did not!

HONEY (*papal gesture*): No, now . . . no.

MARTHA (*to* GEORGE): Well, who do you think did . . . Sexy over there? You think he made his *own* little wife sick?

GEORGE (*helpfully*): Well, you make *me* sick.

MARTHA: THAT'S DIFFERENT!

HONEY: No, now. I . . . I throw up . . . I mean, I get sick . . . occasionally, all by myself . . . without any reason.

GEORGE: Is that a fact?

NICK: You're . . . you're delicate, Honey.

HONEY (*proudly*): I've always done it.

GEORGE: Like Big Ben.

NICK (*a warning*): Watch it!

HONEY: And the doctors say there's nothing wrong with me . . . organically. You know?

NICK: Of course there isn't.

HONEY: Why, just before we got married, I developed . . . appendicitis . . . or everybody *thought* it was appendicitis . . . but it turned out to be . . . it was a . . . (*laughs briefly*) . . . false alarm.

(GEORGE *and* NICK *exchange glances.*)

MARTHA (*to* GEORGE): Get me a drink.

(GEORGE *moves to the bar.*)

George makes everybody sick. . . . When our son was just a little boy, he used to. . . .

GEORGE: Don't, Martha. . . .

MARTHA: . . . he used to throw up all the time, because of George. . . .

GEORGE: I said, don't!

MARTHA: It got so bad that whenever George came into the room he'd start right in retching, and. . . .

GEORGE: . . . the real reason (*spits out the words*) our son . . . used to throw up all the time, wife and lover, was nothing more complicated than that he couldn't stand you fiddling at him all the time, breaking into his bedroom with your kimono flying, fiddling at him all the time, with your liquor breath on him, and your hands all over his. . . .

MARTHA: YEAH? And I suppose that's why he ran away from home twice in one month, too. (*Now to the guests.*) Twice in one month! Six times in one year!

GEORGE (*also to the guests*): Our son ran away from home all the time because Martha here used to corner him.

MARTHA (*braying*): I NEVER CORNERED THE SON OF A BITCH IN MY LIFE!

GEORGE (*handing* MARTHA *her drink*): He used to run up to me when I'd get home, and he'd say, "Mama's always coming at me." That's what he'd say.

MARTHA: Liar!

GEORGE (*shrugging*): Well, that's the way it was . . . you were always coming at him. I thought it was very embarrassing.

NICK: If you thought it was so embarrassing, what are you talking about it for?

HONEY (*admonishing*): Dear . . . !

MARTHA: Yeah! (*To* NICK.) Thanks, sweetheart.

GEORGE (*to them all*): I didn't want to talk about him at all . . . I would have been perfectly happy not to discuss the whole subject. . . . I never want to talk about it.

MARTHA: Yes you do.

GEORGE: When we're alone, maybe.

MARTHA: We're alone!

GEORGE: Uh . . . no, Love . . . we've got guests.

MARTHA (*with a covetous look at* NICK): We sure have.

HONEY: Could I have a little brandy? I think I'd like a little brandy.

NICK: Do you think you should?

HONEY: Oh yes . . . yes, dear.

GEORGE (*moving to the bar again*): Sure! Fill 'er up!

NICK: Honey, I don't think you. . . .

HONEY (*petulance creeping in*): It will steady me, *dear*. I feel a little unsteady.

GEORGE: Hell, you can't walk steady on half a bottle . . . got to do it right.

HONEY: Yes. (*To* MARTHA.) I love brandy . . . I really do.

MARTHA (*somewhat abstracted*): Good for you.

NICK (*giving up*): Well, if you think it's a good idea. . . .

HONEY (*really testy*): I know what's best for me, dear.

NICK (*not even pleasant*): Yes . . . I'm sure you do.

HONEY (GEORGE *hands her a brandy*): Oh, goodie! Thank you (*To* NICK.) Of course I do, dear.

GEORGE (*pensively*): I used to drink brandy.

MARTHA (*privately*): You used to drink bergin, too.

GEORGE (*sharp*): Shut up, Martha!

MARTHA (*her hand over her mouth in a little girl gesture*): Oooooops.

NICK (*something having clicked, vaguely*): Hm?

GEORGE (*burying it*): Nothing . . . nothing.

MARTHA (*she, too*): You two men have it out while we were gone? George tell you his side of things? He bring you to tears, hunh?

NICK: Well . . . no. . . .

GEORGE: No, what we did, actually, was . . . we sort of danced around.

MARTHA: Oh, yeah? Cute!

HONEY: Oh, I love dancing.

NICK: He didn't mean that, Honey.

HONEY: Well, I didn't think he did! Two grown men dancing . . . heavens!

MARTHA: You mean he didn't start in on how he would have amounted to something if it hadn't been for Daddy? How his high moral sense wouldn't even let him *try* to better himself? No?

NICK (*qualified*): No. . . .

MARTHA: And he didn't run on about how he tried to publish a goddam book, and Daddy wouldn't let him.

NICK: A book? No.

GEORGE: Please, Martha. . . .

NICK (*egging her on*): A book? What book?

GEORGE (*pleading*): Please. Just a book.

MARTHA (*mock incredulity*): Just a book!

GEORGE: *Please,* Martha!

MARTHA (*almost disappointed*): Well, I guess you didn't get the whole sad story. What's the matter with you, George? You given up?

GEORGE (*calm . . . serious*): No . . . no. It's just I've got to figure out some new way to fight you, Martha. Guerilla tactics, maybe . . . internal subversion . . . I don't know. Something.

MARTHA: Well, you figure it out, and you let me know when you do.

GEORGE (*cheery*): All right, Love.

HONEY: Why don't we dance? I'd love some dancing.

NICK: Honey. . . .

HONEY: I would! I'd love some dancing.

NICK: Honey. . . .

HONEY: I *want* some! I want some dancing!

GEORGE: All right . . . ! For heaven's sake . . . we'll have some dancing.

HONEY (*all sweetness again. To* MARTHA): Oh, I'm so glad . . . I just love dancing. Don't you?

MARTHA (*with a glance at* NICK): Yeah . . . yeah, that's not a bad idea.

NICK (*genuinely nervous*): Gee.

GEORGE: Gee.

HONEY: I dance like the wind.

MARTHA (*without comment*): Yeah?

GEORGE (*picking a record*): Martha had her daguerreotype in the paper once . . . oh, 'bout twenty-five years ago. . . . Seems she took second prize in one o' them seven-day dancin' contest things . . . biceps all bulging, holding up her partner.

MARTHA: Will you put a record on and shut up?

GEORGE: Certainly, Love. (*To all.*) How are we going to work this? Mixed doubles?

MARTHA: Well, you certainly don't think I'm going to dance with *you,* do you?

GEORGE (*considers it*): Noooooo . . . not with him around . . . that's for sure. And not with twinkle-toes here, either.

HONEY: I'll dance with anyone. . . . I'll dance by myself.

NICK: Honey. . . .

HONEY: I dance like the wind.

GEORGE: All right, kiddies . . . choose up and hit the sack.

(*Music starts. . . . Second movement, Beethoven's 7th Symphony*)

HONEY (*up, dancing by herself*): De, de de *da* da, da-da de, da *da*-da de da . . . wonderful . . . !

NICK: Honey. . . .

MARTHA: All right, George . . . cut that out!

HONEY: Dum, de de da da, da-da de, dum de *da* da da. . . . Wheeeee . . . !

MARTHA: Cut it out, George!

GEORGE (*pretending not to hear*): What, Martha? What?

NICK: Honey. . . .

MARTHA (*as* GEORGE *turns up the volume*): CUT IT OUT, GEORGE!

GEORGE: WHAT?

MARTHA (*gets up, moves quickly, threateningly, to* GEORGE): All right, you son of a bitch. . . .

GEORGE (*record off, at once. Quietly*): What did you say, Love?

MARTHA: You son of a. . . .

HONEY (*in an arrested posture*): You stopped! Why did you stop?

NICK: Honey. . . .

HONEY (*to* NICK, *snapping*): Stop that!

GEORGE: I thought it was fitting, Martha.

MARTHA: Oh you did, hunh?

HONEY: You're always *at* me when I'm having a good time.

NICK (*trying to remain civil*): I'm sorry, Honey.

HONEY: Just . . . leave me alone!

GEORGE: Well, why don't *you* choose, Martha? (*Moves away from the phonograph . . . leaves it to* MARTHA.) Martha's going to run things . . . the little lady's going to lead the band.

HONEY: I like to dance and you don't want me to.

NICK: *I* like you to dance.

HONEY: Just . . . leave me alone. (*She sits . . . takes a drink.*)

GEORGE: Martha's going to put on some rhythm she understands . . . Sacre du Printemps, maybe. (*Moves . . . sits by* HONEY.) Hi, sexy.

HONEY (*a little giggle-scream*): Oooooohhhhh!

GEORGE (*laughs mockingly*): Ha, ha, ha, ha, ha. Choose it, Martha . . . do your stuff!

MARTHA (*concentrating on the machine*): You're damn right!

GEORGE (*to* HONEY): You want to dance with me, angel-tits?

NICK: What did you call my wife?

GEORGE (*derisively*): Oh boy!

HONEY (*petulantly*): No! If I can't do my interpretive dance, I don't want to dance with anyone. I'll just sit here and. . . . (*Shrugs . . . drinks.*)

MARTHA (*record on . . . a jazzy slow pop tune*): O.K. stuff, let's go. (*Grabs* NICK.)

NICK: Hm? Oh . . . hi.

MARTHA: Hi. (*They dance, close together, slowly.*)

HONEY (*pouting*): We'll just sit here and watch.

GFORGE: That's *right!*

MARTHA (*to* NICK): Hey, you *are* strong, aren't you?

NICK: Unh-hunh.

MARTHA: I like that.

NICK: Unh-hunh.

HONEY: They're dancing like they've danced before.

GEORGE: It's a familiar dance . . . they both know it. . . .

MARTHA: Don't be shy.

NICK: I'm . . . not. . . .
GEORGE (*to* HONEY): It's a very old ritual, monkey-nipples . . . old as they come.
HONEY: I . . . I don't know what you mean.

(NICK *and* MARTHA *move apart now, and dance on either side of where* GEORGE *and* HONEY *are sitting; they face each other, and while their feet move but little, their bodies undulate congruently. . . . It is as if they were pressed together.*)

MARTHA: I like the way you move.
NICK: I like the way you move, too.
GEORGE (*to* HONEY): They like the way they move.
HONEY (*not entirely with it*): That's nice.
MARTHA (*to* NICK): I'm surprised George didn't give you his side of things.
GEORGE (*to* HONEY): Aren't they cute?
NICK: Well, he didn't.
MARTHA: That surprises me.

(*Perhaps* MARTHA'*s statements are more or less in time to the music.*)

NICK: Does it?
MARTHA: Yeah . . . he usually does . . . when he gets the chance.
NICK: Well, what do you know.
MARTHA: It's really a very sad story.
GEORGE: You have ugly talents, Martha.
NICK: Is it?
MARTHA: It would make you weep.
GEORGE: Hideous gifts.
NICK: Is that so?
GEORGE: Don't encourge her.
MARTHA: Encourage me.
NICK: Go on.

(*They may undulate toward each other and then move back.*)

GEORGE: I warn you . . . don't encourage her.
MARTHA: He warns you . . . don't encourage me.
NICK: I heard him . . . tell me more.
MARTHA (*consciously making rhymed speech*): Well, Georgie-boy had lots of big ambitions
In spite of something funny in his past. . . .
GEORGE (*quietly warning*): Martha. . . .
MARTHA: Which Georgie-boy here turned into a novel. . . .
His first attempt and also his last. . . .
Hey! I rhymed! I rhymed!
GEORGE: I warn you, Martha.
NICK: Yeah . . . you rhymed. Go on, go on.

MARTHA: But Daddy took a look at Georgie's novel. . . .

GEORGE: You're looking for a punch in the mouth. . . . You know that, Martha.

MARTHA: Do tell! . . . and he was very shocked by what he read.

NICK: He was?

MARTHA: Yes . . . he was. . . . A novel all about a naughty boychild. . . .

GEORGE (*rising*): I will not tolerate this!

NICK (*offhand, to* GEORGE): Oh, can it.

MARTHA: . . . ha, ha!
naughty boychild
who . . . uh . . . who killed his mother and his father dead.

GEORGE: STOP IT, MARTHA!

MARTHA: And Daddy said . . . Look here, I will not let you publish such a thing. . . .

GEORGE (*rushes to phonograph . . . rips the record off*): That's it! The dancing's over. That's it. Go on now!

NICK: What do you think you're doing, hunh?

HONEY (*happily*): Violence! Violence!

MARTHA (*loud: a pronouncement*): And Daddy said . . . Look here, kid, you don't think for a second I'm going to let you publish this crap, do you? Not on your life, baby . . . not while you're teaching here. . . . You publish that goddam book and you're out . . . on your ass!

GEORGE: DESIST! DESIST!

MARTHA: Ha, ha, ha, HA!

NICK (*laughing.*) De . . . sist!

HONEY: Oh, violence . . . violence!

MARTHA: Why, the idea! A teacher at a respected, conservative institution like this, in a town like New Carthage, publishing a book like that? If you respect your position here, young man, young . . . whippersnapper, you'll just withdraw that manuscript. . . .

GEORGE: I will not be made mock of!

NICK: He will not be made mock of, for Christ's sake. (*Laughs.*)

(HONEY *joins in the laughter, not knowing exactly why.*)

GEORGE: I will not!

(*All three are laughing at him.*)

(*Infuriated.*) THE GAME IS OVER!

MARTHA (*pushing on*): Imagine such a thing! A book about a boy who murders his mother and kills his father, and pretends it's all an accident!

HONEY (*beside herself with glee*): An accident!

NICK (*remembering something related*): Hey . . . wait a minute. . . .

MARTHA (*her own voice now*): And you want to know the clincher? You want to know what big brave Georgie said to Daddy?

GEORGE: NO! NO! NO! NO!

NICK: Wait a minute now. . . .

MARTHA: Georgie said . . . but Daddy . . . I mean . . . ha, ha, ha, ha . . . but *Sir,* it isn't a *novel* at all. . . . (*Other voice.*) Not a novel? (*Mimicking* GEORGE'*s voice.*) No, Sir . . . it isn't a novel at all. . . .

GEORGE (*advancing on her*): You will not say this!

NICK (*sensing the danger*): Hey.

MARTHA: The hell I won't. Keep away from me, you bastard! (*Backs off a little . . . uses* GEORGE'*s voice again.*) No, Sir, this isn't a novel at all . . . this is the truth . . . this really happened. . . . TO ME!

GEORGE (*on her*): I'LL KILL YOU!

(*Grabs her by the throat. They struggle.*)

NICK: HEY! (*Comes between them.*)

HONEY (*wildly*): VIOLENCE! VIOLENCE!

(GEORGE, MARTHA, *and* NICK *struggle . . . yells, etc.*)

MARTHA: IT HAPPENED! TO ME! TO ME!

GEORGE: YOU SATANIC BITCH!

NICK: STOP THAT! STOP THAT!

HONEY: VIOLENCE! VIOLENCE!

(*The other three struggle.* GEORGE'*s hands are on* MARTHA'*s throat.* NICK *grabs him, tears him from* MARTHA, *throws him on the floor.* GEORGE, *on the floor;* NICK *over him;* MARTHA *to one side, her hand on her throat.*)

NICK: That's enough now!

HONEY (*disappointment in her voice*): Oh . . . oh . . . oh. . . .

(GEORGE *drags himself into a chair. He is hurt, but it is more a profound humiliation than a physical injury.*)

GEORGE (*they watch him . . . a pause. . . .* ): All right . . . all right . . . very quiet now . . . we will all be . . . very quiet.

MARTHA (*softly, with a slow shaking of her head*): Murderer. Mur . . . der- . . . er.

NICK (*softly to* MARTHA): O.K. now . . . that's enough.

(*A brief silence. They all move around a little, self-consciously, like wrestlers flexing after a fall.*)

GEORGE (*composure seemingly recovered, but there is a great nervous intensity*): Well! That's one game. What shall we do now, hunh?

(MARTHA *and* NICK *laugh nervously.*)

Oh come on . . . let's think of something else. We've played Humiliate the Host . . . we've gone through that one . . . what shall we do now?

NICK: Aw . . . look. . . .

GEORGE: AW LOOK! (*Whines it.*) Awww . . . loooooook. (*Alert.*) I mean, come on! We must know other games, college type types like us . . . that can't be the . . . limit of our vocabulary, can it?

NICK: I think maybe. . . .

GEORGE: Let's see now . . . what else can we do? There are other games. How about . . . how about . . . Hump the Hostess? HUNH?? How about that? How about Hump the Hostess? (*To* NICK.) You wanna play that one? You wanna play Hump the Hostess? HUNH? HUNH?

NICK (*a little frightened*): Calm down, now.

(MARTHA *giggles quietly.*)

GEORGE: Or is that for later . . . mount her like a goddamn dog?

HONEY (*wildly toasting everybody*): Hump the Hostess!

NICK (*to* HONEY . . . *sharply*): Just shut up . . . will you?

(HONEY *does, her glass in mid-air.*)

GEORGE: You don't wanna play that now, hunh? You wanna save that game till later? Well, what'll we play now? We gotta play a game.

MARTHA (*quietly*): Portrait of a man drowning.

GEORGE (*affirmatively, but to none of them*): I am not drowning.

HONEY (*to* NICK, *tearfully indignant*): You told me to shut up!

NICK (*impatiently*): I'm sorry.

HONEY (*between her teeth*): No you're not.

NICK (*to* HONEY, *even more impatiently*): I'm sorry.

GEORGE (*claps his hands together, once, loud*): I've got it! I'll tell you what game we'll play. We're done with Humiliate the Host . . . this round, anyway . . . we're done with that . . . and we don't want to play Hump the Hostess, yet . . . not yet . . . So I know what we'll play. . . . We'll play a round of Get the Guests. How about that? How about a little game of Get the Guests?

MARTHA (*turning away, a little disgusted*): Jesus, George.

GEORGE: Book dropper! Child mentioner!

HONEY: I don't like these games.

NICK: Yeah. . . . I think maybe we've had enough of games, now. . . .

GEORGE: Oh, no . . . oh, no . . . we haven't. We've had only one game. . . . Now we're going to have another. You can't fly on one game.

NICK: I think maybe. . . .

GEORGE (*with great authority*): SILENCE! (*It is respected.*) Now, how are we going to play Get the Guests?

MARTHA: For God's sake, George. . . .

GEORGE: You be quiet!

(MARTHA *shrugs.*)

I wonder. . . . I wonder. (*Puzzles . . . then. . . .*) O.K.! Well . . . Martha . . . in her indiscreet way . . . well, not really indiscreet, because Martha is a naïve, at heart . . . anyway, Martha told you all about my first novel. True or false? Hunh? I mean, true or false that there ever was such a thing. HA! But, Martha told you about it . . . my first novel, my . . . memory book . . . which I'd sort of preferred she hadn't, but hell, that's blood under the bridge. BUT! what she didn't do . . . what Martha didn't tell you about is she didn't tell us all about my *second* novel.

(MARTHA *looks at him with puzzled curiosity.*)

No, you didn't know about that, did you, Martha? About my second novel, true or false. True or false?

MARTHA (*sincerely*): No.

GEORGE: No. (*He starts quietly but as he goes on, his tone becomes harsher, his voice louder.*) Well, it's an allegory, really — probably — but it can be read as straight, cozy prose . . . and it's all about a nice young couple who come out of the middle west. It's a bucolic you see. AND, this nice young couple comes out of the middle west, and he's blond and about thirty, and he's a scientist, a teacher, a scientist . . . and his mouse is a wifey little type who gargles brandy all the time . . . and. . . .

NICK: Just a minute here. . . .

GEORGE: . . . and they got to know each other when they was only teensie little types, and they used to get under the vanity table and poke around, and. . . .

NICK: I said JUST A MINUTE!

GEORGE: This is my game! You played yours . . . you people. This is my game!

HONEY (*dreamy*): I want to hear the story. I love stories.

MARTHA: George, for heaven's sake. . . .

GEORGE: AND! And Mousie's father was a holy man, see, and he ran sort of a traveling clip joint, based on Christ and all those girls, and he took the faithful . . . that's all . . . just took 'em. . . .

HONEY (*puzzling*): This is familiar. . . .

NICK (*voice shaking a little*): No kidding!

GEORGE: . . . and he died eventually, Mousie's pa, and they pried him open, and all sorts of money fell out. . . . Jesus money, Mary money. . . . LOOT!

HONEY (*dreamy, puzzling*): I've heard this story before.

NICK (*with quiet intensity . . . to waken her*): Honey. . . .

GEORGE: But that's in the backwash, in the early part of the book. Anyway, Blondie and his frau out of the plain states came. (*Chuckles.*)

MARTHA: Very funny, George. . . .

GEORGE: . . . thank you . . . and settled in a town just like nouveau Carthage here. . . .

NICK (*threatening*): I don't think you'd better go on, mister. . . .

GEORGE: Do you not!

NICK (*less certainly*): No. I . . . I don't think you'd better.

HONEY: I love familiar stories . . . they're the best.

GEORGE: How right you are. But Blondie was in disguise, really, all got up as a teacher, 'cause his baggage ticket had bigger things writ on it . . . H.I. HI! Historical inevitability.

NICK: There's no need for you to go any further, now. . . .

HONEY (*puzzling to make sense out of what she is hearing*): Let them go on.

GEORGE: We shall. And he had this baggage with him, and part of this baggage was in the form of his mouse. . . .

NICK: We don't have to listen to this!

HONEY: Why not?

GEORGE: Your bride has a point. And one of the things nobody could understand about Blondie was his baggage . . . his mouse, I mean, here he was, pan-Kansas swimming champeen, or something, and he had this mouse, of whom he was solicitous to a point that faileth human understanding . . . given that she was sort of a simp, in the long run. . . .

NICK: This isn't fair of you. . . .

GEORGE: Perhaps not. Like, as I said, his mouse, she tooted brandy immodestly and spent half of her time in the upchuck. . . .

HONEY (*focussing*): I know these people. . . .

GEORGE: Do you! . . . But she was a money baggage amongst other things . . . Godly money ripped from the golden teeth of the unfaithful, a pragmatic extension of the big dream . . . and she was put up with. . . .

HONEY (*some terror*): I don't like this story. . . .

NICK (*surprisingly pleading*): Please . . . please don't.

MARTHA: Maybe you better stop, George. . . .

GEORGE: . . . and she was put up with. . . . STOP? Ha-ha.

NICK: Please . . . please don't.

GEORGE: Beg, baby.

MARTHA: George. . . .

GEORGE: . . . and . . . oh, we get a flashback here, to How They Got Married.

NICK: NO!

GEORGE (*triumphant*): YES!

NICK (*almost whining*): Why?

GEORGE: How They Got Married. Well, how they got married is this. . . . The Mouse got all puffed up one day, and she went over to Blondie's house, and she stuck out her puff, and she said . . . look at me.

HONEY (*white . . . on her feet*): I . . . don't . . . like this.

NICK (*to* GEORGE): Stop it!

GEORGE: Look at me . . . I'm all puffed up. Oh my goodness, said Blondie. . . .

HONEY (*as from a distance*): . . . and so they were married. . . .

GEORGE: . . . and so they were married. . . .

HONEY: . . . and then. . . .

GEORGE: . . . and then. . . .

HONEY (*hysteria*): WHAT? . . . and then, WHAT?

NICK: NO! No!

GEORGE (*as if to a baby*): . . . and then the puff went *away* . . . like magic . . . pouf!

NICK (*almost sick*): Jesus God. . . .

HONEY: . . . the puff went away. . . .

GEORGE (*softly*): . . . pouf.

NICK: Honey . . . I didn't mean to . . . honestly, I didn't mean to. . . .

HONEY: You . . . you told them. . . .

NICK: Honey . . . I didn't mean to. . . .

HONEY (*with outlandish horror*): You . . . told them! You told them! OOOO-HHHH! Oh, no, no, no, no! You couldn't have told them . . . oh, noooo!

NICK: Honey, I didn't mean to. . . .

HONEY (*grabbing at her belly*): Ohhhhh . . . nooooo.

NICK: Honey . . . baby . . . I'm sorry . . . I didn't mean to. . . .

GEORGE (*abruptly and with some disgust*): And that's how you play Get the Guests.

HONEY: I'm going to . . . I'm going to be . . . sick. . . .

GEORGE: Naturally!

NICK: Honey. . . .

HONEY (*hysterical*): Leave me alone . . . I'm going . . . to . . . be . . . sick. (*She runs out of the room.*)

MARTHA (*shaking her head, watching* HONEY'*s retreating form*): God Almighty.

GEORGE (*shrugging*): The patterns of history.

NICK (*quietly shaking*): You shouldn't have done that . . . you shouldn't have done that at all.

GEORGE (*calmly*): I hate hypocrisy.

NICK: That was cruel . . . and vicious. . . .

GEORGE: . . . she'll get over it. . . .

NICK: . . . and damaging . . . !

GEORGE: . . . she'll recover. . . .

NICK: DAMAGING!! TO ME!!

GEORGE (*with wonder*): To you!

NICK: TO ME!!

GEORGE: To you!!

NICK: YES!!

GEORGE: Oh beautiful . . . beautiful. By God, you gotta have a swine to show you where the truffles are. (*So calmly.*) Well, you just rearrange your alliances, boy. You just pick up the pieces where you can . . . you just look around and make the best of things . . . you scramble back up on your feet.

MARTHA (*quietly, to* NICK): Go look after your wife.

GEORGE: Yeah . . . go pick up the pieces and plan some new strategy.

NICK (*to* GEORGE, *as he moves toward the hall*): You're going to regret this.

GEORGE: Probably. I regret everything.

NICK: I mean, I'm going to make you regret this.

GEORGE (*softly*): No doubt. Acute embarrassment, eh?

NICK: I'll play the charades like you've got 'em set up. . . . I'll play in your language. . . . I'll be what you say I am.

GEORGE: You are already . . . you just don't know it.

NICK (*shaking within*): No . . . no. Not really. But I'll *be* it, mister. . . . I'll show you something come to life you'll wish you hadn't set up.

GEORGE: Go clean up the mess.

NICK (*quietly . . . intensely*): You just wait, mister.

(*He exits. Pause.* GEORGE *smiles at* MARTHA.)

MARTHA: Very good, George.

GEORGE: Thank you, Martha.

MARTHA: Really good.

GEORGE: I'm glad you liked it.

MARTHA: I mean. . . . You did a good job . . . you really fixed it.

GEORGE: Unh-hunh.

MARTHA: It's the most . . . life you've shown in a long time.

GEORGE: You bring out the best in me, baby.

MARTHA: Yeah . . . pigmy hunting!

GEORGE: PIGMY!

MARTHA: You're really a bastard.

GEORGE: I? I?

MARTHA: Yeah . . . you.

GEORGE: Baby, if quarterback there is a pigmy, you've certainly changed your style. What are you after now . . . giants?

MARTHA: You make me sick.

GEORGE: It's perfectly all right for you. . . . I mean, you can make your own rules . . . you can go around like a hopped-up Arab, slashing away at everything in sight, scarring up half the world if you want to. But somebody else try it . . . no sir!

MARTHA: You miserable. . . .

GEORGE (*mocking*): Why baby, I did it all for you. I thought you'd like it, sweetheart . . . it's sort of to your taste . . . blood, carnage and all. Why, I thought you'd get all excited . . . sort of heave and pant and come running at me, your melons bobbling.

MARTHA: You've really screwed up, George.

GEORGE (*spitting it out*): Oh, for God's sake, Martha!

MARTHA: I mean it . . . you really have.

GEORGE: (*barely contained anger now*): You can sit there in that chair of yours, you can sit there with the gin running out of your mouth, and you can humiliate me, you can tear me apart . . . ALL NIGHT . . . and that's perfectly all right . . . that's O.K. . . .

MARTHA: YOU CAN STAND IT!

GEORGE: I CANNOT STAND IT!

MARTHA: YOU CAN STAND IT!! YOU MARRIED ME FOR IT!!

(*A silence.*)

GEORGE (*quietly*): That is a desperately sick lie.

MARTHA: DON'T YOU KNOW IT, EVEN YET?

GEORGE (*shaking his head*): Oh . . . Martha.

MARTHA: My arm has gotten tired whipping you.

GEORGE (*stares at her in disbelief*): You're mad.

MARTHA: For twenty-three years!

GEORGE: You're deluded . . . Martha, you're deluded.

MARTHA: IT'S NOT WHAT I'VE WANTED!

GEORGE: I thought at least you were . . . on to yourself. I didn't know. I . . . didn't know.

MARTHA (*anger taking over*): I'm on to myself.

GEORGE (*as if she were some sort of bug*): No . . . no . . . you're . . . sick.

MARTHA (*rises – screams*): I'LL SHOW YOU WHO'S SICK!

GEORGE: All right, Martha . . . you're going too far.

MARTHA (*screams again*): I'LL SHOW YOU WHO'S SICK. I'LL SHOW YOU.

GEORGE (*he shakes her*): Stop it! (*Pushes her back in her chair.*) Now, stop it!

MARTHA (*calmer*): I'll show you who's sick. (*Calmer.*) Boy, you're really having a field day, hunh? Well, I'm going to finish you . . . before I'm through with you. . . .

GEORGE: . . . you and the quarterback . . . you both gonna finish me . . . ?

MARTHA: . . . before I'm through with you you'll wish you'd died in that automobile, you bastard.

GEORGE (*emphasizing with his forefinger*): And you'll wish you'd never mentioned our son!

MARTHA (*dripping contempt*): You. . . .

GEORGE: Now, I said I warned you.

MARTHA: I'm impressed.

GEORGE: I warned you not to go too far.

MARTHA: I'm just beginning.

GEORGE (*calmly, matter-of-factly*): I'm numbed enough . . . and I don't mean by liquor, though maybe that's been part of the process – a gradual, over-the-years going to sleep of the brain cells – I'm numbed enough, now, to be able to take you when we're alone. I don't listen to you . . . or when I *do* listen to you, I sift everything, I bring everything down to reflex response, so I don't really *hear* you, which is the only way to manage it. But you've taken a new tack, Martha, over the past couple of centuries – or however long it's been I've lived in this house with you – that makes it just too much . . . too much. I don't mind your dirty underthings in public . . . well, I *do* mind, but I've reconciled myself to that . . . but you've moved bag and baggage into your own fantasy world now, and you've started playing variations on your own distortions, and, as a result. . . .

MARTHA: Nuts!

GEORGE: Yes . . . you have.

MARTHA: Nuts!

GEORGE: Well, you can go on like that as long as you want to. And, when you're done. . . .

MARTHA: Have you ever listened to your sentences, George? Have you ever listened to the way you talk? You're so frigging . . . convoluted . . . that's what you are. You talk like you were writing one of your stupid papers.

GEORGE: Actually, I'm rather worried about you. About your mind.

MARTHA: Don't you worry about my mind, sweetheart!

GEORGE: I think I'll have you committed.

MARTHA: You WHAT?

GEORGE (*quietly . . . distinctly*): I think I'll have you committed.

MARTHA (*breaks into long laughter*): Oh baby, aren't you something!

GEORGE: I've got to find some way to really get at you.

MARTHA: You've got at me, George . . . you don't have to do anything. Twenty-three years of you has been quite enough.

GEORGE: Will you go quietly, then?

MARTHA: You know what's happened, George? You want to know what's *really happened?* (*Snaps her fingers.*) It's snapped, finally. Not me . . . *it.* The whole arrangement. You can go along . . . forever, and everything's . . . manageable. You make all sorts of excuses to yourself . . . *you* know . . . this is life . . . the hell with it . . . maybe tomorrow he'll be dead . . . maybe tomorrow *you'll* be dead . . . all sorts of excuses. But then, one day, one night, something happens . . . and SNAP! It breaks. And you just don't give a damn any more. I've tried with you, baby . . . really, I've tried.

GEORGE: Come off it, Martha.

MARTHA: I've tried . . . I've really tried.

GEORGE (*with some awe*): You're a monster . . . you *are.*

MARTHA: I'm loud, and I'm vulgar, and I wear the pants in this house because somebody's got to, but I am *not* a monster. I am *not.*

GEORGE: You're a spoiled, self-indulgent, willful, dirty-minded, liquor-ridden. . . .

MARTHA: SNAP! It went snap. Look, I'm not going to try to get through to you any more. . . . I'm not going to try. There was a second back there, maybe, there was a second, just a second, when I could have gotten through to you, when maybe we could have cut through all this crap. But that's past, and now I'm not going to try.

GEORGE: Once a month, Martha! I've gotten used to it . . . once a month and we get misunderstood Martha, the good-hearted girl underneath the barnacles, the little Miss that the touch of kindness'd bring to bloom again. And I've believed it more times than I want to remember, because I don't want to think I'm that much of a sucker. I don't believe you . . . I just don't believe you. There is no moment . . . there is no moment any more when we could . . . come together.

MARTHA (*armed again*): Well, maybe you're right, baby. You can't come together with nothing, and you're nothing! SNAP! It went snap tonight at Daddy's party. (*Dripping contempt, but there is fury and loss under it.*) I sat there at Daddy's party, and I watched you . . . I watched you sitting there, and I watched the younger men around you, the men who were going to go somewhere. And I sat there and I watched you, and *you* weren't *there!* And it snapped! It finally snapped! And I'm going to howl it out, and I'm not going to give a damn what I do, and I'm going to make the damned biggest explosion you ever heard.

GEORGE (*very pointedly*): You try it and I'll beat you at your own game.

MARTHA (*hopefully*): Is that a threat, George? Hunh?

GEORGE: That's a threat, Martha.

MARTHA (*fake-spits at him*): You're going to get it, baby.

GEORGE: Be careful, Martha . . . I'll rip you to pieces.

MARTHA: You aren't man enough . . . you haven't got the guts.

GEORGE: Total war?

MARTHA: Total.

(*Silence. They both seem relieved . . . elated.* NICK *re-enters.*)

NICK (*brushing his hands off*): Well . . . she's . . . resting.

GEORGE (*quietly amused at* NICK*'s calm, off-hand manner*): Oh?

MARTHA: Yeah? She all right?

NICK: I think so . . . now. I'm . . . terribly sorry. . . .

MARTHA: Forget about it.

GEORGE: Happens all the time around here.

NICK: She'll be all right.

MARTHA: She lying down? You put her upstairs? On a bed?

NICK (*making himself a drink*): Well, no, actually. Uh . . . may I? She's . . . in the bathroom . . . on the bathroom floor . . . she's lying there.

GEORGE (*considers it*): Well . . . that's not very nice.

NICK: She likes it. She says it's . . . cool.

GEORGE: Still, I don't think. . . .

MARTHA (*overruling him*): If she wants to lie on the bathroom floor, let her. (*To* NICK, *seriously.*) Maybe she'd be more comfortable in the tub?

NICK (*he, too, seriously*): No, she says she likes the floor . . . she took up the mat, and she's lying on the tiles. She . . . she lies on the floor a lot . . . she really does.

MARTHA (*pause*): Oh.

NICK: She . . . she gets lots of headaches and things, and she always lies on the floor. (*To* GEORGE.) Is there . . . ice?

GEORGE: What?

NICK: Ice. Is there ice?
GEORGE (*as if the word were unfamiliar to him*): Ice?
NICK: Ice. Yes.
MARTHA: Ice.
GEORGE (*as if he suddenly understood*): Ice!
MARTHA: Attaboy.
GEORGE (*without moving*): Oh, yes . . . I'll get some.
MARTHA: Well, go. (*Mugging . . . to* NICK.) Besides, we want to be alone.
GEORGE (*moving to take the bucket*): I wouldn't be surprised, Martha . . . I wouldn't be surprised.
MARTHA (*as if insulted*): Oh, you wouldn't, hunh?
GEORGE: Not a bit, Martha.
MARTHA (*violent*): NO?
GEORGE (*he too*): NO! (*Quietly again.*) You'll try anything, Martha. (*Picks up the ice bucket.*)
NICK (*to cover*): Actually, she's very . . . frail, and. . . .
GEORGE: . . . slim-hipped.
NICK (*remembering*): Yes . . . exactly.
GEORGE (*at the hallway . . . not kindly*): That why you don't have any kids? (*He exits.*)
NICK (*to* GEORGE*'s retreating form*): Well, I don't know that that's . . . (*trails off*) . . . if that has anything to do with any . . . thing.
MARTHA: Well, if it does, who cares? Hunh?
NICK: Pardon?

(MARTHA *blows him a kiss.*)

NICK (*still concerned with* GEORGE*'s remark*): I . . . what? . . . I'm sorry.
MARTHA: I said . . . (*Blows him another kiss.*)
NICK (*uncomfortable*): Oh . . . yes.
MARTHA: Hey . . . hand me a cigarette . . . lover. (NICK *fishes in his pocket.*) That's a good boy. (*He gives her one.*) Unh . . . thanks.

(*He lights it for her. As he does, she slips her hand between his legs, somewhere between the knee and the crotch, bringing her hand around to the outside of his leg.*)

Ummmmmmmm.

(*He seems uncertain, but does not move. She smiles, moves her hand a little.*)

Now, for being such a good boy, you can give me a kiss. C'mon.
NICK (*nervously*): Look . . . I don't think we should. . . .
MARTHA: C'mon, baby . . . a friendly kiss.
NICK (*still uncertain*): Well. . . .
MARTHA: . . . you won't get hurt, little boy. . . .
NICK: . . . not so little. . . .

MARTHA: I'll bet you're not. C'mon. . . .

NICK (*weakening*): But what if he should come back in, and . . . or . . . ?

MARTHA (*all the while her hand is moving up and down his leg*): George? Don't worry about him. Besides, who could object to a friendly little kiss? It's all in the faculty.

(*They both laugh, quietly . . .* NICK *a little nervously.*)

We're a close-knit family here . . . Daddy always says so. . . . Daddy wants us to get to know each other . . . that's what he had the party for tonight. So c'mon . . . let's get to know each other a little bit.

NICK: It isn't that I don't want to . . . believe me. . . .

MARTHA: You're a scientist, aren't you? C'mon . . . make an experiment . . . make a little experiment. Experiment on old Martha.

NICK (*giving in*): . . . not very old. . . .

MARTHA: That's right, not very old, but lots of good experience . . . lots of it.

NICK: I'll . . . I'll bet.

MARTHA (*as they draw slowly closer*): It'll be a nice change for you, too.

NICK: Yes, it would.

MARTHA: And you could go back to your little wife all refreshed.

NICK (*closer . . . almost whispering*): She wouldn't know the difference.

MARTHA: Well, nobody else's going to know, either.

(*They come together. What might have been a joke rapidly becomes serious, with* MARTHA *urging it in that direction. There is no frenetic quality, but rather a slow, continually involving intertwining. Perhaps* MARTHA *is still more or less in her chair, and* NICK *is sort of beside and on the chair.*

GEORGE *enters . . . stops . . . watches a moment . . . smiles . . . laughs silently, nods his head, turns, exits, without being noticed.*

NICK, *who has already had his hand on* MARTHA'*s breast, now puts his hand inside her dress.*)

MARTHA (*slowing him down*): Hey . . . hey. Take it easy, boy. Down, baby. Don't rush it, hunh?

NICK (*his eyes still closed*): Oh, c'mon, now. . . .

MARTHA (*pushing him away*): Unh-unh. Later, baby . . . later.

NICK: I told you . . . I'm a biologist.

MARTHA (*soothing him*): I know. I can tell. Later, hunh?

(GEORGE *is heard off-stage, singing "Who's afraid of Virginia Woolf?"* MARTHA *and* NICK *go apart,* NICK *wiping his mouth,* MARTHA *checking her clothes. Safely later,* GEORGE *re-enters with the ice bucket.*)

GEORGE: . . . of Virginia Woolf,
Virginia Woolf,
Virginia. . . .

. . . ah! Here we are . . . ice for the lamps of China, Manchuria thrown in. (*To* NICK.) You better watch those yellow bastards, my love . . . they aren't amused. Why don't you come on over to our side, and we'll blow the hell out of 'em. Then we can split up the money between us and be on Easy Street. What d'ya say?

NICK (*not at all sure what is being talked about*): Well . . . sure. Hey! Ice!

GEORGE (*with hideously false enthusiasm*): Right! (*Now to* MARTHA, *purring.*) Hello, Martha . . . my dove. . . . You look . . . radiant.

MARTHA (*off-hand*): Thank you.

GEORGE (*very cheerful*): Well now, let me see. I've got the ice. . . .

MARTHA: . . . gotten. . . .

GEORGE: *Got,* Martha. Got is perfectly correct . . . it's just a little . . . archaic, like you.

MARTHA (*suspicious*): What are you so cheerful about?

GEORGE (*ignoring the remark*): Let's see now . . . I've got the ice. Can I make someone a drink? Martha, can I make you a drink?

MARTHA (*bravura*): Yeah, why not?

GEORGE (*taking her glass*): Indeed . . . why not? (*Examines the glass.*) Martha! You've been nibbling away at the glass.

MARTHA: I have not!

GEORGE (*to* NICK, *who is at the bar*): I see you're making your own, which is fine . . . fine. I'll just hootch up Martha, here, and then we'll be all set.

MARTHA (*suspicious*): All set for what?

GEORGE (*pause . . . considers*): Why, I don't know. We're having a party, aren't we? (*To* NICK, *who has moved from the bar.*) I passed your wife in the hall. I mean, I passed the john and I looked in on her. Peaceful . . . so peaceful. Sound asleep . . . and she's actually . . . sucking her thumb.

MARTHA: Awwwwww!

GEORGE: Rolled up like a fetus, sucking away.

NICK (*a little uncomfortably*): I suppose she's all right.

GEORGE (*expansively*): Of course she is! (*Hands* MARTHA *her drink.*) There you are.

MARTHA (*still on her guard*): Thanks.

GEORGE: And now one for me. It's my turn.

MARTHA: Never, baby . . . it's never your turn.

GEORGE (*too cheerful*): Oh, now, I wouldn't say that, Martha.

MARTHA: You moving on the principle the worm turns? Well, the worm part's O.K. . . . cause that fits you fine, but the turning part . . . unh-unh! You're in a straight line, buddy-boy, and it doesn't lead anywhere . . . (*a vague afterthought*) . . . except maybe the grave.

GEORGE (*chuckles, takes his drink*): Well, you just hold that thought, Martha . . . hug it close . . . run your hands over it. Me, I'm going to sit down . . . if you'll excuse me. . . . I'm going to sit down over there and read a book. (*He moves to a chair facing away from the center of the room, but not too far from the front door.*)

MARTHA: You're gonna do *what?*

GEORGE (*quietly, distinctly*): I am going to read a book. Read. Read. Read? You've heard of it? (*Picks up a book.*)
MARTHA (*standing*): Whaddya mean you're gonna read? What's the matter with you?
GEORGE (*too calmly*): There's nothing the matter with me, Martha. . . . I'm going to read a book. That's all.
MARTHA (*oddly furious*): We've got company!
GEORGE (*over-patiently*): I know, my dear . . . (*Looks at his watch.*) . . . but . . . it's after four o'clock, and I always read around this time. Now, you . . . (*dismisses her with a little wave.*) . . . go about your business. . . . I'll sit here very quietly. . . .
MARTHA: You read in the afternoon! You read at four o'clock in the afternoon . . . you don't read at four o'clock in the morning! Nobody reads at four o'clock in the morning!
GEORGE (*absorbing himself in his book*): Now, now, now.
MARTHA (*incredulously, to* NICK): He's going to read a book. . . . The son of a bitch is going to read a book!
NICK (*smiling a little*): So it would seem.

(*Moves to* MARTHA, *puts his arm around her waist.* GEORGE *cannot see this, of course.*)

MARTHA (*getting an idea*): Well, we can amuse ourselves, can't we?
NICK: I imagine so.
MARTHA: We're going to amuse ourselves, George.
GEORGE (*not looking up*): Unh-hunh. That's nice.
MARTHA: You might not like it.
GEORGE (*never looking up*): No, no, now . . . you go right ahead . . . you entertain your guests.
MARTHA: I'm going to entertain myself, too.
GEORGE: Good . . . good.
MARTHA: Ha, ha. You're a riot, George.
GEORGE: Unh-hunh.
MARTHA: Well, I'm a riot, too, George.
GEORGE: Yes you are, Martha.

(NICK *takes* MARTHA'*s hand, pulls her to him. They stop for a moment, then kiss, not briefly.*)

MARTHA (*after*): You know what I'm doing, George?
GEORGE: No, Martha . . . what are you doing?
MARTHA: I'm entertaining. I'm entertaining one of the guests. I'm necking with one of the guests.
GEORGE (*seemingly relaxed and preoccupied, never looking*): Oh, that's nice. Which one?
MARTHA (*livid*): Oh, by God you're funny. (*Breaks away from* NICK . . .

*moves into* GEORGE*'s side-line of vision by herself. Her balance is none too good, and she bumps into or brushes against the door chimes by the door. They chime.*)

GEORGE: Someone at the door, Martha.

MARTHA: Never mind that. I said I was necking with one of the guests.

GEORGE: Good . . . good. You go right on.

MARTHA (*pauses . . . not knowing quite what to do*): Good?

GEORGE: Yes, good . . . good for you.

MARTHA (*her eyes narrowing, her voice becoming hard*): Oh, I see what you're up to, you lousy little. . . .

GEORGE: I'm up to page a hundred and. . . .

MARTHA: Cut it! Just cut it out! (*She hits against the door chimes again; they chime.*) Goddam bongs.

GEORGE: They're chimes, Martha. Why don't you go back to your necking and stop bothering me? I want to read.

MARTHA: Why, you miserable. . . . I'll show *you.*

GEORGE (*swings around to face her . . . says, with great loathing*): No . . . show him, Martha . . . he hasn't seen it. *Maybe* he hasn't seen it. (*Turns to* NICK.) You haven't seen it yet, have you?

NICK (*turning away, a look of disgust on his face*): I . . . I have no respect for you.

GEORGE: And none for yourself, either. . . . (*Indicating* MARTHA.) I don't know what the younger generation's coming to.

NICK: You don't . . . you don't even. . . .

GEORGE: Care? You're quite right. . . . I couldn't care less. So, you just take this bag of laundry here, throw her over your shoulder, and. . . .

NICK: You're disgusting.

GEORGE (*incredulous*): Because *you're* going to hump Martha, *I'm* disgusting? (*He breaks down in ridiculing laughter.*)

MARTHA (*to* GEORGE): You Mother! (*To* NICK.) Go wait for me, hunh? Go wait for me in the kitchen. (*But* NICK *does not move.* MARTHA *goes to him, puts her arms around him.*) C'mon, baby . . . please. Wait for me . . . in the kitchen . . . be a good baby.

(NICK *takes her kiss, glares at* GEORGE *. . . who has turned his back again . . . and exits.*)

(MARTHA *swings around to* GEORGE.) Now you listen to me. . . .

GEORGE: I'd rather read, Martha, if you don't mind. . . .

MARTHA (*her anger has her close to tears, her frustration to fury*): Well, I do mind. Now, you pay attention to me! You come off this kick you're on, or I swear to God I'll do it. I swear to God I'll follow that guy into the kitchen, and then I'll take him upstairs, and. . . .

GEORGE (*swinging around to her again . . . loud . . . loathing*): SO WHAT, MARTHA?

MARTHA (*considers him for a moment . . . then, nodding her head, backing off slowly*): O.K. . . . O.K. . . . You asked for it . . . and you're going to get it.

GEORGE (*softly, sadly*): Lord, Martha, if you want the boy that much . . . have him . . . but do it honestly, will you? Don't cover it over with all this . . . all this . . . footwork.

MARTHA (*hopeless*): I'll make you sorry you made me want to marry you. (*At the hallway.*) I'll make you regret the day you ever decided to come to this college. I'll make you sorry you ever let yourself down. (*She exits.*)

(*Silence.* GEORGE *sits still, staring straight ahead. Listening . . . but there is no sound. Outwardly calm, he returns to his book, reads a moment, then looks up . . . considers. . . .*)

GEORGE: "And the west, encumbered by crippling alliances, and burdened with a morality too rigid to accommodate itself to the swing of events, must . . . eventually . . . fall."

(*He laughs, briefly, ruefully . . . rises, with the book in his hand. He stands still . . . then, quickly, he gathers all the fury he has been containing within himself . . . he shakes . . . he looks at the book in his hand and, with a cry that is part growl, part howl, he hurls it at the chimes. They crash against one another, ringing wildly. A brief pause, then* HONEY *enters.*)

HONEY (*the worse for wear, half asleep, still sick, weak, still staggering a little . . . vaguely, in something of a dream world*): Bells. Ringing. I've been hearing bells.

GEORGE: Jesus!

HONEY: I couldn't sleep . . . for the bells. Ding-ding, bong . . . it woke me up. What time is it?

GEORGE (*quietly beside himself*): Don't bother me.

HONEY (*confused and frightened*): I was asleep, and the bells started . . . they BOOMED! Poe-bells . . . they were Poe-bells . . . Bing-bing-bong-BOOM!

GEORGE: BOOM!

HONEY: I was asleep, and I was dreaming of . . . something . . . and I heard the sounds coming, and I didn't know what it was.

GEORGE (*never quite to her*): It was the sound of bodies. . . .

HONEY: And I didn't want to wake up, but the sound kept coming. . . .

GEORGE: . . . go back to sleep. . . .

HONEY: . . . and it FRIGHTENED ME!

GEORGE (*quietly . . . to* MARTHA, *as if she were in the room*): I'm going to get you . . . Martha.

HONEY: And it was so . . . cold. The wind was . . . the wind was so cold! And I was lying somewhere, and the covers kept slipping away from me, and I didn't want them to. . . .

GEORGE: Somehow, Martha.

HONEY: . . . and there was someone there . . . !

GEORGE: There was no one there.

HONEY (*frightened*): And I didn't want someone there. . . . I was . . . naked . . . !

GEORGE: You don't know what's going on, do you?

HONEY (*still with her dream*): I DON'T WANT ANY . . . NO . . . !

GEORGE: You don't know what's been going on around here while you been having your snoozette, do you.

HONEY: NO! . . . I DON'T WANT ANY . . . I DON'T WANT THEM . . . GO 'WAY. . . . (*Begins to cry.*) I DON'T WANT . . . ANY . . . CHILDREN. . . . I . . . don't . . . want . . . any . . . children. I'm afraid! I don't want to be hurt. . . . PLEASE!

GEORGE (*nodding his head . . . speaks with compassion*): I should have known.

HONEY (*snapping awake from her reverie*): What! What?

GEORGE: I should have known . . . the whole business . . . the headaches . . . the whining . . . the. . . .

HONEY (*terrified*): What are you talking about?

GEORGE (*ugly again*): Does *he* know that? Does that . . . stud you're married to know about that, hunh?

HONEY: About what? Stay away from me!

GEORGE: Don't worry, baby . . . I wouldn't. . . . Oh, my God, that *would* be a joke, wouldn't it! But don't worry, baby. HEY! How you do it? Hunh? How do you make your secret little murders stud-boy doesn't know about, hunh? Pills? PILLS? You got a secret supply of pills? Or what? Apple jelly? WILL POWER?

HONEY: I feel sick.

GEORGE: You going to throw up again? You going to lie down on the cold tiles, your knees pulled up under your chin, your thumb stuck in your mouth . . . ?

HONEY (*panicked*): Where is he?

GEORGE: Where's who? There's nobody here, baby.

HONEY: I want my husband! I want a drink!

GEORGE: Well, you just crawl over to the bar and make yourself one.

(*From off-stage comes the sound of* MARTHA*'s laughter and the crashing of dishes.*)

(*Yelling.*) That's right! Go at it!

HONEY: I want . . . something. . . .

GEORGE: You know what's going on in there, little Miss? Hunh? You hear all that? You know what's going on in there?

HONEY: I don't want to know anything!

GEORGE: There are a couple of people in there. . . .

(MARTHA*'s laughter again.*)

. . . they are in there, in the kitchen. . . . Right there, with the onion skins and the coffee grounds . . . sort of . . . sort of a . . . sort of a dry run for the wave of the future.

HONEY (*beside herself*): I . . . don't . . . understand . . . you . . .

GEORGE (*a hideous elation*): It's very simple. . . . When people can't abide things as they are, when they can't abide the present, they do one of two things . . . either they . . . either they turn to a contemplation of the past, as I have done, or they set about to . . . alter the future. And when you want to change something . . . you BANG! BANG! BANG! BANG!

HONEY: Stop it!

GEORGE: And you, you simpering bitch . . . you don't want *children?*

HONEY: You leave me . . . alone. Who . . . WHO RANG?

GEORGE: What?

HONEY: What were the bells? Who rang?

GEORGE: You don't want to know, do you? You don't want to listen to it, hunh?

HONEY (*shivering*): I don't want to listen to you. . . . I want to know who rang.

GEORGE: Your husband is . . . and you want to know who *rang?*

HONEY: Who rang? Someone rang!

GEORGE (*his jaw drops open . . . he is whirling with an idea*): . . . *Someone. . . .*

HONEY: RANG!

GEORGE: . . . someone . . . rang . . . yes . . . yessss. . . .

HONEY: The . . . bells . . . rang. . . .

GEORGE (*his mind racing ahead*): The bells rang . . . and it was someone. . . .

HONEY: Somebody. . . .

GEORGE (*he is home, now*): . . . somebody rang . . . it was somebody . . . with . . . I'VE GOT IT! I'VE GOT IT, MARTHA . . . ! Somebody with a message . . . and the message was . . . our son . . . OUR SON! (*Almost whispered.*) It was a message . . . the bells rang and it was a message, and it was about . . . our son . . . and the message . . . was . . . and the message was . . . our . . . son . . . is . . . DEAD!

HONEY (*almost sick*): Oh . . . no.

GEORGE (*cementing it in his mind*): Our son is . . . dead. . . . And . . . Martha doesn't know. . . . I haven't told . . . Martha.

HONEY: No . . . no . . . no.

GEORGE (*slowly, deliberately*): Our son is dead, and Martha doesn't know.

HONEY: Oh. God in heaven . . . no.

GEORGE (*to* HONEY . . . *slowly, deliberately, dispassionately*): And you're not going to tell her.

HONEY (*in tears*): Your son is dead.

GEORGE: I'll tell her myself . . . in good time. I'll tell her myself.

HONEY (*so faintly*): I'm going to be sick.

GEORGE (*turning away from her . . . he, too, softly*): Are you? That's nice.

(MARTHA'*s laugh is heard again.*)

Oh, listen to that.

HONEY: I'm going to die.

GEORGE (*quite by himself now*): Good . . . good . . . you go right ahead. (*Very softly, so* MARTHA *could not possibly hear.*) Martha? Martha? I have some . . . terrible news for you. (*There is a strange half-smile on his lips.*) It's about our . . . son. He's dead. Can you hear me, Martha? Our boy is dead. (*He begins to laugh, very softly . . . it is mixed with crying.*)

CURTAIN

## ACT III. THE EXORCISM

MARTHA *enters, talking to herself.*

MARTHA: Hey, hey. . . . Where is everybody . . . ? (*It is evident she is not bothered.*) So? Drop me; pluck me like a goddamn . . . whatever-it-is . . . creeping vine, and throw me over your shoulder like an old shoe . . . George? (*Looks about her.*) George? (*Silence.*) George! What are you doing: Hiding, or something? (*Silence.*) GEORGE!! (*Silence.*) Oh, fa Chri. . . . (*Goes to the bar, makes herself a drink and amuses herself with the following performance.*) Deserted! Abandon-ed! Left out in the cold like an old pussycat. HA! Can I get you a drink, Martha? Why, thank you, George; that's very kind of you. No, Martha, no; why I'd do anything for you. Would you, George? Why, I'd do anything for you, too. Would you, Martha? Why, certainly, George. Martha, I've misjudged you. And I've misjudged you, too, George. WHERE IS EVERYBODY!!! Hump the Hostess! (*Laughs greatly at this, falls into a chair; calms down, looks defeated, says, softly.*) Fat chance. (*Even softer.*) Fat chance. (*Baby-talk now.*) Daddy? Daddy? Martha is abandon-ed. Left to her own vices at . . . (*peers at a clock*) . . . something o'clock in the old A.M. Daddy White-Mouse; do you really have red eyes? Do you? Let me see. Ohhhhh! You do! You do! Daddy, you have red eyes . . . because you cry all the time, don't you, Daddy. Yes; you do. You cry alllll the time. I'LL GIVE ALL YOU BASTARDS FIVE TO COME OUT FROM WHERE YOU'RE HIDING!! (*Pause.*) I cry all the time too, Daddy. I cry alllll the time; but deep inside, so no one can see me. I cry all the time. And Georgie cries all the time, too. We both cry all the time, and then, what we do, we cry, and we take our tears, and we put 'em in the ice box, in the goddamn ice trays (*begins to laugh*) until they're all frozen (*laughs even more*) and then . . . we put them . . . in our . . . drinks. (*More laughter, which is something else, too. After sobering silence.*) Up the drain, down the spout, dead, gone and forgotten. . . . Up the spout, not down the spout; *Up* the spout: THE POKER NIGHT. Up the spout. . . . (*Sadly.*) I've got windshield wipers on my eyes, because I married you . . . baby! . . . Martha, you'll be a song-writer yet. (*Jiggles the ice in her glass.*) CLINK! (*Does it again.*) CLINK! (*Giggles, repeats it several times.*) CLINK! . . . CLINK! . . . CLINK! . . . CLINK!

(NICK *enters while* MARTHA *is clinking; he stands in the hall entrance and watches her; finally he comes in.*)

NICK: My God, you've gone crazy too.
MARTHA: Clink?
NICK: I said, you've gone crazy too.
MARTHA (*considers it*): Probably . . . probably.
NICK: You've all gone crazy: I come downstairs, and what happens. . . .
MARTHA: What happens?
NICK: . . . my wife's gone into the can with a liquor bottle, and she winks at me . . . winks at me! . . .
MARTHA (*sadly*): She's never wunk at you; what a shame. . . .
NICK: She is lying down on the floor again, the tiles, all curled up, and she starts peeling the label off the liquor bottle, the brandy bottle. . . .
MARTHA: . . . we'll never get the deposit back that way. . . .
NICK: . . . and I ask her what she's doing, and she goes: shhhhhh! nobody knows I'm here; and I come back in here, and you're sitting there going Clink! for God's sake. Clink!
MARTHA: CLINK!
NICK: You've all gone crazy.
MARTHA: Yes. Sad but true.
NICK: Where is your husband?
MARTHA: He is vanish-ed. Pouf!
NICK: You're all crazy: nuts.
MARTHA (*affects a brogue*): Awww, 'tis the refuge we take when the unreality of the world weighs too heavy on our tiny heads. (*Normal voice again.*) Relax; sink into it; you're no better than anybody else.
NICK (*wearily*): I think I am.
MARTHA (*her glass to her mouth*): You're certainly a flop in some departments.
NICK (*wincing*): I beg your pardon . . . ?
MARTHA (*unnecessarily loud*): I said, you're certainly a flop in some. . . .
NICK (*he, too, too loud*): I'm sorry you're disappointed.
MARTHA (*braying*): I didn't say I was disappointed! Stupid!
NICK: You should try me some time when we haven't been drinking for ten hours, and maybe. . . .

MARTHA (*still braying*): I wasn't talking about your potential; I was talking about your goddamn performance.

NICK (*softly*): Oh.

MARTHA (*she softer, too*): Your potential's fine. It's dandy. (*Wiggles her eyebrows.*) Absolutely dandy. I haven't seen such a dandy potential in a long time. Oh, but baby, you sure are a flop.

NICK (*snapping it out*): Everybody's a flop to you! Your husband's a flop, *I'm* a flop....

MARTHA (*dismissing him*): You're all flops. I am the Earth Mother, and you're all flops. (*More or less to herself.*) I disgust me. I pass my life in crummy, totally pointless infidelities . . . (*laughs ruefully*) *would*-be infidelities. Hump the Hostess? That's a laugh. A bunch of boozed-up . . . impotent lunk-heads. Martha makes goo-goo eyes, and the lunk-heads grin, and roll their beautiful, beautiful eyes back, and grin some more, and Martha licks her chops, and the lunk-heads slap over to the bar to pick up a little courage, *and* they pick up a little courage, and they bounce back over to old Martha, who does a little dance for them, which heats them all up . . . mentally . . . and so they slap over to the bar again, and pick up a little more courage, and their wives and sweethearts stick their noses up in the air . . . right through the ceiling, sometimes . . . which sends the lunk-heads back to the soda fountain again where they fuel up some more, while Martha-poo sits there with her dress up over her head . . . suffocating – you don't know how *stuffy* it is with your dress up over your head – suffocating! waiting for the lunk-heads; so, *finally* they get their courage up . . . but that's all, baby! Oh my, there is sometimes some very nice potential, but, oh my! My, my, my. (*Brightly.*) But that's how it is in a civilized society. (*To herself again.*) All the gorgeous lunk-heads. Poor babies. (*To* NICK, *now; earnestly.*) There is only one man in my life who has ever . . . made me happy. Do you know that? One!

NICK: The . . . the what-do-you-call-it? . . . uh . . . the lawn mower, or something?

MARTHA: No; I'd forgotten him. But when I think about him and me it's almost like being a voyeur. Hunh. No; I didn't mean him; I meant George, of course. (*No response from* NICK.) Uh . . . George; my husband.

NICK (*disbelieving*): You're kidding.

MARTHA: Am I?

NICK: You must be. Him?

MARTHA: Him.

NICK (*as if in on a joke*): Sure; sure.

MARTHA: You don't believe it.

NICK (*mocking*): Why, of course I do.

MARTHA: You always deal in appearances?

NICK (*derisively*): Oh, for God's sake....

MARTHA: . . . George who is out somewhere there in the dark. . . . George who is good to me, and whom I revile; who understands me, and whom I push off; who can make me laugh, and I choke it back in my throat; who can hold me, at night, so that it's warm, and whom I will bite so there's blood; who keeps learning the games we play as quickly as I can change the rules; who can make me happy and I do not wish to be happy, and yes I do wish to be happy. George and Martha: sad, sad, sad.

NICK (*echoing, still not believing*): Sad.

MARTHA: . . . whom I will not forgive for having come to rest; for having seen me and having said: yes; this will do; who has made the hideous, the hurting, the insulting mistake of loving me and must be punished for it. George and Martha: sad, sad, sad.

NICK (*puzzled*): Sad.

MARTHA: . . . who tolerates, which is intolerable; who is kind, which is cruel; who understands, which is beyond comprehension. . . .

NICK: George and Martha: sad, sad, sad.

MARTHA: Some day . . . hah! some *night* . . . some stupid, liquor-ridden night . . . I will go too far . . . and I'll either break the man's back . . . or push him off for good . . . which is what I deserve.

NICK: I don't think he's got a vertebra intact.

MARTHA (*laughing at him*): You don't, huh? You don't think so. Oh, little boy, you got yourself hunched over that microphone of yours. . . .

NICK: Microscope. . . .

MARTHA: . . . yes . . . and you don't see anything, do you? You see everything but the goddamn mind; you see all the little specks and crap, but you don't see what goes on, do you?

NICK: I know when a man's had his back broken; I can see that.

MARTHA: Can you!

NICK: You're damn right.

MARTHA: Oh . . . you know so little. And you're going to take over the world, hunh?

NICK: All right, now. . . .

MARTHA: You think a man's got his back broken 'cause he makes like a clown and walks bent, hunh? Is that *really* all you know?

NICK: I said, all *right!*

MARTHA: Ohhhh! The stallion's mad, hunh. The gelding's all upset. Ha, ha, ha, HA!

NICK (*softly; wounded*): You . . . you swing wild, don't you.

MARTHA (*triumphant*): HAH!

NICK: Just . . . anywhere.

MARTHA: HAH! I'm a Gatling gun. Hahahahahahahahaha!

NICK (*in wonder*): Aimless . . . butchery. Pointless.

MARTHA: Aw! You poor little bastard.

NICK: Hit out at everything.

(*The door chimes chime.*)

MARTHA: Go answer the door.
NICK (*amazed*): What did you say?
MARTHA: I said, go answer the door. What are you, deaf?
NICK (*trying to get it straight*): You . . . want me . . . to go answer the door?
MARTHA: That's right, lunk-head; answer the door. There must be something you can do well; or, are you too drunk to do that, too? Can't you get the latch up, either?
NICK: Look, there's no need. . . .

(*Door chimes again.*)

MARTHA (*shouting*): Answer it! (*Softer.*) You can be houseboy around here for a while. You can start off being houseboy right now.
NICK: Look, lady, I'm no flunky to you.
MARTHA (*cheerfully*): Sure you are! You're ambitious, aren't you, boy? You didn't chase me around the kitchen and up the goddamn stairs out of mad, driven passion, did you now? You were thinking a little bit about your career, weren't you? Well, you can just houseboy your way up the ladder for a while.
NICK: There's no limit to you, is there?

(*Door chimes again.*)

MARTHA (*calmly, surely*): No, baby; none. Go answer the door. (NICK *hesitates.*) Look, boy; once you stick your nose in it, you're not going to pull out just whenever you feel like it. You're in for a while. Now, git!
NICK: Aimless . . . wanton . . . pointless. . . .
MARTHA: Now, now, now; just do what you're told; show old Martha there's something you *can* do. Hunh? Attaboy.
NICK (*considers, gives in, moves toward the door*): (*Chimes again.*) I'm coming, for Christ's sake!
MARTHA (*claps her hands*): Ha HA! Wonderful; marvelous. (*Sings.*) "Just a gigolo, everywhere I go, people always say. . . ."
NICK: STOP THAT!
MARTHA (*giggles*): Sorry, baby; go on now; open the little door.
NICK (*with great rue*): Christ.

(*He flings open the door, and a hand thrusts into the opening a great bunch of snapdragons; they stay there for a moment.* NICK *strains his eyes to see who is behind them.*)

MARTHA: Oh, how lovely!
GEORGE (*appearing in the doorway, the snapdragons covering his face;*

*speaks in a hideously cracked falsetto*): Flores; flores para los muertos. Flores.

MARTHA: Ha, ha, ha, HA!

GEORGE (*a step into the room; lowers the flowers; sees* NICK; *his face becomes gleeful; he opens his arms*): Sonny! You've come home for your birthday! At last!

NICK (*backing off*): Stay away from me.

MARTHA: Ha, ha, ha, HA! That's the houseboy, for God's sake.

GEORGE: Really? That's not our own little sonny-Jim? Our own little all-American something-or-other?

MARTHA (*giggling*): Well, I certainly hope not; he's been acting awful funny, if he is.

GEORGE (*almost manic*): Ohhhh! I'll bet! Chippie-chippie-chippie, hunh? (*Affecting embarrassment.*) I . . . I brungya dese flowers, Mart'a, 'cause I . . . wull, 'cause you'se . . . awwwwww hell. Gee.

MARTHA: Pansies! Rosemary! Violence! My wedding bouquet!

NICK (*starting to move away*): Well, if you two kids don't mind, I think I'll just. . . .

MARTHA: Ach! You just stay where you are. Make my hubby a drink.

NICK: I don't think I will.

GEORGE: No, Martha, no; that would be too much; he's your houseboy, baby, not mine.

NICK: I'm nobody's houseboy. . . .

GEORGE *and* MARTHA: . . . Now! (*Sing.*) I'm nobody's houseboy now. . . . (*Both laugh.*)

NICK: Vicious. . . .

GEORGE (*finishing it for him*): . . . children. Hunh? That right? Vicious children, with their oh-so-sad games, hopscotching their way through life, etcetera, etcetera. Is that it?

NICK: Something like it.

GEORGE: Screw, baby.

MARTHA: Him can't. Him too fulla booze.

GEORGE: Weally? (*Handing the snapdragons to* NICK.) Here; dump these in some gin. (NICK *takes them, looks at them, drops them on the floor at his feet.*)

MARTHA (*sham dismay*): Awwwwwww.

GEORGE: What a terrible thing to do . . . to Martha's snapdragons.

MARTHA: Is that what they are?

GEORGE: Yup. And here I went out into the moonlight to pick 'em for Martha tonight, and for our sonny-boy tomorrow, for his birfday.

MARTHA (*passing on information*): There is no moon now. I saw it go down from the bedroom.

GEORGE (*feigned glee*): From the bedroom! (*Normal tone.*) Well, there was a moon.

MARTHA (*too patient; laughing a little*): There couldn't have been a moon.
GEORGE: Well, there was. There is.
MARTHA: There is no moon; the moon went down.
GEORGE: There is a moon; the moon is up.
MARTHA (*straining to keep civil*): I'm afraid you're mistaken.
GEORGE (*too cheerful*): No; no.
MARTHA (*between her teeth*): There is no goddamn moon.
GEORGE: My dear Martha . . . I did not pick snapdragons in the stony dark. I did not go stumbling around Daddy's greenhouse in the pitch.
MARTHA: Yes . . . you did. You would.
GEORGE: Martha, I do not pick flowers in the blink. I have never robbed a hothouse without there is a light from heaven.
MARTHA (*with finality*): There is no moon; the moon went down.
GEORGE (*with great logic*): That may very well be, Chastity; the moon may very well have gone down . . . but it came back up.
MARTHA: The moon does *not* come back up; when the moon has gone down it stays down.
GEORGE (*getting a little ugly*): You don't know anything. IF the moon went down, then it came back up.
MARTHA: BULL!
GEORGE: Ignorance! Such . . . ignorance.
MARTHA: Watch who you're calling ignorant!
GEORGE: Once . . . once, when I was sailing past Majorca, drinking on deck with a correspondent who was talking about Roosevelt, the moon went down, thought about it for a little . . . considered it, you know what I mean? . . . and then, POP, came up again. Just like that.
MARTHA: That is not true! That is such a lie!
GEORGE: You must not call everything a lie, Martha. (*To* NICK.) Must she?
NICK: Hell, I don't know when you people are lying, or what.
MARTHA: You're damned right!
GEORGE: You're not supposed to.
MARTHA: Right!
GEORGE: At any rate, I was sailing past Majorca. . . .
MARTHA: You never sailed past Majorca. . . .
GEORGE: Martha. . . .
MARTHA: You were never in the goddamn Mediterranean at all . . . ever. . . .
GEORGE: I certainly was! My Mommy and Daddy took me there as a college graduation present.
MARTHA: Nuts!
NICK: Was this after you killed them?

(GEORGE *and* MARTHA *swing around and look at him; there is a brief, ugly pause.*)

GEORGE (*defiantly*): Maybe.

MARTHA: Yeah; maybe not, too.

NICK: Jesus!

(GEORGE *swoops down, picks up the bunch of snapdragons, shakes them like a feather duster in* NICK'*s face, and moves away a little.*)

GEORGE: HAH!

NICK: Damn you.

GEORGE (*to* NICK): Truth and illusion. Who knows the difference, eh, toots? Eh?

MARTHA: You were never in the Mediterranean . . . truth or illusion . . . either way.

GEORGE: If I wasn't in the Mediterranean, how did I get to the Aegean? Hunh?

MARTHA: OVERLAND!

NICK: Yeah!

GEORGE: Don't you side with her, houseboy.

NICK: I am not a houseboy.

GEORGE: Look! I know the game! You don't make it in the sack, you're a houseboy.

NICK: I AM NOT A HOUSEBOY!

GEORGE: No? Well then, you must have made it in the sack. Yes? (*He is breathing a little heavy; behaving a little manic.*) Yes? Someone's lying around here; somebody isn't playing the game straight. Yes? Come on; come on; who's lying? Martha? Come on!

NICK (*after a pause; to* MARTHA, *quietly with intense pleading*): Tell him I'm not a houseboy.

MARTHA (*after a pause, quietly, lowering her head*): No; you're not a houseboy.

GEORGE (*with great, sad relief*): So be it.

MARTHA (*pleading*): Truth and illusion, George; you don't know the difference.

GEORGE: No; but we must carry on as though we did.

MARTHA: Amen.

GEORGE (*flourishing the flowers*): SNAP WENT THE DRAGONS!!

(NICK *and* MARTHA *laugh weakly.*)

Hunh? Here we go round the mulberry bush, hunh?

NICK (*tenderly, to* MARTHA): Thank you.

MARTHA: Skip it.

GEORGE (*loud*): I said, here we go round the mulberry bush!

MARTHA (*impatiently*): Yeah, yeah; we know; snap go the dragons.

GEORGE (*taking a snapdragon, throwing it, spear-like, stemfirst at* MARTHA): SNAP!

MARTHA: Don't, George.

GEORGE (*throws another*): SNAP!

NICK: Don't do that.

GEORGE: Shut up, stud.

NICK: I'm not a stud!

GEORGE (*throws one at* NICK): SNAP! Then you're a houseboy. Which is it? Which are you? Hunh? Make up your mind. Either way. . . . (*Throws another at him.*) SNAP! *you disgust me.*

MARTHA: Does it matter to you, George!?

GEORGE (*throws one at her*): SNAP! No, actually, it doesn't. Either way . . . I've had it.

MARTHA: Stop throwing those goddamn things at me!

GEORGE: Either way. (*Throws another at her.*) SNAP!

NICK (*to* MARTHA): Do you want me to . . . do something to him?

MARTHA: You leave him alone!

GEORGE: If you're a houseboy, baby, you can pick up after me; if you're a stud, you can go protect your plow. Either way. Either way. . . . Everything.

NICK: Oh for God's. . . .

MARTHA (*a little afraid*): Truth or illusion, George. Doesn't it matter to you . . . at all?

GEORGE (*without throwing anything*): SNAP! (*Silence.*) You got your answer, baby?

MARTHA (*sadly*): Got it.

GEORGE: You just gird your blue-veined loins, girl. (*Sees* NICK *moving toward the hall.*) Now; we got one more game to play. And it's called Bringing Up Baby.

NICK (*more-or-less under his breath*): Oh, for Lord's sake. . . .

MARTHA: George. . . .

GEORGE: I don't want any fuss. (*To* NICK.) You don't want any scandal around here, do you, big boy? You don't want to wreck things, do you? Hunh? You want to keep to your timetable, don't you? Then sit! (NICK *sits.*) (*To* MARTHA.) And you, pretty Miss, you like fun and games, don't you? You're a sport from way back, aren't you?

MARTHA (*quietly, giving in*): All right, George; all right.

GEORGE (*seeing them both cowed; purrs*): Gooooooooood; goooood. (*Looks about him.*) But, we're not all here. (*Snaps his fingers a couple of times at* NICK.) You; you . . . uh . . . you; your little wifelet isn't here.

NICK: Look; she's had a rough night, now; she's in the can, and she's. . . .

GEORGE: Well, we can't play without everyone here. Now that's a fact. We gotta have your little wife. (*Hog-calls toward the hall.*) SOOOWWWIIIEEE!! SOOOWWWIIIEEE!!

NICK (*as* MARTHA *giggles nervously*): Cut that!

GEORGE (*swinging around, facing him*): Then get your butt out of that chair and bring the little dip back in here. (*As* NICK *does not move.*) Now be a good puppy. Fetch, good puppy, go fetch.

(NICK *rises, opens his mouth to say something, thinks better of it, exits.*)

One more game.

MARTHA (*after* NICK *goes*): I don't like what's going to happen.

GEORGE (*surprisingly tender*): Do you know what it is?

MARTHA (*pathetic*):No. But I don't like it.

GEORGE: Maybe you will, Martha.

MARTHA: No.

GEORGE: Oh, it's a real fun game, Martha.

MARTHA (*pleading*): No more games.

GEORGE (*quietly triumphant*): One more, Martha. One more game, and then beddie-bye. Everybody pack up his tools and baggage and stuff and go home. And you and me, well, we gonna climb them well-worn stairs.

MARTHA (*almost in tears*): No, George; no.

GEORGE (*soothing*): Yes, baby.

MARTHA: No, George; please?

GEORGE: It'll all be done with before you know it.

MARTHA: No, George.

GEORGE: No climb stairs with Georgie?

MARTHA (*a sleepy child*): No more games . . . please. It's games I don't want. No more games.

GEORGE: Aw, sure you do, Martha . . . original game-girl and all, 'course you do.

MARTHA: Ugly games . . . ugly. And now this new one?

GEORGE (*stroking her hair*): You'll love it, baby.

MARTHA: No, George.

GEORGE: You'll have a ball.

MARTHA (*tenderly; moves to touch him*): Please, George, no more games; I. . . .

GEORGE (*slapping her moving hand with vehemence*): Don't you touch me! You keep your paws clean for the undergraduates!

MARTHA: (*A cry of alarm, but faint.*)

GEORGE (*grabbing her hair, pulling her head back*): Now, you listen to me, Martha; you have had quite an evening . . . quite a night for yourself, and you can't just cut it off whenever you've got enough blood in your mouth. We are going on, and I'm going to have at you, and it's going to make your performance tonight look like an Easter pageant. Now I want you to get yourself a little alert. (*Slaps her lightly with his free hand.*) I want a little life in you, baby. (*Again.*)

MARTHA (*struggling*): Stop it!

GEORGE (*again*): Pull yourself together! (*Again.*) I want you on your feet and slugging, sweetheart, because I'm going to knock you around, and I want you up for it. (*Again; he pulls away, releases her; she rises.*)

MARTHA: All right, George, What do you want, George?

GEORGE: An equal battle, baby; that's all.

MARTHA: You'll get it!

GEORGE: I want you mad.

MARTHA: I'M MAD!!

GEORGE: Get madder!

MARTHA: DON'T WORRY ABOUT IT!

GEORGE: Good for you, girl; now, we're going to play this one to the death.

MARTHA: Yours!

GEORGE: You'd be surprised. Now, here come the tots; you be ready for this.

MARTHA (*she paces, actually looks a bit like a fighter*): I'm ready for you.

(NICK *and* HONEY *re-enter;* NICK *supporting* HONEY, *who still retains her brandy bottle and glass.*)

NICK (*unhappily*): Here we are.

HONEY (*cheerfully*): Hip, hop. Hip, hop.

NICK: You a bunny, Honey? (*She laughs greatly, sits.*)

HONEY: I'm a bunny, Honey.

GEORGE (*to* HONEY): Well, now; how's the bunny?

HONEY: Bunny funny! (*She laughs again.*)

NICK (*under his breath*): Jesus.

GEORGE: Bunny funny? Good for bunny!

MARTHA: Come on, George!

GEORGE (*to* MARTHA): Honey funny bunny! (HONEY *screams with laughter.*)

NICK: Jesus God. . . .

GEORGE (*slaps his hands together, once*): All right! Here we go! Last game! All sit. (NICK *sits.*) Sit down, Martha. This is a civilized game.

MARTHA (*cocks her fist, doesn't swing. Sits*): Just get on with it.

HONEY (*to* GEORGE): I've decided I don't remember anything. (*To* NICK.) Hello, Dear.

GEORGE: Hunh? What?

MARTHA: It's almost dawn, for God's sake. . . .

HONEY (*ibid*): I don't remember anything, and you don't remember anything, either. Hello, Dear.

GEORGE: You what?

HONEY (*ibid, an edge creeping into her voice*): You heard me, nothing. Hello, Dear.

GEORGE (*to* HONEY, *referring to* NICK): You do know that's your husband, there, don't you?

HONEY (*with great dignity*): Well, I certainly know *that.*

GEORGE (*close to* HONEY*'s ear*): It's just some things you can't remember . . . hunh?

HONEY (*a great laugh to cover; then quietly, intensely to* GEORGE): *Don't* remember; not *can't*. (*At* NICK, *cheerfully*.) Hello, Dear.

GEORGE (*to* NICK): Well, speak to your little wifelet, your little bunny, for God's sake.

NICK (*softly, embarrassed*): Hello, Honey.

GEORGE: Awww, that was nice. I think we've been having a . . . a real good evening . . . all things considered. . . . We've sat around, and got to know each other, and had fun and games . . . curl-up-on-the-floor, for example. . . .

HONEY: . . . the tiles. . . .

GEORGE: . . . the tiles. . . . Snap the Dragon.

HONEY: . . . peel the label. . . .

GEORGE: . . . peel the . . . what?

MARTHA: Label. Peel the label.

HONEY (*apologetically, holding up her brandy bottle*): I peel labels.

GEORGE: We all peel labels, sweetie; and when you get through the skin, all three layers, through the muscle, slosh aside the organs (*an aside to* NICK) them which is still sloshable – (*back to* HONEY) and get down to bone . . . you know what you do then?

HONEY (*terribly interested*): No!

GEORGE: When you get down to bone, you haven't got all the way, yet. There's something inside the bone . . . the marrow . . . and that's what you gotta get at. (*A strange smile at* MARTHA.)

HONEY: Oh! I see.

GEORGE: The marrow. But bones are pretty resilient, especially in the young. Now, take our son. . . .

HONEY (*strangely*): Who?

GEORGE: Our son. . . . Martha's and my little joy!

NICK (*moving toward the bar*): Do you mind if I . . . ?

GEORGE: No, no; you go right ahead.

MARTHA: George. . . .

GEORGE (*too kindly*): Yes, Martha?

MARTHA: Just what are you doing?

GEORGE: Why love, I was talking about our son.

MARTHA: Don't.

GEORGE: Isn't Martha something? Here we are, on the eve of our boy's home-coming, the eve of his twenty-first birfday, the eve of his majority . . . and Martha says don't talk about him.

MARTHA: Just . . . don't.

GEORGE: But I want to, Martha! It's very important we talk about him. Now bunny and the . . . well, whichever he is . . . here don't know much about junior, and I think they should.

MARTHA: Just . . . don't.
GEORGE (*snapping his fingers at* NICK): You. Hey, you! You want to play Bringing Up Baby, don't you!
NICK (*hardly civil*): Were you snapping at me?
GEORGE: That's right. (*Instructing him.*) *You* want to hear about our bouncey boy.
NICK (*pause; then, shortly*): Yeah; sure.
GEORGE (*to* HONEY): And you, my dear? You want to hear about him, too, don't you?
HONEY (*pretending not to understand*): Whom?
GEORGE: Martha's and my son.
HONEY (*nervously*): Oh, you have a child?

(MARTHA *and* NICK *laugh uncomfortably.*)

GEORGE: Oh, indeed; do we ever! Do you want to talk about him, Martha, or shall I? Hunh?
MARTHA (*a smile that is a sneer*): Don't, George.
GEORGE: All rightie. Well, now; let's see. He's a nice kid, really, in spite of his home life; I mean, most kids'd grow up neurotic, what with Martha here carrying on the way she does: sleeping 'til four in the P.M., climbing all over the poor bastard, trying to break the bathroom door down to wash him in the tub when he's sixteen, dragging strangers into the house at all hours. . . .
MARTHA (*rising*): O.K. YOU!
GEORGE (*mock concern*): Martha!
MARTHA: That's enough!
GEORGE: Well, do you want to take over?
HONEY (*to* NICK): Why would anybody want to wash somebody who's sixteen years old?
NICK (*slamming his drink down*): Oh, for Christ's sake, Honey!
HONEY (*stage whisper*): Well, why?!
GEORGE: Because it's her baby-poo.
MARTHA: ALL RIGHT!! (*By rote; a kind of almost-tearful recitation.*) Our son. You want our son? You'll have it.
GEORGE: You want a drink, Martha?
MARTHA (*pathetically*): Yes.
NICK (*to* MARTHA *kindly*): We don't have to hear about it . . . if you don't want to.
GEORGE: Who says so? You in a position to set the rules around here?
NICK (*pause; tight-lipped*): No.
GEORGE: Good boy; you'll go far. All right, Martha; your recitation, please.
MARTHA (*from far away*): What, George?
GEORGE (*prompting*): "Our son. . . ."

MARTHA: All right. Our son. Our son was born in a September night, a night not unlike tonight, though tomorrow, and twenty . . . one . . . years ago.

GEORGE (*beginning of quiet asides*): You see? I told you.

MARTHA: It was an easy birth. . . .

GEORGE: Oh, Martha; no. You labored . . . how you labored.

MARTHA: It was an easy birth . . . once it had been . . . accepted, relaxed into.

GEORGE: Ah . . . yes. Better.

MARTHA: It was an easy birth, once it had been accepted, and I was young.

GEORGE: And I was younger. . . . (*Laughs quietly to himself.*)

MARTHA: And I was young, and he was a healthy child, a red, bawling child, with slippery firm limbs. . . .

GEORGE: . . . Martha thinks she saw him at delivery. . . .

MARTHA: . . . with slippery, firm limbs, and a full head of black, fine, fine hair which, oh, later, later, became blond as the sun, our son.

GEORGE: He was a healthy child.

MARTHA: And I had wanted a child . . . oh, I had wanted a child.

GEORGE: (*prodding her*): A son? A daughter?

MARTHA: A child! (*Quieter.*) A child. And I had my child.

GEORGE: Our child.

MARTHA (*with great sadness*): *Our* child. And we raised him . . . (*laughs, briefly, bitterly*) yes, we did; we raised him. . . .

GEORGE: With teddy bears and an antique bassinet from Austria . . . and *no nurse.*

MARTHA: . . . with teddy bears and transparent floating goldfish, and a pale blue bed with cane at the headboard when he was older, cane which he wore through . . . finally . . . with his little hands . . . in his . . . sleep. . . .

GEORGE: . . . nightmares. . . .

MARTHA: . . . *sleep*. . . . He was a restless child. . . .

GEORGE: . . . (*Soft chuckle, head-shaking of disbelief.*) . . . Oh Lord . . .

MARTHA: . . . sleep . . . and a croup tent . . . a pale green croup tent, and the shining kettle hissing in the one light of the room that time he was sick . . . those four days . . . and animal crackers, and the bow and arrow he kept under his bed. . . .

GEORGE: . . . the arrows with rubber cups at their tip. . . .

MARTHA: . . . at their tip, which he kept beneath his bed. . . .

GEORGE: Why? Why, Martha?

MARTHA: . . . for fear . . . for fear of. . . .

GEORGE: For fear. Just that: for fear.

MARTHA (*vaguely waving him off; going on*): . . . and . . . and sandwiches on Sunday night, and Saturdays . . . (*Pleased recollection.*) . . . and Saturdays the banana boat, the whole peeled banana, scooped out on top, with green grapes for the crew, a double line of green grapes, and along the sides, stuck to the boat with toothpicks, orange slices. . . . SHIELDS.

GEORGE: And for the oar?

MARTHA (*uncertainly*): A . . . carrot?

GEORGE: Or a swizzle stick, whatever was easier.

MARTHA: No. A carrot. And his eyes were green . . . green with . . . if you peered so deep into them . . . so deep . . . bronze . . . bronze parentheses around the irises . . . such green eyes!

GEORGE: . . . blue, green, brown. . . .

MARTHA: . . . and he loved the sun! . . . He was tan before and after everyone . . . and in the sun his hair . . . became . . . fleece.

GEORGE (*echoing her*): . . . fleece. . . .

MARTHA: . . . beautiful, beautiful boy.

GEORGE: Absolve, Domine, animas omnium fidelium defunctorum ab omni vinculo delictorum.[1]

MARTHA: . . . and school . . . and summer camp . . . and sledding . . . and swimming. . . .

GEORGE: Et gratia tua illis succurrente, mereantur evadere judicium ultionis.[2]

MARTHA: (*laughing, to herself*): . . . and how he broke his arm . . . how funny it was . . . oh, no, it hurt him! . . . but, oh, it was funny . . . in a field, his very first cow, the first he'd ever seen . . . and he went into the field, to the cow, where the cow was grazing, head down, busy . . . and he moo'd at it! (*Laughs, ibid.*) He moo'd at it . . . and the beast, oh, surprised, swung its head up and moo'd at him, all three years of him, and he ran, startled, and he stumbled . . . fell . . . and broke his poor arm. (*Laughs, ibid.*) Poor lamb.

GEORGE: Et lucis aeternae beatitudine perfrui.[3]

MARTHA: George cried! Helpless . . . George . . . cried. I carried the poor lamb. George snuffling beside me, I carried the child, having fashioned a sling . . . and across the great fields.

GEORGE: In Paradisum deducant te Angeli.[4]

MARTHA: And as he grew . . . and as he grew . . . oh! so wise! . . . he walked evenly between us . . . (*she spreads her hands*) . . . a hand out to each of us for what we could offer by way of support, affection, teaching, even love . . . and these hands, still, to hold us off a bit, for mutual protection, to protect us all from George's . . . weakness . . . and my . . . necessary greater strength . . . to protect himself . . . and *us*.

GEORGE: In memoria aeterna erit justus: ab auditione mala non timebit.[5]

[1] (Lat.) Absolve, O Lord, the souls of all the faithful departed from every bond of sin (here, as in all the Latin passages that follow, George is quoting from the "Masses for the Dead" in the Roman Catholic *Missal*)

[2] And by the help of Thy grace, let them be found worthy to escape the sentence of vengeance

[3] And to enjoy the full beatitude of the light eternal

[4] May the Angels lead thee into Paradise

[5] The just shall be in everlasting remembrance: he shall not fear the evil hearing

MARTHA: So wise; so wise.
NICK (*to* GEORGE): What is this? What are you doing?
GEORGE: Shhhhh.
HONEY: Shhhhh.
NICK (*shrugging*): O.K.
MARTHA: So beautiful; so wise.
GEORGE (*laughs quietly*): All truth being relative.
MARTHA: It was true! Beautiful; wise; perfect.
GEORGE: There's a real mother talking.
HONEY (*suddenly; almost tearfully*): I want a child.
NICK: Honey. . . .
HONEY (*more forcefully*): I want a child!
GEORGE: On principle?
HONEY (*in tears*): I want a child. I want a baby.
MARTHA (*waiting out the interruption, not really paying it any mind*): Of course, this state, this perfection . . . couldn't last. Not with George . . . not with George around.
GEORGE (*to the others*): There; you see? I knew she'd shift.
HONEY: Be still!
GEORGE (*mock awe*): Sorry . . . mother.
NICK: Can't you be still?
GEORGE (*making a sign at* NICK): Dominus vobiscum.[6]
MARTHA: Not with George around. A drowning man takes down those nearest. George tried, but, oh, God, how I fought him. God, how I fought him.
GEORGE (*a satisfied laugh*): Ahhhhhhh.
MARTHA: Lesser states can't stand those above them. Weakness, imperfection cries out against strength, goodness and innocence. And George tried.
GEORGE: How did I try, Martha? How did I try?
MARTHA: How did you . . . what? . . . No! No . . . he grew . . . our son grew . . . up; he is grown up; he is away at school, college. He is fine, everything is fine.
GEORGE (*mocking*): Oh, come on, Martha!
MARTHA: No. That's all.
GEORGE: Just a minute! You can't cut a story off like that, sweetheart. You started to say something . . . now you say it!
MARTHA: No!
GEORGE: Well, I will.
MARTHA: No!
GEORGE: You see, Martha, here, stops just when the going gets good . . . just

[6] The Lord be with you

when things start getting a little rough. Now, Martha, here, is a misunderstood little girl; she really is. Not only does she have a husband who is a bog . . . a younger-than-she-is bog albeit . . . not only does she have a husband who is a bog, she has as well a tiny problem with spirituous liquors — like she can't get enough. . . .

MARTHA (*without energy*): No more, George.

GEORGE: . . . and on top of all that, poor weighed-down girl, PLUS a father who really doesn't give a damn whether she lives or dies, who couldn't care less *what* happens to his only daughter . . . on top of all that she has a *son*. She has a son who fought her every inch of the way, who didn't want to be turned into a weapon against his father, who didn't want to be used as a goddamn club whenever Martha didn't get things like she wanted them!

MARTHA (*rising to it*): Lies! Lies!!

GEORGE: Lies? All right. A son who would *not* disown his father, who came to him for advice, for information, for love that wasn't mixed with sickness — and you know what I mean, Martha! — who could not tolerate the slashing, braying residue that called itself his MOTHER. MOTHER? HAH!!

MARTHA (*cold*): All right, you. A son who was so ashamed of his father he asked me once if it — possibly — wasn't true, as he had heard, from some cruel boys, maybe, that he was not our child; who could not tolerate the shabby failure his father had become. . . .

GEORGE: Lies!

MARTHA: Lies? Who would not bring his girl friends to the house. . . .

GEORGE: . . . in shame of his mother. . . .

MARTHA: . . . of his father! Who writes letters only to me!

GEORGE: Oh, so you think! To me! At my office!

MARTHA: Liar!

GEORGE: I have a stack of them!

MARTHA: YOU HAVE NO LETTERS!

GEORGE: And you have?

MARTHA: He has no letters. A son . . . a son who spends his summers away . . . away from his family . . . ON ANY PRETEXT . . . because he can't stand the shadow of a man flickering around the edges of a house. . . .

GEORGE: . . . who spends his summers away . . . and he does! . . . who spends his summers away because there isn't room for him in a house full of empty bottles, lies, strange men, and a harridan who. . . .

MARTHA: Liar!!

GEORGE: Liar?

MARTHA: . . . A son who I have raised as best I can against . . . vicious odds, against the corruption of weakness and petty revenges. . . .

GEORGE: . . . A son who is, deep in his gut, sorry to have been born. . . .

(*Both together.*)

MARTHA: I have tried, oh God I have tried; the one thing . . . the one thing I've tried to carry pure and unscathed through the sewer of this marriage; through the sick nights, and the pathetic, stupid days, through the derision and the laughter . . . *God,* the laughter, through one failure after another, one failure compounding another failure, each attempt more sickening, more numbing than the one before; the one thing, the one *person* I have tried to protect, to raise above the mire of this vile, crushing marriage; the one light in all this hopeless . . . *dark*ness . . . our SON.

GEORGE: Libera me, Domine, de morte aeterna, in die illa tremenda: Quando caeli movendi sunt et terra: Dum veneris judicare saeculum per ignem. Tremens factus sum ego, et timeo, dum discussio venerit, atque ventura ira. Quando caeli movendi sunt et terra. Dies illa, dies irae, calamitatis et miseriae; dies magna et amara valde. Dum veneris judicare saeculum per ignem. Requiem aeternam dona eis, Domine: et lux perpetua luceat eis. Libera me Domine de morte aeterna in die illa tremenda: quando caeli movendi sunt et terra; Dum veneris judicare saeculum per ignem.[7]

(*End together.*)

HONEY (*her hands to her ears*): STOP IT!! STOP IT!!

GEORGE (*with a hand sign*): Kyrie, eleison. Christe, eleison. Kyrie, eleison.[8]

HONEY: JUST STOP IT!!

GEORGE: Why, baby? Don't you like it?

HONEY (*quite hysterical*): You . . . can't . . . do . . . this!

GEORGE (*triumphant*): Who says!

HONEY: I! Say!

GEORGE: Tell us why, baby.

HONEY: No!

NICK: Is this game over?

HONEY: Yes! Yes, it is.

GEORGE: Ho-ho! Not by a long shot. (*To* MARTHA.) We got a little surprise for you, baby. It's about sunny-Jim.

MARTHA: No more, George.

GEORGE: YES!

[7] Deliver me, O Lord, from eternal death on that dreadful day when the heavens and the earth shall be moved, and Thou shalt come to judge the world by fire. I am seized with fear and trembling when I reflect upon the judgment and the wrath to come. When the heavens and the earth shall be moved. That day, a day of wrath, of wasting and of misery, a dreadful and exceeding bitter day. When Thou shalt come to judge the world by fire. Eternal rest grant unto them, O Lord, and let perpetual light shine upon them. Deliver me, O Lord, from eternal death on that dreadful day when the heavens and the earth shall be moved, and Thou shalt come to judge the world by fire

[8] Lord, have mercy. Christ, have mercy. Lord, have mercy

NICK: Leave her be!

GEORGE: I'M RUNNING THIS SHOW! (*To* MARTHA.) Sweetheart, I'm afraid I've got some bad news for you . . . for us, of course. Some rather sad news.

(HONEY *begins weeping, head in hands.*)

MARTHA (*afraid, suspicious*): What is this?

GEORGE (*oh, so patiently*): Well, Martha, while you were out of the room, while the . . . two of you were out of the room . . . I mean, I don't know where, hell, you both must have been somewhere. (*Little laugh.*) . . . While you were out of the room, for a while . . . well, Missey and I were sittin' here havin' a little talk, you know: a chaw and a talk . . . and the doorbell rang. . . .

HONEY (*head still in hands*): Chimed.

GEORGE: Chimed . . . and . . . well, it's hard to tell you, Martha. . . .

MARTHA (*a strange throaty voice*): Tell me.

HONEY: Please . . . don't.

MARTHA: Tell me.

GEORGE: . . . and . . . what it was . . . it was good old Western Union, some little boy about seventy.

MARTHA (*involved*): Crazy Billy?

GEORGE: Yes, Martha, that's right . . . crazy Billy . . . and he had a telegram, and it was for us, and I have to tell you about it.

MARTHA (*as if from a distance*): Why didn't they phone it? Why did they bring it; why didn't they telephone it?

GEORGE: Some telegrams you have to deliver, Martha; some telegrams you can't phone.

MARTHA (*rising*): What do you mean?

GEORGE: Martha. . . . I can hardly bring myself to say it. . . .

HONEY: Don't.

GEORGE (*to* HONEY): Do you want to do it?

HONEY (*defending herself against an attack of bees*): No no no no no.

GEORGE (*sighing heavily*): All right. Well, Martha . . . I'm afraid our boy isn't coming home for his birthday.

MARTHA: Of course he is.

GEORGE: No, Martha.

MARTHA: Of course he is. I say he is!

GEORGE: He . . . can't.

MARTHA: He is! I say so!

GEORGE: Martha . . . (*long pause*) . . . our son is . . . dead.

(*Silence.*)

He was . . . killed . . . late in the afternoon. . . .

(*Silence.*)

(*a tiny chuckle*) on a country road, with his learner's permit in his pocket, he swerved, to avoid a porcupine, and drove straight into a. . . .

MARTHA (*rigid fury*): YOU . . . CAN'T . . . DO . . . THAT!

GEORGE: . . . large tree.

MARTHA: YOU CANNOT DO THAT!

NICK (*softly*): Oh my God. (HONEY *is weeping louder.*)

GEORGE (*quietly, dispassionately*): I thought you should know.

NICK: Oh my God; no.

MARTHA (*quivering with rage and loss*): NO! NO! YOU CANNOT DO THAT! YOU CAN'T DECIDE THAT FOR YOURSELF! I WILL NOT LET YOU DO THAT!

GEORGE: We'll have to leave around noon, I suppose. . . .

MARTHA: I WILL NOT LET YOU DECIDE THESE THINGS!

GEORGE: . . . because there are matters of identification, naturally, and arrangements to be made. . . .

MARTHA (*leaping at* GEORGE, *but ineffectual*): YOU CAN'T DO THIS!

(NICK *rises, grabs hold of* MARTHA, *pins her arms behind her back.*)

I WON'T LET YOU DO THIS, GET YOUR HANDS OFF ME!

GEORGE (*as* NICK *holds on; right in* MARTHA*'s face*): You don't seem to understand, Martha; I haven't done anything. Now, pull yourself together. Our son is DEAD! Can you get that into your head?

MARTHA: YOU CAN'T DECIDE THESE THINGS.

NICK: Lady, please.

MARTHA: LET ME GO!

GEORGE: Now listen, Martha; listen carefully. We got a telegram; there was a car accident, and he's dead. POUF! Just like that! Now, how do you like it?

MARTHA (*a howl which weakens into a moan*): NOOOOOOoooooo.

GEORGE (*to* NICK): Let her go. (MARTHA *slumps to the floor in a sitting position.*) She'll be all right now.

MARTHA (*pathetic*): No; no, he is *not* dead; he is not *dead.*

GEORGE: He is dead. Kyrie, eleison. Christe, eleison. Kyrie, eleison.

MARTHA: You can*not.* You may not decide these things.

NICK (*leaning over her; tenderly*): He hasn't decided anything, lady. It's not his doing. He doesn't have the power. . . .

GEORGE: That's right, Martha; I'm not a God. I don't have the power over life and death, do I?

MARTHA: YOU CAN'T KILL HIM! YOU CAN'T HAVE HIM DIE!

HONEY: Lady . . . please. . . .

MARTHA: YOU CAN'T!

GEORGE: There was a telegram, Martha.

MARTHA (*up; facing him*): Show it to me! Show me the telegram!

GEORGE (*long pause; then, with a straight face*): I ate it.

MARTHA (*a pause; then with the greatest disbelief possible, tinged with hysteria*): What did you just say to me?

GEORGE (*barely able to stop exploding with laughter*): I . . . ate . . . it.

(MARTHA *stares at him for a long moment, then spits in his face.*)

GEORGE (*with a smile*): Good for you, Martha.
NICK (*to* GEORGE): Do you think that's the way to treat her at a time like this? Making an ugly goddamn joke like that? Hunh?
GEORGE (*snapping his fingers at* HONEY): Did I eat the telegram or did I not?
HONEY (*terrified*): Yes; yes, you ate it. I watched . . . I watched you . . . you . . . you ate it all down.
GEORGE (*prompting*): . . . like a good boy.
HONEY: . . . like a . . . g-g-g-good . . . boy. Yes.
MARTHA (*to* GEORGE, *coldly*): You're not going to get away with this.
GEORGE (*with disgust*): YOU KNOW THE RULES, MARTHA! FOR CHRIST'S SAKE, YOU KNOW THE RULES!
MARTHA: NO!
NICK (*with the beginnings of a knowledge he cannot face*): What are you two talking about?
GEORGE: I can kill him, Martha, if I want to.
MARTHA: HE IS OUR CHILD!
GEORGE: Oh yes, and you bore him, and it was a good delivery. . . .
MARTHA: HE IS OUR CHILD!
GEORGE: AND I HAVE KILLED HIM!
MARTHA: NO!
GEORGE: YES!

(*Long silence.*)

NICK (*very quietly*): I think I understand this.
GEORGE (*ibid*): Do you?
NICK (*ibid*): Jesus Christ, I think I understand this.
GEORGE (*ibid*): Good for you, buster.
NICK (*violently*): JESUS CHRIST I THINK I UNDERSTAND THIS!
MARTHA (*great sadness and loss*): You have no right . . . you have no right at all. . . .
GEORGE (*tenderly*): I have the right, Martha. We never spoke of it; that's all. I could kill him any time I wanted to.
MARTHA: But why? Why?
GEORGE: You broke our rule, baby. You mentioned him . . . you mentioned him to someone else.
MARTHA (*tearfully*): I did *not.* I never did.
GEORGE: Yes, you did.
MARTHA: Who? WHO?
HONEY (*crying*): To me. You mentioned him to me.
MARTHA (*crying*): I FORGET! Sometimes . . . sometimes when it's night, when it's late, and . . . and everybody else is . . . talking . . . I forget and I . . . want to mention him . . . but I . . . HOLD ON . . . I hold on . . . but I've

wanted to . . . so often . . . oh, George, you've *pushed* it . . . there was no need . . . there was no need for *this.* I *men*tioned him . . . all right . . . but you didn't have to push it over the EDGE. You didn't have to . . . kill him.

GEORGE: Requiescat in pace.[9]

HONEY: Amen.

MARTHA: You didn't have to have him die, George.

GEORGE: Requiem aeternam dona eis, Domine.[10]

HONEY: Et lux perpetua luceat eis.[11]

MARTHA: That wasn't . . . needed.

(*A long silence.*)

GEORGE (*softly*): It will be dawn soon. I think the party's over.

NICK (*to* GEORGE; *quietly*): You couldn't have . . . any?

GEORGE: *We* couldn't.

MARTHA (*a hint of communion in this*): *We* couldn't.

GEORGE (*to* NICK *and* HONEY): Home to bed, children; it's way past your bedtime.

NICK (*his hand out to* HONEY): Honey?

HONEY (*rising, moving to him*): Yes.

GEORGE: (MARTHA *is sitting on the floor by a chair now.*) You two go now.

NICK: Yes.

HONEY: Yes.

NICK: I'd like to. . . .

GEORGE: Good night.

NICK: (*Pause.*) Good night.

(NICK *and* HONEY *exit;* GEORGE *closes the door after them; looks around the room; sighs, picks up a glass or two, takes it to the bar.*
*This whole last section very softly, very slowly.*)

GEORGE: Do you want anything, Martha?

MARTHA (*still looking away*): No . . . nothing.

GEORGE: All right. (*Pause.*) Time for bed.

MARTHA: Yes.

GEORGE: Are you tired?

MARTHA: Yes.

GEORGE: I am.

MARTHA: Yes.

GEORGE: Sunday tomorrow; all day.

MARTHA: Yes.

(*A long silence between them.*)

Did you . . . did you . . . have to?

[9] May he rest in peace
[10] Eternal rest grant unto them, O Lord
[11] And let perpetual light shine upon them

GEORGE (*pause*): Yes.
MARTHA: It was . . . ? You had to?
GEORGE (*pause*): Yes.
MARTHA: I don't know.
GEORGE: It was . . . time.
MARTHA: Was it?
GEORGE: Yes.
MARTHA (*pause*): I'm cold.
GEORGE: It's late.
MARTHA: Yes.
GEORGE (*long silence*): It will be better.
MARTHA (*long silence*): I don't . . . know.
GEORGE: It will be . . . maybe.
MARTHA: I'm . . . not . . . sure.
GEORGE: No.
MARTHA: Just . . . us?
GEORGE: Yes.
MARTHA: I don't suppose, maybe, we could. . . .
GEORGE: No, Martha.
MARTHA: Yes. No.
GEORGE: Are you all right?
MARTHA: Yes. No.
GEORGE (*puts his hand gently on her shoulder; she puts her head back and he sings to her, very softly*):
Who's afraid of Virginia Woolf,
Virginia Woolf,
Virginia Woolf,
MARTHA: I . . . am . . . George. . . .
GEORGE: Who's afraid of Virginia Woolf. . . .
MARTHA: I . . . am . . . George. . . . I . . . am. . . .

(GEORGE *nods, slowly.*)

(*Silence; tableau.*)

CURTAIN

*Who's Afraid of Virginia Woolf?* is a very funny play, but it is also sad, painful, difficult, and of uncertain dramatic integrity. Its spectacle of the family living room as battleground and torture chamber is a match for Strindberg's *The Dance of Death* and O'Neill's *Long Day's Journey Into Night,* and in sordid explicitness and brutality of language it leaves its predecessors far behind. But the verbal sharpshooting slows the dramatic movement, and a night of fun and games is an uneasy vehicle for semi-allegory of religious overtones and inconclusive outcome. There is a tension in the play between the raw realism of a domestic hell and the redemptive ritual that perhaps saves both the marriage and western man. Large, boisterous, loud, lusty, and ruthless, Martha fills the role of Earth Mother, for whom all men are flops, and George, as a critic has suggested, may be a Christ figure because a number of his entries and exits are timed to coincide with somebody using "Jesus Christ" as a profanity. But the Earth Mother is a barren bitch and the Christ figure a cuckold and a child-killer. The imagery is charged, but it fails to make a coherent marriage myth. The imaginary child and the exorcism of it represent a reaching out for a meaning transcending naturalistic psychology, but one that the rest of the play can only doubtfully accommodate. "Hi-jinks and high seriousness fail to fuse," wrote Robert Brustein in his review in *The New Republic* after the Broadway opening in October, 1962. That is too curt a verdict on the structural tension in the play, but Brustein has a point. The tension may be calculated, but it threatens to pull the play apart.

We find the tension in individual scenes as well. There is a strain, not between two dramatic modes but between two motifs, in a little scene in Act II, but there is the same quality of mystifying "significance." George is reading a book while his wife is upstairs making love to their guest. He comes to a sentence he reads aloud to himself: "And the west, encumbered by crippling alliances and burdened with a morality too rigid to accommodate itself to the swing of events, must . . . eventually . . . fall." Then in a fury he hurls the book away. In no other scene have the George-Martha relationship and the "historical inevitability" motif that is the ideological issue between George and Nick been brought more sharply together. Nick is a bright and handsome young scientist on the make, an athlete with brains, "the wave of the future," with visions of a Brave New World managed by eugenicist-technocrats. George, graying and paunchy, is a middle-aged history professor and an academic failure, but a champion of traditional humanistic values and a believer in the "glorious unpredictability . . . the surprise, the multiplexity, the sea-changing rhythm of . . . history." The words he reads discount man's freedom to control events, the efficacy of his moral will, and they prophesy the fall of what George has devoted his professional life to understand. Like Nick, the writer of the sentence is on the side of historical inevitability against George's affirmation of the "endeavor to make communicable sense out of natural order, morality out of the unnatural disorder of man's mind." George's fury, then, is paradoxically both the impotent rage of a man who identifies himself with a losing cause and a scholar's angry impatience with an untenable theory of history. Presumably, it is also an expression of the sexual jealousy he feels for Nick, whom he associates with the mechanistic thought of the passage. (There is a touch of vulgar and ignorant cliché about George's fear of what genetic science is up to these days.) But how do the words he reads relate to his marriage? It is a "crippling alliance" in the sense that it has psychologically emasculated him, but, if so, what is "rigid" about the morality of an adulterous wife and a condoning husband? Do we react to the final game of "Bringing Up Baby" as to a saving act of a flexible imagination because we feel that our entire cultural tradition is behind George's therapeutic game-playing? Does the exorcism vindicate George's values over Nick's in changing the predictable course of events in George's and Martha's marriage toward a final break or disaster and in re-establishing it instead on their joint, humble acceptance of a difficult reality? And is this tentative redemption a parable of some vision Albee has of the spiritual crisis in our culture and its wished-for resolution? Is New Carthage, the academic community, moribund in its emotional and intellectual sterility – like its classical namesake ripe for destruction? In an interview printed in the *Paris Review* in 1966, Albee said he chose the Christian names of George Washington and his wife for his two main characters because the play "contains an attempt to examine the success or failure of American revolutionary principles." This is elliptical, but Albee's point could be that the principles of self-determination, private property rights, and the right of the individual to "life, liberty, and the pursuit of happiness," for which the American Revolution was fought and which have made self-fulfillment the highest value in our national ethos, are incompatible with the virtues of tolerance, humility, and self-abnegation that make marriage viable. Are George and Martha the prototypal American couple? There is more than one reason why one hesitates to answer "yes."

The critical and popular success of the play raises other questions. Here is a play about two unattractive faculty couples having a three-and-a-half hour drunken orgy of obscene violence, playing a series of coarse games in provocation and retaliation. The object of the games is to hurt and humiliate others. In the last of the games an imaginary child is "killed" in Latin litany. The significance of all this is hidden in an abstruse highbrow joke involving Walt Disney's three little pigs and a British stream-of-consciousness novelist. What is the condition of the culture that hails such a play as "brilliant" and "crucial" and turns it into an international box office hit on stage and screen? Of what sort is the "nature" to which the play holds up a "mirror"? What fearful "form and pressure," shaping "the very age and body" of our time, does the mirror reflect?

We have a choice of answers, each reductive. We can say, with the member of the Pulitzer advisory board who vetoed the jury's nomination of the play for the 1962–63 award, that it is "a filthy play" and refuse to be the victims of some sardonic game of Alienate the Audience that Albee is playing for reasons of his own. We can go further and deplore the play's success, saying it proves that we have abandoned standards not just of good taste but of intellectual and dramatic coherence as well, that Hamlet's criteria for meaningful theater sadly no longer apply, and that we have arrived at the age of a theater of pointless cruelty. Or we can take its success as a sign that we have the courage to face some ugly reality in our own lives when we endure the spectacle of the sterile violence of love failed—though cynics will ask whether we do, indeed, "endure" or are simply vulgarly amused. Many, no doubt, have gone to see *Who's Afraid of Virginia Woolf?* in order to be shocked or titillated, or to derive some obscure comfort from observing a marriage worse than their own, or to be thought broadminded, or to keep up with the intelligentsia. Some have come away offended or puzzled or pleased; others as from a vision of their own private purgatory. The play poses questions that are not easily answered and raises controversies in which one does not lightly choose sides. It is more easily described than interpreted and evaluated. Whatever else it may mean, the variety of responses suggests that *Who's Afraid of Virginia Woolf?,* like so many other serious contemporary plays, resists classification by traditional genres and that ours is a drama of uncertain values, the true mirror of a troubled age.

The form of the play is realistic in the sense that we are never required to accept what we see and hear as happening anywhere else than in the real world. The four characters engage in some unusual behavior and talk, but their world is not some grotesque version of a familiar reality, like the living room in *The American Dream,* one of Albee's early, one-act, absurdist parables. The authentic quality of the professorial home is so evident, in fact, that the play has been faulted for not being the fair and accurate picture of the domestic manners and mores in faculty families that the realism of its setting and language seems to imply it is. But the charge is beside the point. Albee is not trying to produce an unretouched sound picture of academic married life as current sociological fact, and he is not telling a story of what typically happens when a college professor and his wife invite fellow guests from a dinner party over for a nightcap. His lines are marvellously speakable, ranging in style from raw expletive and drunken inanity to lonely eloquence and tired monosyllables, but the situation in which they are spoken is so monotonously brutal and limited that their effect is not primarily felt to be realistic. Rather, they represent speech that has been tensed and heightened to aggressive gesture — words as weapons. And violent speech is just one of several images of radical dislocations in social relationships in the play. People play vicious games of mutual insult and injury, betray intimate confidences, throw and smash things, get drunk and sick, leave the party they host, and make loveless love. The incessant and feverish hostility in word and deed in *Who's Afraid of Virginia Woolf?* functions metaphorically like the surrealistic distortions of normal family relationships in *The American Dream*. Both express the reality behind the bland decencies of conventional middle-class family life. Both contain social satire, but both go beyond satire. Compassion comes closer than contempt, than ridicule, than indignation, to define Albee's attitude toward his characters.

That realism for its own sake was not Albee's goal is suggested by a comment he made in the *Paris Review* interview on the Mike Nichols screen version of his play (with Elizabeth Taylor and Richard Burton). He liked the film very much, said Albee, though he felt it slighted the "intellectual" in favor of the "emotional level" of the play. But he did not approve of the film's roadhouse scenes. He did not elaborate on his opinion, but we can guess his reasons. In moving his cameras out of the living room set in the interest of movement and visual change and a broader social scene, Nichols weakened the claustrophobic effect of the play's single setting. The suggestion that George and Martha are trapped in their "dump" was lost in the film. In achieving an added dimension of realism, it frustrated a part of Albee's artistic intent.

Nor was that intent the searching anatomy of a sick marriage that Ibsen and Strindberg established as something of a dramatic subgenre in the closing years of the nineteenth century. Like the two Scandinavians, Albee takes for his subject the conflicts within and between the members of a small middle-class family, and, also like his predecessors, he reveals the origin of the conflicts in retrospective dialogue. Albee's foursome, however, are in various stages of drunkenness, and though the dialogue evidence of this could be said to be a realistic feature, it also means that the quality of their speech is different from that of Strindberg's and particularly Ibsen's characters. Most of it is spontaneous and freewheeling verbal infighting rather than coherent talk about topics and issues. It is vituperative rather than discursive. Except for the narratives in the games passages, it gives the impression, as dialogue never does in Ibsen and Strindberg, of drift rather than of directedness. Also, in older realism the past that is shown to be responsible for the present crisis is supposed to be true history, but George's and Martha's past is a mixture of fact and fantasy. The factual status of George's killing his parents remains ambiguous until the end, and when George "kills" his and Martha's child, he destroys an illusion that has been a reality of their life together. Neither of them has ever believed in the actual existence of the child — they are not psychotics — but their sharing a deliberate fantasy has given their marriage content. The parent game, like all their games, has been deadly serious.

Aeschylus's *Oresteia* begins the tradition of domestic drama written on the premise that tensions in the intimate family group are the source of individual maladjustment. In modern times the premise has been reinforced by Freudian psychology. The central fact of the family situation in *Who's Afraid of Virginia Woolf?* is the absence of an actual child from the archetypal triad of husband/father, wife/mother, and child; or, more accurately, it is the child's imaginary nature. This is neither Aeschylean nor Freudian nor Ibsenite, and it means that what is revealed about George's and Martha's relationship to their respective parents is less important as an explanation of the conditioning past than as a thematic image adjunctive to the imaginary child motif. Incest and adultery, child-killing and parent-killing, do not shape a plot but are metaphors for disruptions of the archetypal patterns of family life. Since Nick and Honey are also childless, the barrenness motif comes to represent an entire emotional climate. The games that make up social life in the play are aggressive responses to barrenness as literal and symbolic fact, and the end of the games is the end of illusion. Significantly, George's and Martha's child dies just before reaching maturity.

A final difference, then, between *Who's Afraid of Virginia Woolf?* and Ibsen's and Strindberg's family dramas is that Albee's play really has little cognitive content as psychology or social realism. It is not, like Ibsen's plays, about the subordination of the wife in bourgeois marriage, or neurotic sex, or the tragic consequences of a husband's choice of vocational over romantic and domestic values; nor does it, like Strindberg's plays, show marriage as a struggle between husband and wife for dominance. George's and Martha's strange and ambivalent relationship does not lend itself to close analysis, and to approach the play as if it were a diagnostic study of an unhappy marriage would be to miss just about every important meaning in it. The ritualization of violent emotion in games of truth and illusion is the real subject of Albee's play, and marriage is its vehicle because it institutionalizes human intimacy.

There is no way of refuting the charge that Albee's play is "filthy." The recent trend toward total permissiveness about what can be said and done on stage may have rendered the charge obsolete, but it has not made it meaningless. We have not abolished the concept of filthy art; we have begun to take it seriously. The way to justify a play like *Who's Afraid of Virginia Woolf?* is to say that the drinking and the promiscuity, the obscenities and the profanities, are ways in which the characters are striking back at an existence of love denied and betrayed. A ritual is a formal act by which private emotion is made communal, and George and Martha achieve a kind of negative communion by taking turns as aggressor and victim, sadist and masochist, in elaborate games of mutual hurt, one of the rules of which is that a player can change the rules without telling the other. Instead of affection there is anger; instead of trust, cheating tricks. But their psychic violence establishes a bond of mutual understanding, even a kind of tenderness, between them. They stay together, because each needs the other as an assurance of his or her own identity. Their ritual of hatred is a form of coexistence. Martha needs George to hurt and to be hurt by, but she can make him "visible" only by turning him into a victim of her braying bitchiness, and George fondles his failures in her sight and invents past guilt in order to make himself available to attack. Victimization means existence, and for Martha the fact that George is there to listen to her saying "If you existed, I'd divorce you" means that she has a husband. It is only when he is not there to hear that she can afford to be sentimental about their relationship:

> George who is out there somewhere in the dark. . . . George who is good to me, and whom I revile; who understands me, and whom I push off; who can make me laugh, and I choke it back in my throat; who can hold me at night, so that it's warm, and whom I will bite so there's blood; who keeps learning the games we play as quickly as I can change the rules; who can make me happy and I do not wish to be happy, and yes I do wish to be happy. George and Martha: sad, sad, sad.

Her verbal assaults are acts of love, pleas for love. The exact psychic process that accounts for this stalemated ambivalence of feeling is not explained, but it is put to work dramatically. Albee's profoundest insight in the play is his scenic demonstration that hatred can be a form of love, and that humiliation, betrayal, adultery, and violence can be efforts to reach another person in a genuine offering of self.

The ritualization of this action of psychological paradox is pervasive, though much of the time it is submerged in the texture of raucuous colloquialism. It is most evident in three formal devices, the first of which Albee imposes on his play by authorial fiat, while the other two are the work of the characters. The first device is the sequence of act titles. "Fun and Games" is a self-explanatory piece of irony. "Walpurgisnacht" is the word for the witches' sabbath in popular German superstition and the title of a scene in part I of Goethe's *Faust,* in which Faust and Mephisto indulge in a blasphemous sexual orgy with young and old witches. The action of "The Exorcism" is the laying to rest of the evil spirits aroused in "Walpurgisnacht." The spiritual action is descending in the first two acts; in the third it rises from the depths of the night of Walpurgis to a scene of forgiveness, reconciliation, acceptance, and tentative communion, as Sunday dawn follows the Night of Wrath and the two couples are left to work out their marital salvation.

Within this inclusive structure of acts is the sequence of the four games George and Martha play with each other and their two guests. The first two games are in the form of revelations that involve, directly or indirectly, betrayal of secrets between husband and wife. The third game is adulterous love-making, ending in an act of uncompleted intercourse off-stage. The fourth begins as a narrative of idyllic parental reminiscence, which gradually grows ugly and ominous and ends in the murder of the imaginary child. Of the three revelations in game one, "Humiliate the Host," the first two (the emblematic boxing match — "it's colored our whole life" — and the story of George's failure as his father-in-law's heir-apparent in the college power structure) are told in Act I. The third (the story of George's novel) is told in Act II. As "Humiliate the Host" is played in both of the first two acts, so "Bringing Up Baby," the fourth and final game, links the last two, for George gets the idea for it at the end of Act II and plays it in Act III. Honey's sickness in the end of Act I and in the middle and end of Act II is a motif that both ties the games together and provides breaks within and between them. The fact that she does not get sick after the fourth game in Act III suggests the restoration of health after George's session of violent therapy. The games are further linked by their alliterative names. Shifting roles in the games weave patterns of psychological action and reaction. In "Humiliate the Host" Martha is aggressor, George victim, and Nick and Honey are passive spectator-listeners. In "Get the Guests" George is aggressor, Nick and Honey are victims, and Martha is spectator-listener. Martha and Nick play "Hump the Hostess" together, but George's attitude toward the initial stages of their love-making leaves it uncertain who is victim and who aggressor in this game, and Honey, off-stage, is not even aware that it is being played. George directs "Bringing Up Baby" against Martha, but the game involves Nick and Honey by analogy. The games occasion uses and abuses of language, and they dramatize the truth-illusion theme by demonstrating that in the games people play they become the roles they assume or are forced to assume: social life is play-acting.

The third ritualizing device is the passage in counterpoint in the exorcism scene in Act III, when George intones the Latin phrases of the Roman Catholic Mass for the Dead against Martha's desperate assertion that their son has been the one pure thing "through the sewer of this marriage," the one thing raised above "the mire of this vile, crushing marriage." It is both a moving and a climactic passage. The beauty of Martha's illusion measures the enormity of her betrayal of her and George's secret child to strangers — she loses the child because she has exposed it — and the solemn Latin phrases sanctify George's act of exorcism, giving religious significance to the psychological rehabilitation it seeks to effect. The counterpoint motif is anticipated at the end of Act I, where it is tied to the verbal and musical leitmotif of the joke about Virginia Woolf.

The exorcism is a form of the "guerilla warfare," the "internal subversion," which represents George's new tactics after "total war" has been declared between him and Martha. By facing her guilt of betrayal, Martha is "subverted" to accept the task George, practicing his profession as teacher, imposes on her – that of confronting "Virginia Woolf."* At the end of "Get the Guests," Nick had been forced to make a similar admission of guilty betrayal, and in "Bringing Up Baby" Honey is forced to recognize the truth about her hysterical pregnancy before her marriage and her self-induced barrenness afterwards and brought to say she wants a child. The last words she and Nick say to one another before their final exit are "Yes. . . . Yes. . . . Yes." There is in this a hint of new life in more than one sense – as if the killing of the invented child in the older marriage may make possible the birth of a real child in the younger marriage.

The final tableau is of George cradling Martha's head as he softly sings the reassuring words of the title song. Martha is tired and afraid; the night's journey has been long and hard. George understands her fears and perhaps shares them, and the words he sings may be foolish, but the tableau itself is that of calm after storm, of rest after battle, of a new promise after the past has been consigned to death. The litany has silenced both brawls and baby talk; and instead of the illusions that barrenness is life, hatred is love, and games are reality, there is the sad wisdom of resignation to uncertainty. "Truth and illusion, George," says Martha when she is on the brink of recognition at the end of Act III. "You don't know the difference."

> GEORGE: No; but we must carry on as though we did.
> MARTHA: Amen.

If her "Amen" is spoken in flippant disbelief, it is ironic. At the end, she must learn to live by George's formula, which gives dignity to and

* In the *Paris Review* interview, Albee said he found the title of his play scrawled in soap on a mirror in a tavern toilet and decided to use it instead of his original title, "The Exorcism," because he felt it was the sort of allusive joke that intellectuals are likely to make and because it could suggest the meaning, "Who is afraid of living life without illusions?" Presumably, Virginia Woolf, the author of *Mrs. Dalloway, To the Lighthouse,* and other novels of journeys through an inner landscape, stands for a courageous and uncompromising realist of the spirit, a scrupulous recorder of the minutest movements of the mind, and, as a suicide in 1941, a rejector of the violence of a world at war. Of Disney's three little pigs, the two younger are foolish illusionists for thinking that their flimsy structures can stand up to the huffing and puffing of the big, bad wolf – they *ought* to be afraid of him – while their older brother, the bricklayer, is the stern and wise realist.

makes moral sense of a life lived in defiance of the process of historical inevitability.

Read thus (and this reading is not offered as final or exhaustive), the ending of *Who's Afraid of Virginia Woolf?* can be taken to signify a stage of new faith in Albee's development, though the content of the faith is not easily defined. (The meaning of the play that followed *Virginia Woolf,* the derivative and dramatically slack *Tiny Alice,* seems unfathomable.) But the ending here certainly departs from, if it does not negate, the nihilism of the short, absurdist plays that preceded *Who's Afraid of Virginia Woolf?* The exorcism of the child is a deliberate spiritual act, and it has consequences. It is an assertion of the moral will against surrendering either to the escapism of a cowardly imagination or to the automated paradise of perfected eugenics. It re-relates life to a supernatural dimension, the very existence of which is denied by the absurdist view of man as a solitary prisoner in a dark void. And as an act of ritual language used redemptively it transcends the breakdown in communication signaled by the incoherence, the non-referential quality, and the dead stereotypes of absurdist dialogue. It seems to say that the human condition is as real as appearances suggest it is, and that, though painful, difficult, and indefinite, it is not hopeless. Small talk, profanity, verbal injury, and the Mass for the Dead are all part of the same, single world of discourse, within which alone human contact is possible.

# LEROI JONES

# Dutchman

CHARACTERS

CLAY, twenty-year-old Negro
LULA, thirty-year-old white woman
RIDERS OF COACH, white and black
YOUNG NEGRO
CONDUCTOR

*In the flying underbelly of the city. Steaming hot, and summer on top, outside. Underground. The subway heaped in modern myth.*

*Opening scene is a man sitting in a subway seat, holding a magazine but looking vacantly just above its wilting pages. Occasionally he looks blankly toward the window on his right. Dim lights and darkness whistling by against the glass. (Or paste the lights, as admitted props, right on the subway windows. Have them move, even dim and flicker. But give the sense of speed. Also stations, whether the train is stopped or the glitter and activity of these stations merely flashes by the windows.)*

*The man is sitting alone. That is, only his seat is visible, though the rest of the car is outfitted as a complete subway car. But only his seat is shown. There might be, for a time, as the play begins, a loud scream of the actual train. And it can recur throughout the play, or continue on a lower key once the dialogue starts.*

*The train slows after a time, pulling to a brief stop at one of the stations. The man looks idly up, until he sees a woman's face staring at him through the window; when it realizes that the man has noticed the face, it begins very premeditatedly to smile. The man smiles too, for a moment, without a trace of self-consciousness. Almost an instinctive though undesirable response. Then a kind of awkwardness or embarrassment sets in, and the man makes to look away, is further embarrassed, so he brings back his eyes to where the face was, but by now the train is moving again, and the face would seem to be left behind by the way the man turns his head to look back through the other windows at the slowly fading platform. He smiles then; more comfortably confident, hoping perhaps that his memory of this brief encounter will be pleasant. And then he is idle again.*

## SCENE I

*Train roars. Lights flash outside the windows.*

LULA *enters from the rear of the car in bright, skimpy summer clothes and sandals. She carries a net bag full of paper books, fruit, and other anonymous articles. She is wearing sunglasses, which she pushes up on her forehead from time to time.* LULA *is a tall, slender, beautiful woman with long red hair hanging straight down her back, wearing only loud lipstick in somebody's good taste. She is eating an apple, very daintily. Coming down the car toward* CLAY.

*She stops beside* CLAY*'s seat and hangs languidly from the strap, still managing to eat the apple. It is apparent that she is going to sit in the seat next to* CLAY, *and that she is only waiting for him to notice her before she sits.*

CLAY *sits as before, looking just beyond his magazine, now and again pulling the magazine slowly back and forth in front of his face in a hopeless effort to fan himself. Then he sees the woman hanging there beside him and he looks up into her face, smiling quizzically.*

LULA: Hello.

CLAY: Uh, hi're you?

LULA: I'm going to sit down. . . . O.K.?

CLAY: Sure.

LULA (*Swings down onto the seat, pushing her legs straight out as if she is very weary*): Oooof! Too much weight.

CLAY: Ha, doesn't look like much to me. (*leaning back against the window, a little surprised and maybe stiff.*)

LULA: It's so anyway.

(*And she moves her toes in the sandals, then pulls her right leg up on the left knee, better to inspect the bottoms of the sandals and the back of her heel. She appears for a second not to notice that* CLAY *is sitting next to her or that she has spoken to him just a second before.* CLAY *looks at the magazine, then out the black window. As he does this, she turns very quickly toward him.*)

Weren't you staring at me through the window?

CLAY (*wheeling around and very much stiffened*): What?

LULA: Weren't you staring at me through the window? At the last stop?

CLAY: Staring at you? What do you mean?

LULA: Don't you know what staring means?

CLAY: I saw you through the window . . . if that's what it means. I don't know if I was staring. Seems to me you were staring through the window at me.

LULA: I was. But only after I'd turned around and saw you staring through that window down in the vicinity of my ass and legs.

CLAY: Really?

LULA: Really. I guess you were just taking those idle potshots. Nothing else to do. Run your mind over people's flesh.

CLAY: Oh boy. Wow, now I admit I was looking in your direction. But the rest of that weight is yours.

LULA: I suppose.

CLAY: Staring through train windows is weird business. Much weirder than staring very sedately at abstract asses.

LULA: That's why I came looking through the window . . . so you'd have more than that to go on. I even smiled at you.

CLAY: That's right.

LULA: I even got into this train, going some other way than mine. Walked down the aisle . . . searching you out.

CLAY: Really? That's pretty funny.

LULA: That's pretty funny. . . . God, you're dull.

CLAY: Well, I'm sorry, lady, but I really wasn't prepared for party talk.

LULA: No, you're not. What are you prepared for? (*Wrapping the apple core in a Kleenex and dropping it on the floor.*)

CLAY (*takes her conversation as pure sex talk. He turns to confront her squarely with this idea*): I'm prepared for anything. How about you?

LULA (*laughing loudly and cutting it off abruptly*): What do you think you're doing?

CLAY: What?

LULA: You think I want to pick you up, get you to take me somewhere and screw me, huh?

CLAY: Is that the way I look?

LULA: You look like you been trying to grow a beard. That's exactly what you look like. You look like you live in New Jersey with your parents and are trying to grow a beard. That's what. You look like you've been reading Chinese poetry and drinking lukewarm sugarless tea. (*Laughs, uncrossing and recrossing her legs.*) You look like death eating a soda cracker.

CLAY (*cocking his head from one side to the other, embarrassed and trying to make some comeback, but also intrigued by what the woman is saying . . . even the sharp city coarseness of her voice, which is still a kind of gentle sidewalk throb*): Really? I look like all that?

LULA: Not all of it. (*She feints a seriousness to cover an actual somber tone.*) I lie a lot. (*Smiling.*) It helps me control the world.

CLAY (*relieved and laughing louder than the humor*): Yeah, I bet.

LULA: But it's true, most of it, right? Jersey? Your bumpy neck?

CLAY: How'd you know all that? Huh? Really, I mean about Jersey . . . and even the beard. I met you before? You know Warren Enright?

LULA: You tried to make it with your sister when you were ten.

(CLAY *leans back hard against the back of the seat, his eyes opening now, still trying to look amused.*)

But I succeeded a few weeks ago. (*She starts to laugh again.*)

CLAY: What're you talking about? Warren tell you that? You're a friend of Georgia's?

LULA: I told you I lie. I don't know your sister. I don't know Warren Enright.

CLAY: You mean you're just picking these things out of the air?

LULA: Is Warren Enright a tall skinny black boy with a phony English accent?

CLAY: I figured you knew him.

LULA: But I don't. I just figured you would know somebody like that. (*Laughs.*)

CLAY: Yeah, yeah.

LULA: You're probably on your way to his house now.

CLAY: That's right.

LULA (*putting her hand on* CLAY*'s closest knee, drawing it from the knee up to the thigh's hinge, then removing it, watching his face very closely, and continuing to laugh, perhaps more gently than before*): Dull, dull, dull. I bet you think I'm exciting.

CLAY: You're O.K.

LULA: Am I exciting you now?

CLAY: Right. That's not what's supposed to happen?

LULA: How do I know? (*She returns her hand, without moving it, then takes it away and plunges it in her bag to draw out an apple.*) You want this?

CLAY: Sure.

LULA (*she gets one out of the bag for herself*): Eating apples together is always the first step. Or walking up uninhabited Seventh Avenue in the twenties on weekends. (*Bites and giggles, glancing at* CLAY *and speaking in loose sing-song.*) Can get you involved . . . boy! Get us involved. Um-huh. (*Mock seriousness.*) Would you like to get involved with me, Mister Man?

CLAY (*trying to be as flippant as* LULA, *whacking happily at the apple*): Sure. Why not? A beautiful woman like you. Huh, I'd be a fool not to.

LULA: And I bet you're sure you know what you're talking about. (*Taking him a little roughly by the wrist, so he cannot eat the apple, then shaking the wrist.*) I bet you're sure of almost everything anybody ever asked you about . . . right? (*Shakes his wrist harder.*) Right?

CLAY: Yeah, right. . . . Wow, you're pretty strong, you know? Whatta you, a lady wrestler or something?

LULA: What's wrong with lady wrestlers? And don't answer because you never knew any. Huh. (*Cynically.*) That's for sure. They don't have any lady wrestlers in that part of Jersey. That's for sure.

CLAY: Hey, you still haven't told me how you know so much about me.

LULA: I told you I didn't know anything about *you* . . . you're a well-known type.

CLAY: Really?

LULA: Or at least I know the type very well. And your skinny English friend too.

CLAY: Anonymously?

LULA (*settles back in seat, single-mindedly finishing her apple and humming snatches of rhythm and blues song*): What?

CLAY: Without knowing us specifically?

LULA: Oh boy. (*Looking quickly at* CLAY.) What a face. You know, you could be a handsome man.

CLAY: I can't argue with you.

LULA (*vague, off-center response*): What?

CLAY (*raising his voice, thinking the train noise has drowned part of his sentence*): I can't argue with you.

LULA: My hair is turning gray. A gray hair for each year and type I've come through.

CLAY: Why do you want to sound so old?

LULA: But it's always gentle when it starts. (*Attention drifting.*) Hugged against tenements, day or night.

CLAY: What?

LULA (*refocusing*): Hey, why don't you take me to that party you're going to?

CLAY: You must be a friend of Warren's to know about the party.

LULA: Wouldn't you like to take me to the party? (*Imitates clinging vine.*) Oh, come on, ask me to your party.

CLAY: Of course I'll ask you to come with me to the party. And I'll bet you're a friend of Warren's.

LULA: Why not be a friend of Warren's? Why not? (*Taking his arm.*) Have you asked me yet?

CLAY: How can I ask you when I don't know your name?

LULA: Are you talking to my name?

CLAY: What is it, a secret?

LULA: I'm Lena the Hyena.

CLAY: The famous woman poet?

LULA: Poetess! The same!

CLAY: Well, you know so much about me . . . what's my name?

LULA: Morris the Hyena.

CLAY: The famous woman poet?

LULA: The same. (*Laughing and going into her bag.*) You want another apple?

CLAY: Can't make it, lady. I only have to keep one doctor away a day.

LULA: I bet your name is . . . something like . . . uh, Gerald or Walter. Huh?

CLAY: God, no.

LULA: Lloyd, Norman? One of those hopeless colored names creeping out of New Jersey. Leonard? Gag. . . .

CLAY: Like Warren?

LULA: Definitely. Just exactly like Warren. Or Everett.

CLAY: Gag. . . .

LULA: Well, for sure, it's not Willie.

CLAY: It's Clay.

LULA: Clay? Really? Clay what?

CLAY: Take your pick. Jackson, Johnson, or Williams.

LULA: Oh, really? Good for you. But it's got to be Williams. You're too pretentious to be a Jackson or Johnson.

CLAY: Thass right.

LULA: But Clay's O.K.

CLAY: So's Lena.

LULA: It's Lula.

CLAY: Oh?

LULA: Lula the Hyena.

CLAY: Very good.

LULA (*starts laughing again*): Now you say to me, "Lula, Lula, why don't you go to this party with me tonight?" It's your turn, and let those be your lines.

CLAY: Lula, why don't you go to this party with me tonight, Huh?

LULA: Say my name twice before you ask, and no huh's.

CLAY: Lula, Lula, why don't you go to this party with me tonight?

LULA: I'd like to go, Clay, but how can you ask me to go when you barely know me?

CLAY: That is strange, isn't it?

LULA: What kind of reaction is that? You're supposed to say, "Aw, come on, we'll get to know each other better at the party."

CLAY: That's pretty corny.

LULA: What are you into anyway? (*Looking at him half sullenly but still amused.*) What thing are you playing at, Mister? Mister Clay Williams? (*Grabs his thigh, up near the crotch.*) What are *you* thinking about?

CLAY: Watch it now, you're gonna excite me for real.

LULA (*taking her hand away and throwing her apple core through the window*): I bet. (*She slumps in the seat and is heavily silent.*)

CLAY: I thought you knew everything about me? What happened?

(LULA *looks at him, then looks slowly away, then over where the other aisle would be. Noise of the train. She reaches in her bag and pulls out one of the paper books. She puts it on her leg and thumbs the pages listlessly.* CLAY *cocks his head to see the title of the book. Noise of the train.* LULA *flips pages and her eyes drift. Both remain silent.*)

Are you going to the party with me, Lula?

LULA (*bored and not even looking*): I don't even know you.

CLAY: You said you know my type.

LULA (*strangely irritated*): Don't get smart with me, Buster. I know you like the palm of my hand.

CLAY: The one you eat the apples with?

LULA: Yeh. And the one I open doors late Saturday evening with. That's my door. Up at the top of the stairs. Five flights. Above a lot of Italians and lying Americans. And scrape carrots with. Also . . . (*looks at him*) the same hand I unbutton my dress with, or let my skirt fall down. Same hand. Lover.

CLAY: Are you angry about anything? Did I say something wrong?

LULA: Everything you say is wrong. (*Mock smile.*) That's what makes you so attractive. Ha. In that funnybook jacket with all the buttons. (*More animate, taking hold of his jacket.*) What've you got that jacket and tie on in all this heat for? And why're you wearing a jacket and tie like that? Did your people ever burn witches or start revolutions over the price of tea? Boy, those narrow-shoulder clothes come from a tradition you ought to feel oppressed by. A three-button suit. What right do you have to be wearing a three-button suit and striped tie? Your grandfather was a slave, he didn't go to Harvard.

CLAY: My grandfather was a night watchman.

LULA: And you went to a colored college where everybody thought they were Averell Harriman.

CLAY: All except me.

LULA: And who did you think you were? Who do you think you are now?

CLAY (*laughs as if to make light of the whole trend of the conversation*): Well, in college I thought I was Baudelaire. But I've slowed down since.

LULA: I bet you never once thought you were a black nigger.

(*Mock serious, then she howls with laughter.* CLAY *is stunned but after initial reaction, he quickly tries to appreciate the humor.* LULA *almost shrieks.*)

A black Baudelaire.

CLAY: That's right.

LULA: Boy, are you corny. I take back what I said before. Everything you say is not wrong. It's perfect. You should be on television.

CLAY: You act like you're on television already.

LULA: That's because I'm an actress.

CLAY: I thought so.

LULA: Well, you're wrong. I'm no actress. I told you I always lie. I'm nothing, honey, and don't you ever forget it. (*Lighter.*) Although my mother was a Communist. The only person in my family ever to amount to anything.

CLAY: My mother was a Republican.

LULA: And your father voted for the man rather than the party.

CLAY: Right!

LULA: Yea for him. Yea, yea for him.

CLAY: Yea!

LULA: And yea for America where he is free to vote for the mediocrity of his choice! Yea!

CLAY: Yea!

LULA: And yea for both your parents who even though they differ about so crucial a matter as the body politic still forged a union of love and sacrifice that was destined to flower at the birth of the noble Clay . . . what's your middle name?

CLAY: Clay.

LULA: A union of love and sacrifice that was destined to flower at the birth of the noble Clay Clay Williams. Yea! And most of all yea yea for you, Clay Clay. The Black Baudelaire! Yes! (*And with knifelike cynicism.*) My Christ. My Christ.

CLAY: Thank you, ma'am.

LULA: May the people accept you as a ghost of the future. And love you, that you might not kill them when you can.

CLAY: What?

LULA: You're a murderer, Clay, and you know it. (*Her voice darkening with significance.*) You know goddamn well what I mean.

CLAY: I do?

LULA: So we'll pretend the air is light and full of perfume.

CLAY (*sniffing at her blouse*): It is.

LULA: And we'll pretend the people cannot see you. That is, the citizens. And that you are free of your own history. And I am free of my history. We'll pretend that we are both anonymous beauties smashing along through the city's entrails. (*She yells as loud as she can.*) GROOVE!

## SCENE II

*Scene is the same as before, though now there are other seats visible in the car. And throughout the scene other people get on the subway. There are maybe one or two seated in the car as the scene opens, though neither* CLAY *nor* LULA *notices them.* CLAY'S *tie is open.* LULA *is hugging his arm.*

CLAY: The party!

LULA: I know it'll be something good. You can come in with me, looking casual and significant. I'll be strange, haughty, and silent, and walk with long slow strides.

CLAY: Right.

LULA: When you get drunk, pat me once, very lovingly on the flanks, and I'll look at you cryptically, licking my lips.

CLAY: It sounds like something we can do.

LULA: You'll go around talking to young men about your mind, and to old men about your plans. If you meet a very close friend who is also with someone like me, we can stand together, sipping our drinks and exchanging codes of lust. The atmosphere will be slithering in love and half-love and very open moral decision.

CLAY: Great. Great.

LULA: And everyone will pretend they don't know your name, and then . . . (*she pauses heavily*) later, when they have to, they'll claim a friendship that denies your sterling character.

CLAY (*kissing her neck and fingers*): And then what?

LULA: Then? Well, then we'll go down the street, late night, eating apples and winding very deliberately toward my house.

CLAY: Deliberately?

LULA: I mean, we'll look in all the shopwindows, and make fun of the queers. Maybe we'll meet a Jewish Buddhist and flatten his conceits over some very pretentious coffee.

CLAY: In honor of whose God?

LULA: Mine.

CLAY: Who is . . . ?

LULA: Me . . . and you?

CLAY: A corporate Godhead.

LULA: Exactly. Exactly. (*Notices one of the other people entering.*)

CLAY: Go on with the chronicle. Then what happens to us?

LULA (*a mild depression, but she still makes her description triumphant and increasingly direct*): To my house, of course.

CLAY: Of course.

LULA: And up the narrow steps of the tenement.

CLAY: You live in a tenement?

LULA: Wouldn't live anywhere else. Reminds me specifically of my novel form of insanity.

CLAY: Up the tenement stairs.

LULA: And with my apple-eating hand I push open the door and lead you, my tender big-eyed prey, into my . . . God, what can I call it . . . into my hovel.

CLAY: Then what happens?

LULA: After the dancing and games, after the long drinks and long walks, the real fun begins.

CLAY: Ah, the real fun. (*Embarrassed, in spite of himself.*) Which is . . . ?

LULA (*laughs at him*): Real fun in the dark house. Hah! Real fun in the dark house, high up above the street and the ignorant cowboys. I lead you in, holding your wet hand gently in my hand . . .

CLAY: Which is not wet?

LULA: Which is dry as ashes.

CLAY: And cold?

LULA: Don't think you'll get out of your responsibility that way. It's not cold at all. You Fascist! Into my dark living room. Where we'll sit and talk endlessly, endlessly.

CLAY: About what?

LULA: About what? About your manhood, what do you think? What do you think we've been talking about all this time?

CLAY: Well, I didn't know it was that. That's for sure. Every other thing in the world but that. (*Notices another person entering, looks quickly, almost involuntarily up and down the car, seeing the other people in the car.*) Hey, I didn't even notice when those people got on.

LULA: Yeah, I know.

CLAY: Man, this subway is slow.

LULA: Yeah, I know.

CLAY: Well, go on. We were talking about my manhood.

LULA: We still are. All the time.

CLAY: We were in your living room.

LULA: My dark living room. Talking endlessly.

CLAY: About my manhood.

LULA: I'll make you a map of it. Just as soon as we get to my house.

CLAY: Well, that's great.

LULA: One of the things we do while we talk. And screw.

CLAY (*trying to make his smile broader and less shaky*): We finally got there.

LULA: And you'll call my rooms black as a grave. You'll say, "This place is like Juliet's tomb."

CLAY (*laughs*): I might.

LULA: I know. You've probably said it before.

CLAY: And is that all? The whole grand tour?

LULA: Not all. You'll say to me very close to my face, many, many times, you'll say, even whisper, that you love me.

CLAY: Maybe I will.

LULA: And you'll be lying.

CLAY: I wouldn't lie about something like that.

LULA: Hah. It's the only kind of thing you will lie about. Especially if you think it'll keep me alive.

CLAY: Keep you alive? I don't understand.

LULA (*bursting out laughing, but too shrilly*): Don't understand? Well, don't look at me. It's the path I take, that's all. Where both feet take me when I set them down. One in front of the other.

CLAY: Morbid. Morbid. You sure you're not an actress? All that self-aggrandizement.

LULA: Well, I told you I wasn't an actress . . . but I also told you I lie all the time. Draw your own conclusions.

CLAY: Morbid. Morbid. You sure you're not an actress? All scribed? There's no more?

LULA: I've told you all I know. Or almost all.

CLAY: There's no funny parts?

LULA: I thought it was all funny.

CLAY: But you mean peculiar, not ha-ha.

LULA: You don't know what I mean.

CLAY: Well, tell me the almost part then. You said almost all. What else? I want the whole story.

LULA (*searching aimlessly through her bag. She begins to talk breathlessly, with a light and silly tone*): All stories are whole stories. All of 'em. Our whole story . . . nothing but change. How could things go on like that forever? Huh? (*Slaps him on the shoulder, begins finding things in her bag, taking them out and throwing them over her shoulder into the aisle.*) Except I do go on as I do. Apples and long walks with deathless intelligent lovers. But you mix it up. Look out the window, all the time. Turning pages. Change change change. Till, shit, I don't know you. Wouldn't, for that matter. You're too serious. I bet you're even too serious to be psychoanalyzed. Like all those Jewish poets from Yonkers, who leave their mothers looking for other mothers, or others' mothers, on whose baggy tits they lay their fumbling heads. Their poems are always funny, and all about sex.

CLAY: They sound great. Like movies.

LULA: But you change. (*Blankly.*) And things work on you till you hate them.

(*More people come into the train. They come closer to the couple, some of them not sitting, but swinging drearily on the straps, staring at the two with uncertain interest.*)

CLAY: Wow. All these people, so suddenly. They must all come from the same place.

LULA: Right. That they do.

CLAY: Oh? You know about them too?

LULA: Oh yeah. About them more than I know about you. Do they frighten you?

CLAY: Frighten me? Why should they frighten me?

LULA: 'Cause you're an escaped nigger.

CLAY: Yeah?

LULA: 'Cause you crawled through the wire and made tracks to my side.

CLAY: Wire?

LULA: Don't they have wire around plantations?

CLAY: You must be Jewish. All you can think about is wire. Plantations didn't have any wire. Plantations were big open whitewashed places like heaven, and everybody on 'em was grooved to be there. Just strummin' and hummin' all day.

LULA: Yes, yes.

CLAY: And that's how the blues was born.

LULA: Yes, yes. And that's how the blues was born. (*Begins to make up a song that becomes quickly hysterical. As she sings she rises from her seat, still throwing things out of her bag into the aisle, beginning a rhythmical shudder and twistlike wiggle, which she continues up and down the aisle, bumping into many of the standing people and tripping over the feet of those sitting. Each time she runs into a person she lets out a very vicious piece of profanity, wiggling and stepping all the time.*) And that's how the blues was born. Yes. Yes. Son of a bitch, get out of the way. Yes. Quack. Yes. Yes. And that's how the blues was born. Ten little niggers sitting on a limb, but none of them ever looked like him. (*Points to* CLAY, *returns toward the seat, with her hands extended for him to rise and dance with her.*) And that's how blues was born. Yes. Come on, Clay. Let's do the nasty. Rub bellies. Rub bellies.

CLAY (*waves his hands to refuse. He is embarrassed, but determined to get a kick out of the proceedings*): Hey, what was in those apples? Mirror, mirror on the wall, who's the fairest one of all? Snow White, baby, and don't you forget it.

LULA (*grabbing for his hands, which he draws away*): Come on, Clay. Let's rub bellies on the train. The nasty. The nasty. Do the gritty grind, like your ol' rag-head mammy. Grind till you lose your mind. Shake it, shake it, shake it, shake it! OOOOweeee! Come on, Clay. Let's do the choo-choo train shuffle, the navel scratcher.

CLAY: Hey, you coming on like the lady who smoked up her grass skirt.

LULA (*becoming annoyed that he will not dance, and becoming more animated as if to embarrass him still further*): Come on, Clay . . . let's do the thing. Uhh! Uhh! Clay! Clay! You middle-class black bastard. Forget your social-working mother for a few seconds and let's knock stomachs. Clay, you liver-lipped white man. You would-be Christian. You ain't no nigger, you're just a dirty white man. Get up, Clay. Dance with me, Clay.

CLAY: Lula! Sit down, now. Be cool.

LULA (*mocking him, in wild dance*): Be cool. Be cool. That's all you know . . . shaking that wildroot cream-oil on your knotty head, jackets buttoning up to your chin, so full of white man's words. Christ. God. Get up and scream at these people. Like scream meaningless shit in these hopeless faces. (*She screams at people in train, still dancing.*) Red trains cough Jewish underwear for keeps! Expanding smells of silence. Gravy snot whistling like sea birds. Clay. Clay, you got to break out. Don't sit there dying the way they want you to die. Get up.

CLAY: Oh, sit the fuck down. (*He moves to restrain her.*) Sit down, goddamn it.

LULA (*twisting out of his reach*): Screw yourself, Uncle Tom. Thomas Woolly-Head. (*Begins to dance a kind of jig, mocking* CLAY *with loud forced humor.*) There is Uncle Tom . . . I mean, Uncle Thomas Woolly-Head. With old white matted mane. He hobbles on his wooden cane. Old Tom. Old Tom. Let the white man hump his ol' mama, and he jes' shuffle off in the woods and hide his gentle gray head. Ol' Thomas Woolly-Head.

(*Some of the other riders are laughing now. A drunk gets up and joins* LULA *in her dance, singing, as best he can, her "song."* CLAY *gets up out of his seat and visibly scans the faces of the other riders.*)

CLAY: Lula! Lula!

(*She is dancing and turning, still shouting as loud as she can. The drunk too is shouting, and waving his hands wildly.*)

Lula . . . you dumb bitch. Why don't you stop it? (*He rushes half stumbling from his seat, and grabs one of her flailing arms.*)

LULA: Let me go! You black son of a bitch. (*She struggles against him.*) Let me go! Help!

(CLAY *is dragging her towards her seat, and the drunk seeks to interfere. He grabs* CLAY *around the shoulders and begins wrestling with him.* CLAY *clubs the drunk to the floor without releasing* LULA, *who is still screaming.* CLAY *finally gets her to the seat and throws her into it.*)

CLAY: Now you shut the hell up. (*Grabbing her shoulders.*) Just shut up. You don't know what you're talking about. You don't know anything. So just keep your stupid mouth closed.

LULA: You're afraid of white people. And your father was. Uncle Tom Big Lip!

CLAY (*slaps her as hard as he can, across the mouth.* LULA'*s head bangs against the back of the seat. When she raises it again,* CLAY *slaps her again*): Now shut up and let me talk.

(*He turns toward the other riders, some of whom are sitting on the edge of their seats. The drunk is on one knee, rubbing his head, and singing softly the same song. He shuts up too when he sees* CLAY *watching him. The others go back to newspapers or stare out the windows.*)

Shit, you don't have any sense, Lula, nor feelings either. I could murder you now. Such a tiny ugly throat. I could squeeze it flat, and watch you turn blue, on a humble. For dull kicks. And all these weak-faced ofays squatting around here, staring over their papers at me. Murder them too. Even if they expected it. That man there . . . (*Points to well-dressed man.*) I could rip that *Times* right out of his hand, as skinny and middle-classed as I am, I could rip that paper out of his hand and just as easily rip out his throat. It takes no great effort. For what? To kill you soft idiots? You don't understand anything but luxury.

LULA: You fool!

CLAY (*pushing her against the seat*): I'm not telling you again, Tallulah Bankhead! Luxury. In your face and your fingers. You telling me what I ought to do. (*Sudden scream frightening the whole coach.*) Well, don't! Don't you tell me anything! If I'm a middle-class fake white man . . . let me be. And let me be in the way I want. (*Through his teeth.*) I'll rip your lousy breasts off! Let me be who I feel like being. Uncle Tom. Thomas. Whoever. It's none of your business. You don't know anything except what's there for you to see. An act. Lies. Device. Not the pure heart, the pumping black heart. You don't ever know that. And I sit here, in this buttoned-up suit, to keep myself from cutting all your throats. I mean wantonly. You great liberated whore! You fuck some black man, and right away you're an expert on black people. What a lotta shit that is. The only thing you know is that you come if he bangs you hard enough. And that's all. The belly rub? You wanted to do the belly rub? Shit, you don't even know how. You don't know how. That ol' dipty-dip shit you do, rolling your ass like an elephant. That's not my kind of belly rub. Belly rub is not Queens. Belly rub is dark places, with big hats and overcoats held up with one arm. Belly rub hates you. Old bald-headed four-eyed ofays popping their fingers . . . and don't know yet what they're doing. They say, "I love Bessie Smith." And don't even understand that Bessie Smith is saying, "Kiss my ass, kiss my black unruly ass." Before love, suffering, desire, anything you can explain, she's saying, and very plainly, "Kiss my black ass." And if you don't know that, it's you that's doing the kissing.

Charlie Parker? Charlie Parker. All the hip white boys scream for Bird. And Bird saying, "Up your ass, feeble-minded ofay! Up your ass." And they sit there talking about the tortured genius of Charlie Parker. Bird would've played not a note of music if he just walked up to East Sixty-seventh Street and killed the first ten white people he saw. Not a note! And I'm the great would-be poet. Yes. That's right! Poet. Some kind of bastard literature . . . all it needs is a simple knife thrust. Just let me bleed you, you loud whore, and one poem vanished. A whole people of neurotics, struggling to keep from being sane. And the only thing that would cure the neurosis would be your murder. Simple as that. I mean if I murdered you, then other white people would begin to understand me. You understand? No. I guess not. If Bessie Smith had killed some white people she wouldn't have needed that music. She could have talked very straight and plain about the world. No metaphors. No grunts. No wiggles in the dark of her soul. Just straight two and two are four. Money. Power. Luxury. Like that. All of them. Crazy niggers turning their backs on sanity. When all it needs is that simple act. Murder. Just murder! Would make us all sane.

(*Suddenly weary.*) Ahhh. Shit. But who needs it? I'd rather be a fool. Insane. Safe with my words, and no deaths, and clean, hard thoughts, urging me to new conquests. My people's madness. Hah! That's a laugh. My people. They don't need me to claim them. They got legs and arms of their own. Personal insanities. Mirrors. They don't need all those words. They don't need any defense. But listen, though, one more thing. And you tell this to your father, who's probably the kind of man who needs to know at once. So he can plan ahead. Tell him not to preach so much rationalism and cold logic to these niggers. Let them alone. Let them sing curses at you in code and see your filth as simple lack of style. Don't make the mistake, through some irresponsible surge of Christian charity, of talking too much about the advantages of Western rationalism, or the great intellectual legacy of the white man, or maybe they'll begin to listen. And then, maybe one day, you'll find they actually do understand exactly what you are talking about, all these fantasy people. All these blues people. And on that day, as sure as shit, when you really believe you can "accept" them into your fold, as half-white trusties late of the subject peoples. With no more blues, except the very old ones, and not a watermelon in sight, the great missionary heart will have triumphed, and all of those ex-coons will be stand-up Western men, with eyes for clean hard useful lives, sober, pious and sane, and they'll murder you. They'll murder you, and have very rational explanations. Very much like your own. They'll cut your throats, and drag you out to the edge of your cities so the flesh can fall away from your bones, in sanitary isolation.

LULA (*her voice takes on a different, more businesslike quality*): I've heard enough.

CLAY (*reaching for his books*): I bet you have. I guess I better collect my stuff and get off this train. Looks like we won't be acting out that little pageant you outlined before.

LULA: No. We won't. You're right about that, at least. (*She turns to look quickly around the rest of the car.*) All right!

(*The others respond.*)

CLAY (*bending across the girl to retrieve his belongings*): Sorry, baby, I don't think we could make it.

(*As he is bending over her, the girl brings up a small knife and plunges it into* CLAY*'s chest. Twice. He slumps across her knees, his mouth working stupidly.*)

LULA: Sorry is right. (*Turning to the others in the car who have already gotten up from their seats.*) Sorry is the rightest thing you've said. Get this man off me! Hurry, now!

(*The others come and drag* CLAY*'s body down the aisle.*)

Open the door and throw his body out.

(*They throw him off.*)

And all of you get off at the next stop.

(LULA *busies herself straightening her things. Getting everything in order. She takes out a notebook and makes a quick scribbling note. Drops it in her bag. The train apparently stops and all the others get off, leaving her alone in the coach.*

*Very soon a young Negro of about twenty comes into the coach, with a couple of books under his arm. He sits a few seats in back of* LULA. *When he is seated she turns and gives him a long slow look. He looks up from his book and drops the book on his lap. Then an old Negro conductor comes into the car, doing a sort of restrained soft shoe, and half mumbling the words of some song. He looks at the young man, briefly, with a quick greeting.*)

CONDUCTOR: Hey, brother!

YOUNG MAN: Hey.

(*The conductor continues down the aisle with his little dance and the mumbled song.* LULA *turns to stare at him and follows his movements down the aisle. The conductor tips his hat when he reaches her seat, and continues out the car.*)

CURTAIN

The setting in *Dutchman* is "the subway heaped in modern myth," and its action is a brief, underground passage to violence, starting all over again as the play ends. In tough, bright, four-letter idiom, the two characters who virtually make up its cast articulate *the* social dialogue in America today. Part polemic, part anecdote, and part allegory, *Dutchman* is the most coherent and the most grimly powerful of LeRoi Jones's first four plays.

"My ideas," says Jones, "revolve around the rotting and destruction of America, so I can't really expect anyone who is part of that to accept my ideas." The remark is depressing, for it automatically incriminates anyone who disagrees with his views. Argue, for example, that *Dutchman* is a defeatist play because it denies the viability of black-white dialogue, or that it only perpetuates attitudes of hatred, or that it oversimplifies the causes of racial conflict by assuming that all oppression is white and all whites oppressors, and you have immediately identified yourself with the forces of destruction and corruption. Discussion is deadlocked the moment it begins.

We should be more discriminating than that about the play, and we can be. Obviously, its "ideas" are a function of the fable about a black man and a white woman and their murderous sexual encounter on a New York subway train. But it is part of the tragedy of our current social situation that the kind of approach suggested by such an observation has become suspect or worse. We are so involved in our racial dilemma that polemics overwhelm the drama. There is a pressure on us to feel that only what the play *says* is important, not what it *is*. Whether this means that *Dutchman* will become dated once our racial tensions are resolved is unimportant today, an issue for some happier America of the future to decide. In the meantime, its social relevance is so appallingly urgent that to deal with it as a literary construct can only seem stupidly frivolous and *ir*relevant. When a house is on fire, the voice and the syntax in which the cry of alarm is raised don't matter. The only responsible way of discussing *Dutchman* is as a black assault on white attitudes toward race. It calls for social action, not for literary criticism. Never mind the art, pay attention to the anger. Time is running out.

But Jones chose to express his anger in drama rather than in some other form. Presumably he did so because he "saw" his subject dramatically and because he hoped a play would reach a larger audience than an essay in a periodical. Whatever his reasons, he has written a play and not a sociological thesis. That Clay's name suggests pliability, that Lula is a seductive apple-eater who is and is not an actress, that much of their talk is about sex, that the setting is subterranean and moving at high speed, that the old Negro conductor calls the second young man "brother," and that the shape of the play is circular are the kind of things we should attend to if we want to find out what Jones is saying. A polemical author does not with impunity decide to use representations of people and their conversation as a medium; that commits him. And if we inspect the commitments his dramatic art makes for him, we are not thereby removing his play to some serene area of esthetics, safely protected from the social crisis; we are sharing the playwright's vision of that crisis, and the vision is polemically more forceful — though it may not be easy to say exactly what we have been told — than an abstracted paraphrase of it in a militant essay. An irresponsible and irrelevant approach to *Dutchman* is one that ignores the stageable particulars of Jones's dramatic imagination and makes a leap for the expected generalizations about black frustration and alienated belligerence. To reduce to stereotypes a play that is about victimization by conceptual and attitudinal stereotypes would be a sad as well as a dangerous paradox.

Clay and Lula meet under circumstances indistinguishable from a casual pickup for quick sex, but the sequel is less sordid and far more serious. The real subject of their edgy, flittering talk is, as Lula soon points out, Clay's manhood. Its overt quality of tentative, mutual seduction is profoundly relevant, for anxieties about sex underlie much of the American mythology about race, and the question of Clay's manhood is a racial question. Clay and Lula are believable characters as strangers meeting accidentally, but they are also figures in a mythical enactment of the confrontation of blacks and whites. The significance of talk and action expands as the realism of the beginning yields to the ritual of the ending. Myth is a concretion in narration, epic or dramatic, of patterns of communal thought and feeling. It is the embodiment in imaginative form of abstracts that distinguish a large social unit (class, nation, culture, race) and control its life and ethos in subtle, sometimes subconscious, ways. *Dutchman* dramatizes the myth of black manhood in America. More specifically, and in Jones's own words, it is about "the difficulty of becoming a man in America."

The archetypal action in this myth is role-playing, the deliberate assumption of identities. But the roles are only partly chosen. Lula stage-manages their play-acting, but her own roles, as well as Clay's, are also imposed by past interracial relationships. The most crucial game Lula wants to play is that of making believe that they are both free from their respective pasts.

> And we'll pretend the people cannot see you. That is, the citizens. And that you are free of your own history. And I am free of my history. We'll pretend that we are both anonymous beauties smashing

> along through the city's entrails. (*She yells as loud as she can.*) GROOVE!

But, as Clay says just before he is killed, the "acting out the little pageant you outlined before" will not come off. Their history *does* hold them and halts the action.

To see exactly why the pageant fails involves a synopsis of Jones's dialogue dialectic. Lula begins their encounter by casting Clay in the role he has already assumed and then mocking his performance. He is the young, middle-class Negro from the suburbs, socially respectable, intellectually ambitious, so anonymous in his trueness to type that Lula can invent facts about him and be right. She rehearses him, giving him lines to speak and gestures to make, in the role he is to play at the party they are going to. They are to be the emancipated, interracial couple, deliberately acting out the old subversive daydreams, flouting dark taboos: the white woman attracted to black virility, the black man cautiously eager for sex with a white woman.

When Clay seems to accept his assigned part in their pageant, Lula changes her tactics. Her game is not to seduce Clay but to challenge him to racial awareness. The arousal to sex is an arousal to black manhood. The roles she gives him to play are meant to confront him with the unreality of what he is trying to be. She denies him the right to the whiteness he presumes to because she wants him to be a "black nigger." She insults him in order to liberate him. She seeks to provoke him into rejecting a way of life and a set of values that are based on a tradition that is no tradition for him: "Boy, those narrow-shoulder clothes come from a tradition you ought to feel oppressed by. . . . Your grandfather was a slave, he didn't go to Harvard." The "black Baudelaire" is a grotesque. By mimicking middle-class white ways Clay has become the "ghost of the future," for the integrated pseudo-white is dead even before he has become what he is trying to become. Clay ought to be the "murderer" his people's past entitles him to be; he ought to act out the suppressed violence of the outraged. Till he accepts his blackness in proud and free defiance, she can see him only as an "escaped nigger" who has "crawled through the wire and made tracks to my side." In Act II, she offers him the role that is his by right: that of the uninhibited and joyous sensualist who dares to join her in her aisle dance, defying social convention. When he hesitates, she taunts him again. "You ain't no nigger, you're just a dirty white man. Get up, Clay. Dance with me, Clay. . . . Get up and scream at these people. . . . Clay, you got to break out. Don't sit there dying the way they want you to die. Get up." When he doesn't, she calls him an Uncle Tom — silly, scared, submissive, smiling, harmless. She rejects him for rejecting the visibility she holds out to him.

But Lula has got Negro history wrong. Clay's grandfather happened to be a night watchman, not a slave, and there were no wires around Southern plantations. She is extrapolating from white images of evil tyranny, as if the evil of slavery was Hitler's evil and not hers. Trapped in the white history she wants to atone for, she needs to believe she understands black psychology. By redeeming his own past on terms she prescribes, Clay is to redeem hers.

In his long answering monologue, Clay makes two points. The first is that blacks are already beyond being the "murderers" she wants them to be. What whites treasure in black culture – everything denoted by "the blues" – is only an alternative to warfare, and so is the black aping of white ways. Blacks already know they are "fantasy people." They are veteran actors, and Lula's coaching is naive presumption. "I sit here," Clay tells her, "in this buttoned-up suit, to keep myself from cutting all your throats." Whether blues-singers or pseudo-white suburbanites, blacks are "a whole people of neurotics, struggling to keep from being sane. . . . Murder! Just murder. Would make us all sane." Clay's second point is that if white liberals keep preaching "rationalism and cold logic" to the blacks, urging them to rise in the name of "the great intellectual legacy" of Western culture, they may find that their pupils have learned their lesson too well. For the logic of that legacy, the lesson of history, is that revolution follows oppression and oppression follows revolution in an endless cycle.

So leave us alone, says Clay. In your own interest, let us continue in our phony mimicry of whiteness, if that is what we opt for. Let us remain as neurotic blues people or as sex maniacs or Uncle Toms or noble militants against a past which you well-meaning whites join us in repudiating because of what it has done to us. The alternative is murder, for hatred is the core of blackness in white America. The old soft-shoeing conductor at the end is engaged in the same subterfuge as other blacks who choose roles in struggling against the sanity of violence. That is why he can greet the young Negro as "brother," though the latter is an intellectual and he is just a menial. "You telling me what I ought to do," says Clay to Lula. " . . . Well, don't! Don't you tell me anything! If I'm a middle-class fake white man . . . let me be. And let me be in the way I want."

Clay's and Lula's "little pageant" ends in murder because Clay refuses to submit to the sexual and ideological seduction she tempts him with. To succumb to the temptation would amount to a fall not from innocence, certainly, but from an experience of American life that at least leaves him the dignity of having a choice of roles. At the end of his tirade, Lula has realized that no dialogue is possible across the gap that separates black and white, and she kills him not so much in fear or hatred, perhaps, as in sheer frustration. The terrible logic of the play compels the conclusion that there is no way to mutual understanding, for Lula is not a bigoted racist or a condescending sentimentalist or an officious assimilationist. She is hard-headed, clever, attractive, and liberal. There is tenderness behind her toughness, a yearning for union: "Dance with me, Clay." If *she* fails, who can hope to succeed?

Like other successful allegories, *Dutchman* is open to other interpretations, though hardly to one that does not recognize the absolute impasse of the ending. Like other modern dramatists Jones is much less interested in accounting for human behavior than in showing it; Clay and Lula are in the play to articulate their feelings, not to reveal their reasons for being pawns in a plot. And so it isn't really very much to the point to ask if Lula is part of a conspiracy involving both whites and blacks (there are blacks among the passengers who help her get rid of Clay's body) to provoke intransigent blacks like Clay to violence in order to justify murdering them. It is more meaningful to ask if Clay's attitude of sly pliancy is meant to represent a passive response to the black struggle for self-fulfillment and if the play is saying that his kind must be eliminated before the struggle can be won. That is, is Clay Jones's hero, or is he the villain? And is Lula the villainess, trying to shape Clay into what, in her bitchy sexiness, she wants him to be, or is she, like Clay, the victim of the racial impasse? These, it could be argued, are genuine ambiguities in the play, but rather than muddling its meaning they darken the problem it poses. That Jones offers no solution is another reason why the play should not be taken to be simple propaganda or polemics. It is, instead, a frightening image of social conflict in play form.

It is also, perhaps, a prophecy. In legend, the Flying Dutchman is a skipper who, frustrated by head winds in his efforts to round Cape Horn, swears he will keep trying even if it takes him all eternity. He is punished for his blasphemy by being taken at his word. His doom is to sail through storms forever, on a ship manned by a crew of dead men who obey his orders but never speak. Superstitious sailors used to say that seeing the Flying Dutchman was an omen of disaster. The analogy between legend and play does not work out as a set of one-to-one correspondences,* but the subway train, like the legendary ship, keeps journeying on, and the spectacle of violence mutely accepted is an omen of things to come that are already on the point of becoming reality.

* But some such correspondences may be suggested. Lula, like the Dutch skipper, is engaged in a futile effort. Today's racial turbulence is the "storm" we are all traveling through toward an uncertain destination. Lula's "crew" are the mute passengers who throw Clay's body off the train on her order. The subway trip with its recurrent violence is "cursed."

PETER WEISS

The Persecution and Assassination of

# Jean-Paul Marat

as Performed by the Inmates
of the Asylum of Charenton
under the Direction of

# The Marquis de Sade

*English Version by Geoffrey Skelton*
*Verse Adaptation by Adrian Mitchell*

## CHARACTERS

MARQUIS DE SADE, Sixty-eight years old, extremely corpulent, grey hair, smooth complexion. He moves heavily, breathes at times with difficulty, as if asthmatic. His clothing is of good quality, but worn. He is wearing white breeches with bows, a wide-sleeved white shirt with ornamental front and lace cuffs and white buckled shoes.

JEAN-PAUL MARAT, In his fiftieth year, suffering from a skin disease. He is draped in a white cloth and has a white bandage round his temples.

SIMONNE EVRARD, Marat's mistress, of indeterminate age. The player of the role is wearing a hospital uniform, with an apron and a headcloth. Her posture is crooked, her movements odd and constrained. When she has nothing to do, she stands wringing a cloth in her hands. She seizes every opportunity to change Marat's bandage.

CHARLOTTE CORDAY, Aged twenty-four. Her clothing consists of a thin white blouse of Empire cut. The blouse does not conceal the bosom, but she wears a flimsy white cloth over it. Her long auburn hair hangs down on the right side of her neck. She wears pink leather boots with high heels, and when she is "on stage" a ribboned hat is tied to her. She is attended throughout by two Sisters, who support her, comb her hair and arrange her clothes. She moves like a somnambulist.

DUPERRET, Girondist Deputy. The player of the role wears, in addition to his hospital shirt, a short waistcoat and the smooth tight trousers of an "Incroyable." His clothing is also white, with some ornamentation. He is held in the mental home as an erotomaniac, and takes advantage of his role as Corday's lover at every suitable opportunity.

JACQUES ROUX, Former priest, radical Socialist. He wears a white hospital shirt with an overall shaped like a monk's robe. The sleeves of his shirt are tied together in front of him over his hands, and he can move only in the limits of this straitjacket.

THE FOUR SINGERS: KOKOL, Bass; POLPOCH, Baritone; CUCURUCU, Tenor; ROSSIGNOL, Soprano, Part crowd types, part comedians. They have decked out their hospital uniforms with grotesque bits of costume and wear the cap of the Revolution. Rossignol, with her tricolour sash and sabre, represents the figure of Marianne. They have singing voices and perform in mime.

PATIENTS, As extras, voices, mimes and chorus. According to need they appear either in their white hospital uniforms or in primitive costumes with strong colour contrasts. Any not required in the play devote themselves to physical exercises. Their presence must set the atmosphere behind the acting area. They make habitual movements, turn in circles, hop, mutter to themselves, wail, scream and so on.

HERALD, Wears a harlequin smock over his hospital shirt. His two-pointed cap is hung with bells and spangles. He is draped with numerous instruments with which he can make a noise as necessary.
He holds in his hand a beribboned staff.

FIVE MUSICIANS, Inmates of the mental home, clad in white. They play harmonium, lute, flute, trumpet and drums.

MALE NURSES, In light grey uniforms with long white aprons which give them the appearance of butchers. They carry batons in the pockets of their aprons.

SISTERS, Also dressed in light grey, with long white aprons, starched collars and large white bonnets. They carry rosaries. The Sisters are played by athletic-looking men.

COULMIER, Director of the mental home, in elegant light grey clothing, with coat and top hat. He wears pince-nez and carries a walking stick. He likes to adopt a Napoleonic pose.

COULMIER'S WIFE and DAUGHTER, Form a composite pattern of colour from pale mauve to pearl grey, sprinkled with jewels and glittering silver.

# ACT I

*The asylum bell rings behind the stage. The curtain rises.*

## 1. Assembly

*The stage shows the bath hall of the asylum. To right and left bathtubs and showers. Against the back wall a many-tiered platform with benches and massage tables. In the middle area of the stage benches are placed for the actors, Sisters and male nurses. The walls are covered with white tiles to a height of about ten feet. There are window openings high up in the side walls. There is a metal framework in front of the platform and around the baths at the sides. Curtains are fixed to each side of the framework before the platform and these can be pulled when the patients are to be hidden. Front stage centre there is a circular arena. To the right of it a dais for* MARAT'*s bath, to the left a dais for* SADE'*s chair. Left front a raised tribunal for* COULMIER *and his* FAMILY. *On another tribunal right front the musicians stand ready.*

SADE *is occupied with last-minute preparations for the entry of the actors.*

*The* MALE NURSES *are completing a few routine operations of bathing and massage. Patients are sitting or lying on the platform at the back.*

SADE *gives a sign. Through a side door at right back the actors enter, led by* COULMIER *and his* FAMILY *and escorted by* SISTERS *and* MALE NURSES.

*The* PATIENTS *rise to their feet. The ceremonious procession comes forward. The asylum bell is still tolling.*

MARAT, *wrapped in a white sheet and accompanied by* SIMONNE, *is led to the bath.* CORDAY, *sunk into herself, is taken to a bench by two Sisters.*

DUPERRET, ROUX *and the* FOUR SINGERS *take up their positions as* COUL-

MIER *reaches the stage. The* HERALD *stands in the middle of the stage.* SADE *stands near his raised chair. The tolling of the bell ceases. The procession moves towards the acting area.*

COULMIER *enters the acting area.*

*The* PATIENTS *in the background stand tensely. One of them adopts an eccentric pose, another comes slowly forward with outstretched arms.*

*FANFARE.*

## 2. Prologue

COULMIER: As Director of the Clinic of Charenton
I would like to welcome you to this salon
To one of our residents a vote
of thanks is due Monsieur de Sade who wrote
and has produced this play for your delectation 5
and for our patients' rehabilitation
We ask your kindly indulgence for
a cast never on stage before
coming to Charenton But each inmate
I can assure you will try to pull his weight 10
We're modern enlightened and we don't agree
with locking up patients We prefer therapy
through education and especially art
so that our hospital may play its part
faithfully following according to our lights 15
the Declaration of Human Rights
I agree with our author Monsieur de Sade
that his play set in our modern bath house won't be marred
by all these instruments for mental and physical hygiene
Quite on the contrary they set the scene 20
For in Monsieur de Sade's play he has tried
to show how Jean-Paul Marat died
and how he waited in his bath before
Charlotte Corday came knocking at his door

## 3. Preparation

HERALD *knocks three times with his staff and gives the orchestra a sign.*

*Ceremonious music begins.* COULMIER *moves to his* FAMILY. SADE *mounts his dais.* MARAT *is placed in his bath.* SIMONNE *puts his bandage straight. The* SISTERS *arrange* CORDAY'S *costume. The* GROUP *assumes the pose of a heroic tableau.*

## 4. Presentation

*The music stops.* HERALD *knocks three times with his staff.*

HERALD: Already seated in his place
here is Marat observe his face

(*points his staff at* MARAT)

Fifty years old and not yet dead
he wears a bandage around his head

(*points staff at bandage*)

His flesh burns it is yellow as cheese 5

(*points at his neck*)

because disfigured by a skin disease
And only water cooling every limb

(*points to bath*)

prevents his fever from consuming him

(MARAT *takes his pen and begins to write.*)

To act this most important role we chose
a lucky paranoic one of those 10
who've made unprecedented strides since we
introduced them to hydrotherapy
The lady who is acting as his nurse

(*points at* SIMONNE. *She bends with a jerky movement over* MARAT, *loosens his bandage and puts on a new one.*)

whose touch certainly makes him no worse
is Simonne Evrard not Charlotte Corday 15
Marat and Evrard united one day
They shared one vision of the just and true
and furthermore they shared her money too
Here's Charlotte Corday waiting for her entry

(*points to* CORDAY *who smooths her clothes and ties her neckcloth*)

She comes from Caen her family landed gentry 20
Her dress is pretty shoes chic and you'll note
she readjusts the cloth around her throat

(*points at it.* CORDAY *adjusts it.*)

Historians agree so it's not lewd in us
to say that she's phenomenally pulchritudinous

(*She draws herself up.*)

Unfortunately the girl who plays the role here 25
has sleeping sickness also melancholia
Our hope must be for this afflicted soul

(*With closed eyes, she inclines her head far backwards.*)

that she does not forget her role

(*with emphasis, turning to* CORDAY)

Ah here comes Monsieur Duperret

(*indicates* DUPERRET)

with silken hose and fresh toupee 30
To the Revolution's murderous insanity
he brings a touch of high urbanity
Though as a well-known Girondist
his name's upon Marat's black list
he's handsome cheerful full of zest 35
and needs more watching than the rest

(DUPERRET *approaches* CORDAY, *pawing her furtively. The* HERALD *raps him on the hand with his staff. A* SISTER *pulls back* DUPERRET.)

Jailed for taking a radical view
of anything you can name the former priest Jacques Roux

(*indicates* ROUX *who pushes out his elbows and raises his head*)

Ally of Marat's revolution but
unfortunately the censor's cut 40
most of his rabble-rousing theme
Our moral guardians found it too extreme

ROUX: Liberty

(*opens his mouth and pushes his elbows out vigorously.* COULMIER *raises his forefinger threateningly.*)

HERALD: Ladies and gentlemen our players
are drawn from many social layers 45

(*He waves his staff over the audience and the group of actors.*)

Our singers for example of these four
each must be classified as bottom drawer

But now they've left the alcoholic mists
of slums and gin cellars our vocalists

(*points to the* FOUR SINGERS)

Cucurucu Polpoch Kokol 50
and on the streets no longer Rossignol

(*Each named changes his pose with a studied bow,* ROSSIGNOL *curtsies.*)

Now meet this gentleman from high society

(*points at* SADE *who turns his back on the public in a bored way*)

who under the lurid star of notoriety
came to live with us just five years ago
It's to his genius that we owe this show 55
The former Marquis Monsieur de Sade
whose books were banned his essays barred
while he's been persecuted and reviled
thrown into jail and for some years exiled
The introduction's over now the play 60
of Jean-Paul Marat can get under way
Tonight the date
is the thirteenth of July eighteen-o-eight
And on this night our cast intend
showing how fifteen years ago night without end 65
fell on that man that invalid

(*points at* MARAT)

And you are going to see him bleed

(*points at* MARAT'*s breast*)

and see this woman after careful thought

(*points at* CORDAY)

take up the dagger and cut him short
Homage to Marat 70

(*Music starts.* CORDAY *is led by the* SISTERS *from the arena to a bench in the background.* SIMONNE *seats herself on the edge of the dais behind* MARAT'*s bath.* SADE *goes to his seat and sits down.* ROUX *and* DUPERRET *withdraw to a bench.*

*The* FOUR SINGERS *take their position for the homage to* MARAT.)

## 5. Homage to Marat

KOKOL & POLPOCH (*recitative*): Four years after the Revolution
and the old king's execution
four years after remember how
those courtiers took their final bow
CHORUS (*singing in the background*): String up every aristocrat 5
Out with the priests and let them live on their fat
CUCURUCU & ROSSIGNOL (*recitative*): Four years after we started fighting
Marat keeps on with his writing
Four years after the Bastille fell
he still recalls the old battle yell 10
CHORUS (*singing in the background*): Down with all of the ruling class
Throw all the generals out on their arse
ROUX: Long live the Revolution

(*The* FOUR SINGERS *and other* PATIENTS *form an adoring group around the bath. A wreath of leaves is held up.*)

PATIENT (*in background*): Marat we won't dig our own bloody graves
PATIENT (*in background*): Marat we've got to be clothed and fed 15
PATIENT (*in background*): Marat we're sick of working like slaves
PATIENT (*in background*): Marat we've got to have cheaper bread
KOKOL (*indicating wreath*): We crown you with these leaves Marat
because of the laurel shortage
The laurels all went to decorate 20
academics generals and heads of state
And their heads are enormous

(*The wreath is placed on* MARAT'*s head, he is lifted from the bath and carried on the shoulders of two patients.*)

CHORUS: Good old Marat
By your side we'll stand or fall
You're the only one that we can trust at all 25

(MARAT *is carried around the arena.* SIMONNE *walks beside him looking up to him anxiously. The* FOUR SINGERS *and the* PATIENTS *in the procession carry out studied gestures of homage.*)

ROSSIGNOL (*naively, taking the play seriously*): Don't scratch your scabs
or they'll never get any better
FOUR SINGERS (*song*): Four years he fought and he fought unafraid
sniffing down traitors by traitors betrayed

Marat in the courtroom Marat underground
sometimes the otter and sometimes the hound 30

Fighting all the gentry and fighting every priest
businessman the bourgeois the military beast
Marat always ready to stifle every scheme
of the sons of the arse-licking dying regime

We've got new generals our leaders are new 35
They sit and they argue and all that they do
is sell their own colleagues and ride on their backs
and jail them and break them or give them all the axe

Screaming in language no man understands
of rights that we grabbed with our own bleeding hands 40
when we wiped out the bosses and stormed through the wall
of the prison they told us would outlast us all

CHORUS & FOUR SINGERS: Marat we're poor and the poor stay poor
Marat don't make us wait any more
We want our rights and we don't care how 45
We want our revolution NOW

(MARAT *is ceremoniously placed back in the bath. The wreath is taken from his head.*

SIMONNE *busily changes his bandages and rearranges the cloth about his shoulders. Music ends.*

SADE *sits unmoving, looking across the stage with a mocking expression on his face.*)

HERALD: The Revolution came and went
and unrest was replaced by discontent

## 6. Stifled Unrest

PATIENT: We've got rights the right to starve
PATIENT: We've got jobs waiting for work
PATIENT: We're all brothers lousy and dirty
PATIENT: We're all free and equal to die like dogs
ROSSIGNOL: And now our lovely new leaders come 5
they give us banknotes which we're told
are money just as good as gold
but they're only good for wiping your bum

(COULMIER *jumps up from his seat.*)

ROUX (*in the middle of the stage*): Who controls the markets
Who locks up the granaries 10

Who got the loot from the palaces
Who sits tight on the estates
that were going to be divided between the poor

(COULMIER *looks around. A* SISTER *pulls* ROUX *back.*)

PATIENTS (*in the background, and beating out the rhythm emphatically*):
Who keeps us prisoner
Who locks us in 15
We're all normal and we want our freedom
CHORUS: Freedom Freedom Freedom

(*The unrest grows.*)

COULMIER (*knocking with his stick on the railing*): Monsieur de Sade

(SADE *takes no notice.*)

It appears I must act as the voice of reason
What's going to happen when right at the start of the play 20
the patients are so disturbed
Please keep your production under control
Times have changed times are different
and these days we should take a subtler view
of old grievances 25

(*The* PATIENTS *are pushed back by the* MALE NURSES.
*Some* SISTERS *place themselves in front of the* PATIENTS *and sing a tranquillizing litany.*)

## 7. Corday Is Introduced

*Midstage,* CORDAY, *who is sitting slumped down on the bench, is being prepared by the* SISTERS *for her entrance.*

HERALD: Here sits Marat the people's choice
dreaming and listening to his fever's voice
You see his hand curled round his pen
and the screams from the street are all forgotten
He stares at the map of France eyes marching from town to town 5

(*Points to the map, which* MARAT *rolls up*)

while you wait

(*Turns round. In the background a whispering begins and spreads.*)

CHORUS (*whispers*): Corday Corday
HERALD: while you wait for this woman to cut him down

(*Points with his staff to* CORDAY. ORCHESTRA *plays the* CORDAY *theme.*)

HERALD (*waiting for the* SISTERS *to complete their preparations*): And none of us

And none of us 10

(CORDAY *is led forward by the* SISTERS)

And none of us can alter the fact do what we will
that she stands outside his door ready and poised to kill

(*he taps the floor three times with his staff.*
CORDAY *is put in position in the arena. This all resembles a ritual act. The music ends. The* SISTERS *step back.*)

CORDAY (*sleepily and hesitantly*): Poor Marat in your bathtub
your body soaked saturated with poison

(*waking up*)

Poison spurting from your hiding place 15
poisoning the people
arousing them to looting and murder
Marat
I have come
I 20
Charlotte Corday from Caen
where a huge army of liberation is massing
and Marat I come as the first of them Marat

(*Pause. A chord on the lute leads in the musical accompaniment.*)

Once both of us saw the world must go
and change as we read in great Rousseau 25
but change meant one thing to you I see
and something quite different to me
The very same words we both have said
to give our ideals wings to spread
but my way was true 30
while for you
the highway led over mountains of dead

Once both of us spoke a single tongue
of brotherly love we sweetly sung
but love meant one thing to you I see 35
and something quite different to me
but now I'm aware that I was blind
and now I can see into your mind
and so I say no
and I go 40
to murder you Marat and free all mankind

(*Music ends.* CORDAY *stands with her head bowed. The* SISTERS *lead her back.*)

## 8. I Am the Revolution

MARAT (*tyrannically*): Simonne Simonne
More cold water
Change my bandage
O this itching is unbearable

(SIMONNE *stands ready behind him and carries out with maniacal movements her rehearsed tasks. She changes his bandage, fans him with the shoulder cloth and tips a jug over the bath.*)

SIMONNE: Jean-Paul don't scratch yourself 5
you'll tear your skin to shreds
give up writing Jean-Paul
it won't do any good
MARAT: My call
My fourteenth of July call 10
to the people of France
SIMONNE: Jean-Paul please be more careful
look how red the water's getting
MARAT: And what's a bath full of blood
compared to the bloodbaths still to come 15
Once we thought a few hundred corpses would be enough
then we saw thousands were still too few
and today we can't even count all the dead
Everywhere you look
everywhere 20

(MARAT *raises himself up in the bath. The* FOUR SINGERS *stretched out on the floor play cards, taking no notice of* MARAT.)

There they are
Behind the walls
Up on the rooftops
Down in the cellars
Hypocrites 25
They wear the people's cap on their heads
but their underwear's embroidered with crowns
and if so much as a shop gets looted
they squeal
Beggars villains gutter rats 30
Simonne Simonne
my head's on fire
I can't breathe

There is a rioting mob inside me
Simonne 35
I am the Revolution

(CORDAY *is led forward by the* SISTERS.)

### 9. Corday's First Visit

HERALD *taps three times with his staff on the floor and points at* CORDAY, *who is led on to the arena.*

DUPERRET *follows* CORDAY *and remains with bent knee at the edge of the arena.* SIMONNE *stands between her and the bath.*

HERALD: Corday's first visit

(ORCHESTRA *plays the* CORDAY *theme.*)

CORDAY: I have come to speak to Citizen Marat
I have an important message for him
about the situation in Caen my home
where his enemies are gathering 5
SIMONNE: We don't want any visitors
We want a bit of peace
If you've got anything to say to Marat
put it in writing
CORDAY: What I have to say cannot be said in writing 10
I want to stand in front of him and look at him

(*amorously*)

I want to see his body tremble and his forehead bubble with sweat
I want to thrust right between his ribs the dagger
which I carry between my breasts

(*obsessively*)

I shall take the dagger in both hands 15
and push it through his flesh
and then I will hear

(*approaches* MARAT)

what he has got to say to me

(*She stands directly in front of the bath. She raises dagger and is poised to strike.* SIMONNE *stands paralysed.* SADE *rises from his seat.*)

SADE: Not yet Corday
You have to come to his door three times 20

(CORDAY *stops short, hides the dagger and withdraws to her bench. The* SISTERS *and* DUPERRET *follow her as she leaves.*)

## 10. Song and Mime of Corday's Arrival in Paris

*As an accompaniment to the song,* PATIENTS *come forward as mimes. They walk singly around the arena. With simple disguises they present types in the streets. One is an "Incroyable," another a "Merveilleuse" or a banner-bearer, a salesman and cutler, an acrobat or flower seller, and there are also some prostitutes.*

CORDAY *circles the arena in the opposite direction. She represents the country girl who has come to town for the first time.*

FOUR SINGERS (*on the edge of the arena, to a musical accompaniment. Song*): Charlotte Corday came to our town
heard the people talking saw the banners wave
Weariness had almost dragged her down
weariness had dragged her down

Charlotte Corday had to be brave 5
She could never stay at comfortable hotels
Had to find a man with knives to sell
had to find a man with knives

Charlotte Corday passed the pretty stores
Perfume and cosmetics powders and wigs 10
unguent for curing syphilis sores
unguent for curing your sores

She saw a dagger its handle was white
walked into the cutlery seller's door
When she saw the dagger the dagger was bright 15
Charlotte saw the dagger was bright

When the man asked her who is it for
it is common knowledge to each of you
Charlotte smiled and paid him his forty sous
Charlotte smiled and paid forty sous 20

(*Mime of the purchase of the knife.* CORDAY *chooses the dagger, takes it and pays. She conceals the dagger under her neckcloth. The* SALESMAN *looks down her bosom with an admiring gesture.*)

Charlotte Corday walked alone
Paris birds sang sugar calls
Charlotte walked down lanes of stone
through the haze from perfume stalls
Charlotte smelt the dead's gangrene 25
Heard the singing guillotine

(*The mime procession grows larger and develops into a dance of death.*

*The music underlines the monotonous rhythm.*

*Two* PATIENTS, *covered with a cloth, represent a horse. They pull a cart in which stand the condemned receiving last rites from a priest.*

*The* PATIENTS *accompanying the cart make ecstatic and contorted movements. Some are seized with convulsions and throw themselves down in fits. One hears stifled giggles and groans and the stamping of feet to music.*)

Don't soil your pretty little shoes
The gutter's deep and red
Climb up climb up and ride along with me
the tumbrel driver said 30

But she never said a word
never turned her head

Don't soil your pretty little pants
I only go one way
Climb up climb up and ride along with me 35
There's no gold coach today

But she never said a word
never turned her head

CORDAY (*in front of the arena, turned to the public. Behind her the stamping continues*): What kind of town is this
The sun can hardly pierce the haze 40
not a haze made out of rain and fog
but steaming thick and hot
like the mist in a slaughterhouse
Why are they howling
What are they dragging through the streets 45
They carry stakes but what's impaled on those stakes
Why do they hop what are they dancing for
Why are they racked with laughter
Why do the children scream
What are those heaps they fight over 50
those heaps with eyes and mouths
What kind of town is this
hacked buttocks lying in the street
What are all these faces

(*Behind her the dance of death takes place. The* FOUR SINGERS *join the dancers.*

*The cart is turned into a place of execution. Two* PATIENTS *represent the guillotine. The execution is prepared in gruesome detail.*

CORDAY *sits slumped at the foremost edge of the arena.*)

Soon these faces will close around me 55
These eyes and mouths will call me to join them

(*The mime depicts the piercing and bursting of the fat belly of the priest. The condemned man leans across the execution block. His hands are sawn off.*)

## 11. Death's Triumph

MARAT (*speaking to the audience*): Now it's happening and you can't stop it happening
The people used to suffer everything
now they take their revenge
You are watching that revenge
and you don't remember that you drove the people to it 5
Now you protest
but it's too late
to start crying over spilt blood
What is the blood of these aristocrats
compared with the blood the people shed for you 10
Many of them had their throats slit by your gangs
Many of them died more slowly in your workshops

(*The hands of the victim fall off. Howls. The executioners start sawing off his head.*)

So what is this sacrifice
compared with the sacrifices the people made
to keep you fat 15
What are a few looted mansions
compared with their looted lives
You don't care
if the foreign armies with whom you're making secret deals
march in and massacre the people 20
You hope the people will be wiped out so you can flourish
and when they are wiped out not a muscle will twitch in your puffy bourgeois faces
which are now all twisted up with anger and disgust

(COULMIER *rises. The head falls off. Triumphant screams. The* PATIENTS *play ball with the head.*)

COULMIER: Monsieur de Sade
we can't allow this 25
you really cannot call this education
It isn't making my patients any better

they're all becoming over-excited
After all we invited the public here
to show them that our patients 30
are not all social lepers

(SADE *does not react. He gazes with a mocking smile across the stage and cues the* HERALD.)

HERALD (*tapping his staff before* COULMIER *has finished speaking*): We only show these people massacred
because this indisputably occurred
Please calmly watch these barbarous displays
which could not happen nowadays 35
The men of that time mostly now demised
were primitive we are more civilised

(HERALD *points with his staff at the execution scene. Trumpet call. Procession of nobles forms quickly, lining up for execution.*)

CORDAY (*rising*): Up there on the scaffold
you stand completely still and stare
farther than your executioners can see 40
That is how I will stand
when it's all over

(*She closes her eyes and appears to be sleeping.*)

SADE: Look at them Marat
these men who once owned everything
See how they turn their defeat into victory 45
Now that their pleasures have been taken away
the guillotine saves them from endless boredom
Gaily they offer their heads as if for coronation
Is not that the pinnacle of perversion

(*The victims kneel in front of the execution block.* SADE *gestures to the whole group to retreat. The* PATIENTS *withdraw. The cart is taken away.* CORDAY *is led to her bench. A curtain is drawn to hide the* PATIENTS.)

## 12. Conversation Concerning Life and Death

*Order is restored at the back. The* SISTERS *murmur a short litany.*

MARAT (*speaking to* SADE *across the empty arena*): I read in your books de Sade
in one of your immortal works
that the basis of all of life is death
SADE: Correct Marat

But man has given a false importance to death 5
Any animal plant or man who dies
adds to Nature's compost heap
becomes the manure without which
nothing could grow nothing could be created
Death is simply part of the process 10
Every death even the cruellest death
drowns in the total indifference of Nature
Nature herself would watch unmoved
if we destroyed the entire human race

(*rising*)

I hate Nature 15
this passionless spectator this unbreakable iceberg-face
that can bear everything
this goads us to greater and greater acts

(*breathing heavily*)

Haven't we always beaten down those weaker than ourselves
Haven't we torn at their throats 20
with continuous villainy and lust
Haven't we experimented in our laboratories
before applying the final solution
Let me remind you of the execution of Damiens
after his unsuccessful attempt to assassinate 25
Louis the Fifteenth (now deceased)
Remember how Damiens died
How gentle the guillotine is
compared with his torture
It lasted four hours while the crowd goggled 30
and Casanova at an upper window
felt under the skirts of the ladies watching

(*pointing in the direction of the tribunal where* COULMIER *sits*)

His chest arms thighs and calves were slit open
Molten lead was poured into each slit
boiling oil they poured over him burning tar wax sulphur 35
They burnt off his hands
tied ropes to his arms and legs
harnessed four horses to him and geed them up
They pulled at him for an hour but they'd never done it before
and he wouldn't come apart 40
until they sawed through his shoulders and hips
So he lost the first arm then the second
and he watched what they did to him and then turned to us

and shouted so everyone could understand
And when they tore off the first leg and then the second leg 45
he still lived though his voice was getting weak
and at the end he hung there a bloody torso with a nodding head
just groaning and staring at the crucifix
which the father confessor was holding up to him

(*In the background a half-murmured litany is heard.*)

That 50
was a festival with which
today's festivals can't compete
Even our inquisition gives us no pleasure
nowadays
Although we've only just started 55
there's no passion in our post-revolutionary murders
Now they are all official
We condemn to death without emotion
and there's no singular personal death to be had
only an anonymous cheapened death 60
which we could dole out to entire nations
on a mathematical basis
until the time comes
for all life
to be extinguished 65

MARAT: Citizen Marquis
you may have fought for us last September
when we dragged out of the gaols
the aristocrats who plotted against us
but you still talk like a grand seigneur 70
and what you call the indifference of Nature
is your own lack of compassion

SADE: Compassion
Now Marat you are talking like an aristocrat
Compassion is the property of the privileged classes 75
When the pitier lowers himself
to give to a beggar
he throbs with contempt
To protect his riches he pretends to be moved
and his gift to the beggar amounts to no more than a kick 80

(*Lute chord.*)

No Marat
no small emotions please
Your feelings were never petty

For you just as for me
only the most extreme actions matter 85

MARAT: If I am extreme I am not extreme in the same way as you
Against Nature's silence I use action
In the vast indifference I invent a meaning
I don't watch unmoved I intervene
and say that this and this are wrong 90
and I work to alter them and improve them
The important thing
is to pull yourself up by your own hair
to turn yourself inside out
and see the whole world with fresh eyes 95

## 13. Marat's Liturgy

*The curtain is drawn open.* PATIENTS *move forward and arrange themselves in a closed group.*

HERALD: Marat's liturgy

MARAT: Remember how it used to be
The kings were our dear fathers
under whose care we lived in peace
and their deeds were glorified 5
by official poets
Piously the simpleminded breadwinners
passed on the lesson to their children

CHORUS (*murmuring in the background as* MARAT *continues*): The kings are our dear fathers
under whose care we live in peace 10
The kings are our dear fathers
under whose care we live in peace

MARAT: And the children repeated the lesson they believed it
as anyone believes
what they hear over and over again 15

(CHORUS *repeats*)

And over and over again the priests said

(*accompanied by chorus of* PATIENTS)

Our love embraces all mankind
of every colour race and creed
Our love is international universal
we are all brothers every one 20

(*continuing alone*)

And the priests looked down into the pit of injustice
and they turned their faces away and said

(*accompanied by chorus of* PATIENTS)

Our kingdom is not as the kingdom of this world
Our life on earth is but a pilgrimage
The soul lives on humility and patience 25

(*continuing alone*)

at the same time screwing from the poor their last centime
They settled down among their treasures
and ate and drank with princes
and to the starving they said

(*accompanied by chorus of* PATIENTS)

Suffer 30
Suffer as he suffered on the cross
for it is the will of God

(*A mime is performed.* PATIENTS *and the* FOUR SINGERS *come forward. Church dignitaries are depicted:* CUCURUCU *carries a cross made of brooms tied together and leads* POLPOCH *with a rope around his neck behind him.* KOKOL *swings a bucket as a censer.* ROSSIGNOL *counts her beads.*
*continuing alone*)

And anyone believes what they hear over and over again
so the poor instead of bread made do with a picture
of the bleeding scourged and nailed-up Christ 35
and prayed to that image of their helplessness
And the priests said

(*Accompanied by chorus of* PATIENTS. *The litanies of the* SISTERS *can also be heard.*)

Raise your hands to heaven bend your knees
and bear your suffering without complaint
Pray for those who torture you 40
for prayer and blessing are the only stairways
which you can climb to Paradise

(*speaking alone*)

And so they chained down the poor in their ignorance
so that they wouldn't stand up and fight their bosses
who ruled in the name of the lie of divine right 45

CHORUS: Amen

COULMIER (*rising and calling above the Amen*): Monsieur de Sade

I must interrupt this argument
We agreed to make some cuts in this passage
After all nobody now objects to the church 50
since our emperor is surrounded by high-ranking clergy
and since it's been proved over and over again
that the poor need the spiritual comfort of the priests
There's no question of anyone being oppressed
Quite on the contrary everything's done to relieve suffering 55
with clothing collections medical aid and soup kitchens
and in this very clinic we're dependent on the goodwill
not only of the temporal government
but even more on the goodness and understanding of the church

HERALD (*raising his staff*): If our performance causes aggravation 60
we hope you'll swallow down your indignation
and please remember that we show
only those things which happened long ago
Remember things were very different then
of course today we're all God-fearing men 65

(*makes the sign of the cross*)

## 14. A Regrettable Intervention

*A* PATIENT, *a clergyman's collar round his neck, detaches himself from the group and hops forward on his knees.*

PATIENT (*stammering incoherently*): Pray pray
O pray to him
Our Satan which art in hell
thy kingdom come
thy will be done 5
on earth as it is in hell
forgive us our good deeds
and deliver us from holiness
Lead us
Lead us into temptation 10
for ever and ever
Amen

(COULMIER *has sprung to his feet.*
MALE NURSES *throw themselves on the* PATIENT, *overpower him, put him under a shower, then bind him and drag him to the back.*)

HERALD (*swinging his rattle*): The regrettable incident you've just seen
was unavoidable indeed foreseen
by our playwright who managed to compose 15
some extra lines in case the need arose

Please understand this man was once the very
well-thought-of abbot of a monastery
It should remind us all that as they say
God moves like man in a mysterious way 20

(*He swings his rattle.*
COULMIER *sits down. The* PATIENTS *retreat and stretch out on the benches, supervised by the* SISTERS *and* MALE NURSES.)

## 15. Continuation of the Conversation Between Marat and Sade

SADE: Before deciding what is wrong and what is right
first we must find out what we are
I
do not know myself
No sooner have I discovered something 5
than I begin to doubt it
and I have to destroy it again
What we do is just a shadow of what we want to do
and the only truths we can point to
are the ever-changing truths of our own experience 10
I do not know if I am hangman or victim
for I imagine the most horrible tortures
and as I describe them I suffer them myself
There is nothing that I could not do and everything fills me with horror
And I see that other people also 15
suddenly change themselves into strangers
and are driven to unpredictable acts
A little while ago I saw my tailor
a gentle cultured man who liked to talk philosophy
I saw him foam at the mouth 20
and raging and screaming attack with a cudgel
a man from Switzerland
a large man heavily armed
and destroy him utterly
and then I saw him 25
tear open the breast of the defeated man
saw him take out the still beating heart
and swallow it

(*A* PATIENT, *in pacing across the stage, comes face to face with* COULMIER *and addresses part of his speech directly to him.*)

PATIENT: A mad animal

Man's a mad animal 30
I'm a thousand years old and in my time
I've helped commit a million murders
The earth is spread
The earth is spread thick
with squashed human guts 35
We few survivors
We few survivors
walk over a quaking bog of corpses
always under our feet
every step we take 40
rotted bones ashes matted hair
under our feet
broken teeth skulls split open
A mad animal
I'm a mad animal 45

(SADE *comes up to him and leads him gently to the back as he continues.*)

Prisons don't help
Chains don't help
I escape
through all the walls
through all the shit and the splintered bones 50
You'll see it all one day
I'm not through yet
I have plans

MARAT: (*Searches for his cue.*)
HERALD (*prompting*): O this itching
MARAT: O this itching this itching (*hesitates*) 55
HERALD (*prompting*): This fever
MARAT: This fever beats in my head like a drum
my skin simmers and scorches
Simonne
Simonne dip the cloth in vinegar and water 60
cool my forehead

(SIMONNE *hastens to him and goes through her motions.*)

SADE: Marat I know
that you'd give up your fame and all the love of the people
for a few days of health
You lie in your bath 65
as if you were in the pink water of the womb
You swim all huddled up
alone with your ideas about the world

which no longer fit the world outside
And why should you care about the world outside 70
For me the only reality is imagination
the world inside myself
The Revolution
no longer interests me

MARAT: Wrong Sade wrong 75
No restless ideas
can break down the walls
I never believed the pen alone
could destroy institutions
However hard we try to bring in the new 80
it comes into being only
in the midst of clumsy deals
We're all so clogged with dead ideas
passed from generation to generation
that even the best of us 85
don't know the way out
We invented the Revolution
but we don't know how to run it
Look everyone wants to keep something from the past
a souvenir of the old regime 90
This man decides to keep a painting
This one keeps his mistress
This man keeps his horse
He (*pointing*) keeps his garden
He (*pointing*) keeps his estate 95
He keeps his country house
He keeps his factories
This man couldn't part with his shipyards
This one kept his army
and that one keeps his king 100
And so we stand here
and write into the declaration of the rights of man
the holy right of property
And now we find where that leads
Every man's equally free to fight 105
fraternally and with equal arms of course
Every man his own millionaire
Man against man group against group
in happy mutual robbery

(*The* PATIENTS *stand up slowly, some step forward. The* SINGERS *take up their positions.*)

And ahead of them the great springtime of mankind 110
the budding of trade and the blossoming of industry
and one enormous financial upsurge
We stand here more oppressed than when we begun

(*points across the auditorium*)

and they think that the Revolution's been won

## 16. The People's Reaction

THE FOUR SINGERS (*with musical accompaniment*): Why do they have the gold
Why do they have all the power
Why do they have friends at the top
Why do they have jobs at the top
We've got nothing always had nothing 5
nothing but holes and millions of them
KOKOL: Living in holes
POLPOCH: Dying in holes
CUCURUCU: Holes in our bellies
ROSSIGNOL: and holes in our clothes 10
THE FOUR SINGERS & CHORUS: Marat we're poor and the poor stay poor
Marat don't make us wait any more
We want our rights and we don't care how
We want our Revolution NOW
HERALD:

(*coming forward quickly, swinging his staff. Music ends. The* FOUR SINGERS *and* CHORUS *withdraw.*)

Observe how easily a crowd turns mob 15
through ignorance of its wise ruler's job
Rather than bang an empty drum
of protest citizens be dumb
Work for and trust the powerful few
what's best for them is best for you 20
Ladies and gentlemen we'd like to see
people and government in harmony
a harmony which I should say
we've very nearly reached today

(DUPERRET *and the* SISTERS *busy themselves with* CORDAY, *who cannot be awakened. They pull her to her feet and hold her up and try to get her moving.*)

### 17. First Conversation Between Corday and Duperret

CORDAY *is led forward by the two* SISTERS, *supporting her under the arms.* DUPERRET *walks behind, supporting* CORDAY'S *back with his hands.*

HERALD (*plays a few runs on his Pan-flute*): And now nobility meets grace
Our author brings them face to face
The beautiful and brave Charlotte Corday

(*turns round in concern, nods in relief and points his staff at* CORDAY)

The handsome Monsieur Duperret

(*With the help of the* SISTERS, CORDAY *enters the arena.* DUPERRET *walks beside her. The* SISTERS *withdraw.* CORDAY *and* DUPERRET *greet each other with exaggerated ceremony.*)

In Caen where she spent the best years of her youth 5
in a convent devoted to the way of truth
Duperret's name she heard them recommend
as a most sympathetic helpful friend

(DUPERRET *uses the scene to make amorous advances to* CORDAY. *The* HERALD *addresses* DUPERRET.)

Confine your passion to the lady's mind
Your love's platonic not the other kind 10

(*He gives the* ORCHESTRA *a sign with his staff.* CORDAY *stands with head held back, eyes closed. The* ORCHESTRA *plays the* CORDAY *theme. The* HERALD *withdraws. He waits a few seconds and watches* CORDAY.)

CORDAY (*with her eyes closed*): Ah dearest Duperret

(*she hesitates then starts again as if singing an aria*)

Ah dearest Duperret what can we do
How can we stop this dreadful calamity
In the streets everyone is saying
Marat's to be 15

(*She hesitates.* DUPERRET *gently caresses her hips and back.*)

Marat's to be tribune and dictator
He still pretends that his iron grip
will relax as soon as the worst is over

But we know what Marat really wants
anarchy and confusion 20

(CORDAY *stands sunk into herself.*)

DUPERRET (*embracing* CORDAY, *also as if singing an aria, but with great ardour*): Dearest Charlotte you must return
return to your friends the pious nuns
and live in prayer and contemplation
You cannot fight
the hard-faced enemies surrounding us 25

(*One of the* SISTERS *approaches* DUPERRET *and pulls back his hand, which he had placed on her bosom.* CORDAY *stands sunk into herself.*)

You talk about Marat but who's this Marat
A street salesman a funfair barker
a layabout from Corsica sorry I mean Sardinia
Marat the name sounds Jewish to me
perhaps derived from the waters of Marah in the Bible 30
But who listens to him
Only the mob down in the streets
Up here Marat can be no danger to us

(DUPERRET *embraces* CORDAY'*s hips.*
*The* FOUR SINGERS *are filling in time with all sorts of pranks, throwing dice and showing each other card tricks.*)

CORDAY (*suddenly awake and full of power*): Dearest Duperret you're trying to test me
but I know what I must do 35

(*Tries to free herself from* DUPERRET'*s embrace. The two* SISTERS *standing behind the podium interfere and pull back* DUPERRET'*s hands.*)

Duperret go to Caen
Barbaroux and Buzot are waiting for you there
Go now and travel quickly
Do not wait till this evening
for this evening everything will be too late 40

DUPERRET (*passionately, in aria style as before*): Dearest Charlotte my place is here

(*throws himself on his knees and hugs her legs*)

How could I leave the city which holds you
Dearest Charlotte
my place is here

(*he forgets himself and becomes wilder in his embracing. The* HERALD *pushes him with his staff and then taps on the floor.*)

HERALD (*prompting*): And why should I run 45
DUPERRET: And why should I run
now when it can't last much longer

(*stroking* CORDAY *vigorously*)

Already the English lie off Dunkirk and Toulon
The Prussians
HERALD (*prompting*): The Spaniards 50
DUPERRET: The Spaniards have occupied Roussillon
Paris
HERALD (*prompting*): Mayence
DUPERRET: Mayence is surrounded by the Prussians
Condé and Valenciennes have fallen to the English 55
HERALD (*correcting*): Austrians
DUPERRET: To the Austrians
The Vendée is up in arms

(*with much ardour and vigorous embraces*)

They can't hold out much longer
these fanatical upstarts 60
with no vision and no culture
They can't hold out much longer
No dear Charlotte here I stay

(*snuggles up to her and puts his head into her lap*)

waiting for the promised day
when with Marat's mob interred 65
France once more speaks the forbidden word
Freedom

(DUPERRET *raises himself, clinging to* CORDAY, *tries to kiss her.* CORDAY *extricates herself, the two* SISTERS *come to her aid, pushing* DUPERRET *away and pulling her back to her bench. The music ends.*)

## 18. Sade Turns His Back on All the Nations

SADE (*shouting to* MARAT): You hear that Marat
Freedom
They all say they want what's best for France
My patriotism's bigger than yours
They're all ready to die for the honour of France 5

Radical or moderate
they're all after the taste of blood

(*rising*)

The luke-warm liberals and the angry radicals
all believe in the greatness of France
Marat 10
can't you see this patriotism is lunacy
Long ago I left heroics to the heroes
and I care no more for this country
than for any other country

COULMIER (*calling over them with raised forefinger*): Take care 15

PATIENT (*in the background*): Long live Napoleon and the nation

(*a shrill laugh in the background*)

KOKOL (*at back calling*): Long live all emperors kings bishops and popes

(*signs of disorder in the background*)

POLPOCH: Long live watery broth and the straitjacket

ROSSIGNOL: Long live Marat

ROUX: Long live the Revolution (*shouting above the disorder*) 20

SADE: It's easy to get mass movements going
movements that move in vicious circles

(*Shrill whistles in background.*
*A* PATIENT *begins to run in a circle, a second and third join in.* MALE NURSES *pursue them and halt them.*)

SADE: I don't believe in idealists
who charge down blind alleys
I don't believe in any of the sacrifices 25
that have been made for any cause
I believe only in myself

MARAT (*turning violently to* SADE): I believe only in that thing which you betray
We've overthrown our wealthy rabble of rulers
disarmed many of them though 30
many escaped
But now those rulers have been replaced by others
who used to carry torches and banners with us
and now long for the good old days
It becomes clear 35
that the Revolution was fought
for merchants and shopkeepers
the bourgeoisie

a new victorious class
and underneath them 40
ourselves
who always lose the lottery

FOUR SINGERS: Those fat monkeys covered in banknotes
have champagne and brandy on tap
They're up to their eyeballs in franc notes 45
We're up to our noses in crap

Those gorilla-mouthed fakers
are longing to see us all rot
The gentry may lose a few acres
but we lose the little we've got 50

Revolution it's more like a ruin
They're all stuffed with glorious food
They think about nothing but screwing
but we are the ones who get screwed

### 19. First Rabble-Rousing of Jacques Roux

ROUX (*springing on a bench in background, shouting*): Pick up your arms
Fight for your rights
Grab what you need and grab it now
or wait a hundred years
and see what the authorities arrange 5

(PATIENTS *approach* ROUX *from the tribunal*)

Up there they despise you
because you never had the cash
to learn to read and write
You're good enough for the dirty work of the Revolution
but they screw their noses up at you 10
because your sweat stinks
You have to sit way down there
so they won't have to see you
And down there
in ignorance and stink 15
you're allowed to do your bit
towards bringing in the golden age
in which you'll all do the same old dirty work
Up there in the sunlight
their poets sing 20
about the power of life

and the expensive rooms in which they scheme
are hung with exquisite paintings
So stand up
Defend yourselves from their whips 25
Stand up stand in front of them
and let them see how many of you there are

(*The* FOUR SINGERS *sit down in the arena and pass a bottle around.*
*The two* SISTERS *grab* ROUX *from behind and pull him down from the dais.*)

COULMIER (*springing up*): Do we have to listen to this sort of thing
We're citizens of a new enlightened age
We're all revolutionaries nowadays 30
but this is plain treachery we can't allow it
HERALD (*sounding a shrill whistle*): The cleric you've been listening to
is that notorious priest Jacques Roux

(*points with his staff at* ROUX)

who to adopt the new religious fashion
has quit the pulpit and with earthier passion 35
rages from soapboxes A well-trained priest
his rhetoric is slick to say the least
'If you'd make paradise your only chance
is not to build on clouds but solid France'
The mob eats from his hand while Roux 40
knows what he wants but not what he should do
Talk's cheap The price of action is colossal
so Roux decides to be the chief apostle
of Jean-Paul Marat Seems good policy
since Marat's heading straight for Calvary 45
and crucifixion all good Christians know
is the most sympathetic way to go
ROUX (*frees himself and jumps forward*): We demand
the opening of the granaries to feed the poor
We demand 50
the public ownership of workshops and factories

(*The* FOUR SINGERS *listen to the disturbance, but soon lose interest. They quarrel for the last drop of the bottle.*)

We demand
the conversion of the churches into schools
so that now at last something useful can be taught in them

(COULMIER *wrings his hands and signifies protest*)

We demand that everyone should do all they can 55
to put an end to war
This damned war
which is run for the benefit of profiteers
and leads only to more wars

(COULMIER *runs across to* SADE *and speaks to him, but* SADE *does not react.*)

We demand 60
that the people who started the war
should pay the cost of it

(*The* FOUR SINGERS *continue their antics.*)

Once and for all
the idea of glorious victories
won by the glorious army 65
must be wiped out
Neither side is glorious
On either side they're just frightened men messing their pants
and they all want the same thing
Not to lie under the earth 70
but to walk upon it
without crutches

COULMIER (*shouting over him*): This is outright defeatism
At this very moment our soldiers are laying down their lives
for the freedom of the world and for our freedom 75

(*turning violently to* SADE)

This scene was cut

SADE (*calling out, without concerning himself with* COULMIER*'s protest*):
Bravo Jacques Roux
I like your monk's habit
Nowadays it's best
to preach revolution 80
wearing a robe

(ROUX *is overpowered by the two* NURSES *and dragged off.* DUPERRET *makes violent passes at* CORDAY, *who remains impassive. The* PATIENTS *come forward restlessly.*)

ROUX (*as he is being strapped to a bench*): Marat
Your hour has come
Now Marat show yourself
Come out and lead the people 85
They are waiting for you

It must be now
For the Revolution
which burns up everything
in blinding brightness 90
will only last as long as a lightning flash

## 20. Monsieur de Sade Is Whipped

ROUX *jumps up, the bench strapped to his back. He is overpowered. The* PATIENTS *are pushed back.* SADE *comes slowly into the arena. He speaks without bothering about the noise.*

SADE: Marat
Today they need you because you are going to suffer for them
They need you and they honour the urn which holds your ashes
Tomorrow they will come back and smash that urn
and they will ask 5
Marat who was Marat
Marat
Now I will tell you
what I think of this Revolution
which I helped to make 10

*(It has become very quiet in the background.)*

When I lay in the Bastille
my ideas were already formed
I sweated them out
under the blows of my own whip
out of hatred for myself 15
and the limitations of my mind
In prison I created in my mind
monstrous representatives of a dying class
who could only exercise their power
in spectacularly staged orgies 20
I recorded the mechanics of their atrocities
in the minutest detail
and brought out everything wicked and brutal
that lay inside me
In a criminal society 25
I dug the criminal out of myself
so I could understand him and so understand
the times we live in
My imaginary giants committed
desecrations and tortures 30

I committed them myself
and like them allowed myself to be bound and beaten
And even now I should like to take
this beauty here

(*pointing to* CORDAY, *who is brought forward*)

who stands there so expectantly 35
and let her beat me
while I talk to you about the Revolution

(*The* SISTERS *place* CORDAY *in the arena.* SADE *hands her a many-stranded whip. He tears off his shirt and offers his back to* CORDAY. *He stands facing the audience.* CORDAY *stands behind him. The* PATIENTS *advance slowly from the background. The ladies on* COULMIER*'s dais stand up expectantly.*)

At first I saw in the Revolution a chance
for a tremendous outburst of revenge
an orgy greater than all my dreams 40

(CORDAY *slowly raises the whip and lashes him.* SADE *cowers.*)

But then I saw
when I sat in the courtroom myself

(*Whiplash.* SADE *gasps.*)

not as I had been before the accused
but as a judge
I couldn't bring myself 45
to deliver the prisoners to the hangman

(*Whiplash.*)

I did all I could to release them or let them escape
I saw I wasn't capable of murder

(*Whiplash.* SADE *groans asthmatically.*)

although murder
was the final proof of my existence 50
and now

(*Whiplash. He gasps and groans.*)

the very thought of it
horrifies me
In September when I saw
the official sacking of the Carmelite Convent 55

I had to bend over in the courtyard
and vomit

(CORDAY *stops, herself breathing heavily.*)

as I saw my own prophecies coming true

(*He falls down on his knees.* CORDAY *stands before him.*)

and women running by
holding in their dripping hands 60
the severed genitals of men

(CORDAY *flogs him again. He groans and falls forward.*)

And then in the next few months

(*hindered by his asthma*)

as the tumbrels ran regularly to the scaffolds
and the blade dropped and was winched up and dropped again

(*Whiplash.*)

all the meaning drained out of this revenge 65
It had become mechanical

(*Another blow. He crumples.* CORDAY *stands very erect.*)

It was inhuman it was dull
and curiously technocratic

(*Whiplash.*)

And now Marat

(*Whiplash.* SADE *breathes heavily.*)

now I see where 70
this Revolution is leading

(CORDAY *stands breathlessly, holding the whip over* SADE. *The two* SISTERS *move forward and pull her back. She does not resist, dragging the whip behind her.*
SADE *continues, lying on his knees.*)

To the withering of the individual man
and a slow merging into uniformity
to the death of choice
to self denial 75
to deadly weakness
in a state

which has no contact with individuals
but which is impregnable
So I turn away 80
I am one of those who has to be defeated
and from this defeat I want to seize
all I can get with my own strength
I step out of my place
and watch what happens 85
without joining in
observing
noting down my observations
and all around me
stillness 90

(*pauses, breathing heavily*)

And when I vanish
I want all trace of my existence
to be wiped out

(*He takes his shirt and returns to his chair, slowly dressing.*)

### 21. Poor Old Marat

MARAT (*bent forward, sunk into himself*): Simonne Simonne

(*staring as if blind*)

Why is it getting so dark
Give me a fresh cloth for my forehead
Put a new towel round my shoulders
I don't know 5
If I am freezing or burning to death

(SIMONNE *stands ready and bends over him with her jerky movements, puts a hand to his brow, changes the cloths, fans him. The* PATIENTS *cower behind the arena.*)

Simonne
Fetch Bas so I can dictate my call
my call to the people of France

(SIMONNE *shakes her head in horror and puts a hand over her mouth.*)

Simonne 10
Where are my papers
I saw them only a moment ago
Why is it so dark

SIMONNE (*pushing the papers lying on the board nearer*): They're here can't you see Jean-Paul

MARAT: Where's the ink 15
Where's my pen

SIMONNE (*indicating*): Here's your pen Jean-Paul
and here's the ink
where it always is
That was only a cloud over the sun 20
or perhaps smoke
They are burning the corpses

(*The* ORCHESTRA *plays. The* FOUR SINGERS *come forward.*)

FOUR SINGERS (*singing to music*): Poor old Marat they hunt you down
The bloodhounds are sniffing all over the town
Just yesterday your printing press 25
was smashed Now they're asking your home address

Poor old Marat in you we trust
You work till your eyes turn as red as rust
but while you write they're on your track
The boots mount the staircase the door's flung back 30

(*together with* CHORUS)

Marat we're poor and the poor stay poor
Marat don't make us wait any more
We want our rights and we don't care how
We want our Revolution NOW

(*Music Finale.* SINGERS *withdraw. The* PATIENTS *close the curtain.*)

### 22. Second Conversation Between Corday and Duperret

*The* SISTERS *and* DUPERRET *busy themselves with* CORDAY. *Together they raise her up. The* SISTERS *arrange her clothes and tie on her hat. The* HERALD *comes forward and knocks his staff on the floor three times.*

HERALD (*plays a few runs on his Pan-flute*): Now that these painful matters have been clarified
let's turn and look upon the sunny side
Fever sores blows not one of them destroys
the universal rule of love's sweet joys
Anger and woe don't give a true reflection 5
of life there's also spiritual affection
Recall this couple and their love so pure

(CORDAY *is led to the centre by* SISTERS. DUPERRET *has his arm around her.*
*The* HERALD *points his staff.*)

she with her neatly-groomed coiffure

(*points to it*)

and her face intriguingly pale and clear

(*points to it*)

and her eyes ashine with the trace of a tear 10

(*points to them*)

her lips sensual and ripe seeming to silently cry for protection

(*points to them*)

and his embraces proving his affection

(*Points to* DUPERRET, *who lifts* CORDAY'*s foot and kisses her shoe, then covers her leg in kisses.* CORDAY *pushes him back.*)

See how he moves with natural grace

(DUPERRET *loses his balance and, without grace, sits on his behind, but rises immediately and strikes a comic amorous pose before* CORDAY, *who turns her face from him in disgust.*)

and how his heart sprints on at passion's pace

(*points to* DUPERRET'*s breast*)

Let's gaze at the sweet blending of the strong and fair sex 15
before their heads fall off their necks

(ORCHESTRA *plays* CORDAY *theme. She hesitates, looking for her words.*
*The* HERALD *prompts her.*)

HERALD: One day it will come to pass
CORDAY (*in the aria style*): One day it will come to pass
Man will live in harmony with himself
and with his fellow-man 20
DUPERRET (*covers her hand and arm with kisses*): One day it will come

(*He strokes her hair, singing in the aria style.*)

a society which will pool its energy
to defend and protect
each person for the possession of each person
and in which each individual 25
although united with all the others

(*putting a hand under* CORDAY'*s dress. She defends herself.*)

only obeys himself
and so stays free

(DUPERRET *tries to kiss* CORDAY'*s mouth. She avoids him.*)

CORDAY: A society
in which every man is trusted with the right 30
of governing himself himself

DUPERRET (*holding* CORDAY *and embracing her violently*): One day it will come
a constitution in which the natural inequalities of man

(CORDAY *leans back.* DUPERRET *jumps after her, continuing.*)

are subject to a higher order
(*breathless*) so that all 35

(*One of the* SISTERS *gets hold of* CORDAY *and leads her back.* CORDAY *is placed in a heroic pose.*)

however varied their physical and mental powers may be
by agreement legally
get their fair share

(*He utters a sigh of relief, and then he also falls into a suitable pose so that they form a pleasant tableau.*)

## 23. These Lies They Tell

MARAT *raises himself up.* CORDAY *is led back by the* SISTERS. DUPERRET *follows her.*

MARAT: These lies they tell about the ideal state
The rich will never give away their property
of their own free will
And if by force of circumstances
they have to give up just a little 5
here and there
they do it only because they know
they'll soon win it back again
The rumour spreads
that the workers can soon expect higher wages 10
Why

(*The head of a* PATIENT *appears from behind the curtain, which is opened from inside.*)

Because this raises production and increases demand
to fill the rich man's gold-chest

Don't imagine
that you can beat them without using force 15

(*The* PATIENTS *rise one by one and advance slowly, listening intently.* CORDAY *lies stretched out on the dais,* DUPERRET *leans over her.*)

Don't be deceived
when our Revolution has been finally stamped out
and they tell you
things are better now
Even if there's no poverty to be seen 20
because the poverty's been hidden
even if you ever got more wages
and could afford to buy
more of these new and useless goods
which these new industries foist on you 25
and even if it seems to you
that you never had so much
that is only the slogan of those
who still have much more than you

(*The* PATIENTS *and* FOUR SINGERS *advance slowly.*)

Don't be taken in 30
when they pat you paternally on the shoulder and say
that there's no inequality worth speaking of
and no more reason
for fighting

(COULMIER *looks around, worried.*)

Because if you believe them 35

(*turns towards the audience*)

they will be completely in charge
in their marble homes and granite banks
from which they rob the people of the world
under the pretence of bringing them culture

(COULMIER *leaves the platform and hurries towards* SADE. *He speaks to him.* SADE *does not react.*)

Watch out 40
for as soon as it pleases them
they'll send you out
to protect their gold
in wars

(SADE *rises and moves to the arena.*)

whose weapons rapidly developed 45
by servile scientists
will become more and more deadly
until they can with a flick of a finger
tear a million of you to pieces

SADE: Lying there 50
scratched and swollen
your brow burning

(COULMIER *nods with satisfaction and returns to the platform.*)

in your world your bath
you still believe that justice is possible
you still believe all men are equal 55
Do you still believe that all occupations
are equally valuable equally satisfying
and that no man wants to be greater than the others
How does the old song go

## 24. Song and Mime of the Glorification of the Beneficiary

*The* FOUR SINGERS *perform a mime, in which they illustrate the cash value of all the things* SADE *names.*

SADE: One always bakes the most delicate cakes
Two is the really superb masseur
Three sets your hair with exceptional flair
Four's brandy goes to the Emperor
Five knows each trick of advanced rhetoric 5
Six bred a beautiful brand-new rose
Seven can cook every dish in the book
And eight cuts you flawlessly elegant clothes
Do you think those eight would be happy
if each of them could climb so high 10
and no higher
before banging their heads on equality
if each could be only a small link
in a long and heavy chain
Do you still think it's possible 15
to unite mankind
when already you see how the few idealists
who did join together in the name of harmony
are now out of tune
and would like to kill each other over trifles 20

MARAT (*raising himself*): But they aren't trifles

They are matters of principle
and it's usual in a revolution
for the half-hearted and the fellow-travellers
to be dropped 25

(*Mime ends.* MARAT *stands up in the bath.*)

We can't begin to build till we've burnt the old building down
however dreadful that may seem to those
who lounge in make-believe contentment
wearing their scruples as protective clothing
Listen 30
Can you hear through the walls
how they plot and whisper

(MARAT *gets out of the bath and stumbles around the arena as if about to faint. Some nurses seize him and put him back into the bath.*)

Do you see how they lurk everywhere
waiting for the chance to strike

THE FOUR SINGERS (*to music accompaniment, singly, speaking in conversational tones while promenading*): What has gone wrong with 35
the men who are ruling
I'd like to know who
they think they are fooling
They told us that torture
was over and gone 40
but everyone knows
the same torture goes on
The king's gone away
The priests emigrating
The nobles are buried 45
so why are we waiting

## 25. Corday's Second Visit

CORDAY *is prepared by the* SISTERS, *who lead her forward.* DUPERRET *follows them.* MARAT *sits waiting in his bath.* SIMONNE *changes his cloths.* SADE *stands in front of his chair.* CORDAY *is placed on the arena in a pose. She holds up her hand as if about to knock. The* SISTERS *stand behind her ready to support her.* DUPERRET *sits down. The* FOUR SINGERS *stop in front of the musicians.*

*The* HERALD *gives* CORDAY *a sign with his staff, she moves her hand as if knocking, and the* HERALD *knocks three times with his staff on the floor.*

*The* ORCHESTRA *plays the* CORDAY *theme.*

HERALD: Now Charlotte Corday stands outside
Marat's front door the second time she's tried

(*points to* CORDAY. SIMONNE *straightens and goes a few steps towards* CORDAY.)

CORDAY (*quietly*): I have come
to deliver this letter

(*draws a letter from her bodice*)

in which I ask again 5
to be received by Marat

(*hesitates*)

I am unhappy
and therefore have a right to his aid

(CORDAY *holds the letter out to* SIMONNE. SIMONNE, *confused, takes a step towards* CORDAY, *returns to the back and begins to change* MARAT'*s bandage.*)

CORDAY (*repeating loudly*): I have a right to his aid

(*She stretches out her hand.* SIMONNE *wavers nervously about, then runs to* CORDAY *and snatches the letter from her.*)

MARAT: Who was that at the door Simonne 10

(SIMONNE *hesitates in confusion between* CORDAY *and* MARAT.)

HERALD (*prompting*): A girl from Caen with a letter
a petitioner

(CORDAY *is now standing sunk into herself.* DUPERRET *rises and puts his arm around her waist. The two* SISTERS *come up.* CORDAY *is led off.*)

SIMONNE (*confused and angry*): I won't let anyone in
They only bring us trouble
All these people with their convulsions and complaints 15
As if you had nothing better to do
than be their lawyer and doctor and confessor

(*She tears the letter up and puts the pieces in her apron. She puts a fresh cloth around* MARAT'*s shoulders.*)

SADE (*goes into the arena and stops near the bath. Musical accompaniment*): That's how it is Marat
That's how she sees your Revolution
They have toothache 20
and their teeth should be pulled

(*The* FOUR SINGERS *mime the characters in his speech. They mime very slowly, with economical gestures illustrating suffering.*)

Their soup's burnt
They shout for better soup
A woman finds her husband too short
she wants a taller one 25
A man finds his wife too skinny
he wants a plumper one
A man's shoes pinch
but his neighbour's shoes fit comfortably
A poet runs out of poetry 30
and desperately gropes for new images
For hours an angler casts his line
Why aren't the fish biting
And so they join the Revolution
thinking the Revolution will give them everything 35
a fish
a poem
a new pair of shoes
a new wife
a new husband 40
and the best soup in the world
So they storm all the citadels
and there they are
and everything is just the same
no fish biting 45
verses botched
shoes pinching
a worn and stinking partner in bed
and the soup burnt
and all that heroism 50
which drove us down to the sewers
well we can talk about it to our grandchildren
if we have any grandchildren

(*Music changes to a quartet with tragic flavour.*)

THE FOUR SINGERS (*taking up their positions*): Marat Marat it's all in vain
You studied the body and probed the brain 55
In vain you spent your energies
for how can Marat cure his own disease

Marat Marat where is our path

or is it not visible from your bath
Your enemies are closing in 60
Without you the people can never win

(MARAT *lays himself wearily across the board.*)

Marat Marat can you explain
how once in the daylight your thought seemed plain
Has your affliction left you dumb
Your thoughts lie in shadows now night has come 65

(*The music changes to a dramatic growling.*
MARAT *is in a fever.* SIMONNE *feels his brow, fans him, changes his bandage.*)

## 26. The Faces of Marat

*The whole stage trembles and roars. The mimes appear with a cart. The cart is drawn by a man and a woman who represent* MARAT'*s parents. The characters in the cart stand for Science, the Army, the Church, the Nouveaux Riches. The priest blesses the owner of the sack of gold looted from the aristocrats. The figures are bedecked with medals and with primitive insignia. The costumes are extremely grotesque.*

MARAT (*raising himself up*): They are coming
Listen to them
and look carefully at
these gathering figures
Listen closely 5
Watch
Yes I hear you
all the voices I ever heard
Yes I see you
all the old faces 10

(*The loud noise continues.*)

HERALD (*tapping his staff*): Ladies and gentlemen silence I pray
Let's hear what these people are aching to say

(*pointing to figures*)

about this man

(*pointing to* MARAT)

whom they all understood

before they bury him for good 15
First the schoolmaster of that charming place

(*points to* SCHOOLMASTER)

in which this man

(*points to* MARAT)

spent his childhood days
SCHOOLMASTER (*sings in falsetto voice*): Even as a child
this Marat 20
made groups of his friends
rush screaming at each other
they fought with wooden swords
but real blood flowed

(*cries are heard in the background*)

and they took prisoners 25
and bound and tortured them
and nobody knew why
HERALD (*pointing to the figure representing* MARAT'*s mother*): Now let us hear this lady for she can
give us the inside story of this man
She smelt him from the very first 30
for from her womb young Marat burst
MOTHER (*in a complaining voice*): Wouldn't eat his food
Lay around for days saying nothing
Broke a lot of canes on his hide we did

(*she laughs shrilly. Laughter is heard in the background, also the sound of whipping.*)

Locked him up in the cellar of course 35
but nothing helped
There was no getting at him
Oh

(*she starts laughing again*)

FATHER (*springing forward, in a hurried voice*): When I bit him he bit back
his own father 40
Threw himself down when I wanted to hang him up
and when I spat at him he lay there stiff as a poker
cold as ice

(*starts to laugh harshly*)

MARAT: Yes I see you
hated father hated mother 45

(*The two figures squat down, still shaking with laughter. They rock to and fro as if sitting in a boat.*)

What's that boat you're rocking in
I see you
I hear you
Why do you laugh like executioners

(*The two figures sit rocking, their laughter dies.*)

SIMONNE (*approaching the bath*): Jean-Paul you're feverish 50
Stop writing Jean-Paul
or it'll kill you
Lie still
You must take more care of yourself
MARAT: I'm not feverish 55
Now I see clearly
those figures were always hallucinations
Why doesn't Bas come
Fetch him
My call to the nation 60
I must write my call
Bas
SCHOOLMASTER (*jumping forward*): When he was five this loudmouth boasted
I can do anything teacher can do
and what's more I know more 65
and at fifteen I've conquered the uni-v-v-v-versities
and outdone all the p-p-professors
and at the age of twenty I've mastered
the entire in-in-in-intellectual cosmos
That's what he boasted 70
as true as I stand here

(*swings his cane*)

MARAT: Simonne
where are my old manuscripts
My novel about the young Count Potovsky
and my book about the chains of slavery 75
SIMONNE (*defensively*): Leave all that stuff
It'll only bring you trouble
MARAT (*raising himself up*): I want to see them

Look for them
bring them to me 80
SCHOOLMASTER: Scribblings of a pickpocket
pilfered thoughts
frivolities tirades
MILITARY REPRESENTATIVE: One book published under the name of a count
The other under the name of a prince 85
Just look at him
this charlatan
greedy for titles and court distinctions
who turned on those he once flattered
only because they did not recognize him 90
A SCIENTIST: What did he do in England this shady Marat
Wasn't he a dandy in the highest society
who had to run away
because he was caught red-handed embezzling and stealing
Didn't he smuggle himself back into well-known circles 95
and get himself appointed physician
to the Count d' Artois
or was it only to his horses
Didn't we see him going about with aristocrats
He charged thirty-six livres for a consultation 100
and on top of that enjoyed the favours of
certain well-born ladies

(COULMIER'*s wife and daughter applaud.*)

A NEWLY RICH: And when at last they let him drop
back to his kind the simple poor
and when he spoke and couldn't stop 105
each word from branding him a boor
and when they found he was a quack
with watered drugs and pills of chalk
and when they threw him on his back
he raised his battered head to squawk 110
Property is Robbery

(*cries in the background*)

Down with all Tyrants

(*The cry is taken up in the background.*)

MARAT: Bas fetch Bas

(VOLTAIRE *emerges from the darkness, suitably masked and with corkscrew curls.*)

CHORUS: Bas
HERALD (*as* VOLTAIRE *advances*): It is a privilege indeed 115
to introduce Voltaire He wrote Candide
VOLTAIRE (*monotonously*): We have received from a certain Marat
a slim volume
entitled Man
This Marat claims in a somewhat revolutionary essay 120
that the soul exists in the walls of the brain
and from that strategic point controls
the hypodraulic mechanism of the body
by means of a network of tinkling nerve threads
At the same time apparently the soul is receiving 125
messages from the mechanamism of the body
messages conveyed by pistons plugs and wires
which the soul transforms into consciousness through separate
centimentrifuges operating asimultaneously
In other words 130
it is the opinion of this gentleman
that a corn fills the corridors of the brain with pain of the soul
and that a troubled soul curdles the liver and kidneys
For this kind of ring-a-ring-a-roses
we can spare not even our laughter 135

(CUCURUCU *and* ROSSIGNOL *laugh ironically Ha Ha Ha. A figure with a palm branch moves forward.*)

HERALD: We're equally happy to welcome today
that eminent scientist Lavoisier

(*points to him*)

LAVOISIER (*monotonously*): The Academy has received from a certain Marat
some theories concerning fire light and electricity
This Marat seems entirely certain 140
that he knows a great deal better than the Academy
For fire he says is not an element
but a liquid fluidium caused by heat
which only ignites because of air
Light he proceeds to say is not light 145
but a path of vibratorating rays
left behind by light
Certainly an extraordinary scientist
He goes further
Heat according to him is not of course heat 150
but simply more vibratoratory rays

which become heat only
when they collide with a body and set in motionability
its minuscule molecules
He wants to pronounce 155
the whole of firm and fixed creation invalid
And instead he wants to introduce
a universe of unbridled activation
in which electrified magnetic forces
whizz about and rub against each other 160
No wonder that the author sits there in his bath
attempting to determine the validity of the proposition
The more you scratch the more you itch

(KOKOL *and* POLPOCH *laugh ironically Ha Ha Ha.* FATHER *and* MOTHER *join in the laughter. The figures mime the attitude of judges about to give a verdict.*)

VOLTAIRE: So this frustrated Newton's eyes
PRIEST: turned to the streets He thought it best 165
SCHOOLMASTER: to join the revolutionaries
NEWLY RICH: and beat his dilettante breast
PRIEST: crying out The oppressed must rise
LAVOISIER: He meant of course I am oppressed

(*Rocking to and fro and laughing, the* FATHER *and* MOTHER *pull back the cart with the figures.* ROUX *hurries to the front, a belated advocate.*)

ROUX: Woe to the man who is different 170
who tries to break down all the barriers
Woe to the man
who tries to stretch the imagination of man
He shall be mocked he shall be scourged
by the blinkered guardians of morality 175
You wanted enlightenment and warmth
and so you studied light and heat

(*unrest in background*)

You wondered how forces can be controlled
so you studied electricity
You wanted to know what man is for 180
so you asked yourself What is this soul
this dump for hollow ideals and mangled morals
You decided that the soul is in the brain

(*The* PATIENTS *form into a group and advance.*)

and that it can learn to think

For to you the soul is a practical thing 185
a tool for ruling and mastering life
And you came one day to the Revolution
because you saw the most important vision
That our circumstances must be changed fundamentally
and without these changes 190
everything we try to do must fail

(COULMIER *jumps up. The* SISTERS *and* MALE NURSES *run towards* ROUX *and pull him into the background.* SADE *stands erect in front of his chair and smiles.* CORDAY *lies sleeping on her bench.* DUPERRET *sits by her on the floor.*)

CHORUS (*to music while the* SISTERS *sing a litany*): Marat we're poor and the poor stay poor
Marat don't make us wait any more
We want our rights and we don't care how
We want our Revolution NOW 195

(*Music ends.*)

HERALD (*swinging his rattle*): The end comes soon Before we watch the crime
let's interpose a drinking thinking time
while you recall that what our cast presents
is simply this a series of events
but that our end which might seem prearranged 200
could be delayed or even changed
We will since it's a play not actual history
postpone it with an interval We guarantee
that after your refreshments and debating
you'll find Marat still in his bathtub waiting 205

(*points to* MARAT)

CURTAIN

## ACT II

*The handbell is rung behind the curtain. Curtain goes up.*

### 27. THE NATIONAL ASSEMBLY

*The setting is the same, but with the following changes:* DUPERRET *sits on the steps leading to* SADE*'s raised chair, between the two* PATIENTS *representing prostitutes. On the left are seated the* PATIENTS *who represent the Girondists in the National Assembly.* SADE *stands underneath* COULMIER'*s platform. The bath has been removed from* MARAT'*s dais. On it are the* FOUR SINGERS *and the* PATIENTS *who represent the Jacobites.* PATIENTS *sit on benches alongside the arena. There are more* PATIENTS *in the background listening. The entire group composes a tableau. The bath, in which* MARAT *stands, is wheeled in through the door at the back right.*

CHORUS *in sections:*

*A drawn-out cat-call.*

*A long monotonous whistle.*

*A muffled trampling of feet.*

MARAT *is pushed in his bath to the centre of the arena. He stands straight and looks towards the* HERALD.

HERALD: Marat is still in his bathtub confined
but politicians crowd into his mind
He speaks to them his last polemic fight
to say who should be tribune. It is almost night

(*He gives the* ORCHESTRA *a sign with his staff. A flourish. The people in the tableau spring to life, stamp their feet, whistle and shout.*)

KOKOL: Down with Marat 5
CUCURUCU: Don't let him speak
ROSSIGNOL: Listen to him he's got the right to speak
POLPOCH: Long live Marat
KOKOL: Long live Robespierre
CUCURUCU: Long live Danton 10
MARAT (*addressing the audience. During his entire speech he never turns to those present on the stage. It is obvious that his speech is imaginary*): Fellow citizens
members of the National Assembly
our country is in danger
From every corner of Europe armies invade us
led by profiteers 15
who want to strangle us
and already quarrel over the spoils
And what are we doing

(*apathetic noises*)

Our minister of war
whose integrity you never doubted 20
has sold the corn meant for our armies
for his own profit to foreign powers

and now it feeds the troops
who are invading us

(*Cries and whistles.*)

KOKOL: Lies 25
CUCURUCU: Throw him out
MARAT: The chief of our army Dumouriez
ROSSIGNOL: Bravo
POLPOCH: Long live Dumouriez
MARAT: against whom I've warned you continually 30
and whom you recently hailed as a hero
has gone over to the enemy
KOKOL: Shame
ROSSIGNOL: Bravo
CUCURUCU: Liar 35

(*shuffling of feet*)

MARAT: Most of the generals
who wear our uniform
are sympathetic with the emigrés
and when the emigrés return
our generals will be out to welcome them 40
KOKOL: Execute them
CUCURUCU: Down with Marat
ROSSIGNOL: Bravo
POLPOCH: Long live Marat
MARAT: Our trusted minister of finance 45
the celebrated Monsieur Cambon
is issuing fake banknotes thus increasing inflation
and diverting a fortune into his own pocket

(*whistles and stamping*)

ROSSIGNOL: Long live free enterprise
MARAT: And I am told 50
that Perregeaux our most intelligent banker
is in league with the English
and in his armoured vaults
is organising a centre of espionage against us
COULMIER (*jumping up to protest*): That's enough 55
We're living in eighteen hundred and eight
and the names which were dragged through the gutter then
have been deservedly rehabilitated
by the command of the Emperor
ROSSIGNOL: Go on 60

KOKOL: Shut up Marat
CUCURUCU: Shut his mouth
POLPOCH: Long live Marat
MARAT (*interrupting*): The people can't pay the inflated price of bread
Our soldiers march in rags 65
The counter-revolution has started a new civil war
and what are we doing
The farms we confiscated from the churches have so far produced nothing
to feed the dispossessed
and years have passed since I proposed these farms 70
should be divided into allotments
and given farm implements and seed
And why have we seen no communal workshops
which were to be started in the old monasteries and country houses
Those who have jobs 75
must sweat for agents stockbrokers and speculators

(*wild cries*)

Fellow citizens
did we fight for the freedom of those
who now exploit us again
KOKOL: Sit down 80
ROSSIGNOL: Hear hear
CUCURUCU: Sit down
POLPOCH: Hear hear
MARAT: Our country is in danger
We talk about France 85
but who is France for
We talk about freedom
but who's this freedom for
Members of the National Assembly
you will never shake off the past 90
you'll never understand
the great upheaval in which you find yourselves

(*whistles and cries of Boo*)

Why aren't there thousands of public seats
in this assembly
so anyone who wants 95
can hear what's being discussed
DUPERRET: What is he trying to do
He's trying to rouse the people again
Look who sits on the public benches
Knitting-women concierges and washer-women 100

with no one to employ them any more
And who has he got on his side
Pickpockets layabouts parasites
who loiter in the boulevards

(*indignation among the onlookers*)

and hang around the cafés 105

CUCURUCU: Wish we could

DUPERRET: Released prisoners
escaped lunatics

(*tumult and whistling*)

Does he want to rule our country
with these 110

MARAT: You are liars
You hate the people

(*cries of indignation*)

ROSSIGNOL: Well done Marat

POLPOCH: That's true

MARAT: You'll never stop talking of the people 115
as a rough and formless mass
Why
Because you live apart from them
You let yourselves be dragged into the Revolution
knowing nothing about its principles 120
Has not our respected Danton himself announced
that instead of banning riches
we should try
to make poverty respectable
And Robespierre 125
who turns white when the word force is used
doesn't he sit at high-class tables
making cultural conversation
by candlelight

(*tongue clicking*)

KOKOL: Shame 130

CUCURUCU: Down with Robespierre

POLPOCH: Long live Marat

ROSSIGNOL: Down with Danton

MARAT: And you still long to ape them
those powdered chimpanzees 135
Necker Lafayette Talleyrand

COULMIER (*interrupting*): That's enough

If you use any more of these passages
we agreed to cut
I will stop your play 140

MARAT (*breaking in*): and all the rest of them
What we need now is a true deputy of the people
one who's incorruptible
one we can trust
Things are breaking down things are chaotic 145
that is good
that's the first step
Now we must take the next step
and choose a man
who will rule for you 150

ROSSIGNOL: Marat for dictator

POLPOCH: Marat in his bathtub

KOKOL: Send him down the sewers

CUCURUCU: Dictator of the rats

MARAT: Dictator The word must be abolished 155
I hate anything to do with masters and slaves
I am talking about a leader
who in this hour of crisis

(*His words are drowned in the mighty tumult.*)

DUPERRET: He's trying to incite them
to new murders 160

MARAT: We do not murder
we kill in self-defence
We are fighting
for our lives

DUPERRET: Oh if only we could have constructive thought 165
instead of agitation
If only beauty and concord could once more replace
hysteria and fanaticism

(*The* FOUR SINGERS *throw themselves on* DUPERRET *and stop his mouth.*)

ROUX (*jumping up in the background*): Look what's happening
Join together 170
Cast down your enemies
disarm them
For if they win
they will spare
not one of you 175

and all that you have won so far
will be lost

(*Enthusiastic calls, whistles and trampling.*)

CALLS (*in spoken chorus, simultaneously*): Marat Marat Marat Marat
Boo
A laurel wreath for Marat 180
Down with Marat
A victory parade for Marat
Down with him
Long live the streets
Long live the lamp-posts 185
Long live the bakers' shops
Long live freedom

(*Disorder and screams. The* PATIENTS *tumble forward.* MARAT*'s bath is pushed on to the platform right.*)

KOKOL & POLPOCH (*dancing*): Hit at the rich until they crash
Throw down their god and divide their cash
CUCURUCU & ROSSIGNOL (*dancing*): We wouldn't mind a tasty meal 190
of paté de foie and filleted eel
CHORUS: Marat Marat Marat Marat Marat

(SADE *raises his hands. They all freeze. Roll of drums and beginning of music.*)

## 28. Poor Marat in Your Bathtub Seat

MARAT *sinks back into his bath. Exhausted, he leans forward on the board.*

*The spectators' benches are pushed back, the* SISTERS *and* NURSES *force back the* PATIENTS. *In front of the arena the* FOUR SINGERS *dance a slow Carmagnole.*

FOUR SINGERS (*accompanied, singing and dancing*): Poor Marat in your bathtub seat
your life on this planet is near complete
Closer and closer to you death creeps
though there on her bench Charlotte Corday sleeps

Poor Marat if she slept too late 5
while dreaming of fairy-tale heads of state
maybe your sickness would disappear
Charlotte Corday would not find you here

Poor Marat stay wide awake
and be on your guard for the people's sake 10

Stare through the failing evening light
for this is the evening before the night

*(Drums. In the background order has been restored after a fashion. The* PATIENTS *should be standing upright, their hands crossed above their heads.* SISTERS *are standing before them, folding their hands and praying. The murmur of prayers can be heard. The* FOUR SINGERS *dance on a while and then stretch themselves out on the arena before* MARAT*'s bath.)*

MARAT *(with fear in his voice)*: What is that knocking Simonne

*(tyrannic again)*

Simonne
more cold water 15

*(*SIMONNE *sits huddled up at the edge of the platform and doesn't react.)*

Simonne
Where is Bas
SADE: Give up Marat
You said yourself
nothing can be achieved by scribbling 20
Long ago I abandoned my masterpiece
a roll of paper thirty yards long
which I filled completely with minute handwriting
in my dungeon years ago
It vanished when the Bastille fell 25
it vanished as everything written
everything thought and planned
will disappear

*(*MARAT *lies with his face on the board and covers his ears with his hands.)*

SADE *(continues)*: Marat
Look at me 30
Marat can you call this living
in your bath
in your mortification

*(By order of the* SISTERS *the* PATIENTS *change their position and stretch up their hands.)*

MARAT *(raising himself up)*: I had time for nothing but work
Day and night were not enough for me 35
When I investigated a wrong it grew branches

and every branch grew twigs
Wherever I turned
I found corruption

(*A* PATIENT *falls over in the ranks. A* NURSE *carries him off.*)

When I wrote 40
I always wrote with action in mind
kept sight of the fact
that writing was just a preparation
When I wrote
I always wrote in a fever 45
hearing the roar of action
When I was preparing
my books on the chains of slavery
I sat for three months
twenty-one hours a day 50
collecting material dreaming of material
paper piling high parchment crackling
until I sank into the swamps of overwork
That manuscript was suppressed
They were always ready 55
to pick up my statements
to slander them maim them
After each pamphlet was published
I had to go into hiding
They came with cannons 60
A thousand men of the National Guard
surrounded my house
And even today
I still wait for the knocking at the door
wait 65
for the bayonet to point at my breast
Simonne
Simonne
Fetch Bas
so that I can dictate my call 70
my fourteenth of July call

SADE: Why all these calls to the nation
It's too late Marat
forget your call
it contains only lies 75
What do you still want from the Revolution
Where is it going
Look at these lost revolutionaries

(*Pointing to the* FOUR SINGERS *who lie stretched out on the floor, scratching themselves, yawning and trying to get the last drop out of the empty bottle.*)

What will you order them to do
Where will you lead them 80

(*In the background the* PATIENTS, *on the* SISTERS' *command, must stand on one leg.*)

Once you attacked the authorities who turned
the law into instruments of oppression
Do you want someone to rule you
to control the words you write
and tell you 85
what work you must do
and repeat to you the new laws
over and over
until you can recite them in your sleep

(*The* PATIENTS *in the background walk in a circle while the* SISTERS *pray. The* FOUR SINGERS *begin to hum unconcernedly, lying at first on the floor with legs waving in the air. Then* ROSSIGNOL *and* CUCURUCU *get up and dance to the hummed melody.*)

MARAT (*falling across the board again*): Why is everything so confused now 90
Everything I wrote or spoke
was considered and true
each argument was sound
And now
doubt 95
Why does everything sound false

THE FOUR SINGERS (*singing and dancing*): Poor old Marat you lie prostrate
while others are gambling with France's fate
Your words have turned into a flood
which covers all France with her people's blood 100

(*Music ends. The* FOUR SINGERS *dance back to the centre of the stage. The* PATIENTS *are led to their platform. The* SISTERS *try to wake* CORDAY. *Loud knocking three times.*)

## 29. Preparations for the Third Visit

HERALD: Corday
wake up

(*Pause. The name* CORDAY *is whispered in the background. The whispering swells up and spreads over the whole stage. The* SISTERS *shake* CORDAY, DUPERRET *calls her name.* SIMONNE *stands awkwardly by the bath and gazes across at* CORDAY.)

CHORUS: Corday
Corday
Corday 5

HERALD (*signals to the orchestra with his staff*): Corday you have an appointment to keep
and there is no more time for sleep
Charlotte Corday awake and stand
Take the dagger in your hand

(*Pause. The* SISTERS *raise* CORDAY *to her feet.* CORDAY *stands with lowered head and wobbly legs. The* SISTERS *support her and lead her slowly forward. Her legs drag along the floor.* DUPERRET *walks behind her with his hands around her hips.*)

HERALD: Come on Charlotte do your deed 10
soon you'll get all the sleep you need

(CORDAY *is pushed into the arena. The two* SISTERS *stand at her side holding her firmly.* DUPERRET, *standing behind her, supports her back. Music ends.*)

CORDAY (*her eyes still closed, speaking, softly, nervously*): Now I know what it is like
when the head is cut off the body
Oh this moment
hands tied behind the back 15
feet bound together
neck bared
hair cut off
knees on the boards
the head already laid 20
in the metal slot
looking down into the dripping basket
The sound of the blade rising
and from its slanting edge
the blood still drops 25
and then the downward slide
to split us in two

(*pause*)

They say
that the head
held high in the executioner's hand 30

still lives
that the eyes still see
that the tongue still writhes
and down below the arms and legs still shudder

DUPERRET (*accompanied by lute. He is still holding his hand on her hip*): Charlotte awaken from your nightmare 35
Wake up Charlotte and look at the trees
look at the rose-coloured evening sky
in which your lovely bosom heaves

(*Pause. He lifts his hand and strokes her on the bosom. He notices the dagger under the cloth.*)

Forget your worries abandon each care
and breathe in the warmth of the summertime air 40
What are you hiding
A dagger
throw it away

(*the music ends*)

CORDAY (*pushes his hand away*): We should all carry weapons nowadays
in self-defence 45

DUPERRET (*beseechingly*): No one will attack you Charlotte
Charlotte throw the dagger away
go away
go back to Caen

CORDAY (*drawing herself up and pushing the* SISTERS' *hands away*): In
my room in Caen 50
on the table under the open window
lies open The Book of Judith
Dressed in her legendary beauty
she entered the tent of the enemy
and with a single blow 55
slew him

DUPERRET: Charlotte
what are you planning

CORDAY (*forlorn again*): Look at this city
Its prisons are crowded 60
with our friends
I was among them just now
in my sleep
They all stand huddled together there
and hear through the windows 65
the guards talking about executions
Now they talk of people as gardeners talk of leaves for burning

Their names are crossed off the top of a list
and as the list grows shorter
more names are added at the bottom 70
I stood with them
and we waited
for our own names to be called

DUPERRET: Charlotte
let us leave together 75
this very evening

CORDAY (*as if she has not heard him*): What kind of town is this
What sort of streets are these
Who invented this
who profits by it 80
I saw peddlers
at every corner
they're selling little guillotines
with tiny sharp blades
and dolls filled with red liquid 85
which spurts from the neck
when the sentence is carried out
What kind of children are these
who can play
with this toy so efficiently 90
and who is judging
who is judging

(PATIENTS *move to a group at centre.* CORDAY *raises her hand to knock.*)

### 30. Corday's Third and Last Visit

*The* HERALD *knocks three times on the floor with his staff while* CORDAY *carries out the knocking movement with her hand.* MARAT *starts up and looks in* CORDAY*'s direction.* SIMONNE *places herself protectively in front of the bath.*

DUPERRET: What do you want at this door
Do you know who lives here

CORDAY: The man
for whose sake I have come here

DUPERRET: What do you want from him 5
Turn back Charlotte

(*goes on his knees before her*)

CORDAY: I have a task

which I must carry out
Go

(*Pushes him with her foot.*)

leave me alone 10

(DUPERRET *embraces her legs. She kicks out at him several times.* DUPERRET *moves back on his knees.*)

HERALD: Now for the third time you observe
the girl whose job it is to serve

(*points to* CORDAY)

as Charlotte Corday stands once more
waiting outside Marat's door
Duperret you see before her languish 15

(*points to* DUPERRET)

prostrated by their parting's anguish

(*raising a forefinger*)

For what has happened cannot be undone
although that might be wished by everyone

(*pointing to* CORDAY)

We tried restraining her with peaceful sleep
and with the claims of a passion still more deep 20
Simonne as well as best she could she tried

(*pointing to* SIMONNE)

but this girl here

(*points to* CORDAY)

would not be turned aside
That man is now forgotten and we can

(*points to* DUPERRET, *who moves backwards on his knees from the dais*)

do nothing more Corday is focussed on this man 25

(*points to* MARAT)

MARAT: No

(*raising himself high*)

I am right
and I will say it once more

Simonne
where is Bas 30
It is urgent
my call

(SIMONNE *moves aside, stops still and stares bewitched at* CORDAY.)

SADE (*approaches the bath*): Marat
what are all your pamphlets and speeches
compared with her 35
she stands there and will come to you
to kiss you and embrace you
Marat
an untouched virgin stands before you and offers herself to you
See how she smiles 40

(CORDAY *stands erect and smiling, throwing her hair aside. She has her hand on the neckcloth in the place where the dagger is hidden.*)

how her teeth shine
how she shakes her auburn hair aside
Marat
forget the rest
there's nothing else 45
beyond the body
Look
she stands there
her breast naked under the thin cloth
and perhaps she carries a knife 50
to intensify the love-play

(CORDAY *moves a step closer to the bath, swaying lightly.* SIMONNE *stands frozen, mechanically wringing the cloth in her hands.*)

MARAT: Simonne Simonne
who was knocking at the door
SADE: A maiden
from the rural desert of a convent 55
Imagine
those pure girls lying on hard floors
in rough shifts
and the heated air from the fields
forcing its way to them through the barred windows 60
Imagine
them lying there
with moist thighs and breasts
dreaming of those
who control life in the outside world 65

(*The* FOUR SINGERS *come forward and begin a copulation mime.* ROSSIGNOL *mounts the strongest of her companions and performs acrobatics with them.*)

SADE (*to musical accompaniment*): And then she was tired of her isolation
and stirred up by the new age
and gathered up in the great tide
and wanted to be part of the Revolution
And what's the point of a revolution 70
without general copulation

CHORUS: And what's the point of a revolution
without general
copulation copulation copulation

(*continues as a round. Mime ends.*)

SADE: Marat 75
as I sat there in the Bastille
for thirteen long years
I learned
that this is a world of bodies
each body pulsing with a terrible power 80
each body alone and racked with its own unrest
In that loneliness
marooned in a stone sea
I heard lips whispering continually
and felt all the time 85
in the palms of my hands and in my skin
touching and stroking
Shut behind thirteen bolted doors
my feet fettered
I dreamed only 90
of the orifices of the body
put there
so one may hook and twine oneself in them

(*A* PATIENT *comes forward on tip-toe and stops behind the arena, listening tensely. Other* PATIENTS *follow.*)

Continually I dreamed of this confrontation
and it was a dream of the most savage jealous 95
and cruellest imagining
Marat
these cells of the inner self
are worse than the deepest stone dungeon
and as long as they are locked 100
all your Revolution remains

only a prison mutiny
to be put down
by corrupted fellow-prisoners

CHORUS (*repeating with musical accompaniment*): And what's the point of a revolution 105
without general copulation

(*Music ends.*)

CORDAY (*to* SIMONNE. *Lute accompaniment*): Have you given my letter to Marat
Let me in it is vital
I must tell him what's happening in Caen
where they are gathering to destroy him 110

MARAT: Who's at the door

SIMONNE: The girl from Caen

MARAT: Let her come in

(SIMONNE *stands aside, shaking her head vigorously. She squats down at the edge of the dais behind the bath and hides her head in her hands.* CORDAY *moves towards the bath, swaying and smiling. Her hand still rests on her neckcloth.* SADE *leaves the arena and goes to his dais, where he remains, standing, watching tensely.*)

CORDAY (*softly*): Marat
I will tell you the names of my heroes 115
but I am not betraying them
for I am speaking to a dead man

MARAT (*raising himself up*): Speak more clearly
I can't understand you
Come closer 120

CORDAY (*coming closer to the bath with a fixed smile, her body slowly swaying. She pushes a hand under her neckcloth*): I name you names
Marat
the names of those
who have gathered at Caen

(*falling into a sing-song*)

I name Barbaroux 125
and Buzot
and Pétion
and Louvet

(*As she speaks the names her face is distorted increasingly by an expression of hate and lust.*)

and Brissot
and Vergniaud 130

and Guadet
and Gensonné

MARAT: Who are you
Come closer

(MARAT *raises himself up high. The cloth falls from his shoulders.* CORDAY *moves closer to him, swaying. Her left hand is stretched out as if to caress. In the right hand she holds the dagger under the neck-cloth.*)

CORDAY (*humming words which sound like caresses*): I am coming Marat 135
You cannot see me Marat
because you are dead

MARAT (*crying out, raising himself up high, half-naked*): Bas
Take this down
Saturday the thirteenth of July seventeen hundred and ninety three 140
A call to the people of France

(CORDAY *stands immediately before* MARAT. *She moves her left hand close to his skin over his chest, his shoulders, his neck.* MARAT *sits arched over the back of the bath, a pen still in his hand.* CORDAY *pulls the dagger from her neckcloth. She holds it with both hands and raises her arms high to strike.*
*The* HERALD *blows shrilly on his whistle.*
*All players remain unmoving in their positions.*
CORDAY *sinks back into herself.* MARAT *sits quietly, leaning forward.*)

31. INTERRUPTUS

HERALD: Now it's a part of Sade's dramatic plan
to interrupt the climax so this man
Marat can hear and gasp with his last breath
at how the world will go after his death
With a musical history we'll bring him up to date 5
From seventeen-ninety-three to eighteen-eight

(*Music starts with very quick military march. The* FOUR SINGERS *sing and perform grotesquely in time to the music. The* HERALD *displays banners showing the date of the events as they are described.*)

FOUR SINGERS: Now your enemies fall
We're beheading them all (*1793*)
Duperret
and Corday 10
executed in the same old way
Robespierre has to get on (*1794*)
he gets rid of Danton

That was spring
comes July 15
and old Robespierre has to die
Three rebellions a year (*1795*)
but we're still of good cheer
Malcontents
all have been 20
taught their lesson by the guillotine
There's a shortage of wheat (*1796*)
We're too happy to eat
Austria
cracks and then 25
she surrenders to our men

Fifteen glorious years
Fifteen glorious years
Years of peace
years of war 30
each year greater
than the year before
Marat
we're marching on

What brave soldiers we've got (*1797*) 35
Now the traitors are shot
Generals
boldly take
power in Paris
for the people's sake 40
Egypt's beaten down flat (*1798*)
Bonaparte did that
Cheer him as
they retreat
even though we lose our fleet 45
Bonaparte comes back (*1799*)
gives our rulers the sack
He's the man (*1800*)
brave and true
Bonaparte would die for you 50
Europe's free of her chains (*1801*)
Only England remains
but we want (*1802*)
wars to cease
so there's fourteen months of peace 55

(PATIENTS *join in, marching on the spot.*)

Fifteen glorious years
Fifteen glorious years
Years of peace
years of war
each year greater 60
than the year before
Marat
we're marching on

England must be insane (*1803*)
wants to fight us again 65
so we march
off to war
Bonaparte is our Emperor (*1804*)
Nelson bothers our fleet
but he's shot off his feet 70
We're on top
yes we are
and we spit on Trafalgar
Now the Prussians retreat (*1806*)
Russia faces defeat (*1807*) 75
All the world
bends its knee
to Napoleon
and his family
Fight on land and on sea (*1808*) 80
All men want to be free
If they don't
never mind
we'll abolish all mankind

Fifteen glorious years 85
Fifteen glorious years
Years of peace
years of war
each year greater
than the one before 90
Marat
we're marching on
behind Napoleon

## 32. The Murder

*The entire cast have resumed their positions exactly as before the song.*

CORDAY *clasps the knife with both hands above her head. Very slowly she lowers it towards* MARAT. SADE *follows her movements precisely, bending from the waist. She kills* MARAT. PATIENTS *let out one single scream.* CORDAY *crumples on the stage.* SADE *stands contemplating the scene.* MARAT *hangs as in David's classical picture, with his right hand over the edge of the bath. In his right hand he still holds his pen, in his left his papers.*

## 33. Epilogue

*The* ORCHESTRA *starts to play soft ceremonious music.*

*The* SISTERS *come forward and take charge of* CORDAY. MARAT *steps out of his bath.* COULMIER *comes forward.*

COULMIER: Enlightened ladies pious gentlemen
let's close the history book and then
return to eighteen-eight the present day
of which though not unclouded we may say
it promises that mankind soon will cease 5
to fear the storms of war the squalls of peace

(*The music turns more and more into a monotonous march. The* PATIENTS *in the background mark time. Their unrest increases.*)

For today we live in far different times
We have no oppressors no violent crimes
and although we're at war anyone can see
it can only end in victory 10
FOUR SINGERS: And if most have a little and few have a lot
you can see how much nearer our goal we have got
We can say what we like without favour or fear
and what we can't say we can breathe in your ear
ROUX (*through the singing*): When will you learn to see 15
When will you learn to take sides
When will you show them
FOUR SINGERS: And though we're locked up we're no longer enslaved
and the honour of France is eternally saved
The useless debate the political brawl 20
are over there's one man to speak for us all
For he helps us in sickness and destitution
he's the leader who ended the Revolution
and everyone knows why we're cheering for
Napoleon our mighty Emperor 25

(*During the song* COULMIER *and his* FAMILY *have congratulated* SADE *and chatted with him.* SADE *presents various members of the cast. At this point the music grows louder. The column of* PATIENTS *begins to march forward.* SISTERS *and* NURSES *try to restrain it. Several times the column advances four paces and takes three paces back. The music and marching rhythm grow in power.* COULMIER *moves anxiously to the side gesticulating.*)

ALL: Led by him our soldiers go
over deserts and through the snow
A victory here and a victory there
Invincible glorious always victorious
for the good of all people everywhere 30

(*The column advances still further, stamping some paces forward and some back. The* HERALD *begins to throw buckets etc. around.* NURSES *try to restrain him.* COULMIER*'s family flee, screaming and shouting.*)

ALL (*in confused but rhythmic shouts in time to the marching*): Charenton Charenton
Napoleon Napoleon
Nation Nation
Revolution Revolution
Copulation Copulation 35

(*The shouting grows. The column reaches the front. The struggle between* NURSES *and* HERALD *develops and catches the attention of the others. Suddenly the whole stage is fighting.* SADE *watches with a faint smile, almost indulgent. The actors have moved to the side. Music, shouting and tramping increase to a tempest. A strong wind blows in through the upper side windows. The huge curtains billow far into the room. The* NURSES *go among the* PATIENTS *wielding their batons.* ROUX *springs forward and places himself before the marchers, his back to them, still with fettered arms.*)

ROUX: When will you learn to see
When will you learn to take sides

(*He tries to force them back, but is drawn in and vanishes from sight in the still advancing ranks.*

*The* PATIENTS *are fully at the mercy of their mad marchlike dance. Many of them hop and spin in ecstasy.* COULMIER *incites the* NURSES *to extreme violence.* PATIENTS *are struck down. The* HERALD *is now in front of the* ORCHESTRA, *leaping about in time to the music.* SADE *stands upright on his chair, laughing triumphantly.*

*In desperation* COULMIER *gives the signal to close the curtain.*)

CURTAIN

At a performance of *Marat/Sade* we watch inmates of the insane asylum at Charenton in 1808 perform Sade's play about the assassination of Marat in Paris in 1793. After the killing, the patient-victim "steps out of his bath," his role done. But Sade's play for his fellow inmates arouses them to riot, and Weiss's play ends in violent confusion. What we have seen is a refraction of the French Revolution through a lunatic theatrical that gets out of hand.

Just about everything that is difficult and meaningful in *Marat/Sade* follows from its refractive structure. Its free verse recitations and songs are never involuted or abstract; it is not a study in intricate character psychology or personal relationships; and if the confrontations of ideologies in Marat's and Sade's conversations do not make a complete and coherent debate on the meaning of revolution, they are not obscure. The play assaults our senses and teases our minds because Sade's ritual reenactment of the past in psychodrama is constantly being subverted by its performers. Irrational acts intrude upon rehearsed histrionics, autocratic systems upon enacted and real revolution, the reality of 1808 upon the imaginary 1793, and our reflections on the intrusions upon our observation of the action.

Saying that Weiss's play has a play-within-a-play structure does not really describe it adequately – certainly not if the term is taken to imply a stable relationship between two levels of action. Rather than one action enclosing another (the way the mousetrap scene in *Hamlet* is framed by the story of Hamlet's revenge, or the way the legend of Grusha in *The Caucasian Chalk Circle* is contained by the kolkhoz action), there is in *Marat/Sade* incessant interflow of an inner action about revolution and an outer action about lunatics. The reversible equation of revolution and lunacy is the insinuated core concept of the play, the historical hero as mad actor its master metaphor, and disorder – in the state (revolution) and in the self (lunacy) – both its subject and its unifying theatrical image. Quite properly, the total stage action reaches us as a cacophony of voices set in a kaleidoscope of pantomimes. The disorder on the stage eludes a firm cognitive grasp. As a play about a disintegrating theatrical performance it could be said to self-destruct, and its proven power over audiences becomes a mordant paradox that reflects on our vision of history as progress and on our sense of a coherent dramatic tradition.

Not much that is of importance can be said about such a play in the traditional vocabulary of drama criticism. Categories of critical analysis like plot structure, dialogue texture, and character motivation become all but irrelevant. Part narrative, part discourse, and part ritual incantation, *Marat/Sade* is above all a play of intense visuality that works by the rationale of theatrical montage. By missing the spectacle, a reader of *Marat/Sade* loses more of the meaning of the play than he does in the reading of most plays. But in the theater he may lose much of the verbal meaning under the powerful spell of the spectacle. Even in an ideally complete experience of the play, its structure is a labyrinth from which there is no carrying away clear meanings in safe and easy exit. It reorders no hierarchy of values, assumes no absolutes, and will not let us rest in any single point of view. One wonders what Molière and Ibsen would have thought of it.

It tells no coherent story about credible characters revealing themselves in the imaginary present tense in which conventional dramatic action occurs. The Charenton bathhouse is an illusionistic set, but the illusion is made precarious by the obvious relevance for the 1960's of Roux's tirades ("We demand that everyone should do all they can / to put an end to war / This damned war / which is run for the benefit of profiteers / and leads only to more wars") and of Coulmier's (and the Herald's) repeated assurances that the Napoleonic, unlike the Revolutionary, era is enlightened, humane, and liberal. Listening to the voice of the 1808 establishment we hear that of our own, benevolently complacent. And in the staging of Sade's play, there is hardly any attempt at illusionism at all. As a piece of equipment that naturally belongs in the bathhouse, Marat's bathtub is an equivocal prop: Corday's first arrival in Paris is staged next to it. The play creates no suspense, for Coulmier's Prologue — if not our memory of the historical facts — tells us that Corday will kill Marat before the play is over. What intervenes between the Prologue and the assassination is not a causally connected sequence of events leading up to and accounting for the assassination, but a succession of choric songs and commentaries, tiradic outbursts, philosophical discussions, and insane pantomime delaying its accomplishment. The result is that Weiss's play is, among other things, about the difficulties of staging Sade's play. Some of the interruptions are impromptu interferences by the on-stage audience of asylum inmates and by Coulmier interfering with the interferers and admonishing Sade to keep his production under control. But others are in Sade's script, so that Sade and Weiss become collaborators in the use of playwriting tactics that continually digress from the straight progress of the nominally central title action. Time shifts not just between 1793 and 1808; there are also the flashback appearances of Marat's parents and other figures from his past, some historical (Voltaire, Lavoisier) and some fictitious (the Schoolmaster). No scene in the play is unaffected by the form of a theater using itself *as* itself rather than as a piece of off-stage space peopled not by actors but by the real-life characters they impersonate. Corday almost disrupts the measured progress of Sade's ritualized version of the murder of Marat by trying to commit the murder prematurely. The Herald, dressed in motley like a medieval court jester or the harlequin figure from the commedia dell'arte of the late Renaissance, introduces a scene between Corday and Duperret by promising us relief from the "painful matters" that have just preceded: the persecution of Marat in a scene replete with imagery of deadly fever, loathsome disease, darkened sun, and burning corpses. What we are to see next will recall for us the couple's "love so pure," "the sweet blending of the strong and fair sex." But what we actually get is a grotesque tableau, mock-heroic and mock-romantic, of an erotomaniac frantically fondling a somnambulist.

The scene illustrates Weiss's main design: the interpenetration of the play about the lunatics at Charenton and the play about the assassination in Paris as mutually ironic commentaries. The modern actor playing Marat impersonates not the revolutionary leader but a paranoiac impersonating Marat. His paranoia is ironically vindicated when he is "killed." Corday is not Corday but a semi-conscious melancholiac who has to be prompted in her part. Sade acts himself but interacts with his fellow patients who are playing the roles of the historical figures his play is about. The Charenton action is a screen between us and the events of the French Revolution, but the idea of the Revolution fills the minds of the Charenton inmates. Their chaotic violence is a parody of the Revolution, but the parody moves by the same emotional dynamic as the Revolution's quest for a perfected social order. The ironic vision of the Revolution as something happening in a madman's brain is balanced by the disturbing vision of a revolt for liberty being suppressed by the post-Revolution establishment — lunacy, as Susan Sontag has observed, being here a metaphor for passion. When the patients usurp the stage in an ending which Sade may or may not have planned, they represent the oppressed people of France, having traded king for emperor, still dispossessed, still not free, and still wanting "Revolution NOW." But their violence is now no longer a programmed dramatization of events that occurred fifteen years earlier, censored and licensed by the director of Charenton for patient "rehabilitation" and audience "delectation." It is a spontaneous actuality in 1808, a revolt against Coulmier's own regime, forcing his family to flee the stage in screaming terror. And the spectacle implicates us, for we are in the seats presumably occupied by the 1808 audience threatened by the bathhouse riot: the fashionable ladies and gentlemen who have come out from Paris to attend one of the notorious Marquis de Sade's theatrical productions "in the 'hiding-place for the moral rejects of civilized society.' "* Coulmier addresses his welcoming Prologue to them, but he is looking at us. Politics and insanity; metaphysics and mad antics; the streets of Paris in 1793 and the bathhouse at Charenton in 1808; the real Marat and Marat the

* From Weiss's "Note on the Historical Background to the Play."

paranoiac; Sade the detached playwright and Sade letting himself be whipped by Corday; Roux, the socialist priest, half in and half out of Sade's play; and the modern audience watching a spectacle that is a threat and an accusation – these are among the shifting constituents in the play's large complex of unresolved tensions.

In an attempt to impose some kind of stable shape on this flux, we may try to distinguish among circles of action, defining each by a separate conflict. Working from the center and out, we find Corday versus Marat, Marat versus Sade, Sade versus Coulmier, patients as performers versus patients as patients, inmates versus audience. But the paradigm collapses when we test it against what actually goes on. Our circles expand and contract and open up, letting characters pass freely from one to another. If we decide we need a separate circle for the Herald and the Four Singers as choric figures, where does it fit in? Their choric functions are not the same. The Herald stage-manages Sade's play about events in Paris in 1793, speaks in ironic echo of Coulmier's self-congratulatory "modern" voice, and is in both capacities presumably Sade's manipulated puppet. The Four Singers, a ribald and unsavory quartet from the Paris gutters, are both spokesmen for and victims of the Revolution, and it is never clear whether or not they perform under Sade's control and whether they realize that they are only members of the asylum cast reenacting Marat's death or think they are witnessing the actual assassination of the real Marat. The characters of the inmost circle arrange themselves in a symmetrical pattern of two complementary couples. The victim Marat, the would-be dictator confined to his bathtub, physically passive but impatient to act, is cared for by the spastic Simonne, urging him to rest. The assassin Corday, nearly passive in her somnolence, is caressed and urged to abstain from action by the hyperactive Duperret. Duperret, the lover, fails to keep Corday from murdering Marat, just as Simonne, Marat's mistress, fails to protect her lover. The assassination itself is both a double martyrdom and – by gesture and verbal image – Corday's act of love. All this is a tidy visualization of historical ironies. But when he debates Sade, Marat moves out of this circle, or, alternatively, we say that Sade enters it, as he does also when he ironically assumes Marat's role as Corday's victim in the whipping scene. Our concept of the play as a system of concentric circles of action is useful only up to a point, because the multi-leveled structure is too fluid and flexible to be held in a fixed paradigm. It cannot, for example, sort out the ambiguities that make up the crucial idea of "audience" in the play.

Weiss himself has said that the "encounter" between Marat and Sade is "the subject" of his play. His remark makes it all the more tempting to turn from the perplexities of the theatricalist form to the drama of ideas which he implies is the reason for the play's being. The encounter is between Marat's passionate commitment to collective action for social reform and Sade's sceptical withdrawal into anarchic individualism. The issue is the utility or futility of revolution. With just as much right as Marat, Sade can claim to "be" the Revolution, since in his prison fantasies he has already acted out its cruelest horrors. His imagination, "the world inside myself," is his "only reality." Alone in its "stillness," he finds in murder "the final proof of my existence."

> In a criminal society
> I dug the criminal out of myself
> so I could understand him and so understand
> the times we live in

Man is a criminal in solitary confinement, for "the cells of the inner self / are worse than the deepest stone dungeons," and consequently (he tells Marat):

> all your Revolution remains
> only a prison mutiny
> to be put down
> by corrupted fellow-prisoners

Because the root of social evil is not in any political and economic system but in man himself, revolution is futile and self-perpetuating violence. The "basis for all life is death," but with the guillotine the Revolution has made dying wholesale and mechanical, passionless and therefore meaningless. In contrast, the ghastly ceremony of the four-hour execution of Damiens, King Louis XV's would-be assassin, was a recognition of the significance of individual suffering. The Revolution leads "To the withering of the individual man / . . . to the death of choice." Sade thinks of himself as "one of those who has to be defeated," for in his chosen stance as alienated observer, passive in his conviction of man's unredeemable depravity, he denies everything the Revolution assumes. For him, as for one of his fellow inmate-prisoners, "man is a mad animal," incapable of progress.

Sade's nihilistic solipsism puts him beyond both indignation and despair. Against it, Marat, the romantic activist, asserts man-made absolutes of value. "What you call the indifference of Nature," he tells Sade, "is your own lack of compassion"; and to Sade's contemptuous "Compassion is the property of the privileged classes," Marat replies:

> Against Nature's silence I use action
> In the vast indifference I invent a meaning
> I don't watch unmoved I intervene
> and say that this and this are wrong
> and I work to alter them and improve them

When Sade says that the leaders of the Revolution "would like to kill each other over trifles," Marat retorts, "But they aren't trifles / They are matters of principle." The Revolution must go on, for the bourgeoisie has set itself up as tyrannical exploiters in the place of the executed king and nobles: "We do not murder / we kill in self-defense / We are fighting for our lives." On the fourth anniversary of the fall of the Bastille, the prison symbol of the old regime where Sade himself was confined for years, Marat is writing still another "call to the people of France" for more bloodshed in the name of freedom and justice. Evil must be eliminated, and it *can* be eliminated, for evil is not in man himself but in what Marat's follower Roux calls "circumstances," in systems and institutions that can be changed. Marat's philosophy is essentially Rousseau's. Man, his position implies, is capable of acting for the good of all, of submerging personal interest in the interest of the community. The ideological clash between Sade and Marat has less to do with politics as the means and ends of social change than with irreconcilable differences between two views of human nature.

*Marat/Sade* ends with Roux's call to the audience for social commitment: "When will you learn to see / When will you learn to take sides." For those for whom the heart of the play is the Marat-Sade debates, Roux's question poses itself as a categorical imperative. But which of the two does Weiss want us to side with: Marat, the social activist who kills from an idealistic belief in a better future; or Sade, the isolated absurdist who inflicts violence only upon himself? Marat, the pre-Marxist; or Sade, the pre-Freudian (in the critic Samuel A. Weiss's illuminating if not exhaustive contrast)? To the extent that we sense the insistent topicality of their encounter, we take sides according to our own convictions about social values and the nature of man, and if the play leaves us neutral or undecided, we feel guilty — the way anyone does who remains uncommitted these days. But if we return the encounter to its place within the turning prism of the lunatic performance, we may begin to doubt the possibility of determining its rights and wrongs, truths and errors. We may come to say with Sade:

> I
> do not know myself
> No sooner have I discovered something
> than I begin to doubt it
> . . . I do not know if I am hangman or victim

or with Marat:

> Why is everything so confused now
> Everything I wrote or spoke
> was considered and true
> each argument was sound
> And now
> I doubt
> Why does everything sound false

It is difficult not to feel that Sade is the more agile and cogent debater, but then we reflect that he is also the presumed author of Marat's lines and may naturally have reserved the best lines for himself. Are the debates, then, only internal dialogues between two sides in Sade's divided mind, the tortured reaching for unreachable truth by a man who has come to doubt his own doubts? How committed is he to his sardonic disengagement? What do we make of the fact that Sade himself is an inmate of Charenton, a certified madman, whose name has become a byword for unspeakable sexual perversions? How seriously are we supposed to take a controversy between two lunatics? Do not the line divisions, which arbitrarily (except, significantly, in the songs) break up units of meaning, serve to subtly remind us that much of the time the characters do not really know what they are saying? Since writing *Marat/Sade,* Weiss has publicly sided with Marat's belief in the value of social revolution. But regardless of his personal political beliefs, his play is not reducible to thesis drama. There is in it no character whom we can safely accept as authoritative spokesman for the playwright. A consideration of the ideologies confronting one another in the Marat-Sade debates may take us to the heart of the labyrinth, but it does not show us the way out. The play is a dramatic inquiry, left unresolved at the end.

This skeptical open-endedness has become something of a signature of contemporary drama on philosophical themes. But of the three names, Luigi Pirandello, Bertolt Brecht, and Antonin Artaud, that first come to mind when we seek to relate *Marat/Sade* to the traditions of modern drama, only the earliest of them, Pirandello, is a confirmed skeptic. Weiss's Pirandellian heritage is evident in his use of the stage as a vehicle for radical relativism: in *Marat/Sade* as in Pirandello, art and life, role and reality, illusion and truth, sanity and insanity, then and now, coalesce in endless and slippery configurations of paradox. As in Pirandello's *Six Characters in Search of an Author,* the primary situation in *Marat/Sade* is a moment from the past frozen in the timeless present of dramatic art. From Brecht, Weiss has taken *Verfremdung* devices, such as choric narrative and a multitude of brief, disjunctive scenes, that keep us from mistaking the theatrical spectacle for realistic mimesis and from losing ourselves in empathy when we should be provoked to thought about human nature and social justice.

But Artaud, the French poet-director and theorist of "the drama of cruelty," is the name that figures most frequently in critical discussions of the influences on *Marat/Sade.* Susan Sontag, for example, sees Weiss's play as representing an unlikely but brilliant marriage of Brecht's "theater of intelligence" and Artaud's "theater of magic, of gesture, of 'cruelty,' of feeling." Artaud's influence on Weiss is real enough. A play about Sade with a play *by* Sade inside it has, not surprisingly, its moments of cruelty, even in the literal sense. And in its escape from the tyranny of the dramatic text, Weiss's play comes close to realizing the "total theater" envisioned by Artaud in *The Theater and Its Double* (1938) – a theater speaking to "total man," "staging events not men," a myth-embodying theater of all the senses, inducing a "delirium" of the spirit, a "mirage," a "virtual reality," prefiguring the primary reality, ecstatic and terrible, that Artaud calls his theater's "double." Artaud wanted to restore the kind of theater that Friedrich Nietzsche postulated as the origin of western drama in *The Birth of Tragedy* (1871, 1886), though Artaud derived his theater from oriental models rather than from Nietzsche's synthesis of Apollonian artifice and the passional wisdom of Dionysus.

But Artaud's influence on *Marat/Sade* is more a matter of form than of substance, and much of it comes filtered through absurdist drama: its restless kinetic energy and its chaotic irrationality. (*Marat/Sade* obviously has nothing in common with the small, claustrophobic, quiescent worlds of Beckett and Pinter.) And in addition to Artaud, not just Pirandello and Brecht but also other, older dramatists and dramas have contributed to Weiss's distinctive use of the theater: the Greek tragic dithyramb and chorus, the medieval passion play with its stylized staging, Shakespeare's panoramic dramaturgy, the improvisations in the Italian commedia dell'arte. The justly celebrated Peter Brook production of Weiss's play was faithful to its Artaudian spirit in making it an occasion for a theater that nearly overwhelms sight and hearing. But the cool and complex intellectualism that never quite lets go its control of the violent spectacles in *Marat/Sade* has no counterpart in Artaud's theater of sensuousness and passion. Not the least vital of the many tensions in Weiss's play is that between its ironic vision of western history and its spectacular physicality.

*Marat/Sade* is a play that seeks to comprehend the diversity of the modern experience in a single artistic form. To that end, it draws upon a variety of old and new dramatic styles and conventions. Its ideological pluralism is both a function of and analogous to the heterogeneity of its sources in earlier traditions of the theater. Its unity strains, but it holds, and without the strain it would have been not just a smaller but a much less relevant play in a world that has become a confused battleground for cultural heritages. That it withholds a final "meaning" seems almost tragically right: it puts before us a mirror image that is grotesque, violent, and perplexing, and which already has become a central item in the modern repertory. It is a good play with which to end an introductory study of drama.

# APPENDIX

## Biographical Notes and Suggested References

Sophocles (?496–406 B.C.) was born in Colonus, then a suburb of Athens. His home town is the setting for *Oedipus at Colonus,* the last of the nearly 120 plays he is said to have written. Only seven are extant today, and only three of these can be dated with any certainty: *Antigone,* 442 B.C.; *Philoctetes,* 409; and *Oedipus at Colonus,* close to 406. Of the others, *Ajax* is thought to be an early play, *Oedipus Rex* is usually dated 430–425, *Electra* is probably later than *Oedipus Rex,* and for *Trachiniae* there is no agreement on date. In the annual competition among playwrights writing for the Dionysiac festival, Sophocles won the prize eighteen times. His trilogies, unlike Aeschylus's, consisted of plays unrelated in subject matter. He was the first tragic writer to put three characters (in addition to the chorus) on stage at the same time.

Chronologically, Sophocles is the second of the three great Athenian tragedians —some thirty years younger than Aeschylus, some fifteen years older than Euripides. His manhood roughly coincides with the flowering of Athenian civilization between the defeat of the Persians in 480 B.C. and the surrender to Sparta at the end of the Peloponnesian War in 404. He was active in political and military affairs. His fame as playwright may have earned him his public employments. Sophocles himself reports that his friend Pericles said that he was a better poet than general. By all accounts, Sophocles was handsome, charming, popular, and well-to-do. Aristophanes, the writer of comedies and Sophocles's younger contemporary, summed up the tenor of his life in calling him "contented among the living, contented among the dead" — a curious but provocative judgment in view of the fact that it concerns one of the greatest of tragic poets.

*Suggested Reading*

Adams, Sinclair M. *Sophocles the Playwright.* Toronto: University of Toronto Press, 1957.

Bieber, Margarete. *The History of the Greek and Roman Theater.* 2nd rev. ed. Princeton, N.J.: Princeton University Press, 1960.

Bowra, C. M. *Sophoclean Tragedy.* Oxford: Clarendon Press, 1944.

Butcher, S. H. *Aristotle's Theory of Poetry and Fine Arts.* New York: Dover Publications, 1951.

Fergusson, Francis. "*Oedipus Rex:* The Tragic Rhythm of Action." In *The Idea of a Theater*. Princeton, N.J.: Princeton University Press, 1949.

Kirkwood, Gordon M. *A Study of Sophoclean Drama*. Ithaca, N.Y.: Cornell University Press, 1958.

Kitto, H. D. F. *Greek Tragedy: A Literary Study*. Garden City, N.Y.: Doubleday (Anchor), 1954.

Knox, Bernard M. W. *The Heroic Temper*. Berkeley: University of California Press, 1964.

Waldock, A. J. A. *Sophocles the Dramatist*. Cambridge, Eng.: Cambridge University Press, 1951.

Whitman, Cedric H. *Sophocles: A Study in Heroic Humanism*. Cambridge, Mass.: Harvard University Press, 1951.

Woodward, Thomas, ed. *Sophocles: A Collection of Critical Essays*. Englewood Cliffs, N.J.: Prentice-Hall, 1966.

*Recordings of* Oedipus Rex

Amherst College Students. Folkway Records (1 record, FL9862, mono).

Campbell, Stratford Players. Caedmon Records (2 records, TC2012, mono).

*Film Versions of* Oedipus Rex

Canadian, 1957. Directed by Tyrone Guthrie (88 min., 16mm, sound, color). Contemporary Films, McGraw-Hill Book Co., 330 W. 42nd St., New York, N.Y. 10036. (Sale or rental.)

American (Encyclopædia Britannica Educational Corp.), 1959 (90 min., 16 mm, sound, color, 3 parts. Encyclopædia Britannica Educational Corp., 425 Michigan Ave., Chicago, Ill. 60611. (Sale, and available on a non-exclusive basis from many rental agencies throughout the U.S. Check local commercial film libraries, public library film collections, and college audio-visual centers.)

Nothing is known about the author of *Everyman,* and scholars disagree on whether it is derived from or the source for *Elckerlijk,* a Flemish morality play printed in 1495. A certain Peter Dorland of Diest has been suggested as the author of the latter.

*Suggested Reading*

Cawley, A. C., ed. *Everyman and Medieval Miracle Plays*. New York: E. P. Dutton, 1959.

Chambers, E. K. *English Literature at the Close of the Middle Ages*. New York: Oxford University Press, 1945.

Cormican, L. A. "Morality Tradition and the Interludes." In *The Age of Chaucer,* edited by Boris Ford. London: Penguin Books, 1954.

Craig, Hardin. *English Religious Drama of the Middle Ages*. Oxford, Eng.: Clarendon Press, 1955.

Ryan, Lawrence V. "Doctrine and Dramatic Structure in *Everyman.*" *Speculum* 22 (1957):722–735.

Williams, Arnold. *The Drama of Medieval England*. East Lansing, Mich.: Michigan State University Press, 1961.

William Shakespeare (1564–1616). Enough is known about Shakespeare, both as citizen and as man of the theater, to refute all speculation that he was not the author of the plays ascribed to him. His life is better documented than that of most of his literary contemporaries. The evidence consists of church and court records and of references, both friendly and unfriendly, to his professional life. The late seventeenth and early eighteenth centuries knew a number of colorful legends about his early life, but these have not been verified by modern scholarship.

He was the son of a substantial tradesman in Stratford-on-Avon. Presumably he received a good grammar-school education (including training in Latin) till he was about sixteen. At eighteen he married Anne Hathaway, who was eight years older than he and with whom he had three children. In the early 1590's he turns up in London as a rising young poet and actor-playwright, a member of the company of the Chamberlain's Men, later (1603) known as the King's Men. When the company built the Globe Theater in 1599, Shakespeare was listed as the second of nine shareholders. In or shortly before 1612 he retired to Stratford, apparently a prosperous man. Friends and colleagues (including Ben Jonson) speak affectionately of him as a witty and cheerful companion.

The First Folio edition of Shakespeare's plays in 1623 established the conventional division of the canon into comedies, histories, and tragedies. (The First Folio includes thirty-six plays, but modern scholars count thirty-seven plays as wholly or almost wholly his.) It is a convenient division, particularly because it is traditional, but it takes no note of Shakespeare's development as a dramatist or of the generic variety within some single plays, and it obscures the range of plays within the same category. *Romeo and Juliet,* from about 1595, is a different kind of tragedy from *King Lear* and *Coriolanus,* from about 1606 and 1608, respectively. A history play like *Richard II* could qualify as tragedy and major parts of *Henry IV,* Part 1 as comedy. And "comedy" is not a very accurate collective term for plays as different as *The Comedy of Errors, A Midsummer Night's Dream, The Merry Wives of Windsor, The Merchant of Venice, Twelfth Night, Measure for Measure,* and *The Tempest.*

The exact chronology of Shakespeare's plays remains uncertain, but there is general agreement that most of the histories were written early, that *Hamlet* is the earliest of the major tragedies and only a little later than such "high" romantic comedies as *As You Like It* and *Twelfth Night,* that the period of "dark" or "problem" comedies of moral ambiguity, like *Troilus and Cressida* and *Measure for Measure,* partly coincides with the period of the mature tragedies, and that the allegorical romances on the themes of forgiveness and reconciliation, like *The Winter's Tale* and *The Tempest,* reflect a post-tragic view of life and are among Shakespeare's last plays.

*Suggested Reading*

Bentley, Gerald E. *Shakespeare: A Biographical Handbook.* New Haven, Conn.: Yale University Press, 1961.

Bradley, A. C. *Shakespearean Tragedy.* New York: Meridian Books, 1955 (first publ. 1904).

Campbell, Oscar J., and Edward G. Quinn. *The Reader's Encyclopedia of Shakespeare.* New York: Thomas Y. Crowell, 1966.

Chute, Marchette. *Shakespeare of London.* New York: E. P. Dutton, 1949.

Dean, Leonard F., ed. *Shakespeare: Modern Essays in Criticism.* New York: Oxford University Press, 1957.

Fergusson, Francis. "*Hamlet, Prince of Denmark:* The Analogy of Action." In *The Idea of a Theater.* Princeton, N.J.: Princeton University Press, 1949.

Granville-Barker, H. *Prefaces to Shakespeare.* Princeton, N.J.: Princeton University Press, 1946.

Granville-Barker, H., and G. B. Harrison. *A Companion to Shakespeare Studies.* Garden City, N.Y.: Doubleday (Anchor), 1960.

Harbage, Alfred, ed. *Shakespeare: The Tragedies: A Collection of Critical Essays.* Englewood Cliffs, N.J.: Prentice-Hall, 1964.

Jones, Ernest. *Hamlet and Oedipus.* New York: W. W. Norton, 1949.

Knight, G. Wilson. *The Wheel of Fire.* London: Methuen, 1949.

Knights, L. C. *An Approach to Hamlet.* Stanford, Cal.: Stanford University Press, 1961.

Levenson, J. C. *Discussions of Hamlet.* Boston: D. C. Heath, 1960.

Mack, Maynard. "The World of *Hamlet.*" *Yale Review* 41 (1952):502–523.

Nagler, A. M. *Shakespeare's Stage.* New Haven, Conn.: Yale University Press, 1964.

Sacks, Claire, and Edgar Whan, eds. *Hamlet: Enter Critic.* New York: Appleton-Century-Crofts, 1960.

Webster, Margaret. *Shakespeare Without Tears.* Rev. ed. Cleveland: World Publishing Company, 1955.

Wilson, J. Dover. *What Happens in Hamlet?* New York: Cambridge University Press, 1951.

## *Recordings of* Hamlet

Complete play:

Richard Burton, Eileen Herlie, Alfred Drake, Hume Cronyn. Columbia Records (4 records, DOL302, mono, and DOS702, stereo).

Marlowe Society. Argo Records (5 records, RG256-60, mono).

Paul Scofield and Cast. Caedmon Records (4 records, SR232, mono, and SRS-232, stereo).

Abridged:

Sir John Gielgud, McGuire, Pamela Brown, Theatre Guild. Victor Records (2 records, LM6007, mono).

Famous scenes:

Burton, Herlie, Drake, Cronyn. Columbia Records (OL8020, mono, and OS2620, stereo).

## *Film Versions of* Hamlet

British (J. Arthur Rank), 1948. Directed by Sir Laurence Olivier (152 min., 16mm, sound, black-and-white). Contemporary Films, McGraw-Hill Book Co., 330 W. 42nd St., New York, N.Y. 10036. (Rental.) Roa's Films, 1696 N. Astor St., Milwaukee, Wis. 52202. (Rental.) Twyman Films, 329 Salem Ave., Dayton, Ohio 45401. (Rental.) Universal Education and Visual Arts (United World Films), 221 Park Ave. S., New York, N.Y. 10003. (Rental.)

American (Encyclopædia Britannica Educational Corp.), 1959 (120 min., 16mm, sound, color, 4 parts). Encyclopædia Britannica Educational Corp., 425 Michigan Ave., Chicago, Ill. 60611. (Sale, and available on a non-exclusive basis from many rental agencies throughout the U.S. Check local commercial film libraries, public library film collections, and college audio-visual centers.)

German, 1964. With Maximilian Schell, directed by Edward Dmytryk and Franz Peter Wirth (127 min., 16mm, sound, black-and-white, dubbed dialogue). Audio Film Center, 34 MacQuesten Pkwy. S., Mount Vernon, N.Y. 10550. (Rental.)

Russian, 1966. Directed by Grigori Kozintsev (148 min., 16mm, sound, black-and-white, subtitles). United Artists, 16729 Seventh Ave., New York, N.Y. 10019. (Rental.)

JEAN BAPTISTE POQUELIN (MOLIÈRE) (1622–1673) was the son of a well-to-do upholsterer attached to the royal court. Both upholstering and law studies proved abortive, and in 1643 young Poquelin co-founded a theatrical company and took the name Molière (its significance is unknown) as a stage name. Unsuccessful in Paris, the company toured the provinces between 1645 and 1658. These were Molière's years of apprenticeship. In 1659 he experienced his first success as a playwright with the brief satire *The Affected Ladies.* In 1661 the company, enjoying royal patronage, established itself in its own theater, the Palais-Royal, in Paris. Until his death, Molière continued to write plays for his company, mainly comedies, and to act, mainly in comic parts. Many of his plays enraged the pious and the learned, and Louis XIV's favor proved fickle. As a result, the fortunes of the company remained insecure, despite Molière's popularity with the enlightened part of his audience. His marriage to a much younger woman appears to have been unhappy, and his children died in infancy. Grim irony attended his death: he suffered a hemorrhage while performing the title role of his own comedy *The Hypochondriac* and died a few hours afterwards.

Like Shakespeare's, the best of Molière's plays belong to world literature. Their farcical plots are vehicles for intimate studies of self-duped eccentrics whose single-minded psychological biases (or "humors") reduce them to stiff human grotesques, unable and unwilling to accommodate themselves to the norms of joyous and healthy social relationships. In Molière's comedies, as in the tragedies of his contemporary Racine, character is destiny. Besides *Tartuffe,* the best known among them are *School for Wives* (1662), *The Misanthrope* (1666), *The Miser* (1668), *The Gentleman Burgher* (1670), and *The Learned Ladies* (1672).

*Suggested Reading*

Fernandez, Ramon. *Molière: The Man Seen Through His Plays.* Translated by Wilson Follet. New York: Hill and Wang (Dramabook), 1958.

Gossman, Lionel. *Men and Masks: A Study of Molière.* Baltimore: Johns Hopkins Press, 1963.

Guicharnaud, Jacques, ed. *Molière: A Collection of Critical Essays.* Englewood Cliffs, N.J.: Prentice-Hall, 1964.

Hubert, Judd D. *Molière and the Comedy of Intellect.* Berkeley: University of California Press, 1962.

Lewis, D. Wyndham. *Molière, the Comic Mask.* London: Eyre and Spottiswoode, 1959.

Moore, Will. *Molière, a New Criticism.* Oxford: Clarendon Press, 1962.

*Recording of* Tartuffe

Willima Hutt, Douglas Rain. Caedmon Records (3 records, 332, stereo).

*Film Version of* Tartuffe

German, 1927. With Emil Jannings, directed by F. W. Murnau (70 min., 8mm, silent, black-and-white). Brandon Films, 221 W. 57th St., New York, N.Y. 10019. (Rental.) Film Classic Exchange, 1926 S. Vermont Ave., Los Angeles, Cal. 90007. (Rental or Sale.)

SIR GEORGE ETHEREGE (?1635–?1691). Very little that is certain is known about Etherege's life. He was probably born at Maidenhead, Berkshire, the son of a Bermuda planter. There is some evidence that he attended Cambridge, lived abroad for a while, and studied law at the Inns of Court. After the success of his plays, he led for some time the life of a fashionable rake, often in the company of the witty and dissolute Earl of Rochester. About 1680 he was knighted and married a wealthy widow. In his later years, he held diplomatic posts in the Hague and in Ratisbon, Germany. His amusing letters to friends in England describe his boredom with life in both places. His improprieties in Ratisbon forced him to leave. He died in Paris, according to one story from injuries he suffered when he fell down a flight of stairs.

Etherege wrote only three plays, *The Comical Revenge, or, Love in a Tub* (1664), *She Would if She Could* (1668), and *The Man of Mode* (1676). Of these, the last is by far the best integrated and most sophisticated, but all three rely heavily on sexual intrigue and witty repartee. *The Comical Revenge* is one of the earliest examples of Restoration comedy of sexual manners, a forerunner of the elegant comedies of manners by Congreve and Sheridan.

*Suggested Reading*

Carnochan, W. B., ed. *The Man of Mode.* Lincoln, Neb.: University of Nebraska Press, 1966.

Fujimura, Thomas H. *The Restoration Comedy of Wit.* New York: Barnes & Noble, 1952.

Holland, Norman. *The First Modern Comedies.* Cambridge, Mass.: Harvard University Press, 1959.

Powell, Jocelyn. "George Etherege and the Form of a Comedy." In *Restoration Theatre,* edited by John Russell and Bernard Harris. New York: St. Martin's Press, 1965.

Rosenfeld, Sybil. *The Letterbook of Sir George Etherege.* London: Oxford University Press, 1928.

Underwood, Dale. *Etherege and the Seventeenth-Century Comedy of Manners.* New Haven, Conn.: Yale University Press, 1957.

HENRIK IBSEN (1828–1906) was born in Skien, a small town in southern Norway. His father, a merchant of some social standing in the town, went bankrupt when the boy was eight, and the family thereafter lived in reduced circumstances. At sixteen Ibsen was apprenticed to a druggist in another small town. Two years later a servant-girl in the household gave birth to his illegitimate child. There is good reason to believe that these early experiences of financial hardship and social disgrace conditioned the shrewd sense of business, the reticence, and the excessive outer propriety that characterized Ibsen in later life, and both financial ruin and bastardy are recurrent motifs in his plays. He wrote his first play in 1848, under the influence of the liberalism of the February revolution in France of that year. Having soon abandoned a plan to study medicine, he was a free-lance journalist for a few years and flirted briefly with political radicalism. In the 1850's and early 1860's he held positions as salaried playwright and director at theaters in Bergen and Christiania (Oslo). Norway's failure to help Denmark in her war against Prussia in 1864 disillusioned him deeply (though he did not himself volunteer for service), and he and his wife and son left Norway for twenty-seven years of self-imposed exile in Italy and Germany. By the time he returned in 1891 he was a world figure. He died in Christiania after several years' illness.

Ibsen's iconoclasm, compact dramaturgy, and use of realistic symbols have earned him his reputation as "the father of modern drama." His canon, however, includes other kinds of plays than those on which, until fairly recently, his reputation was almost exclusively based. Most of his early plays were works of national romanticism, dealing with saga and peasant subject matter. His first popular success was the philosophical dramatic poem *Brand* (1866), which was followed by the complementary, antithetical *Peer Gynt* (1867). Together, these two verse dramas provide a clue to much that has been found obscure in the realistic plays that followed. Ibsen himself considered *Emperor and Galilean* (1873), a ten-act "world-historical drama" about the conflict between paganism and Christianity in the fourth-century Roman emperor Julian the Apostate, his most important work – a judgment no one else has shared. In the late 1870's and 1880's he wrote the social problem plays in prose by which he first attained international fame. The most important of these are *A Doll's House* (1879), *Ghosts* (1881), *An Enemy of the People* (1882), *The Wild Duck* (1884), *Rosmersholm* (1886), and *Hedda Gabler* (1890). Actually, the last three of these subordinate social problematics to individual psychology, and they mark, in some ways, a transition to Ibsen's final phase, in which he continued to anatomize the marriage relationship in heavily symbolic plays of little external action and of some autobiographical import. The most important of his last four plays are *The Master Builder* (1892) and *When We Dead Awaken* (1899).

*Suggested Reading*

Bradbook, Muriel. *Ibsen the Norwegian.* London: Chatto & Windus, 1948.

Downs, Brian W. *Ibsen: the Intellectual Background.* Cambridge, Eng.: Cambridge University Press, 1946.

——. *A Study of Six Plays by Ibsen.* Cambridge, Eng.: Cambridge University Press, 1950.

Fjelde, Rolf, ed. *Ibsen: A Collection of Critical Essays.* Englewood Cliffs, N.J.: Prentice-Hall, 1965.

Lucas, Frank L. *The Drama of Ibsen and Strindberg.* London: Cassell, 1962.

McFarlane, James W., ed. *Discussions of Henrik Ibsen.* Boston: D. C. Heath, 1962.

——, tr. and ed. *Ibsen* [the collected works in English]. London, New York: Oxford University Press, 1960.

——. *Ibsen and the Temper of Norwegian Literature.* London: Oxford University Press, 1960.

Meyer, Michael L. *Henrik Ibsen: The Making of a Dramatist.* London: Hart-Davis, 1967.

Northam, John. *Ibsen's Dramatic Method.* London: Faber and Faber, 1953.

Sprinchorn, Evert, ed. *Ibsen: Letters and Speeches.* New York: Hill and Wang (Dramabook), 1964.

Tennant, P. F. D. *Ibsen's Dramatic Technique.* Cambridge, Eng.: Bowes & Bowes, 1948.

Weigand, Hermann. *The Modern Ibsen.* New York: E. P. Dutton, 1960 (first publ. 1925).

(GEORGE) BERNARD SHAW (1856–1950) was born in Dublin of impoverished English parents. His formal education ended when he was fifteen. In 1876 he arrived in London, and over the next nine years he wrote five unsuccessful novels, joined the Fabian Society, a group of socialist intellectuals, and became a radical journalist. Between 1885 and 1898 he wrote art, music, and drama criticism for leading periodicals. *The Quintessence of Ibsenism* (1891) is enthusiastic propaganda for Ibsen's drama as liberal dialectics, but it says perhaps more about Shaw himself than about Ibsen. The long series of his plays began in 1892 with *Widowers' Houses* and ended in 1948. Once he was established as a playwright, his life was lacking in external events. His biography becomes the biography of a mind and is recorded in his voluminous writings. He married in 1898. In 1905 he setttled in Ayot St. Lawrence in Hertfordshire, where he spent most of his time until his death. He received the Nobel Prize for Literature in 1925. He was a vegetarian and teetotaller and against vivisection and vaccination. He willed the bulk of his estate to a project for English spelling reform.

In a certain sense, the social criticism that informs Shaw's earliest plays remained his deepest concern. His views, however, never became the orthodoxy of any one ideological camp, and many of his plays and his non-dramatic pronouncements on politics have provoked liberals and reactionaries alike. His prefaces to his plays, in impeccably lucid, incisive prose, are often as good clues to his thought as the plays themselves. The plays are drama of dialectics rather than of plot and character, though the best of them have repeatedly proved their ability to hold popular audiences with their dramatic and theatrical craftsmanship. Their distinctive strength is the way in which they wittily and caustically expose all sorts of shams and nonsense in modern thought and feeling. The best of them are more serious than their flamboyant heterodoxy suggests. Of these, the following are the most representative: *Arms and the Man, Candida* (both 1894), *Cæsar and Cleopatra* (1898), *Man and Superman* (1903), *Major Barbara* (1905), *The Doctor's Dilemma* (1906), *Pygmalion* (1912), *Heartbreak House* (1916), *Back to Methuselah* (1921), and *Saint Joan* (1923).

*Suggested Reading*

Bentley, Eric. *Bernard Shaw*. 2nd ed. London: Methuen, 1967.

Chesterton, G. K. *George Bernard Shaw*. New York: Hill and Wang (Dramabook), 1956 (first publ. 1909).

Crompton, Louis. *Shaw the Dramatist*. Lincoln, Neb.: University of Nebraska Press, 1969.

Henderson, Archibald. *George Bernard Shaw: Man of the Century*. New York: Appleton-Century-Crofts, 1956.

Kaufmann, R. J., ed. *G. B. Shaw: A Collection of Critical Essays*. Englewood Cliffs, N.J.: Prentice-Hall, 1965.

Kronenberger, Louis, ed. *George Bernard Shaw: A Critical Survey*. Cleveland: World Publishing Company, 1953.

Meisel, Martin. *Shaw and the 19th-Century Theater*. Princeton, N.J.: Princeton University Press, 1963.

Shaw, Bernard. *Shaw on Theater*. Ed. E. J. West. New York: Hill and Wang (Dramabook), 1958.

*Recording of* Cæsar and Cleopatra

Claire Bloom, Judith Anderson, Max Adrian, Claude Rains, Caedmon Records (2 records, TRM304, mono, and TRS304, stereo).

ANTON PAVLOVICH CHEKHOV (1860–1904) was born in Taganrog on the Sea of Azov in southern Russia, the grandson of a serf and the son of a grocer. A harsh boyhood was followed by medical studies in Moscow. He received his degree in 1884, but he never practiced medicine very regularly and in his last years not at all. In order to pay for his studies and support his family, he began to write and sell small, comical narrative sketches. In 1886, a successful collection of short stories, somewhat in the manner of de Maupassant, brought him acceptance in leading literary circles. His early one-act plays, most of them comedies, were quite successful, his first full-length play, *Ivanov* (1887), somewhat less so, and his next serious dramas failed. In 1890, tired with literary life, he traveled to the penal colony on the island of Sakhalin in the Sea of Okhotsk, off the east coast of Siberia. He returned home by way of Singapore and Ceylon. In 1898, *The Seagull*, which had been a humiliating fiasco in St. Petersburg two years earlier, was a brilliant success in the newly opened Moscow Art Theater, under the direction of Konstantin

Stanislavsky. *The Seagull* established not only Chekhov's reputation as a major playwright but also the success of the Stanislavsky "method" of realistic, inner-motivated acting and the finances of the new theater. Stanislavsky and Chekhov, however, did not always agree on the interpretation of his plays. In 1901 Chekhov married one of the leading actresses in the Moscow Art Theater, but his bad health — he had contracted tuberculosis in his early twenties — forced them to live apart for long periods. While she acted in Moscow, he spent the cold months of the year in Yalta on the Crimea. He wrote three additional plays for the Moscow Art Theater: *Uncle Vanya* (1899, a revision of *The Wood Demon,* which he had written ten years earlier), *The Three Sisters* (1901), and, his greatest success, *The Cherry Orchard* (1904). He died at a sanatorium in southern Germany.

Chekhov's major plays continue both to succeed in the theater and to elude final criticism. The social conditions they reflect are no longer actual, if they ever were. In disjointed dialogue and understated plots they chronicle small and stagnant lives and have no apparent theses. Rather than photographs and stenograms of reality or social problem plays, they are images that reduce to ironic order the unchanneled flow of banality by which most of human life happens.

*Suggested Reading*

Jackson, Robert L. *Chekhov: A Collection of Critical Essays.* Englewood Cliffs, N.J.: Prentice-Hall, 1967.

Magarshack, David. *Chekhov the Dramatist.* New York: Hill and Wang (Dramabook), 1960.

Simmons, Ernest J. *Chekhov.* Boston: Little, Brown, 1962.

Toumanova, Princess Nina Andronikova. *Anton Chekhov: The Voice of Twilight Russia.* New York: Columbia University Press, 1960.

Valency, Maurice J. *The Breaking String: The Plays of Anton Chekhov.* New York: Oxford University Press, 1966.

*Film Version of* The Three Sisters

Russian, 1964. Directed by Samson Samsonov (115 min., 16mm, sound, black-and-white, subtitles). Brandon Films, 221 W. 57th St., New York, N.Y. 10009. (Rental.)

*Recording of* The Three Sisters

Siobhan McKenna and others. Caedmon Records (3 records, TC1221, stereo).

JOHN MILLINGTON SYNGE (1871–1909) came from Protestant Irish landowner stock. He grew up in a Dublin suburb. His mother, widowed a year after the playwright's birth, was deeply religious in a rather dour and puritanical way, and Synge was never attracted to conventional piety. Synge graduated with a B.A. from Trinity College in Dublin in 1892 and went to Germany to prepare himself for a career in music, but in 1895 he moved to Paris to try to make his way as a writer instead. For several years he divided his time between Ireland and Paris. The decisive event in his life as author was his meeting with W. B. Yeats in Paris in 1896. Yeats, poet, playwright, the founder (in 1892) of the Irish Literary Society, and a dynamic leader of an Irish literary revival on native grounds, urged Synge to go to the Aran Islands, three desolate rocks off Ireland's Atlantic coast, for material. The meeting with the hardy community of peasants and fishermen sparked Synge's genius, though of his six plays only *Riders to the Sea* (1902) has an island setting. In 1905 he became, with Yeats and Lady Gregory, one of the directors of the Abbey Theater. His plays had begun to gain him a European reputation even before the violent controversy over *The Playboy of the Western World* in 1907, and the success of *Playboy* on the London stage secured it. He was engaged to Molly Allgood, one of the Abbey actresses, but at the time of his triumph he was already incurably ill with a malignant growth in his neck, and he did not live to marry. When he died he was finishing *Deirdre of the Sorrows,* a lyrical tragedy based on old Irish legend.

*Suggested Reading*

Corkery, Daniel. *Synge and Anglo-Irish Literature.* New York: Russell and Russell, 1965.

Ellis-Fermor, Una M. *The Irish Dramatic Movement.* 2nd ed. London: Methuen, 1954.

Gerstenberger, Donna. *John Millington Synge.* New York: Twayne Publishers, 1965.

Greene, David H., and Edward M. Stephens, *J. M. Synge, 1871–1909.* New York: Macmillan, 1959.

Johnston, Denis. *John Millington Synge.* New York: Columbia University Press, 1965.

Price, Alan. *Synge and Anglo-Irish Drama.* London: Methuen, 1961.

Yeats, W. B. "The Death of Synge." *Dramatis Personae.* London: Macmillan, 1936.

——. "The Irish Dramatic Movement." *Explorations.* London: Macmillan, 1962.

(Johan) August Strindberg (1849–1912) was born in Stockholm, the son of a stolid, middle-class, businessman father and a working-class mother. The couple had children together before their marriage, but the future playwright was born in wedlock. Strindberg tried halfheartedly for an advanced university degree at Uppsala and then for a career in acting. The eight years of his young manhood when he worked as a librarian, became a scholar of some note, and wrote his earliest plays and tales were probably the happiest period in his restless, haunted life. In 1877 he married for the first time. Two years later he made a name for himself with *The Red Room,* a novel of satiric realism. The same year he left Sweden to pursue a writing career abroad. In 1884 he returned home to stand trial on a charge of blasphemy, brought on by *Married,* a collection of short stories. He was acquitted, but the affair strained his hypersensitive nerves. There followed a period of frenetic literary activity, partly in Sweden, partly on the Continent. His thinly disguised autobiographies from the 1880's (*Son of Bondwoman, A Fool's Apology*) and the naturalistic plays *The Father* (1887), *Miss Julie* (1888), and *Creditors* (1888) reflect the tortured ambivalence of his attitude toward women which contributed to the dissolution of his marriage in 1891. Through most of the 1890's Strindberg suffered from a persecution complex, sometimes attended by hallucinations, though authorities disagree as to whether his condition was ever such as to justify calling him a lunatic. Between voluntary stays at mental hospitals he studied and wrote on botany and chemistry — but also on alchemy and demonology. His second marriage failed in 1894. *Inferno* (1897), a somewhat fictionalized autobiography, records the critical years of his psychopathy. From 1902 until his death Strindberg lived in Stockholm, indubitably sane though hardly serene. His third marriage ended in divorce in 1904, but his amazing literary creativity never again left him: plays, novels, tales, short stories, historical writings, and essays on philology, anthropology, politics, and other topics poured from his pen. Among the plays are *To Damascus,* I–III (1898, 1904), an early and moderate experiment in expressionism; *Easter* (1901), a modern parable of Christian expiation; *The Dance of Death,* I–II (1901), an only overtly realistic play of marital horrors; *A*

*Dream Play* (1901), a radically expressionistic descant on the theme that recurs like a refrain throughout: "Human kind is to be pitied"; a long series of Shakespearean chronicle plays with subjects from the lives of Swedish kings from the sixteenth to the eighteenth centuries; and, finally, a group of esoteric, sometimes fantastic "chamber plays" that were performed at the Intimate Theater, Strindberg's own stage in Stockholm, under the management of a younger friend. Of these, in addition to *The Ghost Sonata* (1907), *The Storm* and *The Pelican* (both also 1907) are the most important.

*Suggested Reading*

Brustein, Robert. "August Strindberg." In *The Theatre of Revolt.* Boston: Little, Brown, 1962.

Dahlström, C. E. W. L. *Strindberg's Dramatic Expressionism.* Ann Arbor, Mich.: University of Michigan Press, 1930.

Klaf, Franklin S. *Strindberg: The Origin of Psychology in Modern Drama.* New York: Citadel Press, 1963.

Madsen, Borge Gedso. *Strindberg's Naturalistic Theatre.* Seattle: University of Washington Press, 1962.

Mortensen, Brita M. E., and Downs, Brian W. *Strindberg: An Introduction to His Life and Work.* Cambridge, Eng.: Cambridge University Press, 1949.

Sprigge, Elizabeth. *The Strange Life of August Strindberg.* London: Hamish Hamilton, 1949.

EUGENE O'NEILL (1888–1953), America's most important playwright, was born in a hotel room in New York City, the son of an actor who gained both popularity and wealth from a lifetime career as the title character in a melodramatization of *The Count of Monte Christo.* Home life was disharmonious and unsettled as the family followed the itinerary of his father's acting company. At the end of his freshman year at Princeton, O'Neill was expelled for a prank. For the next five years he drifted — as a gold prospector in Honduras, a sailor on voyages to Europe and South America, a waterfront bum in New York, a bit actor, and a cub reporter. In 1912 he contracted tuberculosis and spent several months in a sanatorium where he read widely in modern drama. Strindberg, particularly, was a revelation. O'Neill began to write one-act plays, enrolled in Professor Baker's famous dramatic workshop at Harvard, and in 1916 saw *Bound East for Cardiff* produced by a group of semi-professionals at Provincetown, Massachusetts. Like most of his early plays, it was based on his sea-going experience. In 1920, his first full-length, professionally produced play, *Beyond the Horizon,* won the Pulitzer Prize. Extremely prolific, he turned out a rapid succession of plays both realistic — *Anna Christie* (1921, second Pulitzer Prize), *Desire Under the Elms* (1924) — and expressionistic — *The Emperor Jones* (1920), *The Hairy Ape* (1922). His plays from the late 1920's were increasingly experimental — *The Great God Brown* (1926), *Marco Millions, Lazarus Laughed* (both 1927). In 1927 he left the "little theater" groups which had produced his early plays and began his long association with the Theater Guild. In 1928 the Guild staged *Strange Interlude,* a long psychological study of a woman in her various life roles which made use of time-stopping, introspective asides and which brought him his third Pulitzer Prize. The trilogy *Mourning Becomes Electra,* a heavily Freudian adaptation of Aeschylus's *Oresteia* set in Civil War America, appeared in 1931. *Ah, Wilderness* (1933), a pleasantly nostalgic piece about adolescent rebellion in small-town New England in the early years of the century is O'Neill's only comedy. In 1936 he received the Nobel Prize for Literature, the first American author to do so. Following the failure of *Days Without End* (1934), O'Neill and his third wife retired to California. He was silent for twelve years until

*The Iceman Cometh* (1946), a wholly naturalistic play making Dr. Relling's point (in Ibsen's *The Wild Duck*) about the necessity for a life of illusions, reinstated him as the leading American playwright. O'Neill's last years were darkened by family tragedies and by ill health. He suffered from a degenerative disorder of the brain that impaired his motor ability and made writing increasingly difficult, but which left his mind clear. Since his death, a few plays that survived his destruction of most of the manuscripts for an enormous tragic cycle dealing with an Irish immigrant family have been produced, without adding much stature to his reputation. *Long Day's Journey Into Night* (published and produced posthumously in 1956), perhaps the best of all his plays, was not intended as part of the cycle. It is a brooding study of the conflicts in a small family, based on the troubled relationships among the young O'Neill (the time is 1912), his parents, and his older brother. It was the fourth of O'Neill's plays to win the Pulitzer Prize.

There is little verbal artistry in O'Neill's plays, and many critics find his most ambitious plays pretentious and overlong. But there is almost no disagreement about his superb sense of theater or about the total commitment he brings, in a variety of dramatic forms, to his quest for meaning in man's anguished existence in a mysterious universe that fails to answer to his desires. Few modern playwrights have pursued the tragic vision more persistently than O'Neill.

*Suggested Reading*

Cargill, Oscar, N. Bryllion Fagin, and William J. Fisher, eds. *O'Neill and His Plays: Four Decades of Criticism.* New York: New York University Press, 1961.

Carpenter, Frederic L. *Eugene O'Neill.* New York: Twayne Publishers, 1964.

Engel, Edwin A. *The Haunted Heroes of Eugene O'Neill.* Cambridge, Mass.: Harvard University Press, 1953.

Falk, Doris V. *Eugene O'Neill and the Tragic Tension.* New Brunswick, N.J.: Rutgers University Press, 1958.

Gassner, John, ed. *O'Neill: A Collection of Critical Essays.* Englewood Cliffs, N.J.: Prentice-Hall, 1964.

Gelb, Arthur, and Barbara Gelb. *O'Neill.* New York: Harper and Row, 1962.

Leech, Clifford. *Eugene O'Neill.* New York: Grove Press, 1963.

BERTOLT BRECHT (1898–1956) was born in the South German town of Augsburg in Bavaria. He studied medicine, served in World War I, began writing expressionistic plays, and in the 1920's was part of a group of avant-garde and leftist poets, playwrights, actors, and artists in Berlin. After becoming a Marxist about 1925, he began writing didactic plays of doctrinaire political content. Artistically, the most successful of these (and the least didactic) is *The Three-Penny Opera* (1928), an adaptation to modern conditions of John Gay's eighteenth-century *Beggar's Opera,* with music by Kurt Weill. In 1928 he married the actress Helene Weigel, who, after World War II, was to create the title role in *Mother Courage.* Brecht and his family fled Germany the day after the Reichstag fire, which initiated the Nazi reign of terror in 1933. He spent the first six years of exile from Hitler's Germany in Denmark. In 1939, when a Nazi invasion of Denmark began to seem likely, he moved to Sweden, and later to Finland. In 1941, when Finland, as Germany's ally, went to war against Russia, the Brechts fled to California, where they remained until 1947. For a while Brecht worked in Hollywood. But the post-war United States did not provide a hospitable climate for a European Marxist, and in 1947 Brecht moved to Zürich where he wrote and produced plays for the National Swiss Theater. In 1949 he moved to East Berlin, ostensibly, at least, supporting the Communist regime. Here he worked with his own ensemble in a theater at Schiffbauerdamm until his death.

In the years of his exile just before and during World War II Brecht wrote his four greatest plays — *Galileo* (1938–39), *Mother Courage* (1941), *The Good Woman of Setzuan* (1943), and *The Caucasian Chalk Circle* (1944–45) — swift, fluid, theatrically inventive, and largely non-illusionistic parables on the dilemmas confronting the embattled human spirit in a world of war, tyranny, corruption, stupidity, and greed. Brecht has been a profound influence on modern theater not only as playwright and director but also as theorist of a new kind of non-Aristotelian drama, in which acting is demonstration rather than impersonation, the mode of the drama episodic narrative rather than unilinear enactment, the proper audience attitude rational observation rather than entranced involvement, and the purpose of the performance the arousal of the audience to social action rather than the release of its empathies in catharsis. But it is possible to argue that his actual practice in his best plays does not conform to his theory. At its greatest, Brecht's art is too spaciously humanistic to be confined by political or esthetic dogma.

*Suggested Reading*

Brecht, Bertolt. "On the Experimental Theatre." *Tulane Drama Review* 6 (1961): 3–17.
——. *Seven Plays by Bertolt Brecht.* Edited and with an introduction by Eric Bentley. New York: Grove Press, 1961.
Demetz, Peter, ed. *Brecht: A Collection of Critical Essays.* Englewood Cliffs, N.J.: Prentice-Hall, 1962.
Esslin, Martin. *Brecht, the Man and His Works.* Garden City, N.Y.: Doubleday (Anchor), 1960.
Ewen, Frederic. *Bertolt Brecht: His Life, His Art, and His Times.* New York: Citadel Press, 1967.
Gray, Ronald. *Bertolt Brecht.* New York: Grove Press, 1961.
Spalter, Max, *Brecht's Tradition.* Baltimore: Johns Hopkins Press, 1967.
Weideli, Walter. *The Art of Bertolt Brecht.* New York: New York University Press, 1963.
Willett, John, ed. and tr. *Brecht on Theatre.* New York: Hill and Wang (Dramabook), 1964.
——. *The Theatre of Bertolt Brecht.* London: Methuen, 1959.

EDWARD FRANKLIN ALBEE (1928– ), one of the first successful practitioners of absurd drama in this country, is the adopted child of a New York family, whose wealth comes from a chain of theaters. He does not know his real parents. By his own account, he was a "problem child," who went through the dismissals from schools (he left Trinity College without a degree) and the sequence of odd jobs (one as a Western Union messenger boy) which in the mind of the public have become obligatory early experience for a successful American writer. In 1958 what Albee himself calls a "creative explosion" led to the writing of *The Zoo Story* in three weeks. It was first produced in Germany in 1959. A later, off-Broadway production received favorable reviews. *The American Dream,* an assault on a whole spectrum of middle-class values, was begun in 1959 but laid aside, completed in 1960, and produced on Broadway early in 1961. In the meantime Albee had written two other short plays, *The Sandbox* (with the same family that appears in *The American Dream*) and the anti-racist *Death of Bessie Smith.* His first full-length play, *Who's Afraid of Virginia Woolf?* (Broadway, 1962), raised a storm of controversy and acclaim both in America and Europe. In 1963 two members of the Pulitzer Prize drama jury resigned in protest against the refusal of the advisory board to make public the jury's nomination and the board's veto of the play for the 1962 award. Hostility to the play centered on its alleged "obscenity." *The Ballad of the Sad Café,* a dramatization of Carson McCullers's novella, was written before *Virginia Woolf* but first produced in 1963. His most recent plays have not added to his already high reputation. They include *Tiny Alice* (1964), a religious allegory-fantasy variously judged and interpreted; two adaptations, *Malcolm* (1966) and *Everything in the Garden* (1967); *A Delicate Balance* (1966), generally favorably received and awarded the Pulitzer Prize; and the two one-acters *Box* and *Quotations from Chairman Mao Tse-tung* (both 1968). The question of his future career is, as one critic has recently said, "no more than the question of the use to which he will put his abilities."

*Suggested Reading*

Albee, Edward F. "Which Theatre Is the Absurd One?" *The New York Times Magazine,* Feb. 25, 1962.

Baxandall, Lee. "The Theatre of Edward Albee." *Tulane Drama Review* 9 (1965):19–40.

Bigsby, C. W. E. *Confrontation and Commitment.* Columbia, Mo.: University of Missouri Press, 1968.

Flanagan, William. "Edward Albee: An Interview." *Paris Review* 10 (1966): 93–121.

Porter, Thomas E. "Fun and Games in Suburbia: *Who's Afraid of Virginia Woolf?*" In *Myth and Modern American Drama.* Detroit: Wayne State University Press, 1969.

Rutenberg, Michael E. *Edward Albee: Playwright in Protest.* New York: DBS Publications, 1969.

*Recording of* Who's Afraid of Virginia Woolf?

Uta Hagen, Arthur Hill. Columbia Records (4 records, DOL287, mono, and DOS687, stereo).

LeRoi Jones (1934– ) was born in Newark, N.J., the son of a postal clerk. Feeling "displaced" at Rutgers, he transferred to Howard University after his freshman year. After post-graduate work at Columbia and the New School for Social Research, he served for a time in the Air Force. Jones thinks of himself primarily as a poet and has published three volumes of verse. In addition to poems and plays, he has also written a history of jazz, *Blues People; Systems of Dante's Hell,* a semi-autobiographical, expressionistic novel; and *Home,* a collection of essays tracing his movement toward black militancy. The first four of his five plays were written in 1964. Only *Dutchman* has received wide critical acclaim. It won the off-Broadway Obie Award and was performed at the Festival of Two Worlds at Spoleto, Italy. *The Baptism* is an incoherent satirical allegory about ritual murder in a white church. In *The Toilet,* set in a dingy institutional latrine, a love relationship between a black and a white boy ends in violence. In *The Slave,* a poet-leader of the blacks, who are fighting a war against the whites, enters the home of his former white wife to get his children back. The setting in *Slave Ship* (1969), a brutal re-enactment of the past, is indicated by the title. Recent critical comments on Jones's work have raised the question of whether the artistic control that marks his best works is being subverted by his racial rage.

*Suggested Reading*

Bigsby, C. W. E. *Confrontation and Commitment.* Columbia, Mo.: University of Missouri Press, 1968.

Costello, Donald P. "LeRoi Jones: Black Man as Victim." *Commonweal* 88 (1968):436–440.

Dennison, George. "The Demagogy of LeRoi Jones." *Commentary* 39 (1965): 67–70.

*Film Version of* Dutchman

British, 1967. Directed by Anthony Harvey (55 min., 16mm, sound, black-and-white). Continental 16, 241 E. 34th St., New York, N.Y. 10016. (Rental.)

PETER WEISS (1916– ) was born in Nowawes near Berlin but has resided in Sweden since fleeing the Nazis just before World War II. He continues to write in German. He began his artistic career as a surrealist painter strongly influenced by Max Ernst and Salvador Dali. Surrealism was the mode of his early film-making as well, but later he turned to documentaries as a means of exploring the theme of personal alienation. Both styles, and their literary corollaries in Franz Kafka and Henry Miller, have continued to influence Weiss, first as novelist and later as playwright.

Though his early work as artist and film producer had attracted attention, Weiss had difficulty finding publishers for his novels, but the award of a literary prize for *Point of Escape* (1963) established his reputation in Germany. His first play, *Night with Guests* (1962), has not yet been produced. His second, *Marat/Sade,* opened in April, 1964, at the Schiller Theater in West Berlin to an enthusiastic reception. The following year the Royal Shakespeare Company, under the direction of Peter Brook, staged the play in London; and in December, 1965, the same production opened in New York, ran for 145 performances, and won the Drama Critics Circle Award for 1965–66. The production has been filmed and has played successfully in art movie houses.

Like *Marat/Sade,* Weiss's later plays also deal with social issues through a combination of visual happenings and documentary technique. *The Investigation* (1966) consists of excerpts from the transcripts of the 1964–65 trial of those responsible for the mass extermination at Auschwitz during the last war. *The Song of the Lusitanian Bogey* (1967) uses verse, discordant melody, and ballet to depict the struggle in Angola between native "primitivism" and Portuguese "civilization." Weiss's latest work, whose title is 46 words long, presents a Marxist interpretation of 2,000 years of Vietnamese history and ends in a presidential order to escalate the war.

*Suggested Reading*

Cohn, Ruby. *"Marat/Sade:* An Education in Theatre." *Educational Theatre Journal* 19 (1967):478–485.

Moeller, Hans Bernard. "German Theatre 1964: Weiss' Reasoning in a Madhouse." *Symposium* 20 (1966):163–173.

Roloff, Michael. "An Interview with Peter Weiss." *Partisan Review* 22 (1965): 220–232.

Sontag, Susan. "Marat/Sade/Artaud." *Partisan Review* 22 (1965):210–219.

Weiss, Samuel A. "Peter Weiss's *Marat/Sade.*" *Drama Survey* 5 (1966–67): 123–30.

*Recording of* Marat/Sade

Royal Shakespeare Company of Great Britain. Caedmon Records (3 records, TR312, stereo).

## SUGGESTED GENERAL REFERENCES

*Theory*

Abel, Lionel. *Metatheatre*. New York: Hill and Wang (Dramabook), 1963.
Artaud, Antonin. *The Theater and Its Double*. Translated by Mary Caroline Richards. New York: Grove Press, 1958.
Barnet, Sylvan, Morton Berman, and William Burto, eds. *Aspects of the Drama: A Handbook*. Boston: Little, Brown, 1962.
Bentley, Eric. *The Life of the Drama*. New York: Atheneum, 1964.
Brereton, Geoffrey. *Principles of Tragedy*. Coral Gables, Fla.: University of Miami Press, 1968.
Brook, Peter. *The Empty Space*. London and New York: Atheneum, 1968.
Brooks, Cleanth, and Robert B. Heilman. *Understanding Drama: Twelve Plays*. New York: Henry Holt, 1948.
Butcher, S. H. *Aristotle's Theory of Poetry and Fine Art*. New York: Dover Publications, 1951.
Calderwood, James L., and Harold E. Toliver, eds. *Perspectives on Drama*. New York: Oxford University Press, 1968.
Clark, Barrett H., ed. *European Theories of Drama, with a Supplement on the American Drama*. New York: Crown Publishers, 1947.
Cole, Toby, ed. *Playwrights on Playwriting: The Meaning and Making of Modern Drama from Ibsen to Ionesco*. New York: Hill and Wang (Dramabook), 1960.
Cook, Albert. *The Dark Voyage and the Golden Mean*. New York: W. W. Norton, 1966.
Corrigan, Robert W., ed. *Comedy: Meaning and Form*. San Francisco: Chandler, 1965.
——, ed. *Tragedy: Vision and Form*. San Francisco: Chandler, 1965.
Corrigan, Robert W., and James L. Rosenberg, eds. *The Context and Craft of Drama*. San Francisco: Chandler, 1964.
Downer, Alan S. *The Art of the Play: An Anthology of Nine Plays*. New York: Henry Holt, 1955.
Drew, Elizabeth. *Discovering Drama*. New York: W. W. Norton, 1937.
Eliot, T. S. *Poetry and Drama*. Cambridge, Mass.: Harvard University Press, 1951.
Ellis-Fermor, Una. *The Frontiers of Drama*. 2nd ed. London: Methuen, 1964.
Ellmann, Richard, and Charles Feidelson, Jr., eds. *The Modern Tradition: Backgrounds of Modern Literature*. New York: Oxford University Press, 1965.
Enck, John J., Elizabeth T. Forter, and Alvin Whitley, eds. *The Comic in Theory and Practice*. New York: Appleton-Century-Crofts, 1960.
Felheim, Marvin, ed. *Comedy, Plays: Theory, and Criticism*. New York: Harcourt, Brace & World, 1962.
Fergusson, Francis. *The Human Image in Dramatic Literature*. Garden City, N.Y.: Doubleday (Anchor), 1957.
——. *The Idea of a Theater*. Garden City, N.Y.: Doubleday (Anchor), 1949.
Frye, Northrop. *Anatomy of Criticism*. Princeton, N.J.: Princeton University Press, 1957.
Guthke, Carl Siegfried. *Modern Tragicomedy*. New York: Random House, 1966.
Heilman, Robert B. *Tragedy and Melodrama: Versions of Experience*. Seattle: University of Washington Press, 1968.
Henn, Thomas R. *The Harvest of Tragedy*. New York: Barnes and Noble, 1966.
Kerr, Walter. *Tragedy and Comedy*. New York: Simon and Schuster, 1967.

Lauter, Paul, ed. *Theories of Comedy*. Garden City, N.Y.: Doubleday (Anchor), 1964.
Levin, Richard, ed. *Tragedy: Plays, Theory, and Criticism*. New York: Harcourt, Brace & World, 1960.
Mandel, Oscar. *A Definition of Tragedy*. New York: New York University Press, 1961.
Nicoll, Allardyce. *The Theatre and Dramatic Theory*. New York: Barnes and Noble, 1962.
———. *The Theory of Drama*. London: G. G. Harrap, 1937.
Nietzsche, Friedrich. *The Birth of Tragedy* and *The Genealogy of Morals*. Translated by Francis Golffing. Garden City, N.Y.: Doubleday (Anchor), 1956.
Olson, Elder. *Tragedy and the Theory of Drama*. Detroit: Wayne State University Press, 1966.
Peacock, Ronald. *The Art of Drama*. London: Routledge & Kegan Paul, 1957.
Raphael, D. D. *The Paradox of Tragedy*. Bloomington, Ind.: Indiana University Press, 1960.
Sewall, Richard B. *The Vision of Tragedy*. New Haven, Conn.: Yale University Press, 1959.
Sewall, Richard B., and Lawrence Michel, eds. *Tragedy: Modern Essays in Criticism*. Englewood Cliffs, N.J.: Prentice-Hall, 1963.
Styan, J. L. *The Dark Comedy*. Cambridge, Eng.: Cambridge University Press, 1962.
———. *The Elements of Drama*. Cambridge, Eng.: Cambridge University Press, 1960.
Thompson, Alan R. *The Anatomy of Drama*. 2nd ed. Berkeley: University of California Press, 1946.
Van Laan, Thomas F. *The Idiom of Drama*. Ithaca and London: Cornell University Press, 1970.
Williams, Raymond. *Modern Tragedy*. Stanford, Cal.: Stanford University Press, 1966.

*History and Criticism*

Bentley, Eric. *In Search of Theater*. New York: Alfred A. Knopf, 1953.
———. *The Playwright as Thinker*. New York: Meridian Books, 1957.
Bogard, Travis, and William I. Oliver, eds. *Modern Drama: Essays in Criticism*. New York: Oxford University Press, 1965.
Brustein, Robert. *The Theatre of Revolt*. Boston: Atlantic-Little, Brown, 1962.
Clark, Barrett H., and George Freedley, eds. *A History of Modern Drama*. New York: D. Appleton-Century, 1947.
Corrigan, Robert W., ed. *Theatre in the Twentieth Century*. New York: Grove Press, 1963.
Dickinson, Hugh. *Myth on the Modern Stage*. Urbana, Ill.: University of Illinois Press, 1969.
Downer, Alan S. *Fifty Years of American Drama*. Chicago: Henry Regnery, 1951.
Esslin, Martin. *The Theatre of the Absurd*. Garden City, N.Y.: Doubleday (Anchor), 1961.
Freedman, Morris, ed. *Essays in the Modern Drama*. Boston: D. C. Heath, 1964.
———. *The Moral Impulse: Modern Drama from Ibsen to the Present*. Carbondale, Ill.: Southern Illinois University Press, 1967.
Gassner, John. *Form and Idea in Modern Theatre*. New York: Dryden Press, 1956.
———. *Masters of the Drama*. 3rd rev. ed. New York: Dover Publications, 1954.
———. *The Theatre in Our Times*. New York: Crown Publishers, 1954.
Grossvogel, David I. *The Blasphemers* (original title: *Four Playwrights and a*

*Postscript: Brecht, Ionesco, Beckett, Genet*). Ithaca, N.Y.: Cornell University Press, 1962.

——. *The Self-Conscious Stage in Modern French Drama*. New York: Columbia University Press, 1958.

Knight, G. Wilson. *The Golden Labyrinth*. New York: W. W. Norton, 1962.

Krutch, Joseph Wood. *"Modernism" in Modern Drama*. Ithaca, N.Y.: Cornell University Press, 1953.

Lucas, Frank L. *The Drama of Chekhov, Synge, Yeats, and Pirandello*. London: Cassell, 1963.

Lumley, Frederick. *Trends in Twentieth Century Drama*. New York: Oxford University Press (Essential Books), 1960.

Nicoll, Allardyce. *World Drama from Aeschylus to Anouilh*. London: G. G. Harrap, 1949.

Porter, Thomas E. *Myth and Modern American Drama*. Detroit: Wayne State University Press, 1969.

Steiner, George. *The Death of Tragedy*. New York: Alfred A. Knopf, 1961.

Valency, Maurice. *The Flower and the Castle: An Introduction to Modern Drama*. New York: Macmillan, 1963.

Wellwarth, George E. *The Theater of Protest and Paradox*. New York: New York University Press, 1964.

Williams, Raymond. *Drama from Ibsen to Eliot*. London: Chatto & Windus, 1952.

*Theater Arts*

Cole, Toby, and Helen Krich Chinoy, eds. *Actors on Acting*. New York: Crown Publishers, 1949.

Goodman, Randolph. *Drama on Stage*. New York: Holt, Rinehart and Winston, 1961.

Gorelik, Mordecai. *New Theatres for Old*. New York: S. French, 1940.

Macgowan, Kenneth, and William Melnitz. *The Living Stage: A History of the World Theater*. New York: Prentice-Hall, 1955. (A shorter version is *The Golden Ages of the Theater,* 1959).

Nicoll, Allardyce. *The Development of the Theatre*. 5th rev. ed. New York: Harcourt, Brace & World, 1966.

Stanislavsky, Constantin. *An Actor Prepares*. Translated by Elizabeth Reynolds Hapgood. New York: Theatre Arts Books, 1936.

*Reference*

Bowman, Walter P., and Robert Hamilton Ball. *Theatre Language: A Dictionary of Terms in English of the Drama and Stage from Medieval to Modern Times*. New York: Theatre Arts Books, 1936.

Gassner, John, and Edward Quinn. *The Reader's Encyclopedia of World Drama*. New York: Thomas Y. Crowell, 1969.

Hartnoll, Phyllis, ed. *The Oxford Companion to the Theatre*. 3rd ed. London: Oxford University Press, 1967.

*Some Useful Collections of Plays*

Bentley, Eric, ed. *The Play: A Critical Anthology*. Englewood Cliffs, N.J.: Prentice-Hall, 1951.

——, ed. *The Modern Theatre,* I–VI. Garden City, N.Y.: Doubleday (Anchor), 1955–1960.

Block, Haskell, and Robert Shedd, eds. *Masters of Modern Drama*. New York: Random House, 1961.

Clayes, Stanley, David Spencer, E. Bradlee Watson, and Benfield Pressey, eds. *Contemporary Drama Series* [five collections]. New York: Charles Scribner's Sons, 1941–1962.
Corrigan, Robert W., ed. *The Modern Theatre.* New York: Macmillan, 1964.
Downer, Alan S., ed. *The Art of the Play.* New York: Henry Holt, 1955.
Gassner, John, ed. *Treasury of the Theatre,* I–II. 3rd ed. New York: Simon and Schuster, 1967.
Grene, David, and Richmond Lattimore, eds. *The Complete Greek Tragedies,* I–IV. Chicago: University of Chicago Press, 1959.
Alvin Kernan, ed. *Character and Conflict: An Introduction to Drama.* 2nd ed. New York: Harcourt, Brace & World, 1969.
——, ed. *Classics of the Modern Theater.* New York: Harcourt, Brace & World, 1965.

*Films*

See *Feature Films on 8 and 16. A Directory of Feature Films Available for Rental, Lease, and Sale in the U.S.* 2nd ed. Compiled and edited by James L. Limbacher. New Haven, Conn.: Readers Press, 1968. For educational films see, *Index to 16mm Educational Films,* National Information Center for Educational Media. New York: University of Southern California, Los Angeles, and McGraw-Hill Book Co., 1967.